United States Tennis Association

OFFICIAL ENCYCLOPEDIA OF TENNIS

United States Tennis Association

1817

OFFICIAL ENCYCLOPEDIA OF TENNIS

CENTENNIAL EDITION

Edited by

Bill Shannon

with the Staff of the USTA

HARPER & ROW, PUBLISHERS, New York

Cambridge, Philadelphia, San Francisco, London,
Mexico City, São Paulo, Sydney

Excerpts of records in Section 5, taken from Official USTA Tennis Yearbook, 1980; copyright 1980 by United States Lawn Tennis Association Inc.

Excerpts in Section 1 on tennis history taken from *Lawn Tennis, its Founders and its Early Days* by George E. Alexander, copyright 1974 by George E. Alexander and United States Lawn Tennis Association Inc. Reprinted by permission of the author.

Excerpts in Section 4 on court courtesy taken from *The Quick and Easy Guide to Tennis,* copyright 1962 by the Crowell-Collier Publishing Company. Reprinted by permission of the publisher, The Macmillan Company.

This work was first published in 1972 under the title *United States Lawn Tennis Association Official Encyclopedia of Tennis.*

For information regarding educational materials, films and official USTA publications, please contact:

USTA Education and Research Center
729 Alexander Road
Princeton, N.J. 08540

Library of Congress Cataloging in Publication Data
Main entry under title:

USTA official encyclopedia of tennis.
    Revision of: Official encyclopedia of tennis.
Rev. and updated 1st ed., c1979.
    Includes index.
    1. Tennis. 2. Tennis—Records. I. Shannon, Bill.
II. United States Tennis Association. III. United
States Tennis Association. Official encyclopedia
of tennis.
GV995.U87 1981   796.342′03   81–47237
ISBN 0-06-014896-9   AACR2

81 82 83 84 85 10 9 8 7 6 5 4 3 2 1

Acknowledgments

This volume, as is true of any book of this type, involved the participation of numerous people. A debt of thanks is owed to George W. Gowen, Ed Fabricius, John Smith, Eve Kraft, John Conroy, and the USTA Education and Research Center staff and Claudette Messuri for their aid in assembling the material for this centennial edition, and to Bill Shannon for compiling and editing the revisions. In many cases, the material from the first and second editions of this book formed the basis for this one. We thank those whose contributions made the original editions possible including Lawrence A. Baker, James H. Van Alen, Edwin S. Baker, Robert S. Malaga, Marjorie Gengler, William Colson, Ron Bookman, F.E. Storer, Barry Lorge, Clifford Sutter, Frances Freese and Alice Valentine. Special thanks are due to Harold O. Zimman and Russ Adams.

We are grateful to Dr. Joanna Davenport, Professor of Physical Education and Women's Athletic Director at Auburn University, for the liberal use of her dissertation, "The History and Interpretation of Amateurism in the United States Lawn Tennis Association." Dr. Davenport, a sport historian, is in the final stages of a book about Eleonora Sears, early sportswoman and former national tennis champion.

Our appreciation is due to George Alexander for his generous permission to use extracts from his book on the early history of the game in America.

To all of these, and many others of the USTA staff, go our sincere thanks.

MICHAEL J. BURNS
Executive Secretary,
United States Tennis Association

Contents

United States Tennis Association

OFFICIAL ENCYCLOPEDIA
OF TENNIS

History of Tennis

For a game which observed only the one hundredth anniversary of its birth in 1973, tennis has shown the most spectacular growth of any popular participant sport in modern recorded history. As the game began its second century, it had become the fastest-growing recreational sport in the world and was probably played by more people in more cultures than any other comparable game. These lavish statements are illustrative of the explosive pattern of growth which began almost immediately following the 1873 introduction of the lawn tennis varietal by Major Walter Clopton Wingfield for the amusement of guests at a pheasant shoot at Nantclwyd Hall in Wales.

Wingfield, now frequently acknowledged as the inventor of the most popular form of tennis, found his game well received at Nantclwyd. Within a few months, he had obtained a patent on the design of the court and published a set of rules for the game. What followed was a rash of imitators, competitors, and litigators. But Wingfield, then retired from the British Army, persevered with his game, altering it and restyling the court.

In just four years from the date of its original introduction, the game was modified and became a competitive tournament sport at the cricket club in Wimbledon. In 1977 the Centennial Wimbledon was a testimony both to the enormous popularity of the game and to the perception of its inventors. One of the most interesting aspects of the Wimbledon Centennial was that a British girl,

Virginia Wade, won the Women's Singles before an audience including Queen Elizabeth II. What followed was an emotional experience for all concerned.

None of this, of course, could have been envisioned by Major Wingfield. However, his general observation that there was a need for an athletic outdoor game in which men and women could compete recreationally was certainly correct.

Tennis, a game of many forms, was not invented by Wingfield. No clear story of the invention of the game in its earliest stages exists. It is likely that it was a development of paddle-and-ball games that have amused mankind since prehistoric times. During the height of the Roman Empire, a variety of ball games were played. At least four of these games have been fairly well identified by drawings and writings. These games have some resemblances to a number of modern games, and it is clear that it is from these roots that today's major ball sports have sprung. It is also not unreasonable to presume that these games themselves had antecedents stretching backward beyond the limits of recorded human sporting activity.

Scholars have devoted a good deal of time and effort attempting to trace connections between the earliest known writings and sketchings of games and their modern counterparts. A good deal of surmise is involved in these endeavors. However, ball games are probably as old as humanity's social organization.

The playing of court tennis was very popular in the sixteenth and seventeenth centuries.

Tennis as a word first appears in a recognizable form in a poem by John Gower, in 1399, in a phrase "Of the tenetz to winne or lose a chase. ..." Even earlier, in 1380, Chaucer had characters speaking of playing "rackets." It should be borne in mind that when writers of this, or almost any, time speak of popular sports and games, they are rarely seeking to leave a record for future historians and researchers. Rather, they are speaking in terms of allusion to elements of everyday life of which they are certain their readers are aware. In much the same way, a contemporary author might make a passing reference to well-known advertising phrases, television situation-comedy characters, local politicians, or current Broadway plays. Behind their comments lies a presumption of knowledge on the part of their readers, who live in the same world they do. Future generations, of course, do not have the advantage of day-to-day contact with the elements of life mentioned in this way. But it is safe to assume that forms of tennis were well known in a sophisticated way in the fourteenth century. These forms of tennis were a long way removed from that which Major Wingfield created.

In France, there are numerous historical references, most revolving around athletically inclined kings, to *paume*. This is a form of handball (palm), which became extremely popular among the French and gradually spread across the English Channel to Britain. *Paume* evolved into indoor and outdoor forms, *short* and *long* as they were termed.

French monastic history from this period is replete with tales of monks playing the game in the courtyards of the monastery. It is evidently with the advent of the indoor form of this game that the racket, or racquet, was introduced for the obvious purpose of extending the reach of the players' arms. At the outset, these rackets were merely bats, known as *battoirs*, in various shapes, lengths, and sizes. In the first known work on tennis, published in Venice in 1555, Antonio Scaino discusses the rackets and suggests that they were shaped to suit the feelings of the individual player. Later, the heads of the rackets were hollowed out.

These hollowed-out heads were filled in with several elements. One of the most popular was parchment, with strings coming as a later development. Naturally, some of the older players stayed with the form of the game which they preferred and played without any racket. Several old references exist in which players with rackets played against ones without.

Eventually *court tennis,* as it became known, was standardized. It remains today as a small, but stubborn, reminder of tennis's past. There are seven court tennis courts in existence in the

United States and a total of less than forty around the world. But an annual championship is held, and several other tournaments are still conducted in the game.

What emerged as the final form of court tennis is an indoor game played on a court which is one of the fascinations of man's sport. A sloping ledge upon which the ball is hit runs around three sides of the court. The ball rolls along the ledge into the other player's side of the court. The floor is marked with stripes, known as "chases," around which much of the game's complex strategy revolves, and the walls are filled with windows and openings into which the ball may be hit. Although the indoor version of court tennis (known variously today as "real" or "Royal" tennis, as well as court tennis) has survived on a limited basis, the outdoor version languished and eventually became passé.

Several other games with some similarity to tennis also remained, however, and some doubtless exercised influence upon Major Wingfield's think-

Court tennis is still played today on approximately 40 courts throughout the world. The above court tennis match in progress was at the Royal Tennis Courts in Melbourne, Australia.

ing. Among these are racquets and badminton. Racquets had a peculiar birth as a diversion for prisoners in London jails. Badminton came by a more conventional method to England. It was a popular game of India that was one of the myriad imports of the Empire.

On October 16, 1833, Walter Wingfield was born into a family which already had an unusual connection with court tennis. Charles d'Orléans, a fifteenth-century tennis player and poet, was imprisoned in Wingfield Castle by young Walter's ancestor, John. Wingfield's father was Clopton Lewis Wingfield, a major in the 66th Foot Regiment. By the time he was thirteen, Walter and his sister, Jane Mary, were orphaned by the death of their father. Within two years, an uncle was proposing the young boy for a commission in the Army. After failing his first examination at Sandhurst, Wingfield finally obtained a commission in the 1st Dragoon Guards, in 1851, at age seventeen.

Wingfield earned a promotion to lieutenant and purchased a promotion to captain shortly before his marriage to Alice Cleveland. His captaincy and wedding came during his service in India, but the family was briefly parted when Wingfield was shipped to China for a short sortie with the 1st Dragoons.

In 1862 he retired from his Army career and returned to England to take up the management of an estate inherited through his paternal grandmother. Rhysnant consisted of some 2,600 acres in the county of Montgomery, Wales. But estate management was not Walter Wingfield's destiny. After earning an appointment as a major in the Montgomeryshire Yeomanry Cavalry, Wingfield moved his family to Belgravia Mansions in the Pimlico section of London in 1873. While he was not especially skilled at anything, Wingfield was well connected on several social levels. Thus was set the stage for his introduction of the new game of lawn tennis.

The game was such a hit when it was introduced at Nantclwyd that Wingfield immediately sought to patent it. He desired an omnibus patent on all aspects of the game but was granted only a patent on the court. Shortly thereafter, Wingfield also received a copyright on the rules which he had newly devised. In its original form, Wingfield's

Major Walter Clopton Wingfield—the man most historians credit with the invention of the modern game of tennis.

game was played on an hourglass-shaped court. A series of rapid changes in the design of the playing area took place over the next few years, and Wingfield was reduced to being a virtual outsider in the game he helped to popularize.

Almost from the outset, Wingfield's rules became a source of much controversy. Within a year after their publication, a convention was called by the Marylebone Cricket Club at Lords to test out competing styles of the game and choose one to be official. Wingfield's style passed this test with flying colors, and he graciously accepted the plaudits of Lords and issued a new code of rules with the club's approval. But the controversy refused to abate. Wingfield's most enduring contribution to the game of tennis was the constant furor he created with his attempts to control the publication and distribution of rules.

In 1870 a group of influential Londoners had formed a club on Worple Road, in the borough of Wimbledon, for the playing of croquet. Then the most popular game of the English lawn party, this diversion led to many a trampled flower bed and disturbed lawn. After a brief search, one group of dedicated croquet players found the plot in Wimbledon and set up the All-England Croquet Club. When .membership began to wane, the club's leaders cast about for something besides croquet for which to use their facility. They found lawn tennis. But immediately the squabble over rules again reared its ugly head. Led by the influential Julian Marshall, the All-England group published a new set of rules of its own, debunked with some thoroughness most of Wingfield's claims, and changed the name of their club to All-England Croquet and Lawn Tennis Club. So popular were the new rules that 7,000 copies of them were sold within a few weeks. Wingfield was out of the picture.

Politics were as much at the bottom of this rather unfair circumstance as anything. Marshall had been joined in his production of the new (and profitable) rule book by C. G. Heathcote. Both were friends of J. W. Walsh and Henry Jones.

Walsh was the editor of *The Field,* a powerful sporting magazine, and Jones was his right-hand man. They were also among the primary backers of the All-England Club. Heathcote happened to be the brother of John Moyer Heathcote, a celebrated but aging champion of court tennis, who had just invented a new ball suitable for the playing of lawn tennis. Covered with white flannel, the new ball was a significant breakthrough for the game. Utilizing the new techniques of vulcanizing rubber, it was both light and lively. With the modifications in the court made by the All-England group, the new ball really produced modern tennis.

With all of this influence arranged against him, poor old Wingfield had little choice but to recede from the situation with as much gentlemanly grace as he could muster. The crowning blow came when the Marylebone added its sanction to the new All-England rules. Then came the establishment of the first tournament at Wimbledon, and tennis was on its way.

The early game of tennis as played in England.

THE FIRST TOURNAMENTS

It was the organization of major tournaments and their appropriate promotion in the sporting publications, as much as anything thereafter, that helped the spread of the game. With *The Field* firmly entrenched behind them, the All-England group moved full steam into their initial tournament in 1877. It was in that august publication that the first public notice of the event appeared, announcing that an all-comers tournament would be held at the All-England Club on July 9 and successive days through July 12.

But subsequent events were to prove that on Monday, July 9, 1877, there was no tennis played at All-England. The club decided to permit a postponement of the event so that most of the members would feel free to attend the annual cricket match between Eton and Harrow. Since most of the members expressed this as their desire, the decision was not much of a decision after all. The referee, as it developed, was none other than *The Field*'s Henry Jones.

He rescheduled the event for Thursday, July 19, instead. A crowd of 200 showed up and paid one shilling each for the privilege of watching the first matches ever played in the All-England tournament. Actually, most of the club's proceeds were derived from the entry fees, which were one pound and one shilling per entrant. W. C. Marshall, C. G. Heathcote, and Julian Marshall were all authorities on the rules they had invented, and there was some dismay when the initial tournament was won not by any of the club's members, who were actively developing the new game, but by Spencer W. Gore, a racquets player. Gore had been a skillful racquets man at Harrow, had only a passing familiarity with the new game, and had almost no familiarity with the new rules.

Gore earned his title the hard way. In the

The lawn tennis meeting at Wimbledon in 1882.

twenty-two-man field, he was forced to beat C. G. Heathcote in the semifinal match and W. C. Marshall, the reigning court-tennis champion, in the final. For his efforts, Gore carted off the gold challenge cup while Marshall got the silver prize and seven guineas, and Heathcote got three guineas. The gold championship trophy was donated by *The Field* and valued at twenty-five guineas (roughly $800 at 1981 rates). Interestingly, especially in light of future confrontations over the problem, no question was raised about the amateur status of the gentlemen who accepted the cash prizes. Given this impetus, tennis began to spread with even greater rapidity.

There remains to this day conflict over who was responsible for introducing the game to the United States. For many years, the proposition had been accepted that the game was introduced to this country by Miss Mary Outerbridge at Staten Island in 1874. Noted sports historian Frank G. Menke first expostulated this theory in 1931 when he cited an interview with a customs agent.

Since that time, Miss Outerbridge had been given credit for introducing the game to the shores of America. The Outerbridge family was one of the most active in the early formation of the United States National Lawn Tennis Association, now the USTA. This fact alone gave considerable weight to Menke's thesis. Prior to 1931, it had generally been assumed that the first lawn tennis set in the United States had been that of William Appleton in Nahant, Massachusetts, where members of the distinguished Dwight and Sears families played the game. It now appears that this first version may be correct.

George E. Alexander has done extensive research on this point and during the early 1970s came to the conclusion that the tennis outfit which Mary Outerbridge brought to Staten Island from Bermuda could not possibly have come there in early 1874. There is, however, no doubt that she did bring a tennis set to Staten Island. It was there that the Outerbridge family set up the first more-or-less public tennis facility in the country, using the grounds of the Staten Island Cricket and Baseball Club in St. George. All other courts were privately held at that time. Further, the Outerbridges set about to promote a tournament

at the club in 1880, which was the first historically significant one ever played in America. Yet it now appears clear that Parisian-born James Dwight was, in fact, the progenitor of American tennis.

It seems that J. Arthur Beebe had picked up a set of the new rules, a net, and other equipment in England and brought it to Nahant as a gift for his in-laws, the Appletons. James Dwight and a friend of the Appleton family, Fred R. Sears, tried the game out in Nahant and shortly began to interest their friends in it. By 1876 they staged a round-robin tournament involving fifteen players in Nahant. Sears and Dwight met in the finals and Dwight won, 12–15, 15–7, 15–13. Fred Sears's younger brother, Richard, was among those attracted to the game, and he entered the summer tournament at Nahant in 1877, although James Dwight was again the tourney winner.

Dr. James Dwight, an early tennis player, who has often been called the "father of American lawn tennis."

The first "National" lawn tennis tournament on September 1, 1880, at Staten Island, New York.

By 1878 the game was not only popular at Nahant and Staten Island but had also spread to Boston, where it was played at the Longwood Cricket Club, and to Newport, Rhode Island. The third Nahant tournament was played that year and Lawrence Curtis won it, but later in the summer Dwight invited players from Newport and Longwood to play at Nahant.

In 1880 E. H. Outerbridge, Mary's brother, convinced his fellows to stage a tournament at Staten Island. James Dwight and Richard Sears were among those entered, as was O. E. Woodhouse. Woodhouse was an Englishman who chanced to be in the United States at the time of the event. He had also been the runner-up in the previous year's All-England. Woodhouse won the tournament with relative ease.

However, there was substantial conflict at the Staten Island event which added to its historical import. The size of the ball used at Staten Island was different from that customarily used in New England and Britain. Partly as a consequence of this problem, Dwight and Sears were knocked out of the doubles competition in the second round. What followed was a request for a standardization of the rules and regulations and the formation of some national body to establish such standards. Clarence M. Clark of the All-Philadelphia Lawn Tennis Committee, and Outerbridge and Dwight representing the Beacon Park A. A. of Boston, signed a statement calling for a meeting to form an association.

This meeting was held in New York at the Fifth Avenue Hotel on May 21, 1881, and its direct result was the formation of the USNLTA. The thirty-six delegates on hand represented nineteen clubs, and another sixteen clubs were represented by proxies. Robert Oliver of the Albany Tennis Club was elected as the first president of the organization. The rules and regulations which had been jointly promulgated by the All-England and the Marylebone clubs in Britain were approved as the United States standards for the game. Later that same year, the first United States National tournament which could truly lay claim to the designation was held by the USNLTA.

Previously, tournaments all claiming to be the National Championship of the United States had been held by various clubs. In 1880 there were at least four such tournaments. But the 1881 event at Newport was, indeed, the National Championship. Dwight was slightly ill at the time of the tournament and played only one round of doubles. But Sears was more than healthy, he was dominating. In 1881 Sears began a reign which encompassed the first seven United States Na-

tional Championship tournaments. It was not until 1888 that anyone else was able to win the event.

Dr. Dwight, however, was zealous in his propagation of the new game. Eventually serving as president of the USNLTA, he was a tireless campaigner for the sport both as a player and an administrator. He had been called a strict constructionist on the rules, and knowledge of his feelings in this area made him the target of an occasional prank. Once, British champion Willie Renshaw packed a box full of ragged old balls while he was umpiring a Dwight match. When Dwight called for new balls, he received the special box. The outburst that followed delighted the spectators who were in on the gag.

One of the things which Dwight immediately sought to promote was international competition, principally between Great Britian and the United States. In America, the sport had been adopted almost exclusively by younger players, which was not the case in England. However, the British had

Tennis as it was played at the Newport Casino in 1881.

many court tennis and racquets players who brought great skill to the lawn tennis game. In the early years of the transatlantic competition, the aggressive play of the young Americans was blunted by the skill and cunning of the older, more experienced Britons. Such was the case when the first Anglo-American series of doubles matches was held.

Since it was evident that Dwight and Sears, as a pair, had only one solid rival in American tennis, it was arranged that they would face the Clark brothers, C. M. and J. S., of Philadelphia, in a pair of matches. The winners of that series would then journey to England for a pair of matches against the finest British players, the Renshaw brothers.

On June 21, 1883, the two United States teams met at Boston; the Clarks won. They repeated their triumph in New York five days later and set sail for England as the United States representatives. In England, the Clarks "did well" in the opinion of *The Field*, "but they were not the equals of the English first rank."

After being beaten by Sears again, 6–2, 6–0, 9–7, in the finals of the third United States National at Newport, Dwight decided to go to England in late 1883 and try his own hand against "the English first rank." After being convincingly beaten by Willie Renshaw, Dwight determined to spend some time with the finest British players and absorb their technique. As a result, he went to Cannes with the Renshaws. During succeeding years he spent much time in the winter in the south of France with the British champions (Willie Renshaw won seven Wimbledons and his brother, Ernest, another), and he formulated sound basic theories about the game by observing their techniques. Partially owing to the substantial amount of time the Renshaws and Dwight spent on the Riviera, that area and neighboring Monte Carlo both became significant strongholds of the new game and remain so to this day.

Meanwhile, the young USNLTA continued to exhibit very strong growth. The first national association in the game (predating England's Lawn Tennis Association by seven years) reported an increase from thirty-four clubs in 1881 to seventy-five plus one regional association by 1890. Associations were being formed by clubs in the same geographic area, and the USNLTA admitted them to membership en masse rather than run the risk that they would form a confederation of their own and challenge the national body for supremacy in the sport. In 1895 the figures had swollen to 106 clubs in membership and ten associations. Shortly thereafter, however, came a sharp drop in membership. Within seven years, the total of clubs and associations in the USNLTA was down to forty-four.

There was some considerable alarm among many of the remaining members. However, the circumstances surrounding this decline appeared to be normal and, for the most part, transitory. Many of the leading players had become involved in the Spanish-American War of 1898, and thus much local leadership was lost either temporarily or permanently. Even more, the impact of the newly popular game of golf was costing the association many member clubs. Shortly, it became evident that the golf fad was going to settle into a responsible pattern, and many clubs rejoined the USNLTA when they found the two games compatible. Many new golf clubs added tennis to their facilities when the members demanded it, and they also became members of the association. A gradual increase in membership began and grew steadily after the low of 1902.

A new area of interest was also adding to the popularity of the game of tennis—women. The first major tournament involving the ladies was staged in 1879, in Dublin, but shortly after a women's tournament was begun in 1884 at Wimbledon. Three years later, the first United States Women's Tournament was held in Philadelphia, with doubles being added to the program in 1890, and mixed doubles, first held in Dublin in 1879, joining the list in 1892.

BALLS, POINTS, AND PLAYERS

One of the controversies surrounding the development of tennis in the United States concerned scoring systems. Prior to the formation of the USNLTA, each club selected a system which it preferred, and they all varied. Many clubs used the straight scoring of one point for each stroke won. Games were often played with the traditional fifteen-point scoring of court tennis, and other variants were introduced along the way.

In court tennis from the beginning of its recorded history, the fifteen-point system was used for individual games. Several theories as to why this happened have been advanced over the years, but the soundest one appears to have a relationship to the sextant of astronomy. The sextant is sixty degrees, or one-sixth of a circle. In early records of the game in France, sets were played to four games. Since sixty degrees make a full circle when multiplied by six, it is thought that matches were six sets of four games each. Therefore, each point was worth fifteen degrees, or points, contributing to the whole. The game concluded when one player completed a full circle of 360 degrees.

Writing in 1555, Scaino informs us that points were scored on the basis of fifteen, thirty, forty-five, and the final point *a una,* when one stroke was needed to win, or *a due* (as in deuce), when two were needed. The final point would, of course, have been sixty. He also notes that the concept of advantage was also used at that time. Most authorities feel that the forty-five was ultimately contracted to forty for the simple reason of ease when the score was called, the "five" just being ignored. In the early 1700s, the set was extended by custom to six games in court tennis.

From that point on, the game of court tennis assumed the shape which was greatly to influence the formation of lawn tennis. The walled court of 110 feet by 38 feet with a net at a height of 5 feet was the custom in England by the start of the Victorian Age. Of course, both the server (striker) and receiver could score points. And use of the walls was paramount to the game, as were the "chases" or floor markings.

Wingfield simplified the game by eliminating many of these latter elements. His concept of simplification did much to popularize the game and broaden its base of participants. It may have been as important to the popularization as the fact that the game was moved outdoors, leaving behind the prohibitively expensive walled court.

One of the impressive advances in the game was the development of the modern ball, as previously noted. In earlier times, balls had been stuffed with hair, cotton, and other material.

When J. M. Heathcote introduced the new flannel-covered ball in England, it was a signal advance.

Another American problem in the early days was team formation. In vogue at one point was to have four players on each side of the net. Gradually, the game evolved into standard singles and doubles, and the teams of three and four to a side virtually vanished after the USNLTA adopted the standard rules of All-England and Marylebone in 1881.

In the process of this standardization on both sides of the Atlantic, another pet of Wingfield's, the name "Sphairistike," also vanished. In an unsuccessful effort to distinguish the game from court tennis, Wingfield used this name for his game in his earliest pamphlets. Since he had obtained patents and sought to profit from the publication of rules, Wingfield was clearly not eager to have the game called "tennis." Many of his friends referred to it as "sticky" by abbreviating his name for it. But when *The Field* group and their All-England compatriots sought to change the game and free it from the Wingfield patents, they pointed to its relationship to court tennis and stated that it should be called "lawn tennis" since it was an outdoor version, modified, of the ancient indoor game. Fortunately for anyone who has to write about it or discuss it, they carried the day on this point. Sphairistike was much too awkward a name, at any rate, to have any degree of general public acceptance, a point which Wingfield eventually acknowledged in good grace but with some remorse.

Wingfield's hourglass court was also a short-lived fantasy. When Julian Marshall, C. G. Heathcote, and Walsh redesigned the game in 1877, they laid out a court twenty-six yards by nine yards, fixing the rectangular shape which the court still retains. They also moved the net posts off the court and placed them three feet outside the edge of the playing area, where they remain. One of the principal differences between the All-England court and the modern one was the height of the net, which was placed at five feet as opposed to today's three feet six inches. As one might imagine, this changed the strategy considerably and made covering the net a much easier task than it is currently.

When Spencer Gore won the first tournament at Wimbledon, he used the side service of racquets with which he was familiar. All of his fellows in the tournament did likewise. In 1878, A. T. Myers introduced the overhead service.

Gore was a progenitor of the net rushing attack, charging up from the baseline to return his opponent's shots until his adversary was worn down. It should also be noted that the courts of the original All-England were a far cry from the carefully manicured lawns of the new club today and the Forest Hills West Side courts. Also, Gore came right up to the net and often hit balls before they even crossed over to his side. After some discussion regarding this tactic, it was decided to permit it. In 1880 the rules were amended to outlaw the practice.

In 1878 P. F. Hadow became the second champion of the Wimbledon Tournament when he developed a simple, but very effective, solution to Gore's tactics. Hadow lobbed over the head of the on-rushing Gore and was skillful enough to drop sufficient shots inside the baseline to win the championship.

With constant exposure, the game began to develop the nuances of offense and defense which have made it a source of constant fascination ever since.

Wimbledon became the center of a rapidly expanding tennis universe. But, thanks to Wingfield, tennis clubs had been established in Scotland, Ireland, Brazil, India, and Germany by the time the first championship was contested at Wimbledon in 1877, as well as several in the United States where courts had been constructed at Nahant, Staten Island, Newport, and Tuxedo, New York. Clubs of one kind or another were subsequently established in France in 1877, Australia, Sweden, Italy, Hungary, and Peru in 1878, Denmark and Switzerland in 1880, and Argentina a year after that. The growth pattern continued with the Netherlands (1882), Jamaica (1883), Greece and Turkey (1885), Lebanon (1889), Egypt and Finland (1890), and South Africa (1892) coming on board shortly thereafter.

One fact was common among all of the groups rushing to join the new tennis rage. The players were almost universally from the well-to-do class in their respective areas. One of the reasons for this was economics. A large lawn had to be available with a minimum of undulations for the game to be played reasonably well. Those with large estates or the financial ability to back a club were the first to join in support of the game.

Emelius H. Outerbridge, brother of Mary, was a scion of a successful and influential Staten Island family. Today one of the major connections with New Jersey is named after the family, the Outerbridge Crossing. It was the impact of this family that helped get the game going in the New York area. The same was, naturally, true of the Dwights, Sears, and others in New England. Because of their fortunate social connections, the tennis-playing families also attracted much more notice in the press than might have been expected. Their diversions were of interest to the general public. They also provided the leadership by example which helped to promote the game quite unconsciously.

During the era of the horse-drawn carriage, when the game came to the United States, the custom was to play in full street clothes. This caused extensive inhibition of movement. Women playing in full hoop skirts with several layers of petticoats didn't move as swiftly as Billie Jean King by a long shot. Clubs commonly posted notices instructing male players not to play in "shirt-sleeves when ladies are present," and many of the early men players played with bowler hats perched atop their heads. The pace of the game was normally not sufficient to disturb the hat.

Even with the addition of a court in Plainfield, New Jersey, the number of U.S. players remained small during the 1870s and early '80s. The addition of Philadelphia to the list of major cities where tennis courts were available, and in 1881 the formation of the USNLTA, started to give the impetus needed to spread the game. Its simplicity was a virtue, and the prosperous and relatively tranquil years of industrial expansion following the Civil War spawned an urge for recreation.

A game of tennis in the earliest days in the United States would only vaguely resemble the high-speed modern game. When four-member teams were common, the eight players would often stand virtually still on the court and pat the ball back and forth across the net without its ever touching the grass. Points were scored slowly when a player muffed a return, and games lasted almost as long as the players felt like playing. Except for the major tournaments and a handful of top players, the game was distinctly a genteel lawn recreation of the wealthy.

Only two basic strokes were common, the slice and the chop. Even though some of the tournament players used the overhead service introduced at Wimbledon in 1878, the majority of the social players stayed with the gentler side service at shoulder level or, sometimes, even underhand.

Another factor in the early days of the game was that a handicapping system was common, with the better players playing from scratch and the lesser ones receiving points. The record of the Nahant tournament in August, 1876, indicates that Dwight and Fred Sears played from scratch while the other eleven players received handicaps ranging up to thirteen points. Dwight played one opponent with a thirteen-point handicap and won, 15–13.

It was due in large measure to these various customs that tennis was treated more seriously by the social press in its early days than by the sporting press. Even some collegiate newspapers contained articles condemning the game. One such article appeared in *The Harvard Crimson* on April 5, 1878:

Allow me a little space to expostulate, not ill-naturedly, I hope, on a kind of athletics that seems to be gaining ground very fast at Harvard. I mean to say Lawn Tennis. There are now four clubs, and perhaps five, that have come into existence here this year. These clubs are generally composed of eight members each; that is, we now have at Harvard from thirty to forty men who devote their leisure hours to Lawn Tennis. Many of these men were formerly seen on the river, forming part of the club fours and sixes; now they have deserted these posts, where as much energy is needed as the College can supply, for a sport that will do themselves little physical good, and can never reflect any credit on the College. Is it not a pity that serious athletics should be set aside by able-bodied men for a game that is at best intended for a seaside pastime? The game is well enough for lazy or *weak* men, but men who have rowed or taken part in a nobler sport should blush to be seen playing Lawn Tennis.

This annoyed penman, a coxswain no doubt, was not entirely atypical, as similar comments were often made about the game at this time. However, the critical point eluded him in his pique. The attraction of the athletically inclined college boys to the game was a major factor in changing the entire nature of the sport. The elements for a fast-paced game were clearly inherent in tennis, they simply weren't being utilized. But they would be.

Growth among the Eastern, mainly Ivy League, colleges continued, and tennis became a major recreation among the students of these schools. It wasn't long before the major Ivy schools—Yale, Harvard, Princeton, and others—formed varsity tennis teams, although they did not compete as a formal league until 1940.

When it was formed, the USNLTA adopted as its purpose the intention "to develop a national scope, to govern the eligibility of clubs, and thus to have control over the qualification of tournament players."

One of the first steps toward these goals was the playing of the National Championship at Newport from August 31 to September 3, 1881. With the numerous victories of Richard Dudley Sears, the tournament became established virtually as a one-man show. It was decided in 1884 to follow the British system and allow the defending champion to "stand out" and meet the winner of the tournament in a Challenge Round for the title. Sears won anyway until 1888, when he did not defend because of an injury. Henry W. Slocum then became the second man to hold the title. Slocum had won the All-Comers Playoff in 1887, but was beaten in the Challenge Round by Sears. When he won it again the next year, he became the champion because of Sears's inability to defend. Incidentally, the Challenge Round was abolished in 1912.

During the years of Sears's reign at Newport, the game was changing. The overhead service became the standard for tournament play and for all of the better amateur sporting types. Lobbing and volleying techniques were improving rapidly as better players were drawn into the game and sought to utilize their athletic skills to the fullest advantage. Human nature exerted its competitive instincts, and the games became more rivalrous and less social. In 1890 Slocum was beaten by Oliver Campbell, who held the title for three years and retired the trophy then in competition. He then retired from competition after his defeat of Fred Hovey in the 1892 final. During the next few years, the dominant player was Bob Wrenn, who made the finals five times between 1893 and 1897.

Wrenn won the crown four times, losing in the final to Hovey in 1895. Malcolm Whitman won the title in 1898 when Wrenn failed to defend. Whitman, likewise, allowed Bill Larned to become the National Singles Champion in 1901 by not defending. Larned was one of the outstanding players of the time, reigning as the intercollegiate champion while at Cornell and finishing as winner of the All-Comers and loser of the Challenge Round four times before 1901.

Larned faced the famous Doherty brothers, Reginald (Big Do) and Hugh (Little Do), in successive years defending his title. In 1902 he beat Big Do, but the next year he lost to Little Do. Holcombe Ward, creator of the innovative "American twist" service, unseated Hugh Doherty in 1904. After Beals Wright and Bill Clothier won the title for a year each, Larned returned in 1907 and won five straight titles. His seven National Singles titles match the record set by Sears and subsequently tied by Big Bill Tilden.

But it was out in California that the next development took place. The game had spread, partially due to its influx into Army bases, to the Pacific Coast not long after its introduction in the United States. Here, unfettered by Eastern con-

Richard Dudley Sears *(left)* and Henry W. Slocum, Jr. *(right)*, the first two United States Singles Champions.

Oliver Campbell defeating Fred Hovey in 1891.

vention, the game had developed, perhaps more roughly in some ways, but into a faster game with almost combative elements.

This was discovered in 1909 when two Californians, Dr. Mel Long and Maurice McLoughlin, came from San Francisco to Newport for the National Singles. Their game was paced to the hard courts of their native Pacific Coast, where the hardness of the court by its very nature speeded up the game. In a thrilling five-set match, they stunned the staid watchers of Newport.

When the National Singles began at Newport, the old Casino was a perfect setting. The matches were played on the flawless lawns next to the Casino itself, and in the first year no grandstands existed. The audience was arrayed around the umpire's chair with the ladies gaily bedecked in their summer finery and quietly reposing under their parasols, while the men stood behind them in full suits, jackets, and starched collars. As the tournament expanded, Newport grew to accommodate it. Grandstands were built and more courts were available for tournament play. By the time Long and McLoughlin had arrived, Newport was the scene of two major sporting events—one was the America's Cup, the periodic world championship of yacht racing, and the other was the National Singles. The National Doubles for men

was played concurrently with the Singles from 1881 to 1889 at Newport, but then was shifted to a different venue as a separate event.

Long and McLoughlin were, unknowingly, spelling the beginning of the end for Newport as the heart of the American tennis universe. During the course of their match, the play became so exciting and intense that the pleasant chat on the verandas and the quiet conversations in the stands ended. The gallery was forced to devote its attention to the match by the sheer energy and excitement of it. At the end, they were standing on their chairs and responded to the finish with warm applause. When the talk resumed, it was about this California style of tennis.

Bill Larned won that 1909 tournament and retained the championship for the next two years as well, but McLoughlin won it in both 1912 and 1913. The face of tennis was changing. One of the most dramatic changes came in 1914 when, after thirty-four tournaments, the last National Singles was played at Newport.

During the years when the American game was growing up at Newport, tennis was also beginning to spread throughout the European continent. It became the favorite of royalty and the nobility in the 1890s and began to organize into competitive form by the turn of the century.

Stars of the early 1900s: *(left to right)* Holcombe Ward, Beals C. Wright, Paul Dalshields, William A. Larned, and William J. Clothier. Incidentally, this group was the United States 1905 Davis Cup team.

was beaten, 5–0. After winning the first Cup round at Boston, the Americans successfully defended at New York in 1902, but were beaten by the British at Boston in 1903. After Britain's defense in 1904, the British Isles defeated the United States two years running and then lost to the Australasians in 1907. For the first time, the Davis Cup was contested in Australia in 1908, with the hosts fending off the United States, 3–2.

Several aspects of the Davis Cup are unique in international sports, but one of the most unusual is that Dwight F. Davis himself was a member of the first two United States teams, winning a singles match in 1900 and losing as a doubles partner in 1903.

The first three matches involved only the United States and the British Isles, but both Belgium and France entered challenges in 1904, Belgium winning the right to face the defender (Britain) by beating the French. The United States did not enter that year, but returned in 1905 only to

Aided probably more than injured by nationalistic feelings then rising in Europe, international matches became popular. Several crowned heads, including the kings of Belgium and Sweden, became both fans and avid players of the outdoor game. Despite the growth of the sport in their countries and in other European powers such as France and Germany, the paramount tennis countries in the years between the turn of the century and World War I were Britain, Australasia, and the United States.

From its inauguration in 1900, the Davis Cup became almost an intramural affair between the United States, the British Isles, and the child of the Empire, Australasia. The last was a combination of Australian and New Zealand talent which was to become a major factor in Cup play. Only once from the first tournament until the suspension in 1915 did any team other than these three play in the Challenge Round. In 1904 Belgium made the final against defending Britain at Wimbledon and

Maurice E. McLoughlin, often called the "California Comet," was a United States star just before World War I.

find itself one of four nations challenging. Thus the Americans had to play through France, captained by the famed Max Decugis, and Australasia, featuring Tony Wilding and Norman Brookes, to get to the Challenge Round.

Brookes and Wilding made a formidable pair, enabling the Australasians to win four straight challenges before being dethroned by the British at Melbourne in 1912. In 1913 the United States regained the Cup for the first time since 1902, with Maurice McLoughlin playing a vital role. After losing in the first round, he won his second singles and teamed with Harold Hackett to win the doubles. Although J. Cecil Parke won both of his singles for the British, the doubles win gave the Americans the Cup, 3–2.

In both 1911 and 1913, the United States team had played preliminary Cup matches at the West Side Tennis Club grounds in New York. The Davis Cup attracted its largest field up to that time with seven challengers in 1913. The United States defeated Australasia, now minus both Brookes and Wilding, 4–1, at New York and then moved to England for the next two matches. In the second round, the United States team met Germany for the first time. The German team was captained by Otto Froitzheim, who happened to be the politically influential chief of police in Wiesbaden.

Froitzheim's influence was of little value as the American team won, 5–0, with four different men participating in the wins. After eliminating Canada, the American team reclaimed the Cup. The

Tony Wilding of New Zealand *(left)* and Norman Brookes of Australia *(right)* were the stars of Wimbledon before World War I. Wilding was killed in action during the war.

(left) The first Davis Cup team *(left to right)* Malcolm Whitman, Dwight F. Davis, and Holcombe Ward and their prize. *(right)* Some thirty years later during USLTA Diamond Jubilee celebration they get together again.

wins at New York and in England stirred press coverage of the Davis Cup and when the 1914 defense was played at West Side, public response was very strong.

So much excitement was created in the New York press for the 1914 Challenge Round against Australasia that the National Singles at Newport became almost an afterthought. Of course, the 1914 challenge for the Davis Cup had a lot going for it. The United States team was headed by the fiery McLoughlin, whose enthusiastic style had captured the public imagination. The Australasian squad included both Brookes and Wilding, two of the big names in international sports. Despite two singles wins by McLoughlin, the Australasian team won the challenge, 3–2.

Tennis at the West Side was played against the backdrop of gathering storm clouds over Europe. Dick Williams won the National Singles later that year at Newport, but the moment was lost in the crush of other events by then.

Still, America in 1915 felt that it would not be drawn into the conflict which was now already worldwide in scale. It was, of course, impossible to have a Davis Cup competition. But that didn't deter the National Singles. In the year of the move to New York, the National title was won by William M. Johnston over McLoughlin in an all-California final.

With almost every other major tennis event in the world suspended due to the "hostilities," the Nationals continued in 1916 with Dick Williams

returning as champion by beating Johnston in the final. Williams thus earned a unique distinction. He is the only man ever to win the National title at both Newport and West Side, where ninety-three of the first ninety-six championships were contested. Williams was also a symbolic link between the old and the new in American tennis. Although the domestic effects of the war were minimal in the United States compared with the physical and political upheaval in Europe, the end of the war brought the beginning of a new era for tennis in the nation.

In this sense, the Patriotic Tournament of 1917 and the National Singles of 1918 were a holding pattern awaiting the dawn of the new era. The only player of reputation available for the competitions in those years was R. Lindley Murray. Many of the top players, including Williams, Johnston, and others, were in the service. Murray was not in combat because he was a chemical engineering graduate of Stanford and was employed by a company producing munitions for the Allied war effort. Despite some severe misgivings on his part about taking time away from his vital job, Murray was convinced to join the tournament in 1917, since the proceeds of the event were to go to the Red Cross for war relief work.

Murray triumphed in the Patriotic Tournament, and as the United States became more deeply involved in the war, his company began to produce explosives for the American government. It was far behind on its orders when the

1918 field was being assembled. Again, however, the proceeds were earmarked for a worthy cause, the Training Camp Activities Fund of the armed services. Murray finally decided to participate again. Although he had only eight days to prepare himself, Murray was the winning finalist. He defeated a young and determined challenger, William T. Tilden, Jr., 6–3, 6–1, 7–5. It was the first of ten Forest Hills finals for Tilden. He would win seven of the next nine.

FIRST NATIONAL CHAMPIONSHIP IN MEN'S SINGLES
Held 1881 at Newport Lawn Tennis Club, Newport, R. I.

First Round	Second Round	Third Round	Semifinal Round	Final Round	Winner
R. D. Sears, Beacon Park Athletic Ass'n, Boston, vs. H. W. Powell, Germantown Cricket Club, Philadelphia	Sears, 6–0, 6–2	Sears, 6–1, 6–2	Sears, 6–3, 6–5	Sears 6–3, 6–0	Sears, 6–0, 6–4, 6–2
Anderson, Staten Island Cricket and B. B. Club, vs. Randolph, Albany Lawn Tennis Club	Anderson, 3–6, 6–5, 6–0				
Nightingale, Providence Lawn Tennis Club, vs. Caldwell, Poughkeepsie Lawn Tennis Club	Nightingale, 6–2, 6–0	Nightingale, 6–4, 6–3			
Barnes, St. George Cricket Club, N.Y., vs. Miller, Newark Lawn Tennis Club	Barnes, 6–2, 1–6, 6–1				
Gray, Beacon Park Athletic Ass'n, Boston, vs. Hines, St. George Cricket Club, N.Y.	Gray, 6–5, 6–3	Gray, 6–0, 6–0	Gray (bye)		
Coggswells, Albany Lawn Tennis Club, vs. Congdon, Providence Lawn Tennis Club	Coggswells, 6–4, 6–5				
T. A. Shaw (bye)	Shaw	Shaw, 6–3, 6–4	Shaw, 3–6, 6–4, 6–1		
Rathbone, Albany Lawn Tennis Club, vs. Saunders, St. George Cricket Club, N.Y.	Rathbone, 6–5, 5–6, 6–5				
Kessler, Staten Island Cricket and B. B. Club, vs. Pruyn, Albany Lawn Tennis Club	Kessler, 6–1, 6–4	Kessler, 6–1, 6–2		Glynn, 6–2, 6–2	
G. M. Smith (bye)	Smith				
W. Gammell, Jr., Providence Lawn Tennis Club, vs. A. Newbold, Young America Cricket Club, Philadelphia	Gammell, 1–6, 6–3, 6–1	Gammell (bye)	Glynn, 6–3, 3–6, 6–4		
R. F. Conover, Newark Lawn Tennis Club, vs. Morse, Poughkeepsie Lawn Tennis Club	Conover, 6–1, 6–1	Glynn, 6–5, 6–2			
Glynn, Staten Island Cricket and B. B. Club, vs. Rives, Newport Lawn Tennis Club	Glynn, 1–6, 6–1, 6–1				

THE ROARING TWENTIES AND BIG BILL TILDEN

Tilden was to become the dominating force in men's tennis during the 1920s, an era often termed (not without reason) "the Golden Age of American sports." With the end of the war, all thoughts turned toward the normalization of life-styles. An ailing President Woodrow Wilson was pushing a League of Nations concept, but the leaders of the victorious European nations instead pushed a vengeful Versailles Treaty upon the defeated countries. The centuries-old Hapsburg and Hohenzollern dynasties collapsed. Prohibition of alcoholic beverages and votes for women became new parts of the United States Constitution.

But America's dramatic and decisive role in the war raised public spirits to new highs. Prosperity was overwhelming America. The old order was changing, the Ford brought efficient transportation to the masses, the tabloid newspapers brought the public giant heroes, and soon radio was to bring the world into living rooms.

Paul Gallico, sports editor of the New York *Daily News*, along with such journalistic giants as Grantland Rice, sought to glamorize sports and glorify its heroes. Babe Ruth burst on the American scene with his towering home runs and mas-sive bravado; Yale gave America Albie Booth, "the watch-fob quarterback"; and tennis contributed Tilden. He was the finest player of his time and was fit and measured for the hero's mantle even though he seldom sought publicity with the eagerness of Ruth or heavyweight champion Jack Dempsey.

But Tilden's contribution to popularizing the game of tennis cannot be underestimated even from the distance of half a century in time. It almost seems that all that had gone before Tilden in tennis was merely a foundation for the construction of his edifice. He caught up the swell of emotions, money, and publicity in the furious pace of the decade that became known as the "Roaring Twenties." He was a larger-than-life character of the Ruth, Dempsey, and golf great Bobby Jones mold. The American public demanded a giant for every sport and Tilden was the man of tennis.

Many of the disparate events leading to this cresting of the tide were, indeed, the very roots of the sport's major events. Dwight Davis and three of his Harvard mates had set out on a tour to California in 1899 for the purpose of playing East versus West amateur tennis matches on an informal basis. A pair of Bostonians—Beals Wright and Malcolm Whitman—Holcombe Ward of Orange,

Lawn tennis stars in service during World War I: *(left to right)* Lt. Col. Dwight Davis, Maj. R. D. Wrenn, Maj. W. A. Larned, Capt. Watson Washburn, Capt. Norris Williams II, Capt. D. S. Walters, Lt. Dean Mathey, and Col. W. C. Johnson.

"Big Bill" Tilden and "Little Bill" Johnston with two USLTA officials looking over the awards before a meet.

New Jersey, and Dwight Davis traveled to the Pacific Coast during the summer recess and played matches against two brother combinations in California. After matches against Sumner and Sam Hardy and George and Robert Whitney, the Crimson foursome returned through the northwest in time for the resumption of fall classes at Cambridge. The trip was evidence enough for young Davis that an international tennis competition was a viable idea.

The Davis Cup was established in February, 1900, and formally contested for the first time that August in Boston. It was to become one of the great forums upon which Tilden would make grand statements with his racket for the benefit of an eager public.

During the 1920s, the United States dominated the Davis Cup to a great extent. Yet the more the Americans won, the more nations sought the chance to beat them. The greater the United States team seemed and the more publicity it generated, all the more eagerly did countries promote the sport to produce a team capable of defeating the Americans.

William (Little Bill) Johnston, who vanquished McLoughlin in the first Forest Hills National Sin-

gles, defeated Tilden in 1919, 6–4, 6–4, 6–3. The United States did not enter the Davis Cup competition that year, although it was resumed with Australasia, captained by the redoubtable Brookes, defeating Britain, 4–1.

In 1920 Tilden and Johnston met again in the finals at the old West Side Club. Tilden took the first set and Johnston the second, both by scores of 6–1. The eerie duplicating pattern continued as the two men again split sets. Tilden took the third, 7–5, and Johnston the fourth, 7–5. Tilden had won the first and third sets and he was able to retain the symmetry by winning the fifth. The 6–3 win gave him the match, three sets to two, and his first United States National Singles.

Both Tilden and Johnston made the maximum contribution as the United States captured the Davis Cup by unseating Australasia. In the first round against France, both won singles matches, and they teamed for the doubles as the United States won, 3–0. Against Britain for the right to challenge, the United States swept to a 5–0 win with Tilden winning twice in singles, Johnston winning twice, and the two pairing again for doubles. At the Domaine Cricket Ground in Auckland, New Zealand, the United States duo re-

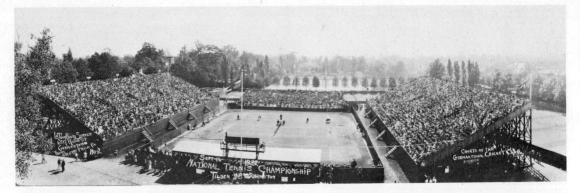

When Tilden and Johnston met, there was always a full house, as shown above during the 1922 National Tennis Championships held at the Germantown Cricket Club.

peated their sweep to recapture the Cup with the loss of only five sets, although Johnston had to rally from a 2–0 deficit in his second singles to beat Brookes three sets to two.

Until 1927 the United States successfully turned back every challenge to its Davis Cup possession, the longest such successful defense in the history of the competition. In 1920 only five nations challenged. By 1923 the number had grown to sixteen, by 1926 it was twenty-three.

Meanwhile, the Germantown Cricket Club in Philadelphia had enlarged its facilities and become a bidder for major tennis events. In 1921 the National Singles were played there for the first time. Tilden retained his title by beating Wallace Johnston in straight sets in the final. He won there again in 1922 and 1923 over Billy Johnston. Then, in 1924, with the completion of the new stadium at Forest Hills, the tournament returned to the West Side Tennis Club, where it was to remain through 1977, being transformed into the United States Open in 1968.

But Tilden remained constant. He defeated Billy Johnston in 1924 in the inaugural of the new courts and again the following year. Tilden had to scramble to win the 1925 title, taking a thrilling five-setter against the never-say-die Johnston. Johnston won the first set and Tilden fought his way to an 11–9 win in the second. He forged a two-set-to-one edge by winning the third, only to have Johnston force a fifth with a 6–4 win before Tilden put it away, 6–3. For six straight years Tilden had now won the final, five times beating

Billy Johnston. Three of the five went five sets. It was classic tennis—Big Bill against Little Bill—and it captured the public imagination.

The slow but steady recovery of Europe from the carnage of the Great War was producing a dynasty of its own in France. In 1924 the Olympics were held in Paris. The first international athletic carnival since the war had been held in Antwerp, Belgium, in 1920, but it was a subdued affair. Paris in the 1920s was a free-wheeling celebration. The Olympics were a jewel in the crown city of the Continent. The Games themselves symbolized the recovery of France from the ravages of war. Tennis was an Olympic sport and the 1924 Games produced a clean sweep of the events for Americans.

What resulted from this was that the sport was dropped from the Olympic roster, where it had been since the start of the modern Olympics in 1896. The winners in that competition gave an indication of American dominance in the early 1920s. They were Vincent Richards in the men's singles, Helen Wills in the women's singles, Mrs. Hazel Wightman and R. Norris Williams in the mixed doubles, Richards and Francis T. Hunter in the men's doubles, and Miss Wills and Mrs. Wightman in the women's doubles. Prior to the five-event sweep in 1924, the only United States winners in Olympic competition had been Beals Wright, who won the singles in 1904 at St. Louis and paired with Edgar Leonard to win the doubles that year.

Tilden's serve had been clocked in his heyday at

Bill **Tilden** was "the" man tennis player of 1920, if not of all time.

124 miles per hour crossing the net. His backhand was nearly as awesome as his forehand. The only player in the world his near-equal at his peak was Billy Johnston, the five-feet six-inch, 121-pound mighty mite.

Tilden was an enormous egocentric and, among other things, a Francophobe. He once said of Jean Borotra, a leading Frenchman of the day, "he achieves first-class results with second-class technique and he has the enchantment, the color, the charm and, most important of all, the insincerity of Paris." It was in Paris, indeed, that the seeds of the destruction of the Tilden-American powerhouse were being sown, even as the United States ran through the Olympics like a knife into warm butter.

Four Frenchmen had been drawn together in 1923 by matches against Ireland in Dublin. By the end of the decade this quartet was to dominate Tilden and Johnston and, thereby, the world of tennis. They were to become known as the "Four Musketeers." Toto Brugnon, Henri Cochet, Jean Borotra, and René Lacoste were Frenchmen with little else in common. They were separated by the full distance of their native land and from the eldest (Brugnon) to the youngest (Lacoste) by a spread of twenty years. But, in combination, they were to bring France to the pinnacle of tennis and give the country the only significant stretch of dominance it has ever enjoyed in the sport.

Although their climb had been a continuous one during the early years of the decade, it had been almost unnoticed by, certainly, the American press and public until 1926. That year, the gallery of West Side was somewhat uneasy in witnessing an all-French final to the United States Nationals. Lacoste disposed of Borotra in straight sets to become the first non-American to win at Forest Hills. Even more startling was to be his victory in 1927 when Lacoste, then twenty-two, defeated Tilden, 11–9, 6–3, 11–9, to repeat his triumph with an impressive trump.

To make the French tennis demonstration even more impressive, Lacoste failed to defend successfully in 1928, but he was succeeded by Henri Cochet, who downed Francis Hunter in a tough five-set final. Tilden recouped somewhat in 1929 when he won his record-equaling, seventh United States title by downing the luckless Hunter, who lost another five-set heartbreaker. Tilden, in totaling seven wins at Forest Hills and Germantown, produced what is probably the most incredible record in the history of United States singles play. Although he tied the record previously set by Richard Sears and W. A. Larned, Tilden achieved his mark under much greater handicaps. Sears won the first seven National Tournaments at Newport and played against smaller fields composed almost entirely of native talent. Also, his last four titles (from 1884) were won in a challenge-round circumstance.

Under that formation, the defender "stood out" of the tournament while the remainder of the field played through the draw in an "all-comers" competition to determine which one had the right to challenge the defender for the title. Therefore, Sears won four of his seven crowns by the playing (and winning) of a single match against an opponent who had just finished a full

Tennis was popular in the 1920s, as witnessed by the gathering in New York's Central Park for an exhibition between Vinny Richards and Bill Johnston.

draw. Larned was likewise the beneficiary of smaller fields and the Challenge Round. He won his last title in 1911, the final year of the Challenge Round.

Tilden won all of his titles by playing through the entire draw, generally against an all-star field including the best foreign competition. Tilden also won three times at Wimbledon, including two of the so-called "world championship on grass" tournaments in 1920 and 1921. At the time of its establishment in 1913, the International Lawn Tennis Federation (ILTF) sought to reward Wimbledon for its service as the cradle of the modern game. Therefore, it bestowed this lofty title upon the All-England tournament at Wimbledon.

Tilden was also unique in that he did not become a world-class player in the true sense of the word until he was twenty-eight. In 1920, when he won both Forest Hills and Wimbledon, Tilden was virtually a self-resurrection project. First ranked as America's Number One in 1915, he was unable to win big matches in major tournaments because of his feeble backhand, which was a weak chop. After losing the 1919 United States final to Johnston, Tilden retired to Providence, where he spent an entire year working on his backhand

until it was the equal of his forehand or, put simply, the best in the world. From that point forward, he was the world's top player.

It is possible that the moody Tilden could have won even more titles at Wimbledon had he tried to do so. After 1925 he remained more and more land-bound in the United States, almost defying would-be challengers to come and find him in his lair. There was also a political motivation involved here. Tilden and the USNLTA (which dropped its "N" in 1920 and became the USLTA) had been conducting an uneasy arm's-length truce for several years.

Tilden opened himself to charges of commercialism by lending his name to several journalistic endeavors which ran him afoul of the USLTA. He was also under constant pressure from the Association to maintain some kind of records to support the large expense vouchers he submitted for trips abroad for Davis Cup defenses and other competitions. At one point, the USLTA flatly refused to pay his extravagant expenses.

In retrospect, it is perhaps easy now to say that Tilden should have been entitled to a private cabin for his transatlantic crossings. But Association officials felt that he should not be shown undue favoritism because of his stature. The rightness or wrongness of this attitude is not at issue since it was, indeed, the fact.

But the journalism problem was much more severe than the constant bickering about accommodations and expenses. The matter of Tilden's writings caused rules governing amateurism in tennis to be rewritten. One writer said, "No player has ever flouted the amateur rule with the persistence —and success—of Bill Tilden." Yet Tilden, for his part, was more honest than many of his successors, who privately accepted sub rosa payments for their services in the years of "shamateurism," before open tennis cleansed this festering sore.

It was long abundantly clear that Tilden was making considerable profit from his newspaper and syndicated writing ventures about tennis. The USLTA felt that this constituted a violation of the amateur code which forebade a player "from profiting directly or indirectly from the game."

Tilden's counter-claim was in two parts. One was that he was a writer before he was a tennis champion, and the second was that he interpreted the rule to prohibit teaching of tennis for money by championship players, not writing about matches in which he was playing. The Association met these objectives head-on in 1924 when it revised its rules on the recommendation of its Amateur Rules Committee. The new rule stated that no player could write about tennis in any publication if he was compensated for so doing.

There was considerable squirming both within the Association and among the players over this ruling. Up to that time most of the substantial writing about tennis in magazines, books, and newspapers had been done by the players. In fact, it was clear that the writings of the players themselves had done much to progress the game and spread its popularity. In addition to creating a class of people known as "tennis writers," as distinct and apart from the players, the new rule was also a direct hit at Tilden. But it turned out that Tilden did not have to fight this battle at the outset. Such was the furor over the new ruling about writing, that a committee of seven was set up to study the player-official controversy.

Among the members of the committee was Grantland Rice, who remarked that "it's a matter of taste, not amateurism" as to whether a player writes about tennis or not. In 1925 the committee came back with a compromise recommendation which was tailored to fit Tilden as an outcast without prohibiting writing about tennis by players in general. The rule was also ameliorated to the extent that its breech did not constitute professionalism per se, but rather exposed the violator to suspension for a period of time. The new rule was stated in these terms:

1. A player was not allowed after February, 1925, "the use of his titles or statement of his reputation won on the tennis courts in connection with books, newspaper, magazine or other written articles, motion pictures of himself, lectures or radio talks, for which he is to receive any payment or compensation."

Two of France's great players of the 1920s and '30s: Jean Borotra *(left)* and Henri Cochet *(right)*.

Vincent Richards was one of the all-time great doubles players.

2. A player was not permitted to write "for pay or for a consideration, current newspaper articles covering a tournament or match in which he is entered as a competitor."

Tilden at this time was estimated to be making an average of $25,000 a year from the Philadelphia *Public Ledger* and its syndicate for his writings on tournaments in which he participated. Tilden almost immediately wrote an article about a tournament in which he was playing following the promulgation of the new rule. A meeting of the Executive Committee of the USLTA was called to debate this transgression on August 1, 1925. After generating 117 pages of minutes, the Committee decided to put Tilden on notice that any further violation on his part would result in a suspension.

All of this controversy tended to obscure some of the goings-on taking place on the court. But by 1926, it was no longer possible to obscure the steady rise of the French "Musketeers," who posed a strong threat to American domination of the Davis Cup. France had been beaten back in 1925, 5–0, at Germantown, and the following year

lost again but reduced the margin to 4–1 when Lacoste defeated Tilden in four sets in the fourth singles after the United States had clinched the Cup.

Then came the climactic confrontation of 1927. Again, the venue was Germantown. After the playdown of the twenty-three challenging nations had once again produced France as the challenger, the United States met the Frenchmen for the third straight year. On the first day, Lacoste defeated Billy Johnston and Tilden beat Cochet in four sets. On the second day, it all came apart for the Americans. Tilden split sets with Lacoste, but the Frenchman then won the third and fourth, 6–3, 6–2. Needing only to win the next singles for the long-coveted Cup, France got the win from Cochet. He, too, split sets with Johnston and won the next two, 6–2, 6–4. The United States won the doubles to make the final margin 3–2, but the Cup was on its way to Paris.

With the longest dominance in the history of the competition at an end, the Americans set out to regain the Cup. But another squabble between Tilden and the USLTA intervened. In its wake it was to leave an aura of bad publicity for both parties, which lasted for many years.

In June, 1928, Tilden (then captain of the Davis Cup team) was competing at Wimbledon, and while there he filed daily press reports back to the United States on the tournament. Almost immediately, an executive committee meeting was called for July 17. The first meeting failed to resolve the matter. It was clear to most members that Tilden had taken a direct affront to their amateur rule, and that a suspension was mandatory. However, the prestige of Tilden was enormous and suspending him was tantamount to throwing away the upcoming challenge for the Davis Cup. A second meeting, on August 24, was called and it was determined to suspend Tilden forthwith. The Davis Cup team was en route to Italy for its final match for the right to challenge. The United States had won over Mexico, China, and Japan earlier in the year with Tilden captaining and leading the squad.

Tilden did not face Italy. He was removed as the playing captain and replaced by Joseph Wear. With Francis Hunter and John Hennessey carrying the major burdens, the United States managed to defeat the Italians 4–1 as Hunter made his first Cup appearance that year and won a pivotal first singles over Placido Gaslini, 6–1, 6–1, 6–0. Hennessey then won his two singles and teamed with George Lott to take the doubles. But the French were something else altogether, and everybody connected with the United States team knew it. There was also another problem.

By winning over the Italians, the battling second-line American players had unwittingly kept the controversy alive. The United States press was bannering the story on page one as a daily occurrence, pushing aside many heavy international stories. There were two reasons for this. One, Tilden was a major American hero and a man with an enormous public reputation. Two, he was seen by much of the press as one of their own. After all, he was being punished for writing newspaper articles.

In short order, the situation became a major international cause célèbre. Tensions between the French and American governments became acute over the matter. America's ambassador in Paris, Myron T. Herrick, caused the State Department to appeal to the USLTA to repeal the ban. After the application of this pressure, the Association rescinded the suspension for the duration of the Davis Cup Challenge Round. The French, who had constructed the new Stade Roland Garros in Paris for the matches, were fearful that Tilden's absence would seriously damage the gate receipts and were relieved when the suspension was lifted.

However, the ban was reinstated when Tilden returned to the United States after the French successfully defended the Cup with a 4–1 victory. The only United States win was Tilden's first singles over Lacoste. Tilden was suspended for six months after his return and was granted reinstatement on February 8, 1929, at which time he was also restored to the United States Davis Cup team.

During the next two years, Tilden again resumed his position of dominance, winning his final Forest Hills in 1929 and his third and last Wimbledon in 1930. But still another incident was to spice his final years as an "amateur." He agreed to a contract for $3,000 to cover the 1930 Davis Cup matches.

This last hurdle was cleared when a compromise was worked out whereby Tilden was permitted to write reflective comments on the matches after they had been completed. Following the major events of the 1930 season, Tilden turned professional and severed his connection with the USLTA and the problems of amateur tennis. Before departing the international amateur scene, however, Tilden took one more fling at regaining the Davis Cup for America, but it was unsuccessful as the French again beat back the United States challenge, 4–1, in 1930. Once more, the lone United States point was scored when Tilden won his first singles match against Borotra.

France retained the Cup in 1931 by defeating a British squad and in 1932 turned back a United States challenge before being beaten in 1933 by Great Britain. But the 1932 United States team at Roland Garros was reflective of the changes in the American tournament tennis scene after the removal of Tilden. The 1932 American squad was built around the talented Ellsworth Vines and Wilmer Allison. The California game came to the fore with Tilden's departure and John Doeg, a nephew of May Sutton Bundy, was the Forest Hills titlist in 1930, followed by Vines for the next two years.

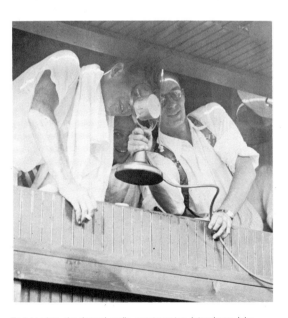

Ted Husing, the famed radio sportscaster, interviews John Doeg after his 1930 victory, in the press box at Forest Hills.

Vines was ranked eighth in the United States in 1930, but shot to the top of the rankings with his successive wins at West Side. He defeated Davis Cupper George Lott for his first championship and steamrollered Cochet in the 1932 final, winning in straight sets, all by 6–4 scores. Vines repeated his win over Cochet in the 1932 Davis Cup challenge, winning an epic five-setter, but was beaten by Borotra in singles, and the French kept the Cup, 3–2.

Fred Perry, a popular and energetic British star, was the next pretender to the throne vacated by Tilden. Perry won at Forest Hills in 1933 and 1934. He defeated Jack Crawford of Australia for his first United States National title and Allison for his second. Perry also led the British team to its victory over the French for possession of the Davis Cup in 1933. Having ended the six-year reign of the French team in Cup play, the British fought off American challenges in 1934 and 1935 and an Australian one in 1936 before the United States in 1937 finally brought the Cup back to the country of its origin for the first time in more than a decade.

It was Don Budge, when he was on the verge of becoming the first man ever to score the Grand Slam in tennis, who was responsible for the return of the Davis Cup to the United States. But Budge

Ellsworth Vines was one of the most powerful players in the history of tennis.

George Lott *(left)* and Lester Stoefen *(right)* were considered by many as one of the greatest doubles teams.

first had to struggle to displace Perry as the best player in the world. In 1935 Perry sought his third straight Forest Hills crown and was knocked out in an early round by Allison, who went on to win the championship in a surprise. Perry suffered a heavy fall in his match against Allison and was shaken up to the degree that it may have affected his play. Regardless, Allison eventually defeated fellow American Sidney Wood in the final. A year later, Perry came back to Forest Hills and won there for the third time in four years, defeating young Budge in the final.

However, the final match was a heroic confrontation that was to give an indication of things to come. Budge won the first set, 6–2, and after Perry won the next two to go up 2–1, Budge stormed back with a convincing 6–1 win in the fourth set. In the decisive fifth, Perry ultimately prevailed, 10–8, in a finish that left the crowd limp by the end of the match.

Once more, the world was beginning, grudgingly, to face the possibility of another worldwide war. But in 1937, the final acceptance of this realization was still ahead. That year, Budge became the first American finalist at Wimbledon since the losing Ellsworth Vines in 1933. He faced perhaps the finest player ever produced in Germany, the

Baron Gottfried von Cramm, winner of the 1934 and 1936 French finals, making his third straight appearance in the All-England championship match. The pair had met previously in the Interzone Davis Cup final in 1935, when Budge won in four sets. The American repeated this win with even more gusto, sweeping von Cramm in straight sets, 6–3, 6–4, 6–2, to win his first Wimbledon. In the 1937 Davis Cup final for the right to challenge Britain for the Cup, the two met again in the match which would decide the challenger.

Both von Cramm and Budge had won their first singles. The Americans had taken the doubles and Henner Henkel defeated Bitsy Grant of the United States in the other singles. The von Cramm–Budge match would determine the challenger to Britain's hold on the Cup. Since the British team was considered ripe for the picking, the winner of the United States–German match was rated odds-on to win the Cup. Wimbledon's famed Centre Court was the site. It was a scene which appeared to be a disaster for the American right from the first. Von Cramm swept through the first two sets, 8–6 and 7–5. Then with the match and, probably, the Davis Cup within his grasp, von Cramm began to fade. Budge won the third set, 6–4. The American evened the match by taking the fourth, 6–2. With the world watching and many observers pinning heavy political im-

pact on the outcome, the two men prepared for the start of the fifth set. Germany sought the potential propaganda edge that the Davis Cup might bring. Adolf Hitler was still smarting under the sting administered by Jesse Owens in the 1936 Berlin Olympics. Radio carried the match around the globe.

Von Cramm was under heavy pressure from Berlin. Budge was under no political pressure whatever, which probably made matters worse. He bore the burden of American hopes and he knew it. In the tenseness of this almost unbearable pressure, Budge battled to an 8–6 win in the fifth set. By winning the last three sets, he had won his match, the right to challenge, and, as events proved, the Cup. The Americans ran over the undermanned British, 4–1, in the Challenge Round, with Budge winning two singles matches and teaming with Gene Mako on the winning doubles pair. Budge did engage in a marathon 15–13 set with Charles Hare in his first singles, but otherwise he was almost invincible against the British, dropping only one singles set.

In 1938 Budge scaled a height never before achieved and unequaled for nearly a quarter of a century thereafter: the traditional Grand Slam. He won the Australian, French, Wimbledon, and United States singles titles in the same year. Not until 1962, when Rod Laver first did it, was any

Both sides in World War II lost good tennis players, but two of the greatest killed in action were Joseph Hunt of the United States *(left)* and Henner Henkel of Germany *(right)*.

Ted Schroeder slips after making a difficult return to Bobby Riggs in the 1941 Nationals. Riggs went on to defeat Frank Kovacs in the final.

other conflagration with Germany and no championships were held in either country. Adrian Quist won the Australian and Don McNeill outlasted Riggs in five sets to win at Forest Hills.

Meanwhile, the United States conducted a successful defense of the Davis Cup in 1938, with Budge again in the forefront. He defeated John Bromwich and Quist in his two singles as the United States stood off an Australian challenge, 3–2, at Germantown. But, in 1939, without Budge, the Americans once more lost the Cup. Australia won it at Philadelphia's Merion Cricket Club after a peculiar sequence in which Americans Riggs and Frank Parker won both singles on the first day and then lost both on the third day. In between the Australian pair defeated the United States tandem of Jack Kramer and Joe Hunt in doubles and the Cup went down under. For Quist and Bromwich, the win was a vindication of their loss the prior year. For the United States, it was an indication of the value of the retired Budge. With the outbreak of the Second World War, the Cup went into storage until competition was resumed in 1946.

other man able to accomplish this unique sweep. Jack Crawford had come perhaps closest to achieving the Slam before Budge. He led Perry, two sets to one, in the Forest Hills final of 1933 after having won the three earlier championships. But Perry won the final two sets, the match, and the United States crown. In 1934 Perry himself missed winning only at Roland Garros. But Budge won them all. In fact, compared to the struggles of 1937, the Grand Slam was almost too easy for Budge. After easy wins in Australia and France, he defeated Henry Austin at Wimbledon in straight sets and fellow American Gene Mako, often his Davis Cup doubles partner, in four at Forest Hills.

Within the next year, political events took center stage. The 1939 championships saw the emergence of Bobby Riggs as the American star to succeed Budge. When Budge did not defend at Wimbledon, Riggs won there. He defeated Elwood Cooke in five sets to win the All-England and then routed S. Welby Van Horn in three sets to take his Forest Hills championship. But by 1940, England and France were engulfed in an-

MAY, HAZEL, SUZANNE, AND THE TWO HELENS

Almost from the outset, women were a major part of the American competitive tennis picture. But it took them much longer to become accepted as a spectator attraction comparable to their male counterparts.

One of the earliest of the top-notch women players was Adeline King Robinson of Staten Island, who won the first ladies' championship played at the Staten Island Cricket Club in 1878. For the next decade, she was a formidable force in women's tennis, both in singles and with a variety of partners in doubles and mixed doubles.

Miss Robinson scored a notable victory over Ellen Roosevelt, 6–0, 6–4, at Hastings-on-Hudson in 1887. In that same tournament, she played on winning teams in doubles (with Alice Smith) and mixed doubles (with her brother). Earlier that summer, she swept all three titles at the Long Island championship played at the Meadow Club.

The "Big Four of the Belmont Cricket Club of Philadelphia":
(left to right) Bertha Townsend, Margaret Ballard, Louise
Allderdice, and Ellen Hansell.

By 1888, Miss Robinson's game was on the down slide, but she still reached the finals of the Narragansett tournament that year in mixed doubles (with H. A. Taylor) before losing to Ellen Roosevelt, her old rival, who was partnered with Oliver S. Campbell of Columbia University, the National Singles champion in 1890–91–92. She also made the finals of the mixed doubles in the women's nationals at Philadelphia in 1888 but then faded from the scene.

In part, of course, the slow development of women's tennis was the result of inhibiting social mores. The demure ladies of the 1880s and 1890s, for the most part, were much too prim in their approach to tennis to have their game be treated as much more than a social recreation. On the other hand, the men's game at that time wasn't all that much better.

Not all of the ladies were demure in their approach to the game, however, and much of the impetus for the first women's national tournament came from Philadelphia where the so-called "Big Four" of the Belmont Cricket Club—Ellen Hansell, Margaret Ballard, Bertha Townsend, and Louise Allderdice—pushed for the development of a full program for women.

It was no surprise that they got it, although when the first women's tournament was organized at the Philadelphia Cricket Club in September, 1887, it was not recognized by the USNLTA. That barrier was breached two years later.

Of the four pioneers, Misses Hansell and Townsend proved to be the best players. Miss Hansell won the first singles championship of the United States at the age of seventeen in 1887, defeating Laura Knight in the final match, 6–1, 6–0. Miss Townsend (who, as Mrs. Toulmin, made the semifinals as late as 1906) was the titlist the following year, downing Marion Wright in the all-comers final, 6–2, 6–2, and her friend and clubmate, Miss Hansell, in the challenge round.

Miss Townsend successfully defended in the challenge round a year later. One of the factors that made Bertha so difficult to defeat was that she played lefthanded. By virtue of this, she is today generally credited with having discovered the backhand. Ellen Roosevelt played her way through the field in 1890 and discovered a way to counter Miss Townsend's southpaw style to win, 6–2, 6–3, in the challenge round, a form which was not eliminated from the tournament until 1919. Prior to that year, the defending champion was allowed to "stand out" until a survivor among all other players had been determined. Then the defender played one match against that survivor.

With her second victory, Miss Townsend took two legs on the trophy which was then the prize of women's tennis, a silver tennis girl upholding a silver platter with the whole in the form of a small epergne. But that trophy was not, in fact, to be retired by any of the "Big Four." It was to go into the permanent possession of the first girl to win three titles. This honor fell to Juliette P. Atkinson in 1898. But the "Big Four" dominance ended well before that. In 1890 two sisters from outside the Philadelphia clique that started women's tennis history in the United States, Grace and Ellen Roosevelt of New York, cracked the tournament by winning the doubles, and Ellen captured the singles.

Mabel Cahill came close to beating Miss Atkinson and winning the silver tennis girl. She won the singles for two years running and lost the final to Aline Terry in 1893 when she defaulted due to illness. After single-year reigns by Miss Terry and

Four of the better-known lady players at the turn of the century: *(left to right)* Helen Gilleandeau, Marie Wagner, Elizabeth Moore, and Grace Gilleandeau.

Helen Helwig, Miss Atkinson won her first singles in 1895. She repeated in 1897 and 1898 and made the final four straight times between 1895 and 1898.

Juliette Atkinson was easily the superior player of her day. She was a smallish, wiry girl who was outstanding at all of the outdoor sports of the time. In 1894 she won her first major titles, teaming with Edwin Fischer to take the National Mixed Doubles and with Miss Helwig to win the Ladies' Doubles. She won the doubles with Miss Helwig again the next year and won the singles final against her doubles partner. In 1896 she paired up with Elizabeth Moore to win the doubles and lost to Miss Moore, 6–4, 4–6, 6–3, 6–2, in the singles final.

Seven times in nine years Juliette Atkinson was a member of the winning doubles combination and achieved this distinction with five different partners. She won her last doubles title in 1902, but by that time she had already been supplanted as the reigning queen of singles by Elizabeth Moore, her one-time doubles partner. Miss Moore defeated Miss Atkinson for the Singles Championship in 1896 and by 1905 had won a total of four singles plus two mixed doubles titles in partnership with Wylie C. Grant.

Already the base of women's tennis was beginning to broaden, even if only slightly, and the principal competition for the two top Easterners in the closing years of the century was Marion Jones, the best of the Pacific Coast. She invaded the East in 1899 and twice won the singles, adding

a doubles with Juliette Atkinson in 1902 and a mixed doubles with Raymond Little in 1901.

In England, tennis was also showing an accelerated growth on the distaff side. The British produced two top female players before the end of the century—Charlotte Dod and Blanche Bingley. Miss Dod won the Wimbledon title five times from 1887 to 1893 and Miss Bingley, as Mrs. W. G. Hillyard, was the champion six times between 1886 and 1900. In 1898 a British writer said, "Miss Dod was by far the best lady player that the lawn tennis world has yet seen." It was to see much better, but Lottie Dod was a pioneer. She showed heretofore uncommon volleying power, as well as outstanding baseline power. Mrs. Hillyard was noted for her groundstrokes and what one observer called "the most indomitable resolution." Miss Dod won her first Wimbledon at the age of fifteen and remains as one of the youngest competitors in the history of the event, although her record was approached by America's Tracy Austin in 1977. Just to show that her athletic ability was not a one-dimensional thing, Miss Dod was also a top golfer and won the British Ladies' Golf championship in 1904.

May G. Sutton was the next outstanding product of the Pacific Coast, and she won both the singles and doubles in 1904. But she achieved a most singular distinction the following year when she became the first American to win a Wimbledon title, defeating the defending titleholder Dorothea Douglas in the final. Miss Douglas, later

May G. Sutton was the first American to win at Wimbledon

A section of the gallery at the 1908 Women's National Championships at the Philadelphia Cricket Club.

famous as Mrs. Lambert Chambers, won seven Wimbledon finals between 1903 and 1914. Miss Sutton defeated her in the 1905 title match, 6–3, 6–4, and then unseated Mrs. Lambert Chambers again in 1907, 6–1, 6–4. Ironically, May Sutton was born in England but raised in California. She derived her inspiration for tennis from that famous 1899 tour of the Harvard boys led by Dwight Davis. Following her marriage to Thomas Bundy, she remained active in tennis, and Mrs. Bundy was a member of the 1925 Wightman Cup team that defeated Great Britain, 4–3, at the West Side Tennis Club.

It was California that was to produce the next two outstanding women players in America—Hazel Hotchkiss and Mary K. Browne. Hazel Hotchkiss was nothing short of outstanding and burst upon the American tennis scene somewhat as her fellow Californian, Maurice McLoughlin, had done in the men's game. Starting in 1909, she swept the singles, doubles, and mixed doubles for three straight years, pairing twice with Edith Rotch and once with Eleanora Sears in the doubles. Her mixed doubles partners were Wallace Johnston in 1909 and 1911 and Joseph Carpenter, Jr., in 1910. In 1915, after her marriage to George W. Wightman of Boston, she again made the finals in singles, losing to Molla Bjurstedt.

She made the finals in 1919 and won this time, becoming the only woman to win the event from 1915 to 1922 except for the dominant Molla Bjurstedt. Mary K. Browne duplicated the feat of Miss Hotchkiss by winning the singles, doubles, and mixed doubles three years running in 1912, 1913, and 1914. She also earned the distinction of being the Number One player on the first official USNLTA rankings ever issued for women in 1913.

But in 1915, Molla Bjurstedt came onto the scene and was the most prominent woman player for the balance of the decade. She became the first to win four tournaments in a row with her victory in 1918. However, the 1917 triumph was in the Patriotic Tournament held that year in lieu of the Nationals. But in the course of winning four straight years over all competition, she defeated four different opponents in the finals, giving some indication of her dominance.

After being displaced by Mrs. Wightman in 1919, she came back as Mrs. Mallory and won three more years in succession—1920, 1921, 1922 —again defeating different opponents in the finals. Mrs. Mallory's seven triumphs, including the Patriotic of 1917, came at the expense of seven different women, not one having been faced more than once. Among her victims in the finals were Mary K. Browne in 1921 and Helen Wills in 1922.

But the 6–3, 6–1 triumph of 1922 was merely staving off momentarily the ultimate emergence of Helen Wills. The following year, the final was a rematch between Mrs. Mallory and Miss Wills. This time, Miss Wills made short work of the defending champion, defeating her 6–1, 6–4.

Like all human endeavors, the following triumphs of Helen Wills Moody and Helen Jacobs were built on a foundation. As in all cases, this foundation was built by the hardy pioneers who preceded them and blazed the trails. The "Big Four" of Philadelphia, whose enthusiasm and persistence won a place on the sports calendar of America for women's tennis, began the process. The great champions of the last decade of the nineteenth century, principally Juliette Atkinson and Elisabeth Moore, set a level of competition for

Hazel Hotchkiss after she captured her third straight title in 1911.

her long-distance walks, Miss Sears was a member of a respected family who showed that women could participate in many varied athletic activities without causing revolutions or losing their essential femininity. Tennis was only a part of her contribution to the American scene, but she made the finals in singles in 1912, losing to young Californian Mary K. Browne, and played on winning teams both in doubles and mixed doubles. She played on four winning doubles combinations, two with Hazel Wightman and two others with Molla Mallory. She played on the 1916 winning team in mixed doubles with Willis E. Davis. Aside from tennis, Eleanora Sears was outstanding in swimming, squash, riflery, and golf. Then there were her famous walks from Boston to various points around the country, often in the company of college boys and her lady friends, or both. She was an advocate of exercise for women and showed its undeniable value at a time in which much controversy was being expended over the

their time ranked high among these. Mrs. Wightman made a unique contribution in the form of her lifelong dedication to the sport and her donation in 1923 of the Wightman Cup, an international team trophy for women. This was originally intended as a counterpart of the Davis Cup, but after the successful defense against Britain in 1923 at the new stadium of the West Side Tennis Club, it was decided to restrict it to competition between the women of the two great English-speaking nations. May Bundy gave American women world tennis status with her victory in the Wimbledon championships and made an even more permanent psychological impression with her victory over Dorothea Lambert Chambers in 1907, showing that an American woman could win a major foreign event on skill, not as a fortunate one-year happenstance.

But it was probably Eleanora Sears who had the most profound influence, not just on tennis but on all sports for women in this country. Famous for

Mary K. Browne *(left)* and Molla Bjurstedt *(right)* were America's two leading players before World War I stopped tournament play.

franchise for women. Her lasting contribution was perhaps best summarized in *Pictorial History of American Sports* by Durant and Bettman:

At first the daring young woman horrified New England conservatives with her tomboyish activities. But she demonstrated that a woman could play men's games without causing a revolution. She won her cause and was a prime liberator of women in sports.

In the process of improving the caliber of their play, the tennis players also moved away from the early encasements of costume as well as custom. Marie Wagner, a five-time indoor champion, once described the turn-of-the-century standard clothing in the following terms: "No girl would appear unless upholstered with a corset, a starched petticoat, a starched skirt, heavily buttoned-trimmed blouse, a starched shirtwaist with long sleeves and cufflinks, a high collar and four-in-hand necktie, a belt with silver buckle, and sneakers with large silk bows."

By 1920 the ladies had rid themselves of most of the starch, and the ever-growing interest among them in the sport was beginning to produce more and more world-class players. Perhaps foremost among these was Helen Wills, the losing finalist to Molla Mallory in 1922. After her triumph the following year, she was to win six more National Singles titles, the last in 1931. Her entrance came at the height of the Golden Age of Sports and made her name nearly as well known as that of Big Bill Tilden. Her principal competitor during her early years remained Mrs. Mallory, but Helen Wills was generally the favorite of the galleries due to her American origins. Although she became an American citizen as Mrs. Franklin Mallory, Molla Mallory was a Norwegian who had won that country's singles title eight times before coming to the United States in 1914. As a transplanted Yankee, she originally worked as a masseuse and played tennis as a hobby. While Molla Mallory gave American women's tennis an immeasurable lift during World War I and the years immediately following, Miss Wills made it truly American.

Interestingly, Molla Mallory played mixed doubles on many occasions with Tilden, and the pair twice won the National title. She played a number of memorable matches, including her victory over "Bunny" Ryan in the 1926 Forest Hills finale. But Miss Wills became the first American woman to win the French championship and the first United States woman since May Sutton Bundy to win at Wimbledon. She won eight All-England titles, never losing in a final match. Despite her many triumphs at Wimbledon, Helen Newington Wills, later Mrs. Moody, remained indelibly associated with Forest Hills and, more particularly, the new stadium at West Side which was opened in 1923.

The Philadelphia Cricket Club was the host of the Women's Nationals from their inception in 1887 until 1920. The singles and doubles were

Helen Wills is considered by many the greatest woman player ever.

The famous Moody–Jacobs contest which Miss Jacobs won.

transferred to Forest Hills in 1921. With the opening of the new stadium, the men's events, which had been held at the Germantown Cricket Club for two years, returned to Forest Hills. The women's events were staged in August with the men following in September.

In her first appearance in the finals, Helen Wills was a fifteen-year-old starlet who captured the heart of the crowd. With the opening of the new stadium, the girl who came to be known as "Little Miss Poker Face" captured the title as well as defeated Mrs. Mallory, who annexed her final title in 1926 when Miss Wills did not defend. In her first three finals, Helen Wills defeated Mrs. Mallory twice and Kathleen McKane once, losing only one set in three years. But her invincible streak came to an end when she did not compete in 1926, but returned the following year and resumed her usual pattern of destroying her opposition.

"Little Miss Poker Face," as her nickname might indicate, played a cool game with an almost total absence of flair. She was a mechanical perfectionist who was a genius at placement and unerringly accurate with her shots. She steadily wore down an opponent without any seeming sign of emotion regardless of the outcome of a point, set, or match.

Betty Nuthall, later to become the first non-American to win the title at Forest Hills, was beaten in the 1927 final and then came one of the

long succession of confrontations with Miss Wills's arch-rival from California, Helen Jacobs. Between them, the two Helens were to virtually dominate women's tennis for more than a decade on both

Fred Perry and Helen Jacobs ruled the lawn tennis world in the mid-1930s.

sides of the Atlantic. From 1923 to 1938, the pair combined to win eleven United States national singles, nine Wimbledon singles, four French, and one Italian, or a total of twenty-five major singles titles. Of these, Helen Wills Moody accounted for nineteen, but six times faced Helen Jacobs in the finals of major tournaments, winning five of the six.

Immediately following World War I, a young French girl, Suzanne Lenglen, became the hottest European name in tennis. She won the first postwar Wimbledon in 1919. And then she won the first postwar French title in 1920, repeating at Wimbledon the same year. She won both the British and French crowns four straight years before missing at Wimbledon in 1924 when her finals victim of the year before, Kathleen (Kitty) McKane, won by beating Miss Wills in the final. Miss Lenglen then won both crowns again in 1925 and the French for the seventh year running in 1926. This remarkable run gave her a total of thirteen out of fifteen Women's Singles Championships at Wimbledon and France. Suzanne Lenglen was an international name in tennis. In 1926 she turned professional and made a rather disappointing world tour, largely against the aging Mary K. Browne.

It is possible that Miss Lenglen could have also won both of the Wimbledon tournaments during this time. In 1924 she was incapacitated by the illness which also prevented her participation in the Olympic Games in Paris. It was the Olympics of Antwerp in 1920 that had helped rocket her to international stardom as she rode through to the ladies' title by winning sixty of sixty-four games in her matches. Her final Wimbledon appearance in 1926 was a bizarre series of misunderstandings heavily larded with prima donna emotionalism. When her second-round singles match was rescheduled for the benefit of Queen Mary, the French star arrived four hours late, causing an Anglo-French uproar. Rain then postponed another match and the upset Miss Lenglen resigned from the tournament, returned to France, and signed a professional contract with Charles C. Pyle, the American promoter. She died of leukemia at the age of thirty-nine, mourned as a national heroine in France.

Miss Lenglen made only one appearance at Forest Hills, and that was perhaps a misguided mistake when she was in less than good health. She was beaten by Mrs. Mallory in 1921. One observer of the match at the old Central Court of West Side that day wrote an engaging description of Lenglen. "She spoke in an animated fashion with all those who crowded around her. She impressed me, especially when I saw her with her six rackets. Her short-sleeved tennis outfit, with its short skirt,

Betty Nuthall of Great Britain was the first non-American to win the Women's Singles title.

was the first seen in the States. Her black hair was held in place with a brightly colored headband, and her figure was delicate with very slim ankles. The white of her shoes was dazzling as she sped about the court. As soon as I had seen that match, I knew what my goal would be, and what kind of tennis I wanted to play." The writer of these words? Helen Wills. She had won the Girls' 18 Singles tournament that year at Forest Hills and was rewarded with a seat at the Lenglen–Mallory match as a prize.

Helen Wills later did a good deal of writing for both newspapers and wire services and wrote a novel and a charming biography. Her writings tend to belie the stolid nature of her on-court decorum, which bordered on stiffness. She remained aloof throughout her career as a player and was in many ways better received at Wimbledon than at Forest Hills, the British having somewhat more of an appreciation for natural reserve in personality than do Americans.

One of the classic confrontations in the history of tennis promotion was the famous match between Miss Lenglen and Miss Wills at the Carlton Club in Cannes in 1926. After weeks of worldwide publicity, which included numerous stories somewhat long on imagination and short on fact, the two played in a mixed doubles match against one another and then faced off in what was to be a two-match series of singles.

With fans packed into every cranny of the tiny club and hundreds seated on rooftops, Miss Lenglen won the first set, 6–3, and appeared to have won the second when the crowd swarmed onto the court. However, the match was officiated by a full crew of senior officials from England, and linesman Lord Charles Hope finally fought his way through the swarming mass to the umpire's chair and denied that he had made the match-ending "out" call. The second set was then resumed after the confusion subsided. Ultimately, the tiring Miss Lenglen won the second, 8–6, and then retired to a kiosk constructed for the event, drained both emotionally and physically.

Remaining on the court, the still-fresh Miss Wills was all but ignored by the excited spectators. One, however, went straight to her. Freddie Moody proposed to Helen Wills on the court and the two were ultimately married in 1930. Regret-tably, Miss Wills suffered a sudden attack of appendicitis and was unable to compete at Wimbledon. Nearly lost in the confusion of the Wills illness and the Lenglen furor was the victory in the fiftieth anniversary of Wimbledon by Kitty McKane, now Mrs. Godfree.

With Lenglen having turned professional, Miss Wills won the next four Wimbledons, twice defeating little Lili Alvarez, bettering Helen Jacobs in 1929, and Bunny Ryan in 1930. Of their four meetings in Wimbledon finals, Miss Wills defeated Miss Jacobs in all four and, all told, Miss Jacobs won only once in their fifteen head-to-head matches. That victory came in the 1933 Forest Hills final and was marred by Mrs. Moody's retiring at 8–6, 3–6, 3–0, due to the pain of her dislocated lumbar vertebra.

Her withdrawal caused a massive public outcry and she said later that on sober reflection she "would have rather passed out on the court." Indeed, it appeared that that might be the next thing to happen when she painfully walked to the umpire's chair and withdrew. The default enabled Miss Jacobs to retain the Forest Hills title she had won for the first time the previous year. It was also the final appearance in a United States final for Mrs. Moody. Her nine finals had begun with a loss in 1922 and ended with another in 1933. In between, she had won seven titles. Although she never won again at Forest Hills, Mrs. Moody continued to win at Wimbledon. She took the title there in 1933, 1935, and again in 1938. She won a record eight championships at the All-England and also played on three winning doubles teams and one mixed doubles championship pair. In France, Mrs. Moody won the singles in 1928, 1929, 1930, and again in 1932.

Helen Jacobs, a lifelong enemy of Mrs. Moody, was her precise opposite in terms of performing personality. She was lively and energetic. As a result, she became one of the most popular of all United States women champions. But Helen Wills, with her international exploits and her daring challenge of the great Lenglen, had raised women's tennis to a point where it was considered to be one of the major sports and earned it coverage on a par with that of the men's game around the world. Miss Jacobs capitalized on this new condition with vigorous play and championship per-

The first non-American finals for the Women's title occurred when Anita Lizana of Chile *(left)* and Jadwiga Jedrzejowska of Poland *(right)* met in 1937. Miss Lizana won.

formances at Forest Hills in 1932, 1933, 1934, and 1935. She also played on three doubles championships and one mixed doubles winner. At Wimbledon, she was much less fortunate, winning only once (1936) and losing five times in the finals, four of them to Mrs. Moody. Helen Jacobs never won at Roland Garros but did take the Italian title in 1934.

Still another Californian, Alice Marble, broke the Jacobs string at four in 1936. She was unable to repeat the next year and a unique occasion took place as a result. Forest Hills had its first final in the women's singles in which no American was involved; Anita Lizana defeated Poland's Jadwiga Jedrzejowska. But the Alice Marble story was more important. Thought at one time to be suffering from tuberculosis, Miss Marble, one of America's most promising tennis talents, was removed from the game. With the help of her tennis teacher, Eleanor Tennant, she fought her way back into competitive shape after it was learned that she was actually suffering from pleurisy complicated by anemia. She was also buoyed by a letter from famous actress Carole Lombard, who told her of her own fight back to her career after

it had apparently been ended by illness. After stumbling in 1937, Miss Marble came charging back to take the United States title in 1938, 1939, and 1940, beating Helen Jacobs in the final at Forest Hills in each of the last two years. Miss Marble also won at Wimbledon in 1939 by whipping Kay Stammers, 6–2, 6–0.

But the 1939 Wimbledon was the last held before the onslaught of still another war. The war years removed almost all foreign competition from the field, and with the greats of the previous decade no longer a factor, the Forest Hills title was taken by Mrs. Sarah Palfrey Cooke in 1941 and 1945, with Pauline Betz winning three straight titles in between Mrs. Cooke's victories. With informal encouragement from the Roosevelt administration, Forest Hills, like most major American sporting events, kept going on a limited but spirited level during the war. Louise Brough and Margaret Osborne joined with Miss Betz and Mrs. Cooke in producing exciting matches.

One of the highlights of the period between the wars was the increasing popularity of the Wightman Cup matches, which were to remain for four decades the major international team competi-

Alice Marble was one of the finest women players.

Molla Mallory and Mrs. May Sutton Bundy played as a doubles team in 1925, and Mrs. Mallory was a singles player in each of the first three matches.

In 1923 the United States swept the first series, 7–0, at the new stadium of the West Side Tennis Club. The following year, the series moved to Wimbledon and made its first appearance at the new Wimbledon created by Captain Stanley Peach. The new Centre Court had been opened initially for the 1922 championships.

Increasingly, the demand for tickets had been rising far beyond the ability of the old Centre Court on Worple Road to handle. Thousands were annually turned away during the fortnight's second week, when the majority of the matches were contested in the main stand. In the "new" facility, the Centre Court had a capacity of about 14,750 and its principal auxiliary, Court 1, could hold 5,000. It should be noted that in the ensuing years

tion for women in the tennis world. Wightman Cup matches became one of the annual highlights of the calendar at Forest Hills and Wimbledon during the 1920s and 1930s, as the championship alternated back and forth between the United States and Great Britain. Since the two nations produced a majority of the finest caliber female players, the competition often produced exciting and historic matches.

Almost all of the outstanding stars of women's tennis participated in these matches to some extent. Part of the reason for this was the expanded format in comparison to the Davis Cup. The men played four singles and one doubles for a total of five matches. The women played five singles matches and two doubles, which produced different combinations in doubles and had the natural effect of expanding the teams on both sides.

Mrs. Wightman herself was among the legendary early players in women's tennis in the twentieth century to have played in the first few matches in this series. She captained the first United States teams in 1923 and 1924 and played on winning doubles combinations both years. Mrs.

Mrs. Sarah Palfrey Cooke during the late 1930s and early 1940s won many events.

Suzanne Lenglen, one of the most outstanding women players.

The turnabout was achieved simply for Britain by a remarkable reversal of almost all individual results, Helen Wills and Mrs. Mallory both going down to two defeats in singles to Phyllis Covell, who had not even played singles in the first meeting the year before.

After a 4–3 win by Britain at Forest Hills in 1925, the entire United States team was restructured, and by 1926 no players from the first team in 1923 played at Wimbledon for the Americans. The United States pulled out the victory by a 4–3 win when Mary K. Browne and Bunny Ryan won the second doubles on the final day over Mrs. Kitty McKane Godfree and Evelyn Colyer, 3–6, 6–2, 6–4.

After the first eight matches were evenly divided, the United States began a nine-match streak in the series in 1931. By 1939 the United States had a lead of 13–4 in the Wightman Cup when the war suspended the competition. When play was resumed in 1946, the United States team, including Pauline Betz, Margaret Osborne, Louise Brough, and Doris Hart, blasted to successive 7–0 triumphs and a 6–1 victory in 1948 as Mrs. Wightman captained the team for the thir-

further expansions were made that raised the capacity of Centre Court to 15,000 by the 1970s and that of Court 1 to 7,500. At its opening on June 26, 1922, King George V made the formal dedication and the affair was a high social occasion. The weather, however, was most uncooperative and rain bedeviled the tournament throughout that year.

Still smarting from its shutout defeat in the inaugural, the British team rebounded with a spectacular 6–1 win in the second Wightman Cup competition in 1924 at the new Wimbledon. The teams for the first series the previous year included Helen Wills, Mrs. Mallory, Eleanor Goss, and Mrs. Wightman for the United States and Kitty McKane, Mrs. R. C. Clayton, Mrs. W. Geraldine Beamish, and Mrs. B. C. Covell for Britain. In 1924 the teams were essentially the same for the United States with only Mrs. Marion Zinderstein Jessup, a member of four winning Forest Hills doubles teams, added. The British women also added to their doubles contingent, with Mrs. D. C. Shepherd-Barron and Evelyn Colyer joining it.

Kitty McKane, later Mrs. Godfree, was one of Great Britain's great women stars of the late 1920s.

The first all-German final at Wimbledon occurred in 1931 when Cilli Aussem *(left)* met Hilda Krahwinkel *(right)*. Miss Aussem won, but Miss Krahwinkel (as Mrs. Sperling) won many of Europe's leading titles.

teenth and final time. In 1949 it was another 7–0 victory for the United States squad. The Americans won twenty-one straight times before the British halted the streak, 4–3, at Wimbledon in 1958, the first win for Great Britain since 1930.

The British won again in 1960 at Wimbledon before the United States won twelve of the next thirteen. After two more British wins in 1974 and 1975—the first back-to-back defeats for the Americans since 1924 and 1925—the United States extended its dominance by winning the next two meetings, 5–2 and 7–0. The 1975 loss at Cleveland was the first defeat for the American team on United States soil since 1925 at West Side, but the victory two years later at Oakland, California, was the first shutout by a United States team since 1954 and the first 7–0 shutout since 1953. In 1974 the series moved indoors and left the traditional venue of Wimbledon and the outdoor stadiums of the United States. The popularity of this move was best illustrated by the Oakland crowd of 11,317 for the final 1977 matches, the largest ever for Wightman Cup play in the United States.

TENNIS CUPS RUNNETH OVER

In the 1920s and 1930s, the concept of the Davis and Wightman cups led to a host of cup competitions in restricted areas and classes such as the Federation Cup, the Mitre Cup, the Prentice Cup, the King of Sweden's Cup, and the Butler Cup. In recent years, more such competitions have begun with the World Cup, the Dubler Cup, the Bell Cup, and the Stevens Cup. There are others of lesser interest as well.

The Mitre Cup is the Davis Cup of South America. It has stimulated development of the game in that continent. Originated in 1920, it was donated by an Argentinian sportsman whose family boasted a president of Argentina and founders of the famous newspaper *La Nacion*. Virtually every South American player of note has appeared in this competition or in the Patino Cup Tournament, the South American Junior Championships.

In 1936 the King of Sweden's Cup was endowed by Gustav V. It was the indoor version of the Davis Cup for Continental Europe and in 1975 came under the control of the European Tennis Association. The next year, it developed into a league format. Under the original formula, the Cup was won seven times by Sweden, six times by Denmark, four times by Britain, and three times by France. Other countries having won at least once were Yugoslavia, Italy (two), Czechoslovakia, and Spain. Play was suspended from 1939 to 1951 as a result of World War II and its aftermath.

Play for the Butler Cup, or more properly Cups, was also begun in the period between the two world wars by American George Butler, who was a regular winter resident of the French Riviera. The Cups are played for annually in a variety of classes, one of which is doubles. In the men's doubles competition, the entering teams must be composed of two players of the same nationality.

A proliferation of new competitions began after the end of the Second World War, including the Galea Cup (1950) for boys under twenty-one in Europe; the Annie Soisbault Cup (1965) for girls under twenty-one in Europe; the BP Cup (1975), a European team competition for both boys and girls twenty and under; and the World Cup (1970) and Bell Cup (1972), which are team competitions between Australia and the United States for, re-

President Harding meets with the 1921 United States Davis Cup team: *(left to right)* A. Y. Leach, F. S. Myrick (president of USLTA), Watson M. Washburn, Col. C. O. Sherrell (aide to the President), Samuel Hardy (captain of Davis Cup team), President Harding, Wallace F. Johnson, R. N. Williams II, William T. Tilden II, and C. Christian (Secretary to the President).

spectively, men and women.

One of the more interesting of the postwar cups is the Dubler (1958), which is often called "the Davis Cup for Veterans." It is a senior men's competition originally presented by Switzerland's Leon Dubler and conducted by the Veteran's International Tennis Association (VITA) on a challenge-round basis. Italy dominated the early play, winning the Cup seven times in its first ten years. In 1968 the United States entered the Association and promptly won the Cup five straight years, losing it to Australia in 1973, regaining it the next year, and losing it again to Australia in 1975. Italy won its eighth Cup in 1976 and the United States its seventh in 1977.

Richard Stevens of Buzzards Bay, Massachusetts, donated the Stevens Cup (1961) and it, too, is an international team competition for senior men. The United States has dominated competition for this trophy since its inception, winning it the first eleven years it was in play. Canada, five times a runner-up to the United States, finally broke this dominance in 1976. This Cup honors the memory of Mr. Stevens's father, Richard, Sr., who ranked in the first ten nationally eight times between 1892 and 1905.

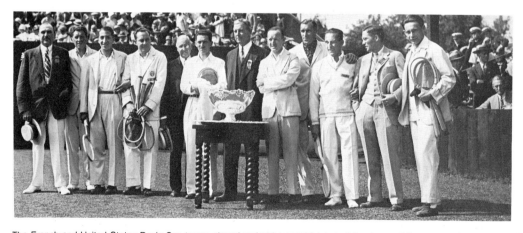

The French and United States Davis Cup teams played under the watchful eye of the donor of the cup.

In pre–World War II days, the Davis Cup team traveled by boat. The 1934 United States team of Frank Shields, L. R. Stoefen, and Sydney Wood practice aboard the S.S. *Paris*.

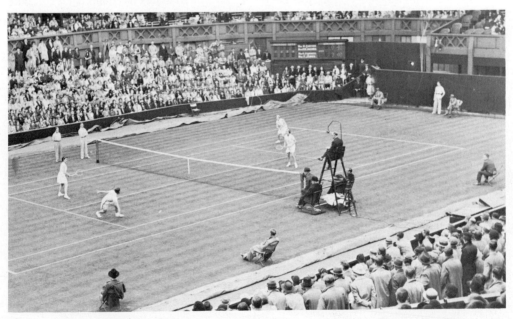

The deciding match of the 1936 Wightman Cup matches played at Wimbledon. Helen Jacobs (going for the ball) and Mrs. Sarah Palfrey Cooke defeated Kay Stammers and Freda Jones 1–6, 6–3, 7–5, and the United States retained the Cup 4 matches to 3.

Early United States *(top)* and British *(bottom)* Wightman Cup teams.

In 1928, Bill Tilden and Wilbur Coen (nearest the camera) of the United States defeated Bunny Austin and C. H. Kingsley of Great Britain in the Butler Cups final at Monte Carlo. The famed clubhouse and terraces of this beautiful tennis complex are in the background.

AMERICANS, THE ILTF, AND THE OLYMPICS

One of the unique records in Olympic sports is that of the United States and tennis. Americans have won every event in tennis in which they have been formally entered. Like all records of this kind, of course, numerous complications and an involved trail of events surround it.

When the Olympics were revived at Athens in 1896, men's singles and doubles were the only events on the program, and the United States did not enter a team. In 1900, when the Games were held in Paris for the first time, the United States not only did not enter but the USNLTA passed a resolution opposing entry into the competition. The events turned out to be a tour de force for Britain's Doherty brothers, who won men's singles (Hugh doing the honors), mixed doubles (Reggie with Charlotte Cooper), and men's doubles.

In 1904, however, the Games were held in St. Louis, and since they were in this country, the Association allowed participation. Beals Wright, then the United States Doubles Champion with Holcombe Ward, made an appearance at St. Louis and won the singles. He then teamed with E. W. Leonard to win the doubles competition. Since there were no other events on the schedule, the United States had a clean sweep of the available honors. The sport then was reduced to a women's singles in 1908 (won by Mrs. Dorothea Lambert Chambers of Britain), but reappeared in full flower in 1912. The Association did not formally participate in the Stockholm Games, but did approve the entry of individual players who might want to play on their own. But the absence of a formal entry diminished interest.

With the 1916 Games canceled due to World War I, the next Olympics were those held in 1920 in Antwerp. Again, a peculiar circumstance arose, one with which tennis was to become all too familiar in the years ahead. The United States Nationals and the Olympic tennis program were to be held on conflicting dates. By now, the wartime experience had broadened the scope of Americans and the entire country was more oriented toward international competition. Thus the USNLTA made a request to the Olympic officials in Belgium that the dates of the tennis competition be advanced to July. The Belgians responded that they were unable to make such a change in the schedule since the program and planning were already too far developed. As a result, the Association was unable to enter the 1920 Games, although thirteen tennis nations did send teams. The best-known result of the Antwerp Olympics in tennis was the performance of Suzanne Lenglen. Having already won the 1919 Wimbledon, the young French star was sensational in the Olympics. She not only swept the singles title but also won the mixed doubles with Max Decugis.

Then came the 1924 Olympiad at Paris where, possibly aided by the indisposition of Miss Lenglen, the Americans swept all five events on the program. The results were as follows:

Men's Singles—Vincent Richards (US) def. Henri Cochet (France), 6–4, 6–4, 5–7, 4–6, 6–2.

Women's Singles—Helen Wills (US) def. Diddie Vlasto (France), 6–2, 6–2.

Men's Doubles—Vincent Richards and Francis Hunter (US) def. Henri Cochet and Toto Brugnon (France), 4–6, 6–2, 6–3, 2–6, 6–3.

Women's Doubles—Helen Wills and Mrs. Hazel Wightman (US) def. Mrs. Phyllis Covell and Kitty McKane (Great Britain), 7–5, 8–6.

Mixed Doubles—Mrs. Wightman and R. Norris Williams (US) def. Mrs. Marion Zinderstein Jessup and Vincent Richards (US), 6–2, 6–3.

Watson Washburn, Lillian Scharman, and Edith Sigourney were also members of the United States team, but they did not make the finals in any of the events.

One of the great ironies of the scenario here is that a major reason for the dropping of the tennis program at the Olympics was a conflict between the Games' organizers, the International Olympic Committee, and the International Lawn Tennis Federation. In itself, there was a strange twist to the formation of the ILTF. The idea for an international organization for the sport was originally generated by an American, Duane Williams. It was clear, he stated, that the growth of tennis would be worldwide, and thus there should be an

America's victorious Olympic tennis team: *(left to right, seated)* Edith Sigourney, Eleanor Goss, Mrs. Marion Zinderstein Jessup, Mrs. Hazel Wightman (captain), Helen Wills, and Lillian Scharman. *(standing)* Watson Washburn, Dr. Sumner Hardy (President of the California Lawn Tennis Association), Vincent Richards, Francis T. Hunter, Richard Norris Williams (captain), and Julian Myrick (Chairman of Davis Cup and International Committee of the United States Lawn Tennis Association).

organization of international stature to help regulate that growth. But when the organizational meeting of the group was held in Paris and the ILTF formed in 1913, the United States was not represented. Williams had spoken to the Secretary of the Swiss LTA who in turn presented the idea to Henry Wallet, the influential president of the French LTF. Wallet greeted the idea with great enthusiasm and set about organizing a meeting of the world's national associations for the purpose of banding them together in such an organization as Williams had envisioned. While there was no reasonable dispute as to the concept, the USNLTA had some serious differences with the new group.

One of the problems was inherent in the American group's support of the Davis Cup. The USNLTA was reluctant to back any movement which might detract from the Cup which the United States authorities felt was the championship of the world. Another problem was the desire of the member nations joining the new group to reward Britain for being the cradle of the game. They intended to award Britain a perpetual "world championship on grass" event to be held at Wimbledon. There was also a controversy about the strictness of amateur rules. The proposed rules of the new Federation were somewhat tighter than those in use in the United States, and the USNLTA declined to alter its own code.

Over a period of years, these disputes were discussed on an almost annual basis, but it wasn't until 1923 that action to resolve them was taken. The USLTA passed a resolution in which it stated that if at any time the ILTF would abandon the award of the world's championship on grass event to Britain (or any country for that matter), it would join the international body. In March, 1923, the ILTF met and made some sweeping changes in its rules. It abolished the World's Championship, adopted universal playing rules, and also recognized the national tournaments of Britain, France, Australia, and the United States as the "Big Four" events annually. Thus mollified, the USLTA promptly ended its decade-long holdout and joined the ILTF, making it a truly representative international tennis organization.

In one of its first major moves after the Americans joined it, the ILTF presented a set of demands to the International Olympic Committee regarding further tennis competition in the Games. The demands were:

1. The ILTF to be granted at least one representative on the IOC.
2. The ILTF be permitted to cooperate in the technical and material organization of lawn tennis at the Games.
3. The amateur definition of the ILTF to be adopted by the IOC for governing participation in tennis at the Games.
4. The holding of the Olympics in any one year would not be construed to cancel or supersede the holding during that year of any officially recognized lawn tennis championships or competition.
5. The Olympics not be regarded as "a championship of the world in lawn tennis."

Swiftly, the IOC rejected these demands and dropped tennis from the Olympic program. In 1968 the sport was returned to the program on a nonmedal basis, with Manuel Santana defeating Manuel Orantes in an all-Spanish final for the men's singles exhibition, and Helga Niessen (now Mrs. Masthoff) of West Germany defeating Peaches Bartkowicz of the United States, 6–4, 6–2, for the women's singles. A United States mixed doubles pair, Herb Fitzgibbon and Julie Heldman, won that competition in the Mexico City Games.

In the 1970s, efforts were undertaken to have tennis restored to the Olympic event list on a medal basis. Officially, the ITF (which removed "Lawn" from its title in 1977), sought to have the sport restored in time for the 1984 Olympics in the event that an accommodation could be worked out to the satisfaction of both the IOC and ITF.

A move in the direction of having tennis as a part of major international sports competitions was the inclusion of the game in the Pan American Games. This inclusion produced a sweep of honors for the United States entries in the 1975 Games, but it also demonstrated that the world of tennis, changing as it was, could work with international competitions.

PEACE, SCHISMS, AND TURMOIL

With the end of the war in both Europe and the South Pacific, a degree of normalcy returned to the tennis firmament. It also brought with it the winds of change. Of all major sports, tennis was perhaps most resolute in its resistance to the postwar explosion of professional sports. The history of the game from 1945 well into the 1960s was largely one of the movement toward professionalism and open tennis.

At first, tennis and professionalism moved on corollary but distinctly separate paths. During the formative years of the game, few major stars had ever turned professional and none had done so at the peak of his career. Even Big Bill Tilden, the giant of them all, turned professional only after many years of brilliant play in the major tournaments of the world and at a time when his skills were beginning to erode with advancing age. Tilden, of course, had begun his career extremely late in life by normal standards for such things, and he was well into his 30s before turning professional.

Consumed by a drive to maintain the purity of their game, the ruling class of tennis officials in the major nations actually created three classes of players. The first was the basic recreational tennis player: leisure-seeking businessmen, homemakers, students, and part-time club players. The second was the outright professional who toured in a tight-knit unit with a small number of his own fellows, almost outcasts from the general world of tennis. The third was that group of amateur players who continued to perform regularly on the approved circuit of nonprofessional events and major tournaments.

It was in this last class that the real difficulty arose. The principal players of this group traveled around the world for the prestigious events at Wimbledon, Roland Garros, Forest Hills, and Australia as well as the lesser, but growing, ones in Italy, Monte Carlo, South Africa, the Caribbean, New Zealand, and Canada. They also played in regular events at Sea Bright, New Jersey, Newport, and other similar spas of the well-to-do. These events were generally held under the sponsorship of one or more wealthy patrons.

Over the years, it became abundantly clear that these players had little, if any, other visible means of support besides tennis playing. Since they were not professional, they could not play tournaments for prize money. What arose from this was a system of sub rosa payments often disguised as lavish "expense" allowances and often simply disguised. The term *shamateurism* was coined by the American press to describe this state of affairs. Early on, most major officials refused to acknowledge that such a situation even existed. Thus conditions were frozen in an impasse for nearly a generation.

A new group of tennis leaders came into gradual control in the years after the middle 1960s. Accustomed to the flow of money into tennis, they saw the need to recognize the problem and agreed that it existed. Some even began pushing for some sort of recognition of professionalism as a fact of life in tennis. This was at first a minority view, but one which rapidly gained ground in the United States and Great Britain. Against much resistance, these countries pushed to the forefront movements to open tournament play and Davis Cup competition to professional players. The eventual and, some would say inevitable, triumph of their viewpoint brought about the open era and the game's greatest growth explosion.

In 1945 tennis in the United States was prepared to welcome the return of players from other nations around the world. Within a year, the international tennis circuit was restored to nearly its prewar status, and the major events which had been suspended by the war were among the first events to return.

Sports on all levels experienced a spectator growth unrivaled in the history of the nation during the first few years after the war. Building booms spurred the economy and returning servicemen found only slight difficulty in becoming reemployed. Leisure time on a scale never before imagined became the standard in America. The acceleration of mechanization forced by the full industrial mobilization of the war years reduced the requirement for manpower. Unions, their power at new peaks, maintained wage levels in the face of steadily declining work weeks. With prosperity and free time, Americans turned to spectator sports in record numbers.

Baseball attendance boomed to record levels, college football enjoyed a renaissance which restored it to its halcyon days of the 1920s, a new major league professional basketball circuit was formed, two professional football leagues competed for spectator dollars. Horse racing, its companion harness racing, stock cars, hockey, and other forms of amusement experienced explosive growth in both interest and participation. Tennis was in the forward legion of this growth. Fans began turning out to watch Davis Cup matches and major events at Forest Hills in ever-increasing throngs.

During the war, diminished fields continued the great traditions of Forest Hills, and the National Singles remained one of the major annual events in American sports. Many premier players were in military service during the war, but most of the leading ones were able to arrange leave time for the two-week competition at Forest Hills. In 1942 Ted Schroeder defeated Frank Parker in a wild five-set final to win his only National Singles crown. The next year, Lieutenant Joe Hunt defeated Seaman Jack Kramer to win the title. Kramer, later to become one of the most influential of all early players in burgeoning professional tennis, had teamed with Schroeder in both 1940 and 1941 to win the doubles.

Parker, now an Army sergeant, returned in 1944 and 1945 to win successive titles, beating Billy Talbert both times. Talbert, an insulin-supported diabetic, lost in four sets to Parker in 1944 and went out in three in 1945, but not until he engaged Parker in a 14–12 first set, one of the longest in a Forest Hills final.

With Parker, Kramer, Schroeder, Talbert, and Gardnar Mulloy as a base, the United States was fairly well stocked with talented players at the end of the war. Talbert and Mulloy proved to be one of the outstanding American doubles pairs, winning the Forest Hills title in 1942, 1945, 1946, and 1948, losing the final in 1947, 1950, and 1953. Talbert, especially, was a gifted doubles man and was a finalist in doubles at Forest Hills nine times with four different partners in his career. His only singles finals were the two wartime losses to Parker. Later, Talbert became one of the prime movers in open tennis and served as a distinguished tournament director for the United States

Open at Forest Hills for several years and later returned to that post after a two-year hiatus when the event was shifted into the new USTA (the "Lawn" having been dropped in 1976) National Tennis Center. He was also a Davis Cup player, winning six zone doubles matches without a loss and twice appearing in Challenge Rounds.

Now out of the Navy Kramer, came into the 1946 tournament at the peak of his game and ran over Tom Brown in three sets in the final after a brief 9–7 struggle in the opening set. Kramer won again in 1947, but this time it was a battle against the wily Parker. The 1947 final was also a signal event at Forest Hills in that it attracted the largest crowd before the advent of open tennis. The audience, reportedly more than 14,000, literally overflowed the stadium. It watched a tense and exciting match between two of the best American men. Kramer appeared virtually out of the match after dropping the first two sets to Parker, 6–4, 6–2. But he rallied brilliantly in the next two, winning the third, 6–1, and the fourth, 6–0, to deadlock the match. In the decisive fifth, Kramer completed the successful defense of his title with a 6–3 victory. A standing ovation from the packed stands followed.

What came shortly thereafter was even more startling than Kramer's splendid finish against Parker. He turned professional and went on a cross-country tour. But his place was taken by a young, gangly, black-maned Californian, Richard ("Pancho") Gonzales. Gonzales, perhaps the finest player produced in the United States since Tilden, was an incredible bundle of energy with amazing extension, solid strokes, and a burning competitive fire. Gonzales became the third man in a row to win two straight titles at Forest Hills by capturing the 1948 final against South Africa's Eric Sturgess in three sets and the 1949 final over Schroeder in five. The confrontation between Schroeder and Gonzales was another memorable moment at Forest Hills, with the eventual loser taking the first two sets. In almost a mirror image of Kramer, Gonzales fought back to sweep the next three. Even more amazing, perhaps, was that Schroeder's first set win was by 18–16, the longest set ever in a final.

Then Gonzales did something which was also an emulation of Kramer. He turned professional.

Gonzales was to go on to create the greatest record in the history of touring professional tennis in the United States.

In 1941 Bobby Riggs, a finalist three straight years at Forest Hills and the Singles Champion in 1939 and 1941, turned professional. It was he who formulated the postwar tour, signing Jack Kramer as his leading star name. It was also he who signed Gonzales. Riggs, one of the irrepressible characters of tennis, had doubtless accepted the yawning abyss of pro tennis for several reasons. Given his nature, the most obvious was money. Riggs was not only an outstanding athlete, he was also an outstanding promoter of almost anything.

Riggs was also a notorious gambler. He would wager on anything at any time, it was said. But it wasn't said with total accuracy. Riggs also knew *how* to wager and on *what.* He became famous for virtually bankrupting a well-known London bookmaker in 1939. He had wagered, at astronomical odds, that he would win not only the men's singles, but the doubles and the mixed doubles as well. He disposed of Elwood Cooke in the singles final, teamed with Cooke to win the doubles, and paired with Alice Marble to take the mixed. Riggs then collected a massive payoff from the unfortunate bookie who had underestimated his talent and overestimated his ego.

Having been modestly successful in a tour with Kramer, Riggs induced Gonzales to undertake a 123-match cross-country marathon against Kramer, then the reigning pro champion. Kramer won the tour, ninety-six matches to twenty-seven, but Gonzales earned $75,000. What followed was Gonzales's rise to the top of the pro tennis heap and then virtual inactivity. After failing as a teacher, Gonzales sought to return to the pro tour only to be rebuffed by Riggs. But Riggs, and other players signed by him, boycotted the United States Pro Indoor Tournament and Gonzales won it. In 1953 Kramer had supplanted Riggs as the major domo of American pro tennis, and he added Gonzales to a troupe which then consisted of Australians Ken McGregor and Frank Sedgman and the ubiquitous Pancho Segura.

This tour had done most of its best business in Australia, not surprisingly. If nothing else, Gonzales was about to prove that professional tennis was at least honest. He ran through the series of 1954 with fifteen victories against McGregor, who failed to beat him even once, adding sixteen wins over Sedgman in twenty-five matches and making a shambles of the whole business. Kramer almost had to retire him to restore some semblance of competition. At twenty-six, Pancho Gonzales, the poor Mexican-American from Los Angeles, was the greatest tennis player in the world. He was also unemployed.

When Dinny Pails was persuaded to play another tour against Gonzales in Australia, the American won forty-five of the fifty-two matches. "I can't put you out on the court," Kramer told Gonzales at this point, "until I get (Tony) Trabert, (Ken) Rosewall, or (Lew) Hoad."

This, then, was the pattern that was emerging. With American and Australian talent dominating the postwar world of tennis, Kramer would wait for the finest talents to win the major tournaments and then try to induce them to come away and join his tour, facing the invincible Gonzales. While Kramer would diligently seek to sign up the game's top names for his tour, Gonzales would lurk impatiently in the wings. All of Kramer's targets (Trabert, Rosewall, and Hoad) eventually succumbed to his sales pitch and his money.

Following Gonzales's departure into the pro ranks, Art Larsen won the 1950 National Singles at Forest Hills with a final win over Herb Flam. In 1951 a non-American won the men's crown for the first time since Fred Perry in 1936 when Frank Sedgman, an Australian, took it. Sedgman, nicknamed "the Gentleman" for his court deportment, successfully defended in 1952, becoming the fourth man in nine years to win the title twice in succession. Like his immediate two predecessors in this accomplishment—Kramer and Gonzales—he then joined the pro tour.

It was an all-American Forest Hills final in 1953 when Tony Trabert defeated Vic Seixas, and Seixas won the following year at Forest Hills by downing Australian Rex Hartwig. The Australians had the final all to themselves in 1955 when Trabert won his second title by beating Ken Rosewall in straight sets. Rosewall and Lew Hoad repeated the act in 1956 with Rosewall winning.

Australian supremacy was then in the ascendancy. It was to dominate the world for the rest of the decade of the 1950s and most of the early

1960s. Behind the explosive presence of the Australians was their nonplaying Davis Cup captain, Harry Hopman. Hopman tutored his charges for the purpose of winning the Cup for Australia. The fact that they won titles in all of the world's major tournaments with alarming consistency was a pleasant by-product.

Meanwhile, Hopman was achieving his aim. In 1946 the first postwar Davis Cup Challenge Round was held in Australia (by virtue of the Australians' win of the last prewar challenge in 1939). The United States, captained by the wily Walter Pate, won the Cup with a impressive 5–0 sweep of their hosts. Jack Kramer led the victory by winning two singles and teaming with Ted Schroeder to take the doubles over John Bromwich and Adrian Quist.

At the West Side Tennis Club in 1947, the script was nearly the same. Jack Kramer again won twice in singles and the Americans defended, 4–1. The only loss came in doubles. It was Forest Hills again for the Challenge Round in 1948 and again the United States put the Australians to rout, 5–0. Kramer was gone to the pros, but Frank Parker

and Ted Schroeder took two singles apiece and the tough team of Talbert and Mulloy won in the doubles. For the fourth year running, the Australians played their way through the draw and emerged as the challengers in 1949. And, for the fourth year running, the United States defeated them, this time 4–1, at Forest Hills. This win was notable in that it included the first appearance of Gonzales, who wiped out Sedgman and Bill Sidwell in straight sets to win his two singles. It was, as subsequent events were to prove, also his last appearance in the Davis Cup.

Hopman came on the scene in 1950. He brought the Australians through the draw again despite the fact that the entry list had grown from eighteen nations in the first postwar year of 1946 to twenty-five. Sedgman won his opening singles against Tom Brown, Jr., and McGregor likewise defeated Schroeder on the first day. Australia regained the Cup with a doubles win on the second day for an insurmountable 3–0 lead. Brown won his singles, but Sedgman defeated Schroeder to send the Australians home with a 4–1 win and the Cup.

Jack Kramer receives his award from the King and Queen in the Royal Box at Wimbledon after his 1947 victory.

For the next four years, the Challenge Rounds were to be held in Australia. They produced record crowds, among the largest in the history of tennis. There were several reasons for this phenomenon. One was the general popularity of Americans in postwar Australia. Another was the enthusiastic self-pride of the Australians and their delight in taking the measure of their large and powerful friends and allies.

Crowds of 16,100 showed up on each of the three days during the first Challenge Round played in Australia in 1951. They saw their team retain the Cup in a thrilling finish when Sedgman and McGregor won the doubles on the final day over Schroeder and Trabert, 6–2, 9–7, 6–3. In 1952 Sedgman and McGregor avoided the last-minute heroics, taking the first three singles and defending, 4–1. The Americans were back for another try the next year at Kooyong Stadium in Melbourne. This time another new attendance record (17,500) was set. Even more remarkable was the fact that Hopman rebuilt his team entirely in the intervening year. Both Sedgman and McGregor had signed with Kramer. The Australian captain replaced them with Rosewall and Hoad. Australia won, 3–2, but the United States won a singles and tied the match by winning the doubles before the Cup was clinched by Rosewall's win in the last singles match.

Although thirty nations entered the competition in 1954, the United States (with Seixas and Trabert) again emerged from the draw as the challenger. This time, the Americans won the challenge at White City in Sydney before the largest crowds in the history of Cup competition. A capacity audience of 25,578 turned out each day during the week between Christmas and New Year's. Trabert beat Hoad in the crucial first singles and Seixas then defeated Rosewall. Both lost on the second day but they combined for a 6–2, 4–6, 6–2, 10–8 win over the Australian pair in the doubles to bring the Cup back to the United States. But it didn't remain there long. In 1955 Australia showed up for the challenge at Forest Hills and ran through the United States like a buzzsaw, romping home with a 5–0 sweep.

During the years immediately following the Second World War, the resumption of major tournaments in Europe brought with it a dominance by American men. This was notably true at Wimbledon, where the Americans were almost total in their domination. The resumption of play at the All-England began almost immediately after the end of the fighting in Europe. The famed Centre Court had been partly smashed by a bomb, huge holes ripped in its roof and its courts made unplayable. Court 1, however, remained generally unscathed and was put to almost instant use as two international tournaments were staged in celebration of the Allied victory. With the return of tennis came the end to Mrs. Norah Cleather's agricultural endeavors. The acting secretary of the All-England, she had raised chickens on the club grounds to aid the war effort.

Crowds turned out in abundance for the postwar matches. Players turned up from everywhere. Many people who had built casual acquaintances with fellow soldiers suddenly learned that their wartime compatriots were tennis players of some magnitude in private life. The war had other effects, too. Lieutenant Joe Hunt, the 1943 Forest Hills winner, disappeared in his Air Corps plane shortly after his victory. Almost at the same time, Henner Henkel, the German Davis Cupper, was to vanish in the action at Stalingrad. The famed stadium of Roland Garros in Paris became a concentration camp during the Nazi occupation. Henkel's Davis Cup partner, the celebrated Baron von Cramm, had his political difficulties with the German government, was shipped to the Eastern front as a raw recruit, wounded, and saved from probable extermination by the S.S. through the tacit protection of King Gustav V, Sweden's tennis-playing monarch.

At the first Wimbledon of the postwar era, 1946, some ripple effects remained. Some entries were refused, including that of France's Jean Borotra. Borotra had been Minister of Sport under the Pétain Vichy government. Although he had resigned in 1942 and was captured trying to escape to North Africa, the allegations of cooperation with the Nazis brought about the rejection of his application. Yvon Petra, the giant Frenchman, was the first postwar Wimbledon winner, defeating Geoff Brown in the final. Petra had been a prisoner of war two years earlier. One of the most touching of all Wimbledon scenes with respect to the war actually came a couple of years later when Austrian

Hans Redl, who had lost an arm in combat, was allowed to enter. Redl lofted the ball with his racquet so that he could serve it. When he made his first appearance, the game was stopped by a standing ovation from the British fans. If peace is forgiveness, the war had perhaps finally, if not ended, at least receded. But before the tears replaced the curses, Americans compiled their most impressive Wimbledon record.

Jack Kramer was among the favorites in the 1946 bracket with Riggs, the last prewar winner, already among the pros. But both Kramer and the strongest Australian, Dinny Pails, fell out along the way despite the fact that the general level of play was somewhat below the Wimbledon norm. But in 1947, Kramer returned at the top of his game and performed as expected. One of the things that had hampered Kramer the previous year was severe blisters on his right hand. They became so severe that he could hardly hold the racket. When he was eliminated by Jaroslav Drobny, shaking the winner's hand was a painful experience. He was healthy in 1947 and it showed. Kramer ran through his first three matches in straight sets. In the semifinal he dropped one set to Pails, 6–1, 3–6, 6–1, 6–0, and then clubbed Tom Brown, 6–1, 6–3, 6–2, in the final.

Kramer also won the doubles with fellow Californian Bob Falkenberg, the 1946 collegiate champion from the University of Southern California, and then correctly forecast that Falkenberg would win the singles in 1948. Kramer's departure for the professional ranks made Falkenberg's win a possibility. No singles winner has aroused more critical comment in the process of his win than Falkenberg. He incurred the ire of the fans and officials with his long rests on the court each time he fell—and he fell many times during the fortnight. Two years later it was discovered that he was suffering from a severe thyroid deficiency and it had been little short of a miracle that he had won at all, rests or no rests.

"Lucky" Ted Schroeder came, saw, and conquered in 1949 after one of the most eventful passages in the history of Wimbledon. Down 2–5 in the fifth set to veteran Gardnar Mulloy in the first round, he rallied for a stunning win. He then saved several match points against Australia's Sedgman and was taken to five sets by both South African Sturgess and, in the final, by Drobny whom he finally subdued, 3–6, 6–0, 6–3, 4–6, 6–4.

Budge Patty succeeded Schroeder in 1950 and Dick Savitt took over from Patty in 1951. These were high days for United States power, for neither Patty nor Falkenberg ever played Davis Cup for their country, although Falkenberg did later represent Brazil. Of course, the thinning out of the ranks by steady defections to the pros also helped many a cause. It is doubtful that Falkenberg, Patty, Savitt, or perhaps even Schroeder could have taken either Kramer or Gonzales in those days.

Sedgman became the first Australian winner in decades by taking the 1952 final from Drobny in five sets.

In 1930 Wilmer Allison had reached the final despite being omitted from the seeding list. Kurt Nielsen became the second man to achieve this in 1953 and then gave an encore in 1955, losing to Vic Seixas the first time and Trabert the second.

In between came the 1954 victory of one of the most popular of all Wimbledon winners, Drobny, who beat Ken Rosewall and became champion sixteen years after his appearance in 1938. No winner before or since has enjoyed such sustained applause as when the self-exiled Czech finally triumphed at long last. Drobny received the warmest welcome of all non-British champions when the winners were reassembled for the 1977 Centennial Wimbledon.

After Trabert's 1955 win, the Australians, who had been pounding at the door for half a decade, came to the fore. In fact, it was an all-Aussie final the next year when Lew Hoad downed Rosewall. Hoad gave an astonishing display in the final the following year against Ashley Cooper. Cooper lasted only fifty-seven minutes and won a meager five games. A final-day appearance by Queen Elizabeth II gave the championship a new dimension of importance. But the occasion was somewhat marred by the intrusion onto the court of a woman carrying a semipolitical banner. She was quickly escorted away by the referee, Colonel John Legg.

One of the greatest impacts of Hoad's second successive win in 1957 was what happened immediately thereafter. Less than twenty-four hours

Tony Trabert *(left)* held the Men's Singles title in the United States in 1953 and 1955; Vic Seixas *(right),* the oldest first-time winner of the United States title, held it in 1954.

after his victory, Hoad turned professional. His signing meant that Rosewall, Sedgman, Gonzales, Pancho Segura, and Hoad were all in the same camp and all were ineligible for future Wimbledon, Forest Hills, Roland Garros, and Australian championships. The pro inroad was becoming international and had the effect of continually stripping away the top stars of tennis from the top events.

It was becoming clear that some solution for this problem had to be found. But that solution remained more than a decade in the future—although that future was beginning to be limited by some observers who made the revolutionary suggestion that pros and amateurs be allowed to compete in the same tournaments.

Meanwhile, the Australian combine of Harry Hopman seemed to be capable of providing an almost inexhaustible supply of talent. In 1957 Mal Anderson defeated Ashley Cooper in the Forest Hills final, making the second straight year that both finalists had been Australian. Neale Fraser became the third straight United States National

winner from Down Under in the following fall when he finished off Peruvian Alex Olmedo. Fraser won for the second year running in 1960, defeating young Rod Laver in straight sets, 6–4, 6–4, 9–7, though the match was tougher than the score indicated.

Roy Emerson arrived as a world class player in 1961 and took the measure of Laver in the final at Forest Hills. At Wimbledon, the Australians were also eclipsing the American preeminence. Cooper, the easy victim of Hoad in 1957, came back the following year to win All-England, beating Fraser in the final. Olmedo carried away top honors in 1959 and Fraser regained the title for Australia a year later. In 1961 Laver played in the final for the third straight year and finally won, defeating Chuck McKinley, the first American finalist since Trabert. The next year, Laver was not to be denied anywhere in the world.

For the first time since Budge in 1938, the tennis world had a Grand Slam champion as Laver swept everything and everyone before him in the Australian, Wimbledon, Roland Garros, and Forest Hills tournaments. For good measure, he threw in victories in the Italian and German championships.

It was hardly a surprise when Laver turned pro after completing this devastation. In fact, to many of the other players it was doubtless a relief. But it was a continuing cause for concern among officials of the major tournaments.

Regardless, Laver's defection opened up the field a bit and Mexico's Rafael Osuna took advantage by winning at Forest Hills over Frank Froehling, the first American to make the last two since 1955. Roy Emerson, in 1964, returned the United States title to the Australian camp with a victory over countryman Fred Stolle in a virtual repeat of their Wimbledon final earlier in the year.

But the United States had some good news from Wimbledon in 1963 when stocky Chuck McKinley battled his way to the final for the second time in three years and then took out Stolle to win after a tense 9–7 first set. Neither McKinley nor any other United States player was able to stop the foreign domination at Forest Hills, however, as Spain's Manuel Santana succeeded to the title in 1965 in another all-foreign final, beating South

Darlene Hard of the United States and Neale Fraser of Australia captured the majority of the silverware at the 1960 Nationals. Miss Hard won the singles and doubles, while Fraser took the singles and mixed doubles.

African Cliff Drysdale, 6–2, 7–9, 7–5, 6–1. Emerson, who was in the process of winning the Australian title six times in seven years, captured his second successive Wimbledon title in 1965, again outlasting Stolle in the final. For his part, Stolle won the French title.

After regaining the Davis Cup with their 5–0 sweep at Forest Hills in 1955, the Australians repeated their defense with another sweep over the United States at Adelaide in 1956 and retained the Cup again the next year at Melbourne with a 3–2 win. Then came a surprising, and slightly controversial, United States win in 1958. Alex Olmedo, the Peruvian who was to be a Forest Hills finalist a year later, was a college student in the United States at the University of Southern California. As such, he played for the United States Davis Cup team.

With Olmedo winning both of his singles and pairing with Ham Richardson on the winning doubles combination, the United States defeated the Australians, 3–2, to recover the Cup. The next year, the Challenge Round was held at Forest Hills for the final time. It was also one of the most exciting of the finals as the Australian team survived the thirty-nine-nation challenge playoffs and then won the Cup. After dividing the four singles matches, the challenge came down to the doubles. Roy Emerson and Neale Fraser represented the Australians and Olmedo and Butch Buchholz the United States. The Emerson-Fraser team won, 7–5, 7–5, 6–4. It was the third time since 1950 that Australia had come to Forest Hills and won the Cup. In each of the next two years, the United States was knocked out in the Interzone final by Italy, and both times the Australians turned back the Italian challenge to retain the Cup. In 1962 the United States was upset in the American zone by Mexico behind the strong performances of Antonio Palafox and Rafael Osuna. But the Mexicans were swept by Australia in the Challenge Round, 5–0.

The largest challenging field in the history of the competition up to that time, forty-eight nations, entered in 1963 and the United States fought its way through Iran, Venezuela, Mexico, Britain, and India, losing only one match along the way, to make the challenge against Australia. The Americans—Chuck McKinley and Dennis Ralston

The victorious 1958 United States Davis Cup team: *(left to right)* Bernard Bartzen, Alex Olmedo, Perry Jones (captain), Barry MacKay, and Earl Buchholz, Jr.

—each won once in singles and then combined for the doubles. They recaptured the Cup by defeating Emerson and Fraser in the doubles, winning the decisive final set, 11–9. When the Challenge Round was held in the United States in 1964, it was staged at the Harold T. Clark Courts in Cleveland, Ohio. Roy Emerson was the Australian hero, defeating both Ralston and McKinley in singles, while Stolle won once in singles, and Australia again became the Cup holder, 3–2.

When the Americans were beaten by Spain in 1965, the Australians routed the Spaniards, 4–1, in the challenge and repeated a similar exercise against India in 1966 and Spain again the following year.

When the United States was finally able to again reach the Challenge Round in 1968, it made the trip worthwhile by defeating Australia, 4–1, at Adelaide. Clark Graebner won both of his singles, Arthur Ashe split his two, and the doubles combination of Bob Lutz and Stan Smith defeated John Alexander and Ray Ruffels in straight sets. No other team was ever to win a Challenge Round. The United States staged successful defenses in 1969 and 1970 at Cleveland and in 1971 at Charlotte, North Carolina. Thereafter, the Challenge Round was abolished and the defender was required to play through the draw into a final which matched the two interzonal winners. Continued growth in tennis was exhibited by the steady expansion of the field of challenging nations in Davis Cup play. The total of challengers hit the fifty mark for the first time in 1969. It reached fifty-six in 1974 and fifty-eight in 1976.

DAWN OF THE OPEN ERA

Fred Stolle was the Australian tennis player of the era about whom everybody had heard but about whom, somehow, no one really knew anything. He lived constantly in the shadow of the superior compatriots named Laver, Rosewall, and Newcombe. Stolle finally broke out into the limelight, even if only briefly, in 1966. That was the year he won the United States title at Forest Hills. What made the win even more delightful for Stolle was that he was able to defeat his better-known countryman, Newcombe, 4–6, 12–10, 6–3, 6–4, in the final. He retreated into the shadows shortly thereafter, however, and Newcombe won the title the next year by routing American Clark Graebner, 6–4, 6–4, 8–6.

Although it was not clear at the moment, the 1967 Forest Hills final was a signal event. It was the last of the National Amateur finals to be staged at the West Side Tennis Club. By 1968 open tennis was a fact. The amateur event was shifted to Boston's Longwood Cricket Club and Forest Hills was the site of the new United States Open, with its $100,000 prize money. Easily the supreme irony of the whole open business was that the first United States Open was won by an amateur who did not collect the prize money. Indeed, the winner of the Amateur and the Open turned out to be Arthur Ashe, even though both tournaments were held within the space of about two weeks.

For several years, the major tennis nations, notably the United States, Britain, and Australia, had pressed for a declaration of open tennis, erasing the lines of distinction between amateurs of any variety and outright professionals. In 1967 they once more brought the issue to a vote at the International Lawn Tennis Federation and, once again, their efforts were thwarted as the proposal was voted down by the membership. However, this time the reaction was different. The British took the fore and declared that, irrespective of the ILTF decision, all tournaments staged in Britain during 1968 would cease to make the discrimination between amateur and professional players. The events would be open to all, and therefore, open in tennis terms.

What followed was a hastily reconvened meeting of the ILTF membership. With the strong support of USLTA president Bob Kelleher, a compromise package was pushed through which provided for the immediate sanctioning of a dozen open events (designated in advance) and the commitment to negotiate with the pro promoters to resolve the continuing crisis. In 1969 the number of open events was enlarged to thirty.

One aspect of the compromise created plenty of confusion on its own. This was the so-called "registered player" category which provided for certain players to receive prize money in certain events (the open ones) and to play as amateurs in other tournaments where no prize money was offered. This situation was created largely due to the insistence that the major international team competitions—Davis Cup, Wightman Cup, and Federation Cup—were to remain closed to professionals. In order to retain their top players for these events, several nations pushed for the "registered player" concept to allow their better players to collect major prizes and still preserve their amateur standings.

Within a year, the USLTA created a new category which permitted players turning nineteen to earn available prizes without losing their recognition by the Association. Within a decade, the distinction between amateur and professional was to virtually disappear, although there were to be many bumps along the way.

Having been rated for three years as the Number Two man in America, Ashe rose to the top of the ratings with his outstanding year in 1968. He accomplished some of his finest feats while serving in the United States Army and playing for the United States Davis Cup team at the same time. He was, however, an amateur throughout it all. That made him eligible for the new National Amateur competition at Longwood, and he made the most of the opportunity by eliminating the top Australian hope, Alan Stone, in the quarterfinals and defeating lefty Jim McManus in the semifinals. McManus was the last unseeded player in the tournament.

Meanwhile, Ashe's Davis Cup partner, Charles Pasarell, gained the semifinals and took out veteran Clark Graebner in straight sets. In the final, Ashe turned back Pasarell, 4–6, 6–3, 8–10, 6–0, 6–4, fighting off three break points which would have prolonged the fifth set even further. The marathon was nothing new for Pasarell. Earlier in the year, he had been involved in the longest match ever played in an American championship. In the doubles quarterfinal of the National Indoors, Pasarell and Ronnie Holmberg were beaten by Englishmen Mark Cox and Bobby Wilson, 26–24, 17–19, 30–28.

It was the sandy-haired young Cox who had stolen the headlines at the world's first recognized Open in April, 1968, at Bournemouth, England. On the raw, rainy Monday, April 21, the first event in which professionals lawfully mingled and competed with amateurs in tennis began. The pros slid through the opening-day matches with some close calls but no losses. It was Cox who struck the first blow, taking out thirty-nine-year-old Pancho Gonzales in a five-set thriller in the second round.

Gonzales swept through the first set, 6–0, Cox held up in the second, 6–2, and then Gonzales won the third, 6–4. Cox's natural edge in age then began to take hold, and he won the final two sets for the match, 6–3, 6–3. Cox performed what was an even bigger surprise to most experts the next day when he knocked off Roy Emerson and handed the long-time Australian champ one of his worst defeats in the process, 6–0, 6–1, 7–5.

However, form finally prevailed as Laver restored the pros' respectability by defeating Cox in the semifinals. Ken Rosewall became the winner of the first open event by downing Laver in the final, 3–6, 6–2, 6–0, 6–3, to claim the British Hard Court title. Despite the attention focused on the hard courts, it was not a completely true test on either side. Only one of the two professional groups then functioning—the National Tennis League, headed by George McCall—entered at Bournemouth. Further, many of the top amateurs were wary of risking their reputations and also stayed away. No Americans played in the event.

But as the summer wore on, things warmed up. The other pro tour—World Championship Tennis—showed up for its first open at the Queen's Club in London in June. Most of the top amateurs entered the French championships, also an open for the first time, that month. Ken Rosewall won the French title.

Wimbledon offered a total of only $62,000 for its first venture into the world of open tennis but attracted virtually every name tennis player who was permitted to enter. Laver was to win at Wimbledon, knocking off another pro and fellow Australian, Tony Roche, in the final. Laver collected the grand sum of $4,800 for his 6–3, 6–4, 6–2 triumph but said the money didn't really matter. "I never thought about it," he was quoted afterward. "Just being back here was enough."

That brought the leading players back to New York where many of them had played the previous spring when the USLTA staged a giant weeklong indoor championship at Madison Square Garden. Ashe was also the winner of the men's title in that event, defeating Emerson in the final. It was Emerson's final amateur appearance.

At Forest Hills, the largest open purse then offered included $14,000 for the men's winner. Ashe played in the Open for $20 per day in expenses as an amateur. He got into his first big match against Emerson, now a pro, needing a win for a berth in the quarterfinal round. Emerson's status did nothing to change his game, and Ashe beat him again to make the round of eight.

But it was the veteran Gonzales, now past his fortieth birthday, who captured the early cheers from the crowd. His play belied his age as Gonzales, seeded thirteenth largely on sentiment,

Many experts believe that if "open" tennis had come in the early 1950s Pancho Gonzales would have been ranked as the world's greatest player.

reached the quarterfinals, too, and knocked off Wimbledon finalist Roche on the way (in straight sets).

Gonzales finally went out in the quarters but not before another thrilling display. He took on trim Tom Okker, the pride of the Netherlands, and amazingly outlasted him in a marathon thirty-game first set, 16–14. But then age once more took its toll and Okker prevailed by winning the next three sets, 6–3, 10–8, 6–3. Ashe disposed of South African Cliff Drysdale, the 1965 losing finalist, in the quarterfinals and then beat Clark Graebner in the semis. When Okker eliminated Rosewall in their semifinal match, the Dutchman was automatically entitled to the first prize money since Ashe was unable to collect it. Playing the final match more for pride than anything else, Ashe and Okker locked up in a five-set thriller. Ashe won the first, 14–12, and Okker took the second, 7–5.

Ashe gained the upper hand by taking the pivotal third set, 6–3, and after losing the fourth, won the decisive fifth by the same score. For the first time since Tony Trabert in 1955, an American had won the final at Forest Hills. Coupled with the 4–1 win over Australia at Memorial Drive in the Davis Cup Challenge Round, Ashe's wins at Longwood and Forest Hills made the year an outstanding one for the United States, although the open events were to have a longer-lasting impact on the game.

One of the more startling things about the 1968 United States Open, besides the mere fact of its existence, was that the public response was outstanding. The event drew 97,294 fans in twelve sessions, an increase of probably 30,000 over the final National Singles the year before. It was clear that the presence of the pros had a distinct appeal to the United States tennis public, even if none of the so-called "big names" even made it to the semifinals. Rosewall was the only touring pro among the final four. What seemed to matter was that all of the players, regardless of their status, had the chance to win the championship. Ashe's victory at Longwood rated scant attention in the general press, but his win at Forest Hills was page one news in much of the country.

It was then abundantly evident that open tennis was a fact of life in the sport. It only remained to determine what form it would take over the ensuing years. "The open tennis question has been a big one for us," USLTA president Alastair B. Martin wrote, "and we certainly felt that open tennis should be put into effect and brought about in an orderly fashion." A strong positive vote on this question at the annual meeting that year in Coronado, California, was reflective of this position.

"We also felt," Martin continued, "that more realistic amateur rules should be enacted. We know that the charge of 'shamateurism'—often accurate—has hurt the game's reputation and we want the players to know exactly where they stand. We realize that they desire to be governed by fair, enforceable rules, and we are working on such rules now. We intend them to be reasonable and we intend to enforce them."

Martin, writing in late 1968, then went on to suggest that professional tennis was a distinct asset to the game as a whole. "A sound professional game," he said, "would benefit tennis in furnishing a career opportunity for our leading players just as pro football and basketball did for post-college-age athletes of top-flight ability." These comments were the latest development in an uneasy relationship between the amateur game as represented by the original ideals of the USTA's founding fathers and professional tennis in its various aspects that spanned over four decades.

In 1927 the Professional Lawn Tennis Association was formed after a series of meetings had taken place in New York involving primarily teachers of the game. One of the objectives of the PLTA was to ensure that the USLTA understood where the teachers stood in relation to the touring professional players. At the time, a famous American promoter—Charles C. Pyle—was in the process of forming the first serious touring pro group. Pyle, who was the manager and guiding light behind football star Red Grange, promoted the rather unsuccessful tour matching of Suzanne Lenglen against Mary K. Browne. A statement was issued after the formation of the new group which said, in part:

> For some time past there has been a very strong feeling among lawn tennis professionals that there is a need for some organization to assist them in obtaining a proper and recog-

nized status in the tennis world. A meeting was accordingly held September 23 (1927) and it was decided to form an Association. This meeting was followed by others at which the following regulations were agreed upon:

An initiation fee of $10 will be charged all new members.

Dues are to be $5 annually.

An executive committee has been elected and a constitution adopted. It is the desire of this executive committee to have all tennis professionals of accepted standards become members of the Association.

The same year, the USLTA formed its first official position with respect to professionals. It acknowledged the sometimes sharp difference between the teaching professional and the touring professional, but it also struggled with the problem of players who crossed that line, as many did many times. In its policy on pros, the Association published a three-part resolution which (1) gave recognition to the Professional Lawn Tennis Association, (2) discouraged the recognition of individual promoters of individual pro matches and events involving both pro and amateurs, and (3) required all member clubs holding events involving professionals, either alone or with amateurs or members, to request permission from the Association to do so.

Shortly thereafter, the Longwood Cricket Club asked for permission to stage pro-amateur exhibitions in conjunction with the National Championships. This permission was denied. The matter came to a sharper head when the Palm Beach Tennis Club permitted its facilities to be used for a professional event. On March 17, 1928, a lengthy meeting was held by the USLTA executive committee but no clear-cut solutions were found. It was evident that some members of the executive committee were concerned about pushing the rules too far.

But on February 13, 1931, following Bill Tilden's decision to turn pro, a resolution that had previously been tabled was enacted stating that "no exhibition matches between amateurs and professionals would be authorized" for member clubs. Subsequently, this injunction was modified slightly to permit exhibitions under certain conditions such as bona fide charity benefits.

As for the touring pros themselves, Pyle struck his first strong blow against the amateur ranks when he signed Vincent Richards in 1926. He then added well-known Frenchman Paul Feret and two other Americans, Harvey Snodgrass and Howard Kinsey. Kinsey was a part of the United States Doubles Championship team of 1926, and Snodgrass was a well-known teaching pro who had often been ranked. Kinsey was ranked sixth nationally in 1926 and Snodgrass had been sixth the year before. The signing of the three standouts was the action which prodded the USLTA to take its first official stance on professionalism.

Pyle's tour, however, was less than successful. Richards, although omitted from the 1926 rankings, was in the top four each of the prior five years and was as superior to his opponents as Lenglen was to hers. On October 9, 1926, the first professional tour began at Madison Square Garden, but the superiority of Richards and Miss Lenglen shortly wore out the public interest. The tour expired after the first year when the temperamental Suzanne refused to tour again. Vinny Richards, along with Kinsey and Snodgrass, tried to revive interest by staging a professional tournament involving mostly teaching pros. However, the teachers were no match for the touring players and Richards won the event easily. The next major thrust for the pro game came in 1930.

After years of sniping and battling with the USLTA Tilden turned pro and formed Tilden's Tennis Tours, Inc. He enlisted Richards and signed Czechoslovakian standout Karel Koseluth. His first American tour and a subsequent jaunt through Europe were markedly successful. But thereafter, the interest waned as Tilden continued to demonstrate his superiority. The picture changed radically in 1937 when both Ellsworth Vines of the United States and Fred Perry of England opted for professionalism. Thereafter, virtually a steady flow of talent into the pro ranks made the touring pros a real factor in tennis.

Among those who turned pro in the years immediately before, during, and shortly after World War II were Don Budge, Alice Marble, Bobby Riggs, Mary Hardwick, Frank Kovacs, Pauline Betz, and Gussie Moran. Riggs took over promotion of the main tour for several years, but it was the coming of Jack Kramer that really revolutionized the professional game.

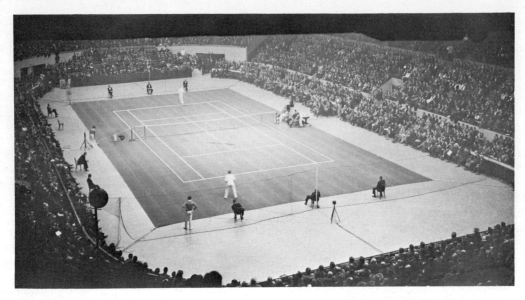

Madison Square Garden (New York) was the scene of the first United States professional matches in 1926.

Kramer, in addition to being a top name and a powerful player, was a skilled promoter who knew how to balance his talent and milk the maximum publicity out of the events they played. He also was a smooth salesman who talked many an amateur star into signing a pro contract while still at the peak of his game and marketability. Kramer also had Pancho Gonzales, perhaps the finest player ever on the pro circuit.

Until Tilden in 1930, at the end of the so-called Golden Age of Sport, no player who had won the United States or Wimbledon titles turned professional. After 1946, five of the seven winners at Forest Hills and three other Wimbledon winners signed pro contracts in the decade ending in 1957. Kramer was effective—of that there was no doubt!

Almost from the outset, the leaders of the USLTA and their All-England counterparts recognized the problem posed by the potential of professional tennis. It was this very recognition, in fact, that led to problems. Although indoor arenas such as New York's Madison Square Garden, the Boston Garden, and the Chicago Stadium were certainly venues which could be utilized for occasional pro tour events, it was a virtual certainty that courts of member clubs would be sought as sites for pro events. What the Association was at-

tempting to do when it required clubs to seek permission for pro events was to get control of the scheduling of such events. The initial thought was not to outlaw pro events or even make a concerted effort to prevent the development of a pro field. Open tournaments were, almost from the very start, considered a positive thing by the governing body of the game in America.

The philosophy of the resolution regarding pros approved in 1927 was discussed in the annual meeting in 1928 by President Samuel Collom. His comment is instructive:

The intention of the resolution was to recognize the same principle, in tennis, as does exist in golf. You have amateur championships and professional championships and eventually, as that develops, you will have open championships.

In the context of his time, Collom was expounding a very pregnant thought. Golf's major open events, the United States and British, had flourished since 1895 and 1860, respectively, and were still considered half of the Grand Slam along with their amateur counterparts. In 1930 Bobby Jones won the four, both opens and both amateurs, and retired. It seemed perfectly logical to United States officials that tennis would inevitably take the same course. They were right. Except, of course, there was one major difference in tennis and therein lay the tale of four decades of struggle.

With the golf experience before them, the United States and Britain well saw what the future would be for tennis. However, both groups were loyal members of the International Lawn Tennis Federation and were determined to remain members. In 1930 the financially strapped Germantown Cricket Club applied for permission to stage a professional tournament in Philadelphia. The permission was granted with the proviso that the ILTF had no objection. At the subsequent meeting of the international body, it developed that there was more than a little objection. Led by Belgium's Chevalier de Borman, the resolution approving the Germantown request was crushed, with only the United States and Britain supporting it in the vote. "The day we open our gates to the professionals," de Borman declared, "all our points of view will change." That he, as one of the founders of the international organization, was opposed is to put the fact somewhat mildly. His ringing denunciation of the pros became the rallying cry for the opposition.

A rather peculiar sequence of events led to an even stronger ILTF position against professionals in 1933. With the Germantown club repeating its request, the USLTA once again granted permission. Under Rule 23, the statute in question, the Association president, Louis J. Carruthers, ruled, "there was nothing in Rule 23 which forbade the holding of an open tournament if the member nation wished to hold one." Carruthers was on sound legal ground, but he failed to reckon with the power of international politics, even in the sports field. Ample publicity was given to the USLTA decision to allow Germantown to hold an open event. Before it was played, however, the annual meeting of the ILTF was held in London. Inexplicably, the USLTA failed to send any representative to the meeting. Instead, the United States was represented by John MacVeagh, second secretary of the United States embassy in London.

What transpired in London was an outpouring against the USLTA position, and the result was a resolution which plugged up the loophole Car-

ruthers had discovered. It stated: "neither Rule 23 nor any other Rule permits the holding of such tournaments."

Now the lines had been clearly drawn. The USLTA was not going to oppose the ILTF on this ruling. The smaller nations with less of a commercial orientation than the United States and Britain were unalterably opposed to allowing the professionals under the sanctioning umbrella. Instead, they sought to ostracize them. It was the fear of most smaller nations that big monied sports interests in the English-speaking countries would lure away their national stars and strip their Davis Cup teams of talent after the national associations had worked, in many cases, years to develop a player of international caliber. Thus the USLTA was

The Czechoslovakian star Karel Koseluth was a big winner on the pro tour of the early 1930s.

forced to deal harshly with a member club in 1937 when the Greenbriar Golf and Tennis Club held an event billed as "The First United States Open Tennis Championship." It withdrew the club's membership and barred the six amateur players who had competed in the tournament from future participation in USLTA events. The next year, the LTA of India sought to get ILTF approval to have each member nation hold one open tournament annually. The United States then resubmitted its resolution stating that each nation had the right to determine for itself whether or not to hold such events. The resolution was defeated, 118 to 51, with the USLTA resolution as an amendment.

During the Second World War, certain exhibitions for charity involving pros (such as Tilden) were permitted by the ILTF for war relief charities, but there was no further movement toward true open tennis until 1957 when the Florida LTA recommended that the United States resubmit its 1938 amendment to the ILTF.

Meanwhile, the impact of Kramer's pro activity was beginning to be felt in the USLTA treasury. Income from Forest Hills dropped steadily with the decline in attendance. The almost total defection of the top stars to the pro tour was diminishing the value of international competition, and the major nations once more began to apply pressure, mildly at first, to the ILTF. At the annual ILTF meeting of 1960, it was expected that an amendment permitting a limited number of open events was to be approved for the following year. However, the amendment was surprisingly defeated, 107–102, and the ILTF decided to set up another committee to study the matter and report back in 1962. At the 1962 meeting, three propositions were put forth on the question of amateur versus professional tennis and open tournaments:

1. To abolish from the ILTF rules any references to "amateurs" and "professionals" as such, leaving it as the national associations' local option.
2. To retain the present rules and organize a central ILTF "control" to insure compliance throughout the world.
3. To retain present rules but to delegate to each national association the responsibility of defining allowable expenses and enforcement of the rules.

Since only the first proposition really created any hope of open tennis, the question of open tournaments was put on the agenda as a fourth question, with the USLTA retaining its historic position for local option. The first two proposals were defeated, as was the one concerning open tournaments. The third was held over for "further study." A stalemate had been reached. The smaller nations plus the Soviet bloc and Australia remained opposed to open tennis, while the British, Americans, and French favored it. Then, surprisingly, the USLTA reversed itself and adopted a position opposed to open tournaments. This turn of events came at a time when pro tennis was showing steady growth in the United States.

In 1967 the ILTF at its annual meeting voted down a British proposal to abolish the distinction between amateurs and professionals by a vote of 139 to 83, with the USLTA voting with the majority. Then came the most startling confrontation in the history of international tennis politics. The Council of the Lawn Tennis Association voted to hold the 1968 Wimbledon tournament as an open event "come hell or high water." The British threw down the gauntlet and brazenly defied the will of the ILTF. It was the greatest rebellion tennis officialdom had ever known. On December 14, 1967, the British carried the matter a step further. By a vote of 295 to 5, the LTA voted not only to hold an open at Wimbledon but to eliminate the distinction among players effective April 22, 1968, the first day of play at Bournemouth in the British Hard Court Championships.

In the United States, the news hit like a bombshell. USLTA president Bob Kelleher quickly assessed the situation. It became apparent that the leading American players, both amateur and professional, intended to play Wimbledon regardless of the ruling by the ILTF. For its part, the world body's president, Giorgio di Stefani of Italy, announced that the British LTA would be expelled from the ILTF on April 22 if it carried through its intentions. Kelleher then began to formulate a campaign to reverse the stand of the USLTA. Knowing that the British could not carry the day without allies, he also was aware that United States support was of utmost importance. Kelleher further sensed that the opportunity to end the hypocrisy surrounding tennis was at hand and, once gone, might not return again. He and his agents began explaining the position to delegations from USLTA sections and pushing for acceptance of the national autonomy position that had long been the USLTA stance.

Kelleher did not favor the British position on the abolition of the line between amateur and professionals, but he did support their desire for open play and wanted the United States to have a right to stage open tournaments as well. Despite the division of the ranks on the matter of amateur definition, Kelleher was able to get the leadership of the USLTA to accept the basic principle of national autonomy. On February 3, 1968, the meeting at Coronado, California, took place at which the USLTA membership took a strong positive position on open tournaments and national self-determination regarding the staging of these events. It rejected the British position on amateur and professional distinctions, but authorized Kelleher, as the USLTA delegate to the ILTF, to withdraw from the international group if individual nations were not granted the privilege of determining for themselves their right to stage open tournaments.

Sweden, meanwhile, entered a call for a special ILTF meeting on the British crisis. The meeting was held on March 30, 1968, in Paris. Kelleher made it obvious that the United States was prepared to take a hard line on the matter of national autonomy. The French already tacitly supported the British position and Australia also did an about face at this point. While disapproving of the British methods, the Australians agreed with the principle of open tournaments and the single classification of players. Australia affirmed its loyalty to the ILTF and questioned America's none-too-subtle threat to withdraw from the organization. But, regardless of the shades of difference among the nations, it was apparent that the overwhelming sentiment of the delegates was for open tournaments. At the meeting, a compromise proposal was approved without a single dissenting vote, permitting twelve open tournaments for 1968 including the British Hard Courts, Wimbledon, the French, and United States opens.

Thus at dawn on April 22, 1968, at the West Hants Lawn Tennis Club, came the start of the long-awaited open era of tennis. Owen Davidson of Australia was the first pro to face an amateur. He lost his first point to young Englishman John Clifton, but went on to win the match. Tennis history was being made. On the first day, pro Fred Stolle struggled to beat amateur Pete Curtis and then remarked, "we pros are bloody nervous. We have reputations to uphold and the amateurs have nothing to lose."

Within a decade, however, tennis had become more popular than at any time in its history and was the fastest-growing sport in the world. Nobody was any longer interested in which of its players were paid. The major question was how much did they make? Players earned as much as $100,000 for winning a major tournament, and the Wimbledon prize kitty grew from $64,000 in 1968 to more than $500,000 in 1978. Jimmy Connors of the United States won nearly $1,000,000 in 1977 alone without winning titles at either Wimbledon or Forest Hills.

For the USLTA and other national associations, the open era brought with it undreamed-of riches. The USTA signed a multimillion-dollar national television contract and built its own National Tennis Center in New York. Attendance at the United States Open surpassed all previous records at an astronomical rate. It was a long way from the lament voiced by USLTA president George Barnes in a letter to former president Julian Myrick in 1961:

> ... the income from our National Singles Championship has been gradually diminishing until the USLTA income in 1960, as you know, was nil. To rebuild our name players, we need money, to get money we need more spectators and to get more spectators we need name players. So it is ring-around-the-rosie! Which comes first, the spectators, the name players, or the money?

In the final analysis, the public demanded the name players—all the top players—competing together for the great tournament championships. As soon as tennis delivered that package, it boomed. Open tennis brought the big name players back from the pro touring troupes to the place from which they came, the national associations, and everybody benefited. It was only a pity that the prescience of Samuel Collom had not made its full impact four decades earlier.

LITTLE MO, BILLIE JEAN, AND GRAND SLAMS

Partly due to a combination of circumstances that included disinterest in many cases, no woman had ever achieved the Grand-Slam and only one, Mrs. Helen Wills Moody Roarke, had even come as close as winning three of the four major titles. In both 1928 and 1929, she missed by the margin of the Australian titles during the height of her dominance. Don Budge (1938) had achieved it among the men, and two others, Australia's Jack Crawford (1933) and England's Fred Perry (1934), missed it by one. In the years immediately following World War II, it was beginning to look as though a woman's Grand Slam was still far off in the future of the game. Two of the dominant players in the field, Sarah Palfrey Cooke and Pauline Betz, turned professional in 1946.

In the late 1940s, the major titles were split up among four Americans—the so-called "Big Four" —Margaret Osborne duPont, A. Louise Brough, Shirley Fry, and Doris Hart. Of this quartet, none was so clearly dominant over the others as to present a good chance at a Grand Slam. At Forest Hills, Miss Brough won in 1947 and Mrs. duPont in 1948 (beating Miss Brough in the final), repeating in 1949 and 1950 by downing Miss Hart both times in the final. Doris Hart won the Australian in 1949 and Louise Brough in 1950. From 1946 to 1952, Mrs. duPont won twice at Roland Garros, Miss Hart twice, and Miss Fry once (1951). Louise Brough played consistently better at Wimbledon than did the others, collecting thirteen titles between 1948 and 1955, including four singles crowns.

American women stars of late 1940s and early 1950s: *(left to right)* Mrs. Margaret Osborne duPont, A. Louise Brough, Doris Hart, and Shirley Fry.

As a group, the Americans dominated. In the All-England finals, Margaret Osborne defeated Doris Hart in the 1947 final, Louise Brough defeated Miss Hart in the 1948 final, Miss Brough defeated Mrs. duPont in both 1949 and 1950, and Miss Hart won in 1951 over Miss Fry. Miss Brough and Mrs. duPont won the doubles five times, Miss Brough also winning four mixed doubles championships (two with John Bromwich and one each with Tom Brown, Jr., and Eric Sturgess).

But in 1949, a petite Californian named Maureen Connolly made her first tentative effort at national recognition by winning the National Girls' 18 title at age fourteen. She turned the same trick the following year and then, in 1951, surprised the tennis world by defeating Shirley Fry, 6–3, 1–6, 6–4, to win the United States National title at Forest Hills before she reached seventeen. She was the second-youngest winner ever, missing by only a few days the record for youngest National champion set by May Sutton Bundy in 1904.

Overnight, "Little Mo," as she was dubbed by the press, became an American hero, the darling of the tennis set, and known to sports fans who didn't even follow the game. She also proved to be the dominant player of the world women's tennis scene. In 1952 she expanded her horizons with a first attempt at Wimbledon. She won it, stopping Louise Brough, 6–4, 6–3, for the championship.

Her career was brief, meteoric, and not entirely a happy experience for her. She was once asked by a reporter to relate her funniest moment in tennis and replied, "I never had any." Maureen Connolly was, however, the best women's player in the world during the span of her playing career. She added a second successive Forest Hills title to her Wimbledon in 1952.

For Miss Connolly, the remarkable string of victories was a reward for her hours on the tennis court, her years of practice under the watchful eye of Eleanor Tennant, coach of an earlier Californian woman whiz, Alice Marble. But they were also the realization of a dream her mother had nurtured for her since she was abandoned by her father as an infant in San Diego. Mrs. Connolly, frustrated in her own desire to become a concert pianist, turned to playing the organ. She then pushed her daughter into dancing and singing.

But an inept tonsillectomy ended hopes of a singing career for Maureen. The young girl's fondest wish was for a horse, but her family's economic status made it impossible.

She quite by chance came across an aggressive tennis stylist, named Gene Garret, using the courts in her neighborhood. She became infected with the idea that tennis would serve as a substitute for horseback riding. Then under Eleanor Tennant's guidance, she began to bloom rapidly, relying on her iron will and superb ground strokes. Miss Connolly was also often fueled by the belief that her opponents disliked her and that she, therefore, disliked them. This thought, often given credence by her mother and her teacher, gave her the driven look on the court that earned her the nickname "Little Mo." The sobriquet was applied by a San Diego tennis writer, not as a truncation of her first name, but rather due to her likeness, in the writer's mind, to the famed battleship *Missouri,* its decks bristling with unfriendly armament.

In 1953 Maureen Connolly became the first woman ever to win the Grand Slam. She started modestly enough by defeating Julie Sampson, 6–3, 6–2, in the Australian final. Then she played Doris Hart. Doris Hart played as fine tennis that year as she had ever played. Although hampered throughout her career by a deformed knee as the result of a childhood infection, Miss Hart was a strong all-around player. She wore long skirts, unfashionable even then, to mask her damaged knee, which restricted her movement to a rapid dancelike gait. Despite this difficulty, she was to win the Italian championship in 1953 and make the finals at Roland Garros, Wimbledon, and Forest Hills. It was her misfortune to play Maureen Connolly in those finals. At Paris, Miss Connolly won handily, 6–2, 6–4. Wimbledon was the best match of all, although it went to Maureen in straight sets, 8–6, 7–5. At Forest Hills, Miss Connolly won her third successive United States title and completed the Grand Slam, 6–2, 6–4.

A year later, she played the European circuit, winning the Italian singles, the French singles and doubles (with Mrs. H. C. Hopman), and her third Wimbledon singles. She never lost a match at Wimbledon and, in fact, lost only four during her entire career as a world-class player. She was beaten twice by Doris Hart, once by Shirley Fry, and once by Mrs. Beverly Fleitz. Following her return from Wimbledon, Miss Connolly indulged herself in the horseback riding of which she was so fond and suffered an accident which damaged her leg. It prevented her defense at Forest Hills and virtually ended her career, although she played professionally for a short time. In all, she won twelve major international titles and all nine of her matches in Wightman Cup play. Remarkably, Maureen Connolly accomplished all this before her twentieth birthday. In June, 1969, she tragically died of cancer at thirty-five.

Maureen Connolly's court brilliance not only eclipsed the performances of Margaret duPont, Louise Brough, Doris Hart, and Shirley Fry, but also the often-sensational exploits of Gussie Moran. Nicknamed "Gorgeous Gussie," Miss Moran's game was glamour—a quality she possessed in abundance.

Easily the most attractive of the players in the immediate postwar era in America, she was a sensation in the press if not always on the court. She often sported brief undershorts cut from leopard skin and generally appeared with peekaboo lace beneath, though not too far beneath, her short skirts. In 1949 she was good enough to earn a Centre Court match at Wimbledon and her attire created a positive scandal in the Royal Box. She later became a modestly successful radio and television sports commentator.

Following Maureen Connolly's retirement, Doris Hart snapped up two straight Forest Hills titles in 1954 and 1955, and her close friend Shirley Fry won the United States title in 1956. Miss Fry's 1956 victory marked the first appearance in the final for a black woman at Forest Hills—New Yorker Althea Gibson. Although she was beaten that year, 6–3, 6–4, Miss Gibson came back to win the next two years in a culmination of one of the sport's most heart-rending stories.

During her childhood on Harlem streets, Althea Gibson was often beaten by her father, a former boxer, and lived for some time in a publicly supported home. She triumphed against some of the greatest barriers ever hurdled in the world of sports, and was greatly helped when Alice Marble wrote a magazine article comparing her trial to the furor created by Gussie Moran's shorts, clearly

a much less important social question.

When Althea Gibson won her first Forest Hills title in 1957, she triumphed over Louise Brough. Miss Brough was making her sixth (and last) appearance in the United States final, and she had won only once. In 1958 Miss Gibson was the winner again, but not without a tough struggle against Darlene Hard, 3–6, 6–1, 6–2. Already thirty-one, age was working against her, and Althea Gibson never made the finals again.

Her game was built principally around strength and reach, but at her height she was a tireless competitor. Her first major international title was the Italian in 1956 (when she was twenty-nine). That summer, Miss Gibson also won the French singles and doubles (with Angela Buxton). In 1957 and 1958, she paralleled her Forest Hills wins

In her very short career, few, if any, tennis players have approached Maureen Connolly's record.

with singles victories at Wimbledon, although the British crowds were not what one might call warm to her triumphs.

In 1958 she also won the Wimbledon doubles, pairing with the next dominant face on the international women's circuit, Maria Bueno. Miss Bueno succeeded Miss Gibson as the champion at Forest Hills in 1959 and a year later lost a marathon final to Darlene Hard, 6–4, 10–12, 6–4. Miss Hard also won in 1961, defeating Britain's Ann Haydon, 6–4, 6–3. She made the final for the third straight time in 1962, but once again the Grand Slam was in the wind if not on the line. Margaret Smith of Australia was to be one of the top international players for the next decade, and she was warming to her task by winning the Australian and French titles in 1962. Miss Smith lost at Wimbledon, but defeated Darlene Hard, 9–7, 6–4, to win Forest Hills and complete a three-quarter slam. Four times in her career she was to win three of the four major titles. But she also was to become the second woman to win a Grand Slam, in 1970.

In 1963 Maria Bueno returned from a severe illness to win her second Forest Hills and earned her third the next year. The emergence in the late 1950s of Althea Gibson and Maria Bueno changed the direction of women's tennis and made it a more serious affair than it had been in the earlier postwar years. Perhaps influenced by Gussie Moran, tennis had spawned a group of glamour girls in the late 1940s and early 1950s. Included in this group were the likes of Lea Pericoli of Italy, tabbed "La Divina" by the popular press, and Karol Fageros, an American famed for her gold lamé panties. Although Miss Fageros won both the Canadian singles and doubles in 1954, the major contribution of these players often came at the Monte Carlo tennis show then staged by Gloria Butler, daughter of the donor of the Butler Cup for doubles.

Maria Bueno was perhaps the combination of beauty and skill that appealed, especially to European audiences. But she was a serious and talented tennis player. In her wake were to come two of the finest the game has ever known, Margaret Smith Court and Billie Jean Moffitt King.

Margaret Smith served notice on the tennis world by winning the championship of her native Australia seven straight years starting in 1960. Winning the doubles at Forest Hills in 1961, she first appeared at Wimbledon the same year and was beaten in the quarterfinals of the singles by Christine Truman. The following year, she was the Number One seed among the women at Wimbledon. In her first match, she faced a precocious young American, Billie Jean Moffitt. After the match, the American was no longer an unknown; she had knocked Margaret Court out of the tournament with an astonishing victory after rallying twice from match point.

Raised in Long Beach, California, the daughter of a fireman, Billie Jean Moffitt began her early tennis training at the Los Angeles Tennis Club after showing promise in local tournaments. One of her experiences there helped mold her later attitudes. Long the domain of Perry Jones, the club denied her a place in a formal photograph of winners because she did not have the "appropriate" tennis clothing (whites).

Actually, it was a bit unfair to class Billie Jean as an "unknown" at Wimbledon. Miss Moffitt had made her first appearance and won her first title there the year before. In 1960 she was ranked fourth in the United States at the age of sixteen and in 1961 had gone to Wimbledon where she teamed with Mrs. Karen Susman to win the doubles.

Yet this background did not detract from the magnitude of her upset victory over Margaret Smith. Billie Jean, too, was eliminated in a subse-

Maria Bueno was the first non-American player to break the United States' monopoly on National and Wimbledon titles after World War II.

quent round and her doubles partner, Karen Susman, won the singles in 1962. But over the final years before the advent of open play, the Misses Smith and Moffitt were to virtually monopolize the women's singles. Margaret Smith won it in 1963 and 1965 with Maria Bueno the champion in between. Following her 1965 marriage to attorney Larry King, Billie Jean returned in 1966 and won her first singles crown at the All-England, defeating Miss Bueno in the final.

At Forest Hills in 1965, Margaret Smith won her second United States title and achieved it by defeating Billie Jean, 8–6, 7–5. Maria Bueno won for the fourth and final time in 1966 by downing the United States Number Two, Nancy Richey, in the final. In 1967 Billie Jean King won both her second successive Wimbledon and her first Forest Hills. She defeated Britain's Ann Haydon Jones in both finals.

In 1968 the USLTA staged an International Indoor Tournament at Madison Square Garden for both men and women. It contained one of the most remarkable women's matches played in recent years. Mrs. King met Miss Richey, long her archrival, in the semifinal and quickly built a 5–1 edge in the second set after winning the first, 6–4, and was playing for match point. She smashed an overhead that angled sharply for the right sideline.

Surprisingly, Miss Richey reached it and returned a high lob that Billie Jean inexplicably botched into the net. Suddenly, the match completely reversed itself as the Garden crowd sat in stunned silence. Miss Richey won thirty-nine of the next fifty-one points, sweeping twelve straight games and winning the match. The next night she defeated Australia's Judy Tegart for the tournament title. After this strange collapse, Mrs. King signed a professional contract with the National Tennis League, headed by former United States Davis Cup captain George MacCall. Arthur Ashe won the men's crown in that event (over Roy Emerson, 6–4, 6–4, 7–5) and also turned pro.

With the open revolution now at hand, Mrs. King gleefully headed for England, freed from the shackles of amateur restraint to defend her Wimbledon championship. Despite having been tired by a strenuous schedule and having just recovered from a mild illness, she reached the semifinals

with relative ease. Then it appeared that she had come a cropper. Ann Haydon Jones, whom she had beaten in the final the previous year, won the first set, 6–4, and served for the match leading the second, 5–4. At 15–all, however, Mrs. King denied her, broke her service and ran off a thirteen-point string that carried her to 1–0 in the third set. Mrs. King then won it, 4–6, 7–5, 6–2, after having been three points from elimination.

Meanwhile, Miss Tegart was knocking out Billie Jean's major competition, defeating Margaret Smith Court and Nancy Richey. But when the pair met in the finals, Mrs. King halted Miss Tegart's upset string with a 9–7, 7–5 victory for her third straight All-England singles. She also teamed with Rosemary Casals to win the doubles, and thus earned her first two major international titles as a professional. In her amateur career, she had won thirty-one national championships, including fourteen American titles, by age twenty-four.

With Forest Hills now set to host the first United States Open, the National Singles titles were shifted to Boston's venerable Longwood, where Margaret Smith Court won the singles by defeating Maria Bueno in the final. At Forest Hills, Mrs. King was trying to rule again over the mixed bag of amateurs, "players," and contract pros who made up the field. She was able to master all but one. In the final, she was beaten by Virginia Wade of Britain, who played one of the finest matches of her career to win, 6–4, 6–2.

Mrs. Margaret Smith Court, with her Wimbledon win shown here, was the second woman to accomplish the Grand Slam.

Although she was denied the Forest Hills championship, it had been an eventful and worthwhile year for Mrs. King. She was the top money winner among the women pros, she had matched Maureen Connolly's streak of three straight Wimbledon singles titles and, most importantly, she had achieved professional status and could make her living from tennis. Billie Jean King was later to become as much a social activist as a tennis star, providing much of the impetus for the first real women's pro tour, pressing publicly and vigorously for the ideals of the "women's liberation" movement and helping to form the Women's Tennis Association, the international counterpart of the men players' group (the ATP).

One of the finest mixed-doubles teams was Billy Talbert and Mrs. Margaret Osborne duPont.

TENNIS MOVES INTO ITS SECOND CENTURY

With the reaffirmation of the open era, 1969 brought an expanded schedule of open events and marked the entrance of the professional players into almost all of the major world-class events except for the Davis Cup, Wightman Cup, and other similar tournaments for national teams.

It also brought tennis its first pro Grand Slam. Rod Laver, who had turned the trick as an amateur in 1962, swept through the four traditional major events. He defeated Andres Gimeno, 6–3, 6–4, 7–5, in Australia; Ken Rosewall, 6–4, 6–3, 6–4, at Roland Garros; and John Newcombe, 6–4, 5–7, 6–4, 6–4, at Wimbledon. Laver completed the Slam by defeating fellow Australian lefthander Tony Roche at Forest Hills, 7–9, 6–1, 6–3, 6–2. The big crowd drawn by Laver for the United States Open final raised the tournament's attendance to 101,496. By 1975 this figure more than doubled.

In 1971 former United States Davis Cup captain and doubles champion Bill Talbert was named tournament director at the Open. In the five years of his stewardship, the attendance rose from 122,-996 in 1970 to 153,287 in 1974 and leaped to 216,683 in 1975 when night play was introduced at the West Side Tennis Club for the first time.

After Virginia Wade won the first United States Open title in 1968, she was succeeded for two years by Margaret Smith Court. In 1969 Mrs. Court defeated American Nancy Richey and the following year turned back Rosemary Casals to complete her women's Grand Slam. In her 1970 Grand Slam, she had defeated Kerry Melville, 6–1, 6–3, for the Australian title; Ann Haydon Jones, 6–1, 4–6, 6–3, for the French; and Billie Jean King, 14–12, 11–9, for the Wimbledon. Roche, loser to Laver the year before, made the Forest Hills final again in 1970, but again lost, this time to Ken Rosewall in four sets.

Wimbledon's second attempt at an Open in 1969 produced, in addition to Laver's victory in the men's final, a title for Ann Haydon Jones, who defeated Billie Jean King for the women's championship. In 1970 Margaret Court won her third All-England singles crown en route to the Grand Slam, and John Newcombe took the first of his two straight Wimbledon men's championships. Evonne Goolagong shared the 1971 honors at Wimbledon with Newcombe, winning the final over the defending Mrs. Court, 6–4, 6–1.

At Forest Hills in 1971, Chris Evert made her debut, which equaled the excitement generated by Miss Goolagong's triumph at the All-England. Having won forty-six straight amateur matches coming into the tournament, Christine Marie Evert of Fort Lauderdale, Florida, reached the semifinals at age sixteen before losing to Mrs. King in a match played before a sellout crowd on a Friday afternoon.

Chris Evert had been a junior champion of note, winning the United States fourteen-and-under title at thirteen in 1968. By 1971 she was ranked sixteenth nationally by the USLTA and trounced Virginia Wade, 6–1, 6–1, in her Wightman Cup debut. In the process she became the youngest girl ever to play a Wightman Cup match. After declining more than $50,000 in prize money, she turned professional on her eighteenth birthday in December, 1972. Miss Evert was then ranked third in the United States. She became the top women's player in the world by 1974, when she won 103 of 110 matches played and captured the titles at the Italian, French, and Wimbledon championships.

"Chrissie," as she was then known, created a sensational press excitement and public response upon her Forest Hills debut, and it almost overshadowed the ultimate victories of Stan Smith over Jan Kodes and Mrs. King over Rosemary Casals. From the very onset of her career, Miss Evert was possessed of a calm on-court demeanor of self-control and confidence. Off the court, she demonstrated a bright, often cheerful, countenance to the public that softened what sometimes seemed to be an ice-water playing concentration and the killer-instinct of a champion.

Stan Smith became the first American to win at Wimbledon since 1963, when he defeated Ilie Nastase in the 1972 final, although defender Newcombe was not among the field. Billie Jean King captured the women's title by unseating Miss Goolagong, the charming Australian aborigine, then twenty, in the final, 6–3, 6–3.

Nastase salvaged some semblance of stature by beating Arthur Ashe for the United States Open championship and also winning the Grand Prix Masters at Barcelona over Smith, 6–3, 6–2, 3–6, 2–6, 6–3. Mrs. King won for the second straight year over Kerry Melville in the women's final.

In 1973 Mrs. King repeated at Wimbledon and Jan Kodes captured the men's final in the midst of the ATP boycott, which cut most of the leading pros out of the men's field. Nastase won the Grand Prix Masters for the third year running and Mrs. King, ranked Number One in the world by general consensus on her 1972 record, was upset by Mrs. Court in the Forest Hills championship match. Newcombe, who stayed out of Wimbledon due to the boycott, won at Forest Hills by defeating Kodes in a tough five-set final.

Jimmy Connors burst onto the world scene in 1974 by winning at Australia, Wimbledon, and Forest Hills, downing the veteran Rosewall at the All-England, 6–1, 6–1, 6–4, and at the United States Open, 6–1, 6–0, 6–1. Miss Evert was the dominant force in women's tennis but lost the Virginia Slims final (and its record women's prize of $32,000) to Evonne Goolagong, 6–3, 6–4. Miss Goolagong had reached the Slims final by upsetting Mrs. King in the semis. But Billie Jean won at Forest Hills and took some revenge against Miss Goolagong, rallying after dropping the first set to win, 3–6, 6–3, 7–5.

Guillermo Vilas of Argentina became a world-class player by winning the Grand Prix Masters title over three-time winner Nastase, 7–6, 6–2, 3–6, 3–6, 6–4. Nastase gained the Masters title for the fourth time in five years in 1975 by defeating Swedish sensation Bjorn Borg in the final, 6–2, 6–2, 6–1, at Stockholm. John Newcombe turned back Jimmy Connors in the Australian final while Borg and Vilas met in the French championship with the Swede winning, 6–2, 6–3, 6–4. At Wimbledon, it was the first all-American final since Jack Kramer and Tom Brown in 1947, and Arthur Ashe won over Jimmy Connors, 6–1, 6–1, 5–7, 6–4.

Connors also made the final at Forest Hills and also lost. This time he was beaten by old pro Manuel Orantes in the last grass tournament championship, 6–4, 6–3, 6–3. A synthetic surface (Hartru) was then installed at the behest of the ATP. The change left Wimbledon as the major tournament in the world still contested on natural grass.

Among the women, 1975 saw Chris Evert win

Rod Laver winning his first of four Wimbledon titles. The Duchess of Kent made the presentation.

a staggering sixteen of the twenty-four tournaments she entered, including the final eight that year. She finished the year with thirty-five straight matches won and wound up with the Virginia Slims championship, the United States Clay Court title for the fourth straight year, and more than $350,000 in earnings. Miss Evert also won at Forest Hills. Evonne Goolagong was a losing finalist for the third year in a row, 5–7, 6–4, 6–2. Miss Evert, however, was not a party to the Wimbledon final, as Billie Jean King defeated Miss Goolagong (now Mrs. Roger Cawley), 6–0, 6–1.

The advent of open tennis as a universal fact of the tennis world brought about a wide range of disputes both off court and on, gave new measuring standards for the status of players, and engendered the greatest growth in the history of the game. In 1971 a major administrative crisis came to the fore when the ILTF threatened to ban players under contract to the Dallas-based World Championship Tennis pro circuit backed by oilman Lamar Hunt. The ILTF decreed that after January 1, 1972, WCT contract professionals would be prohibited from playing in events sanctioned by the ILTF and its member associations or at clubs belonging to those groups. The confrontation came about through conflicts in scheduling between the WCT and the ILTF's Grand Prix, begun in 1970 under the international sponsorship of the Pepsi-Cola organization. The two groups were unable to agree on conditions under which the thirty-two men then contracted to WCT would compete in ILTF Grand Prix events. The ban affected such players as Grand Slam winners Rod Laver, Ken Rosewall, John Newcombe, and Arthur Ashe.

At the root of the dispute was the desire of Hunt and his tournament managers to have a voice in the scheduling, conduct, and financial affairs of tournaments and a share of the profits from events in which players under contract to them played. The USLTA expressed strong opposition to the ILTF decree and considered it contrary to the best interests of tennis. By 1972 the dispute between the ILTF and the WCT took another turn, this time in the direction of compromise when the ILTF and the WCT agreed to schedule two separate tours from January to May each year.

But the year 1972 was marked most significantly by organizational movements among the players who sought more influence over their own destinies. In September, a group of tournament players organized themselves, with Cliff Drysdale of South Africa as president, as the "Association of Tennis Professionals." Jack Kramer, a long-time promoter of pro tours in the United States and a former standout player, was named executive director of the organization. The ATP began with fifty-six members paying $400 dues each. Also, action began to intensify on the women's front.

Gladys M. Heldman, publisher of an American tennis magazine, *World Tennis,* began forming a group of touring women pros, and a ruling by the United States government almost threw a sponsor into her lap. After 1971 cigarette advertising was banned on United States television. What followed was the Virginia Slims Circuit, supported by the Phillip Morris organization as a promotional outlet for its cigarette targeted primarily at women. The Slims began tentatively with two tournaments in 1971, but formed a full-fledged

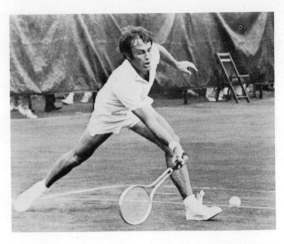

John Newcombe of Australia won the Men's title in 1967, 1970, and 1971.

circuit the next year. Ultimately, it was to grow into a tour encompassing more than a dozen tournaments a year and its final became one of the major women's events.

In mid-1973, the women formed their own group, the Women's Tennis Association, with Billie Jean King as its president. A controversy over the Virginia Slims circuit flared when the ILTF threatened to bar the players on the unsanctioned tour from competing in most of the world's major tournaments, including Grand Prix events.

An immediate outgrowth of this was a lawsuit against the United States Lawn Tennis Association brought in early 1973 by Mrs. Heldman, organizer of the original women's tour which became the Slims Circuit. She was subsequently joined in the action by Mrs. King. Seeking a preliminary injunction against the USLTA, they alleged antitrust violations and interference with contractual rights. The suit, in effect, challenged the Association's power to sanction tournaments.

Justice Milton Pollack in the New York Federal District Court denied the motion for injunction and ruled in favor of the USLTA. Subsequently, the Virginia Slims Circuit applied for, and received, USLTA sanction for its tournaments. During the course of the dispute, the USLTA organized its own tour—the Women's Prize Money Circuit—which featured such players as Chris Evert, Virginia Wade, and Evonne Goolagong. In

Chuck McKinley in 1963 was the most recent American to win a Men's Singles title at Wimbledon.

the aftermath of the suit and after Slims' request for USLTA sanction, players on the USLTA circuit joined the Slims tour.

This move gave women's tennis an important boost as a professional spectator attraction, since it presented all of the top stars in the same package. Meanwhile, the men's tour was fragmented into two or three different groupings playing at the same time at different sites, and still another group, led by American star Jimmy Connors, played independently of both WCT and the Grand Prix. Connors's manager, Bill Riordan, structured his own minicircuit as a showcase for Connors and several other men pros.

Since its formation in 1913, the ILTF had ruled the world of tennis and, having survived its spat with the WCT, seemed to be on firm ground once more. But in 1973, it faced what was in some ways an even more difficult challenge from the ATP. The dispute was ignited by a shot fired in the Balkans when Nikki Pilic of Yugoslavia was suspended by his national association for failing to play for the Yugoslavian Davis Cup team. The ILTF reduced the term of the initial suspension, but it was still of sufficient duration to exclude Pilic from the Italian and French opens and the All-England. The Italians defied the ILTF and permitted Pilic to enter the event, but the British denied his entry on the grounds of the suspension. The ATP then sued on Pilic's behalf.

It had been anticipated by the ATP that only a face-saving pro forma defense would be offered by the All-England Club. However, when a full and successful defense was presented by the stubborn British, the ATP called for a boycott of the Wimbledon event by all of its members. As a result, over eighty of the leading men players refused to play and only a trio of ATP members were in the Wimbledon men's field (Briton Roger Taylor, Rumanian Ilie Nastase, and Australian Ray Keldie). The unprecedented boycott was reinforced when Taylor and Nastase were ostensibly fined $5,000 each by the ATP for participating and Keldie was dunned $1,000. Despite the absence of the ATP players, Wimbledon attracted its usual sellout crowds.

Nonetheless, adverse public and press reaction placed pressure on the All-England Club and an accord was finally reached later in the year when the ILTF agreed to allow the ATP some say in the affairs of the major tournaments in which its members competed.

Czechoslovakian Jan Kodes, the 1970 French champion, won the men's title against the reduced field at Wimbledon by beating Russian Number One Alex Metreveli in the final. It was the only final for either at the All-England.

Earlier in the same year, the World Team Tennis league was formed in the United States and began its first season in 1974 with sixteen clubs playing a truncated single-set version of tennis, with men's and women's singles and doubles and a mixed doubles match comprising each night's play. The league devised a weighted scoring system which discarded standard tennis concepts and used a format of five sets consisting of at least six games but not more than thirteen. Both the ILTF and ATP were hostile to the WTT.

During its first season of 1974, World Team Tennis claimed attendance of 833,966 for its sixteen teams, each playing a forty-four-game schedule. However, in 1975, the league was reduced to ten franchises in two divisions (Eastern and Western). The Denver Racquets won the 1974 playoff championship and then moved to Phoenix. Succeeding WTT champions were: 1975, Pittsburgh Triangles; 1976, New York Sets; 1977, New York Apples; 1978, Los Angeles Strings. Many noted players joined WTT teams for all or part of their respective schedules during the league's early years, including Billie Jean King, playing coach of the Philadelphia Freedoms and later with New York. In November, 1974, Mrs. King's husband, Larry, became the fourth president of the league.

When, in 1974, Jimmy Connors and Evonne Goolagong signed contracts with WTT teams, they were barred by the Italian and French federations from playing in the open championships in those countries. Connors and Miss Goolagong immediately sought legal relief in the courts. By being denied entry into the French Open, Connors, having won at Australia, Wimbledon, and Forest Hills that year, was not permitted a chance for the traditional Grand Slam. Alleging a conspiracy to monopolize the game, Connors sued the ATP, Jack Kramer, the French federation, and others. The matter was settled out of court, but its impact was to make federations wary of attacking players due to their affiliation with WTT. By merely surviving until 1978, the WTT illustrated the enormous influence of American economic weight on the growth of the game during the open era.

One of the outgrowths of the constant struggle between tennis administrators and pro players was the formation of the Men's International Professional Tennis Council in 1974 with representatives from the players, promoters, and the national associations. A year later, the Women's International Professional Tennis Council was also formed in conjunction with the ILTF. Both men and women pros won several other points at issue during 1974, including the formal adoption by the ILTF of the twelve-point form of the tie-breaker over the nine-point playoff which was unpopular with the players (though favored by the USLTA and a majority of fans). The nine-point system, however, was retained by the Virginia Slims Circuit. The ladies achieved equal prize money when the United States Open granted them parity with the men on a round-by-round basis in the $270,-000 prize kitty offered at Forest Hills in 1974. However, this set off a battle with the men, who claimed that the parity was really an inequality against them.

The male pros said that they played longer matches, more of them, and were the primary box-office attraction for major tournaments. Neither the women nor the United States Open agreed and equal prize money was retained at the Open, where the total purse rose to over $500,000 in 1978.

By the mid-1970s, relative stabilization had been reached after a decade of jockeying between players, promoters, and administrators. However, the formation of the International Professional Tennis Councils had handed over to the players, promoters, and national associations much of the authority previously held by the ILTF.

Television became a major factor in the world of tennis, with all three major American networks scheduling hours of live coverage of major events such as Wimbledon (via satellite), Forest Hills, the Grand Prix Masters, Virginia Slims finals, and the WCT's principal tournaments. Another difficulty presented itself when, in 1977, it was revealed that a series of televised matches on a winner-

take-all basis were, in fact, nothing of the sort. All players had, indeed, been guaranteed a minimum prize.

While this revelation did not turn into a major scandal, it did provoke a Congressional inquiry into television sports and, more importantly, illustrated that the dangers were present for such problems in the future. The USTA, WCT, and other interested parties took steps to avoid a repetition of this situation. The USTA had negotiated a lucrative television contract for the Open, and, armed with this support, broke away from the long-time relationship with the West Side Tennis Club in New York, in 1977, with the declaration that it was constructing a new $6 million National Tennis Center in New York on the former site of the 1939 and 1964 World's Fairs in Flushing Meadow.

This project involved the rebuilding of the city-owned Armstrong Stadium (originally Singer Bowl) and had a 20,000-seat facility ready for the 1978 United States Open. Included in this project were public courts and an indoor facility.

By constructing a new home for the Open (and such other events as major Davis Cup ties), the USTA confirmed its place as the major national association in the open era. New York's Madison Square Garden became the home for the Grand Prix Masters in 1978. That event had been played in the United States only once before, in 1976 when Manuel Orantes won the title by defeating Wojtek Fibak, 5–7, 6–2, 0–6, 7–6, 6–1, with a startling comeback.

Other 1976 major titles included a surprise win in the Australian championship by Mark Edmondson over John Newcombe in four sets, Adriano Panatta's win over Guillermo Vilas in the Italian final in four sets, including two 7–6 tie-breakers, and Panatta's win over American Harold Solomon in the final at Roland Garros. At Wimbledon, Roscoe Tanner knocked Jimmy Connors out with a straight-set win in the quarterfinals, and Bjorn Borg then beat Tanner in the semifinal and Nastase in the final to win. Borg and Connors met in the Forest Hills final and Connors won a tense match, 6–4, 3–6, 7–6, 6–4, to lay claim to the world's Number One ranking. He finished with $687,335 in winnings for the year.

Chris Evert was once again the big winner

among the women with $343,165 in earnings. Miss Evert snapped a twenty-five-match winning streak by Evonne Goolagong Cawley at Wimbledon to win the final, 6–3, 4–6, 8–6, after having lost the Virginia Slims final to her in another three-set battle at Los Angeles earlier in the year. Miss Evert also won her second consecutive Forest Hills, defeating Mrs. Cawley, 6–3, 6–0. In addition, she defeated Françoise Durr of France for the $45,000 first prize in the Colgate Inaugural at Palm Springs, California.

The new events were making more and more of an impact on the prize money lists as well as the new financial standard for judging the leading players. While certain tennis officials and organizations, notably the ITF, hung tenaciously onto the traditional concepts, it was clear that things had changed with the open era. Among them was the Grand Slam concept.

For all practical purposes, the original Grand Slam of Australia, France, Wimbledon, and the United States titles was no longer valid. The former two tournaments had diminished somewhat in luster and were often passed up by the leading players. Both the men and women among the world-class players felt that Wimbledon and the United States Open, the two tournaments with the largest prize-money offerings among the major world events, were definitely events worthy of Grand Slam stature. But for most of the women the Virginia Slims final and the Colgate World Series supplanted Australia and France in the rank of importance. For the men, the peer status of Australia and France was considered much less than that of the WCT final and the Grand Prix Masters. Both of these events were the culmination of a season of competition, and players shared with many fans the belief that they were the most valid measures of championship play.

In 1970 the Grand Prix Masters began in Tokyo and the next year the Dallas-based WCT finals were held for the first time. Some basis for the players' feelings could be seen in the fact that from 1971 through 1977, no man had ever won more than two of the four events. Ilie Nastase did it in 1972, Connors in both 1974 and 1977, Arthur Ashe in 1975, and Bjorn Borg in 1976.

Chris Evert won three of four among the

Professional tennis has come a long way since 1926. You will note above that Rod Laver collected $35,000 for victory in the finals of the 1970 Tennis Champion Classic. In 1971 he received $170,000 for winning all fourteen matches in the 1971 Classic.

women in both 1976 and 1977, failing to win only the Virginia Slims final the first year and Wimbledon the second. After winning the Slims crown in 1975, Miss Evert lost to the 1974 champ, Evonne Goolagong, in 1976.

International team competition was also opened up by the elimination of the Challenge Round in the Davis Cup. Starting in 1972, when the defender had to play through the draw for the first time, five different nations won the Cup in five years although political considerations somewhat marred the event.

In 1972 the United States played through the draw and successfully defended the Cup by defeating Romania, 3–2, in a wild final held at the Progresul Club in Bucharest. The United States had voluntarily given choice of grounds to the Romanians but still won the Cup, clinching on Stan Smith's final day singles win over Ion Tiriac. The key win was the doubles when Smith and Erik van Dillen swept Tiriac and Ilie Nastase in straight sets. Tiriac later became Guillermo Vilas's coach and confidant.

A year later, the United States again made the final but was swept out, 5–0, before the onslaught of Australia's two-man team of Rod Laver and John Newcombe. Final restrictions against contract pro players were dropped the next year but politics became an even bigger issue. Largely through a series of defaults, the South African team qualified for the final. They then won the Cup by default when India's government refused its team permission to play in the final.

The Cup was won on the court again in 1975 when Sweden, led by young wunderkind Bjorn Borg, defeated Czechoslovakia in the first indoor final (played at Stockholm). Swedish captain Lennart Bergelin, a former player for his nation, subsequently became Borg's manager. In 1976 Italy defeated Chile in the final, 4–1, as Adriano Panatta won two singles and teamed with Paoli Bertolucci on the winning doubles team. In 1977 Australia won again, taking its twenty-fourth Cup win, beating Italy at Sydney, 3–1, with one match abandoned.

It was 1978 before 1977 tennis came to a close, and there was even some disagreement as to that point. But most of the disagreement centered around who was the top male player in the world during 1977. Guillermo Vilas made a valid claim by winning eighty-five of eighty-six matches in one stretch including a defeat of Jimmy Connors in the round-robin phase of the Grand Prix Masters in early January, 1978.

But Vilas was injured in that match and his left ankle forced him out of the tournament after he withdrew from his last round-robin match and then lost to Bjorn Borg in the semifinals. Connors, meanwhile, won his semifinal over Brian Gottfried and beat Borg for the Masters title.

Connors was easily the year's biggest money winner and claimed to be the Number One after defeating Borg in the Masters. He had also won the WCT final over Dick Stockton, 6–7, 6–1, 6–4, 6–3, earlier in the year. But Borg had defeated Connors in the 1977 Pepsi Grand Slam final and also topped him to win the Wimbledon singles. Vilas, for his part, beat Connors in the Forest Hills final as well as in the classic match in the Masters' round robin. In itself, the match between Connors and Vilas was a marvel. It attracted a massive crowd of 18,690, the largest ever for an indoor tournament match in the United States, and Vilas finally outlasted Connors, 6–4, 3–6, 7–5, with tennis that had the big crowd cheering throughout.

There was little argument as to the Number One among the women. It was Chris Evert. She won the Virginia Slims final, earned $503,134 ($200,000 more than runner-up Martina Navratilova), and reigned as singles champion of the women's World Series (defeating Navratilova, 6–3, 7–6) and the United States Open, where she won for the third straight year in 1977. She thus had three quarters of the new Grand Slam, missing only Wimbledon.

But Grand Slam concepts weren't all that had changed. During the decade following the approval of open competition, a massive growth in prize-money events had pushed the kitty available for professional players to over $12 million per year. The vast majority of this money was contributed by United States–based corporations. ITF officials and European federations began to see American money dominating the sport and detracting from their authority.

Mrs. Billie Jean King of the United States won the Wimbledon in 1968.

As a practical matter, the huge pro tours were already beyond the grasp of the ITF but, in 1977, the international group sought to extract large sanction fees for major events sponsored by corporations. A particular bone of contention was the $250,000 Grand Slam event conducted in Boca Raton, Florida, and sponsored by Pepsi-Cola. USTA president W. E. (Slew) Hester threatened to withdraw the American association from the ITF if the demands were pushed.

Early in 1978, the ITF announced that it was forming a panel to name the world's top ten players at the end of the year. Previously, world top ten lists had been produced by major tennis writers with the London *Daily Telegraph*'s list, chosen by the respected Lance Tingay, given the most credence. The ITF named a three-man panel of former champions (Don Budge, Lew Hoad, and Fred Perry) to pick the world's Number One man after a dispute arose over who could claim that title for 1977. ITF head Phillip Chatrier announced the formation of the panel and said in his statement that it was rightfully the job of the ITF to select the Number One in the world. Many of the leading players felt that this move was merely an effort by the ITF to reimpose itself in the professional territory instead of the playing rules and amateur affairs areas with which it had been left by the dynamics of the new open era.

"If they would come around every week," said the outspoken Connors, "and see the players every week, that would be good. But I don't think anybody should have a job sitting around their house reading the results in the paper."

As the open era had unfolded, policy decisions in major matters gradually came under the control of councils composed of the players' associations, tournament directors, and national associations, with the ITF given little say in how the money was to be distributed and receiving little of the booty. When, in November, 1977, it sought to require United States tournaments to pay a percentage of their gross receipts to the ITF, Hester informed the world body that it would force the USTA out of the group if it persisted.

One sign of growing dominance of American money in tennis was the signing of the three-year agreement to stage the Grand Prix Masters at Madison Square Garden in January, beginning in

Virginia Wade of Great Britain won the first United States Women's Open title.

1978, under the sponsorship of Colgate Palmolive, a multinational company headquartered in New York.

Pepsi-Cola's continued staging of the Grand Slam in Florida was another sign of this trend. When Bjorn Borg defeated Connors, 7–6, 3–6, 6–1, for the second straight year in the 1978 final, he carted away $125,000. The other three men in the field divided a like amount with Connors getting $60,000, third-place finisher Brian Gottfried $40,000, and fourth-place man Vitas Gerulaitis $25,000.

But Connors started faster than anyone in 1978, winning the Grand Prix Masters' final over Borg at the Garden and claiming the $100,000 winner's purse. After losing to Borg in the Grand Slam, he appeared a week later in the finals of the $225,000 United States Indoors at Philadelphia against Roscoe Tanner. Connors won the title with a straight-set victory over Tanner. The tournament was an ironic reversal of the Wimbledon two years earlier where Tanner knocked Connors out of the quarterfinals and lost the semifinal to Borg. In the United States Pro Indoor event in 1978, Tanner eliminated Borg in the quarterfinals and made the final only to lose to Connors.

Meanwhile, Martina Navratilova, the twenty-one-year-old former Czechoslovakian champion who was seeking United States citizenship, exploded on the women's circuit. She started 1978 by winning seven of the first ten Virginia Slims tournaments, including her first triumph over Billie Jean King in five tries. Miss Navratilova defeated Mrs. King, 1–6, 6–2, 6–2, at Houston. In part, the early 1978 surge by Miss Navratilova was due to the 122-day vacation taken by Chris Evert beginning late in 1977.

But Miss Evert returned in March and made the finals in the last two events on the Virginia Slims Circuit (at Boston and Philadelphia), winning in her second tournament. In April, she annexed her fifth straight Family Circle Cup title, defeating Kerry Reid in the final, 6–2, 6–0. That win extended her clay-court victory string to 118 matches in succession, encompassing twenty-four winning tournaments.

Miss Navratilova, after a brief vacation of her own, won the Slims championship by defeating Evonne Goolagong, 7–6, 6–4, at Oakland. She easily finished as the top singles player on the eleven-tournament circuit. The 1978 Virginia Slims attracted 406,881 fans for its tournaments plus the $150,000 final at Oakland, but its future was very much in doubt.

Martina Navratilova dominated women's play during most of the year, winning at Wimbledon over Chris Evert after Miss Evert had eliminated defending champion Virginia Wade.

But as the year progressed, 1978 became more a stage for the virtuoso performance of Bjorn Borg. He won the Italian Open by defeating Adriano Panatta in the final, took the French Open by routing Guillermo Vilas in the final, and won his third successive Wimbledon title with a decisive 6–2, 6–2, 6–3 final win over Jimmy Connors. Borg thus became the first man since England's Fred Perry to win the crown three straight years. Perry did it in 1934, 1935, and 1936.

Subsequent to the Oakland final in April, a major schism developed between Virginia Slims and the Women's Tennis Association. The WTA voted to reject the Slims' offer of eleven $120,000 events for 1979 plus a $400,000 final at New York's Madison Square Garden. The Association sought instead to widen the base of its sponsorship with individual underwriters for each of its 1979 tournaments.

But the major development of 1978 was the opening of the USTA National Tennis Center in New York's Flushing Meadow. Formal ceremo-

nies were held on the evening of August 29 and two matches played in the 20,000-seat Stadium. The following day, a full order of play was staged using the field courts and the 6,000-seat Grandstand.

Jimmy Connors made the 1978 U.S. Open a tour de force for his aggressive style on the fast DecoTurf courts. He won the title with a straight-set, 6–4, 6–2, 6–2, win over Bjorn Borg in the final. Connors had taken out young John McEnroe in the semis while Borg had eliminated Vitas Gerulaitis to reach the final meeting with Connors.

Chris Evert won her fourth straight women's Open singles crown over the surprise of the tournament, 16-year-old Pam Shriver, 7–5, 6–4. Miss Shriver had reached the final with a stunning upset of Martina Navratilova in the semis after beating Leslie Hunt and eighth-seed Kerry Reid in the two previous rounds.

Despite the loss of one night's play to rain, the total attendance for the tournament was a record 275,300 with an overflow crowd of 19,537 on hand for the singles finals, both of which were staged on the same day for the first time.

For players, spectators and USTA officials, the new National Tennis Center was virtually an unqualified success.

Another pleasant surprise came a month later when the U.S. Davis Cup team edged Sweden, 3–2, on Arthur Ashe's third-day singles win, overcoming two wins by Sweden's Borg. Great Britain unseated the defending Australians, 3–2, in the other semifinal to set up the first U.S.–Britain final since 1937, which the U.S. won handily, 4–1.

Another Davis Cup, the country's twenty-sixth, was recorded the following year when the American team rolled through Italy, 5–0. But in 1980, the U.S. squad was knocked out of the Cup competition in the quarterfinal round by Argentina.

In 1981, the Davis Cup format underwent some significant changes, with the zonal system being eliminated for the top sixteen teams. In the first major adjustment of the competition since 1923 (other than the dropping of the Challenge Round in 1972), the first sixteen were seeded against each other in a top division. They then engaged in a knock-out tournament to determine the winner. Four of the first sixteen were subject to relegation after 1981, to be replaced by the four nations with the best performance in the zonal rounds played among those not eligible for the Cup that calendar year.

As to 1978 competition in the major tournaments, Jimmy Connors was the Grand Prix top point producer during the year but failed to qualify for the $300,000 bonus money. That went, instead, to third-place finisher Eddie Dibbs. In any case, John McEnroe strengthened his case for greatness with a win in the Grand Prix Masters at the end of the 1978 season.

In 1978, Martina Navratilova was the dominant force in the Virginia Slims' final season. In 1979, the major women's indoor circuit was taken over by Avon Products.

Bjorn Borg continued to control the prize money in the major tournaments. In 1978, he won his third straight singles crown at Wimbledon and also captured both the French and Italian crowns. The only major title that managed to elude him was the U.S. Open. In its first year at the spectacular new site, Borg was beaten by Connors in the final.

Borg extended his Wimbledon singles streak to five successive years by winning again in 1979 (over Roscoe Tanner) and in 1980 (over John McEnroe).

McEnroe, who won the U.S. Open in 1979, denied Borg a chance at the Grand Slam with a victory over the Swedish star at Flushing the next year. Both the 1980 Wimbledon final, won by Borg, and the return match at the U.S. Open, were epic five-setters. The split between the two men was an equitable result.

Meanwhile, Chris Evert, who married British Davis Cupper John Lloyd, returned to the women's wars in 1979 after a brief honeymoon and picked up her third successive French singles (where Borg also won the men's). Tracy Austin gained her first major European title in 1979 in the Italian championships.

A year later, Mrs. Lloyd was the Italian champion and repeated in the French, downing Rumania's Virginia Ruzici in both finals. Borg won at Roland Garros but young Yannick Noah was the Italian winner.

McEnroe finished as the top player for the year on the Grand Prix circuit in both 1979 and 1980.

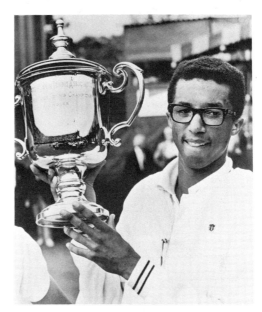

Arthur Ashe won both the United States Men's National and Open titles in 1968.

But, both times, Borg came on to win the Masters playoff at New York's Madison Square Garden.

Prize money generally was escalating at amazing rates. In 1979, both Borg and McEnroe earned over $1 million, and Martina Navratilova led the world's women with nearly $750,000 in winnings. For 1981, the USTA assembled a $1 million purse for the events at the U.S. Open alone. That was an increase of almost 50 percent from the 1980 figure to $685,000 available to winners at the Open.

But the attendance and television interest were keeping pace with the growth of prize money. In 1980, the U.S. Open attracted 331,140 paid customers at the new National Tennis Center.

It was clear that, peripheral considerations aside, tennis had grown into a massive international spectator sport and television attraction as a direct result of the revolt inspired by the British and supported by the Americans in 1968. The decade that followed, the first ten years of the open era, was an exciting one filled with thrilling matches, burgeoning tournament schedules, and the rise of new stars.

In the recreational area, tennis displayed an equally impressive record of growth. In 1968 it was estimated that ten million recreational play-

The professionals even have their own Davis Cup type of competition called the World Cup. Australia won it in 1970 and the United States in 1971. The key to the 1971 victory was the team of Arthur Ashe and Dennis Ralston winning over Australians Tony Roche and John Newcombe *(forecourt)*.

ers were active in the United States. By 1976 the estimate had grown to twenty-nine million with no end in sight. Between 1973 and 1977, the growth rate of participants was 45 percent, a figure unapproached by any other American recreational sport. The USTA distributed over three-quarters of a million dollars to its seventeen sections for developmental use in 1981 alone.

Although the creation and expansion of the professional tennis circuits had reduced the power of the ITF, it had also contributed enormously to the spread of tennis as a recreational game. Since its introduction in Major Wingfield's version at Nantclwyd in 1873 and its subsequent modification at Wimbledon, tennis has come an enormous distance.

As impressive as it was, the first decade of the open era was a natural building upon the solid foundation of the earlier years. As the game moved into its second century, the 1980s held out a promise of even more energetic growth and excitement.

One of the first steps on that road was the opening of the National Tennis Center in New York as a new home for the United States Open. The new Center incorporated the technological improvements which came with the rise of tennis in the fifty-five years since the opening of the West Side Tennis Club Stadium and also superseded it as the largest arena ever built in the United States for tennis. There is little doubt that it proved to be an impressive launching pad for the second century.

USTA PRESIDENTS

Since its founding on May 21, 1881, at New York's old Fifth Avenue Hotel, the USTA has had thirty-five presidents. Several of them have been distinctive in various ways.

Dr. James Dwight of Boston served as head of the organization for twenty years, easily the longest such service in USTA history and a total encompassing one fifth of its first century of existence. When he finally retired due to ill health in 1912, his successor stated that he was "a reluctant candidate" because he wished Dr. Dwight would continue to serve.

Dr. Dwight was the USTA's second president. Its first, Gen. Robert Shaw Oliver of Albany, N.Y., was elected at the meeting in 1881 at which the organization was formed and served until the following year.

Four presidents of the Association have been former winners of the National Singles championship—a condition perhaps unique in all major sports organizations in America where former great players have become executive heads of the organization on a frequent basis.

Richard D. Sears won the first seven singles championships ever contested and was elected president of what was then known as the USNLTA in 1887. He won his final singles championship the same year that he began serving as president.

Henry W. Slocum, Jr. twice won the singles title (succeeding Sears) and served as president in 1892–93.

Robert D. Wrenn, the man who followed the redoubtable Dr. Dwight in 1912, served four years as USTA president and had previously won four National Singles crowns. Holcombe Ward won the singles championship in 1904 and was elected president in 1937, eventually serving for eleven years—the second longest term in USTA history.

USTA Presidents

1881–82	Gen. Robt. Shaw Oliver (Albany, N.Y.)	1948–51	Lawrence A. Baker (Washington)
1882–85	Dr. James Dwight (Boston)	1951–53	Russell B. Kingman (Roselle, N.J.)
1885–87	Thomas K. Fraser (New York)	1953–56	James H. Bishop (Culver, Ind.)
1887–89	Richard D. Sears (Boston)	1956–58	Renville H. McMann (New York)
1889–92	Joseph S. Clark (Philadelphia)	1958–60	Victor Denny (Seattle, Wash.)
1892–94	Henry W. Slocum, Jr. (New York)	1960–62	George E. Barnes (Chicago)
1894–1912	Dr. James Dwight (Boston)	1962–64	Edward A. Turville (St. Petersburg, Fla.)
1912–16	Robert D. Wrenn (Boston)	1964*	James B. Dickey (Ft. Lauderdale, Fla.)
1916–20	George T. Adee (New York)	1964–67	Martin L. Tressel (Pittsburgh)
1920–23	Julian S. Myrick (New York)	1967–69	Robert J. Kelleher (Beverly Hills, Calif.)
1923–24	Dwight F. Davis (Washington)	1969–71	Alastair B. Martin (New York)
1924–25	George Wightman (Boston)	1971–73	Robert B. Colwell (Seattle, Wash.)
1925–28	Jones W. Mersereau (New York)	1973–75	Walter Elcock (Brookline, Mass.)
1928–30	Samuel H. Collom (Philadelphia)	1975–77	Stanley Malless (Indianapolis, Ind.)
1930–31	Louis B. Dailey (New York)	1977–79	W.E. Hester, Jr. (Jackson, Miss.)
1931–33	Louis J. Carruthers (New York)	1979–81	Joseph E. Carrico (Chicago)
1933–34	Harry S. Knox (Chicago)	1981–	Marvin P. Richmond (Kansas City, Mo.)
1934–37	Walter Merrill Hall (New York)		
1937–48	Holcombe Ward (New York)		

*died in office, October 12, 1964.

MEN WHO HAVE WON NATIONAL SINGLES CHAMPIONSHIP AND SERVED AS USTA PRESIDENT

Player	Champion (Years)	President (Years)
Richard D. Sears	1881–87 (7)	1887–89 (2)
Henry W. Slocum, Jr.	1888–89 (2)	1892–93 (1)
Robert D. Wrenn	1893–94–96–97 (4)	1912–16 (4)
Holcombe Ward	1904 (1)	1937–48 (11)

Longest-serving presidents: Dr. James Dwight, 20 years; Holcombe Ward, 11; Robert D. Wrenn and George T. Adee, 4 years each.

Slocum was elected as the first treasurer of the USTA in 1888, the same year he won his first singles title. He went on to become the first man ever to serve in all four major elective offices—president, vice president, secretary, and treasurer. Subsequently, George W. Wightman (whose wife donated the Wightman Cup) also served in all four posts.

Dwight Filley Davis, donator of the Davis Cup for international men's competition, also served as president of the USTA after having filled two prior (though separated) terms as vice president.

Lawrence A. Baker, though never a National Singles champion, achieved distinction as an administrator. He served in all five elected positions in the USTA—president, first vice-president, second vice-president, secretary, and treasurer—after the second vice-presidency was added in 1930. He then was USTA legal counsel for many years after the completion of his distinguished law career.

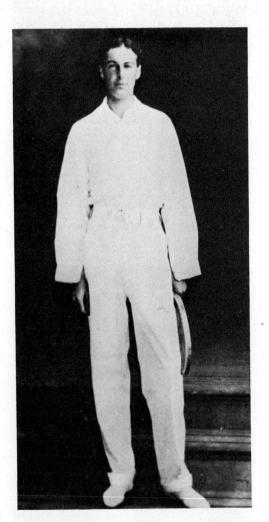 

The famed Doherty brothers, Reginald *(left)* and Hugh *(right)*.

Tennis Equipment

Before you can play tennis, there are certain "tools of the trade" that you will need. These include tennis balls, a racket, and suitable clothing. In addition you need a court to play on.

THE TENNIS BALL

The balls used in court tennis were, in the oldest times, made of strips of cloth rolled together and stitched with thread. Later, for a period, they were made of leather stuffed with wool, feathers, bran, and other materials. In fact, some of the manufacturers in France began using inferior materials, so that in 1480 an ordinance was passed by Louis XI prohibiting the making of tennis balls except in a certain manner and threatening confiscation of all those made in any other way. There was a time when it was quite popular to stuff tennis balls with human hair. William Shakespeare, in his time, comments: ". . . the barber's man hath been seen with him; and the old ornament of his cheek hath already stuffed tennis balls."

The present type of tennis ball was invented by John Heathcote, one of the most famous of British sportsmen. An interesting account of his invention appeared in the British publication *Spectator:*

In a very characteristic English country house there is preserved as an historical relic—it may become an heirloom—the first, the very first, covered lawn-tennis ball. It was invented within the family circle of Mr. John Heathcote, for very many years champion of real tennis, a great player and a great sportsman. When the new game was invented (in the early 1870's) he found the uncovered ball over light—to a player of the court game it must have felt light indeed—and between the genius of himself and his wife the pattern of two globular strips of flannel, which would completely envelope a sphere, was worked out, and the flannel bandage applied. The invention was made public property.

Various improvements in tennis balls, of course, have been made from this early time.

Specifications

For many years little effort was made to standardize the balls, but now the rules of tennis not only specify their size and weight, but even go so far as to define with great accuracy their resilience. The International Tennis Federation has succeeded in standardizing the balls used throughout the world to such an extent that there is hardly any difference noticeable when players of one country play in the tournaments of others.

The official ITF rules require that the ball

. . . shall have a uniform outer surface and shall be white in color. If there are any seams they shall be stitchless. The ball shall be more than 2½ inches (6.35 centimeters) and less than 2⅝

85

inches (6.67 centimeters) in diameter, and more than 2 ounces (56.7 grams) and less than 2¹/₁₆ ounces (58.5 grams) in weight. The ball shall have a bound of more than 53 inches (135 centimeters) and less than 58 inches (147 centimeters) when dropped 100 inches (254 centimeters) upon a concrete base. The ball shall have a forward deformation (or change of shape) of more than .230 inch (.58 centimeter) and less than .290 inch (.74 centimeter) and a return deformation of more than .355 inch (.90 centimeter) and less than .425 inch (1.08 centimeters) at 18 pounds (8.165 kilograms) load. The two deformation figures shall be the averages of three individual readings along three axes of the ball and no two individual readings shall differ by more than .030 inch (.08 centimeter) in each case.

Tennis balls marked "Meets USTA (ITF) specifications" or "Approved by USTA" are manufactured according to these specifications and should provide standard performance. Approved balls are clearly stamped. Other balls not approved by this organization might be of improper size and off weight, causing inaccurate flight and bounce.

How Balls Are Made

To produce tennis balls worthy of meeting USTA or ITF specifications, generally about sixteen manufacturing operations are involved.

Prior to the manufacture of the ball itself, the rubber mill room processes the crude or synthetic rubber into cylindrical slugs of solid rubber measuring about an inch in diameter and 1¼ inches long.

From the mill room the rubber slugs are sent to the tennis-ball department. Each slug is then placed in a press where it is molded to form a shell which will become one-half of a ball center. When taken from the press, each hemisphere has an unnecessary appendage called the flash—a lip around the entire edge of the section where a mate will be joined to form the whole center. The flash is removed by workers operating cutting machines, after which the shell edges are buffed before receiving a coating of cement.

In preparing the shells for vulcanizing, the shells are placed into molds, the edges coated with cement, then two molds are set facing each other.

Several sets of molds are arrayed in a line, then moved into a drum-shaped vulcanizer. Here, in addition to the vulcanizing itself, an important process occurs. So that a tennis ball will bounce properly when it lands on a tennis court, its center must contain the correct amount of air pressure—about 10 to 15 pounds. Air is therefore introduced into the vulcanizer and thus into the center of the balls. As the air pressure is applied, a ram within the vulcanizer squeezes each set of molds together as one unit. After the shells have been forced together within their molds—and simultaneously inflated with air—actual curing in the vulcanizer takes place.

Withdrawn from the vulcanizer and removed from the molds, the now completely spherical balls are buffed at the flash line (or joint line) to remove any excess cement. The centers are next tumbled in a large drum in order to rough up slightly the entire surface for later application of cover cement. Then they are sent through a washer to a gauging bin, where they are measured to determine conformance within maximum and minimum limitations of size. Any centers found to be outside the official size limitations are rejected.

The rubber centers are next placed on a vertically rotating rack which dips the balls through a coating of cement. Removed from the rack after their cement bath, the centers are hung in a drying room to give the adhesive a "tackier" property. When dried to the proper degree, the centers are ready to receive their covers.

During these operations, other workers have been cutting out covers for tennis balls from huge rolls of nylon-dacron-wool fabric, using a knife-edged device shaped in the form of a cover panel. Nylon and dacron are used for strength and durability and wool for fluffiness.

The balls are now placed in a final mold in which the covers are "cured" to the ball. Upon completion of the curing, the balls are sent through a steamer, which brings out the fluffiness of the wool in the cover. Then the balls are forwarded on conveyors to inspectors who thoroughly examine each ball to make certain it meets a rigid standard of perfection for a tennis ball.

Following final inspection, brand names are stamped on each ball, utilizing a stencil which transfers the name to the cover. After stamping, three balls are pressure-packed in a can which is hermetically sealed to preserve the factory freshness of each ball.

An important new development in tennis balls is the so-called "pressureless" ball. Very special properties are necessary in the cores of such balls. The wall of the core must provide the required bounce and compression unaided by any internal pressure. This means in practical terms that the wall of the core must be thicker and yet the core must be no heavier than the weight of a normal pressurized core.

The main basic production techniques are similar to those for a conventional ball except that special molds (to give a thicker wall) are used for the core and no core inflation takes place. The nylon-dacron-wool cover used on the pressureless ball is about the same as that used on the conventional pressurized one.

The difference between pressureless and pressurized tennis balls can be detected by some players but not by others. In general, top-class players can detect a difference, due to the fact that they are particularly sensitive to the feel of the ball on the racket and its response to their stroke. Other players seem unable to distinguish between them. The major advantage of the pressureless ball appears to be increased storage and playing life. But, up to the present time, this new type of ball has not been acceptable in the higher levels of tennis.

Buying and Caring for Balls

As previously stated, the USTA tests and approves balls that meet ITF specifications. These are the ones you should purchase in most cases.

There are balls designed for special uses, too. For instance, so-called heavy-duty balls are covered with more felt or fuzz and are supposed to last longer on hard-surface courts. Other balls are made especially for clay and indoor composition courts, while still others are built specifically for better action on grass courts. There are even balls designed to give normal playing action at elevations above 5,000 feet.

At one time all tennis balls were white. Today, yellow balls are used in virtually all major tournaments played on synthetic surfaces, and red balls

are employed in "nonofficial" play at night and other times where high visibility is required. Thus, you can purchase tennis balls for almost any type of play.

No tennis ball will last for an indefinite period of time. Advanced players like to start a match with new balls, but they will use old balls for rallying or practicing on the backboard. Balls can be used for three to eight sets, although they are pretty well worn at the end of three sets on concrete. Most advanced players will use balls three to five sets. Balls that are older can be employed for backboard and service practice.

A tin of tennis balls will, of course, last the inexperienced player a longer time, but they should not be used when the felt covering is worn thin, or the fuzz is knocked off. This covering gives balls the necessary grip with the stringing at impact. As the felt wears, this grip is gradually lost, the bounce increases considerably, and the flight of the ball becomes more erratic. With this resultant loss of ball control, it becomes most difficult to make the proper tennis strokes and the game becomes less interesting. Also remember that once the pressure has escaped from the can, the balls will soon lose some of their bounce.

Since dampness and extreme temperature are the greatest enemies of tennis balls, never store them in locations where these conditions exist. Also do not play with balls that are wet or damp. After a day's play, a light brushing of the ball with a stiff brush will help rough up the nap, insuring more sets of accurate play.

THE TENNIS RACKET

While the *Rules of Lawn Tennis* (Rule 3) give detailed specifications for the ball used in the game, there are no specifications for the racket or any description thereof in the rules. In the *Glossary of Technical Terms Used in the Game of Lawn Tennis,* published by the USTA and printed in Section 7, the racket is described as "the implement used to strike the ball."

In the playing rules, the first reference to the racket is in Rule 6, which reads in part as follows: "The server shall then project the ball by hand into the air in any direction and before it hits the ground strike it with his *racket* and the delivery shall be deemed to have been completed at the moment of the impact of the racket and the ball."

In the 1950s there appeared in *American Lawn Tennis* magazine an editorial entitled "What Is a Racket?" For further enlightenment on this subject the editorial is reprinted in part:

The appearance in an English tournament of a player using a racket in each hand occasioned surprise recently. Upon investigation, it was found that there is no rule forbidding such action. Some people think this strange. It is nothing of the kind. A player can use as many rackets, and as many kinds, as he desires; just as he may play with a racket in either his right or his left hand, or with both. He does not even have to use a racket, as the term is generally understood. He can use anything that by any stretch of the imagination can be described as a racket. Indeed, there have been cases where, as a special stunt, instead of a racket a barrel stave was used, and even a soda bottle.

The laws, properly enough, are not concerned with the kind of racket used; it can be of any size or shape.

Summed up, a player can use to hit the ball any implement that can be regarded as complying with the term racket. About the only thing that cannot legally be used to hit the ball is a player's hand or arm.

Since there are no *rule* standards, manufacturers have set a variety of racket-frame specifications with regard to length and same size of head. Rackets may also vary in six other aspects: weight, balance, size of handle, frame material, flexibility, and type of strings.

Weight of the Racket

Racket-frame weights are classified light (12 to 12¾ ounces); medium (12¾ to 13½ ounces); and heavy (13½ to 14¾ ounces). A few especially designed rackets go into the extra-heavy class (above 14¾ ounces). These weight designations are determined by weighing on a scale without regard to balance. The strings of rackets weigh approximately ¾ ounce, but are *not* figured into the manufacturer's weight classification.

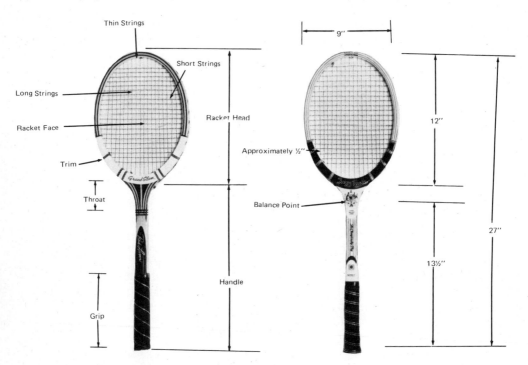

Parts and dimensions of a typical tennis racket.

The difference between a light and a heavy frame is less than 3 ounces, but it will result in a great difference in playing characteristics. The proper racket weight, however, is largely a question of feel and individual preference. But remember that while you employ your muscles to start the stroke, it is the momentum (or weight) of the racket that gives the necessary follow-through. If the racket is too light, it is difficult to obtain a smooth follow-through and there will be a certain amount of unnecessary strain and wear on the racket as well as on arm muscles. On the other hand, a racket that is too heavy generally results in slow stroking and an unnatural tiredness of the playing arm. The following can be used as a guide to the range you should consider:

	Weight in Ounces
Children*	12 to 12¾
Junior girls	12½ to 13
Junior boys	12¾ to 13½
Women	12½ to 13¾
Men	13⅜ to 14½

*Small children may use a junior-size racket, which is 1 or 2 inches shorter than standard size, is lighter, and has a smaller handle. The racket head, however, is standard size.

Balance of the Racket

The weight of a tennis racket may be distributed in three ways: evenly; handle-heavy, or light in head and top; or head-heavy. Since the balance of a racket is seldom indicated, the player must determine the balance for himself.

The most common balancing point, or axis, you can use to determine a racket's balance is a finger. A ruler or straightedge, however, is much better. To determine the balance axis, the racket is supported on a straightedge and moved along until a position is found where it is balanced. This point should be marked with a felt-tipped pen. Next the racket length should be determined with a yardstick, and the distance from the bottom of the racket to the balance mark measured. For example, if the overall length of a tennis racket is 27 inches, and if the balance point is at 13½ inches from the bottom, the racket is said to be evenly, or well, balanced. If the balance axis is 14½ inches from the bottom, the racket is said to be head-heavy by 1 inch; conversely, if the axis is 12½ inches from the bottom, the racket is said to be handle-heavy by 1 inch.

The majority of today's players prefer a racket that is either evenly balanced or slightly handle-heavy, or head-light. Except in the hands of an experienced player, the top-, or head-, heavy racket is hard to manipulate when volleying and has the tendency to permit an average player to swing through too fast on ground strokes.

Size of Handle

The size of the tennis racket's octagonally shaped handle (a few expert players prefer special shapes —round, square, or built up in some other fashion) usually depends on the size of your hand and fingers. *Standard* handle sizes vary, in ⅛-inch steps, from 4 to 5 inches (i.e., 4, 4⅛, 4¼, etc.). When the racket is gripped, the handle should feel quite comfortable with the fingers lightly spread around it. Many experts suggest the use of a handle which is large enough for the thumb of

  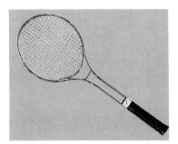

The three types of racket frames: *(left to right)* wood, aluminum, and stainless steel.

the hand to overlap the tip of the third finger. This is a matter of preference; some like a smaller handle and others select a larger one.

There are several types of racket-handle coverings, or, as they are more commonly called, grips, used today. While the selection of the grip is again a matter of individual preference, the leather covering is usually recommended. Perforations in the covering are desirable since they help to absorb perspiration moisture and prevent racket slippage.

Some of the leading players in the 1970s have the following preferences as to weight, balance, and handle size:

In all, as many as eighteen pieces of wood are permanently bonded together to create a perfect union of all parts. The present-day laminated system neutralizes opposing stresses and strains and provides greatest resistance to splitting and warping while insuring symmetrically perfect shape and uniform performance.

To the well-known long-fiber woods of ash and hickory, which had always been used, have been added beech for strength and attractive grain, and maple for resiliency and lustrous finish. Other woods such as mahogany, sycamore, basswood, and bamboo are also used for more diversified and attractive appearances. It is in the careful selec-

Player	Weight (ounces)	Balance	Handle (inches)
Rod Laver	14¼	Heavy handle	4⅝
Tony Roche	13⅝	Heavy handle	4⅝
Roy Emerson	14	Evenly balanced	4⅝
John Newcombe	14¼	Heavy head	4⅝
Margaret Court	13⅝	Evenly balanced	4⅝ (square built)
Lew Hoad	13⅜	Heavy handle	4¹¹⁄₁₆ tapering to 4⅜
Ilie Nastase	13½	Heavy handle	4⅝ tapering to 4⁷⁄₁₆
Tom Okker	13¼	Heavy handle	4⅝ tapering to 4½
Virginia Wade	13⅜	Heavy handle	4⁹⁄₁₆ tapering to 4⁷⁄₁₆
Sharon Walsh	13	Heavy handle	4⅝
Mary Ann Curtis	13½	Evenly balanced	4¾ rounded handle

Frame Material

The racket may be made from either wood or metal. Just before World War II, the laminated type of wood racket frames started to replace the single bend construction. This change brought an end to the 150-year reign of the old frame, which was steam-bent from one piece of stock to the desired shape of the finished product. With its varying degrees of resiliency, this single strip was no stronger than its weakest section and was susceptible to severe warping. To eliminate these defects, the modern laminated frame features eight to twelve long, thin, individual strips which form the basic racket frame and run in a continuous length from the handle around the bow and back down the handle. A triangular throat wedge, inside and outside shoulder reinforcements, and the long handle wedge strengthen the racket to give maximum performance and wear at all stress points.

tion of wood that the secret of lamination lies. The long, laminated strips are chosen from stock that is free from knots and flaws. They must have even grain running their entire length. All other wood assemblies are also free from any imperfections that could cause weakness, especially at points of greatest strain.

When the parts have been cut and selected, adhesive is applied and they are assembled in the bending jig, a process requiring only 45 seconds, so perfectly do all parts fit. The clamps are then tightened, and the complete bending jig is placed in a kiln at controlled heat and humidity conditions suitable to the adhesives used in the bonding operation. One of the greatest improvements of modern laminated construction has been achieved by technical advances in the bonding and gluing operation. Water-soluble animal glues have been replaced by insoluble synthetic-resin adhesives to make the wood joints and plies virtually weatherproof.

From the bending jig, the racket begins its course through the wood room, where it is planed, drilled, grooved, and shaped. Fiber faces also are applied during this stage to provide flexible reinforcement over critical glue joints of the throat and handle wedges. These fiber faces prevent lacquer cracks where the lacquer itself is not as flexible as the wood. It is at this point that the handles are built up to the desired size with basswood overlays, called flakes. Expert woodworkers complete the operation, giving the entire frame a cabinet finish.

Now the frame is ready for one of the most important operations in the whole fabrication of a top-quality racket: weighing and balancing. A ¾-inch hole is drilled 6 inches into the handle, into which is placed a high-gravity, leaded rubber plug. The weight and the positioning of the plug in the handle locates the balance point. This is the all-important operation that gives a racket that intangible quality of "feel" so eagerly sought by all players.

After weighing and balancing, the frames continue into the finishing department, where they receive three full spray coats of highest-quality clear lacquer. Between coats, decorative and identifying decals as well as the bindings are applied. After the finish coat, the grips are individually wrapped by skilled craftsmen.

Metal rackets—both aluminum and steel—have been extremely popular in the last few years with better players. These players claim that a metal racket gives them added zip on their serves and volley; they say it provides more power on ground strokes with far less effort; and they claim it cures (or at least eases) the pain of tennis elbow (Section 4). They do admit, however, that some minor adjustments are necessary to get used to a metal racket, such as timing and the length of the backswing. Metal rackets are also more expensive than the wood types.

Metal rackets are manufactured in various ways, and the exact techniques of bending and shaping of the steel and aluminum in racket shapes is still a trade secret. However, if you wish to purchase a metal racket—and this holds good for wood ones—buy from a reliable manufacturer and carefully examine the construction. Neatness in the making of the joints, fastening of the grip,

etc., all show good workmanship as well as a good racket.

Remember that the racket you select should be a good one, although not necessarily expensive. There are many good, inexpensive rackets available at your local sporting goods dealer or tennis pro shop. Unfortunately, however, there are also inferior frames that can have a serious effect on your game. While these rackets may cost a little less originally, they will not hold their strings tight and will lose their shape in a comparatively short time.

Flexibility of the Racket

Although wood and metal (aluminum and steel) racket frames appear rigid enough when picked up in the hand, during play quite large stresses are set up in the frame, which result in a certain amount of flexing. This is not a drawback, since it is desirable that the racket frame "give" to some extent. However, there are some rackets that are noticeably stiffer than others.

Of the three frame materials, steel is the most flexible, while wood is the least. In most cases the more flexible a racket is, the greater the speed that can be obtained, since the less a ball is compressed when hit, the faster it will fly. But this greater speed is at the sacrifice of control. In other words, the stiff racket permits better control of the ball when making a shot. Like the other points of selection, the amount of flexibility is largely a question of individual preference. Players must decide, based on their own experience, when to use a flexible racket and when to use a stiff one.

Type of Strings

Tennis strings today fall into two categories: gut and nylon.

Genuine gut strings are made from animal intestines. Although the name "cat-gut" is still occasionally heard, no cats are or ever were involved in the process. The raw material for the finest genuine gut tennis strings comes from young, healthy lambs. Hog gut is also used for tennis strings, but it does not have the resiliency of lamb gut.

As a rule, gut strings are preferred by tournament players because of somewhat greater resiliency. They have the disadvantage of considerably higher cost and susceptibility to damage by moisture. The moderately priced multi-ply nylon strings are impervious to moisture and possess playing qualities which can be recommended to the great majority of tennis players.

Strings are made in two thicknesses, 15 and 16 gauge. Sixteen gauge is the thinner string, which has greater resilience but wears through faster. Fifteen gauge, the thicker string, lasts longer but does not quite match the 16 gauge for resilience. For this reason 16 gauge is preferred for tournament play, while 15 gauge is better for the average player.

High-quality rackets should be purchased unstrung. This will permit a greater selection of frames as well as wider choice of type of string for the racket. Rackets may be strung with the desired tension on the strings. Prestrung rackets are usually not strung as tightly as good play requires; however, most prove satisfactory for beginners. Tensions between 55 and 65 pounds provide excellent playing characteristics.

Care of the Racket

Taking proper care of your tennis racket insures maximum life and top playing at all times. Even metal rackets, which do not warp like wood, require a little care.

When outdoors and not playing, keep the racket head covered in a waterproof case. Many of these cases or covers are made with a pocket for tennis balls, eliminating some extra carrying.

After you finish play, dry off the grip and check your racket to be certain that it is clean. Indoors, metal rackets can be kept in a case, but wooden ones should be kept in a press. A press is exactly what its name implies, a metal or wooden frame that slides over the racket head and then is secured tightly in place. The type with a centered lever arrangement is preferable to that with four corner screws, as it is not always possible to obtain equal tension on the frame with the latter. A press is essential to avoid warping of a wooden racket. Also always store the racket in a place that is at room temperature, never in a location where there is dampness or extreme heat.

TENNIS CLOTHING

There is nothing in the *Rules of Lawn Tennis* that states you cannot romp around the court in pink tights or blue denim overalls. Traditionally, however, the basic principle of proper tennis dress is that *white is right.* While the custom of wearing white is more rigidly observed at some tennis clubs, resorts, and hotels than at others (most public parks and municipal courts usually have no restrictions on the color or type of clothing worn), it is always reassuring to know that in white you are right wherever you might play.

Actually, there are some practical reasons behind this old tennis tradition: white reflects, rather than absorbs, heat, thus aiding the player to stay cool. In addition, the uniform wearing of white is not distracting to other players, as bright colors might be.

Some other general suggestions for proper dress are that your outfit should be clean, neat, comfortable, and always within the bounds of good taste. Bathing suits, while frequently convenient, are usually frowned upon, and not always the most comfortable tennis dress in any case.

Shoes and Socks

Shoes can be considered the most important part of your tennis outfit. Flat-soled, heelless, canvas-topped or leather, white tennis sneakers or shoes are the accepted rule both for your own comfort and out of consideration for other players, since heeled or heavy shoes do not improve the surface of most types of courts. Be sure the pair you select is lightweight, durable, comfortable, well-fitting, and well-constructed with smoothly molded soles for skidproof traction. Do *not* substitute basketball or other sports shoes—you can easily find many brands made solely for tennis playing. Actually, many tennis shoes have a cushioned support arch and heel.

Have your shoes laced tightly enough for comfort and do not have any loose ends hanging. After playing for the day, be sure to clear out any grit which has lodged in the soles, otherwise you may have some problem the next time you play.

Socks are also important. White cotton or thick woolen ones are the most absorbent and are most

Women's tennis clothes have changed greatly in the twentieth century: *(left to right)* early 1900s, 1920s, and 1970s.

comfortable. Be sure that your socks do not have any holes, since these could cause blisters. Also make certain that your socks are clean. Aside from the hygienic aspect, dirt is an abrasive substance and constant movement will make your feet sore. When playing on hard court surfaces, some players wear two pairs of socks.

Suggested Women's Outfits

The woman's outfit should have as few frills as possible. The most highly recommended is the typical one-piece tennis dress with abbreviated, pleated skirt. Sharkskin, piqué, poplin, nylon, polyester, cotton, and combinations of these materials are all good-looking, practical, and washable. Shorts and shirt or blouse combinations are also a good choice if you have the figure for the former. And that brings up another point. The clinging type of outfit that covers you like a coat of paint might do wonders for your physical form, but your tennis form will suffer. While your outfit should not "bag," it should be loose enough so that it does not bind your swing or otherwise cramp your style. Today, women's tennis outfits—both the dresses and shirt-and-shorts combinations— are so attractive that some women have been known to take up the game just to wear one.

While you might prefer to play bareheaded, a white peaked hat or tennis visor helps to keep the sun off your eyes and your hair in place. Remember that hair flopping all over the place is a distraction and hinders your vision. If you do not wear a hat, a hair ribbon will keep your hair under control.

"Flappy" jewelry also has a tendency to interfere with your play. It is better left in a safe place where it will not get lost or broken.

In cooler weather a white cardigan sweater is eminently correct and comfortable, either off court or on. As a matter of fact, a medium-weight sweater or jacket comes in handy after you finish playing in any weather. It will help keep you from catching a cold or stiffening up while cooling off after the match.

Suggested Men's Outfits

Although in cool climates, slacks of flannel or gabardine are still worn occasionally, the usual attire for men, both in tournament and informal play, now consists of a white T-shirt, polo shirt, or sport shirt with a collar, and white tailored shorts of duck, cotton, nylon, or similar material. The standard undershirt is not correct on the court. Also you may be tempted in hot weather to tan your manly torso, to shed your shirt and play barechested. This is not a major sin but there are many places where it is considered more polite to "keep your shirt on." And the fact of the matter is you will probably be more comfortable anyhow with some kind of covering to absorb the perspiration. Remember that neatness is important in tennis— shirts hanging sloppily out of shorts are taboo.

The white peaked hat or tennis visor is again practical for shading the eyes. In cooler weather a white pullover sweater will come in very handy.

Knitted sweatbands are often worn by both ladies and men around their wrists to keep perspiration from running down their arms into their hands, making the racket slippery and difficult to hold. On hot days a band of some type of absorbent material worn around the forehead will prevent misting of the lenses in the case of players who wear glasses.

For male players, it is also important to wear an athletic supporter during a match. Like all sports, the activity in tennis places a physical strain on the body. An athletic supporter can help prevent a painful hernia and pulled groin muscles, particularly when one is chasing balls that require reaching and lunging.

In the racket or tennis bag that you take on court, it is a good idea to have a towel so that you can dry off between games. Other helpful items that you may have in that bag could include salt tablets to avoid cramps, safety pins for broken shoulder straps (for women), bandages for blisters and small cuts, rosin for gripping moist rackets, and so on. Maybe you do not have to have all these items, but if an emergency arises, it is nice to have them.

PRACTICE DEVICES

Tennis requires as much practice as you can give it (see Section 3). While practicing with a partner is ideal, a partner unfortunately cannot always be found. Here are several devices that may be employed to practice without another player.

Practice Board

Many tennis clubs, municipal courts, and playgrounds have backboards to practice on. Building a practice board requires the construction of a backboard—wood or concrete is preferable—high enough to maintain a steady rhythm during a practice session. Here are instructions for building a typical practice board:

The framework is made of four 12-foot 4 by 4-inch hemlock posts which will be set 6 feet apart and 3 feet into the ground. The actual work on the board is done with the whole thing laid flat on the ground. The four posts are laid on the ground first and on top of these are laid the five 18-foot 2 by 4's flat side down and securely spiked on the posts, which makes them parallel to the ground. Every joint is painted before putting the pieces together so as to make the whole thing as weather- and waterproof as possible. On top of this is laid (as it lies on the ground) a floor of ordinary 3-inch matched fir flooring. Each edge of each board is painted also before it is laid so that when the assembly is finished, there is no joint that is exposed to the elements. (Three-quarter-inch exterior-grade plywood can be substituted for the flooring if desired.) This makes a board which is 18 feet long and 9 feet high with the boards laid vertical. As the boards run this way, there is no piecing of the floor as the longest piece is only 9 feet long. The practice board is then raised into place and secured by using four 2 by 4 planks as braces. These braces are spiked to the top of the practice board and then to four 4 by 4-inch posts set 3 feet into the ground at the rear of the board to form a triangular support arrangement.

On top of this board is a headpiece which makes a sort of roof over the width of the board and forms a drip edge on the back side to prevent the water from running down the full height of the boards. Above all this is a screen of 2 by 4's which slants out over the front of the board at an angle of about 30 degrees from the perpendicular. The long pieces are 6 feet long and are extended down the back side to join the main 2 by 4 braces to which they are spiked. The top end is joined by another 2 by 4 spiked to the ends of the long pieces. While common poultry wire is often used on this type of board it usually does not prove at all satisfactory, as the force of the balls which hit it breaks through it in a few days. Inasmuch as the width of the board is half the width of a tennis court, you can hang in place of the poultry wire an old net cut in half. One part of this is hung along the extreme outer edge of the frame and the other piece about halfway down the slant of the frame. As these are fastened only at top and on the extreme ends, there is enough "give" to it so that there is not the wear and tear on them that there was on the netting, which was stretched taut. On either side there are wings which extend for 12 feet at about 45 degrees. These are of the same construction as the frame on top of the board itself, as netting, etc., soon gives way under the constant pounding of the balls.

The whole board is then painted a grass green. On this is painted a white line indicating the proper position that the net takes on the court, that is, 3 feet high at the center and rising toward the edges. The playing surface should, of course, be the same as that on the courts themselves.

Rebound Net

The rebound net has several advantages over the fixed backboard. Its mobility and quiet are foremost among these, and in addition the net is adjustable to permit various types of rebound. The net is stretched over a well-braced frame which can be set up anywhere. Depending on the amount of use and outside exposure, the netting may have to be replaced possibly as often as each year. The rebound from such tension-strung netting is more like a ball struck by a racket than the rebound from a wood or concrete surface, and thus a player may better learn how to handle an opponent's "pace."

Ball-Throwing Machine

There are a number of mechanical devices on the market for throwing tennis balls for practice purposes. All of these perform more or less on the catapult principle and are capable of various adjustments for both speed and trajectory. A number of balls are placed in a storage rack and then fed individually into position to be hit by a wood or metal paddle toward the player. These electrically operated machines are readily moved around the surface of the court, and from the opposite side of a tennis net go far toward creating actual game conditions. Ball-throwing machines are of inestimable value in clinics as well as in individual teaching and practicing.

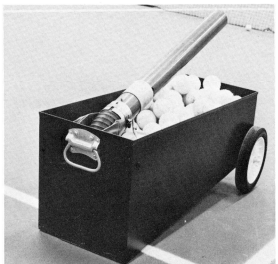

Two types of ball-throwing machines.

Typical rebound net in action.

A rebound ball device such as this is ideal for home use.

Rebound Ball

There are several automatic ball-return devices on the market. Several of them may be used in the home or in the backyard. For example, one of these rebound ball devices is a standard tennis ball on the end of an 8½-foot nylon cord attached to a 5-foot heavy rubber band. The end of the rubber is connected to a solid base. You stand a step behind the base and stroke out at the ball, in a similar manner as with the paddle-ball toy. The ball travels about 16 feet and rebounds to the front of the stand, where it can be restroked.

The use of the various practice devices—backboards, rebound nets, ball-throwing machines, and rebound balls—is fully discussed in Section 3.

THE TENNIS COURT

In brief, the rules state that the court for the "singles game" shall be a rectangle 78 feet long and 27 feet wide. It shall be divided across the middle by a net the ends of which shall be attached, or pass over, the tops of two posts, 3 feet 6 inches high, which shall stand 3 feet outside the court on each side. The height of the net shall be 3 feet at the center.

The first tennis court in the United States is often considered to be this one at Staten Island, New York, which was illustrated in the September 24, 1881, issue of *Harper's Weekly.*

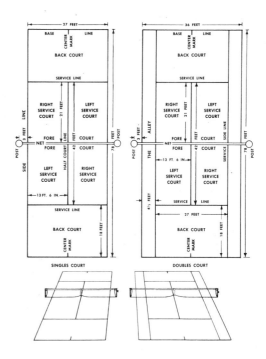

Diagram and dimensions of official singles and doubles courts.

The lines bounding the ends and sides of the court shall respectively be called the "base lines" and the "side lines." On each side of the net, at a distance of 21 feet from it and parallel with it, shall be drawn the "service lines." The space on each side of the net between the service line and the side lines shall be divided by the "center service line" into two equal parts called the "service courts." There are other details pertaining to the width of the lines, band on the net, etc.

Rule 31 relates to the "doubles game." For this game the court shall be 36 feet in width, there being an "alley" 4½ feet wide on each side of the court. The service courts stay the same for the doubles game. It will be seen that the posts in singles shall be 3 feet outside the singles court and in doubles 3 feet outside the doubles court.

But what happens when you play a singles game on a doubles court with the net posts set up for doubles, as they are on most club courts? The rules say nothing about this except that in Rule 20 of the ITA a note under the rule mentions "if for the sake of convenience a doubles court is to be used for singles play, it should be equipped with singles posts for the purposes of the singles game." Where the posts can be easily moved, as on grass courts, the rule can be taken care of. On other courts singles or net sticks can be placed at the proper distance, raising the net a little over an inch at a point 3 feet outside the singles side lines. The exact measurement is 1.29 inches. But thousands of games and matches are played without these

singles sticks with the result that the players have a lower net to play over for side-line shots.

How to Lay Out a Tennis Court

Most-accurate results are obtained if a tennis court is laid out by a civil engineer or competent surveyor using proper surveying instruments. However, if such services are not readily available, adequate accuracy can be obtained with the proper use of two good 50-foot tapes.

It is desirable for courts to be laid out for both singles and doubles play. However, since the same lines—except for the side-line extensions for doubles play—are required for each, it is best to lay out the singles court first, establishing the lines shown in the accompanying diagram. Courts should be laid out with the long way north and south if possible. First establish the net or center line. This is done by driving a nail at point *A,* then a second nail—27 feet from *A*—at point *B.* Then

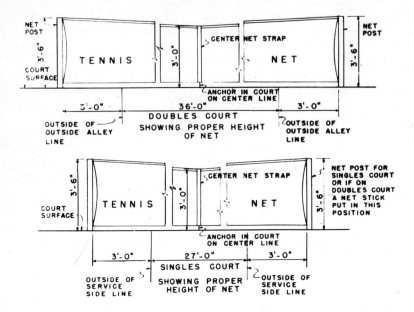

take the two 50-foot tapes and attach their respective ends to the nails *A* and *B*. On the first, which will determine the side line *A-E,* measure off 39 feet and on the second, which will determine the diagonal *B-E,* measure off 47 feet 5¼ inches; pull taut in such directions that at these distances they meet at point *E.* Drive a nail at *E.* Then establish point *D* in a similar manner. (Note that the distance from *E* to *D* should be 27 feet—the same as from *A* to *B.*)

Check this for accuracy before driving a nail at *D.* Point *F* (21 feet from *A*) and point *C* (21 feet from *B*) should then be established and nails driven at these points. This gives you the lower (or south) half of the court. The upper (or north) half is determined in a similar manner. This completes the boundaries for the singles court. The doubles-court boundaries are established by prolonging the base lines (from points *E* and *D* on lower half and similarly for the upper half) 4 feet 6 inches in each direction and joining the four new points to establish the side lines for the doubles court. (Note that the doubles court is actually 9 feet wider than the singles court, with side lines parallel to those of the singles court.)

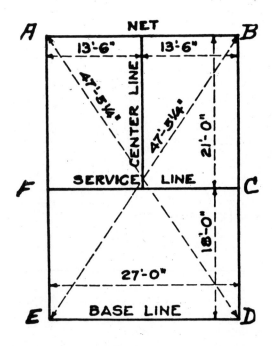

Method of laying out a tennis court.

Note the inside face of the net posts 3 feet outside the doubles side line and other details given. For championship play, the space behind the base line—i.e., between the base line and fence (or wire netting)—should be not less than 21 feet and the space between the side lines and the fence not less than 12 feet. Lines are a maximum of 2 inches in width, with the exception of the base line, which may vary from 2 to 4 inches, and the center line, which must be 2 inches in width.

For tournament play when a doubles court is used for a singles match, net sticks should be placed exactly 3 feet outside the service side line to support the top of the net at exactly 3 feet 6 inches above the court.

Court Material

There are almost as many different tennis-court surfaces as there are countries. However, for the purpose of the *Encyclopedia of Tennis*, we shall use general classifications.

First of all, note that well over 90 percent of the courts in the world are of clay, or of a surface so comparable to clay that they can be grouped under this heading. Throughout Europe, for example, one may look a long time before discovering any other type of outdoor court surface. The game was first played upon grass and, while the number of grass courts total but a fraction of the total number of clay courts, grass courts are to be found in England, the eastern seaboard of the United States, and in Australia.

Cement courts are mostly in America and in the state of California particularly, where one must look long for a court other than cement. Other sections of America have their cement courts but not to the extent one finds in California.

Certain sections of Europe, notably Sweden, possess many indoor courts with a wood surface. And there has been a great increase in the number of indoor courts in the United States in recent years.

There can be no real understanding of the playing qualities of the various surfaces, or any intelligent approach to how best to play on the various surfaces, without an understanding of one all-important fact. Some court surfaces play "fast" and some play "slow." There persists a complete misunderstanding on the part of a great majority of players as to just what is meant by this. In what manner is it judged that a certain court possesses fast or slow playing qualities? What exactly is the gauge of measurement?

The speed of the game (is the court fast or slow?) is determined by the amount of time which elapses between the moment the ball meets the court the first time and the moment it hits, or would hit if allowed to bounce again, the court the second time. The length of that period of time between bounces is the time one has to reach and hit the ball. The longer this period of time, the slower the game and, conversely, the shorter this period of time, the faster the game. (The subject of how to "play" the various court surfaces is fully covered in Section 3.)

Selection of Tennis-Court Surfaces. The selection of the tennis-court surface depends on a variety of factors. Among the factors to be considered are climate; the amount of money available for construction, upkeep, and maintenance; the preference of the players who will be using the court; and the reputation, experience, and availability of the court installer. Other than grass, most porous surfaces (ones which permit water to filter through the surface) use some type of tape for lines rather than marking the lines daily. Tapes often affect a ball bounce differently from the rest of the surface and require maintenance; and if not properly maintained they create tripping hazards.

One of the main factors to be considered is the amount of supervision to be provided at the court location. The cushioned-type tennis-court surface and the fast-drying tennis-court surface, and other surfaces such as clay and grass, should never be constructed in an area where anyone except tennis players, wearing tennis shoes, is to be allowed. Should courts using these types of surfaces be constructed in an area where constant supervision is not provided, children with street shoes, bicycles, etc., could do a great amount of damage. In general, tennis courts with these surfaces are found in country clubs and tennis clubs, where supervision is provided constantly by someone, such as the tennis professional, who sees that the courts are properly cared for. These types of courts can also be installed in parks and in schools provided that the authorities in these places supply the supervision necessary to insure that the tennis surfaces are not abused.

Tennis courts to be constructed in areas such as parks or schools where supervision cannot be provided should have surfaces of the noncushioned type. This type of court, such as hot plant-mix asphalt, concrete, or job-mixed asphaltic composition, is sturdier and stronger and can take some abuse without damage.

Climate may affect choice of courts. Extreme heat may produce softening of certain surfaces, glare, heat radiation, or cracking of surface. Extreme cold and frost action may be more likely to damage certain surfaces unless specific precautions are taken by an experienced court builder and maintenance personnel.

The following is a discussion of the "pros" and "cons" for each surface, and these factors should be carefully considered in the selection of the tennis-court surface.

Grass Courts. It is on grass, perhaps, that the full range of tennis skill can best be employed. That is, grass courts in good condition provide one of the most luxurious of all surfaces. The Wimbledon matches are held on grass. There is great resilience under foot, and grass lends itself to the largest variety and perfection of stroking of any surface. It is a cool, clean surface, free of dust and glare. Owing to climate and soil requirements, grass courts cannot be grown everywhere. The installation costs are high, as is the daily care required to keep these courts in playable condition. Therefore if you are concerned about cost, consider something other than this most luxurious of surfaces.

It is essential that the installer be an expert in turf construction. The drainage lines and porous beds below the surface must be perfectly installed. Over this must be a minimum of 6 inches of specially prepared, tested, fertile soil. Specially selected grass seed must be expertly sown and maintained.

Daily care is a must with grass courts. They need watering, top dressing, fertilizing, mowing, and reseeding or sodding. The court needs moving periodically to rest the most abused grass. In addition, there is rolling, fungus control, aerification, grub and worm control, additions of chemi-cals, and brushing to maintain a grass court properly. Its high initial and maintenance cost, lack of uniform bounce when not in nearly perfect condition, relatively slow drying after a moderate rain, slipperiness when damp, discoloring of balls, and the need for experts to maintain the court are the major disadvantages. Remember that grass varies a great deal even at clubs in the same geographical area. Different types of grass combinations can be used. Some grass courts are kept close-cropped and are heavily rolled. Others are maintained in an entirely different manner because of differences in grass types. Local conditions such as the amount of rainfall, presence of certain fungi, or even the preference of groundsmen or club officials must be taken into consideration when selecting a grass surface. The differences between the courts at such world-famous clubs as Wimbledon's All-England Club and Forest Hills' West Side Tennis Club are quite pronounced.

In most cases, however, grass courts are considered fast, since the ball does not rise appreciably from the surface and one has a minimum of time to reach the ball and execute the necessary stroke.

Clay Courts. These courts and so-called claylike surfaces are many times more numerous than all the other surfaces combined. From almost the beginning of tennis upon the continent, the standard or popular court has carried the name of its maker. What this "maker" produced was a gritty top dressing for a court. It was usually dark red in color, which made it most pleasant to the eye and which served as a fine background. This top dressing, or court surface, was quite porous and was applied on top of a carefully installed foundation which allowed quick drainage.

There are today many such top dressings on the market and they usually bear the name of the manufacturer. There are thousands of such courts in this country, and they fall definitely within our term of "clay" courts. In fact, the U.S. National Clay Court Championships are played upon these courts. Their advantage lies in the fact that they drain much more quickly than regular clay and, as a rule, the maintenance is much less than clay. They are seen more often in this country in a green color, while Europe prefers the dark red. Sometimes this top dressing mentioned is applied on top of a clay court in this country simply to add color to the court. As to real clay, the color and substance varies in different sections and so do the courts. Some clay courts are light in color and others quite dark. Some may be more dirt than clay.

Advantages of clay courts are that materials for construction are available in most parts of the country. They can be built with relatively inexperienced labor. With reasonable maintenance, one can have relatively uniform ball bounce. Repairs are rather inexpensive. Because the player can slide on this surface, it is easy on the feet and legs. Clay courts are the least expensive to construct.

One disadvantage of a clay court is that it may take a day to be playable after a moderately heavy rain. Depending on the color and nature of the clay, it also may stain the balls and create a glare in the player's eyes. Daily maintenance is required to keep the courts in reasonably playable condition. Painted lines must be marked freshly every day—or at least cleaned. If there are leaded or other types of lines, they can create irregular ball bounce or possible tripping hazards and they must be kept clean to be seen.

On clay surfaces, the ball usually bounces up higher than on grass, its forward speed is slowed more by contact with the surface than in the case of grass, and one has much more time in which to reach the ball and make the necessary stroke. Of course, clay courts have many variations. An extreme example might be some sun-baked courts in the mid–United States as compared with a fast-drying type of court in France. The ball bounces high on sun-baked clay and, of course, much lower on the fast-drying type. The latter sometimes gives the impression that the ball is almost hanging in air, so much does surface check bounce.

In the construction of the clay court today there is nationally used and constructed a clay-base composition installation. This construction utilizes the binding of clay and eliminates the slow drying properties of the clay material by introducing certain composition aggregates into the clay and surfacing over the clay. These courts, constructed in either red or green, afford excellent playing qualities and are at least 50 percent faster in drying than the old clay court. However, they still require maintenance, which should be given daily

and which usually consists of dragging, watering, and rolling.

In recent years there has been an increased use of the fast-drying composition installation, which usually is constructed in green and which affords an excellent playing surface. This court features a porous cushion base over which is laid an approximate 1 to 1½ inches of fast-drying green composition surface (usually patented). This type of court dries off almost immediately after rains, therefore affording almost uninterrupted play during the season. However, it is put out of commission by frost action, and in the northern sections of the country usually has to be covered during the winter months to prevent deterioration of the surface. This fast-drying court presents very fine playing qualities and has great player acceptance. These courts are relatively expensive to construct because drainage through the surface and into the base is necessary and because of the problem of transporting surfacing materials from the sources of supply to the site of the installation.

Concrete and Asphalt Courts. For some years concrete courts were to be found only in California. Of recent years, court-construction companies have found that by far the greatest growth and demand, by percentage, has been with this type of court. Now they are found in all sections. There are several reasons for this. Perhaps one of the leading reasons is economics. Once a cement court is installed, the only upkeep is that of brushing the court clear of dirt and occasionally repainting the lines or restaining the surface. In these days of soaring labor costs, the maintenance problem has become no small item.

On concrete, the ball is not slowed appreciably by contact with the surface, but it bounces much higher than on grass. It is definitely a fast surface. In addition, one generally doesn't think of variations on concrete court surfaces. However, for some time two of California's biggest tournaments were played within a week of each other and upon courts which varied a great deal as to speed. The answer can be found in the method of finishing the concrete surface: a smooth-finished concrete as compared with a concrete finished with certain whorls, or a slight degree of coarseness, which to a certain extent may somewhat slow the bounce of the ball.

Concrete courts, while they present no great problem of maintenance, do present a problem of abrasiveness and rigidity which creates such undesirable features as shock to the feet and legs and wearing out of tennis shoes and tennis balls. In recent years, great strides have been made in so-called "all-weather," nonmaintenance types, which fall within the concrete category but also include some added features. Each company seems to have its own name or names for these surfaces, but they are quite alike in that they have produced a solid-surfaced court with some "give" and spring.

By "all-weather" we mean that the surface of the court is ready for play whenever weather conditions permit. This means that play would be interrupted only during the actual periods of rain or snow on the court area. The "nonmaintenance" features of this court mean that the surface requires no daily maintenance, although there is a certain degree of refinishing required approximately every five to six years, depending upon the type of court installed and the location relative to climatic and weather conditions.

Most all-weather, nonmaintenance courts built today have a semiresilient to resilient surface and usually consist of asphalt compositions. These compositions consist of an asphalt mixture with mineral aggregate, fibers, cork, granules, asbestos, and other ingredients which tend to give a certain degree of resiliency to the court. This court usually presents a sealed surface, which means that all drainage is taken care of off the surface of the court and not through to the base of the construction. The surfaces vary from regular black finish to green compositions using asphalt and acrylic mixtures. There are also rubber-composition installations.

The all-weather, or so-called "hard," court affords the school, college, playground, municipality, and club a tennis-court surface which requires no daily maintenance, has excellent player acceptance, and (because the surface is not easily damaged) generally requires no supervision. These are definite assets, and because of the resiliency of the surface and the development of nondiscoloring rubberized finishes make these courts the most desirable and acceptable. The all-weather courts play much the same as concrete.

Wood Courts. The use of wooden courts indoors, has, of course, been quite extensive in tennis-loving Sweden and, to a much lesser extent, in other countries where long and hard winters are the rule. These wooden courts vary too, but to a lesser extent than some of the other surfaces. Upon occasion, wooden courts may be found with canvas stretched over the surface.

Wood is the fastest of all court surfaces. The ball skids upon contact with the surface, remains low, and the player has the absolute minimum of time in which to react.

Other Surfaces. Currently, other surfaces are being tested and in some cases have been in use for some time, particularly abroad. One such imported material is sheet cork. This material requires a solid sub-base over which the sheet cork can be laid. Therefore the cost will be relatively high. At present, available information is not sufficient to evaluate the material.

Another "new" method of cushioned construction is the so-called asphalt-bound system. Favorable features of these especially designed asphalt courts are: superb playability, true ball bounce, true plane surface, nonabrasive surface which is easy on players as well as tennis balls and shoes, all-weather and all-year availability, nonglaring surface in a choice of many standard nonstaining colors, low pro-rated yearly maintenance cost, no daily upkeep, rapid drying after a rain, and a cushioned surface with sure footing and no skidding. These courts are used for championship play and are recommended for tennis clubs and varsity play where protection (fence and gates) is provided.

These courts require little maintenance. If the colored surface is the full acrylic system, a new top dressing may be required after four to six years. If the colored surface is not the full acrylic system, but asphalt emulsion and acrylic, a new top dressing may be required after three to six years. To keep the color vivid, the surface should be occasionally flushed with water and swept to remove dust or dirt.

In the past few years a number of artificial or synthetic court surfaces have been placed on the market. There have been a number of carpetlike materials; grass-like surfaces; sheet plastics in a variety of colors, patterns, and thicknesses; and waffle-like plastic placed over a thin layer of foam rubber.

There are numerous other synthetic surfaces being manufactured in the United States. They play similar to grass, but because of their synthetic nature, they play more consistent than grass. The actual speed of the court, however, can be regulated by spraying the courts or shaving the fibers.

Many of these surfaces have been tried indoors and outdoors. Since all of these surfaces must be placed over a base, the court is only as true as the base. Also the cost is relatively high when the cost of the base is added to the cost of the synthetic surface. This type of surface might be considered when only the playing surface needs to be replaced and the base is in good condition. The advantages are pleasant colors, uniform bounce, easy maintenance, comfort for the feet, and easy replacement of worn places. But a number of synthetic court materials have been withdrawn from the market because of one or a number of problems, such as lack of durability, color stability, dimensional stability, quick-drying ability, or adherence to surface below, or the surface is too fast or too slow, seams pull apart, or it is too costly. Therefore it is recommended that the would-be purchaser of a synthetic surface check very thoroughly with a previous user of this same surface and that he play on it, particularly if it is to be used outdoors, and be sure the installer is willing to make repairs if necessary.

Actually, there are now available throughout the country contractors who specialize in tennis-court construction, or who have an organization available to construct properly installed tennis courts. Anyone interested in the construction of a court whether for private use or for clubs, schools, colleges, municipalities, or parks departments would do well first to consult such an organization in order to obtain the benefit of its experience along this line. The United States Tennis Association will furnish a list of such contractors either local or those with a nation-wide construction organization specializing in the installation, resurfacing, and reconstruction of tennis courts. In this way accurate and complete information can be obtained which will assist the prospective court owners in proper site selection, orientation, and construction procedure, and also help them to decide the type of court, surfacing, and equipment required for the particular installation.

WHERE TO PLAY

In today's age of booming tennis popularity, there are few cities, towns, or villages where tennis courts are not available to the public either free of charge or for a nominal hourly rental. There are also many private tennis clubs throughout the United States. These clubs vary in size, services, activities, and costs. Some are informal groups which pool their resources to buy land and build courts, and provide only an old shed in which to store the nets and other gear. They seek new members to reduce individual costs or to get equipment that all can use. Then there are the huge, nonprofit organizations with million-dollar properties that include stadiums, swimming pools, and luxurious clubhouses. Membership in such tennis clubs is rather expensive and exclusive. For most beginners, however, it is best to get the feel of tennis first on public park and municipal courts or on private rental courts. Later after they learn the sport, they can join private tennis clubs, either large or small.

Locating a place to play in a town where you are a stranger is usually a relatively simple matter. Rental courts will probably be listed in the classified telephone directory. Local sporting-goods dealers frequently can supply further information. Or a phone call to the local YMCA or Junior Chamber of Commerce should give you the desired information. The latter organization, incidentally, has been responsible for developing both extensive new tennis facilities and widespread interest in the game in many areas throughout the country. If public tennis facilities are inadequate in your area, perhaps it might prove helpful to contact your local Junior Chamber of Commerce and enlist its support. A complete list of USTA member clubs can be had by writing to USTA.

Winter Tennis

The growth of winter tennis as a sport can be attributed to the new facilities, surfaces, and inter-

Night tennis is increasing the popularity of the sport. Above is the installation at Stowe Stadium, Kalamazoo College, Kalamazoo, Michigan.

est generated by playing year round. The new facilities include such devices as synthetic "bubbles," which can be blown up and used as coverings on outdoor courts during the winter.

The opportunities for winter tennis are improving. Owing to the limited facilities, many courts have been reserved in the past on a three- or four-month basis at prices few players can afford. As more facilities continue to be established and renovated for winter play, the fees will undoubtedly be reduced. When playing winter tennis, several points should be remembered:

1. Check the lights and background in the facil-

ity. Nothing can replace natural sunlight. Playing indoors can affect your serve, volley, and return of serve.
2. Check the surface. Is it faster or slower than the surface you normally play on outdoors? Adjust your game accordingly.
3. Give yourself sufficient warmup time to avoid injuries or pulled muscles.
4. Be on time for your game. Indoor courts are not as plentiful as outdoor facilities.
5. If you are changing from outdoors to indoors, approach your game gradually; do not expect too much the first time out.

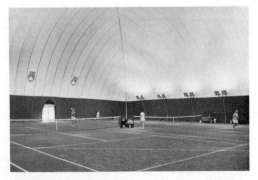

Inflated building structures, such as this one of the courts of the DuPont Country Club in Wilmington, Del., have made winter tennis possible to many more players.

TENNIS CAMPS AND
THEIR SELECTION

A few years ago, the idea of a camp specializing in tennis was a radical concept. Today, the present popularity of the tennis camp is based on three ingredients: 1) top flight instruction and facilities; 2) readily available stiff competition; and 3) the fun and camaraderie of being together with others of the same age and interest for a period of time.

The tennis camp results are invariably impressive and parents are quick to recognize this, as well as their children's enthusiasm for the game and the camp. Today's youngsters want to specialize and are anxious to get away from the old-styled camp routine of riflery, swimming, canoeing, sailing, arts and crafts, and so forth. Teenagers get their fill of this type of hourly routine during the school year and cannot wait for the opportunity to channel their efforts into a single chosen field of endeavor whether it be tennis, golf, basketball, hockey, swimming, or music.

What should parents look for in helping their child select a tennis camp? There are some who feel that the objective of the tennis camp should be to produce winners. We take exception to that viewpoint, for it is obvious everyone cannot be a winner. Furthermore, there are more important objectives worth striving for. The young player will discover that through tennis he can expand such qualities as perseverance, courtesy, courage, and sportsmanship.

Tennis should develop not only a winning spirit, but control over one's body, mind, and emotions. The tennis camp should help campers discover these inner resources, in addition to acquiring to the fullest of their individual abilities a lifetime sport of challenge and enjoyment.

Tennis is reportedly the fastest growing sport in the country. This is primarily the result of today's youth who have been challenged by the game, and have seen the long-range value of acquiring an individual sport that they can play for the rest of their lives. Let us hope that the tennis camps can continue to play a leading role in assisting the youngsters on their long and enjoyable careers as lifetime tennis players. Here are some discernible

Tennis at the 7th Regiment Armory, New York—An artist's conception, *Harper's Weekly,* December 10, 1881.

Fine community tennis programs such as the one at Princeton, N.J., help to develop an interest in the game as well as many fine young players.

factors parents should look for in selecting a tennis camp for their youngsters:

AGE: Generally 12 to 16 years of age for a boarding camp, and from 8 to 18 years of age for a day camp when on a lesson basis, and only then if there is sufficient interest, attention span, strength, and ability to concentrate for the duration of the lesson.

INTEREST: It is essential that the youngster who plans to attend camp have a keen interest in learning the game rather than just playing. *Parents please* do not push children into such highly specialized instruction, but rather wait for them to request the opportunity.

COED: This is an individual preference. The youngsters understandably seem to favor the idea and it tends to produce a more enjoyable and socially rounded summer. The problems one associates with the coed situation can be realistically dealt with by experienced supervision.

LENGTH: Camps range from one week to eight. We have tried three-, four-, and six-week sessions, and find that the four-week session is the most ideal from the standpoint of maximum learning and enjoyment, as well as family vacations. Any period less than two weeks has an extremely limited value, except for the most experienced players.

STAFF: An extremely important factor, particularly if one holds by the educational theory of developing the whole child while at camp. There should be a good mix of Professional Tennis Association coaches and college or tournament players. An instructor to pupil ratio of 1 to 6–8, and an overstaff to camper ratio of 1 to 4–6 are advisable.

FACILITIES: These will vary widely among educational campuses, hotel-motel complexes, and large family homes. Accommodations tend to be luxurious by the old camp standards, with two or more in a room having an adjoining bath. The really important factor is the camper-to-court ratio which should be 4–6 campers per tennis court. There should be adequate backboard space and other teaching aides. Particularly helpful are video-tape replay equipment or slow-motion movies, which, when used in conjunction with a film editor and viewer, permit the camper and his instructor to analyze on a frame-by-frame basis the individual problems before and after instruction.

FOOD: Tennis campers need the best of foods, and the camp should go to extremes to provide carefully balanced training meals of high-protein content. Campers prefer good plain food and plenty of it.

SUPERVISION: Paramount to a productive summer is careful planning and thoughtful organization that leaves sufficient free time for bull sessions, summer reading, pick-up games of ping pong, volleyball, and so forth. Weekend trips to state and national tournaments, summer stock theater, polo or baseball games, as well as nearby points of interest provide welcome relief from the daily routine.

OTHER ACTIVITIES: To balance out the high degree of physical activity during the day, many camps have an evening activity program ranging from such academically helpful courses as typing and speed-reading to guitar, musical theater, art, or chess.

INSTRUCTION: The key to the success of tennis camps rests on both imaginative and productive instruction on as well as off the court. The program should follow four basic steps: 1) analyze and identify the specific problems of each camper; and 2) convince the camper, with the help of instant replay video tape or slow-motion stop-action movies, of his specific faults that need correction. At the same time, show films of proper stroking so as to give the camper a proper mental fix as to what to emulate; 3) arrange a four-hour-a-day instructional program best suited to the individual needs of each camper. Six to eight campers in a group under the full-time guidance of one instructor has proved most beneficial. The group and instructor come on a regular rotation basis before the professional master teachers who constantly oversee the whole program of instruction and drills; and 4) competitive play needs to be carefully arranged to minimize the tendency, when under pressure, to revert to familiar but improper habits. Competition should be varied and equally matched to produce best results. Davis Cup team-styled play and individual ladder play have proved more effective than elimination tournaments in this regard.

Tennis camp programs are one of the fastest ways for young people to learn the game.

Tips for Parents

The great tennis controversy currently raging in the United States no longer concerns open tennis, the footfault rule, the Davis Cup captain, the next president of the USTA or the financing of the National Championships. It is being fought over the role of the parent in the development of young tennis players. People are either "for" parents or "against" them; most of us are "for" the good ones and "against" the bad ones. If you are a mother or a father and you think you are encouraging your offspring, check the following DOs and DON'Ts to see if your conduct toward your child is irreproachable and encourages interest in the game:

1. If you play well, make yourself available for your child as an opponent or a partner. Never coach or offer helpful hints. Leave this up to his pro.

2. When your son or daughter takes a lesson, do not sit on the sidelines and watch.

3. The only time you ever give pointers on strategy to your child is when he literally begs you to do so. Your comments then should be brief, encouraging, and to the point. If he asks you a vague question, such as "What did I do wrong?", do not answer in detail; let it go with a brief commiseration and encouragement for the future.

4. Never watch your child (in practice or in a tournament) unless he specifically requests your presence. Do not call lines, applaud, berate the opponent, discuss the match with the umpire or expound on the match with fellow spectators. You are the epitome of the Silent Observer.

5. When your child enters a tournament, he is on his own. Do not go up to the tournament desk for any reason, unless your child wishes to introduce you to the committee. Do not comment on the seedings, the draw, the scheduling or the court assignments.

6. When people tell you how well your child is playing, you reply "Thank you," and let it go at that. Never go into the Department of Fuller Explanations, Expostulations or Exhortations, including such "modest" declamations as "We really don't care just how good he gets as long as he enjoys the game" or "We leave it all up to him because . . ."

7. When your child has lost, never ask "what happened?" or "what went wrong?" If he wishes to tell you, he will and you should silently commiserate. He knows he can talk to you because you are interested and because he will not face either an inquisition, a lecture or a series of stories on matches *you* played.

8. If your child wants to play a tournament, give him every help you can in getting there. You do not fill out his entry blank but you do provide the entry fee. Never *suggest* that he enter a tournament.

9. Do not arrange practice games for your child but do help him get to the courts if he asks for help.

10. Display your child's trophies because you are proud of his achievements. If someone comments on them, thank them but do not then proceed to identify every cup and medal.

11. Be content about the amount of practice (or lack thereof) given to the game by your child. Forcing a youngster to practice will never make a champion. If you want a champion in the family, try to be one yourself; do not force your child to be one for you.

12. The only time to interfere is when your child has thrown his racket, screamed, yelled or otherwise behaved outrageously on the court.

13. Do not insist that your child train. This is up to him and perhaps he does not care as much about the game as you do.

14. If your child has a "bad year," simply encourage him and explain (once) that every great player has had a bad loss, a bad season or a bad year. Overcoming these defeats is what makes the champion.

15. When your child's forehand goes "off" or he chokes in a match or he gets stale, let him work it out for himself. If he is capable of playing in a tournament, he is capable of deciding what he is going to do with regard to his forehand, his choking or his staleness. If he requests your advice, ask him his solution before you give him your own. After all, you cannot hit the ball for him.

Principles of Tennis

FUNDAMENTALS OF TENNIS

Tennis is a basically simple game which involves opposing players who stroke the ball back and forth over a net into the court. Play continues until one of the players hits the ball out of the court, into the net, or does not stroke the ball before it bounces twice.

Play is started when one player (the server) stands behind the base line and to the right of the center mark and puts the ball in play by tossing it in the air and striking it with his racket so that it lands in the right service court on the opposite side of the net. This player has then "served" the ball to his opponent.

The opposing player (the receiver) must let the served ball bounce and then must hit it into his opponent's court, between the side lines, the base line, and the net. Balls are hit alternately until one of the players fails to return the ball into his opponent's court. After the service, balls can be played before they have bounced or on the first bounce. Points are scored according to the official United States Tennis Association (USTA) rules*(see Section 4). After the first point is completed, the server moves to the left of the center mark and serves into his opponent's left service court. Subsequently, he alternates service courts for every point. A designated number of points makes up a game; games make up a set, and sets, a match.

In doubles, two players on one side oppose two players on another side. The idea of the game, however, remains essentially the same as in singles. Players serve in turn in doubles, first a member of one team, then a member of the other team, and so on. However, players need not take turns hitting the ball after it is in play following a return of service.

Spinning to determine who serves first.

109

Three basic grips: *(left to right)* Eastern, Continental, and Western.

As in all sports there are basic fundamentals. In tennis these are a good grip and proper tennis form. The latter includes the swing and hitting the ball, footwork, and timing.

The Grip

The fundamentals of lawn tennis are affected more perhaps by the player's grip of the racket than anything else that is within his control. His playing position, his swing, the twist the ball receives, all depend on the grip he has on his racket when he hits the ball.

There has been controversy over the best methods of gripping the racket almost since the birth of the game. There have been three distinct schools, each of which has its merits, and beyond these a half dozen eccentric styles of holding the racket have earned more or less success. But while we find that certain methods of gripping have apparent advantages for certain strokes, they lose in other strokes as much or more than is gained. It is not practicable to change the hold for every stroke, so some set style must be adopted that gives the most advantage for all the strokes required.

A slight shifting, for instance, in the position of the hand gives a much better hold for the rolling backhand drive, but only for this stroke, and so it

is available only for those players who use this stroke regularly. If this is adopted, then other strokes on the backhand side must be adapted to this hold or suffer in consequence.

There are three *major* different types of grips: the Eastern, the Continental, and the Western. The basic difference between the three is position of the palm of the hand. In the Western grip, the palm is under the handle; in the Continental, it is over it; while in the Eastern, the palm is behind the handle.

Eastern Grip. This is the most popular grip today, being used by over 70 percent of American players. It is recommended for the novice by most experts. It is equally good for dealing with high, waist-high, or very low shots.

The Eastern grip is made by holding the racket at the throat with the left hand and extending it comfortably in front of you with the butt end of the handle toward your body. The face of the racket should be at right angles to the ground. Grasp the racket with the right hand so that the back knuckle of the thumb is directly on top of the racket, about an eighth of an inch to the left of center. This means that the V or wishbone formed between the forefinger and the thumb should be above the top plane of the handle. The butt of the racket should rest easily on the heel of the hand. The thumb is wrapped around the racket and the fingers extended comfortably along the handle. The palm of the hand should be against the back plane of the handle. This grip is often described as "shaking hands with the racket." A lefthanded player should do the above procedure by holding the racket with the right hand and grasping it with the left.

The backhand grip can be obtained from the Eastern forehand grip by shifting the hand to the left (counterclockwise) about one quarter of a turn. This should bring the back knuckle of the first finger directly on top of the racket. Now, the V between the thumb and forefinger will come just at the inner edge of the handle and your thumb will point diagonally across the handle. By having part of the thumb behind the racket, this grip gives added support and control to the stroke. The change from the forehand to the backhand is made by using the left hand to help guide the racket. This can be accomplished while you are in the anticipatory position or during the backswing.

Continental Grip. For the Continental grip, the handle is rotated about an eighth of a turn (counterclockwise by righthanders, clockwise by lefthanders) from the Eastern grip. Since the Continental grip is halfway between the Eastern forehand and backhand grips, it is good for either of these two basic groundstrokes without the necessity of shifting the hand grip. It also facilitates making short cross-court shots and, in addition, is excellent for dealing with low bounces. However, unless your wrist is very strong, you will find it difficult to control high-bounding balls.

The Continental grip is made by standing the racket on one edge and then simply picking it up from that position. In so doing, the palm of the hand is virtually on top of the racket and the thumb extends across the front of the handle.

Many top Australian players use the Continental grip because of their emphasis on net play even in the beginning stages of learning. The no-change feature of the grip makes it especially suitable for the fast action required there, and doubtless many players have simply transferred their net grips into back-court play.

Western Grip. This grip is very good for dealing with high shots and suitable for waist-high balls, but is difficult to use on very low shots. In other words, it is not as good an all-around grip as the other two, and hence is the least used of the three.

The Western grip is obtained by laying the racket face down on the ground and then picking it up in the same manner as the Continental. This places the palm of the hand underneath the handle when the racket head is brought into a vertical or hitting position.

There is no general agreement as to precisely when the hand has left the range of the Eastern grip to become, let us say, a Continental or, if moved in the other direction, a Western. This is simply a matter of semantics. Actually, some players, over the years, have used variations or combinations of these grips and some have even used unorthodox ones. For example, Pancho Segura—who had one of the best forehand drives—used an unorthodox two-handed grip. Likewise, John Bromwich, the Australian great, used both hands on the handle for the backhand. A few players have used no backhand at all. They shifted the racket from right hand to left and played forehands on either side. Such a style has a major disadvantage when it comes to rapid net play.

Whether you use an Eastern, a Continental, or a Western grip, there is only one way to hold the racket—with firm fingers. The racket is your weapon and it must move the ball; if you hold it loosely, the ball will twist the racket in your hand and you will have no control.

Many players, when trying to grip the racket firmly, will tighten up the whole arm. The arm itself should be relaxed. All strokes (with the exception of the moment of impact on serve and overhead) are hit with a bent arm. On groundstrokes, the arm wheels freely from shoulder and elbow on the backswing, and the arm is bent slightly on the hit. It becomes almost straight only on the follow-through. It becomes stiff only when one stretches wide for a ball almost out of reach. The arm is also bent on the volley, again the only exception being the side ball.

Learning to keep the fingers firm and the arm relaxed is a prerequisite to good tennis. At first the arm will always stiffen. It is like learning to pat your stomach with your left hand and rub your head with a circular motion with your right hand; in the beginning both hands will perform the same motion, and it takes concentration to make them act out different motions simultaneously.

The wrist should be as firm as the fingers. Beginners and intermediates should practice hitting the ball with a wrist that is absolutely locked during the hit. If the wrist is loose, the ball moves the racket instead of the racket moving the ball. Wrist and arm are practically one straight line on the backhand groundstroke and volley; wrist and arm form a 20-degree angle on forehand groundstroke and volley. The wrist snaps only on the service and overhead.

The player should be well past the intermediate stage before he ever tries to put wrist action into his groundstrokes. When he has learned to stroke the ball well with firm fingers, locked wrist, and relaxed arm, he can introduce "wrist" shots into his game. The "wrist" movements are necessary for slice, drop shots, chops, and the angle or touch game; if they are acquired too soon, the player may never learn a solid set of groundstrokes.

When wrist is introduced into a player's repertoire, he is at a stage when he understands that the wrist moves the ball, not the ball the wrist. To hit groundstrokes with such an action, the wrist must be strong as iron and the timing must be perfect. It is not a shot for a beginner.

To rest the hand from the fatigue of constant tight gripping, relax the grip between the strokes, and if necessary help to carry the weight by resting the neck of the racket in the left hand between shots.

Always grip the racket by the very end; never shorten the grip. This is the hardest thing to impress on the beginner's mind, because he finds it more difficult to swing the racket at first with the full length of the handle, and he is very reluctant to do this, when the shorter grip gives him a quicker control and permits him to hit the ball with a jerky half swing. At first the beginner swings his racket only a foot or two in striking, making more of a push than a blow of his stroke, and this lets him delay striking until the last second, and the stroke seems easier to be made in this way. But the error of this method is that it depends on the strength of the player's arm for success, and this is the first great fallacy by which the novice is led into bad habits of play. The arm's strength has little to do with the good tennis stroke; it depends almost entirely on the momen-

tum of the racket, and at the moment of impact little or no strength is exerted by the arm.

As in golf, the player "presses" as soon as he uses his muscles too much. The racket and the golf club really do the work required, and it is only necessary for the player to start them in the right direction, and increase their momentum and speed by the swing of the body and arm until they reach the maximum when the ball is hit. He need only guide the racket or club, rather than push it along.

The length of the racket is increased by every inch of the handle that is extended beyond the gripping hand, so that its leverage and the power of its swing under momentum increase fast with this extension. As it is difficult to shift the grip after first habits are formed, it is doubly important to begin with the long grip, even though it seems more difficult at first.

The reluctance of most beginners to grip the handle by the extreme end comes from the difficulty of making a successful stroke with only a half swing and a long grip. The novice hesitates to make a full swing because he cannot calculate at first so far ahead where the ball is going to bound and how high and how deep it will jump up in front of him. He fears to draw his racket far back to make the stroke because he expects to make only a half swing.

The leather "button," or binding at the end of the handle helps to prevent the racket from slipping from the hand, and also warns the player, without his needing to look down, when his hand has reached the end of the handle. This leather end should rest against the fleshy part of the hand at the base of the thumb, and, if the full-length grip is cultivated, it will rest very comfortably there while in play.

The size of the handle is an important point. There is a tendency to have it too large. It should be of such diameter that it fills the hand but allows the fingers to work. If it is too large this is impossible. The smaller the handle the quicker is the work of hand and fingers. On the other hand, there is the principle that the handle should be large enough to act as a strut in the hand, and so keep the wrist firm. The best size, as previously stated in Section 2, is that which makes the thumb and middle finger overlap to the extent of about an inch, not less in any case, but very little more.

Tennis Form

Good form in any sport is one of those elusive qualities that are hard to describe, and often harder to adopt. Briefly defined, good form, so far as it applies to lawn tennis, may be said to be the manner and method of playing which will produce in the hands of the average man the greatest percentage of success. It is that method of using the body, the arms, and the legs which gives the greatest freedom and the best ability to make successful strokes.

There have been many players and some experts who have won high honors despite bad form, and too often have these men been followed as models simply because it was thought that their success vindicated their methods. But this is an empty fallacy, for such a player may have certain mental or physical qualities that are entirely foreign to the average player. Abnormal length of arms or legs may affect his manner of swinging his racket or the position he assumes during play. The same methods adopted by a player of a different mold would not give the same results.

Three of the elements of good tennis form are sound strokes, perfect balance, and proper timing. A well-founded stroke gives the player the equipment to deal with the ball, good balance enables the player to hit with the full force of his weight and regain his ready position immediately thereafter, and fine timing allows the player to meet the ball at the right moment. There are other factors in the good player's repertoire—anticipation, footwork, stamina, a cool head, the will to win, strategy, and so on—but these are the refinements of match play and are developed as the player moves to higher levels. First the player must acquire good strokes, good balance, and good timing.

The Swing and Hitting the Ball. Whether you make a forehand or backhand, a lift or slice stroke, the general principles involved are much the same, and a thorough study of these will help.

Three distinct actions must be kept in mind, although they frequently all run into one with such rapidity that it is hard to separate them. First we have the backswing in preparation for the stroke; then the act of hitting the ball, and finally the follow-through.

To hit the ball properly, the eyes should be kept on the ball until it is hit, and in calling attention to this, it should be pointed out that "keeping the eye on the ball" means actually focusing the eyes on the ball as it approaches. A player should have a sense of bringing the focus in as the ball comes toward him. By so doing, the inside muscles of the eyes will become tired sooner, but the effort will be worthwhile. Most beginning players fail to do this and too often look through the ball. This means that as the ball leaves the opponent's racket the eyes are fixed on it but as it comes toward the player he does not bring the focus in with the advance of the ball. Most persons can unconsciously gauge with great accuracy their distance from an object on which the eyes are properly focused. Nothing will help you to hit the ball with the center of the racket as much as will this matter of focusing and, if a ball is not hit with the center of the racket, the shot is generally flubbed, or at least, is ineffective. Therefore, all through the stroke, be careful to keep your head down and your eye on the ball.

During play there are times when it is necessary to see where an opponent is, and to glance at the court and its boundary lines. Expert players also use a special finesse in the higher art of expert play, in which they look away from the ball just before they hit it, in order to direct a placed shot more accurately. But this kind of technique is not for beginners, and should be put aside entirely until the player is well on the road to expert skill.

Only by watching the ball constantly will it be possible to calculate the angle of its flight, the distance it will travel before striking, and how high and how far it will bound before you must hit it. The ball in any sharp light offers a fine mark, and the eye can be focused on it no matter how fast it may fly through the air. Whether it is coming or going, so long as the play continues, it must be followed constantly if one is to play well.

The anticipatory, or readiness, position should be somewhat crouching, with bent knees, shoulders thrown well forward, and the weight carried up on the toes. Ready to spring in any direction on the instant, the player in this position is wonderfully able to reach the return that may be placed in some other part of the court. He should always be ready to move quickly, and even when the ball comes directly toward him, he should jump forward in striking. The greatest power in making any stroke comes from leaning to meet the ball, which brings all the player's weight into the blow.

As soon as your opponent hits the ball you should as quickly as possible determine the direction of the ball, then determine whether you are going to receive it on the forehand or backhand. Immediately upon making this decision you should carry the racket back into position for the stroke, whether on forehand or backhand. In the event of an overhead smash, it is well to get the racket back and up in position well ahead of time.

The reasons for this precaution are very sound, as well as obvious. If the racket is in position to make the stroke when the ball reaches you, you can go through with the stroke easily, without hurrying, without jerking, and the stroke is more than likely to be well timed and sound. If you await the arrival of the ball before getting the racket in position, you must take the backswing and return to the point of contact with the ball so quickly that accuracy is very difficult. If you get your racket back as soon as your opponent hits the ball, you are more than likely to be able to handle the position of your feet. In running to receive the ball, at the same time get the racket back, or up in case of a smash, in position to make the stroke.

A good test to see if you are getting the racket back early enough in anticipation of the stroke and getting it back properly is to note whether you have started for position on balls which your opponent has hit toward your court, but which have been stopped by the net. If you have started toward the correct position before the ball hits the net, you will know that you are anticipating reasonably well. If you have not started before the ball is netted, you will know that your anticipation is bad.

As soon as you know the ball is coming to your forehand or your backhand, swing your shoulders to the right or to the left, as the case may be, so that the shoulders are at right angle to the net. You should be able to tell whether the ball is going to be on the forehand or the backhand before the ball in flight is on your side of the net. If you swing your shoulders in time your feet will have the tendency to move more easily and to cooperate more smoothly so you may be in correct position

for a proper stroke. Taking advantage of all the time available for getting into proper position assures you ample time to make your shot unhurried. Shots made in a great hurry cannot consistently be good shots.

A full and free backswing is most essential. It is not necessary, as in golf, to wrap your arm and racket around your neck in order to get the full impetus necessary for a hard drive, but a stroke that starts only a foot or two back of the point of impact with the ball is unlikely to have any great power. In fact, the power of a tennis stroke depends almost entirely on the momentum of the racket, and this is gained largely by the swing that adds the weight of the body to the force. Little if any muscle is required to make a good stroke. The well-timed swing of the arm and racket, accelerated by body swing, and the all-important "follow-through" are what do the work. Not only is the swing of the body before the ball is hit needed to produce a good stroke, but it should be carried far beyond that point, following the ball long after it has left the racket. This follow-through, so much talked of in golf, is equally important in tennis, and the fastest strokes of expert players are the result of perfect timing to secure the maximum momentum in the racket, added to a full follow-through of the body weight.

A good player starts his windup when he runs. He does not wait until he gets to the ball. If he has to run wide on his forehand, he starts his semicircular (or straight-back) backswing immediately. By the time he has reached the ball, the racket has begun its forward motion. The only time a player can start his backswing after his feet are planted for the shot is against a soft hitter. The more pace the opponent has on his ball, the sooner the windup must begin.

Beginners invariably start their backswing after the ball has cleared the net; advanced players start as soon as the ball leaves the opponent's racket. Players in the intermediate category frequently show a tendency to be late either on forehand windup, backhand windup, or on the backswing when running for a short ball or drop shot.

A top player always looks ready because he starts his windup in plenty of time; a lesser player always looks rushed because he waits too long to begin the stroke.

At the back of its preliminary swing the racket must pause anyway and lose its momentum before starting forward, so that it can be checked for a slightly longer period if necessary, if you should unintentionally swing too early for the stroke. It is far better to err on this side than on the other, so it is a safe rule to keep swinging back earlier until you find you must noticeably check the racket before starting the forward swing for the stroke. This pause at the end of the backswing has an inclination to steady the stroke, but it can easily be exaggerated and it then has a tendency, particularly when marked, to expose the direction of the attack.

The total absence of any pause may result in hurrying the stroke too much, and the tendency to "snap" on the ball which follows this habit invariably results in a loss of control. If full time is not allowed and the forward swing is hurried, the slightest deviation of the ball from the expected flight will result in a bad stroke, as there is no time left to correct the swing to meet this shift.

At the end of the reach backward, you will notice that the arm swings naturally either upward or sidewise behind you. By all means, select the upward motion. This keeps the racket in the direct line of flight and avoids the side motion that is so apt to throw off the accuracy of the stroke as well as the body's poise during the forward stroke. You should also increase somewhat the arc of this circle in the backswing by turning slightly with the shoulders so that you have the longest reach possible without getting out of position for a free stroke. The shoulders at the end of the backswing should be parallel with the feet and the line of flight of the ball. The weight of the body, too, should be shifted full on the back foot and when making a strong stroke, it should be swung back as far as possible to preserve the balance.

If you find that you run well on either side but that you make too many errors when running in for short balls or drop shots, the fault may lie in the fact that you are not ready. Start your windup as you run forward. The backswing is not only completed but the racket should actually be moving forward when you reach the ball. Errors are corrected by exaggerations in the other direction. If you have been late on your windup, get your racket back the moment the ball leaves the opponent's racket, even if it makes you too early for the ball.

When the time is right to begin the forward swing, that is, to make the stroke, the body turns on the hips, the right shoulder comes forward, followed by the upper arm, and then the forearm; and finally just before the ball is hit, the wrist adds the snap of a whiplash to the blow and the full weight of the body shifts quickly forward from the backward to the forward foot, so that at the moment of impact all possible energy is concentrated in the blow.

Now comes the greatest difficulty that is found in the play of most players. They are inclined to stop here. After hitting the ball, they feel that is as far as they can control it, and they make no effort to follow through, recovering the balance as quickly as possible in the most convenient way. But this is all wrong. Just as in golf, the follow-through is most important. While it is true that after the ball has once left the racket, it is impossible to further affect its movements, the after swing of the player does affect the whole stroke most materially. It is impossible to make a true stroke without it, since any effort to cut short the swing infallibly affects the stroke itself and draws the racket away from its work before its maximum power has been exerted.

The racket should not only follow the ball itself just as far as you can normally reach, but you should also bend the whole body as far as the balance will allow to lengthen the swing of the arm. The entire body should be turned on the hips, the bent knees allowing it to move forward with the stroke and extend the swing of the racket. At the end of this following swing, the body should turn still further around, the shoulders pulling in, the arm and the wrist bending to allow the racket's impetus to be checked with a short swing like the *moulinet* of the swordsman.

For the most exaggerated groundstrokes, the weight of the body is thrown so violently forward in the follow-through that the balance is frequently checked by carrying the back foot forward to a further advanced position. Indeed this style is not at all uncommon, and where well practiced it almost invariably increases the body swing, the follow-through, and the power of the stroke. It is an excellent habit to allow the weight to draw the back foot forward to a new position, and the habit of taking this forward step in making the stroke will add greatly to the vigor of the attack.

This method should be used sparingly when the player is well forward in his court, for if the weight is thrown too far forward when in the volleying position, it is easy to lose the balance forward and become exposed to an overhead attack by a lob before the balance can be recovered.

Now, through all these three motions of the stroke, one cardinal rule should always be kept in mind. Every motion should be as far as possible in the direct line of the ball's flight; every motion that is off this line tends to lessen or check the power of the stroke and to lessen its accuracy. Side motion of any kind only weakens the swing.

It is not an uncommon fault among beginners to see the player bend his body backward away from the ball, particularly in making the forehand groundstroke. This only serves to detract from the body swing by checking the forward motion of the weight. Swinging the racket across the face of the ball to exaggerate the cut checks the forward force of the stroke and sometimes loses more in speed than it gains in the twist.

The more directly every motion can be kept in line with the flight intended for the ball, the more accurate will be the aim of the player and the more power there will be in the stroke. Side motions of the racket and arm almost invariably mean lost power and cause poor direction as well. The player who swings his racket across the path of the ball, rather than directly after it in the same plane, is generally wild in his returns and finds it difficult to control the ball as he should.

It is practically impossible to make a good stroke when the ball is played from close to the body. One should keep away from it in every direction. As it approaches, keep further back than you think necessary, and then jump forward to meet it, which gives the much-needed body weight in the stroke. Sidewise, also, never let the ball approach directly toward your body. Rather keep it off to one side and lean out to meet it, again using the balance of the body to add weight to the stroke. When a ball comes straight at you, step to one side or the other or your stroke will be ruined.

The elbow becomes bent and cramped when the ball gets in close to the player's body, and there is little or no power in a stroke made from such a position. If the ball bounds to the right or left of what was expected, the difference can be taken up by the bend of the elbow if well extended, but when cramped, all chance to correct the error in calculating the ball's flight is lost.

The idle arm should be used as a counterbalance. With it extended far out in the opposite direction from that carrying the racket, the balance can be preserved much better, and it also permits the player to lean farther out to meet the ball and to use his body weight in the stroke.

Watch a man run and you will see that whenever his right leg goes forward, his right arm swings back, and the same with the left. Without the arms swinging as counterbalances, it would not be possible for him to run nearly so fast, as the efforts of his legs would throw him off his balance with no help from the arm on the opposite side. It is the same thing in tennis, and the value of the idle arm as a counterbalance in fast play cannot be overestimated.

In all groundstrokes, where a full swing is called for, and in most others, the player should turn his side toward the net when he makes the stroke. This gives a free swing for the racket and brings the feet into line so that the weight can be shifted from one to the other during the stroke to increase the body swing that is so necessary for speed. In stepping into this position, the player moves forward with one foot or backward with the other, according to whether the next ball is coming short or deep into his court.

Except while making a few volleys at the net, it is best to loosen up the joints so that the swing of the racket is not jerky. A pliable wrist is a great help, and the "flick" of the racket just before the ball is hit, by which experts add so much to their speed, all comes from the wrist. The more the whole arm from shoulder to wrist can be treated like a whiplash, the smoother and more powerful will be the stroke. The arm acts like a jointed rod, but the smoother the joints work, the better will be the stroke.

Another important point for the beginner to keep in mind is the necessity of preparing for the next stroke the instant the ball has been hit. Do not wait to see where your return is going before you start, but begin instantly to recover your balance and move to the best position for the next stroke. Anticipation of this kind is one of the greatest advantages an experienced player has over the novice.

Footwork. Footwork is the means of perfect weight control and balance, while timing is the transference of the player's weight into his stroke, thus giving "pace" to the ball. Actually, good footwork is the secret of success in boxing, baseball, tennis, football, dancing, and many other sports, for by this medium the punch of the boxer, the carrying power of the batter, the pace of the tennis player, the distance of the punter, or the balance of the dancer is determined. There is a fraction of a second when ball and body are in such a juxtaposition that if the ball is struck then, the speed and pace are increased by the maximum leverage of the body. That is the moment when the weight of the body crosses the center of balance in a forward movement, and simultaneously the ball in its flight meets the racket. Only by this forward movement of striking the ball is it possible to acquire the maximum power. That is perfect timing.

Good footwork in tennis is as important as sound groundstrokes or a big serve. Without the proper footwork, a player may find his weight moving backward or sideways rather than forward. He may plant his feet too late or too early, block himself from moving into the ball, or find himself glued to the ground when he should be taking a step forward or sideways. Good footwork can mean speed in reaching the ball, balance when meeting it, and power on the hit.

The basic requirements for proper tennis footwork are: (1) the weight should be on the balls of the feet rather than the heels; (2) the hop-skip motion should be used when necessary to wind up on the correct foot; and (3) the player should step toward the net with the left foot on the forehand and the right foot on the backhand.

When the player is in the ready position, his weight should be evenly distributed on the toes of both feet. He should feel "bouncy" rather than flatfooted. His feet are well spread and his knees are bent, but he is not leaning over so far that he loses his balance. The "bouncier" he is, the more ready he is to move. When the ball leaves his opponent's racket, he makes his move: he pushes off with his left foot if he is moving toward his right (he lets his weight go onto the heel of his left foot, which is used as the "pusher"). If he does not have far to go, he simply skips sideways, with his body still facing the net. When a ball comes to his backhand, the action is reversed: he pushes off with his right foot to move toward his left. He skips toward balls that he can reach easily but runs toward balls that are wide or very short.

If the opponent hits a short ball that can be reached without difficulty, the player skips forward (the right foot on the forehand is always one step closer to the net than the left). If the ball comes directly to the player rather than to his side, he hop-skips one step toward the backhand so that he can play the ball naturally on his forehand.

The skip is used to prevent a player from getting glued to the ground, to make it easy for him to step toward the net with the proper foot, and to make last-minute adjustments if he misjudged the bounce. The run is always used instead of the skip to reach a difficult ball, but you will often see good players run toward the ball, then skip on the last step (if there is time) so that their footwork will be correct for the hit.

The proper footwork on the hit is neither the open stance with body facing the net nor the closed stance with left foot crossing toward the right alley (or right foot crossing toward the left alley).

The wide-open stance does not make it easy to put one's weight into the ball, and the extreme closed stance prevents the weight from moving forward (it is, instead, moving sideways). Correct footwork is to step toward the net—with the left foot on the forehand and the right foot on the backhand. The stance is slightly open on the forehand, but the right side is toward the net on the backhand.

There are times when the player must use the wide-open or the extreme closed stance. One does not have time to adjust footwork against a cannonball serve (one simply turns the left shoulder toward the net on the forehand and the right shoulder toward the net on the backhand). Again, when one is running for a very wide ball, one may end up in an extreme closed stance. In the latter case, the shot cannot be an attacking one since the weight is moving in the wrong direction.

If you have been having problems with footwork, review the three basic requirements for the proper approach: (1) on your toes, (2) hop-skip whenever possible, (3) step toward the net with left foot on forehand and right foot on backhand. This may be the answer to bettering your balance and increasing your speed and your power.

Timing. A player with good timing knows when to commence his stroke so that he will meet the ball at the proper moment. A player with poor timing may plan to hit the ball slightly in front of him but may catch it behind him. The two factors which will enable the player to improve his timing are: a consideration of the stroke involved (a forehand is timed differently from a backhand) and very early preparation.

Even if a match is played on a perfect court with no bad bounces, and the opponent hits every ball with exactly the same amount of pace, the player still must adjust his timing to the particular stroke involved. The timing on a groundstroke is different from that on a volley, and the timing on an overhead is different from that on a serve. Forehands are hit a fraction of a second earlier than backhands. Often a player's timing will be "off" on his forehand but perfect on his backhand: occasionally he will have a good backhand day but his forehand will be "off." The stroke did not come apart suddenly: the timing did. The first stage of the cure is to recognize that the timing on forehands is different from that on backhands, that the timing on volleys is different from that on groundstrokes.

In all strokes one must decide at what point one wishes to meet the ball. The serve should be hit to the side of and slightly in front of the body; volleys should be met 12 to 18 inches in front of the body; groundstrokes should be met several inches in front of the body (for beginners) or several feet in front of the body (for advanced players). Once the desired point of contact is established, the stroke should be practiced until this contact is met with more and more regularity. The stroke gets grooved to meet the ball at a particular point.

The easiest way to develop good timing is to play a soft hitter. You are not being rushed and so you can always meet the ball at the point in front of you which you have decided is most desirable. The harder your opponent's pace, the more rapid your preparation must be. One must still try to meet the ball in front of the body, and so the windup must begin as soon as the opponent hits the ball. Never compromise when playing a hard hitter by taking the ball late; keep to the desired point of contact, which is in front of your body.

A change-of-pace artist may throw your timing off. His object is to prevent you from getting a rhythm: he will try to make you hit late by throwing in an occasional hard ball and to make you hit too early by giving you an occasional softer ball. Your own concentration will defeat his strategy of spins, cannonballs, and drop shots since you will be aware immediately of the change in his plan and you can alter your own preparation at once to adjust to the shot.

Awareness of early preparation, the desired point of contact, and your opponent's style will help you develop good timing. This "awareness," which allows you to make adjustments in your own game, will enable you to change from a slow court to a fast one, from soft balls to hard ones, and from ideal conditions to windy ones.

TENNIS STROKES

Tennis strokes can be divided into three categories: groundstrokes, volleys, and service strokes.

Groundstrokes are those you play after the ball has bounced on your side of the net and include the drive (forehand and backhand), the lob, the drop shot, the half volley, and the overhead smash.

The volley strokes are shots played when the ball is in flight, before it has bounced on your side of the net, and include horizontal volley (forehand and backhand), the overhead volley, the smash, the lob volley and the stop volley.

The service stroke is the one employed to put the ball in play during an actual game. Now let us take a closer look at each of these three categories of strokes.

The basic forehand drive from the anticipatory position to the completed follow-through.

Forehand Groundstrokes

The forehand drive "off the ground" is the commonest stroke in the game, so you should learn to make it before you go on to any other. It is the foundation of both attack and defense; and it must be thoroughly mastered if you are to become a good player.

It is the commonest stroke in the game because, first, the number of strokes off the ground is never less than 50 percent even when both players are volleyers by temperament, and rises to considerably over 90 percent when both players are baseliners; and second, because three-quarters of all these groundstrokes are forehand strokes, owing to everybody's natural preference for, if possible, taking the ball forehanded rather than back-

handed. The purpose of the forehand is to return a ball on the racket side of the body (the right side of a righthanded player or the left of a lefthanded player) after it has bounced once. It should be used to keep the ball and the opponent deep in the opposite court. That is, a deep drive into your opponent's court gives you more time to reach the net and materially reduces the possibility of being successfully passed or lobbed. To accomplish this, a ball hit by the forehand drive must be placed near the top of the net (low), near the opponent's base line (deep), and should carry speed (flat or topspin). Fortunately, this most important stroke is the easiest and the most natural to learn.

To make a forehand stroke properly, it is most important to get into the proper position to hit the ball right. This means to run to a position in the court about 2 or 3 feet to the left of where the ball will come up from its bound. You should be well back of the spot where it hits the ground so as to allow room for the bound, and also to permit you to meet it as your weight is thrown forward or toward the ball itself. When this position is reached your left foot should be forward or toward the net and the right back of it nearly in direct line with the flight of the ball.

As the ball strikes the ground, your racket should start to move in the backswing, and should pass around behind your body and slightly upward, extended at the full reach of the arm. As previously stated, most beginners find it very difficult to start the backswing early enough, and a late start shortens the backswing and makes the stroke jerky and poorly executed, lacking power. In the forehand drive, the swing should be as continuous as possible, with no stopping of the racket at the end of the backswing, but a slight turn and an immediate forward swing without checking the headway of the racket. To pull back the racket only a foot or so, stop it to gauge the flight of the ball, and then start it forward to hit will never accomplish anything in tennis. The momentum of the racket must be kept up from the start back until long after the ball has been hit, for that, not the strength in the arm, is what gives power to the stroke.

The racket should act as simply an extension of the forearm, and be kept as far away from the body as possible. The upper arm, forearm, and racket all three act as a jointed rod that strikes like a flail, and if the wrist is added to the movement it becomes like a whiplash in its action, imparting a powerful blow. At all times avoid getting your elbow cramped up close to the body.

As the backswing is made the body should be turned or pivoted around on the hips and both the shoulders and the hips turned to follow the racket back and make its swing easier. The weight should be evenly balanced between the two legs when the backswing is started and then transferred back onto the right foot to carry the weight back evenly without losing balance.

As the ball starts to rise from the ground, the forward, or hitting, swing starts, and the unwinding of the backward coil reverses its first action. The hips turn first, then the shoulders, followed by

the upper arm, forearm, and wrist as the racket sweeps forward to meet the ball. In this forward swing, the weight is again shifted back from the right foot to the even center when the ball is met and then continued on until it ends entirely on the left foot.

The ball should be met at a height between the knee and waist and as nearly as possible opposite the center of the body. The racket must be guided so that the ball strikes the center of the strings of the racket, the nearer the center the better. Meeting the ball off center is likely to turn the racket in the hand and always reduces the strength as well as the accuracy of the shot.

The head of the racket should be perpendicular to the ground at the moment when the ball is hit —that is, the top part of the frame should be no farther forward or back than the lower part. This gives what is known as an "open" racket and the greatest accuracy and strength in the stroke. The handle of the racket should be very nearly parallel to the ground.

From the point of impact, there are three variations of the end of the stroke, all having their own uses and advantages, and the player can select any style he pleases, and vary the style of shot, if he can control several styles, for different results.

The Flat Forehand Drive. The ideal forehand drive is a flat drive which skims the net and yet is able to keep your opponent deep in his court. But flat drives are too difficult to control, especially on low bounces; for if the ball crosses the net higher than 6 inches or so above the net cord, it will land out of court. This margin of safety is too small. Topspin, on the other hand, enables you to drive the ball 2 or more feet above the net and also deep to your opponent's base line. Your margin of safety above the net is much greater than with the flat drive; and the forward downspin, aided by gravitation, pulls the ball downward within the court after it has crossed the net. You should therefore make fewer errors.

The term *flat* as it is used in tennis means a ball hit without spin. A ball hit *totally* without twist or spin would naturally travel in the same direction in which it starts until its momentum is spent and gravity alters its course. But it is almost impossible to hit a tennis ball without giving it some spinning motion. The strings of the racket cling very close to its rough surface, and the slightest motion of the racket that is off the straight line tends to wipe or brush them across the surface of the ball, and makes it revolve before it loses contact.

Topspin on the Forehand. Topspin enables a player to hit with more pace, depth, and control. A stroke without spin depends on gravity alone to bring the ball into court. Topspin makes a hard-hit ball dip after it clears the net comfortably; under the same circumstances, a flat ball would sail out. A stroke with topspin is the ideal passing shot since the spin pushes the ball down, thus forcing the volleyer to hit a low ball; a stroke with underspin is the most dangerous passing shot since the underspin causes the ball to rise, thus allowing the volleyer to hit down on a high ball.

In topspin (or overspin or loop), the top edge of the tennis ball is turning in the direction of the opponent while the bottom edge is moving away from him. In underspin (or backspin), the bottom edge of the ball is spinning toward the opponent. The topspin ball tends to drop to the ground faster than a ball without spin, while the underspin ball tends to hang in the air.

Topspin is achieved by the upward motion of the racket with respect to the ball. Therefore the racket must approach the ball from below ball level (this does not mean that the racket head should be dropped). A player can still take a high backswing if he so chooses, but he must then develop a circular or figure-8 swing so that his racket will be below ball level just before the hit. The racket face can be either slightly closed, absolutely perpendicular to the ground, or slightly open. However, if the face is too closed, the ball will go short or into the net; if the face is too open, the player will have to pull up sharply with his racket (use an enormous amount of topspin) to bring the ball into court.

The follow-through on a topspin shot must be higher than the level at which the ball is hit. In other words, the racket starts below ball level and ends above ball level. It is not necessary to roll the face of the racket over after the ball has been hit. This action has no effect on the ball since the moment of impact is already over. Some players do roll the face of the racket over, but it is just a matter of personal idiosyncrasy—just as a big backswing or a small backswing are matters of personal idiosyncrasy.

Players with Eastern, Western, or Continental grips can hit topspin shots. The Continental grip is usually hit with a cocked wrist (the racket head points upward). Continental players who try topspin will pull up sharply with the arm as the ball is hit. The movement is therefore upward rather than forward, and this makes for a rather erratic action. In the Western style, the wrist is laid way back, the elbow is bent, and the racket ends up very high. The topspin is pronounced, but the grip makes it difficult to handle low balls because the wrist must be bent around so much. The Eastern grip is ideal for the topspin shot since it can be used on low, medium, or high balls. The wrist is laid back on the backswing but is firm at the moment of impact. Beginners and intermediates should use as little wrist action as possible since topspin with the Eastern grip can be achieved by racket trajectory alone (the racket starts below ball level and ends above ball level). Wrist action or wrist snap can be developed later by good players who want to add a little variety to their game.

The amount of topspin given to any shot depends to a degree on the hitting position of the ball. For example, a ball that is higher than the waist (which is higher than the net) requires less spin and can be hit almost flat. But when a ball is lower than the waist (below the net), it requires some lifting. Where one has to lift, one is required to put something on the ball to bring it down again. Thus more topspin is required on a low shot than on a high one. To do this, the face of the racket must be kept slightly open (you must reconcile the angle of your racket face with the angle of your hitting), and you must start your stroke lower than where the ball will be hit. In other words, you use topspin in different degrees as the situation demands to control shots. This knowledge comes only by trial and error and plenty of practice.

Slice and Chop Strokes. There is still a third variation of making the forehand groundstroke with an underspin or backspin. The predominating feature of these is the underspin on the ball that is imparted, for a slice stroke (sometimes called a *cut shot*) or chop stroke always makes the ball spin *backward* in a direction opposite to that used in the drop stroke. The spinning motion is against the flight of the ball through the air, the top moving backward and the bottom forward, which is again exactly opposite to what happens when the topspin is used.

All of these strokes are made by striking the ball with a glancing blow, the bottom edge of the racket being forward and the strings touching more of the under side of the ball than the top. In order to prevent such a blow underneath from lifting the ball up too high, the swing must be made with a downward angle. The racket starts high and ends low, very different from the drop stroke, and the head is dragged across the ball sharply while the strings are still in contact with its cover.

The chop stroke is used primarily as a defensive weapon to change the pace of the game, or against a player who does not like to run or to handle a stroke with spin. There are two distinct types of chop shots: the deep chop and the soft chop.

The deep chop, or underspin drive, is used as a change upon the topspin drive and is played from the same position on the court. This chop also is highly effective as a means of returning the wide-bounding American twist service. As a rule, you should restrict its use to only high-bounding balls where you have a straight angle down over the net. On low-bounding balls, those below the level of the net, this shot has the tendency to sail out of the court.

The soft chop shot (known also as the *dink* or *softie*) is used only when you are up close (never more than 5 feet from the net) and your opponent is playing deep. Then it is aimed to drop closely over the net and should be played on a cross-court angle. For if you play it straight down the court, nine out of ten times the shot will go too deep and be recovered. Therefore, you must angle the ball away from your opponent.

In making the chop stroke, the player crouches even more than in any of the other strokes, the bend from the hips forward being more pronounced. The racket is swung back slower than in the drop shot and not nearly so far. Few of the slice-stroke players carry their rackets in the preliminary swing back farther than behind the shoulder. As the swing is shorter, it can be made later with greater accuracy than with the drop shot. This is the feature that generally appeals to

beginners, the short swing, and many adopt the chop-stroke style at first and change afterward when they learn of its limitations. It is much wiser to begin with the other stroke and learn that properly to avoid the necessary change in style later.

The position of the feet for the chop stroke also is slightly different from the others, as the shorter swing does not depend so much on momentum, and the right foot is extended as a rule farther forward to steady the player as he strikes. This stroke is made off the right foot, while the drop stroke is made off both feet, the weight being pretty equally divided during the stroke. As the racket is brought sharply down to meet the ball, the shoulders straighten up a little to take some of the bend out of the elbow, but at no time in the stroke is the arm as straight as in the other strokes. There is an inclination to bend the elbow somewhat in making all chop strokes, and this bend is not fully straightened out with most players until the very end of the stroke.

When the ball is met, all of the body weight is suddenly exerted in the racket, the shoulders doing more than the hips, and the wrist adds to the "drag" of the racket across the ball to give it the necessary twist. As the stroke is finished, all of the weight is thrown over to the forward foot and the arm and racket end their swing with the downward thrust still further pronounced. The racket finishes out in front of the left knee, extended at the full length of the arm, and the shoulders turned around completely in their effort to check its swing without losing the balance.

The greatest difficulty the player has to overcome in using the chop stroke is its tendency to drive the ball out of court. In order to prevent this, the stroke must be played slower and with less power so it will not go too far, and this necessity robs the stroke of the virtue of speed that other strokes possess. As against this drawback, however, it must be conceded that the short backswing and the more constrained position permit greater accuracy, and as a rule chop-stroke players have a closer control of their slow returns than do drop-stroke players of their faster shots. The player can delay longer before striking, and this allows him to change his swing later if a bad bound or a change in the opponent's position makes it necessary.

On the other hand again, it is much easier for the opposing player to volley an undercut ball at the net than a drop shot, for its underspinning motion makes the ball twist downward and go away from his racket faster. The revolution of a top-spinning ball tends to make it leave a volleyer's racket slower and jump upward when volleyed. For this reason, the cut strokes are less effective against an opponent who is at the net ready to volley, and the drop strokes are the best against such an opponent. Conversely, the drop stroke is best against a net player and weakest against an opponent at the back of his court.

As has been previously mentioned, it is a distinct advantage to play the ball from as high in the air as possible, but the upward motion of the racket makes it difficult to do this when making a drop shot. The motion of the racket in the chop stroke just reverses this, being in the downward direction, so that these strokes can be played from a much higher bound than the others.

Often the disadvantage of the underspin which keeps the ball up in its flight can be overcome by striking it from a higher point and consequently closer to the net, which will sometimes take the volleyer by surprise and pass him with the slower ball this stroke affords, because it is played with more of a downward angle which allows it to travel nearly as fast as the other and still remain inside the court lines.

The slice, or side-twist shot, causes the ball to bounce low and to curve to the side on which the spin is applied. It can be hit either forehand or backhand and is good on low-bounding balls. Actually, the slice and chop are executed in exactly the same manner from the standpoint of grip, position, and stance. However, in the slice, instead of hitting down on the back of the ball, you hit down and to the outside of it, imparting under- and side-spin. When making the forward swing for a forehand slice, the racket, starting outside and above the ball, is brought down through the air at an angle almost 45 degrees to your left, and as it moves in this almost forward-sideward diagonal path, the racket cuts across the bottom of the ball. This severe right-to-left cut causes the ball to curve to your right. For the backhand slice, the cut is from the left to your right, which causes the ball to rotate in the same direction and curve in

its flight to your left. As you could expect, these strokes require strong wrist action, an open-face racket, and a follow-through that will extend naturally in the direction of the shot.

Some players succeed in using side twists with either a topspinning or an undercut ball. When hit with a horizontal racket these are only possible by advancing the wrist well ahead of the ball and drawing the racket in toward the body while in contact, which gives the ball an out twist as well as an underspin or a topspin according to whether the racket travels upward or downward when it meets the ball. These side twists are used most in the services, however, which are made with a racket that is more nearly perpendicular, and therefore allows the motion to be sidewise without interfering with the body swing, by the use of the wrist. This will be taken up later in this section under the heading of Services.

The backspinning shots, both of them, carry less speed than the flat-hit or the topspinning shot and are therefore more used for defense than for attack. But with any tennis stroke, do not try for speed in your drives until you have mastered the stroke. Remember, in tennis, science is often more important than strength. Do not try to "knock the cover off the ball," or "blast your opponent off the court." Placing the ball in the right spot at the right time is more important.

Actually, learning to drive a tennis ball fast is something like driving an automobile. You will come to grief if you drive at eighty miles per hour before you have learned to control the car at a speed of forty. Apply the same principle when learning to drive a tennis ball. If you are a beginner, do not drive too fast. As your control improves, gradually increase your speed. When you have so mastered the forehand stroke that you do not need to think about your footwork or your swing, then drive as fast as you like, provided you do not sacrifice control for speed, and provided further that increased speed warrants the increased risk. Therefore, as you develop your forehand, concentrate first on control. Power, speed, and deception will come naturally, if you learn first the fundamentals of control.

Backhand Groundstrokes

The backhand groundstrokes are used to return balls which have bounced once on the court to the left of a righthanded player or to the right of a lefthander. Their importance cannot be overemphasized. The opportunity of playing the backhand drive should never be avoided by moving position to play the ball on your stronger and generally more reliable forehand. Such a practice not only reveals a major weakness to your opponent, but it also leaves an area of the court unprotected. In other words, one may prefer the forehand stroke and use it on every possible occasion, but no chain is stronger than its weakest link, and if there is a distinct weakness in the backhand play, the defense will be vulnerable whenever attacked by a "heady" player.

There is no question that the forehand stroke is the easier way to play the ball. It is the natural

The regular Eastern backhand grip.

way, and the arm and elbow are less embarrassed when swinging the racket on the right side of the body than when they must be crossed over to reach a ball on the other side. That is, in forehand play, the backswing is clear of the body and the turn as the blow is delivered keeps the arm free, but in backhand play the arm must swing across the body, and the pushing muscles of the upper arm rather than those that pull are used in making the stroke. The grip of the hand too allows all the power to be *behind* the racket for a forehand shot, while on the other side the necessary grip forces the hand *above,* and in the Continental style, a little *ahead* of the racket, giving the effort more of a pull than a push. The shoulder is seldom behind the ball and the turning of the body for the follow-through is never so pronounced in backhand play, because the striking arm is already far advanced when the stroke begins and it is difficult to shift so that the ball can be followed as long as in forehand play.

The methods of gripping the racket, which vary distinctly for this stroke from all the others, have been fully covered earlier in this section, and the general elements of good form also bear strongly on this stroke. But in addition to these, there are a good many points which apply only to backhand strokes; the beginner should study these carefully before going deeper into the play.

As in the forehand stroke, there are the same options regarding the best way of hitting the ball and the exact amount of twist to put on it. One can play the ball nearly straight with little or no twist, by using a perfectly straight follow-through; he can put topspin on the ball and give it the same dropping tendency already recommended for the forehand stroke, or he can use a chop stroke that will make the ball spin backward in its flight through the air.

In the backhand stroke the proper stance and backswing should be coordinated even more closely than in the forehand. From the anticipatory or readiness position, with the right hand relaxed on the handle and the left lightly cradling the throat, you begin the backswing of your body and racket immediately when the ball is seen to be coming toward your backhand.

Start the stroke by turning your right shoulder toward the net. This turning movement begins as

The basic backhand drive stroke from the anticipatory position to the completed follow-through.

the racket head starts swinging back at hip level. The left hand guides the racket back and the right hand makes a change to the backhand grip. With the racket still coming back, pivot to the left on the ball of your left foot. As the backswing nears its completion, the racket should be well back and behind you, knees flexed, the eyes and head forward, and the body and shoulders rotated away from the net. Actually, your body should be swung around to the left far enough so that your back is almost half turned to it. Watch the flight of the oncoming ball over your right shoulder and keep the racket head above the wrist at all times during the backswing. The weight of your body should be on the back, or left foot. Thus, the pivot in the backhand stroke is much more emphatic than in the forehand drive. Many inexperienced players

do not turn their bodies nearly enough; in consequence, the racket arm meets with resistance by not being able to swing past the body. If there is any doubt of the importance of the turn of the body, stand sideways facing the net and, without turning the body, see how far the racket can be taken back. Then try it again, but on this occasion turn your hips away from the net, and you will quickly find that your racket arm has a much smoother swing.

During the backswing, the racket's path can be either an almost horizontal flat arc kept at hip level on its trip back or it can be circular with its peak at about shoulder height and with the racket head tilted slightly backward. The flat-arc backswing, similar to the horizontal straight-back motion in the forehand stroke, is usually recommended for beginners. Once you have the footwork and timing mastered, you can use the circular backswing. But with either backswing, the left hand should be kept on the racket until you start the forward swing.

In the completed backswing position your weight is back on the rear foot, left knee loose and bent, right knee sagged; and you are looking over your right shoulder, eyes glued on the oncoming ball. Having "wound" yourself up into such a position, you must now reverse the action into and through the ball. Release the left hand from the throat of the racket and swing the right arm and racket toward the net in an almost flat arc in line with the oncoming ball or slightly below it. In the latter case, the racket head will help to give the ball its necessary topspin, but do not exaggerate the upward movement or too much spin will occur. As the racket comes closer to the point of impact, the weight of the body is gradually transferred to the front, right foot. Your wrist should be

straight and your elbow kept slightly bent and close to your body until the ball has been hit.

The ball should be met at a point from 10 to 15 inches in advance of the right hip and the right hip should be drawn in. The mechanics of the backhand drive make it next to impossible to execute the shot consistently unless impact occurs before the ball reaches a point opposite the body. Actually, there is no feature in connection with the execution of any stroke in tennis as important as this. Also keep away from the ball. All too many players hit the ball with a backhand stroke too close to the body, which cramps the shot and results in less power and speed. Keeping away from the ball makes for free, confident, hard hitting and will materially help to eliminate errors.

At the moment of impact, the complete momentum of your swing should have reached its maximum speed with the body turned into the ball by swinging the left shoulder well around. The weight of the body should now all be on the

The two-handed backhand stroke of Franjo Puncec, Yugoslavian star of the 1930s (left). Some players, such as Peaches Bartkowicz (right), continue to use it today.

right foot. The right knee should be bent while the left knee should be sagged and turned inward, with the rear foot steadying your body for balance. Do not use any type of push-off action with this foot to help the shot. Your grip should be gradually tightening on the racket handle so that at impact the wrist is firm or locked. Your arm should be straightened well out from the body as you swing through the ball.

While it is best to stroke a ball at waist level, your opponents do not always oblige by hitting the ball so that it bounces to this height. Therefore, you must learn to make the backhand swing at all levels. For a low shot, one below waist level, you follow the same procedure as for low forehand strokes. That is, you bend your knees so that you bring your waist level down to the level of the ball. Except for the bending of the knees, the backhand stroke is executed in the same manner as that used on a waist-level ball. For balls that have a very low bounce, those just off your shoe top, the hitting should be a little upward, with the racket face slightly tilted back. This open face will lift the ball to the proper height over the net. Remember that it is usually advantageous to hit the ball on the rise—at least it should be hit before it begins to fall. This means that your opponent will have less time to get into position and your shot may be concealed to a greater extent.

Topspin and Underspin. As stated earlier, topspin and backspin can be applied to backhand drives. The topspin backhand starts low and ends high; the underspin backhand starts high and ends low. In the topspin shot, the face of the racket is perpendicular to the ground at the moment of impact; in the underspin or slice shot, the racket face is open at the hit. That is, by rolling the racket backward and allowing the racket to pass under the ball, a backspin is given, and we have an undercut that has a tendency to keep the ball up in the air long and make its bound low. It is a good stroke for straight side-line shots, when the distance to the base line or diagonally to where the ball would go out of court is so long that the stroke can be played fast without danger; but for cross-court shots it is generally difficult to play fast and hold in court. This stroke is easy to volley at the net, too, so that it is seldom as good a passing stroke against a volleyer. With the opponent at the base line, however, when only driving must be considered, it is very useful, because its slow "hop" is a mean, lifeless ball to handle off the ground.

For the chop and slice stroke, the racket should finish low, generally at about the height of the waist, but for the topspinning, rolling lift stroke, the racket's swing should end much higher, generally above the shoulder. The same principles of meeting the ball and imparting the twist apply as in the forehand stroke, and some experts get the same variations here by increasing their follow-through and imparting the twist with a turn of the wrist at the last moment before the ball leaves the racket.

The forehand chop shot from the backswing to the completed follow-through.

The backhand slice stroke from the backswing to the completed follow-through.

As the player becomes better and the competition stiffer, he will find it more difficult to hit backhand topspin shots down the line. The ball is coming hard and deep, and if the player's preparation is the least bit late, he will err on the down-the-line. He therefore has two choices: to slice or to prepare earlier. The latter is the wiser decision although frequently he will slice for better control. But the backhand stroke without any twist at all, the straight hit ball, is perhaps more valuable for general play than either of the others. As in forehand drives, however, control is the most important consideration in your backhand stroke production. Uncontrolled speed loses more points than it wins; it is where you place the ball that counts.

Lobbing

The lob was, originally, almost entirely a defensive groundstroke. It consists of hitting the ball up high in the air, so that it will pass high over the head of your opponent if he is forward in the court and drop far back by his base line. It was, and still is, of great use in getting yourself out of a disadvantageous position and giving you time to assume an advantageous one, or perhaps only to give you breathing time, if you are being run about a great deal from one end to the other of your base line. Its two main objects are to drive your opponent away from the net and to enable you to get there yourself. To attain these objects, two kinds of lob are in use: the fast, comparatively low, one, which is played just over the top of your opponent's reach; and the high toss, which is intended to hit right at the back of his court. There is one essential common to both forms: they must be deep. You must aim to hit right on his base line, or at most a foot inside it. A short lob is, or ought to be, fatal. The most useful lob is one to your opponent's backhand corner; but, of course, you should not lob repeatedly to the same place.

The development of the lob into an effective weapon of attack was introduced by American international players in the late 1920s. Actually, it is a valuable means of dislodging a volleyer from the net. No volleyer can stay at the net against a good lob, and there are very few players who can smash a deep lob, or, at any rate, who can go on doing so. Sooner or later the strain of watching— and hitting—the ball tells; the ball goes into the net, and the patient lobber gets his reward.

Like other groundstrokes, lobs can be made either forehand or backhand. In addition, many of the same rules apply here as in the groundstroke drives. The ball must not be taken in front of the body, nor with the wrong foot or shoulder forward. The body should be turned with the side toward the net to allow a full swing as in a good drive and the same freedom of the arm and shoulder is required.

The forehand lob stroke from the anticipatory position to the completed follow-through.

The lob is a slower stroke and much more deliberate than any other groundstroke. The backswing is shorter and the body motion in the actual stroke less pronounced, while the follow-through is very much reduced. The racket should be dropped with the head distinctly below the wrist, and the stroke has an upward swing that is absent in the other groundstroke. With the head of the racket hanging downward at an angle of 45 degrees, the same free sweep of the arm is made, with the ball well off to the side so that the shoulder can be brought into the stroke. The same grips are used as previously mentioned for groundstroke drives.

The sweep of the racket must be long and smooth, not jerky like the stab of a chop stroke. The ball is met with even less impact than in other groundstrokes and is swept away rather than hit with a sharp blow. The slower the stroke can be made, the better are the results likely to be. No other stroke in the game is made with such deliberate movements.

The most dangerous error for the beginner to counteract, however, is the desire to strike the ball from underneath and drive it straight upward in the air. On the contrary, the ball must be hit clearly from behind, with a forward sweep, the upward turn coming just before the racket meets the ball. The bevel of the face of the racket can be depended on almost as much as the upward swing to direct the ball high enough to pass over the opponent's head. Except when it is played for the purpose of gaining time to recover position in court or to get a resting spell when the player is

The backhand lob stroke from the start of the backswing to the completed follow-through.

hard pressed, a lob should not be driven any higher in the air than is necessary to keep clear of the opponent's reach. With the other man at the net ready to smash, which is generally his position when the lob is used, it is only necessary for the ball to pass a foot or two above the highest point he can reach by jumping, and the lower it can safely pass him the better. If only a little out of reach, the stroke will have a flatter trajectory and more forward motion on the ball, and will greatly reduce the other man's chances of turning and running back to make the return.

The angle of the bound of a low lob also makes it much more difficult to return than a high straight ball. From every point of view then, it is desirable to keep lobbed balls as low as is safe, and for this reason as much forward motion as possible should be put into the swing of the racket. If a purely upward swing is used for the lob, it will be difficult to avoid raising the ball unnecessarily high in the air, even when the low lob is very much to be desired.

For the backhand lob, the same general rules hold good as for the backhand drive. The body should be turned around so that the playing shoulder is toward the net and the feet are lined up almost in the direction that the ball is to be sent. As the upward swing of the racket requires it to start very low in the forward swing, the body should be bent somewhat away from the net; the left knee bends a little to let the shoulder drop.

With the racket turned slightly backward in the grip, as in the forehand lob, and the thumb extended behind its handle for support, the stroke is inclined to be even a little more upward in direction than the forehand lob. The ball should be met further forward than on the other side, and this makes it more difficult to swing as straight and still lift the ball as in the other stroke.

The finish of the stroke in both cases is in an upward direction, and the racket should be allowed to follow after the ball as long as possible. The body swing cannot be pronounced, as the forward motion is not long enough. The elbow should be bent more than in the groundstrokes, but the ball must be kept well clear of the body.

Even after a lob, it is necessary as in every other stroke of the game to recover position quickly and prepare at once for the next stroke no matter what it may be. It is as dangerous to stand and watch a lobbed ball sail through the air as it is to watch a drive until the opponent has returned it. In either case, you are very likely to be caught out of position and not ready for the next stroke.

Many a lob that was started with good intentions of being kept out of the antagonist's reach is ultimately smashed hard in return. Except for very low lobs that are well timed and well placed so as to catch the opponent so close to the net that he is unable to back away fast enough to volley them, the chances are very strong that any lobbed ball will be returned and will come back fast.

The stroke itself is of necessity slow enough to allow the other man in most cases time to reach it, and it only depends on how deep the lob has been placed whether it will be smashed or returned only moderately hard. In either case it behooves the lobber to hurry to his best defensive position immediately after every lob has been sent up.

As already explained, a short lob is like throwing the point away, but what constitutes a short lob is not quite so easy to state. Against the average player, any ball that will fall inside the service line should be considered a short lob, and most players will have long odds in favor of their being able to kill the ball, if they can smash from within 15 feet of the net. Some players are able to kill even from back of the service line, or at least to smash hard enough to keep the lobber in constant trouble unless he gets better length than this.

To be out of danger, safe from hard smashing, a lob should not fall more than 10 feet inside the base line of the court. Except when the opponent is caught "anchored" at the net and passed overhead with a low lob, any lobbed ball is defensive and the lobber can hardly expect to win, except through an error by his opponent, until he is able to turn the attack against him.

A deep lob will often drive the other man back far enough to open his court for a drive on the next play, and the lob therefore will often turn the attack against a volleyer unless he is very quick at recovering his position at the net again after each smash.

The lob is best used as a surprise stroke against a volleyer. To lob repeatedly to your antagonist often means that he will soon become used to the stroke and, preparing himself in position and swing, will shortly be able to smash successfully. If he is given lobs only occasionally, he will be less likely to handle them well and they are more likely to be successful.

When the server runs in constantly to the net and takes a position very close up to volley, it is often a good plan to lob regularly to dislodge him; and such a campaign will often break up his net attack, so that he is forced to give it up. When he does stop running in, however, that should be the signal to stop lobbing at once and go to driving at his feet.

Placing a lob generally increases its attacking power, and the backhand corner near the base line is almost invariably the best spot to aim for. It is doubly difficult to smash lobs over the backhand shoulder, so a lobbing attack in the backhand corner is always the hardest to meet.

The success of any lob, of course, does not depend on speed or hitting power but rather on the touch and feel of the racket in the lift of the ball. It should be so finely judged that it just misses the head of your opponent's racket when he jumps up to intercept it. Insufficient height and distance render lobs ineffective. It is usually better to make the highest point of the ball loop closer to the net than to you (the lobber). Disguise the position of the racket almost to the moment of impact so that your opponent will not suspect the nature of the stroke. This deception is of the utmost importance, particularly when using the lob as an offensive weapon. If you betray your intentions before making the stroke, your opponent will have sufficient time to retreat near the base line and get ready for a countering return smash.

Volleying

The volley (both forehand and backhand) is the stroke used to hit the ball before it bounces. This stroke is employed chiefly when you are playing the net—the primary objective of an attacking player. It is often called a finishing shot because its principal purpose is to win the point and put an end to a rally.

Originally, all strokes in tennis were made after the ball had bounded, and it was not until some years after the game had reached England from its native home in India that the idea of striking the ball in the air, "on the fly" as we used to say in baseball, came into vogue. But it was only a short time after this that the value of the new stroke was well appreciated. The famous Renshaw brothers, among the earliest English champions, introduced the volley stroke and revolutionized the early development of the game.

Two distinct advantages are offered by the volley: time and angle of attack. A ball hit in the air, particularly when close in toward the net, offers a much wider range of the antagonist's court for attack than when hit off the ground. In addition to

The forehand volley stroke from the anticipatory position to the completed follow-through.

this, much valuable time is gained by using the stroke, since the player on the other side has less time to anticipate the volleyed stroke than one played from the back of the court. This element of time is of far greater importance than is understood by most players. A tennis player forced to one side of his court to make a return requires a certain amount of time to recover a safe position in the center, from which he can reach any stroke that his adversary may deliver to him. If he is badly hurried, his stroke falters, and he suffers soon from fast breathing, which also hurts his play immediately. To keep an opponent in such a condition is to maintain a constant attack that keeps him on the defensive.

Primarily, then, the volleying position at the net is the best position for attack, and by the volleying position we mean anywhere in front of the service line, for it is next to impossible in fast play to hit a ball off the ground from in front of the service line. Now, two players cannot survive long with both at the net against each other because the closeness of their positions does not afford either time enough to anticipate the other's attack, and one or the other must lose at once. Hence, it is necessary that one of them retire to the back of his court and assume the defensive when his adversary outgenerals him and gains the coveted net position. But you must not reason from this that it is always safe to make a dash for the net if the other man has not anticipated you. On the contrary, a very dangerous attack can be maintained from the base line, and blindly rushing to the net is as short-sighted as camping indefinitely at the back of the court. There are correct principles which should be learned to show how and when it is safe to take the volleying position. This subject will be fully covered later in this section under Position Play.

Horizontal Volleying. There are two distinctly different types of volleys with sharply defined lines to identify them. First, there are the volleys of a horizontal ball, one that is coming straight at the player, and generally pretty fast; and second, the volleys of dropping balls, which are most often distinguished as smashes. There are several variations of these two basic types.

The correct horizontal-volleying position is from 6 to 15 feet back of the net, but it also has its own relation to the position of the ball as well. The volleyer should be directly opposite his opponent only if the ball is in the center of the court. The playing center is not always the middle of the net, for if the ball is far out to the right in your opponent's territory, your own court will be open to attack on the same side more than on the other, and you should move over a little more in that direction to protect yourself against the next stroke.

Having assumed the right position in court— whether by running up immediately after serving or by gradually working up during a long rally makes no difference—the actual position of the body differs somewhat from that assumed for groundstrokes. The volleyer does not have time to change position from backhand to forehand volleys or vice versa, and he must be ready at all times to handle either kind of ball. His position at the net therefore must be squared around more, his feet almost parallel with the net.

For the fastest kind of volleying, it is better to have the right foot extended slightly behind the left, but with the legs spread well apart and the weight carried low to give the player the advantage of an instant start in any direction. Not to keep one foot a little behind the other makes it slower to get started back for a lob, and the opponent can often catch a volleyer napping at the net and win an easy point by lobbing over his head, if the position of his feet does not guard him against such a surprise attack. To anticipate a sharp drive at either side, the volleyer must be ready to jump sidewise on the instant and the racket must be

balanced in front of his body, as when waiting for the return of the service. The "splice," or "wedge," at the throat should be balanced in the left hand well out in front and the player will then be ready to shift it to either side without a second's hesitation to meet the ball. Bent knees and the weight carried up on the toes, as in the other strokes, are also essential to quick starting.

When the direction of the oncoming ball is known and the actual stroke starts, the racket is swung out on that side of the body and back with a short, quick swing that is less deliberate and more snappy than that used for the groundstrokes. The backswing is shorter because there is *very* little follow-through required and less time to make it. The racket is kept nearly horizontal, except when the ball comes higher or lower than the waist, and then, of course, its angle must be accommodated to the height of the ball.

The face of the racket should be beveled slightly backward to strike a glancing upward blow, but the amount of this angle depends largely on the height of the ball. For a low ball, which is below the level of the net when hit, the racket must be beveled enough to raise it back over the net, while balls that are met well above the height of the net require little or none of this cut, for the racket can meet them almost square. In other words, high volleys are hit downward; low volleys, which are to be hit up and over the net, are approached with an open racket face so that the underspin will carry the ball upward. The knees are slightly flexed on high volleys; the knees are bent deeply on low ones. High and low volleys are both hit in front of the body with the feet comfortably apart. The racket head should never point downward; instead the volleyer gets down to the ball.

The stroke itself is much shorter and sharper than a groundstroke. There is less swing, both forward and backward, and there is less follow-through. The ball is met with an almost stiff wrist, the flexibility of the groundstroke not being required here. The short swing is more like a sweep than a blow, but the racket follows only a short distance, being quickly swung back into line and recovered in the former position for waiting, balanced in front of the player. The body should be swung forward slightly as the blow is struck, but the squared position makes it impossible to follow far after the ball without losing the balance. That is, the ball is merely pushed or punched, and the racket head is brought back with the elbow slightly bent and the wrist cocked. The racket head, both in the movement back and in the shot itself, should never be permitted to fall below the wrist, and the wrist should remain firm or locked throughout the entire stroke.

As a rule you should use the same grips for the forehand and backhand volleys as you do for the forehand and backhand drives. But efficient changing from the forehand grip to backhand and vice versa can be acquired only by practice and, when volleying, this change must be quick and automatic. For this reason, many players use the Continental grip—this can be used for either type of shot—because they find that they cannot change their grip from one to the other fast

enough. When first starting to volley, however, it is generally best to use the two conventional grips. When you are more experienced you can then switch to the grip or grips that best suit your style of volleying. To volley successfully, you need very accurate timing and a strong wrist. If you think that your wrists are weak, choke up on the racket handle a little. While this is not necessary to perform the volley stroke, it may give you confidence when you first start using it.

It is always dangerous, of course, to stand too close to the net, and beginners who find it difficult to get back fast enough to smash lobs will do better to stand 3 or 4 feet back of the position from which they expect to volley, and then step forward to meet the ball when the time comes to make the stroke. Stepping forward like this as you strike increases the power of any volley stroke, as well as acting as a safeguard against overhead at-

The backhand volley stroke from the anticipatory position to the completed follow-through.

tack by a lob.

Always take a volley shot as high as possible and direct the ball downward in order to place your opponent at the greatest possible disadvantage. This can be achieved by opening up the racket face so that the ball will bite the ground quicker and will not bounce up to any degree. The direction of your shot can also be controlled or angled (this is called an *angle volley*) off and away from an opponent by regulating the timing of your stroke. For a straight-down-the-middle shot, the ball should be hit just in front of your forward foot. If you wish the ball to angle to your left, punch it slightly earlier than you would for the shot straight down the court. To push the ball off to your right, time your punch a fraction later or hit the ball a little farther out from your left foot.

As was stated earlier, little follow-through is needed in making most volley strokes and that which occurs is largely from the action of your wrist. Actually, when volleying close to the net on a hard-hit ball, all that is needed at impact is a tightening of your grip on the racket, letting the racket remain still. The resulting effect is the same as if the ball were to hit a solid wall. But it is very important that the ball strike the center of your racket so that it will have enough force to carry it back over the net.

When volleying a slow- or medium-speed ball, you can increase the length of your backswing and follow-through. This type of shot is called a *drive volley* and is made for a kill. In the drive volley, the racket head should not go much farther back than your right shoulder, but there should be a follow-through to give the shot speed. Contact should be made with an open-face racket, and the ball should be hit down. The wrist may be bent slightly as the racket is drawn back, but it should be firm and locked at impact. The racket shoulder should turn toward the net as the ball is punched over, and the extent of the follow-through is controlled by the locked wrist. Remember that the drive-volley shot can be compared with the close-in body punch or jab of a boxer—a compact punch with a great deal of power behind it.

You can control the direction or angle of a backhand volley by the positioning of your left foot and by regulating the point of impact. For a volley shot straight down the court, the point of impact

should be well in front of the body. The left foot should be parallel to the net and directly in back of the right. For a volley shot that you wish to angle off to your right, punch at the ball a little earlier than for the straight shot and at the same time the back foot should be brought forward. For a shot to your left, you should punch at the ball a fraction later (closer to your body) and the rear foot, if possible, should be a little farther back. The backhand drive volley is played in the same manner as for the forehand style except that the procedure is reversed.

Special effort should always be made to meet the ball at a point higher than the net whenever possible. A volley becomes more defensive than aggressive when struck from lower down, as in that case the ball must be lifted back over the net, and this robs it of its attacking power. Actually, the low volley, especially one just a few inches above the court, should be employed only when it is impossible to play the ball off the ground (after the bounce). Low volleying is a purely defensive weapon and, unless perfectly played, is rarely effective even as good defense since the stroke all too often results in a pop-up. This, of course, gives your opponent a chance for a kill.

Regarding the placing of volleys, everything depends on the position of the antagonist. First, the volley should always be deep back into the other court, unless a short stroke is certain to end the rally. To let the opponent reach the ball in close to you spells disaster every time, for the volleyer has very little time to prepare for his stroke under the most favorable conditions, and, if the opponent is close to him, this will be so short that he must often miss the stroke from lack of time to swing on the ball even though it comes straight at him.

The unexpected point is always the best attack against the opponent, but, other things being equal, the extreme backhand corner is perhaps the most vulnerable spot. From that position it is most difficult to pass a volleyer at the net, and this offers the most profitable point for attack, as a rule.

But there are other considerations than power of attack. Often a volleyer himself is in trouble and needs defense. He may be hard pressed, jumping from side to side so fast that he is in imminent

How to smash.

danger of being passed on the next play. Then the middle of the court is the safest place to direct a volley stroke. From the middle of the court, the opponent will find the angles for passing more difficult than from the sides, and a deep volley down the center of the court to near his base line is generally a safe return. The ball can be directed best with the swing of the arm, but the wrist also can be bent slightly and deflect the ball to one side or the other at will. Some good players swing the whole body around to place a ball across the court on the volley, but this style generally defeats its own object by showing the opponent which way the ball is going.

Smashing and Overhead Volleying. The distinction between overhead volleying, or smashing, and the horizontal volley lies chiefly in the angle at which the ball is taken. For these strokes the ball is met higher up and driven downward. With the head of the racket above the arm and shoulder, ready to meet a dropping ball, the stroke is completely altered from that used in horizontal strokes, and even more closely resembles the blow of a woodsman's ax than the service.

There is much more freedom in this position, and a longer swing and follow-through are permitted. For the smash the player can put all his power in the stroke and hit the ball as hard as he is able. The horizontal volley is apt to be a cramped, punched stroke, while overhead the play is freedom itself.

The smash is primarily a killing stroke. It is intended to end the rally every time, and the player, if he is fairly close to the net, calculates, as a rule, that he will be able to kill the ball with that stroke. He does not expect another return and the smash is therefore played with great abandon. Some players even lose their balance at the end of the stroke and make little or no effort to recover position to be ready for another, in case the unexpected should happen and the adversary return the ball they intended to kill. These are poor tactics, however, and dangerous always.

The smash is a stroke that is properly used only on a lob, for no other return provides the dropping lifeless ball needed for its execution. On a short lob, that is, a ball that falls within 12 or 15 feet of the net, the risk of error is small, and even this risk decreases rapidly as the distance to the net is lessened. When within 10 feet of the net, it is always safe to hit the ball hard, and when so close as this it is seldom difficult to earn a clean ace by smashing the ball right "through" the other man.

The deeper the ball to be smashed, the more difficult it is to handle; the danger of missing increases very rapidly, and when a lob drops back of the service line, it depends entirely on the individual skill of the player whether it's better to smash than to volley the return. To ease up on a smash generally results in ruining the stroke. If the full power and speed cannot be risked, it is generally better to change the stroke to a volley and wait for a better opening for the attempt to kill.

Making the smash requires the fullest action possible. The racket should start well behind the back with a full backswing and come forward with rapidly increasing energy, striking the ball with a sharp impact. The entire body weight should be thrown into the blow, and there should be a full body swing and follow-through to add to the power of the stroke. No other stroke of the game is played so "wide open," for as this shot is expected to end the rally nine times out of ten, the attitude is one of finality that permits the player literally to throw himself at the ball regardless of what may follow.

The ball should always be met with an "open" racket, that is, with the full face of the stringing exposed, the face being at right angles to the direction of the ball, and it is essential that the ball should be struck in the center of the strings. Twist is almost unnecessary, although some players have an inclination to wrap the racket around the ball slightly, as in the service, and this has a tendency to keep the ball somewhat better under control.

The position of the player for a smash or an overhead volley is very important. He must be directly under the ball for a smash, and nearly as far forward for the volley. Nothing will ruin an otherwise good smash so quickly as to stand too far back for the ball. As in the service, this position is almost sure to bring it down into the net instead of over into the adversary's court.

For a hard smash, the player should stand so directly under the ball that, if he should miss it, the ball would fall on his head, but the whole body should be bent somewhat forward so the head would be slightly in front of the rest of the body. For a less severe volley, the ball can be slightly in front of the player's position, but under no circumstances should it be forward enough to make him reach out far for it. This is a fault that is almost certain to bring failure.

One of the most common mistakes of beginners is to try to smash every high ball that they can reach. The smash is a stroke that is used far more than is necessary, both because it wastes the player's strength and because it often entails an unnecessary risk. Hosts of overhead balls, even

The low forehand volley stroke from the anticipatory position to the point of impact.

short lobs at the net, can be killed quite as effectually with a well-directed volley as by a smash, and this stroke results in fewer errors.

It is a safe rule to remember, when you have a dropping ball to handle, that it should be smashed only when you feel certain that you will not miss the shot. If the opponent is off to one side of the court, even then it is not necessary, as a sharp volley to the other side will be just as effective and more easily made.

If the opponent is close to you, play the ball straight at him fast and he will have little or no chance of returning it, but if he is at the back of his court and ready for a ball in the center, smash to the edges if you feel sure of the stroke, or volley off to one side. As mentioned earlier, on a deep lob, the smash is almost always dangerous, and a deep volleyed return will generally give you another chance at the ball, with perhaps better chances for success on a shorter return. The

player who takes few risks with deep lobs and patiently waits for an easy ball to kill generally wins out in the end, while the dashing swashbuckler who wants to bury every ball in the ground is always found among the losers.

In some cases, the overhead smash can be a groundstroke. That is, it can be executed when a ball bounces high in the air. The mechanics of this smash are the same as the overhead volley smash just described.

The overhead volley of a horizontal ball calls for a full swing, a sharp impact with less twist than any other stroke of the game (unless it be the lob), and a medium follow-through. The success of the shot depends more on direction than on the mere execution of the play. It is an easy stroke to make and not difficult to direct. If the adversary has left an opening, it should afford an ace on the next play, but if he is well covered up and the ball is over the center of the net, a deep volley into one

The low backhand volley stroke from the anticipatory position to the point of impact.

The forehand stop-volley stroke from the backswing to the completed follow-through.

corner will often open up the way for a clean ace on the next return. This stroke is so simple and affords so many chances to kill that the experienced player seldom offers his opponent such an opening.

Overhead volley strokes are made with much the same motions as the smash, except with less speed or abandon and with more caution to control the ball. That is, you will lessen the backswing, and stop the racket behind the head, hitting with a slower motion. Sometimes a slight bevel on the face of the racket, to overcome the dropping angle of the ball, will lessen the danger of missing from far back in the court. Also the finish differs slightly. With the overhead volley, the racket is stopped out in front of the player, about opposite the waist as a rule, and it is quickly recovered at the finish to a safe position for the next stroke, no

matter what may come. For the smash, remember that the racket is allowed to follow after the ball as far as it will go and generally ends close to the ground at the end of the swing.

The Lob Volley. The lob volley, in which the ball is pushed up over the head of your opponent at the net, is another very useful variant of the volley, especially in doubles. It is not, however, easy to play. It must obviously be made sufficiently high to be sure of being out of your opponent's reach, and at the same time sufficiently fast to make it impossible for him to get back in time to take it off the ground. Otherwise he gets an easy smash.

Since this lob shot is usually played in much the same manner as the low volley shots (both forehand and backhand), all instructions for these strokes (see page 118) apply here. The only major

The forehand drop shot from the anticipatory position to the completed follow-through.

difference is that in the case of the lob volley, the racket face is opened to a greater angle. You still need the same backspin to control the ball but little or no follow-through is necessary. The weight should be on the forward foot at impact.

The Stop Volley. The stop volley (also called a *drop volley*) is another very effective form of the volley. It is a volley stroke, hit either forehand or backhand, in which the ball barely drops over the net. To execute it, you should be right up to the net. Hold your racket upright, and, just as the ball comes to it, move it either upward, with a dragging action, or downward, with a digging action. However fast the ball is coming to you it will drop

The forehand half-volley stroke from the anticipatory position to the completed follow-through.

The backhand half-volley stroke from the backswing to the completed follow-through.

quietly, very dead, just over the net. Indeed, the harder your opponent's drive, the more effective the stop volley. Fingers and wrist, here again, must be very delicately employed. Actually, the stop volley's aim is to keep the ball away from your opponent. Its success depends on the deftness and delicacy of your touch. At impact, the wrist should be loose and flexible. The purpose is to stop the flight of the oncoming ball and to drop it just over the net with a minimum bounce. While it is a rather simple stroke and is fairly easy to perform, there is considerable danger that the return will either fail to clear the net or go too far over; in the latter case your opponent will return it and either pass or lob you, leaving you standing helpless at the net.

The Drop Shot. This shot closely resembles the stop volley, but it is a groundstroke (see page 000). While its execution is much the same, it is very much more difficult to make. It requires greater delicacy of touch than any other stroke in tennis, and the faster the ball approaches the more difficult it is to make. Its success depends on your ability to hit the ball with considerable backspin and just enough forward motion to clear the net.

To accomplish this, the racket is held loosely and its forward motion results from a flick of the wrist. The face of the racket should be opened at an angle of 45 degrees or more from the vertical —the forward part of the rim being the lowest part of the racket face. The racket moves downward as well as forward, the downward motion being about equal to the forward motion. No follow-through is needed. The result of this stroke is a miniature lob with plenty of backspin. Because of the lower bounce, drop shots are much more effective on grass than on a hard or fast court.

A drop shot should be used only when made from a position inside the service line and a stop volley only when practically on top of the net; and in both cases only when your opponent is very deep or so hopelessly out of position that he has no chance whatsoever to retrieve the return. If he can reach and return either shot, you will both be so close to the net that your court will be wide open and the point very likely his. To be most effective, both the stop volley and the drop shot should be disguised to resemble something else. For example, the stop volley should be masked as a drive volley, while the drop shot's preparation should be made to resemble that of a forehand or backhand drive.

The Half Volley. The half volley is, technically, also a groundstroke, the ball being hit when it has risen only an inch or two from the ground. It is usually a defensive stroke used either when you are caught out of position or against balls that bounce at your feet. As you have so little time in which to make the stroke, it is a rather difficult shot to play. The half volley may be hit either forehand or backhand.

The technique of the half-volley stroke (sometimes called a *pickup shot*) is very much the same as that for the low volley; that is, the same grip, same stance, and a short backswing are employed, with short follow-through. Since the ball is played near the ground and very soon after it has bounced, you should bend from the knees and waist to keep the wrist stiff and the racket head from hitting the ground. The ball should not be stroked but should merely be blocked by placing the head of the racket a foot or so behind the point at which you judge it will hit the ground; the momentum of the ball provides the power for the return. While on a few occasions the racket face should be open as in a low volley, the majority of the time the ball should be hit with a closed-face racket. (This means the racket face is tilted forward at the top, producing a natural overspin or topspin.)

The closing of the racket face is not a wrist action, but rather it is a rolling over of the entire arm in the same manner as for the forehand drive. This rolling over is very important since if you do not do it, the ball will sail out of court, while if you just move your wrist, the ball will probably end up in the net. The impact point should be slightly ahead of your forward foot, but often you will be caught without time to place your body correctly. At these times the ball still is met out in front of the body, but to the side. Keep your head down as the racket follows through on its up-and-over course. This will steer the ball where you want it to go.

It is a most important consideration in lawn tennis to keep the eye on the ball until it has left the racket and never to make strokes with the body too erect, the follow-through being better accomplished with a slight leaning of the body with the stroke. In the half volley, the follow-through is a quicker process than in ordinary groundstrokes.

The Service Stroke

The service, as previously mentioned, is the stroke used in putting the ball in play. It is the only stroke in tennis in which the player has complete control over the ball—as well as the only shot made which the ability of your opponent does not affect. Thus, it is a wise player who takes full advantage of his serve. For instance, a good service immediately puts your opponent (the receiver) on the defensive by forcing him out of position or playing to his weakness. This gives you the opportunity to obtain the maximum benefit from the rest of your shots. Remember that if you always win your service games, you never will lose a set or a match.

There are, however, many varieties of the ser-

vice stroke, and no two of the best players use *exactly* the same style of delivery. More than any other stroke of the game, the mechanics of this particular play are left almost entirely to the individuality of the player. It opens up a lot of possibilities for this service stroke, to be told simply that you may stand at almost any point you please behind the base line and hit a ball into the opposite court in any way you please, when you please.

You have time to wait and think out your motions before you hit the ball, and your originality has much more chance for play here than in the heat of battle where the action is much faster, with less time to think of the stroke. It is very evident that many players have put their minds on this problem, with varying results that have developed many kinds of deliveries. But in spite of this fact, there are three principal types of service: the slice; the American twist; and the flat serve, or cannonball. All three follow the same basic techniques of grip, stance, and delivery, but vary in how the racket head strikes the ball and in the follow-through.

The service stroke itself is usually a long, free, rhythmic swing in a continuous motion. It is similar, to a degree, to that of the overhead volley stroke. Like the other strokes of tennis, the service requisites are good footwork, smooth body action, and correct method of hitting the ball. All of the very good servers follow closely the same set of fundamentals.

The Grip. The grip for the service is again a matter of individual preference. Most experts, however, seem to prefer the Continental grip. But, for the beginner it is usually best to use the same grip that he uses for the forehand drive stroke. After he has learned to make his toss and delivery correctly, and has gotten his timing, he can try the Continental serving grip.

The major difference between the modified Continental serving grip and the basic Continental is that the fingers are spread out more, the forefinger extending up the handle like a trigger finger. This permits more flexibility of the wrist, which is necessary to impart the various spins employed in serving.

The Stance. In taking the proper readiness position for the service, the left foot should be forward and about 3 to 6 inches behind the base line.

The angle of the left foot depends on the individual. Most professional tennis instructors believe that the best form is to place the toe so that a slight pivot in serving will bring the foot around to a position perpendicular to the net. The right foot should be 12 to 18 inches behind the left, depending on the height of the player, and approximately parallel to the base line. In this position, an imaginary line drawn across the toes of both feet should point in the direction the ball will travel; thus, for serving into the opponent's right service court, the left foot should be drawn back slightly from the right foot, and vice versa when serving into the left court. (This is a righthanded world, and lefthanders, as usual, will have to adjust accordingly.)

To complete the readiness position for a serve, hold the racket out toward the net so that your wrist is at approximately chest level and the racket head is about level with the face. The left hand should hold the balls. Be sure that the stance is comfortable and the body is as relaxed as possible in a position that is sideways to the net. The left shoulder should be directed toward the court into which the service is to be made. The weight is evenly distributed on the toes at the beginning of the stroke. As the toss is made and the backswing started, the weight falls back on the right foot. The forward swing brings all the weight rhythmically into the ball and onto the toes of the left foot. This is exactly the same procedure that a pitcher goes through in throwing a baseball. The serve is a combined arm and body swing.

When serving, remember that you play the first point from the right of the center mark and serve the ball diagonally across the court to your left into the opponent's right service court. The next point is served from the left of the center mark into your opponent's left service court, and then alternately right and left until the game is finished. While the tennis rules say that you can stand anywhere between the center mark and side line, the base of all good servers is near the center mark. (About 1 to 3 feet to the side of it—behind the base line, of course—is a good distance for the beginner.) The server who stands at a distance from the center mark leaves too much of the court open into which the opponent can place the return of the service.

It is very important for a beginner to avoid the error of foot-faulting. The player must keep the left foot behind the base line. He must not swing his right foot over the line before he hits the ball. Many fine players have had great trouble breaking themselves of the foot-fault habit. A serve illegally delivered is just as much a fault according to the rules as a ball hit outside the service court. The causes of foot-faulting are much easier to correct at the time the serve is being learned than afterward.

The Ball Toss. To serve, the ball is tossed into the air and hit. But throwing the ball consistently in the same place and at the same height requires practice and, to make it even more difficult, you have to swing your racket at the same time. The ball is held in the fleshy parts of the fingers. It is customary to hold two balls—the second ready for use if the first service is a fault or a let. (Some players even hold three balls.) This second ball should be held between the ring and little fingers and the lower fleshy part of the thumb. The other ball is held between the first two fingers and the thumb.

The ball should be released by opening the first two fingers and thumb when the arm is slightly above shoulder height. For better control of the ball, toss with relaxed fingers and thumb, not the palm, and let the hand follow through after it has been released. The upward motion of the arm should have sufficient momentum to send the ball above the right eye, high enough for a comfortable reach with a fully extended arm, and enough to enable you to hit it as it starts to drop. To establish that height for yourself, hold the racket straight up above your shoulder with your arm bent at the elbow only enough to be comfortable. Now, toss one ball up just to the top of the racket, so that, if allowed to fall to the ground, it hits just off the point of your forward toe. Remember that it is much better to toss the ball too high and be able to hit it as it falls, than to toss it too low and hit it with the edge of the racket or miss it altogether.

Practice the toss for both proper height and direction for a while without hitting the ball. To check the toss direction, place the racket on the ground directly in front of the left foot. Then as you toss the ball to the proper hitting height, let it drop to see if it drops directly on the face of the racket on the ground. Many beginners toss the ball either too far behind them or too far toward the net. In order to reach a ball in the latter case without falling forward, the player swings his leg around and the foot passes over the base line before impact. When the ball is too far behind, the smooth rhythm so necessary in a serve cannot be obtained, resulting in a poor stroke. Remember that if you do not think your toss is straight to the point where you want it, you do not have to hit the ball. You can allow it to fall, catch it, and start your toss again.

The Swing. You should start your toss and backswing at the same time. To accomplish this easily, the two hands should be close together at the start in a position in front of the waist. As the left hand goes up, the right takes the racket down and backward to a point where the arm is completely extended. After the racket has reached this low ebb, it is brought up with increasing momentum to perform a loop behind the head. From this loop the forward swing is made and the ball is hit. That is, from the serving readiness position, swing the left arm downward against the left thigh and, at the same time, draw the right arm down so that the racket head swings close to the body, past the right knee, over the shoe tops, and then backward away from the net. As it passes the right leg, the wrist will turn outward naturally, turning the racket over completely. (You can feel the natural turn outward in the bones of your forearm.) Also as the racket passes the right foot, transfer the weight to the rear (right) foot and raise the heel of the front (left) foot, keeping the toes of the front foot on the ground and the knee slightly bent.

The racket should continue to move backward and upward in a circular arc until its head is about shoulder high, behind you, and pointing away from the net. It is now that the elbow should be bent in almost a 45-degree angle, dropping the racket behind the shoulders in an almost backscratching position. In this cocked position (the racket behind the back with its head pointing downward toward the ground), keep the elbow, forearm, and both shoulders in direct line with one another. This is the point in your swing that you release the ball upward. Remember that the

important error to avoid in making the backswing is that of pausing during the procedure. The long swing is necessary to get the weight properly into the ball. Any break in the rhythm of the stroke defeats this purpose.

The upward movement of the left arm starts as the racket head passes the shoe tops. Be sure that the release is smooth—not a jerky pitch—and as the ball leaves the fingers, watch its upward flight very closely. While the ball is traveling upward and after the racket has made a small looping swing behind the back, the wrist and elbow are snapped upward into a fully extended position overhead with the wrist, arm, and racket in line as one long lever. The ball should be overhead and slightly toward the net side of the forward foot. The ball should be hit at arm's length above the head, so that even in the case of a short player, it can be brought down into the service court. At the moment of impact, the top of the racket should be closer to the net than the lower edge or throat. The degree of this angle depends on the individual player. Obviously a very tall man would probably strike the ball with a more pronounced tilt to his racket than a short one. The player must use his own sense of touch. If the majority of his serves tend to find the net, the angle is too abrupt. If the serves tend to have too much length, the reverse holds true.

Actually, beginners often strike the ball in front of the head or off to the side at a height opposite

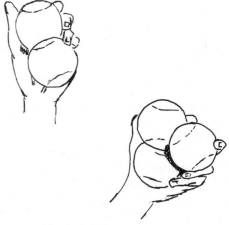

The method of holding the balls for a serve.

the face, but it is not possible to make a really good service without a higher position to strike from. Hitting too far forward will cause the ball to go into the net, as a rule, while a ball that is hit too far back will more often go out of court by traveling too far over the net.

The forward swing of the racket that makes the actual stroke must be started before the ball reaches the point at which you have calculated to hit it. The wrist begins the movement, starting the racket directly upward, and the elbow next straightens out its bend so that the arm and handle are extended to their full reach by the time the racket approaches the ball. Then the body and shoulder take up the work and the full force of the weight is added to the momentum of the racket so that it is traveling at top speed when the ball is met. Everything depends on great momentum in the racket in order to secure speed in the stroke. But the ball must not be met squarely with the racket, as many beginners are inclined to believe. The overhead service stroke is even more of a glancing blow than the drive groundstrokes. The face of the racket should be turned in the hand so that the racket passes outside of the ball, the right edge of the frame, as it appears up in the air, being forward and the other side beveling sharply backward.

As the racket leaves the ball, all the weight of the server's body and all the power of his shoulders are brought to play, so that the ball gains great momentum from the stroke. The speed of the racket pulls the player ahead rapidly, and before the racket can be checked, he is generally forced to take a step forward, even if he does not start at once to run in to the net to volley the next return of the antagonist.

The end of the racket's swing should be far out in front of the left foot and slightly to the right of it—more or less to the right according to the amount of side motion the racket carried to give the ball the spinning motion. The racket should be allowed to swing forward until it nearly touches the ground, and it is a serious mistake that ruins the service to attempt to check the swing at a point much higher than this.

The follow-through is as important in the service as in the groundstrokes, and it is with both shoulders and body weight in this last end of the swing that it is most useful. Without the necessary following of the racket, the ball loses both power and speed, and it also becomes more difficult to control its direction accurately.

The feet and legs play a very important function in the swing. The legs maintain your balance while the weight is being shifted first to the back foot and then to the front. The forward thrust of your body will cause your front heel to rise from the ground during the forward swing, and the right foot, once the ball has been struck, should follow it across the base line. Failure to move the right foot into the court during the follow-through handicaps you in recovering your balance in case of a quick return of your service. Also allow the back foot to follow across the base line and into the court so that you can assume the anticipatory position from which you are ready to begin the next stroke. But, when moving your feet, be careful you do not foot-fault.

The swing of a serve should be a long, free, continuous rhythmic motion. Racket arm, ball arm, and body must all be carefully synchronized so that there are no stops or hitches in your swing. Power in the serve comes from your body, your arm, and your wrist—it is the only tennis stroke that employs wrist snap.

The Slice Service. The differences between the three major types of services—slice, flat, and twist—are the way the racket meets the ball at impact and the method of follow-through. The slice service is the simplest to learn and execute and the one that should first be mastered. The ball is tossed slightly to the right of the head and shoulder, and the racket is brought around the outside of the ball and slightly over it. The racket face is beveled slightly to aid the swing in imparting the side spin that adds control and from which the service takes its name. The swing is down and across the body to the left, completing the act of applying the spin to the ball. That is, the racket passes over the upper right-hand surface of the ball as the ball is hit down upon in a right-to-left twist of the racket. The racket must be whipped into the ball with a sharp wrist snap and smooth follow-through. This type of service causes the ball to spin in a sideways direction when it leaves the racket. The sideways spin on the ball makes it curve to the left during its flight in much the same manner as a ball curves in when a pitcher throws it.

In hitting the slice service you rotate the racket slightly during the swing so that its frame is inclined diagonally toward the right side line. This permits your racket strings to hit the ball a glancing blow, cutting across from left to right to get a slight slice that causes the ball to curve downward in its flight. Let the racket follow through down across your body to the left.

The slice service is the easiest to learn and control and can be accomplished with the least effort, and most women and beginners use it because it is not too tiring and the ball has plenty of action. When properly controlled, the curve of the sliced ball is downward over the net and to the left, away from the receiver's forehand. This means that your opponent cannot attack or hit an aggressive return of your service. If the spin is too great, of course, the ball will curve out of the service court.

The slice serve from the ready position to the completed follow-through.

But this can be easily compensated for by aiming as far to the right as necessary to adjust for the curve of your service. It does not require too much practice to determine how much curve you actually are getting on your service, and from that point all that is necessary is for you to control it by proper placement.

The Flat Service. The flat, or cannonball, service is a powerhouse delivery and is the one in which the ball blasts down into the receiver's court in an almost straight line. When properly placed, it is very difficult for the receiver to handle. But this serve is a very risky one to employ since it must clear the net cord by at most a few

The flat, or cannonball, service from the ready position to the completed follow-through.

inches or it will land out of court. The margin of safety is very small. Therefore it should only be used occasionally on the first ball and then only by players of well above average height. Actually, the cannonball should be used as a mixer and sparingly. Let the sudden and unexpected blast of this flat serve be employed to catch your opponent off guard and perhaps worry him somewhat. But for most players, this serve is not a percentage shot, which means if you employ it too often you are going to lose your service somewhere along the line.

The flat service is much like the slice service except that the toss is more to the left, but still a bit to the right of the head, and the flat face of the racket is exposed to the ball, as the name of the service implies, rather than a beveled racket face as in the slice or twist service. The follow-through is to the left of the body, about the same as the slice service. This service should be used as a first service only and, if missed, followed by the safer slice or twist service for a second ball.

The Twist Service. The American twist service is the most difficult of all serves to learn, and is probably the toughest and most physically demanding shot in tennis. It definitely is not a service recommended for most women. But, once learned, the twist is a good change of pace since the ball curves to the server's left and bounces toward the receiver's backhand, or away from the direction in which it was curving. The flight of the ball describes a comparatively high arc, allowing the server ample time in which to get set for the return or to reach the net if he desires. This service is usually played to an opponent's backhand, and it is difficult to return effectively because of the excessive spin and the high bounce. This is accomplished by moving the racket upward and across the ball, imparting spin to it, which causes it to bounce high when it lands in the service court.

The American twist service is started the same as the other services, with the weight on the back foot and the body sideways to the net. In tossing the ball, the body is turned more decidedly until the back is almost turned to the net, the feet remaining in position. The ball is tossed slightly farther back and to the left. The weight is handled very much the same as in the other services. It is shifted from the back foot to the front foot. There is a greater arch in the back at the most backward point in the backswing. The racket is whipped up from its low position and comes across the inside and left of the ball, and up, imparting the twist to the shot. As the weight is shifted to the front foot, the racket comes through, starts in its downward motion, and finishes down and, in the case of a righthander, to the right of the body instead of to the left of the body as in the slice and flat services. This service has not the speed of the flat or slice service, as a rule, but carries much more spin. There should be much more wrist action in this service than the others, which aids in imparting the great spin necessary to an effective twist service.

Service Strategy. Two services of average speed for first and second delivery are much stronger than one terrific "swipe" and a weak "pop" second delivery. The man who keeps a good average fast pace on his first service has to make less shift in his method of hitting for the second and is less likely to double-fault. The practice of the first delivery also helps him to gauge his error and he is able to keep fair speed on the second ball with less danger of a double fault. In short, the extremely fast first ball is so radically different from an easy second delivery that it does not help the player in gauging his second delivery, and he consequently takes no chances playing close to the net or to the court lines, and makes such an easy service that the ball is frequently killed outright, and generally the attack is turned against him on the next stroke.

Now, having acquired a fairly fast overhead, twist delivery that is well under control, and a second delivery that is of the same style but just a trifle slower and a trifle higher to be sure of clearing the net, every player should practice both until he is reasonably certain of avoiding the deadly pitfall of double faults. The next point is the control of the direction. This is of the utmost importance, and no style of service should be adopted that does not permit of the most perfect control.

The average player of little experience considers his duty done in serving when the ball is safely delivered into the opponent's court; he does not see the far greater possibilities of attack in placing the service. To be sure, the latitude for placing is small, but there is ample range to outwit the adversary in even the small space allowed, as his time is short in which to shift position to meet the attack.

Before making the delivery, the position of the adversary should be carefully noted, and the position of his arm and racket to see whether he is anticipating a backhand or a forehand stroke. If you have studied your adversary or are familiar with his play, you may already know his favorite strokes and what his attitudes mean. If he is a better player of forehand than backhand strokes, naturally his weak spot will be on the other side, while the reverse will sometimes be the case. Possibly he will habitually lean in one direction or the other in anticipating the service, to be in position for the stroke he prefers, and this at once should give the signal to place the ball on the opposite side of the court.

When the server is running in to volley, new problems that must be taken into consideration complicate the service. If the receiver is weak on the backhand side, the server should consistently place the service to his backhand side until he finds that it is being anticipated. The receiver may run around the backhand attack to get the ball on his forehand, or he may anticipate this attack by bringing his racket over into position for this return so that he is able to handle it better. Then an occasional service placed to the other extreme edge of the court will bring him back into a normal receiving position again, or possibly win an ace outright by the very unexpectedness of the play.

If the opponent is found to select one direction regularly for his return from a given position, this in itself can be anticipated often with success. For instance, the receiver may cross-court five balls for every one that he plays down the line from a backhand return. In this case, you should serve to the backhand and watch for the cross-court return, leaning a little to that side of the center of the court at the risk of the unexpected line pass. Or the opposite may be the case and can be anticipated similarly.

The center theory is perhaps of more value to the server than at any other point of the play. The most difficult problem the server has to solve is to get to the net safely in order to secure the volleying position. The center theory is more fully covered later in this section on position play, but so far as it refers to the service, it is the principle of placing the service in the center of the court (that is, in the corners of the service courts nearest the center of the whole court) in order to keep the opponent in the center of his court, directly in front of you as you stand at the middle of the net to volley. This shuts off his chances for fast sideline drives, because from the center any fast ball that will pass you must be aimed out of court, and a slow ball will give you more time to reach it.

Adopting this center theory, which is most valuable in a volleying net attack, the server should always stand very close to the center of his base line to serve. By shifting a yard to the right or left he can serve into the left or right court and still keep his delivery right down the center by placing each ball close to the dividing line of his opponent's service courts.

Against a righthanded player, this will bring his backhand presented to the delivery always in the right court and his forehand in the left court. If his backhand is weak, this will make the right court the more productive and the left court always dangerous if his forehand stroke is severe. However, this attack can be varied whenever one finds that an opponent is handling these deliveries in an embarrassing manner. If the left-court service is being pounded with a forehand drive that is too fast to handle, an occasional service far out to the adversary's backhand toward the extreme edge of the court will often catch him by surprise, and if it does not score a clean ace will embarrass his return in consequence so that an easy chance for a kill will result.

Often the backhand weakness of an antagonist will make it advisable to work on the center theory only in the righthand court where it attacks his backhand, and to place the service far to the edge of the court regularly in the left court. In this case the path of the server in running in must be further to his right to cover the dangerous opening along his right side line, unless the opponent has shown a marked tendency to cross-court his backhand returns.

Always keep an opponent guessing and off balance. For example, the first serve may be to the

The twist service from the ready position to the completed follow-through.

opponent's backhand and the next to his forehand. By using such a strategy, you will play your opponent's strong stroke often enough to prevent him from covering up his weakness. This makes for larger openings on his weak side and permits possible aces, or shots that he cannot reach.

When placing a serve, generally make your opponent move to meet the ball. Occasionally, however, it may be good strategy to serve directly at him, thus throwing him off balance. When planning to play the point near your base line, place the ball near his side line to pull the opponent out of position, thus opening up his court for the return. Serve a flat, fast service only occasionally, as a surprise ace or to keep your opponent from edging in or over too much.

If planning to rush the net after serving the ball, a good forcing serve, one which will enable the server to get beyond his service line before the ball can be returned, is essential. The best serve of this type is one with plenty of spin, which insures control and retards the ball sufficiently in its flight to enable the server to reach the net quickly with the least effort. Either a slice serve with some topspin or an American twist will permit you to vary your placement, and if you can serve both, your service attack will be greatly strengthened by varying the direction of the break and the height of the bounce. Speaking of the height of the bounce, watch whether your opponent prefers high or low balls. If he handles low-bounding services well, give him a high-bounding American twist serve. If he prefers high-bounding balls, hit a well-placed sliced serve that will bounce low. Do not overdo this strategy and likewise do not rush the net after each serve. Again, keep him guessing.

Regardless of your strategy, serve from the same spot behind the base line. Do not stand close to the center mark one time, and then near the side line the next. Select one spot on either side of center mark (one for serving to the left service court and one for the right), and develop your serve from these spots. The best players generally stand pretty close to the center mark since that puts them in good defensive position for the opponent's return.

The Return of the Serve

The return of serve is the second most important stroke in tennis; only the serve takes priority. Basically it must have consistency, since you are bound to lose every game in which you receive if 50 percent of your returns are errors. Remember that the receiver of service is heavily handicapped by the rules of the game. He is forced to stand back and await the attack of the server. He is forbidden to volley the ball, and his first return must often be made under the disconcerting conditions of an opponent thundering up to the net behind a twisting service that makes the ball curve in the air and bound crooked. This advantage of the server over his opponent in the opening duel is responsible for the records which show that a very large proportion of all games in tournament tennis are won by the side having service.

In order to offset this advantage and to get the ball into general play so that the receiver may get back on even terms with his adversary, every ingenuity of the player must be brought into play. But at least he has one thing in his favor, for the server is limited closely in the area that he can use for placing the ball, so the receiver need not move far out of his waiting position in order to reach the ball. For these reasons it is as well, perhaps, to consider the first return as a play in itself and treat it separately from the other groundstrokes of the game.

But every precaution must be used to anticipate the service. Even though the service court is small, it is no easy task to cover all of it, and the striker-out should be keyed up to the highest pitch for instant action. The anticipatory, or readiness, position requires the legs spread well apart, the body bent forward from the hips and carried up on the toes, while the racket should be balanced in front, with the idle hand braced against its "throat" so that it can help start the backswing in any direction that the approaching ball requires.

As the forehand is usually the strongest weapon of offense, it should be slightly favored by the receiver. In other words, he should stand a little bit to the left of the center of the service court. This means that the server has a smaller portion of court in which to find his opponent's weakest shot off the ground. It also allows the receiver to run around any slow serves to his backhand, take them on his forehand, and often make a good forcing return.

The distance at which the player stands from the service line to receive depends on several factors. The speed of the service, the amount of spin on the service, the intention of the receiver and the quickness of his reflexes, all have an important bearing on the issue. If the service is of average speed and the ability of the receiver about average, the best position is either on or slightly to either side of the base line.

Against a powerful straight service it is often wise to back up slightly. This gives the receiver a little extra time to judge and handle the ball. A service that is sharply angled and carries lots of spin presents a different problem. The ball breaks away from the court and the player. The farther back the receiver stands, the greater amount of court he has to cover. Against this service it is best to stand in closer. If the receiver is keen to take the ball on the rise and make an offensive thrust off each serve, he must also be in closer. Some players prefer to set up a defense against powerful serves by standing in close and blocking the ball back. The reflexes of the individual are his own problem. The individual must experiment in order to estimate the quickness of his own reflexes. When these factors are added together, the receiver usually finds himself anywhere between the base line and a spot 3 or 4 feet in front of it.

Taking the ball on the rise in returning service is a dangerous practice. It is hard to perfect one's timing to master the return of service when there is less time to get properly set. To make matters more difficult, the receiver must line the ball up so that it is on his direct path to the net, as he is usually forced to advance to the net after such a return, in order to cover his court. He would otherwise be badly out of position. He must therefore have both a first-class net game and wonderful anticipation to use this style of taking the ball on the rise successfully.

There are several advantages to the procedure, including a certain psychological edge over the server. He feels that he must make harder and better-placed deliveries to maintain the offensive. A net-rushing server, for instance, is constantly hurrying to get in to the net to keep from having to handle shots at his feet.

On the other side of the picture, we find that this policy results in more errors and bad positions on the part of the receiver. Although often giving a player a brilliant attack, it can also result in the exact opposite, making for inconsistency. Most teaching professionals' advice is to take the ball at the top of the bounce until the return is consistent. Then possibly learn to play it on the rise occasionally—for the psychological effect on the opponent, if for nothing else.

Most players use a safer method of delivery on their second serve. This may take the form either of less pace or a greater amount of spin. The receiver, therefore, has a better chance to take over the offensive on the easier second serve. If you move in closer, this usually will worry the server a little and enable you to get to the net quicker, should you succeed in making a forcing return.

When the serve is placed well out of the reach of the receiver, he is often forced into some mad scrambling to retrieve it. Some exponents of the game are in favor of a jump or lunge to cover the necessary distance. In most cases, however, it is best to keep both feet on the ground and run or slide and stretch to get the shot. When you lunge or jump, you are apt to destroy your sense of balance.

Actually, when considering the best method of handling a service, it is necessary to examine the matter in two different situations: first, when the server runs up to the net, and second, when he does not. Against the volleyer, who is fast on his feet and well settled in position to handle the first return, the receiver has four plays open to him. He can pass down the line, he can pass across the court, he can lob over the server's head to drive him back, or he can drive toward the adversary with a low dropping stroke that is kept close to the net or drops soon after crossing it so that it leaves no chance for a killing volley.

The pass down the line is always easier (for a righthanded player) in the right court, where his forehand drive can be brought into play. If the service is directed toward the edge of the court, this stroke will generally offer the best chance, for the cross-court pass is then more difficult and the line more open for attack. For a player with a fine control of the backhand drive, the line pass is also open in the left court when the service comes toward the side.

But when the server works on the center theory, or, without that plan of action, keeps his service well centered, the line pass is not open for a fast ball, and is more difficult for a slow ball.

From the center of the court, the dropping ball is often the best attack against a good smasher to whom it is dangerous to lob. The cross-court shot can be played slow from the center to either side, but the receiver is always in trouble against a fast

How a John Newcombe serve looks to his opponent.

server who centers his service and closes the alleys to attack from a pass up the side lines.

Occasionally, a short cross-court pass will be found very useful from the outside edge across in front of the server as he runs up to volley. A return from a wide position allows a sharper angle and more speed because of the greater distance the ball must travel, and while difficult to execute, it is a most valuable attack for occasional use. This shot should not be played often because it will give the server an easy chance to kill if he is able to anticipate it and lean toward the cross-court position to intercept it. Your own position at the side of the court will make it impossible for you to defend against his volley and the court will be open to him; such a shot must win outright or it won't win at all.

But another side of this stroke is its value as a surprise and to keep the volleyer in the center of the court. If the cross-court return of service is never used, an experienced server will find it easy to direct his attack to the far edge of your service court and lean toward the same side to intercept your attempts at passing along the side lines. This is when the cross-court shot is most valuable, and one or two successes with this stroke will bring

him back to his correct position and give you an even chance once more for the line pass, unless he centers his service.

If you fail to find the necessary opening for any passing shot, a dropping ball down the center of the court will make the volleyer block the ball upward again over the net, if you succeed in making it low enough and drop quickly enough for the purpose. Your second shot may offer a better chance for a winning pass, and often does. At least it brings the striker back on more nearly even terms with the server if the latter does not make a very aggressive stroke from such a return of his service.

The lob is often a good answer to a difficult service, and varied with passing strokes or drop strokes at the feet of the server it is doubly valuable. To lob regularly to a server is to court destruction, for he will soon be able to anticipate the shot and then only the deepest and straightest dropping balls will not be killed; even they are likely to be volleyed back so deep as to drive you out of court to handle them. But worked occasionally with the other variations, the lobbing return has a tendency to keep the server from coming in close, which opens up his position in turn for the dropping attack. Particularly is this valuable from the extreme left of the left service court, where the backhand is attacked, and the server is running up diagonally to meet the return. A lob diagonally to his backhand corner then will be very difficult for him to reach, and may make him turn and give you the attack.

Lobbing the service is generally better toward the end of a hard match, rather than at the start when the adversary is fresh and strong. When he begins to show signs of fatigue, particularly if you are stronger than he at the end, a lobbing attack generally produces good results. Perhaps the most dangerous lob of all for the server is one that is made with the same motion used in playing a passing stroke. It is quite possible to swing the arm forward as though to drive the ball, and turn it at the last instant and lob with the face of the racket beveled back. The server is almost certain to lunge forward, if this stroke is concealed well, in order to volley the next stroke, and he will then be caught off balance for a probable ace.

The server who remains on the base line presents a different problem. The receiver has more of an opportunity to put the ball in play and to bide his time to go to the net. As a general rule, the return should be a deep, well-placed shot, usually to the weaker side of the server. In this way, he may be forced into making a shot which offers a better opportunity for a sally to the net than his service did. Against a base-liner, as well, the returns must be varied; no set program is practical.

The best way to cope with a base-liner is either to attack from the net or draw him in to it. The former practice is usually considered best for most players but it often pays to refrain from becoming overanxious to attack. It is best to rally with your opponent until he makes a shot well inside the base line. The tactics must depend on the soundness of the server in the different departments. Sometimes, in the case of a player whose serve is less severe, it is better to try the forcing shot from the service return, as that is more apt to be an easier shot than would result from a base-line exchange.

Whatever method the receiver uses, he should remember to mix his shots, and confuse and surprise his opponent whenever possible. Make the server run, and by all means take the offensive away from him at every opportunity.

Changing and Correcting a Stroke

The only time to change a stroke is when it will not do the job. This is not something to be done lightly; no matter how grooved the new stroke becomes, you may lapse back into old habits as soon as the stroke is put under pressure. As a result, you may end up with a new stroke that is even worse than the old one.

The only reasons for altering a grooved stroke are: (1) you cannot be consistent with the old one; (2) you have no control with it; or (3) it lacks power. Since a change must be made, make the change as simple as possible. In the case of groundstrokes, stick with your old grip. Do not throw away a Western forehand just because a group of Continental stylists regard it disparagingly, and do not switch from Continental to Eastern simply because the Eastern is the thing to do. It is reasonably easy to make a service or volley grip change; it is almost impossible for most play-

ers to make a successful forehand groundstroke alteration.

The best way to change a stroke is to understand what you have been doing and why it has prevented you from hitting the ball in court consistently, with control or with power. If you do not understand where your stroke has failed you, the transformation will be that much harder. But if, for example, you can see that you have closed the face of your racket and that therefore too many balls have been netted, it will be easier to learn to open it. You do not then need a complete new stroke; you simply concentrate on an exaggerated "open" racket face.

Never change a stroke just because someone says it does not look right. Some of the greatest strokes in the game have been the most unorthodox. No one ever had a less classical backhand volley than Jean Borotra, but no one ever hit it better or harder. Do not change a topspin backhand to an undercut; a pretty but ineffectual shot —unless your ideal is to look good while losing. The criterion for changing a stroke is: lack of consistency, control, or power.

Never change a natural sidespin forehand to topspin. You can, if you wish, add a topspin forehand to your repertoire. Never change an awkward but effective stroke so you can acquire underspin as an additional shot to your game. Do not throw all your strokes out the window because they are "different." If they are preventing you from improving, alter them only as necessary.

Take the case of the player who hits the ball with so much wrist action that his timing has to be perfect. If he has a good edge and if he practices regularly, the stroke may be eminently satisfactory for him. He should not change it simply because it is wristy. However, if he feels his timing will never be good enough to handle such a stroke with consistency, he can decide to eliminate some of the wrist and to hold the face of the racket on the ball a little longer. His own understanding of the situation makes it that much easier to handle the transformation.

The pro who automatically alters a pupil's strokes simply because he is not conforming to the pro's ideas is performing an action that boosts his own ego but does not necessarily help his pupil. With pupils who are not yet grooved, changes are easy, but with those who have played regularly for one or two years or more, any major alterations are traumatic and should only be made after long and careful deliberation. This is not to say a pro should not make any number of minor changes such as cutting down the backswing or follow-through, teaching better balance, the bending of the knees, a wider stance, or hitting the ball on the top of the bounce, on the rise, or further in front of the body. The major changes on groundstrokes are a different grip, windup, wrist action, and spin. When the position of arm and/or wrist and/or racket with regard to the ball is changed, the transformation must be major.

A player with a weak service or a tendency to double-fault should analyze what he has before throwing away the whole action. The fault may lie in the toss or in poor transference of weight. If the fewest possible changes are made, the player can accomplish them without too much difficulty. Adding slice to a serve is relatively easy; changing the entire windup is extremely difficult. It is not, "How much of my stroke can I toss out?" but, "How much can I retain?"

When a service is unsound in every department but the player is grooved in his serving, the changes should be made gradually. One cannot in one hour learn a new toss, transference of weight, windup, hit, and follow-through. At least two things will go wrong every time because with each serve the player must concentrate on five different ideas. If, therefore, the player can keep his old windup, no matter how strange it looks, he may be able to acquire a better serve by making only one or two changes—and there will be less likelihood of the whole action falling apart.

The beginners and the intermediates (and very often the advanced players) do not know what they want in the way of a stroke. Too often a player thinks he would like to "hit hard and look good," but when he starts playing in top tournament level, he wants a lot less and a lot more—he will skip the looks and much of the pace to go for steadiness and control. He finds that points are won on the other fellow's errors, that a classical game can be beaten by an unorthodox one, and that there is more to the game than just strokes.

Whether the new stroke means a complete overhaul of the old one or two adjustments only, the same formula is used in discarding past reflexes and learning new ones. First, the player must understand what he has been doing and more important, what he is now trying to do. He must be willing to give ample time to the learning process, he must not expect to acquire the new stroke in one day, one week, or one month, and he must never revert back to the old habit. In other words, he must be mentally attuned to the program.

Second, he must learn to perform the stroke (or that segment of the stroke which he is learning) without a ball—i.e., in front of a mirror or, if he has professional help, to the satisfaction of his coach. If he cannot execute the stroke well without a ball, how can he do it well with one? The beginner will work on one phase of the stroke only; the advanced player has a less difficult job, although "unlearning" can be as frustrating as learning.

Third, the player now tests his stroke with a ball, but in the simplest possible manner. If it is a forehand, he learns to play it by dropping a ball and then hitting it or by having a coach or friend "feed" him balls. Once the concept is firmly set in his mind, he can utilize the backboard to best advantage. He practices the stroke itself, with the emphasis not on getting the ball back or on hitting it hard but on memorizing a process.

Fourth, once the new stroke is firmly established, the player can rally with anyone or play sets against those players who will not "press" his newly acquired series of habits; the weaker the opposition, the more confidence he achieves in his new weapon and the less likely he is to revert to the old stroke.

Fifth, when the new stroke appears to "work" against lesser players, he can test it out against a better, more forceful caliber of opposition. But the player must have the right mental outlook; he is practicing and learning, and the emphasis should be on hitting the new stroke properly, not on winning.

Sixth, when the new stroke is an integral part of the player's repertoire, the intermediate or advanced player is ready to use it in tournaments. This can take anywhere from 3 months to 6 months, provided the player has been practicing regularly and conscientiously. The novice or beginner can also enter tournaments in his own classification; his game is far from polished, but when segments of his stroke are grooved, he also is ready to use them in competition.

COURT TACTICS AND STRATEGY

The game of tennis combines skill in execution of the shots with a good deal of thinking on the part of the player. This thinking has to do with where the ball should be hit, how it should be hit, and from what position in the court it should be played. Strokes are not sufficient, by themselves, to produce top-grade tennis. Many players possessing beautiful stroke production are constantly defeated by opponents who are distinctly inferior in this department. To enjoy the most success a player must arrive at a combination of good stroke production and good court tactics.

The subject of court tactics cannot be dismissed with a fixed set of rules and regulations. Instead, the player must consider the different possibilities and organize them as he sees fit. He must use standard strokes, but must vary the depth and pace of his shots in order to enjoy the most success. The game has progressed so much in the last decade that the player must be able to apply these fundamentals from any position in the court. For this reason, the all-court style of play is the only one that completely fills the bill. I would advise the young player to set this as his goal. A game built on base-line play or on net-rushing tactics alone can be broken up by an expert strategist. On the other hand, an all-court game keeps the opponent guessing.

Player Position and the Placement of the Ball

The very foundation of court tactics is to play a purposeful game. You should determine before each stroke whether you are going to try to win a point, or whether you are merely keeping the ball in play and returning a defensive stroke so as to get yourself in better position. Purposeless tennis is the cause of much grief. The player should not strive for a forcing shot or winner on every return. As a matter of fact, he should not strive for this unless and until he is able satisfactorily to get himself into position to reasonably expect a placement, or unless he is striving to pull his opponent out of position for a point shot later.

Perhaps the most important theory of purposeful position play was first laid down by Wilfred Balleley of England in the book which he wrote on the game in the 1890s, when he and his brother were at the height of their fame. This is: The part of the court which lies between the base line and the service line is "forbidden territory." You ought never to come to rest in it; it should only be used as a means either of getting up to the net from the base line, or of getting back behind the base line from the net. If you take up your position, either for attack or defense, in the "forbidden territory," it is long odds that you will lose the ace against an opponent of equal stroke-playing capability. Your opponent will either drive hard at your feet—the most difficult stroke of all to return —or, more probably, drive right past you so deep that you will be unable to get back in time to reach the ball; and even if you do, you will be trying to return it over a net from which you are running away—an almost hopeless endeavor. Against a better player you are never likely to win an ace at all in that position. Do not stop there. There are two purposeful places from which you should conduct your campaign. One is the volleying position—the position of attack—for which you should always be between the net and the service line, and as near the net as you can get. The other is the groundstroke position—the position of defense—for which you should always be behind the base line. If you should be drawn into the "forbidden territory" to make a stroke, leave it instantly the stroke is made, to regain either the net or the base-line position, according to whether you see opportunity for attack or recognize that you must act on the defensive.

After the service has been delivered, the server may run in to volley the next return of his opponent, or he may stay back and wait to play it after the bound. The latter method is much the better until a considerable degree of skill has been gained. If one runs in, he must be prepared to jump very quickly to the right or the left to intercept a wide return, and he must be able to hit on the run, for there will be no time when volleying at the net to get set for the stroke or to deliberate long on which stroke to play.

But whether you decide to run in or stay back,

remember the "forbidden territory" rule just given: Go all the way in or stay all the way back. Do not hesitate halfway in the matter, for nothing is more deadly than to be caught part of the way up toward the net and meet the ball at your feet. As was stated, this general rule applies to all strokes in the game. After each stroke that you have made, either stay back at the base line or run all the way in to within 10 or 15 feet of the net. Against an opponent who drives a swift ball, it is better to stay well behind the base line in awaiting the next return, for you can get better force in your stroke if you are moving forward to meet the ball when you hit it than if you stand still or move backward.

Expert players often stand 10 feet outside the court at the back awaiting the fast drives of their adversaries, and when they do run in to volley, go up to within 6 or 8 feet of the net. To be caught halfway back means that you must volley a dropping ball, which is much more difficult to play than one flying horizontally over the net, and you must also hit it harder and further in your volleyed return.

Sidewise also, one must be very careful not to be caught in the wrong position, as this will offer the adversary a fine opening to place the ball out of your reach with his next stroke. If you have to run over to one side of the court to make a stroke, you should immediately return to the center (of the base line, not of the whole court itself) to be ready for the next return no matter where it may be placed.

Establish a base of operations in your mind, and after each play return to this central base without waiting to watch the result of your shot. If you hesitate, the delay may prove fatal, and the next return be placed far to the other side before you will have time to recover and reach the ball.

If you are volleying at the net, there is the same necessity to return to the center of the court near the net and ready for the next volley. If smashing and drawn back for a lob, the instant it has been hit, you must return to the volleying position near the net or retire to the base line for defensive play, else the next ball may be driven at your feet and the point lost. The most difficult returns of all are those that must be made when the ball strikes close to the feet.

In any case, one must take into consideration the position of the adversary, for if he has been drawn off far to one side you will be in more danger of being "passed" on that side than the other, and the "playing center" will be a little away from the actual center of the court. At the net this is even more important than at the base line, but there too some allowance must be made for the adversary's position when he is hitting the ball. If the opponent is far off to your right, move a little over toward this side of the court, and vice versa if he is off at your left. This can easily be overdone, however, and tempts the other man to try a short cross-court passing shot that will be a sure winner if it is successful. The sharply angled return is more difficult to reach, and the difficulty is increased if you are caught standing off at one side of the court, particularly if you happen to be at the same side as the player.

The return of service is almost invariably made from one side or the other of the court, as the server is by law required to serve somewhat diagonally and often does exaggerate this to a sharp angle to draw you out of position. The instant this first stroke has been made, the player should run to the center of the court to await the next return, and here again the playing position should be planned in advance, either at the back of the court or at the net. There are few chances to take the net position, however, immediately after the first return.

If the server is running up behind his service to volley the first return, as is sometimes the case, it is dangerous to return far back of the base line, because from the net position it is quite possible for him to play a stop volley, as its bound is almost always low. With the opponent at the net, it is doubly important to keep well up on the toes and ready for an instant start.

You must use good judgment in going to the net; for no matter how good you may be at the volley and smash, your net attack will fail if you give your opponent a setup. If, for example, the drive which you follow in is soft, short, and high-bouncing, you will almost certainly be passed. If you drive a very fast, flat ball or if you start to run in from far behind your base line, you will not be able to get beyond your service line, and you will then give your opponent an excellent opportunity to drive the ball at your feet, forcing you to half-volley or to low-volley, thus enabling him to pass you on his next return. As a general rule, follow in the return if driving from inside the base line; stay back when driving from behind your base line.

To reach a volleying position quickly and safely, it is generally wise to play a forcing stroke. Do not confuse an ace with a forcing stroke, however. If you get a setup or if your opponent is out of position, drive hard to a corner for an ace. But if he is in position, play a forcing shot: drive deep to the center of his court with some topspin, not too close to the net cord, and follow in without hesitation. The object here is not to win the point outright, as it would be with a clean ace, but to force the opponent to make a comparatively weak return which can be volleyed or smashed. By driving deep to the center of his court, the possibility of an opponent driving straight down the side line is eliminated and this forces him, if he drives, to drive within a narrower angle; thus you limit his choice of drives and reduce the amount of unprotected court you must cover. The topspin will sufficiently retard the flight of the ball to enable you to reach the net before the opponent has returned the ball.

As previously mentioned, if the opponent's drive is short, falling more than several feet within the base line, there is a chance to capture the net behind a forcing stroke. But when his drive lands within a foot or so of the base line, or when driven out of position, do not attempt to go in; for you will have to run too far to get beyond your own service line before your opponent has returned your drive. His deep drive has put you temporarily on the defensive and you should wait for a more favorable opportunity to go in. To attempt to win the point by an ace unless he is out of position is usually also a waste of effort. This is the time for patience, not for a wild, impetuous drive—the time for you to use your head and try to maneuver him out of position or force him to make the weak return which will enable you to seize the net on your next return.

As soon as you have returned the opponent's deep drive, hurry into the anticipatory position for your next shot. Do not wait to see where your return will land; do not stand still, assuming that you will make an ace or that your opponent will make an error. You should know where your opponent will logically play his shot and get in position to return that shot; at the same time keep in mind that he may play an illogical shot to an unexpected spot to catch you off guard.

If your opponent has hit a good shot or you have made an error in judgment and are off balance, try to make your return as deep as possible, but be sure to get that ball back into your opponent's court. If your opponent stays on the base line, do not be afraid to hit the ball with less speed, well above the net, and as deep as you can without making an error. He will not often force you after a deep return that has a high bounce. On the contrary, his return is likely to lose its sting or even become weak, permitting you to take the offensive.

Remember that it is necessary to anticipate in tennis. It is a bad move to wait until the ball has already covered a certain part of its trajectory before going to meet it. In such an event you must run faster or hurry your stroke, which results in loss of breath, increased fatigue, and greater opportunity for errors. Certain players never give the impression of running on the court, yet they are always in the right position. Others are constantly on the move, always darting at full speed, and are easily played out. The former know how to anticipate.

Anticipation demands a certain mental alertness and an instinctive understanding of the game. One must not start until the ball leaves the opponent's racket. To start exactly at that moment, the mind must have made its decision in advance, one must already have an idea where the shot will land. Thus one gains a fraction of a second, and all these fractions added together at the end of a match represent the extent of time during which you have set the cadence of the play.

One must not start too soon, for this would allow your stratagem to be discovered and turned against you. Neither must you start too late. The interval is very short—it is between the moment when the opponent is sufficiently set so as no longer to be able to change the stroke and the moment when the ball is hit.

It goes without saying that from the moment when anticipation becomes a natural part of your game, you must take account of it in your method of placing the ball. Let us call the "closed side" of the court that part to which the previous shot has drawn the opponent, that is to say, where he tends to stay momentarily, and the "open side" that part of the court which is least well protected. The most elementary tactic will lead you to play always toward the open side so as to put the opponent out of position in the easiest possible way. When you play twice in succession to the same side, that is, to the closed side on the second shot, you have attempted a deception. Between two players of equal strength and whose strokes have an equal speed, the side to aim for becomes a sort of game of "odd or even." The better psychologist ought to win.

The study of anticipation and deception includes a second step, false anticipation. A pretended start in one direction naturally incites the opponent to try a deceptive shot to the opposite side—which fails because the start was a false one.

There are two ways of making a deceptive shot, in depth or width. It is an error to believe that this tactic can only be applied on shots placed to right and left. A deceptive lob, over an opponent rushing for the net, is one of the most effective shots. Again, a very short drop shot to surprise a player retreating toward the base line almost always wins the point. For a deception attempted laterally it is a good thing to play short, shorter if possible than the first ball. A short cross-court shot is very effective, especially if it is deceptive. It will be noticed that the more one imposes one's game on an opponent, the easier it is to anticipate. Indeed a superiority in tactics or in cadence reduces the opponent's means of reply and one's own problems are less complex.

To repeat, your position in the court must be governed chiefly by the position of the ball first, then by the position of the opponent, and finally by the known characteristics of his play. If your return has carried the ball far over to the right of the other man's court, your waiting position must be correspondingly to your own left to anticipate his next shot. Similarly, you must lean toward your own right when you have played the ball far out to the left side of your opponent's court.

The "Center Theory." Speaking generally, you are safer on sharp cross-court angles the farther you are from the net, and the more in danger the nearer you approach the net. Conversely, you are more or less safe in the net position according to how near the center of your opponent's court the ball is placed when he is ready to make his next return. This is the basis of what is known as the "center theory," and those who study it most closely find it one of the better means of strengthening their net attack. This theory, with or without its name, was used by "expert" players for a great number of years. James Dwight of the United States was one of the first to make it his style of play.

The "center theory" is this: A volleyer is in a better position to command the court and so maintain his position at the net if he volleys *down the middle of the court rather than to the sides.* If he volleys down the middle, his opponent must be in the middle of his court to return the ball. If his opponent is in the middle, he will have less chance to drive the ball past the volleyer on either side than if he were driving from a corner of his base line. Less chance, because, if driving from either corner, he can drive hard down the side line, for he has the full length of the court to keep his shot in court; but, if he is in the middle of the court, he cannot drive so hard to either side line as he can when driving straight down the side line, because of the danger of the ball going out of court owing to the angle at which it is traveling. Since he cannot drive so hard, the ball travels more slowly, and therefore the volleyer has more time to intercept it. The only hard drive that can be made from the middle of the base line is down the middle of the court; and this drive, however fast, is generally quite easily dealt with by a volleyer in position.

Both in attack and defense the player who has made a study of the "center theory" has a good pull over one who has not. In defense (in a base-line duel) when you yourself are playing from the base line and your opponent's backhand is not sufficiently weak to make it worthwhile to keep on hammering at it, you should keep the ball down the middle of the court and as deep as possible, because your opponent will find fewer chances of making a winning stroke from the middle of his own base line, or of making a shot that will even drive you so far out of position that he will be safe in running up to the net. But if he does get to the net, remember that the "center theory" is temporarily useless. You must either lob or try to pass him. In attack, or rather as a means of preparing for attack, it is also most useful; for when you have driven your opponent, let us say, out to the side of his court at one corner, a deep drive down the middle will give you a straight instead of a slanting run in to the net, at the same time lessening the danger of being passed. Once settled safely at the net, the center theory is still a splendid defense of your position if you do not get the opportunity at once to end the play by killing the ball. There are many times when a man is volleying that he can return the ball but cannot kill it, and then the part of wisdom is to keep the other man from passing and wait for a better opening for the kill you are playing for. Again the center theory is needed, for the volley that does not kill is better in the center of the court so that the next return shall not turn the tables against you and put you on the defensive.

Thus, from every viewpoint, the center theory is a help to defense and a greater help to safety while attacking. For the man who wants to throw all caution to the winds and rip and slash his way through all opposition, perhaps the better course is to adopt only the sharpest angles for all his strokes, but this opens him up to even greater dangers than he is hoping to ensnare his antagonist with, and unless he is very skillful at this style of game, the safer man on the other side of the net is likely to beat him. Remember that the net position enables the skillful volleyer to dominate the court, and thus it is worth some risk to gain that advantage. By going to the net you force your opponent to make errors by the very fact that if he fails to be accurate, he will give you an opportunity to win the point. This mental hazard is of very real value in a long, hard match. You must expect to be passed now and then; but do not let an occasional pass discourage you from continuing your attack.

If the other man tries to dislodge you from the net by lobbing, then you must get back quickly to smash, and if your smash is not an outright kill, you must return to the net position instantly. The slightest hesitation or delay after smashing a lob means that it will be too late to get up close again,

and the next return will be at your feet. You will be forced to stay back in your court and the adversary may take that opportunity to take the net attack into his own hands.

When lobbing yourself, place your lobs far back. It is better to risk putting the ball out of court than to lob short. That is sure death, and the moral effect of a smashed ace gives the enemy more confidence. If there is any choice, it is better to lob to the backhand corner of the other man's court than to his forehand side. Few players can smash from the backhand side, for the stroke is much easier when made with the ball over the right shoulder. On the left side, the player is generally forced outside of the court to smash, and if he does not kill outright, then his court is wide open for the next return.

The lob is often the best defense against a good net player who gets in close, but it should be varied. If you lob too much, the other man will get used to handling that stroke and soon begin to kill it. On the other hand, watch for the first time he fails to follow up his smash quickly to the net and try to get the next return at his feet before he comes in close enough to volley. That is the turning point and often wins a long rally.

In smashing one of your opponent's lobs, select the part of his court that seems least covered, but if the ball is falling short so you are not far from the net when you hit it, the direction is not so important and sheer speed alone will generally kill. It is sometimes more effective to smash directly at the other man's feet, particularly if he is fairly close to you. He will hardly have time enough to get his racket into position to make a return from a hard smash right at him, and this is sometimes more embarrassing than a hard-hit ball a little way off, as it gives less room in which to swing the racket.

Depth and Net Clearance. Top players automatically know when depth is important and when it is necessary to hit a ball with a large margin of net clearance. But beginners and intermediates are confused: they try for depth at the wrong times, and they cannot judge the proper moment to aim for net clearance.

The two subjects must be taken together because one goes with the other. In order to hit a deep ball, one should clear the net by 2 to 8 feet.

A ball that whistles past the tape will fall short, whereas a ball with a great deal of net clearance is much more likely to land near the base line.

Depth is important when the opponent is on the base line. A short ball (or one that skims the net) gives the opponent the opportunity to make a forcing shot and to take the net position. Therefore all efforts in base-line exchanges should be toward keeping the opponent pinned back. One only hits a short ball (a net skimmer) when the opponent has been worked out of position. A sharply angled short shot can then be a winner. When playing from the base line, there is another consideration other than depth. The idea is to force the opponent, but not to the point where forcing shots become errors, and to prevent the opposition from getting grooved. For this reason, base-line exchanges should clear the net by different margins—by 8 to 10 feet when one is retrieving a very deep ball, and by 2 to 3 feet when one is trying for added pace.

Depth is unimportant when the opponent is at net. Now one tries only to keep the ball low, for a high ball to a net player is a setup. The ball should clear the net by the narrow margin of 3 inches to a foot. If the ball is dropping quickly (falling short), the opponent will have to volley up, which is the aim of the defender.

There is a third consideration. Should one try for depth on return of serve against a net-rusher? A few servers come in so fast that they can make their first volley from inside the service line. The return against them should be low and short (a net-skimmer to prevent them from hitting down on volleys and a fast-dropping ball to force them to volley up). However, many big servers take their first volley at a point several feet behind the service line. The ideal riposte is a ball which will land at the server's feet. This means a certain amount of depth, but basically the ball must be dropping fast when it reaches the area immediately behind the service line. A ball with high net clearance (6 to 8 feet) will not drop fast enough, and it is therefore better to try for 2 feet of clearance. This gives the receiver a safety margin while insuring a reasonably deep return. But whatever you do, do not stick to one pattern, and always avoid a high return to the net player. Skim an occasional one from the base line in a back-court exchange, go for high, looping bouncers at other times which clear the net by 10 feet, and see how your change of pace will break up your opponent's rhythm and make your hard shots seem harder.

Playing on Different Surfaces

As was stated in Section 2, there are many tennis court surfaces, and each and every one of them requires a different technique and strategy. For instance, the man who is trained on clay always has trouble his first year on grass. Clay players develop an accurate base-line game, and power on attack is not important. It is necessary instead to run down the ball, to keep it in court, to lob very high, and to get back into position. This steady, accurate clay-court champion is lost on grass, where the premium is on speed and attack at any cost.

Grass is a game of moving forward, forward, forward. A stab volley is liable to be a winner, whereas on clay the stab volley is almost a sure loser since the player gets passed on the return. One needs only a big serve and volley on grass; the groundstrokes are far less important. Conversely, one need not have a big serve or volley on clay; groundstrokes that have depth, consistency, and accuracy are all-important. Bad grass is the greatest equalizer, for a man with a big serve and stab volley has a chance against the champion who has not only a big serve and volley but good groundstrokes as well. Games follow serve, and with a few bad breaks (rough bounces) against him, the champ is out.

There are numerous synthetic court surfaces being used today. Most of these surfaces are made of acrylic fibers, rubber, or a synthetic plastic grass, and play about as fast as grass. Because of their synthetic nature, they play more consistently than grass, but the speed of the court can be regulated by spraying the courts or shaving the fibers.

The cement player has a wider choice of games. One can become good on cement with an attacking game, but this surface can also develop excellent retrievers. One can be a base-liner or a net-rusher, and one can win with a good serve or beat a big server with one's excellent groundstrokes.

Cement is much faster than clay and it has a truer bounce than grass, but the ball bounces high, which gives one a chance to retrieve it. The cement player is usually better rounded than the clay or grass devotee; he is more likely to have both good groundstrokes and a good volley, and he realizes the importance of a big serve.

Aggressive cement players make the transition to grass faster than to clay; steady cement players adjust more quickly to clay. The average cement player is more aggressive than steady since speed pays off and so does a well-founded attack.

Grass is an unusual surface for training. Grass players have real trouble adjusting to clay and a certain amount of difficulty in responding to the high bounces on cement. Grass is not only fast, but a hard ball tends to slither away from the opponent. It is difficult to groove one's strokes on this surface.

Wood is like fast cement. The trouble is that most wood courts are not well lit, and this adds another dimension to the difficulties of learning the surface. A big serve is vital, but one does have a chance to get a good swing at the ball because the bounce is true. Scandinavian indoor courts are excellent because they are well lit. A cement or grass player can adjust to them very quickly.

Most professionals teach their pupils to hit groundstrokes with their side to the net. As they hit the ball, the front leg is supposed to move into the shot, i.e., toward the net. This always holds true when there is plenty of time to get to a ball and the footing is sure. On clay, composition, or grass, the player moving toward a ball runs several steps less, then slides into the shot. This saves energy for the long matches and means that the player does not have to be in perfect position to hit a ball since he has to slide at the last minute.

The slide when running to the forehand side finds the player hitting with an open stance. If the player is righthanded, he plants his left foot and slides his right foot sideways to meet the ball. If he were to slide his left foot, he would be too twisted in relation to the net to effect a good shoulder turn and powerful shot. Normally the foot slides 2 or 3 feet. When our righthanded friend changes direction and goes forward, it is his left foot that slides; the shot usually looks like a classical hard-surface forehand, with the left leg a little more extended

than usual. This spreading of the feet when moving forward is very good since the player hits the ball more in front of his body and, consequently, gets more power. The open stance usually results in a more defensive shot than the closed stance unless there is a good weight shift at the last minute, since the weight is not being moved from back to front foot unless the shoulder comes through well. Therefore the open-stance forehand is seen more frequently on clay or composition courts than on grass since on the latter surface most players are always moving into net (as the player moves to net behind a ball, he generally turns his left shoulder in and the stance is seldom completely open).

There are few if any open-stance backhands that are satisfactory. In other words, a righthanded player cannot slide his left foot to meet a ball on his backhand side. He is then unable to turn his right shoulder because he is facing the net and it has already been turned. When he moves forward, his right foot also slides because he must keep his right shoulder toward the net until he makes contact with the ball and turns it.

Because footing is sure on cement and the surface is so hard, players changing to clay or grass are afraid to slide or fall. But sliding on clay or grass is necessary, and falling properly is seldom dangerous on grass. A last-minute flat-out lunge often wins a point. However, such acrobatic action should not be overdone unless the player would prefer to be a circus performer rather than a tennis star.

A great, aggressive champion can attack on clay and win; a great defensive champ can parry a grass attack and come out ahead. The real champion is good on all surfaces. Usually he adjusts his game to the court, attacking more on the fast and defending more on the slow.

Playing the Wind

One cannot always play under ideal conditions. Many times the court will be rough, the background glaring, the underfooting wet, the gallery noisy, the backstops too short, the lighting poor, or the wind hazardous. The winner will have the better mental attitude and the better plan, and he will be oblivious to outside distractions. He will welcome the challenge of poor conditions because he knows that he can surmount them better than his opponent. The loser will be distraught; it is one of the facts of tournament tennis that the man who trails is the man who complains, while the winner takes everything in stride.

There are three kinds of wind. It can blow against you on one side of the net so that your best shots go short, and with you on the other so that all your lobs sail out. It can blow from one side to the other so that anticipated forehands come into your backhand. Or, hardest of all to master, it can be gusty, sweeping the ball in any direction just as you are set for it.

If you look on the wind as a challenge, you have won half the battle. You are fighting an opponent and the elements, but so is he. If you recognize the fact that not only your best shots but his, too, will be only adequate on a windy day, you automatically have the edge. The chances are that his attitude will not be as good as yours.

Topspin is the master wind shot. When the wind is blowing behind you, only topspin will make the ball drop into court. Do not try for depth; try for pace with topspin. This is not only a good base-line weapon when the wind is with you, but it is an ideal passing shot. Use enormous quantities of backspin on your lobs to enable you to lob high and yet keep the ball in court. Slice all your serves to prevent them from sailing. On the other side of the net, you are fighting the wind. Slug a little more than your wont and the ball will still go in. Lob with twice the strength of your usual lob. On this side of the net, you can be a "steady slugger." Overhit your serve; the wind will bring it in.

When the wind is bringing forehands into your body, watch for the wild bounce. Hit every ball wide to the opponent's backhand. Lob only to his backhand. When you hit a forehand cross-court (or a backhand down the line), do not try for too sharp an angle or to hit too close to the line. Reverse the preceding when you change sides on the odd game.

Gusty winds are the most difficult to play. Shorten the toss on your serve to prevent the wind from taking the ball away from you. (This, of course, necessitates a speedup in the service stroke.) Watch the ball like a hawk and be light on your feet so that you can play a ball that either moves away from or into you. Be conscious of the changes in the wind. When it lets up, revert to your normal game. When it is with you, use topspin; when it is against you, hit out.

Tennis Strategy and Psychology

Tennis strategy and psychology are closely connected. The psychological element wins or loses as many matches as stroke production. The game between two well-matched opponents becomes similar to a series of chesslike maneuvers, each player trying to outsmart the other. The ability of one player to excel the other in quickness of combining physical and mental reflexes usually decides the match. The one who can immediately grasp and sense the right play during a rally stands the best chance to win. The element of surprise is of particular advantage; it can do more to break up the opponent's game than any other factor.

The first and obvious rule of good court strategy is: Place the ball where the opponent cannot reach it. The second half of that rule: Be right at the spot to which the opponent directs his return. It stands to reason, however, that if the opponent's game is equal to or better than your own, you can hardly expect to score with every shot. So be patient. Do not try to win a point with every stroke. Bide your time by keeping the ball in play until some hole in his court opens up through which you can drive a scoring ace. Be satisfied to lose at first if such losses point the way to a final win. Often by keeping the ball in play without attempting kills, you can get a little rest when driven hard, can conserve your strength for your own offensive attack and the crucial moments of the battle. When your own offense fails, fall back on a steady defensive campaign and let your opponent make the errors.

Placing shots is the first consideration. Pacing the shots is only secondary. Speed under control is an asset but it may prove a boomerang when up against a player who can absorb the pace and use speed to his own ends. Often it pays to soften your own game and make the other fellow manufacture the speed. You have less pace to deal with and he is likely to make more errors. If you use speed continually you are serving your opponent with a steady diet and he soon accustoms himself to it; whereas if you mix your pace, you disturb his stroking. It is confusing to have a ball hit your racket like a thunderbolt at one time and like a feather the next. Remember that you cannot rely alone on either speed or strategy for success. Rather, you must arrive at a combination of both factors.

You must consider what effect you seek. If your opponent is well off court, you can score a placement by hitting the ball with a slight amount of pace. An opponent who maintains good court position can only be dislodged by a more severe shot. A player should mix up the pace and hit no harder than will permit a good margin of safety on all shots. By that it is not meant that you should rely on a minimum amount of speed. You should hit the ball hard enough, but should not sacrifice safety for too much speed.

There are two ways of playing the game—to your own strength or to your opponent's weakness. If your forehand cross-court is your strength but your opponent's backhand is his weakness, do you hit your forehand cross-court or do you hit it down the line to the weak spot of the opposition? If your game is based on rushing the net after service and your opponent's game is based on superb passing shots, do you continue to attack or do you try to bring your opponent to net where he is least at home? If you like to hit hard from the base line and your opponent dreads only soft, high loops deep to his backhand, do you hit crisply each time or do you lift the ball soft and easy?

The true tennis artist can adjust his game to play his strength when the opportunity rises but to play to the weakness of the opponent as well. But analyzing the opponent is a fascinating process. When you know what his weakness is, you may not have the equipment to make use of your knowledge. As an example, you may be a baseliner who hits with reasonable force and accuracy but who does not quite have the power to deal with a steady, fast retriever. You win a number of points but you lose more than 50 percent of the games. You are far too unsure of your volley to attack regularly. Your opponent, on the record, is not as good as you but he beats you. Now here is a good solution: your weakness (which you avoid and never hit) may be superior to his weakness, so

try a net attack. Do not serve and come in. Wait for the short ball. Then drive it or chip it or sidespin it on your forehand deep to his backhand and come to net. He will probably hit up and you will actually learn confidence in a volley because the weakness is so apparent.

If he is a lefty, slice every short backhand you get deep down the line, and then close in at net. Again, your confidence in your volley will grow because his return is short. Playing an opponent's weakness will be your best chance to overcome what had heretofore been your weakness. It will also give you greater enjoyment for you will learn to think and improve instead of simply hitting by rote.

Before leaving the subject of playing to an opponent's weakness, here is an important point to remember: do so discriminately. Plans of this nature do not always succeed. The opponent may be adept at covering his weaknesses and cause you an anxious afternoon. Preconceived plans are fine but they should be made quite flexible. Some opponents will hit to certain spots time after time when finding themselves in particular positions in the court. It is wise to study these methods and base your plans on an attempt to take advantage of them when you discover them. For instance, when playing a good base-liner, it is often good strategy to lure him to the net with the intent of passing him for the point, Since he is a base-liner by choice, he probably is weak at the net. To draw him in and away from his favorite base-line position with a shot that has to be played close to the net would be, in this case, a sound tactical move.

Keep in mind that you should always change a losing game and never change a winning one. However, too many players believe that there are only two strategies—hitting hard or soft-balling. Some of the suggestions below may help you to develop a "thinking" game in which you make the most of your strokes and of your opponent's weaknesses.

If you have been losing in a match in which base-line play has predominated, try coming to net more or pulling in your opponent. Increase your depth or try alternating long with short. See if stepping up the pace will help or if soft, high balls are more effective. Play one side repeatedly to probe for a weakness. Discover any weakness in your opponent's passing-shot game. If depth does not produce errors, perhaps change of pace will do it or, as an alternative, heavy spins.

If you have been losing while playing an attacking game, change your method of attack. Your approach shots may be short, you may be coming in on "nothing" balls, or you may be playing to your opponent's strength. Perhaps there is a forehand weakness in the opponent's passing shots, or he may be susceptible to an attack down the center. Possibly he is grooved to your approach, so mix them up.

If your opponent has been winning by a successful attack, try lobbing more (to the backhand). If you have been hitting your passing shots hard, try soft, dipping balls. He may have been outguessing you; do not hit cross-courts (or down-the-lines) exclusively. A counterattack may take the play away from him.

If your serve has not been an effective weapon, try hitting it harder or, if your first serve has not been going in, throw in your second serve first. If your opponent has been stepping around your serve to the backhand, try a wide slice to the forehand. If you have stayed back, vary your tactics by coming in. Change of pace can be as effective on the serve as it is on groundstrokes if you use your head.

It is fairly easy to understand the reason for changing one's game when losing. The next step is to know at what time the change should take place if it becomes necessary. In three-set matches, the loss of the first set due to a single breakthrough service is no sign that your game may not prevail —stick to it. However, the loss of the first set plus another breakthrough or a lead against you of 3–1 or 4–2 is convincing enough to indicate that your game is a losing one—change. In a five-set match, it requires a bit more time to prove that your tactics may not be the winning ones. Actually, great care should be taken and careful study should be given to this change. In some cases, for instance, like the one mentioned above, when you are down 1 set and trailing 3–1 in the second, it would be foolish to change your game if, let us say, you had based your tactics on steady base-line play to exhaust your opponent in a three-set match, and he was beginning to show the strain of the long rallies imposed upon him. In that case, the

3–1 lead would be offset by the fact that in all probability the opponent could not physically hold the pace that had given him this lead. Be sure the time is at hand to change by a clear concise summary of the effect which your efforts are having upon your opponent's game as well as the score.

Next let us consider the importance of the various sets, games, and points in the course of a match. Many players of ability play each point to the limit from the first to the last of a match, with the idea that a point is a point wherever you can get it.

Nothing could be further from the truth—no two points are of exactly the same value, and the keenest players sense this, doling out their resources, mental and physical, so as to be able to give every effort to those points considered vital to success. This has been known as playing to the score.

First, in regard to sets. In a three-set match every effort should be bent on winning the initial set. The shorter the scheduled course of the match, the more important becomes the advantage of an early and definite lead. Up goes the confidence of the leader, off falls that of his opponent. In a five-set match, many players do not take the loss of the first set too seriously, but attempt to win two of the first three, with the second considered the most important. In games, the seventh game of the set is usually considered the most important, although the fifth to the seventh are always vital. With a lead of 3–1, the player should go all out in an attempt to get to 4–1, which usually means the set. To see the importance of this particular game, the fifth, let us say the server is 3–1 and fails to hold. The opponent needs then only to hold service to be level 3–all. (Another point to consider is the fact that a service break usually means the loss of a two-game lead and not just one.) Following the same reasoning, it can be seen that at 4–2, holding means 5–2, a good lead, while losing results in 4–3. It is true these leads of two games appear large. They are. But it is here that every effort must be bent to hold and add to this lead instead of letting up.

Second, in regard to points. The third point of a game is usually the most important—closely followed in importance by the second. Usually these points spell the difference between 40–0 and 30–15, or between 30–0, a huge allowance, and 15–all. Do not risk too much at 30–0, just because you realize you lead. At 40–0 treat the point in the same manner. If you lose it for 40–15, take more of a chance here, then more carefully at 40–30. Play two of the points carefully to one more risky when holding a lead for the game. Trailing 0–40 or 15–40, take a chance. Coming up to 30–40, do not disregard the effort you have made and play more conservatively before hitting for the winner. Take your chances when you are way down; you will not be any worse off and you may score. On the top, with everything to lose, do not throw it away; await your opening.

When playing a better player, there is always a tendency to "press." Actually, pressing means trying too hard, overhitting, going for the big shots, and, often, playing jerkily. The solution to the problem lies in getting ready more quickly. The better player hits harder and/or deeper and/or attacks more. The lesser player feels his only ripostes are harder returns and outright winners on passing shots. But instead of increasing his pace (which results in more errors) or going for the shots with too little margin, he would do better to prepare more quickly. As soon as the ball leaves his opponent's racket he must make his move; before the ball bounces, his own racket is coming forward for the hit.

The harder the opponent hits, the earlier the windup must be. If one prepares in time and meets the ball in front of the body, one can utilize the opponent's speed. A player who cannot generate his own pace against a soft hitter will find he has "natural pace" if he can meet the ball solidly in front of him against a hard hitter.

The better the opponent, the more closely one must follow the ball. Lapses of concentration are not as dangerous when one is playing a weak opponent who does not force, but one can never take one's eye off the ball when one is up against a better player. This is particularly true against the net-rusher; one must look at the ball, not the opponent.

The time to try a new stroke or to increase one's pace or to change one's style is against a lesser player; one must stick with one's own equipment and forget experimentation against a better player. Do not go for "the big winners" when you are losing; use the pace that is natural to you, but prepare earlier. This does not mean you cannot work out a tactical plan, but overhitting should never be part of it.

You cannot compensate for a weakness in your own strokes by "blasting" the ball. If your opponent is murdering your relatively innocuous serve, the riposte is not to try to murder his relatively effective delivery. Neither is it to go for cannonballs on your first serve. You use what you have as effectively as you can; if your serve is relatively weak, you try for accuracy, depth, and spin —not for aces. If your opponent is forcing you on your weak side, you try for consistency, accuracy, and change of pace by preparing early; you do not go for the big winners. One avoids "pressing" by early preparation, intense concentration, and utilizing one's own equipment. One can still lose simply because the opponent is better, but there is a much better chance of getting into the match and of playing one's best if these three precepts are followed. You may still be overpowered, but you will be ready for many more balls and you will be "in" many more points.

It is often foolish to try to outlast an opponent in a marathon duel if the weather is excessively warm, unless the heat particularly favors you. Some players lose energy quickly in the heat, while others thrive on it. One must also consider side winds and back winds when choosing tactics. The ball may travel a considerable distance from its intended line of flight due to a strong wind, and the player must adjust his shots to these conditions of play. A player must try to avoid becoming upset during a match because of bad bounces, decisions, or other adverse conditions.

Exhaustion or excess physical strain is to be avoided whenever possible. It may cause the loss of that particular match or of matches to follow in the tournament. Try to relax completely between points to accomplish this end. Another important factor in this connection is to avoid running yourself out on unimportant points. It is easy to tear about the court to make unusual gets, and find yourself winded on the next two or three points to follow.

There are some players who are willing to waste time and points on shots that just will not click on that day. This is a foolish practice. Some other shot should be substituted to gain the necessary result if a favorite continues to fail to come off after a reasonable trial.

You must decide whether to assume the offensive or to content yourself with defensive methods. The latter are sometimes quite effective against an opponent using great speed, with a good percentage of accompanying errors. Try to size up the opponent and find which styles of play are most effective against him. It may be that he is weak against a net attack or a combination of short shots and lobs. If these weaknesses, or others, can be found, force the issue. On the other hand, if he is erratic and has trouble keeping the ball in play, rally with him and give him opportunities to make mistakes. By all means avoid playing the game of your adversary. If he wants speed, slow-ball him. If he wants to bring you into the net, change tactics and make him come in. Base your tactics on the style that upsets and surprises your rival most effectively.

The best base for an attacking style is the net position. This saves considerable time, distance, and energy, and is most disconcerting to an opponent. If you are planning to attack, do not hesitate to advance to the net at every opportunity. Another offensive method is to draw your opponent to the net in an attempt to pass or lob over him, or run him from the base line with a sharply angled return.

The best method of defense is to exchange shots from the base line to force your opponent into error. It is a safer base because it offers the maximum territory of the opponent's court as a target.

Deception and the element of surprise are also important. They consist of doing the unexpected and hitting the ball to the least obvious place. The opponent who expects a shot in his backhand corner is often the victim of a placement ace when a tantalizing drop shot floats over the net. The best way to worry an adversary is to keep him guessing as to what will come next. There is nothing that will wear the opponent out like making him chase into a far corner for an unexpected drive, or causing him to change his direction to go back after a ball in a corner that he has just left. Actually, in the game of tennis, deception can take two forms: (1) concealment of your stroke

and the direction you are going to hit the ball; and (2) not letting your opponent know where you are going to be in the court. Disguise the stroke and the direction of the ball as much as possible. Also, by feinting with your body—by leaning to the left or right at the correct moment—it is sometimes possible to draw the shot of the opponent where you want it to come. In other words, create a false opening. The use of deception requires extra practice on your part, but it generally pays dividends.

Do not be afraid to take a chance. If you play all your shots safe, right down the middle of the court, your opponent will have no trouble with you because you are not giving him any. Try placing some of the shots inches from the side line or the base line. Try dropping them a foot over the net. Try fast topspin drives, those high twisting lobs, those sudden rushes to the net. You may lose plenty of points in the process, but practice makes perfect, and you will soon find your shots dropping where you want them. Then you have a good tennis attack. Remember that one of the cardinal rules of all sport is never alter a winning combination. The same is true of tennis. If the tide is against you, you must take chances to gamble for possible victory. In such a case, change your game, change your strokes, pace, and method of attack. But never change a winning game unless you believe your adversary has discovered your plan of attack and has mustered an adequate defense against it.

Match Play. The difference between a game with friends and a tournament match is pressure. There is no way to simulate competitive play, and the only way to get tournament experience is simply by entering as many tournaments as possible and learning from your errors. There is not enough tension in practice, and therefore your development as a player will be limited if you cannot compete against others under tournament conditions.

Tension produces fatigue. A player in good condition may get exhausted in the third game of the first set of a tournament match. Top players therefore try to avoid prematch exertions which do not pay off. They may practice hard in the morning or have a hit just before playing, but they do not sit in the sun, do gymnastics, swim, or drive until after the match is over.

Each player is an individual and each will have his own method of training which is best for him. However, none will change their routine just before a tournament. If a player regularly goes to bed at 11:00, he should not suddenly go to bed at 9:00. If he eats lightly before playing, he should not switch to heavy meals when he enters a tournament. The one addition to his routine is salt pills, since players are susceptible to cramps because of match strain.

A good competitor goes into a match with a plan. He does not change it after he loses one point or one game; he does not stick to it if he has been badly beaten in the first set. It is good to be flexible, to play more aggressively on a wet, fast court, to serve short and wide against a receiver who plays too far back, to lob more against a player with a shaky overhead stroke, to play steadily on a slow court but to switch to another tactic if the plan is not succeeding.

The mental attitude of the match player is a function of his own personality. He needs confidence in his own game but respect for his opponent's abilities as well. The unconfident player will tighten on his strokes or will resort to retrieving or overhitting as a desperation measure. The overconfident player expects his opponent to fall over as soon as he steps on the court.

The temperament of a player can win or lose for him. If he cannot control his anger when he errs on a big point, the match will slip away from him. Anger against an opponent can be just as hazardous. If one expects misbehavior or mistakes on the part of the opposition, the crowd, and an occasional linesman, one is only pleasantly surprised if all goes well. The old tournament hand is not upset by stalling or any of the other gambits of gamesmanship whose object is to make him lose control. He takes the calls as they come and he does not fly into a tantrum when a linesman or umpire proves to be fallible. He is too good a competitor to let a partisan crowd get under his skin; he welcomes the opportunity of demonstrating his skill and his poise under the worst of circumstances. However, he sticks to his guns when it is a question of the rules.

Among the "don'ts" of competitive play: Don't listen to advice from well-wishers, don't gulp water on the odd games (sip it), don't worry about lost points, don't run for a ball that is going out (it is the mark of a rabbit), don't think of what you will say to your opponent after you have won, don't count the gallery, don't let extraneous thoughts come into your mind, and don't rush yourself out of the match. Among the "do's": When the nervous strain is great, try deep breathing; when fatigue overwhelms you, stay on your toes; when your strokes fail you, go back to fundamentals; when you are down two sets to one and are playing badly, take the intermission; and when you win or lose the match, be gracious. More on the etiquette of tennis can be found in Section 4.

Practice. The player who moans and groans the least on the court is the one who is in the best shape for his ability—i.e., the man who practices the most and who gets the most out of his practice. He will have his bad days, but the hours he has spent on the court have shown him how to play when reflexes or strokes are not what they should be. Only a few devotees of the game can spend unlimited time on the courts, but it is not just the number of hours but how they are spent that counts.

To the champion, who at one time spent five hours a day, seven days a week, learning the game, match play is far more important than practice. Two or three tough matches a week are all he needs, and if he is in the finals of each tournament, that is exactly what he will get—three easy early rounds and two or three real tests—until he comes to the major championships, where he can expect at least three or four hard matches. His worry is usually not whether he can get enough tough matches in the season but whether he will get over-tennised before the end of the year.

The lesser tournament player—the one who is nationally ranked but who is generally "out" by the quarterfinals—has a problem that is particular to himself. Why is he losing repeatedly to players ranked above him and how can he improve? Does he lack a tactical plan, is he overhitting, does he have a service weakness, is he too unaggressive, is his return of serve faulty, does he understand the surface? A player of this level must learn self-analysis, since all the good advice in the world will have far less meaning than the discovery of a fault by himself. Once he sees it, he can cure it with diligent, intelligent practice.

The poor tournament player who has the desire but lacks the weapons to achieve victory is the man who must practice the most. His weaknesses are many. He needs no less than two hours a day (often four or five) to reach his goal. He is the reasonably good college player who beats the local talent but whose aims are much higher. He is the first or second rounder on the grass-court circuit (although often his entry is not accepted). He wants to be a tournament player, but his failings are many. Nine times out of ten this player is not giving tennis enough time and his practice is haphazard. He does not work on the backboard, he does not practice his serve, he does not give it full effort when he plays practice sets, he will only work against certain players, he starts the season too late and he is afraid to enter the lesser tournaments. He will be a loser until all these defects are corrected.

The club or parks player has a much more limited time schedule, but he, too, can make vast improvements by regular workout periods used intelligently. He may have been playing twenty years or more, and if so probably is not looking for sensational victories. The most profitable method for him to improve is not by stroke changes, which are senseless for a grooved player, but by regularity of practice and self-study. Every time he skips a week his game will fluctuate, but he can get his occasional good days without so many bad ones by sticking to a twice-a-week schedule and by analyzing the game through looking, reading, and discussing. Analysis is infinite: Does he fail to lob? Is he taking the ball late? Can he start sooner? Is his first serve going in? Is he watching the ball? Is he drop-shotting enough or too often? etc.

Beginner and intermediate players should be on the court no less than twice a week (more often if they can) and should have professional help as well. Desire and concentration will make every practice session worthwhile and more enjoyable. These two factors will enable players to absorb what the pro is telling them, and the regularity with which they practice will keep them from forgetting the newly acquired nuances of their game. The more hours of concentrated effort they can give to it, the faster they will improve.

No player can ever get better without working at the game. Practice aids are fully discussed in Section 2.

Taking a Tennis Lesson

Skill in tennis develops more quickly from systematic, meaningful practice than from random hitting. True, you will improve through endless hours of casual rallying and play, but supervised practice under the watchful eye of a good instructor will be far more economical of your time and effort. Regardless of your present level of development, whether you are a beginner, intermediate, or advanced player, and whether you have played continually all winter long or are starting over again after a long layoff, taking lessons from a competent professional is the logical way to proceed. There are many good teachers scattered across the land. A description of the teaching-learning process as conducted by experienced tennis professionals is presented here.

Kinds of Lessons. Lessons can be classified as private (individual) or group (more than one person). For a private lesson, the pro works with only one person and the lessons run for a half to one hour. This is the most expensive of all lessons. The fee for group lessons, in which two or more people are taught at the same time, depends on the number in the group. In the case of large groups—twenty or thirty—the fee may be very small. Some pros offer a series of lessons, often ten, for less than the cost of that number of separate lessons. It is economical for the learner and it permits the pro to plan his teaching in a way that provides full coverage of all essential parts of the game. For these reasons, the best approach to the problem of learning is to contract for a full series of lessons regardless of whether you prefer group or individual instruction.

When talking with the pro, describe your tennis background and ask what length and spacing of lessons he suggests. He will probably ask some questions also. He will want to know your aim in tennis, how much you intend to practice, and how many lessons you plan to take. He will need to know your level of aspiration and your degree of commitment before he can plan your learning program.

The Teacher's Methods. Most experienced professionals use the *show-and-tell, watch-and-praise* method of teaching. In this plan the pro first demonstrates and describes the action to be learned. He tells you step-by-step what to do and how to do it, and he demonstrates slowly as he explains his moves. He points out the important parts of the stroke that you should work on and he tells you what to notice in his demonstration. He stresses cue words to direct action, and he explains the sequence of moves. Last, he demonstrates the end result, the immediate goal you are working for. He makes a few shots, showing the speed and trajectory he wants you to imitate.

He then lets you try to do what he has demonstrated and described. Probably he will first have you make several "dummy" swings at an imaginary ball: if you cannot make the proper swing at an imaginary ball, you certainly should not expect to make it at a real ball. While you are swinging, he analyzes your stroke. If he is a skilled teacher, he will first tell you what you are doing right. He will offer praise and encouragement to help "nail down" these good moves. At the same time he will try to build around them to correct mistakes you are making; he will describe, demonstrate, and possibly even guide you manually through your moves and positions in your swing.

When you swing reasonably well with consistency, he will let you move ahead. He may then take you to "fixed ball" practice in which you swing at a ball suspended on a cord or string. In this practice you will not have to time or judge the flight of a moving ball and so you will be able to focus all your attention on the mechanical act of swinging.

After you get the feel of hitting these stationary balls, you are ready to apply your stroke to a moving ball. For this practice, your pro will toss or hit softly to you, giving you the easiest kinds of balls to hit. He stands close to the net and feeds balls accurately enough to let you concentrate fully on your form; he will practically hit the racket for you. As you improve he will gradually move farther and farther from you and feed you more difficult balls to hit. If, at some point, play becomes too difficult for you—if you become confused and have to struggle to hit—he will realize he moved you too fast. He will take you backwards a step or two to review teaching points or to present new and different ones. Temporary way-stops such as these are often necessary. The pro will always have you hitting at balls appropriate for your level. In this way he hopes to move you along gradually. Eventually you will be able to rally with him from full length at your best speed.

Learning Takes Time. Do not be alarmed if the corrections suggested by the pro do not feel right immediately. A new grip or a new kind of swing may feel strange for a while. As you work on the changes, they will begin to feel more comfortable. Finally the corrections will have replaced the old faulty habits.

Kinds of Practice. Besides acting as a practice partner for you, your pro will tell you what kind of practice to do on your own. He may suggest "dummy" swing drills, possibly in front of a mirror where you can see your form. He may demonstrate how he wants you to practice against a background or a suitable substitute such as your garage door. He may want you to rally across the net with your friends or with someone he provides for that purpose. If so, he will explain the procedure for these.

Most pros consider this separate practice to be essential for learning. Their lessons are merely the starting point from which learning takes place. By demonstration, explanation, and hand guidance, they try to give the learner an understanding of good form. In addition, they provide the learner with some practice under conditions as near perfect as possible. But they all feel that the important task of establishing good habits of form falls to the learner. When it is attained, it is due as much to proper practice away from the pro as it is to practice done directly under his supervision.

Understanding the Learning Process. If practice is to be efficient, it cannot be done carelessly. Learning to hit a tennis ball is not merely a matter of meaningless repetition until a habit is formed. It is a process of conscious effort by which you try to make changes and corrections. Working under the pro's directions, you try to do as he suggests. But you do not always do it right the first time and so you try again. You attempt to correct mistakes indicated by the pro, changing a part of the swing here or there and noting whether or not the change makes any difference in the end result.

In order to make these changes permanent, you must learn to respond to cues of "feel" resulting from the movement of your hands, your arms, and your legs. In order to arrive at a point where you can respond to these cues of feel without thinking about them—when you can do that, you have learned what it is you are practicing—you must first concentrate on and learn to react to other cues, mainly voice cues offered by your pro. The cues, of course, will be carefully selected by him, and will be in keeping with the method of stroking recommended by him. "Point to the top of the fence," for example, could be a valuable guide to you if you continue to turn the racket face over despite the pro's advice to finish with the racket face perpendicular to the ground. Usually the ability to feel the stroke consistently comes only after many repetitions of voice cues by the pro or after manual guidance by him or after the repetition of voice cues by the learner.

You may be able to speed the transition of voice cues to cues of feel by describing to yourself what it is you are trying to do. Even though the pro uses carefully chosen cues, they do not always mean the same thing to all learners. Some of his cues may not have registered with you. Putting the action into your own words often makes certain parts stand out more clearly, and often these parts will be the most important parts for you.

Putting it into your own words also calls attention to the difference between good and bad shots. Try to describe how it feels when you make a good shot or when the pro commends you for good form. Remember the description and carry it over into your private practice. Describe how it feels when you make a bad shot. This emphasizes errors and directs your attention to what should be avoided.

It may also help if you ask the pro to describe how it feels to him when he strokes correctly. Ask about the sequence of his moves. Make him define his terms so you understand exactly what part of the stroke he is referring to. If his explanation sounds too complicated, tell him so and ask for a simpler explanation with emphasis on the parts that confuse you. Repeat the description as you try to imitate his stroke. Do not just look at what he is doing: talk about it.

This sequence of watching the pro demonstrate while he explains, after which you imitate and put the action into your own words, can be summed up to provide a useful guide to learning to play: *see it—hear it, say it—do it.* Follow this sequence in your lessons. In this way, you will be using several senses and you will be responding to several cues. This is the efficient way to learn.

When practicing on your own afterward, try not only to duplicate the right motion and movements described by the pro but also to eliminate all unnecessary movements. In other words, keep it simple. Do not confuse yourself by adding fancy flourishes and flashy moves. Concentrate on the essential parts pointed out by the pro. Think about your lessons when you are away from the pro. It may help if you write down what you remember about each lesson immediately afterward. Many pros do this, keeping a file catalog of each pupil so they can keep track of the work done in each lesson. But putting it down for yourself, in your own words, will help you see your problems and your objectives more clearly. Try to summarize the lesson in a clear and orderly way. If you can do so, the pro has done the job well. But you have only started to learn. You must continue to review the teaching points and to apply them in your practice. There are no shortcuts or magic words, except good, hard practice. If you have learned what and how to practice, your money was well spent.

DOUBLES PLAY

The game for pairs differs greatly from the singles game that has just been discussed in detail. Not only is the court larger and the number of players doubled, but the tactics are a great deal different. In singles play it is possible to score a great many points from the base line. In doubles, practically all of the scoring is done from the net position.

Doubles play also injects another element: teamwork. (Two players make up a team in doubles—both of the same sex or one of each. The latter is called *mixed* doubles.) In fact, the essential basis of good doubles play is good teamwork and complete sympathy between the partners. Two inferior players who "pull well" together will nearly always defeat a pair who are perhaps better individually, but whose play and demeanor are selfish and egotistical. Your aim should be to help your partner in every possible way, giving confidence and encouragement when things are going badly, and keeping a cool and determined head in the hour of victory. Because of your proximity and the fact that you are only two in a team, your mental outlook on the ensuing match inevitably reacts on your partner, and it is up to you to see that it is a helpful, optimistic aspect.

A double fault or a badly missed setup by you at a critical moment may do more harm to your side than the actual losing of one point, because it may quite unsettle your partner, who in his or her turn may also become erratic. A consistently bad return of service is one of the most demoralizing faults from your colleague's point of view that you can have—because however steady he or she may be, the game cannot be won if you repeatedly miss your return. In singles you can make mistakes, go out for winners, try the most impossible shots, and you have only yourself to consider—but in a double your partner must be your first consideration—even as you should be his or hers. To combine well, you must know by instinct or by experience what your partner's movements are likely to be, so that you neither clash nor leave part of the court unprotected.

Whether you are pairing up for men's doubles, mixed doubles, or ladies' doubles, you should try to find a partner whose type of game fits in with your own. If you prefer the right court, it is no use starting a partnership with another right-court player. If you are inclined to be brilliant but erratic in your play, then choose a partner who is steady and imperturbable—one who will have a restraining influence on your impetuousness. But above all choose somebody with whom you can be in complete sympathy on the court—this is the most important point of all, if you are to have a successful and enjoyable career as a doubles pair.

As a general rule the stronger player should take the left court, because he or she is in a better position to take more of the game than when in the right court—the center-court balls being on his forehand. Also the even points—the second, fourth, etc., in a game—are more important than the odd—because on them depends the winning

or losing of games. Hence the return of service of the player in the left court is of vital importance. Find out as soon as possible in which court you return the service the best, and then always play in it, and persevere with your returns until you bring them up to a very high degree of consistency. If you specialize in one court you should in time become quite expert. You may, of course, have to change your court to fit in with your different partners.

There are two distinct formations in the doubles game, either both up at the net, or one up and one back. (The former is called the *parallel formation*, while the latter is the *echelon formation*.) In these days when nearly everyone can volley, you generally see the former combination in action, and it is certainly more effective and greater fun. Two good volleyers will as a rule beat a "one up and one back" partnership, except where the baseline player is *exceptionally* good.

The objective in doubles, as pointed out earlier, is to get to the net and hold that position successfully. The position should be just as close to the net as possible, with the knowledge that any lob must be covered. This closeness depends on the height of the player in question. The most effective shots against a pair at the net are the low, well-concealed lobs and fast-dropping "loop-drives." Lobs are used to drive them away, while the drives may force them to volley up and allow you to challenge

Close cooperation is required in doubles play, and this 1970 Austrian championship team of Karen Krantzcke and Kerry Melville do it well.

their position. Good care must be taken to defend against either of these shots when you yourself are in position at the net.

When serving, a slice or twist service enables you to reach the net immediately. The volley and smash permit you to stay there and win the point. Sharply angled volleys and smashes are brought into play because of the extra width of the doubles court and because of your position at the net to the right or left of the half-court line. But when the opponents are serving, a clean passing shot is extremely difficult unless you can maneuver them out of position, because each opponent has 9 feet less court to protect than in singles. To win the point capturing the net is usually necessary, and the best way to do that is either to lob or to play a short shot, usually cross-court, directly at your opponent's feet. So important is it for you to steal the net that you are warranted in taking risks in going to the net. Quick thinking, good judgment, and daring are at a premium in forcing the net from your opponents.

The official rules of doubles play are given in Section 4.

Mrs. Carole Graebner prepares for a backhand stroke while Judy Tregart rushes to back her up.

Service Strategy

In doubles, it is very difficult to break through service. One break may cost the set. In protecting the service, the position of the server's partner is important. He should station himself as far inside the court as possible, allowing himself only enough margin to be able to cover all but the last outside foot or two of the alley; shots in this space are the exception rather than the rule. (About 6 to 8 feet from the net and about 9 to 12 feet from the doubles side line is usually considered a good net-man's position. He should, of course, face the receiver.) Next, he must be in as close as possible, giving himself enough room to be able to cover any lob. This position forces a cross-court return of service beyond the reach of the net player, or a defensive lob which may be dealt with summarily. If your opponents have been able to win points by hitting cross-court placements against the server or have been returning the service at his feet, his partner can eliminate this by standing near the center of the net on the same half of the court on which the server stands. This defensive shifting of

position is called the *Australian formation*, and when employed the receiver cannot make a cross-court return without giving the net man a volley and therefore must play his return down the side line. It is a simple matter for the server to run to the net up through the vacant half of the court, covering the alley as he goes.

Since the server must get to the net as quickly as possible, the most successful service in doubles is the twist or slice with a medium-paced delivery. This should be placed to the weakest point in the receiver's game, with sufficient spin and pace to keep him from running around the shot. The server should place special emphasis on getting the first service in the court. By the use of medium pace he is able to control the serve better as well as to have more time to gain the net. However, many good doubles servers believe in throwing in an occasional fast service to give a change of pace. Actually, the serve should be of good length and varied, so that the receiver is kept guessing. The down-the-middle serve, of course, is always a good one in doubles since it will limit the angle at which the receiver can return the ball. When the service is across the court, the server's partner must be prepared for a shot possibly down his alley and should move slightly in that direction.

The purpose of the server is to get in to volley as high a shot as possible. He should try to avoid having to make low or half-volleys. No matter where he makes the first volley from, he should keep bearing in to the net. The center theory here works to better advantage. A good first volley down the center of the court draws one of the opposition, if not both, to that point, and may leave an opening for a placement in either corner. If a lob is put up, the server and partner must deal with it and recover the net position immediately. That is, as you run up to volley the return you will not have much time to think, but must make up your mind in a flash what you are going to do with the ball. Speaking broadly, there are two courses open to you. If the return is a good low dipping drive, which you will have to volley upward, send it back from whence it came because in that quarter it will be fairly safe, the opponent of necessity still being back. If the return is an easy volley, fairly high over the net, then go for a winner, by playing it downward at the opponent at the net, who at such close quarters has very little chance of returning it. The nearer you can get to the net before you have to volley the return, the easier the stroke, and the more chance of winning the point.

If you decide not to come in on your service at all, you must try with your next stroke to make an opening to enable you to join your partner. But always remember that the longer you stay back, the better opportunities you give your opponents for attacking from the net position.

Return-of-Service Strategy

A team that can return service well can do much to destroy a good doubles combination. A return of serve seldom wins the point outright, but it can set up a less forceful return or it can open up the court to the defenders. Basically, there are three possible returns, speaking directionally—the cross-court to the incoming server, the lob over the backhand of the net man, and the down-the-line in the net man's alley.

Of the three returns, the topspin cross-court drive is the safest return and should be used more frequently than the other two. The length of this drive should vary according to the movements of the server. Should the server follow up the service, then the return should be a dipping shot, aimed to bounce at his feet, giving a very difficult low volley. Another good return to the oncoming server is a sharply angled ball, low over the net, and toward the alley—this shot if accurately played will often win the point outright. It is far more effective to return a well-placed dipping ball at the advancing server than just to hit hard, because a good volleyer never minds a hard ball if it is high over the net. If, however, the server remains on the base line, then a good length drive, deep into the corner, will give you the opportunity to join your partner at the net and you will have gained the attacking position.

A successful lob is a very difficult stroke to play. It must be a good length, and well disguised, otherwise the opponents will see what your intention is and will have plenty of time to get back and "smash" it.

The drive straight down the side line is risky, but if brought to perfection will win many points outright. Even if it is not successful and you lose the point, it is well worth trying because you will have conveyed to your opponent the fact that you are thinking of the shot, and in consequence he will keep in position and allow more cross-court drives to pass unmolested. It should also be used occasionally if one of the opponents is inclined to poach (to take the shots that normally belong to his partner) and to keep him from edging too much over to the center, to "keep him in his place." If, however, your opponents adopt the so-called Australian formation when they are serving, your cross-court drive must be eliminated, and you must either drive straight down the side line or lob.

A good man in the receiver's court will alternate his returns, but his decisions will be based not on the shots themselves but on the talents of the opposition. Remember, too, that it is most important to keep the ball in play when you return the service. Inexperienced teams waste too many points in trying to drive hard for a clean ace. A short, low drive is much more important than speed. In fact, a drive with moderate speed is usually more difficult to volley than a fast return. A clean pass off the service is so difficult that your errors will probably more than offset your aces.

Do not allow the opponents' activities at the net to fluster you and put you off your aim. The tendency is to have one eye on the volleyer and one on the ball, and the result is fatal. Watch the ball and concentrate and make up your mind—but not obviously—what you are going to do, and unless the adversary moves before you have hit the ball, he or she will not be in time to intercept a good shot. And if the volleyer does move before you strike the ball, you have only to change your direction and push it quite gently straight down the side line to win the point.

The return of service resolves itself into a battle of wits between the receiver and the opponent at the net—the former trying to avoid the latter, and the latter endeavoring to intercept the drives of the former.

It is difficult to define the best position for you to take when your partner is receiving the service, but it generally depends on two things: the movements of the server and the general quality of your partner's return. When the server remains back you should certainly stand up at the net, because you are in the attacking position. Also, if your partner has a good return of service you should stand close to the net irrespective of what the server is doing, as you may have an opportunity of intercepting the server's return. Only when your partner is having great difficulty with the service, and more often than not putting the ball on to the opponents' rackets, should you stand back, because under these circumstances your position at the net is useless, whereas if you are back you have a chance of picking up the opponents' volleys. If there is any doubt as to which position is better, the simplest thing is to ask your partner's opinion as to where you should stand while this particular service is in progress.

To return service well in doubles, one needs concentration to a superb degree, mental relaxation, anticipation to handle flat, hard serves, and a knowledge of service spins for control in returning slices and twists. The lefthanded slice or the righthanded American twist will bounce, then move toward your left. The sooner you take slice or twist, the less effective they will be; therefore you stand in as much as possible for spin serves. The later you take flat, hard serves, the less the

forward pace on them; therefore you want to take them from behind the base line, particularly on a fast court. And so you stay on your toes in anticipation of moving forward for slices and twists or of jumping backward for flat cannonballs.

Strategy During Rallies

In volley, the first objective, when serving, is to force a weak return from your opponents or to draw them out of position—in either case, you can then volley or smash for the point. If, for example, either opponent is standing on or inside his base line, volley deep, directly at him and as near to his feet as possible, so as to force a comparatively weak return which you can kill. Or, if you volley deep to the center of their base line, you will draw at least one, possibly both, of your opponents to the center, which may give you an opportunity to volley to a corner for an ace. Or you may volley deep to one corner, drawing your opponents apart, and then volley or smash between them through the opening you have made.

The sharply angled cross-court volley to the alley is often effective for an ace, but if it fails, you will probably give your opponents a setup. The extra width of the doubles court and your position to the side of the half-court line provide wide angles and frequent chances to kill a ball by a short, sharp, wide volley; you should, however, volley to kill. The stop volley is often effective, especially on grass courts. Somewhat similar tactics apply to the smash as to the volley. Eventually, you may learn to kill a lob from almost any part of the court; but for the beginner a good general rule is to smash for a kill when you are near the service line, but not when you are near your base line. Do not let lobs drop, however, no matter how deep they may be, or you will lose the net position. If the lobbers run in, smash at their feet; if they stay back, smash deep; and in either case, get back into a volleying position quickly. Your partner should tell you if your opponents are following in their lobs; he should also watch the lob and should call if it is going out.

Actually, an important matter about which you must have a definite understanding with your partner is the taking of lobs. Many points are lost on this score, not because the lobs are untakable

—but because the partners muddle one another. Here again, so long as you understand each other, you can adopt what method you like, but as a general rule it is easier for the partner standing at the net to retrieve the deep lobs, when the server is running in. It is obviously easier to get off the mark quickly from a stationary position than to have to stop, turn, and retrace your steps. In fact it is almost impossible for the server, if he or she is concentrating on getting right up to the net as quickly as possible, to cope with the deep lobs that go over either head, and pitch within an inch of the base line. On the other hand, the player at the net has only to watch the receiver's racket carefully to anticipate the lob, and will then have plenty of time to take the necessary action. Here is another important reason why the server should maintain a strict rule with regard to following up the service. The partner at the net must know what the server's movements are going to be if he or she is to deal satisfactorily with the lobs. If the server is coming in, the net player must not poach —but must be ready to fly back and retrieve the lobs.

When both partners are up at the net, they will of course each retrieve their own lobs. During a rally if one has to run back, the other should move back as well, so as to be on a level. There are fewer "gaps" in the court when the partners are in line with one another.

Your reply to the deep lob (one that you cannot kill) must depend on the movements of your opponents. If they follow their lob up to the net—as they should—then your only chance is to send back a lob, high and deep, one that they cannot reach to smash and which gives you the opportunity of reaching the net position again. If, however, the opponents do not advance to the net when they have lobbed over your heads, then a good-length drive will give you a chance of reaching the net once more. But always remember that when either you or your partner has to lob, if it is not a good one, it will be "killed," and your best chance of picking up a "kill" is by taking up your position outside the base line.

With regard to the short lob which can be smashed, each player should be responsible for those in his or her court, and those in the center should be dealt with by the partner in the left court, because they fall on the forehand—whereas they are on the backhand of the right court player, and therefore almost impossible to "kill."

A short, low cross-cut drive should always be attempted if your opponents are slow in regaining the net after smashing one of your deep lobs. If this squeeze play is well executed and followed in without the slightest hesitation, you can steal the net from the servers. It is demoralizing for your opponents to have the net taken away from them in this manner, and you only need to bring it off a few times in one game to break through their service and win a commanding lead in the set. This is, of course, a risky play; unless your drive is low, you will lose the point. But it is so all-important for your team to capture the net, and chances of winning the point from the back court are so much against you that it pays to take chances—not by driving blindly with all your strength, but by finesse.

The lob comes into its own in doubles and can occasionally turn defense into attack if it is not abused. An effective attack sometimes is to alternate deep lobs and short drives, being constantly on your toes to follow in your short drive when possible. Persistent lobbing sometimes will break down all but the strongest attack. If one of your opponents is not too strong on smashing, you can sometimes steal the net by lobbing deep, preferably to his backhand, and following in. If your opponent lets your lob drop near his base line, take the net.

Poaching is often sound strategy in doubles. When you are serving, for example, your partner, from his net position, can often get a possible volley shot on a ball returned to your side of court, and in such a case, he should take it. Partners who have played together for a long time almost know instinctively when each will poach on the other, but it is a good idea to call out or signal a poach whenever possible. Too much poaching, however, may ruin the game—as well as leave one side of the court open for the opponents to drive over a winning point. A good rule to follow is to poach only when you can execute a decisive stroke.

While shots down the center usually belong to the partner on whose forehand they come, there should be a prearranged understanding about this and certain other types of shots. In a quick en-

Position is important in doubles play. Here Rex Hartwig backhands the ball back to the team of Tony Trabert and Vic Seixas, while Lew Hoad is ready for their return.

counter at the net, the partner who has just played the ball generally continues to finish the point if possible. He is warmed up and in close contact with the exchange. However, when this is the case the player not handling the shot or shots must move swiftly to cover any section of the court exposed by his partner's action.

In doubles, when all the players are volleying, many balls are taken which if left alone would go out. There is so little time for your partner to judge the pace and elevation of the ball that he or she has to volley, but you are in a better position and should call "out" clearly and distinctly. Again, if there is any doubt in your mind as to which of you is going to take a certain ball, a quick "yours" or "mine" will prevent you from hampering one another.

Doubles Tips

The game of doubles is much more than serve, return of serve, and volley. It is a game of skill, tactics, and headwork. Here are suggestions for good doubles:

1. The partner who is winning his serve more easily should start serving first in each set.
2. Lefties should serve on the sunny side since it is *not* the sunny side for them.
3. Lefties are generally better in the right court since it gives them an opportunity to poach off the forehand.
4. When in doubt, hit down the center.
5. Do not baby setups; hit them!
6. Lob frequently; drop-volley rarely; drop-shot never.
7. Vary your returns of serve and disguise them.
8. If you never poach, your opponents need be less careful about their returns.
9. Never be angry with a partner who is passed when he poaches.
10. Do not moan or look unhappy when your partner misses.
11. When you have pulled the opponent wide to the backhand court, you and your partner should cover your forehand alley and the center, leaving your backhand alley open. The reverse holds true on a wide ball to the forehand court.
12. Play the weaker opponent and play his weakness.
13. Practice the doubles shots you do not know —except in a match.
14. When a lob goes over your head and your partner goes back for it, cross over quickly so that you are not both caught on the same side.
15. Show good manners: do not call shots on your opponent's side (unless asked), do not quick-serve, do not stall, and do not blame your partner if you lose.

Mixed Doubles

Mixed doubles is a branch of the game which calls for some principles very different from those used in either singles or men's doubles. The same methods of play that are used in other doubles do not often hold good and frequently cannot be

A lob to the backcourt can cause problems in doubles play.

brought into use because of the inequality of the two partners in this kind of a game. That is, the principle of the weaker link of a chain applies very strongly here, and it is very difficult to prevent the opposing players from selecting the woman on your side of the net for attack and by directing their strokes to her, to reduce the opposing strength to the level of the weaker player's game. To prevent this only one way seems practicable, and that is to get the woman up to the net at the first opportunity and then to direct your strokes, if you be the man partner, so as to support her in that position where she can be of the most value to her team.

The woman is usually more valuable to her side at the net and the man at the back of her court, unless he can work his way in and support his partner in the volleying position, when both might hold the attack safely together. The difficulty is in getting the woman up to the net safely. When her man partner serves, there is no question but that her place is at the net, and she can take up her stand there before the ball is put into play. Similarly, when he is the receiver, she can take the same position safely and he can support her by his first return.

But when the woman serves and when she is

the receiver, the man's place generally is at the middle of the base line to cover any return that the other side can make. For the dangerous run that the woman must make toward the net without being caught halfway up with the ball at her feet, a strategic stroke must be made that will give her the needed time, and this is not always afforded by the return of the adversaries. If both of the opponents are back in their court, perhaps the safest way to secure the desired position is to drive deep into the woman's corner on the other side and have your partner run up behind this drive.

If the other woman is on the same side of the court as your partner, this can be done at the first opening, but if they are diagonally opposite, it is always safer to have her cross over to the side opposite her woman opponent, and then make the run to the net on the first deep drive into the woman's corner. If the woman on the other side is playing at the net, this chance is not open, and the next alternative is to lob deep over the woman's head and your partner can then run in under this lob unless the man on the other side is an exceptionally good smasher, when it might be dangerous to lob at all. However that may be, one of these two devices should be used and maneuvered for until your partner can reach the net safely, after which a new situation presents itself.

With the woman at the net, this tactical position is usually sound, and if the other woman has also reached the net, then it is a matter of better tennis on even terms or better strategy that ought to win. With the woman against you at the base line and your partner at the net, the odds are all in your favor, of course, so long as you can prevent the opposing woman from running in. Unless she be exceptionally clever at passing, a deep drive into her corner ought to let you follow it up safely, and with both yourself and your partner at the net together, victory is almost certain with the ball kept on the woman's side of the court, and about even if the opposing man gets a chance at the play.

With both women in the volleying position, the play between the two men generally is diagonally across the court, and it should be the aim of the clever player to keep his drives well over in front of his partner, so that from her position she will be able to cover as much territory as possible. To play to the other corner leaves the "open diagonal" of the court wide open and limits the partner's usefulness to covering a very small sector of the court.

When the opponent follows the same tactics and simply tries to outdrive you, a splendid variation is to work him far out to the outside of his court to meet a diagonal drive and then to lob deep and low over his partner's head and follow the play up to the net. The effect of this play is to bring the man on the other side directly behind his partner, leaving them doubled up and the other side of the court entirely unguarded.

If you follow this play up to the net quickly, the court will be wide open for a kill and nothing but a lob or a brilliant passing stroke will save the other side from losing. The greatest danger of this play is that the man opponent will be able to cross quickly enough to smash, but if the lob is low and well placed to the side of the court, he will find it very difficult to get there in time, especially if he was far over to the other side before.

When volleying with all four at the net it is in most cases best to aim at the woman, for she is likely to be not only less strong in the wrist for the return, but less able to keep up a series of short crisp shots. She may volley finely, but she has not the endurance of the man. Do not think, however, that she will be slower at chasing lobs or less reliable when dealing with them. She will not be so punishing overhead, but she will be as well, possibly better, able to deal with them after the bounce, and swifter to reach a good position for that purpose.

There are many other variations of play for mixed doubles, but success in this game depends largely on getting your woman partner up to the net, and keeping her there safely so her position covers as much of the court as possible. Naturally, the woman who volleys well is much the stronger partner, and to select one who volleys badly is to court defeat.

The service is a big advantage in mixed doubles, and the man should always serve first as he ought to win his own service game 70 percent of the time with evenly matched teams. The struggle usually develops around the winning of the games in which the women serve and both of the men are expected to win their own service games.

Rules and Etiquette of Lawn Tennis

The United States Tennis Association—in this, its own "official" book—has been, of course, mentioned many times. Its early history was fully covered in Section 1. Now let us take a look at the activities of the organization itself.

UNITED STATES TENNIS ASSOCIATION (USTA)

The United States Tennis Association is a nationwide, noncommercial membership organization devoted to the development of tennis as a means of healthful recreation and physical fitness and to the maintenance of high standards of amateurism, fair play, and sportsmanship. The oldest amateur sport-governing body in the United States, it is a nonprofit organization, consisting of seventeen geographical sectional associations, many of which contain district associations. Organization and promotional work for and through the over 2,000 affiliated clubs composing the National Association are directed by close to 700 officers and committeemen throughout the entire country. All such activities are conducted by elective or voluntary workers without remuneration, supervised from the various sectional headquarters or the National Executive Office in New York City, which includes the only recompensed staff within the USTA.

One of the main functions of the USTA has been to establish or alter rules for the benefit of the sport and players. Most of the legislation concerning rules of the game occurred during the early years of the Association. Beginning with the first meeting, three rules were adopted which have not been changed over the years. The most important decree concerned the method of keeping score. The present system of counting was chosen and thus the old system of racquets scoring that was being used by some clubs was outlawed. The present dimension of 21 feet between the service line and the net was established as the official measurement for a tennis court. Also, to avoid disputes in tournaments, it was ruled that the decision of the umpire was to be final.

In the fall of 1881, the Association published a book of rules with some additional changes. The server was to stand with one foot behind the base line, although the other foot could be on or over the base line. A good service delivered when the receiver was not ready was not to count, a "let" on the service was no longer to be in play, the net and posts were not to be touched, and the ball was not to be volleyed before it passed the net. If the umpire wished, he could direct the players to change sides after every game, either throughout the match or in the deciding set. Court regulations were to the effect that the service court in doubles was to be reduced to the same size as in singles.

Other major rule changes occurred in 1891. A rest was provided for in a match, although it was only 7 minutes instead of the present period of 10 minutes. There was to be a referee for every tournament and an umpire for every match. By 1895 most of the rules of tennis were well established and these have lasted through the years. A few minor changes have been made since, which concern the action of the server. In 1898 it was ruled that the server must keep both feet behind the base line. In 1955 it was stated that while both feet must be behind the base line during service, one foot may swing over the line so long as it does not touch the ground before the ball is struck. The present USTA tennis rules are given later in this section.

The United States Tennis Association not only formulates standard tennis rules but also sanctions national tournaments and the rules of organization. As previously stated in Section 1, the first United States national tournament was held at Newport, R.I., in 1881. This contest included men's singles and men's doubles. Presently the national USTA championships are: The USTA Open Championship; United States Amateur Championship; United States Clay-court Championship; United States Hard-court Championship; United States Father-Son Championship; United States Mother-Daughter Championship; United States Husband-Wife Championship; United States 18, 16, 14, and 12-and-under championships; United States Interscholastic Championship; and National Collegiate Championship (men and women). In all veterans' championships, divisions are junior veterans 35 and 40, senior 45 and 50, senior 55, 60, 65, 70, 75, and 80; in women's competition, there is women's 35, 40, and 45; senior, and senior 50, 55, 60, 65, and 70. Greater detail on these tournaments is given in Section 5. In 1980, over 14,000 tournaments were held throughout the United States under the auspices of the USTA.

As the number of tournaments and players increased, it was necessary to make official regulations for the organization of tournaments. As was the case with the rules of the game, most of the laws were laid down during the early years of the Association. For instance, in 1884 the Bagnall-Wild system of draw was adopted for tournaments. This innovation eliminated "byes" after the first round. Prior to this, a new draw had been made after each round, and byes had occurred in any round. Also in 1884, a novel step was introduced to make tournaments fairer and more interesting. It was decided that the present champion of a tournament should not compete in the matches until the last day of the contest. This meant that the champion would "stand out" and defend his title against the winner among the other players. This system was used until 1912, when it was abolished in favor of the present system by which all contestants play throughout the tournament.

In 1885 the first official rankings of players were made, whereby the ten most skilled men in the country were rated in order of ability as shown by their tournament records. In 1910 the list grew to include 100 players, but this proved to be too large a number and the next year the list was reduced to 35 players. These rankings have continued to be made each year, and at present approximately 35 players in each division and age group are ranked by the USTA. More on ranking can be found in Section 6.

The USLTA in 1922 inaugurated "seeding a draw" for tournaments. Previously players had been placed in a draw at random and consequently the two best players often had to play against each other before the final round. The principle behind seeding was to place the best players in different sections of the draw so that they would not meet each other in the early rounds. Today seeding is done in all tournaments, whether local or national.

In 1922, after years of negotiations, the USLTA joined the International Lawn Tennis Federation (ILTF), which had been founded in 1913. Then, as today, this body encompassed all the lawn tennis associations in the world in an endeavor to provide standard regulations everywhere for the game of tennis. Thus, as a member of the Federation, the USTA is an effective factor in supervision and changes of the worldwide playing rules, maintaining high standards in the production of tennis balls, rackets, and all other playing paraphernalia.

The USTA is probably the most active and enthusiastic member of the International Federation in developing and expanding junior tennis in its many phases. Actually, the promotion of junior development is one of the most important programs in the United States Tennis Association. Clinics, a series of tournaments, and the encouragement of travel opportunities are among some of the benefits to be derived from junior development. The junior development program offers such opportunities as:

1. A summer tour and practice program on the Junior Davis Cup team, from which future Davis Cup players are selected.
2. The chance for international competition on the junior level in such top tournaments as the Orange Bowl Championships, held annually in Miami Beach, and the Sunshine Cup, or Junior Davis Cup, also held in Miami Beach, and the Junior Wightman Cup for girls.
3. A comprehensive group of national tournaments for players in the junior (18-and-under, 16, 14, and 12) divisions, in both girls' and boys' competition.
4. Clinics and instructional programs through various tournaments. Several leading tournaments in the U.S. donate part of their proceeds to junior development in underprivileged areas.
5. The chance for financial aid to deserving young players, who show a need and desire to improve themselves.
6. The formation of foundations in various states and by certain sectional associations to help deserving players meet the financial responsibility that goes with traveling to top tournaments.

Annual reports are submitted to the USTA by a Junior Development Committee on the progress of programs. Interested parents should contact the USTA National Executive Office, 51 East 42 Street, New York, N.Y. 10017, or their sectional association for information on junior development programs available in their area.

In the beginning years of the Association, tennis was a young sport and only engaged in by a very small minority of the population. Consequently, the structure of the organization was simple and its problems were relatively few. Though a small group it had unchallenged authority as the na-

tional body for the game of tennis from its inception. It undertook projects that had far-reaching results, such as selection of a standard ball, adoption of a common method of scoring, issuance of standard rules, and so forth. It is important to keep in mind that in its first years the Association did not have on its membership rolls all those clubs playing tennis. Yet, as the game developed and the functions of the Association became more numerous, it became more of a necessity for a club to belong to the national body in order to receive certain privileges. The early years of the Association received these comments from J. Parmly Paret in his 1904 book on tennis:

The USNLTA is the controlling body, but its membership includes only a small proportion of the tennis clubs of the country. There are many smaller sectional associations through the West, and some also in the East, few of which hold membership in the USNLTA. The policy of the National Association has not been aggressive, and no attempt is made to outlaw players who compete in tournaments under other auspices, or to insist on the enforcement of its laws outside of its own membership.

However, it should be pointed out that since the very first national tournament in 1881 many tournaments were open only to those players who belonged to clubs which had membership in the USLTA.

As tennis grew in popularity and the responsibilities of the Association toward the game became more numerous, it is natural that the organization itself became larger and more complex in order to carry out its functions. A brief examination of some of the developments and changes in structure illustrates this point.

The governing body within the USTA has always been an Executive Committee. In 1881 the Executive Committee consisted of six people: President, Vice-President, Secretary-Treasurer, and three delegates. Furthermore, it is recorded in its very first year that there were several committees, notably a Tournament Committee and a Prize Committee. Today the USTA has an Executive Committee (numbering 42 people) which consists of the officers and delegates. In addition, there are 52 national committees. Each of the 17 sectional associations has a somewhat similar

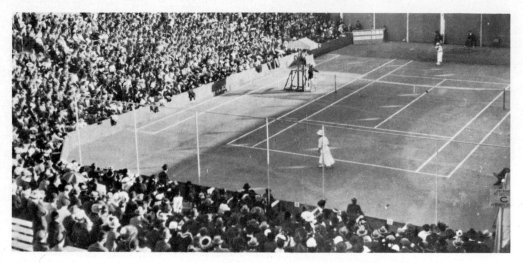

Resort areas were among the first to install tennis courts. Here is a partial view of the capacity audience watching the famous match between May Sutton and Molla Bjurstedt on the Hotel Virginia courts at Long Beach, Calif., in 1914. Miss Sutton was the winner.

setup. Thus, it will be seen that several thousand tennis enthusiasts, many of them famous national and international champions of the past, voluntarily devote many thousand hours each year to coordinating and improving tennis playing conditions, and the maintenance of the high amateur standards which have always been the keynote of the game. More than ten million players, who annually tread the thousands of courts throughout the United States, benefit by this promotional work, whether they play on school, public park, small community, or famous club courts with many years of history and tradition back of them, such as the West Side Tennis Club of New York, the Los Angeles Club, Town and Country Club of Chicago, and the historic clubs along the Atlantic Coast, the birthplace of American tennis, such as Seabright, Longwood, Newport, Germantown, Merion, Chevy Chase, and others, where first the turf was marked with the introduction of the game in America in 1874.

USTA Sectional Associations

Here is a listing of the seventeen sectional associations of USTA:

EASTERN—comprising the state of New York and those parts of Connecticut and New Jersey within 35 miles of New York City Hall.

FLORIDA—comprising the state of Florida.

HAWAII—comprising the state of Hawaii.

INTERMOUNTAIN—comprising the states of Colorado, that part of Idaho south of the 45th parallel of latitude, Montana, Nevada (except for the counties of Washoe and Ormsby in the state of Nevada), Utah, Wyoming.

MIDDLE ATLANTIC—comprising District of Columbia and the states of Maryland, Virginia (except city of Bristol), and West Virginia, except the following counties therein: Boone, Cabell, Calhoun, Jackson, Kanawha, Lincoln, Logan, Mason, Mingo, Pleasants, Putnam, Ritchie, Roane, Wayne, Wirt and Wood.

MIDDLE STATES—comprising the states of New Jersey (except that part within 35 miles of New York City Hall), Pennsylvania, Delaware.

MISSOURI VALLEY—comprising the states of Iowa, Kansas, Missouri, Nebraska, Oklahoma, that part of Illinois known as Rock Island County and that part of Illinois within a 30-mile radius of St. Louis City Hall.

NEW ENGLAND—comprising the states of Connecticut (except that part within 35 miles of New York City Hall), Maine, Massachusetts, New Hampshire, Rhode Island, Vermont.

NORTHERN CALIFORNIA—comprising the counties of Alameda, Alpine, Amador, Butte,

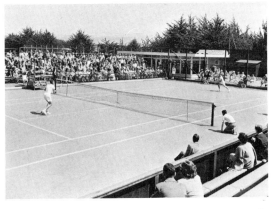

Famous resort courts in widely separated parts of the United States: *(top, left)* Arizona Inn, Tucson, Ariz.; *(top, right)* Spruce Point Inn, Boothbay, Me.; *(bottom, left),* Del Monte Lodge, Pebble Beach, Calif.; *(bottom, right)* Boca Raton Hotel and Club, Boca Raton, Fla.

Calaveras, Colusa, Contra Costa, Del Norte, El Dorado, Fresno, Glenn, Humboldt, Inyo, Kings, Lake, Lassen, Madera, Marin, Mariposa, Mendocino, Merced, Modoc, Mono, Monterey, Napa, Nevada, Placer, Plumas, Sacramento, San Benito, San Francisco, San Joaquin, San Mateo, Santa Clara, Santa Cruz, Shasta, Sierra, Siskiyou, Solano, Sonoma, Stanislaus, Sutter, Tehama, Trinity, Tulare, Tuolumne, Yolo and Yuba in the state of California, and the counties of Washoe and Ormsby in the state of Nevada.

NORTHWESTERN—comprising the states of Minnesota, North Dakota, South Dakota.

PACIFIC NORTHWEST, comprising the states of Alaska, Oregon, Washington, and that part of Idaho north of the 45th parallel of latitude, and the province of British Columbia.

PUERTO RICO—comprising Puerto Rico and U.S. Virgin Islands of St. Thomas, St. Croix and St. John.

SOUTHERN—comprising the states of Alabama, Arkansas, Georgia, Kentucky (except Boone, Campbell and Kenton counties), Louisiana, Mississippi, North Carolina, South Carolina, Tennessee and city of Bristol, Virginia.

SOUTHERN CALIFORNIA—comprising the counties of Imperial, Kern, Los Angeles, Orange, Riverside, San Bernardino, San Diego, San Luis Obispo, Santa Barbara, Ventura.

SOUTHWESTERN—comprising the states of Arizona and New Mexico, together with El Paso County, Texas.

TEXAS—comprising the state of Texas, except El Paso County.

(left) Tennis courts on the island of Bermuda (Elbow Beach Surf Club) and *(right)* Nassau (Emerald Beach Plantation and Hotel).

WESTERN—comprising the states of Illinois (except Rock Island County and that part of Illinois within a 30-mile radius of St. Louis City Hall), Indiana, Michigan, Ohio, Wisconsin, that portion of Kentucky included in the counties of Boone, Campbell and Kenton, and that portion of West Virginia included in the counties of Boone, Cabell, Calhoun, Jackson, Kanawha, Lin

coln, Logan, Mason, Mingo, Pleasants, Putnam, Ritchie, Roane, Wayne, Wirt and Wood.

Since the addresses frequently change with the elections of new secretaries, addresses of these sectional associations as well as a list of clubs holding direct membership in the USTA may be obtained by writing to the USTA Executive Office, 51 East 42 Street, New York, New York 10017.

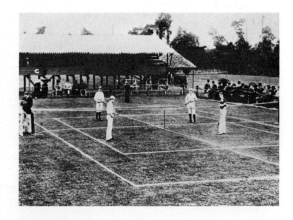 

The Nationals at Newport in the 1880s and in the 1970s at West Side Tennis Club in Forest Hills. There is some difference in the size of the crowd!

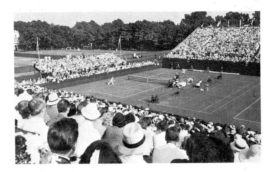

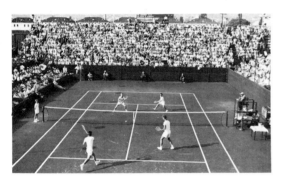 

Three of the United States' most famous tennis stadiums: *(top)* Merion Cricket Club, Ardmore, Pa.; *(bottom, left)* Los Angeles Tennis Club, Los Angeles, Calif.; *(bottom, right)* The Harold T. Clark Courts, Cleveland Heights, Ohio.

INTERNATIONAL TENNIS FEDERATION (ITF)

The International Tennis Federation, which is located at Church Road, Wimbledon, London SW19 5TF, Great Britain, is considered the governing body of world tennis. According to the rules of the ITF, its objects are as follows:

1. To uphold the Rules of Lawn Tennis as at present adopted, and to make and maintain such alterations and additions thereto from time to time as may appear necessary or desirable.
2. To print and publish in the English language from time to time as occasion may require the official and decisive text of the Rules of Lawn Tennis.
3. To print and publish from time to time as occasion may require the official and decisive text of these Rules.
4. To check, and if necessary correct, the translation of the Rules of Lawn Tennis and interpretation of these Rules into any other language prior to the same being recognized as accurate by the Federation, such translation having been first made by any nation or nations using such language and having been then submitted to the Federation for checking.
5. To recognize and uphold the regulations for the time being in force for the International Tennis Championships (Davis Cup and Federation Cup).
6. To award official lawn tennis championships recognized by the Federation.
7. To draw up a calendar of official championships, tournaments open to all categories, and major tournaments open to amateurs and professionals.
8. To promote and encourage the teaching of lawn tennis.
9. To employ the funds of the Federation in such manner as shall be deemed expedient.

The fourth Madison Square Garden in New York has hosted many of the leading professional and open indoor matches since its opening in 1968.

10. To strengthen the bonds of friendship between the existing associations and to encourage the formation of new associations.
11. To give associations by joint action a greater influence in their dealings with the governing bodies of other sports.
12. To enforce the observation of these rules in all national and international competitions.

13. To uphold the principles on which the Federation is founded and generally to take such measures as may appear expedient for advancing the interests of lawn tennis from an international point of view.
14. To preserve its independence in all matters concerning the game of lawn tennis without the intervention of any outside authority in its relations with its affiliated associations.

Addresses of affiliated associations—those with voting rights in the ITF—are as follows:

ALGERIA—Federation Algerienne de Tennis, O.C.O., B.P. 10 El-Bar, Algiers.

ARGENTINA—Asociacion Argentina de Tennis, Avenida Presidente Julio A. Roca, 546–7° Piso 1067, Buenos Aires.

AUSTRALIA—L.T.A. of Australia, Box 343, South Yarra, Victoria 3141.

AUSTRIA—Osterreichischer Tennisverband, Hainburgerstrasse 36/4 A 1030 Vienna.

BELGIUM—Federation Royale Belge de Tennis, 71–75, rue des Aduatiques, 1040 Brussels.

BOLIVIA—Federacion Boliviana de Tennis, Apartado postal 20887–6959, La Paz.

BRAZIL—Confederacao Brasileira de Tenis, Rua Anfilofio de Carvalho No. 29, Grupo 407/8—ZC-20.030-P. Centro, Rio de Janeiro.

BULGARIA—Bulgarian Lawn Tennis Federation, Boul. Tolboukhine, 18, Sofia 1000.

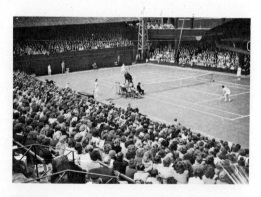

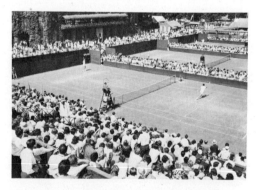

Wimbledon, headquarters of the All-England Club. *(left)* The famed Centre Court and *(right)* some of the 17 outer grass courts.

CAMEROON—Fédération Camerounaise de Lawn-Tennis, B.P. 1121, Yaoundé

CANADA—Canadian Lawn Tennis Association, National Sports and Recreation Centre, 333 River Rd., Ottawa, Ontario, KIL 8B9.

CHILE—Federacion de Lawn Tennis de Chile, Casilla 1149, Santiago.

COLOMBIA—Asociacion Colombiana de Tennis, Apartado aereo 10.917, Calle 26, Bogota 1.

CUBA—Federacion Amateur Cubana de Tennis, Calle 13 Y.C., Havana.

CZECHOSLOVAKIA—Ceskoslovenska Tenisova Asociace, Na Porici 12, Prague 1.

DENMARK—Dansk Tennis Forbund, Idraettens Hus, Brondby Stadion 20, DK 2600 Glostrup.

ECUADOR—Asociacion Ecuatoriana de Tennis, Box 6264, Centro Comercial Inaquito, Quito.

EGYPT—Egyptian L.T.A., 13 Kasr el Nil, Cairo.

FINLAND—Suomen Tennisliitto, Box 25202, Helsinki 25.

FRANCE—Federation Française de Tennis, Stade Roland Garros, 2 Ave. Gordon Bennett, 75016 Paris.

GERMAN DEMOCRATIC REPUBLIC— Deutscher Tennis-Verband der DDR, Storkower Strasse, 118, 1055, Berlin.

GERMAN FEDERAL REPUBLIC—Deutscher Tennis Bund, Zeiss-Strasser 13, 3000 Hannover 81.

GREAT BRITAIN—The Lawn Tennis Association, Barons Court, West Kensington, London, W 14 9EG.

GREECE—Federation Hellenique de Lawn Tennis, 8 rue Omirou (133), Athens.

HUNGARY—Magyar Tenisz Szovetseg, Rosenberg Hold utca 1, 1054 Budapest.

INDIA—All India L.T.A., 3 Alipore Ave., Calcutta 27.

INDONESIA—Indonesian Lawn Tennis Association, P.O. Box 303, Jakarta.

IRAN—Iranian Tennis Federation, Sports Federations Joint Bureau, P.O. Box 11-1642, Teheran.

IRAQ—Iraqi Tennis Federation, Box 22, Baghdad.

IRELAND—Irish L.T.A., 15 Cilleanna, Raheny, Dublin 5.

ISRAEL—Israel Tennis Federation, P.O. Box 20073, Tel Aviv.

ITALY—Federazione Italiana Tennis, Viale Tiziano 70, 00100 Rome.

JAMAICA—Jamaica L.T.A., 2A Piccadilly Road, P.O. Box 175, Kingston 5.

JAPAN—Japan Lawn Tennis Association, 1-1-1 Jinnan, Shibuya-ku, Tokyo 150.

KENYA—Kenya L.T.A., P.O. Box 43184, Nairobi.

KOREA—Korean L.T.A., Room 706, Sports Building, 19 Makyo-Dong, Chungku, Seoul.

LEBANON—Federation Libanaise de Lawn Tennis, P.O. Box 113–5591, Hamra, Beirut.

LIBYA—General Libyan Arab Lawn Tennis Federation, 154 September St., P.O. Box 879, Tripoli.

LUXEMBOURG—Federation Luxembourgeoise de Tennis, C.P. 2659, Luxembourg 1.

MALAYSIA—L.T.A. of Malaysia, No. 11, Jalan, 6/18, Petaling Jaya, Selangor.

MEXICO—Federacion Mexicana de Tenis A.C., Durango No. 225–301, Mexico 7, D.F.

MONACO—Federation Monegasque de Lawn Tennis, 46 rue Grimaldi, Monaco.

MOROCCO—Federation Royale Marocaine de Lawn-Tennis, Maison des Sports, Parc de la Ligue Arabe, Casablanca.

NETHERLANDS—Koninklijke Nederlandsche Lawn Tennis Bond, Box 107, 1200 AC Hilversum.

NEW ZEALAND—New Zealand L.T.A., G.P.O. Box 1645, Wellington, C.I.

NIGERIA—Nigeria L.T.A., P.O. Box 145, Lagos.

NORWAY—Norges Tennisforbund, Hauger Skolevei 1, 1351 Rud.

PAKISTAN—All Pakistan L.T.A., 263 Shabbir Sharif Rd., Rawalpindi Cantt, Punjab.

PERU—Federacion Peruana de Lawn Tennis, Casilla 2243, Lima.

PHILIPPINES—Philippine Lawn Tennis Association, Box 4143, Manila.

POLAND—Polski Zwiazek Tenisowy, ul., Marszalkowska, 2, IIIrd floor, 00–581 Warsaw.

PORTUGAL—Federacao Portuguesa de Tennis, Rua do Arco do Cego, 90–6° Esq., Lisbon 1.

RUMANIA—Federatia Romana de Tenis, Vasile Conta 16, Bucharest.

SOUTH AFRICA—The South African Tennis Union, Box 2211, Johannesburg 2000.

SPAIN—Real Federacion Española de Tenis, Avda. Generalisimo Franco 618 3D, Barcelona (15).

SRI LANKA—Sri Lanka L.T.A., 45 Sir Marcus Fernando Mawatha, Colombo 7.

SUDAN—Sudan Lawn Tennis Association, P.O. Box 1553, Khartoum.

SWEDEN—Svenska Tennisforbundet, Lidingovagen 75, S 115 37 Stockholm.

SWITZERLAND—Association Suisse de Tennis, House of Sports, C.P. 3000 Berne.

TAIWAN—Republic of China Tennis Association, 6th floor, Tai Tze Building, 20 Pa-Teh Road, 3rd Section, Taipei (105) Taiwan.

THAILAND—The Lawn Tennis Association of Thailand, 125/1 Tiwanon Road, Soi Romchit Petkrai, Nontaburi.

TRINIDAD and TOBAGO—L.T.A. of Trinidad and Tobago, P.O. Box 601, Port-of-Spain, Trinidad, W.I.

TUNIS—Federation Tunisienne de Lawn Tennis, 65 Avenue de la Liberté, Tunis.

TURKEY—Turkiye Tenis Federasyonu, Ulus Is Hani, Ankara.

U.S.A.—United States T.A., 51 East 42 Street (Suite 1001), New York, N.Y. 10017.

U.S.S.R.—Lawn Tennis Federation of the U.S.S.R., Skatertnyi pereulok 4, Moscow 69.

URUGUAY—Associacion Uruguaya de Lawn Tennis, Calle Pablo de Maria 1063 Montevideo.

VENEZUELA—Federacion Venezolana de Tennis, Altamira Tennis Club, Chacao, Edo. Miranda, Caracas.

VIET-NAM—Federation de Lawn Tennis du Viet-Nam, 135 Hai Ba Trung St., Saigon.

YUGOSLAVIA—Tenis Savez Yugoslavije, Terazije 35, Belgrade.

Addresses of associate members—those without voting rights in ITF—are as follows:

AFGHANISTAN—Afghanistan L.T.A., c/o National Olympic Committee, National Stadium, Kabul.

BAHAMAS—Bahamas Lawn Tennis Association, P.O. Box N–8333, Nassau.

BAHRAIN—Bahrain Lawn Tennis, Table Tennis and Squash Federation, P.O. Box 5074, Bahrain.

BANGLADESH—Bangladesh L.T.A., Officer's Club, 26 Bailey Road, Dacca.

BARBADOS—Barbados L.T.A., P.O. Box 615C, Bridgetown.

BERMUDA—Bermuda L.T.A., P.O. Box 341, Hamilton 5.

BURMA—Burma Tennis Federation, Aungsan Stadium, Rangoon.

CONGO—Federation Congolaise de Lawn-Tennis, B.P. 2092, Brazzaville.

CYPRUS—Cyprus L.T.A., Egypt Ave., Nicosia.

DAHOMEY—Federation Dahomeene de Lawn-Tennis, Ecole Urbaine de Foun-Foun, Porto-Novy, Dahomey.

DOMINICAN REPUBLIC—Federacion Dominicana de Tennis, Santo Domingo Tennis Club, Apartado 330, Santo Domingo.

GHANA—Ghana L.T.A., Sports Council of Ghana, P.O. Box 1272, Accra.

GUATEMALA—Federacion Nacionale de Tenis, Apartado Postal 371, Ciudad de Guatemala.

GUYANA—Guana L.T.A., P.O. Box 88, Georgetown.

HAITI—Federation Haitienne De Tennis, P.O. Box 1728, 1377 Rue Carlstroem, Port-au-Prince.

HONG KONG—Hong Kong L.T.A., Room 911, Queen Elizabeth Stadium, Oi Kwan Road, Hong Kong.

KHMER REPUBLIC (Cambodia)—Federation Cambodgienne de Tennis, 98, Vithei Dekcho Damdin, Phnom-Penh.

KOREA (North)—L.T.A. of the Democratic People's Republic of Korea, Munsin-Dong 2, Dongdewon District, Pyongyang.

KUWAIT—Kuwait Tennis Association, Ahmad Al-Mehri Building, Fahad Al-Salem Street, P.O. Box 20496, Kuwait.

LIBERIA—Liberia Tennis Association, National Sports & Athletic Commission, P.O. Box 502, Broad Street, Monrovia.

MALAWI—Lawn Tennis Association of Malawi, P.O. Box 1417, Blantyre.

MAURITIUS—Mauritius L.T.A., Rue Dr. Ferriere, Port-Louis.

NEPAL—All Nepal Lawn Tennis Association, c/o National Sports Council, Bagh Durbar, Kathmandu.

NETHERLANDS ANTILLES—Nederlands Antilliaanse Tennis Bond, P.O. Box 1941, Willemstad, Curacao.

PARAGUAY—Associacion Paraguaya de Lawn Tennis, Casilla Correo 26, Asuncion.

PUERTO RICO—Puerto Rico Tennis Association, Box 40456–Minillas Station, Santurce, Puerto Rico 00940.

SAN MARINO—Federazione Sammarinese Tennis, 47031 Republic of San Marino.

SAUDI ARABIA—Saudia Arabian Tennis Federation, P.O. Box 4674, Riyadh.

SENEGAL—Federation Senegalaise de Lawn-Tennis, B.P. 510, Dakar.

SINGAPORE—Singapore Lawn Tennis Association, Sports House (Room 23), Rutland Road, Singapore 0821.

SOMALIA—Somalia Amateur Tennis Association, P.O. Box 523, Mogadiscio.

SURINAM—Surinaamse Tennis Bond, P.O. Box 2632, Paramaribo.

SYRIA—Syrian Tennis Federation, P.O. Box 421, Damascus.

TANZANIA—Tanganyika Lawn Tennis Association, P.O. Box 965, Dar es Salaam.

TOGO—Federation Togolaise de Lawn-Tennis, B.P. 2596 Lome.

UGANDA—Uganda L.T.A., P.O. Box 2107, Kampala.

ZAIRE—Federation de Tennis du Zaire, B.P. 2596, Kinshasa.

ZIMBABWE—Tennis Association of Zimbabwe, 14 St. Dominic Road, P.O. Belvedere, Salisbury.

Rules of Tennis and Cases and Decisions

Explanatory Note

The appended Code of Rules and Cases and Decisions is the Official Code of the International Tennis Federation, of which the United States Tennis Association is a member.

Italicized EXPLANATIONS, EXAMPLES, NOTES and COMMENTS have been prepared by the USTA Rules Interpretations Committee to amplify and facilitate interpretation of the formal code.

SPECIAL NOTE: In 1978, 1979 and 1980 the ITF has made changes in several rules and added some new Cases and Decisions. Appearing for the first time in this year's printing are, of especial note: A new Case 1 of Rule 17 and, related to it, a new Case 1 under Rule 30. Also, Rule 32 has been rewritten. All changes for these three years are shown in bold-face type.

The Singles Game

RULE 1

Dimensions and Equipment

The court shall be a rectangle 78 feet (23.77m) long and 27 feet (8.23m) wide.

It shall be divided across the middle by a net suspended from a cord or metal cable of a maximum diameter of one-third of an inch (0.8cm), the ends of which shall be attached to, or pass over, the tops of two posts, **which shall be not more than 6 inches (15cm) square or 6 inches (15cm) in diameter. The centers of the posts shall be 3 feet (0.91m) outside the court on each side and the height of the posts shall be such that the top of the cord or metal cable shall be 3 feet 6 inches (1.07m) above the ground.**

When a combined doubles (see Rule 35) and singles court with a doubles net is used for singles, the net must be supported to a height of 3 feet 6 inches (1.07cm) by means of two posts, called "singles sticks" which shall be not more than 3 inches (7.5cm) square or 3 inches (7.5cm) in diameter. The centers of the singles sticks shall be 3 feet (0.91m) outside the singles court on each side.

The net shall be extended fully so that it fills completely the space between the two posts and shall be of sufficiently small mesh to prevent the ball's passing through. The height of the net shall be 3 feet (0.914m) at the center, where it shall be held down taut by a strap not more than 2 inches (5cm) wide and completely white in color. There shall be a band covering the cord or metal cable and the top of the net of not less than 2 inches (5cm) nor more than 2½ inches (6.3cm) in depth on each side and completely white in color.

There shall be no advertisement on the net, strap, band or singles sticks.

The lines bounding the ends and sides of the Court shall respectively be called the Baselines and the Sidelines. On each side of the net, at a distance of 21 feet (6.40m) from it and parallel with it, shall be drawn the Service lines. The space on each side of the net between the service line and the sidelines shall be divided into two equal parts, called the service courts, by the center service line, which must be 2 inches (5cm) in width, drawn half-way between, and parallel with, the sidelines. Each baseline shall be bisected by an imaginary continuation of the center service line to a line 4 inches (10cm) in length and 2 inches (5cm) in width called the center mark, drawn inside the Court at right angles to and in contact with such baselines. All other lines shall be not less than 1 inch (2.5cm) nor more than 2 inches (5cm) in width, except the baseline, which may be 4 inches (10cm) in width, and all measurements shall be made to the outside of the lines.

If banners are placed at the back of the court they may not contain white, yellow or any other light color.

Note — In the case of the International Tennis Championship (Davis Cup) or other Official Championships of the International Federation, there shall be a space behind each baseline of not less than 21 feet (6.4m), and at the sides of not less than 12 feet (3.66m).

It is important to have a stick 3 feet, 6 inches long, with a notch cut in at the 3-foot mark for the purpose of measuring the height of the net at the posts and in the center. These measurements always should be made before starting to play a match.

RULE 2

Permanent Fixtures

The permanent fixtures of the Court shall include not only the net, posts, cord or metal cable, strap and band, but also, where there are any such, the back and side stops, the stands, fixed or movable seats and chairs around the Court, and their occupants, all other fixtures around and above the Court, and the Chair Umpire, Net Umpire, Line Umpires and Ball Boys when in their respective places.

Diagram and Dimensions of Tennis Court

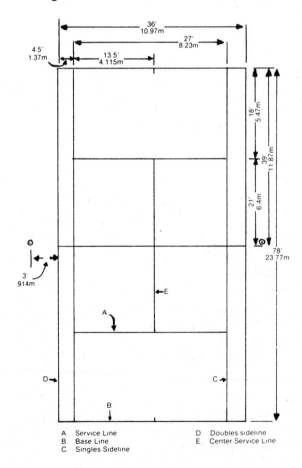

A. Service Line
B. Base Line
C. Singles Sideline
D. Doubles sideline
E. Center Service Line

RULE 3

Ball — Size, Weight and Bound
   The ball shall have a uniform outer surface and shall be white or yellow in color. If there are any seams they shall be stitchless. The ball shall be more than two and a half inches (6.35cm) and less than two and five-eighths inches (6.67cm) in diameter, and more than two ounces (56.7 grams) and less than two and one-sixteenth ounces (58.5 grams) in weight. The ball shall have a bound of more than 53 inches (135cm) and less than 58 inches (147cm) when dropped 100 inches (254cm) upon a concrete base. The ball shall have a forward deformation of more than .220 of an inch (.56cm) and less than .290 of an inch (.74cm) and a return deformation of more than .350 of an inch (.89cm) and less than .425 of an inch (1.08cm) at 18 lbs. (8.165 kg) load. The two deformation figures shall be the averages of three individual readings along three axes of the ball and no two individual readings shall differ by more than .030 of an inch (.08cm) in each case.
   Regulations for conducting tests for bound, size and deformation of balls may be found on **page 515** of the 1979 USTA Yearbook or obtained from USTA in New York.

   "How often may the player have new balls?"
   The ball-change pattern is specified by the Referee before the match is started. According to Tournament Regulations the Chair Umpire may call for a ball change at other than the prescribed time when in his opinion abnormal conditions warrant so doing. In a non-officiated match the players should agree beforehand on this matter.

RULE 4

The Racket
   The racket shall consist of a frame and a stringing. The frame may be of any material, weight, size or shape.
   The strings must be alternately interlaced or bonded where they cross, and each string must be connected to the frame. If there are attachments, they must be used only to prevent wear and tear and must not alter the flight of the ball. The density in the center must be at least equal to the average density of the stringing. The stringing must be made so that the moves between the strings will not exceed that which is possible, for instance, with 18 mains and 18 crosses uniformly spaced and interlaced in a stringing area of 75 square inches.
   Note — The spirit of this rule is to prevent undue spin on the ball that would result in a change in the character of the game.

RULE 5

Server and Receiver
   The Players shall stand on opposite sides of the net; the player who first delivers the ball shall be called the Server, and the other the Receiver.
   Case 1. Does a player, attempting a stroke, lose the point if he crosses an imaginary line in the extension of the net, (a) before striking the ball (b) after striking the ball?
   Decision. He does not lose the point in either case by crossing the imaginary line provided he does not enter the lines bounding his opponent's court. (Rule 20 (e.)) In regard to hindrance, his opponent may ask for the decision of the umpire under Rules 21 and 25.
   Case 2. The Server claims that the Receiver must stand within the lines bounding his court. Is this necessary?
   Decision. No. The Receiver may stand wherever he pleases on his own side of the net.

RULE 6

Choice of Ends and Service
   The choice of ends and the right to be Server or Receiver in the first game shall be decided by toss. The player winning the toss may choose, or require his opponent to choose:
   (a)   The right to be Server or Receiver, in which case the other player shall choose the end; or
   (b)   The end, in which case the other player shall choose the right to be Server or Receiver.
   Note — *These choices should be made promptly, and are irrevocable.*

RULE 7

Delivery of Service
   The service shall be delivered in the following manner. Immediately before commencing to serve, the Server shall stand with both feet at rest behind (i.e. farther from the net than) the base-line, and within the imaginary continuations of the center-mark and side-line. The Server shall then project the ball by hand into the air in any direction and before it hits the ground strike it with his racket, and the delivery shall be deemed to have been completed at

the moment of the impact of the racket and the ball. A player with the use of only one arm may utilize his racket for the projection.

Case 1. May the Server in a singles game take his stand behind the portion of the base-line between the sidelines of the singles court and the doubles court?

Decision. No.

Case 2. If a player, when serving, throws up two or more balls instead of one, does he lose that service?

Decision. No. A let should be called, but if the umpire regards the action as deliberate he may take action under Rule 21.

Case 3. May a player serve underhand?

Decision. Yes. There is no restriction regarding the kind of service which may be used; that is, the player may use an underhand or overhand service at his discretion.

RULE 8

Foot Fault

The Server shall throughout the delivery of the service:

(a) Not change his position by walking or running.

(b) Not touch, with either foot, any area other than that behind the baseline within the imaginary extensions of the center-mark and sideline.

EXPLANATION: The service begins when the Server takes a ready position and ends when his racket makes contact with the ball, or when he misses the ball in attempting to serve it.

Note: The following interpretation of Rule 8 was approved by the International Federation on 9th July, 1958:

(a) The Server shall not, by slight movements of the feet which do not materially affect the location originally taken up by him, be deemed "to change his position by walking or running."

(b) The word "foot" means the extremity of the leg below the ankle.

COMMENT: This rule covers the most decisive stroke in the game, and there is no justification for its not being obeyed by players and enforced by officials. No tournament official has the right to request or attempt to instruct any umpires to disregard violations of it. It is the prerogative of the Receiver, or his partner, to call a foot fault or faults, but only after all efforts (appeal to the server, requests for monitoring help, etc.) have failed, and the foot faulting is so flagrant as to be clearly perceptible from the Receiver's side.

RULE 9

From Alternate Courts

(a) In delivering the service, the Server shall stand alternately behind the right and left Courts, beginning from the right in every game. If service from a wrong half of the Court occurs and is undetected, all play resulting from such wrong service or services shall stand, but the inaccuracy of the station shall be corrected immediately it is discovered.

(b) The ball served shall pass over the net and hit the ground within the Service Court which is diagonally opposite, or upon any line bounding such Court, before the Receiver returns it.

COMMENT: The Receiver is not allowed to volley a served ball, i.e., he must allow it to strike in his court first. (See Rule 18(a)).

RULE 10

Faults

The Service is a fault:

(a) If the Server commits any breach of Rules 7, 8 or 9-b;

(b) If he misses the ball in attempting to strike it;

(c) If the ball served touches a permanent fixture (other than the net, strap or band) before it hits the ground.

Case 1. After throwing a ball up preparatory to serving, the Server decides not to strike at it and catches it instead. Is it a fault?

Decision. No.

Case 2. In serving in a singles game played on a doubles court with doubles and singles net posts, the ball hits a singles stick and then hits the ground within the lines of the correct service court. Is this a fault or a let?

Decision. In serving it is a fault, because the singles stick, the doubles post, and that portion of the net, strap or band between them are permanent fixtures. (Rules 2 and 10, and note to Rule 24).

EXPLANATION: The significant point governing Case 2 is that the part of the net and band "outside" the singles sticks is not part of the net over which this singles match is being played. Thus such a serve is a fault under the provisions of Article (c) above . . . By the same token, this would be a fault also if it were a singles game played with permanent posts in the singles position. (See Case 1 under Rule 24 for difference between "service" and "good return" with respect to a ball's hitting a net post.)

NOTE: In matches played without umpires it is customary for the Receiver to determine whether the service is good or a fault. Indeed each player makes the calls for all balls hit to his side of the net. (In doubles, the Receiver's partner makes the calls with respect to the service line.)

RULE 11

Service After a Fault

After a fault (if it be the first fault) the Server shall serve again from behind the same half of the Court from which he served that fault, unless the service was from the wrong half, when, in accordance with Rule 9, the Server shall be entitled to one Service only from behind the other half. A fault may not be claimed after the next service has been delivered.

Case 1. A player serves from a wrong court. He loses the point and then claims it was a fault because of his wrong station.

Decision. The point stands as played and the next service should be from the correct station according to the score.

Case 2. The point score being 15 all, the Server, by mistake, serves from the left-hand court. He wins the point. He then serves again from the right-hand court, delivering a fault. The mistake in station is then discovered. Is he entitled to the previous point? From which court should he next serve?

Decision. The previous point stands. The next service should be from the left-hand court, the score being 30/15, and the Server has served one fault.

RULE 12

Receiver Must Be Ready

The Server shall not serve until the Receiver is ready. If the latter attempts to return the service, he shall be deemed ready. If, however, the Receiver signifies that he is not ready, he may not claim a fault because the ball does not hit the ground within the limits for the service.

Note: The Server must wait until the Receiver is ready for the second service as well as the first, and if the Receiver claims to be not ready and does not make any effort to return a service, the Server may not claim the point, even though the service was good.

RULE 13

A Let

In all cases where a let has to be called under the rules, or to provide for an interruption to play, it shall have the following interpretations:

Note: A service that touches the net in passing yet falls into the proper court (or touches the receiver) is a let. This word is used also when, because of an interruption while the ball is in play, or for any other reason, a point is to be replayed.

(a) When called solely in respect of a service, that one service only shall be replayed.

(b) When called under any other circumstance, the point shall be replayed.

Note: A spectator's outcry (of "out," "fault" or other) is not a valid basis for replay of a point, but action should be taken to prevent a recurrence.

Case 1. A service is interrupted by some cause outside those defined in Rule 14. Should the service only be replayed?

Decision. No, the whole point must be replayed.

EXPLANATION: The phrase "in respect of a service" in (a) means a let because a served ball has touched the net before landing in the proper court, OR because the Receiver was not ready . . . Case 1 refers to a second serve, and the decision means that if the interruption occurs during delivery of the second service, the Server gets two serves.

EXAMPLE: On a second service a Linesman calls "fault" and immediately corrects it (the Receiver meanwhile having let the ball go by). The Server is entitled to two serves, on this ground: The corrected call means that the Server has put the ball into play with a good service, and once the ball is in play and a let is called, the point must be replayed . . . Note, however, that if the serve were an unmistakable ace — that is, the Umpire was sure the erroneous call had no part in the Receiver's inability to play the ball — the point should be declared for the Server.

Case 2. If a ball in a play becomes broken, should a let be called?

Decision. Yes.

Note: A ball shall be regarded as having become "broken" if, in the opinion of the Chair Umpire, it is found to have lost compression to the point of being unfit for further play, or unfit for any reason, and it is clear the defective ball was the one in play.

RULE 14

The Service Is A Let

The service is a let:

(a) If the ball served touches the net, strap or band, and is otherwise good, or, after touching the net, strap or band, touches the Receiver or anything which he wears or carries before hitting the ground.

(b) If a service or a fault is delivered when the Receiver is not ready (see Rule 12).

In case of a let, that particular service shall not count, and the Server shall serve again, but a service let does not annul a previous fault.

COMMENT: Note that a let called on second service because the Receiver was not ready does not annul the first-service fault. Second service to come.

RULE 15

When Receiver Becomes Server

At the end of the first game the Receiver shall become the server, and the Server Receiver; and so on alternately in all the subsequent games of a match. If a player serves out of turn, the player who ought to have served shall serve as soon as the mistake is discovered, but all points scored before such discovery shall be reckoned. If a game shall have been completed before such discovery, the order of service remains as altered. A fault served before such discovery shall not be reckoned.

Note: If an error in serving sequence occurs and is discovered during a TIE-BREAKER game the serving sequence should be adjusted immediately so as to bring the number of points served by each player into the fairest possible balance. All completed points shall count.

RULE 16

When Players Change Ends

The players shall change ends at the end of the first, third and every subsequent alternate game of each set, and at the end of each set unless the total number of games in such set be even, in which case the change is not made until the end of the first game of the next set.

If a mistake is made and the correct sequence is not followed the players must take up their correct station as soon as the discovery is made and follow their original sequence.

RULE 17

Ball in Play Till Point Decided

A ball is in play from the moment at which it is delivered in service. Unless a fault or let be called, it remains in play until the point is decided.

COMMENT: A point is not "decided" simply when, or because, a good shot has clearly passed a player, nor when an apparently bad shot passes over a baseline or sideline. An outgoing ball is still definitely "in play" until it actually strikes the ground, backstop or a permanent fixture, or a player. The same applies to a good ball, bounding after it has landed in the proper court. A ball that becomes imbedded in the net is out of play.

Case 1. A player fails to make a good return. No call is made and the ball remains in play. May his opponent later claim the point after the rally has ended?

Decision. No. The point may not be claimed if the players continue to play after the error has been made, provided the opponent was not hindered.

Explanation: If a shot by Player A is out but is not promptly called out, and the rally continues with A ultimately winning the point, Player B has no right to claim the point even though an official confirms that A's shot had, indeed, been out. (The "out" call, to be valid, must be made almost simultaneously with the return — by B — of the ball that was out, certainly before Player A makes, or attempts, another return.) (See also Case 1 under Rule 30.)

Case 2. A ball is played into the net; the player on the other side, thinking that the ball is coming over, strikes at it and hits the net. Who loses the point?

Decision. If the player touched the net while the ball was still in play, he loses the point.

RULE 18

Server Wins Point

The Server wins the point:

(a) If the ball served, not being a let under Rule 14, touches the Receiver or anything which he wears or carries, before it hits the ground;

(b) If the Receiver otherwise loses the point as provided by Rule 20.

RULE 19

Receiver Wins Point

The Receiver wins the point:

(a) If the Server serves two consecutive faults;

(b) If the Server otherwise loses the point as provided by Rule 20.

RULE 20

Player Loses Point

A player loses the point if:

(a) He fails, before the ball in play has hit the ground twice consecutively, to return it directly over the net (except as provided in Rule 24 (a) or (c)); or

(b) He returns the ball in play so that it hits the ground, a permanent fixture, or other object, outside any of the lines which bound his opponent's Court (except as provided in Rule 24 (a) and (c)); or

(c) He volleys the ball and fails to make a good return even when standing outside the Court; or

(d) **In playing the ball he deliberately carries or catches it on his racket or deliberately touches it with his racket more than once; or**

EXPLANATION: Only when there is a definite "second push" by the player does his shot become illegal, with consequent loss of point. It should be noted that the word "deliberately" is the key word in this Rule and that two hits occurring in the course of a single continuous stroke would not be deemed a double hit.

(e) He or his racket (in his hand or otherwise) or anything which he wears or carries touches the net, post (single stick, if they are in use), cord or metal cable, strap or band, or the ground within his opponent's Court at any time while the ball is in play (touching a pipe support running across the court at the bottom of the net is interpreted as touching the net); [See Note at Rule 23]; or

(f) He volleys the ball before it has passed the net; or

(g) The ball in play touches him or anything that he wears or carries, except his racket in his hand or hands; or

Note: *that this loss of point occurs regardless of whether the player is inside or outside the bounds of his court when the ball touches him. A player is considered to be "wearing or carrying" anything that he was wearing or carrying at the beginning of the point during which the touch occurred.*

(h) He throws his racket at and hits the ball.

EXAMPLE: Player has let racket go out of his hand clearly before racket hits ball, but the ball rebounds from his racket into proper court. This is not a good return; player loses point.

(i) He deliberately and materially changes the shape of his racket during the playing of a point.

Case 1. In delivering a first service which falls outside the proper court, the Server's racket slips out of his hand and flies into the net. Does he lose the point?

Decision. If his racket touches the net while the ball is in play, the Server loses the point (Rule 20 (e)).

Case 2. In serving, the racket flies from the Server's hand and touches the net before the ball has touched the ground. Is this a fault, or does the player lose the point?

Decision. The Server loses the point because his racket touched the net while the ball was in play. (Rule 20 (e)).

Case 3. A and B are playing against C and D. A is serving to D. C touches the net before the ball touches the ground. A fault is then called because the service falls outside the service court. Do C and D lose the point?

Decision. The call "fault" is an erroneous one. C and D have already lost the point before "fault" could be called, because C touched the net while the ball was in play. (Rule 20 (e)).

Case 4. May a player jump over the net into his opponent's court while the ball is in play and not suffer penalty?

Decision. No; he loses the point. (Rule 20 (e)).

Case 5. A cuts the ball just over the net, and it returns to A's side. B, unable to reach the ball, throws his racket and hits the ball. Both racket and ball fall over the net on A's court. A returns the ball outside of B's court. Does B win or lose the point?

Decision. B loses the point. (Rule 20 (e) and (h)).

Case 6. A player standing outside the service court is struck by the service ball before it has touched the ground. Does he win or lose the point?

Decision. The player struck loses the point (Rule 20 (g), except as provided under Rule 14 (a)).

EXPLANATION: The exception referred to is that of a served ball that has touched the net en route into the Receiver's court; in that circumstance it is a let service, not loss of point. Such a let does not annul a previous (first service) fault; therefore if it occurs on second service, the Server has one serve coming.

Case 7. A player standing outside the court volleys the ball or catches it in his hand and claims the point because the ball was certainly going out of court.

Decision. In no circumstance can he claim the point;

(1) If he catches the ball he loses the point under Rule 20 (g).

(2) If he volleys it and makes a bad return he loses the point under Rule 20 (c).

(3) If he volleys it and makes a good return, the rally continues.

RULE 21

Player Hinders Opponent

If a player commits any act which hinders his opponent in making a stroke, then, if this is deliberate, he shall lose the point or if involuntary, the point shall be replayed.

Case 1. Is a player liable to a penalty if in making a stroke he touches his opponent?

Decision. No, unless the Umpire deems it necessary to take action under Rule 21.

Case 2. When a ball bounds back over the net, the player concerned may reach over the net in order to play the ball. What is the ruling if the player is hindered from doing this by his opponent?

Decision. In accordance with Rule 21, the Umpire may either award the point to the player hindered, or order the point to be replayed. (See also Rule 25.)

USTA Interpretation: Upon appeal by a competitor that an opponent's action in discarding a "second ball" after a rally has started constitutes a distraction (hindrance), the Umpire, if he deems the claim valid, shall require the opponent to make some other and satisfactory disposition of the ball. Failure to comply with this instruction may result in loss of point(s) or disqualification.

Case 3. Does an involuntary double hit constitute an act which hinders an opponent within Rule 21?

Decision: No.

RULE 22

Ball Falling on Line — Good

A ball falling on a line is regarded as falling in the Court bounded by that line.

COMMENT: In matches played without officials, it is customary for each player to make the calls on all balls hit to his side of the net, and if a player cannot call a ball out with surety he should regard it as good.

RULE 23

Ball Touching Permanent Fixture

If the ball in play touches a permanent fixture (other than the net, posts, cord or metal cable, strap or band) after it has hit the ground, the player who struck it wins the point; if before it hits the ground his opponent wins the point.

Case 1. A return hits the Umpire or his chair or stand. The player claims that the ball was going into court.
Decision. He loses the point.
NOTE: A ball in play that after passing the net strikes a pipe support running across the court at the base of the net is regarded the same as a ball landing on clear ground. See also Rule 20 (e).

RULE 24

Good Return

It is a good return:

(a) If the ball touches the net, post (singles stick, if they are in use), cord or metal cable, strap or band, provided that it passes over any of them and hits the ground within the Court; or

(b) If the ball, served or returned, hits the ground within the proper Court and rebounds or is blown back over the net, and the player whose turn it is to strike reaches over the net and plays the ball, provided that neither he nor any part of his clothes or racket touch the net, post (singles stick), cord or metal cable, strap or band or the ground within his opponent's Court, and that the stroke is otherwise good; or

(c) If the ball is returned outside the post or singles stick, either above or below the level of the top of the net, even though it touches the post or singles stick, provided that it hits the ground within the proper Court; or

(d) If a player's racket passes over the net after he has returned the ball, provided the ball passes the net before being played and is properly returned; or

(e) If a player succeeds in returning the ball, served or in play, which strikes a ball lying in the Court [i.e. on his court when the point started; if the ball in play strikes a ball, rolling or stationary, that has come from elsewhere after the point started, a let should be called.].

Note: If, for the sake of convenience, a doubles court is equipped with singles posts for the purpose of a singles game, then the doubles posts and those portions of the net, cord or metal cable and band outside such singles posts shall be regarded as "permanent fixtures *other than* net, post, strap or band," and therefore *not* posts or parts of the net of that singles game.

A return that passes under the net cord between the singles stick and adjacent doubles post without touching either net cord, net or doubles post and falls within the area of play is a good return. (But in doubles this would be a "through" — loss of point.)

Case 1. A ball going out of court hits a net post and falls within the lines of the opponent's court. Is the stroke good?
Decision. If a service; no, under Rule 10 (c). If other than a service; yes, under Rule 24 (a).
Case 2. Is it a good return if a player returns the ball holding his racket in both hands?
Decision. Yes.
Case 3. The service, or ball in play, strikes a ball lying in the court. Is the point won or lost thereby? (A ball that is touching a boundary line is considered to be "lying in the court".)
Decision. No. Play must continue. If it is not clear to the Umpire that the right ball is returned a let should be called.
Case 4. May a player use more than one racket at any time during play?
Decision. No: the whole implication of the rules is singular.
Case 5. Must a player's request for the removal of a ball or balls lying in the opponent's court be honored?
Decision. Yes, but not while the ball is in play.

RULE 25

Interference

In case a player is hindered in making a stroke by anything not within his control except a permanent fixture of the Court, or except as provided for in Rule 21, the point shall be replayed.

Case 1. A spectator gets into the way of a player, who fails to return the ball. Is the player entitled to a let?
Decision. Yes, if in the Umpire's opinion he was obstructed by circumstances beyond his control, but not if due to permanent fixtures of the Court or the arrangements of the ground.
Case 2. A player is interfered with as in Case 1, and the Umpire calls a let. The Server had previously served a fault. Has he the right to two services?

Decision. Yes; as the ball was in play, the point, not merely the stroke, must be replayed as the rule provides.

Case 3. Is a player entitled to a let under Rule 25 because he thought his opponent was being hindered, and consequently did not expect the ball to be returned?

Decision. No.

Case 4. Is a stroke good when a ball in play hits another ball in the air?

Decision. A let should be called unless the other ball is in the air by the act of one of the players, in which case the Umpire will decide under Rule 21.

Case 5. If an Umpire or other judge erroneously calls "fault" or "out" and then corrects himself, which of the calls shall prevail?

Decision. A let must be called, unless, in the opinion of the Umpire, neither player is hindered in his game, in which case the corrected call shall prevail.

Case 6. If the first ball served — a fault — rebounds, interfering with the Receiver at the time of the second service, is the Receiver entitled to a let?

Decision. Yes. But if he had an opportunity to remove the ball from the court and negligently failed to do so, he may not claim a let.

Case 7. Is it a good stroke if the ball touches a stationary or moving object on the court?

Decision. It is a good stroke unless the stationary object came into court after the ball was put into play in which case a "let" must be called. If the ball in play strikes an object moving along or above the surface of the court a "let" must be called.

Case 8. What is the ruling if the first service is a fault, the second service correct, and it becomes necessary to call a let under the provisions of Rule 25 or if the Umpire is unable to decide the point?

Decision. The fault shall be annulled and the whole point replayed.

COMMENT: See Rule 13 and Explanation thereto.

RULE 26

The Game

If a player wins his first point, the score is called *15* for that player; on winning his second point, the score is called *30* for that player; on winning his third point, the score is called *40* for that player, and the fourth point won by a player is scored *game* for that player except as below:

If both players have won three points, the score is called *deuce*; and the next point won by a player is called *advantage for that player*. If the same player wins the next point, he wins the game; if the other player wins the next point the score is again called *deuce;* and so on until a player wins the two points immediately following the score at deuce, when the game is scored for that player.

COMMENT: In matches played without an umpire the Server should announce, in a voice audible to his opponent and spectators, the set score at the beginning of each game, and (audible at least to his opponent) point scores as the game goes on. Misunderstandings will be averted if this practice is followed.

RULE 27

The Set

A player (or players) who first wins six games wins a set; except that he must win by a margin of two games over his opponent and where necessary a set shall be extended until this margin be achieved. NOTE: See The Tiebreaker System at the back of this book.

RULE 28

Maximum Number of Sets

The maximum number of sets in a match shall be 5, or, where women take part, 3.

RULE 29

Rules Apply to Both Sexes

Except where otherwise stated, every reference in these Rules to the masculine includes the feminine gender.

RULE 30

Decisions of Umpire and Referee

In matches where a Chair Umpire is appointed his decision shall be final; but where a Referee is appointed an appeal shall lie to him from the decision of a Chair Umpire on a question of law, and in all such cases the decision of the Referee shall be final.

In matches where assistants to the Chair Umpire are appointed (Line Umpires, Net Umpire) their decisions shall be final on questions of fact, **except that if, in the opinion of the Chair Umpire, a clear mistake has been made, he shall have the right to change the decision of an assistant or order a let to be played.**

When such an assistant is unable to give a decision he shall indicate this immediately to the Chair Umpire who shall give a decision. When the Chair is unable to give a decision on a question of fact he shall order a let to be played.

In Davis Cup or other team matches where a Referee is on court, any decision can be changed by the Referee, who may also instruct the Chair Umpire to order a let to be played.

The Referee, in his discretion, may at any time postpone a match on account of darkness or the condition of the ground or the weather. In any case of postponement the previous score and previous occupancy of courts shall hold good, unless the Referee and the players unanimously agree otherwise.

Case 1. May an Umpire overrule a Linesman at the end of a rally if, in his opinion, a clear mistake has been made during the course of the rally?

Decision: No, unless he does so promptly after the mistake has occurred, or if, in his opinion, the opponent was hindered.

NOTE: For definition of "promptly" see Case 1 under Rule 17.

RULE 31

Play shall be continuous from the first service till the match is concluded:

(a) Notwithstanding the above, after the third set, or when women take part the second set, either player is entitled to a rest, which shall not exceed 10 minutes, or, in countries situated between Latitude 15 degrees north and Latitude 15 degrees south, 45 minutes, and furthermore when necessitated by circumstances not within the control of the players the Chair Umpire may suspend play for such a period as he may consider necessary.

If play is suspended and not resumed until a later day the rest may be taken only after the third set (or when women take part the second set) of play on such later day, completion of an unfinished set being counted as one set.

If play is suspended and not resumed until 10 minutes have elapsed in the same day, the rest may be taken only after three consecutive sets have been played without interruption (or when women take part two sets), completion of an unfinished set being counted as one set.

Any nation is at liberty to modify this provision or omit it from its regulations governing tournaments, matches or competitions held in its own country, other than the International Tennis Championships (Davis Cup and Federation Cup).

(b) Play shall never be suspended, delayed or interfered with for the purpose of enabling a player to recover his strength or his breath.

(c) **A maximum of 30 seconds shall elapse from the end of one point to the time the ball is served for the next point, except that when changing ends a maximum of one minute 30 seconds shall elapse from the last point of one game to the time when the ball is served for the first point of the next game.**

These provisions shall be strictly construed. The Chair Umpire shall be the sole judge of any suspension, delay or interference and after giving due warning he may disqualify the offender.

Note: A tournament committee has discretion to decide the time allowed for a warmup period prior to a match. It is recommended that this not exceed five minutes.

USTA Rules Regarding Rest Periods in Age-Limited Categories:

Regular MEN's and WOMEN's, and MEN's 21 and WOMEN's 21 — Paragraph (a) of Rule 31 applies, except that a tournament using tie-breakers may eliminate rest periods provided advance notice is given.

BOYS' 18 — All matches in this division shall be best of three sets with NO REST PERIOD, except that in interscholastic, state, sectional and national championships the FINAL ROUND may be best-of-five. If such a final requires more than three sets to decide it, a rest of 10 minutes after the third set is mandatory. Special Note: In severe temperature-humidity conditions a Referee may rule that a 10-minute rest may be taken in a Boys' 18 best-of-three. However, to be valid this must be done before the match is started, and as a matter of the Referee's independent judgment.

BOYS' 16, 14 and 12, and GIRLS' 18, 16, 14 and 12 — All matches in these categories shall be best of three sets. A 10-minute rest before the third set is MANDATORY in Girls' 12, 14 and 16, and BOYS' 12 and 14. The rest period is OPTIONAL in GIRLS' 18 and BOYS' 16. (Optional means at the option of any competitor).

All SENIOR divisions (35's, 40's, 45's, 50's and up), and Father-and-Son: Under conventional scoring, all matches best-of-three, with rest period optional.

When 'NO-AD' scoring is used in a tournament... A tournament committee may stipulate that there will be no rest periods, even in some age divisions where rest periods would be optional under conventional scoring. These divisions are: regular Men's (best-of-five) and Women's... Men's 21 (best-of-five) and Women's 21... Men's 35... Seniors (men 45 and over)... Father-and-Son.

N.B. Two conditions of this stipulation are: (1) Advance notice must be given on entry blanks for the event, and (2) The Referee is empowered to reinstate the normal rest periods for matches played under unusually severe temperature-humidity conditions; to be valid, such reinstatement must be announced before a given match or series of matches is started, and be a matter of the Referee's independent judgment.

COMMENT: When a player competes in an event designated as for players of a bracket whose rules as to intermissions and length of match are geared to a different physical status, the player cannot ask for allowances based on his or her age, or her sex. For example, a female competing in an intercollegiate (men's) varsity team match would not be entitled to claim a rest period in a best-of-three-sets match unless that were the condition under which the team competition was normally held.

Case 1. A player's clothing, footwear, or equipment (excluding racket) becomes out of adjustment in such a way that it is impossible or undesirable for him to play on. May play be suspended while the maladjustment is rectified?

Decision. If this occurs in circumstances **outside the control of the player, a suspension may be allowed. The Umpire shall be the judge of whether a suspension is justified and the period of the suspension.**

Case 2. If, owing to an accident, a player is unable to continue immediately, is there any limit to the time during which play may be suspended?

Decision. No allowance may be made for natural loss of physical condition. Consideration may be given by the Umpire for accidental loss of physical ability or condition.

COMMENT: Case 2 refers to an important distinction that should be made between a disability caused by an accident during the match, and disability attributable to fatigue, illness or exertion (examples: cramps, muscle pull, vertigo, strained back). Accidental loss embodies actual injury from such mishaps as collision with netpost or net, a cut from a fall, contact with chair or backstop, or being hit with a ball, racket or other object. A legitimate toilet visit is permissible and is not regarded as natural loss of physical condition.

Even in case of accident, no more than three minutes should be spent in diagnosis/prognosis, and if bandaging or medication is going to require more than that, the decision as to whether any additional time is to be allowed should be reached by the Referee after considering the recommendation of the Chair Umpire; and, of course, taking into account the need for being fair to the non-injured player. In no case should the injured player be permitted to leave the court area, nor should more than approximately 15 minutes total elapse before either play is resumed or a default declared.

Case 3. During a doubles game, may one of the partners leave the court while the remaining partner keeps the ball in play?

Decision. Yes, so long as the Umpire is satisfied that play is continuous within the meaning of the rules, and that there is no conflict with Rules 36 and 37. (See Case 1 of Rule 36).

Note: When a match is resumed following an interruption necessitated by weather conditions, it is allowable for the players to engage in a "re-warm-up" period. It may be of the same duration as the warm-up allowed at the start of the match; may be done using the balls that were in play at the time of the interruption, and the time for the next ball change shall not be affected by this.

RULE 32

Coaching

During the playing of a match in a team competition, a player may receive coaching from a team captain who is sitting on the court only when he changes ends at the end of a game, but not when he changes ends during a tie-break game.

A player may not receive coaching during the playing of any other match.

The provisions of this rule must be strictly construed. After due warning, an offending player may be disqualified.

Case 1. Should a warning be given, or the player be disqualified, if the coaching is given by signals in an unobtrusive manner?

Decision: No. Action should be taken only if play is interrupted, or if the player's opponent is distracted, or if coaching is given verbally.

Case 2. Should the Umpire or the Referee ask the coach to stop coaching?

Decision. No. It is for the player to take this action, as it is the player who will be penalized. The player may, however, ask the Umpire for his assistance.

Case 3. Can a player receive coaching during the 10-minute rest in a five-set match, or when play is interrupted and he leaves the court?

Decision: Yes. In these circumstances, when the player is not on the court, there is no restriction on coaching.

NOTE: The word "coaching" includes any advice or instruction.

USTA Interpretation: The gist of this rule is that, except in team competitions, a player MAY NOT RECEIVE (except during an authorized intermission) any coaching other than that which is done unobtrusively, by signals, and in a manner that is not distracting to the opponent. But in team competition a player MAY receive instruction, but only from a captain who is sitting courtside, and only during court changeovers or an authorized intermission.

See also Tournament Regulation 9(a) and (b).

RULE 33

Ball Change Error

In matches where balls are changed after an agreed number of games, if the balls are not changed in the correct sequence the mistake shall be corrected when the player, or pair in the case of doubles, who should have served with the new balls is next due to serve.

THE DOUBLES GAME

RULE 34

The above Rules shall apply to the Doubles Game except as below.

RULE 35

Dimensions of Court

For the Doubles Game the Court shall be 36 feet (10.97m) in width, i.e. 4½ feet (1.37m) wider on each side than the Court for the Singles Game, and those portions of the singles sidelines which lie between the two service lines shall be called the service sidelines. In other respects, the Court shall be similar to that described in Rule 1, but the portions of the singles sidelines between the baseline and the service line on each side of the net may be omitted if desired.

Case 1. In doubles the Server claims the right to stand at the corner of the court as marked by the doubles sideline. Is the foregoing correct or is it necessary that the Server stand within the limits of the center mark and the singles sideline?

Decision. The Server has the right to stand anywhere back of the baseline between the center mark extension and the doubles sideline extension.

RULE 36

Order of Service

The order of serving shall be decided at the beginning of each set as follows:

The pair who have to serve in the first game of each set shall decide which partner shall do so and the opposing pair shall decide similarly for the second game. The partner of the player who served in the first game shall serve in the third; the partner of the player who served in the second game shall serve in the fourth, and so on in the same order in all subsequent games of a set.

EXPLANATION: It is not required that the order of service, as between partners, carry over from one set to the next. Each team is allowed to decide which partner shall serve first for it, in each set. This same option applies with respect to the order of receiving service.

Case 1. In doubles, one player does not appear in time to play, and his partner claims to be allowed to play single-handed against the opposing players. May he do so?

Decision. No.

RULE 37

Order of Receiving

The order of receiving the service shall be decided at the beginning of each set as follows:

The pair who have to receive the service in the first game shall decide which partner shall receive the first service, and that partner shall continue to receive the first service in every odd game, throughout the set. The opposing pair shall likewise decide which partner shall receive the first service in the second game and that partner shall continue to receive the first service in every even game throughout that set. Partners shall receive the service alternately throughout each game.

EXPLANATION: The receiving formation of a doubles team may not be changed during a set; only at the start of a new set. Partners must receive throughout each set on the same sides of the court which they originally select when the set began. The first Server is not required to receive in the right court; he may select either side, but must hold this to the end of the set.

Case 1. Is it allowable in doubles for the Server's partner to stand in a position that obstructs the view of the Receiver?

Decision. Yes. The Server's partner may take any position on his side of the net in or out of the court that he wishes. (The same is true of the Receiver's partner).

RULE 38

Service Out of Turn

If a partner serves out of his turn, the partner who ought to have served shall serve as soon as the mistake is discovered, but all points scored, and any faults served before such discovery shall be reckoned. If a game shall have been completed before such discovery the order of service remains as altered.

RULE 39

Error in Order of Receiving

If during a game the order of receiving the service is changed by the receivers it shall remain as altered until the end of the game in which the mistake is discovered, but the partners shall resume their original order of receiving in the next game of that set in which they are receivers of the service.

RULE 40

Ball Touching Server's Partner Is Fault

The service is a fault as provided for by Rule 10, or if the ball served touches the Server's partner or anything which he wears or carries; but if the ball served touches the partner of the Receiver or anything which he wears or carries, not being a let under Rule 14 (a), before it hits the ground, the Server wins the point.

RULE 41

Ball Struck Alternately

The ball shall be struck alternately by one or other player of the opposing pairs, and if a player touches the ball in play with his racket in contravention of this Rule, his opponents win the point.

EXPLANATION: This means that, in the course of making one return, only one member of a doubles team may hit the ball. If both of them hit the ball, either simultaneously or consecutively, it is an illegal return. The partners themselves do not have to "alternate" in making returns. (Mere clashing of rackets does not make a return illegal, if it is clear that only one racket touched the ball.)

Should any point arise upon which you find it difficult to give a decision or on which you are in doubt as to the proper ruling, immediately write, giving full details, to John Stahr, U.S.T.A. Rules Interpretation Committee, 65 Briarcliff Rd., Larchmont, N.Y. 10538, and full instructions and explanations will be sent to you.

Reproduced with permission of publisher.

SCORING

Shortly after Major Wingfield received his patent for a game called "Sphairistike" in 1874, suggestions for improvement were proffered and a number were adopted. The name was changed to lawn tennis, the hourglass court was transformed into a rectangle, the net measurement was altered from 7 feet to 3 feet, and tennis enthusiasts began to play not only on lawns but on dirt, clay, cement, and even boards. The original fan-shaped racket became oval and the ball was improved by welding the seams. After the first few years changes in the rules were extremely rare, and for the most part they were concerned with the definition of a foot fault.

But suggestions never stopped pouring in for more alterations. More than twenty years ago Gardnar Mulloy proposed that the scoring be changed from "love," "15," "30," and "40" to "0," "1," "2," and "3." Cleveland's Jack March experimented with a 21-point table tennis scoring which he used in his World Pro Championships. As the game got faster, tennis players recommended that (1) only one serve be allowed, (2) the balls be softened, and (3) servers be required to stand 3 feet behind the base line. Jack Kramer, then the promoter of the pro tour, introduced the "3-bounce" rule, which restricted the server from volleying until the third return, and the pro set, in which the preliminary tour match was reduced to one long set. Then James H. Van Alen, a devotee of the short match, appeared on the scene, and has dedicated much time to the promulgation of the Van Alen Simplified Scoring System (VASSS). VASSS offered several new styles of scoring—a 31-point game, a 21-point game, and a no-ad set of otherwise regular scoring—plus a "one-serve" rule and an alternative serving requirement of

standing 3 feet behind the base line. VASSS was used in the Consolation event at the Newport Invitation and in the Newport Pro Championships. Eventually it spread to other Consolation tournaments and even to college matches. However, neither the Jack March, the Jack Kramer, nor the James Van Alen system received ILF approval, and so any matches played under these rules were not considered for ranking purposes. Nevertheless, the pro set and VASSS continued to grow in popularity; in the summer of 1970 the Eastern Grass Court Championships at Orange used pro sets in the early rounds when rain delayed play, and the 1969 U.S. Open ran a Consolation event along VASSS lines.

In 1968 the Middle States section of the USTA adopted a sudden-death rule to prevent marathon matches. When the set score reached 5-all, only one more game was played. Van Alen considered that this was unfair to the receiver and he therefore proposed a VASSS sudden-death tie-breaker of 9 points which is described later in this section.

The pros adopted a sudden-death play-off in their 1970 $10,000 Classic. Some 14,000 spectators at Madison Square Garden watched Pancho Gonzalez win a tie-breaker set against Rod Laver. The Philadelphia Open also utilized a sudden-death system which was a variation of the VASSS tie-breaker. At 6-all in games, the players alternated serves until one of them reached 7 points. If the score got to 6 points all, play continued until one of them won by 2 points. There were small confusions since serve changed with every point, and occasionally a player forgot whether he or she was to serve in the forehand or the backhand court. Still it was tremendously exciting, and players and spectators would flock into the auditorium

General Robert S. Oliver (left) of Albany, N.Y., the first president of what is now the USTA, and Dr. James Dwight of Boston, the second president, were active in directing the young Association into the standardization of playing rules. Dr. Dwight, especially, became one of the early international authorities on uniform rules for tennis and his dictums were generally considered the "law of the game."

from the lounges, locker rooms, and dining areas whenever the word was passed that a sudden-death tie-breaker was about to begin.

The sudden-death system used by Philadelphia was, unfortunately, specifically prohibited by International Lawn Tennis Federation (ILTF) rules. The Philadelphia promoters were notified by the USLTA at the end of the first day's play that the tie-breaker rule must be abandoned. The promoters, however, continued to use sudden-death, and as a consequence the ILTF fined USLTA $500.

The ILTF earlier in the summer of 1970 approved a nine-point sudden-death tie-breaker sequence for use experimentally in several major tournaments, of which the United States Open was the largest and most prestigious. In 1971 the USLTA authorized use of the 7-out-of-12 as well as the 5-out-of-9 point method as permitted options for any tournament wishing to use the tie-breaker. Today, the 7-out-of-12-point tie-breaker is the only ITF-authorized tie-break system for tournaments requiring ITF sanction. Likewise, all USTA-sanctioned tournaments must use only the 12-point tie-breaker, except in any set played under No-Ad. Further details will be found on page 208.

Conventional Scoring System

Although tennis scoring seems to have its basis more in tradition than in practical mathematics, once mastered it is a relatively simple system. There are four units of scoring: point, game, set, and match. The *point* is the smallest unit of scoring.

Scoring the Game. If a player wins his first point, his score is 15; on winning his second point, his score is 30; on winning his third point, his score is 40; on winning his fourth point he has won the game. The exception to this is when each player has scored three points (40-40); the score is then called *deuce*. The next point after deuce is called *advantage*. If the player with the advantage scores the following point, he wins the game. However, if the other player wins the following point, the score again becomes deuce. This continues until a player wins the two points immediately following a score at deuce; then the game is scored for that player. A score of zero is called *love*.

To avoid any misunderstandings it is considered good practice for the server to call the point score for confirmation at the end of every point played. In so doing, it is standard for the server to call his own score first. For example, if the server should lose the first point of the game, he would call the score, "love-15." Should he win the first point, he would call the score "15-love." When the score is even (15-15, 30-30), it is called *all* or *up*. For example, the server would call the score "15-all," "30-all." If the score is tied at 40-40, the call is "deuce." When the server has the advantage, he calls "server's advantage," or "ad in"; when the receiver has it, the call is "receiver's advantage," or "ad out."

Scoring the Set. The player who first wins six games wins a *set*. If each player won five games, however, the score is called *games all*, and the next game won is scored *advantage* game for that player. If the same player wins the next game, he wins the set. However, if his opponent wins the next game, the score is again called games all, and so on until a player wins two games more than his opponent. Set scores may range from 6-0 to any combination of numbers (6-2, 6-4, 7-5, 12-10, 17-15, etc.).

The score in games should be called by the server at the end of each game, or whenever the players change sides of the court. Players should do this at the end of the first, third, and every subsequent alternate game of each set, and at the end of each set unless the total number of games in such a set be even, in which case the change is not made until the end of the first game of the next set. The change of sides is intended to equalize such factors as sun and wind.

Scoring the Match. A match consists of the best two out of three sets, although in national tournament competition (men only) it is the best three out of five sets. While cards vary slightly in arrangement, a typical one is reproduced here. It shows that in the first game the score ran, and would have been called: "15-love, 30-love, 30-15, 40-15, 40-30, game Mr. A." In the second game it

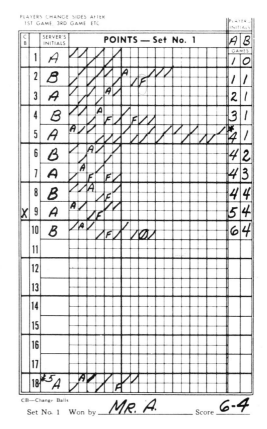

Typical tennis score card.

was: "love-15, 15-all, 15-30, 30-all, 40-30, deuce, advantage B, deuce, advantage A, deuce, advantage B, game Mr. B."

In recent years a number of members of the Tennis Umpires Association have adopted some extra touches to (1) aid themselves in keeping track of things, and (2) provide more information for the contestants, their coaches or pros, the sports writers, or anyone interested. Here is an excerpt from a typical card of this kind:

The "3:48/4:20" figures show the starting and finishing times for the set. The placing of the server's initials shows from which end of the court (from umpire's viewpoint) the serve is delivered: quite useful, especially in doubles, or in case of intermission or interruption. The letters in the point-score boxes stand for: A—an ace; P—a placement; O—an out; N—netted ball, or one that fails to reach the net; F—double fault; H—player hit by ball in play. (The large X in the left margin calls attention quickly to the fact that this game was a breakthrough service.) Further refinements could include: a minus sign after an A or a P, to designate a serve or shot that is "all but" an outright ace or placement; Pl—placement scored on a lob; Pd —placement via drop shot; Pn—placement, but thanks to a net cord!

The heavy lines at the bottom of the game box (Game 9, right) on both the server's initial side and the running-score side are a means of avoiding the embarrassment of overlooking a ball change. The lines mean you change balls *after* that game.

It should be made clear that there is nothing mandatory about the codified type of scorekeeping shown in the illustration at right. Any umpire is entitled to make his scorecard as simple or as complicated as suits his inclinations, and many will possibly prefer to make some variations on the symbols shown here. The principle, though, is sound. At least the recording of the starting and finishing times is very much to be recommended; and markings that make possible a recapitulation of—at least—the service aces and double faults often prove very useful.

The Point Penalty System

1. Use of the USTA Point Penalty System is mandatory in any sanctioned tournament at District or Sectional Championship level or above. In other tournaments its use is at the discretion of the Referee, who may, before the start of the tournament or of any round or match, order its use.

2. The purposes of the system are: (1) to deter unsportsmanlike conduct, (2) to ensure compliance with the continuous-play rule, and (3) to ensure on-time appearance for matches. The objective of the Point Penalty System is not to punish, but to secure compliance with the rules.

3. The imposition of penalties is primarily a function of the Chair Umpire, but the Referee may impose penalties in any umpired or non-umpired match on the basis of his own observations or those of his designated assistants.

4. While normally the imposition of penalties will be in accordance with the basic table, a

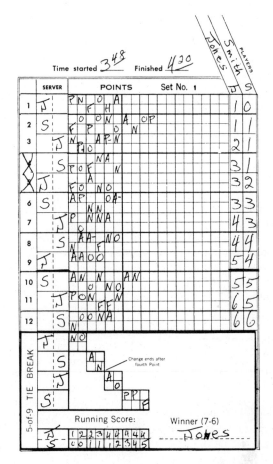

Method of scoring in nine-point tie-breaker game.

flagrantly unsportsmanlike act may result in the imposition of an immediate penalty, even a default, for a first offense. Such a default, if declared by a chair umpire or referee's assistant, is appealable to the Referee; if imposed by the Referee it is appealable to the Tournament Committee.

5. A player may not appeal to the Referee a point penalty imposed by the Chair Umpire until a third one has been imposed on that player or that team. A penalty on a member of a doubles team is considered to have been imposed on the team. Penalties are cumulative within each of the Time and Conduct categories, except the Warmup penalty.

6. All penalties under PPS are treated as though the points or games actually had been played so far as serving order, court occupancy and ball change are concerned. Exception: As the chart indicates, a player penalized for LATENESS also loses his option with respect to service or end for the first game *played;* the first ball change shall be reckoned from this first game *played.*

7. A game penalty imposed during a game means the loss of the game in progress, regardless of the point score at the time; there is no carry-over of points to the next game. A penalty imposed between games or prior to the start of a match will apply to the next point or game scheduled to be played.

8. A point penalty is scored as though the player had played and lost what would have been the next point.

9. A player who is the beneficiary of a penalty imposed upon his opponent may not, in the best interests of the game, decline to accept it any more than he could decline to accept a point for a double fault by his opponent. A player who disobeys the instructions of an official in such a case is himself liable for default.

10. In any match where point or game penalties have been imposed—especially any for unsportsmanlike conduct—the Chair Umpire has the obligation to report all of them to the Referee, who will in turn report any of these that resulted in a default or that he considers serious breaches to the Sectional or higher grievance committee.

11. Nothing in the Point Penalty System rules out a subsequent imposition of monetary fines, suspensions or other disciplinary actions by whatever governing body has jurisdiction.

The Tie-Break System

A tournament committee must announce before the start of its tournament the details regarding what, if any, tie-break systems will be employed in the tournament. The tie-break system may be put into effect in any round of the tournament at either 6-games all or 8-games all in any set or it may be used in all sets of a match except the identifiable final set when an ordinary advantage set will be played.

A tournament that has been authorized by the USTA or by a USTA Section to use VASSS No-Ad scoring may use the 9-point tie-breaker in any set played under No-Ad. It may change to the 7-of-12 tie-breaker in its later rounds. Also, No-Ad scoring, with the 9-point tiebreaker, is authorized for consolation matches in any tournament (including third-place playoffs). *Other than the foregoing exceptions, all sanctioned tournaments using tiebreakers will use only the 12-point tie-breaker.*

If a ball change is due on a tie-breaker game, it will be deferred until the second game of the next set. A tie-breaker game counts as one game in reckoning ball changes.

The score of a tie-breaker set will be written 7–6 (x) or 6–7 (x) or 9–8 (x) or 8–9 (x) with score of the winner of the *match* entered first with the result of the tie-break set shown in parentheses (as indicated by *x* above).

There is never a racket spin to determine the server in a set following a tie-breaker. Changes of ends during a tie-breaker are to be made with delay and within the 30 seconds normally allowed between points.

The 12-point Tie-Breaker. *Singles:* A, having served the first game of the set, serves the first point from the right court. B serves the next two points (points 2 and 3) left and right. A serves points 4 and 5 (left and right). B serves point 6 (left) and, after the players change ends, B also serves point 7 (right). A serves points 8 and 9 (left and right). B serves points 10 and 11 (left and

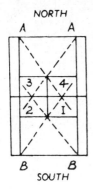

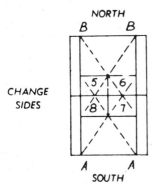

Tie-breaker diagram for the VASSS system. If tied at 4-4, A has the right to receive the 9th and final point either right or left.

first game of the set. A serves the first point (right court). C serves points 2 and 3 (left and right). B serves points 4 and 5 (left and right). D serves point 6 (left) and the teams change ends. D serves point 7 (right). A serves points 8 and 9 (left and right). C serves points 10 and 11 (left and right). B serves point 12 (left). A team that wins 7 points during these first 12 points wins the game and set. If the score has reached 6-all, the teams change ends. B then serves point 13 (right) and they continue until one team has established a 2-point margin and thus wins the game and set. As in singles, they change ends for one game to start a following set with team C-D to serve first.

The 9-point Tie-Breaker. *Singles:* With A having served the first game of the set, he serves points 1 and 2 (right court and left). Then B serves points 3 and 4 (right and left). The players then change ends. A serves points 5 and 6 (right and left). B serves points 7 and 8 (right and left). If the score reached 4 points all, B serves point 9 (right court or left at the election of A). The first player to win 5 points wins the game and set. The players stay for one game to start the next set and B is the first server.

Doubles: The same format as in singles applies. Each player serves from the same end of the court in the tie-breaker game that he served from during the set. (Note that this operates to alter the sequence of serving by the partners on the *second*-serving team.)

With A-B versus C-D, if the serving sequence during the set was A-C-B-D, the sequence in the tie-breaker becomes A-D-B-C.

VASSS (Van Alen Simplified Scoring System)
VASSS No-Ad Scoring. The No-Ad scoring procedure is simply what its name implies. Developed by James Van Alen (hence the name, which stands for Van Alen Simplified Scoring System), the VASSS game gives the win to the first player to reach 4 points. The seventh point of a game becomes a game point for each player. The receiver has the choice of advantage court or deuce court to which the service is to be delivered on the seventh point. If a No-Ad set reaches 6-games all, a tie-breaker shall be used, which is normally the 9-point tiebreaker. Note that in VASSS No-Ad, the

right) and A serves point 12 (left). A player who reaches 7 points during these first 12 points wins the game and the set.

If the score has reached 6 points all, the players change ends and continue in the same pattern until one player established a margin of 2 points, which gives him the game and the set. Note that the players change ends every 6 points. Also note that the player who serves the last point of one of these 6-point segments also serves the first point of the next segment (from the right court). For a following set, the players change ends and B serves the first game.

Doubles: This follows the same sequence, with partners preserving their serving sequence. Assume A-B versus C-D with A having served the score may be called either in conventional terms or in simple numbers, i.e., "zero, one, two, three, game," etc.

Cautionary Note. Any ITF-sponsored tournament should get special authorization from the ITF before using the No-Ad system of scoring.

Rules of VASSS "Single Point." This method permits an efficient way to handicap accurately and consists of the following:

1. It is scored as in table tennis—1-2-3-4. . . .
2. The serve changes from A to B every 5 points (5, 10, 15, . . .). This 5-point sequence is called a "hand." Serve also changes at the end of the set.
3. The first point in each "hand" (1, 6, 11, 16, . . .) is served into the right, or forehand, court.
4. Sides are changed on the odd 5-point "hand" (5, 15, and 25).
5. The official set is fixed at 31 points. But where time is at a premium, 21 points may be used.
6. If there is no umpire the server is required to *call score loud and clear* after each point.
7. The winner of the set must lead by at least 2 points (31-29). Maximum number of points 69, playing time 25 to 30 minutes.

Nine-Point VASSS Tie-Breaker Rule. In the event the score is tied in "no-ad" at 6 games all or in "single point" at 30 points all, player A who would normally serve the thirteenth game in "no-ad" or the sixty-first point in "single point" shall serve points 1, 2, 5, 6, of the 5-out-of-9-point tie-breaker. Sides shall be changed after the first 4 points. Player B in the tie-breaker game shall serve points 3 and 4, 7 and 8, and if the score shall reach 4 points all, he serves the ninth point into either the right or left court. Each player shall serve 2 points in succession, right-left, 1 and 2, 3 and 4, etc. At the end of the tie-breaker game player B in the first set (he who served points 3, 4, 7, 8, and 9 of the tie-breaker) shall commence serving in the second set. In the event the score is again tied in the second set, 6 games all, or 30 points all respectively, he shall serve points 1, 2, 5, and 6 of the tie-breaker game, etc., etc. The

advantage enjoyed by Player B who serves the ninth point, providing the score is tied at 4-4, is offset by the fact that his opponent, Player A, serves 4 out of the first 6 points, namely, 1, 2, 5, and 6, and the fact that the ninth point may never be reached.

In doubles, the same player on team A serves points 1 and 2, his partner 5 and 6. On team B one player serves points 3 and 4 and his partner points 7, 8, and 9. Each player shall serve from the side from which he served during the preceding games in the set.

In regular VASSS play, a match may be either 2 sets or 4 sets with the 9-point tie-breaker to decide the winner if sets are divided, or the regular 2 out of 3 or 3 out of 5 set match formula may be used.

Handicapping in Tennis

In early court tennis games, handicapping was by means of what was known as a "bisque." This was equivalent to a stroke (point as we say in the United States) claimed at pleasure by the recipient subject to certain limitations as to when it could not be taken. It is uncertain when this was introduced into the game but it was probably about the end of the fourteenth century.

Early lawn tennis rules also called for the using of the bisque. In 1888 a movement was made in England toward the abolition of the bisque and the substitution of a system of handicapping by means of fractions of fifteen. A committee was appointed and reported that the value of a bisque was not ascertainable and that it would be for the best interests of the game that the bisque should be discarded. The quarter system was recommended and finally adopted in 1890.

Even this was not entirely satisfactory, and finally in 1894 the method of handicapping by sixths of 15 was adopted. In the case of received odds this works out as follows:

In each series of six games,

$\frac{1}{6}$ of 15, one point received in the 2nd game of the series

$\frac{2}{6}$ of 15, one point received in the 2nd and 4th games

$\frac{3}{6}$ of 15, one point received in the 2nd, 4th, and 6th games

⁴⁄₆ of 15, one point received in the 2nd, 4th, 5th, and 6th games

⁵⁄₆ of 15, one point received in the 2nd, 3rd, 4th, 5th, and 6th games

A handicap of 15 (i.e., ⁶⁄₆ of 15) would be one point in each game of the set.

For example, a player receiving four-sixths of fifteen receives nothing in the first and third games, and fifteen in the second, fourth, fifth, and sixth games of a set. In the next and every succeeding six games of a set the odds recur in the same order. At the start of a new set, of course, you start again with a new series of six games.

With a handicap over fifteen, one point per game is added to the handicap shown above. For example, with a handicap of 15⁴⁄₆, the player would receive 15 in the first game, 30 in the second game, 15 in the third, 30 in the fourth, fifth, and sixth games, repeating this order in each series of six games until the set is ended.

When the sixth system was devised, complex handicap tables were formulated. But the tables and mathematics required to figure out the proper handicap between two players was far too complicated and unwieldy. Unfortunately, the so-called "official" system, as well as some of the peculiar rules otherwise affecting handicapping, have prevented handicap tennis tournaments from being overly popular in the United States. The inability of the average player or official to understand and apply the handicap tables is the principal drawback.

In actual practice, most clubs which have handicap tournaments deviate from the official system in that they compute the differentials by direct subtraction. For most practical purposes, there seems to be little objection to this procedure other than its lack of official sanction.

Other handicap systems can be employed, such as by either spotting a player a certain number of points per game, say one point, or the first point (15); or a certain number of games per set, if the difference in level between the players is noticeably great. Other handicaps can be used by moving the service line 3 feet farther back to give the opponent more time to return serve, or by allowing the weaker player more serves per game to help him hold service and thus stay in the match.

VASSS Handicap Rules. Handicaps are not as effective in the conventional scoring system as they are when using the VASSS single-point method described earlier in this section. On March 2, 1968, Gene Scott, a top-ranking male amateur player, beat Billie Jean King, the then No. 1 women's player in the United States, 21-17, in a tennis match at the Long Island indoor tennis tournament in Old Brookville, N.Y. Scott spotted Mrs. King 10 points in a 21-point set played under VASSS scoring rules. On the basis of this, 10 points in a 21-point game would be a suitable man-to-woman ratio, while the man-to-man handicap would be lower, ranging anywhere from 1 to 10—again depending on the quality level of the players established in earlier matches.

In the VASSS handicap system, play proceeds as if the points of the handicap had actually been played. For example:

(a) Handicap 2 points: Server commences, serving point 3 into right, or forehand, court. Service and side both change after 3 points (2 + 3 = 5).

(b) Handicap 6 points: Server commences serving point 7 into the left, or backhand, court. Service changes after 4 points (6 + 4 = 10). Sides are changed after 9 points (6 + 9 = 15).

The giver of the handicap shall have the choice of service and side in the opening set, choice of service only in subsequent sets. At the conclusion of the set players do not change sides.

To estimate handicap points to be received at 30-30 in the nine-point tie-breaker, the following should be used:

First to third points, no points handicap; fourth to seventh points, 1-point handicap; eighth to fourteenth points, 2-point handicap; fifteenth to twenty-first points, 3-point handicap; twenty-second to thirtieth points, 4-point handicap.

In the nine-point tie-breaker handicap, points shall be considered as if already played. Examples: 1-point handicap, A shall serve point 2 into left, or backhand, court; 2-point handicap, B shall serve point 3 into right, or forehand, court.

Par Tennis

Par tennis is a new game developed by Dan Sullivan, the pro and part owner of The Racquet Club in St. Petersburg, Florida. The game follows the same idea of conventional tennis except that the scoring system and playing procedures are different.

In par tennis, Sullivan starts a certain number of players on a specific number of courts, say ten playing on five courts, or eight on four courts. Each of the players plays a 10-point match, and the lowest number of errors in each game wins. Each player meets every other player in his group once. After these players finish, Sullivan puts another ten on the courts and the same procedure is followed.

To establish a total of 18 matches in a day, or the figure that will correspond to a round of 18 holes in golf, Sullivan repeats the procedure, either rotating his groups or playing the same ten in the round-robin.

At the end of a weekend, the players have played 36 matches, or if the tournament is over three or four days, they can play 72 matches. Par is considered four errors per 10-point match or 72 for an 18-match series, similar to the par 72 of many golf courses. Thus, if a player finishes all of his 18 matches with only three errors, he is deemed to have scored 3 under par, or 69 for the tournament. Naturally, the player with the lowest score wins. Sullivan has clocked his groups and figures that it takes 80 minutes for all 10 players to complete a round. The scoring system can be revised so that the highest number of points, rather than fewest errors, are used to determine a winner.

The par system is particularly effective for club tournaments or events that may entice players to participate knowing they will not be eliminated in the first round, since each player will complete an entire 18-, 36-, 54-, or 72-match series, or whatever figure is established .

COMPETITION AND TOURNAMENTS

One of the best ways to improve your game of tennis, and to gain experience, is by playing against a variety of opponents, especially those who are better at the game than you are. It is a well-known fact that if you play with people whose game is more advanced than your own, you will gradually improve, until you reach their standard, and conversely, if you consistently play with weaker players, your standard of play will deteriorate. Therefore, it is up to you to get as much play as you can against those who excel at the game, always remembering that an occasional game with weaker players will help them on and should do you no harm. It is not an easy matter for the "rabbit"—a term that was commonly used at one time to describe a beginner or weak player—to obtain practice against the more advanced exponents, because they hardly like to suggest a game themselves, and the "stars" perhaps do not think of fixing one up. Remember that all tennis champions were in the "rabbit" class at the very beginning of their careers.

Types of Tournaments

There are various types of tournaments held during the tennis year. They are generally classified as follows:

1. *Surface.* National championships are held in the United States on grass, clay, hard court, and indoors. The actual locations of these tournaments are determined by the United States Tennis Association.

2. *Categories.* Each tournament is broken down into playing categories: men's singles, women's singles, men's doubles, women's doubles, senior singles, mixed doubles, junior veterans, boys' singles, etc.

3. *Age.* National junior championships are held in the United States in age groups. The age breakdown is 18, 16, 14, and 12 and under, in singles and doubles, and for boys and girls; in addition to general men's and women's groups, there are junior veterans (35 and up) and seniors (45 and up).

4. *Section.* Each section of the United States has its own state and sectional championships. These tournaments, besides being broken down into surfaces if more than one type of surface is used in the section, are further defined by divisions (men's singles, women's singles, junior singles, etc.).

5. *Open.* These are tournaments in which amateur and professional players are allowed to compete. The concept of open tennis is not new. As early as the 1930s, promoters were discussing the blending of amateur and professional. But not until 1968 did open tennis become a reality; when it did, it surpassed even the dreams of its early proponents.

A complete listing of national USTA championships, including winners and qualifications, is given in Section 5.

USTA Amateur-Player Ruling

At its Annual Meeting February 8, 1969, the USTA amended Article III of its Constitution to create new definitions of categories for players under its jurisdiction, as follows:

Section 1: The following categories of tennis players are recognized as within the jurisdiction of the USTA:
   a. Amateurs
   b. Players
Section 2: Any tennis player is an *Amateur* who does not receive and has not received, directly or indirectly, pecuniary advantage by the playing, teaching, demonstrating or pursuit of the game, except as expressly permitted by the USTA.

An *Amateur* will not be deemed to have received pecuniary advantage by reason of: (1) Being reimbursed for reasonable expenses actually incurred by him in connection with his participation in a tournament, match or exhibition, or (2) being the recipient of a scholarship or other benefits authorized by his school (high school, college or university) which does not affect his eligibility as a tennis player for such school.
Section 3: Any tennis player who is still eligible to play in any age category under 19 years of age will be permitted to participate in a tournament, match or exhibition only if he is in good standing under amateur regulations.
Section 4: All other tennis players who accept the authority of, and who are in good standing with the USTA shall be designated as *Players.*

Section 5: Both *Amateurs* and *Players* shall play only in tournaments, matches or exhibitions which are sanctioned or approved by the USTA, and both *Amateur* and *Player* may compete in all such sanctions; provided, that *Players* may not participate in tournaments, matches or exhibitions expressly limited to *Amateurs.*

Essentially what these rules do is this: They divide USTA tennis players into two basic categories:

1. Those who play tennis for the love of the game and for its healthful recreational benefits, i.e., the *Amateur* who derives no pecuniary advantage from the game.
2. Those who play tennis to earn money therefrom, i.e., the nonamateur, designated, *Player.*

The new rules do not attempt to regulate the touring professionals who are under contract to the promoters, except to recognize that such touring professionals may play in ITF-sanctioned open tournaments.

A *Player* is eligible to play in all the events for which an amateur is eligible except for tournaments for amateurs only. A *Player:*

May be given this status only after reaching the age of 19 years.

May receive any total of living and traveling expenses.

May receive prize money without limit.

Further effects of the new rules are to permit:

The sanction by USTA of tournaments (other than ITF-approved opens) at which prize money is offered for which *Players* may compete.

The sanction of USTA tournaments for amateurs only.

Enrollment in the USTA. *Anyone* can enroll in the USTA and all players, officials, committee members, patrons, spectators, and commentators regardless of age or degree of skill can be a part of this nationwide organization through the Enrollment Program. Each receives a numbered identification card which entitles him to apply for entry in USTA-sanctioned tournaments anywhere, to have his record considered for ranking, and to be placed on the official mailing list. It is a positive requirement for participants under USTA tournament regulations; a privilege for enthusiasts. The fees are $6 (including subscription to the Official Magazine) for adult enrollees (21 years of age and over) and $2 for junior enrollees (under 21 years of age). Juniors who subscribe to the magazine pay another $2, total fee $4. Life Enrollment fee is $100, which is tax deductible. Checks for $100 should be made out to National Tennis Education Fund, and sent to 51 East 42 Street, New York, N.Y. 10017.

One half of every enrollment fee goes right back to the section in which it was collected for promotion and conduct of tennis in that area.

All tournament entry blanks should provide a line for the applicant's current enrollment number. If he has none, an application must be filled out; the appropriate fee must be paid and a receipt given prior to his first match. All cards are issued by USTA, 51 East 42 Street, New York, N.Y. 10017. Information on the enrollment program can also be obtained from this address.

USTA Championship Tournament Regulations

Each USTA Championship Committee is authorized to select from its own membership a subcommittee to pass upon the qualifications of the applicants for entry, to make the draw, and determine the seeding, in accordance with USTA Tournament Regulations and such Committee shall select the referee of the event.

In addition to meeting the requirements stated in the following regulations, every applicant for entry in a USTA Championship (or other event sanctioned by the USTA) must qualify as an amateur and meet other eligibility requirements as set forth in the Constitution, By-Laws and Standing Orders of the USTA.

Entries for all USTA Championship events shall close on a published date at least five (5) days prior to the beginning of play. The Committee in charge of each Championship shall have the power to include other players for proper reasons, prior to the making of the draw.

Entries shall be considered from players in good standing, belonging to clubs affiliated with the USTA or the recognized association of a foreign country; from players of schools and colleges who are otherwise eligible; and from such other players as are acceptable to the Committee.

In 1978, it was ruled that nonresident foreign players would no longer be eligible to compete in junior events.

Entries should be made through the Secretary of the player's club or through the properly constituted authorities of the player's school or college and, in the case of foreign entrants, through the National Association of the player's country.

All players who wish to have their entries considered for the National Championships must submit their complete tournament records from October of last year to the date of filing entry in the current year. This information should cover dates, location and scores of all matches played in sanctioned tournaments, domestic and foreign. Give singles data if entering singles; doubles data if entering doubles.

The USTA Committee in charge of each Championship shall have authority to exercise its judgment in accepting or rejecting entries. In the case of domestic entries, lack of membership in a club affiliated with the USTA shall be sufficient reason for rejection. The foregoing rules are supplemented by the following special limitations for certain Championships.

USTA Men's and Women's Singles Championships

1. Players are eligible for consideration whose entries are acceptable to the Committee by reason of unusual promise of skill in the case of young players, or the recommendation of the player's Sectional Associations.

2. Each duly accredited Sectional Association shall be entitled to have accepted the entry of either its first or second ranked player.

3. The first four United States seeded men and the first four United States seeded women players in the Singles Championships shall be entitled to receive a daily expense allowance not in excess of the amount which, under existing regulations, may be received as a per diem allowance under Standing Order IV (8) nor shall such expense be allowed seeded players who are residents of the city or its immediate environs where the Championships are held.

USTA Men's and Women's Doubles Championships

If applicants are otherwise qualified, the following entries shall be accepted:

1. Members of the team which won the current Sectional Doubles Championship. If the winners cannot compete, the runners-up may take their places. If neither the winners nor the runners-up can compete, the Sectional Association may in its discretion appoint one of the semifinalist teams to take their places, it being intended that each duly accredited Sectional Association shall be entitled to a Doubles Championship entry.

2. In the case of the Men's Doubles Championship the winning team of the two No. 1 teams in the Army, Navy, Air Force and Marine Corps Leech Cup Matches of the current year.

3. The first two United States seeded men's teams and the first two United States seeded women's teams shall be entitled to receive a daily expense allowance not in excess of the amount which, under existing regulations, may be received as a per diem allowance under Standing Order IV (8) nor shall such expense be allowed seeded players who are residents of the city or its immediate environs where the Championships are held.

USTA Mixed Doubles Championship

The USTA Mixed Doubles Championship is restricted to 48 teams.

USTA Men's 35 and 40 Championships (Singles and Doubles)

The USTA Men's 35 and 40 Championships in Singles and Doubles are open to men 35 (or 40) years of age or who become 35 (or 40) years of age during the year of competition.

USTA Husband and Wife Championship

The USTA Husband and Wife Championship is to be held annually and is restricted to approximately 32 teams.

USTA Men Seniors' Championships (Singles and Doubles)

1. The USTA Seniors' Championships in Singles and Doubles are open to men 45 years of age or who become 45 years of age during the year of competition.

  (a) The Seniors' Singles Championship is restricted to 64 players and the Seniors' Doubles Championship to approximately 32 teams.

2. The USTA Seniors' 50, 55, 60, 65, 70, 75, & 80 Championships in Singles and Doubles are open to men 50, 55, 60, 65, 70, 75 & 80 years of age or who become 50, 55, 60, 65, 70, 75, & 80 years of age respectively during the year of competition.

USTA Women's 35 Championships (Singles and Doubles)

The USTA Women's Championships in Singles and Doubles are open to women of 35 years of age or who become 35 years of age during the year of competition.

USTA Women Seniors' Championships (Singles and Doubles)

The USTA Women Seniors' Championships in Singles and Doubles are open to women of 40 years of age or who become 40 years of age during the year of competition.

USTA Women Seniors' 45, 50, 55, 60, 65 & 70 Championships (Singles and Doubles)

The USTA Women Seniors' 45, 50, 55, 60, 65 & 70 Championships in Singles and Doubles are open to women of 45, 50, 55, 60, 65 & 70 years of age or who become 45, 50, 55, 60, 65 & 70 years of age during the year of competition.

USTA Father and Son Championship

The USTA Father and Son Championship is to be held annually and is restricted to approximately 32 teams composed of father and son of blood relationship, or son adopted by order or judgment of a court of competent jurisdiction.

USTA Mother and Daughter Championship

The USTA Mother and Daughter Championship is to be held annually and is restricted to approximately 32 teams composed of mother and daughter of blood relationship, or daughter adopted by order or judgment of a court of competent jurisdiction.

USTA Indoor Championships

The USTA Indoor Championships are subject to the entry and management rules and regulations for the corresponding outdoor events.

USTA Interscholastic Championships

1. The competition shall be known as "The USTA Interscholastic Tennis Championships."
2. Such championships shall be played annually, the time and place to be determined by a standing committee of the USTA (par. 8).
3. To be eligible to compete a player must be the semifinalist in a qualifying interscholastic tournament which must be held in the United States by or under the direction of a college, university, school or USTA Sectional Association, hereinafter referred to as the "Holder."
4. Notice of intention to hold a qualifying tournament shall be filed prior to the event by the Holder with the Executive Secretary, USTA, 51 East 42nd St., New York, N.Y. 10017. Written approval of the Executive Office of the USTA must be obtained before any qualifying tournament may be scheduled.
5. The Holder shall admit to competition, under such rules and limitations as the Holder may prescribe, students certified by a responsible school official to have been in good standing at a preparatory school or high school located within the United States, or within any foreign country, during the current school year.

Entries shall not be accepted from high schools affiliated with the National Federation of State High School Athletic Associations, unless such entries have been approved by the Federation.

A semifinalist in Singles and/or Doubles in any preceding qualifying tournament held during the currently qualifying period shall not be eligible for re-entry in a succeeding qualifying tournament for the current championships.
6. The Holder shall immediately communicate the results of all matches to the Executive Secretary, USTA, and the Chairman of the Interscholastic Tennis Tournament Committee of the institution holding the championship event, and such communication shall in every case include the home address of the semifinalists in each completed competition, together with the certificates of responsible school officials as to such semifinalists, as required by par. 5 above.
7. The Holder shall be permitted to charge an entry fee to such Qualifying Tournaments to provide whatever revenue may be necessary to cover the purchase of balls and other tournament expenses. Neither the USTA nor its Sectional Associations shall be liable for financial deficits arising from the operations of a Qualifying Tournament.
8. A standing committee of the USTA shall promote and be responsible for the championship competitions. Such committee shall have power to accept entry of outstanding schoolboy players who actually had no opportunity to attend a Qualifying Tournament, and who are recommended by Sectional Associations or by individuals whose opinions should carry weight. Although a player may qualify in all respects and be eligible to enter a championship competition, the Championship Committee shall have full power in its discretion to reject any entry or limit the number of entries. The Committee shall, from its membership if practicable, appoint a Referee and an Assistant Referee for the USTA Interscholastic Championships, Singles and Doubles. The Committee shall select a date when entries will close.
9. All matches in the Championship competitions shall consist of best two of three sets in all rounds excepting the final round which may consist of best of five sets.
10. Entry to qualifying Doubles competitions shall be limited to teams nominated as such by individual schools, and members of a doubles team must be schoolmates representing the same school. Qualifiers in Doubles may be permitted at the discretion of the Committee, to play in both Singles and Doubles.
11. Points for the team score shall be awarded for each event (singles and doubles) on the following basis:

1 point for each match won. In the case of a bye or a default in the first round no point shall be awarded unless the player or double team shall win the next round match, in which case 2 points shall be awarded, one for the bye or default and one for the next round match win.
12. No school may enter more than four singles players and two doubles teams.

USTA Junior Davis Cup Sectional Team Championship

1. The event shall be known as the USTA Junior Davis Cup Sectional Team Championships.

2. This event will be held annually.

3. The competition is open to teams representing each of the Sections comprising the United States Tennis Association. Each of said sections shall be represented by one team which shall consist of male players only.

4. Membership on each Sectional Team shall be by arbitrary selection of the section and the Junior Davis Cup Chairman in each section shall select the sectional team for his own section; the president of each section shall act in case his section does not have a sectional Chairman. The method of selection for membership on the sectional team may be as each section elects, either on the basis of ranking lists, center tournaments, regional center playoffs, inter-city Junior Davis Cup matches, tournaments, elimination try-outs, round-robins, character, sportsmanship and availability, or any combination of these factors.

5. Players selected for membership on each Sectional Team must be permanent residents of their respective sections. Each team member shall not have reached his 21st birthday as of the first day of January of the year of the tournament and each player is required to possess a current annual USTA enrollment card.

6. The number of players on a Sectional Team shall be a maximum of four. (Maximum two singles players and one doubles team for scoring purposes.)

7. The referee of the tournament shall be the National Chairman of the Junior Davis Cup Committee of the USTA or the person designated as referee by him.

8. All matches shall be played under the laws and rules of lawn tennis as sanctioned and interpreted by the USTA. The tournament shall consist of both singles and doubles play. Points shall be earned in both singles and doubles as follows: Winner—5 points; Finalists—4 points; Semifinalists—3 points; Quarterfinalists—2 points. A consolation tournament for singles only shall be conducted at the same time and place as the tournament herein provided and first-round losers shall automatically be entered in the consolation round and shall play in it. Points in the consolation round shall be at one-half the value of the main tournament. The Sectional Team scoring the most points in the main tournament plus the points earned by its players in the consolation event, shall be declared the winner of the event. In case of ties, the two Sectional Teams earning the same number of points shall be declared co-holders of the place earned by their point scores.

Regulations for USTA Junior, Boys' 16, 14 & 12, Girls' 18, 16, 14 & 12 Chps., and Girls' Intersectional Team Matches

1. Age Limit Eligibility—The following are the correct USTA titles for age classifications and they should be used at all times:

Junior refers to 18 and under boys.
Girls' 18 refers to 18 and under girls.
Boys' 16 refers to 16 and under boys.
Girls' 16 refers to 16 and under girls.
Boys' 14 refers to 14 and under boys.
Girls' 14 refers to 14 and under girls.
Boys' 12 refers to 12 and under boys.
Girls' 12 refers to 12 and under girls.

Junior Championship tournaments shall be open only to players who have not reached their eighteenth birthday before October 1st in the year of competition but who have reached their sixteenth birthday before October 1st in that year. Any player winning the Boys' 16 Championships shall be eligible to compete in the Junior Championships the following year even though still eligible for the Boys' 16 Championships; however, he cannot play in both.

Boys' 16, Boys' 14, Boys' 12 and Girls' 18, Girls' 16, Girls' 14 and Girls' 12 tournaments shall be open to players in these divisions who have not reached the maximum age limit before October 1st in the year of competition.

An individual or doubles team holding a USTA Championship title in any of the age divisions may compete for a subsequent similar title without further qualification while remaining within the age limit of such age division, and winners (singles and doubles) of a lower age division in their final year of age limitation in their respective age divisions shall be eligible to play in the next higher age division the following year without further qualification for all USTA Championships played under these regulations.

2. Duration of Matches—Matches for Boys' 14, Boys' 12, Girls' 16, Girls' 14 and Girls' 12 shall be the best of three sets and there shall be

a ten-minute rest period after the second set. Matches for Boys' 16 and Girls' 18 shall be the best of three sets, but at the request of any player a rest period of ten minutes may be taken at the conclusion of the second set. Matches for Juniors shall be the best of three sets, except in the final round of a USTA Championship tournament when at the discretion of the referee the best of five sets may be required to decide the winner. When such a final round of competition requires more than three sets, there shall be a ten-minute rest period after the third set.

3. Qualifying Tournaments—Sectional, State, District, Tennis Center Tournaments and sanctioned State Jaycee (Championship) Tournaments shall be qualifying tournaments for the USTA Junior, Boys' 16, Boys' 14, Boys' 12, Girls' 18, Girls' 16, Girls' 14 and Girls' 12 Championships.

From these qualifying tournaments the USTA Sectional Associations will select players and alternates whose legal residence must be in that section to represent such section. These players must be qualified and be recommended by their respective sections. A Sectional Association may, at its discretion, waive the necessity of local qualifications for players who were ranked nationally the preceding year and who are still playing in the same age division during the current year. The Girls' 18 players selected to represent their sections in the "Girls' Intersectional Team Matches" played prior to the Girls' 18 USTA Championships shall be accepted for entry in said Girls' 18 Championships and also any girls who have played in the Girls' 16 USTA Championships and who have been recommended by the Girls' 16 USTA Championship Committee. In the event an applicant is denied the right to participate in a qualifying tournament in his or her own section, the USTA Championships Chairmen may accept such entry at their discretion.

A. Sanction for qualifying tournaments must be obtained by application to the Executive Secretary, USTA, 51 E. 42nd St., New York, N.Y. 10017, or by application to a Sectional Association where such Sectional Association compiles its own schedules.

B. Registration—Qualifying Tournament Committees shall accept as entrants only those who present a USTA Enrollment Card with their entry fee and also an "age

identification card" if the player's home Sectional Association requires such a card. Sectional Associations or District Associations may at their discretion issue "age identification cards" and charge a fee therefore. If a fee is charged the fee shall not exceed One Dollar ($1.00) per card or Fifty Cents (50¢) for duplicating issuance of card.

C. It shall be the duty of the Qualifying Tournament Committee to properly publicize the tournament and to report the results promptly to a designated Sectional official.

D. This designated Sectional official shall list those qualified or eligible players in their proper order, whenever specified for the limitation of a USTA Championship.

E. Any Junior, Boy 16, Boy 14, Boy 12, Girl 18, Girl 16, Girl 14, or Girl 12 who qualified in either singles or doubles is eligible for selection by his or her Sectional Association for either or both events in the applicable USTA Championship.

(1) Junior, Boys' 16, Boys' 14 and Boys' 12 finalists in qualifying tournaments shall be eligible for selection by their respective Sectional Associations for the USTA Championships in their respective classes.

(2) Semifinalists in Girls' 18, Girls' 16, Girls' 14 and Girls' 12 District, Sectional and State qualifying tournaments shall be eligible for selection by their respective Sectional Association for the USTA Championships for which they were able to qualify. Finalists in Tennis Center qualifying tournaments shall be eligible for selection by their respective Sectional Association for the USTA Championships of the same age group in which they have qualified.

F. Tennis Center Tournaments will be held in the cities listed herein which have been designated as Tennis Centers.

(1) Tennis Centers—(see list of Tennis Centers on pages 220–221).

(2) Entry to Tennis Center Championships shall be restricted to residents of the section wherein such Tennis Centers are located unless the Sectional Association designates other limitations within that section.

(3) A Sectional Association shall be authorized to rule that no player who has

previously qualified for the USTA Junior, Boys' 16, Boys' 14, Boys' 12, Girls' 18, Girls' 16, Girls' 14 and Girls' 12 Championships through any one of the two qualifying methods or tournaments shall be permitted to enter another qualifying Tennis Center Tournament during the same calendar year.

G. The USTA will present gold and silver medalettes to properly registered winners and runners-up of qualifying tournaments upon application in accordance with the rulings below.

(1) These tournaments must be completed after January 1st at least two weeks prior to the date of the beginning of the USTA Championships of the current year in the classification specified.

(2) These tournaments shall have had not less than eight bona fide entries in singles and not less than four bona fide teams in doubles in each classification.

(3) The Chairman of the Junior Tennis Programs Committee shall have the authority to use his discretion and judgment to the extent that he may authorize the award of tennis center medalettes to winners and runners-up in qualifying tournaments which began in time to finish prior to two weeks before the USTA Championship but which, because of weather conditions or other unusual circumstances, were not completed as originally scheduled.

(4) The Chairman of the Sectional Junior Programs Committee shall apply to the Executive Secretary of the USTA, through the Secretary of the Sectional Association, before May 1st, for the required number of medalettes for the current year.

(a) The medalettes will be sent to the Secretary of the Sectional Association who will see that they reach the committee of the qualifying tournament before the completion of the event.

(b) A certification that medalettes have been distributed in accordance with USTA regulations shall be sent in with the report of the qualifying tournament's results to the Secretary of the Sectional Association who shall then forward it to the Executive Secretary of the USTA.

4. Entries for all USTA Junior, Boys' 16, Boys' 14, Boys' 12, Girls' 18, Girls' 16, Girls' 14 and Girls' 12 Championships must be in the hands of the Championships Committee fourteen days prior to the dates scheduled for the beginning of play. Each entry must be accompanied by an entry fee of not less than Two Dollars ($2.00) nor more than Six Dollars ($6.00) for each single entry and not less than Three Dollars ($3.00) nor more than Eight Dollars ($8.00) for each doubles team entry. The fees are to be set forth on the entry blanks and the entry blanks to USTA Championships shall bear the signature of the officer of the Sectional Association who recommends the player for play in the Championship. (These entry fee rates shall not be construed as applying to or for the USTA Junior, Boys' 16, Girls' 18 or Girls' 16 Indoor Championships.)

A. Each USTA Junior Championships Committee shall accept as entrants only those players whose ages qualify them according to the age limit eligibility regulations.

B. Any Boy 16 eligible to compete in the USTA Junior and Boys' 16 Championships may compete in the Boys' 16 class only.

C. No Junior, Boy 16, Boy 14, Boy 12, Girl 18, Girl 16, Girl 14 or Girl 12 shall be permitted to enter a USTA Championship unless he or she shall have first been officially registered in the office of the Sectional (or District) Association in which the player lives and also possesses a USTA identification card.

D. Quarterfinalists in the USTA Girls' 16 Championships or players who have been recommended by the USTA Girls' 16, Girls' 14 or Girls' 12 Committee shall be eligible for the USTA Girls' 18 Championships.

5. No players shall be eligible to compete for the Singles or Doubles Championships except those qualifying under the foregoing regulations; but the Championship Committee may accept the entries of foreign players who do not qualify under these regulations and who are within the established age limits, and the Championship Committee may, at its discretion, accept the entry of any Junior, Boy 16, Boy 14, Boy 12, Girl 18, Girl 16, Girl 14 or Girl 12 whose record in its judgment warrants; provided such entrant has the endorsement of his or her Sectional Association.

A. Each Sectional Association shall name a qualified official, one who is thoroughly familiar with the playing record of the boys and juniors in his Section, who shall send to the Chairman of each of the following Championship Committees, namely, Junior and Boys' 16, and Boys' 14 and 12, a list of the qualified players whose entries are recommended by said Sectional Association.

B. Each Sectional Association shall name a qualified official, preferably a woman, one who is thoroughly familiar with the playing record of the girls in her Section, who shall send to the Chairman of each of the following Championship Committees, namely, Girls' 18, Girls' 16, and Girls' 14 and 12, a list of the qualified players whose entries are recommended by said Sectional Association.

6. These Annual USTA Championship tournaments shall be held upon courts of the type of surface selected by the respective Championship Committee with the approval of the USTA Junior Tennis Development Committee.

7. The Championships Committee of the USTA Junior and Boys' 16 Championships may require:

A. Entrants to report not later than a full day preceding start of play;

B. That entrants be requested not to play in Men's Tournament Events the week preceding the USTA Junior and Boys' 16 Championships;

C. That all members of USTA holding Junior and Boys' 16 Tournaments during the week preceding the USTA Junior and Boys' 16 Championships be requested to complete such tournaments at least two full days before the opening of the USTA Junior and Boys' 16 Championships.

8. The number of entries in the USTA Junior Championship shall be limited to one hundred twenty-eight with eight alternates and the number of entries in the USTA Boys' 16 Championship shall be limited to 128 with eight alternates, provided, however, that the Chairman of the Championships Committee may, at his discretion, from time to time, or at any time, enlarge the aforesaid quotas, the entries to be distributed equitably among the sections, as set forth in the following paragraph, subject to acceptance by the USTA Junior and Boys' 16 Championships Committee. In the event of cancellation for any cause, the alternates may be placed in the draw. In the event of no cancellations, the alternates will be permitted to play doubles.

The minimum allocation of entries to each section shall be based upon the ratio that the total number of its enrolled Juniors bear to the total number of enrolled Juniors in the entire USTA; said ratio to be multiplied by one hundred twenty to determine the minimum allocation for Juniors; and the ratio determined as aforesaid to be multiplied by 120 to determine the minimum allocation for Boys' 16 (16 & under). Enrollment as aforesaid shall be based upon the aggregate totals in each section and the cumulative totals throughout the USTA, as of December 31st in each preceding calendar year, commencing in 1961. The term "enrolled juniors" shall be construed to mean all boys and girls who will not reach or pass their nineteenth birthday during the calendar year of their enrollment. The final decision as to the number of entries, their acceptance and all other matters pertaining to these Championships, will rest within the discretion of the USTA Junior and Boys' 16 Championships Committee.

Each player will send his entry to the Championship Committee in the usual way.

9. The USTA Girls' 18 and Girls' 16 Championships shall each have a draw of ninety-six if that number of qualified entrants are received by the Championship Committee.

A. The Sectional official in charge of reporting the list of qualified players shall have the responsibility of listing and ranking said qualified players in the order in which the Sectional official believes that their records place them.

(1) Preference in listing shall be shown to players who have qualified in tournaments in the following order: Sectional, State, State Jaycees, District and Tennis Center.

(2) The complete records of all players shall be included with the list.

B. The USTA Girls' 18 Championship Committee shall accept at least six girls from each Sectional Association who are recommended by their respective Sectional Association.

C. The remainder of the draw shall be filled by qualified players from Sectional Associations already represented and by foreign entries.

D. The Sectional official may change the order of his qualified players at any time until the entry closes, and this order must be retained unless additional data is received by the Championship Committee when it may change the order.

E. Entry blanks for the USTA Girls' 18 Championship shall be sent to the Presidents of the Sectional Associations with the request that the blanks be forwarded to the Sectional official in charge for distribution to the players.

(1) The players shall fill out the blanks and return them to their Sectional Association accompanied by their entry fees.

(2) The Sectional Association shall check all entry blanks to see that the individual membership numbers are listed and that each blank has a complete and correct record.

(3) The Sectional Association shall send in the previously mentioned list of qualified players promptly and then send in the entry blanks and fees to the USTA Girls' 18 Championship Committee before the entry closes.

10. The draws for the Junior, Boys' 16, Boys' 14, Boys' 12, Girls' 18, Girls' 16, Girls' 14 and Girls' 12 Championships are to be made so as to avoid, if possible, the presence in the same quarter of more than one of the first four players representing the same Sectional Association.

Tennis Center Designations as of January 1, 1981

The following cities listed by Sectional Associations have been designated as tennis centers:

Alaska—Anchorage.
Hawaii—Honolulu.
Puerto Rico—Piedras.

EASTERN

Connecticut—Stamford.
New Jersey—Arlington, East Orange, Glen Ridge, Hackensack, Hoboken, Maplewood, Montclair, Orange, Short Hills, Westfield.
New York—Albany, Andes, Ardsley-on-Hudson, Bayside, Binghamton, Bronxville, Brooklyn, Buffalo, Elmira, Garden City, Great Neck, L.I., Great Kills, S.I., Hartsdale, Jackson Heights, L.I., Mamaroneck, New Rochelle, New York City, North Tarrytown, Rochester, Scarsdale, Syracuse, Schenectady, Tannersville, Utica, Woodmere, L.I., Yonkers.

FLORIDA

Florida—Coral Gables, Daytona Beach, Delray Beach, Ft. Lauderdale, Fort Walton Beach, Hollywood, Jacksonville, Lakeland, Miami, Miami Beach, Ocala, Orlando, Sarasota, St. Petersburg, Tampa.

INTERMOUNTAIN

Colorado—Denver, Ft. Collins, Pueblo, Colorado Springs.
Idaho—Boise.
Montana—Butte, Billings, Great Falls, Missoula.
Nevada—Las Vegas.
Utah—Lehi, Salt Lake City, Ogden.

MIDDLE ATLANTIC

D.C.—Washington.
Maryland—Baltimore, Bethesda-Chevy Chase, Cumberland, Hagerstown, Salisbury.
Virginia—Arlington County, Charlottsville, Hilton Village, Lynchburg, Norfolk, Richmond.
West Virginia—Alderson, Beckley, Bluefield, Princeton, Wheeling.

MIDDLE STATES

Delaware—Wilmington, New Castle.
New Jersey—Haddonfield, Ocean City, Woodbury, Princeton, Lawrenceville, Trenton.
Pennsylvania—Allentown, Altoona, Bethlehem, Cynwyd, Drexel Hills, Erie, Harrisburg, Haverford, Lancaster, Norristown, North Philadelphia, Philadelphia, Pittsburgh, Reading, Scranton, Williamsport, Huntington Valley, Bloomsburg, Wyomissing, Eagles Mere, Narbeth, Hershey, Carnegie, York.

MISSOURI VALLEY

Iowa—Ames, Burlington, Cedar Rapids, Keokuk, Des Moines, Red Oak.
Kansas—Arkansas City, Winfield.
Missouri—Kansas City, St. Louis.

NEW ENGLAND

Connecticut—Bridgeport, Hamden, Hartford, New Haven, Westport.
Maine—Portland, York.

Massachusetts—Boston, Osterville, Quincy, Springfield, Wianno, Winchester, Worcester.

New Hampshire—Concord, Hanover, Portsmouth, Rye Beach.

Rhode Island—Newport, Providence.

Vermont—Brattleboro, Burlington.

NORTH CALIFORNIA

California—Fresno, Monterey, Sacramento, San Francisco.

Nevada—Reno.

NORTHWESTERN

Minnesota—Duluth, Minneapolis, Rochester, St. Paul.

North Dakota—Fargo.

South Dakota—Sioux Falls.

PACIFIC NORTHWEST

British Columbia—Duncan, Vancouver, Victoria.

Oregon—Eugene, Portland, Klamath Falls, Corvallis.

Washington—Bellingham, Bremerton, Burien, Everett, Hoquiam, Seattle, Spokane, Tacoma, Wenatchee, Yakima.

SOUTHERN

Alabama—Anniston, Birmingham, Huntsville, Mobile.

Arkansas—Little Rock.

Georgia—Atlanta, Augusta, Columbus, Macon, Rome, Savannah.

Kentucky—Louisville.

Louisiana—New Orleans, Shreveport.

Mississippi—Jackson.

North Carolina—Asheville, Chapel Hill, Charlotte, Goldsboro, Greensboro, Raleigh.

South Carolina—Belton, Charleston, Clinton, Columbia, Greenville.

Tennessee—Chattanooga, Knoxville, Memphis, Nashville, Sewanee.

SOUTHERN CALIFORNIA

California—La Jolla, Los Angeles, San Diego.

SOUTHWESTERN

Arizona—Phoenix, Tucson.

New Mexico—Albuquerque.

Texas—El Paso.

TEXAS

Texas—Austin, Beaumont, Brownsville, Corpus Christi, Dallas, Fort Worth, Galveston, Greenville, Houston, San Antonio, Tyler, Waco, Wichita Falls.

WESTERN

Illinois—Aurora, Chicago, Danville, Decatur, Dixon, Evanston, Fox River Valley, Hinsdale, Joliet, North Shore, Oak Park, Pekin, Peoria, Quincy, Rockford, South Chicago, Urbana, West Suburban Chicago.

Indiana—Bloomington, Calumet, Culver, Elkhart, Evansville, Fort Wayne, Hammond, Gary, Goshen, Indianapolis, La Porte, Mishawaka, New Paris, Plymouth, South Bend, Terre Haute.

Michigan—Allen Park, Ann Arbor, Battle Creek, Bay City, Berrien Springs, Birmingham, Bloomfield Hills, Highland Park, Dearborn, Detroit, East Detroit, Flint, Grand Haven, Grand Rapids, Grosse Pointe, Holland, Hubbell, Iron Mountain, Kalamazoo, Lansing, Marquette, Midland, Monroe, Muskegon, Niles, Pontiac, Saginaw, St. Joseph, South Haven, Traverse City, Trenton, Wyandotte.

Ohio—Akron, Cincinnati, Cleveland, Columbus, Dayton, Hamilton, Lakeside, Lima, Mt. Vernon, Middletown, Newark, Springfield, Toledo, Youngstown.

W. Virginia—Charleston, Huntington, Parkersburg.

Wisconsin—Appleton, Ashland, Beaver Dam, Chippewa Falls, Delafield, Eau Claire, Green Bay, Janesville, Kenosha, La Crosse, Madison, Manitowoc, Menasha, Milwaukee, Milwaukee Suburbs, Oshkosh, Platteville, Rhinelander, Stevens Point, Superior, Waukesha, Wausau, Wauwatosa.

The administrative Committee may, in its discretion, add to the number of centers.

How to Make the Draw

The USTA, as previously stated, employs the Bagnall-Wild system of making a drawing. The object of this method of drawing is to place the byes, if any, in the first round, both for convenience and still more because a bye is of less value in the first round than later in the tournament.

By the method used for making the draw of a tournament during the early days of the game, it was possible for a player to have a bye in the semifinal round; he could then rest and watch two players hammering away at each other for hours to decide which should meet him in the final. The Bagnall-Wild system precluded that by placing all the byes, if any, in the first round, so that in subsequent rounds the number of players in each round would be a power of 2; after each round the number of players remaining would be half as many as in the preceding round.

When the total number of entires is 2, or a power of 2 (4, 8, 16, 32, 64, and so on), then all the names can be written down in a single column, and two of the players will meet in the finals. It is when the total is not a power of 2 that difficulties arise. It is then necessary to so arrange the first round that the number of players thereafter will equal a power of 2. This is done by placing a certain proportion of players in the second round without having played a match in the first round. These are the byes and have one less match to play than the other competitors.

In making the draw, first determine the number of byes by subtracting the total number of entries from the next higher power of 2. For example, if you have 41 entries you subtract 41 from the next higher power of 2, which is 64. This leaves 23 byes, 11 of which should be placed in the upper half of the draw and 12 at the bottom. This leaves 18 players in the first round, and after these men have played, 9 of them will be advanced to the second round, in line with the 23 byes. We now have 23 plus 9, or 32 players in the second round, and as 32 is a power of 2, there will be no byes during the remainder of the tournament, and only two men can meet in the final round.

G. A. Bagnall-Wild was the secretary and treasurer of the Bath Lawn Tennis Club of England and delegate to the meeting of secretaries that used to be convened annually by the All-England Club in the early days of the game in England. Early in 1883 a meeting to discuss the formation of a Lawn Tennis Association was held in London, but the result was inconclusive. A proposal was made and carried that a conference on the subject should be held with the All-England Club. That club, in declining the conference, offered to institute an annual meeting of secretaries of clubs with power to arrange fixtures and to discuss matters affecting the game; and a second meeting for the discussion of the question of an association turned down the project by a very small majority. The offer of the All-England Club was then accepted, and thenceforth until 1888 a meeting of lawn tennis representatives was annually held under the presidency of the secretary of the All-England Club.

Bagnall-Wild first brought his system before the delegates' meeting in the winter of 1883, but he was not allowed to move its adoption on the ground that he had failed to give due notice of his intention to do so. However, in the winter of 1884 Bagnall-Wild got his system adopted with the difference that whereas he put the byes at the bottom, the All-England Club decided to draw matches and byes alternately, putting the surplus,

A 32-place draw sheet ready for a tournament with 27 entries.

if any, of byes or matches at the bottom. The top and bottom method of drawing byes was adopted in England in 1886. As mentioned earlier, the USNLTA Executive Committee adopted the Bagnall-Wild system of drawing in 1884, at its meeting on July 7. It took quite a number of years for the top and bottom method, when adopted, to become the general practice, and the draws in even the championships were very much mixed up until about the year 1890.

Even today the theory does not seem to be understood by some tournament committees, and from time to time some weird methods of drawings are to be seen. In recent years the method of making the draw has been further complicated by various systems of seeding and placing of entries. Some seeding was done in the championship held at Newport in 1895 and again in 1896; but not thereafter until the present seeding regulations were adopted on February 4, 1922.

In the Senior championships the committees are authorized to "place" the same number of players in the draw as they are allowed to seed. In the Girls' USTA championship the normal procedure is to place players of high rank from the same Sectional Associations in different quarters of the draw. In competitions between nations, states, cities, clubs, colleges, schools, and similar bodies, when the competition is really between such bodies and not between the players as individuals, the players may be placed in such manner as agreed upon by the management of the competition.

Seeding the Draw

In order to prevent the best players from meeting each other during the early rounds of a tournament, it is common practice to place, or seed, them in the draw. Seeding is usually determined by ranking, record, and reputation. When seeding the draw, three principal points should be kept in mind:

1. USTA Tournament Regulations stipulate that, in a sanctioned tournament, not more than 1 player in every 4 may be seeded. Note that this stipulation is permissive, not mandatory. In many tournaments the tournament committee may feel that less liberal seeding is preferable. (Obviously, the further down the line one goes in selecting

seeds, the more difficult the judgments.) There is no minimum specified. One in eight is the most usual pattern.

2. Every seeded position is drawn by lot. You draw to determine whether No. 1 goes on the very top, or the very bottom; then No. 2 gets the opposite position. The same principle is followed for the rest of the seeds. (Note that each seeded player drawn to a spot in the lower half of the draw is placed on the bottom line of whatever segment he draws.)

3. USTA Tournament Regulations make no provision for showing seeded players any special consideration in "giving" them first-round byes (where there is a less than full bracket). Thus, in a tournament with 27 entries the byes would be opposite Seeds 1 and 2—on Lines 2 and 31—and also on Lines 4 and 29, and Line 27. This would mean that Seeds 3 and 4 would not get byes, while the players who happen to be drawn to Lines 3, 28, and 30 would get them. But in club, league, and invitation tournaments the tournament committee has the option of distributing byes among seeded players (in case of a less than full bracket).

Where the Seeds Go. Here are how the seeds should be placed in the draw:

For a 16-player draw, with two seeds: One goes on line 1, the other on line 16. Decide by drawing

For a 32-player draw, with four seeds: Seeds 1 and 2 draw for lines 1 and 32, seeds 3 and 4 draw for lines 9 and 24.

For a 64-player draw, with eight seeds: Seeds 1 and 2 draw for lines 1 and 64; seeds 3 and 4 draw for lines 17 and 48; seeds 5, 6, 7, and 8 draw for lines 9, 56, 25, and 40.

For a 128-player draw, with 16 seeds (two 64-line draw sheets, Upper and Lower): Seeds 1 and 2 draw for lines U-1 and L-64 (or 128).* Seeds 3 and 4 draw for lines U-33 and L-32 (96). Seeds 5, 6, 7, and 8 draw for lines U-17, L-48 (112), U-49, and L-16 (80). Seeds 9, 10, 11, 12, 13, 14, 15, and 16 draw for lines U-9, L-56 (120), U-25, L-40 (104), U-41, L-24 (88), U-57, and L-8 (72).

If your number of entries is only a few over the number for an even bracket—say, 37—you might find it less confusing to "build up" from a 32-line

*Numbers in parentheses apply if you have renumbered the second sheet 65 to 128.

sheet than to "build down" from 64. To do this you start at the middle and create two-line (two-player) pairings at each of several lines until you have provided as many lines as you have players. When doing it this way, remember that if you have an uneven number of these "extra" matches to chart, the top half of the draw gets the odd one (just the opposite of the disposition of the odd bye).

The Rest of the Draw. Once you have filled in the lines to be occupied by seeded players, and marked those lines that represent byes, the rest of the draw is filled in by drawing the names of all the rest of the competitors and writing them on the remaining unoccupied lines, in the order in which they are drawn.

When this drawing procedure operates to bring together, for their first match, players of the same family, same school or college, or same foreign country, the tournament committee may, at its discretion, place the second player so drawn in the same relative position in the next quarter of the draw. (This is in accord with the procedure followed in making the draw for USTA National Championships.)

"Foreign" Seeds. In recent years there has been a strong trend away from having separate seeding lists for "foreign" and domestic players—along with a trend toward minimizing the total number of seeds. However, in some situations it may be deemed desirable to have such separate lists.

Procedure: (1) The domestic seeds should be only half as many as the total seeds planned; (2) draw these domestic seeds according to the pattern indicated above, and insert the names on the lines to which they are drawn; (3) the No. 1 foreign seed is then placed at the opposite end of the same half of the draw as the No. 2 domestic seed, while, conversely, the No. 2 foreign seed is placed at the opposite end of the half to which the No. 1 domestic seed was drawn; (4) foreign seeds Nos. 3 and 4 are drawn by lot and placed in the two quarters that do not already have foreign seeds 1 and 2, the one drawn to the top half going to the bottom line of the first quarter, the other one going to the top line of the fourth quarter.

For example, in a 64 draw, with 4 domestic seeds and 4 foreign seeds, assume that the No. 1 domestic seed is drawn for line 1 on the draw sheet. Domestic seed No. 2 would be on line 64, and domestic Nos. 3 and 4 would be drawn for lines 17 and 48. Then foreign seed No. 1 would go on line 33, and foreign seed No. 2 would go on line 32 . . . and foreigns 3 and 4 would be drawn for lines 16 and 49. This would mean that each of the eight 8-line segments would have a seeded player, alternating, top to bottom, between domestic and foreign.

Obviously, it is desirable, for simplicity's sake, to have an even number of seeded positions. However, if an odd number of players is to be seeded, the determination of which half of the draw gets the "extra" seed should be made by lot.

Rankings. Most local, sectional, and national tennis associations issue an annual list of rankings for players in each division. Rankings are based solely on tournament won-lost records for that year. Generally, a player must compete in a specific number of sanctioned tournaments before being eligible for a ranking.

Other Types of Competitions

There are several different types of competitive events that can be used by tennis clubs and similar groups to provide stimulating competition. The most popular types of events are: single elimination, double elimination, consolation, handicap, move-up move-down, round-robin, pyramid, and ladder. The first five of these competitions are generally used to determine a champion and runner-up, and when the tournament is to be of short duration.

The round-robin tournament requires a great deal of time but is used to give each member of a group an opportunity to play every other member. Frequently it is used early in a course to determine the positions of the players on a challenge ladder or pyramid.

The ladder and pyramid events are used to maintain a flexible or changing ranking list over a prolonged time period. The handicap tournament can be used as a single elimination, double elimination, consolation, or round-robin event.

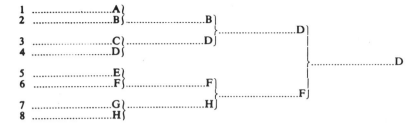

Diagram of a single elimination tournament.

Single Elimination Tournament. The simplest type of tournament is the single elimination tournament, in which the winner of each match advances in the tournament and the loser is eliminated. As the name implies, one loss eliminates a player; no provision is made for an off day or bad luck occurring to a player. This type of draw is most convenient with a large number of contestants and only a short time available for play.

If all players are of equal ability or their ability is unknown, all names are placed in a hat and drawn blindly for positions on the draw sheet. The first name drawn is placed on the first line of the draw, the second name drawn is placed on the second line, and so on, assuming, of course, that proper provision has been made for the number of byes required. The single elimination tournament type is used in all USTA events, but the drawing and seeding is as described earlier.

Double Elimination Tournament. The double elimination tournament, in which a player must lose twice before he is eliminated, is superior to the single elimination tournament when a small number of contestants is involved (less than eight) for it makes allowances for players having off days. Byes are given for less than eight players. If more than eight players are entered, two separate tournaments can be held and the winners can meet for the championship.

Consolation Tournament. The consolation tournament is generally used only when the number of entries is eight or sixteen. Here, the losers in the first round of play compete with each other for the consolation title. First-round winners advance to the right and compete for the championship.

Round-Robin Tournament. In a round-robin tournament, each player plays every other player once, and the final standing is determined on a percentage basis.

For an even number of players: Assign each player a number. Schedule matches according to the following (for eight entries):

1-8	1-7	1-6	1-5	1-4	1-3	1-2
2-7	8-6	7-5	6-4	5-3	4-2	3-8
3-6	2-5	8-4	7-3	6-2	5-8	4-7
4-5	3-4	2-3	8-2	7-8	6-7	5-6

Note that number 1 remains stationary and the other numbers revolve around it in a counterclockwise direction.

For an odd number of players: Assign each player a number. Schedule matches according to the following (for nine entries):

9	8	7	6	5	4	3	2	1
1-8	9-7	8-6	7-5	6-4	5-3	4-2	3-1	2-9
2-7	1-6	9-5	8-4	7-3	6-2	5-1	4-9	3-8
3-6	2-5	1-4	9-3	8-2	7-1	6-9	5-8	4-7
4-5	3-4	2-3	1-2	9-1	8-9	7-8	6-7	5-6

Note that all figures revolve, and one player has a bye in each round.

Handicap Tournament. The handicap tournament can be run as a single or double elimination, consolation, or round-robin event. Handicaps can be determined as previously discussed or in such other manner as decided by the club. The best player gets the lowest handicap, the most inferior player gets the highest handicap.

Move-Up Move-Down Tournament. In this type of tournament the players move up a court (from court 5 to 4 to 3, etc.) when they win. Each player strives to reach court 1 and to remain there throughout the tournament. It provides much fun in a group situation.

Players are paired as opponents and assigned to numbered courts. All start play on a signal from the tournament chairman. After some arbitrary length of time, play is halted. The number of games won by each player is then recorded. The winner on each court "moves up" to the next lower-numbered court. The loser on each court "moves down" one court. The winner on court 1 can go nowhere, so he stays there; the loser on the last court also stays on that court (the highest-numbered court). Another round is played, after which changes in position are again made. In doubles, players change partners after they change courts.

Ladder Tournament. In a ladder tournament, players are listed according to ability or ranking, with the best player at the top of the list. Competition is arranged by challenge, and a player is allowed to challenge either of the two players above him on the ladder. If the challenger wins, he takes the place of the loser and the loser moves down one rung on the ladder as do all intervening players. If the challenged player wins, he is allowed to challenge someone above him before he must accept another challenge. All challenges must be accepted and played before a definitely agreed time. Specific rules should be posted concerning the ladder tournament in order to avoid disputes and to keep the tournament running smoothly. This type of tournament is ideal for maintaining a continuous ranking of players over a long period of time.

Pyramid Tournament. The pyramid tournament, like the ladder tournament just described, maintains continuous, prolonged competition. It allows for more challenging and participating and can include a larger number of participants than the ladder tournament. After the original drawings are made, any player may challenge any other player in the same horizontal row. If he wins, he can challenge any player in the row above him. When a player loses to someone on the row below him, he changes places with the winner. Again, as in the ladder tournament, clear, concise, and specific rules should be posted with the challenge board in order to avoid disputes about challenge matches.

VASSS Round-Robin Medal Play. This round-robin tournament follows the same basic schedule as given earlier for conventional round-robin play except that VASSS Single-Point system of scoring is employed. In addition, a round-robin in this VASSS-type tournament may be any multiple of 20 (40, 60, 80) total points of one 31-point set. The winner shall receive a 5-point bonus for the win, plus the unplayed points in the set (e.g.: A player wins 31-10, his score for that round will be 31 + 5 + 20 = 56 points). The winner of the tournament is the player with the most points at the end of the round-robin schedule.

Individual handicaps are estimated against scratch for the number of points in a round, as decided by the tournament committee. A tournament doubles-team handicap is the sum of the individual players' handicaps.

Team Matches

Here are some general guidelines regarding formats for team matches:

Any scholastic, college, industrial, or club league is entitled to choose its own format for the matches. The larger universities usually play six singles and three doubles, and individuals are allowed to compete in both.

A popular format for industrial leagues, clubs, high schools, and smaller colleges is four singles, three doubles. Many have found that the schedul-

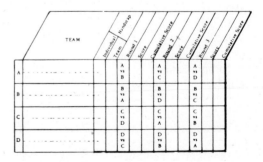

The VASSS round-robin score sheet.

ing is easier, and the playing opportunities better distributed, if players are confined to playing either singles or doubles, but not both.

Singles matches always are first on the schedule. The scoring is simple: each match, whether singles or doubles, counts one point; a tie counts a half point for each side.

First Aid on the Courts

During a tournament—or actually any other time during a game—an accident may occur that requires first aid. Here is some general information that may help should any of the following situations occur:

SCRATCHES, BLISTERS: Clean wounds thoroughly before applying medicine or bandages. For blisters, cease playing immediately in order to avoid aggravation (wear two pairs of socks to avoid blisters).

BLEEDING: Do not wash wound. Press down on bleeding point, wrap with handkerchief, piece of shirt, towel, etc. If bleeding won't stop, apply pressure above wound, or make tourniquet, tie around limb with half knot, place stick over it; tie another knot over stick and twist. Be sure to loosen frequently. Send for doctor.

TWISTED ANKLES, CRAMPS: Stay off ailing legs and seek immediate medical attention. With cramps, sit down and rub affected area toward heart; do not resume activity without medical approval.

BROKEN BONE: Whether simple or compound, do *not* move victim. Send for doctor. Make victim lie still.

ARTIFICIAL RESPIRATION: If victim is not breathing, apply mouth-to-mouth breathing at once. Lay victim on back. Clear mouth and throat. Tilt head back. Pull chin up. Pull jaw forward with thumb. Place mouth over victim's, pinch victim's nostrils, take deep breath, blow hard enough to make victim's chest rise. Remove mouth, let victim's chest fall. Repeat at rate of 12 breaths a minute (20 for children) until victim breathes naturally.

LIGHTNING: If victim is not breathing, apply mouth-to-mouth breathing. Send for doctor. Make victim comfortable.

FAINTING: Have victim sit with head between knees or lie down with head lower than feet. Sprinkle water on face. Do not give stimulant. Send for doctor.

HEART ATTACK: Send for doctor. Make victim comfortable. Loosen tight clothing. Keep victim warm. Do not give stimulant. Suggest slow, deep breaths.

SUN STROKE: Lay victim on back in shade with head slightly elevated. Cool head and body with water. Rub arms and legs toward heart. Send for doctor.

TENNIS ELBOW: One of the most discussed but still medically vague problems on the court is the "tennis elbow." Thousands of players complain annually of pains in the elbow area around the arm, and doctors offer consoling words of wisdom without any real cure. A tennis elbow can be detected by pain, throbbing, or stiffness in the area on top of and around the elbow of your racket hand. Generally, the tennis elbow is a result of (1) overworking the arm with too much tennis in too short a period of time; (2) a gradual age level, where the player is not physically able to participate as freely as he formerly did; or (3) racket strung too tightly puts undue pressure back into the elbow.

Doctors say the best remedy for the tennis elbow is rest. Painkillers and aspirin may be a temporary answer, but they may lead to more serious problems. With rest, doctors may be able to restore the elbow to normalcy and a gradual program of tennis can be incorporated. Continually overworking the arm may lead to complications in the shoulder and other areas of the body. Heat treatments, massages and whirlpools are other means of relaxing the arm and relieving some of the pain, off the court.

Other medical ailments such as "trick knees," stiff wrists, or stiff shoulders require more delicate handling. Many players with knee problems find doubles an easier outlet than singles. They also play more on clay courts than cement or hard courts because the sliding eases the stop-and-start irregularities.

It is only safe to say that a player's health is more important than winning or losing; for without it, the player never gets the chance even to walk on the court.

DUTIES AND JURISDICTIONS OF OFFICIALS

Umpires and linesmen have been a familiar sight on the courts since the earliest annals of the sport. An old photograph of one of the early Wimbledon tournaments shows the umpire in a gray top hat seated in a chair raised on a table near the net, and linesmen in their positions opposite the lines. Evidently it was found this early that men to call the score and judge the lines relieved the players, added to the enjoyment of the gallery, and insured fairness of play for any match. Actually, it is the duty of every player to become an efficient umpire or linesman, and although it is rather an irksome task, a really good official is much admired and is of great value to the game of lawn tennis. Even if as a player you have not studied the rules of the game, as an umpire it is essential that you should know them. It is amazing what a number of obscure and unique points arise at different times, questions which the umpire has to decide. If, however, you are uncertain of some technicality, you should refer the matter to the referee, whose decision shall be final.

When playing in an open tournament, you must always be ready to do your share of umpiring, and there are often occasions in ordinary club tournaments and matches when umpires and linesmen are badly needed. The only time when it is not advisable to take on a match is if you yourself are due to play immediately afterward. Officiating is apt to tire your eyes and sitting in one position for a long time stiffens your muscles, so avoid umpiring just before you are going to play.

Duties of Referee, Umpire, and Linesman

By far the question most often asked of a tennis official—usually by a spectator who has just watched a close match that might have been decided by one questionable call—is: Can the umpire overrule a linesman's call?

The answer is no. But let us not just drop it there. Good, experienced umpires—and good, experienced linesmen—know the rest of the answer, the practical solution in those unhappy instances where, as they say, "Everybody knew it was out, but. . . ."

In such a situation it is possible for the umpire to help avoid an injustice. If the umpire is sure the call was erroneous he can refrain from repeating the linesman's call as he normally would, and this, coupled with a quietly inquiring look, gives the linesman a cue and an opportunity to volunteer either a "correction" or a "not sure." Thereupon the umpire can make the amended call or call a let, whichever in his discretion is the fairest solution. The above refers, of course, to calls based on matters of fact, not on interpretations of the rules. If, for instance, a linesman calls a foot fault for "hopping" (no longer prohibited), it is within the umpire's province to reverse such a call (and to make sure all his linesmen know all the rules!).

There are three basic groups of officials involved in the play of lawn tennis, and their duties are as follows:

Referee. The referee is *ex officio* a member of the tournament committee. He should be present at the making of the draw, and should be on the premises at all times that tournament play is going on. If he must be absent he must appoint a *pro tem* referee. Any time the referee plays in or officiates in a tournament match, he must appoint a *pro tem* referee.

The referee shall have power to appoint and remove umpires and linesmen, to assign courts, and decide starting times for matches. He shall decide any point of law (but not a question of fact) which an umpire may be unable to decide—or which may be referred to him on appeal from the decision of an umpire.

Generally the referee—in cooperation with the tournament chairman—decides such matters as the number of games between ball changes, and the number of balls per change, and whether or not spikes will be permitted.

It is the referee's decision as to whether any match, once started, shall be postponed because of weather conditions—rain, darkness, etc. Note this distinction: An umpire may *suspend* play—as in the event of rain—but actual *postponement* may be ordered only by the referee.

The referee has the authority to declare a competitor defaulted for failure to be ready when his match is called. Usually such a default is declared after consultation between the referee and the tournament committee, but the referee is the ultimate authority. USTA tournament regulations provide that the umpire may default a player who, in the opinion of the umpire, deliberately ignores and/or refuses to follow his directions with respect to the player's conduct in a match. Discerning umpires make a distinction between the words "default" and "retired" in recording the outcome of a match. The former term is applicable in cases of a player's failing to appear for a match, or of being defaulted for misconduct, whereas once a match has been started and a player is unable to continue because of illness or other cause, the outcome should show the actual score so far as the match progressed, followed by "retired." The situations could logically be reported this way: (1) player failed to appear—"John Doe *won from* Richard Roe by default"; (2) player defaulted for misconduct—"John Doe *defeated* Richard Roe, 3-3, default"; (3) player unable to continue—"John Doe *defeated* Richard Roe, 6-4, 3-3, retired."

There is a fundamental distinction to be made between the roles of the referee and the tournament committee chairman: The referee is primarily responsible for judgment decisions regarding fairness of conditions of actual play, whereas the tournament committee's responsibility is primarily that of seeing to it that proper and adequate physical facilities are available.

In the matter of equipment for the umpires' chairs, the referee and the umpires themselves have the primary responsibility—the referee first, the umpires as a "check." Here is a basic list of equipment with which the umpires' chairs should be stocked:

Towels
Salt tablets
Mercurochrome or iodine
Smelling salts
Wrist sweat bands
Water and cups
Aspirin
Rosin or sawdust
Rubber bands
Safety pins
Adhesive bandages
Adhesive tape
Scissors
Yardsticks and singles sticks

Score cards are also, basically, the responsibility of the referee, but the responsibility for obtaining them and preparing them, with names and descriptions for particular matches, is usually delegated to a chairman of umpires.

Umpire. The umpire has general oversight of the conduct of a match. Primarily this entails making optimum disposition of the linesmen that are available; introducing the players; keeping the running score on his score card and calling it after each point, game, and set (and at other times when requested by a competitor). Other specific duties of the umpire are:

1. To ascertain that the net be the right height before the start of play, and to measure and adjust the net after each set or at other suitable intervals.
2. To repeat "out" or "fault" calls of linesmen (or make those calls himself with respect to lines for which he has assumed responsibility, in a match not fully staffed with linesmen).
3. To see that the competitors change sides at the proper times, and serve and receive in proper rotation.
4. To see that play is resumed promptly at the expiration of time allowed for a rest period.
5. To see that play is "continuous" within the generally accepted meaning of the term. The rules now have a time limit of 60 seconds on court changes. This means the players should be "in position and ready to resume play" within 60 seconds.
6. To suspend play (subject to confirmation by the referee) when weather or other conditions make this advisable.
7. To request the presence of the referee when confronted with a question of tournament procedure on which he, the umpire, does not have authority (for example, the question of whether a competitor shall be allowed to put on spikes).
8. To complete the score card, sign it, and deliver it, at the conclusion of the match, to the authorized person or desk.

A competitor who wishes to have a linesman removed must make such a request to the umpire in charge of the match, and it is the umpire's decision whether the request shall be referred to the referee for decision. If the competitor's request is that the umpire himself be removed, it must be communicated to the referee for decision. In either case it is generally desirable that no such request bring about an interruption of play—and the umpire has the authority to decide whether there shall be any suspension while the request is relayed to the referee. The latter should give full consideration to the known and assumed reasons for the requested removal—and act only if they are well founded, not simply on a competitor's objection.

As for the umpire's procedure, most persons learn tennis umpiring techniques largely by following the examples of established officials. For those who have little or no opportunity to do this —and as a checklist for even those who have had some experience—here follows a set of recommended procedures:

Upon getting your assignment and score card, make sure you understand the basic facts about the match, such as name of the tournament, division (men's, women's singles, doubles, etc.), the round, best of ? sets, correct names and residences of the contestants, and the ball change. All of this should be on your score card when it is handed to you, but if it is not, you should write it in. Be sure you have two eraser-equipped pencils in good working order.

When you go onto the court (preferably accompanying the contestants, although that is not always possible), check these matters first: height of the net; singles sticks properly placed—or removed, as the case may be; adequate supply of balls; other equipment for the umpire's chair.

If there are linesmen who have been assigned to your match but have not been given specific line assignments, it is your function to deploy them in the way that gives you best coverage, considering the nature of the contest, the setting, the type of court, and the known capabilities of the available linesmen. Have the players spin for choice of service or court, etc., then mark that part of your score card accordingly, noting at least the first ball change.

If there are ball boys, be sure they understand the players' preferences regarding clearing balls on missed first services, or any special arrangements that need to be made; also that they under-

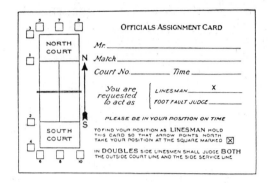

A typical official's assignment card.

stand about quickly moving all balls to the server's end of the court. Make sure you know how each player prefers to have his name pronounced. If there is a warmup time limit indicated, "inviting" the players to take their practice serves is a polite way of reminding them it's about time to get started. Allow about 45 seconds for this.

While there is no requirement that every person umpiring a tennis match must use exactly the same phrases in given situations, it is true that over the years a well-standardized pattern of announcements has evolved through pursuit of the "A-B-C" ideal of Accuracy, Brevity, and Clarity— plus another C, Courtesy. Here is the way it goes:

Starting the match: "Ladies and gentlemen, your attention, please. This is a third-round match in the Eastern Grass Court Championships, men's singles. On my right (or, in the court nearer the boxes), from Denmark, Mr. Torben Ulrich; on my left (or, in the far court), from Evanston, Illinois, Mr. Martin Riessen. . . . This will be the best of three sets. Mr. Ulrich won the toss and elected to receive, so Mr. Riessen will serve first." (Glance to see that all linesmen are ready) "Ready? Play!" (Announce each player as he serves for the first time: "Mr. Ulrich serving.")

Always use Mr. and Miss or Mrs. in introductions, and in the call at the conclusion of a game, set, or match: "Game, Mr. Smith." However, it is not necessary to use the "Mr." when calling advantage points for male players; often it occurs so repetitiously in a long deuced game as to be tiresome. "Advantage, Smith" suffices. But always use the player's name on these calls, not such terms as striker, or server, or receiver, or "advantage in" or "advantage out." (In doubles, because of the awkwardness of calling both partners' names on every advantage point, most experienced umpires use the server's name for all advantage-point calls for that side, and sort of "divide up" the identifications of the receiving side, being in part guided by the action that gave the receivers advantage.)

Call games as follows: "Game, Mr. Smith; he wins the first game." In sets other than the first set, make it "Game, Mr. Smith; leads three games to two, first set." Or "Game, Mr. Jones. Three games to two, Mr. Smith leads, first set." . . . "Game, Mr. Jones; games are three-all, first set."

Note: In the game mentioned above where Mr. Jones won the game but nevertheless still trailed in the score, there is a full-stop period after the name Jones. *Then* the score is given, and then Mr. Smith's name occurs. This sequence is used to avoid the slight confusion that might result if one phrase ended in "Mr. Jones" and the next one started with "Mr. Smith."

Call sets as follows: "Game and third set, Mr. Smith, seven games to five. Mr. Jones leads in sets, two to one."

Note: It is desirable for the umpire to be alert to game points and set points—and of course match point—and that he make his call promptly when those points are concluded. Delay (except to allow applause to subside) gives rise to lack of confidence in the official. But *do not ever* announce that an upcoming point is "set point" or "match point."

In matches where players take an intermission, it is the umpire's responsibility to see that they are back on the court ready to resume play at the specified time. At resumption of play the umpire's announcement is: "With Mr. Jones leading, two sets to one, Mr. Smith will serve first in the fourth set . . . Ready? Play!"

Linesman. It is the duty of a linesman to decide every question of fact regarding the line to which he is assigned. Primarily this means making the decision as to whether any ball falling near that line is good or out . . . but questions regarding foot faulting also will present themselves to base-linesmen, and occasionally also to center service-linesmen and side-linesmen.

The linesman's only cries are "out" and "fault," the latter being the call on any served ball that

clears the net but falls outside any of the service-box lines. Use of hand signals, in moderation, can be helpful in supplementing voice calls—but beware of starting a hand signal "too soon," lest you decide, a split second later, that the ball was not out, after all!

The calls of the linesman must be prompt, loud, and decisive. He should make an audible call on every ball that is "out" on his line, even those that go flying many feet beyond the line. That is because, properly, the umpire cannot make an "out" call on any line that is covered by a linesman unless he gets a call from that linesman or gets a signal from the linesman that he was "unsighted" and unable to make a decision. Never call a ball "out" until the ball has actually struck. The call on an out ball is "out"—not "outside."

If a linesman, in his effort to make his call quickly, calls a ball "out" and then instantly realizes it was good, he must immediately get the attention of the umpire and indicate a correction. The umpire will take it from there. If the umpire calls the score or makes a call at variance with the linesman's decision—possibly through failure to hear a call—the linesman should call the umpire's attention to the error.

Linesmen calling the side lines should be alert to the probability that they will have to stand, moving a few feet "outside" their chair's position, in order to get an unobstructed view of services coming toward that side line. The linesman has the obligation also of being alert to the possibility of his being called upon for an opinion on an occasional ball falling near a line not "his own," and should give his opinion—only when asked—and only if he is positive about the ball.

The linesman should quickly inform the umpire by signal (both hands in front of eyes) or voice if for any reason he is unable to make a call on a ball falling near his line. . . . It is *not* a linesman's duty to catch (or try to catch), or to retrieve, any ball. Do not be a ball boy.

Although white is the traditional color of clothing for tennis players, it is not desirable in the garments of linesmen.

Net Umpire. In important matches such as the finals and semifinals of a major tournament, a net-cord umpire is added. The net-cord umpire usually keeps one hand on the net cord to ascertain service lets by touch. It is the duty of the net umpire to:

1. Keep his own score card as a double check on the chair umpire.
2. Measure the net before the start of the match and at changeover games at the start of each set (and at other times when in his judgment and that of the umpire it would be advisable).
3. Make sure the umpire knows any time a served ball touches the net in passing.
4. Call attention to any instance where a player or anything he wears or carries touches the net while the ball is still in play, or where the ball in play touches a player or anything he wears or carries, other than his racket held in his hand or hands.
5. Help the umpire keep track of ball changes, etc.
6. When requested by the umpire, be responsible for calling "not up." (This should be the sole responsibility of either the umpire or the net umpire. Whose responsibility it is should be clearly understood before the match starts.)

Foot-Fault Judge. The foot-fault judge is seldom used today. In most tournaments the calling of infractions of the foot-fault rule is left to the linesmen—primarily the base-linesman, although it is possible for players to violate the center mark and side line, also, and when this happens the linesmen on center service and the side line make the call. However, in some events it is deemed desirable to have a separate foot-fault judge. The purpose of this, originating in earlier times, when there was more of an element of "interpretation" involved in judging whether a foot fault was committed, is to insure that interpretation is the same at each end of the court. To a lesser extent, this still is the purpose, so a match should have only one foot-fault judge, if it has any.

The foot-fault judge has a chair at either end of the court. If the physical layout permits, it may be desirable for these chairs to be at the opposite end of each base line from the chairs of the base-linesmen. Regardless of which side his chairs are on, the foot-fault judge should remember that he "changes on the even" instead of the odd—and

should make his move quickly so that the players never have to wait for him.

The Tennis Umpires' Association

The Tennis Umpires' Association is an organized group which furnishes officials of training and experience for tournament tennis. The early judges were generally men intimately connected with the tournament; the linesmen were almost always players, and the umpire was perhaps some official of the home club conducting the event. They were picked up in haphazard fashion by an overworked referee if they could be persuaded to serve. But, because of the supply of such individuals being limited, only the very important matches were ever graced by their presence.

These conditions, with only minor improvements, existed down to the last ten years. As more men became interested, the available candidates for umpires and linesmen increased; but with the growth of the game, tournaments advanced in entries, so that it was still unusual to find any but feature matches properly umpired and lined. This was true of the championships, for even here where tennis enthusiasts gathered in numbers, the supply of umpires and linesmen by no means equaled the demand. Some of these old umpires were just as good as we have today. No one could umpire a match better and be heard more clearly by the gallery than Fred S. Mansfield, the dean of umpires, who for many years handled the principal events at Newport and Longwood. Unfortunately, there were not many like him and good linesmen were even more scarce, for it developed that judging the lines was not the easy job that it would seem and that some men were very much more accurate than others.

Finally the demand became insistent. Players who had enjoyed the benefit of an umpire wanted one whenever a match seemed likely to be close, and they wanted an experienced umpire and competent linesmen, for careless ones were worse than useless. About this time the singles championship was moved from the Newport Casino to the West Side Tennis Club at Forest Hills and the men of the club determined that this feature of the tournament could be improved. They selected E. C. Conlin, who had had experience in a Davis Cup Challenge Round, to handle the umpiring, and to him is largely due the credit of inaugurating a Tennis Umpires' Association. Other men had suggested such an organization, but Conlin's energy put it into being. He planned a national body of umpires and for their training conceived the idea of an umpires' manual which gave not only the rules and regulations but complete instructions for umpires and their handling of situations during tournaments, as well as many hints on the management of tournaments and the tennis spectators.

The original idea was to have an integral organization with chapters in all tennis centers, but after trial it was found better to affiliate with USTA. The Association still exists, but now as a committee of USTA, although the old name is retained. The parent body does the secretarial work, keeps the umpires' lists, and takes care of the expenses, such as printing the manual and tournament stationery.

Once started, the idea grew rapidly; it has spread over all of the important tennis centers of the United States and has even invaded foreign countries. All of the championships in this country are played under its regulations and its work has made for the smooth running of these prominent events as well as innumerable smaller tournaments.

The average spectator little realizes the detail that applies to the selection of the best man for officiating at championship matches. A very brief outline may be interesting. All of the umpires in adjacent tennis sections are called upon, through the mailing list, to serve in the tournament and the applications are listed on a card system. From this card list, daily before the play starts, men are assigned for every match, and a card is given each man designating the match, number of the court, the time, and his exact position. This removes all confusion; the men know their positions and take them when the players go to the court.

A fully staffed tennis match requires the services of an umpire and ten or eleven linesmen. For these duties it is not necessary to have been an ex-regional or national tennis champion. The job is available to anyone with good eyesight who either knows or is ready to learn the rules of lawn tennis, and who has the ability to make accurate and instantaneous decisions as to the outcome of a match.

Applicants for these positions must pass a written test and serve as an umpire or linesman in a "friendly" match under the guidance of a member of the Tennis Umpire's Association. After these and a final test, the aspirants are accepted to sectional membership and are given their cards in the Tennis Umpire's Association. Any match held under the sanction of USTA is open for holders of these cards to serve as umpire or linesman. They are entitled to present themselves or be invited. For information, write the USTA at their New York office.

TENNIS ETIQUETTE

Good sportsmanship, good manners, and the generally accepted customs that constitute the social graces of court play are the lifeblood of tennis. While it is true that tennis is a competitive game and can be a tough and grueling sport, it is one in which the niceties are cherished. The majority of the tennis matches that you will participate in, at least until you reach tournament status, will be friendly get-togethers where the fun of playing is as important as winning.

Many of the manners and customs of the game are not included in the official rules given earlier in this section. They have come about from the experience of players through the years and are now considered as part of the game of tennis. Since some of the suggestions contained herein may seem obvious to the veteran player, it should be pointed out that one of the basic objectives of the following "Twelve Rules of Good Courtmanship" is to start the *beginner* off in the right direction. By learning these rules you and your fellow players will be able to realize the fullest measure of sporting pleasure from the game.

Twelve Rules of Good Courtmanship

The following twelve rules are reprinted here by courtesy of Ashaway Products, Inc.:

1. PROPER ATTITUDE. Your attitude toward the game can add to or detract considerably from both your own and your fellow players' enjoyment of it. Enthusiasm, naturally, is always a plus factor. Even if you are "stuck" with an opponent you outclass completely, it's in poor taste to act bored and superior. The good sport will maintain his interest and offer encouragement whenever possible. In general, it is traditional in tennis to praise good shots or plays made by either a doubles partner or an opponent. However, this *can* be overdone—to the point where it no longer seems sincere or is open to misinterpretation. For example, should you serve an obvious ace and follow it up with a too vehement "Nice try," it really turns into praise for your own shot.

As in any other sport, knowing how to lose in tennis is also an accomplishment. The alibi artist and the Jonah whose "game is way, way off today" can quickly and unfairly take the edge off a hard-won victory. It is not necessary to hurdle across the net to do it, but a sincere word of congratulation for the winner, and the trite but traditional "Nice game" for the loser always add to the general good feeling.

Before you play, greet your opponent, or opponents, in a friendly manner and introduce yourself. Spin your racquet or toss a coin to decide choice of side or serve. Rally to warm up and then ask if your opponent wishes to take any practice serves before starting the match. "First one in" should not be used to start a match.

All of your equipment, incidentally, should be kept in good condition—so you will not be tempted to use it as an alibi, and also because it means far more enjoyment from your game.

2. KNOW THE RULES. To avoid embarrassment to yourself and to those with whom you play, learn and know the official rules of the game. While you do not need to know all the finer points involved in the rules, you should learn the basic ones. This speeds up play and allows more time for concentration on improving your game.

3. DRESS THE PART. White is comfortable and sharp—to wear it on the court marks you as right for the occasion. It has been the standard tennis attire for years, so to look your best, white is right. (More details on dressing the part can be found in Section 2.)

4. MEET YOUR MATCH. No matter how you play or with whom you play, any kind of tennis is better than no tennis at all. However, everyone enjoys it more if opponents are at least somewhere near the same level of playing ability.

In club play, it is standard practice to try to improve your ranking by challenging opponents several notches up the ladder. An eager beginner, on the other hand, would be way out of line to try to set up a match with the club champion. However, if the champ himself suggests the match, that is something else again, and by all means hop to it. In fact if you consider yourself among the better players in a tennis group, it is good practice to invite a match with a lesser opponent now and then to avoid the tag of snob.

The doubles game quite frequently offers the ideal situation in that it makes it easier to distribute the talent evenly on both sides of the court.

5. AVOID STALLING. Because a faster tennis game is more fun to play, and also, since wearing down an opponent is a legitimate and frequently used tennis strategy, it is considered bad form to stall for a breather during a match. While it is hardly necessary to sprint around the court retrieving balls for the server, it is not considered good form to be a "creeper" either. You should get back into position for receiving the next serve as soon as possible after a point is completed.

Because it helps to keep play moving, it is the receiver's duty after each point has been played to retrieve all balls on his side of the court so that the server has two or three in hand to start each serve. This eliminates delay in case of a let and helps the server zero in.

6. CALLING SERVES. In lieu of an umpire it falls upon the receiver of the service to plainly call close serves either good or out. And, in the case of doubt, it is, of course, good tennis manners to give your opponent the benefit of the call. Strictly speaking, the receiver really should not touch any service which does not fall good. However, in most friendly games it has become accepted practice to stop bad serves with the racket to keep balls off adjoining courts and reduce mileage rolled up in chasing them. Return balls directly to the server when he is waiting to serve.

In case of any delayed or misunderstood call, or any circumstance outside of normal play which throws the server off his balance, it is customary for the *receiver* to offer replay of the point. Lets should also be clearly called in accordance with the official rules.

Unless your match has the benefit of an umpire, it is the responsibility of the server to call the score after each point. Do not wrangle over decisions or behave like a spoiled child.

During a rally, you are the linesman (in lieu of an official linesman) for all balls that land on your side of the net. Do not call the good balls, just the outs. Again, if any question arises, replay the point. Also, offer to replay the point if during a rally there is interference caused by a ball rolling on your court from an adjoining one or by a piece of paper blowing around.

7. REPLAY OF FAST SERVICE. Before delivering the service, it is the responsibility of the server to be sure the receiver is ready—and to offer replay of the service if any doubt exists. This is worthy of special note by players who are in the habit of delivering a fast second serve right on top of a first-service fault.

When receiving, do not return the ball unless the serve was good and you intended to play the point.

8. CROSSING COURTS. When one of your balls wanders over into an adjoining court where play is in progress, never attempt to retrieve it during play. Even though you might not interfere with the action itself, your presence is distracting. Wait until the point is completed; then retrieve the ball quickly, or if it is convenient to a player on the other court, ask for it with a polite, "Thank you!"

In the same regard, if a ball from another court turns up on yours, it is proper for you to return it at the first break in your own play.

To avoid confusion on crowded public courts, if balls are not already marked it is a good idea to do so by inking on some identifying symbol.

9. OTHERS ARE WAITING. On crowded club and public courts where others are waiting to play, it is both thoughtless and selfish to hog a court. Unless you have hired a court for a specific period of time, it is considered proper to vacate it upon completion of the set.

When the players waiting outnumber the courts available, it is often an easy and polite solution to suggest a doubles match so that more players may participate. Practice outside the playing area—not on the side lines between courts.

Another sacrifice you may be called upon to make at times is to forego the pleasures of play completely when courts are wet and soft. Al-though this does not apply, of course, to concrete and some composition courts, wet-weather play on other types of surfaces will chew them up considerably and spoil the fun.

10. DON'T ARGUE. If an umpire and a linesman have been assigned to your match, show them consideration and treat them with courtesy. In every match, you and your opponent will probably believe that one or more inaccurate decisions have been made; but as a general rule the linesman is in a better position than you are to make close decisions.

When you get a questionable decision, do not bang the ball against the backstop or high in the air or show your irritation in any other way. Accept all decisions in a sportsmanlike manner. This ability to take it is a test of your sportsmanship.

11. CONTROL YOUR TEMPER. Keep your temper under control; do not allow things to distract or annoy you. Keep your mind concentrated on the game. Keep on fighting until the last point has been scored, whether you are winning or losing. Remember that self-control is one of the most important attributes of sportsmanship and successful play. Shake hands with your opponent and thank him for the match.

12. SIDE-LINE ETIQUETTE. While you are waiting for a court, it is not hard at all to make a nuisance of yourself. Loud conversation, shouting to someone down the line, bouncing balls, or jumping around at the side of the court will all help to distract the players. Also, kibitzing a match with uninvited umpiring, or unasked advice, no matter how expert it might be, will win you few tennis friends.

On the other hand, you can sometimes be quite helpful while you are watching or waiting. It is a nice gesture, for example, for a spectator to chase balls hit out of the court so that play can continue without interruption.

Another thing to remember is that when you are walking to your court to start your match you should never walk behind another match while play is in progress. Even at a distance you can be a distraction. And it is not any major sacrifice to wait a moment or two until the point is completed.

Etiquette for the Gallery

When you are a spectator at a tennis match, you are one of the "gallery" which has assembled to see good tennis played. There are well-defined (although unwritten) laws of conduct for the gallery, which are as binding upon them as the laws of tennis are upon the players and officials. Only by your cooperation in observing these unwritten laws can the perfect playing conditions be secured which make for the successful conduct of a tournament and your enjoyment of the matches you witness.

The spirit of good sportsmanship and correct behavior that tennis demands on the court is no less important on the part of the gallery. Whenever tournaments are played and there is promise of keen competition between players, onlookers will be found on the side lines. The tennis audience has always been supposed to be a discreet and refined one. There are correct times for applause if a shot or rally has been particularly brilliant. No one boos the umpire or hurls pop bottles. Tennis has thrills for the onlookers, but no noisy thrills. It is with this in mind that the following suggestions are made:

A moving background is the most disturbing condition that a player can experience; it makes perfect play of the ball next to impossible. For this reason you should not move about when opposite the end of a court, except when it is absolutely necessary to do so.

If you are in a stand that faces more than one court, do not move from one match to the other while the play is on; it is fatal to good play. If you want to watch the other match, wait until a set is finished before moving.

Do not applaud or give vocal expression of your feelings while a rally is on, but wait until the point has been played out and then applaud all you want to.

Do not applaud errors; your approval should be given to good strokes only. Do not applaud a shot that goes out of court or into the net, even if it gives a point to the player you want to win.

Do not coach the players. Never call "good," "out," "let it go," "hit it," etc., because thereby you are influencing a player's judgment, which is a factor in the outcome of the match. Coaching interferes with the fair playing of a match and may become extremely disconcerting by causing doubt as to whether some particular call came from a spectator or was an official's decision.

Never talk to an umpire, linesman, or player while a match is in progress.

If you do not agree with the decisions as they are given, withhold your disapproval; remember that the linesmen and umpires are in a better position to judge the play than you are and that the committee has selected the most competent men available for these duties.

Do not throw a stray ball into the court while play is on; wait until a stroke is finished and then roll it in.

Refrain from talking loudly while a match is on, as a player hears you and frequently takes it as a call from a linesman and does not play a good ball.

Under no circumstances walk or stand so near a court that you obstruct a contestant; this is inexcusable.

Do not walk or stand on the playing surface of a court before or after a match, as the heels of your shoes make holes in the surface that cause the ball to take bad bounds when a match is played.

Just before a match, do not try to renew an old acquaintanceship or express your wishes for victory to a player. Leave him alone; he has enough on his mind at that time. See him after the match; he has more time then and you will find him more cordial.

If you have to bring a dog with you, see that he watches the match from the side lines. All players are fond of dogs—after the match.

Know your neighbors at a tennis match before you criticize a player—friends and relatives frequently attend.

Read and know the rules; it will add to your enjoyment of the matches.

And last, do what you can to help the committee, for they are working for your pleasure. While the etiquette of the gallery at tennis may seem conservative, it is based on sane and logical reasons. Tennis is a conservative and dignified sport. The etiquette of both gallery and court conforms to the spirit of the game.

Results of Major Tournaments and Championships

USTA OPEN CHAMPIONS

National champions of the United States Lawn Tennis Association were provided for when that body was organized, May 21, 1881. Prior to that time so-called national championships had been held, in some cases several being contested in one year, but conditions varied at each tournament and the implements and equipment of the game had not become standardized.

The first championship of the United States under uniform conditions, open to all comers and sanctioned by the National Association, was held at The Casino, Newport, R.I., in August, 1881 (with a singles field of 24 men), and for 34 years without interruption the championship was held there. From 1915 to 1920 the West Side Tennis Club staged the tournament at Forest Hills, N.Y., and from 1921 to 1923 it was held at the German-town Cricket Club, Philadelphia. In 1924, after the completion of the West Side Tennis Club Sta-dium, the championship returned to Forest Hills, and was held there through 1977.

In 1968, two championships were held—one for amateurs at Boston's Longwood and another, the first U.S. Open, at Forest Hills. After 1969, the "National Singles" amateur event, per se, was dis-continued. Championships have been held each year since 1881 with the exception of 1917. In that year and only in that year Patriotic Tournaments were sanctioned by the National Association, be-cause of the participation of the United States in World War I.

A challenge round was instituted in 1884 and abandoned after the 1911 championship. During those years the champion "stood out"—in other words did not play through the tournament—eventually meeting the winner of the All Comers' in a challenge round for the championship.

The USTA National Tennis Center in Flushing Meadow (New York City) contains the stadium where the Open and its allied events have been staged since 1978.

USTA CHAMPIONS—MEN'S SINGLES

Year	Winner	Runner-up	Score
1881	Richard D. Sears	W. E. Glyn	6–0, 6–3, 6–2
1882	Richard D. Sears	C. M. Clark	6–1, 6–4, 6–0
1883	Richard D. Sears	J. Dwight	6–2, 6–0, 9–7
1884	Richard D. Sears	H. A. Taylor	6–0, 1–6, 6–0, 6–2
1885	Richard D. Sears	G. M. Brinley	6–3, 4–6, 6–0, 6–3
1886	Richard D. Sears	R. L. Beeckman	4–6, 6–1, 6–3, 6–4
1887	Richard D. Sears	H. W. Slocum, Jr.	6–1, 6–3, 6–2
1888*	Henry W. Slocum, Jr.	H. A. Taylor	6–4, 6–1, 6–0
1889	Henry W. Slocum, Jr.	Q. A. Shaw	6–3, 6–1, 4–6, 6–2
1890	Oliver S. Campbell	H. W. Slocum, Jr.	6–2, 4–6, 6–3, 6–1
1891	Oliver S. Campbell	C. Hobart	2–5, 7–5, 7–9, 6–1, 6–2
1892	Oliver S. Campbell	F. H. Hovey	7–5, 3–6, 6–3, 7–5
1893*	Robert D. Wrenn	F. H. Hovey	6–4, 3–6, 6–4, 6–4
1894	Robert D. Wrenn	M. F. Goodbody	6–8, 6–1, 6–4, 6–4
1895	Fred H. Hovey	R. D. Wrenn	6–3, 6–2, 6–4
1896	Robert D. Wrenn	F. H. Hovey	7–5, 3–6, 6–0, 1–6, 6–1
1897	Robert D. Wrenn	W. V. Eaves	4–6, 8–6, 6–3, 2–6, 6–2
1898*	Malcolm D. Whitman	D. F. Davis	3–6, 6–2, 6–2, 6–1
1899	Malcolm D. Whitman	J. P. Paret	6–1, 6–2, 3–6, 7–5
1900	Malcolm D. Whitman	W. A. Larned	6–4, 6–1, 6–2, 6–2
1901*	William A. Larned	B. C. Wright	6–2, 6–8, 6–4, 6–4
1902	William A. Larned	R. F. Doherty	4–6, 6–2, 6–4, 8–6
1903	Hugh L. Doherty	W. A. Larned	6–0, 6–3, 10–8
1904*	Holcombe Ward	W. J. Clothier	10–8, 6–4, 9–7
1905	Beals C. Wright	Holcombe Ward	6–2, 6–1, 11–9
1906	William J. Clothier	B. C. Wright	6–3, 6–0, 6–4
1907*	William A. Larned	Robert LeRoy	6–2, 6–2, 6–4
1908	William A. Larned	B. C. Wright	6–1, 6–2, 8–6
1909	William A. Larned	W. J. Clothier	6–1, 6–2, 5–7, 1–6, 6–1
1910	William A. Larned	T. C. Bundy	6–1, 5–7, 6–0, 6–8, 6–1
1911	William A. Larned	M. E. McLoughlin	6–4, 6–4, 6–2
1912†	Maurice E. McLoughlin	Wallace F. Johnson	3–6, 2–6, 6–2, 6–4, 6–2
1913	Maurice E. McLoughlin	R. N. Williams	6–4, 5–7, 6–3, 6–1
1914	Richard N. Williams	M. E. McLoughlin	6–3, 8–6, 10–8
1915	Wm. M. Johnston	M. E. McLoughlin	1–6, 6–0, 7–5, 10–8
1916	Richard N. Williams	Wm. M. Johnston	4–6, 6–4, 0–6, 6–2, 6–4
1917‡	Richard L. Murray	N. W. Niles	5–7, 8–6, 6–3, 6–3
1918	R. Lindley Murray	Wm. T. Tilden II	6–3, 6–1, 7–5
1919	Wm. M. Johnston	Wm. T. Tilden II	6–4, 6–4, 6–3
1920	Wm. T. Tilden II	Wm. M. Johnston	6–1, 1–6, 7–5, 5–7, 6–3
1921	Wm. T. Tilden II	Wallace F. Johnson	6–1, 6–3, 6–1
1922	Wm. T. Tilden II	Wm. M. Johnston	4–6, 3–6, 6–2, 6–3, 6–4
1923	Wm. T. Tilden II	Wm. M. Johnston	6–4, 6–1, 6–4
1924	Wm. T. Tilden II	Wm. M. Johnston	6–1, 9–7, 6–2
1925	Wm. T. Tilden II	Wm. M. Johnston	4–6, 11–9, 6–3, 4–6, 6–3
1926	Jean René Lacoste	Jean Borotra	6–4, 6–0, 6–4
1927	Jean René Lacoste	Wm. T. Tilden II	11–9, 6–3, 11–9
1928	Henri Cochet	Francis T. Hunter	4–6, 6–4, 3–6, 7–5, 6–3
1929	Wm. T. Tilden II	Francis T. Hunter	3–6, 6–3, 4–6, 6–2, 6–4
1930	John H. Doeg	Francis X. Shields	10–8, 1–6, 6–4, 16–14
1931	H. Ellsworth Vines, Jr.	George M. Lott, Jr.	7–9, 6–3, 9–7, 7–5
1932	H. Ellsworth Vines, Jr.	Henri Cochet	6–4, 6–4, 6–4
1933	Frederick J. Perry	John H. Crawford	6–3, 11–13, 4–6, 6–0, 6–1
1934	Frederick J. Perry	Wilmer L. Allison	6–4, 6–3, 3–6, 1–6, 8–6
1935	Wilmer L. Allison	Sidney B. Wood	6–2, 6–2, 6–3
1936	Fred Perry	J. Donald Budge	2–6, 6–2, 8–6, 1–6, 10–8

(above) Frank Sedgman was the first of a long line of Australians who won the Men's Singles National Championship after World War II.

(right) Rod Laver with the USLTA Open Trophy, which he won in 1969.

Year	Winner	Runner-up	Score
1937	J. Donald Budge	Baron G. von Cramm	6–1, 7–9, 6–1, 3–6, 6–1
1938	J. Donald Budge	C. Gene Mako	6–3, 6–8, 6–2, 6–1
1939	Robert Riggs	S. Welby Van Horn	6–4, 6–2, 6–4
1940	Donald McNeill	Robert L. Riggs	4–6, 6–8, 6–3, 6–3, 7–5
1941	Robert L. Riggs	Francis Kovacs II	5–7, 6–1, 6–3, 6–3
1942	Frederick R. Schroeder, Jr.	Frank Parker	8–6, 7–5, 3–6, 4–6, 6–2
1943	Lt. Joseph R. Hunt	Seaman John A. Kramer	6–3, 6–8, 10–8, 6–0
1944	Sgt. Frank A. Parker	William F. Talbert	6–4, 3–6, 6–3, 6–3
1945	Sgt. Frank A. Parker	William F. Talbert	14–12, 6–1, 6–2
1946	John A. Kramer	Tom Brown, Jr.	9–7, 6–3, 6–0
1947	John A. Kramer	Frank A. Parker	4–6, 2–6, 6–1, 6–0, 6–3
1948	Richard A. Gonzalez	Eric W. Sturgess	6–2, 6–3, 14–12
1949	Richard A. Gonzalez	Frederick R. Schroeder, Jr.	16–18, 2–6, 6–1, 6–2, 6–4
1950	Arthur Larsen	Herbert Flam	6–3, 4–6, 5–7, 6–4, 6–3
1951	Frank Sedgman	E. Victor Seixas, Jr.	6–4, 6–1, 6–1
1952	Frank Sedgman	Gardnar Mulloy	6–1, 6–2, 6–3
1953	Tony Trabert	E. Victor Seixas, Jr.	6–3, 6–2, 6–3
1954	E. Victor Seixas, Jr.	Rex Hartwig	3–6, 6–2, 6–4, 6–4
1955	Tony Trabert	Ken Rosewall	9–7, 6–3, 6–3
1956	Kenneth Rosewall	Lewis Hoad	4–6, 6–2, 6–3, 6–3
1957	Malcolm J. Anderson	Ashley J. Cooper	10–8, 7–5, 6–4
1958	Ashley J. Cooper	Malcolm J. Anderson	6–2, 3–6, 4–6, 10–8, 8–6
1959	Neale Fraser	Alejandro Olmedo	6–3, 5–7, 6–2, 6–4
1960	Neale Fraser	Rodney Laver	6–4, 6–4, 9–7
1961	Roy Emerson	Rodney Laver	7–5, 6–3, 6–2
1962	Rodney Laver	Roy Emerson	6–2, 6–4, 5–7, 6–4
1963	Rafael Osuna	Frank Froehling III	7–5, 6–4, 6–2
1964	Roy Emerson	Fred Stolle	6–4, 6–1, 6–4
1965	Manuel Santana	Cliff Drysdale	6–2, 7–9, 7–5, 6–1
1966	Fred Stolle	John Newcombe	4–6, 12–10, 6–3, 6–4
1967	John Newcombe	Clark Graebner	6–4, 6–4, 8–6
1968	Arthur Ashe	Robert Lutz	4–6, 6–3, 8–10, 6–0, 6–4
1969	Stanley R. Smith	Robert Lutz	9–7, 6–3, 6–1

*No challenge round played.   †Challenge round abolished.   ‡National Patriotic Tournament.

USTA OPEN CHAMPIONS—MEN'S SINGLES

Year	Winner	Runner-up	Score
1968	Arthur Ashe	Tom Okker	14–12, 5–7, 6–3, 3–6, 6–3
1969	Rod Laver	Tony Roche	7–9, 6–1, 6–3, 6–2
1970	Ken Rosewall	Tony Roche	2–6, 6–4, 7–6, 6–3
1971	Stanley R. Smith	Jan Kodes	3–6, 6–3, 6–2, 7–6
1972	Ilie Nastase	Arthur Ashe	3–6, 6–3, 6–7, 6–4, 6–3
1973	John Newcombe	Jan Kodes	6–4, 1–6, 4–6, 6–2, 6–2
1974	Jimmy Connors	Ken Rosewall	6–1, 6–0, 6–1
1975	Manuel Orantes	Jimmy Connors	6–4, 6–3, 6–3
1976	Jimmy Connors	Bjorn Borg	6–4, 3–6, 7–6, 6–4
1977	Guillermo Vilas	Jimmy Connors	2–6, 6–3, 7–6, 6–0
1978	Jimmy Connors	Bjorn Borg	6–4, 6–2, 6–2
1979	John McEnroe	Vitas Gerulaitis	7–5, 6–3, 6–3
1980	John McEnroe	Bjorn Borg	7–6, 6–1, 6–7, 5–7, 6–4

USTA Champions—Women's Singles

The national women's championships were held at the Philadelphia Cricket Club from 1887 to 1920 inclusive. From 1921 to 1977 they were held at Forest Hills. Originally the mixed doubles and women's doubles were played in connection with the Women's Singles Championship Tourna-ment. In 1921 the mixed doubles and in 1935 the women's doubles were transferred and made part of the National Doubles Championship program. From 1942, the women's and mixed doubles were played in connection with the men's championships at Forest Hills, transferring with them to the USTA National Tennis Center in 1978.

USTA CHAMPIONS—WOMEN'S SINGLES

Year	Winner	Runner-up	Score
1887	Ellen Hansell	Laura Knight	6–1, 6–0
1888	Bertha L. Townsend	Ellen Hansell	6–3, 6–5
1889	Bertha L. Townsend	Louise D. Voorhees	7–5, 6–2
1890	Ellen C. Roosevelt	Bertha L. Townsend	6–2, 6–3
1891	Mabel Cahill	Ellen C. Roosevelt	6–4, 6–1, 4–6, 6–3
1892	Mabel Cahill	Elizabeth Moore	5–7, 6–3, 6–4, 4–6, 6–2
1893*	Aline Terry	Alice Schultz	6–1, 6–3
1894	Helen Helwig	Aline Terry	7–5, 3–6, 6–0, 3–6, 6–3
1895	Juliette P. Atkinson	Helen Helwig	6–4, 6–2, 6–1
1896	Elizabeth Moore	Juliette Atkinson	6–4, 4–6, 6–3, 6–2
1897	Juliette Atkinson	Bessie Moore	6–3, 6–3, 4–6, 3–6, 6–3
1898	Juliette Atkinson	Marion Jones	6–3, 5–7, 6–4, 2–6, 7–5
1899*	Marion Jones	Maud Banks	6–1, 6–1, 7–5
1900*	Myrtle McAteer	Edith Parker	6–2, 6–2, 6–0
1901	Elizabeth Moore	Myrtle McAteer	6–4, 3–6, 7–5, 2–6, 6–2
1902	Marion Jones	Elizabeth Moore	6–1, 1–0, default
1903	Elizabeth Moore	Marion Jones	7–5, 8–6
1904	May Sutton	Elizabeth Moore	6–1, 6–2
1905*	Elizabeth Moore	Helen Homans	6–4, 5–7, 6–1
1906*	Helen Homans	Mrs. Maud Barger-Wallack	6–4, 6–3
1907*	Evelyn Sears	Carrie B. Neely	6–3, 6–2
1908	Mrs. Maud Barger-Wallach	Evelyn Sears	6–2, 1–6, 6–3
1909	Hazel Hotchkiss	Mrs. Barger-Wallach	6–0, 6–1
1910	Hazel Hotchkiss	Louise Hammond	6–4, 6–2

Molla Bjurstedt playing Eleanor Goss in 1918 for the Women's National Championship. Miss Bjurstedt won 6-4, 6-3, for one of seven titles.

Year	Winner	Runner-Up	Score
1911	Hazel Hotchkiss	Florence Sutton	8-10, 6-1, 9-7
1912*	Mary K. Browne	Eleanora Sears	6-4, 6-2
1913	Mary K. Browne	Dorothy Green	6-2, 7-5
1914	Mary K. Browne	Marie Wagner	6-2, 1-6, 6-1
1915*	Molla Bjurstedt	Mrs. Hazel H. Wightman	4-6, 6-2, 6-0
1916	Molla Bjurstedt	Mrs. Louise H. Raymond	6-0, 6-1
1917†	Molla Bjurstedt	Marion Vanderhoef	4-6, 6-0, 6-2
1918	Molla Bjurstedt	Eleanor E. Goss	6-4, 6-3
1919†	Mrs. Hazel H. Wightman	Marion Zinderstein	6-1, 6-2
1920	Mrs. Molla B. Mallory	Marion Zinderstein	6-3, 6-1
1921	Mrs. Molla B. Mallory	Mary K. Browne	4-6, 6-4, 6-2
1922	Mrs. Molla B. Mallory	Helen Wills	6-3, 6-1
1923	Helen Wills	Mrs. M. Mallory	6-2, 6-1
1924	Helen Wills	Mrs. M. Mallory	6-1, 6-2
1925	Helen Wills	Kathleen McKane	3-6, 6-0, 6-2
1926	Mrs. Molla B. Mallory	Elizabeth Ryan	4-6, 6-4, 9-7
1927	Helen Wills	Betty Nuthall	6-1, 6-4
1928	Helen Wills	Helen H. Jacobs	6-2, 6-1
1929	Helen Wills	Mrs. M. Watson	6-4, 6-2
1930	Betty Nuthall	Mrs. L. A. Harper	6-4, 6-1
1931	Mrs. Helen Wills Moody	Mrs. E. B. Whittingstall	6-4, 6-1
1932	Helen H. Jacobs	Carolin A. Babcock	6-2, 6-2
1933	Helen H. Jacobs	Mrs. Helen Wills Moody	8-6, 3-6, 3-0, default
1934	Helen H. Jacobs	Sarah H. Palfrey	6-1, 6-4
1935	Helen H. Jacobs	Mrs. Sarah P. Fabyan	6-1, 6-4
1936	Alice Marble	Helen H. Jacobs	4-6, 6-3, 6-2
1937	Anita Lizana	Jadwiga Jedrzejowska	6-4, 6-2
1938	Alice Marble	Nancy Wynne	6-0, 6-3
1939	Alice Marble	Helen H. Jacobs	6-0, 8-10, 6-4
1940	Alice Marble	Helen H. Jacobs	6-2, 6-3
1941	Mrs. Sarah Palfrey Cooke	Pauline Betz	6-1, 6-4
1942	Pauline Betz	A. Louise Brough	4-6, 6-1, 6-4
1943	Pauline Betz	A. Louise Brough	6-3, 5-7, 6-3
1944	Pauline Betz	Margaret Osborne	6-3, 8-6
1945	Mrs. Sarah P. Cooke	Pauline Betz	3-6, 8-6, 6-4

*No Challenge Round Played.
†National Patriotic Tournament.

USTA CHAMPIONS—WOMEN'S SINGLES (cont.)

Year	Winner	Runner-up	Score
1946	Pauline Betz	Mrs. Patricia Canning	11–9, 6–3
1947	A. Louise Brough	Margaret Osborne	8–6, 4–6, 6–1
1948	Mrs. Margaret Osborne du Pont	A. Louise Brough	4–6, 6–4, 15–13
1949	Mrs. Margaret Osborne du Pont	Doris Hart	6–4, 6–1
1950	Mrs. Margaret Osborne du Pont	Doris Hart	6–3, 6–3
1951	Maureen Connolly	Shirley Fry	6–3, 1–6, 6–4
1952	Maureen Connolly	Doris Hart	6–3, 7–5
1953	Maureen Connolly	Doris Hart	6–2, 6–4
1954	Doris Hart	A. Louise Brough	6–8, 6–1, 8–6
1955	Doris Hart	Patricia Ward	6–4, 6–2
1956	Shirley J. Fry	Althea Gibson	6–3, 6–4
1957	Althea Gibson	A. Louise Brough	6–3, 6–2
1958	Althea Gibson	Darlene Hard	3–6, 6–1, 6–2
1959	Maria E. Bueno	Christine Truman	6–1, 6–4
1960	Darlene R. Hard	Maria E. Bueno	6–4, 10–12, 6–4
1961	Darlene R. Hard	Ann Haydon	6–3, 6–4
1962	Margaret Smith	Darlene Hard	9–7, 6–4
1963	Maria E. Bueno	Margaret Smith	7–5, 6–4
1964	Maria E. Bueno	Mrs. Carole C. Graebner	6–1, 6–0
1965	Margaret Smith	Billie Jean Moffitt	8–6, 7–5
1966	Maria E. Bueno	Nancy Richey	6–3, 6–1
1967	Mrs. Billie Jean King	Mrs. Ann H. Jones	11–9, 6–4
1968	Mrs. Margaret S. Court	Maria E. Bueno	6–2, 6–2
1969	Mrs. Margaret S. Court	Virginia Wade	4–6, 6–3, 6–0

USTA OPEN CHAMPIONS—WOMEN'S SINGLES

Year	Winner	Runner-up	Score
1968	Virginia Wade	Mrs. Billie Jean King	6–4, 6–2
1969	Mrs. Margaret S. Court	Nancy Richey	6–2, 6–2
1970	Mrs. Margaret S. Court	Rosemary Casals	6–2, 2–6, 6–1
1971	Mrs. Billie Jean King	Rosemary Casals	6–4, 7–6
1972	Mrs. Billie Jean King	Kerry Melville	6–3, 7–5
1973	Mrs. Margaret S. Court	Evonne Goolagong	7–6, 5–7, 6–2
1974	Mrs. Billie Jean King	Evonne Goolagong	3–6, 6–3, 7–5
1975	Chris Evert	Evonne Goolagong	5–7, 6–4, 6–2
1976	Chris Evert	Mrs. Evonne G. Cawley	6–3, 6–0
1977	Chris Evert	Wendy Turnbull	7–6, 6–2
1978	Chris Evert	Pam Shriver	7–5, 6–4
1979	Tracy Austin	Mrs. Chris Evert Lloyd	6–4, 6–3
1980	Mrs. Chris Evert Lloyd	Hana Mandlikova	5–7, 6–1, 6–1

USTA Champions—Men's Doubles

Prior to 1890 the national doubles championship was played in conjunction with the singles tournament. From 1890 to 1906 tournaments were held in the East and West, and the sectional winners at these meets then played off for the privilege of meeting the standing-out champions in the challenge round. In 1907 there were three sections competing in preliminary doubles, and this number was increased in subsequent years. In 1917 a play-through Patriotic Tournament was held, as no championships were sanctioned that year. The 1918 championship meet was also a play-through tournament, the sectional and preliminary doubles and the challenge round having been done

The result of the 1969 Open Championship can be seen on the scoreboard. Mrs. Court *(right)* defeated Miss Richey *(left)* 6-2, 6-2.

away with. In 1919 the plan of qualifying sectional winners was restored, although an exception was made in the case of the Australian teams, which were on a visit to the United States at that time, and the last challenge round in national doubles was played that year. Since 1920 there have been few changes in the conditions that now prevail. The mixed doubles championship was contested

in conjunction with the women's national tournament until 1921, after which it was added to the men's doubles competition. In 1935 the Women's Doubles Championship was added to the Doubles Championship Tournament, and the Mixed Doubles Championship was added to the Singles Championship Tournament.

USTA CHAMPIONS—MEN'S DOUBLES

Year	Winners	Runners-up
1881	C. M. Clark and F. W. Taylor	A. Van Rensselaer and A. E. Newbold
1882	Richard D. Sears and James Dwight	W. Nightingale and G. M. Smith
1883	Richard D. Sears and James Dwight	A. Van Rensselaer and A. E. Newbold
1884	Richard D. Sears and James Dwight	A. Van Rensselaer and W. V. R. Berry
1885	Richard D. Sears and Joseph S. Clark	H. W. Slocum, Jr. and W. P. Knapp
1886	Richard D. Sears and James Dwight	H. A. Taylor and Godfrey M. Brinley
1887	Richard D. Sears and James Dwight	H. A. Taylor and H. W. Slocum, Jr.
1888	Oliver S. Campbell and Valentine G. Hall	Clarence Hobart and E. P. MacMullen
1889	Henry W. Slocum, Jr. and Howard A. Taylor	V. G. Hall and O. S. Campbell
1890	Valentine G. Hall and Clarence Hobart	Charles W. Carver and John A. Ryerson
1891	Oliver S. Campbell and Robt. Huntington, Jr.	V. G. Hall and Clarence Hobart
1892	Oliver S. Campbell and Robert. Huntington, Jr.	V. G. Hall and Edward L. Hall
1893	Clarence Hobart and Fred H. Hovey	O. S. Campbell and Robt. P. Huntington, Jr.
1894	Clarence Hobart and Fred H. Hovey	Carr B. Neel and Samuel R. Neel
1895	Malcolm G. Chace and R. D. Wrenn	John Howland and A. E. Foote
1896	Carr B. Neel and Samuel R. Neel	Robert D. Wrenn and M. G. Chace
1897	Leo E. Ware and Geo. P. Sheldon, Jr.	Harold S. Mahony and Harold A. Nisbet
1898	Leo E. Ware and Geo. P. Sheldon, Jr.	Holcombe Ward and Dwight F. Davis
1899	Holcombe Ward and Dwight F. Davis	Leo E. Ware and Geo. P. Sheldon, Jr.
1900	Holcombe Ward and Dwight F. Davis	Fred B. Alexander and Raymond D. Little
1901	Holcombe Ward and Dwight F. Davis	Leo E. Ware and Beals C. Wright
1902	Reginald F. Doherty and Hugh L. Doherty	Holcombe Ward and Dwight F. Davis

USTA CHAMPIONS—MEN'S DOUBLES (cont.)

Year	Winners	Runners-up
1903	Reginald F. Doherty and Hugh L. Doherty	Kreigh Collins and L. Harry Waidner
1904	Holcombe Ward and Beals C. Wright	Kreigh Collins and Raymond D. Little
1905	Holcombe Ward and Beals C. Wright	Fred B. Alexander and Harold H. Hackett
1906	Holcombe Ward and Beals C. Wright	Fred B. Alexander and Harold H. Hackett
1907	Fred B. Alexander and Harold H. Hackett	William A. Larned and William J. Clothier
1908	Fred B. Alexander and Harold H. Hackett	Raymond D. Little and Beals C. Wright
1909	Ferd B. Alexander and Harold H. Hackett	Maurice E. McLoughlin and George J. Janes
1910	Fred B. Alexander and Harold H. Hackett	Thos. C. Bundy and Trowbridge W. Hendrick
1911	Raymond D. Little and Gustave F. Touchard	Fred B. Alexander and Harold H. Hackett
1912	Maurice E. McLoughlin and Thos. C. Bundy	Raymond D. Little and Gustave F. Touchard
1913	Maurice E. McLoughlin and Thos. C. Bundy	John R. Strachan and Clarence J. Griffin
1914	Maurice E. McLoughlin and Thos. C. Bundy	George M. Church and Dean Mathey
1915	William M. Johnston and Clarence J. Griffin	Maurice E. McLoughlin and Thos. C. Bundy
1916	William M. Johnston and Clarence J. Griffin	Maurice E. McLoughlin and Ward Dawson
1917*	Fred B. Alexander and Harold A. Throckmorton	Harry C. Johnson and Irving C. Wright
1918	William T. Tilden II and Vincent Richards	Fred B. Alexander and Beals C. Wright
1919	Norman E. Brookes and Gerald Patterson	William T. Tilden, II and Vincent Richards
1920	William M. Johnston and Clarence J. Griffin	Willis F. Davis and Roland E. Roberts
1921	William T. Tilden II and Vincent Richards	R. N. Williams, II and W. M. Washburn
1922	William T. Tilden II and Vincent Richards	Gerald L. Patterson and Pat O'Hara Wood
1923	William T. Tilden II and Brian I. C. Norton	R. N. Williams II and W. M. Washburn
1924	Howard Kinsey and Robert Kinsey	Gerald L. Patterson and Pat O'Hara Wood
1925	R. Norris Williams II and Vincent Richards	Gerald Patterson and John B. Hawkes
1926	R. N. Williams II and Vincent Richards	Wm. T. Tilden, II and Alfred H. Chapin, Jr.
1927	Wm. T. Tilden II and Francis T. Hunter	Wm. M. Johnston and R. Norris Williams, Jr.
1928	George M. Lott, Jr. and John Hennessey	Gerald L. Patterson and John B. Hawkes
1929	George M. Lott, Jr. and John H. Doeg	Berkeley Bell and Lewis N. White
1930	George M. Lott, Jr. and John H. Doeg	John Van Ryn and Wilmer Allison
1931	Wilmer Allison and John Van Ryn	Gregory Mangin and Berkeley Bell
1932	H. Ellsworth Vines and Keith Gledhill	Wilmer Allison and John Van Ryn
1933	George M. Lott, Jr. and Lester R. Stoefen	Francis X. Shields and Frank A. Parker
1934	George M. Lott, Jr. and Lester R. Stoefen	Wilmer L. Allison and John Van Ryn
1935	Wilmer L. Allison and John Van Ryn	J. Donald Budge and C. Gene Mako
1936	J. Donald Budge and C. Gene Mako	Wilmer L. Allison and John Van Ryn
1937	Baron G. von Cramm and Henner Henkel	J. Donald Budge and C. Gene Mako
1938	J. Donald Budge and C. Gene Mako	Adrian K. Quist and John Bromwich
1939	Adrian K. Quist and John Bromwich	John A. Crawford and Harry C. Hopman
1940	John A. Kramer and Frederick T. Schroeder, Jr.	Gardnar Mulloy and Henry J. Prussoff
1941	John A. Kramer and Frederick T. Schroeder, Jr.	Wayne Sabin and Gardnar Mulloy

*National Patriotic Tournament.

Year	Winners	Runners-up
1942	Lt. Gardnar Mulloy and William Talbert	Frederick Schroeder, Jr. and Sidney B. Wood, Jr.
1943	J. A. Kramer and Frank A. Parker	William Talbert and David Freeman
1944	Lt. W. Donald McNeill and Robert Falkenburg	William Talbert and Francisco Segura
1945	Lt. Gardnar Mulloy and William Talbert	Robert Falkenburg and Jack Tuero
1946	Gardnar Mulloy and William Talbert	Donald McNeill and Frank Guernsey
1947	John A. Kramer and Frederick T. Schroeder, Jr.	William Talbert and William Sidwell
1948	Gardnar Mulloy and William Talbert	Frank A. Parker and Frederick T. Schroeder, Jr.
1949	John Bromwich and William Sidwell	Frank Sedgman and George Worthington
1950	John Bromwich and Frank Sedgman	William Talbert and Gardnar Mulloy
1951	Kenneth McGregor and Frank Sedgman	Don Candy and Mervyn Rose
1952	Mervyn Rose and E. Victor Seixas, Jr.	Kenneth McGregor and Frank Sedgman
1953	Rex Hartwig and Mervyn Rose	Gardnar Mulloy and William F. Talbert
1954	E. Victor Seixas, Jr. and Tony Trabert	Lewis Hoad and Ken Rosewall
1955	Kosei Kamo and Atsushi Miyagi	Gerald Moss and William Quillian
1956	Lewis Hoad and Kenneth Rosewall	Hamilton Richardson and E. Victor Seixas, Jr.
1957	Ashley J. Cooper and Neale Fraser	Gardnar Mulloy and Budge Patty
1958	Alex Olmedo and Hamilton Richardson	Sam Giammalva and Barry MacKay
1959	Neale Fraser and Roy Emerson	Alex Olmedo and Earl Buccholz, Jr.
1960	Neale Fraser and Roy Emerson	Rod Laver and Bob Mark
1961	Charles McKinley and Dennis Ralston	Rafael Osuna and Antonio Palafox
1962	Rafael Osuna and Antonio Palafox	Charles McKinley and Dennis Ralston
1963	Charles McKinley and Dennis Ralston	Rafael Osuna and Antonio Palafox
1964	Charles McKinley and Dennis Ralston	Graham Stilwell and Mike Sangster
1965	Roy Emerson and Fred Stolle	Frank Froehling III and Charles Pasarell
1966	Roy Emerson and Fred Stolle	Clark Graebner and Dennis Ralston
1967	John Newcombe and Tony Roche	William Bowrey and Owen Davidson
1968	Robert Lutz and Stan Smith	Robert Hewitt and Ray Moore
1969	Richard Crealy and Alan Stone	William Bowrey and Charles Pasarell

USTA OPEN CHAMPIONS—MEN'S DOUBLES

Year	Winners	Runners-Up
1968	Robert Lutz and Stan Smith	Arthur Ashe and Andres Gimeno
1969	Ken Rosewall and Fred Stolle	Charles Pasarell and Dennis Ralston
1970	Pierre Barthes and Nicki Pilic	Roy Emerson and Rod Laver
1971	John Newcombe and Roger Taylor	Stan Smith and Eric van Dillen
1972	Cliff Drysdale and Roger Taylor	Owen Davidson and John Newcombe
1973	Owen Davidson and John Newcombe	Rod Laver and Ken Rosewall
1974	Bob Lutz and Stan Smith	Pat Cornejo and Jaime Fillol
1975	Jimmy Connors and Ilie Nastase	Tom Okker and Marty Riessen
1976	Marty Riessen and Tom Okker	Paul Kornk and Cliff Letcher
1977	Bob Hewitt and Frew McMillan	Raul Ramirez and Brian Gottfried
1978	Bob Lutz and Stan Smith	Marty Riessen and Sherwood Stewart
1979	John McEnroe and Peter Fleming	Bob Lutz and Stan Smith
1980	John McEnroe and Peter Fleming	

USTA Champions—Women's Doubles

1887 Ellen Hansell and Laura Knight
1888–89 not held
1890 Ellen C. Roosevelt and Grace W. Roosevelt
1891 Mabel E. Cahill and Mrs. W. Fellowes Morgan
1892 Mabel E. Cahill and A. M. McKinley
1893 Aline M. Terry and Hattie Butler
1894 Helen R. Helwig and Juliette P. Atkinson
1895 Helen R. Helwig and Juliette P. Atkinson
1896 Elisabeth H. Moore and Juliette P. Atkinson
1897 Juliette P. Atkinson and Kathleen Atkinson
1898 Juliette P. Atkinson and Kathleen Atkinson
1899 Jane W. Craven and Myrtle McAteer
1900 Edith Parker and Hallie Champlin
1901 Juliette P. Atkinson and Myrtle McAteer
1902 Juliette P. Atkinson and Marion Jones
1903 Elisabeth H. Moore and Carrie B. Neely
1904 May G. Sutton and Miriam Hall
1905 Helen Homans and Carrie B. Neely
1906 Mrs. L. S. Coe and Mrs. D. S. Platt
1907 Marie Weimer and Carrie B. Neely
1908 Evelyn Sears and Margaret Curtis
1909 Hazel V. Hotchkiss and Edith E. Rotch
1910 Hazel V. Hotchkiss and Edith E. Rotch
1911 Hazel V. Hotchkiss and Eleanora Sears
1912 Dorothy Green and Mary K. Browne
1913 Mary K. Browne and Mrs. R. H. Williams
1914 Mary K. Browne and Mrs. R. H. Williams
1915 Mrs. Hazel Hotchkiss Wightman and Eleonora Sears
1916 Molla Bjurstedt and Eleanora Sears
1917* Molla Bjurstedt and Eleanora Sears
1918 Marion Zinderstein and Eleanor Goss
1919 Marion Zinderstein and Eleanor Goss
1920 Marion Zinderstein and Eleanor Goss
1921 Mary K. Browne and Mrs. R. H. Williams
1922 Mrs. Marion Zinderstein Jessup and Helen N. Wills
1923 Kathleen McKane and Mrs. B. C. Covell
1924 Mrs. Hazel Hotchkiss Wightman and Helen N. Wills

1925 Mary K. Browne and Helen N. Wills
1926 Elizabeth Ryan and Eleanor Goss
1927 Mrs. Kathleen McKane Godfree and Ermyntrude Harvey
1928 Mrs. Hazel Hotchkiss Wightman and Helen N. Wills
1929 Mrs. Phoebe Watson and Mrs. L. R. C. Michell
1930 Betty Nuthall and Sarah Palfrey
1931 Betty Nuthall and Mrs. Eileen Bennett Whittingstall
1932 Helen Jacobs and Sarah Palfrey
1933 Betty Nuthall and Freda James
1934 Helen Jacobs and Sarah Palfrey
1935 Helen Jacobs and Mrs. Sarah Palfrey Fabyan
1936 Mrs. Marjorie Gladman Van Ryn and Carolin Babcock
1937 Mrs. Sarah Palfrey Fabyan and Alice Marble
1938 Mrs. Sarah Palfrey Fabyan and Alice Marble
1939 Mrs. Sarah Palfrey Fabyan and Alice Marble
1940 Mrs. Sarah Palfrey Fabyan and Alice Marble
1941 Mrs. Sarah Palfrey Cooke and Margaret E. Osborne
1942 A. Louise Brough and Margaret E. Osborne
1943 A. Louise Brough and Margaret E. Osborne
1944 A. Louise Brough and Margaret E. Osborne
1945 A. Louise Brough and Margaret E. Osborne
1946 A. Louise Brough and Margaret E. Osborne
1947 A. Louise Brough and Margaret E. Osborne
1948 A. Louise Brough and Mrs. Margaret Osborne du Pont
1949 A. Louise Brough and Margaret Osborne du Pont
1950 A. Louise Brough and Mrs. Margaret Osborne du Pont

*National Patriotic Tournament.

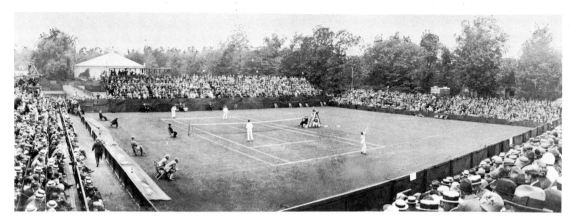

The National Doubles Championships were held at the Longwood Courts near Boston for many years.

1951	Shirley Fry and Doris Hart
1952	Shirley Fry and Doris Hart
1953	Shirley Fry and Doris Hart
1954	Shirley Fry and Doris Hart
1955	A. Louise Brough and Mrs. Margaret Osborne du Pont
1956	A. Louise Brough and Mrs. Margaret Osborne du Pont
1957	A. Louise Brough and Mrs. Margaret Osborne du Pont
1958	Jeanne M. Arth and Darlene R. Hard
1959	Jeanne M. Arth and Darlene R. Hard
1960	Maria E. Bueno and Darlene R. Hard
1961	Darlene R. Hard and Lesley Turner
1962	Darlene R. Hard and Maria E. Bueno
1963	Robyn Ebbern and Margaret Smith
1964	Billie Jean Moffitt and Mrs. Karen H. Susman
1965	Mrs. Carole Caldwell Graebner and Nancy Richey
1966	Maria E. Bueno and Nancy Richey
1967	Rosemary Casals and Mrs. Billie Jean King
1968	Maria E. Bueno and Mrs. Margaret S. Court
1969	Mrs. Margaret S. Court and Virginia Wade

USTA Open Champions—Women's Doubles

1968	Maria E. Bueno and Mrs. Margaret S. Court
1969	Françoise Durr and Darlene Hard
1970	Mrs. Margaret S. Court and Judy Dalton
1971	Rosemary Casals and Judy Dalton
1972	Francoise Durr and Betty Stove
1973	Mrs. Margaret Smith Court and Virginia Wade
1974	Mrs. Billie Jean King and Rosemary Casals
1975	Mrs. Margaret Smith Court and Virginia Wade
1976	Linky Boshoff and Ilana Kloss
1977	Martina Navratilova and Betty Stove
1978	Mrs. Billie Jean King and Martina Navratilova
1979	Betty Stove and Wendy Turnbull
1980	Mrs. Billie Jean King and Martina Navratilova

USTA Champions—Mixed Doubles

1887	Virginia Stokes and Joseph S. Clark
1888	Marion Wright and Joseph S. Clark
1889	not held

USTA Champions—Mixed Doubles *(cont.)*

1890 Mabel E. Cahill and R.V. Beach
1891 Mabel E. Cahill and M.R. Wright
1892 Mabel E. Cahill and Clarence Hobart
1893 Ellen C. Roosevelt and Clarence Hobart
1894 Juliette P. Atkinson and Edwin P. Fischer
1895 Juliette P. Atkinson and Edwin P. Fischer
1896 Juliette P. Atkinson and Edwin P. Fischer
1897 Laura Henson and D. L. Magruder
1898 Carrie B. Neely and Edwin P. Fischer
1899 Elizabeth J. Rastall and Albert L. Hoskins
1900 Margaret Hunnewell and Alfred Codman
1901 Marion Jones and Raymond D. Little
1902 Elizabeth H. Moore and Wylie C. Grant
1903 Helen Chapman and Harry F. Allen
1904 Elisabeth H. Moore and Wylie C. Grant
1905 Mrs. Alice S. Hobart and Clarence Hobart
1906 Sarah Coffin and Edward B. Dewhurst
1907 May Sayres and Wallace F. Johnson
1908 Edith E. Rotch and Nathaniel W. Niles
1909 Hazel V. Hotchkiss and Wallace F. Johnson
1910 Hazel V. Hotchkiss and Joseph R. Carpenter, Jr.
1911 Hazel V. Hotchkiss and Wallace F. Johnson
1912 Mary K. Browne and R. N. Williams II
1913 Mary K. Browne and William T. Tilden II
1914 Mary K. Browne and William T. Tilden II
1915 Mrs. Hazel Hotchkiss Wightman and Harry C. Johnson
1916 Eleonora Sears and Willis E. Davis
1917* Molla Bjurstedt and Irving C. Wright
1918 Mrs. Hazel Hotchkiss Wightman and Irving C. Wright
1919 Marion Zinderstein and Vincent Richards
1920 Mrs. Hazel Hotchkiss Wightman and Wallace F. Johnson
1921 Mary K. Browne and William Johnston
*National Patriotic Tournament.

1922 Mrs. Molla Bjurstedt Mallory and William T. Tilden II
1923 Mrs. Molla Bjurstedt Mallory and William T. Tilden II
1924 Helen N. Wills and Vincent Richards
1925 Kathleen McKane and John B. Hawkes
1926 Elizabeth Ryan and Jean Borotra
1927 Eileen Bennett and Henri Cochet
1928 Helen N. Wills and John B. Hawkes
1929 Betty Nuthall and George M. Lott, Jr.
1930 Edith Cross and Wilmer L. Allison
1931 Betty Nuthall and George M. Lott, Jr.
1932 Sarah Palfrey and Frederick Perry
1933 Elizabeth Ryan and H. Ellsworth Vines, Jr.
1934 Helen H. Jacobs and George M. Lott, Jr.
1935 Mrs. Sarah Palfrey Fabyan and Enrique Maier
1936 Alice Marble and C. Gene Mako
1937 Mrs. Sarah Palfrey Fabyan and J. Donald Budge
1938 Alice Marble and J. Donald Budge
1939 Alice Marble and Harry C. Hopman
1940 Alice Marble and Robert L. Riggs
1941 Mrs. Sarah Palfrey Cooke and John A. Kramer
1942 A. Louise Brough and Frederick R. Schroeder, Jr.
1943 Margaret Osborne and William F. Talbert
1944 Margaret Osborne and William F. Talbert
1945 Margaret Osborne and William F. Talbert
1946 Margaret Osborne and William F. Talbert
1947 A. Louise Brough and John Bromwich
1948 A. Louise Brough and Thomas P. Brown, Jr.
1949 A. Louise Brough and Eric Sturgess
1950 Mrs. Margaret Osborne du Pont and Kenneth McGregor
1951 Doris Hart and Frank Sedgman
1952 Doris Hart and Frank Sedgman
1953 Doris Hart and E. Victor Seixas, Jr.
1954 Doris Hart and E. Victor Seixas, Jr.
1955 Doris Hart and E. Victor Seixas, Jr.
1956 Mrs. Margaret Osborne du Pont and Kenneth Rosewall

1957 Althea Gibson and Kurt Nielsen
1958 Mrs. Margaret Osborne du Pont and
    Neale Fraser
1959 Mrs. Margaret Osborne du Pont and
    Neale Fraser
1960 Mrs. Margaret Osborne du Pont and
    Neale Fraser
1961 Margaret Smith and Robert Mark
1962 Margaret Smith and Fred Stolle
1963 Margaret Smith and Ken Fletcher
1964 Margaret Smith and John Newcombe
1965 Margaret Smith and Fred Stolle
1966 Mrs. Donna Floyd Fales and Owen
    Davidson
1967 Mrs. Billie Jean King and Owen
    Davidson
1968 Mary Ann Eisel and Peter Curtis
1969 Patti Hogan and Paul Sullivan

USTA Open Champions—Mixed Doubles

1969 Mrs. Margaret S. Court and Martin Riessen
1970 Mrs. Margaret S. Court and Martin
    Riessen
1971 Mrs. Billie Jean King and Owen
    Davidson
1972 Mrs. Margaret Smith Court and Marty
    Riessen
1973 Mrs. Billie Jean King and Owen
    Davidson
1974 Pam Teeguarden and Geoff Masters
1975 Rosemary Casals and Dick Stockton
1976 Mrs. Billie Jean King and Phil Dent
1977 Betty Stove and Frew McMillan
1978 Betty Stove and Frew McMillan
1979 Greer Stevens and Bob Hewitt
1980 Wendy Turnbull and Marty Riessen

USTA Champions—Junior Singles

1916 Harold A. Throckmorton
1917 Charles S. Garland
1918 Harold L. Taylor
1919 Vincent Richards
1920 Vincent Richards
1921 Vincent Richards
1922 Arnold W. Jones
1923 George M. Lott, Jr.

Dennis Ralston won the USLTA Junior Singles title on his way to Davis Cup fame.

1924 George M. Lott, Jr.
1925 Cranston M. Holman
1926 John Doeg
1927 Francis X. Shields
1928 Francis X. Shields
1929 Keith Gledhill
1930 Wilmer Hines
1931 Jack Lynch
1932 Frank Parker
1933 Donald Budge
1934 C. Gene Mako
1935 Robert Riggs
1936 Julius Heldman
1937 Joseph R. Hunt
1938 David Freeman
1939 Frederick R. Schroeder, Jr.
1940 Robert D. Carrothers, Jr.
1941 J. Edward (Budge) Patty
1942 J. Edward (Budge) Patty
1943 Robert Falkenburg
1944 Robert Falkenburg
1945 Herbert Flam
1946 Herbert Flam
1947 Herbert Behrens

USTA Champions—Junior Singles *(cont.)*

1948	Gilbert A. Bogley
1949	Gilbert A. Bogley
1950	Hamilton Richardson
1951	Ted Rogers
1952	Jack Frost
1953	John Lesch
1954	Gerald Moss
1955	Esteban Reyes
1956	Rodney Laver
1957	Alan Roberts
1958	Earl Buchholz, Jr.
1959	Dennis Ralston
1960	William Lenoir
1961	Charles Pasarell
1962	Mike Belkin

1963	Cliff Richey
1964	Stanley R. Smith
1965	Robert Lutz
1966	Stephen Avoyer
1967	Jeff Borowiak
1968	Robert McKinley
1969	Erik Van Dillen
1970	Brian Gottfried
1971	Raul Ramirez
1972	Patrick DuPre
1973	Bill Martin
1974	Ferdi Taygan
1975	Howard Schoenfeld
1976	Larry Gottfried
1977	Van Winitsky
1978	David Dowlen
1979	Scott Davis
1980	Sammy Giammalva

USTA OPEN CHAMPIONS—JUNIOR SINGLES

Year	Boys	Girls
1973	Billy Martin	
1974	Billy Martin	Ilana Kloss
1975	Howard Schoenfield	Natasha Chmyreva
1976	Ricardo Ycaza	Marise Krueger
1977	Van Winitsky	Claudie Casablanca
1978	Per Hjertquist	Linda Siegel
1979	Scott Davis	Alycia Moulton
1980	Mike Folberg	Susan Mascarin

USTA Champions—Junior Doubles

1918	Vincent Richards and Harold L. Taylor
1919	Frank T. Anderson and J. Cecil Donaldson
1920	Harold Godshall and Robert Hinckley
1921	Arnold W. Jones and William W. Ingraham
1922	Arnold W. Jones and William W. Ingraham
1923	George M. Lott, Jr. and Julius Sagalowsky

1924	George M. Lott, Jr. and Thomas McGlinn
1925	Malcolm T. Hill and Henry L. Johnson, Jr.
1926	Berkeley Bell and James Quick
1927	C. Alphonso Smith and Edward Jacobs
1928	Francis X. Shields and W. Barry Wood
1929	Ellsworth Vines and Keith Gledhill
1930	Wilmer Hines and Judge L. Beaver
1931	Kendall Cram and Judge L. Beaver
1932	Jack Lynch and C. Gene Mako
1933	C. Gene Mako and Ben Dey

1934 C. Gene Mako and Lawrence Nelson
1935 Robert Riggs and Joseph R. Hunt
1936 Joseph R. Hunt and Julius Heldman
1937 Joseph R. Hunt and John Moreno, Jr.
1938 David Freeman and S. Welby Van Horn
1939 John A. Kramer and C. E. Olewine
1940 R. D. Carrothers, Jr. and D. C.
        Woodbury
1941 James A. Evert and Robert Smidl
1942 J. E. (Budge) Patty and Robert
        Falkenburg
1943 Robert Falkenburg and James Brink
1944 Robert Falkenburg and John Shea
1945 Herbert Flam and Hugh Stewart
1946 Herbert Flam and Hugh Stewart
1947 Herbert Behrens and Richard Mouledous
1948 Richard Mouledous and Keston Deimling
1949 Gilbert A. Bogley and Richard Squires
1950 Whitney Reed and Norman Peterson
1951 Donald Flye and William Quillian
1952 Francisco Contreras and Sam Giammalva
1953 Jon Douglas and Myron Franks
1954 Earl Baumgardner and Gerald Moss
1955 Gregory Grant and Juan Jose
1956 Rodney Laver and James Shaffer
1957 Robert H. R. Delgado and Allen Fox
1958 Earl Buchholz, Jr. and Charles McKinley
1959 Charles McKinley and Martin Riessen
1960 William Lenoir and Frank Froehling
1961 Charles Pasarell and Clark Graebner
1962 Jackie Cooper and Martin Schad
1963 Jack Jackson and John Pickens
1964 Dean Penero and Jeff Brown
1965 Marcelo Lara and Jasjit Singh
1966 Alberto Carrero and Stanley Pasarell
1967 Zan Guerry and Tony Ortiz
1968 Robert McKinley and F. D. Robbins
1969 Richard Stockton and Erik Van Dillen
1970 Brian Gottfried and Alex Mayer, Jr.
1971 James Delaney and Chip Fisher
1972 Stephen Mott and Brian Teacher
1973 Bill Martin and Trey Waltke
1974 Francisco Gonzalez and Rocky Maguire
1975 Tony Giammalva and Bill Scanlon
1976 Larry Gottfried and John McEnroe
1977 Robert Van't Hof and Van Winitsky
1978 Scott Bondurant and Blaine Willenborg
1979 Mike DePalmer and Rodney Harmon
1980 Ben Testerman and Scott Davis

USTA Champions—Junior Singles (Grass)

1966 James Rombeau
1967 Mike Estep
1968 F. D. Robbins
1969–74 not held
1975 Jai DiLouie
1976 Larry Gottfried
1977 Mel Purcell
1978 David Siegler
1979 Scott Davis
1980 Scott Davis

USTA Champions—Junior Doubles (Grass)

1966 Stephen Avoyer and James Rombeau
1967 Mike Estep and Zan Guerry
1968 Robert McKinley and F. D. Robbins
1969–74 not held
1975 Chris Delaney and Peter Rennert
1976 Larry Gottfried and John McEnroe
1977 Peter Rennert and Martin Davis
1978 David Dowlen and Billy Nealon
1979 Scott Davis and Fabio Thiou-Bet
1980 Scott Davis and Ben Testerman

USTA NATIONAL CHAMPIONS

USTA Champions—Boys' 12 Singles

1962 Richard Stockton
1963 Richard Stockton
1964 Brian Gottfried
1965 Jake Warde
1966 Jake Warde
1967 Eugene Mayer
1968 Eugene Mayer
1969 Ben McKown
1970 Juan Farrow
1971 Teddy Staren
1972 Blaine Willenborg
1973 Peter Herrmann
1974 Ben Testerman
1975 Chris Huff
1976 James Arias
1977 Richard Leach
1978 Richey Reneberg
1979 Neville Williams
1980 Al Parker

USTA Champions—Girls' 12 Singles

1962	Connie Capozzi
1963	Connie Capozzi
1964	Patty Ann Reese
1965	Marcelyn Louie
1966	Christine Bartkowicz
1967	Ann Kiyomura
1968	Marna Louie
1969	Jeanne Evert
1970	Lynn Epstein
1971	Sherry Acker
1972	Mareen Louie
1973	Linda Siegel
1974	Tracy Austin
1975	Shelly Solomon
1976	Susan Mascarin
1977	Andrea Jaeger
1978	Margaret Hopkins
1979	Kathy Rinaldi
1980	Marianne Werdel

USTA Champions—Boys' 12 Doubles

1962	Rick Devereaux and Richard Stockton
1963	Brian Gottfried and Richard Stockton
1964	Brian Gottfried and James Connors
1965	James Hagey and Paul Lockwood
1966	Fred DeJesus and Jake Warde
1967	David Bohrnstedt and Dave Sherbeck
1968	Billy Martin and Eugene Mayer
1969	Pem Guerry and Howard Schoenfield
1970	Juan Farrow and Chip Hooper
1971	Teddy Staren and Dave Pelisek
1972	Bobby Berger and Blaine Willenborg
1973	Paul Crozier and Boyd Bryan
1974	John Davis and Howard Sands
1975	Greg Holmes and Derk Pardoe
1976	James Arias and Bobby Banck
1977	Jimmy Brown and Richey Reneberg
1978	Robby Weiss and Aaron Krickstein
1979	Robby Weiss and Aaron Krickstein
1980	John Boytim and Stephen Enochs

USTA Champions—Girls' 12 Doubles

1962	Jane Lawson and Connie Capozzi
1963	Connie Capozzi and Gene Shapiro
1964	Marcelyn Louie and Karin Benson
1965	Karin Benson and Marcelyn Louie
1966	Susan Epstein and Chrissie Evert
1967	Lisa Barry and Laurie Jo Fleming
1968	Kathy May and Gretchen Galt
1969	Judy Gfroerer and Jeanne Evert
1970	Susan Wright and Susan Hagey
1971	Sherry Acker and Lea Antonoplis
1972	Mareen Louie and Sue Rasmussen
1973	Betty Newfield and Caroline Stoll
1974	Tracy Austin and Kelly Henry
1975	Susan Mascarin and Ann Van Walleghem
1976	Andrea Jaeger and Beverly Bowes
1977	Andrea Jaeger and Beverly Bowes
1978	Kathy Rinaldi and Nicole Stafford
1979	Ginny Purdy and Lynn Nabors
1980	Clare Evert and Raka Raychaudhuri

USTA Champions—Boys' 14 Singles

1962	Alberto Carrero
1963	Zan Guerry
1964	Mac Claflin
1965	Richard Stockton
1966	Randall Thomas
1967	Bob Kreiss
1968	Fred DeJesus
1969	William Martin
1970	William Martin
1971	Ben McKown
1972	Juan Farrow
1973	Larry Gottfried
1974	Blaine Willenborg
1975	Peter Herrmann
1976	Ben Testerman
1977	Jimmy Arias
1978	Tim Pawsat
1979	Matthew Frooman
1980	Aaron Krickstein

USTA Champions—Girls' 14 Singles

1962	Jane Bartkowicz
1963	Jane Bartkowicz
1964	Linda Tuero
1965	Connie Capozzi
1966	Patty Ann Reese
1967	Karin Benson
1968	Chris Evert
1969	Laurie Fleming
1970	Marita Redondo
1971	Jeanne Evert

1972 Robin Tenney
1973 Zenda Liess
1974 Jennifer Balent
1975 Tracy Austin
1976 Tracy Austin
1977 Shelly Solomon
1978 Andrea Jaeger
1979 Beverly Bowes
1980 Lisa Bonder

USTA Champions—Boys' 14 Doubles

1962 Zan Guerry and Richard Howell
1963 Zan Guerry and George Taylor
1964 Richard Stockton and George Taylor
1965 Richard Stockton and Erik Van Dillen
1966 Jimmy Connors and Brian Gottfried
1967 Fred DeJesus and Jake Warde
1968 Fred DeJesus and Jake Warde
1969 Mark Joffey and Chris Sylvan
1970 Earl Hassler and Eugene Mayer
1971 Gary Taxman and Percy Wright
1972 Walter Redondo and Donald Paulson
1973 John McEnroe and Van Winitsky
1974 Bobby Berger and Blaine Willenborg
1975 George Tanase and Tom Warneke
1976 Scott Davis and Ben Testerman
1977 Chris Huff and Bruce Herzog
1978 Pat Harrison and Tim Siegel
1979 Brad Ackerman and Jimmy Brown
1980 Tom Bender and John Schmitt

USTA Champions—Girls' 14 Doubles

1962 Paulette Verzin and Patsy Rippy
1963 Jane Bartkowicz and Ginger Pfeiffer
1964 Patricia Montano and Kristy Pigeon
1965 Marjorie Gengler and Alice
      deRochemont
1966 Karin Benson and Marcelyn Louie
1967 Whitney Grant and Janet Newberry
1968 Chris Evert and Susan Epstein
1969 Ann Kiyomura and Susan Kraft
1970 Marita Redondo and Gretchen Galt
1971 Jeanne Evert and Judy Gfroerer
1972 Beth Bondurant and Lynn Epstein
1973 Jamie Baisden and Berta McCallum
1974 Jennifer Balent and Mareen Louie
1975 Betty Newfield and Caroline Stoll

1976 Ellen March and Joanie Holzschuh
1977 Susan Mascarin and Anna Walleghem
1978 Andrea Jaeger and Beverly Bowes
1979 not completed
1980 Lisa Bender and Joni Urban

USTA Champions—Boys' 16 Singles

1962 Clifford Richey
1963 Bill Harris
1964 Alberto Carrero
1965 Zan Guerry
1966 Erik Van Dillen
1967 Richard Stockton
1968 Jimmy Connors
1969 James Hagey
1970 Fred De Jesus
1971 William Martin
1972 Bill Maze
1973 Ben McKown
1974 Walter Redondo
1975 Larry Gottfried
1976 Tim Wilkison
1977 Robert Krishnan
1978 Ben Testerman
1979 Matt Anger
1980 Jimmy Brown

USTA Champions—Girls' 16 Singles

1962 Kathy Blake
1963 Jane Bartkowicz
1964 Jane Bartkowicz
1965 Jane Bartkowicz
1966 Linda Tuero
1967 Kristy Kemmer
1968 Janet Newberry
1969 Eliza Pande
1970 Chris Evert
1971 Laurie Fleming
1972 Marita Redondo
1973 Betsy Nagelson
1974 Zenda Liess
1975 Lea Antonopolis
1976 Mareen Louie
1977 Linda Siegel
1978 Tracy Austin
1979 Kathleen Horvath
1980 Zina Garrison

The 1964 Girls' 16 Champions *(left to right),* Paulette Verzin, Mary Hardwick Hare (former British star), Patsy Rippy, and Jane "Peaches" Bartkowicz. Peaches defeated Patsy for the singles; Patsy and Paulette won the doubles title. Miss Bartkowicz was generally considered United States' best girl champion in the 1960s.

USTA Champions—Boys' 16 Doubles

1962	James Hobson and Steven Tidball
1963	Roy Barth and Robert Lutz
1964	William Davidson and James Rombeau
1965	Mike Estep and George Taylor
1966	Richard Stockton and Erik Van Dillen
1967	Mike Machette and Richard Stockton
1968	James Hagey and Robert Kreiss
1969	James Delaney and Chip Fisher
1970	Fred DeJesus and John Whitlinger
1971	William Martin and Trey Waltke
1972	Bruce Manson and Perry Wright
1973	Nial Brash and Matt Mitchell
1974	Jeff Robbins and Van Winitsky
1975	Larry Gottfried and John McEnroe
1976	Murray Robinson and Tom Wilkison
1977	Sean Brawley and David Siegler
1978	Scott Davis and Ben Testerman
1979	Sam Giammalva and Bill Quigley
1980	Rick Leach and Tim Pawsat

USTA Champions—Girls' 16 Doubles

1962	Stephanie DeFina and Jean Danilovich
1963	Rosemary Casals and Pixie Lamm
1964	Paulette Verzin and Patsy Rippy
1965	Jane Bartkowicz and Valerie Ziegenfuss

1966	Connie Capozzi and Linda Tuero
1967	Gail Hansen and Patty Ann Reese
1968	Kris Kemmer and Janet Newberry
1969	Susan Epstein and Chris Evert
1970	Barbara Downs and Ann Kiyomura
1971	Carrie Fleming and Susan Mehmedbasich
1972	Jeanne Evert and Kathy Kuykendall
1973	Susan Mehmedbasich and Robin Tenney
1974	Sherry Acker and Anne Smith
1975	Lea Antonopolis and Berta McCallum
1976	Lucia Fernandez and Trey Lewis
1977	Tracy Austin and Maria Fernandez
1978	Pam Shriver and Barbara Potter
1979	Kathleen Horvath and Pilar Vasquez
1980	Andrea Leand and Susan Mascarin

USTA Champions—Girls' 18 Singles

1918	Katherine Porter
1919	Katherine Gardner
1920	Louise Dixon
1921	Helen N. Wills
1922	Helen N. Wills
1923	Helen Hooker
1924	Helen Jacobs
1925	Helen Jacobs
1926	Louise McFarland
1927	Marjorie Gladman
1928	Sarah Palfrey
1929	Sarah Palfrey
1930	Sarah Palfrey
1931	Ruby Bishop
1932	Helen Fulton
1933	Bonnie Miller
1934	Helen Pedersen
1935	Patricia Henry
1936	Margaret Osborne
1937	Barbara Winslow
1938	Helen I. Bernhard
1939	Helen I. Bernhard
1940	A. Louise Brough
1941	A. Louise Brough
1942	Doris Hart
1943	Doris Hart
1944	Shirley J. Fry
1945	Shirley J. Fry
1946	Helen Pastall
1947	Nancy Chaffee

1948	Beverly J. Baker
1949	Maureen Connolly
1950	Maureen Connolly
1951	Anita Kanter
1952	Julia Ann Sampson
1953	Mary Ann Ellenberger
1954	Barbara N. Breit
1955	Barbara N. Breit
1956	Miriam Arnold
1957	Karen J. Hantze
1958	Sally M. Moore
1959	Karen J. Hantze
1960	Karen J. Hantze
1961	Victoria Palmer
1962	Victoria Palmer
1963	Julie Heldman
1964	Mary Ann Eisel
1965	Jane Bartkowicz
1966	Jane Bartkowicz
1967	Jane Bartkowicz
1968	Kristy Pigeon
1969	Sharon Walsh
1970	Sharon Walsh
1971	Chris Evert
1972	Ann Kiyomura
1973	Carrie Fleming
1974	Rayni Fox
1975	Beth Norton
1976	Lynn Epstein
1977	Tracy Austin
1978	Tracy Austin
1979	Andrea Jaeger
1980	Kate Gompert

Helen Wills winning her first Girls' Championship in 1921.

USTA Champions—Girls' 18 Doubles

1919	Elizabeth Warren and Penelope Anderson
1920	Virginia L. Carpenter and Helen Sewell
1921	Virginia L. Carpenter and Ceres Baker
1922	Helen N. Wills and Helen Hooker
1923	Helen Hooker and Elizabeth Hilleary
1924	Frances Curtis and Margaret P. Palfrey
1925	Marjorie Morrill and Louise Slocum
1926	Mianne Palfrey and Sarah Palfrey
1927	Marjorie Gladman and Jo Cruickshank
1928	Mianne Palfrey and Sarah Palfrey
1929	Mianne Palfrey and Sarah Palfrey
1930	Helen Marlow and Mercedes Marlow
1931	Alice Marble and Bonnie Miller
1932	Gracyn Wheeler and Katharine Winthrop
1933	Bonnie Miller and Frances Herron
1934	May Hope Doeg and Priscilla Merwin
1935	Hope Knowles and Patricia Cumming
1936	Margaret Osborne and Elinor Dawson
1937	Helen Bernhard and Patricia Cumming
1938	Margaret Jessee and Joan Bigler
1939	Patricia Canning and Marguerita Madden
1940	Doris Hart and Neillie Sheer
1941	A. Louise Brough and Gertrude A. Moran
1942	M. R. Donnelly and Barbara A. Brooke
1943	Doris Hart and Shirley J. Fry
1944	Margaret Varner and Jean E. Doyle
1945	Margaret Varner and Jean E. Doyle
1946	Barbara Wilkins and Mary Cunningham
1947	Nancy Chaffee and Beverly J. Baker
1948	Beverly J. Baker and Marjorie McCord
1949	Maureen Connolly and Lee Van Keuren
1950	Maureen Connolly and Patricia Zellmer
1951	Elaine Lewicki and Bonnie MacKay
1952	Mary Ann Ellenberger and Linda Mitchell
1953	Nancy Dwyer and Mary Ann Ellenberger
1954	Barbara N. Breit and Darlene Hard
1955	Barbara N. Breit and Diane Wootton
1956	Mary Ann Mitchell and Rosa Maria Reyes
1957	Sally M. Moore and Helene J. Weill
1958	Karen J. Hantze and Helene J. Weill
1959	Karen J. Hantze and Kathy Chabot

USTA Champions—Girls' 18 Doubles *(cont.)*

1960	Karen J. Hantze and Kathy Chabot
1961	Victoria Palmer and Judy Alvarez
1962	Jane Albert and Mary Arfaras
1963	Jane Albert and Stephanie DeFina
1964	Mary Ann Eisel and Wendy Overton
1965	Jane Bartkowicz and Valerie Ziegenfuss
1966	Jane Bartkowicz and Valerie Ziegenfuss
1967	Jane Bartkowicz and Valerie Ziegenfuss
1968	Kristy Pigeon and Denise Carter
1969	Gail Hansen and Patty Ann Reese
1970	Nancy Ornstein and Kris Kemmer
1971	Janet Newburg and Eliza Pande
1972	Marita Redondo and Laurie Tenney
1973	Susan Boyle and Kathy May
1974	Anne Bruning and Barbara Hallquist
1975	Lea Antonopolis and Berta McCallum
1976	Sherry Acker and Ann Smith
1977	Lea Antonopolis and Kathy Jordan
1978	Tracy Austin and Maria Fernandez
1979	Andrea Jaeger and Susy Jaeger
1980	Louise Allen and Marian Kremer

USTA Champions—Men's 21 Singles

1976	Bruce Manson
1977	Bruce Manson
1978	Mel Purcell
1979	Jay Lapidus
1980	Blaine Willenborg

USTA Champions—Women's 21 Singles

1976	Barbara Hallquist
1977	Stacy Margolin
1978	Barbara Jordan
1979	Kathy Horvath
1980	Ann Hendricksson

USTA Champions—Men's 21 Doubles

1976	Bill Maze and Chris Lewis
1977	Bill Maze and Bruce Nichols
1978	Mel Purcell and Jeff Robbins
1979	Robert Van't Hof and Peter Meister
1980	David Dowlen and Bill Nealon

USTA Champions—Women's 21 Doubles

1976	Gretchen Galt and Ann Bruning

1977	Sherry Acker and Diane Morrison
1978	Sherry Acker and Barbara Jordan
1979	Trey Lewis and Kathy O'Brien
1980	Lisa Levins and Betty Newfield

USTA Champions—Father and Son (Grass)

1918	Alfred H. Chapin and Alfred H. Chapin, Jr.
1919	Fred G. Anderson and Fred C. Anderson
1920	Fred G. Anderson and Fred C. Anderson
1921	Fred G. Anderson and Fred C. Anderson
1922	J. D. E. Jones and Arnold W. Jones
1923	Joseph W. Wear and W. Potter Wear
1924	Alfred H. Chapin and Alfred H. Chapin, Jr.
1925	J. D. E. Jones and Arnold W. Jones
1926	Donald M. Hill and Malcolm T. Hill
1927	John Barton and Horace Barton
1928	J. D. E. Jones and Arnold W. Jones
1929	J. D. E. Jones and Arnold W. Jones
1930	J. D. E. Jones and Arnold W. Jones
1931	J. D. E. Jones and Arnold W. Jones
1932	J. D. E. Jones and Arnold W. Jones
1933	R. N. Watt and M. Laird Watt
1934	R. N. Watt and M. Laird Watt
1935	Wm. J. Clothier and Wm. J. Clothier II
1936	Wm. J. Clothier and Wm. J. Clothier II
1937	R. N. Watt and M. Laird Watt
1938	F. J. Sulloway and A. W. Sulloway
1939	R. B. Mulloy and Gardnar Mulloy
1940	L. R. Gay and F. R. Gay
1941	R. B. Mulloy and Gardnar Mulloy
1942	R. B. Mulloy and Lt. (j. g.) Gardnar Mulloy
1943–45	not held
1946	Arthur Nielsen and Arthur Nielsen, Jr.
1947	G. Diehl Mateer and G. Diehl Mateer, Jr.
1948	Arthur Nielsen and Arthur Nielsen, Jr.
1949	G. Diehl Mateer and G. Diehl Mateer, Jr.
1950	G. Diehl Mateer and G. Diehl Mateer, Jr.
1951	G. Diehl Mateer and G. Diehl Mateer, Jr.
1952	Karl Kamrath and Karl Kamrath, Jr.
1953	Roger Richardson and Hamilton Richardson

1954	Roger Richardson and Hamilton Richardson	1921	Philip B. Hawk
1955	J. Andrew Crane and Michael Crane	1922	Philip B. Hawk
1956	Sidney Wood, Jr. and Sidney Wood III	1923	Philip B. Hawk
1957	Harry Hoffmann and Harry Hoffmann, Jr.	1924	Craig Biddle
1958	Henry Hoffmann and Harry Hoffmann, Jr.	1925	Alfred J. Cawse
1959	F. A. Froehling, Jr. and F. A. Froehling III	1926	Alfred J. Cawse

1954 Roger Richardson and Hamilton Richardson
1955 J. Andrew Crane and Michael Crane
1956 Sidney Wood, Jr. and Sidney Wood III
1957 Harry Hoffmann and Harry Hoffmann, Jr.
1958 Henry Hoffmann and Harry Hoffmann, Jr.
1959 F. A. Froehling, Jr. and F. A. Froehling III
1960 Harry Hoffmann and Harry Hoffmann, Jr.
1961 H. William Bond and William Bond
1962 F. A. Froehling, Jr. and F. A. Froehling III
1963 F. A. Froehling, Jr. and F. A. Froehling III
1964 Robert Ralston and Dennis Ralston
1965 F. A. Froehling, Jr. and F. A. Froehling III
1966 Chauncey D. Steele, Jr. and C. D. Steele III
1967 Leslie Fitz Gibbon and Herbert Fitz Gibbon
1968 Chauncey D. Steele, Jr. and C. D. Steele III
1969 Chauncey D. Steele, Jr. and C. D. Steele III
1970 Chauncey D. Steele, Jr. and C. D. Steele III
1971 Frederick McNair III and Frederick McNair IV
1972 Frederick McNair III and Frederick McNair IV
1973 Frederick McNair III and Frederick McNair IV
1974 Alan Fleming and Peter Fleming
1975 Hugh Hyde and Hugh Hyde Jr.
1976 Stephen Potts and Stephen Potts Jr.
1977 Richard Karzen and Jerry Karzen
1978 Richard Karzen and Jerry Karzen
1979 Sam Giammalva and Sammy Giammalva
1980 Stephan Potts and Stephan Potts, Jr.

USTA Champions—Men Seniors' Singles

1918 Ross Burchard
1919 Clarence Hobart
1920 William A. Campbell

1921 Philip B. Hawk
1922 Philip B. Hawk
1923 Philip B. Hawk
1924 Craig Biddle
1925 Alfred J. Cawse
1926 Alfred J. Cawse
1927 Alfred J. Cawse
1928 Henry H. Bassford
1929 Clarence M. Charest
1930 Henry H. Bassford
1931 Fred C. Baggs
1932 Clarence M. Charest
1933 Clarence M. Charest
1934 Raymond B. Bidwell
1935 Raymond B. Bidwell
1936 Raymond B. Bidwell
1937 Cedric A. Major
1938 Henry H. Bassford
1939 Percy W. Guilford
1940 Watson Washburn
1941 Arthur W. Macpherson
1942 William L. Nassau
1943 not held
1944 J. Gilbert Hall
1945 J. Gilbert Hall
1946 J. Gilbert Hall
1947 J. Gilbert Hall
1948 J. Gilbert Hall
1949 J. Gilbert Hall
1950 J. Gilbert Hall
1951 Harold T. MacGuffin
1952 Harry Hopman
1953 William A. Maxwell
1954 David L. Freed
1955 R. Philip Hanna
1956 Bryan M. Grant, Jr.
1957 Bryan M. Grant, Jr.
1958 Gardnar Mulloy
1959 J. Hal Surface, Jr.
1960 Gardnar Mulloy
1961 Gardnar Mulloy
1962 Gardnar Mulloy
1963 Gardnar Mulloy
1964 Gardnar Mulloy
1965 Robert V. Sherman
1966 Jaroslav Drobny
1967 Jaroslav Drobny
1968 Gardnar Mulloy
1969 Robert Riggs

USTA Champions—Men Seniors' Singles *(cont.)*

1970	Torsten Johansson
1971	Torsten Johansson
1972	Bobby Riggs
1973	L. Straight Clark
1974	Don Gale
1975	Dell Sylvia
1976	Russell Seymour
1977	Russell Seymour
1978	Russell Seymour
1979	Russell Seymour
1980	Russell Seymour

USTA Champions—Men Seniors' Doubles

1921	J. D. E. Jones and Arthur Ingraham
1922	Holcombe Ward and Dwight F. Davis
1923	A. Wallis Myers and Samuel Hardy
1924	Walter L. Pate and Samuel Hardy
1925	Walter L. Pate and Samuel Hardy
1926	Albert J. Gore and Claude J. Butlin
1927	Fred C. Baggs and Dr. William Rosenbaum
1928	Irving C. Wright and Harry C. Johnson
1929	Fred C. Baggs and Dr. William Rosenbaum
1930	S. Jarvis Adams and Henry H. Bassford
1931	Fred C. Baggs and Dr. William Rosenbaum
1932	S. Jarvis Adams and Henry H. Bassford
1933	G. P. Gardner, Jr. and Richard Bishop
1934	Fred C. Baggs and Dr. William Rosenbaum
1935	Raymond B. Bidwell and Richard Bishop
1936	William Clothier and Dwight F. Davis
1937	Lawrence A. Baker and John G. McKay
1938	Dr. William Rosenbaum and Fred C. Baggs
1939	Dr. G. Colket Caner and Cornelius C. Felton
1940	Watson Washburn and Hugh Kelleher
1941	Jacques Brugnon and Meade Woodson
1942	W. M. Washburn and A. W. Macpherson
1943	not held
1944	Watson Washburn and A. W. Macpherson
1945	J. Gilbert Hall and Sidney Adelstein

1946	J. Gilbert Hall and Sidney Adelstein
1947	J. Gilbert Hall and Sidney Adelstein
1948	Mel Gallagher and John Woodall
1949	Wilmer Allison and J. Gilbert Hall
1950	Wilmer Allison and J. Gilbert Hall
1951	Sidney Adelstein and Bernard Clinton
1952	Pierre Harang and Harry Hopman
1953	Edward Chandler and Gerald Stratford
1954	Edward Chandler and Gerald Stratford
1955	Edward Chandler and Gerald Stratford
1956	Jean Borotra and Harry Hopman
1957	Edward Jacobs and C. Alphonso Smith
1958	Leonard Prosser and J. Hal Surface, Jr.
1959	Harry Hoffmann and W. E. Hester, Jr.
1960	Jean Borotra and Adrian Quist
1961	Clifford Sutter and Ernest Sutter
1962	Gardnar Mulloy and Mike McLaney
1963	Gardnar Mulloy and William F. Talbert
1964	Gardnar Mulloy and William F. Talbert
1965	Gardnar Mulloy and William F. Talbert
1966	Robert J. Freedman and Robert V. Sherman
1967	Gardnar Mulloy and William F. Talbert
1968	Ellis Slack and Richard C. Sorlien
1969	Gardnar Mulloy and Robert Riggs
1970	Gary Hippenstiel and Chauncey Steele, Jr.
1971	Lennart Bergelin and Torsten Johansson
1972	Lacy Leginstein and Torsten Johansson
1973	Gardnar Molloy and Tony Vincent
1974	Homer Richards and Richard C. Sorlien
1975	L. Straight Clark and Hal Burrows
1976	Jason Morton and Russell Seymour
1977	Jason Morton and Russell Seymour
1978	Jason Morton and Russell Seymour
1979	Jason Morton and Russell Seymour
1980	John Been and Richard Shuette

USTA Clay Court Champions—Men's Singles

1910	Melville H. Long
1911	Walter T. Hayes
1912	R. Norris Williams II
1913	John R. Strachan
1914	Clarence J. Griffin
1915	R. Norris Williams II
1916	Willis E. Davis

1917	Samuel Hardy	1946	Frank A. Parker
1918	William T. Tilden II	1947	Frank A. Parker
1919	William Johnston	1948	Richard A. Gonzales
1920	Roland Roberts	1949	Richard A. Gonzales
1921	Walter T. Hayes	1950	Herbert Flam
1922	William T. Tilden II	1951	Tony Trabert
1923	William T. Tilden II	1952	Arthur Larsen
1924	William T. Tilden II	1953	E. Victor Seixas, Jr.
1925	William T. Tilden II	1954	Bernard Bartzen
1926	William T. Tilden II	1955	Tony Trabert
1927	William T. Tilden II	1956	Herbert Flam
1928	not held	1957	E. Victor Seixas, Jr.
1929	Emmett Paré	1958	Bernard Bartzen
1930	Bryan M. Grant, Jr.	1959	Bernard Bartzen
1931	H. Ellsworth Vines, Jr.	1960	Barry MacKay
1932	George M. Lott, Jr.	1961	Bernard Bartzen
1933	Frank Parker	1962	Charles R. McKinley
1934	Bryan M. Grant, Jr.	1963	Charles R. McKinley
1935	Bryan M. Grant, Jr.	1964	Dennis Ralston
1936	Robert L. Riggs	1965	Dennis Ralston
1937	Robert L. Riggs	1966	Cliff Richey
1938	Robert L. Riggs	1967	Arthur Ashe
1939	Frank A. Parker	1968	Clark Graebner
1940	Donald McNeill	1969	Zeljko Franulovic
1941	Frank A. Parker		
1942	Seymour Greenberg		
1943	Seymour Greenberg		
1944	Francisco Segura		
1945	William F. Talbert		

Billy Talbert and Gardnar Mulloy won the National Doubles in 1945, 1946, and 1948. They teamed up again in 1963, 1964, 1965, and 1967 to win the Seniors' Doubles.

USTA Clay Court Champions—Women's Singles

1912	May Sutton
1913	not held
1914	Mary K. Brown
1915	Molla Bjurstedt
1916	Molla Bjurstedt
1917*	Ruth Sanders
1918	Carrie B. Neely
1919	Corinne Gould
1920	Marion Zinderstein
1921	Mrs. B. E. Cole
1922	Mrs. Lois Moyes Bickle
1923	Mayme MacDonald
1924–39	not held
1940	Alice Marble
1941	Pauline M. Betz
1942	not held
1943	Pauline M. Betz
1944	Dorothy M. Bundy

*Patriotic Tournament.

USTA CLAY COURT OPEN CHAMPIONS—MEN'S SINGLES

Year	Winner	Runner-up	Final Score
1970	Cliff Richey	Stan Smith	6–2, 10–8, 3–6, 6–1
1971	Zeljko Franulovic	Cliff Richey	6–3, 6–4, 0–6, 6–3
1972	Bob Hewitt	Jimmy Connors	7–6, 6–1, 6–2
1973	Manuel Orantes	Raul Ramirez	6–4, 6–1, 6–4
1974	Jimmy Connors	Bjorn Borg	5–7, 6–3, 6–4
1975	Manuel Orantes	Arthur Ashe	6–2, 6–2
1976	Jimmy Connors	Wojtek Fibak	6–2, 6–4
1977	Manuel Orantes	Jimmy Connors	6–1, 6–3
1978	Jimmy Connors	Jose Higueras	7–5, 6–1
1979	Jimmy Connors	Guillermo Vilas	6–1, 2–6, 6–4
1980	Jose Luis Clerc	Mel Purcell	7–5, 6–3

USTA Clay Court Champions—Women's Singles *(cont.)*

1945	Mrs. S. Palfrey Cooke
1946	Barbara Krase
1947	Mrs. Mary A. Prentiss
1948	Mrs. Magda Rurac
1949	Mrs. Magda Rurac
1950	Doris Hart
1951	Dorothy Head
1952	Anita Kanter
1953	Maureen Connolly
1954	Maureen Connolly
1955	Mrs. Dorothy H. Knode
1956	Shirley J. Fry
1957	Althea Gibson
1958	Mrs. Dorothy H. Knode
1959	Sally M. Moore
1960	Mrs. Dorothy H. Knode
1961	Edda Buding
1962	Donna Floyd
1963	Nancy Richey
1964	Nancy Richey
1965	Nancy Richey
1966	Nancy Richey
1967	Nancy Richey
1968	Nancy Richey
1969	Mrs. Gail S. Chanfreau

Emmett Paré was the 1929 National Clay Court Singles Champion.

USTA CLAY COURT OPEN CHAMPIONS—WOMEN'S SINGLES

Year	Winner	Runner-up	Final Score
1970	Linda Tuero	Mrs. Gail S. Chanfreau	7–5, 6–1
1971	Mrs. Billie Jean King	Linda Tuero	6–4, 7–5
1972	Chris Evert	Evonne Goolagong	7–6, 6–1
1973	Chris Evert	Veronica Burton	6–4, 6–3
1974	Chris Evert	Mrs. Gail S. Chanfreau	6–0, 6–0
1975	Chris Evert	Dianne Fromholtz	6–3, 6–4
1976	Kathy May	Brigitte Cuypers	6–4, 4–6, 6–2
1977	Laura DuPont	Nancy Richey	6–4, 6–3
1978	Dana Gilbert	Viviana Gonzalez	6–2, 6–3
1979	Mrs. Chris Evert Lloyd	Mrs. Evonne G. Cawley	6–4, 6–3
1980	Mrs. Chris Evert Lloyd	Andrea Jaeger	6–4, 6–3

USTA Clay Court Champions—Men's Doubles

1910 Fred G. Anderson and Walter T. Hayes
1911 J. Horner Winston and Hugh C. Whitehead
1912 Harold H. Hackett and W. Merrill Hall
1913 John R. Strachan and Clarence J. Griffin
1914 Nat Browne and Claude Wayne
1915 George M. Church and Dean Mathey
1916 George M. Church and Dean Mathey
1917* Charles S. Garland and Samuel Hardy
1918 Charles S. Garland and Samuel Hardy
1919 William Johnston and Samuel Hardy
1920 Vincent Richards and Roland Roberts
1921 Clifton B. Herd and Walter T. Hayes
1922 Ralph H. Burdick and Fred Bastian
1923 Howard Kinsey and Robert Kinsey
1924 Howard Kinsey and Robert Kinsey
1925 Harvey Snodgrass and Walter Wesbrook
1926 Lewis N. White and Louis Thalheimer
1927 John Hennessey and Lucien E. Williams
1928 not held
1929 J. Gilbert Hall and Frederic Mercur
1930 J. Gilbert Hall and Frederic Mercur
1931 H. Ellsworth Vines, Jr. and Keith Gledhill
1932 George M. Lott, Jr. and Bryan M. Grant, Jr.
1933 Jack Tidball and C. Gene Mako
1934 J. Donald Budge and C. Gene Mako
1935 J. Gilbert Hall and Berkeley Bell
1936 Robert L. Riggs and Wayne Sabin
1937 John McDiarmid and Eugene McCauliff

*Patriotic Tournament.

1938 Joseph R. Hunt and Lewis Wetherell
1939 Frank Parker and C. Gene Mako
1940 Robert Harman and Robert C. Peacock
1941 John A. Kramer and F. R. Schroeder, Jr.
1942 William F. Talbert and William Reedy
1943 Earl Cochell and Robert Kimbrell
1944 Francisco Segura and William F. Talbert
1945 Francisco Segura and William F. Talbert
1946 William F. Talbert and Gardnar Mulloy
1947 Frederick R. Schroeder, Jr. and Jack Tuero
1948 Samuel Match and Tom Chambers
1949 E. Victor Seixas, Jr. and Samuel Match
1950 Herbert Flam and Arthur Larsen
1951 Hamilton Richardson and Tony Trabert
1952 Grant Golden and Arthur Larsen
1953 Bernard Bartzen and Grant Golden
1954 E. Victor Seixas, Jr. and Tony Trabert
1955 Hamilton Richardson and Tony Trabert
1956 Francisco Contreras and Alejandro Olmedo
1957 Ashley J. Cooper and Neale Fraser
1958 Samuel Giammalva and Barry MacKay
1959 Bernard Bartzen and Grant Golden
1960 Bob Hewitt and Martin Mulligan
1961 Charles McKinley and Dennis Ralston
1962 Ramsey Earnhart and Martin Riessen
1963 Clark Graebner and Martin Riessen
1964 Charles McKinley and Dennis Ralston
1965 Clark Graebner and Martin Riessen
1966 Clark Graebner and Dennis Ralston
1967 Clark Graebner and Martin Riessen
1968 Robert Lutz and Stan Smith
1969 Bill Bowrey and Clark Graebner

USTA Clay Court Open Champions—Men's Doubles

1970   Arthur Ashe and Clark Graebner
1971   Jan Kodes and Zeljko Franulovic
1972   Bob Hewitt and Frew McMillan
1973   Bob Carmichael and Frew McMillan
1974   Jimmy Connors and Ilie Nastase
1975   Juan Gisbert and Manuel Orantes
1976   Brian Gottfried and Raul Ramirez
1977   Pat Cornejo and Jaime Fillol
1978   Gene Mayer and Hank Pfister
1979   Gene Mayer and John McEnroe
1980   Kevin Curran and Steve Denton

USTA Clay Court Champions—Women's Doubles

1914   Mary K. Brown and Mrs. Robert Williams
1915–16   not held
1917*   Mrs. Charles Gregg and Ruth Sanders
1918   Bobbie Esch and Mrs. Ralph Fields
1919   Carrie Neely and Katherine Voorhees
1920   Eleanor Tennant and Florence Ballin
1921   not held
1922   Leslie Bancroft and Mrs. Frank Godfrey
1923   Edith Sigourney and Mrs. Ream Leachman
1924–39   not held
1940   Alice Marble and Mary Arnold
1941   Mrs. Jane S. Gallagher and Barbara Bradley
1942   not held
1943   Pauline M. Betz and Nancy Corbett
1944   Pauline M. Betz and Doris Hart
1945   Pauline M. Betz and Doris Hart
1946   Shirley Fry and Mrs. Mary Arnold Prentiss
1947   Mrs. Mary A. Prentiss and Gertrude Moran
1948–49   not held
1950   Shirley Fry and Doris Hart
1951   Mrs. Magda Rurac and Mrs. Pat C. Todd
1952   Mrs. Lucille Davidson and Doris Popple
1953   Anita Kanter and Mrs. Thelma Long
1954   Maureen Connolly and Doris Hart
1955   Mrs. Dorothy H. Knode and Janet Hopps
1956   Shirley J. Fry and Mrs. Dorothy H. Knode

1957   Althea Gibson and Darlene R. Hard
1958   Karol Fageros and Mrs. Dorothy H. Knode
1959   Sandra Reynolds and Renée Schuurman
1960   Darlene R. Hard and Billie Jean Moffitt
1961   Justina Bricka and Carol Hanks
1962   Darlene Hard and Susan Behlmar
1963   Maria Bueno and Darlene Hard
1964   Mrs. Carole C. Graebner and Nancy Richey
1965   Mrs. Carole C. Graebner and Nancy Richey
1966   Karen Krantzcke and Kerry Melville
1967   Karen Krantzcke and Kerry Melville
1968   Nancy Richey and Valerie Ziegenfuss
1969   Mrs. L. T. Bowrey and Mrs. G. S. Chanfreau

USTA Clay Court Open Champions—Women's Doubles

1970   Rosemary Casals and Mrs. G. S. Chanfreau
1971   Mrs. Billie J. King and Judy Dalton
1972   Evonne Goolagong and Lesley Hunt
1973   Patti Hogan and Sharon Walsh
1974   Gail Chanfreau and Julie Heldman
1975   Fiorella Bonicelli and Isabel Fernandez
1976   Linky Boshoff and Ilana Kloss
1977   Linky Boshoff and Ilana Kloss
1978   Helena Anliot and Helle Sparre-Viragh
1979   Kathy Jordan and Anne Smith
1980   Paula Smith and Anne Smith

USTA Clay Court Champions—Mixed Doubles

1912   May Sutton and Fred Harris
1915   Mrs. Hazel H. Wightman and Harry Johnson
1916   Molla Bjurstedt and George Church
1917*   Ruth Sanders and Howard Cordes
1919   Marion Leighton and Elwood Cooke
1923   Mayme McDonald and A. J. Castle
1945   Mrs. Sarah P. Cooke and Elwood Cooke
1977   Sheila McInerney and Drew Gitlin
1978   not held
1979   Kim Jones and Mike Bauer
1980   not held

*Patriotic Tournament without championship.

USTA Amateur Clay Court Champions—Men's Singles

1970 Roscoe Tanner
1971 Harold Solomon
1972 Ross Walker
1973 Pat DuPre
1974 Victor Amaya
1975 Victor Amaya
1976 Francisco Gonzales
1977 Bruce Foxworth
1978 Gabriel Mattes
1979 Lloyd Bourne
1980 Mike DePalmer

USTA Amateur Clay Court Champions—Women's Singles

1970 Linda Tuero
1971 Janice Metcalf
1972 Janice Metcalf
1973 Janice Metcalf
1974 Lynn Epstein
1975 Jo Anne Russell
1976 Candy Reynolds
1977 Sheila McInerney
1978 Kathy Jordan
1979 Sheila McInerney
1980 Ann White

USTA Amateur Clay Court Champions—Men's Doubles

1970 Lito Alvarez and Modesta Vasquez
1971 Alex Mayer and Roscoe Tanner
1972 Raz Reid and Fred McNair
1973 Vitas Gerulaitis and Brian Teacher
1974 Nick Saviano and Peter Fleming
1975 Butch Walts and Bill Maze
1976 Bill Maze and Eric Fiedler
1977 Gary Plock and John Rast
1978 Mike Harrington and Doug Adler
1979 Blaine Willenborg and Scott Bondurant
1980 Mike DePalmer and Ben Testerman

USTA Amateur Clay Court Champions—Women's Doubles

1970 Pam Austin and Margaret Cooper
1971 Pam Farmer and Janice Metcalf
1972 Pat Bostrom and Ann Lebedeff
1973 Janice Metcalf and Jane Stratton
1974 Sue Boyle and Lindsay Morse
1975 Mary Hamm and Diane Desfor
1976 Nancy Yeargin and Candy Reynolds
1977 Sheila McInerney and Barbara Hallquist
1978 Kathy Jordan and Wendy White
1979 Sheila McInerney and Lucy Gordon
1980 Ann White and Lucia Fernandez

USTA Clay Court Champions—Junior Singles

1923 George Lott
1924–66 not held
1967 Zan Guerry
1968 Bill Colson
1969 Danny Birchmore
1970 Harold Solomon
1971 John Whitlinger
1972 Vitas Gerulaitis
1973 Ferdi Taygan
1974 Ben McKown
1975 Jai DiLouie
1976 John McEnroe
1977 John Corse
1978 Tim Mayotte
1979 Ben Testerman
1980 Sammy Giammalva

USTA Clay Court Champions—Junior Doubles

1967 Jeff Borowiak and Erik Van Dillen
1968 Paul Gerken and Ron Cornell
1969 Brian Gottfried and Roscoe Tanner
1970 John Whitlinger and Gary Groslimond
1971 unfinished
1972 Pat DuPre and Victor Amaya
1973 Bill Maze and Butch Walts
1974 Bruce Manson and Perry Wright
1975 Tony Giammalva and Bill Scanlon

USTA Clay Court Champions—Junior Doubles *(cont.)*

1976 Larry Gottfried and John McEnroe
1977 Mel Purcell and Chip Hooper
1978 Blaine Willenborg and Scott Bondurant
1979 Mike DePalmer and Rodney Harmon
1980 Scott Davis and Ben Testerman

USTA Clay Court Champions—Boys' 12
Singles

1976 Jim Bauman
1977 Doug Pielet
1978 Richey Reneberg
1979 Robby Weiss
1980 Stephen Enochs

USTA Clay Court Champions—Boys' 12
Doubles

1976 Jimmy Brabb and Mark Styslinger
1977 Steve Herzog and Chip Leighton
1978 Craig Johnson and Brad Pearce
1979 Keith Burford and Jim Williams
1980 Stephan Enochs and John Boytim

USTA Clay Court Champions—Girls' 12
Singles

1976 Marlin Noriega
1977 Kathy Horvath
1978 Lisa Bonder
1979 Kathy Rinaldi
1980 Carling Bassett

USTA Clay Court Champions—Girls' 12
Doubles

1976 Marlin Noriega and Gigi Fernandez
1977 Carol Heynen and Leigh Ann Eldredge
1978 Margaret Hopkins and Ginny Purdy
1979 Debbie Sprece and Marianne Werdel
1980 Carling Bassett and Marianne Werdel

USTA Clay Court Champions—Boys' 14
Singles

1976 Ben Testerman
1977 Chris Huff
1978 Tim Siegel
1979 Matt Freeman
1980 Eric Amend

USTA Clay Court Champions—Boys' 14
Doubles

1976 Ben Testerman and Scott Davis
1977 Chris Huff and Bruce Herzog
1978 Bobby Banck and Michael Kures
1979 Jamie Harty and Simone Youl
1980 Ron Woodbridge and Mark Kratzman

USTA Clay Court Champions—Girls' 14
Singles

1976 Kelly Henry
1977 Bettina Bunge
1978 Kathy Horvath
1979 Heather Hairston
1980 Kathy Rinaldi

USTA Clay Court Champions—Girls' 14
Doubles

1976 Jackie Geller and Carol Christian
1977 Robin White and Shelly Solomon
1978 Amy Holton and Lori Kosten
1979 Leigh Ann Eldredge and Janet Lagasse
1980 Joni Urban and Lisa Bonder

USTA Clay Court Champions—Boys' 16
Singles

1967 Woody Blocher
1968 Gery Groslimond
1969 Fred DeJesus
1970 John Whitlinger
1971 William Martin

1972 Ferdi Taygan
1973 Howard Schoenfield
1974 Jai DiLouie
1975 John McEnroe
1976 Tim Wilkison
1977 Paul Crozier
1978 Bruce Brescia
1979 George Bezecny
1980 Jimmy Brown

USTA Clay Court Champions—Boys' 16 Doubles

1967 Woody Blocher and Richard Stockton
1968 Emilio Montano and Larry Loeb
1969 Fred DeJesus and John Whitlinger
1970 Gray King and Patrick Dupree
1971 Horace Reid and William Martin
1972 Gene Mayer and Howard Schoenfield
1973 Ben McKown and Ferdi Taygan
1974 Daniel Gerken and Curtis Stadler
1975 Larry Gottfried and John McEnroe
1976 Bobby Berger and Blaine Willenborg
1977 Michael Fancutt and Ben Testerman
1978 Greg Holmes and Mark McKeen
1979 Greg Holmes and Todd Witsken
1980 John Letts and Matt Frooman

USTA Clay Court Champions—Girls' 18 Singles

1967 Linda Tuero
1968 Linda Tuero
1969 Kristen Kemmer
1970 Sue Stap
1971 Sue Stap
1972 Robin Tenney
1973 Kathy May
1974 Barbara Jordan
1975 Sheila McInerney
1976 Lea Antonopolis
1977 Linda Siegel
1978 Tracy Austin
1979 Andrea Jaeger
1980 Kathy Horvath

USTA Clay Court Champions—Girls' 18 Doubles

1967 Carol Hunter and Ginger Pfeiffer
1968 Whitney Grant and Kristen Kemmer
1969 Whitney Grant and Kristen Kemmer
1970 Nancy Ornstein and Kristen Kemmer
1971 Sandy Stap and Sue Stap
1972 Jill Schwikert and Joy Schwikert
1973 Betsy Nagelson and Jo Anne Russell
1974 Rayni Fox and Kathy May
1975 Sherry Acker and Anne Smith
1976 Sherry Acker and Anne Smith
1977 Mary Lou Piatek and Wendy Burkhart
1978 Tracy Austin and Maria Fernandez
1979 Mary Lou Piatek and Anne White
1980 Felicia Rachiatore and Shelly Solomon

USTA Amateur Clay Court Champions—Girls' 16 Singles

1975 Jennifer Balent
1976 Zenda Liess
1977 Tracy Austin
1978 Andrea Jaeger
1979 Kathy Horvath
1980 Carol Heynen

USTA Amateur Clay Court Champions—Girls' 16 Doubles

1975 Sherry Acker and Anne Smith
1976 Ilene Fernandez and Susan Henricksson
1977 Tracy Austin and Laura Starr
1978 Andrea Jaeger and Susy Jaeger
1979 Kathy Horvath and Beverly Bowes
1980 Zina Garrison and Lori McNeil

USTA Clay Court Champions—Men's 21 Singles

1978 Andy McCurry
1979 Andy McCurry
1980 Mike Bauer

USTA Clay Court Champions—21 Mixed Doubles

1979　Susan Gibson and Paul Bernstein
1980　Ann White and Jack Kruger

USTA Clay Court Champions—Men's 21 Doubles

1978　Gabriel Mattos and Rodney Young
1979　Andy McCurry and Paul Bernstein
1980　Jean Desdunes and Gregg Cooper

USTA Clay Court Champions—Women's 21 Singles

1978　Julie Pressly
1979　Lucy Gordon
1980　Ilene Friedland

USTA Clay Court Champions—Women's 21 Doubles

1978　Tracy Tanner and Barbara Barnes
1979　Lucy Gordon and Shannon Gordon
1980　Paula Scheb and Mrs. Colleen O'Brien McCabe

USTA Clay Court Champions—Father and Son

1949　Kirk Reid, Sr. and Kirk Reid, Jr.
1950　Edward Kaiser and Donald Kaiser
1951　Everett Hicks and David Hicks
1952　Cecil Powless and John Powless
1953　Bernard Leightheiser and Bernard Leightheiser, Jr.
1954　Harry Hoffmann and Harry Hoffmann, Jr.
1955　Clarence E. Sledge and Clarence E. Sledge, Jr.
1956　Clarence E. Sledge and Clarence E. Sledge, Jr.
1957　Cecil Powless and John Powless
1958　Cecil Powless and John Powless
1959　Frank Froehling, Jr. and Frank Froehling III
1960　Ward Parker and Jim Parker
1961　Hugh Lynch, Jr. and Hugh Lynch III
1962　Ward Parker and Jim Parker

1963　Chauncey D. Steele, Jr. and Chauncey D. Steele III
1964　Harry Hoffmann and Harry Hoffmann, Jr.
1965　Fred McNair III and Fred McNair IV
1966　Alex Guerry and Zan Guerry
1967　Fred McNair III and Fred McNair IV
1968　Fred McNair III and Fred McNair IV
1969　Glenn Hippenstiel and Gary Hippenstiel
1970　Fred McNair III and Fred McNair IV
1971　Alex Guerry and Zan Guerry
1972　Fred McNair III and John McNair
1973　Richard Gonzalez and Richard Gonzalez, Jr.
1974　David Brown and Dave Brown
1975　Harrison Straley and Chuck Straley
1976　Eldon Rowe and Brad Rowe
1977　Richard Karzen and Jerry Karzen
1978　Steve Potts and Dek Potts
1979　John Mangan and John Mangan, Jr.
1980　Richard Leach and Ricky Leach

USTA Clay Court Champions—Men's 35 Singles

1964　Tony Vincent
1965　Tony Vincent
1966　Tony Vincent
1967　Bob Barker
1968　Tony Vincent
1969　Gardnar Mulloy
1970　Paul Cranis
1971　King Van Nostrand
1972　Eugene L. Scott
1973　Eugene L. Scott
1974　Eugene L. Scott
1975　Eugene L. Scott
1976　Adrian Bey
1977　Cliff Drysdale
1978　Bob Carmichael
1979　Butch Newman
1980　Fred Stolle

USTA Clay Court Champions—Men's 35 Doubles

1964　Tom Falkenburg and Nolan Touchstone
1965　Bill Tully and King Lambert
1966　Gardnar Mulloy and Tony Vincent

1967   Bob Barker and Bill Tully
1968   Sidney Schwartz and Tony Vincent
1969   Sidney Schwartz and Tony Vincent
1970   Paul Cranis and Ed Rubinoff
1971   Paul Cranis and Hamilton Richardson
1972   Paul Cranis and Hamilton Richardson
1973   Sam Giammalva and Tony Vincent
1974   Mike Green and Ned Weld
1975   Eugene L. Scott and Fred Stolle
1976   Eugene L. Scott and Barry MacKay
1977   Bob Carmichael and Cliff Drysdale
1978   Bob Carmichael and Eugene L. Scott
1979   Butch Newman and Jim Parker
1980   Fred Stolle and Eugene L. Scott

1974   Bob Barker
1975   Dell Sylvia
1976   Jason Morton
1977   Allen Morris
1978   Allen Morris
1979   Russell Seymour
1980   Dell Sylvia

USTA Clay Court Champions—Men Seniors' Singles

1946   Karl Hodge
1947   William L. Nassau
1948   Fritz Mercur
1949   L. F. Kruger
1950   Larry Simmons
1951   Mel Dranga
1952   Mel Dranga
1953   Knute Krassenstein
1954   Jack Staton
1955   Bryan M. Grant, Jr.
1956   Bryan M. Grant, Jr.
1957   Harry R. Hoffmann
1958   Gardnar Mulloy
1959   Bryan M. Grant, Jr.
1960   Bryan M. Grant, Jr.
1961   Bryan M. Grant, Jr.
1962   Chauncey D. Steele, Jr.
1963   Bryan M. Grant, Jr.
1964   Julius Heldman
1965   Bob V. Sherman
1966   George Ball
1967   Lou Schopfer
1968   Bob V. Sherman
1969   Lou Schopfer
1970   Gustavo Palafox
1971   Gustavo Palafox
1972   Gustavo Palafox
1973   Frank Sedgman

USTA Clay Court Champions—Men Seniors' Doubles

1946   Kirk Reid and Martin Tressel
1947   Karl Hodge and Martin Tressel
1948   Fritz Mercur and Percy Kynaston
1949   William L. Nassau and L. F. Kruger
1950   John Woodall and W. F. Widen
1951   Bernard Clinton and John Hoff
1952   Bernard Clinton and John Hoff
1953   Sidney Adelstein and Victor Heuser
1954   John Dorr and Monte L. Ganger
1955   Mal C. Courts and Bryan M. Grant, Jr.
1956   David L. Freed and Leonard Prosser
1957   W. E. Hester, Jr. and Alex Wellford
1958   Len Prosser and Hal Surface
1959   C. Alphonso Smith and Hugh Lynch
1960   Bryan M. Grant, Jr. and Larry Shippey
1961   Bryan M. Grant, Jr. and Larry Shippey
1962   Bryan M. Grant, Jr. and Larry Shippey
1963   Bryan M. Grant, Jr. and Larry Shippey
1964   Frank Thompson and Randy Gregson
1965   Bryan M. Grant, Jr. and Larry Shippey
1966   Bryan M. Grant, Jr. and Larry Shippey
1967   Fred McNair III and Richard Sorlien
1968   Glenn Hippenstiel and Joseph Woolfson
1969   George Druliner and Bob Stuckert
1970   Jay Freedman and Gustavo Palafox
1971   Robert L. Riggs and Tony Vincent
1972   Gustavo Palafox and Jay Freedman
1973   Richard A. Gonzalez and Hugh Stewart
1974   Leonard Brose and Homer Richards
1975   Tom Falkenberg and Tom Bartlett
1976   Russell Seymour and Jason Morton
1977   Jason Morton and Russell Seymour
1978   Allen Morris and John Powless
1979   Allen Morris and John Powless
1980   Jason Morton and John Powless

USTA Clay Court Champions—Men Seniors' 50 Singles

1968 Gardnar Mulloy
1969 Gardnar Mulloy
1970 Bobby L. Riggs
1971 Bobby L. Riggs
1972 Al Doyle
1973 Gustavo Palafox
1974 Gustavo Palafox
1975 Gustavo Palafox
1976 Gustavo Palafox
1977 Gustavo Palafox
1978 Gustavo Palafox
1979 Gustavo Palafox
1980 Jason Morton

USTA Clay Court Champions—Men Seniors' 50 Doubles

1968 Tom Bird and Bryan M. Grant, Jr.
1969 Bryan M. Grant, Jr. and Jack Rogers
1970 Bobby L. Riggs and Chauncey D. Steele, Jr.
1971 Tom Bird and Henry Crawford
1972 Bobby Riggs and Jack Rodgers
1973 Jay Freedman and Gustavo Palafox
1974 Jay Freedman and Gustavo Palafox
1975 Jay Freedman and Gustavo Palafox
1976 Jay Freedman and Gustavo Palafox
1977 Jay Freedman and Gustavo Palafox
1978 Jay Freedman and Gustavo Palafox
1979 Ed Kauder and Dick Meehan
1980 Leonard Brose and James Zeron

USTA Clay Court Champions—Men Seniors' 55 Singles

1964 C. Alphonso Smith
1965 Bryan M. Grant, Jr.
1966 Bryan M. Grant, Jr.
1967 Bryan M. Grant, Jr.
1968 Bryan M. Grant, Jr.
1969 Bryan M. Grant, Jr.
1970 Gardnar Mulloy
1971 Harry Hoffmann

1972 Al Doyle
1973 Al Doyle
1974 Don Manchester
1975 Al Doyle
1976 Harry Hoffman
1977 Buck Archer
1978 Buck Archer
1979 Gustavo Palafox
1980 Gustavo Palafox

USTA Clay Court Champions—Men Seniors' 55 Doubles

1964 Jack Staton and Jim Hodgkins
1965 Charles Brooke and Alphonso Smith
1966 Clayton Burwell and N. E. Powel
1967 W. E. Hester and Harry Hoffmann
1968 Gardnar Mulloy and C. Alphonso Smith
1969 Len Prosser and Harry Crawford
1970 Tom Bird and Larry Shippey
1971 Charles Swanson and Howard Sprague
1972 Tom Bird and Henry Crawford
1973 Charles Lass and George Peebles
1974 Jim Gilchrist and Howard Sprague
1975 Tom Avirett and Charles Swanson
1976 Tom Avirett and Charles Swanson
1977 Buck Archer and John Rodgers
1978 Warren Drake and William Shivar
1979 Buck Archer and Tom Falkenberg
1980 Gustavo Palafox and George Pendley

USTA Clay Court Champions—Men Seniors' 60 Singles

1967 Ike Macy
1968 Emil Johnson
1969 Jack Staton
1970 Gene Short
1971 Bryan M. Grant, Jr.
1972 Harry Hoffman
1973 Harry Hoffman
1974 Chauncey D. Steele, Jr.
1975 Friedrich Klein
1976 Chauncey D. Steele, Jr.
1977 Chauncey D. Steele, Jr.
1978 Bobby Riggs
1979 Bobby Riggs
1980 Bob Sherman

USTA Clay Court Champions—Men Seniors' 60 Doubles

1967	Dave Freeborn and Monte Ganger
1968	Bernard Clinton and Monte Ganger
1969	Frank Goeltz and C. Alphonso Smith
1970	Frank Goeltz and C. Alphonso Smith
1971	Frank Goeltz and C. Alphonso Smith
1972	Bryan M. Grant, Jr., and Henry Crawford
1973	W. E. Hester, Jr., and Harry Hoffman
1974	John Shelton and William Smith
1975	Harry Hoffman and Charles Swanson
1976	Harry Hoffman and Charles Swanson
1977	Harris Everett and Charles Swanson
1978	Bobby Riggs and Jack Davis
1979	Bobby Riggs and Harold DeMoody
1980	Bobby Riggs and Harold DeMoody

USTA Clay Court Champions—Men Seniors' 65 Singles

1968	A. L. Enloe
1969	Bernard Clinton
1970	Tom Sherbourne
1971	Frank Goeltz
1972	Dick Skeen
1973	Erling Jensen
1974	Frank Goeltz
1975	Jack Staton
1976	Bryan M. Grant, Jr.
1977	Bryan M. Grant, Jr.
1978	Harry Hoffman
1979	Gardnar Mulloy
1980	Gardnar Mulloy

USTA Clay Court Champions—Men Seniors' 65 Doubles

1968	A. L. Enloe and Hobart Wrobbel
1969	A. L. Enloe and Bernard Clinton
1970	A. L. Enloe and Thomas Marshall
1971	Frank Goeltz and Ted Wellman
1972	Sam Shore and Dave Freeborn
1973	Monte Ganger and Frank Goeltz
1974	Frank Goeltz and C. Alphonso Smith
1975	M. O. Christopher and Erling Jensen

1976	Bryan M. Grant, Jr. and Len Prosser
1977	Col. N. E. Powel and Leonard Prosser
1978	John Shelton and Verne Hughes
1979	Harry Hoffman and Charles Swanson
1980	Chauncey D. Steele, Jr., and Frank Thompson

USTA Clay Court Champions—Men Seniors' 70 Singles

1970	Frank G. Roberts
1971	Walter Wesbrook
1972	Arthur L. Enloe
1973	Arthur L. Enloe
1974	Kenneth Beer
1975	Wilfred Jones
1976	Frank Goeltz
1977	Frank Goeltz
1978	Frank Goeltz
1979	Frank Goeltz
1980	Bill Conel

USTA Clay Court Champions—Men Seniors' 70 Doubles

1970	Frank G. Roberts and Farnham Warriner
1971	Clarence Chaffee and Clarke Kaye
1972	Clarence Chaffee and Clarke Kaye
1973	Clarence Chaffee and Clarke Kaye
1974	Arthur L. Enloe and Herschel Hyde
1975	Kenneth Beer and Wilfred Jones
1976	Frank Goeltz and Monte Ganger
1977	Sam Shore and Wilfred Jones
1978	Frank Goeltz and Erling Jensen
1979	Hugh Weckerly and Bill Seidel
1980	Leonard Prosser and Jack Staton

USTA Clay Court Champions—Men Seniors' 75 Singles

1973	Stephen Graves
1974	Stephen Graves
1975	William Mallery
1976	Clarence Chaffee
1977	Mal Clarke
1978	Clarence Chaffee
1979	Clarence Chaffee
1980	Ken Beer

USTA Clay Court Champions—Men Seniors' 75 Doubles

1973 Eldon Roark and Bryan Hamlin
1974 Gordon Steele and DeWitt Redgrave
1975 Stephen Graves and Thomas Jefferson Glover
1976 Clarence Chaffee and Revel Ritz
1977 Mal Clarke and Clarence Chaffee
1978 Mal Clarke and Ted Wellman
1979 Mal Clarke and Steve Harris
1980 Mal Clarke and Clarence Chaffee

USTA Clay Court Champions—Men Seniors' 80 Singles

1977 John L. Giegerich
1978 Albert Leitch
1979 Albert Leitch
1980 DeWitt Redgrave

USTA Clay Court Champions—Men Seniors' 80 Doubles

1977 Eldon Roark and Henry Doyle
1978 Albert Leitch and Kirk Reid
1979 DeWitt Redgrave and Stephen Graves
1980 Albert Leitch and Kirk Reid

USTA Clay Court Champions—Women's 35 Singles

1971 Evelyn Houseman
1972 Betty Washington
1973 Nancy Reed
1973 Nancy Reed
1975 Arlene Cohen
1976 Arlene Cohen
1977 Mrs. Owen McHaney
1978 Judy Alvarez
1979 Mrs. Nancy Richey Gunter
1980 Judy Alvarez

USTA Clay Court Champions—Women's 35 Doubles

1971 Ruth Gross and Nancy Neeld
1972 Ruth Gross and Nancy Neeld

1973 Evelyn Houseman and Mrs. Betty R. Pratt
1974 Mrs. June E. Gay and Diana Gai
1975 Arlene Cohen and Karen Knoche
1976 Susan Anawalt and Arlene Cohen
1977 Darlene Hard and Nancy Neeld
1978 Judy Alvarez and Norma Veal
1979 Mrs. Nancy Richey Gunter and Cathie Anderson
1980 Judy Alvarez and Charleen Hillebrand

USTA Clay Court Champions—Women Seniors' Singles

1971 Mrs. Betty R. Pratt
1972 Nancy Neeld
1973 Barbara Weigandt
1974 Nancy Reed
1975 Nancy Reed
1976 Nancy Reed
1977 Nancy Reed
1978 Mrs. Owen McHaney
1979 Paula Ferguson
1980 Nancy Reed

USTA Clay Court Champions—Women Seniors' Doubles

1971 Evelyn Houseman and Louise B. Clapp
1972 Louise B. Clapp and Barbara Weigandt
1973 Louise B. Clapp and Barbara Weigandt
1974 Jane Crofford and Betty Gray
1975 Nancy Neeld and Nancy Reed
1976 Sally Bondurant and Maria Ayala
1977 Charlene Grafton and Gloria Payne
1978 Sally Bondurant and Barbara Fullwood
1979 Carol Wood and Eleanor Wright
1980 Billie Oxrieder and Eleanor Wright

USTA Clay Court Champions—Women's 45 Singles

1974 Barbara Weigandt
1975 Barbara Weigandt
1976 Olga Palafox
1977 Nancy Neeld
1978 Nancy Reed
1979 Nancy Reed
1980 Jane Crofford

USTA Clay Court Champions—Women's 45 Doubles

1974 Barbara Weigandt and Louise B. Clapp
1975 Rhoda Herron and Marjorie Kohler
1976 Olga Palafox and Charlene Grafton
1977 Olga Palafox and Charlene Grafton
1978 Nancy Neeld and Evelyn Houseman
1979 Nancy Neeld and Charlene Grafton
1980 Jane Crofford and Olga Palafox

USTA Clay Court Champions—Women's 50 Singles

1974 Nancy Penson
1975 Mrs. Betty R. Pratt
1976 Mrs. June E. Gay
1977 Mrs. June E. Gay
1978 Mrs. Betty R. Pratt
1979 Mrs. Betty R. Pratt
1980 Mrs. Betty R. Pratt

USTA Clay Court Champions—Women's 50 Doubles

1974 Sally Fuller and Amy Yee
1975 Mrs. Betty R. Pratt and Rhoda Herron
1976 Nancy Swenson and Nancy Penson
1977 Mrs. June E. Gay and Mrs. F. A. C. Vosters
1978 Mrs. Dorothy B. Chency and Mrs. Betty R. Pratt
1979 Mrs. Betty R. Pratt and Vilma Gordon
1980 Mrs. June E. Gay and Jeanne Dattan

USTA Clay Court Champions—Women's 55 Singles

1977 Mrs. Dorothy B. Cheney
1978 Mrs. Dorothy B. Cheney
1979 Mrs. Dorothy B. Cheney
1980 Mrs. Betty R. Pratt

USTA Clay Court Champions—Women's 55 Doubles

1977 Marge Skolil and Florence Tout
1978 Mrs. Dorothy B. Cheney and Amy Yee
1979 Mrs. Dorothy B. Cheney and Phyllis Adler
1980 Mrs. Dorothy B. Cheney and Phyllis Adler

USTA Clay Court Champions—Women's 60 Singles

1975 Sally Lang
1976 Ann Hoffman
1977 Mrs. Dorothy B. Cheney
1978 Mrs. Dorothy B. Cheney
1979 Mrs. Dorothy B. Cheney
1980 Mrs. Dorothy B. Cheney

USTA Clay Court Champions—Women's 60 Doubles

1975 Sally Lang and Catherine Semple
1976 Thelma Merker and Ann Hoffman
1977 Edna Maynard and Sheila Evans
1978 Thelma Merker and Ann Hoffman
1979 Mrs. Dorothy B. Cheney and Margo Mahoney
1980 Mrs. Dorothy B. Cheney and Margo Mahoney

USTA Clay Court Champions—Women's 65 Singles

1979 Margo Mahoney
1980 Wilma Smith

USTA Clay Court Champions—Women's 65 Doubles

1979 Evelyn Davis and Ann Hoffman
1980 Mercelina Parker and Margo Mahoney

USTA Clay Court Champions—Mother and Daughter

1976 Mrs. F. A. C. Vorsters and Mrs. Gretchen Spruance
1977 Mrs. F. A. C. Vosters and Mrs. Gretchen Spruance
1978 Mrs. F. A. C. Vosters and Mrs. Gretchen Spruance
1979 Mrs. F. A. C. Vosters and Mrs. Gretchen Spruance
1980 Mrs. F. A. C. Vosters and Mrs. Gretchen Spruance

USTA Indoor Champions—Men's Singles

1898	Leo Ware	1932	Gregory S. Mangin
1899	not held	1933	Gregory S. Mangin
1900	J. Appleton Allen	1934	Lester R. Stoefen
1901	Holcombe Ward	1935	Gregory S. Mangin
1902	J. Parmly Paret	1936	Gregory S. Mangin
1903	Wylie C. Grant	1937	Frank Parker
1904	Wylie C. Grant	1938	Donald McNeill
1905	Edward B. Dewhurst	1939	Wayne Sabin
1906	Wylie C. Grant	1940	Robert L. Riggs
1907	Theodore R. Pell	1941	Frank L. Kovacs II
1908	Wylie C. Grant	1942–45	not held
1909	Theodore R. Pell	1946	Francisco Segura
1910	Gustave F. Touchard	1947	John A. Kramer
1911	Theodore R. Pell	1948	William F. Talbert
1912	Wylie C. Grant	1949	Richard A. Gonzales
1913	Gustave F. Touchard	1950	Donald McNeill
1914	Gustave F. Touchard	1951	William F. Talbert
1915	Gustave F. Touchard	1952	Richard Savitt
1916	R. Lindley Murray	1953	Arthur D. Larsen
1917	S. Howard Voshell	1954	Sven Davidson
1918	S. Howard Voshell	1955	Tony Trabert
1919	Vincent Richards	1956	Ulf Schmidt
1920	William T. Tilden II	1957	Kurt Nielsen
1921	Frank T. Anderson	1958	Richard Savitt
1922	Francis T. Hunter	1959	Alejandro Olmedo
1923	Vincent Richards	1960	Barry MacKay
1924	Vincent Richards	1961	Richard Savitt
1925	Jean Borotra	1962	Charles R. McKinley
1926	Jean René Lacoste	1963	R. Dennis Ralston
1927	Jean Borotra	1964	Charles R. McKinley
1928	William Aydelotte	1965	Jan Erik Lundquist
1929	Jean Borotra	1966	Charles Pasarell
1930	Francis T. Hunter	1967	Charles Pasarell
1931	Jean Borotra	1968	Cliff Richey
		1969	Stan Smith
		1970	Stan Smith

USTA NATIONAL INDOOR OPEN CHAMPIONS—MEN'S SINGLES

Year	Winner	Runner-up	Final Score
1970	Ilie Nastase	Cliff Richey	6–8, 3–6, 6–4, 9–7, 6–0
1971	Clark Graebner	Cliff Richey	2–6, 7–6, 1–6, 7–6, 6–0
1972	Stan Smith	Ilie Nastase	5–7, 6–2, 6–3, 6–4
1973	Jimmy Connors	Karl Meiler	7–6, 7–6, 6–3
1974	Jimmy Connors	Frew McMillan	6–4, 7–5, 6–3
1975	Jimmy Connors	Vitas Gerulaitis	5–7, 7–5, 6–1, 3–6, 6–0
1976	Ilie Nastase	Jimmy Connors	6–2, 6–3, 7–6
1977	Bjorn Borg	Brian Gottfried	6–4, 6–3, 4–6, 7–5
1978	Jimmy Connors	Tim Gullickson	7–6, 6–3
1979	Jimmy Connors	Arthur Ashe	6–4, 5–7, 6–3
1980	John McEnroe	Jimmy Connors	7–6, 7–6

(Held at Salisbury, Md., 1970–76; Memphis, Tenn., since 1977)

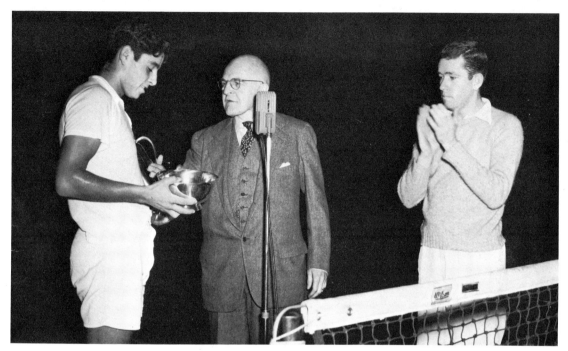

Pancho Gonzales receiving the Indoor Championship trophy from Walter Merrill Hall, chairman of the USTA Indoor Championships Committee, while Billy Talbert, runner-up for the title, which he won in 1948, applauds the new champion.

USTA Indoor Champions—Women's Singles

1907	Elisabeth H. Moore	1923	Mrs. Benjamin E. Cole II
1908	Marie Wagner	1924	Mrs. Marion Zinderstein Jessup
1909	Marie Wagner	1925	Mrs. Marion Zinderstein Jessup
1910	Mrs. Frederick G. Schmitz	1926	Elizabeth Ryan
1911	Marie Wagner	1927	Mrs. Hazel Hotchkiss Wightman
1912	not held	1928	Edith Sigourney
1913	Marie Wagner	1929	Margaret Blake
1914	Marie Wagner	1930	Mianne Palfrey
1915	Molla Bjurstedt	1931	Marjorie Sachs
1916	Molla Bjurstedt	1932	Marjorie Morrill
1917	Marie Wagner	1933	Dorance Chase
1918	Molla Bjurstedt	1934	Norma Taubele
1919	Mrs. Hazel Hotchkiss Wightman	1935	Jane Sharp
1920	Helen Pollak	1936	Mrs. Marjorie Gladman Van Ryn
1921	Mrs. Molla Bjurstedt Mallory	1937	Mme. Sylvia Henrotin
1922	Mrs. Molla Bjurstedt Mallory	1938	Virginia Hollinger
		1939	Pauline M. Betz
		1940	Mrs. Sarah Palfrey Fabyan

USTA Indoor Champions—Women's Singles *(cont.)*

1941 Pauline M. Betz
1942 Mrs. Patricia Canning Todd
1943 Pauline M. Betz
1944 Katharine Winthrop
1945 Mrs. Helen Pedersen Rihbany
1946 Mrs. Helen Pedersen Rihbany
1947 Pauline M. Betz
1948 Mrs. Patricia Canning Todd
1949 Gertrude Moran
1950 Nancy Chaffee
1951 Nancy Chaffee
1952 Mrs. Nancy Chaffee Kiner
1953 Mrs. Thelma Long
1954 Mrs. Dorothy W. Levine
1955 Katharine Hubbell
1956 Lois Felix
1957 Mrs. Dorothy W. Levine
1958 Nancy O'Connell
1959 Lois Felix
1960 Carole Wright
1961 Janet Hopps
1962 Carole Wright
1963 Carol Hanks
1964 Mary Ann Eisel
1965 Nancy Richey

Mrs. Marion Zinderstein Jessup won many USTA titles in the 1920s.

1966 Mrs. Billie Jean King
1967 Mrs. Billie Jean King
1968 Mrs. Billie Jean King
1969 Mrs. M. A. E. Curtis
1970 Mrs. M. A. E. Curtis
1971 Mrs. Billie Jean King
1972 not held

USTA NATIONAL INDOOR OPEN CHAMPIONS—WOMEN'S SINGLES

Year	Winner	Runner-up	Final Score
1973	Evonne Goolagong	Virginia Wade	6–4, 6–4
1974	Mrs. Billie Jean King	Chris Evert	6–3, 3–6, 6–2
1975	Martina Navratilova	Evonne Goolagong	6–2, 4–6, 6–3
1976	Virginia Wade	Betty Stove	5–7, 7–5, 7–5
1977	not held		
1978	Chris Evert	Virginia Wade	6–7, 6–2, 6–4
1979	Mrs. Evonne G. Cawley	Dianne Fromholtz	6–3, 6–4
1980	Tracy Austin	Dianne Fromholtz	6–1, 2–6, 6–2

USTA Indoor Champions—Men's Doubles

1900 Calhoun Cragin and J. P. Paret
1901 Calhoun Cragin and O. M. Bostwick
1902 W. C. Grant and R. LeRoy
1903 W. C. Grant and R. LeRoy
1904 W. C. Grant and R. LeRoy
1905 T. R. Pell and H. F. Allen
1906 H. H. Hackett and F. B. Alexander

1907 H. H. Hackett and F. B. Alexander
1908 H. H. Hackett and F. B. Alexander
1909 W. C. Grant and T. R. Pell
1910 G. F. Touchard and C. R. Gardner
1911 F. B. Alexander and T. R. Pell
1912 F. B. Alexander and T. R. Pell
1913 W. C. Grant and G. C. Shafer

1914 W. C. Grant and G. C. Shafer
1915 G. F. Touchard and W. M. Washburn
1916 A. M. Lovibond and W. Rosenbaum
1917 F. B. Alexander and W. Rosenbaum
1918 G. C. Shafer and K. Smith
1919 W. T. Tilden II and V. Richards
1920 W. T. Tilden II and V. Richards
1921 V. Richards and S. H. Voshell
1922 F. T. Anderson and S. H. Voshell
1923 V. Richards and F. T. Hunter
1924 V. Richards and F. T. Hunter
1925 J. Borotra and A. W. Asthalter
1926 W. T. Tilden II and F. C. Anderson
1927 J. Borotra and J. Brugnon
1928 W. Aydelotte and P. G. Rockafellow
1929 W. T. Tilden II and F. T. Hunter
1930 P. G. Rockafellow and M. Cutler
1931 J. Borotra and C. Boussus
1932 G. M. Lott, Jr. and J. Van Ryn
1933 C. Cutter and E. McCauliff
1934 G. M. Lott, Jr. and L. R. Stoefen
1935 G. S. Mangin and B. Bell
1936 K. Schroder and J. G. Hall
1937 F. A. Parker and G. S. Mangin
1938 F. J. Bowden and J. Pitman
1939 E. McCauliff and C. Sutter
1940 R. L. Riggs and E. T. Cooke
1941 W. D. McNeill and F. D. Guernsey, Jr.
1942–45 not held
1946 W. D. McNeill and F. D. Guernsey, Jr.
1947 J. A. Kramer and R. Falkenburg
1948 J. Borotra and M. Bernard
1949 W. F. Talbert and W. D. McNeill
1950 W. F. Talbert and W. D. McNeill
1951 W. F. Talbert and W. D. McNeill
1952 W. F. Talbert and W. D. McNeill
1953 A. D. Larsen and K. Nielsen
1954 W. F. Talbert and T. Trabert
1955 E. V. Seixas, Jr. and T. Trabert
1956 S. Giammalva and E. V. Seixas, Jr.
1957 G. Golden and B. MacKay
1958 G. Golden and B. MacKay
1959 B. MacKay and A. Olmedo
1960 Andres Gimeno and Manuel Santana
1961 C. R. Crawford and R. Holmberg
1962 R. Laver and C. R. McKinley
1963 C. R. McKinley and R. D. Ralston
1964 Manuel Santana and Jose Luis Arilla
1965 C. R. McKinley and R. D. Ralston

1966 Robert Lutz and Stan Smith
1967 Arthur Ashe and Charles Pasarell
1968 Thomas Koch and Tom Okker
1969* Robert Lutz and Stan Smith
1970 Arthur Ashe and Stan Smith
1971 Ilie Nastase and Ion Tiriac
1971 Juan Gisbert and Manuel Orantes
1972 Andres Gimeno and Manuel Orantes
1973 Jurgen Fassbender and Juan Gisbert
1974 Jimmy Connors and Frew McMillan
1975 Jimmy Connors and Ilie Nastase
1976 Sherwood Stewart and Fred McNair
1977 Sherwood Stewart and Fred McNair
1978 Brian Gottfried and Raul Ramirez
1979 Tom Okker and Wojtek Fibak
1980 John McEnroe and Brian Gottfried

*Open champions.

USTA Indoor Champions—Women's Doubles

1908 Mrs. Helen Helwig Pouch and Elisabeth H. Moore
1909 Elisabeth H. Moore and Erna Marcus
1910 Marie Wagner and Clara Kutroff
1911 Elizabeth C. Bunce and Barbara Fleming
1912 not held
1913 Marie Wagner and Clara Kutroff
1914 Mrs. S. F. Weaver and Clare Cassel
1915 Mrs. Helen Homans McLean and Mrs. S. F. Weaver
1916 Molla Bjurstedt and Marie Wagner
1917 Marie Wagner and Margaret T. Taylor
1918 Eleanor Goss and Mrs. S. F. Weaver
1919 Mrs. Hazel Hotchkiss Wightman and Marion Zinderstein
1920 Mrs. L. Gouverneur Morris and Helene Pollak
1921 Mrs. Hazel Hotchkiss Wightman and Marion Zinderstein
1922 Mrs. Frank Godfrey and Mrs. Marion Zinderstein Jessup
1923 Mrs. Benjamin E. Cole II and Mrs. Frank Godfrey
1924 Mrs. Hazel Hotchkiss Wightman and Mrs. Marion Zinderstein Jessup

USTA Indoor Champions—Women's Doubles *(cont.)*

1925 Mrs. William Endicott and Mrs. J. Dallas Corbiere
1926 Elizabeth Ryan and Mary K. Browne
1927 Mrs. Hazel Hotchkiss Wightman and Mrs. Marion Zinderstein Jessup
1928 Mrs. Hazel Hotchkiss Wightman and Sarah Palfrey
1929 Mrs. Hazel Hotchkiss Wightman and Sarah Palfrey
1930 Mrs. Hazel Hotchkiss Wightman and Sarah Palfrey
1931 Mrs. Hazel Hotchkiss Wightman and Sarah Palfrey
1932 Marjorie Morrill and Mrs. Marjorie Gladman Van Ryn
1933 Mrs. Hazel Hotchkiss Wightman and Sarah Palfrey
1934 Norma Taubele and Jane Sharp
1935 Mrs. Dorothy Andrus and Mme. Sylvia Henrotin
1936 Mrs. Dorothy Andrus and Mme. Sylvia Henrotin
1937 Mrs. Dorothy Andrus and Mme. Sylvia Henrotin
1938 Mrs. Virginia Rice Johnson and Katharine Winthrop
1939 Norma Taubele and Grace Surber
1940 Mrs. Gracyn Wheeler Kelleher and Norma Taubele
1941 Pauline M. Betz and Dorothy M. Bundy
1942 Katharine Winthrop and Mrs. Virginia Rice Johnson
1943 Pauline M. Betz and Mrs. Hazel H. Wightman
1944 Katharine Winthrop and Mrs. Virginia Rice Johnson
1945 Katharine Winthrop and Mrs. Virginia Rice Johnson
1946 Mrs. Helen Petersen Rihbany and Ruth Carter
1947 Doris Hart and Barbara Scofield
1948 Doris Hart and Barbara Scofield
1949 Gertrude Moran and Mrs. Marjorie Gladman Buck
1950 Nancy Chaffee and Mrs. Marjorie Gladman Buck

1951 Mrs. Marjorie Gladman Buck and Nancy Chaffee
1952 Mrs. Nancy Chaffee Kiner and Mrs. Patricia Canning Todd
1953 Mrs. Thelma Long and Mrs. Barbara Scofield Davidson
1954 Mrs. Dorothy W. Levine and Mrs. Barbara W. Ward
1955 Ruth Jeffery and Katharine Hubbell
1956 Lois Felix and Katharine Hubbell
1957 Mrs. Dorothy W. Levine and Nancy O'Connell
1958 Carol Hanks and Nancy O'Connell
1959 Lois Felix and Katharine Hubbell
1960 Mrs. Marjorie Gladman Buck and Ruth Jeffery
1961 Janet Hopps and Katharine Hubbell
1962 Belmar Gunderson and Ruth Jeffery
1963 Carol Hanks and Mary Ann Eisel
1964 Mary Ann Eisel and Kay Hubbell
1965 Mrs. Carol Hanks Aucamp and Mrs. Mary Ann Eisel
1966 Rosemary Casals and Mrs. Billie Jean King
1967 Mrs. Carol H. Aucamp and Mary Ann Eisel
1968 Mrs. Billie Jean King and Rosemary Casals
1969* Mary Ann E. Curtis and Valerie Ziegenfuss
1970* Nancy Richey and Peaches Bartkowicz
1971* Mrs. Billie Jean King and Rosemary Casals
1972* not held
1973* Marina Kroshina and Olga Morozova
1974* not held
1975* Rosemary Casals and Mrs. Billie Jean King
1976* Francoise Durr and Rosemary Casals
1977* not held
1978* Mrs. Kerry M. Reid and Wendy Turnbull
1979* Mrs. Billie Jean King and Martina Narratilova
1980* Ann Kiyomura and Candy Reynolds

*Open champions.

USTA Indoor Champions—Mixed Doubles

1921 Mrs. M. Bjurstedt Mallory and William T. Tilden II
1922 Mrs. M. Bjurstedt Mallory and William T. Tilden II
1923 Mrs. H. Hotchkiss Wightman and Burnham N. Dell
1924 Mrs. H. Hotchkiss Wightman and William T. Tilden II
1925 Mrs. M. Zinderstein Jessup and Karl S. Pfaffman
1926 Mrs. H. Hotchkiss Wightman and G. Peabody Gardner, Jr.
1927 Mrs. H. Hotchkiss Wightman and G. Peabody Gardner, Jr.
1928 Mrs. H. Hotchkiss Wightman and Henry L. Johnson, Jr.
1929 Margaret Blake and Richard Harte
1930 Margaret Blake and Richard Harte
1931 Sarah Palfrey and Lawrence B. Rice
1932 Marjorie Morrill and G. Colket Caner
1933 Sarah Palfrey and G. Holmes Perkins
1934 Norma Taubele and Frank J. Bowden
1935 Jane Sharp and Gregory S. Mangin
1936 Mrs. Sylvia Henrotin and Kalle Schroder
1937 Mrs. Sylvia Henrotin and Frank J. Bowden
1938 Norma Taubele and Frank J. Bowden
1939 Pauline M. Betz and Wayne Sabin
1940 Pauline M. Betz and Robert L. Riggs
1941 Pauline M. Betz and Albert H. Stitt
1942 Katharine Winthrop and Albert H. Stitt
1943 Pauline M. Betz and Albert H. Stitt
1944 Judy Atterbury and Albert H. Stitt
1945 Mrs. Norma T. Barber and Robert Stewart
1946 Mrs. Helen Pedersen Rihbany and Geo. W. Mandell
1947 Doris Hart and William F. Talbert
1948 Doris Hart and William F. Talbert
1949 Gertrude Moran and Richard Gonzalez
1950 Nancy Chaffee and Budge Patty
1951 Beverly Baker and Straight Clark
1952–53 not held
1954 Lois Felix and Winslow Blanchard
1955 Ruth Jeffery and Wallace McIntyre
1956 Ruth Jeffery and Dever Hobbs
1957 Mildred Thornton and Dr. Donald Manchester
1958 Mildred Thornton and Dr. Donald Manchester
1959 Mrs. Mildred Thornton Johnson and Dr. Donald Manchester
1960 Lois Felix and Dr. Donald Manchester
1961 Janet Hopps and Arthur (Bud) Collins
1962 Carole Wright and Chauncey D. Steele, Jr.
1963 Carol Hanks and Chauncey D. Steele III
1964 Belmar Gunderson and Chauncey D. Steele III
1965 Mary Ann Eisel and Chauncey D. Steele III
1966 Mrs. Billie Jean King and Paul Sullivan
1967 Mrs. Billie Jean King and Paul Sullivan
1968 Mary Ann Eisel and Chauncey D. Steele III
1969–80 not held

USTA Indoor Champions—Junior Singles

1915 Elliott H. Binzen
1916 Elliott H. Binzen
1917 E. H. Hendrickson
1918 Vincent Richards
1919 Vincent Richards
1920 Vincent Richards
1921 Edgar F. Dawson
1922 John F. W. Whitbeck
1923 Kenneth Appel
1924 Horace G. Orser
1925 Julius Seligson
1926 Julius Seligson
1927 Francis X. Shields
1928 Richard Murphy
1929 William Jacobs
1930 Mark Hecht
1931 Mark Hecht
1932 Mark Hecht
1933 Frank Parker
1934 Gilbert A. Hunt
1935 Alfred L. Jarvis, Jr.
1936 Donald McNeill
1937 Joseph Fishbach
1938 Joseph Fishbach
1939 William Umstaedter
1940 James Evert
1941–44 not held
1945 Sidney Schwartz

USTA Indoor Champions—Junior Singles *(cont.)*

1946 Leonard Steiner
1947 Sidney Schwartz
1948 Tony Trabert
1949 Jerry DeWitts
1950 Hamilton Richardson
1951 Samuel Giammalva
1952 Samuel Giammalva
1953 Albert E. Harum, Jr.
1954 Alphonse Holtman
1955 Ronald Holmberg
1956 Earl Buchholz, Jr.
1957 Charles McKinley
1958 Charles McKinley
1959 Charles McKinley
1960 Arthur Ashe, Jr.
1961 Arthur Ashe, Jr.
1962 Gary Rieser
1963 Cliff Richey
1964 Frank Conner
1965 Armistead Neely
1966 Jeff Borowiak
1967 Don Lutz
1968 Robert McKinley
1969 Roscoe Tanner
1970 Brian Gottfried
1971 James Delaney
1972 Victor Amaya
1973 Howard Schoenfield
1974 Howard Schoenfield
1975 Tony Giammalva
1976 Rick Cowden
1977 Jeff Turpin
1978 Scott Davis
1979 Scott Davis
1980 Michael Kures

USTA Indoor Champions—Junior Doubles

1915 James Weber and R. C. Rand
1916 Willard Botsford and R. C. Haines
1917 Gerald B. Emerson and Herman F. Dornheim
1918 Frank T. Anderson and H. B. Kaltenbach
1919 Vincent Richards and Frank T. Anderson
1920 Vincent Richards and P. S. McHugh
1921 Jerome Lang and Edgar F. Dawson
1922 Kenneth Appel and John Van Ryn

1923 Malcolm T. Hill and Henry L. Johnson, Jr.
1924 Malcolm T. Hill and Henry L. Johnson, Jr.
1925 Malcolm T. Hill and Henry L. Johnson, Jr.
1926 Malcolm T. Hill and Henry L. Johnson, Jr.
1927 Francis X. Shields and Julius Seligson
1928 Richard Murphy and Samuel P. Hayes, Jr.
1929 Richard Downing and S. E. Davenport
1930 Kendal H. Cram and Frank M. Shore
1931 Bernard Friedman and Lester Kabacoff
1932 Giles Verstraten and John Nogrady
1933 Gilbert A. Hunt and Sumner Rodman
1934 Gilbert A. Hunt and Charles Mattmann
1935 Melvin L. Lapman and Marvin Kantrowitz
1936 Charles T. Mattmann and Peter Lauck
1937 Robert A. Low and Marvin Kantrowitz
1938 Joseph Fishbach and Dave Johnsen
1939 Richard E. Shipp and Fred V. Krais, Jr.
1940 James Evert and Richard J. Bender
1941–44 not held
1945 Richard Savitt and Leonard L. Steiner
1946 Pvt. Hugh Steward and Alex Hetzeck
1947 Sidney Schwartz and Alex Hetzeck
1948 Tony Trabert and Dixon Osburn
1949 Jerry DeWitts and Jack Turpin
1950 Hamilton Richardson and Bob Sierra
1951 Edward Daily and Samuel Giammalva
1952 Samuel Giammalva and Richard Schuette
1953 Mike Green and Richard Schuette
1954 David Harum and Wayne Pearce
1955 Arthur Andrews and Crawford Henry
1956 Earl Buchholz, Jr. and C. Edward Sledge
1957 Earl Buchholz, Jr. and Charles McKinley
1958 Charles McKinley and Raymond Senkowski
1959 Charles McKinley and Cliff Buchholz
1960 Frank Froehling III and Butch Newman
1961 Cliff Buchholz and Butch Newman
1962 B. H. Brown and Gary Rieser
1963 B. H. Brown and Gary Rieser
1964 John Good and Brian Marcus
1965 Richard Dell and George Turner
1966 Jeff Borowiak and Mike Estep

1967 John Fort and Don Lutz
1968 Robert McKinley and Richard Stockton
1969 Brian Gottfried and Richard Stockton
1970 Brian Gottfried and Alex Mayer, Jr.
1971 James Delaney and John Whitlinger
1972 Michael Nissley and Bruce Manson
1973 Ferdi Taygan and Howard Schoenfield
1974 John Austin and Tony Graham
1975 Jai DiLouie and Tony Giammalva
1976 Leland Putterman and Dan Weber
1977 Jeff Turpin and Scott Bondurant
1978 Scott Davis and Ben Testerman
1979 Fabio Mion-Bet and Paul Chamberlin
1980 Anthony Emerson and Jorge Lozano

USTA Indoor Champions—Boys' 16 Singles

1962 Cliff Richey
1963 Chuck Brainard
1964 Jasjit Singh
1965 Jeff Borowiak
1966 George Taylor
1967 Richard Stockton
1968 Robert Kreiss
1969 John Whitlinger
1970 John Whitlinger
1971 Kenneth Walts
1972 Howard Schoenfield
1973 Juan Farrow
1974 Larry Gottfried
1975 John Corse
1976 Billy Nealon
1977 Ben Testerman
1978 Sammy Giammalva
1979 Jonathan Canter
1980 Jimmy Brown

USTA Indoor Champions—Boys' 16 Doubles

1962 Cliff Brown and Steve Stockton
1963 Chuck Brainard and John Towner
1964 Leo Estopare and Dan Oram
1965 Bob Alloo and Leo Estopare
1966 Robin Sandage and Jack Hughes
1967 Mike Machette and Richard Stockton
1968 Timmy Connors and Brian Gottfried
1969 Randall Schneider and Brian Teacher
1970 William Martin and Patrick Dupre
1971 William Martin and Trey Waltke

1972 Howard Schoenfield and Perry Wright
1973 Jai DiLouie and Rick Meyers
1974 Eliot Teltscher and Clark Diehl
1975 Scott Bondurant and John Corse
1976 Scott Davis and Ben Testerman
1977 Ben Testerman and Scott Davis
1978 Eric Korita and Eric Weiss
1979 Rick Leach and Tim Pawsat
1980 Jimmy Brown and Doug Pielet

USTA Indoor Champions—Boys' 14 Singles

1972 Van Winitsky
1973 John Corse
1974 Paul Crozier
1975 Bruce Brescia
1976 Jimmy Arias
1977 Mitchell Perkins
1978 Rick Leach
1979 Robby Weiss
1980 Aaron Krickstein

USTA Indoor Champions—Boys' 14 Doubles

1972 John McEnroe and Van Winitsky
1973 John Corse and David Dowlan
1974 Eric Korita and Danny Weiss
1975 Scott Davis and Ben Testerman
1976 Alan Racko and Martin Wostenholme
1977 Mitchell Perkins and E. C. Morgan
1978 Brad Ackerman and Jimmy Brown
1979 Patrick McEnroe and Ricky Peck
1980 Aaron Krickstein and Robby Weiss

USTA Indoor Champions—Boys' 12 Singles

1972 Paul Crozier
1973 Bruce Brescia
1974 Robby Palmer
1975 James Arias
1976 Robby Weiss
1977 Richey Reneberg
1978 Robby Weiss
1979 Michael Briggs
1980 Al Parker

USTA Indoor Champions—Boys' 12 Doubles

1972 Boyd Bryan and Paul Crozier
1973 George Myers and David Perlmutter
1974 Boyd Bryan and Paul Crozier
1975 Todd Witsken and Mark Styslinger
1976 Jeff Karp and Keith Thomas
1977 Marc Fishman and Eric Amend
1978 Robby Weiss and Aaron Krickstein
1979 David Gllob and Stephen Hentschel
1980 Al Parker and Chris Garner

USTA Indoor Champions—Girls' 18 Singles

The USLTA Indoor Girls' Championships were held in the late winter or early spring from the time of the first tournament in 1920 (with the exception of three years, 1921, 1922, and 1923, when the tournament was not held) up to and including 1930.

Instead of holding the next tournament in the spring of 1931 as customary, the tournament was held in December, 1930, during the Christmas holidays. Thus, two tournaments were held in the same year. Since and including 1930, the Indoor Girls' Championships have been held regularly in December. In 1969 the tournament was held Thanksgiving weekend.

1920 Martha Bayard
1921–23 not held
1924 Elizabeth Hilleary
1925 Alice C. Francis
1926 Marjorie Morrill
1927 Sarah Palfrey
1928 Sarah Palfrey
1929 Mianne Palfrey
1930 Katharine Winthrop
1930 Sarah Palfrey
1931 Katharine Winthrop
1932 Helen Grawn
1933 Millicent Hirsh
1934 Virginia Hollinger
1935 Virginia Hollinger
1936 Helen Bernhard
1937 Helen Bernhard
1938 Marguerita Madden
1939 Marguerita Madden
1940 Dorothy Wightman
1941 Lillian Lopaus
1942 Lillian Lopaus
1943 Shirley J. Fry
1944 Barbara Wilkins
1945 Barbara Wilkins
1946 Barbara Wilkins
1947 Laura Lou Jahn
1948 Laura Lou Jahn
1949 Elaine Lewicki
1950 Edith Ann Sullivan
1951 Elaine Lewicki
1952 Mary Slaughter
1953 June Stack
1954 June Stack
1955 Nancy O'Connell
1956 Nancy O'Connell
1957 Nancy O'Connell
1958 Bonnie Mencher
1959 Justina Bricka
1960 Sue Behlmar
1961 Alice B. Christer
1962 Yale Stockwell
1963 Yale Stockwell
1964 Carolyn Clarke
1965 Vicky Rogers
1966 Judy Dixon
1967 Andrea Voikos
1968 Andrea Voikos
1969 Linda Rupert
1970 Andrea Voikos
1971 Susan Stap
1972 Susan Graham
1973 Patty Shoolman
1974 Zenda Liess
1975 Anne Smith
1976 Stacy Margolin
1977 Maria Rothschild
1978 Mary Lou Piatek
1979 Kelly Henry
1980 Andrea Leand

USTA Indoor Champions—Girls' 18 Doubles

1926 Marjorie Morrill and Lee Palfrey
1927 Mianne Palfrey and Sarah Palfrey
1928 Mianne Palfrey and Sarah Palfrey
1929 Mianne Palfrey and Sarah Palfrey
1930 Hilda Boehm and Helen Boehm
1930 Sarah Palfrey and Joanna Palfrey
1931 Katharine Winthrop and Helen Jones

1932	Louise Harding and Marion Wood
1933	Millicent Hirsh and Helen Grawn
1934	Virginia Hollinger and Helen Bernhard
1935	Virginia Hollinger and Helen Bernhard
1936	Helen Bernhard and Virginia Kollinger
1937	Helen Bernhard and Dorothy Wightman
1938	Helen Bernhard and Dorothy Wightman
1939	Marguerita Madden and Dorothy Wightman
1940	Lillian Lopaus and Betty Rosenquest
1941	Lillian Lopaus and Betty Rosenquest
1942	Judy Atterbury and Norma Meister
1943	Shirley J. Fry and Norma Meister
1944	Mary DeYoung and Jean Pipes
1945	Sylvia Knowles and Nina Irwin
1946	Barbara Wilkins and Anne Wofford
1947	Laura Lou Jahn and Adrienne Goldberg
1948	Laura Jahn and Mrs. A. Goldbert Ayares
1949	Elaine Lewicki and Edith Ann Sullivan
1950	Elaine Lewicki and Bonnie MacKay
1951	Susan Bralower and Elaine Lewicki
1952	Belmar Gunderson and Mary Slaughter
1953	Patricia Sullivan and Carroll Wendell
1954	Lorraine Jake and June Stack
1955	Virginia Connolly and Nancy O'Connell
1956	Donna Floyd and Nancy O'Connell
1957	Nancy O'Connell and Virginia Hesse
1958	Susan Behlmar and Bonnie Mencher
1959	Justina Bricka and Susan Behlmar
1960	Susan Behlmar and Heidi Lincoln
1961	Virginia Gilbane and Joanne Swanson
1962	Duane Horan and Joanne Swanson
1963	Yale Stockwell and Roberta Zimman
1964	Carolyn Clarke and Susan Mabrey
1965	Carolyn Clarke and Charlotte Atwater
1966	Evelyn Haase and Bonnie Logan
1967	Connie Capozzi and Marjorie Gengler
1968–69	not held
1970	Karin Benson and Andrea Voikos
1971	Claude Smith and Andrea Voikos
1972	Carrie Meyer and Claudia Smith
1973	Judy Acker and Sherry Acker
1974	Susan Hagey and Mary Carillo
1975	Sherry Acker and Anne Smith
1976	Kathy Jordan and Anne Smith
1977	Maria Rothschild and Mary Lou Piatek
1978	Mary Lou Piatek and Anne White
1979	Susan Pendo and Linley Tanner
1980	Zina Garrison and Lori McNeil

USTA Indoor Champions—Girls' 16 Singles

1962	Yale Stockwell
1963	Marilyn Aschner
1964	Carolyn Clarke
1965	Vicki Rogers
1966	Andrea Voikos
1967	Andrea Voikos
1968	Andrea Voikos
1969	Clare Schmoyer
1970	Susan Pritula
1971	Gretchen Galt
1972	Susan Mehmedbasich
1973	Susan Hagey
1974	Anne Smith
1975	Charlene Murphy
1976	Tracy Austin
1977	Tracy Austin
1978	Kathrin Keil
1979	Pamela Casele
1980	Amy Holton

USTA Indoor Champions—Girls' 16 Doubles

1962	Debbie King and Gery Wolf
1963–64	not held
1965	Hannabeth Jackson and Jade Schiffman
1966–69	not held
1970	Una Keyes and Claudia Smith
1971	Nancy Anderson and Leslie Vyce
1972	Sheryl Maskell and Thayer Wendell
1973	Sheryl Maskell and Susie Brown
1974	Sherry Acker and Anne Smith
1975	Anne White and Lisa Kearney
1976	Tracy Austin and Kelly Henry
1977	Tracy Austin and Kelly Henry
1978	Joy Cummings and Jane Jarosz
1979	Penny Barg and Carol Heynen
1980	Lisa Bonder and Joni Urban

USTA Indoor Champions—Girls' 14 Singles

1972	Zenda Liess
1973	Jennifer Balent
1974	Tracy Austin
1975	Tracy Austin
1976	Carol Christian
1977	Susan Mascarin
1978	Carol Heynen
1979	Joni Urban
1980	Eileen Tell

USTA Indoor Champions—Girls' 14 Doubles

1972 Jan Devereaux and Zenda Liess
1973 Jennifer Balent and Laura Starr
1974 Betty Newfield and Caroline Stoll
1975 Tracy Austin and Kelly Henry
1976 Nancy Talley and Carol Christian
1977 Susan Mascarin and Andrea Leand
1978 Lori Kosten and Kathy Foxworth
1979 Joni Urban and Lisa Bonder
1980 Terry Phelps and Sonia Hahn

USTA Indoor Champions—Girls' 12 Singles

1972 Toni Moss
1973 Tracy Austin
1974 Shelly Solomon
1975 Susan Mascarin
1976 Lori Kosten
1977 Margaret Hopkins
1978 Kathy Rinaldi
1979 Marianne Werdel
1980 Jill Galiene

USTA Indoor Champions—Girls' 12 Doubles

1972 Toni Moss and Caroline Stoll
1973 Tracy Austin and Kelly Henry
1974 Susan Mascarin and Anna Van
       Walleghem
1975 Susan Mascarin and Robin White
1976 Leigh Van Eldredge and Carol Heynen
1977 Colette Kavanaugh and Cari Hagey
1978 Kathy Rinaldi and Nicole Stafford
1979 Marianne Werdel and Carling Bassett
1980 Jennifer Santrock and Kerri Reiter

USTA Indoor Champions—Men Seniors' Singles

1951 Karl Hodge
1952 Willard Roeder
1953 John E. Sisson
1954 not held
1955 R. Philip Hanna
1956 Reginald S. Weir
1957 Reginald S. Weir
1958 Gardnar Mulloy
1959 Reginald S. Weir
1960 Gardnar Mulloy
1961 C. D. Steele, Jr.
1962 George H. Ball
1963 Gardnar Mulloy
1964 Julius Heldman
1965 Julius Heldman
1966 Robert Galloway
1967 Emery Neale
1968 Robert Sherman
1969 Robert Sherman
1970 Robert Sherman
1971 Ed Doane
1972 Richard Mechem
1973 Hugh Stewart
1974 Joe Ignatius
1975 King Lambert
1976 Russell Seymour
1977 Russell Seymour
1978 Russell Seymour
1979 King Van Nostrand
1980 Larry Huebner

USTA Indoor Champions—Men Seniors' Doubles

1951 Monte Ganger and Karl Hodge
1952 John English and Willard Roeder
1953 John E. Sisson and Arthur LeVan Zerbe
1954 not held
1955 Edwards Jacobs and C. Alphonso Smith
1956 R. Berkeley Bell and R. Philip Hanna
1957 R. Berkeley Bell and R. Philip Hanna
1958 R. Berkeley Bell and Edgar B. Nye
1959 Gardnar Mulloy and M. H. Robineau
1960 Robert Hagey and Frank A. Thompson,
       Jr.
1961 George H. Ball and Reginald Weir
1962 George H. Ball and Reginald Weir
1963 Gardnar Mulloy and William Talbert
1964 George MacCall and Al Martini
1965 Randolph Gregson and Frank Thompson
1966 Robert Galloway and Robert Hagey
1967 Samuel Lee and Emery Neale
1968 Robert Freedman and Robert Sherman
1969 Emery Neale and Robert Sherman
1970 Butch Krikorian and Joseph Woolfson
1971 Robert Sherman and Richard Metteer
1972 Homer Richards and Robert Sherman
1973 Hugh Stewart and George Yardley

1974 John Fleitz and Al Martini
1975 Richard Metteer and Ed Kauder
1976 William Davis and Dell Sylvia
1977 Russell Seymour and Jason Morton
1978 Russell Seymour and Jason Morton
1979 Russell Seymour and Jason Morton
1980 Clif Mayne and Hugh Ditzler

USTA Indoor Champions—Men's 35 Singles

1967 Mike Oberlander
1968 Vladmir Petrovic
1969 S. L. Shafner
1970 Dell Sylvia
1971 Jim Ladin
1972 King Van Nostrand
1973 Eugene L. Scott
1974 Jim Landin
1975 Hank Jungle
1976 Horst Ritter
1977 Adrian Bey
1978 Butch Newman
1979 Butch Buchholz
1980 Jim Osborne

USTA Indoor Champions—Men's 35 Doubles

1967 Eldon Rowe and Don White
1968 Whitney Reed and Steven Voydat
1969 Ollie Gresham and S. L. Shafner
1970 John Been and Richard Schuette
1971 Sam Park and Ed. Kauder
1972 John Been and Richard Shuette
1973 John Been and Richard Shuette
1974 Ron Livingston and George Yardley
1975 Clif Mayne and Hugh Ditzler
1976 Horst Bitter and Dick Leach
1977 Frank Froehling and Bill Higgins
1978 Jim Parker and Butch Newman
1979 Peter Van Lingen and Keith Diepraam
1980 Jim Parker and Butch Newman

USTA Indoor Champions—Men's 50 Singles

1971 Robert Sherman
1972 Robert Sherman
1973 Joe Woolfson
1974 Robert Sherman
1975 Robert Perez

1976 Robert Perez
1977 Ed Kauder
1978 Ed Kauder
1979 Hugh Stewart
1980 Russell Seymour

USTA Indoor Champions—Men's 50 Doubles

1971 Robin Hippenstiel and Verne Hughes
1972 Robin Hippenstiel and Verne Hughes
1973 Butch Krikorian and Joe Woolfson
1974 Nolan McQuown and Roy McQuown
1975 William Crosby and Robert Perez
1976 Robert Perez and Richard Metteer
1977 Ed Kauder and Richard Metteer
1978 Ed Kauder and Richard Metteer
1979 Hugh Stewart and Bill Davis
1980 Russell Seymour and Jason Morton

USTA Indoor Champions—Men Seniors' 55 Singles

1966 Bryan M. Grant
1967 Robert Shepherd
1968 Bill Lurie
1969 Chauncey Steele, Jr.
1970 Chauncey Steele, Jr.
1971 William Smith
1972 William Smith
1973 Al Doyle
1974 Charles Lass
1975 Alan Cheesebro
1976 Bob Sherman
1977 Robert Sherman
1978 Robert Sherman
1979 Robert Sherman
1980 Robert Sherman

USTA Indoor Champions—Men Seniors' 55 Doubles

1966 N. E. Powel and Len Prosser
1967 N. E. Powel and Len Prosser
1968 Gardnar Mulloy and C. Alphonso Smith
1969 Bitsy Grant and Henry Crawford
1970 Len Prosser and Henry Crawford
1971 Robin Hippenstiel and Verne Hughes
1972 Robin Hippenstiel and Verne Hughes
1973 Tom Bird and Henry Crawford

USTA Indoor Champions—Men Seniors' 55 Doubles *(cont.)*

1974 Bob Galloway and Al Martini
1975 Robin Hippenstiel and Verne Hughes
1976 Ed Doane and Glenn Hippenstiel
1977 Alan Cheesebro and Bob Galloway
1978 Dave Martin and Bob Galloway
1979 Keith Larsen and Vince Fotre
1980 L. Straight Clark and Richard Metteer

USTA Indoor Champions—Men Seniors' 60 Singles

1967 Kenneth Beer
1968 Kenneth Beer
1969 C. Alphonso Smith
1970 Len Prosser
1971 N. E. Powel
1972 John Faunce
1973 John Faunce
1974 William Smith
1975 Chauncey D. Steele, Jr.
1976 Chauncey D. Steele, Jr.
1977 J. B. Cantrell
1978 Bobby Riggs
1979 Bobby Riggs
1980 Robert Sherman

USTA Indoor Champions—Men Seniors' 60 Doubles

1967 Robert Abnot and Les Wanee
1968 Edward G. Chandler and Gerald Stratford
1969 Edward Chandler and Gerald Stratford
1970 Len Prosser and Charles Brooke
1971 Len Prosser and N. E. Powel
1972 Col. N. E. Powel and Leonard Prosser
1973 Verne Hughes and Leonard Prosser
1974 Leonard Prosser and William Smith
1975 Bob Hagey and John Shelton
1976 Robin Hippenstiel and Victor Hughes
1977 Robin Hippenstiel and Verne Hughes
1978 Bobby Riggs and Joe Davis
1979 Robin Hippenstiel and George Peebles
1980 Robin Hippenstiel and Verne Hughes

USTA Indoor Champions—Men Seniors' 65 Singles

1968 Carl Busch
1969 Ken Beer
1970 Tom Sherburne
1971 Frank Goeltz
1972 Dick Skeen
1973 Erling Jensen
1974 Frank Goeltz
1975 Jack Staton
1976 Col. N. E. Powel
1977 Harry Hoffman
1978 Harry Hoffman
1979 Chauncey D. Steele, Jr.
1980 Bill Lurie

USTA Indoor Champions—Men Seniors' 65 Doubles

1968 Carl Busch and Joe Ciano
1969 Joe Ciano and Carl Busch
1970 Edward Chandler and Gerald Statford
1971 Frank Goeltz and Ted Wellman
1972 Marion Hawks and Herschel Hyde
1973 Marshall Christopher and Dave Freeborn
1974 Frank Goeltz and C. Alphonso Smith
1975 Leonard Prosser and Charles Brooke
1976 Col. N. E. Powel and Leonard Prosser
1977 Col. N. E. Powell and Leonard Prosser
1978 John Shelton and Verne Hughes
1979 Harry Hoffman and Charles Swanson
1980 Harry Hoffman and Charles Swanson

USTA Indoor Champions—Men Seniors' 70 Singles

1970 Frank G. Roberts
1971 Joseph T. Ciano
1972 Joseph T. Ciano
1973 Ken Beer
1974 Clarence Chaffee
1975 Clarence Chaffee
1976 Frank Goeltz
1977 Frank Goeltz
1978 Frank Goeltz
1979 Fran Manis
1980 Bill Conel

USTA Indoor Champions—Men Seniors' 70 Doubles

1970 Frank G. Roberts and Bryan Hamlin
1971 Joseph T. Ciano and Clarke Kaye
1972 Joe Ciano and Clarke Kaye
1973 Clarence Chaffee and Ted Wellman
1974 Ken Beer and Richard Bourne
1975 Clarence Chaffee and Herschel Hyde
1976 Lee Wanee and Stan Maloney
1977 Frank Goeltz and Bill Seidel
1978 Erling Jensen and Frank Goeltz
1979 Erling Jensen and L. A. Barnes
1980 Leonard Prosser and Elbert Lewis

USTA Indoor Champions—Men Seniors' 75 Singles

1976 Stephen Graves
1977 Clarence Chaffee
1978 Mal Clarke
1979 Mal Clarke
1980 Clarence Chaffee

USTA Indoor Champions—Men Seniors' 75 Doubles

1976 Stephen Graves and DeWitt Redgrave
1977 Mal Clarke and Clarence Chaffee
1978 Mal Clarke and Clarence Chaffee
1979 Mal Clarke and Stephen Harris
1980 Clarence Chaffee and Ed Chandler

USTA Indoor Champions—Men Seniors' 80 Singles

1978 Albert Leitch
1979 Stephen Graves
1980 DeWitt Redgrave

USTA Indoor Champions—Men Seniors' 80 Doubles

1978 Albert Leitch and Kirck Reid
1979 Stephen Graves and Bill Mallery
1980 Kirk Reid and Bill Mallery

USTA Indoor Champions—Father and Son Doubles

1977 Pancho Gonzalez and Richard Gonzalez
1978 Pancho Gonzalez and Richard Gonzalez
1979 Pancho Segura and Spencer Segura
1980 Roy Emerson and Anthony Emerson

USTA Indoor Champions—Women's 35 Singles

1975 Arlene Cohen
1976 Arlene Cohen
1977 Arlene Cohen
1978 Judy Alvarez
1979 Susan Starrett
1980 Alice Middleton

USTA Indoor Champions—Women's 35 Doubles

1975 Susan Anawalt and Arlene Cohen
1976 Susan Anawalt and Arlene Cohen
1977 Susan Anawalt and Arlene Cohen
1978 Susan Anawalt and Arlene Cohen
1979 Susan Starrett and Judy Alvarez
1980 Kathy Graeter and Carol Schmidt

USTA Indoor Champions—Women Seniors' Singles

1970 Mrs. June E. Gay
1971 Dodo Cheney
1972 Mrs. Dorothy B. Cheney
1973 Evelyn Houseman
1974 Janet Adkisson
1975 Amy Yee
1976 Mrs. June E. Gay
1977 Janice Stwins
1978 Pat Welles
1979 not held
1980 Julia Hayward

USTA Indoor Champions—Women Seniors' Doubles

1970 Mrs. June E. Gay and Rhoda Herron
1971 Barbara Hultgren and S. Fuller
1972 Evelyn Houseman and Mary A. Prentiss
1973 Evelyn Houseman and Marge Kohler

USTA Indoor Champions—Women Seniors' Doubles
(cont.)

1974 Evelyn Houseman and Mrs. June E. Gay
1975 Mary Ann Shelton and Florence Tout
1976 Mrs. June E. Gay and M. Appel
1977 Charlene Grafton and Mrs. Dorothy B. Cheney
1978 Mrs. June B. Gay and Pat Welles
1979 not held
1980 Julia Hayward and Helen Perez

USTA Indoor Champions—Women's 45 Singles

1974 Susie Hublitz
1975 Nancy Penson
1976 Nancy Neeld
1977 Charlene Grafton
1978 Charlene Grafton
1979 Betsy Roberti
1980 Kathy Henry

USTA Indoor Champions—Women's 45 Doubles

1974 Catherine Duke and Carol Schneider
1975 Vilma Gordon and Mae Mayer
1976 Mrs. Dorothy B. Cheney and Carol Schneider
1977 Lucille Davidson and Jeane Harrison
1978 Mary Ann Plante and Nancy Reed
1979 Mary Ann Plante and Nancy Reed
1980 Betty Claus and Polly Hoff

USTA Indoor Champions—Women's 50 Singles

1976 Mrs. Dorothy B. Cheney
1977 Mrs. Dorothy B. Cheney
1978 Mrs. Dorothy B. Cheney
1979 Kathy Rothfels
1980 Helen Perez

USTA Indoor Champions—Women's 50 Doubles

1976 Lucille Davidson and Doris Popple
1977 Lucille Davidson and Doris Popple
1978 Mrs. Dorothy B. Cheney and Phyllis Adler

1979 Mrs. Dorothy B. Cheney and Jeanne Dalton
1980 Mrs. Dorothy B. Cheney and Mrs. June E. Gay

USTA Indoor Champions—Women's 55 Singles

1976 Sally Fuller
1977 Mrs. Dorothy B. Cheney
1978 Mrs. Dorothy B. Cheney
1979 Mrs. Dorothy B. Cheney
1980 Mrs. June E. Gay

USTA Indoor Champions—Women's 55 Doubles

1976 Pat Maloney and Sally Fuller
1977 Georgia Buechley and Paige Shunny
1978 Amy Yee and Sally Fuller
1979 Lucille Davidson and Doris Popple
1980 Lucille Davidson and Doris Popple

USTA Indoor Champions—Women's 60 Singles

1978 Pat Yoemans
1979 Mrs. Dorothy B. Cheney
1980 Mrs. Dorothy B. Cheney

USTA Indoor Champions—Women's 60 Doubles

1978 Pat Yoemans and Elizabeth Dudley
1979 Pat Yoemans and Maxine King
1980 Mrs. Dorothy B. Cheney and Margo Mahoney

USTA Indoor Champions—Seniors' Mixed Doubles

1969 C. Alphonso Smith and Sarah Danzig
1970 Kitty Prince and Charles Brooke
1971 Mrs. Dorothy B. Cheney and C. Alphonso Smith
1972 Evelyn Houseman and John Faunce
1973 Evelyn Houseman and Verne Hughes
1974 Evelyn Houseman and Leonard Prosser
1975 Mrs. Mary Ann Shelton and John Shelton

1976 Mary Jane Hedreen and Jimmie
     McDaniel
1977 Mrs. Dorothy B. Cheney and George
     Peebles
1978 Mrs. Dorothy B. Cheney and George
     Peebles
1979 not held
1980 Lucille Davidson and Verne Hughes

USTA Hard Court Champions—Men's Singles

1948 Frederick R. Schroeder, Jr.
1949 Frederick R. Schroeder, Jr.
1950 Arthur Larsen
1951 Frederick R. Schroeder, Jr.
1952 Arthur Larsen
1953 Tony Trabert
1954 Gilbert J. Shea
1955 Herbert Flam
1956 Alejandro Olmedo
1957 Thomas P. Brown, Jr.
1958 Thomas P. Brown, Jr.
1959 Ramanathan Krishnan
1960 Whitney Reed
1961 Allen E. Fox
1962 Rafael Osuna
1963 Arthur Ashe
1964 Dennis Ralston
1965 Dennis Ralston
1966 Stan Smith
1967 Stan Smith
1968 Stan Smith
1969 Clark Graebner
1970 not held
1971 Robert Lutz
1972–80 not held

USTA Hard Court Champions—Men's Doubles

1948 F. R. Schroeder, Jr. and E. Victor Seixas, Jr.
1949 Frederick R. Schroeder, Jr. and Eric
     Sturgess
1950 Thomas P. Brown, Jr. and Tony Trabert
1951 Jerry DeWitts and Harry Likas
1952 Thomas P. Brown, Jr. and Arthur D.
     Larsen

1953 Thomas P. Brown, Jr. and Tony Trabert
1954 William Crosby and Robert T. Perez
1955 Early Baumgardner and Hugh Stewart
1956 Noel Brown and Gilbert J. Shea
1957 Myron J. Franks and Alejandro Olmedo
1958 Noel Brown and Hugh Stewart
1959 Ramanathan Krishnan and Hugh Stewart
1960 Chris Crawford and Whitney Reed
1961 Wm. Hoogs, Jr. and James McManus
1962 Ramsey Earnhart and Rafael Osuna
1963 William Bond and Tom Edlefsen
1964 Dennis Ralston and William Bond
1965 Tom Edlefsen and Dennis Ralston
1966 Robert Lutz and Stan Smith
1967 Jim McManus and Jim Osborne
1968 Richard Leach and Rafael Osuna
1969 Robert Lutz and Erik Van Dillen
1970 not held
1971 Jim McManus and Jim Osborne
1972–80 not held

USTA Hard Court Champions—Women's Singles

1948 Gertrude Moran
1949 Doris Hart
1950 Mrs. Patricia C. Todd
1951 Mrs. Patricia C. Todd
1952 Mrs. Mary A. Prentiss
1953 Anita Kanter
1954 Mrs. Beverly B. Fleitz
1955 Miriam Arnold
1956 Mrs. Nancy C. Kiner
1957 Mrs. Beverly B. Fleitz
1958 Mrs. Beverly B. Fleitz
1959 Sandra Reynolds
1960 Katherine D. Chabot
1961 Nancy Richey
1962 Carol Hanks
1963 Darlene Hard
1964 Kathy Harter
1965 Rosemary Casals
1966 Mrs. Billie J. King
1967 Jane Bartkowicz
1968 Maryna Godwin
1969 Eliza Pande
1970–80 not held

Among her many titles, Rosemary Casals holds the 1965 Hard Court championship.

USTA Hard Court Champions—Women's Doubles

1948   A. Louise Brough and Mrs. M. O. du Pont
1949   Mrs. Virginia Kovacs and Gertrude Moran
1950   Mrs. Pat Todd and Barbara Scofield
1951   Anita Kanter and Julia Sampson
1952   Mrs. M. Arnold Prentiss and Julia Sampson
1953   Barbara Lum and Doris Popple
1954   Mrs. Dorothy B. Cheney and Darlene R. Hard
1955   Mrs. Gracyn W. Kelleher and Mrs. Patricia C. Todd
1956   Mrs. Nancy C. Kiner and Mrs. Patricia C. Todd
1957   Mrs. Beverly B. Fleitz and Mrs. Patricia C. Todd
1958   Sally M. Moore and Gwyneth Thomas
1959   Sandra Reynolds and Renée Schuurman
1960   Carole A. Caldwell and Katherine D. Chabot
1961   Mrs. D. H. Knode and Mrs. M. A. Prentiss
1962   Marilyn Montgomery and Mrs. J. Hopps Adkisson
1963   Darlene Hard and Paulette Verzin
1964   Mimi Arnold and Barbara Benigni
1965   Kathy Harter and Sue Shrader
1966   Rosemary Casals and Mrs. Billie J. M. King
1967   Stephanie Grant and Valerie Ziegenfuss
1968   Patti Hogan and Maryna Godwin
1969   Pam Austin and Tam O'Shaugnessy
1970–80 not held

USTA Hard Court Champions—Mixed Doubles

1948   Mrs. M. Osborne du Pont and Thomas P. Brown, Jr.
1949   Doris Hart and Eric Sturgess
1950   Mrs. Magda Rurac and Arnold Beisser
1951   Anita Kanter and Whitney Reed
1952   Julia Ann Sampson and Hugh Stewart
1953 not held
1954   Mrs. Patricia C. Todd and William Crosby
1955   Mrs. Patricia C. Todd and Gardnar Mulloy
1956   Mrs. Patricia C. Todd and Gardnar Mulloy
1957   Sally M. Moore and Michael G. Davies
1958   Sally M. Moore and Hugh Stewart
1959   Sandra Reynolds and Whitney Reed
1960   Carole A. Caldwell and Chris Crawford
1961   Mrs. M. A. Prentiss and Richard Leach
1962   Carol Hanks and James McManus
1963   Darlene Hard and Hugh Stewart
1964 not held
1965 not held
1966   Rosemary Casals and Ian Crookenden
1967   Kristy Pigeon and William Demas
1968   Mrs. Dorothy Cheney and Richard Leach
1969   Sharon Walsh and Mike Machette
1970–80 not held

USTA Amateur Hard Court Champions—Men's Singles

1978   John Sadri
1979   Robby Venter
1980   Brad Gilbert

USTA Amateur Hard Court Champions—Men's Doubles

1978 John Sadri and Tony Graham
1979 Hall Bernstein and Mike Bauer and Hall Bernstein
1980 Mike Bauer and Dane Chapin

USTA Amateur Hard Court Champions— Women's Singles

1978 Stacy Margolin
1979 Wendy White
1980 Heather Ludloff

USTA Amateur Hard Court Champions— Women's Doubles

1978 Kay McDaniel and Felicia Hutnick
1979 Wendy White and Kelly Kruk
1980 Heather Ludloff and Donna Rubin

USTA Hard Court Champions—Men's 21 Singles

1978 Larry Gottfried
1979 Jay Lapidus
1980 Andy Andrews

USTA Hard Court Champions—Men's 21 Doubles

1978 Chip Hooper and Mel Purcell
1979 Jay Lapidus and Robert Van't Hof
1980 David Dowlen and Joel Hoffman

USTA Hard Court Champions—Women's 21 Singles

1978 Barbara Jordan
1979 Pilar Vasquez
1980 Betsy Heidenberger

USTA Hard Court Champions—Women's 21 Doubles

1978 Kim Steinmetz and Ann Broyles
1979 Vickie Vasieck and Catherine Yellverton
1980 Jane Jarosz and Jennifer Goodling

USTA Hard Court Champions—Mixed 21 Doubles

1978 Drew Meyers and Ebie Taylor
1979 Germaine Ohaco and Richard Acuna
1980 Jane Jarosz and Ron Kowal

USTA Hard Court Champions—Junior Singles

1946 Hugh Stewart
1947 Lorne Main
1948 Jerry DeWitts
1949 Hamilton Richardson
1950 Fred Hagist
1951 Herschel Hyde
1952 Mike Franks
1953 Franklin Johnson
1954 Dale Junta
1955 Gregory Grant
1956 Roger Werksman
1957 Joseph Cowley
1958 Thomas Edlefsen
1959 Dennis Ralston
1960 Paul Palmer
1961 Gary Rose
1962 Jerry Cromwell
1963 Gary Rose
1964 Stan Smith
1965 Stephen Avoyer
1966 Stephen Avoyer
1967 Jeff Borowiak
1968 F. D. Robbins
1969 Roscoe Tanner
1970 Jim Connors
1971 Raul Ramirez
1972 Brian Teacher
1973 Trey Waltke
1974 Ferdi Taygan
1975 Howard Schoenfield
1976 Robert Van't Hof
1977 Andy Kohlberg
1978 Fritz Buehning
1979 Scott Davis
1980 Tomm Warneke

USTA Hard Court Champions—Junior Doubles

1946 Hugh Stewart and Vincent Schneider
1947 Matt Murphy and Jerry DeWitts
1948 Jerry DeWitts and Ernest duBray

USTA Hard Court Champions—Junior Doubles *(cont.)*

1949	Robert Perry and Reynolds McCabe
1950	Norman Peterson and Jacque Grigry
1951	Herschel Hyde and Cliff Mayne
1952	John Lesch and Alan Call
1953	Brooke Grant and Franklin Johnson
1954	Earl Baumgardner and Dick Peters
1955	Edward Atkinson and Robert Delgado
1956	Chris Crawford and George Stoesser
1957	Michael Crane and Rudy Hernando
1958	Michael Crane and Michael Farrel
1959	Dennis Ralston and Ramsey Earnhart
1960	Paul Palmer and Henry Kamakana
1961	Rodney Kop and James Osborne
1962	Jeff Brown and Dean Penero
1963	John Tidball and Steve Tidball
1964	Jim Hobson and Steve Tidball
1965	Marcelo Lara and Jasjit Singh
1966	Stephen Avoyer and Don Lutz
1967	Jeff Borowiak and Erik Van Dillen
1968	Richard Stockton and Erik Van Dillen
1969	Brian Gotfried and Roscoe Tanner
1970	Jim Connors and Bob Kreiss
1971	James Hagey and Raul Ramirez
1972	Pat DuPre and Victor Amaya
1973	Peter Pearson and Chris Sylvan
1974	Bruce Manson and Perry Wright
1975	Dan Gerken and Curt Stalder
1976	Christian Dunk and Curt Stalder
1977	Fritz Buehning and Andrew Chase
1978	David Dowlen and Bill Nealon
1979	Mike DePalmer and Rodney Harmon
1980	Scott Davis and Ben Testerman

USTA Hard Court Champions—Boys' 16 Singles

1962	Jeff Brown
1963	Carlos Carriedo
1964	Jim Rombeau
1965	Zan Guerry
1966	Erik Van Dillen
1967	Mike Kreiss
1968	Brian Gottfried
1969	Chico Hagey
1970	John Whitlinger
1971	William Martin
1972	Gene Mayer
1973	Matt Mitchell
1974	Jai DiLouie

1975	Van Winitsky
1976	Andrew Chase
1977	Scott Davis
1978	Scott Davis
1979	Sammy Giammalva
1980	Todd Witsken

USTA Hard Court Champions—Boys' 16 Doubles

1962	Jeff Brown and Dean Penero
1963	Roy Barth and Robert Lutz
1964	Jim Rombeau and Jim Davidson
1965	Zan Guerry and Don Lutz
1966	Richard Bohrnstedt and Randy Verdieck
1967	Jeff Austin and Tim Ott
1968	Jim Connors and Brian Gottfried
1969	John Burrman and Jeff Cowan
1970	Steve Mott and Brian Teacher
1971	Steward Keller and Bruce Nichols
1972	Bruce Manson and Perry Wright
1973	Tracy DeLatte and Pem Guerry
1974	Don Paulson and Walter Redondo
1975	Jeff Robbins and Van Winitsky
1976	Doug Crawford and Jeff Turpin
1977	Gary Lemon and Eric Van't Hof
1978	Scott Davis and Fabio Mion-Bet
1979	Eric Korita and Danny Weiss
1980	Tim Pawsat and Rick Leach

USTA Hard Court Champions—Boys' 14 Singles

1962	Steve Turpin
1963	Don Lutz
1964	Richard Bohrnstedt
1965	Erik Van Dillen
1966	Randy Thomas
1967	Bob Kreiss
1968	Jake Warde
1969	Bruce Nichols
1970	Tom Kreiss
1971	Matt Mitchell
1972	Walter Redondo
1973	Larry Gottfried
1974	John Corse
1975	David Siegler
1976	Bruce Brescia
1977	Chris Huff

1978 Bobby Banck
1979 Jonathan Canter
1980 Eric Amend

USTA Hard Court Champions—Boys' 14
Doubles

1962 Stephen Fiske and James Rombeau
1963 Mac Claflin and Paul Marienthal
1964 Bud Bioun and Rick Ellsworth
1965 Clyde LeBaron and Dan Chadbourne
1966 James Hagey and Kent Woodard
1967 James Hagey and Bob Kreiss
1968 Stephen Mott and Bruce Nichols
1969 William Maze and Michael Nissley
1970 Drew Sweet and Ferdi Taygen
1971 Don Paulsen and Walter Redondo
1972 Don Paulson and Walter Redondo
1973 Larry Gottfried and Eliot Teltscher
1974 John Corse and David Dowlin
1975 Paul Crozier and Boyd Bryan
1976 Michael Fallberg and Mike Turner
1977 Chris Huff and Bruce Herzog
1978 Bobby Banck and Michael Kures
1979 Jonathan Canter and Ricky Leach
1980 Tom Bender and John Schmitt

USTA Hard Court Champions—Boys' 12
Singles

1962 Mac Claflin
1963 Erik Van Dillen
1964 Randall Thomas
1965 Jake Warde
1966 Jake Warde
1967 Ken Walts
1968 William Maze
1969 Howard Schoenfield
1970 Walter Redondo
1971 Jeff Robbins
1972 Jeff Arons
1973 David Dowlin
1974 Ben Testerman
1975 Peter Mako
1976 Jim Arias
1977 Ricky Leach
1978 Richey Reneberg
1979 Jim Williams
1980 Michael Briggs

USTA Hard Court Champions—Boys' 12
Doubles

1962 Mac Claflin and Erik Van Dillen
1963 Barry Laing and Ronnie Marston
1964 Steve Derian and James Hagey
1965 James Hagey and Jake Warde
1966 Dave Sherbeck and Brian Teacher
1967 William Maze and Dave Sherbeck
1968 Tom Kreiss and William Maze
1969 Matt Mitchell and Jeff Robinson
1970 Don Paulsen and Walter Redondo
1971 James Curley and Eliot Teltscher
1972 Mike Lee and Jeff Arons
1973 Peter Herrmann and David Siegler
1974 John Davis and Howard Sands
1975 Derk Pardoe and Greg Holmes
1976 Mitchell Perkins and Todd Witsken
1977 Ricky Leach and Brad Ackerman
1978 Richey Reneberg
1979 Robby Weiss and Aaron Krickstein
1980 Michael Briggs and Chris Toomey

USTA Hard Court Champions—Girls' 18
Singles

1922 Carolyn Swartz
1923 Avery Follett
1924 Edith Cross
1925 Dorothea Swartz
1926 Dorothea Swartz
1927 Louise McFarland
1928 Dorothy Weisel
1929 Charlotte Miller
1930 Helen Marlowe
1931 Alice Marble
1932 Gracyn Wheeler
1933 Claire Buckner
1934 Gussie Raegener
1935 Margaret Osborne
1936 Eleanor Dawson
1937 Margaret Jessee
1938 Patricia Canning
1939 Patricia Canning
1940 Shirley Catton
1941 Barbara Krase
1942 Shirley Catton
1943 Dorothy Head
1944 E. Louise Snow

USTA Hard Court Champions—Girls' 18 Singles *(cont.)*

1945 Nancy Chaffee
1946 Helen Pastall
1947 Beverly Baker
1948 Laura Lou Jahn
1949 Anita Kanter
1950 Diane Kostial
1951 Mary Ann Eilenberger
1952 Patricia Naud
1953 Patricia Naud
1954 Barbara Benigni
1955 Mary Ann Mitchell
1956 Sally M. Moore
1957 Sally M. Moore
1958 Barbara Benigni
1959 Victoria Palmer
1960 Victoria Palmer
1961 Jean Danilovich
1962 Jane Albert
1963 Kathy Harter
1964 Rosemary Casals
1965 Rosemary Casals
1966 Pixie Lamm
1967 Roylee Bailey
1968 Denise Carter
1969 Marcelyn Louie
1970 Eliza Pande
1971 Laurie Tenney
1972 Ann Kiyomura
1973 Carrie Meyer
1974 Stephanie Tolleson
1975 Beth Norton
1976 Mareen Louie
1977 Mareen Louie
1978 Kathy Jordan
1979 Mary Lou Piatek
1980 Kelly Henry

USTA Hard Court Champions—Girls' 18
Doubles

1927 Betty Fitch and Margaret Smith
1928 Violet Doeg and Doris Doeg
1929 Ida Cross and Alice Marble
1930 Marian Hunt and Alice Marble
1931 Katherine Wood and Gracyn Wheeler
1932 Bonnie Miller and May Doeg
1933 Gussie Raegener and Margaret Osborne
1934 Margaret Osborne and Gussie Raegener
1935 Jane Stanton and Patricia Henry
1936 Janet Hartzell and Patsy Hiller
1937 Patricia Canning and Barbara Duncan
1938 Patricia Canning and Barbara Duncan
1939 Daphne Buckell and Dorothy Buckell
1940 Helen Gurley and Dorothy Head
1941 Barbara Krase and Shirley Catton
1942 Dorothy Head and Barbara Scofield
1943 Dorothy Head and Barbara Scofield
1944 E. Louise Snow and Jean E. Doyle
1945 Nancy Chaffee and Margaret Varner
1946 Nancy Chaffee and Katherine Smith
1947 Beverly Baker and Marjorie McCord
1948 Marjorie McCord and Bea Springer
1949 Mariane Hertel and Mihan Rumwell
1950 Gertrude Beall and Joan Merciadis
1951 Mary Ann Eilenberger and Linda Mitchell
1952 Jacquelyn Halleck and Lynn Wall
1953 Pat Naud and Mardel Railey
1954 Elspeth Bennett and Lynn Wall
1955 Audrey Arnold and Linda Vail
1956 Barbara Benigni and Mary Thompson
1957 Barbara Benigni and Farel Footman
1958 Barbara Benigni and Farel Footman
1959 Barbara Browning and Pam Davis
1960 Victoria Palmer and Laurie Callaway
1961 Jan Conroy and Andria Miller
1962 Rosemary Casals and Gloria Segerquist
1963 Kathy Harter and Kathy Blake
1964 Rosemary Casals and Toni Alford
1965 Lynne Abbes and Valerie Ziegenfuss
1966 Lynne Abbes and Valerie Ziegenfuss
1967 Gail Hansen and Debbie John
1968 Denise Carter and Pam Richmond
1969 Ann Lebedeff and Tam O'Shaugnessy
1970 Janet Newberry and Eliza Pande
1971 Ann Kiyomura and Jane Stratton
1972 Jill Schwikert and Joy Schwikert
1973 Bee Kilgore and Carrie Meyer
1974 Susan Mehmedbasich and Stephanie Tolleson
1975 Susan Hagey and Elizabeth Smith
1976 Sherry Acker and Anne Smith
1977 Sherry Acker and Anne Smith
1978 Mareen Louie and Trey Lewis
1979 Mary Lou Piatek and Anne White
1980 Elizabeth Evans and Susan Pendo

USTA Hard Court Champions—Girls' 16
Singles

1962 Jane Albert
1963 Lynne Abbes
1964 Lynne Abbes
1965 Peggy Michel
1966 Kristy Pigeon
1967 Marcelyn Louie
1968 Marcelyn Louie
1969 Eliza Pande
1970 Ann Kiyomura
1971 Laurie Tenney
1972 Susan Mehmedbasich
1973 Susan Hagey
1974 Lea Antonopolis
1975 Mareen Louie
1976 Charlene Murphy
1977 Kelly Henry
1978 Bettina Bunge
1979 Pilar Vasquez
1980 Carol Heynen

USTA Hard Court Champions—Girls' 14
Singles

1962 Rosemary Casals
1963 Lynne Abbes
1964 Pam Teeguarden
1965 Pam Teeguarden
1966 Kris Kemmer
1967 Marcelyn Louie
1968 Barbara Downs
1969 Ann Kiyomura
1970 Vickie Jensen
1971 Susan Mehmedbasich
1972 Susan Hagey
1973 Lea Antonopolis
1974 Mareen Louie
1975 Linda Siegel
1976 Tracy Austin
1977 Joy Cummings
1978 Carol Heynen
1979 Beverly Bowes
1980 Joni Urban

USTA Hard Court Champions—Girls' 16
Doubles

1962 Kathleen Blake and Kathy Harter
1963 Margaret Fredericks and Wendy Overton
1964 Paulette Verzin and Robyn Berrey
1965 Stephanie Grant and Lea Trumbull
1966 Kris Kemmer and Ann Lebedeff
1967 Patty Reese and Cindy Thomas
1968 Whitney Grant and Karen Demmer
1969 Barbara Downs and Ann Kiyomura
1970 Barbara Downs and Ann Kiyomura
1971 Vicki Jensen and Kathy May
1972 Marna Louie and Stephanie Tolleson
1973 Susan Mehmedbasich and Robin Tenney
1974 Lea Antonopolis and Karen Krajewski
1975 Sherry Acker and Anne Smith
1976 Mareen Louie and Susan Rasmussen
1977 Maria Fernandez and Lucia Fernandez
1978 Felicia Raschiatore and Shelly Solomon
1979 Zina Garrison and Lori McNeil
1980 Zina Garrison and Lori McNeil

USTA Hard Court Champions—Girls' 14
Doubles

1962 Kristen Stewart and Pixie Lamm
1963 Patti Hogan and Margaret Michel
1964 Stephanie Grant and Lea Trumbull
1965 Gaye Harris and Teresa Thomas
1966 Marcelyn Louie and Karin Benson
1967 Whitney Grant and Janet Newberry
1968 Ann Kiyomura and Janet Thomas
1969 Kathy May and Gretchen Galt
1970 Kathy May and Vickie Jensen
1971 Susan Mehmedbasich and Susan Zaro
1972 Susan Hagey and Susan Wright
1973 Lea Antonopolis and Sandra Collins
1974 Mareen Louie and Shannon Anderson
1975 Toni Moss and Linda Siegel
1976 Tracy Austin and Kelly Henry
1977 Beverly Bowes and Andrea Jaeger
1978 Elizabeth Evans and Robin White
1979 Beverly Bowes and Stephanie Savides
1980 Joni Urban and Lisa Bonder

USTA Hard Court Champions—Girls' 12 Singles

1962 Pamela Teeguarden
1963 Gail Hansen
1964 Marcelyn Louie
1965 Marcelyn Louie
1966 Barbara Downs
1967 Ann Kiyomura
1968 Kathy May
1969 Susan Mehmedbasich
1970 Tobin Tenney
1971 Lea Antonopolis
1972 Mareen Louie
1973 Linda Siegel
1974 Kelly Henry
1975 Carol Sue Lloyd
1976 Carol Heynen
1977 Carol Heynen
1978 Cari Hagey
1979 Kathy Rinaldi
1980 Marianne Werdel

USTA Hard Court Champions—Girls' 12 Doubles

1962 Pamela Teeguarden and Jane Miller
1963 Karin Benson and Cindy Bridges
1964 Marcelyn Louie and Karin Benson
1965 Whitney Grant and Marcelyn Louie
1966 Anita May and Lori Sherbeck
1967 Sue Boyle and Ann Kiyomura
1968 Gretchen Galt and Kathy May
1969 Susan Mehmedbasich and Susan Zaro
1970 Susan Hagey and Susan Wight
1971 Dana Gilbert and Moreen Lorie
1972 Mareen Louie and Susan Rasmussen
1973 Kelly Henry and Shelly Stillman
1974 Robin White and Kimberly Wilson
1975 Robin White and Amy Olmedo
1976 Lynn Lewis and Cheryl Jones
1977 Carol Heynen and Leigh Ann Eldredge
1978 Marianne Werdel and Debbie Spence
1979 Marianne Werdel and Debbie Spence
1980 Melissa Gurney and Stephanie Rehe

USTA Hard Court Champions—Father and Son

1959 Guadelupe and Robert Delgado
1960 H. William and William Bond
1961 H. William and William Bond
1962 Robert and R. Dennis Ralston
1963 H. William and William Bond
1964 Frank A. Jr. and Frank A. Froehling III
1965 George and Steven Meyerson
1966 H. William and William Bond
1967 H. William and William Bond
1968 Glenn E. and Gary Hippenstiel
1969 W. E. and William Canning
1970 Robert and James Hagey
1971 Robert and James Hagey
1972 Kenneth and Kenneth Walts, Jr.
1973 Kenneth and Kenneth Walts, Jr.
1974 Kenneth and Kenneth Walts, Jr.
1975 Eldon and Brad Rowe
1976 Eldon and Brad Rowe
1977 Vladimir and Glen Petrovic
1978 Roy and Anthony Emerson
1979 Richard and Ricky Leach

USTA Hard Court Champions—Mother and Daughter

1980 Mrs. Julie DuVall and Jeanne DuVall

USTA Hard Court Champions—Men Seniors' Singles

1948 John Murio
1949 John Murio
1950 George Rice
1951 not held
1952 Mel Dranga
1953 William A. Maxwell
1954 John E. Sisson
1955 Edgar D. Yeomans
1956 John E. Sisson
1957 Edgar D. Yeomans
1958 Gardnar Mulloy
1959 J. Hal Surface, Jr.
1960 William Lurie
1961 William Lurie
1962 C. D. Steele, Jr.
1963 Gardnar Mulloy
1964 Robert L. Galloway

1965	Robert V. Sherman
1966	Emery W. Neale
1967	Emery W. Neale
1968	Emery W. Neale
1969	Thomas Brown, Jr.
1970	Thomas Brown, Jr.
1971	Robert L. Riggs
1972	Pancho Segura
1973	Hugh Stewart
1974	Hugh Stewart
1975	Vladimir Petrovic
1976	Russell Seymour
1977	Russell Seymour
1978	Clif Mayne
1979	Jim Perley
1980	Marty Devlin

USTA Hard Court Champions—Men Seniors' Doubles

1948	Earl Ehlers and Eli H. Bashor
1949	William Catton and Edwin McCord
1950	George Rice and Herschel Hyde
1951	not held
1952	James Hodgkins and Edward Leonard
1953	Mel Gallagher and William A. Maxwell
1954	Alan Herrington and John E. Sisson
1955	Alan Herrington and John E. Sisson
1956	Alan Herrington and John E. Sisson
1957	Edward G. Chandler and Gerald Stratford
1958	Robert J. Kelleher and Elbert R. Lewis
1959	Robert J. Kelleher and Elbert R. Lewis
1960	Robert J. Kelleher and Elbert R. Lewis
1961	H. William Bond and C. D. Steele, Jr.
1962	Robert J. Kelleher and Elbert R. Lewis
1963	Gardnar Mulloy and Alphonso Smith
1964	George MacCall and Al Martini
1965	Robert J. Freedman and Robert V. Sherman
1966	Emery Neale and Chauncey D. Steele, Jr.
1967	Robert L. Galloway and David E. Martin
1968	Robert L. Galloway and David E. Martin
1969	Emery Neale and Robert L. Riggs
1970	Sam Match and Robert L. Riggs
1971	Ron Dunas and Pancho Segura
1972	Ronald Dunas and Pancho Segura
1973	Ronald Dunas and Sam Match

1974	Hugh Stewart and George Yardley
1975	King Lambert and Sam Match
1976	Jerry DeWitts and Russell Seymour
1977	Jerry DeWitts and Russell Seymour
1978	Robert Perry and Richard Doss
1979	Robert Perry and Richard Doss
1980	King Lambert and Ed Kauder

USTA Hard Court Champions—Women Seniors' Singles

1953	Mrs. Marion Raful
1954	Mrs. Gracyn W. Kelleher
1955	Mrs. Gracyn W. Kelleher
1956	Mrs. Mary A. Prentiss
1957	Mrs. Dorothy B. Cheney
1958	Mrs. Dorothy B. Cheney
1959	Mrs. Dorothy B. Cheney
1960	Mrs. Dorothy B. Cheney
1961	Mrs. Dorothy B. Cheney
1962	Mrs. Dorothy B. Cheney
1963	Mrs. Dorothy B. Cheney
1964	Mrs. Dorothy B. Cheney
1965	Mrs. Dorothy B. Cheney
1966	Mrs. Dorothy B. Cheney
1967	Mrs. Dorothy B. Cheney
1968	Mrs. Dorothy B. Cheney
1969	Mrs. Dorothy B. Cheney
1970	Mrs. Nancy A. Neeld
1971	Mrs. Barbara Weigandt
1972	Mrs. Barbara Weigandt
1973	Mrs. Barbara Weigandt
1974	Mrs. Barbara Weigandt
1975	Mrs. Barbara Weigandt
1976	Mrs. Barbara Weigandt
1977	Mrs. Barbara Weigandt
1978	Donna Balchios
1979	Louella Lipson
1980	Charleen Hillebrand

USTA Hard Court Champions—Women Seniors' Doubles

1953	Dorothy DeVries and Florence D. Nebauer
1954	Mrs. Gracyn W. Kelleher and Mrs. Marion Raful
1955	Mrs. Gracyn W. Kelleher and Mrs. Gretl Dupont

USTA Hard Court Champions—Women Seniors' Doubles *(cont.)*

1956   Mrs. Gracyn W. Kelleher and Mrs. Estelle Kristenson

1957   Mrs. Dorothy B. Cheney and Mrs. Janet Robbins

1958   Mrs. Gracyn W. Kelleher and Mrs. Mary Arnold Prentiss

1959   Mrs. Gracyn W. Kelleher and Mrs. Mary Arnold Prentiss

1960   Mrs. Gracyn W. Kelleher and Mrs. Mary Arnold Prentiss

1961   Mrs. Gracyn W. Kelleher and Mrs. Mary Arnold Prentiss

1962   Mrs. Gracyn W. Kelleher and Mrs. Mary Arnold Prentiss

1963   Mrs. Dorothy B. Cheney and Mrs. Mary Arnold Prentiss

1964   Mrs. Dorothy B. Cheney and Mrs. Helen McDowell

1965   Mrs. Dorothy B. Cheney and Mrs. Helen McDowell

1966   Mrs. Gracyn W. Kelleher and Mrs. Mary Arnold Prentiss

1967   Mrs. Gracyn W. Kelleher and Mrs. Mary Arnold Prentiss

1968   Mrs. Dorothy B. Cheney and Mrs. June E. Gay

1969   Mrs. Dorothy B. Cheney and Mrs. June E. Gay

1970   Mrs. Gracyn W. Kelleher and Mrs. Mary Arnold Prentiss

1971   Mrs. Louise B. Clapp and Mrs. Barbara G. Weigandt

1972   Mrs. Evelyn Houseman and Mrs. Mary Arnold Prentiss

1973   Mrs. Dorothy B. Cheney and Marcia Hodges

1974   Mrs. Dorothy B. Cheney and Marcia Hodges

1975   Mrs. Louise B. Clapp and Mrs. Barbara Weigandt

1976   Mrs. Dorothy B. Cheney and Mrs. Evelyn Houseman

1977   Mrs. Dorothy B. Cheney and Mrs. Evelyn Houseman

1978   Jill Leach and Yoko Taylor

1979   Patricia McCabe and Norma Veale

1980   Julie Hayward and Dorothy Mathiessen

USTA Hard Court Champions—Seniors' Mixed Doubles

1955   Mrs. Gracyn Kelleher and A. D. Herrington

1956   Mrs. Mary A. Prentiss and Joseph T. Ciano

1957   Mrs. Gracyn W. Kelleher and Jack Tidball

1958   Mr. and Mrs. Robert J. Kelleher

1959   Mrs. Janet Robbins and Clifford Robbins

1960   Mr. and Mrs. Robert J. Kelleher

1961   Mrs. Helen Watanabe and Verne Guertin

1962   Mrs. Mary A. Prentiss and Len Prosser

1963   Mrs. Corky Olerich and William Smith

1964   Mr. and Mrs. Robert J. Kelleher

1965   Mrs. Corky Olerich and Al Martini

1966   Mrs. Corky Olerich and Ralph E. Wyer

1967   Mrs. Phylis Adler and Merwin Miller

1968   Mrs. Dorothy B. Cheney and Vern Hughes

1969   Mrs. Dorothy B. Cheney and David Martin

1970   Mrs. A. Dalton and B. Press

1971   Mrs. Dorothy B. Cheney and Robert L. Riggs

1972   Mrs. Evelyn Houseman and Merwin Miller

1973   Mrs. Jeanne Datton and Ben Press

1974   Mrs. Evelyn Houseman and Len Prosser

1975   Mrs. Dorothy B. Cheney and Jerry DeWitts

1976   Mrs. Evelyn Houseman and Richard Metteer

1977   Mrs. Julie S. Hayward and George Yardley

1978   Mrs. Dorothy B. Cheney and Hugh Stewart

1979 not held

1980   Helen Perez and L. Straight Clark

USTA Hard Court Champions—Men's 35 Singles

1959   Joseph Woolfson

1960   Joseph Woolfson

1961   Butch Krikorian

1962   Emery Neale

1963 Hugh Stewart
1964 Vladimir Petrovic
1965 Hugh Stewart
1966 Vladimir Petrovic
1967 Don Gale
1968 Clif Mayne
1969 Jacques Grigry
1970 Clif Mayne
1971 Don Kierbow
1972 Jim Landin
1973 Barry MacKay
1974 Don Kierbow
1975 Barry MacKay
1976 Adrian Bey
1977 Fred Stolle
1978 Butch Newman
1979 Keith Diepraam
1980 not finished

USTA Hard Court Champions—Men's 35 Doubles

1959 Jack Bowker and John Williams
1960 Merwin Miller and George MacCall
1961 George MacCall and Merwin Miller
1962 George MacCall and Al Martini
1963 Emery Neale and Merwin Miller
1964 Clint Arbuckle and Joe Woolfson
1965 Don Gale and Butch Krikorian
1966 Merill Ehmke and Milt Richardson
1967 Hugh Ditzler and Ed Kauder
1968 Don Gale and Butch Krikorian
1969 Ed Kauder and Jerry Dewitts
1970 Hugh Ditzler and Clif Mayne
1971 Don Kierbow and Whitney Reed
1972 Don Kierbow and Whitney Reed
1973 Don Kierbow and Whitney Reed
1974 Don Kierbow and Whitney Reed
1975 Hugh Ditzler and Clif Mayne
1976 Adrian Bey and Jim Schmidt
1977 Adrian Bey and Jim Schmidt
1978 Butch Newman and Jim Parker
1979 Butch Newman and Jim Parker
1980 not finished

USTA Hard Court Champions—Men Seniors' 50 Singles

1968 Charles Lass
1969 Ed Doane

1970 Robert Sherman
1971 Robert Sherman
1972 Bobby Riggs
1973 David Martin
1974 Glenn Hippenstiel
1975 Bob Perez
1976 Bob Sherman
1977 Ed Kauder
1978 Ed Kauder
1979 Jason Morton
1980 Hugh Stewart

USTA Hard Court Champions—Men Seniors' 50 Doubles

1968 Ed Doane and Len Prosser
1969 Bob Galloway and Bob Hagey
1970 Merwin Miller and Don White
1971 Glenn Hippenstiel and Milt Richardson
1972 Bobby Riggs and Bob Sherman
1973 Butch Krikorian and Joe Woolfson
1974 Butch Krikorian and Joe Woolfson
1975 Bob Sherman and Joe Ignatius
1976 Bob Sherman and Joe Ignatius
1977 Bob Sherman and Joe Ignatius
1978 Ed Kauder and Dick Metteer
1979 Ed Kauder and Jason Morton
1980 Hugh Stewart and Bill Davis

USTA Hard Court Champions—Men Seniors' 55 Singles

1964 C. Alphonso Smith
1965 C. Alphonso Smith
1966 Jack Staton
1967 N. E. Powel
1968 Eugene Short
1969 William Smith
1970 William Smith
1971 William Smith
1972 Bob Hill
1973 Charles Lass
1974 Charles Lass
1975 Ed Doane
1976 Alan Cheesebro
1977 Clyde Hippenstiel
1978 Bob Sherman
1979 Bob Sherman
1980 Bob Sherman

USTA Hard Court Champions—Men Seniors' 55 Doubles

1964 C. Alphonso Smith and Eddie Jacobs
1965 Clayton Burwell and C. Alphonso Smith
1966 Charles Brooke and Len Prosser
1967 N. E. Powel and Len Prosser
1968 Len Prosser and Vern Hughes
1969 Len Prosser and Vern Hughes
1970 Len Prosser and Vern Hughes
1971 G. Hippenstiel and Vern Hughes
1972 Robin Hippenstiel and Verne Hughes
1973 Ed Doane and Len Prosser
1974 Robin Hippenstiel and Verne Hughes
1975 Robin Hippenstiel and Verne Hughes
1976 Alan Cheesebro and Bob Galloway
1977 Charles Lass and Bob Galloway
1978 Charles Anderson and Merwin Miller
1979 Milton Richardson and Jack Bowker
1980 Vincent Fotre and Keith Larsen

USTA Hard Court Champions—Men Seniors' 60 Singles

1966 Les Wanee
1967 Monte Ganger
1968 Kenneth Beer
1969 C. Alphonso Smith
1970 Jack Staton
1971 Francis Manis
1972 John Faunce
1973 John Faunce
1974 Chauncey D. Steele, Jr.
1975 Bill Smith
1976 Bill Smith
1977 Alex Swetka
1978 George Peebles
1979 Bobby Riggs
1980 Bob Sherman

USTA Hard Court Champions—Men Seniors' 60 Doubles

1966 Bernard Clinton and Monte Granger
1967 Bernard Clinton and Monte Granger
1968 Bernard Clinton and Monte Granger
1969 Marshall Christopher and Monte Granger
1970 Charles Brooke and Jack Staton
1971 H. Hoff and Herschel Hyde

1972 Col. N. E. Powel and Len Prosser
1973 Tom Bird and Henry Crawford
1974 Len Prosser and Bill Smith
1975 Len Prosser and Bill Smith
1976 Robin Hippenstiel and Verne Hughes
1977 Robin Hippenstiel and Verne Hughes
1978 Charles Lass and Bob Galloway
1979 Robin Hippenstiel and George Peebles
1980 Robin Hippenstiel and Verne Hughes

USTA Hard Court Champions—Men Seniors' 65 Singles

1970 Ken Beer
1971 Bud Goltz
1972 Dick Skeen
1973 Erling Jensen
1974 Jack Staton
1975 Jack Staton
1976 Bitsy Grant
1977 Harry Hoffman
1978 Harry Hoffman
1979 Chauncey D. Steele, Jr.
1980 Chauncey D. Steele, Jr.

USTA Hard Court Champions—Men Seniors' 65 Doubles

1970 M. Hawks and W. Westbrook
1971 Les Wanee and Stanley Maloney
1972 Frank Goeltz and Ted Wellman
1973 Erling Jensen and Jack Staton
1974 Frank Goeltz and C. Alphonso Smith
1975 Eugene Short and Jack Staton
1976 Col. N. E. Powel and Len Prosser
1977 Col. N. E. Powel and Len Prosser
1978 John Shelton and Verne Hughes
1979 Harry Hoffman and Charles Swanson
1980 Harry Hoffman and Charles Swanson

USTA Hard Court Champions—Men Seniors' 70 Singles

1970 Steve Graves
1971 Joseph T. Ciano
1972 Joseph T. Ciano
1973 Joseph T. Ciano
1974 Herschel Hyde
1975 Clarence Chaffee

1976 Frank Goeltz
1977 Bill Seidel
1978 Emil Johnson
1979 Frank Goeltz
1980 Jack Staton

USTA Hard Court Champions—Men Seniors' 70 Doubles

1970 Frank Roberts and Carl Busch
1971 Joseph T. Ciano and Clarke Kaye
1972 Joe Ciano and Clarke Kaye
1973 Clarence Chaffee and Ted Wellman
1974 Clarence Chaffee and Ted Wellman
1975 Clarence Chaffee and Ted Wellman
1976 Walter Westbrook and Frank Goeltz
1977 L. A. Barnes and Paul Needles
1978 Emil Johnson and Dave Freeborn
1979 Frank Goeltz and C. Alphonso Smith
1980 Len Prosser and Elbert Lewis

USTA Hard Court Champions—Men Seniors' 75 Singles

1974 Stephen Graves
1975 Stephen Graves
1976 Stephen Graves
1977 Mal Clarke
1978 Clarence Chaffee
1979 Ken Beer
1980 Ken Beer

USTA Hard Court Champions—Men Seniors' 75 Doubles

1974 Stephen Graves and Walter Westbrook
1975 Stephen Graves and Carl Busch
1976 Abby Leitch and Clarke Kaye
1977 Mal Clarke and Clarence Chaffee
1978 Ted Wellman and Lou Burgle
1979 Herschel Hyde and Win Morris
1980 Will Jones and Frank Matheson

USTA Hard Court Champions—Men Seniors' 80 Singles

1978 Walter Wesbrook
1979 Walter Wesbrook
1980 Kirk Reed

USTA Hard Court Champions—Men Seniors' 80 Doubles

1978 Stephen Graves and Carl Busch
1979 Walter Wesbrook and Bill Mallery
1980 Kirk Reed and Bill Mallery

USTA Hard Court Champions—Women's 35 Singles

1970 Evelyn Hansen
1971 Diana Gai
1972 Mrs. Evelyn Houseman
1973 Charlene Grafton
1974 Mrs. Evelyn Houseman
1975 Mrs. Mimi Wheeler
1976 Mrs. Charlene Hillebrand
1977 Arlene Cohen
1978 Judy Alvarez
1979 Cathie Anderson
1980 Judy Louie

USTA Hard Court Champions—Women's 35 Doubles

1970 Charlene Grafton and Anita Kappe
1971 Mary A. Prentiss and Evelyn Houseman
1972 Mrs. Evelyn Houseman and Mrs. Mary Arnold Prentiss
1973 Charlene Grafton and Gloria Payne
1974 Charlene Grafton and Gloria Payne
1975 Mrs. Evelyn Houseman and Mrs. Dorothy B. Cheney
1976 Charlene Grafton and Gloria Payne
1977 Susan Starrett and Janice Stevens
1978 Susan Anawalt and Arlene Cohen
1979 Marlene Poletti and Julie Hill
1980 Norma Veal and Pat McCabe

USTA Hard Court Champions—Women Seniors' 45 Singles

1972 Mrs. June B. Gay
1973 Mrs. June B. Gay
1974 Vilma Gordon
1975 Helen Perez
1976 Helen Perez
1977 Mrs. Nancy Neeld
1978 Charlene Grafton
1979 Charlene Grafton
1980 Louella Parsons

USTA Hard Court Champions—Women
Seniors' 45 Doubles

1972   Mrs. June B. Gay and Mrs. Mary Arnold Prentiss
1973   Mary Ann Sheldon and Frances Wakefield
1974   Lucille Davidson and Doris Popple
1975   Lucille Davidson and Jean Ann Harrison
1976   Lucille Davidson and Jean Ann Harrison
1977   Charlene Grafton and Nancy Neeld
1978   Charlene Grafton and Nancy Neeld
1979   Charlene Grafton and Nancy Neeld
1980   Evelyn Robards and Donna Myers

USTA Hard Court Champions—Women
Seniors' 50 Singles

1970   Pat Yeomans
1971   Dodo Cheney
1972   Rhoda Herron
1973   Amie Yee
1974   Nancy Penson
1975   Mrs. Dorothy B. Cheney
1976   Mrs. June E. Gay
1977   Mrs. June E. Gay
1978   Vilma Gordon
1979   Mrs. June E. Gay
1980   Nancy Neeld

USTA Hard Court Champions—Women
Seniors' 50 Doubles

1970   Ruby Bixler and Pat Yeomans
1971   S. Fuller and Pat Mahoney
1972   June Micklewait and Gertrude Amelina
1973   June Micklewait and Gertrude Amelina
1974   Phyllis Adler and Corky Murdock
1975   Phyllis Adler and Corky Murdock
1976   Phyllis Adler and Mrs. Dorothy B. Cheney
1977   Phyllis Adler and Mrs. Dorothy B. Cheney
1978   Phyllis Adler and Jeanne Dattan
1979   Gerry Carter and Marianne Hanley
1980   Jill Leach and Yoko Taylor

USTA Hard Court Champions—Women
Seniors' 55 Singles

1976   Mrs. Dorothy B. Cheney
1977   Mrs. Dorothy B. Cheney
1978   Mrs. Dorothy B. Cheney
1979   Mrs. Dorothy B. Cheney
1980   Mrs. Dorothy B. Cheney

USTA Hard Court Champions—Women
Seniors' 55 Doubles

1976   Rhoda Herron and Florence Tout
1977   Marge Skolil and Florence Tout
1978   Arline Barker and Betty Cookson
1979   Mrs. Dorothy B. Cheney and Barbara Clark
1980   Alice Reeve and Betty Brink

USTA Hard Court Champions—Women
Seniors' 60 Singles

1979   Mrs. Dorothy B. Cheney
1980   Mrs. Dorothy B. Cheney

USTA Hard Court Champions—Women
Seniors' 60 Doubles

1979   Pat Yoemans and Gertrude Amling
1980   Barbara Clark and Eleanor Harbula

USTA Hard Court Champions—Women
Seniors' 65 Singles

1979   Ann Hoffman
1980   Shelia Evans

USTA Hard Court Champions—Women
Seniors' 65 Doubles

1979   Ann Hoffman and Evelyn Davis
1980   Louise Andrews and Wilma Smith

USTA Amateur Champions (Grass)

With the institution of the U.S. Open in 1968 as the major American championship, separate tournaments were established for amateur players in several categories. Since 1970, these events have been designated as the USTA Amateur Championships (Grass) and the champions in various classes follow:

MEN'S SINGLES

Year	Winner	Runner-up	Final Score
1969	George Seewagen	Zan Guerry	9–7, 6–3, 1–6, 2–6, 6–4
1970	Roscoe Tanner	Haroon Rahim	3–6, 2–6, 6–1, 8–6, 10–8
1970*	Haroon Rahim	John Gardner	6–3, 6–4, 1–6, 11–13, 6–4
1971	John Gardner	Raul Ramirez	1–6, 4–6, 6–3, 7–5, 6–4
1972	Alex Mayer	Vitas Gerulaitis	6–3, 6–3, 6–2
1973	Jim Delaney	Nick Saviano	6–4, 7–6, 6–1
1974	Chico Hagey	Peter Fleming	6–5, 3–6, 6–2, 6–3
1975	Gonzalo Nunez	Eric Friedler	6–3, 3–6, 6–5, 5–3 (ret.)
1976	Chris Lewis	Bill Maze	6–3, 6–4
1977–80	not held		

WOMEN'S SINGLES

Year	Winner	Runner-up	Final Score
1969	Linda Tuero	Gwyneth Thomas	4–6, 6–1, 6–2
1970	Linda Tuero	Laura DuPont	7–5, 6–3
1970*	Eliza Pande	Sharon Walsh	3–6, 9–7, 6–2
1971	Marita Redondo	Barbara Downs	6–0, 6–3
1972	Marita Redondo	Laurie Fleming	7–5, 3–6, 6–2
1973	Candy Reynolds	Kathy May	1–6, 7–6, 6–0
1974	not held		
1975	Lele Farood	Mary Hamm	6–5, 3–6, 5–4
1976	Diane Desfor	Paula Smith	6–5, 6–1
1977–80	not held		

*First year (Grass).

DOUBLES

Year	Men	Women	Mixed
1969	Tom Leonard and Eric van Dillen	Emilie Burrer and Pam Richmond	Pam Richmond and Joaquin Loyo-Mayo
1970	Lito Alvarez and Modesto Vasquez	Pam Austin and Margaret Cooper	not held
1970*	Robert McKinley and Dick Stockton	Gail Hansen and Sharon Walsh	not held
1971	Gene Scott and Vitas Gerulaitis	Pam Farmer and Janice Metcalf	not held
1972	Jim Hagey and Raul Ramirez	Pat Bostrom and Ann Lebedeff	not held
1973	Victor Amaya and Pat DuPre	Sally Greer and Linda Rupert	not held
1974	Rand Evert and DeArmond Briggs	not held	not held
1975	Steve Morris and Chris Gunning	Lele Farood and JoAnne Russell	Mary Hamm and Bill Scanlon
1976	Tim Garcia and Colon Numez	Barb Halliquist and Barbara Jordan	Cindy Thomas and Chris Lewis
1977–80	not held	not held	not held

*First year (Grass).

USTA Open Champions—Men Seniors' Doubles

1968 Torsten Johansson and Gardnar Mulloy
1969 Emery Neale and Robert Riggs
1970 L. Straight Clark and E. Victor Seixas
1971 L. Straight Clark and E. Victor Seixas
1972–80 not held

USTA Grass Court Champions—Men's 35 Singles

1967 Brian R. Tobin
1968–70 not held
1971 Sam Giammalva
1972 Mal Anderson
1973 Eugene L. Scott
1974 Eugene L. Scott
1975 Bob Hewitt
1976 Marty Riessen
1977–78 not held
1979 Robert Siska
1980 Jim Osborne

USTA Grass Court Champions—Men Seniors' 50 Singles

1979 Jason Morton
1980 Russell Seymour

USTA Grass Court Champions—Men Seniors' 50 Doubles

1979 Bobby Riggs and Richard Sorlien
1980 Ed Kauder and Kingman Lambert

USTA Grass Court Champions—Men Seniors' 55 Singles

1965 Bryan M. Grant
1966 Bryan M. Grant
1967 Bryan M. Grant
1968 Bryan M. Grant
1969 Gardnar Mulloy
1970 Chauncey D. Steele, Jr.
1971 Chauncey D. Steele, Jr.
1972 Chauncey D. Steele, Jr.
1973–74 not held
1975 Torsten Johansson
1976 Torsten Johansson

1977 Warren Drake
1978 Richard Sorlier
1979 Ken Wilson
1980 L. Straight Clark

USTA Grass Court Champions—Men Seniors' 55 Doubles

1965 Charles Brooke and C. Alphonso Smith
1966 Clayton Burewell and N. E. Powel
1967 N. E. Powel and Len Prosser
1968 Tom Bird and Bryan M. Grant
1969 Gardnar Mulloy and C. Alphonso Smith
1970 Chauncey D. Steele, Jr. and Frank Thompson
1971 Chauncey D. Steele, Jr. and Frank Thompson
1972 Tom Bird and Henry Crawford
1973–74 not held
1975 Glenn Hippenstiel and Bob Galloway
1976 Alan Cheesebro and Bob Galloway
1977 Buck Archer and Jack Rodgers
1978 Buck Archer and Jack Rodgers
1979 Jerry Laroque and Newton Meade
1980 Buck Archer and Tom Falkenberg

USTA Grass Court Champions—Men Seniors' 60 Singles

1968 Bernard Clinton
1969 C. Alphonso Smith
1970 Leonard Prosser
1971 N. E. Powel
1972 Harry Hoffman
1973 Gardnar Mulloy
1974 Gardnar Mulloy
1975 Gardnar Mulloy
1976 Gardnar Mulloy
1977 George Peebles
1978 Gardner Mulloy
1979 Bobby Riggs
1980 Bob Sherman

USTA Grass Court Champions—Men Seniors' 60 Doubles

1968 Monte Ganger and Crawford Christopher
1969 C. Alphonso Smith and Edward Tarangioli

1970 Charles Brooke and Leonard Prosser
1971 N. E. Powel and Leonard Prosser
1972 Bryan M. Grant and Henry Crawford
1973 Tom Bird and Henry Crawford
1974 Col. Nicholas E. Powel and Leonard Prosser
1975 Gardnar Mulloy and Jack Dreyfus
1976 Harry Hoffman and Charles Swanson
1977 George Peebles and Howard Sprague
1978 George Peebles and Tom Chambers
1979 George Peebles and Robin Hippenstiel
1980 Harry Hoffman and Charles Swanson

USTA Grass Court Champions—Men Seniors' 65 Singles

1969 Bernard Clinton
1970 Edward Chandler
1971 Frank Goeltz
1972 Milton Bush
1973 Frank Goeltz
1974 Frank Goeltz
1975 Jack Staton
1976 Len Prosser
1977 Harry Hoffman
1978 Harry Hoffman
1979 Gardnar Mulloy
1980 Fritz Klein

USTA Grass Court Champions—Men Seniors' 65 Doubles

1969 Bernard Clinton and Ted Wellman
1970 Edward Chandler and Ted Wellman
1971 Frank Goeltz and Kahl Spriggs
1972 Glen Sherar and Daniel Paul
1973 Marshall Christopher and Monte Ganger
1974 Frank Goeltz and C. Alphonso Smith
1975 Len Prosser and Charles Brooke
1976 Len Prosser and Bitsy Grant
1977 Len Prosser and N. E. Powel
1978 Harry Hoffman and Charles Brooke
1979 Harry Hoffman and Charles Swanson
1980 Harry Hoffman and Charles Swanson

USTA Grass Court Champions—Men Seniors' 70 Singles

1970 Frank G. Roberts
1971 Reul Ritz

1972 Arthur Enloe
1973 Clarence Chaffee
1974 Clarence Chaffee
1975 Wilfred Jones
1976 Frank Goeltz
1977 Frank Goeltz
1978 Earling Jensen
1979 Earling Jensen
1980 Leonard Prosser

USTA Grass Court Champions—Men Seniors' 70 Doubles

1970 Frank G. Roberts and Farham Warriner
1971 Richard Dole and DeWitt Redgrave
1972 Clarence Chaffee and Perry Rockafellow
1973 Clarence Chaffee and Perry Rockafellow
1974 Herschel Hyde and Clark Kaye
1975 Herschel Hyde and Arthur Enloe
1976 Monte Ganger and Frank Goeltz
1977 Monte Ganger and Frank Goeltz
1978 Mal Clarke and Ted Wellman
1979 Mal Clarke and Stephen Harris
1980 Leonard Prosser and Jack Staton

USTA Grass Court Champions—Men Seniors' 75 Singles

1974 Bill Mallery
1975 Dewitt Redgrave
1976 Clarence Chaffee
1977 Clarence Chaffee
1978 Mal Clarke
1979 Clarence Chaffee
1980 Wilfred Jones

USTA Grass Court Champions—Men Seniors' 75 Doubles

1974 Dewitt Redgrave and Gordon Steele
1975 Bill Mallery and T. J. Glover
1976 Clarence Chaffee and Perry Rockafellow
1977 Clarence Chaffee and Percy Rockafellow
1978 Mal Clarke and Ted Wellman
1979 Mal Clarke and Stephen Harris
1980 Wilfred Jones and Frank Matheson

USTA Grass Court Champions—Men Seniors' 80 Singles

1978 Kirk Reid
1979 Kirk Reid
1980 Kirk Reid

USTA Grass Court Champions—Men Seniors' 80 Doubles

1978 Kirk Reid and Albert Leitch
1979 Kirk Reid and Albert Leitch
1980 Kirk Reid and Albert Leitch

USTA Grass Court Champions—Women Seniors' Singles

1938 Mrs. William V. Hester
1939 Mrs. Walter Blumenthal
1940 Mrs. Gretl Dupont
1941 Mrs. William V. Hester
1942 Mrs. Gretl Dupont
1943 not held
1944 Mrs. Philip Theopold
1945 Mrs. Gretl Dupont
1946 Mrs. Philip Theopold
1947 Mrs. Alice Wanee
1948 Mrs. Muriel Bostwick
1949 Mrs. Richard Buck
1950 Mrs. Richard Buck
1951 Mrs. Richard Buck
1952 Mrs. Richard Buck
1953 Mrs. Richard Buck
1954 Mrs. Nell Hopman
1955 Mrs. Nell Hopman
1956 Mrs. Richard Buck
1957 Mrs. Richard Buck
1958 Mrs. Richard Buck
1959 Mrs. Merceina Parker
1960 Mrs. Charlotte Lee
1961 Kay Hubbell
1962 Kay Hubbell
1963 Mrs. Baba M. Lewis
1964 Mrs. Dorothy B. Cheney
1965 Mrs. Lucille Davidson
1966 Mrs. Betty R. Pratt
1967 Mrs. Dorothy B. Cheney
1968 Mrs. Betty R. Pratt

1969 Mrs. Betty R. Pratt
1970 Mrs. Nancy Neeld
1971 Mrs. Betty R. Pratt
1972 Mrs. Betty R. Pratt
1973 Nancy Reed
1974 Mrs. Betty R. Pratt
1975 Evelyn Houseman
1976 Shirley Irvin
1977 Nancy Reed
1978 Nancy Reed
1979 Nancy Reed
1980 Nancy Reed

USTA Grass Court Champions—Women Seniors' Doubles

1938 Mrs. Elizabeth B. Corbiere and Mrs. Henry R. Guild
1939 Eleanora R. Sears and Mme. Sylvia Henrotin
1940 Mrs. Hazel Hotchkiss Wightman and Mrs. Edith Sigourney
1941 Mrs. Hazel Hotchkiss Wightman and Mrs. Edith Sigourney
1942 Mrs. Hazel Hotchkiss Wightman and Mrs. Molly T. Fremont-Smith
1943 not held
1944 Mrs. Hazel Hotchkiss Wightman and Mrs. Edith Sigourney
1945 Mrs. Philip Theopold and Mrs. John B. Pierce
1946 Mrs. Hazel Hotchkiss Wightman and Mrs. Edith Sigourney
1947 Mrs. Hazel Hotchkiss Wightman and Mrs. Edith Sigourney
1948 Mrs. Hazel Hotchkiss Wightman and Mrs. Marion Zinderstein Jessup
1949 Mrs. Hazel Hotchkiss Wightman and Mrs. Richard Buck
1950 Mrs. Hazel H. Wightman and Mrs. Richard Buck
1951 Mrs. Richard Buck and Mrs. Edward Pinkhan
1952 Mrs. Richard Buck and Mrs. Hazel H. Wightman
1953 Mrs. Richard Buck and Mrs. Nell Hopman

1954 Mrs. Nell Hopman and Mrs. Hazel Wightman

1955 Mrs. Richard Buck and Mrs. Q. A. Shaw McKean

1956 Mrs. Walter Mahony and Mrs. Clarence Warner

1957 Mrs. Richard Buck and Mrs. Q. A. Shaw McKean

1958 Mrs. Richard Buck and Mrs. Q. A. Shaw McKean

1959 Mrs. Richard Buck and Mrs. Q. A. Shaw McKean

1960 Mrs. Richard Buck and Mrs. Q. A. Shaw McKean

1961 Mrs. Richard Buck and Mrs. Q. A. Shaw McKean

1962 Mrs. Richard Buck and Mrs. Q. A. Shaw McKean

1963 Mrs. Charlotte M. Lee and Katharine Hubbell

1964 Mrs. Richard Buck and Mrs. Q. A. Shaw McKean

1965 Katharine Hubbell and Mrs. Charlotte Lee

1966 Mrs. Baba M. Lewis and Mrs. Betty R. Pratt

1967 Mrs. Shirley F. Irwin and Mrs. Betty R. Pratt

1968 Mrs. Gloria E. Dillenbeck and Mrs. Betty R. Pratt

1969 Mrs. Dorothy B. Cheney and Mrs. June E. Gray

1970 Mrs. Nancy Neeld and Mrs. Betty R. Pratt

1971 Mrs. Nancy Neeld and Mrs. Betty R. Pratt

1972 Mrs. Nancy Neeld and Mrs. Betty R. Pratt

1973 Mrs. Betty R. Pratt and Nancy Reed

1974 Mrs. Betty R. Pratt and Mrs. F. A. C. (Bunny) Vosters

1975 Mrs. Betty R. Pratt and Nancy Reed

1976 Mrs. Dorothy B. Cheney and Evelyn Houseman

1977 Mrs. Dorothy B. Cheney and Evelyn Houseman

1978 Carol Wood and Eleanor Wright

1979 Mary Ann Plante and Nancy Reed

1980 Mary Ann Plante and Nancy Reed

USTA Grass Court Champions—Women's 35 Singles

1978 Judy Alvarez
1979 Judy Alvarez
1980 Judy Alvarez

USTA Grass Court Champions—Women's 35 Doubles

1978 Judy Alvarez and Charleen Hillebrand
1979 Judy Alvarez and Marion Archard
1980 Erol Agnos and Helen Johnson

USTA Grass Court Champions—Women's 40 Singles

1980 Laurella Lipson

USTA Grass Court Champions—Women's 40 Doubles

1980 Julie Hayward and Dorothy Mattiessen

USTA Grass Court Champions—Women's 50 Singles

1975 Mrs. Betty R. Pratt
1976 Mrs. Betty R. Pratt
1977 Mrs. Betty R. Pratt
1978 Mrs. Betty R. Pratt
1979 Mrs. Betty R. Pratt
1980 Vilma Gordon

USTA Grass Court Champions—Women's 50 Doubles

1975 Mrs. Betty R. Pratt and Mrs. F. A. C. (Bunny) Vosters
1976 Mrs. Betty R. Pratt and Betty McIlwaine
1977 Mrs. Dorothy B. Cheney and Carol Schneider
1978 Shirley Irvin and Joan Garrett
1979 Shirley Irvin and Joan Garrett
1980 Mrs. Dorothy B. Cheney and Margo Mahoney

USTA Grass Court Champions—Women's 55 Singles

1978 Mrs. Dorothy B. Cheney
1979 Phyllis Adler
1980 Mrs. Betty R. Pratt

USTA Grass Court Champions—Women's 55 Doubles

1978 Mrs. Dorothy B. Cheney and Florence Tout
1979 Mrs. Dorothy B. Cheney and Phyllis Adler
1980 Mrs. Dorothy B. Cheney and Phyllis Adler

USTA Grass Court Champions—Women's 60 Singles

1979 Mrs. Dorothy B. Cheney
1980 Mrs. Dorothy B. Cheney

USTA Grass Court Champions—Women's 60 Doubles

1979 Mrs. Dorothy B. Cheney and Margo Mahoney
1980 Mrs. Dorothy B. Cheney and Margo Mahoney

USTA Champions—Mother and Daughter

1967 Mrs. F. A. C. Vosters and Gretchen
1968 Mrs. F. A. C. Vosters and Gretchen
1969 Mrs. F. A. C. Vosters and Gretchen
1970 Mrs. F. A. C. Vosters and Gretchen
1971 Mrs. F. A. C. Vosters and Gretchen
1972 Mrs. Suzanne Sutter and Cindy
1973 Mrs. F. A. C. Vosters and Mrs. Gretchen Spruance
1974 Mrs. F. A. C. Vosters and Mrs. Gretchen Spruance
1975 Mrs. F. A. C. Vosters and Nina Moyer
1976 Mrs. Dorothy B. Cheney and Chris Putnam
1977 Mrs. F.A.C. Vosters and Mrs. Gretchen Spruance
1978 Mrs. F. A. C. Vosters and Mrs. Gretchen Spruance
1979 Mrs. F. A. C. Vosters and Mrs. Gretchen Spruance
1980 Mrs. F. A. C. Vosters and Mrs. Gretchen Spruance

Church Cup

The Church Cup was donated by George Myers Church in 1918 for competition between teams of men representing Boston, New York, and Philadelphia, and it continued in that format until 1932. In 1946 the competing teams represented three Sectional Associations, New England, Eastern, and Middle States. In 1947 the Middle Atlantic Section was admitted to the competition. The record of previous Church Cup matches is as follows:

Date	No. of Teams	Winner	Runner-up	Score
1918	3	New York	Philadelphia	6–3
1919	3	Boston	Philadelphia	6–3
1920	3	New York	Boston	5–3
1921	3	New York	Philadelphia	6–2
1922	not held			
1923	3	New York	Philadelphia	6–3
1924	3	New York and Philadelphia tied		2–2

Date	No. of Teams	Winner	Runner-up	Score
1925	3	Boston	New York	5–4
1926	3	Philadelphia	New York	6–3
1927	3	Philadelphia	New York	5–4
1928	3	Boston	Philadelphia	5–4
1929	3	New York	Philadelphia	7–2
1930	3	New York	Philadelphia	6–3
1931	3	New York	Boston	7–2
1932	3	New York	Philadelphia	7–2
1933–45	not held			
1946	3	Eastern	Middle States	5–4
1947	4	Middle Atlantic	New England	5½–3½
1948	4	Middle States	Eastern	7–2
1949	4	Eastern	Middle States	6–2
1950	4	Middle States	New England	7–2
1951	not held			
1952	4	New England	Middle States	6–3
1953	4	Middle States	Eastern	6–3
1954	4	Eastern	Middle States	6–3
1955	4	Middle States	New England	7–1
1956	4	Middle States	Middle Atlantic	6–3
1957	4	Eastern	Middle Atlantic	5–4
1958	4	Middle States	Eastern	5–4
1959	4	Middle States	Eastern	5–2
1960	4	Middle Atlantic	New England	5–4
1961	4	Middle States	Eastern	5–4
1962	4	Middle States	Middle Atlantic	9–0
1963	4	Middle States	Eastern	5–4
1964	4	Eastern	New England	8–1
1965	4	Eastern	Middle Atlantic	5–2
1966	4	Middle Atlantic	New England	7–2
1967	4	Middle Atlantic	Middle States	6–3
1968	4	Middle States	Middle Atlantic	5–4
1969	4	New England	Eastern	5–4
1970	4	New England	Eastern	5–4
1971	4	New England	Eastern	5–4
1972	4	Eastern	New England	7–2
1973	4	Eastern	Middle Atlantic	6–3
1974	3	Eastern	Middle States	4–3
1975	4	Middle Atlantic	Eastern	6–3
1976	4	New England	Eastern	6–3
1977	4	New England	Eastern	6–3
1978	4	Middle Atlantic	Middle States	5–4
1979	4	Eastern	New England	8–1
1980	4	Eastern	New England	5–4

Note: When 3 teams participated the runner-up listed was one of the finalists on the second day of play.

Sears Cup

The Sears Cup, named in honor of Eleanora Sears —a great woman player of the early 1900s—is the women's counterpart of the Church Cup. It started in 1927, but unlike the men's trophy it has had a continuous life. The record of previous Sears Cup matches is as follows:

Date	No. of Teams	Winner	Runner-up	Score
1927	3	New England	Eastern	5–2
1928	4	New England	Eastern	9–0
1929	4	New England	Eastern	5–4
1930	4	New England	Eastern	6–3
1931	4	New England	Eastern	6–3
1932	4	Eastern	Middle States	7–2
1933	3	New England	Eastern	5–4
1934	4	Eastern	Middle States	7–2
1935	4	Eastern	New England	6–3
1936	3	Eastern	Middle States	5–4
1937	4	New England	Eastern	6–3
1938	4	Eastern	New England	7–2
1939	4	New England	Eastern	5–4
1940	4	Eastern	New England	5–4
1941	3	New England	Eastern	8–1
1942	3	Eastern	Middle States	9–0
1943	2	Eastern	Middle States	8–1
1944	3	Eastern	New England	7–2
1945	3	Eastern	Middle States	9–0
1946	3	Eastern	Middle Atlantic	8–1
1947	4	Eastern	New England	6–3
1948	4	Middle States	New England	6–3
1949	4	Eastern	New England	8–1
1950	4	Eastern	New England	5–2
1951	3	New England	Middle States	5–4
1952	4	New England	Eastern	6–3
1953	4	Middle States	New England	9–0
1954	4	New England	Eastern	6–3
1955	4	Middle States	New England	6–3
1956	4	New England	Middle States	6–3
1957	4	Middle States	New England	7–2
1958	4	New England	Middle States	6–3
1959	4	Middle States	New England	5–0
1960	4	Middle States	Middle Atlantic	9–0
1961	3	Middle States	Middle Atlantic	7–2
1962	4	New England	Middle Atlantic	6–3
1963	4	Middle States	Middle Atlantic	8–1
1964	4	Middle States	Middle Atlantic	6–3
1965	4	Middle States	New England	6–1
1966	4	Eastern	New England	5–4
1967	4	Middle States	Eastern	6–3
1968	4	Middle Atlantic	Eastern	5–4
1969	3	Middle States	Middle Atlantic	6–3
1970	4	Eastern	Middle Atlantic	5–4
1971	4	Middle States	Eastern	7–2
1972	4	Eastern	Middle Atlantic	5–4
1973	4	Eastern	Middle States	5–4
1974	4	Middle States	Eastern	9–0
1975	4	Middle Atlantic	Eastern	7–2
1976	4	Middle States	Middle Atlantic	6–3
1977	4	Middle States	Middle Atlantic	6–3
1978	4	Middle States	Middle Atlantic	5–4
1979	4	Eastern	Middle Atlantic	5–4
1980	4	Eastern	New England	5–4

Note: When 3 teams participated the runner-up listed was one of the finalists on the second day of play.

Eleanora Randolph Sears Challenge Bowl (U.S.T.A. Girls' Intersectional Team Matches)

1943—Eastern L.T.A.; 1944—Western L.T.A.; 1945—No competition; 1946—California T.A.; 1947—California T.A.; 1948—Texas T.A.; 1949—Western L.T.A.; 1950—Western L.T.A.; 1951—Western L.T.A.; 1952—Southern California T.A.; 1953—Southern California T.A.; 1954—Northern California T.A.; 1955—Southern California T.A.; 1956—Southern California T.A.; 1957—Southern California T.A.; 1958—Southern California T.A.; 1959—Southern California T.A.; 1960—Southern California T.A.; 1961—Southern California T.A.; 1962—Northern California T.A.; 1963—Florida T.A.; 1964—Northern California T.A.; 1965—Northern California T.A.; 1966—Northern California T.A.; 1967—Southern California T.A.; 1968—Northern California T.A.; 1969—Southern California T.A.; 1970—Southern California T.A.; 1971—Northern California T.A.; 1972—Florida T.A.; 1973—Southern California T.A.; 1974—Southern California T.A.; 1975—Southern California T.A.; 1976—Southern California T.A.; 1977—Southern California T.A.; 1978—Northern California T.A.; 1979—Western T.A.; 1980—Florida T.A.

OTHER AMERICAN CHAMPIONSHIPS

USPTA National Professional Champions

The first National Professional Championships were held in America under the leadership of the Professional Lawn Tennis Association of the United States. In the 1930s this group joined with United States Professional Lawn Tennis Association (see page 00) in sponsoring the Championship. In 1970 USPLTA decided to drop the word "Lawn" from their name and became United States Professional Tennis Association (USPTA). Here are the winners of the National Professional Championships since their start in 1927:

Mike Davies *(left)* and Sam Giammalva *(right)* were consistently outstanding pro players in the 1960s. At the right, Giammalva is receiving his award from the great teaching professional Bill Lufler.

USPTA National Men's Singles Champions

1927	Vincent Richards
1928	Vincent Richards
1929	Karel Kozeluh
1930	Vincent Richards
1931	William T. Tilden II
1932	Karel Kozeluh
1933	Vincent Richards
1934	Hans Nusslein
1935	William T. Tilden II
1936	Joseph Whalen
1937	Karel Kozeluh
1938	Frederick J. Perry
1939	H. Ellsworth Vines
1940	J. Donald Budge
1941	Frederick J. Perry
1942	J. Donald Budge
1943	Bruce Barnes
1944	not held
1945	Welby Van Horn
1946	Robert L. Riggs
1947	Robert L. Riggs
1948	Jack Kramer
1949	Robert L. Riggs
1950	Francisco Segura
1951	Francisco Segura
1952–1961	not held
1962	Bernard J. Bartzen
1963	Bernard J. Bartzen
1964	Samuel A. Giammalva
1965	Michael Davies
1966	Francisco Segura
1967	Samuel A. Giammalva
1968	not held
1969	Billy Higgins
1970	Samuel A. Giammalva
1971	Billy Higgins
1972	Ian Crookenden
1973	Mark Shires
1974	Pancho Walthall
1975	Pancho Walthall
1976	Jim Parker
1977	Zdravko Mincek
1978	Armistead Neely
1979	Armistead Neely
1980	Larry Loeb

Vincent Richards and Bill Tilden won their first doubles title in 1918 when Richards was only 15. Here they are shown after winning their last major title—USPTA Doubles Championship —in 1945.

USPTA National Women's Singles Champions

1972	Alice Tym
1973	Carol Weymuller
1974	Susan Eastman
1975	Owen McHaney and Betsy Butler (co-champions)
1976	Anne Borders
1977	Christine Koutras
1978	Bunnie Miller
1979	Astrid Suurbeek
1980	Susan Shelby Torrence

USPTA National Men's Doubles Champions

1929	Vincent Richards and Karel Kozeluh
1930	Vincent Richards and Howard O. Kinsey
1931	Vincent Richards and Howard O. Kinsey
1932	William T. Tilden II and Bruce Barnes
1933	Vincent Richards and Charles M. Wood
1934	Bruce Barnes and Emmeth Pare
1935	George M. Lott, Jr. and Lester Stoefen
1936	Charles M. Wood and Harold Blauer

1937 Vincent Richards and George M. Lott, Jr.
1938 Vincent Richards and Frederick J. Perry
1939 Bruce Barnes and Keith Gledhill
1940 J. Donald Budge and Frederick J. Perry
1941 J. Donald Budge and Frederick J. Perry
1942 J. Donald Budge and Robert L. Riggs
1943 Bruce Barnes and Gene Mako
1944 not held
1945 Vincent Richards and William T. Tilden II
1946 Frank L. Kovacs and Frederick J. Perry
1947 J. Donald Budge and Robert L. Riggs
1948 Jack Kramer and Francisco Segura
1949 J. Donald Budge and Frank L. Kovacs
1950 Welby Van Horn and Frank L. Kovacs
1951 Francisco Segura and Richard Gonzalez
1952–1961 not held
1962 Samuel A. Giammalva and Eugene Gerrett
1963–1964 not held
1965 Michael Davies and Allan Quay
1966 Francisco Segura and Michael Davies
1967 Samuel A. Giammalva and Jason Morton
1968 not held
1969 Richard N. Leach and Robert A. Potthast
1970 Richard N. Leach and Robert A. Potthast
1971 Ramsey Earhart and Walter Johnson
1972 Dick Leach and Robert Potthast
1973 Greg Hillary and Bob Steck
1974 Dick Leach and Tom Leonard
1975 Jim Parker and Larry Parker Bill Lofgren and George Amaya (co-champions)
1976 Pancho Walthall and Jim Parker
1977 Bill Lofgren and George Amaya
1978 not held
1979 Pat Cramer and Steve Siegel
1980 Brian Marcus and Rob Casterri

USPTA Intersectional Men's Team—Match Champions

1964 Eastern
1965 New England
1966 New England
1967 Florida
1968 Midwest
1969 Florida

1970 Florida
1971 Florida
1972 Florida
1973 Texas
1974 Southern
1975 California
1976 Southern
1977 Texas
1978 Texas and Florida (tie)
1979 Texas
1980 Texas

USPTA National Women's Doubles Champions

1972 Janice Rapp and Alice Tym
1973 Charlene Grafton and Carol Weymuller
1974 Susan Eastman and Alice Tym
1975 Carol Weymuller and Betsy Butler
1976 Ann Borders and Janet Talley
1977 Christine Koutras and Sherry Bedingfield
1978 not held
1979 Yvonne Gallop and Joyce Tabor
1980 Wendy Overton and Astrid Suurbeek

USPTA National Men Seniors' Over-35 Singles Champions

1967 Juan F. Weiss
1968 not held
1969 Ben Press
1970 Robert A. Potthast
1971 Jason Morton
1972 Robert Potthast
1973 Roy Garrido
1974 not held
1975 Bill Tym
1976 Bill Tym
1977 Bill Tym
1978 Billy Higgins
1979 Steve Wilkinson
1980 Jim Parker

USPTA National Men Seniors' Over-35 Doubles Champions

1967 Juan F. Weiss and Emilio Posada
1968 not held
1969 Ben Press and Alex Gordon
1970 Ed Kauder and Hal H. Miller
1971 Jason Morton and James Schmidt
1972 Jayson Morton and Patricio Apey

USPTA National Men Seniors' Over-35 Doubles *(cont.)*

1973 Ben Press and Alex Gordon
1974 not held
1975 Bill Tym and Dick Leach
1976 Jerry Walters and Roy Garrido
1977 Billy Higgins and Luis Ayala
1978 not held
1979 Rob Cadwallader and John Stock
1980 Dick Johnson and Tim Heckler

USPTA Men's Over-45 Singles Champions

1970 Gustavo Palafox
1971 Ben Press
1972 Armando Vierra
1973 Don Martin
1974 Dell Sylvia
1975 Dell Sylvia
1976 Dell Sylvia
1977 Dell Sylvia
1978 Dell Sylvia
1979 Dell Sylvia
1980 Dell Sylvia

USPTA Men's Over-45 Doubles Champions

1970 Gustavo Palafox and Juan F. Weiss

1971 Alex Gordon and Ben Press
1972 Alex Gordon and Ben Press
1973 Bob Luxenberg and Paul Lynner
1974 Tom Falkenberg and Paul Lynner
1975 Tom Bartlett and Dell Sylvia
1976 Dell Sylvia and Bob Luxenberg
1977 Tom Bartlett and Don Kaiser
1978 not held
1979 Rey Garrido and Dell Sylvia
1980 Rey Garrido and Dell Sylvia

USPTA National Men's Over-55 Singles Champions

1967 Leonard Hartman
1968 not held
1969 Frank M. Goeltz
1970 not held
1971 John Faunce
1972 John Faunce
1973 Bob Galloway
1974 not held
1975 Warren McMillan
1976 Ernie Spiller
1977 Bob Stubbs
1978 Leon Wilson
1979 Leon Wilson
1980 Tom Falkenburg

U.S. PRO INDOOR MEN'S SINGLES CHAMPIONS

Year	Champion	Runner-up	Final Score
1962	Jon Douglas	Ron Holmberg	5–7, 3–6, 6–1, 6–2, 7–5
1963	Whitney Reed	Frank Froehling	4–6, 6–1, 8–6, 6–4
1964	Chuck McKinley	Rafael Osuna	6–3, 8–6, 5–7, 4–6, 6–3
1965	Charles Pasarell	Ian Crookenden	6–8, 11–9, 8–6, 6–4
1966	Charles Pasarell	Arthur Ashe	13–11, 6–2, 2–6, 9–7
1967	Arthur Ashe	Charles Pasarell	7–5, 9–7, 6–3
1968	Manuel Santana	Jan Leschly	8–6, 6–3
1969	Rod Laver	Tony Roche	6–3, 8–6, 6–2
1970	Rod Laver	Tony Roche	7–5, 6–4, 6–4
1971	John Newcombe	Rod Laver	7–6, 7–6, 6–4
1972	Rod Laver	Ken Rosewall	4–6, 6–2, 6–2, 6–2
1973	Stan Smith	Bob Lutz	7–6, 7–6, 4–6, 1–6, 6–4
1974	Rod Laver	Arthur Ashe	6–1, 6–4, 3–6, 6–4
1975	Marty Riessen	Vitas Gerulaitis	7–6, 5–7, 6–2, 6–7, 6–3
1976	Jimmy Connors	Bjorn Borg	7–6, 6–4, 6–0
1977	Dick Stockton	Jimmy Connors	3–6, 6–4, 3–6, 6–1, 6–2
1978	Jimmy Connors	Roscoe Tanner	6–4, 6–2, 6–3
1979	Jimmy Connors	Arthur Ashe	6–3, 6–4, 6–1
1980	Jimmy Connors	John McEnroe	6–3, 2–6, 6–3, 3–6, 6–4

(Tournament played annually at Philadelphia)

USPTA National Men's Over-55 Doubles Champions

1967 Leonard Hartman and William C. Lufler
1968–69 not held
1970 Garnet W. Glenney and William Millikan
1971 Garnet W. Glenney and William Millikan
1972 John Faunce and Gar Glennery
1973 Allie Ritzenberg and Charles Swanson
1974 not held
1975 Warren McMillan and Earl Meyers
1976 Warren McMillan and Leo LaBorde
1977 Bob Stubbs and Jack Cook
1978 not held
1979 Jack Cook and Frank Froehling
1980 Tom Falkenburg and J P Feigenbaum

U.S. PRO INDOOR MEN'S DOUBLES CHAMPIONS

Year	Winner	Year	Winner
1962	not played	1971	not completed
1963	Ron Holmberg and Mike Green	1972	Arthur Ashe and Bob Lutz
1964	Thomas Koch and Arthur Ashe	1974	Mike Estep and Pat Kramer
1965	Luis Arilla and Nicki Kalo	1975	Brian Gottfried and Raul Ramirez
1966	Charles Pasarell and Arthur Ashe	1976	Rod Laver and Dennis Ralston
1967	Bob Lutz and Mark Cox	1977	Bob Hewitt and Frew McMillan
1968	Charles Pasarell and Arthur Ashe	1978	Bob Hewitt and Frew McMillan
1969	Marty Riessen and Tom Okker	1979	Wojtek Fibak and Tom Okker
1970	Ilie Nastase and Ion Tiriac	1980	John McEnroe and Peter Fleming

Althea Gibson was the first ATA Champion to win the National title.

American Tennis Association Champions

In 1916 the American Tennis Association, the governing body for black players, was formed, and singles championships for men and women were held in 1917, with other divisions—juniors, doubles, veterans, etc., constantly being added as in USTA play. Several players in the ATA have made notable records in the sport. Dr. Reginald Weir earned high Eastern rankings in the USTA, and, in 1956, he won the national senior's indoor championship to become the first member of his race to win a USTA championship. Since that time, Althea Gibson and Arthur Ashe, Jr.—both former ATA singles champions—have won United States National Championships. Here are the winners of the ATA's major divisions:

ATA Men's Singles Champions

1917 Tally Holmes
1918 Tally Holmes
1919 Sylvester Smith
1920 B. M. Clark

ATA Men's Singles Champions *(cont.)*

1921	Tally Holmes
1922	Edgar G. Brown
1923	Edgar G. Brown
1924	Tally Holmes
1925	Theodore Thompson
1926	Eyre Saitch
1927	Theodore Thompson
1928	Edgar G. Brown
1929	Edgar G. Brown
1930	Douglas Turner
1931	Reginald Weir
1932	Reginald Weir
1933	Reginald Weir
1934	Nathaniel Jackson
1935	Franklin Jackson
1936	Lloyd Scott
1937	Reginald Weir
1938	Franklin Jackson
1939	Jimmie McDaniel
1940	Jimmie McDaniel
1941	Jimmie McDaniel
1942	Reginald Weir
1943	not held
1944	Lloyd Scott
1945	Lloyd Scott
1946	Jimmie McDaniel
1947	George Stewart
1948	George Stewart
1949	unfinished*
1950	Oscar Johnson
1951	George Stewart
1952	George Stewart
1953	George Stewart
1954	Earthna Jacquet
1955	Robert Ryland
1956	Robert Ryland
1957	George Stewart
1958	Wilbert Davis
1959	Wilbert Davis
1960	Arthur Ashe, Jr.
1961	Arthur Ashe, Jr.
1962	Arthur Ashe, Jr.
1963	Wilbert Davis
1964	George Stewart
1965	Luis Glass
1966	Wilbert Davis
1967	Wilbert Davis
1968	Robert Binns
1969	Marty Gool
1970	Gene Fluri
1971	John Wilkerson
1972	Horace Reid
1973	Arthur Carrington
1974	Roger D. Guedes
1975	Benny Sims
1976	Terrance Jackson
1977	Terrance Jackson
1978	Rodney Harmon
1979	Warwick Jones
1980	Kelvin Belcher

*Reginald Weir and Harold Mitchell were finalists. The score stood at two (2) sets all, Mitchell leading in the fifth set 1–0, when due to heavy rain they were unable to resume play.

ATA Women's Singles Champions

1917	Lucy Slowe
1918	M. Rae
1919	M. Rae
1920	M. Rae
1921	Lucy Slowe
1922	Isadore Channels
1923	Isadore Channels
1924	Isadore Channels
1925	Lulu Ballard
1926	Isadore Channels
1927	Lulu Ballard
1928	Lulu Ballard
1929	Ora Washington
1930	Ora Washington
1931	Ora Washington
1932	Ora Washington
1933	Ora Washington
1934	Ora Washington
1935	Ora Washington
1936	Lulu Ballard
1937	Ora Washington
1938	Mrs. Flora Lomax
1939	Mrs. Flora Lomax
1940	Mrs. Agnes Lawson
1941	Mrs. Flora Lomax
1942	Mrs. Flora Lomax
1943	not held
1944	Roumania Peters
1945	Mrs. Kathryn Irvis
1946	Roumania Peters
1947	Althea Gibson

1948	Althea Gibson
1949	Althea Gibson
1950	Althea Gibson
1951	Althea Gibson
1952	Althea Gibson
1953	Althea Gibson
1954	Althea Gibson
1955	Althea Gibson
1956	Althea Gibson
1957	Gwendolyn McEvans
1958	Mary E. Fine
1959	Gwendolyn McEvans
1960	Mimi Kanarek
1961	Carolyn Williams
1962	Carolyn Liguori
1963	Ginger Pfiefer
1964	Helen Watanabe
1965	Helen Watanabe
1966	Bonnie Logan
1967	Doris Harrison
1968	Dorothy Kornegay
1969	Dorothy Kornegay
1970	Dorothy Kornegay
1971	Alphonda Edwards
1972	Lorraine Bryant
1973	Mimi Kanarek
1974	Jean Burnett
1975	Diane Morrison
1976	Kim Sands
1977	Leslie Allen
1978	Joann Jacobs
1979	Zina Harrison
1980	Zina Harrison

ATA Men's Doubles Champions

1917	Tally Holmes and Sylvester Smith
1918	D. Monroe and Percy Richardson
1921	Tally Holmes and Sylvester Smith
1922	Tally Holmes and Sylvester Smith
1923	J. L. McGriff, Sr. and E. D. Downing
1924	Tally Holmes and Theodore Thompson
1925	Tally Holmes and Theodore Thompson
1926	Eyre Saitch and Theodore Thompson
1927	Tally Holmes and Theodore Thompson
1928	Eyre Saitch and Sylvester Smith
1929	Eyre Saitch and Sylvester Smith
1930	J. L. McGriff, Sr. and E. D. Downing
1931	Nathaniel Jackson and Franklin Jackson

1932	Richard Hudlin and Douglas Turner
1933	Nathaniel Jackson and Franklin Jackson
1934	Nathaniel Jackson and Franklin Jackson
1935	Nathaniel Jackson and Franklin Jackson
1936	Nathaniel Jackson and Franklin Jackson
1937	James Stocks and Thomas Walker
1938	Nathaniel Jackson and Franklin Jackson
1939	Jimmie McDaniel and Richard Cohen
1940	Clifford Russell and Howard Minnis
1941	Jimmie McDaniel and Richard Cohen
1942	Clifford Russell and Howard Minnis
1943	not held
1944	Ronald Fieulleteau and Howard Minnis
1945	Lloyd Scott and Louis Graves
1946	Jimmie McDaniel and James L. Stocks
1947	John Chandler and Harold Mitchell
1948	George Stewart and Hubert Eaton
1949	George Stewart and Hubert Eaton
1950	James Stocks and Oscar Johnson
1951	George Stewart and Hubert Eaton
1952	Jimmie McDaniel and Eartha Jacquet
1953	unfinished
1954	Eartha Jacquet and Wilbert Davis
1955	Clyde Freeman and Harold Freeman
1956	George Stewart and Hubert Eaton
1957	George Stewart and John Chandler
1958	Wilbur Jenkins and Thomas Calhoun
1959	Joe Pierce and Shaw Emmons
1960	Wilbur Jenkins and Thomas Calhoun
1961	Arthur Ashe and Ronald Charity
1962	Wilbert Davis and Robert Davis
1963	Howard Minnis and William Monroe
1964	Luis Glass and Lenward Simpson
1965	Luis Glass and Lenward Simpson
1966	John Mudd and Arthur Carrington
1967	John Mudd and Arthur Carrington
1968	Marty Gool and Gregory Morton
1969	Marty Gool and Gregory Morton
1970	Gene Fluri and Tom Fluri
1971	William Heinbecker and Jerry Johnson
1972	Arthur Carrington and Gregory Morton
1973	Sheri Anadan and Luis Glass
1974	Bruce Foxworth and Roger D. Guedes
1975	M. Andrew and Lawrence King
1976	T. Scott and Terrance Jackson
1977	Weldon Rogers and Marel Harmon
1978	Rodney Harmon and M. Harmon
1979	M. McCurley and O. Ongunrinde
1980	M. Delande and G. Williams

ATA Women's Doubles Champions

1924 Isadore Channels and Emma Leonard
1925 Ora Washington and Lulu Ballard
1926 Ora Washington and Lulu Ballard
1927 Ora Washington and Lulu Ballard
1928 Ora Washington and Lulu Ballard
1929 Ora Washington and Lulu Ballard
1930 Ora Washington and Blanche Winston
1931 Ora Washington and Blanche Winston
1932 Ora Washington and Lulu Ballard
1933 Ora Washington and Anita Gant
1934 Ora Washington and Lulu Ballard
1935 Ora Washington and Lulu Ballard
1936 Ora Washington and Lulu Ballard
1937 Bertha Isaacs and Lilyan Spencer
1938 Margaret Peters and Roumania Peters
1939 Margaret Peters and Roumania Peters
1940 Margaret Peters and Roumania Peters
1941 Margaret Peters and Roumania Peters
1942 Lillian Van Buren and Flora Lomax
1943 not held
1944 Margaret Peters and Roumania Peters
1945 Margaret Peters and Roumania Peters
1946 Margaret Peters and Roumania Peters
1947 Margaret Peters and Roumania Peters
1948 Margaret Peters and Roumania Peters
1949 Margaret Peters and Roumania Peters
1950 Margaret Peters and Roumania Peters
1951 Margaret Peters and Roumania Peters
1952 Margaret Peters and Roumania Peters
1953 Margaret Peters and Roumania Peters
1954 Evelyn George and Ivy C. Ransey
1955 Eva F. Bracy and Mary E. Fine
1956 Angela Imala and Lorraine Williams
1957 Eva F. Bracy and Mary E. Fine
1958 Eva F. Bracy and Mary E. Fine
1959 Marlene Everson and Darnella Everson
1960 Bessie A. Stockard and Carolyn Williams
1961 Carloyn Williams and Marreline Faggett
1962 Mimi Kanarek and Carolyn Liguori
1963 Mimi Fry and Ginger Pfiefer
1964 Sylvia Hooks and Bonnie Logan
1965 Jean Eichardson and Helen Watanabe
1966 Bonnie Logan and Bessie Stockard
1967 Sylvia Hooks and Bessie Stockard
1968 Ann Koeger and Bessie Stockard
1969 T. Rueter and S. Beauchamp
1970 T. Rueter and S. Beauchamp
1971 Pamela Stienmetz and Bunny Wall
1972 Elaine Busch and Jean Burnett
1973 Arvelia Meyers and Jean Burnett
1974 Bessie Stockard and Barbara Faulkner
1975 S. Dancy and Lisa Rapfogel
1976 M. Tiff and B. Richardson
1977 Karen Hardin and Brenda Richards
1978 Jean Burnett and Brenda Richards
1979 Jean Burnett and C. Watson
1980 Zina Harrison and L. McNeil

ATA Mixed Doubles Champions

1924 Nellie Nicholson and B. M. Rhetta
1925 C. O. Seames and L. C. Downing
1926 E. Robinson and E. Cole
1927 Blanche Winston and Louis Jones
1928 Blanche Winston and W. A. Kean
1929 Anita Gant and O. B. Williams
1930 Anita Gant and O. B. Williams
1931 Anne Roberts and Theodore Thompson
1932 Martha Davis and Henry Williams
1933 Emma Leonard and C. O. Hilton
1934 Emma Leonard and C. O. Hilton
1935 not held
1936 not held
1937 Flora Lomax and William H. Hall
1938 Lulu Ballard and Gerald Norman, Jr.
1939 Ora Washington and Sylvester Smith
1940 Flora Lomax and William H. Hall
1941 Eoline Thornton and Harold Mitchell
1942 Kathryn Jones and William E. Jones
1943 not held
1944 Lillian Van Buren and Delbert Russell
1945 Lillian Van Buren and Delbert Russell
1946 Ora Washington and George Stewart
1947 Ora Washington and George Stewart
1948 Althea Gibson and R. Walter Johnson
1949 Althea Gibson and R. Walter Johnson
1950 Althea Gibson and R. Walter Johnson
1951 Mary Etta Fine and Leo Fine
1952 Althea Gibson and R. Walter Johnson
1953 Althea Gibson and R. Walter Johnson
1954 Althea Gibson and R. Walter Johnson
1955 Althea Gibson and R. Walter Johnson
1956 G. McEvans and W. A. Campbell
1957 Doris Harrison and Ernie Ingram
1958 Gwen McEvans and Clyde Freeman
1959 Gwen McEvans and Clyde Freeman
1960 Elaine Busch and George Stewart

1961	Mimi Kanarek and Ernest Ingram		1951	Wade Herren
1962	Mimi Kanarek and Ernest Ingram		1952	Linn Rockwood
1963	Lucy McEvans and Charles Berry		1953	Clyde Hippenstiel
1964	Bessie Stockard and Charles Berry		1954	Clyde Hippenstiel
1965	Sylvia Hooks and William Morton, Jr.		1955	Clyde Hippenstiel
1966	Sylvia Hooks and William Morton, Jr.		1956	Linn Rockwood
1967	Bonnie Logan and Lenward Simpson		1957	Linn Rockwood
1968	Bonnie Logan and Lenward Simpson		1958	Noel Brown
1969	Bonnie Logan and Lenward Simpson		1959	Alan Tong
1970	Bonnie Logan and Lenward Simpson		1960	John Evans
1971	Beverly Hassel and Alberto Loney		1961	Gardnar Mulloy
1972	L. Stavins and Chris Scott		1962	Fred Drilling
1973	Ann Koger and Tyrone Mapp		1963	Gerald Dubie
1974	Ann Koger and Tyrone Mapp		1964	Bob Potthast
1975	R. Harris and D. Stuart		1965	David Reed
1976	M. Superville and Jesse Holt		1966	Rod Susman
1977	Wila Bentley and Willis Thomas Jr.		1967	Rod Susman
1978	S. Elam and Jesse Holt, Jr.		1968	Gary Johnson
1979	S. Elam and Jesse Holt, Jr.		1969	William Tym
1980	Sally Middleton and Jesse Holt, Jr.		1970	Larry Paker
			1971	Mike Anderson
			1972	Ken Stuart

National Public Parks Champions—Men's Singles

			1973	Robert Hetherington
			1974	Lawrence King
1923	Cranston W. Holman		1975	Steve Wilkinson
1924	Theodore R. Drewes		1976	Orlando Agudelo
1925	Theodore R. Drewes		1977	Juan Farrow
1926	Theodore R. Drewes		1978	Mark Andrews
1927	Theodore R. Drewes		1979	Mike Rose
1928	George J. Jennings, Jr.			
1929	George J. Jennings, Jr.			
1930	George J. Jennings, Jr.			
1931	George J. Jennings, Jr.			
1932	Arnold Simons			
1933	Arnold Simons			
1934	Barnard Welsh			
1935	Barnard Welsh			
1936	Lewis Wetherell			
1937	Lewis Wetherell			
1938	Willis Anderson			
1939	Willis Anderson			
1940	Richard McKee			
1941	Willis Anderson			
1942–45	not held			
1946	Richard Hainline			
1947	Fred Kovaleski			
1948	Willis Anderson			
1949	Myron McNamara			
1950	Clyde Hippenstiel			

The outstanding University of Southern California team of Stan Smith *(left)* and Bob Lutz *(right)* won the Intercollegiate doubles title in 1967 and 1968. In the latter year, they also won the United States Open and National doubles crown as well as helping the United States to win the Davis Cup.

National Public Parks Champions—Women's Singles

1930	Mrs. Virginia B. Bueker
1931	Mary Z. McHale
1932	Helen Germaine
1933	Ruth Bailey
1934	Mrs. Ruth Bailey Prosser
1935	Elizabeth Deike
1936	Elizabeth Deike
1937	Mary Arnold
1938	Catherine Malcolm
1939	Marta M. Barnett
1940	Helen Germaine
1941	Muriel Magnuson
1942–45	not held
1946	Beverly J. Baker
1947	Mrs. Mary Arnold Prentiss
1948	Mrs. Mary Arnold Prentiss
1949	Mrs. Lucile Davidson
1950	Mrs. Mary Arnold Prentiss
1951	Mrs. Mary Arnold Prentiss
1952	Mrs. Mary Arnold Prentiss
1953	Mrs. Mary Arnold Prentiss
1954	Mrs. Mary Arnold Prentiss
1955	June Stack
1956	Mrs. Mary Arnold Prentiss
1957	Mrs. Mary Arnold Prentiss
1958	Mrs. Mary Arnold Prentiss
1959	Joyce Pniewski
1960	Joan Johnson
1961	Joan Johnson
1962	Joan Johnson
1963	Jane Bartkowicz
1964	Mimi Arnold
1965	Susan Dykes
1966	Eileen Rahlens
1967	Pat Cody
1968	Mrs. Janie Albert Freeman
1969	Alice Tym
1970	Joan Johnson
1971	Pat Cody
1972	Jan Hasse
1973	Sue Eastman
1974	Pat Cody
1975	Karen Dawson
1976	Karen Dawson
1977	Pat Cody
1978	Andrea Whitmore
1979	Tina Mochizuki
1980	Pamela Jung

National Public Parks Champions—Men's Doubles

1923	Elmer Schwartz and Ted Heuerman
1924	Frank Regan and Cranston W. Holman
1925	Charles Lejeck and Leo Lejeck
1926	Gabriel Lavine and Gus Amsterdam
1927	Ralph Rice and George J. Jennings, Jr.
1928	Ralph Rice and George J. Jennings, Jr.
1929	G. J. Jennings, Jr. and Robert B. Considine
1930	George J. Jennings, Jr. and Jack DeLara
1931	George J. Jennings, Jr. and Gordon L. Braudt
1932	Gordon L. Braudt and Carl Ireneus
1933	William Schommer and Charles Britzius
1934	William Schommer and Charles Britzius
1935	Barnard Welsh and Ralph McElvenny
1936	Ted Drewes and Robert Norton
1937	Willis Anderson and Ronald Lubin
1938	Elbert R. Lewis and Willis Anderson
1939	Julius Heldman and Willis Anderson
1940	Willis Anderson and Jerry Crowther
1941	Dr. W. F. Widen and Ed Olson
1942–45	not held
1946	Willis Anderson and Geo. Druliner
1947	Fred Kovaleski and Gene Russell
1948	Nolan McQuown and Myron McNamara
1949	Myron McNamara and Nolan McQuown
1950	Bobby Curtis and Clayton Benham
1951	Thomas Chambers and Clyde Hippenstiel
1952	Nolan McQuown and Roy McQuown
1953	Nolan McQuown and Roy McQuown
1954	Thomas Chambers and Clyde Hippenstiel
1955	Glenn Basset and Clyde Hippenstiel
1956	Ralph Dudgeon and Allen Schmidt
1957	Wayne Pearce and Linn Rockwood
1958	Noel Brown and Ramsey Earnhart
1959	George MacCall and Marsh Miller
1960	Mickey Schad and Roddy McNerney
1961	Ed Foster and Don Schmidt
1962	Dick Horwitz and Jerry Johnson
1963	Gary Russell and Wayne Collett
1964	Bob Potthast and Dick Leach

1965 Gary Johnson and David Reed
1966 Jerry Johnson and Jim Parker
1967 Jerry Johnson and Rod Susman
1968 Bob Kreiss and Mike Kreiss
1969 Jerry Van Linge and Ed Grubb
1970 Larry Paker and Paul Tobin
1971 Robert Hetherington and Charles
       Garfinkel
1972 Dave Bohannon and Eddie Scott
1973 Charles Garfinkel and Robert
       Hetherington
1974 Chris Sadkowski and Dirk Dugan
1975 Steve Wilkinson and Terry Noyce
1976 Tom Rittenmeir and Rick Rozen
1977 Steve Wilkinson and Kevin Ylinen
1978 Curt Condon and Rick Rozen
1979 Steve Wilkinson and Kevin Ylinen
1980 Brian McQuown and Keith Simpson

National Public Parks Champions—Women's Doubles

1930 Ethel Haas and Elizabeth Kaiser
1931 Mary Zita McHale and Mary McQuiston
1932 Mrs. V. B. Ducker and Mrs. A.
       Linderman
1933 Mrs. Ruth Prosser and Mrs. Ella
       Felbinger
1934 Helen Rose and Mrs. Andree Russell
1935 Constance O'Donovan and Esther
       Politzer
1936 Edna Smith and Irene David
1937 Mary Arnold and Mrs. Gertrude
       Dockstader
1938 Mrs. Gertrude Dockstader and Mary
       Arnold
1939 Marta Barnett and Mrs. Catherine
       Sample
1940 Mrs. Merceina Parker and Frances
       Jacobson
1941 Muriel Magnuson and Beverly Pawlak
1942–45 not held
1946 Mrs. Wilma Smith and Mrs. Merceina
       Parker
1947 Mrs. Mary Prentiss and Mrs. June Crow
1948 Mrs. Mary Prentiss and Mrs. Alice
       Wanee
1949 Mrs. Nora Prosser and Mrs. Lucile
       Davidson

1950 Mrs. Nora Prosser and Mrs. Lucile
       Davidson
1951 Mrs. Lucile Davidson and Mrs. Nora
       Prosser
1952 Joan Johnson and Mary Hernando
1953 Joan Johnson and Mary Hernando
1954 Joan Johnson and Geralyn Shepard
1955 Mrs. Mary Prentiss and Barbara
       Talmadge
1956 Muriel Cooper and Joan Warner
1957 Joan Johnson and Geralyn Shepard
1958 Joan Johnson and Geralyn Shepard
1959 Winnie McCoy and Pat Moseley
1960 Winnie McCoy and Pat Moseley
1961 Joan Johnson and Geralyn Shepard
1962 Joan Johnson and Geralyn Shepard
1963 Joan Johnson and Geralyn Shepard
1964 Joan Johnson and Geralyn Shepard
1965 Marilyn Mueller and Lydia Weiberg
1966 Pat Cody and Barbara Grubb
1967 Marilyn Mueller and Lydia Wieberg
1968 Evelyn Houseman and Carol Schneider
1969 Pat Cody and Vicki Smouse
1970 Mrs. Mary A. Prentiss and Lenny Yee
1971 Mrs. Mary A. Prentiss and Pat Cody
1972 Jan Hasse and Doreen Irish
1973 Jan Hasse and Doreen Irish
1974 Hilary Hilton and Charlotte Dial
1975 Hilary Hilton and Karen Dawson
1976 Hilary Hilton and Rita Torres
1977 Jan Hasse and Lori Anderson
1978 Andrea Whitmore and Ashara Moranon
1979 Tina Mochizuki and Rita Agassi
1980 Aschara Moranon and Cherise Dadian

National Public Parks Champions—Mixed Doubles

1961 Geralyn Shepard and Sam Plancia
1962 Joan Johnson and Barry Pelton
1963 Joan Johnson and Gary Russell
1964 Betsy Roberti and Ed Kauder
1965 Mary A. Prentiss and Gary Johnson
1966 Eileen Rahlens and Gary Johnson
1967 Mrs. Karne H. Susman and Rod Susman
1968 Janie Freeman and Sam Plancia
1969 Pat Cody and Mike Baer
1970 Joan Johnson and Charles Pate

National Public Parks Champions—Mixed Doubles *(cont.)*

1971 Suzanne Gray and Ross Helft
1972 Mickie Thomas and John Norgauer
1973 Doreen Irish and Tony Esquire
1974 Hilary Hilton and Mike Duran
1975 Liane Marquez and Larry King
1976 Karen Dawson and Tom Rittenmeir
1977 Andrea Whitmore and Keith Simpson
1978 Andrea Whitmore and Neil Bessent
1979 Hillary Marold and Charles Marold
1980 Pamela Jung and Graham Espley-Jones

National Public Parks Champions—Junior Singles

1948 Oscar Johnson
1949 Allen Cleveland
1950 James Reed
1951 Richard Doss
1952 Robert Jacobs
1953 not held
1954 Alex Olmedo
1955 Forrest Stewart
1956 Richard Leach
1957 Norman Karns
1958 Marcus Carriedo
1959 Marcus Carriedo
1960 Eltinge Brown
1961 Doug Sykes
1962 Joe Huey
1963 Edward Grubb
1964 Brian Cheney
1965 Ron Teeguarden
1966 Maurice Poirier
1967 Dale Fritz
1968 Gualberto Escudero
1969 Dan Lambert
1970 Grant Smith
      Banoo Nunna
1972 Earl Lund
1973 Henri Elkins
1974 James Harper
1975 Mark Johnson
1976 John Steele
1977–80 not held

National Public Parks Champions—Junior Doubles

1961 Rodney Kop and Antonio Sison
1962 Dennis Law and Steve Rosen

1963 Ed Grubb and Robert Eisenberg
1964 Brian Cheney and Erick Baer
1965 Joel Ostroff and John Levin
1966 Rich Westphaln and Maurice Poirier
1967 Jim Logan and Bill Long
1968 Chuck Nachand and Paul Vodak
1969 D. Lambert and P. Lambert
1970 D. Lambert and P. Lambert
1971 Bhanu Murthy and Larry Belinsky
1972 Earl Lund and Tim O'Reilly
1973 Paul Ruben and Chris Smith
1974 Chris Layer and Carlos Hassey
1975 Patrick Tom and Macurio Pascual
1976 Kalavid Moranon and Ron Booth
1977–80 not held

National Public Parks Champions—Boys' 16 Singles

1962 Ron Willens
1963 Jim Rombeau
1964 Brian Parrott
1965 Robert Hill
1966 Mike Tesman
1967 Jim Armstrong
1968 Jeff Cowan
1969 Chris Kane
1970 Nick Saviano
1971 Mike Greenberg
1972 Lloyd Dixon
1973 Piya Moranon
1974 Paul Bernstein
1975 Bill Nardi
1976 Guillermo Stevens
1977–80 not held

National Public Parks Champions—Boys' 16 Doubles

1962 Ron Willens and Rick Reed
1963 Lowell Chatburn and Brad Cornell
1964 Erich Wise and Richard Dauben
1965 Robert Hill and Jim Logan
1966 Jeff Austin and Mike Shires
1967 Jim Armstrong and Richard Ley
1968 Tom McArdle and Paul Novacek
1969 John Bennett and Chris Kane
1970 Steve Hahn and Nick Saviano
1971 Jeff Williams and Brad Rose

1972   Bob Dellar and Bill Bartlett
1973   Macarid Pasual and Pat Nava
1974   Ed Sena and Paul Bernstein
1975   Curt Ensign and Nelson Char
1976   Guillermo Stevens and Juan Ceron
1977–80   not held

National Public Parks Champions—Boys' 14 Singles

1962   Tom Leonard
1963   Richard Bohrnstedt
1964   Christopher Chapin
1965   Steve Derian
1966   Steve Derian
1967   Jim McNairy
1968   Ted Hagey
1969   Michael Nissky
1970   Michael Edles
1971   Alan Winkler
1972   Bela Betyar
1973   Robert Vanthof
1974   Kevin McClinton
1975   Stanley Benoit
1976   Eduardo Arredondo
1977–80   not held

National Public Parks Champions—Boys' 12 Singles

1965   James Hagey
1966   Joe Edles
1967   Michael Nissley
1968   Richard Grant
1969   Piya Moranon
1970   Ron Hightower
1971   Adam Cioth
1972   Eddie Buggs
1973   Stanley Benoit
1974   John Tsumas
1975   Ricky Leach
1976   Jimmy Pugh
1977–80   not held

National Public Parks Champions—Girls' 18 Singles

1948   Julie Sampson
1949   Anita Kanter
1950   Anita Kanter
1951   Mary Ann Eilenberger
1952   Darlene Hard
1953   not held
1954   Lorna Raymond
1955   Karen Hantze
1956   Patricia Cushman
1957   Carol Ann Loop
1958   Judy Minna
1959   Judy Minna
1960   Annette Stoesser
1961   Andria Miller
1962   Penny Myrell
1963   Jean Inez
1964   Barbara Strong
1965   Mary Anna Poiset
1966   Mary Anna Poiset
1967   Jane Richardson
1968   Gloria Pananides
1969   Gale Litton
1970   Rill Culver
1971   Sue Ince
1972   Nancy Parker
1973   Margie Strode
1974   Diane Cronk
1975   Kim McCarthy
1976   Helen Park
1977–80   not held

National Public Parks Champions—Girls' 18 Doubles

1961   Andria Miller and Jane Conrol
1962   Karen Haase and Penny Myrell
1963   Cynthia Raymond and Linda Cushing
1964   Pam Teeguarden and Peggy Michel
1965   Cathy Apple and Stephanie Berger
1966   Sheryl Jorgenson and Cynde Haffner
1967   Debbie Brown and Jane Richardson
1968   Gloria Pananides and Dawn Crossen
1969   Diane Miller and Mary Miller
1970   Kevan Dignam and J. Wright
1971   Nancy Parker and Helen Parker
1972   Robin Kahn and Penny Johnson
1973   Carolyn Tom and Margie Strode
1974   Jeannette Reading and Eve Collins
1975   Aschara Moranon and Julie Filkoff
1976   Aschara Moranon and Hilda Gonzales
1977–80   not held

National Public Parks Champions—Girls' 16 Singles

1962 Sherrie Pruitt
1963 Robyn Berrey
1964 Valerie Ziegenfuss
1965 Diane Driscall
1966 Sharon Guthrie
1967 Janice Metcalf
1968 Christine Cheney
1969 Joy Schwikers
1970 Gloria Thomas
1971 Terry Holladay
1972 Diane Morrison
1973 Patricia Vargas
1974 Cherise Dadian
1975 Valerie Cates
1976 Blair Townsend
1977–80 not held

National Public Parks Champions—Girls' 16 Doubles

1962 Jean Inez and Patti Hogan
1963 Kathy Apple and Robyn Berrey
1964 Valerie Ziegenfuss and Ann Chaboudy
1965 Mary Poiset and Ann Chaboudy
1966 Sharon Guthrie and Pam Austin
1967 Wendy Appleby and Christine Cheney
1968 Molly Tyson and Tracy Macnair
1969 Jill Schwikert and Joy Schwikert
1970 Gloria Thomas and Diane Desfor
1971 Terry Holladay and Susan Hagey
1972 Diane Morrison and Kim Nilsson
1973 Aschara Moranon and Kim Greenhouse
1974 Lisa Albano and Charmaine Dadian
1975 Kimberly Wilson and Shelly Stillman
1976 Christina Ortega and Maria Llamas
1977–80 not held

National Public Parks Champions—Girls' 14 Singles

1962 Kristen Stewart
1963 Patti Hogan
1964 Betty Ann Grubb
1965 Ann Lebedeff
1966 Janet Newberry
1967 Lori Sherbeck
1968 Diane Desfor
1969 Lindsay Morse
1970 Tina Tsumas
1971 Susan Hagey
1972 Trey Lewis
1973 Cherise Dadian
1974 Tracy Austin
1975 Caryn Copeland
1976 Maria Elena Llamas
1977–80 not held

National Public Parks Champions—Girls' 12 Singles

1965 Janet Newberry
1966 Abbe Wise
1967 Gretchen Gelt
1968 Marita Redondo
1969 Kimberly Nilsson
1970 Lea Antonopolis
1971 Judi Jacobi
1972 Tracy Austin
1973 Tracy Austin
1974 Jena Strozier
1975 Amy Olmedo
1976 Andrea Gonzalez
1977–80 not held

National Public Parks Champions—Men's 35 Singles

1969 Alan Schwartz
1970 Alan Schwartz
1971 Melvin Lewis
1972 Melvin Lewis
1973 not held
1974 Bill McClung
1975 Dave Weber
1976 John Noraguer
1977 John Norgauer
1978 Jim Nelson
1979 Steve Wilkinson
1980 Mirceau Morariu

National Public Parks Champions—Men's 35 Doubles

1969 Seymour Greenberg and Alan Schwartz
1970 John Foreman and Alan Schwartz
1971 Melvin Lewis and Larry Ross

1972 Gary Russell and Tom Springer
1973 not held
1974 Charles Garfinkle and Bill McClung
1975 Dave Weber and Harry Taylor
1976 Alan Schwartz and Bob Haung
1977 Dick Horwitz and Jerry Johnson
1978 Bob Huang and Bill Williams
1979 Gary Thorn and Terry McMahon
1980 Charles Morold and Wally Piekarski

National Public Parks Champions—Men Seniors' Singles

1959 Ed di Leone
1960 Ed di Leone
1961 Norman MacDonald
1962 Alex Swetka
1963 Ed di Leone
1964 William Smith
1965 William Lurie
1966 Bob Weinstock
1967 Bob Galloway
1968 Dave Martin
1969 Seymour Greenberg
1970 Bob Thompson
1971 Chris Scott
1972 Al Ruda
1973 Chuck Hubbard
1974 Harry Brown
1975 Mel Lewis
1976 Grant Golden
1977 Harry Brown
1978 Frank Keister
1979 Mel Lewis
1980 Charles Karabell

National Public Parks Champions—Men Seniors' Doubles

1961 Gardnar Mulloy and Homer Shoop
1962 Ed di Leone and Courtney Bock
1963 Courtney Bock and Ed di Leone
1964 Francis Gay and Robert Hill
1965 Courtney Bock and Ed di Leone
1966 Harry Burrus and Bob Weinstock
1967 Bob Galloway and Dave Martin
1968 Bob Galloway and Dave Martin
1969 George Lott and Sam Fields
1970 Dick McFarland and Bob Thompson

1971 Dick McFarland and Bob Thompson
1972 Charles Lass and H. M. Wammack
1973 Harold Becker and Glenn Miller
1974 Vito Grybanskas and Wally Pierkarski
1975 Bill Kuross and Ken Boyum
1976 Seymour Greenberg and Grant Golden
1977 Gardnar Larned and David Muir
1978 Ed Saunders and Gil Mayer
1979 Gardnar Larned and David Muir
1980 John Sahratian and Charles Karabell

National Public Parks Champions—Men's 50 Singles

1975 Ken Boyum
1976 Seymour Greenberg
1977–78 not held
1979 Ken Boyum
1980 Roy McQuown

National Public Parks Champions—Men's 50 Doubles

1975 Al Gross and Bill Maul
1976 Al Valiquet and Steve Morgan
1977–78 not held
1979 Gardnar Larned and David Muir
1980 Roy McQuown and Frank Simmons

National Public Parks Champions—Women Seniors' Singles

1964 Mrs. Mary Arnold Prentiss
1965 not held
1966 Mrs. Merceina Parker
1967 not held
1968 Mrs. Mary Arnold Prentiss
1969 Marilyn Mueller
1970 Joan Johnson
1971 Mrs. Mary Arnold Prentiss
1972 Mrs. Mary Arnold Prentiss
1973 Dee Dolny
1974 Ruth Aucott
1975 Betty Claus
1976 Mary Lou McCaslin
1977 Ada Cowen
1978 Klara Betyar
1979 Laurie King
1980 Winnie McCoy

National Public Parks Champions—Women
Seniors' Doubles

1964 Mrs. Mary Arnold Prentiss and Gertie Irish
1965 not held
1966 Muriel Cooper and Jean Warner
1967 not held
1968 Phyllis Adler and Carol Schneider
1969 Marilyn Mueller and Jane Pratt
1970 Joan Johnson and J. Prentiss
1971 Phyllis Yambrack and Alphonzice
      Edwards
1972 Nora Prosser and Lucille Davidson
1973 Dee Wilden and Corine Barnes
1974 Gwen Mitchel and Dee Dolny
1975 Betty Claus and Polly Hoff
1976 Marilyn Mueller and Mrs. Betty R. Pratt
1977 Joan Killen and Ada Cowen
1978 Winnie McCoy and Susie Sasa
1979 Ellie Peden and Dee Dolny
1980 Laurie King and Jean Richardson

Francisco (Pancho) Segura while at the University of Miami won the National Intercollegiate Championship three years in a row (1943–45). The only other player to do this was M. G. Chace (1893–95) while at Brown and Yale.

NATIONAL INTERCOLLEGIATE CHAMPIONS—
Men's Singles

Year	Winner	School	Year	Winner	School
1883	H. A. Taylor (fall)	Harvard	1900	R. D. Little	Princeton
1883	J. S. Clark (spring)	Harvard	1901	Fred B. Alexander	Princeton
1884	W. P. Knapp	Yale	1902	William J. Clothier	Harvard
1885	W. P. Knapp	Yale	1903	E. B. Dewhurst	U. of Penn.
1886	G. M. Brinley	Trinity	1904	Robert LeRoy	Columbia
1887	P. S. Sears	Harvard	1905	E. B. Dewhurst	U. of Penn.
1888	P. S. Sears	Harvard	1906	Robert LeRoy	Columbia
1889	R. P. Huntington, Jr.	Yale	1907	G. P. Gardner, Jr.	Harvard
1890	F. H. Hovey	Harvard	1908	Nat W. Niles	Harvard
1891	F. H. Hovey	Harvard	1909	W. F. Johnson	U. of Penn.
1892	W. A. Larned	Cornell	1910	R. A. Holden, Jr.	Yale
1893	M. G. Chace	Brown	1911	E. H. Whitney	Harvard
1894	M. G. Chace	Yale	1912	G. M. Church	Princeton
1895	M. G. Chace	Yale	1913	Richard N. Williams II	Harvard
1896	M. D. Whitman	Harvard	1914	G. M. Church	Princeton
1897	S. G. Thomson	Princeton	1915	R. N. Williams II	Harvard
1898	L. E. Ware	Harvard	1916	G. Colket Caner	Harvard
1899	Dwight Davis	Harvard	1917–18	not held	

Year	Winner	School	Year	Winner	School
1919	C. S. Garland	Yale	1950	Herbert Flam	U. of Cal., L.A.
1920	L. M. Banks	Yale	1951	Tony Trabert	Univ. of Cincinnati
1921	Philip Neer	Stanford	1952	Hugh Stewart	U. of So. Cal.
1922	Lucien E. Williams	Yale	1953	Hamilton Richardson	Tulane
1923	Carl H. Fischer	Phila. Osteo.	1954	Hamilton Richardson	Tulane
1924	Wallace Scott	U. of Wash.	1955	Jose Aguero	Tulane
1925	E. G. Chandler	California	1956	Alejandro Olmedo	U. of So. Cal.
1926	E. G. Chandler	California	1957	Barry MacKay	U. of Mich.
1927	Wilmer Allison	Texas	1958	Alejandro Olmedo	U. of So. Cal.
1928	Julius Seligson	Lehigh	1959	Whitney Reed	San Jose State
1929	Berkeley Bell	Texas	1960	Larry Nagler	U. of Cal., L.A.
1930	Clifford Sutter	Tulane	1961	Allen Fox	U. of Cal., L.A.
1931	Keith Gledhill	Stanford	1962	Rafael Osuna	U. of So. Cal.
1932	Clifford Sutter	Tulane	1963	Dennis Ralston	U. of So. Cal.
1933	Jack Tidball	U. of Cal., L.A.	1964	Dennis Ralston	U. of So. Cal.
1934	C. Gene Mako	U. of So. Cal.	1965	Arthur Ashe	U. of Cal., L.A.
1935	Wilbur Hess	Rice Institute	1966	Charles Pasarell	U. of Cal., L.A.
1936	Ernest Sutter	Tulane	1967	Robert Lutz	U. of So. Cal.
1937	Ernest Sutter	Tulane	1968	Stanley Smith	U. of So. Cal.
1938	Frank D. Guernsey	Rice Institute	1969	Joaquin Loyo-Mayo	U. of So. Cal.
1939	Frank D. Guernsey	Rice Institute	1970	Jeff Borowiak	U. of Cal., L.A.
1940	Donald McNeill	Kenyon College	1971	Jim Connors	U. of Cal., L.A.
1941	Joseph R. Hunt	U.S. Naval Acad.	1972	Dick Stockton	Trinity (Tex.) Univ.
1942	Frederick R. Schroeder, Jr.	Stanford	1973	Alex Mayer, Jr.	Stanford
			1974	John Whitlinger	Stanford
1943	Francisco Segura	Univ. of Miami	1975	Bill Martin	U. of Cal., L.A.
1944	Francisco Segura	Univ. of Miami	1976	Bill Scanlon	Trinity (Tex.) Univ.
1945	Francisco Segura	Univ. of Miami	1977	Matt Mitchell	Stanford
1946	Robert Falkenburg	U. of So. Cal.	1978	John McEnroe	Stanford
1947	Gardnar Larned	Wm. & Mary	1979	Kevin Curren	U. of Texas
1948	Harry E. Likas	U. San Francisco	1980	Robert Van't Hof	U. of So. Cal.
1949	Jack Tuero	Tulane			

NATIONAL INTERCOLLEGIATE CHAMPIONS—
Men's Doubles

Year	Winner	School	Year	Winner	School
1883	J. S. Clark and H. A. Taylor (spring)	Harvard	1888	V. G. Hall and O. S. Campbell	Columbia
1883	H. A. Taylor and R. E. Presbrey (fall)	Harvard	1889	O. S. Campbell and A. E. Wright	Columbia
1884	W. P. Knapp and W. V. S. Thorne	Yale	1890	Q. A. Shaw, Jr. and S. T. Chase	Harvard
1885	W. P. Knapp and A. L. Shipman	Yale	1891	F. H. Hovey and R. D. Wrenn	Harvard
1886	W. P. Knapp and W. L. Thacher	Yale	1892	R. D. Wrenn and F. B. Winslow	Harvard
1887	P. S. Sears and Q. A. Shaw, Jr.	Harvard	1893	M. G. Chace and C. R. Budlong	Brown

Jimmy Connors, a left-handed star for the UCLA team, was the intercollegiate singles champion in 1971 and then won the first of his U.S. Open titles in 1974.

NATIONAL INTERCOLLEGIATE CHAMPIONS—MEN'S DOUBLES *(cont.)*

Year	Winner	School	Year	Winner	School
1894	M. G. Chace and A. E. Foote	Yale	1923	L. N. White and Louis Thalheimer	Texas
1895	M. G. Chace and A. E. Foote	Yale	1924	L. N. White and Louis Thalheimer	Texas
1896	L. E. Ware and W. M. Scudder	Harvard	1925	Gervais Hills and Gerald Stratford	California
1897	L. E. Ware and M. D. Whitman	Harvard	1926	E. G. Chandler and Tom Stow	California
1898	L. E. Ware and M. D. Whitman	Harvard	1927	John Van Ryn and Kenneth Appel	Princeton
1899	Holcombe Ward and D. F. Davis	Harvard	1928	Ralph McElvenny and Alan Herrington	Stanford
1900	F. B. Alexander and R. D. Little	Princeton	1929	Benjamin Gorchakoff and Arthur Kussman	Occidental
1901	H. A. Plummer and S. L. Russell	Yale	1930	Dolf Muehleisen and Robert Muench	California
1902	W. J. Clothier and E. W. Leonard	Harvard	1931	Bruce Barnes and Karl Kamrath	U. of Texas
1903	B. Colston and E. Clapp	Yale	1932	Keith Gledhill and Joseph Coughlin	Stanford
1904	K. H. Behr and G. Bodman	Yale	1933	Joseph Coughlin and Sam Lee	Stanford
1905	E. B. Dewhurst and H. B. Register	Pennsylvania	1934	C. Gene Mako and G. Philip Castlen	U. of So. Cal.
1906	E. B. Wells and A. Spaulding	Yale	1935	Paul Newton and Richard Bennett	California
1907	N. W. Niles and A. S. Dabney	Harvard	1936	W. Bennet Dey and Wm. Seward	Stanford
1908	H. M. Tilden and A. Thayer	Pennsylvania	1937	Richard Bennett and Paul Newton	California
1909	W. F. Johnson and A. Thayer	Pennsylvania	1938	Joseph R. Hunt and Lewis Wetherell	U. of So. Cal.
1910	D. Mathey and B. N. Dell	Princeton	1939	Douglas Imhoff and Robert Peacock	California
1911	D. Mathey and C. T. Butler	Princeton	1940	Laurence A. Dee and James Wade	Stanford
1912	G. M. Church and W. H. Mace	Princeton	1941	Charles E. Olewine and Charles H. Mattmann	U. of So. Cal.
1913	W. M. Washburn and J. J. Armstrong	Harvard	1942	Frederick R. Schroeder, Jr. and Laurence Dee	Stanford
1914	R. N. Williams II and Richard Harte	Harvard	1943	John Hickmann and Walter Driver	Univ. of Texas
1915	R. N. Williams II and Richard Harte	Harvard	1944	John Hickman and Felix Kelley	Univ. of Texas
1916	G. C. Caner and Richard Harte	Harvard	1945	Francisco (Pancho) Segura and Tom Burke	Univ. of Miami
1917–18	not held		1946	Robert Falkenburg and Tom Falkenburg	U. of So. Cal.
1919	C. S. Garland and K. N. Hawkes	Yale	1947	Sam Match and Bobby Curtis	Rice Institute
1920	A. Wilder and L. Wiley	Yale	1948	Fred Kovaleski and Bernard Bartzen	Wm. & Mary
1921	J. B. Fenno, Jr. and E. W. Feibleman	Harvard	1949	Jim Brink and Fred Fisher	U. of Wash.
1922	James Davies and Philip Neer	Stanford			

NATIONAL INTERCOLLEGIATE CHAMPIONS—MEN'S DOUBLES *(cont.)*

Year	Winner	School	Year	Winner	School
1950	Herbert Flam and Gene Garrett	U. of Cal., L.A.	1966	Ian Crookenden and Charles Pasarell	U. of Cal., L.A.
1951	Earl Cochell and Hugh Stewart	U. of So. Cal.	1967	Robert Lutz and Stan Smith	U. of So. Cal.
1952	Hugh Ditzler and Clifton Mayne	Univ. of Calif.	1968	Robert Lutz and Stan Smith	U. of So. Cal.
1953	Lawrence Huebner and Robert Perry	U. of Cal., L.A.	1969	Joaquin Loyo-Mayo and Marcella Lara	U. of So. Cal.
1954	Ronald Livingston and Robert Perry	U. of Cal., L.A.	1970	Pat Cramer and Luis Garcia	U. of Miami
1955	Francisco Contreras and Joaquin Reyes	Univ. So. Calif.	1971	Jeff Borowiak and Haroon Rahim	U. of Cal., L.A.
1956	Francisco Contreras and Alejandro Olmedo	Univ. So. Calif.	1972	Alex Mayer, Jr., and Roscoe Tanner	Stanford
1957	Crawford Henry and Ronald Holmberg	Tulane	1973	Alex Mayer, Jr., and Jim Delaney	Stanford
1958	Edward Atkinson and Alejandro Olmedo	Univ. So. Calif.	1974	John Whitlinger and Jim Delaney	Stanford
1959	Ronald Holmberg and Crawford Henry	Tulane	1975	Bruce Manson and Butch Walts	U. of So. Cal.
1960	Larry Nagler and Allen Fox	U. of Cal., L.A.	1976	Peter Fleming and Ferdi Taygan	U. of Cal., L.A.
1961	Rafael Osuna and Ramsey Earnhart	U. of So. Cal.	1977	Chris Lewis and Bruce Manson	U. of So. Cal.
1962	Rafael Osuna and Ramsey Earnhart	U. of So. Cal.	1978	John Austin and Bruce Nichols	U. of Cal., L.A.
1963	Rafael Osuna and Dennis Ralston	U. of So. Cal.	1979	Erick Iskersky and Ben McCowan	Trinity (Tex.)
1964	William Bond and Dennis Ralston	U. of So. Cal.	1980	Mel Purcell and Rodney Harmon	Tennessee
1965	Arthur Ashe and Ian Crookenden	U. of Cal., L.A.			

Colleges Winning Intercollegiate Championships—Men's Singles

Brown, 1893
Columbia, 1904, 1906
Cornell, 1892
Harvard, 1883 (Spring), 1883 (Fall), 1887, 1888, 1890, 1891, 1896, 1898, 1899, 1902, 1907, 1908, 1911, 1913, 1915, 1916
Kenyon, 1940
Lehigh, 1928
Philadelphia College of Osteopathy, 1923
Princeton, 1897, 1900, 1901, 1912, 1914
Rice Institute, 1935, 1938, 1939
San Jose State College, 1959
Stanford, 1921, 1931, 1942, 1973, 1974, 1977, 1978
Texas, 1927, 1929, 1979
Trinity (Conn.), 1886
Trinity (Tex.), 1972, 1976
Tulane, 1930, 1932, 1936, 1937, 1949, 1953–1955
University of California, 1925, 1926
University of California (L.A.), 1933, 1950, 1960, 1961, 1965, 1966, 1970, 1971, 1975
University of Cincinnati, 1951
University of Miami, 1943–1945
University of Michigan, 1951
University of Pennsylvania, 1903, 1905, 1909
University of San Francisco, 1948
University of Southern California, 1934, 1946, 1952, 1956, 1958, 1962–1964, 1967–1969, 1980
University of Washington, 1924
U.S. Naval Academy, 1941
William & Mary, 1947
Yale, 1884, 1885, 1889, 1894, 1895, 1910, 1919, 1920, 1922

Total Individual Championships by Colleges (1883 through 1980)

Harvard—16; Univ. of Southern California—12; Yale and Univ. of California, Los Angeles—9 each; Tulane—8; Stanford—7; Princeton—5; Rice, Texas, Miami (Fla.) and Pennsylvania—3 each; Columbia and Trinity (Tex.)—2; Brown, Cornell, Kenyon, Lehigh, Philadelphia College of Os-

teopathy, Trinity (Conn.), Cincinnati, Michigan, San Francisco, Navy and William & Mary—1 each.

NCAA Team Champions—Division I

1946	U. of So. California
1947	William and Mary
1948	William and Mary
1949	U. of San Francisco
1950	U. of Cal. (L.A.)
1951	U. of So. California
1952	U. of Cal. (L.A.)
1953	U. of Cal. (L.A.)
1954	U. of Cal. (L.A.)
1955	U. of So. California
1956	U. of Cal. (L.A.)
1957	Michigan
1958	U. of So. California
1959	Tulane and Notre Dame (tie)
1960	U. of Cal. (L.A.)
1961	U. of Cal. (L.A.)
1962	U. of So. California
1963	U. of So. California
1964	U. of So. California
1965	U. of Cal. (L.A.)
1966	U. of So. California
1967	U. of So. California
1968	U. of So. California
1969	U. of So. California
1970	U. of Cal. (L.A.)
1971	U. of Cal. (L.A.)
1972	Trinity (Tex.)
1973	Stanford
1974	Stanford
1975	U. of Cal. (L.A.)
1976	U. of Cal. (L.A.) and U. of So. California (tie)
1977	Stanford
1978	Stanford
1979	U. of Cal. (L.A.)
1980	Stanford

Team Championships: U. of California, Los Angeles—13; University of Southern California—12; Stanford—5; William and Mary—2; University of San Francisco, University of Michigan, Tulane, Notre Dame and Trinity (Tex.) University—1 each.

WINNERS OF BOTH INTERCOLLEGIATE CHAMPIONSHIPS AND NATIONAL SINGLES (Men's Singles)

Winner	Intercollegiate	National
Fred H. Hovey	1890, 1891	1895
William A. Larned	1892	1901, 1902, 1907–1911
Malcolm D. Whitman	1896	1898, 1899, 1900
William J. Clothier	1902	1906
Richard N. Williams II	1913, 1915	1914, 1916
Wilmer L. Allison	1927	1935
W. Donald McNeill	1940	1940
Joseph R. Hunt	1941	1943
Frederick R. Schroeder, Jr.	1942	1942
Tony Trabert	1951	1953, 1955
Rafael Osuna	1962	1963
Arthur Ashe	1965	1966, 1968*
Stanley Smith	1968	1969, 1971*
Jim Connors	1971	1974,* 1976,* 1978*
John McEnroe	1978	1979,* 1980*

*U. S. Open.

One of many Intercollegiate Champions who went on to greater heights in both tennis and learning was Rhodes scholar Hamilton Richardson.

USTA Women's Intercollegiate Team Champions

1968	Trinity (Tex.) Univ.
1969	Trinity (Tex.) Univ.
1970	Odessa (Tex.) Coll.
1971	Arizona State U.
1972	Arizona State U.
1973	Trinity (Tex.) Univ.
1974	Arizona State U.
1975	Trinity (Tex.) Univ.
1976	Trinity (Tex.) Univ.
1977	So. California
1978	So. California
1979	event discontinued

AIAW National Champions—Singles

1977	Lindsay Morse	U. of Cal., Irvine
1978	Jeanne DuVall	U. of Cal., L.A.
1979	Kathy Jordan	Stanford
1980	Wendy White	Rollins

AIAW National Champions—Doubles

1977	Sue Hagey and Diane Morrison	Stanford
1978	Kathy Jordan and Barbara Jordan	Stanford
1979	Kathy Jordan and Alycia Moulton	Stanford
1980	Trey Lewis and Anne White	U. of So. California

AIAW Team Champions—Large College

1977	U. of So. California
1978	Stanford
1979	U. of So. California
1980	U. of Cal., L.A.

AIAW Team Champions—Small College

1977	U. of Tenn. (Chattanooga) and Calif. St. (Bakersfield), tie.
1978	U. of Tenn. (Chattanooga)
1979	U. of Tenn. (Chattanooga)
1980	Div. II—Calif. Poly (Pomona)
	Div. III—U. of Calif., Davis

USTA Women's Collegiate Champions—Singles

1958	Darlene R. Hard	Pomona
1959	Donna Floyd	William & Mary
1960	Linda Vail	Oakland City College
1961	Tory Ann Fretz	Occidental
1962	Roberta Alison	U. of Alabama
1963	Roberta Alison	U. of Alabama
1964	Jane Albert	Stanford
1965	Mimi Henreid	UCLA
1966	Cecilia Martinez	San Francisco State
1967	Patsy Rippy	Odessa Junior College
1968	Emilie Burrer	Trinity (Tex.) University
1969	Emilie Burrer	Trinity (Tex.) University
1970	Laura DuPont	North Carolina
1971	Pam Richmond	Arizona State
1972	Janice Metcalf	Redlands Univ.
1973	Janice Metcalf	Redlands Univ.
1974	Carrie Meyer	Marymount College
1975	Stephanie Tolleson	Trinity (Tex.) Univ.
1976	Barbara Hallquist	U. of So. California
1977	Barbara Hallquist	U. of So. California
1978	Stacy Margolin	U. of So. California
1979	event discontinued	

USTA Women's Collegiate Champions—Doubles

1958	Sue Metzger and	St. Mary's Notre Dame
	Erika Puetz	Webster
1959	Joyce Pniewski and	Mich. State Univ.
	Phyllis Saganski	Mich. State Univ.
1960	Susan Butt and	Univ. of British Columbia
	Linda Vail	Oakland City College
1961	Tory Ann Fretz and	Occidental College
	Mary Sherar	Yakima Valley Jr. College
1962	Linda Yeomans and	Stanford
	Carol Hanks	Stanford
1963	Roberta Alison and	Univ. of Alabama
	Justina Bricka	Washington (Mo.) Univ.
1964	Connie Jaster and	
	Carol Loop	California State at Los Angeles
1965	Nancy Falkenberg and	
	Cynthia Goeltz	Mary Baldwin College
1966	Yale Stockwell and	
	Libby Weiss	U. of So. California
1967	Jane Albert and	
	Julie Anthony	Stanford
1968	Emilie Burrer and	
	Becky Vest	Trinity (Tex.) University
1969	Emilie Burrer and	
	Becky Vest	Trinity (Tex.) University
1970	Pam Farmer and	
	Connie Capozzi	Odessa Junior College
1971	Pam Richmond and	
	Peggy Michel	Arizona State
1972	Peggy Michel and	
	Pam Richmond	Arizona State Univ.
1973	Cathy Beene and	
	Linda Rupert	Lamar
1974	Ann Lebedeff and	
	Karen Reinke	San Diego State
1975	JoAnne Russell and	
	Donna Stockton	Trinity Univ.
1976	Susan Hagey and	
	Diane Morrison	Stanford
1977	Jodi Applebaum and	
	Terry Salganik	U. of So. California
1978	Sherry Acker and	
	Judy Acker	U. of Florida
1979	event discontinued	

USTA INTERSCHOLASTIC CHAMPIONS—BOYS' SINGLES

Year	Player	School
1891	Robert D. Wrenn	Cambridge (Mass.) Latin
1892	M.G. Chace	Providence (R.I.) University Grammar
1893	C. R. Budlong	Providence (R.I.) High
1894	W. G. Parker	Tutor Schl., New York
1895	Leo F. Ware	Roxbury (Mass.) Latin
1896	Reginald Fincke	Hotchkiss, Lakeville, Conn.
1897	Reginald Fincke	Hotchkiss, Lakeville, Conn.
1898	Beals C. Wright	Hopkinson, Boston
1899	Beals C. Wright	Hopkinson, Boston
1900	Beals C. Wright	Hopkinson, Boston
1901	E. P. Larned	Lawrenceville (N.J.) Schl.
1902	H. H. Whitman	Nobles, Boston
1903	Karl H. Behr	Lawrenceville (N.J.) Schl.
1904	N. W. Niles	Boston Latin
1905	N. W. Niles	Boston Latin
1906	J. A. Ross	Hyde Park High, Chicago
1907	William F. Johnson	Haverford (Pa.) Schl.
1908	Dean Mathey	Pingry Schl.
1909	Maurice E. McLaughlin	San Francisco High
1910	E. H. Whitney	Stone's Schl., Boston
1911	George M. Church	Irving Schl.
1912	C. B. Herd	Exeter Acad.
1913	G. C. Caner	St. Mark's
1914	Leonard Beekman	Pawling (N.Y.) Schl.
1915	H. A. Throckmorton	Woodridge High
1916–22	not played	
1923	John F. W. Whitbeck	Loomis Schl.
1924	Horace Orser	Stuyvesant, New York
1925–35	not held	
1936	Robert A. Low	Choate, Wallingford, Conn.
1937	William E. Gillespie	Scarborough Schl.
1938	John A. Kramer	Scarborough Schl.
1939	Charles E. Olewine	Santa Monica (Calif.) High
1940	Robert D. Carothers, Jr.	Coronado (Calif.) High
1941	E. Victor Seixas, Jr.	Wm. Penn Charter
1942	Robert Falkenburg	Fairfax High, Los Angeles
1943	Charles W. Oliver	Perth Amboy (N.J.) High
1944	Bernard Bartzen	San Angelo (Tex.) High
1945	Herbert Flam	Beverly Hills (Calif.) High
1946	High Sewart	So. Pasadena (Calif.) High
1947	Herbert Behrens	Ft. Lauderdale (Fla.) High
1948	G. A. Bogley	Landon Schl., Chevy Chase, Md.
1949	Keston Deimling	Oak Park (Ill.) High
1950	Hamilton Richardson	University High, Baton Rouge, La.
1951	Herbert Browne	Dreher High, Columbia, S.C.
1952	Edward Rubinoff	Miami Beach (Fla.) High
1953	Mike Green	Miami Beach (Fla.) High
1954	Gregory Grant	So. Pasadena (Calif.) High
1955	Crawford Henry	Grady High, Atlanta, Ga.
1956	C. E. Sledge, Jr.	Highland Park (Tex.) High
1957	Earl Buchholz, Jr.	Burroughs High, St. Louis, Mo.
1958	Raymond Senkowski	Hamtramck (Mich.) High
1959	William Lenoir	Tucson (Ariz.) High
1960	William Lenoir	Tucson (Ariz.) High
1961	Arthur Ashe	Sumner High, St. Louis, Mo.
1962	Jackie Cooper	Xavier High, Louisville, Ky.

USTA INTERSCHOLASTIC CHAMPIONS—BOYS' SINGLES *(cont.)*

Year	Player	School
1963	Mike Belkin	No. Miami Beach (Fla.) High
1964	Bob Goeltz	Landon Schl., Bethesda, Md.
1965	Bob Goeltz	Landon Schl., Bethesda, Md.
1966	Bob Goeltz	Landon Schl., Bethesda, Md.
1967	Zan Guerry	Baylor Schl., Chattanooga, Tenn.
1968	Charles Owen	Tuscaloosa (Ala.) High
1969	Fred McNair	Landon Schl., Bethesda, Md.
1970	Harold Solomon	Springbrook (Md.) High
1971	John Whitlinger	Shattuck High, Neenah, Wisc.
1972	Bill Matyastik	University High, Baton Rouge, La.
1973	David Parker	Galesburg (Ill.) High
1974	Chris Delaney	Georgetown Prep, Md.
1975	Pem Guerry	Baylor Schl., Chattanooga, Tenn.
1976	Jim Hodges	Landon Schl., Bethesda, Md.
1977	Jay Lapidus	Lawrenceville (N.J.) Schl.
1978	Jeff Turpin	St. Mark's High, Dallas, Tex.
1979	Mike DePalmer	Bradenton (Fla.) High
1980	Mike DePalmer	Bradenton (Fla.) High

USTA INTERSCHOLASTIC CHAMPIONS—GIRLS' SINGLES

Year	Player	School
1968	Linda Tuero	St. Martin's, Metaire, La.
1969	Connie Capozzi	Hillsdale Schl., Ohio
1970–77	not held	
1978	Mary Lou Piatek	Whiting (Ind.) High
1979	Connie Yowell	Southboro (Mass.) High
1980	Beverly Bowes	Deerfield (Ill.) High

USTA Interscholastic Champions—Boys' Doubles

1936	Robert A. Low and Henry H. Daniels
1937	M. C. Hooper and Bob Patterson
1938	Don Buffington and Wm. Gillespie
1939	Bill McMurry and Carl Mitchell
1940	E. Victor Seixas, Jr. and William T. Vogt
1941	Blair Hawley and John Moses
1942	Robert Falkenburg and Thomas Falkenburg
1943	Macdonald Mathey and Dean W. Mathey
1944	Macdonald Mathey and Dean W. Mathey
1945	F. Burton Smith and Dean W. Mathey
1946	Macdonald Mathey and Dean W. Mathey
1947	Herbert Behrens and George King
1948	Gilbert A. Bogley and Jack Yates
1949	Charles Atherton and Edward Dailey
1950	Gilmore Rothrock and Roger Young
1951	Tim Coss and Ted Rogers
1952	Gerald Moss and Edward Rubinoff
1953	David Harum and Edward White
1954	Jeffrey Arnold and Robert Macy
1955	Robert Macy and John Skogstad
1956	Richard Ogden and Edward Simmons
1957	Gerald Dubie and Raymond Senkowski
1958	Frank Froehling III and John Karabasz
1959	Frank Froehling III and John Karabasz
1960	William Lenoir and Hal Lowe
1961	Jackie Cooper and Martin Schad
1962	Jackie Cooper and Martin Schad
1963	Linn Foss and Richard Dell
1964	Bob Goeltz and Richard Dell
1965	Bob Goeltz and Richard Dell
1966	Mac Claflin and Bill Monan
1967	Zan Guerry and Tony Oritz
1968	Mac Claflin and Bill Colson
1969	Roscoe Tanner and David Dick

1970 Joe Garcia and David Dick
1971 William Brock and Hunt Harris
1972 David Dick and Buzz Willett
1973 Chris Delaney and Tim Delaney
1974 Jim Hodges and Tim Jenkins
1975 Pem Guerry and Wesley Cash
1976 Jim Hodges and Dek Potts
1977 Andy Andrews and Lever Stewart
1978 Jeff Turpin and Brad Stoffel
1979 Dan McLaughlin and Todd Ryska
1980 Pat Mehaffy and Mike Smith

USTA Interscholastic Champions—Girls' Doubles

1968 Patti Miller and Kathy Dombos
1969 Karen Corter and Alice DeRochemont
1970–77 not held
1978 Laura Garner and Sheri Slobin
1979 Debbie Robb and Linley Tanner
1980 Beverly Bowes and Barbara Bramlett

Virginia Slims—Finals

1972 (Boca Raton, Fla.)—(Sf)—Chris Evert def. Billie Jean King, 6-4, 6-2; Kerry Melville Reid def. Francoise Durr, 6-2, 6-3. (F)—Evert def. Melville Reid, 7-5, 7-4.
1973 (Boca Raton, Fla.)—(Sf)—Nancy Richey def. Francoise Durr, 6-2, 6-1; Chris Evert def. Kerry Melville Reid, 6-1, 6-2. (F)—Evert def. Richey, 6-3, 6-3.
1974 (Los Angeles)—(Sf)—Chris Evert def. Virginia Wade, 6-4, 6-2; Evonne Goolagong def. Billie Jean King, 6-2, 4-6, 6-3. (F)—Goolagong def. Evert, 6-3, 6-4.
1975 (Los Angeles)—(F)—Chris Evert def. Martina Navratilova, 6-4, 6-2. (3rd)—Virginia Wade def. Evonne Goolagong, 8-5.
1976 (Los Angeles)—(F)—Evonne Goolagong def. Chris Evert, 6-3, 5-7, 6-3. (3rd)—Rosemary Casals def. Martina Navratilova, 8-5.
1977 (New York)—(F)—Chris Evert def. Sue Barker, 2-6, 6-1, 6-1. (3rd)—Martina Navratilova def. Rosemary Casals, 8-5.
1978 (Oakland, Calif.)—(F)—Martina Navratilova def. Evonne Goolagong Cawley, 7-6, 6-4. (3rd)—Wendy Turnbull def. Rosemary Casals, 7-6, 6-3.

Avon Championships—Finals

1979 (New York)—(F)—Martina Navratilova def. Tracy Austin, 6-3, 3-6, 6-2. (3rd)—Sue Barker def. Dianne Fromholtz, 6-2, 6-2. (D/F)—Françoise Durr and Betty Stove def. Steve Barker and Ann Kiyomura, 7-6, 7-6.
1980 (New York)—(F)—Tracy Austin def. Martina Navratilova, 6-2, 2-6, 6-2. (3rd)—Evonne Goolagong Cawley def. Billie Jean King, default. (D/F)—Billie Jean King and Martina Navratilova def. Wendy Turnbull and Rosemary Casals, 6-3, 4-6, 6-3.

World Championship of Tennis—Finals (all Finals at Dallas)

1971 (Sf)—Rod Laver def. Arthur Ashe, 6-3, 1-6, 6-3, 6-3; Ken Rosewall def. Tom Okker, 6-3, 6-3, 6-1. (F)—Rosewall def. Laver, 6-4, 1-6, 7-6, 7-6.
1972 (Sf)—Rod Laver def. Marty Riessen, 4-6, 4-6, 6-1, 6-2, 6-0; Ken Rosewall def. Arthur Ashe, 6-4, 6-3, 7-6. (F)—Rosewall def. Laver, 4-6, 6-0, 6-3, 6-7, 7-6. (3rd)—Ashe def. Riessen, 6-3, 6-1.
1973 (Sf)—Stan Smith def. Rod Laver, 4-6, 6-4, 7-6, 7-5; Arthur Ashe def. Ken Rosewall, 6-4, 6-2, 5-7, 1-6, 6-2. (F)—Smith def. Ashe, 6-3, 6-3, 4-6, 6-4. (3rd)—Rosewall def. Laver, 6-3, 6-2.
1974 (Sf)—John Newcombe def. Stan Smith, 6-1, 3-6, 7-6, 6-2; Bjorn Borg def. Jan Kodes, 4-6, 6-4, 6-3, 6-2. (F)—Newcombe def. Borg, 4-6, 6-3, 6-3, 6-2. (3rd)—Smith def. Kodes, 6-4, 7-6.
1975 (Sf)—Arthur Ashe def. John Alexander, 3-6, 6-1, 6-3, 6-4; Bjorn Borg def. Rod Laver, 7-6, 3-6, 5-7, 7-6, 6-2. (F)—Ashe def. Borg, 3-6, 6-4, 6-4, 6-0. (3rd)—Laver def. Alexander, 6-4, 6-2.
1976 (Sf)—Bjorn Borg def. Harold Solomon, 7-5, 6-0, 6-3; Guillermo Vilas def. Dick Stockton, 7-5, 6-4, 6-1. (F)—Borg def. Vilas, 1-6, 6-1, 7-5, 6-1. (3rd)—Solomon def. Stockton, 6-7, 6-3, 6-2.
1977 (Sf)—Jimmy Connors def. Eddie Dibbs, 6-4, 7-5, 6-1; Dick Stockton def. Vitas Gerulaitis, 7-6, 3-6, 6-7, 6-3, 6-3. (F)—Connors def. Stockton, 6-7, 6-1, 6-4, 6-3. (3rd)—Dibbs def. Gerulaitis, 7-6, (ret).
1978 (Sf)—Vitas Gerulaitis def. Bjorn Borg, default; Eddie Dibbs def. Corrado Barazzutti, 6-2, 7-6, 6-4. (F)—Gerulaitis def. Dibbs, 6-3, 6-2, 6-1. (3rd)—Barazzutti def. Borg, default.

World Championship of Tennis—Finals *(cont.)*

1979 (Sf)—John McEnroe def. Jimmy Connors, 6-1, 6-4, 6-4; Bjorn Borg def. Vitas Gerulaitis, 7-5, 7-6, 2-6, 6-2. (F)—McEnroe def. Borg, 7-5, 4-6, 6-2, 7-6.

1980 (Sf)—John McEnroe def. Johan Kriek, 6-4, 4-6, 7-6, 6-3; Jimmy Connors def. Ivan Lendl, 6-4, 7-5, 6-3. (F)—Connors def. McEnroe, 2-6, 7-6, 6-1, 6-2. (D/F)—Peter McNamara and Paul McNamee def. Butch Walts and Andy Pattison, 6-4, 6-4, 7-6.

MAJOR INTERNATIONAL CHAMPIONSHIPS

All-England Championships (Wimbledon Championships)

The following record indicates the final match by which the championship was decided. From 1877 to 1921 the men's singles was decided on a challenge-round system, the previous year's winner standing out until a winner of the so-called All Comers' event qualified to challenge. The same system applied in the women's singles and the men's doubles from 1886 to 1921. It never applied in the women's and mixed doubles. In those years the presence of the previous year's winner in the last match means that the title was decided in a challenge round.

Lew Hoad displays the "prize" of tennis, the Wimbledon Cup, which he won in both 1956 and 1957.

The Championships were staged at the All-England Club, Worple Road, Wimbledon, London, from 1877 to 1921, when the club moved to Church Road, Wimbledon. Partial seeding by placing overseas competitors was introduced in 1924, full merit seeding in 1927. Wimbledon became Open in 1968.

ALL-ENGLAND CHAMPIONSHIPS—MEN'S SINGLES

Year	Winner	Runner-Up	Score
1877	Spencer W. Gore	W. C. Marshall	6–1, 6–2, 6–4
1878	P. F. Hadow	Spencer W. Gore	7–5, 6–1, 9–7
1879	J. T. Hartley	V. "St. Leger" Gould	6–2, 6–4, 6–2
1880	J. T. Hartley	H. F. Lawford	6–0, 6–2, 2–6, 6–3
1881	William Renshaw	J. T. Hartley	6–0, 6–2, 6–1
1882	William Renshaw	Ernest Renshaw	6–1, 2–6, 4–6, 6–2, 6–2
1883	William Renshaw	Ernest Renshaw	2–6, 6–3, 6–3, 4–6, 6–3
1884	William Renshaw	H. F. Lawford	6–0, 6–4, 9–7
1885	William Renshaw	H. F. Lawford	7–5, 6–2, 4–6, 7–5
1886	William Renshaw	H. F. Lawford	6–0, 5–7, 6–3, 6–4
1887	H. F. Lawford	Ernest Renshaw	1–6, 6–3, 3–6, 6–4, 6–4
1888	Ernest Renshaw	H. F. Lawford	6–3, 7–5, 6–0
1889	William Renshaw	Ernest Renshaw	6–4, 6–1, 3–6, 6–0
1890	W. J. Hamilton	William Renshaw	6–8, 6–2, 3–6, 6–1, 6–1

Year	Winner	Runner-Up	Score
1891	Wilfred Baddeley	Joshua Pim	6–4, 1–6, 7–5, 6–0
1892	Wilfred Baddeley	Joshua Pim	4–6, 6–3, 6–3, 6–2
1893	Joshua Pim	Wilfred Baddeley	3–6, 6–1, 6–3, 6–2
1894	Joshua Pim	Wilfred Baddeley	10–8, 6–2, 8–6
1895	Wilfred Baddeley	Wilberforce V. Eaves	4–6, 2–6, 8–6, 6–2, 6–3
1896	H. S. Mahoney	Wilfred Baddeley	6–2, 6–8, 5–7, 8–6, 6–3
1897	Reggie F. Doherty	H. S. Mahoney	6–4, 6–4, 6–3
1898	Reggie F. Doherty	H. Laurie Doherty	6–3, 6–3, 2–6, 5–7, 6–1
1899	Reggie F. Doherty	Arthur W. Gore	1–6, 4–6, 6–2, 6–3, 6–3
1900	Reggie F. Doherty	Sidney H. Smith	6–8, 6–3, 6–1, 6–2
1901	Arthur W. Gore	Reggie F. Doherty	4–6, 7–5, 6–4, 6–4
1902	H. Laurie Doherty	Arthur W. Gore	6–4, 6–3, 3–6, 6–0
1903	H. Laurie Doherty	Frank L. Riseley	7–5, 6–3, 6–0
1904	H. Laurie Doherty	Frank L. Riseley	6–1, 7–5, 8–6
1905	H. Laurie Doherty	Norman E. Brookes	8–6, 6–2, 6–4
1906	H. Laurie Doherty	Frank L. Riseley	6–4, 4–6, 6–2, 6–3
1907	Norman E. Brookes	Arthur W. Gore	6–4, 6–2, 6–2
1908	Arthur W. Gore	H. Roper Barrett	6–3, 6–2, 4–6, 3–6, 6–4
1909	Arthur W. Gore	M. G. J. Ritchie	6–8, 1–6, 6–2, 6–2, 6–2
1910	Anthony F. Wilding	Arthur W. Gore	6–4, 7–5, 4–6, 6–2
1911	Anthony F. Wilding	H. Roper Barrett	6–4, 4–6, 2–6, 6–2 def.
1912	Anthony F. Wilding	Arthur W. Gore	6–4, 6–4, 4–6, 6–4
1913	Anthony F. Wilding	Maurice E. McLoughlin	8–6, 6–3, 10–8
1914	Norman E. Brookes	Anthony F. Wilding	6–4, 6–4, 7–5
1915–18	not held		
1919	Gerald L. Patterson	Norman E. Brookes	6–3, 7–5, 6–2
1920	William T. Tilden II	Gerald L. Patterson	2–6, 6–3, 6–2, 6–4
1921	William T. Tilden II	Brian I. C. Norton	4–6, 2–6, 6–1, 6–0, 7–5
1922	Gerald L. Patterson	Randolph Lycett	6–3, 6–4, 6–2
1923	William M. Johnston	Francis T. Hunter	6–0, 6–3, 6–1
1924	Jean Borotra	Jean René Lacoste	6–1, 3–6, 6–1, 3–6, 6–4
1925	Jean René Lacoste	Jean Borotra	6–3, 6–3, 4–6, 8–6
1926	Jean Borotra	Howard Kinsey	8–6, 6–1, 6–3
1927	Henri Cochet	Jean Borotra	4–6, 4–6, 6–3, 6–4, 7–5
1928	Jean René Lacoste	Henri Cochet	6–1, 4–6, 6–4, 6–2
1929	Henri Cochet	Jean Borotra	6–4, 6–3, 6–4
1930	William T. Tilden II	Wilmer Allison	6–3, 9–7, 6–4
1931	Sidney Wood	Frank X. Shields	default
1932	Ellsworth Vines	Wilfred Austin	6–4, 6–2, 6–0
1933	Jack Crawford	Ellsworth Vines	4–6, 11–9, 6–2, 2–6, 6–4
1934	Fred J. Perry	Jack Crawford	6–3, 6–0, 7–5
1935	Fred J. Perry	Gottfried von Cramm	6–2, 6–4, 6–4
1936	Fred J. Perry	Gottfried von Cramm	6–1, 6–1, 6–0
1937	Donald Budge	Gottfried von Cramm	6–3, 6–4, 6–2
1938	Donald Budge	Wilfred Austin	6–1, 6–0, 6–3
1939	Bobby Riggs	Elwood Cooke	2–6, 8–6, 3–6, 6–3, 6–2
1940–45	not held		
1946	Yvon Petra	Geoff E. Brown	6–2, 6–4, 7–9, 5–7, 6–4
1947	Jack Kramer	Tom P. Brown	6–1, 6–3, 6–2
1948	Bob Falkenburg	John Bromwich	7–5, 0–6, 6–2, 3–6, 7–5
1949	Ted Schroeder	Jaroslav Drobny	3–6, 6–0, 6–3, 4–6, 6–4
1950	Budge Patty	Frank Sedgman	6–1, 8–10, 6–2, 6–3
1951	Dick Savitt	Ken McGregor	6–4, 6–4, 6–4
1952	Frank Sedgman	Jaroslav Drobny	4–6, 6–3, 6–2, 6–3
1953	Vic Seixas	Kurt Nielsen	9–7, 6–3, 6–4
1954	Jaroslav Drobny	Ken Rosewall	13–11, 4–6, 6–2, 9–7
1955	Tony Trabert	Kurt Nielsen	6–3, 7–5, 6–1

ALL-ENGLAND CHAMPIONSHIPS—MEN'S SINGLES *(cont.)*

Year	Winner	Runner-Up	Score
1956	Lew Hoad	Ken Rosewall	6–2, 4–6, 7–5, 6–4
1957	Lew Hoad	Ashley Cooper	6–2, 6–1, 6–2
1958	Ashley Cooper	Neale Fraser	3–6, 6–3, 6–4, 13–11
1959	Alex Olmedo	Rod Laver	6–4, 6–3, 6–4
1960	Neale Fraser	Rod Laver	6–4, 3–6, 9–7, 7–5
1961	Rod Laver	Chuck McKinley	6–3, 6–1, 6–4
1962	Rod Laver	Martin Mulligan	6–2, 6–2, 6–1
1963	Chuck McKinley	Fred Stolle	9–7, 6–1, 6–4
1964	Roy Emersom	Fred Stolle	6–4, 12–10, 4–6, 6–3
1965	Roy Emerson	Fred Stolle	6–2, 6–4, 6–4
1966	Manuel Santana	Dennis Ralston	6–3, 6–1, 6–1
1967	John Newcombe	Wilhelm Bungert6–3, 6–1, 6–1	
1968*	Rod Laver	Tony Roche	6–3, 6–4, 6–2
1969*	Rod Laver	John Newcombe	6–4, 5–7, 6–4, 6–4
1970*	John Newcombe	Ken Rosewall	5–7. 6–3, 6–2, 3–6, 6–1
1971*	John Newcombe	Stan Smith	6–3, 5–7, 2–6, 6–4, 6–4
1972*	Stan Smith	Ilie Nastase	4–6, 6–3, 6–3, 4–6, 7–5
1973*	Jan Kodes	Alex Metreveli	6–1, 9–7, 6–3
1974*	Jimmy Connors	Ken Rosewall	6–1, 6–1, 6–4
1975*	Arthur Ashe	Jimmy Connors	6–1, 6–1, 5–7, 6–4
1976*	Bjorn Borg	Ilie Nastase	6–4, 6–2, 9–7
1977*	Bjorn Borg	Jimmy Connors	3–6, 6–2, 6–1, 5–7, 6–4
1978*	Bjorn Borg	Jimmy Connors	6–2, 6–2, 6–3
1979*	Bjorn Borg	Roscoe Tanner	6–7, 6–1, 3–6, 6–3, 6–4
1980*	Bjorn Borg	John McEnroe	1–6, 7–5, 6–3, 6–7, 8–6

*Open Championship

ALL-ENGLAND CHAMPIONSHIPS—WOMEN'S SINGLES

Year	Winner	Runner-Up
1884	Maud Watson	Lillian Watson
1885	Maud Watson	Blanche Bingley
1886	Blanche Bingley	Maud Watson
1887	Lottie Dod	Blanche Bingley
1888	Lottie Dod	Mrs. Blanche Bingley Hillyard
1889	Mrs. Blanche Bingley Hillyard	L. Rice
1890	L. Rice	L. Jacks
1891	Lottie Dod	Mrs. Blanche Bingley Hillyard
1892	Lottie Dod	Mrs. Blanche Bingley Hillyard
1893	Lottie Dod	Mrs. Blanche Bingley Hillyard
1894	Mrs. Blanche Bingley Hillyard	L. Austin
1895	Charlotte Cooper	H. Jackson
1896	Charlotte Cooper	Mrs. W. H. Pickering
1897	Mrs. Blanche Bingley Hillyard	Charlotte Cooper
1898	Charlotte Cooper	L. Martin
1899	Mrs. Blanche Bingley Hillyard	Charlotte Cooper
1900	Mrs. Blanche Bingley Hillyard	Charlotte Cooper
1901	Mrs. Charlotte Cooper Sterry	Blanche Bingley Hillyard
1902	M. E. Robb	Charlotte Cooper Sterry
1903	Dorothea Douglas	E. W. Thompson
1904	Dorothea Douglas	Charlotte Cooper Sterry
1905	May Sutton	Dorothea Douglas
1906	Dorothea Douglas	May Sutton

Year	Winner	Runner-Up
1907	May Sutton	Dorothea Douglas Lambert Chambers
1908	Mrs. Charlotte Cooper Sterry	A. M. Morton
1909	Dora Boothby	A. M. Morton
1910	Mrs. Dorothea Douglas Lambert Chambers	Dora Boothby
1911	Mrs. Dorothea Douglas Lambert Chambers	Dora Boothby
1912	E. W. Thomson Larcombe	Charlotte Cooper Sterry
1913	Mrs. Dorothea Douglas Lambert Chambers	Mrs. R. J. McNair
1914	Mrs. Dorothea Douglas Lambert Chambers	E. W. Thomson Larcombe
1915–18	not held	
1919	Suzanne Lenglen	Dorothea Douglas Lambert Chambers
1920	Suzanne Lenglen	Dorothea Douglas Lambert Chambers
1921	Suzanne Lenglen	Elizabeth Ryan
1922	Suzanne Lenglen	Mrs. Molla B. Mallory
1923	Suzanne Lenglen	Kitty McKane
1924	Kitty McKane	Helen Wills
1925	Suzanne Lenglen	Joan Fry
1926	Kitty McKane Godfree	Lili Alvarez
1927	Helen Wills	Lili Alvarez
1928	Helen Wills	Lili Alvarez
1929	Helen Wills	Helen Jacobs
1930	Mrs. Helen Wills Moody	Elizabeth Ryan
1931	Cilly Aussem	Hilda Krahwinkel
1932	Mrs. Helen Wills Moody	Helen Jacobs
1933	Mrs. Helen Wills Moody	Dorothy Round
1934	Dorothy Round	Helen Jacobs
1935	Mrs. Helen Wills Moody	Helen Jacobs
1936	Helen Jacobs	Hilda Krahwinkel Sperling
1937	Dorothy Round	Jadwiga Jedrzejowska
1938	Mrs. Helen Wills Moody	Helen Jacobs
1939	Alice Marble	Kay Stammers
1940–45	not held	
1946	Pauline Betz	A. Louise Brough
1947	Margaret Osborne	Doris Hart
1948	A. Louise Brough	Doris Hart
1949	A. Louise Brough	Mrs. Margaret Osborne du Pont
1950	A. Louise Brough	Mrs. Margaret Osborne du Pont
1951	Doris Hart	Shirley Fry
1952	Maureen Connolly	A. Louise Brough
1953	Maureen Connolly	Doris Hart
1954	Maureen Connolly	A. Louise Brough
1955	A. Louise Brough	Mrs. Beverly Baker Fleitz
1956	Shirley Fry	Angela Buxton
1957	Althea Gibson	Darlene Hard
1958	Althea Gibson	Angela Mortimer
1959	Maria Bueno	Darlene Hard
1960	Maria Bueno	Sandra Reynolds
1961	Angela Mortimer	Christine Truman
1962	Karen Hantze Susman	Vera Puzejova Sukova
1963	Margaret Smith	Billie Jean Moffitt
1964	Maria Bueno	Margaret Smith
1965	Margaret Smith	Maria Bueno
1966	Mrs. Billie Jean Moffitt King	Maria Bueno
1967	Mrs. Billie Jean Moffitt King	Maria Bueno
1968*	Mrs. Billie Jean Moffitt King	Judy Tegart
1969*	Mrs. Ann Haydon Jones	Mrs. Billie Jean Moffitt King
1970*	Mrs. Margaret Smith Court	Mrs. Billie Jean Moffitt King
1971*	Evonne Goolagong	Mrs. Margaret Smith Court

The famed men's doubles team of Fred Stolle and Bob Hewitt.

When Angela Mortimer won the Ladies' Singles Championship in 1961 from Christine Truman, she was the first Briton to do so since 1937.

ALL-ENGLAND CHAMPIONSHIPS—WOMEN'S SINGLES (cont.)

Year	Winner	Runner-Up
1972*	Mrs. Billie Jean Moffitt King	Evonne Goolagong
1973*	Mrs. Billie Jean Moffitt King	Chris Evert
1974*	Chris Evert	Olga Morozova
1975*	Mrs. Billie Jean Moffitt King	Evonne Goolagong
1976*	Chris Evert	Mrs. Evonne Goolagong Cawley
1977*	Virginia Wade	Betty Stove
1978*	Martina Navratilova	Chris Evert
1979*	Martina Navratilova	Chris Evert
1980*	Mrs. Evonne Goolagong Cawley	Mrs. Chris Evert Lloyd

*Open championships.

ALL-ENGLAND CHAMPIONSHIPS—MEN'S DOUBLES (Played from 1879 to 1883 at Oxford)

Year	Winner	Runner-Up
1879	L. R. Erskine and H. F. Lawford	F. Durant and G. E. Tabor
1880	William and Ernest Renshaw	O. E. Woodhouse and C. J. Cole
1881	William and Ernest Renshaw	W. J. Down and H. Vaughan
1882	J. T. Hartley and R. T. Richardson	J. G. Horn and C. B. Russell
1883	C. W. Grinstead and C. E. Welldon	C. B. Russell and R. T. Milford
1884	William and Ernest Renshaw	E. W. Lewis and E. L. Williams
1885	William and Ernest Renshaw	C. E. Farrar and A. J. Stanley
1886	William and Ernest Renshaw	C. E. Farrar and A. J. Stanley
1887	Herbert W. Wilberforce and P. B. Lyon	J. Hope Crispe and Barrat Smith
1888	William and Ernest Renshaw	Herbert Wilberforce and P. B. Lyon
1889	William and Ernest Renshaw	E. W. Lewis and G. W. Hillyard
1890	Joshua Pim and F. O. Stoker	E. W. Lewis and G. W. Hillyard
1891	Wilfred and Herbert Baddeley	Joshua Pim and F. O. Stoker

Year	Winner	Runner-Up
1892	E. W. Lewis and H. S. Barlow	Wilfred and Herbert Baddeley
1893	Joshua Pim and F. O. Stoker	E. W. Lewis and H. S. Barlow
1894	Wilfred and Herbert Baddeley	H. S. Barlow and C. H. Martin
1895	Wilfred and Herbert Baddeley	E. W. Lewis and W. V. Eaves
1896	Wilfred and Herbert Baddeley	R. F. Doherty and H. A. Nisbet
1897	Reggie F. and H. Laurie Doherty	Wilfred and Herbert Doherty
1898	Reggie F. and H. Laurie Doherty	H. A. Nisbet and C. Hobart
1899	Reggie F. and H. Laurie Doherty	H. A. Nisbet and C. Hobart
1900	Reggie F. and H. Laurie Doherty	H. Roper Barrett and H. A. Nisbet
1901	Reggie F. and H. Laurie Doherty	Dwight Davis and Holcombe Ward
1902	Sidney H. Smith and Frank Riseley	Reggie F. and H. Laurie Doherty
1903	Reggie F. and H. Laurie Doherty	H. S. Mahoney and M. G. J. Ritchie
1904	Reggie F. and H. Laurie Doherty	Sidney H. Smith and Frank Riseley
1905	Reggie F. and H. Laurie Doherty	Sidney H. Smith and Frank Riseley
1906	Sidney H. Smith and Frank Riseley	Reggie F. and H. Laurie Doherty
1907	Norman E. Brookes and Anthony Wilding	Beals C. Wright and Karl Behr
1908	Anthony Wilding and M. G. J. Ritchie	Arthur W. Gore and H. R. Barrett
1909	Arthur W. Gore and H. R. Barrett	Stanley Doust and H. A. Parker
1910	Anthony Wilding and M. G. J. Ritchie	Arthur W. Gore and H. R. Barrett
1911	André Gobert and Max Décugis	Anthony Wilding and M. G. J. Ritchie
1912	H. R. Barrett and Charles Dixon	André Gobert and Max Décugis
1913	H. R. Barrett and Charles Dixon	F. W. Rahe and H. Kleinschroth
1914	Norman E. Brookes and Anthony Wilding	H. R. Barrett and Charles Dixon
1915–18	not held	
1919	R. V. Thomas and Pat O'Hara Wood	Randolph Lycett and R. W. Heath
1920	R. N. Williams and C. S. Garland	A. R. F. Kingscote and J. C. Parke
1921	Randolph Lycett and Max Woosnam	Arthur H. and Frank G. Lowe
1922	J. O. Anderson and Randolph Lycett	Gerald Patterson and Pat O'Hara Wood
1923	Leslie A. Godfree and Randolph Lycett	Count deGomar and E. Flaquer
1924	Frank Hunter and Vincent Richards	R. N. Williams and W. M. Washburn
1925	Jean Borotra and Jean René Lacoste	J. Hennessey and R. Casey
1926	Jacques Brugnon and Henri Cochet	H. Kingsley and Vincent Richards
1927	Frank Hunter and William Tilden II	Jacques Brugnon and Henri Cochet
1928	Jacques Brugnon and Henri Cochet	Gerald Patterson and J. B. Hawkes
1929	Wilmer Allison and John Van Ryn	J. Colin Gregory and Ian G. Collins
1930	Wilmer Allison and John Van Ryn	John H. Doeg and George M. Lott
1931	George M. Lott and John Van Ryn	Jacques Brugnon and Henri Cochet
1932	Jean Borotra and Jacques Brugnon	Fred J. Perry and G. Pat Hughes
1933	Jean Borotra and Jacques Brugnon	R. Nunoi and J. Satoh
1934	George M. Lott and Lester R. Stoefen	Jean Borotra and Jacques Brugnon
1935	Jack Crawford and Adrian Quist	Wilmer Allison and John Van Ryn
1936	G. Pat Hughes and Raymond Tuckey	Charles Hare and Frank Wilde
1937	Don Budge and Gene Mako	G. Pat Hughes and Raymond Tuckey
1938	Don Budge and Gene Mako	Henner Henkel and G. von Metaxa
1939	Ellwood Cooke and Bobby Riggs	Charles Hare and Frank Wilde
1940–45	not held	
1946	Tom Brown and Jack Kramer	Geoff Brown and Dinny Pails
1947	Bob Falkenburg and Jack Kramer	Tony Mottram and O. W. Sidwell
1948	John Bromwich and Frank Sedgman	Tom Brown and Gardnar Mulloy
1949	Richard Gonzales and Frank Parker	Gardnar Mulloy and Ted Schroeder
1950	John Bromwich and Adrian Quist	Geoff Brown and O. W. Sidwell
1951	Ken McGregor and Frank Sedgman	Jaroslav Drobny and Eric Sturgess
1952	Ken McGregor and Frank Sedgman	Vic Seixas and Eric Sturgess
1953	Lew Hoad and Ken Rosewall	Rex Hartwig and Mervyn Rose
1954	Rex Hartwig and Mervyn Rose	Vic Seixas and Tony Trabert
1955	Rex Hartwig and Lew Hoad	Neale Fraser and Ken Rosewall
1956	Lew Hoad and Ken Rosewall	Nicola Pietrangeli and O. Sirola

ALL-ENGLAND CHAMPIONSHIPS—MEN'S DOUBLES *(Played from 1879 to 1883 at Oxford) (cont.)*

Year	Winner	Runner-Up
1957	Budge Patty and Gardnar Mulloy	Neale Fraser and Lew Hoad
1958	Sven Davidson and Ulf Schmidt	Ashley Cooper and Neale Fraser
1959	Roy Emerson and Neale Fraser	Rod Laver and Bob Mark
1960	Rafael Osuna and Dennis Ralston	Mike Davies and Bobby Wilson
1961	Roy Emerson and Neale Fraser	Bob Hewitt and Fred Stolle
1962	Bob Hewitt and Fred Stolle	Boro Jovanovic and Nikki Pilic
1963	Rafael Osuna and Antonio Palafox	Jean C. Barclay and Pierre Darmon
1964	Bob Hewitt and Fred Stolle	Roy Emerson and Ken Fletcher
1965	John Newcombe and Tony Roche	Ken Fletcher and Bob Hewitt
1966	Ken Fletcher and John Newcombe	Bill Bowrey and Owen Davidson
1967	Bob Hewitt and Frew McMillan	Roy Emerson and Ken Fletcher
1968*	John Newcombe and Tony Roche	Ken Rosewall and Fred Stolle
1969*	John Newcombe and Tony Roche	Tom Okker and Marty Riessen
1970*	John Newcombe and Tony Roche	Ken Rosewall and Fred Stolle
1971*	Roy Emerson and Rod Laver	Dennis Ralston and Arthur Ashe
1972*	Bob Hewitt and Frew McMillan	Stan Smith and Erik van Dillen
1973*	Jimmy Connors and Ilie Nastase	John Cooper and Neale Fraser
1974*	John Newcombe and Tony Roche	Bob Lutz and Stan Smith
1975*	Vitas Gerulaitis and Alex Mayer	Colin Dowdeswell and Allan Stone
1976*	Brian Gottfried and Raul Ramirez	Ross Case and Geoff Masters
1977*	Ross Case and Geoff Masters	John Alexander and Phil Dent
1978*	Bob Hewitt and Frew McMillan	John McEnroe and Peter Fleming
1979*	John McEnroe and Peter Fleming	Brian Gottfried and Raul Ramirez
1980*	Peter McNamara and Paul McNamee	Stan Smith and Bob Lutz

*Open championships.

ALL-ENGLAND CHAMPIONSHIPS—WOMEN'S DOUBLES

Year	Winners	Runners-Up
1913	Mrs. R.J. McNair and Doro Boothby	Charlotte Cooper Sterry and Dorothea Douglas L. Chambers
1914	A.M. Morton and Elizabeth Ryan	E.W. Thomson Larcombe and G. Hannam
1915–18	not held	
1919	Suzanne Lenglen and Elizabeth Ryan	E.W. Thomason Larcombe and Dorothea Douglas L. Chambers
1920	Suzanne Lenglen and Elizabeth Ryan	E. W. Thomson Larcombe and Dorothea Douglas L. Chambers
1921	Suzanne Lenglen and Elizabeth Ryan	Geraldine Beamish and Mrs. G. Peacock
1922	Suzanne Lenglen and Elizabeth Ryan	Kitty McKane and Mrs. A. D. Stocks
1923	Suzanne Lenglen and Elizabeth Ryan	Joan Austin and Edith Colyer
1924	Hazel Wightman and Helen Wills	Phyllis Covel and Kitty McKane
1925	Suzanne Lenglen and Elizabeth Ryan	Mrs. A. V. Bridge and Mrs. C. G. McIlquham
1926	Mary K. Browne and Elizabeth Ryan	Kitty McKane Godfree and Edith Colyer

Year	Winner	Runner-Up
1927	Helen Wills and Elizabeth Ryan	Mrs. G. Peacock and Bobie Heine
1928	Peggy Saunders and Phyllis Watson	Ermyntrude Harvey and Eileen Bennett
1929	Peggy Michell and Phyllis Watson	Phyllis Covel and Dorothy Shepherd Barron
1930	Helen Wills Moody and Elizabeth Ryan	Eleanor Cross and Sarah Palfrey
1931	Phyllis Mudford and Dorothy Shepherd Barron	Doris Metaxa and Josane Sigart
1932	Doris Metaxa and Josane Sigart	Helen Jacobs and Elizabeth Ryan
1933	Simone Mathieu and Elizabeth Ryan	Freda James and Billie Yorke
1934	Simone Mathieu and Elizabeth Ryan	Dorothy Andrus and Sylvia Henrotin
1935	Freda James and Kay Stammers	Simone Mathieu and Hilda Krahwinkel Sperling
1936	Freda James and Kay Stammers	Helen Jacobs and Sarah Palfrey Fabyan
1937	Simone Mathieu and Billie Yorke	Phyllis Mudford King and Elsie Pittman
1938	Sarah Palfrey Fabyan and Alice Marble	Simone Mathieu and Billie Yorke
1939	Sarah Palfrey Fabyan and Alice Marble	Helen Jacobs and Billie Yorke
1940–45	not held	
1946	A. Louise Brough and Margaret Osborne	Pauline Betz and Doris Hart
1947	Pat Todd and Doris Hart	A. Louise Brough and Margaret Osborne
1948	A. Louise Brough and Margaret Osborne du Pont	Pat Todd and Doris Hart
1949	A. Louise Brough and Margaret Osborne du Pont	Pat Todd and Gussie Moran
1950	A. Louise Brough and Margaret Osborne du Pont	Doris Hart and Shirley Fry
1951	Doris Hart and Shirley Fry	A. Louise Brough and Margaret Osborne du Pont
1952	Doris Hart and Shirley Fry	A. Louise Brough and Maureen Connolly
1953	Doris Hart and Shirley Fry	Julie Sampson and Maureen Connolly
1954	A. Louise Brough and Margaret Osborne du Pont	Doris Hart and Shirley Fry
1955	Angela Mortimer and Anne Shilcock	Shirley Bloomer and Pat Ward
1956	Angela Buxton and Althea Gibson	Daphne Seeney and Fay Muller
1957	Althea Gibson and Darlene Hard	Thelma Long and Mary Hawton
1958	Maria Bueno and Althea Gibson	Margaret Osborne du Pont and Margaret Varner
1959	Jean Arth and Darlene Hard	Beverly Baker Fleitz and Christine Truman
1960	Maria Bueno and Darlene Hard	Sandra Reynolds and Renée Schuurman
1961	Karen Hantze and Billie Jean Moffitt	Ian Lehane and Margaret Smith
1962	Billie Jean Moffitt and Karen Hantze Susman	Sandra Reynolds Price and Renée Schuurman
1963	Maria Bueno and Darlene Hard	Robyn Ebbern and Margaret Smith
1964	Margaret Smith and Lesley Turner	Billie Jean Moffitt and Karen Hantze Susman
1965	Maria Bueno and Billie Jean Moffitt	Françoise Durr and Janine Lieffrig
1966	Maria Bueno and Nancy Richey	Margaret Smith and Judy Tegart
1967	Rosemary Casals and Billie Jean Moffitt King	Maria Bueno and Nancy Richey
1968*	Rosemary Casals and Billie Jean Moffitt King	Françoise Durr and Ann Haydon Jones
1969*	Margaret Smith Court and Judy Tegart	Patti Hogan and Peggy Michell
1970*	Rosemary Casals and Billie Jean Moffitt King	Françoise Durr and Virginia Wade
1971*	Rosemary Casals and Billie Jean Moffitt King	Margaret Smith Court and Evonne Goolagong
1972*	Billie Jean Moffitt King and Betty Stove	Judy Tegart Dalton and Francoise Durr
1973*	Billie Jean Moffitt King and Rosemary Casals	Francoise Durr and Betty Stove
1974*	Evonne Goolagong and Peggy Michel	Helen Gourlay and Karen Krantzcke
1975*	Ann Kiyomura and Kazuko Sawamatsu	Francoise Durr and Betty Stove
1976*	Chris Evert and Martina Navratilova	Billie Jean Moffitt King and Betty Stove
1977*	Helen Gourlay Cawley and JoAnn Russell	Martina Navratilova and Betty Stove
1978*	Wendy Turnbull and Kerry M. Reid	Virginia Ruzici and Mima Jausovec
1979*	Bille Jean King and Martina Navratilova	Betty Store and Wendy Turnbull
1980*	Kathy Jordon and Anne Smith	Rosemary Casals and Wendy Turnbull

*Open championships.

ALL-ENGLAND CHAMPIONSHIPS—MIXED DOUBLES

Year	Winners	Runners-up
1913	J. Hope Crispe and Mrs. C.O. Tuckey	J.C. Parke and E.W. Thomson Larcombe
1914	J.C. Parke and E.W. Thomson Larcombe	Anthony F.
1953	Vic Seixas and Doris Hart	Enrique Morea and Shirley Fry
1954	Vic Seixas and Doris Hart	Ken Rosewall and Margaret Osborne du Pont
1955	Vic Seixas and Doris Hart	Enrique Morea and A. Louise Brough
1956	Vic Seixas and Shirley Fry	Gardnar Mulloy and Althea Gibson
1957	Mervyn Rose and Darlene Hard	Neale Fraser and Althea Gibson
1958	Bob Howe and Loraine Coghlan	Kurt Nielsen and Althea Gibson
1959	Rod Laver and Darlene Hard	Neale Fraser and Maria Bueno
1960	Rod Laver and Darlene Hard	Bob Howe and Maria Bueno
1961	Fred Stolle and Lesley Turner	Bob Howe and Edda Buding
1962	Neale Fraser and Margaret Osborne du Pont	Dennis Ralston and Ann Haydon
1963	Ken Fletcher and Margaret Smith	Bob Hewitt and Darlene Hard
1964	Fred Stolle and Lesley Turner	Ken Fletcher and Margaret Smith
1965	Ken Fletcher and Margaret Smith	Tony Roche and Judy Tegart
1966	Ken Fletcher and Margaret Smith	Dennis Ralston and Billie Jean Moffitt King
1967	Owen Davidson and Billie Jean Moffitt King	Ken Fletcher and Maria Bueno
1968*	Ken Fletcher and Margaret Smith Court	Alex Metreveli and Olga Morozova
1969*	Fred Stolle and Ann Jones	Tony Roche and Judy Tegart
1970*	Ilie Nastase and Rosemary Casals	Alex Metreveli and Olga Morozova
1971*	Owen Davidson and Billie Jean Moffitt King	Marty Riessen and Margaret Smith Court
1972*	Ilie Nastase and Rosemary Casals	Evonne Goolagong and Kim Warwick
1973*	Billie Jean Moffitt King and Owen Davidson	Janet Newberry and Raul Ramirez
1974*	Billie Jean Moffitt King and Owen Davidson	Lesley Charles and Mark Farrell
1975*	Margaret Smith Court and Marty Riessen	Betty Stove and Allan Stone
1976*	Francoise Durr and Tony Roche	Rosemary Casals and Dick Stockton
1977*	Greer Stevens and Bob Hewitt	Betty Stove and Frew McMillan
1978*	Frew McMillan and Betty Stove	Ray Ruffels and Billie Jean King
1979*	Bob Hewitt and Greer Stevens	Frew McMillan and Betty Stove
1980*	John Austin and Tracy Austin	Mark Edmondson and Dianne Fromholtz

*Open championships.

Rosemary Casals and Mrs. Billie Jean King won the Ladies' Doubles Championship in 1967, 1968, 1970, 1971. Mrs. King also won the title with Karen Hantze (1961) and Maria Bueno (1965).

Lining up before their 1970 Wimbledon final in the Veterans' Doubles are: *(left to right)* George MacCall, Pancho Segura, Bobby Riggs, and Jaroslav Drobny. Match was won by Drobny and Riggs in straight sets.

French Championships—Men's Singles

1891 J. Briggs
1892 J. Schopfer
1893 L. Riboulet
1894 A. Vacherot
1895 A. Vacherot
1896 A. Vacherot
1897 P. Ayme
1898 P. Ayme
1899 P. Ayme
1900 P. Ayme
1901 A. Vacherot
1902 A. Vacherot
1903 Max Décugis
1904 Max Décugis
1905 M. Germot
1906 M. Germot
1907 Max Décugis
1908 Max Décugis
1909 Max Décugis
1910 M. Germot
1911 A. H. Gobert
1912 Max Décugis
1913 Max Décugis
1914 Max Décugis
1915–19 no competition
1920 A. H. Gobert
1921 J. Samazeuith
1922 Henri Cochet
1923 P. Blanchy
1924 Jean Borotra
1925* Jean René Lacoste
1926 Henri Cochet
1927 Jean René Lacoste
1928 Henri Cochet
1929 Jean René Lacoste
1930 Henri Cochet
1931 Jean Borotra
1932 Henri Cochet
1933 John H. Crawford
1934 Gottfried von Cramm
1935 Fred J. Perry
1936 Gottfried von Cramm
1937 Henner Henkel
1938 J. Donald Budge
1939 W. Donald McNeill

*Entries accepted from all countries.

France's Marcel Bernard won his country's title in 1946.

Czechoslovakia's Jan Kodes took the French title in both 1970 and 1971.

French Championships—Men's Singles *(cont.)*

1940	no competition
1941†	Bernard Destreman
1942†	Bernard Destreman
1943†	Yvon Petra
1944†	Yvon Petra
1945†	Yvon Petra
1946	Marcel Bernard
1947	Josef Asboth
1948	Frank A. Parker
1949	Frank A. Parker
1950	Budge Patty
1951	Jaroslav Drobny
1952	Jaroslav Drobny
1953	Kenneth Rosewall
1954	Tony Trabert
1955	Tony Trabert
1956	Lewis Hoad
1957	Sven Davidson
1958	Mervyn Rose
1959	Nicola Pietrangeli
1960	Nicola Pietrangeli
1961	Manuel Santana
1962	Rodney Laver
1963	Roy Emerson
1964	Manuel Santana
1965	Fred Stolle
1966	Tony Roche
1967	Roy Emerson
1968‡	Ken Rosewall
1969‡	Rodney Laver
1970‡	Jan Kodes
1971‡	Jan Kodes
1972‡	Andres Gimeno
1973‡	Ilie Nastase
1974‡	Bjorn Borg
1975‡	Bjorn Borg
1976‡	Adriano Panatta
1977‡	Guillermo Vilas
1978‡	Bjorn Borg
1979‡	Bjorn Borg
1980‡	Bjorn Borg

†From 1941–45 the championship was called the "Tournoi de France."
‡Open championship.

French Championships—Women's Singles

1897	F. Masson
1898	F. Masson
1899	F. Masson
1900	Mrs. J. Provost
1901	P. Girod
1902	F. Masson
1903	F. Masson
1904	K. Gillou
1905	K. Gillou
1906	Mrs. K. Fenwick
1907	Mrs. C. de Kermel
1908	Mrs. K. Fenwick
1909	J. Mattey
1910	J. Mattey
1911	J. Mattey
1912	J. Mattey
1913	M. Broquedis
1914	M. Broquedis
1915–19	no competition
1920	Suzanne Lenglen
1921	Suzanne Lenglen
1922	Suzanne Lenglen
1923	Suzanne Lenglen
1924	D. Vlasto
1925	Suzanne Lenglen
1926	Suzanne Lenglen
1927	K. Bouman
1928	Helen Wills
1929	Helen Wills
1930	Mrs. H. Wills Moody
1931	C. Aussem
1932	Mrs. H. Wills Moody
1933	M. C. Scriven
1934	M. C. Scriven
1935	Mrs. H. Sperling
1936	Mrs. H. Sperling
1937	Mrs. H. Sperling
1938	Mrs. R. Mathieu
1939	Mrs. R. Mathieu
1940	no competition
1941	A. Weiwers
1942	A. Weiwers
1943	Mrs. N. Lafargue
1944	L. Veber
1945	Mrs. L. Dodille Payot
1946	Margaret Osborne
1947	Mrs. Patricia C. Todd
1948	Mrs. N. Landry
1949	Mrs. Margaret O. du Pont
1950	Doris Hart

1951	Shirley Fry
1952	Doris Hart
1953	Maureen Connolly
1954	Maureen Connolly
1955	Angela Mortimer
1956	Althea Gibson
1957	Shirley Bloomer
1958	Mrs. S. Koermoczi
1959	Christine Truman
1960	Darlene Hard
1961	Ann Haydon
1962	Margaret Smith
1963	Lesley Turner
1964	Margaret Smith
1965	Lesley Turner
1966	Mrs. A. H. Jones
1967	Françoise Durr
1968	Nancy Richey
1969	Mrs. Margaret Smith Court
1970	Mrs. Margaret Smith Court
1971	Evonne Goolagong
1972	Mrs. Billie Jean King
1973	Mrs. Margaret Smith Court
1974	Chris Evert
1975	Chris Evert
1976	Sue Barker
1977	Mima Jausovec
1978	Virginia Ruzici
1979	Mrs. Chris Evert Lloyd
1980	Mrs. Chris Evert Lloyd

At nineteen years of age, Evonne Goolagong won both the French and Wimbledon championships in 1971.

French Championships—Men's Doubles

1891	B. Desjoyau and T. Legrand
1892	J. Havet and D. Albertini
1893	J. Schopfer and F. Goldsmith
1894	L. Brosselin and J. Lesage
1895	A. Vacherot and C. Winzer
1896	F. N. Warden and J. Wynn
1897	P. Ayme and T. Lebreton
1898	A. Vacherot and X. E. Casdagli
1899	P. Ayme and T. Lebreton
1900	P. Ayme and T. Lebreton
1901	A. Vacherot and M. Vacherot
1902	M. Décugis and J. Worth
1903	M. Décugis and J. Worth
1904	M. Décugis and M. Germot
1905	M. Décugis and J. Worth
1906	M. Décugis and M. Germot
1907	M. Décugis and M. Germot
1908	M. Décugis and M. Germot
1909	M. Décugis and M. Germot
1910	M. Décugis and M. DuPont
1911	M. Décugis and M. Germot
1912	M. Décugis and M. Germot
1913	M. Décugis and M. Germot
1914	M. Décugis and M. Germot
1915–19	no competition
1920	M. Décugis and M. Germot
1921	A. H. Gobert and W. H. Laurentz
1922	J. Brugnon and M. DuPont
1923	P. Blanchy and J. Samarzeuilh
1924	Jean Borotra and Jean René Lacoste
1925	Jean Borotra and Jean René Lacoste
1926	Vincent Richards and H. Kinsey
1927	Henri Cochet and J. Brugnon
1928	Jean Borotra and J. Brugnon
1929	Jean Borotra and Jean René Lacoste
1930	Henri Cochet and J. Brugnon
1931	George M. Lott and John Van Ryn
1932	Henri Cochet and J. Brugnon
1933	G. P. Hughes and F. J. Perry
1934	Jean Borotra and J. Brugnon
1935	Jack Crawford and Adrian Quist
1936	Jean Borotra and Marcel Bernard

French Championships—Men's Doubles *(cont.)*

1937 Gottfried von Cramm and Henner Henkel
1938 Bernard Destremau and Yvon Petra
1939 Don McNeill and C. R. Harris
1940 no competition
1941† Bernard Destremau and C. Boussus
1942† Bernard Destremau and Yvon Petra
1943† Marcel Bernard and Yvon Petra
1944† Marcel Bernard and Yvon Petra
1945† Henri Cochet and P. Pellizza
1946 Marcel Bernard and Yvon Petra
1947 Eustace Fannin and Eric Sturgess
1948 Lennart Bergelin and Jaroslav Drobny
1949 Frank Parker and Richard Gonzales
1950 William Talbert and Tony Trabert
1951 Kenneth McGregor and Frank Sedgman
1952 Kenneth McGregor and Frank Sedgman
1953 Lewis Hoad and Kenneth Rosewall
1954 E. Victor Seixas, Jr. and Tony Trabert
1955 E. Victor Seixas, Jr. and Tony Trabert
1956 Don Candy and Robert Perry
1957 Malcolm J. Anderson and Ashley J. Cooper
1958 Ashley J. Cooper and Neale Fraser
1959 Nicola Pietrangeli and Orlando Sirola
1960 Neale Fraser and Roy Emerson
1961 Roy Emerson and Rodney Laver
1962 Roy Emerson and Neale Fraser
1963 Roy Emerson and Manuel Santana
1964 Roy Emerson and Ken Fletcher
1965 Roy Emerson and Fred Stolle
1966 Clark Graebner and Dennis Ralston
1967 John Newcombe and Tony Roche
1968* Ken Rosewall and Fred Stolle
1969 John Newcombe and Tony Roche
1970 Ilie Nastase and Ion Tiriac
1971 Arthur Ashe and Marty Riessen
1972 Bob Hewitt and Frew McMillan
1973 John Newcombe and Tom Okker
1974 Dick Crealy and Onny Parun
1975 Brian Gottfried and Raul Ramirez
1976 Fred McNair and Sherwood Stewart
1977 Brian Gottfried and Raul Ramirez
1978 Hank Pfister and Gene Mayer

*Open championship.
†From 1941–45, the championship was called the "Tournoi de France."

1980 Hank Pfister and Victor Amaya
1979 Sandy Mayer and Gene Mayer

French Championships—Women's Doubles

1925 S. Lenglen and D. Vlasto
1926 S. Lenglen and D. Vlasto
1927 Mrs. T. Peacock and E. L. Heine
1928 Mrs. J. Watson and E. Bennett
1929 L. de Alvarez and K. Bouman
1930 Mrs. H. Wills Moody and Elizabeth Ryan
1931 Mrs. Whittingstall and Betty Nuthall
1932 Mrs. H. Wills Moody and Elizabeth Ryan
1933 Mrs. R. Mathieu and Elizabeth Ryan
1934 Mrs. R. Mathieu and E. Ryan
1935 M. C. Scriven and K. Stammers
1936 Mrs. R. Mathieu and A. M. Yorke
1937 Mrs. R. Mathieu and J. Jedrzekowska
1938 Mrs. R. Mathieu and A. M. Yorke
1939 Mrs. R. Mathieu and J. Jedrzekowska
1940 no competition
1941* A. Weiwers and D. St. Omer Roy
1942 A. Weiwers and D. St. Omer Roy
1943 A. Weiwers and D. St. Omer Roy
1944 Mrs. B. Grosbois and Mrs. J. Manescau
1945 Mrs. N. Lafargue and Mrs. P. Fritz
1946 A. Louise Brough and Margaret Osborne
1947 A. Louise Brough and Margaret Osborne
1948 Doris Hart and Mrs. Pat C. Todd
1949 Mrs. M. O. du Pont and A. Louise Brough
1950 Doris Hart and Shirley Fry
1951 Doris Hart and Shirley Fry
1952 Doris Hart and Shirley Fry
1953 Doris Hart and Shirley Fry
1954 Maureen Connolly and Mrs. N. Hopman
1955 Mrs. B. B. Fleitz and Darlene Hard
1956 Angela Buxton and Althea Gibson
1957 Shirley Bloomer and Darlene Hard
1958 Rosie Reyes and Yola Ramirez
1959 Sandra Reynolds and Renée Schuurman
1960 Maria Bueno and Darlene Hard
1961 Sandra Reynolds and Renée Schuurman
1962 Sandra Reynolds and Renée Schuurman
1963 Mrs. A. H. Jones and Renée Schuurman
1964 Margaret Smith and Lesley Turner
1965 Margaret Smith and Lesley Turner
1966 Judy Tegart and Margaret Smith
1967 Françoise Durr and Gail Sheriff
1968 Françoise Durr and Mrs. A. H. Jones

1969 Françoise Durr and Mrs. A. H. Jones
1970 Mrs. C. S. Chanfreau and Françoise Durr
1971 Mrs. C. S. Chanfreau and Françoise Durr
1972 Mrs. Billie Jean King and Betty Stove
1973 Mrs. Margaret S. Court and Virginia
      Wade
1974 Chris Evert and Olga Morozova
1975 Chris Evert and Martina Navratilova
1976 Florella Bonicella and Gail Lovera
1977 Regina Marsikova and Pam Teegarden
1978 Mima Jausovec and Virginia Ruzici
1979 Betty Stove and Wendy Turnbull
1980 Anne Smith and Kathy Jordan

*Open championships.

French Championships—Mixed Doubles

1925 S. Lenglen and J. Brugnon
1926 S. Lenglen and J. Brugnon
1927 Mrs. M. Bordes and Jean Borotra
1928 E. Bennett and Henri Cochet
1929 E. Bennett and Henri Cochet
1930 C. Aussen and William T. Tilden II
1931 Betty Nuthall and P. D. Spence
1932 Betty Nuthall and Fred J. Perry
1933 M. C. Scriven and Jack H. Crawford
1934 C. Rosambert and Jean Borotra
1935 L. Pavot and M. Bernard
1936 A. M. Yorke and M. Bernard
1937 Mrs. R. Mathieu and Y. Petra
1938 Mrs. R. Mathieu and D. Mitic
1939 Mrs. S. P. Fabyan and Elwood T. Cooke
1940–45 no competition
1946 Pauline Betz and Budge Patty
1947 Mrs. S. Summers and Eric W. Sturgess
1948 Mrs. P. C. Todd and Jaroslav Drobny
1949 Mrs. S. Summers and Eric W. Sturgess
1950 Barbara Sudfield and Enrique Morea
1951 Doris Hart and Frank Sedgman
1952 Doris Hart and Frank Sedgman
1953 Doris Hart and E. Victor Seixas, Jr.
1954 Maureen Connolly and Lew Hoad
1955 Darlene Hard and Gordon Forbes
1956 Mrs. T. C. Long and Luis Ayala
1957 V. Puzejova and J. Javorsky
1958 Shirley Bloomer and Nicoli Pietrangeli
1959 Yola Ramirez and William Knight
1960 Maria Bueno and Robert Howe

1961 Darlene Hard and Rod Laver
1962 Renée Schuurman and Robert Howe
1963 Margaret Smith and Ken Fletcher
1964 Margaret Smith and Ken Fletcher
1965 Margaret Smith and Ken Fletcher
1966 Annette van Zyl and Frew McMillan
1967 Mrs. B. J. King and Owen Davidson
1968* Françoise Durr and Jean Claude Barclay
1969* Mrs. M. S. Court and Martin Riessen
1970* Mrs. B. J. King and Jean Claude Barclay
1971* Françoise Durr and Jean Claude
      Barclay
1972* Evonne Goolagong and Kim Warwick
1973* Françoise Durr and Jean Claude
      Barclay
1974* Martina Navratilova and Ivan Molina
1975* Fiorella Bonicelli and Thomas Koch
1976* Ilana Kloss and Kim Warwick
1977* Mary Carillo and John McEnroe
1978* Renata Tomanova and Pavel Slozil
1979* Wendy Turnbull and Bob Hewitt
1980* Anne Smith and Billy Martin

*Open championship.

Australian Championships—Men's Singles

1905 R. W. Heath
1906 Tony Wilding
1907 H. M. Rice
1908 Fred Alexander
1909 Tony Wilding
1910 R. W. Heath
1911 Norman Brookes
1912 J. C. Parke
1913 E. F. Parker
1914 Pat O'Hara Wood
1915 F. G. Lowe
1916–18 no competition
1919 R. F. Kingscote
1920 Pat O'Hara Wood
1921 R. G. Gemmell
1922 James Anderson
1923 Pat O'Hara Wood
1924 James Anderson
1925 James Anderson
1926 John Hawkes
1927 Gerald Patterson
1928 Jean Borotra
1929 J. C. Gregory

Adrian Quist *(left)* won the Australian Championship in 1936, 1940, and 1948, while Viv McGrath *(right)* took it in 1937.

Australian Championships—Men's Singles *(cont.)*

1930	E. F. Moon
1931	Jack Crawford
1932	Jack Crawford
1933	Jack Crawford
1934	Fred Perry
1935	Jack Crawford
1936	Adrian Quist
1937	Viv McGrath
1938	Don Budge
1939	John Bromwich
1940	Adrian Quist
1941–45	no competition
1946	John Bromwich
1947	Dinny Pails
1948	Adrian Quist
1949	Frank Sedgman
1950	Frank Sedgman
1951	Richard Savitt
1952	Ken McGregor
1953	Ken Rosewall
1954	Merv Rose
1955	Ken Rosewall
1956	Lew Hoad
1957	Ashley Cooper
1958	Ashley Cooper
1959	Alex Olmedo
1960	Rodney Laver
1961	Roy Emerson
1962	Rodney Laver
1963	Roy Emerson
1964	Roy Emerson
1965	Roy Emerson
1966	Roy Emerson
1967	Roy Emerson
1968	Bill Bowrey
1969*	Rodney Laver
1970*	Arthur Ashe
1971*	Ken Rosewall
1972*	Ken Rosewall
1973*	John Newcombe
1974*	Jimmy Connors
1975*	John Newcombe
1976*	Mark Edmonson
1977* (Jan.)	Roscoe Tanner
1977* (Dec.)	Vitas Gerulaitis
1978*	Guillermo Vilas
1979*	Guillermo Vilas
1980*	Brian Teacher

*Open championship.

Australian Championships—Women's Singles

1922	Mrs. M. Molesworth
1923	Mrs. M. Molesworth
1924	S. Lance
1925	D. Akhurst
1926	D. Akhurst
1927	E. F. Boyd
1928	D. Akhurst
1929	D. Akhurst
1930	D. Akhurst
1931	Mrs. C. Buttsworth
1932	Mrs. C. Buttsworth
1933	Joan Hartigan
1934	Joan Hartigan
1935	Dorothy Round
1936	Joan Hartigan
1937	Nancye Wynne
1938	D. M. Bundy
1939	Mrs. V. Westacott
1940	Nancye Wynne
1941–45	no competition
1946	Mrs. Nancye W. Bolton
1947	Mrs. Nancye W. Bolton
1948	Mrs. Nancye W. Bolton
1949	Doris Hart
1950	A. Louise Brough
1951	Mrs. Nancye W. Bolton
1952	Mrs. Thelma C. Long
1953	Maureen Connolly
1954	Mrs. Thelma C. Long
1955	Beryl Penrose
1956	Mary Carter
1957	Shirley J. Fry
1958	Angela Mortimer
1959	Mrs. M. Reitano
1960	Margaret Smith
1961	Margaret Smith
1962	Margaret Smith
1963	Margaret Smith
1964	Margaret Smith
1965	Margaret Smith
1966	Margaret Smith
1967	Nancy Richey
1968	Mrs. Billie J. King
1969*	Mrs. Margaret S. Court
1970*	Mrs. Margaret S. Court
1971*	Mrs. Margaret S. Court
1972*	Virginia Wade
1973*	Mrs. Margaret Smith Court
1974*	Evonne Goolagong
1975*	Evonne Goolagong
1976*	Mrs. Evonne Goolagong Cawley
1977*	Mrs. Evonne Goolagong Cawley
1978*	Mrs. Evonne Goolagong Cawley
1978*	Chris O'Neill
1979*	Barbara Jordan
1980*	Hana Mandlikova

*Open championship.

Australian Championships—Men's Doubles

1905	T. Tachell and R. Lycett
1906	Tony Wilding and R. W. Heath
1907	H. A. Parker and W. A. Gregg
1908	Fred Alexander and Alfred Dunlop
1909	E. F. Parker and J. P. Keane
1910	H. Rice and A. Campbell
1911	R. W. Heath and R. Lycett
1912	J. C. Parke and C. P. Dixon
1913	E. F. Parker and A. H. Hedemann
1914	A. Campbell and Gerald Patterson
1915	H. M. Rice and C. V. Todd
1916–18	no competition
1919	Pat O'Hara Wood and R. V. Thomas
1920	Pat O'Hara Wood and R. V. Thomas
1921	R. H. Gennell and R. V. Thomas
1922	Gerald Patterson and John Hawkes
1923	Pat O'Hara Wood and C. B. St. John
1924	Norman Brookes and James Anderson
1925	Gerald Patterson and Pat O'Hara Wood
1926	Gerald Patterson and John Hawkes
1927	Gerald Patterson and John Hawkes
1928	Jean Borotra and Jacques Brugnon
1929	Jack Crawford and Harry Hopman
1930	Jack Crawford and Harry Hopman
1931	D. Donohoe and R. Dunlop
1932	Jack Crawford and E. F. Moon
1933	Ellsworth Vines and Keith Gledhill
1934	Fred Perry and Geroge Hughes
1935	Jack Crawford and Viv McGrath
1936	Adrian Quist and D. P. Turnbull
1937	Adrian Quist and D. P. Turnbull
1938	Adrian Quist and John Bromwich
1939	Adrian Quist and John Bromwich
1940	Adrian Quist and John Bromwich
1941–45	no competition

Pat O'Hara Wood *(left)* and Gerald L. Patterson *(right)* were famed doubles players of the 1920s.

Australian Championships—Men's Doubles *(cont.)*

1946	Adrian Quist and John Bromwich
1947	Adrian Quist and John Bromwich
1948	Adrian Quist and John Bromwich
1949	Adrian Quist and John Bromwich
1950	Adrian Quist and John Bromwich
1951	Frank Sedgman and Ken McGregor
1952	Frank Sedgman and Ken McGregor
1953	Lew Hoad and Ken Rosewall
1954	Rex Hartwig and Merv Rose
1955	Vic Seixas and Tony Trabert
1956	Lew Hoad and Ken Rosewall
1957	Lew Hoad and Neale Fraser
1958	Ashley Cooper and Neale Fraser
1959	Rodney Laver and Bob Mark
1960	Rodney Laver and Bob Mark
1961	Rodney Laver and Bob Mark
1962	Roy Emerson and Neale Fraser
1963	Bob Hewitt and Fred Stolle
1964	Bob Hewitt and Fred Stolle

1965	John Newcombe and Tony Roche
1966	Roy Emerson and Fred Stolle
1967	John Newcombe and Tony Roche
1968	Dick Crealy and Allen Stone
1969*	Roy Emerson and Rodney Laver
1970*	Robert Lutz and Stan Smith
1971*	John Newcombe and Tony Roche
1972*	Owen Davidson and Ken Rosewall
1973*	Mal Anderson and John Newcombe
1974*	Ross Case and Geoff Masters
1975*	John Alexander and Phil Dent
1976*	John Newcombe and Tony Roche
1977* (Jan.)	Brian Gottfried and Raul Ramirez
1977* (Dec.)	Ray Ruffels and Allan Stone
1978*	Wojtek Fibak and Kim Warwick
1979*	Peter McNamara and Paul McNameo
1980*	Mark Edmondson and Kim Warwick

*Open championships.

Australian Championships—Women's Doubles

1922	E. F. Boyd and M. Mountain
1923	E. F. Boyd and S. Lance
1924	D. Akhurst and S. Lance
1925	Mrs. R. R. Harper and D. Akhurst
1926	Mrs. P. O'Hara Wood and E. F. Boyd
1927	Mrs. P. O'Hara Wood and L. Bickerton
1928	D. Akhurst and E. F. Boyd
1929	D. Akhurst and L. Bickerton
1930	Mrs. M. Molesworth and E. Hood
1931	Mrs. D. A. Cozens and L. Bickerton
1932	Mrs. C. Buttsworth and Mrs. J. H. Crawford
1933	Mrs. M. Molesworth and Mrs. V. Westacott
1934	Mrs. M. Molesworth and Mrs. V. Westacott
1935	E. Dearman and N. Lyle
1936	T. Coyne and N. Wynne
1937	T. Coyne and N. Wynne
1938	T. Coyne and N. Wynne
1939	T. Coyne and N. Wynne
1940	T. Coyne and N. Wynne
1941–45	no competition
1946	J. Fetch and M. Bevis
1947	Mrs. T. C. Long and Mrs. N. W. Bolton
1948	Mrs. T. C. Long and Mrs. N. W. Bolton
1949	Mrs. T. C. Long and Mrs. N. W. Bolton

Four Australian women stars of the 1930s and 1940s *(left to right):* Dot Stevenson, Nancye Wynne (later Mrs. Bolton), Mrs. Nell Hopman, and Thelma Coyne (Mrs. Long).

1976* Evonne Goolagong and Helen Gourlay
1977* Dianne Fromholtz and Mrs. Helen G. Cawley
1977* (Dec.) Evonne Goolagong Cawley and Mrs. Helen G. Cawley
  and Kerry M. Reid and Mona Guerrant (co-champions, final match abandoned, rain)
1978* Betsy Nagelson and Renata Tomanova
1979* Judy Chaloner and Dianne Evers
1980* Betsy Nagelson and Martina Navratilova

*Open championship.

1950   A. Louise Brough and Doris Hart
1951   Mrs. T. C. Long and Mrs. N. W. Bolton
1952   Mrs. T. C. Long and Mrs. N. W. Bolton
1953   Maureen Connolly and Julia Sampson
1954   Mrs. M. Hawton and Beryl Penrose
1955   Mrs. M. Hawton and Beryl Penrose
1956   Mrs. M. Hawton and Mrs. T. C. Long
1957   Althea Gibson and Shirley Fry
1958   Mrs. M. Hawton and Mrs. T. C. Long
1959   Renée Schuurman and Sandra Reynolds
1960   Maria Bueno and Christine Truman
1961   Mrs. M. Reitano and Margaret Smith
1962   Margaret Smith and Robyn Ebbern
1963   Margaret Smith and Robyn Ebbern
1964   Judy Tegart and Lesley Turner
1965   Margaret Smith and Lesley Turner
1966   Mrs. C. C. Graebner and Nancy Richey
1967   Lesley Turner and Judy Tegert
1968   Karen Krantzcke and Kerry Melville
1969* Mrs. M. S. Court and Judy Tegart
1970* Mrs. M. S. Court and Mrs. J. T. Dalton
1971* Mrs. M. S. Court and Evonne Goolagong
1972* Kerry Harris and Helen Gourlay
1973* Margaret Smith Court and Virginia Wade
1974* Evonne Goolagong and Peggy Michel
1975* Evonne Goolagong and Peggy Michel

Australian Championships—Mixed Doubles

1922   E. F. Boyd and John B. Hawkes
1923   S. Lance and Horace M. Rice
1924   D. Akhurst and John Willard
1925   D. Akhurst and John Willard
1926   E. F. Boyd and John B. Hawkes
1927   E. F. Boyd and John B. Hawkes
1928   D. Akhurst and Jean Borotra
1929   D. Akhurst and E. F. Moon
1930   N. Hall and Harry C. Hopman
1931   Mr. and Mrs. John H. Crawford
1932   Mr. and Mrs. John H. Crawford
1933   Mr. and Mrs. John H. Crawford
1934   J. Hartigan and E. F. Moon
1935   L. M. Bickerton and C. Boussus
1936   Mr. and Mrs. Harry C. Hopman
1937   Mr. and Mrs. Harry C. Hopman
1938   M. Wilson and John Bromwich
1939   Mr. and Mrs. Harry C. Hopman
1940   N. Wynne and Colin Long
1941–45   no competition
1946   Mrs. N. Bolton and Colin Long
1947   Mrs. N. Bolton and Colin Long
1948   Mrs. N. Bolton and Colin Long
1949   Doris Hart and Frank Sedgman
1950   Doris Hart and Frank Sedgman
1951   Mrs. C. Long and George Worthington
1952   Mrs. C. Long and George Worthington
1953   Julia Sampson and Rex Hartwig
1954   Mrs. C. Long and Rex Hartwig
1955   Mrs. C. Long and George Worthington
1956   Beryl Penrose and Neale Fraser
1957   Fay Muller and Mal Anderson

Australian Championships—Mixed Doubles *(cont.)*

1958 Mrs. Mary Hawton and Bob Howe
1959 Sandra Reynolds and Bob Mark
1960 Jan LeHane and Trevor Fancutt
1961 Jan LeHane and Bob Hewitt
1962 Lesley Turner and Fred Stolle
1963 Margaret Smith and Ken Fletcher
1964 Margaret Smith and Ken Fletcher
1965 unfinished
1966 Judy Tegart and Tony Roche
1967 Lesley Turner and Owen Davidson
1968 Mrs. Billie J. King and Dick Crealy
1969–80 not held

Italian Championships—Men's Singles

1930 William T. Tilden II
1931 Pat Hughes
1932 André Merlin
1933 Emanuele Sertorio
1934 Giovanni Palmieri
1935 Wilmer Hines
1936–49 not held
1950 Jaroslav Drobny
1951 Jaroslav Drobny
1952 Frank Sedgman
1953 Jaroslav Drobny
1954 J. Edward Patty
1955 Fausto Gardini
1956 Lewis Hoad
1957 Nicola Pietrangeli
1958 Mervyn Rose
1959 Luis Ayala
1960 Barry MacKay
1961 Nicola Pietrangeli
1962 Rodney Laver
1963 Martin Mulligan
1964 Jan Erik Lundquist
1965 Martin Mulligan
1966 Tony Roche
1967 Martin Mulligan
1968 Tom Okker
1969* John Newcombe
1970* Ilie Nastase
1971* Rodney Laver
1972* Manuel Orantes
1973* Ilie Nastase
1974* Bjorn Borg

1975* Raul Ramirez
1976* Adriano Panatta
1977* Vitas Gerulaitis
1978* Bjorn Borg
1979* Vitas Gerulaitis
1980* Guillermo Vilas

Italian Championships—Women's Singles

1930 Lili Alvarez
1931 Lucia Valerio
1932 Ada Adamoff
1933 Elizabeth Ryan
1934 Helen Jacobs
1935 Hilda Sperling
1936–49 not held
1950 Angela Bossi
1951 Doris Hart
1952 Susan Partridge
1953 Doris Hart
1954 Maureen Connolly
1955 Patricia Ward
1956 Althea Gibson
1957 Shirley Bloomer
1958 Maria Bueno
1959 Christine Truman
1960 Mrs. S. Kormoczi
1961 Maria E. Bueno
1962 Margaret Smith
1963 Margaret Smith
1964 Margaret Smith
1965 Maria Bueno
1966 Mrs. A. H. Jones
1967 Lesley Turner
1968 Mrs. L. T. Bowrey
1969* Julie M. Heldman
1970* Mrs. B. J. King
1971* Virginia Wade
1972* Linda Tuero
1973* Evonne Goolagong
1974* Chris Evert
1975* Chris Evert
1976* Mima Jausovec
1977* Janet Newberry
1978* Regina Marsikova
1979* Tracy Austin
1980* Mrs. Chris Evert Lloyd

*Open championship.

Italian Championships—Men's Doubles

1930 William T. Tilden II and Wilbur Coen
1931 Alberto Del Bono and Pat Hughes
1932 Giorgio De Stefani and Pat Hughes
1933 J. Lesuer and Martin Legeay
1934 G. Palmieri and George Rogers
1935 Jack Crawford and Viv McGrath
1936–49 not held
1950 Bill Talbert and Tony Trabert
1951 Jaroslav Drobny and Dick Savitt
1952 Jaroslav Drobny and Frank Sedgman
1953 Lewis Hoad and Kenneth Rosewall
1954 Jaroslav Drobny and Enrique Morea
1955 Arthur Larsen and Enrique Morea
1956 Jaroslav Drobny and Lewis Hoad
1957 Lewis Hoad and Neale Fraser
1958 Kurt Nielsen and Anton Jansco
1959 Neale Fraser and Roy Emerson
1960 not completed
1961 Neale Fraser and Roy Emerson
1962 Rodney Laver and John Fraser
1963 Bob Hewitt and Fred Stolle
1964 Bob Hewitt and Fred Stolle
1965 John Newcombe and Tony Roche
1966 Roy Emerson and Fred Stolle
1967 Bob Hewitt and Frew McMillan
1968 Tom Okker and Martin Riessen
1969 not completed
1970* Ilie Nastase and Ion Tiriac
1971* John Newcombe and Tony Roche
1972* Ilie Nastase and Ion Tiriac
1973* John Newcombe and Tom Okker
1974* Brian Gottfried and Raul Ramirez
1975* Brian Gottfried and Raul Ramirez
1976* Brian Gottfried and Raul Ramirez
        and John Newcombe and Geoff Masters
        (co-champions)
1977* Brian Gottfried and Raul Ramirez
1978* Victor Pecci and Belus Prajoux
1979* Peter Fleming and Tomas Smid
1980* Mark Edmondson and Kim Warwick

Italian Championships—Women's Doubles

1930 Lucia Valerio and Lili Alvarez
1931 Anna Luzzatti and R. Gagliardi
1932 C. Rosambert and Lolette Payot
1933 Mrs. D. Burke and I. Adamoff
1934 Helen Jacobs and Elizabeth Ryan
1935 Evelyn Dearman and Nancy Lyle
1936–49 not held
1950 Jean Quertier and Mrs. Jean
        Walker-Smith
1951 Doris Hart and Shirley Fry
1952 Mrs. T. Long and Mrs. Nell Hopman
1953 Maureen Connolly and Julia Sampson
1954 Patricia Ward and E. M. Watson
1955 Patricia Ward and Christine Marcelis
1956 Mrs. T. C. Long and Mrs. M. Hawton
1957 Mrs. T. C. Long and Mrs. M. Hawton
1958 Shirley Bloomer and Christine Truman
1959 Yola Ramirez and Rosie Reyes
1960 Yola Ramirez and Rosie Reyes
1961 Lesley Turner and Jan LeHane
1962 Maria Bueno and Darlene Hard
1963 Margaret Smith and Robyn Ebbern
1964 Margaret Smith and Lesley Turner
1965 Madonna Schacht and Annette van Zyl
1966 Norma Baylon and Annette van Zyl
1967 Rosemary Casals and Lesley Turner
1968 Mrs. M. S. Court and Virginia Wade
1969* Françoise Durr and Mrs. Ann H. Jones
1970* Rosemary Clark and Mrs. B. J. M. King
1971* Mrs. H. N. Masthoff and Virginia Wade
1972* Lesley Hunt and Olga Morozova
1973* Virginia Wade and Olga Morozova
1974* Chris Evert and Olga Morozova
1975* Chris Evert and Martina Navratilova
1976* Linky Boshoff and Ilana Kloss
1977* Brigitte Cuypers and Marise Kruger
1978* Virginia Ruzici and Mima Jausovec
1979* Betty Stove and Wendy Turnbull
1980* Renata Tomanova and Hana
        Mandlikova

Italian Championships—Mixed Doubles

1930 Lili Alvarez and J. L. DeMorpurgo
1931 Lucia Valerio and Pat Hughes
1932 Lolette Payot and J. Bonte
1933 Mrs. Dorothy Burke and Martin Legeay
1934 Elizabeth Ryan and Henry Culley
1935 Jadwiga Jedrzejowska and Harry
        Hopman
1936–49 not held
1950 not completed

*Open championships.

Italian Championships—Mixed Doubles *(cont.)*

1951	Shirley Fry and Felicissimo Ampon
1952	Arvilla McGuire and Kurt Nielsen
1953	Doris Hart and E. Victor Seixas, Jr.
1954	divided
1955	divided
1956	Mrs. T. C. Long and Luis Ayala
1957	Mrs. T. C. Long and Luis Ayala
1958	Shirley Bloomer and Giorgio Fachini
1959	Rosie Reyes and Francisco Contreras
1960	not played
1961	Margaret Smith and Roy Emerson
1962	Lesley Turner and Fred Stolle
1963	canceled
1964	Margaret Smith and John Newcombe
1965	Carmen Coronado and Edison Mandarino
1966	not played
1967	Lesley Turner and William Bowrey
1968	Mrs. M. S. Court and Martin Riessen
1969–80	not played

German Championships—Men's Singles

1892	W. Bonne
1893	G. Winzer
1894	G. Voss
1895	G. Voss
1896	G. Voss
1897	Geroge W. Hillyard
1898	S. M. Mahony
1899	C. Hobart
1900	Geroge W. Hillyard
1901	Max Décugis
1902	Max Décugis
1903	M. G. J. Ritchie
1904	M. G. J. Ritchie
1905	M. G. J. Ritchie
1906	M. G. J. Ritchie
1907	Otto Froitzheim
1908	M. G. J. Ritchie
1909	Otto Froitzheim
1910	Otto Froitzheim
1911	Otto Froitzheim
1912	Otto von Muller
1913	H. Schomburgk
1914–19	no competition
1920	Otto Kreuzer
1921	Otto Froitzheim
1922	Otto Froitzheim
1923	H. Landmann
1924	B. von Kehrling
1925	Otto Froitzheim
1926	Hans Moldenhauer
1927	Hans Moldenhauer
1928	Dann D. Prenn
1929	C. Boussus
1930	C. Boussus
1931	Roderick Menzel
1932	Gottfried von Cramm
1933	Gottfried von Cramm
1934	Gottfried von Cramm
1935	Gottfried von Cramm
1936	no competition
1937	Henner Henkel
1938	O. Szigeti
1939	Henner Henkel
1940–47	no competition
1948	Gottfried von Cramm
1949	Gottfried von Cramm
1950	Jaroslav Drobny
1951	Lennart Bergelin
1952	E. W. Sturgess
1953	Budge Patty
1954	Budge Patty
1955	Art Larsen
1956	Lew A. Hoad
1957	Mervyn G. Rose
1958	Sven Davidson
1959	W. A. Knight
1960	Nicola Pietrangeli
1961	Rod Laver
1962	Rod Laver
1963	Martin F. Mulligan
1964	Wilhelm P. Bungert
1965	E. Cliff Drysdale
1966	Fred S. Stolle
1967	Roy Emerson
1968	John D. Newcombe
1969*	Tony D. Roche
1970*	Tom Okker
1971*	Andres Gimeno
1972*	Manuel Orantes
1973*	Eddie Dibbs
1974*	Eddie Dibbs

*Open championship.

1975* Manuel Orantes
1976* Eddie Dibbs
1977* Paolo Bertolucci
1978* Guillermo Vilas
1979* Jose Higueras
1980* Harold Solomon

German Championships—Women's Singles

1896 M. Thomsen
1897 Mrs. G. W. Hillyard
1898 E. Lane
1899 C. Cooper
1900 Mrs. G. W. Hillyard
1901 T. Lowther
1902 C. Ross
1903 V. Pinckney
1904 E. Lane
1905 E. Lane
1906 L. Berton
1907 F. de Madarasz
1908 F. de Madarasz
1909 D. Heimann
1910 M. Rieck
1911 M. Rieck
1912 D. Koring
1913 D. Koring
1914–19 no competition
1920 Mrs. I. Friedleben
1921 Mrs. I. Friedleben
1922 Mrs. I. Friedleben
1923 Mrs. I. Friedleben
1924 Mrs. I. Friedleben
1925 Mrs. N. Neppach
1926 Mrs. I. Friedleben
1927 Cilly Aussem
1928 D. Akhurst
1929 Mrs. Paula S. von Reznicek
1930 Cilly Aussem
1931 Cilly Aussem
1932 L. Payot
1933 Hilda Krahwinkel
1934 Mrs. Hilda K. Sperling
1935 Mrs. Hilda K. Sperling
1936 no competition
1937 Mrs. Hilda K. Sperling
1938 Mrs. Hilda K. Sperling
1939 Mrs. Hilda K. Sperling
1940–47 no competition

1948 U. Rosenow
1949 Mrs. M. Weiss
1950 Dorothy Head
1951 Mrs. Nancye W. Bolton
1952 Dorothy Head
1953 Mrs. Dorothy H. Knode
1954 Mrs. A. J. Mottram
1955 Berle Penrose
1956 Mrs. N. C. Long
1957 Y. Ramirez
1958 L. Coghlan
1959 Edda Buding
1960 Sandra Reynolds
1961 Sandra Reynolds
1962 Mrs. Sandra R. Price
1963 Renee Schuurman
1964 Margaret Smith
1965 Margaret Smith
1966 Margaret Smith
1967 Francoise Durr
1968 Mrs. Anette du Plooy
1969* Judy A. M. Tegart
1970* Mrs. H. Hoesl
1971* Mrs. Billie Jean King
1972* Mrs. Helga N. Masthoff
1973* Mrs. Helga N. Masthoff
1974* Mrs. Helga N. Masthoff
1975* Renata Tomanova
1976* Sue Barker
1977* Laura du Pont
1978* Mima Jausovec
1979* Caroline Stoll
1980* Tracy Austin

German Championships—Men's Doubles

1902 Max Décugis and M. Germot
1903 R. Kinzl and C. von Wessely
1904 M. G. J. Ritchie and W. E. Lane
1905 A. F. Wilding and E. Spitz
1906 M. G. J. Ritchie and G. F. Adler
1907 L. Trasenster and O. Froitzheim
1908 O. von Muller and H. Schomburgk
1909 F. W. Rahe and C. Bergmann
1910 O. von Muller and H. Schomburgk
1911 Otto Froitzheim and F. Pipes
1912 L. Transenster and L. M. Heyden

*Open championship.

German Championships—Men's Doubles *(cont.)*

1913 R. Kinzl and C. von Wessely
1914–19 not held
1920 G. Salm and O. Kruezer
1921 L. M. Heyden and H. Schomburgk
1922 Otto Froitzheim and O. Kreuzer
1923 F. W. Rahe and B. von Kehrling
1924 F. W. Rahe and B. von Kehrling
1925 Otto Froitzheim and O. Kreuzer
1926 F. W. Rahe and B. von Kehrling
1927 D. M. Greig and M. V. Summerson
1928 R. O. Cummings and E. F. Moon
1929 Jacques Brugnon and C. Boussus
1930 J. B. Crawford and E. F. Moon
1931 W. Dessart and E. Nourney
1932 J. B. Crawford and H. Hopman
1933 J. Satoh and R. Nuoni
1934 E. Maier and A. Quist
1935 Henner Henkel and H. Denker
1936 not held
1937 J. B. Crawford and V. McGrath
1938 Yvon Petra and J. Lesueur
1939 Henner Henkel and R. Menzel
1940–47 no competition
1948 G. von Cramm and J. E. Harper
1949 G. von Cramm and J. E. Harper
1950 A. Quist and O. W. Sidwell
1951 K. Nielsen and T. Ulrich
1952 J. Drobny and W. Avre
1953 G. von Cramm and B. Patty
1954 G. von Cramm and B. Patty
1955 G. von Cramm and B. Patty
1956 Lew Hoad and D. Candy
1957 M. G. Rose and D. Candy
1958 F. Contreras and M. Llamas
1959 L. Ayala and D. Candy
1960 Roy Emerson and N. Fraser
1961 Bob Hewitt and F. S. Stolle
1962 Bob Hewitt and M. F. Mulligan
1963 Bob Hewitt and F. S. Stolle
1964 J. L. Arilla and M. Santana
1965 Ingo Buding and C. Kuknke
1966 F. S. Stolle and T. Ulrich
1967 Bob Hewitt and F. McMillan
1968 Tom Okker and M. Riessen
1969* Tom Okker and M. Riessen
1970* R. Hewitt and F. McMillan
1971* A. Gimeno and J. Alexander
1972* Jan Kodes and Ilie Nastase

Germany's two best pre–World War II players, Heinrich Henkel *(left)* and Baron Gottfried von Cramm *(right)*.

1973* Jurgen Fassbender and Hans Pohmann
1974* Jurgen Fassbender and Hans Pohmann
1975* Juan Gisbert and Manuel Orantes
1976* Fred McNair and Sherwood Stewart
1977* Bob Hewitt and Karl Meiler
1978* Tom Okker and Wojtek Fibak
1979* Jan Kodes and Tomas Smid
1980* Hans Gildemeister and Andres Gomez

*Open championship

German Championships—Women's Doubles

1925 Mrs. N. Neppach and Mrs. H. Kaeber
1926 Mrs. M. Galvao and E. Hoffmann
1927 Mrs. N. Neppach and Mrs. H. Petery
     Varady
1928 D. Akhurst and E. Boyd
1929 J. Fry and M. V. Chamberlain
1930 Mrs. L. A. Godfree and Mrs. H. Watson
1931 Mrs. L. A. Godfree and N. Trentham
1932 H. Krahwinkel and A. Peitz

1933 Mrs. J. B. Pittmann and K. Stammers
1934 E. M. Dearman and N. M. Lyle
1935 Mrs. A. Schneider and Mrs. M. Rollin
Conquerque
1936 no competition
1937 Mrs. H. K. Sperling and Mrs. M. Rollin
Conquerque
1938 N. Wynne and T. Coyne
1939 Mrs. H. K. Sperling and Mrs. A.
Schneider
1940–47 no competition
1948 Mrs. M. Dietz and T. Heidtmann
1949 Mrs. A. von Tarnay and T. Zehden
1950 Mrs. J. Pohmann and D. Head
1951 Mrs. N. W. Bolton and Mrs. M. Procter
1952 D. Head and Mrs. A. J. Mottram
1953 Mrs. D. H. Knode and Mrs. A. J.
Mottram
1954 Mrs. E. Vollmer and Mrs. A. J. Mottram
1955 B. Penrose and M. Carter
1956 E. F. Muller and B. Seeney
1957 A. Mortimer and P. Ward
1958 M. Hawton and Mrs. N. C. Long
1959 Y. Ramirez and R. M. Reyes
1960 E. Buding and C. Truman
1961 S. Reynolds and R. Schuurman
1962 L. R. Turner and J. Lehane
1963 L. Hunt and A. M. van Zyl
1964 M. Smith and L. R. Turner
1965 M. Smith and L. R. Turner
1966 M. Smith and Mrs. A. H. Jones
1967 J. Tegart and L. R. Turner
1968 Mrs. A. M. duPlooy and P. Walkden
1969* H. Niessen and J. Tegart
1970* K. Krantzcke and K. Melville
1971* Mrs. B. J. King and R. Casals
1972* Helga N. Masthoff and Heidi Orth
1973* Helga N. Masthoff and Heidi Orth
1974* Helga Hoesl and Raquel Giscafre
1975* Dianne Fromholtz and Renata
Tomanova
1976* Linky Boshoff and Ilana Kloss
1977* Linky Boshoff and Ilana Kloss
1978* Mima Jausovec and Virginia
Ruzici
1979* Wendy Turnbull and Rosemary Casals
1980* Hana Mandlikova and Betty Stove

*Open championships.

German Championships—Mixed Doubles

1906 N. Schmoller and O. Kreuzer
1907 Mrs. G. Neresheimer and L. Trasenster
1908 K. Osery and L. Trasenster
1909 M. Rieck and M. Galvao
1910 Mrs. G. Neresheimer and F. C. Uhl
1911 Mrs. G. Neresheimer and F. C. Uhl
1912 D. Koering and H. Schomburgk
1913 D. Koering and H. Schomburgk
1914–19 no competition
1920 Mrs. J. Friedleben and O. Kreuzer
1921 Mrs. H. Schomburgk and H. Schomburgk
1922 E. de Alvarez and L. M. Heyden
1923 E. de Alvarez and L. M. Heyden
1924 Mrs. N. Neppach and H. Kleinschroth
1925 Mrs. Neppach and A. Ludke
1926 C. Aussem and H. Moldenhauer
1927 J. Kallmeyer and D. M. Greig
1928 C. Aussem and R. R. Boyd
1929 E. L. Colyer and H. G. N. Lee
1930 Mrs. L. A. Godfree and J. C. Gregory
1931 L. Payot and H. C. Fisher
1932 H. Krahwinkel and G. von Cramm
1933 H. Krahwinkel and G. von Cramm
1934 Mrs. H. K. Sperling and G. von Cramm
1935 C. Aussem and H. Henkel
1936 no competition
1937 M. L. Horne and H. Denker
1938 N. Wynne and J. Lesueur
1939 G. Wheeler and M. Smith
1940–47 no competition
1948 V. Rosenow and E. Buchholz
1949 Mrs. J. Pohmann and T. Koch
1950 Mrs. M. Dietz and O. W. Sidwell
1951 Mrs. N. W. Bolton and J. Borotra
1952 D. Head and E. W. Sturgess
1953 P. Ward and A. J. Mottram
1954 Mrs. E. Vollmer and H. W. Stewart
1955 Mrs. E. Vollmer and H. W. Stewart
1956 Mrs. T. C. Long and L. Ayala
1957 E. Buding and M. G. Rose
1958 Y. Ramirez and J. Jansco
1959 Y. Ramirez and W. A. Knight
1960 S. Reynolds and I. Vermaak
1961 S. Reynolds and R. Hewitt
1962 L. R. Turner and K. Fletcher
1963 L. R. Turner and F. S. Stolle
1964 H. Schultze and N. Pilic
1965 M. Smith and N. Fraser

German Championships—Mixed Doubles *(cont.)*

1966   M. Smith and J. Newcombe
1967   C. Sheriff and T. Okker
1968   Mrs. A. M. du Plooy and F. McMillan
1969* J. Tegart and M. Riessen
1970* J. T. Dalton and F. McMillan
1971   not held
1972* Heidi Orth and Jurgen Fassbender
1973* Pat Pretorius and Hans Pohmann
1974* Heidi Orth and Jurgen Fassbender
1975–80   not played

South African Championships—Men's Singles

1891   L. A. Richardson
1892   L. A. Richardson
1893   W. L. Edwards
1894   L. Giddy
1895   L. Giddy
1896   L. Giddy
1897   L. Giddy
1898   L. Giddy
1899   L. G. Heard
1900–02   no competition
1903   R. W. G. Clarke
1904   P. W. Sherwell
1905   H. A. Kitson
1906   J. Richardson
1907   Dr. A. Rowan
1908   H. A. Kitson
1909   R. F. Doherty
1910   A. F. Wilding
1911   H. A. Kitson
1912   G. H. Dodd
1913   H. A. Kitson
1914   C. L. Winslow
1915–19   no competition
1920   B. I. C. Norton
1921   L. Raymond
1922   L. Raymond
1923   L. Raymond
1924   L. Raymond
1925   I. J. Richardson
1926   J. Condon
1927   no competition
1928   G. Eaglestone
1929   C. J. J. Robbins
1930   L. Raymond

1931   L. Raymond
1932   Max Bertram
1933   C. J. J. Robbins
1934   N. G. Farquharson
1935   N. G. Farquharson
1936   N. G. Farquharson
1937   J. Palada
1938   N. G. Farquharson
1939   E. W. Sturgess
1940   E. W. Sturgess
1941–45   no competition
1946   E. W. Sturgess
1947   E. Fannin
1948   E. W. Sturgess
1949   E. W. Sturgess
1950   E. W. Sturgess
1951   E. W. Sturgess
1952   E. W. Sturgess
1953   E. W. Sturgess
1954   E. W. Sturgess
1955   W. R. Seymour
1956   J. C. Vermaak
1957   E. W. Sturgess
1958   U. Schmidt
1959   G. L. Forbes
1960   E. Buchholz
1961   G. L. Forbes
1962   R. Mark
1963   Wilhelm Bungert
1964   A. Segal
1965   Cliff Drysdale
1966   Roy Emerson
1967   Manuel Santana
1968   Tom Okker
1969* Rod Laver
1970* Rod Laver
1971* Ken Rosewall
1972* Cliff Richey
1973* Jimmy Connors
1974* Jimmy Connors
1975* Harold Solomon
1976* Harold Solomon
1977* Guillermo Vilas
1978* Tim Gullikson
1979* Andrew Pattison
1980* Kim Warwick

*Open championships.

South African Championships—Women's Singles

1891	H. Grant
1892	H. Grant
1893	H. Grant
1894	H. Grant
1895	R. Biddulph
1896	Mrs. H. Green
1897	N. Hickman
1898	N. Hickman
1899	N. Hickman
1900–02	no competition
1903	F. Kuys
1904	Mrs. H. A. Kirby
1905	Mrs. H. A. Kirby
1906	Mrs. H. A. Kirby
1907	Mrs. H. A. Kirby
1908	B. Kelly
1909	Mrs. G. Washington
1910	Mrs. H. A. Kirby
1911	Mrs. G. Washington
1912	Mrs. H. A. Kirby
1913	M. Coles
1914	G. Mathias
1915–19	no competition
1920	Mrs. C. L. Winslow
1921	N. Edwards
1922	Mrs. T. MacJannett
1923	Mrs. M. Pitt
1924	Mrs. I. E. Peacock
1925	Mrs. I. E. Peacock
1926	Mrs. I. E. Peacock
1927	no competition
1928	E. L. Heine
1929	Mrs. MacJannett
1930	R. D. Tapscott
1931	E. L. Heine
1932	Mrs. E. L. H. Miller
1933	Mrs. C. J. J. Robbins
1934	Mrs. C. J. J. Robbins
1935	Mrs. A. Allister
1936	Mrs. E. L. H. Miller
1937	Mrs. E. L. H. Miller
1938	Mrs. C. J. J. Robbins
1939	Mrs. O. Craze
1940	Mrs. O. Craze
1941–45	no competition
1946	Mrs. M. Muller
1947	Mrs. M. Muller
1948	Mrs. S. P. Summers
1949	Mrs. S. P. Summers
1950	Shirley J. Fry
1951	Mrs. S. P. Summers
1952	Doris J. Hart
1953	Mrs. H. Redick-Smith
1954	Mrs. H. Redick-Smith
1955	Mrs. H. Redick-Smith
1956	D. Kilian
1957	Mrs. H. Brewer
1958	B. Carr
1959	Sandra Reynolds
1960	Mrs. V. Vucovich
1961	Sandra Reynolds
1962	Mrs. A. Segal
1963	Annette Van Zyl
1964	Darlene Hard
1965	Christine C. Truman
1966	Mrs. Billie Jean M. King
1967	Mrs. Billie Jean M. King
1968	Mrs. Margaret S. Court
1969*	Mrs. Billie Jean M. King
1970*	Mrs. Margaret S. Court
1971*	Mrs. Margaret S. Court
1972*	Evonne Goolagong
1973*	Chris Evert
1974*	Kerry Melville
1975*	Mrs. Annette DuPlooy
1976*	Brigette Cuypers
1977*	Linky Boshoff
1978*	Bridget Cuypers
1979*	Bridget Cuypers
1980*	Lesley J. Charles

Canadian Championships—Men's Singles

1890	E. E. Tanner
1891	F. S. Mansfield
1892	F. H. Hovey
1893	H. E. Avery
1894	R. W. P. Matthews
1895	W. A. Larned
1896	R. D. Wrenn
1897	L. E. Ware
1898	L. E. Ware
1899	M. D. Whitman
1900	M. D. Whitman
1901	W. A. Larned
1902	B. C. Wright

*Open championship.

Canadian Championships—Men's Singles *(cont.)*

1903	B. C. Wright
1904	B. C. Wright
1905	no tournament
1906	I. C. Wright
1907	J. F. Foulkes
1908	T. Y. Sherwell
1909	J. F. Foulkes
1910	J. F. Foulkes
1911	B. P. Schwengers
1912	B. P. Schwengers
1913	R. Baird
1914	T. M. Sherwell
1915–18	no tournament
1919	Seijchiro Kashio
1920	Paul Bennett
1921	W. J. Bates
1922	Frank Anderson
1923	W. L. Rennie
1924	George M. Lott
1925	W. F. Crocker
1926	L. DeTurenne
1927	J. A. Wright
1928	Wilmer Allison
1929	J. A. Wright
1930	G. Lyttleton
1931	Jack Wright
1932	Frank Parker
1933	John Murio
1934	Marcel Rainville
1935	Eugene Smith
1936	Jack Tidball
1937	Walter Senior
1938	Frank Parker
1939	P. Morey Lewis
1940	Don McDiarmid
1941–45	no tournaments
1946	P. Morey Lewis
1947	James Evert
1948	William Tully
1949	Henri Rochon
1950	Brendan Macken
1951	Tony Vincent
1952	Richard Savitt
1953	Mervyn Rose
1954	Bernard Bartzen
1955	Robert Bedard
1956	Noel Brown

1957	Robert Bedard
1958	Robert Bedard
1959	Reynaldo Garrido
1960	Ladislav Legenstein
1961	Whitney Reed
1962	Juan Couder
1963	Whitney Reed
1964	Roy Emerson
1965	Ronald Holmberg
1966	Allen Fox
1967	Manuel Santana
1968	Ramanathan Krishnan
1969*	Cliff Richey
1970	Mike Belkin
1970*	Rod Laver
1971	Peter Burwash
1971*	John Newcombe
1972*	Ilie Nastase
1973*	Tom Okker
1974*	Guillermo Vilas
1975*	Manuel Orantes
1976*	Guillermo Vilas
1977*	Jeff Borowiak
1978*	Eddie Dibbs
1979*	Bjorn Borg
1980*	Ivan Lendl

Canadian Championships—Women's Singles

1919	Marion Zinderstein
1920	Mrs. H. Bickle
1921	Mrs. H. Bickle
1922	Mrs. H. Bickle
1923	F. Best
1924	Mrs. H. Bickle
1925	M. Leeming
1926	M. Leeming
1927	C. Swartz
1928	Marjorie Gladman
1929	Olive Wade
1930	Olive Wade
1931	Edith Cross
1932	Olive Wade
1933	Gracyn Wheeler
1934	Caroline Deacon
1935	Margaret Osborne
1936	Dr. Esther Bartosh
1937	Evelyn M. Dearman

*Open championships.

1938	Mrs. R. Bolte
1939	Elizabeth Blackman
1940	Eleanor Young
1941–45	no tournament
1946	Mrs. B. Lewis
1947	Mrs. G. Kelleher
1948	Patricia Macken
1949	Mrs. B. Lewis
1950	Barbara Knapp
1951	Mrs. L. Davidson
1952	Melita Ramirez
1953	Melita Ramirez
1954	Karol Fageros
1955	Mrs. H. Sladek
1956	Jean Laird
1957	Mrs. L. Brown
1958	Eleanor Dodge
1959	Mary Martin
1960	Donna Floyd
1961	Ann Haydon
1962	Ann Barclay
1963	Ann Barclay
1964	Benita Senn
1965	Julie M. Heldman
1966	Rita Bentley
1967	Kathy Harter
1968	Jane Bartkowicz
1969*	Faye Urban
1970	André Martin
1970*	Mrs. Margaret S. Court
1971	Vicki Berner
1971*	Françoise Durr
1972*	Evonne Goolagong
1973*	Evonne Goolagong
1974*	Chris Evert
1975*	Marcie Louie
1976*	Mima Jausovec
1977*	Regina Marsikova
1978*	Regina Marsikova
1979*	Laura DuPont
1980*	Mrs. Chris Evert Lloyd

Canadian Championships—Men's Doubles

1919	G. D. Holmes and P. Bennett
1920	P. Bennett and F. W. Leistikow
1921	C. V. Todd and N. Peach
1922	F. T. and F. G. Anderson
1923	W. F. Crocker and Jack Wright

1924	G. M. Lott and Sam Hardy
1925	W. F. Crocker and Jack Wright
1926	L. DeTurenne and John Proctor
1927	B. Harrison and S. Lockwood
1928	J. Van Ryn and Wilmer Allison
1929	J. A. Wright and W. F. Crocker
1930	Fred Mercur and J. G. Hall
1931	Jack Wright and Marcel Rainville
1932	George Lott and Marcel Rainville
1933	John Murio and Martin Kenneally
1934	Harold Surface and Philip Castlen
1935	Worth Oswold and Charles Weesner
1936	Jack Tidball and Charles Church
1937	Walter Martin and D. N. Jones, Jr.
1938	W. L. Allison, Jr. and Frank Parker
1939	P. M. Lewis and F. A. Froehling
1940	Ross Wilson and Phil Pearson
1941–45	no tournament
1946	Jim Macken and Brendan Macken
1947	James Evert and Jerry Evert
1948	Edgar Lanthier and Gordon MacNeil
1949	Edgar Lanthier and Gordon MacNeil
1950	Robert Abdesselam and Jean Ducos
1951	Brendan Macken and Lorne Main
1952	Kurt Nielsen and Richard Savitt
1953	Rex Hartwig and Mervyn Rose
1954	Luis Ayala and Lorne Main
1955	Robert Bedard and Donald Fontana
1956	Earl Baumgardner and Noel Brown
1957	Robert Bedard and Donald Fontana
1958	Robert Howe and Whitney Reed
1959	Robert Bedard and Donald Fontana
1960	Peter School and Ladislav Legenstein
1961	Whitney Reed and Michael Sangster
1962	Bill Hoogs and Jim McManus
1963	Joaquin Loyo-Mayo and Marcelo Lara
1964	Roy Emerson and Fred Stolle
1965	Ronald Holmberg and Lester Sack
1966	Keith Carpenter and Mike Carpenter
1967	Roy Emerson and Manuel Santana
1968	Harry Fauquier and John Sharpe
1969*	John Newcombe and Ron Holmberg
1970	Bob Bedard and Bob Puddicombe
1970*	William Bowrey and Martin Riessen
1971	Peter Burwash and Ken Binnis
1971*	Tom Okker and Martin Riessen
1972*	Ilie Nastase and Ion Tiriac

*Open championships.

Canadian Championships—Men's Doubles *(cont.)*

1973* Rod Laver and Ken Rosewall
1974* Manuel Orantes and Guillermo Vilas
1975* Cliff Drysdale and Ray Moore
1976* Bob Hewitt and Raul Ramirez
1977* Bob Hewitt and Raul Ramirez
1978* Wojtek Fibak and Tom Okker
1979* John McEnroe and Peter Fleming
1980* Bruce Manson and Brian Teacher

Canadian Championships—Women's Doubles

1919 Mrs. H. Bickle and F. Best
1920 Mrs. H. Bickle and F. Best
1921 Mrs. H. Bickle and F. Best
1922 Mrs. H. Bickle and F. Best
1922 Mrs. H. Bickle and F. Best
1923 Mrs. H. Bickle and F. Best
1924 Mrs. H. Bickle and F. Best
1925 M. Leeming and K. Tatlow
1926 Mrs. D. Bourque and L. Fraser
1927 C. Swartz and Edith Cross
1928 Mrs. A. H. Chapin, Jr. and Marjorie
        Gladman
1929 Mrs. O. E. Gray and Olive Wade
1930 M. Leeming and H. Leeming
1931 Edith Cross and Mrs. D. Perow
1932 M. Leeming and Mrs. K. J. Salmond
1933 Mrs. H. V. Wilson and Mary Campbell
1934 Caroline Deacon and Eleanor Young
1935 Mrs. C. Rose and Mrs. M. Laird
1936 Mrs. G. M. Gross and Jean Milne
1937 Evelyn Dearman and J. Ingram
1938 Mrs. Frank Fisher and Mrs. W. Walson,
        Jr.
1939 E. and L. Blackman
1940 E. Young and E. Milne
1941–45   no tournaments
1946 Mrs. B. Lewis and Noreen Haney
1947 Mrs. G. Wheeler Kelleher and June
        Crow
1948 Mrs. Frank Fisher and Mary Green
1949 Mrs. B. Lewis and Edyth A. Sullivan
1950 Isabel Troccole and Carol Liguori
1951 Mrs. L. Davidson and Doris Popple
1952 Doris Ell and Melita Ramirez
1953 Mrs. Thelma Long and Melita Ramirez
1954 Karol Fageros and Ethel Norton

American Julie Heldman won, among her many honors, the Canadian and Italian championships.

1955 C. Bowan and Ann Barclay
1956 Mrs. J. Lee and Pat Miller
1957 Mrs. L. Brown and Mrs. H. Doleschell
1958 Barbara Browning and Pam Davis
1959 Mrs. D. Head Knode and Mary Martin
1960 Donna Floyd and Belmar Gunderson
1961 M. Bundy and Eleanor Dodge
1962 Ann Barclay and Mrs. L. Brown
1963 Susan Butt and Vicki Berner
1964 Mrs. A. Tym and Hedy Rutzezeck
1965 Brenda Nunns and Faye Urban
1966 Vicki Berner and Faye Urban
1967 Vicki Berner and Faye Urban
1968 not held
1969* Vicki Berner and Faye Urban
1970 Andre Martin and Jane O'Hara
1970* Mrs. M. S. Court and Rosemary Casals
1971 Andre Martin and Jane O'Hara

*Open championships.

1971* Rosemary Casals and Françoise Durr
1972* Mrs. Margaret Court and Evonne Goolagong
1973* Evonne Goolagong and Peggy Michel
1974* Gail Chanfreau and Julie Heldman
1975* Mrs. Margaret Court and Julie Anthony
1976* Cynthia Doerner and Janet Newberry
1977* Linky Boshoff and Ilana Kloss
1978* Regina Marsikova and Pam Teagaurden
1979* Lea Antonopolis and Dianne Evers
1980* Regina Marsikova and Andrea Jaeger

Canadian Championships—Mixed Doubles

1919 Marion Zinderstein and H. Taylor
1920 G. Maxwell and P. Bennett
1921 Mrs. H. Bickle and W. Bates
1922 G. Hutchings and L. K. Verley
1923 Mr. and Mrs. H. F. Wright
1924 P. Grierson and Sam Hardy
1925 M. Leeming and John Proctor
1926 D. Seaker and C. W. Aikman
1927 C. Swartz and S. Lockwood
1928 Mrs. A. H. Chaplin, Jr. and John Doeg
1929 tie, not decided
1930 M. Leeming and John Proctor
1931 Edith Cross and L. Driscod
1932 Olive Wade and Grant McLean
1933 Gracyn Wheeler and M. Kenneally
1934 Mrs. H. L. Beer and George Leclerc
1935 Mrs. M. Laird and Ray Casey
1936 Dr. Esther Bartosh and Verne Hughes
1937 Evelyn Dearman and M. Laird Watt
1938 Mr. and Mrs. Wilmer Allison
1939 E. Young and Wm. H. Pedlar
1940 Jean Milne and Phil Pearson
1941–45 no tournament
1946 Mr. and Mrs. Morey Lewis
1947 Mr. and Mrs. Robert Kelleher
1948 Mrs. P. Robinson and R. Buser
1949 Mrs. B. Lewis and Blair Hawley
1950 Barbara Knapp and Lorne Main
1951 Doris Popple and Paul Willey
1952 Melita Ramirez and Gustavo Palafox
1953 Melita Ramirez and Francisco Contreras
1954 Ethel Norton and Dan Sullivan
1955 canceled
1956 Jean Laird and Paul Willey

1957 Mrs. Anne Bagge Vieira and Robert Howe
1958 Farel Footman and Whitney Reed
1959 Marietta Laframboise and Robert Bedard
1960 Deirdre Catt and Michael Sangster
1961 Ann Haydon and Michael Sangster
1962 Eleanor Dodge and Keith Carpenter
1963 Vicki Berner and Keith Carpenter
1964 Mrs. Alice Tym and Owen Davidson
1965 Faye Urban and Tom Body
1967 Kathy Harter and Ray Keldie
1968 not held
1969 Andre Martin and Bill Higgins
1970–80 not held

Irish Championships—Men's Singles

1879 V. "St. Leger" Gould
1880 W. Renshaw
1881 W. Renshaw
1882 W. Renshaw
1883 E. Renshaw
1884 H. F. Lawford
1885 H. F. Lawford
1886 H. F. Lawford
1887 E. Renshaw
1888 E. Renshaw
1889 W. J. Hamilton
1890 E. W. Lewis
1891 E. W. Lewis
1892 E. Renshaw
1893 J. Pim
1894 J. Pim
1895 J. Pim
1896 W. Baddeley
1897 W. V. Eaves
1898 H. S. Mahony
1899 R. F. Doherty
1900 R. F. Doherty
1901 R. F. Doherty
1902 H. L. Doherty
1903 W. S. Drapes
1904 J. C. Parke
1905 J. C. Parke
1906 F. L. Riseley
1907 M. G. J. Ritchie
1908 J. C. Parke

*Open championship.

Irish Championships—Men's Singles *(cont.)*

1909 J. C. Parke
1910 J. C. Parke
1911 J. C. Parke
1912 J. C. Parke
1913 J. C. Parke
1914 C. J. Tindell Green
1915–18 no competition
1919 C. Campbell
1920 V. Miley
1921 C. Campbell
1922 no competition
1923 G. F. Mackay
1924 L. A. Meldon
1925 C. F. Scroope
1926 H. Landry
1927 G. R. O. Crole-Rees
1928 G. L. Rogers
1929 J. S. Oliff
1930 H. G. N. Lee
1931 E. A. McGuire
1932 S. B. Wood
1933 D. N. Jones
1934 C. E. Malfroy
1935 A. C. Stedman
1936 G. L. Rogers
1937 G. L. Rogers
1938 O. Anderson
1939 M. D. Deloford
1940–45 no competition
1946 D. Pails
1947 A. J. Mottram
1948 E. W. Sturgess
1949 N. Cockburn
1950 H. Weiss
1951 A. Segal
1952 N. Kumar
1953 N. Kumar
1954 H. Stewart
1955 H. Stewart
1956 B. Patty
1957 A. J. Cooper
1958 N. A. Fraser and M. G. Davies divided
1959 J. W. Frost
1960 R. D. Ralston
1961 W. Bond
1962 R. Laver
1963 R. K. Wilson

1964 R. K. Wilson
1965 A. D. Roche
1966 J. Cromwell
1967 K. Wooldridge
1968* Tom Okker
1969* Bob Hewitt
1970* Tony D. Roche
1971* Cliff Drysdale
1972* Bob Hewitt
1973* Mark Cox
1974* Sherwood Stewart
1975* Alvin Gardner
1976* not held
1977* Sean Sorenson
1978* Bob Carmichael
1979* Paul Kronk
1980* Matt Doyle

*Open championship.

Irish Championships—Women's Singles

1879 M. Langrishe
1880 D. Meldon
1881 no competition
1882 H. Abercrombie
1883 M. Langrishe
1884 M. Watson
1885 M. Watson
1886 M. Langrishe
1887 C. Dod
1888 Mrs. G. W. Hillyard
1889 L. Martin
1890 L. Martin
1891 L. Martin
1892 L. Martin
1893 L. Stanuell
1894 Mrs. G. W. Hillyard
1895 C. Cooper
1896 L. Martin
1897 Mrs. G. W. Hillyard
1898 C. Cooper
1899 L. Martin
1900 L. Martin
1901 M. E. Robb
1902 L. Martin
1903 L. Martin
1904 W. A. Longhurst
1905 W. A. Longhurst

1906	W. A. Longhurst		1963	B. J. Moffitt
1907	M. Garfit		1964	M. E. Bueno
1908	M. Garfit		1965	M. E. Bueno
1909	M. Garfit		1966	M. Smith
1910	A. Holder		1967	A. Soady
1911	Mrs. D. R. Barry		1968*	Mrs. Margaret S. Court
1912	Mrs. A. Larcombe		1969*	Mrs. Billie Jean King
1913	A. Barry		1970*	Virginia Wade
1914	I. Clarke		1971	Virginia Wade
1915–18	no competition		1972*	Evonne Goolagong
1919	E. Ryan		1973*	Margaret Smith Court
1920	E. Ryan		1974*	Gail S. Chanfreau
1921	E. Ryan		1975*	Sue Mappin
1922	no competition		1976*	not held
1923	H. Ryan		1977*	not held
1924	H. Wallis		1978*	Mary Sawyer
1925	E. Boyd		1979*	Pam Whytcross
1926	H. Wallis		1980*	Pam Whytcross
1927	Mrs. M. Watson			

British Hard Courts—Men's Singles

1928	Mrs. Blair White			
1929	E. L. Heine		1924	R. Lycett
1930	H. Wallis		1925	P. D. B. Spence
1931	Mrs. Blair White		1926	Jacques Brugnon
1932	J. Jedrzejowska		1927	J. R. Lacoste
1933	H. Wallis		1928	J. R. Lacoste
1934	Mrs. H. K. Sperling		1929	H. W. Austin
1935	S. G. Chuter		1930	H. G. N. Lee
1936	A. Lizana		1931	C. Boussus
1937	T. R. Jarvis		1932	Fred J. Perry
1938	Mrs. H. W. Moody		1933	Fred J. Perry
1939	A. Marble		1934	Fred J. Perry
1940–45	no competition		1935	Fred J. Perry
1946	A. L. Brough		1936	Fred J. Perry
1947	Mrs. E. W. A. Bostock		1937	H. W. Austin
1948	Mrs. S. Summers		1938	Kho Sin Kie
1949	Mrs. T. C. Long		1939	Kho Sin Kie
1950	H. Weiss		1940–45	no competition
1951	E. F. Lombard		1946	J. E. Harper
1952	M. Connolly		1947	E. W. Sturgess
1953	A. Mortimer		1948	E. W. Sturgess
1954	M. Connolly		1949	P. Masip
1955	Mrs. J. Fleitz		1950	Jaroslav Drobny
1956	S. J. Bloomer		1951	Jaroslav Drobny
1957	S. Reynolds		1952	Jaroslav Drobny
1958	Mrs. D. H. Knode		1953	E. Morea
1959	Mrs. R. Schuurman		1954	A. J. Mottram
1960	Mrs. D. H. Knode		1955	Sven Davidson
1961	A. S. Haydon			
1962	M. Schacht			

*Open championships.

British Hard Courts—Men's Singles *(cont.)*

1956 Budge Patty
1957 Jaroslav Drobny
1958 W. A. Knight
1959 L. A. Gerrard
1960 M. G. Davies
1961 Roy Emerson
1962 Rod Laver
1963 W. A. Knight
1964 W. A. Knight
1965 J. E. Lundquist
1966 Ken N. Fletcher
1967 J. E. Lundquist
1968* Ken R. Rosewall
1969* John D. Newcombe
1970* Mark Cox
1971* Gerald Battrick
1972* Bob Hewitt
1973* Adriano Panatta
1974* Ilie Nastase
1975* Manuel Orantes
1976* Wojtek Fibak
1977* not held
1978* Jose Higueras
1979* not held
1980* Angel Gimenez

The finalists in 1930 British Hard Court Championship: Mrs. M. List *(left)* and Joan Fry *(right)*. Miss Fry took the title.

British Hard Courts—Women's Singles

1924 Elizabeth Ryan
1925 Elizabeth Ryan
1926 J. Fry
1927 Betty Nuthall
1928 E. A. Goldsack
1929 E. L. Heine
1930 J. Fry
1931 Mrs. R. Mathieu
1932 Mrs. R. Mathieu
1933 Dorothy E. Round
1934 Dorothy E. Round
1935 K. E. Stammers
1936 K. E. Stammers
1937 A. Lizana
1938 M. C. Scriven
1939 K. E. Stammers
1940–45 no competition
1946 Mrs. E. W. A. Bostock

1947 Mrs. N. Bolton
1948 Mrs. B. E. Hilton
1949 P. J. Curry
1950 P. J. Curry
1951 Doris Hart
1952 Doris Hart
1953 Doris Hart
1954 Doris Hart
1955 Angela Mortimer
1956 Angela Mortimer
1957 Shirley J. Bloomer
1958 Shirley J. Bloomer
1959 Angela Mortimer
1960 Christine C. Truman
1961 Angela Mortimer
1962 R. Schuurman
1963 Mrs. A. H. Jones

*Open championships.

1964 Mrs. A. H. Jones	1972* Evonne Goolagong	
1965 Mrs. A. H. Jones	1973* Virginia Wade	
1966 Mrs. A. H. Jones	1974* Virginia Wade	
1967 Virginia Wade	1975* Janet Newberry	
1968* Virginia Wade	1976* Mrs. Helga Masthoff	
1969* Mrs. Margaret S. Court	1977* not held	
1970* Mrs. Margaret S. Court	1978* Iris Riedel	
1971* Mrs. Margaret S. Court	1979–80 not held	

*Open championships.

GRAND PRIX CIRCUIT—
Masters Playoff Champions

1970—Stan Smith	1974—Guillermo Vilas	1978 John McEnroe
1971—Ilie Nastase	1975—Ilie Nastase	1979 Bjorn Borg
1972—Ilie Nastase	1976—Manuel Orantes	1980 Bjorn Borg
1973—Ilie Nastase	1977—Jimmy Connors	

YEARLY LEADERS SINCE 1970

Year	(Men)	Pts.	Bonus
1970	Cliff Richey	60	$25,000
1971	Stan Smith	187	25,000
1972	Ilie Nastase	659	50,000
1973	Ilie Nastase	610	55,000
1974	Guillermo Vilas	797	100,000
1975	Guillermo Vilas	850	100,000
1976	Raul Ramirez	938	150,000
1977	Guillermo Vilas	2,047	300,000
1978	Jimmy Connors	2,030	—
1979	John McEnroe	2,414	300,000
1980			
	(Women)		
1971	Billie Jean King	181	$ 10,000
1972	Billie Jean King	719	22,500
1973	Chris Evert	710	23,750
1974	discontinued		

COLGATE SERIES CHAMPIONSHIP—Finals

Year	Winner	Runner-up	Final Score
1977	Chris Evert	Billie Jean King	6–2, 6–2
1978	Chris Evert	Martina Navratilova	6–3, 6–3
1979	Martina Navratilova	Tracy Austin	6–2, 6–1
1980	Tracy Austin	Andrea Jaeger	6–2, 6–2

FAMILY CIRCLE CUP—Women's Singles

Year	Winner	Year	Winner
1973	Rosemary Casals	1977	Chris Evert
1974	Chris Evert	1978	Chris Evert
1975	Chris Evert	1979	Tracy Austin
1976	Chris Evert	1980	Tracy Austin

Professional World Tournament

While professional tournaments in the United States started in 1926 (see Section II), they were played in Europe soon after World War I. (The French Professional Championship started in 1920.) But the oldest contested *international* world tournament was the one held at Wembley Stadium in England. Here are the results from the first tournament in 1934 to the last in 1972.

PROFESSIONAL WORLD SINGLES TOURNAMENT

Year	Winner	Runner-up
1934	H. Ellsworth Vines	Hans Nusslein
1935	H. Ellsworth Vines	William T. Tilden II
1936	H. Ellsworth Vines	William T. Tilden II
1937	Hans Nusslein	William T. Tilden II
1938	Hans Nusslein	William T. Tilden II
1939–45	not held	
1946	not held	
1947	Donald Budge	Robert L. Riggs
1948	Robert L. Riggs	Donald Budge
1949	John A. Kramer	Robert L. Riggs
1950	Richard A. Gonzales	Welby Van Horn
1951	Richard A. Gonzales	Francisco Segura
1952	Richard A. Gonzales	John A. Kramer
1953	Frank A. Sedgman	Richard A. Gonzales
1954–55	not held	
1956	Richard A. Gonzales	Frank A. Sedgman
1957	Kenneth Rosewall	Francisco Segura
1958	Frank A. Sedgman	M. Anthony Trabert
1959	Malcolm J. Anderson	Francisco Segura
1960	Kenneth Rosewall	Francisco Segura
1961	Kenneth Rosewall	Lewis Hoad
1962	Kenneth Rosewall	Lewis Hoad
1963	Kenneth Rosewall	Lewis Hoad
1964	Rodney Laver	Kenneth Rosewall
1965	Rodney Laver	Andres Gimeno
1966	Rodney Laver	Kenneth Rosewall
1967	Rodney Laver	Kenneth Rosewall
1968	Kenneth Rosewall	John Newcombe
1969	Kenneth Rosewall	John Newcombe
1970	Rodney Laver	Kenneth Rosewall
1971	Ilie Nastase	Rodney Laver
1972	Cliff Richey	Clark Graebner

(Event Discontinued)

Professional World Doubles Tournament

1934 William T. Tilden II and H. Ellsworth Vines

1935 William T. Tilden II and H. Ellsworth Vines

1936 William T. Tilden II and H. Ellsworth Vines

1937 William T. Tilden II and Henri Cochet

1938 William T. Tilden II and H. Ellsworth Vines

1939–46 not held

1947 not available

1948 Fred Perry and Donald Budge

1949 Fred Perry and Donald Budge

1950 Richard A. Gonzales and Donald Budge

1951 Richard A. Gonzales and Francisco Segura

1952   Richard A. Gonzales and Francisco
          Segura
1953   Frank A. Sedgman and Donald Budge
1954–55   not held
1956   Richard A. Gonzales and M. Anthony
          Trabert
1957   Lewis Hoad and Kenneth Rosewall
1958   Richard A. Gonzales and Kenneth
          Rosewall
1959   Lewis Hoad and M. Anthony Trabert
1960   Frank A. Sedgman and Kenneth
          Rosewall
1961   Lewis Hoad and Kenneth Rosewall
1962   Lewis Hoad and Kenneth Rosewall
1963   Frank A. Sedgman and Alex Olmedo
1964   Lewis Hoad and Kenneth Rosewall
1965   Rodney Laver and Earl Buchholz
1966   Lewis Hoad and Kenneth Rosewall
1967   Rodney Laver and Andres Gimeno
1968   John Newcombe and Tony Roche
1969   John Newcombe and Tony Roche
1970   John Newcombe and Tony Roche
1971   not held
1972   Clark Graebner and Tom Gorman

Andres Gimeno after he won the 1968 Madison Square Garden Challenge Trophy.

MAJOR TOURNAMENT RESULTS

VIRGINIA SLIMS CIRCUIT

1970 Tournaments

HOUSTON—Rosemary Casals def. Judy Tegart Dalton, 5-7, 6-1, 7-5

RICHMOND—Billie Jean King def. Nancy Richey, 6-3, 6-3

1971 Tournaments

SAN FRANCISCO—Billie Jean King def. Rosemary Casals, 6-3, 6-4

LONG BEACH—Billie Jean King def. Rosemary Casals, 6-1, 6-2

MILWAUKEE—Billie Jean King def. Rosemary Casals, 6-3, 6-2

OKLAHOMA CITY—Billie Jean King def. Rosemary Casals, 1-6, 7-6, 6-4

CHATTANOOGA—Billie Jean King def. Ann Hayden Jones, 6-4, 6-1

PHILADELPHIA—Rosemary Casals def. Françoise Durr, 6-3, 3-6, 6-2

FT. LAUDERDALE—Francoise Durr def. Billie Jean King, 6-3, 3-6, 6-3

BOSTON—Billie Jean King def. Rosemary Casals, 4-6, 6-2, 6-3

DETROIT—Billie Jean King def. Rosemary Casals, 3-6, 6-1, 6-2

NEW YORK—Rosemary Casals def. Billie Jean King, 6-4, 6-4

SAN JUAN—Ann Hayden Jones def. Nancy Richey, 6-4, 6-4

LAS VEGAS—Ann Hayden Jones def. Billie Jean King, 7-5, 6-4

ST. PETERSBURG—Chris Evert def. Julie Heldman, 6-1, 6-2

SAN DIEGO—Billie Jean King def. Rosemary Casals, 3-6, 7-5, 6-1

HOUSTON—Billie Jean King def. Kerry Melville Reid, 6-4, 4-6, 6-1

CHICAGO—Françoise Durr def. Billie Jean King, 6-4, 6-2

NEWPORT—Kerry Melville Reid def. Françoise Durr, 6-3, 6-7, 7-6

LOUISVILLE—Billie Jean King def. Rosemary Casals, 6-1, 4-6, 6-3

PHOENIX—Billie Jean King def. Rosemary Casals, 7-5, 6-1

1972 Tournaments

SAN FRANCISCO—Billie Jean King def. Kerry Melville Reid, 7-6, 7-6

LONG BEACH—Rosemary Casals def. Françoise Durr, 6-2, 6-7, 6-3

BOSTON—Virginia Wade def. Françoise Durr, 6-3, 7-5

FT. LAUDERDALE—Chris Evert def. Billie Jean King, 6-1, 6-0

OKLAHOMA CITY—Rosemary Casals def. Valerie Ziegenfuss, 6-4, 6-1

WASHINGTON, D.C.—Nancy Richey def. Chris Evert, 7-6, 6-2

BIRMINGHAM, MICH.—Kerry Melville Reid def. Rosemary Casals, 6-3, 6-7, 6-4

DALLAS—Nancy Richey def. Billie Jean King, 7-6, 6-1

RICHMOND—Billie Jean King def. Nancy Richey, 6-3, 6-4

SAN JUAN—Nancy Richey def. Chris Evert, 6-1, 6-3

JACKSONVILLE—Marie Neumannova def. Billie Jean King, 6-4, 6-3

ST. PETERSBURG—Nancy Richey def. Chris Evert, 6-3, 6-4

TUCSON—Billie Jean King def. Françoise Durr, 6-0, 6-3

INDIANAPOLIS—Billie Jean King def. Nancy Richey, 6-3, 6-3

COLUMBUS—Rosemary Casals def. Françoise Durr, 6-7, 7-6, 6-0

DENVER—Nancy Richey def. Billie Jean King, 1-6, 6-4, 6-4

NEWPORT—Margaret Smith Court def. Billie Jean King, 6-4, 6-1

CHARLOTTE—Billie Jean King def. Margaret Smith Court, 6-2, 6-2

ALBANY, CALIF.—Margaret Smith Court def. Billie Jean King, 6-4, 6-1

PHOENIX—Billie Jean King def. Margaret Smith Court, 7-6, 6-3

1973 Tournaments

SAN FRANCISCO—Margaret Smith Court def. Kerry Melville Reid, 6-3, 6-3

LOS ANGELES—Margaret Smith Court def. Nancy Richey, 7-5, 6-7, 7-5

WASHINGTON, D.C.—Margaret Smith Court def. Kerry Melville Reid, 6-1, 6-2

MIAMI—Margaret Smith Court def. Kerry Melville Reid, 4-6, 6-1, 7-5

INDIANAPOLIS—Billie Jean King def. Rosemary Casals, 5-7, 6-2, 6-4

DETROIT—Margaret Smith Court def. Kerry Melville Reid, 7-6, 6-3

CHICAGO—Margaret Smith Court def. Billie Jean King, 6-2, 4-6, 6-4

RICHMOND—Margaret Smith Court def. Janet Newberry, 6-2, 6-1

TUCSON—Kerry Melville Reid def. Nancy Richey, 6-3, 6-3

PHILADELPHIA—Margaret Smith Court def. Kerry Harris, 6-1, 6-0

BOSTON—Margaret Smith Court def. Billie Jean King, 6-2, 6-4

JACKSONVILLE—Margaret Smith def. Rosemary Casals, 5-7, 6-3, 6-1

HILTON HEAD—Rosemary Casals def. Nancy Richey, 3-6, 6-1, 7-5

DENVER—Billie Jean King def. Betty Stove, 6-4, 6-2

NASHVILLE—Margaret Smith Court def. Billie Jean King, 6-3, 4-6, 6-2

ALLAIRE, N.J.—Margaret Smith Court def. Lesley Hunt, 4-6, 6-2, 6-3

NEWPORT—Margaret Smith Court def. Julie Heldman, 6-3, 6-2

ST. LOUIS—Rosemary Casals def. Karen Krantzcke, 6-4, 6-7, 6-0

HOUSTON—Françoise Durr def. Rosemary Casals, 6-4, 1-6, 6-4

COLUMBUS—Chris Evert def. Margaret Smith Court, default.

PHOENIX—Billie Jean King def. Nancy Richey, 6-1, 6-3

1974 Tournaments

SAN FRANCISCO—Billie Jean King def. Chris Evert, 7-6, 6-2

MISSION VIEJO, CALIF.—Chris Evert def. Billie Jean King, 6-3, 6-1

WASHINGTON, D.C.—Billie Jean King def. Kerry Melville Reid, 6-0, 6-2

FT. LAUDERDALE—Chris Evert def. Kerry Melville Reid, default.

DETROIT—Billie Jean King def. Rosemary Casals, 6-1, 6-1

CHICAGO—Virginia Wade def. Rosemary Casals, 2-6, 6-4, 6-1

DALLAS—Chris Evert def. Virginia Wade, 7-5, 6-2

AKRON—Billie Jean King def. Nancy Richey, 6-3, 7-5

NEW YORK—Billie Jean King def. Chris Evert, 6-3, 3-6, 6-2

SARASOTA, FLA.—Chris Evert def. Evonne Goolagong, 6-4, 6-0

ST. PETERSBURG—Chris Evert def. Kerry Melville Reid, 6-0, 6-1

PHILADELPHIA—Olga Morozova def. Billie Jean King, 7-6, 6-1

NEWPORT—Chris Evert def. Betsy Nagelson, 6-4, 6-3

ORLANDO—Martina Navratilova def. Julie Heldman, 7-6, 6-4

DENVER—Evonne Goolagong def. Chris Evert, 7-5, 3-6, 6-4

HOUSTON—Chris Evert def. Virginia Wade, 6-3, 5-7, 6-1

PHOENIX—Virginia Wade def. Helen Gourlay, 6-1, 6-2

1975 Tournaments

SAN FRANCISCO—Chris Evert def. Billie Jean King, 6-1, 6-1

SARASOTA—Billie Jean King def. Chris Evert, 6-2, 6-3

WASHINGTON, D.C.—Martina Navratilova def. Kerry Melville Reid, 6-3, 6-1

AKRON—Chris Evert def. Margaret Smith Court, 6-4, 3-6, 6-3

CHICAGO—Margaret Smith Court def. Martina Navratilova, 6-3, 3-6, 6-2

DETROIT—Evonne Goolagong def. Margaret Smith Court, 6-3, 3-6, 6-3

BOSTON—Martina Navratilova def. Evonne Goolagong, 6-2, 4-6, 6-3

HOUSTON—Chris Evert def. Margaret Smith Court, 6-3, 6-2

DALLAS—Virginia Wade def. Martina Navratilova, 2-6, 7-6, 4-3 (ret.)

PHILADELPHIA—Virginia Wade def. Chris Evert, 7-5, 6-4

1976 Tournaments

HOUSTON—Martina Navratilova def. Chris Evert, 6-3, 6-4

WASHINGTON, D.C.—Chris Evert def. Virginia Wade, 6-2, 6-1

CHICAGO—Evonne Goolagong Cawley def. Virginia Wade, 3-6, 6-3, 6-2

AKRON—Evonne Goolagong Cawley def. Virginia Wade, 6-2, 3-6, 6-2

DETROIT—Chris Evert def. Rosemary Casals, 6-4, 6-2

SARASOTA—Chris Evert def. Evonne Goolagong Cawley, 6-3, 6-0

SAN FRANCISCO—Chris Evert def. Evonne Goolagong Cawley, 7-5, 7-6

DALLAS—Evonne Goolagong Cawley def. Martina Navratilova, 6-1, 6-1

BOSTON—Evonne Goolagong Cawley def. Virginia Wade, 6-2, 6-0

PHILADELPHIA—Evonne Goolagong Cawley def. Chris Evert, 6-3, 7-6

1977 Tournaments

WASHINGTON—Martina Navratilova def. Chris Evert, 6-2, 6-3

HOLLYWOOD, FLA.—Chris Evert def. Margaret Smith Court, 6-3, 6-4

HOUSTON—Martina Navratilova def. Sue Barker, 7-6, 7-5

MINNEAPOLIS—Martina Navratilova def. Sue Barker, 6-0, 6-1

SEATTLE—Chris Evert def. Martina Navratilova, 6-2, 6-4

CHICAGO—Chris Evert def. Margaret Smith Court, 6-1, 6-3

LOS ANGELES—Chris Evert def. Martina Navratilova, 6-2, 2-6, 6-1

DETROIT—Martina Navratilova def. Sue Barker, 6-4, 6-4

SAN FRANCISCO—Sue Barker def. Virginia Wade, 6-3, 6-4

DALLAS—Sue Barker def. Terry Holladay, 6-1, 7-6

PHILADELPHIA—Chris Evert def. Martina Navratilova, 6-4, 4-6, 6-3

1978 Tournaments

WASHINGTON—Martina Navratilova def. Betty Stove, 7–5, 6-4

HOLLYWOOD, FLA.—Evonne Goolagong Cawley def. Wendy Turnbull, 6-2, 6-3

HOUSTON—Martina Navratilova def. Billie Jean King, 1-6, 6-2, 6-2

LOS ANGELES—Martina Navratilova def. Rosemary Casals, 6-3, 6-2

CHICAGO—Martina Navratilova def. Evonne Goolagong Cawley, 6-7, 6-2, 6-2

SEATTLE—Martina Navratilova def. Betty Stove, 6-1, 1-6, 6-1

DETROIT—Martina Navratilova def. Dianne Fromholtz, 6-3, 6-2

KANSAS CITY—Martina Navratilova def. Billie Jean King, 7-5, 2-6, 6-3

DALLAS—Evonne Goolagong Cawley def. Tracy Austin, 4-6, 6-0, 6-2

BOSTON—Evonne Goolagong Cawley def. Chris Evert, 4-6, 6-1, 6-4

PHILADELPHIA—Chris Evert def. Billie Jean King, 6-0, 6-4

AVON CIRCUIT

1979 Tournaments

WASHINGTON—Tracy Austin def. Martina Navratilova, 6-3, 6-2

OAKLAND, CALIF.—Martina Navratilova def. Chris Evert, 7-5, 7-5

HOUSTON—Martina Navratilova def. Virginia Wade, 6-3, 6-2

HOLLYWOOD, FLA.—Greer Stevens def. Dianne Fromholtz, 6-4, 2-6, 6-4

CHICAGO—Martina Navratilova def. Tracy Austin, 6-4, 6-3

SEATTLE—Chris Evert def. Renee Richards, 6-1, 3-6, 6-3

LOS ANGELES—Chris Evert def. Martina Navratilova, 6-3, 6-4

DETROIT—Wendy Turnbull def. Virginia Ruzici, 7-5, 1-6, 7-6

DALLAS—Martina Navratilova def. Chris Evert, 6-4, 6-4

PHILADELPHIA—Wendy Turnbull def. Virginia Wade, 5-7, 6-3, 6-2

BOSTON—Dianne Fromholtz def. Sue Barker, 6-2, 7-6

1980 Tournaments

CINCINNATI—Tracy Austin def. Chris Evert Lloyd, 6-2, 6-1

KANSAS CITY—Martina Navratilova def. Greer Stevens, 6-0, 6-2

CHICAGO—Martina Navratilova def. Chris Evert Lloyd, 6-4, 6-4

SEATTLE—Tracy Austin def. Virginia Wade, 6-2, 7-6

LOS ANGELES—Martina Navratilova def. Tracy Austin, 6-2, 6-0

OAKLAND, CALIF.—Martina Navratilova def. Evonne Goolagong Cawley, 6-1, 7-6

DETROIT—Billie Jean King def. Evonne Goolagong Cawley, 6-3, 6-0

HOUSTON—Billie Jean King def. Martina Navratilova, 6-1, 6-3

DALLAS—Martina Navratilova def. Evonne Goolagong Cawley, 6-3, 6-2

BOSTON—Tracy Austin def. Virginia Wade, 6-2, 6-1

WORLD CHAMPIONSHIP TENNIS

1971 Tournaments (Autumn)

QUEBEC CITY—Tom Okker def. Rod Laver, 6-3, 7-6, 6-7, 6-1

FORT WORTH—Rod Laver def. Marty Riessen, 2-6, 6-4, 3-6, 7-5, 6-3

SAN FRANCISCO—Rod Laver def. Ken Rosewall, 6-4, 6-4, 7-6

VANCOUVER—Ken Rosewall def. Tom Okker, 6-2, 6-2, 6-4

COLOGNE, W. GERMANY—Bob Lutz def. Jeff Borowiak, 6-3, 6-7, 6-3, 6-2

BARCELONA, SPAIN—Manuel Orantes def. Bob Lutz, 6-4, 6-3, 6-4

STOCKHOLM OPEN—Arthur Ashe def. Jan Kodes, 6-3, 3-6, 6-2, 1-6, 6-4

ITALIAN INDOOR, BOLOGNA—Rod Laver def. Arthur Ashe, 6-3, 6-4, 6-4

1972 Tournaments (Spring)

RICHMOND—Rod Laver def. Cliff Drysdale, 2-6, 6-3, 7-5, 6-3

TORONTO—Rod Laver def. Ken Rosewall, 6-1, 6-4

MIAMI—Ken Rosewall def. Cliff Drysdale, 3-6, 6-2, 6-4

CHICAGO—Tom Okker def. Arthur Ashe, 4-6, 6-2, 6-3

HOUSTON—Rod Laver def. Ken Rosewall, 6-2, 6-4

QUEBEC CITY—Marty Riessen def. Rod Laver, 7-5, 6-2, 7-5

CHARLOTTE—Ken Rosewall def. Cliff Richey, 2-6, 6-2, 6-2

DENVER—Rod Laver def. Marty Riessen, 4-6, 6-3, 6-4

LAS VEGAS—John Newcombe def. Cliff Drysdale, 6-3, 6-4

1972 Tournaments (Autumn)

ST. LOUIS—John Newcombe def. Nikki Pilic, 6-3, 6-3

WASHINGTON, D.C.—Tony Roche def. Marty Riessen, 3-6, 7-6, 6-4

LOUISVILLE—Arthur Ashe def. Mark Cox, 6-4, 6-4

CLEVELAND—Mark Cox def. Ray Ruffels, 6-3, 4-6, 4-6, 6-3, 6-4

FT. WORTH—John Newcombe def. Ken Rosewall, 5-7, 1-6, 7-5, 6-5, 6-4

MONTREAL—Arthur Ashe def. Roy Emerson, 6-1, 3-6, 6-2, 7-5

SAN FRANCISCO—John Newcombe def. Cliff Drysdale, 6-4, 6-1, 7-5

VANCOUVER—John Newcombe def. Marty Riessen, 6-7, 7-6, 7-6, 7-5

ESSEN, W. GERMANY—Nikki Pilic def. Bob Lutz, 4-6, 6-4, 7-6

GOTHENBERG, SWEDEN—John Newcombe def. Roy Emerson, 6-0, 6-3, 6-1

ROTTERDAM—Arthur Ashe def. Tom Okker, 3-6, 6-2, 6-1

AUTUMN PLAYOFF AT ROME—(1R) Bob Lutz def. John Newcombe, 6-7, 7-6, 6-3; Cliff Drysdale def. Mark Cox, 6-4, 6-3; Tom Okker def. Marty Riessen, 7-6, 6-4; Arthur Ashe def. Nikki Pilic, 7-6, 6-1; (Sf)—Lutz def. Drysdale, 6-4, 6-4; Ashe def. Okker, 6-7, 6-3, 6-3; (F)—Ashe def. Lutz, 6-2, 3-6, 6-3, 3-6, 7-6; (3rd)—Okker def. Drysdale, 6-3, 7-5.

1973 Tournaments

(GROUP A)

LONDON—Brian Fairlie def. Mark Cox, 2-6, 6-2, 6-2, 7-6

MILAN—Marty Riessen def. Roscoe Tanner, 7-6, 6-0, 7-6

COPENHAGEN—Roger Taylor def. Marty Riessen, 6-2, 6-3, 7-5

COLOGNE, W. GERMANY—Jan Kodes def. Brian Fairlie, 6-1, 6-3, 6-1

CHICAGO—Arthur Ashe def. Roger Taylor, 3-6, 7-6, 7-6

WASHINGTON, D.C.—Tom Okker def. Arthur Ashe, 6-3, 6-7, 7-6

VANCOUVER—Tom Gorman def. Jan Kodes, 3-6, 6-2, 7-5

HOUSTON—Ken Rosewall def. Fred Stolle, 3-6, 6-2, 7-5

CLEVELAND—Ken Rosewall def. Roger Taylor, 6-3, 6-4

CHARLOTTE—Ken Rosewall def. Arthur Ashe, 6-3, 7-6

DENVER—Mark Cox def. Arthur Ashe, 6-1, 6-1

(GROUP B)

MIAMI—Rod Laver def. Dick Stockton, 7-6, 6-3, 7-5

LACOSTA—Colin Dibley def. Stan Smith, 6-3, 7-6

RICHMOND—Rod Laver def. Roy Emerson, 6-4, 6-3

TORONTO—Rod Laver def. Roy Emerson, 6-3, 6-4

ATLANTA—Stan Smith def. Rod Laver, 6-3, 6-4

ST. LOUIS—Stan Smith def. Rod Laver, 6-4, 3-6, 6-4

MUNICH, W. GERMANY—Stan Smith def. Cliff Richey, 6-1, 7-5

BRUSSELS—Stan Smith def. Rod Laver, 6-2, 6-4, 6-1

JOHANNESBURG—Brian Gottfried def. Jaimie Fillol, default.

GOTHENBERG, SWEDEN—Stan Smith def. John Alexander, 5-7, 6-4, 6-2

DOUBLES PLAYOFFS AT MONTREAL—Roy Emerson-Rod Laver def. Terry Addison-Colin Dibley, 6-4, 7-5, 6-1; Bob Lutz-Stan Smith def. Nikkie Pilic-Allan Stone, 7-6, 6-3, 3-6, 7-6; Tom Okker-Marty Riessen def. Mark Cox-Graham Stilwell, 6-7, 6-7, 7-6, 6-2, 6-2; Ken Rosewell-Fred Stolle def. Arthur Ashe-Roscoe Tanner, 6-1, 6-7, 6-4, 7-6. (Sf)—Lutz-Smith def. Laver-Emerson, 7-6, 4-6, 7-6, 7-6; Okker-Riessen def. Rosewall-Stolle, 6-2, 6-3, 6-7, 2-6, 6-3; (F)—Lutz-Smith def. Okker-

1973 Tournaments, Group B (*cont.*)

Riessen, 6-2, 7-6, 6-0; (3rd)—Laver-Emerson def. Rosewall-Stolle, 6-3, 6-3.

1974 Tournaments

(RED GROUP)

RICHMOND—Ilie Nastase def. Tom Gorman, 6-2, 6-3
TORONTO—Tom Okker def. Ilie Nastase, 7-6, 6-2
MIAMI—Cliff Drysdale def. Tom Gorman, 6-4, 7-5
WASHINGTON, D.C.—Ilie Nastase def. Tom Okker, 6-3, 6-3
ROTTERDAM—Tom Okker def. Tom Gorman, 4-6, 7-6, 6-1
MUNICH, W. GERMANY—Frew McMillan def. Nikkie Pilic, 5-7, 7-6, 7-6
MONTE CARLO—Andrew Pattison def. Ilie Nastase, 5-7, 6-3, 6-4
JOHANNESBURG—Andrew Pattison def. John Alexander, 6-3, 7-5

(BLUE GROUP)

ST. PETERSBURG, FLA.—John Newcombe def. Alex Metreveli, 6-0, 7-6
HEMPSTEAD, N.Y.—Stan Smith def. John Newcombe, 6-4, 3-6, 6-3
LACOSTA, CALIF.—John Newcombe def. Stan Smith, 6-2, 6-4, 6-4
ATLANTA—Dick Stockton def. Jiri Hrebec, 6-2, 6-1
NEW ORLEANS—John Newcombe def. Jeff Borowiak, 6-4, 6-2
ORLANDO—John Newcombe def. Jaimie Fillol, 6-2, 6-3, 6-3
CHARLESTON—Jeff Borowiak def. Dick Stockton, 6-4, 5-7, 7-6
ST. LOUIS—Stan Smith def. Alex Metreveli, 6-4, 6-4

(GREEN GROUP)

BOLOGNA—Arthur Ashe def. Mark Cox, 6-4, 7-5
LONDON—Bjorn Borg def. Mark Cox, 6-7, 7-6, 6-4
BARCELONA—Arthur Ashe def. Bjorn Borg, 6-4, 3-6, 6-3
SÃO PAULO—Bjorn Borg def. Arthur Ashe, 6-2, 3-6, 6-3

PALM DESERT—Rod Laver def. Roscoe Tanner, 6-4, 6-2
TOKYO—Rod Laver def. Juan Gisbert, 5-7, 6-2, 6-0
HOUSTON—Rod Laver def. Bjorn Borg, 7-6, 6-2
DENVER—Roscoe Tanner def. Arthur Ashe, 6-2, 6-4

(DOUBLES CHAMPIONSHIP)

MONTREAL—(1R)—Owen Davidson-John Newcombe def. Clark Graebner-Charles Pasarell, 7-5, 7-6, 6-2; Bob Lutz-Stan Smith def. John Alexander-Phil Dent, 7-6, 6-3, 6-3; Arthur Ashe-Roscoe Tanner def. Ross Case-Geoff Masters, 7-6, 3-6, 7-6, 7-5; Bob Hewitt-Frew McMillan def. Ove Bengston-Bjorn Borg, 6-4, 7-6, 3-6, 6-3. (Sf)—Davidson-Newcombe def. Lutz-Smith, 6-4, 6-4, 6-7, 7-6; Hewitt-McMillan def. Ashe-Tanner, 7-5, 6-4, 6-4. (F)—Hewitt-McMillan def. Davidson-Newcombe, 6-2, 6-7, 6-1, 6-2.

1975 Tournaments

(RED GROUP)

TORONTO—Harold Solomon def. Stan Smith, 6-4, 6-1
FT. WORTH—John Alexander def. Dick Stockton, 7-6, 4-6, 6-3
SAN ANTONIO—Dick Stockton def. Stan Smith, 7-5, 2-6, 7-6
WASHINGTON, D.C.—Mark Cox def. Dick Stockton, 6-2, 7-6
MEMPHIS—Harold Solomon def. Jiri Hrebec, 2-6, 6-1, 6-4
ATLANTA—Mark Cox def. John Alexander, 6-3, 7-6
TOKYO—Bob Lutz def. Stan Smith, 6-4, 6-4
HOUSTON—Ken Rosewall def. Cliff Drysdale, 6-3, 3-6, 6-1

(BLUE GROUP)

ST. PETERSBURG, FLA.—Raul Ramirez def. Roscoe Tanner, 6-0, 1-6, 6-2
LACOSTA, CALIF.—Rod Laver def. Allan Stone, 6-2, 6-2
SÃO PAULO—Rod Laver def. Charles Pasarell, 6-4, 6-4
CARACAS—Rod Laver def. Raul Ramirez, 7-6, 6-2
ORLANDO—Rod Laver def. Vitas Gerulaitis, 6-3, 6-4

ST. LOUIS—Vitas Gerulaitis def. Roscoe Tanner, 2-6, 6-2, 6-3

DENVER—Jimmy Connors def. Brian Gottfried, 6-3, 6-4

CHARLOTTE—Raul Ramirez def. Roscoe Tanner, 3-6, 6-4, 6-3

(GREEN GROUP)

RICHMOND—Bjorn Borg def. Arthur Ashe, 4-6, 6-4, 6-4

BOLOGNA—Bjorn Borg def. Arthur Ashe, 7-6, 4-6, 7-6

BARCELONA—Arthur Ashe def. Bjorn Borg, 7-6, 6-3

ROTTERDAM—Arthur Ashe def. Tom Okker, 3-6, 6-2, 6-4

MUNICH, W. GERMANY—Arthur Ashe def. Bjorn Borg, 6-4, 7-6

MONTE CARLO—Manuel Orantes def. Bob Hewitt, 6-2, 6-4

JOHANNESBURG—Buster Mottram def. Tom Okker, 6-4, 6-2

STOCKHOLM—Arthur Ashe def. Tom Okker, 6-4, 6-2

(DOUBLES CHAMPIONSHIP)

MEXICO CITY—(1R)—Brian Gottfried-Raul Ramirez def. Vijay Amritraj-Anand Amritraj, 6-3, 6-2, 7-6; Arthur Ashe-Tom Okker def. John Alexander-Phil Dent, 4-6, 6-3, 7-6, 6-3; Ross Case-Geoff Masters def. Dick Stockton-Eric Van Dillen, 2-6, 6-4, 6-2, 6-4; Mark Cox-Cliff Drysdale def. Bob Lutz-Stan Smith, 7-6, 6-7, 7-6, 7-6. (Sf)—Gottfried-Ramirez def. Ashe-Okker, 7-6, 7-6, 7-6; Cox-Drysdale def. Case-Masters, 6-4, 6-7, 6-1, 3-6, 7-6. (F)—Gottfried-Ramirez def. Cox-Drysdale, 7-6, 6-7, 6-2, 7-6. (3rd)—Case-Masters def. Ashe-Okker, 6-3, 7-6, 6-1.

(WORLD DOUBLES CHALLENGE)

DALLAS—Brian Gottfried-Raul Ramirez def. Bob Hewitt-Frew McMillan, 7-5, 6-3, 4-6, 2-6, 7-5.

1976 Tournaments

COLUMBUS—Arthur Ashe def. Andrew Pattison, 3-6, 6-3, 7-6

INDIANAPOLIS—Arthur Ashe def. Vitas Gerulaitis, 6-2, 6-7, 6-4

ATLANTA—Ilie Nastase def. Jeff Borowiak, 6-2, 6-4

BARCELONA—Eddie Dibbs def. Cliff Drysdale, 6-1, 6-1

RICHMOND—Arthur Ashe def. Brian Gottfried, 6-2, 6-4

LAGOS, NIGERIA—Dick Stockton def. Arthur Ashe, 6-3, 6-2

TORONTO—Bjorn Borg def. Vitas Gerulaitis, 2-6, 6-3, 6-1

ST. LOUIS—Guillermo Vilas def. Vijay Amritraj, 4-6, 6-0, 6-4

ROME—Arthur Ashe def. Bob Lutz, 6-2, 0-6, 6-3

ROTTERDAM—Arthur Ashe def. Bob Lutz, 6-3, 6-3

FT. WORTH—Guillermo Vilas def. Phil Dent, 6-7, 6-1, 6-1

MEMPHIS—Vijay Amritraj def. Stan Smith, 6-2, 0-6, 6-0

MEXICO CITY—Raul Ramirez def. Eddie Dibbs, 7-6, 6-2

WASHINGTON, D.C.—Harold Solomon def. Onny Parun, 6-3, 6-1

JACKSON, MISS.—Ken Rosewall def. Raul Ramirez, 6-3, 6-3

SÃO PAULO—Bjorn Borg def. Guillermo Vilas, 7-6, 6-2

CARACAS—Raul Ramirez def. Ilie Nastase, 6-3, 6-4

JOHANNESBURG—Onny Parun def. Cliff Drysdale, 7-6, 6-3

HOUSTON—Harold Solomon def. Ken Rosewall, 6-4, 1-6, 6-1

MONTE CARLO—Guillermo Vilas def. Wojtek Fibak, 6-1, 6-1, 6-4

CHARLOTTE—Tony Roche def. Vitas Gerulaitis, 6-3, 3-6, 6-1

DENVER—Jimmy Connors def. Ross Case, 7-6, 6-2

STOCKHOLM—Wojtek Fibak def. Ilie Nastase, 6-4, 7-6

(DOUBLES CHAMPIONSHIP)

KANSAS CITY—(1R)—Brian Gottfried-Raul Ramirez def. Vijay Amritraj-Anand Amritraj, 6-2, 7-6, 4-6, 6-4; Wojtek Fibak-Karl Meiler def. Ross Case-Geoff Masters, 7-6, 7-6, 7-5; Arthur Ashe-Tom Okker def. John Alexander-Phil Dent, 4-6, 6-3, 6-4, 7-6; Bob Lutz-Stan Smith def. Eddie Dibbs-Harold Solomon, 6-1, 6-3, 6-4. (Sf)—Fibak-Meiler def. Gottfried-Ramirez, 6-4, 6-4, 4-6, 4-6, 6-4; Lutz-Smith def. Ashe-Okker, 6-2, 7-6, 2-6, 7-6. (F)—Fibak-

1976 Tournaments, Doubles Championship (*cont.*)

Meiler def. Lutz-Smith, 6-3, 2-6, 3-6, 6-3, 6-4. (3rd)—Ashe-Okker def. Gottfried-Ramirez, 6-3, 3-6, 6-1.

1977 Tournaments

BIRMINGHAM, ALA.—Jimmy Connors def. Bill Scanlon, 6-3, 6-3

RICHMOND—Tom Okker def. Vitas Gerulaitis, 3-6, 6-3, 6-4

MEXICO CITY—Ilie Nastase def. Wojtek Fibak, 4-6, 6-2, 7-6

TORONTO—Dick Stockton def. Jimmy Connors, 5-6, (ret.)

MONTERREY, MEX.—Wojtek Fibak def. Vitas Gerulaitis, 6-4, 6-3

ST. LOUIS—Jimmy Connors def. John Alexander, 7-6, 6-2

ROTTERDAM—Dick Stockton def. Ilie Nastase, 2-6, 6-3, 6-3

LONDON—Eddie Dibbs def. Vitas Gerulaitis, 7-6, 6-7, 6-4

MONTE CARLO—Bjorn Borg def. Corrado Barazzutti, 6-3, 7-5, 6-0

HOUSTON—Adriano Panatta def. Vitas Gerulaitis, 7-6, 6-7, 6-1

CHARLOTTE—Corrado Barazzutti def. Eddie Dibbs, 7-6, 6-0

(DOUBLES CHAMPIONSHIP)

KANSAS CITY—(F)—Vijay Amritraj-Dick Stockton def. Vitas Gerulaitis-Adriano Panatta, 7-6, 7-6, 4-6, 6-3.

GRAND PRIX CIRCUIT

1973 Tournaments
Grand Prix Masters Playoff

(BOSTON)

ROUND-ROBIN: (Blue Group)—Ilie Nastase and John Newcombe, 2-1, Jan Kodes and Tom Gorman, 1-2; (White Group)—Tom Okker, 3-0, Jimmy Connors, 2-1, Stan Smitg, 1-2; Manuel Orantes, 0-3; (Sf)—Nastase def. Connors, 6-3, 7-5; Okker def. Newcombe, 3-6, 7-5, 3-5 (ret.). (F)—Nastase def. Okker, 6-3, 7-5, 4-6, 6-3

1974 Tournaments

BRITISH HARD (Bournemouth)—Ilie Nastase def. Paolo Bertolucci, 6-1, 6-3, 6-2; Virginia Wade def. Julie Heldman, 6-1, 6-3, 6-1

SWEDISH OPEN (Bastaad)—Bjorn Borg def. Adiano Panatta, 6-3, 6-0, 6-7, 6-3; Sue Barker def. Marijke Schaar, 6-1, 7-5

SWISS OPEN (Gstaad)—Guillermo Vilas def. Manuel Orantes, 6-1, 6-2

IRISH OPEN (Dublin)—Sherwood Stewart def. Colin Dowdeswell, 6-3, 9-8; Gail Chanfreau def. Raquel Giscafre, 6-4, 6-1

WELSH OPEN (Newport)—Armistead Neeley def. Michael Collins, 6-2, 6-4; Julie Heldman def. Sue Mappin, 6-3, 6-4

CHICAGO—Stan Smith def. Marty Riessen, 3-6, 6-1, 6-4

WASHINGTON, D.C.—Harold Solomon def. Guillermo Vilas, 1-6, 6-3, 6-0

LOUISVILLE—Guillermo Vilas def. Jaime Fillol, 6-4, 7-5

CINCINNATI—Marty Riessen def. Bob Lutz, 7-6, 7-6

BRETTON WOODS, N.H.—Rod Laver def. Harold Solomon, 6-4, 6-3

COLUMBUS, O.—Raul Ramirez def. Roscoe Tanner, 3-6, 7-6, 6-4

SO. ORANGE, N.J.—Alex Metreveli def. Jimmy Connors, default

JAPAN OPEN (Tokyo)—John Newcombe def. Ken Rosewall, 3-6, 6-2, 6-3

JEAN BECKER OPEN (Paris)—Brian Gottfried def. Eddie Dibbs, 6-3, 5-7, 8-6, 6-0

LONDON—Jimmy Connors def. Brian Gottfried, 6-2, 7-6

MERION, PA.—John Lloyd def. John Whitlinger, 6-0, 4-6, 6-3, 7-5

STOCKHOLM OPEN—Arthur Ashe def. Tom Okker, 6-2, 6-2

SOUTH AMERICAN (Buenos Aires)—Guillermo Vilas def. Manuel Orantes, 6-3, 0-6, 7-5, 6-2; Raquel Giscafre def. Beatriz Araujo, 7-5, 1-6, 6-2

NETHERLANDS (Hilversum)—Guillermo Vilas def. Barry Phillips-Moore, 6-4, 6-2, 1-6, 6-3

PERSPECTUS, N.J.—Ilie Nastase def. Juan Gisbert, 6-4, 7-6

LOS ANGELES—Jimmy Connors def. Harold Solomon, 6-3, 6-1

ALAMO, CALIF.—Ross Case def. Arthur Ashe, 6-3, 5-7, 6-4

Grand Prix Masters Playoff

(KOOYONG, AUSTRALIA)

ROUND-ROBIN: (Blue Group)—Guillermo Vilas, 3-0, John Newcombe, 2-1, Bjorn Borg, 1-2, Onny Parun, 0-3; (White Group)—Ilie Nastase, 3-0, Raul Ramirez, 2-1, Manuel Orantes, 1-2, Harold Solomon, 0-3. (Sf)—Vilas def. Ramirez, 4-6, 6-3, 6-2, 7-5; Nastase def. Newcombe, 6-3, 7-6, 6-2. (F)—Vilas def. Nastase, 7-6, 6-2, 3-6, 3-6, 6-4.

GRAND PRIX CIRCUIT

1975 Tournaments

(Not including events listed elsewhere)

BAVARIAN (Munich)—Guillermo Vilas def. Karl Meiler, 2-6, 6-0, 6-2, 6-1

BRITISH HARD (Bournemouth)—Manuel Orantes def. Patrick Prosy, 6-3, 4-6, 6-2, 7-5; Janet Newberry def. Terry Holladay, 7-9, 7-5, 6-3

AGFA CUP—Jaime Fillol def. Jan Kodes, 6-4, 1-6, 6-0, 7-5

NOTTINGHAM, ENG.—Tom Okker def. Tony Roche, 6-1, 3-6, 6-3

SWEDISH OPEN (Bastaad)—Manuel Orantes def. Jose Higueras, 6-0, 6-3; Sue Barker def. Helga Masthoff, 6-4, 6-0

SWISS OPEN (Gstaad)—Ken Rosewall def. Karl Meiler, 6-4, 6-4, 6-3; Glynis Coles def. Linky Boshoff, 9-7, 2-6, 8-6

AUSTRIAN (Kitzbuhel)—Adriano Panatta def. Jan Kodes, 2-6, 6-2, 7-5, 6-4; Sue Barker def. Pam Teegarden, 6-4, 6-4

NETHERLANDS (Hilverum)—Guillermo Vilas def. Zeljko Franulovic, 6-4, 6-7, 6-2, 6-3

CHICAGO—Roscoe Tanner def. John Alexander, 6-1, 6-7, 7-6

WASHINGTON, D.C.—Guillermo Vilas def. Harold Solomon, 6-1, 6-3

LOUISVILLE—Guillermo Vilas def. Ilie Nastase, 6-4, 6-3

CINCINNATI—Tom Gorman def. Sherwood Stewart, 7-5, 2-6, 6-4

NORTH CONWAY, N.H.—Jimmy Connors def. Ken Rosewall, 6-2, 6-2

GROVE CITY, O.—Vijay Amritraj def. Bob Lutz, 6-4, 7-5

SO. ORANGE, N.J.—Ilie Nastase def. Bob Hewitt, 7-6, 6-1

LOS ANGELES—Arthur Ashe def. Roscoe Tanner, 3-6, 7-5, 6-3

ALAMO, CALIF.—Arthur Ashe def. Guillermo Vilas, 6-0, 7-6

MAUI, HAWAII—Jimmy Connors def. Alex Mayer, 6-1, 6-0

MADRID—Jan Kodes def. Adriano Panatta, 6-2, 3-6, 7-6, 6-2

SOUTH PACIFIC—Brian Gottfried def. Harold Solomon, 6-2, 7-6, 6-1

DENVER—Martina Navratilova def. Carrie Mayer, 4-6, 6-4, 6-3

SPANISH OPEN—Bjorn Borg def. Adriano Panatta, 1-6, 7-6, 6-3, 6-2

1974 LEADING MONEY WINNERS

Men		Women	
1. Jimmy Connors	$281,309	1. Chris Evert	$261,460
2. Guillermo Vilas	274,327	2. Billie Jean King	173,225
3. John Newcombe	273,299	3. Evonne Goolagong	102,506
4. Bjorn Borg	215,229	4. Virginia Wade	85,389
5. Ilie Nastase	190,752	5. Rosemary Casals	72,389
6. Arthur Ashe	165,194	6. Julie Heldman	60,511
7. Stan Smith	163,326		
8. Manuel Orantes	139,857		
9. Rod Laver	134,600		
10. Raul Ramirez	127,425		
11. Tom Okker	114,649		
12. Marty Riessen	101,137		

Grand Prix Circuit—1975 Tournaments *(cont.)*

AUSTRALIAN INDOOR—Stan Smith def. Bob Lutz, 7-6, 6-2

ARYAMEHR CUP—Eddie Dibbs def. Ivan Molina, 1-6, 6-4, 7-5, 6-4

PERTH—Harold Solomon def. Alex Mayer, 6-2, 7-6, 7-5

PHILIPPINE (Manila)—Ross Case def. Corrado Barazzuti, 6-2, 6-1

FRENCH INDOOR (Lyon)—Tom Okker def. Arthur Ashe, 6-3, 2-6, 6-3, 3-6, 6-4

STOCKHOLM—Adriano Panatta def. Jimmy Connors, 4-6, 6-3, 7-5; Virginia Wade def. Francoise Durr, 6-3, 4-6, 7-5

JAPAN OPEN (Tokyo)—Raul Ramirez def. Manuel Orantes, 6-4, 7-5, 6-3

LONDON—Eddie Dibbs def. Jimmy Connors, 1-6, 6-1, 7-5; Virginia Wade def. Evonne Goolagong, 6-3, 6-2

CITIZENS CLASSIC—Tom Gorman def. Alex Mayer, 6-3, 6-1, 6-1

SOUTH AMERICAN (Buenos Aires)—Guillermo Vilas def. Adriano Panatta, 6-1, 6-4, 6-4

INDIAN CHAMPIONSHIPS (Calcutta)—Vijay Amritraj def. Manuel Orantes, 7-5, 6-3.

Grand Prix Masters Playoff

(STOCKHOLM)

ROUND-ROBIN: (Blue group)—Guillermo Vilas, 3-0; Bjorn Borg, 2-1; Harold Solomon, 1-2; Raul Ramirez, 0-3; (White Group)—Arthur Ashe, 3-0; Ilie Nastase, 2-1; Manuel Orantes, 1-2; Adriano Panatta, 0-3. (Sf)—Borg def. Ashe, 6-4, 3-6, 6-2, 6-2; Nastase def. Vilas, 6-0, 6-3, 6-4. (F)—Nastase def. Borg, 6-2, 6-2, 6-1.

GRAND PRIX CIRCUIT

1976 Tournaments

ROMIKA CUP—Manuel Orantes def. Karl Meiler, 6-1, 6-4, 6-1

BRITISH HARD (Bournemouth)—Wojtek Fibak def. Manuel Orantes, 6-2, 7-9, 6-2, 6-2

AGFA CUP—Bjorn Borg def. Manuel Orantes, 6-2, 6-2, 6-0

NOTTINGHAM, ENG.—Jimmy Connors and Ilie Nastase, tied (rain)

BERLIN OPEN—Victor Pecci def. Hans Pohmann, 6-1, 6-2, 5-7, 6-3

SWEDISH OPEN (Bastaad)—Antonio Zugarelli def. Corrado Barazzutti, 3-6, 7-5, 6-2; Renata Tomanova def. Helena Anliot, 6-3, 6-2

SWISS OPEN (Gstaad)—Raul Ramirez def. Adriano Panatta, 7-5, 6-7, 6-1, 6-3; Michele Gurdal def. Gail Lovera, 4-6, 6-2, 6-3

AUSTRIAN (Kitzbuhel)—Manuel Orantes def. Jan Kodes, 7-6, 6-2, 7-6; Wendy Turnbull def. Virginia Ruzici, 6-4, 5-7, 6-3

CINCINNATI—Roscoe Tanner def. Eddie Dibbs, 7-6, 6-3

NETHERLANDS (Hilversum)—Balazs Taroczy def. Ricardo Cano, 6-7, 2-6, 6-1, 6-3, 7-5

WASHINGTON, D.C.—Jimmy Connors def. Raul Ramirez, 6-2, 6-4

LOUISVILLE—Harold Solomon def. Wojtek Fibak, 6-2, 7-5

NORTH CONWAY, N.H.—Jimmy Connors def. Raul Ramirez, 7-6, 4-6, 6-3

GROVE CITY, O.—Roscoe Tanner def. Stan Smith, 6-4, 7-6

SO. ORANGE, N.J.—Ilie Nastase def. Roscoe Tanner, 6-4, 6-2; Marise Kruger def. Lea Antonopolis, 6-3, 6-2

BERMUDA (Hamilton)—Cliff Richey def. Gene Mayer, 7-6, 6-2

LOS ANGELES—Brian Gottfried def. Arthur Ashe, 6-2, 6-2

SAN FRANCISCO—Roscoe Tanner def. Brian Gottfried, 4-6, 7-5, 6-1

MAUI, HAWAII—Harold Solomon def. Bob Lutz, 6-3, 5-7, 7-5

ARYAMEHR CUP—Manuel Orantes def. Raul Ramirez, 7-6, 6-0, 2-6, 6-4

TROFEO GILETTE—Manuel Orantes def. Eddie Dibbs, 7-6, 6-2, 6-1

AIR INDIA/BP CLASSIC—Mark Edmondson def. Phil Dent, 3-6, 6-4, 6-4, 6-4

SPANISH OPEN (Madrid)—Manuel Orantes def. Eddie Dibbs, 6-1, 2-6, 2-6, 7-5, 6-4

AUSTRALIAN INDOOR—Geoff Masters def. Jim Delaney, 4-6, 6-3, 7-6, 6-3

JEAN BECKER OPEN—Eddie Dibbs def. Jaime Fillol, 5-7, 6-4, 6-4, 7-6

FISCHER GRAND PRIX—Wojtek Fibak def. Raul Ramirez, 6-7, 6-3, 6-4, 2-6, 6-1

Four outstanding young American men players: *(top, left to right)* Tom Gorman and Erik Van Dillen. *(bottom, left to right)* Jeff Borowiak and Jimmy Connors.

Grand Prix Circuit—1976 Tournaments *(cont.)*

HITACHI CLASSIC—Ray Ruffels def. Phil Dent, 6-0, 4-6, 2-6, 6-3, 6-2

LONDON—Raul Ramirez def. Manuel Orantes, 6-3, 6-4; Virginia Wade def. Chris Evert, 6-2, 6-2

JAPAN OPEN (Tokyo)—Roscoe Tanner def. Corrado Barazzutti, 6-3, 6-2; Wendy Turnbull def. Michele Gurdal, 6-1, 6-1

COLOGNE, W. GERMANY—Jimmy Connors def. Frew McMillan, 6-2, 6-3

STOCKHOLM OPEN—Mark Cox def. Manuel Orantes, 4-6, 7-5, 7-6

HONG KONG OPEN—Ken Rosewall def. Ilie Nastase, 1-6, 6-4, 7-6, 6-0

BENSON & HEDGES—Jimmy Connors def. Roscoe Tanner, 3-6, 7-6, 6-4

PHILADELPHIA INTERNATIONAL—Brian Fairlie def. Ray Ruffels, 7-5, 6-7, 7-6

BRAZIL OPEN—Guillermo Vilas def. Jose Higueras, 6-3, 6-0

SOUTH AMERICAN (Buenos Aires)—Guillermo Vilas def. Jaime Fillol, 6-2, 6-2, 6-3

INDIAN OPEN (Bangalore)—Kim Warwick def. Shashi Menon, 6-1, 6-1

Grand Prix Masters Playoff

(HOUSTON, TEXAS)

ROUND-ROBIN: (Blue Group)—Harold Solomon, Guillermo Vilas, Brian Gottfried, 2-1, Raul Ramirez, 0-3; (White Group)—Manuel Orantes, Wojtek Fibak, 2-1, Eddie Dibbs, Roscoe Tanner, 1-2; (Sf)—Orantes def. Solomon, 6-4, 6-4, 6-4; Fibak def. Vilas, 6-2, 6-2, 5-7, 3-6, 8-6. (F)—Orantes def. Fibak, 5-7, 6-2, 0-6, 7-6, 6-1.

GRAND PRIX CIRCUIT

1977 Tournaments

SYDNEY—Tony Roche def. Dick Stockton, 6-3, 3-6, 6-3, 6-4

ADELAIDE—Victor Amaya def. Brian Teacher, 6-1, 6-4, 6-2

BALTIMORE—Brian Gottfried def. Guillermo Vilas, 6-3, 7-6

DAYTON—Jeff Borowiak def. Buster Mottram, 6-3, 6-3

LITTLE ROCK—Sandy Mayer def. Haroon Rahim, 6-2, 6-4

MIAMI BEACH—Raul Ramirez def. Eddie Dibbs, 6-0, 6-3

SPRINGFIELD, MASS.—Guillermo Vilas def. Stan Smith, 6-1, 3-6, 6-3

SAN JOSE, CALIF.—Jiri Hrebec def. Sandy Mayer, 3-6, 6-4, 7-5

PALM SPRINGS, CALIF.—Brian Gottfried def. Guillermo Vilas, 2-6, 6-1, 6-3

MEMPHIS—Bjorn Borg def. Brian Gottfried, 6-4, 6-3, 4-6, 7-5

HAMPTON, VA.—Sandy Mayer def. Stan Smith, 4-6, 6-3, 6-2, 1-6, 6-3

JOHANNESBURG—Guillermo Vilas and Bjorn Borg, co-winners (rain)

WASHINGTON, D.C.—Brian Gottfried def. Bob Lutz, 6-2, 6-1

HELSINKI—Mark Cox def. Kjell Johansson, 6-3, 6-3

NICE—Bjorn Borg def. Guillermo Vilas, 6-4, 1-6, 6-2, 6-0

LACOSTA, CALIF.—Brian Gottfried def. Marty Riessen, 6-3, 6-2

LOS ANGELES—Stan Smith def. Brian Gottfried, 6-4, 2-6, 6-3

MURCIA, SP.—Jose Higueras def. Buster Mottram, 6-4, 6-0, 6-3

DENVER—Bjorn Borg def. Brian Gottfried, 7-5, 6-2

BAVARIAN (Munich)—Zeljko Franulovic def. Victor Pecci, 6-1, 6-1, 6-7, 7-5

DUSSELDORF—Wojtek Fibak def. Ray Moore, 6-1, 5-7, 6-2

NOTTINGHAM—Jaime Fillol and Tim Gullikson, co-winners (rain)

BRUSSELS—Harold Solomon def. Karl Meiler, 7-5, 3-6, 2-6, 6-3, 6-4

LONDON—Raul Ramirez def. Mark Cox, 9-7, 7-5

BERLIN—Paolo Bertolucci def. Jiri Hrebec, 6-4, 5-7, 4-6, 6-2, 6-4

FLORENCE—Paolo Bertolucci def. John Feaver, 6-4, 6-1, 7-5

LAS VEGAS—Jimmy Connors def. Raul Ramirez, 6-4, 5-7, 6-2

SWEDISH OPEN (Bastaad)—Corrado Barazzutti def. Balazs Taroczy, 7-6, 6-7, 6-2

Four young lady American players: *(top, left to right)* Valerie Ziegenfuss, Chris Evert. *(bottom, left to right)* Patti Hogan and Kristy Pigeon.

Grand Prix Circuit—1977 Tournaments *(cont.)*

SWISS OPEN (Gstaad)—Jeff Borowiak def. Jean-Francois Caujolle, 2-6, 6-1, 6-3

LONDON—Raul Ramirez def. Mark Cox, 9-7, 7-5

BERLIN—Paolo Bertolucci def. Jiri Hrebec, 6-4, 4-6, 6-2, 6-4

BRUSSELS—Harold Solomon def. Karl Meiler, 7-5, 3-6, 2-6, 6-3, 6-4

NOTTINGHAM, ENG.—Tim Gullikson and Jaime Fillol (final abandoned, title shared)

SWISS OPEN (Gstaad)—Jeff Borowiak def. Jean Caujolle, 2-6, 6-1, 6-3; Lesley H. Hanbuechen def. Helen Gourlay, 4-6, 7-5, 6-1

SWEDISH OPEN (Bastaad)—Corrado Barazzutti def. Balazs Taroczy, 7-6, 6-7, 6-2; Florenta Mihai def. Mary Struthers, 6-4, 6-4

NEWPORT—Tim Gullikson def. Hank Pfister, 6-4, 6-4, 5-7, 6-2

BOSTON—Manuel Orantes def. Eddie Dibbs, 7-6, 7-5, 6-4

COLUMBUS, O.—Guillermo Vilas def. Brian Gottfried, 6-2, 6-1

CARACAS—Guillermo Vilas def. Ilie Nastase, 6-2, 6-2

PERTH—Vitas Gerulaitis def. Geoff Masters, 6-3, 6-4, 6-2

COLOGNE—Bjorn Borg def. Wojtek Fibak, 2-6, 7-5, 6-3

JAPAN OPEN (Tokyo)—Manuel Orantes def. Kim Warwick, 6-2, 6-1

PARIS—Guillermo Vilas def. Christophe Roger-Vasselin, 6-2, 6-1, 7-6

DUTCH OPEN (Hilversum)—Patrick Proisy def. Lito Alvarez, 6-0, 6-2, 6-0

KITZBUHEL—Guillermo Vilas def. Jan Kodes, 5-7, 6-2, 4-6, 6-3, 6-2; Renata Tomanova def. Katja Ebbinghaus, 6-3, 7-5

CINCINNATI—Harold Solomon def. Mark Cox, 6-2, 6-3

WASHINGTON—Guillermo Vilas def. Brian Gottfried, 6-4, 7-5

LOUISVILLE—Guillermo Vilas def. Eddie Dibbs, 1-6, 6-0, 6-1

SO. ORANGE—Guillermo Vilas def. Roscoe Tanner, 6-4, 6-2; Lindsey Beaven def. Renee Richards, 1-6, 7-6, 6-1

NO. CONWAY—John Alexander def. Manuel Orantes, 2-6, 6-4, 6-4

COLUMBUS, O.—Guillermo Vilas def. Brian Gottfried, 6-2, 6-1

STOCKHOLM OPEN—Sandy Mayer def. Ray Moore, 6-2, 6-4

HONG KONG—Ken Rosewall def. Tom Gorman, 6-3, 5-7, 6-4, 6-4

BOGOTA, COL.—Guillermo Vilas def. Jose Higueras, 6-1, 6-2, 6-3

MANILA—Karl Meiler def. Manuel Orantes, default

SANTIAGO, CHILE—Guillermo Vilas def. Jaime Fillol, 6-0, 2-6, 6-4

WEMBLEY OPEN (London)—Bjorn Borg def. John Lloyd, 6-4, 6-4, 6-3

OVIEDO, SP.—Eddie Dibbs def. Raul Ramirez

ARGENTINA OPEN (Buenos Aires)—Guillermo Vilas def. Jaime Fillol, 6-2, 7-5, 3-6, 6-3

TAIPEI—Tim Gullikson def. Ismail El Shafei, 6-7, 7-5, 7-6, 6-4

INDIAN OPEN (Bombay)—Vijay Amritraj def. Terry Moor, 7-6, 6-4

1977 LEADING MONEY WINNERS

Men		Women	
1. Guillermo Vilas	$800,642	1. Chris Evert	$453,134
2. Jimmy Connors	622,657	2. Martina Navratilova	275,317
3. Brian Gottfried	478,988	3. Billie Jean King	274,149
4. Bjorn Borg	345,661	4. Betty Stove	229,162
5. Dick Stockton	311,856	5. Virginia Wade	193,476
6. Ilie Nastase	296,956	6. Sue Barker	180,458
7. Eddie Dibbs	283,691	7. Kerry Melville Reid	139,567
8. Vitas Gerulaitis	274,324	8. Rosemary Casals	126,139
9. Raul Ramirez	245,007	9. Wendy Turnbull	98,568
10. Roscoe Tanner	239,456	10. Françoise Durr	92,703

Grand Prix Masters Playoff

(NEW YORK—MADISON SQUARE GARDEN)

ROUND-ROBIN: (Blue group)—John McEnroe, 3–0; Arthur Ashe, 2-1; Jimmy Connors, 1-2; Harold Solomon, 0-3; (Red group)—Brian Gottfried, 3-0; Eddie Dibbs, 2-1; Raul Ramirez, 1-2; Corrado Barazzutti, 0-3. (Sf)—McEnroe def. Dibbs, 6-1, 6-4; Ashe def. Gottfried, 7-5, 3-6, 6-3. (F)—McEnroe def. Ashe, 6-7, 6-3, 7-5.

GRAND PRIX CIRCUIT

1978 Tournaments

(Not including events listed elsewhere)

SYDNEY—Roscoe Tanner def. Brian Teacher, 6–3, 3–6, 6-3, 6-7, 6-4; Evonne Goolagong Cawley def. Sue Barker, 6-2, 6-3.

ADELAIDE—Tim Gullickson def. Chris Lewis, 3-6, 6-4, 3-6, 6-2, 6-4.

ST. LOUIS—Sandy Meyer def. Eddie Dibbs, 7-6, 6-4.

SPRINGFIELD, MASS.—Heinz Gunthardt def. Harold Solomon, 6-3, 3-6, 6-2.

RICHMOND, VA.—Vitas Gerulaitis def. John Newcombe, 6-3, 6-4.

LITTLE ROCK, ARK.—Dick Stockton def. Hank Pfister, 6-4, 5-3 ret.

MEXICAN OPEN (Mexico City)—Raul Ramirez def. Pat DuPre, 6-4, 6-1.

SARASOTA, FLA.—Tomaz Smid def. Nick Saviano, 7-6, 0-6, 7-5.

BALTIMORE—Cliff Drysdale def. Tom Gorman, 7-5, 6-3.

MIAMI—Ilie Nastase def. Tom Gullickson, 6-3, 7-5.

DENVER—Jimmy Connors def. Stan Smith, 6-2, 7-6.

OCEAN CITY, MD.—Balasz Taroczy def. Ray Moore, 6-4, 6-4.

GOTHENBORG—Bjorn Borg def. Vitas Gerulaitis, 6-4, 1-6, 6-3.

MONTE CARLO—Raul Ramirez def. Tomas Smid, 6-3, 6-3, 6-4.

GUADALAJARA—Sandy Meyer def. John Newcombe, 6-3, 6-4.

ROTTERDAM—Jimmy Connors def. Raul Ramirez, 7-5, 7-5.

JOHANNESBURG—Cliff Richey def. Colin Dowdeswell, 7-5, 7-6.

DAYTON, O.—Brian Gottfried def. Eddie Dibbs, 2-6, 7-5, 7-6

MILAN—Bjorn Borg def. Vitas Gerulaitis, 6-3, 6-3.

WASHINGTON, D.C.—Brian Gottfried def. Raul Ramirez, 7-5, 7-6.

LAS VEGAS—Harold Solomon def. Corrado Barazzutti, 6-1, 3-0 ret.

TULSA, OKLA.—Eddie Dibbs def. Pat DuPre, 6-7, 6-2, 7-5

NICE—Jose Higueras def. Yannick Noah, 6-3, 6-4, 6-4

SAN JOSE, CALIF.—Arthur Ashe def. Bernie Mitton, 6-7, 6-1, 6-2.

HOUSTON—Brian Gottfried def. Ilie Nastase, 3-6, 6-4, 6-1.

FLORENCE—Jose-Luis Clerc def. Patrice Dominguez, 6-4, 6-2, 6-1.

NEWPORT—Bernie Mitton def. John James, 6-1, 3-6, 7-6.

BRUSSELS—Werner Zirngibl def. Ricardo Cano, 1-6, 6-3, 6-4, 6-3.

HAMBURG—Vladmir Zednik def. Harold Eischenbroich, 6-4, 7-5, 6-2.

BIRMINGHAM, ENG.—Jimmy Connors def. Raul Ramirez, 6-3, 6-1, 6-2.

LONDON—Tony Roche def. John McEnroe, 8-6, 9-7.

CINCINNATI—Eddie Dibbs def. Raul Ramirez, 5-7, 6-3, 6-2.

GSTAAD—Guillermo Vilas def. Jose-Luis Clerc, 6-3, 7-6, 6-4.

WASHINGTON, D.C.—Jimmy Connors def. Eddie Dibbs, 7-5, 7-5.

BASTAD—Bjorn Borg def. Corrado Barazzutti, 6-1, 6-2.

STUTTGART—Uli Pinner def. Kim Warwick, 6-2, 6-2, 7-6.

LOUISVILLE—Harold Solomon def. John Alexander, 6-2, 6-2.

HILVERSUM—Balazs Taroczy def. Tom Okker, 2-6, 6-1, 6-2, 6-4.

NO. CONWAY, N.H.—Eddie Dibbs def. John Alexander, 6-4, 6-4.

SO. ORANGE, N.J.—Guillermo Vilas def. Jose-Luis Clerc, 6-1, 6-3.

NEW ORLEANS—Roscoe Tanner def. Victor Amaya, 6-3, 7-5.

Grand Prix Circuit—1978 Tournaments *(cont.)*

COLUMBUS, O.—Arthur Ashe def. Bob Lutz, 6-3, 6-4.

STOWE, VT.—Jimmy Connors def. Tim Gullickson, 6-2, 6-3.

CLEVELAND—Peter Fiegl def. Van Winitsky, 4-6, 6-3, 6-3.

ATLANTA—Stan Smith def. Eliot Teltscher, 4-6, 6-1, 2-1 ret.

WOODLAND, TEX. (Doubles)—Wojtek Fibak and Tom Okker def. Sherwood Stewart and Marty Riessen, 7-6, 3-6, 4-6, 7-6, 6-3

LOS ANGELES—Arthur Ashe def. Brian Gottfried, 6-2, 6-4.

HARTFORD, CONN.—John McEnroe def. Johann Kriek, 6-2, 6-4.

BOURNEMOUTH—Jose Higueras def. Paulo Bertolucci, 6-2, 6-1, 6-3.

SAN FRANCISCO—John McEnroe def. Dick Stockton, 3-6, 7-6, 6-2.

AIX-EN-PROVENCE—Guillermo Vilas def. Jose-Luis Clerc, 6-3, 6-0, 6-3.

MEXICO OPEN, FALL (Mexico City)—Vijay Amritraj def. Raul Ramirez, 6-4, 6-4.

MAUI, HAWAII—Bill Scanlon def. Peter Fleming, 6-2, 6-0.

TORNEO GILLETTE, SP.—Jose Higueras def. Tomas Smid, 6-7, 6-3, 6-3, 6-4.

BARCELONA—Balasz Taroczy def. Ilie Nastase, 1-6, 7-5, 4-6, 6-3, 6-4.

SYDNEY INDOOR—Jimmy Connors def. Geoff Masters, 6-0, 6-0, 6-4.

JAPAN OPEN (Osaka)—Adriano Panatta def. Pat DuPre, 6-3, 6-3.

VIENNA—Stan Smith def. Balasz Taroczy, 4-6, 7-6, 7-6, 6-3.

BASLE—Guillermo Vilas def. John McEnroe, 6-3, 5-7, 7-5, 6-4.

COLOGNE—Wojtek Fibak def. Vijay Amritraj, 6-2, 0-1 ret.

PARIS—Bob Lutz def. Tom Gullickson, 6-2, 6-2, 7-6.

HONG KONG—Eliot Teltscher def. Pat DuPre, 6-4, 6-3, 6-2.

STOCKHOLM OPEN—John McEnroe def. Tim Gullickson, 6-2, 6-2.

LONDON (Wembley)—John McEnroe def. Tim Gullickson, 6-7, 6-4, 7-6, 6-2.

BOGOTA, COL.—Victor Pecci def. Rolf Gehring, 6-4, 4-6, 6-3, 6-3.

TAIPEI, TAIWAN—Brian Teacher def. Tom Gorman, 6-3, 6-3, 6-3.

Grand Prix Masters Playoff

(NEW YORK—MADISON SQUARE GARDEN)

ROUND-ROBIN: (Blue group)—John McEnroe, 3-0; Arthur Ashe, 2-1; Jimmy Connors, 1-2; Harold Solomon, 0-3; (Red group)—Brian Gottfried, 3-0; Eddie Dibbs, 2-1; Raul Ramirez, 1-2; Corrado Barazzutti, 0-3. (Sf)—McEnroe def. Dibbs, 6-1, 6-4; Ashe def. Gottfried, 7-5, 3-6, 6-3. (F)—McEnroe def. Ashe, 6-7, 6-3, 7-5.

1978 LEADING MONEY WINNERS

Men		Women	
1. Eddie Dibbs	$582,872	1. Martina Navratilova	$450,757
2. Raul Ramirez	450,110	2. Chris Evert	354,486
3. John McEnroe	445,024	3. Virginia Wade	270,027
4. Wojtek Fibak	383,843	4. Kerry Melville Reid	208,766
5. Ilie Nastase	367,422	5. Wendy Turnbull	189,583
6. Vitas Gerulaitis	359,095	6. Betty Stove	177,243
7. Harold Solomon	354,732	7. Evonne Goolagong Cawley	160,844
8. Jimmy Connors	353,307	8. Virginia Ruzici	151,379
9. Bjorn Borg	348,386	9. Billie Jean King	149,492
10. Brian Gottfried	312,205	10. Regina Marsikova	88,894

GRAND PRIX CIRCUIT

1979 Tournaments

AUCKLAND—Tim Wilkison def. Peter Feigl, 6–3, 6–7, 6-4, 2-6, 6-2.

BIRMINGHAM, ALA.—Jimmy Connors def. Eddie Dibbs, 6-2, 3-6, 7-5.

BALTIMORE—Harold Solomon def. Marty Riessen, 7-5, 6-4.

RICHMOND, VA.—Bjorn Borg def. Guillermo Vilas, 6-3, 6-1.

LITTLE ROCK—Vitas Gerulaitis def. Butch Walts, 6-2, 6-2.

PALM SPRINGS, CALIF.—Roscoe Tanner def. Brian Gottfried, 6-4, 6-2.

SARASOTA, FLA.—Johann Kriek def. Rick Meyer, 7-6, 6-2.

DENVER—Wojtek Fibak def. Victor Amaya, 6-4, 6-1.

LAGOS, NIGERIA—Hans Kary def. Peter Feigl, 6-4, 3-6, 6-2.

WASHINGTON, D.C.—Roscoe Tanner def. Brian Gottfried, 6-4, 6-4.

NEW ORLEANS—John McEnroe def. Roscoe Tanner, 6-4, 6-2.

NANCY, FRANCE—Yannick Noah def. Jean Haillet, 6-2, 5-7, 6-1, 7-5.

SAN JOSE, COSTA RICA—Bernie Mitton def. Tom Gorman, 6-4, 6-1, 6-3.

MILAN—John McEnroe def. John Alexander, 6-4, 6-3.

STUTTGART—Wojtek Fibak def. Guillermo Vilas, 6-2, 6-2, 3-6, 6-2.

DAYTON, O.—Butch Walts def. Marty Riessen, 6-3, 6-4.

ROTTERDAM—Bjorn Borg def. John McEnroe, 6-4, 6-2.

NICE—Victor Pecci def. John Alexander, 6-3, 6-2, 7-5.

MONTE CARLO—Bjorn Borg def. Vitas Gerulaitis, 6-2, 6-1, 6-3.

TULSA, OKLA.—Jimmy Connors def. Eddie Dibbs, 6-7, 7-5, 6-1.

CAIRO—Peter Feigl def. Carlos Kirmayr, 7-5, 3-6, 6-1.

RIVER OAKS, HOUSTON—Jose Higueras def. Gene Mayer, 6-3, 2-6, 7-6.

JOHANNESBURG—Jose-Luis Clerc def. Deon Joubert, 6-2, 6-1.

SANTA CLARA, CALIF.—John McEnroe def. Peter Fleming, 7-6, 7-6.

LAS VEGAS—Bjorn Borg def. Jimmy Connors, 6-3, 6-2.

HAMBURG—Jose Higueras def. Harold Solomon, 3-6, 6-1, 6-4, 6-1.

FLORENCE—Raul Ramirez def. Karl Meiler, 6-4, 1-6, 3-6, 7-5, 6-0.

MUNICH—Manuel Orantes def. Wojtek Fibak, 6-3, 6-2, 6-4.

LONDON—John McEnroe def. Victor Pecci, 6-7, 6-1, 6-1.

BRUSSELS—Balasz Taroczy def. Ivan Lendl, 6-1, 1-6, 6-3.

BERLIN—Peter McNamara def. Patrice Dominguez, 6-4, 6-0, 6-7, 6-2.

SURBITON, ENG.—Victor Amaya def. Mark Edmondson, 6-4, 7-5.

WASHINGTON, D.C.—Guillermo Vilas def. Victor Pecci, 7-6, 7-6.

LOUISVILLE—John Alexander def. Terry Moor, 7-6, 6-7, 3-3 ret.

NO. CONWAY, N.H.—Harold Solomon def. Jose Higueras, 5-7, 6-4, 7-6.

SO. ORANGE, N.J.—John McEnroe def. John Lloyd, 6-7, 6-4, 6-0.

LAFAYETTE, LA.—Marty Riessen def. Pat DuPre, 6-4, 5-7, 6-2.

COLUMBUS, O.—Brian Gottfried def. Eddie Dibbs, 6-3, 6-0.

TORONTO—Bjorn Borg def. John McEnroe, 6-3, 6-3.

STOWE, VT.—Jimmy Connors def. Mike Cahill, 6-0, 6-1.

CLEVELAND—Stan Smith def. Ilie Nastase, 7-6, 7-5. Woodlands, Tex. (Doubles)—Marty Riessen and Sherwood Stewart def. Bob Carmichael and Tim Gullikson, 6-3, 2-2 ret.

ATLANTA—Eliot Teltscher def. John Alexander, 6-3, 4-6, 6-2.

LOS ANGELES—Peter Fleming def. John McEnroe, 6-4, 6-4.

SAN FRANCISCO—John McEnroe def. Peter Fleming, 4-6, 7-5, 6-2.

KAANAPALI, HAWAII—Bill Scanlon def. Peter Fleming, 6-1, 6-1.

TOKYO—Bjorn Borg def. Jimmy Connors, 6-2, 6-2.

COLOGNE—Gene Mayer def. Wojtek Fibak, 6-3, 3-6, 6-1.

Grand Prix Circuit—1979 Tournaments *(cont.)*

PARIS—Harold Solomon def. Corrado Barazzutti, 6-3, 2-6, 6-3, 6-4.

TOKYO—Terry Moor def. Pat DuPre, 3-6, 7-6, 6-2.

BARCELONA—Hans Gildemeister def. Eddie Dibbs, 6-4, 6-3, 6-1.

BASLE—Brian Gottfried def. Johann Kriek, 7-5, 6-1, 4-6, 6-3.

SYDNEY—Vitas Gerulaitis def. Guillermo Vilas, 4-6, 6-3, 6-1, 7-6.

VIENNA—Stan Smith def. Wojtek Fibak, 6-4, 6-0, 6-2.

BRISBANE—Phil Dent def. Ross Case, 7-6, 6-2, 6-3.

TEL AVIV—Tom Okker def. Per Hjertquist, 6-4, 6-3.

BORDEAUX—Yannick Noah def. Harold Solomon, 6-0, 6-7, 6-1, 1-6, 6-4.

QUITO—Victor Pecci def. Jose Higueras, 2-6, 6-4, 6-2.

HONG KONG—Jimmy Connors def. Pat DuPre, 7-5, 6-3, 6-1.

STOCKHOLM OPEN—John McEnroe def. Gene Mayer, 6-7, 6-3, 6-3.

BOGOTA—Victor Pecci def. Jairo Velasco, 6-3, 6-4.

TAIPEI, TAIWAN—Bob Lutz def. Pat DuPre, 6-3, 6-4, 2-6, 6-3.

LONDON—John McEnroe def. Harold Solomon, 6-3, 6-4, 7-5.

INDIAN OPEN (Bombay)—Vijay Amritraj def. Peter Elter, 6-1, 7-5.

BOLOGNA—Butch Walts def. Gianni Ocleppo, 6-3, 6-2.

SOUTH AMERICAN OPEN (Buenos Aires)—Guillermo Vilas def. Jose-Luis Clerc, 6-1, 6-2, 6-2.

SANTIAGO—Hans Gildemeister def. Jose Higueras, 7-5, 5-7, 6-4.

JOHANNESBURG—Andrew Pattison def. Victor Pecci, 2-6, 6-3, 6-3.

SYDNEY—Phil Dent def. Hank Pfister, 6-4, 6-4, 7-5.

Grand Prix Masters Playoff

(NEW YORK—MADISON SQUARE GARDEN)

ROUND-ROBIN: (Blue group)—Vitas Gerulaitis, 2-1; John McEnroe, 2-1; Harold Solomon, 1-2; Guillermo Vilas, 1-2; (Red group)—Bjorn Borg, 3-0; Jimmy Connors, 2-1; Roscoe Tanner, 1-2; Jose Higueras, 0-3. (Sf)—Gerulaitis def. Connors, 7-5, 6-2; Borg def. McEnroe, 6-7, 6-3, 7-6. (F)—Borg def. Gerulaitis, 6-2, 6-2.

1979 LEADING MONEY WINNERS

Men		Women	
1. Bjorn Borg	$1,019,345	1. Martina Navratilova	$747,548
2. John McEnroe	1,005,238	2. Chris Evert Lloyd	564,398
3. Jimmy Connors	701,340	3. Tracy Austin	541,676
4. Vitas Gerulaitis	414,515	4. Wendy Turnbull	317,463
5. Guillermo Vilas	374,195	5. Dianne Fromholtz	265,990
6. Peter Fleming	353,315	6. Billie Jean King	185,804
7. Roscoe Tanner	263,433	7. Betty Stove	182,006
8. Eddie Dibbs	249,293	8. Sue Barker	175,452
9. Wojtek Fibak	234,452	9. Evonne Goolagong Cawley	171,573
10. Harold Solomon	222,078	10. Virginia Wade	146,283

GRAND PRIX CIRCUIT

1980 Tournaments

HOBART—Shlomo Glickstein def. Robert Van't Hof, 7-6, 6-4.

AUCKLAND, N.Z.—John Sadri def. Tim Wilkison, 6-4, 3-6, 6-3, 6-4.

BIRMINGHAM, ALA.—Jimmy Connors def. Eliot Teltscher, 6-3, 6-2.

BALTIMORE—Harold Solomon def. Tim Gullikson, 7-6, 6-0.

RICHMOND, VA.—John McEnroe def. Roscoe Tanner, 6-1, 6-2.

SAN JUAN, P.R.—Paul Ramirez def. Phil Dent, 6-3, 6-2.

SARASOTA, FLA.—Eddie Dibbs def. Andres Gomez, 6-1, 6-3.

DENVER—Gene Mayer def. Victor Amaya, 6-2, 6-2.

LAGOS, NIGERIA—Peter Feigl def. Harry Fritz, 6-2, 6-3, 6-2.

WASHINGTON, D.C.—Victor Amaya def. Ivan Lendl, 6-7, 6-4, 7-5.

CAIRO—Corrado Barazzutti def. Paolo Bertolucci, 6-4, 6-0.

ROTTERDAM—Heinz Gunthardt def. Gene Mayer, 6-2, 6-4.

STUTTGART—Tomas Smid def. Mark Cox, 6-1, 6-3, 5-7, 1-6, 6-4.

COSTA RICA—Jose-Luis Clerc def. Jimmy Connors, 4-6, 2-6, ret.

FRANKFURT—Stan Smith def. Johan Kriek, 2-6, 7-6, 6-2.

METZ, FR.—Gene Mayer def. Gianni Ocleppo, 6-3, 6-3, 6-0.

MILAN—John McEnroe def. Vijay Amritraj, 6-1, 6-4.

NICE—Bjorn Borg def. Manuel Orantes, 6-2, 6-0, 6-1.

DAYTON, O.—Wojtek Fibak def. Bruce Manson, 7-6, 6-3.

MONTE CARLO—Bjorn Borg def. Guillermo Vilas, 6-1, 6-0, 6-2.

NEW ORLEANS—Wojtek Fibak def. Eliot Teltscher, 6-4, 7-5.

PALM HARBOR—Paul McNamee def. Stan Snith, 6-4, 6-3.

RIVER OAKS, HOUSTON—Ivan Lendl def. Eddie Dibbs, 6-1, 6-3.

JOHANNESBURG—Heinz Gunthardt def. Victor Amaya, 6-4, 6-4.

TULSA, OKLA.—Howard Schoenfield def. Trey Waltke, 5-7, 6-1, 6-0.

LOS ANGELES—Gene Mayer def. Brian Teacher, 6-3, 6-2.

LAS VEGAS—Bjorn Borg def. Harold Solomon, 6-3, 6-1.

BERLIN—Harold Solomon def. Guillermo Vilas, 6-7, 6-2, 6-4, 2-6, 6-3.

FLORENCE—Adriano Panatta def. Raul Ramirez, 6-2, 6-4, 6-4.

MUNICH—Rolf Gehring def. Christophe Freyss, 6-2, 0-6, 6-2, 6-2.

LONDON—John McEnroe def. Kim Warwick, 6-3, 6-1.

BRUSSELS—Peter McNamara def. Barazs Taroczy, 7-6, 6-3, 6-0.

SURBITON, ENG.—Brian Gottfried def. Sandy Mayer, 6-3, 6-3.

VIENNA—Angel Gimenez def. Tomas Smid, 1-6, 1-1 ret.

NEWPORT, R.I.—Vijay Amritraj def. Andrew Pattison, 6-1, 5-7, 6-3.

GSTAAD—Heinz Gunthardt def. Kim Warwick, 4-6, 6-4, 7-6.

SWEDISH OPEN (Bastad)—Balazs Taroczy def. Sammy Giammalva, 6-3, 7-5, 3-6, 7-6.

STUTTGART—Vitas Gerulaitis def. Wojtek Fibak, 6-2, 7-5, 6-2.

WASHINGTON, D.C.—Brian Gottfried def. Jose-Luis Clerc, 7-5, 4-6, 6-4.

HILVERSUM—Balazs Taroczy def. Haroon Ismail, 6-3, 6-2, 6-1.

KITZBUHEL—Guillermo Vilas def. Ivan Lendl, 6-3, 6-2, 6-2.

NO. CONWAY, N.H.—Jimmy Connors def. Eddie Dibbs, 6-3, 5-7, 6-1.

SO. ORANGE, N.J.—Jose-Luis Clerc def. John McEnroe, 6-3, 6-2.

COLUMBUS, O.—Bob Lutz def. Terry Rocavert, 6-4, 6-3.

STOWE, VT.—Bob Lutz def. Johan Kriek, 6-3, 6-1.

CLEVELAND—Gene Mayer def. Victor Amaya, 6-2, 6-1.

ATP FINALS (Cincinnati)—Harold Solomon def. Francisco Gonzalez, 7-6, 6-3.

ATLANTA—Eliot Teltscher def. Terry Moor, 6-2, 6-2.

PALERMO—Guillermo Vilas def. Paul McNamee, 6-4, 6-0, 6-0.

BOURNEMOUTH, ENG.—Angel Gimenez def. Shlomo Glickstein, 3-6, 6-3, 6-3.

SAN FRANCISCO—Gene Mayer def. Eliot Teltscher, 6-2, 2-6, 6-1.

GENEVA—Balazs Taroczy def. Adriano Panatta, 6-3, 6-2.

BORDEAUX—Mario Martinez def. Gianni Ocleppo, 6-0, 7-5, 7-5.

MADRID—Jose-Luis Clerc def. Guillermo Vilas, 6-3, 1-6, 1-6, 6-4, 6-2.

Grand Prix Circuit—1980 Tournaments *(cont.)*

HONOLULU, HAWAII—Eliot Teltscher def. Tim Wilkison, 7-6, 6-3.

BARCELONA—Ivan Lendl def. Guillermo Vilas, 6-4, 5-7, 6-4, 4-6, 6-1.

TEL AVIV—Harold Solomon def. Shlomo Glickstein, 6-2, 6-3.

BRISBANE—John McEnroe def. Phil Dent, 6-3, 6-4.

SYDNEY—John McEnroe def. Vitas Gerulaitis, 6-3, 6-4, 7-5.

BASLE—Ivan Lendl def. Bjorn Borg, 6-3, 6-2, 5-7, 0-6, 6-4.

CANTON—Jimmy Connors def. Eliot Teltscher, 6-2, 6-4.

TOKYO—Ivan Lendl def. Eliot Teltscher, 3-6, 6-4, 6-0.

MELBOURNE—Vitas Gerulaitis def. Peter McNamara, 7-5, 6-3.

VIENNA—Brian Gottfried def. Balazs Taroczy, 6-2, 6-4, 6-3.

TOKYO—Jimmy Connors def. Tom Gullikson, 6–1, 6–2.

COLOGNE—Bob Lutz def. Nick Saviano, 6-4, 6-0.

PARIS—Brian Gottfried def. Adriano Panatta, 4-6, 6-3, 6-1, 7-6.

STOCKHOLM OPEN—Bjorn Borg def. John McEnroe, 6-3, 6-4.

HONG KONG—Ivan Lendl def. Brian Teacher, 5-7, 7-6, 6-3.

QUITO—Jose-Luis Clerc def. Victor Pecci, 6-4, 1-6, 10-8.

LONDON INDOOR—John McEnroe def. Gene Mayer, 6-4, 6-3, 6-3.

TAIPEI, TAIWAN—Ivan Lendl def. Brian Teacher, 6-7, 7-3, 6-3, 7-6.

BOGOTA—Dominique Bedel def. Carlos Kirmayr, 6-4, 7-6.

SOUTH AMERICAN OPEN (Buenos Aires)—Jose-Luis Clerc def. Rolf Gehring, 6-7, 2-6, 7-5, 6-0, 6-3.

BOLOGNA—Tomas Smid def. Paolo Bertolucci, 7-5, 6-2.

BANGKOK—Vijay Amritraj def. Brian Teacher, 6-3, 7-5.

JOHANNESBURG—Kim Warwick def. Fritz Buehning, 6-2, 6-1, 6-2.

SANTIAGO—Victor Pecci def. Christophe Freyss,

4-6, 6-4, 6-3.

SYDNEY—Fritz Buehning def. Brian Teacher, 6-3, 6-7, 7-6.

SOFIA—Per Hjertquist def. Vadim Borisov, 6-3, 6-2, 7-5.

Grand Prix Masters Playoff

(NEW YORK—MADISON SQUARE GARDEN)

ROUND-ROBIN (Blue group)—Gene Mayer, 3-0; Bjorn Borg, 2-1; Jose-Luis Clerc, 1-2; John McEnroe, 0-3; (Red group)—Jimmy Connors, 3-0; Ivan Lendl, 2-1; Harold Solomon, 1-2; Guillermo Vilas, 0-3. (Sf)—Borg def. Connors, 6-4, 6-7, 7-3; Lendl def. Mayer, 6-3, 6-4. (F)—Borg def. Lendl, 6-4, 6-2, 6-2.

DOUBLES: (Sf)—John McEnroe and Peter Fleming def. Kevin Curren and Steve Denton, 6-2, 6-2; Peter McNamara and Paul McNamee def. Stan Smith and Bob Lutz, 0-6, 6-3, 6-4. (F)—McEnroe and Fleming def. McNamara and McNamee, 6-4, 6-3.

COLGATE SERIES—1978

TOKYO—Virginia Wade def. Betty Stove, 6–4, 7–6.

SAN ANTONIO, TEX.—Stacy Margolina def. Yvonne Vermaak, 7-5, 6-1.

MONTREAL—Carolina Stoll def. Francoise Durr, 6-3, 6-2.

ATLANTA—Chris Evert def. Martina Navratilova, 7-6, 0-6, 6-3.

PHOENIX, ARIZ.—Martina Navratilova def. Tracy Austin, 6-4, 6-2.

BRIGHTON, ENG.—Virginia Ruzici def. Betty Stove, 5-7, 6-2, 7-5.

EAST LAKE WOODLANDS, FLA.—Virginia Wade def. A. Maria Fernandez, 6-4, 7-6.

SYDNEY—Dianne Fromholtz def. Kerry M. Reid, 6-1, 1-6, 6-2.

ADELAIDE—Kerry M. Reid def. Beth Norton, 7-5, 6-7, 6-1.

COLGATE SERIES—1979

CARLSBAD, CALIF.—Kerry M. Reid def. Sue Barker, 6-3, 6-7, 7-6.

VIENNA—Chris Evert Lloyd def. Caroline Stoll, 6-1, 6-1.

BERLIN—Caroline Stoll def. Regina Marsikova, 7-6, 6-0.

CHICHESTER, ENG.—Evonne Goolagong Cawley def. Sue Barker, 6-1, 6-4.

EASTBOURNE, ENG.—Chris Evert Lloyd def. Martina Navratilova, 7-5, 5-7, 13-11.

SAN DIEGO—Tracy Austin def. Martina Navratilova, 6-4, 6-2.

RICHMOND, VA.—Martina Navratilova def. Kathy Jordan, 6-1, 6-3.

TORONTO—Laura DuPont def. Brigette Cuypers, 6-4, 6-7, 6-3.

MAHWAH, N.J.—Chris Evert Lloyd def. Tracy Austin, 6-7, 6-4, 6-1.

TOKYO—Billie Jean King def. Evonne Goolagong Cawley, 6-4, 7-5.

PITTSBURGH—Sue Barker def. Renee Richards, 6-3, 6-1.

ATLANTA—Martina Navratilova def. Wendy Turnbull, 7-6, 6-4.

MINNEAPOLIS—Evonne Goolagong Cawley def. Dianne Fromholtz, 6-3, 6-4.

PHOENIX—Martina Navratilova def. Chris Evert Lloyd, 6-1, 6-3.

OLDSMAR, FLA.—Evonne Goolagong Cawley def. Virginia Wade, 6-0, 6-3.

STOCKHOLM OPEN—Bille Jean King def. Betty Stove, 6-3, 6-7, 7-5.

STUTTGART—Tracy Austin def. Martina Navratilova, 6-2, 6-0.

BRIGHTON, ENG.—Martina Navratilova def. Chris Evert Lloyd, 6-3, 6-3.

MELBOURNE—Hana Mandlikova def. Wendy Turnbull, 6-3, 6-2.

KYOTO—Betsy Nagelson def. Naoko Sato, 6-3, 6-4.

TOKYO—Betsy Nagelson def. Naoko Sato, 6-1, 3-6, 6-3.

SYDNEY—Sue Barker def. Rosalyn Fairbank, 6-0, 7-5.

ADELAIDE—Hana Mandlikova def. Virginia Ruzici, 7-5, 2-2 ret.

COLGATE SERIES—1980

CHICHESTER, ENG.—Chris Evert Lloyd def. Evonne Goolagong Cawley, 6-3, 6-7, 7-5.

EASTBOURNE, ENG.—Tracy Austin def. Wendy Turnbull, 7-6, 6-2.

MONTREAL—Martina Navratilova def. Greer Stevens, 6-2, 6-1.

KITZBUHEL—Virginia Ruzici def. Hana Mandlikova, 3-6, 6-1, ret.

RICHMOND, VA.—Martina Navratilova def. Mary Lou Piatek, 6-3, 6-0.

SAN DIEGO—Tracy Austin def. Wendy Turnbull, 6-1, 6-3.

MAHWAH, N.J.—Hana Madlikova def. Andrea Jaeger, 6-7, 6-2, 6-2.

SALT LAKE CITY—Virginia Ruzici def. Ivanna Madruga, 6-1, 6-3.

TOKYO—Billie Jean King def. Terry Holladay, 7-5, 6-4.

LAS VEGAS—Andrea Jaeger def. Hana Mandlikova, 7-5, 4-6, 6-3.

ATLANTA—Hana Mandlikova def. Wendy Turnbull, 6-3, 7-5.

1980 LEADING MONEY WINNERS

Men		Women	
1. John McEnroe	$1,026,383	1. Tracy Austin	$683,787
2. Bjorn Borg	723,212	2. Martina Navratilova	674,400
3. Jimmy Connors	604,641	3. Chris Evert Lloyd	427,705
4. Ivan Lendl	568,911	4. Hana Mandlikova	376,430
5. Gene Mayer	384,719	5. Billie Jean King	321,309
6. Guillermo Vilas	378,601	6. Wendy Turnbull	315,573
7. Vitas Gerulaitis	344,666	7. Andrea Jaeger	258,431
8. Wojtek Fibak	319,887	8. Evonne Goolagong Cawley	210,080
9. Brian Gottfried	294,579	9. Virginia Ruzici	194,113
10. Jose-Luis Clerc	277,234	10. Pam Shriver	182,649

Other 1974 Tournaments

DALLAS—Billie Jean King and Owen Davidson def. Rosemary Casals and Marty Riessen, 6-2, 4-6, 6-3, 6-4

ROANOKE—Jimmy Connors def. Karl Meiler, 6-4, 6-3

OMAHA—Karl Meiler def. Jimmy Connors, 6-3, 1-6, 6-1

BALTIMORE—Sandy Mayer def. Clark Graebner, 6-2, 6-1

DAYTON—Raul Ramirez def. Brian Gottfried, 6-1, 6-4, 7-6

LITTLE ROCK—Jimmy Connors def. Karl Meiler, 6-2, 6-1

BIRMINGHAM, ALA.—Jimmy Connors def. Sandy Mayer, 7-5, 6-3

SALISBURY, MD.—Jimmy Connors def. Frew McMillan, 6-4, 7-5, 6-3

PARAMUS, N.J.—Sandy Mayer def. Jurgen Fassbender, 6-1, 6-3

HAMPTON, VA.—Jimmy Connors def. Ilie Nastase, 6-4, 6-4

SALT LAKE CITY—Jimmy Connors def. Vitas Gerulaitis, 4-6, 7-6, 6-3

JACKSON, MISS.—Sandy Mayer def. Karl Meiler, 7-6, 7-5

TUCSON—John Newcombe def. Arthur Ashe, 6-3, 7-6

TEMPE, ARIZ.—Jimmy Connors def. Vijay Amritraj, 6-1, 6-2

WASHINGTON, D.C.—Vijay Amritraj def. Karl Meiler, 6-4, 6-3

PORTLAND, ME.—Ilie Nastase def. Roger Taylor, 4-6, 6-1, 6-4

LAS VEGAS—Rod Laver def. Marty Riessen, 6-2, 6-2

HILTON HEAD, S.C.—Chris Evert def. Kerry Melville Reid, 6-1, 6-3

ROANOKE, VA.—Roger Taylor def. Vitas Gerulaitis, 7-6, 7-6

LITTLE ROCK—Billy Martin def. George Hardie, 6-2, 7-6

SALISBURY, MD.—Jimmy Connors def. Vitas Gerulaitis, 5-7, 7-5, 6-1, 3-6, 6-0

BOCA RATON, FLA.—Jimmy Connors def. Jurgen Fassbender, 6-4, 6-2

RIDGEFIELD, CONN.—Roger Taylor def. Sandy Mayer, 7-5, 5-7, 7-6

SHREVEPORT, LA.—(Doubles)—Juan Gisbert and Bill Brown def. Janos Benyik and Bob Machan, 6-4, 6-4

HAMPTON, VA.—Jimmy Connors def. Jan Kodes, 3-6, 6-3, 6-0

NEW YORK—Vitas Gerulaitis def. Jimmy Connors, default.

JACKSON, MISS.—Ken Rosewall def. Butch Buchholz, 7-5, 4-6, 7-6

TUCSON—John Alexander def. Ilie Nastase, 7-5, 6-2

WASHINGTON, D.C.—Alex Metreveli def. Haroon Rahim, 6-3, 7-5

AUSTIN, TEXAS—Chris Evert def. Billie Jean King, 4-6, 6-3, 7-6

AMELIA ISLAND, FLA.—Chris Evert def. Martina Navratilova, 7-5, 6-4

LAS VEGAS—Roscoe Tanner def. Ross Case, 5-7, 7-5, 7-6

RYE, N.Y.—Chris Evert def. Virginia Wade, 6-0, 6-1

ATLANTA—Chris Evert def. Martina Navratilova, 2-6, 6-2, 6-0

MISSION VIEJO, CALIF.—Chris Evert def. Cynthia Doerner, 6-1, 6-3

PHOENIX—Nancy Richey Gunter def. Virginia Wade, 4-6, 7-5, 6-4

ORLANDO, FLA.—Chris Evert def. Martina Navratilova, default.

Other 1975 Tournaments

FREEPORT—Jimmy Connors def. Karl Meiler, 6-0, 6-2

BALTIMORE (Towson, Md.)—Brian Gottfried def. Allan Stone, 3-6, 6-2, 6-3

BIRMINGHAM, ALA.—Jimmy Connors def. Billy Martin, 6-4, 6-3

DAYTON—Brian Gottfried def. Geoff Masters, 6-4, 4-6, 6-4

Other 1976 Tournaments

AUSTIN, TEXAS—Chris Evert def. Evonne Goolagong Cawley, 6-3, 7-6

BIRMINGHAM, ALA.—Jimmy Connors def. Roscoe Tanner, 6-4, 3-6, 6-1

DAYTON—Jaime Fillol def. Andrew Pattison, 7-5, 6-7, 6-4

BOCA RATON, FLA.—Butch Walts def. Cliff Richey, 3-6, 6-4, 6-4

SALISBURY, MD.—Ilie Nastase def. Jimmy Connors, 6-2, 6-3, 7-6

LITTLE ROCK—Haroon Rahim def. Colin Dibley, 6-4, 7-5

HAMPTON, VA.—Jimmy Connors def. Ilie Nastase, 6-2, 6-2, 6-2

LACOSTA, CALIF.—Ilie Nastase def. Jimmy Connors, 4-6, 6-0, 6-1

PALM SPRINGS, CALIF.—Jimmy Connors def. Roscoe Tanner, 6-4, 6-4

TOWSON, MD.—Vitas Gerulaitis def. Sherwood Stewart, 6-3, 6-4

SACRAMENTO, CALIF.—Tom Gorman def. Brian Carmichael, 6-2, 7-6

AMELIA ISLAND, FLA.—Chris Evert def. Kerry Melville Reid, 6-2, 6-2

LAS VEGAS—Jimmy Connors def. Ken Rosewall, 6-1, 6-3

MYRTLE BEACH, S.C.—Ilie Nastase def. Manuel Orantes, 6-4, 6-3

ATLANTA—Virginia Wade def. Betty Stove, 5-7, 7-5, 7-5

NEWPORT—Vijay Amritraj def. Brian Teacher, 6-3, 4-6, 6-3, 6-1

PHOENIX—Chris Evert def. Dianne Fromholtz, 6-1, 7-5

MISSION HILLS, CALIF.—Chris Evert def. Francoise Durr, 6-1, 6-2

Other 1977 Tournaments

EDINBURGH—Ken Revie def. Hank Roulston, 6-3, 3-6, 6-1; Martina Navratilova def. Kristien Shaw, 2-6, 9-8, 7-5

RYE, N.Y.—Guillermo Vilas def. Ilie Nastase, 6-2, 6-0

CHARLOTTE, N.C.—Martina Navratilova def. Mima Jausovec, 3-6, 6-2, 6-1

FT. WAYNE, IND.—Sally Greer def. Donna Ganz, 4-6, 6-1, 6-0

LAS VEGAS—Jimmy Connors def. Roscoe Tanner, 6-2, 5-6, 3-6, 6-2, 6-5

SYDNEY, AUST.—Evonne Goolagong Cawley def. Kerry Reid, 6-1, 6-3

TOKYO—Ken Rosewall def. Ilie Nastase, 4-6, 7-6, 6-4; Billie Jean King def. Martina Navratilova, 7-5, 5-7, 6-1

MELBOURNE—Evonne Goolagong Cawley def. Wendy Turnbull, 6-4, 6-1

RYE, N.Y.—Guillermo Vilas def. Ilie Nastase, 6-2, 6-0

CHARLOTTE, N.C.—Martina Navratilova def. Mima Jausovec, 3-6, 6-2, 6-1

BASEL, SWITZ.—Bjorn Borg def. John Lloyd, 6-4, 6-2, 6-3

VIENNA—Brian Gottfried def. Wojtek Fibak, 6-1, 6-1

SAN JUAN, P.R.—Billie Jean King def. Janet Newberry, 6-1, 6-3

PALM SPRINGS—Chris Evert def. Billie Jean King, 6-2, 6-2

PARIS (Indoor)—Corrado Barazzutti def. Brian Gottfried, 7-6, 7-6, 6-7, 3-6, 6-4

TUCSON—Chris Evert def. Martina Navratilova, 6-3, 7-6

VIRGINIA BEACH—Guillermo Vilas def. Ilie Nastase, 6-2, 4-6, 6-2

PT. WASHINGTON, N.Y.—Billie Jean King def. Caroline Stoll, 6-1, 6-1

RIVER PLATE (Buenos Aires)—Guillermo Vilas def. Wojtek Fibak, 6-4, 6-3, 6-0

Other 1978 Tournaments

SCANDINAVIAN CUP (Gothenburg)—Bjorn Borg def. Vitas Gerulaitis, 6-4, 1-6, 6-3.

NEW YORK INVITATIONAL—Vitas Gerulaitis def. Ilie Nastase, 6-2, 6-0.

TOKYO—Tracy Austin def. Martina Navratilova, 6-1, 6-1.

MONTEGO BAY—Ilie Nastase def. Peter Fleming, 2-6, 5-6, 6-2, 6-4, 6-4.

PARADISE ISLAND—Billy Martin def. Victor Pecci, 6-4, 1-6, 7-6.

KYOTO, JAPAN—Ross Case def. Jun Kuki, 6-1, 6-7, 6-1.

SOUTH AMERICAN OPEN (Buenos Aires)—Jose-Luis Clerc def. Victor Pecci, 6-4, 6-4.

MANILA—Yannick Noah def. Peter Feigl, 7-6, 6-0.

ITALIAN INDOOR (Bologna)—Peter Fleming def. Adriano Panatta, 6-2, 7-6.

JOHANNESBURG—Tim Gullikson def. Harold Solomon, 2-6, 7-6, 7-6, 6-7, 6-4.

SANTIAGO—Jose-Luis Clerc def. Victor Pecci, 3-6, 6-3, 6-1.

CALCUTTA—Yannick Noah def. Pascal Portes, 6-3, 6-2.

PONTE VEDRA, FLA.—Bob Lutz def. Dick Stockton, 6-4, 6-1.

Other 1979 Tournaments

LACOSTA, CALIF.—Chris Evert Lloyd def. Dianne Fromholtz, 3-6, 6-3, 6-1.

NEW YORK INVITATIONAL—Eddie Dibbs def. Harold Solomon, 6-7, 7-6, 6-3.

NEWPORT, R.I.—Brian Teacher def. Stan Smith, 1-6, 6-3, 6-4.

GSTAAD—Uli Pinner def. Peter McNamara, 6-2, 6-4, 7-5.

STUTTGART—Tomas Smid def. Uli Pinner, 6-4, 6-0, 6-2.

SWEDISH OPEN (Bastad)—Bjorn Borg def. Balazs Taroczy, 6-1, 7-5.

HILVERSUM—Balasz Taroczy def. Tomas Smid, 6-2, 6-2, 6-1.

KITZBUHEL—Vitas Gerulaitis def. Pavel Slozil, 6-2, 6-2, 6-4.

ATP FINAL (Cincinnati)—Peter Fleming def. Roscoe Tanner, 6-4, 6-2.

PALERMO—Bjorn Borg def. Corrado Barazzutti, 6-4, 6-0, 6-4.

MADRID—Yannick Noah def. Manuel Orantes, 6-3, 6-7, 6-3, 6-2.

MONTREAL—Bjorn Borg def. Connors, 6-4, 6-2, 2-6, 6-4.

Other 1980 Tournaments

PUERTO RICO—Mark Cox def. Humphrey Hose, 7-6, 6-0.

CURACAO—Humphrey Hose def. Carlos Kirmayr, 6-4, 2-6, 6-4.

PANAMA CITY—Mark Cox def. Victor Pecci, 6-2, 6-4.

BOGOTA—Victor Pecci def. Mark Cox, 6-3, 6-4.

BOCA RATON, FLA.—Bjorn Borg def. Vitas Gerulaitis, 6-1, 5-7, 6-1.

SALISBURY, MD.—Bjorn Borg def. Vijay Amritraj, 7-5, 6-1, 6-3.

NEW YORK INVITATIONAL—Vitas Gerulaitis def. John McEnroe, 2-6, 6-3, 6-0.

MONTREAL—Bjorn Borg def. Jimmy Connors, 6-4, 6-2, 2-6, 6-4.

INTERNATIONAL TEAM COMPETITIONS

International Challenge Trophy (Davis Cup)

In 1900 Dwight Filley Davis of St. Louis, Missouri, then a 21-year-old just graduated from Harvard College, and a leading American player, put into competition the International Lawn Tennis Challenge Trophy. He envisioned a yearly tournament that would advance friendship and goodwill internationally among sportsmen who visited one another's country for matches.

The success of his idea was almost immediate, and quickly the sterling silver bowl became known simply as the Davis Cup. A total of 63 nations have appeared in the competition, but only eight have won: The United States (26 times), Australia (24), Great Britain (9), France (6), South Africa (1), Sweden (1), Italy (1), and Czechoslovakia (1). Through 1971, the champion nation stood out, meaning that the victor of one year defends the Cup the following year in the grand final called the Challenge Round against the nation which wins its way through an elimination tournament involving four zones: European Zones A and B, American Zone, and Eastern Zone. A challenging nation must usually win five or six matches to reach the Challenge Round. In 1971 the Challenge Round was dropped in favor of all-comers format.

Eight nations, besides the eight winners, have appeared in the Challenge or Final Round: Belgium, Japan, Mexico, Spain, India, Romania, West Germany, and Chile.

Beginning in 1981, a new format was adopted. In this plan, the top 16 nations conduct a single-elimination (or "knock out") competition for the Davis Cup. Other nations competing play in zonal divisions with the four nations winning the zonal play advancing into the top 16 the following year, replacing the first four eliminated the previous year.

Those nations eliminated can, of course, return to the top 16 again by winning in the zonal play of the next year and earning a promotion in a cycle intended to continually repeat itself with four teams going up and four coming down each year.

Davis Cup matches were inaugurated in 1900, and with the exception of 1901 and 1910, contests were held annually until 1914, the challenge round of that year being played just prior to the outbreak of World War I. Competition was suspended during the war and was not resumed until 1919. In 1904, 1912, and 1919 the United States did not compete. There was no Cup play during 1940–1945, due to World War II.

British Isles (now Great Britain) was the only nation to challenge for the Cup in 1900, and the first match was played at Dwight Davis's club, Longwood Cricket Club in Boston, August 8, 9, and 10. Davis captained the United States team and won a singles match as well as the decisive doubles (with Holcombe Ward) in a 3-0 triumph. Until 1904 the British were the only challengers. Then France and Belgium entered the tournament. In 1905 the nation that would compile the best record, Australia, came in, known until 1924 as Australasia (a combination of Australia and New Zealand).

The International Lawn Tennis Challenge Trophy is under the jurisdiction of the Davis Cup nations. The representatives of these Davis Cup nations (nations entered in the current competition and/or having played in one or more of the five last preceding competitions and which are still eligible to compete) meet annually in London during the period between June 14 and July 31. Each nation may be represented at the Annual General Meeting (and at any general meeting that may be held from time to time at the discretion of the champion nation or upon request to the champion nation by not less than one-third of the nations and within six months after receipt of such request by the champion nation) by not more than two accredited representatives, and each nation is entitled to one vote.

Davis Cup competition is conducted by the Committee of Management appointed annually by the lawn tennis association (for an example), or corresponding organization of the champion nation. This committee has power to co-opt other persons for the purpose of carrying out all or any of its duties and to set up a Zonal Committee of Management to manage the zones or sections of the competition in the geographical area in which the champion nation is not situated, with a special committee being appointed for the European Zone.

The rules of lawn tennis, as adopted by the International Tennis Federation, govern Davis Cup play. While having full authority over the Davis Cup competition, the Davis Cup nations recognize the ITF's interest in all international competition by providing in the Davis Cup regulations that the Committee of Management of the ITF may nominate an additional representative to membership of the Davis Cup Committee of Management. This representative may attend all meetings of the Davis Cup Committee of Management and the annual general meeting of the Davis Cup nations.

The format is a three-day match of two singles the first day, a doubles the second, and two singles the third.

The challenge round format was dropped after 1971 competition and the all-comers' type has replaced it. Competition is divided into four geographic zones: two European Zones (all European

The Davis Cup as it appeared in the early 1900s *(left)* and as it appears today *(right).*

nations, Middle East, and Africa); American Zone (both North and South America plus the nations of the Caribbean); and Eastern Zone (the nations of Asia, plus Australia and New Zealand). The choice of site for the finals is determined by the ITF, but no nation may be the host for two consecutive years. The venue date and surface of the court will be decided by the home nation.

Davis Cup Challenge Rounds

1900—UNITED STATES d. BRITISH ISLES, 3-0
Longwood Cricket Club, Boston, Massachusetts
(Captains: British Isles, Arthur W. Gore; U.S., Dwight F. Davis)
British Isles was the only challenger.
Malcolm D. Whitman (U.S.) d. Arthur W. Gore, 6-1, 6-3, 6-2; Dwight F. Davis (U.S.) d. E. D. Black, 4-6, 6-2, 6-4, 6-4; Malcolm D. Whitman (U.S.) d. E. D. Black, unplayed; Dwight F. Davis (U.S.) d. Arthur W. Gore, 9-7, 9-9, unfinished; Holcombe Ward and Dwight F. Davis (U.S.) d. E. D. Black and H. Roper Barrett, 6-4, 6-4, 6-4.
1901—no match
1902—UNITED STATES d. BRITISH ISLES, 3-2
Crescent Athletic Club, Brooklyn, N.Y.
(Captains: British Isles, William H. Collins; U.S., Malcolm D. Whitman).
British Isles was the only challenger.
Reginald F. Doherty (B.I.) d. William A. Larned, 2-6, 3-6, 6-3, 6-4; Malcolm D. Whitman (U.S.) d. Dr. Joshua Pim, 6-1, 6-1, 1-6, 6-0; William A. Larned (U.S.) d. Dr. Joshua Pim, 6-3, 6-2, 6-3; Malcolm D. Whitman (U.S.) d. Reginald F. Doherty, 6-1, 7-5, 6-4; Reginald F. Doherty and Hugh L. Doherty (B.I.) d. Holcombe Ward and Dwight F. Davis, 3-6, 10-8, 6-3, 6-4.
1903—BRITISH ISLES d. UNITED STATES, 4-1
Longwood Cricket Club, Boston, Massachusetts
(Captains: British Isles, William H. Collins; U.S., William A. Larned).
British Isles was the only challenger.
Hugh L. Doherty (B.I.) d. Robert D. Wrenn, 6-0, 6-3, 6-4; William A. Larned (U.S.) d. Reginald F. Doherty, default; Hugh L. Doherty (B.I.) d. William A. Larned, 6-3, 6-8, 6-0, 2-6, 7-5; Reginald F. Doherty (B.I.) d. Robert D. Wrenn, 6-4, 3-6, 6-3, 6-4; Reginald F. Doherty and Hugh L. Doherty

(B.I.) d. Robert D. Wrenn and George L. Wrenn, 7-5, 9-7, 2-6, 6-3.
1904—BRITISH ISLES d. BELGIUM, 5-0
Wimbledon, London
(Captains: Belgium, Paul de Borman; British Isles, William H. Collins).
Two challenging nations entered competition.
Hugh L. Doherty (B.I.) d. Paul de Borman, 6-4, 6-1, 6-1; Frank L. Riseley (B.I.) d. W. Lemaire, 6-1, 6-4, 6-2; Hugh L. Doherty (B.I.) d. William Lemaire, default; Frank L. Riseley (B.I.) d. Paul de Borman, 4-6, 6-2, 8-6, 7-5; Reginald F. Doherty and Hugh L. Doherty (B.I.) d. Paul de Borman and W. Lemaire, 6-0, 6-1, 6-3.
1905—BRITISH ISLES d. UNITED STATES, 5-0
Wimbledon, London
(Captains: U.S., Paul Dashiell; British Isles, William H. Collins)
Four challenging nations entered competition.
Hugh L. Doherty (B.I.) d. Holcombe Ward, 7-9, 4-6, 6-1, 6-2, 6-0; Sidney H. Smith (B.I.) d. William A. Larned, 6-4, 6-4, 5-7, 6-4; Sidney H. Smith (B.I.) d. William J. Clothier, 4-6, 6-1, 6-4, 6-3; Hugh L. Doherty (B.I.) d. William A. Larned, 6-4, 2-6, 6-8, 6-4, 6-2; Reginald F. Doherty and Hugh L. Doherty, (B.I.) d. Holcombe Ward and Beals C. Wright, 8-10, 6-2, 6-2, 4-6, 8-6.
1906—BRITISH ISLES d. UNITED STATES, 5-0
Wimbledon, London
(Captains: U.S., Beals Wright; British Isles, William H. Collins)
Two challenging nations entered competition.
Sidney H. Smith (B.I.) d. Raymond D. Little, 6-4, 6-4, 6-1; Hugh L. Doherty (B.I.) d. Holcombe Ward, 6-2, 8-6, 6-3; Sidney H. Smith (B.I.) d. Holcombe Ward, 6-1, 6-0, 6-4; Hugh L. Doherty (B.I.) d. Raymond D. Little, 3-6, 6-3, 6-8, 6-1, 6-3; Reginald F. Doherty and Hugh L. Doherty (B.I.) d. Holcombe Ward and Raymond D. Little, 3-6, 11-9, 9-7, 6-1.
1907—AUSTRALASIA d. BRITISH ISLES, 3-2
Wimbledon, London
(Captains: Australasia, Norman E. Brookes; British Isles, S. A. E. Hickson)
Two challenging nations entered competition.

Norman E. Brookes (A) d. Arthur W. Gore, 7-5, 6-1, 7-5; Anthony F. Wilding (A) d. H. Roper Barrett, 1-6, 6-4, 6-3, 7-5; Norman E. Brookes (A) d. H. Roper Barrett, 6-2, 6-0, 6-3; Arthur W. Gore (B.I.) d. Anthony F. Wilding, 3-6, 6-3, 7-5, 6-2; Arthur W. Gore and H. Roper Barrett (B.I.) d. Norman E. Brookes and Anthony F. Wilding, 3-6, 4-6, 7-5, 6-2, 13-11.

1908—AUSTRALASIA d. UNITED STATES, 3-2
Warehousemen's Grounds, Melbourne, Australia
(Captains: U.S., Beals Wright; Australasia, Norman E. Brookes)
Two challenging nations entered competition.

Norman E. Brookes (A) d. Fred B. Alexander, 5-7, 9-7, 6-2, 4-6, 6-3; Beals C. Wright (U.S.) d. Anthony F. Wilding, 3-6, 7-5, 6-3, 6-1; Anthony F. Wilding (A) d. Fred B. Alexander, 6-3, 6-4, 6-1; Beals C. Wright (U.S.) d. Norman E. Brookes, 0-6, 3-6, 7-5, 6-2, 12-10; Norman E. Brookes and Anthony F. Wilding (A) d. Beals C. Wright and Fred B. Alexander, 6-4, 6-2, 5-7, 1-6, 6-4.

1909—AUSTRALASIA d. UNITED STATES, 5-0
Double Bay Grounds, Sydney, Australia
(Captains: U.S., Maurice E. McLoughlin; Australasia, Norman E. Brookes)
Two challenging nations entered competition.

Norman E. Brookes (A) d. Maurice E. McLoughlin, 6-2, 6-2, 6-4; Anthony F. Wilding (A) d. Melville H. Long, 6-2, 7-5, 6-1; Norman E. Brookes (A) d. Melville H. Long, 6-4, 7-5, 8-6; Anthony F. Wilding (A) d. Maurice E. McLoughlin, 3-6, 8-6, 6-2, 6-3; Norman E. Brookes and A. F. Wilding (A) d. Maurice E. McLoughlin and Melville H. Long, 12-10, 9-7, 6-3.

1910—no match

1911—AUSTRALASIA d. UNITED STATES, 5-0
Hagley Park, Christchurch, New Zealand

The 1920 United States Davis Cup team: *(left to right)* William M. Johnston, R. N. Williams II, Samuel Hardy (captain), William T. Tilden II, Charles S. Garland, and Watson Washburn.

Davis Cup Challenge Rounds—1911 (cont.)

(Captains: U.S., William A. Larned; Australasia, Norman E. Brookes)
Two challenging nations entered competition.
Norman E. Brookes (A) d. Beals C. Wright, 6-4, 2-6, 6-3, 6-3; Rodney W. Heath (A) d. William A. Larned, 2-6, 6-1, 7-5, 6-2; Norman E. Brookes (A) d. Maurice E. McLoughlin, 6-4, 3-6, 4-6, 6-3, 6-4; Rodney W. Heath (A) d. Beals C. Wright. Default. Norman E. Brookes and Alfred W. Dunlop (A) d. Beals C. Wright and Maurice E. McLoughlin, 6-4, 5-7, 7-5, 6-4.

1912—BRITISH ISLES d. AUSTRALIA, 3-2
Warehousemen's Grounds, Melbourne, Australia
(Captains: British Isles, Charles P. Dixon; Australasia, Norman E. Brookes)
Two challenging nations entered competition.
J. Cecil Parke (B.I.) d. Norman E. Brookes, 8-6, 6-3, 5-7, 6-2; Charles P. Dixon (B.I.) d. Rodney W. Heath, 5-7, 6-4, 6-4, 6-4; J. Cecil Parke (B.I.) d. Rodney W. Heath, 6-2, 6-4, 6-4; Norman E. Brookes (A) d. Charles P. Dixon, 6-2, 6-4, 6-4; Norman E. Brookes and Alfred W. Dunlop (A) d. J. Cecil Parke and Alfred E. Beamish, 6-4, 6-1, 7-5.

1913—UNITED STATES d. BRITISH ISLES, 3-2
Wimbledon, London
(Captains: U.S., Harold H. Hackett; British Isles, Roger J. McNair)
Seven challenging nations entered competition.
J. Cecil Parke (B.I.) d. Maurice E. McLoughlin, 8-10, 7-5, 6-4, 1-6, 7-5; R. Norris Williams II (U.S.) d. Charles P. Dixon, 8-6, 3-6, 6-2, 1-6, 7-5; Maurice E. McLoughlin (U.S.) d. Charles P. Dixon, 8-6, 6-3, 6-2; J. Cecil Parke (B.I.) d. R. Norris Williams II, 6-2, 5-7, 5-7, 6-4, 6-2; Harold H. Hackett and Maurice E. McLoughlin (U.S.) d. H. Roper Barrett and Charles P. Dixon, 5-7, 6-1, 2-6, 7-5, 6-4.

1914—AUSTRALASIA d. UNITED STATES, 3-2
West Side Tennis Club, Forest Hills, N.Y.
(Captains: Australasia, Norman E. Brookes; U.S., Maurice E. McLoughlin)
Six challenging nations entered competition.

Norman E. Brookes (A) d. R. Norris Williams II, 6-1, 6-2, 8-10, 6-3; Maurice E. McLoughlin (U.S.) d. Anthony F. Wilding, 6-2, 6-3, 2-6, 6-2; Anthony F. Wilding (A) d. R. Norris Williams II, 7-5, 6-2, 6-3; Maurice E. McLoughlin (U.S.) d. Norman E. Brookes, 17-15, 6-3, 6-3; Norman E. Brookes and A. F. Wilding (A) d. Maurice E. McLoughlin and Thomas C. Bundy, 6-3, 8-6, 9-7.

1915–18—no match
1919—AUSTRALASIA d. BRITISH ISLES, 4-1
Double Bay Grounds, Sydney, Australia
(Captains: British Isles, Algernon R. F. Kingscote; Australasia, Norman E. Brookes).
Four challenging nations entered competition.
Gerald L. Patterson (A) d. Arthur H. Lowe, 6-4, 6-3, 2-6, 6-3; Algernon R. F. Kingscote (B.I.) d. James O. Anderson, 7-5, 6-2, 6-4; Gerald Patterson (A) d. Algernon R. F. Kingscote, 6-4, 6-4, 8-6; James O. Anderson (A) d. Arthur H. Lowe, 6-4, 5-7, 6-3, 4-6, 12-10; Norman E. Brookes and Gerald L. Patterson (A) d. Algernon R. F. Kingscote and Alfred E. Beamish, 6-0, 6-0, 6-2.

1920—UNITED STATES d. AUSTRALASIA, 5-0
Domain Cricket Ground, Auckland, New Zealand
(Captains: U.S., Sam Hardy; Australasia, Norman E. Brookes).
Five challenging nations entered competition.
William T. Tilden II (U.S.) d. Norman E. Brookes, 10-8, 6-4, 1-6, 6-4; William M. Johnston (U.S.) d. Gerald L. Patterson, 6-3, 6-1, 6-1; William T. Tilden II (U.S.) d. Gerald L. Patterson, 5-7, 6-2, 6-3, 6-3; William M. Johnston (U.S.) d. Norman E. Brookes, 5-7, 7-5, 6-3; William T. Tilden II and William M. Johnston (U.S.) d. Norman E. Brookes and Gerald L. Patterson, 4-6, 6-4, 6-0, 6-4.

1921—UNITED STATES d. JAPAN, 5-0
West Side Tennis Club, Forest Hills, N.Y.
(Captains: Japan, Ichiya Kumagae; U.S., R. Norris Williams II)
Eleven challenging nations entered competition
William T. Tilden II (U.S.) d. Zenzo Shimizu, 5-7, 4-6, 7-5, 6-2, 6-1; William M. Johnston (U.S.) d. Ichiya Kumagae, 6-2, 6-4, 6-2; William T. Tilden II (U.S.) d. Ichiya Kumagae, 9-7, 6-4, 6-1; William M.

President Calvin Coolidge making the initial draw in the 1924 Davis Cup drawings in the presence of diplomatic representatives and Dwight F. Davis on the White House lawn.

Johnston (U.S.) d. Zenzo Shimizu, 6-3, 5-7, 6-2, 6-4; R. Norris Williams II and Watson M. Washburn (U.S.) d. Zenzo Shimizu and Ichiya Kumagae, 6-2, 7-5, 4-6, 7-5.

1922—UNITED STATES d. AUSTRALASIA, 4-1
    West Side Tennis Club, Forest Hills, N.Y.
    (Captains: Australasia, James O. Anderson;
        U.S., R. Norris Williams II)
    Ten challenging nations entered competition.
William T. Tilden II (U.S.) d. Gerald L. Patterson, 7-5, 10-8, 6-0; William M. Johnston (U.S.) d. James O. Anderson, 6-1, 6-2, 6-3; William M. Johnston (U.S.) d. Gerald L. Patterson, 6-2, 6-2, 6-1; William T. Tilden II (U.S.) d. James O. Anderson, 6-4, 5-7, 3-6, 6-4, 6-2; Gerald L. Patterson and Pat O'Hara Wood (A) d. William T. Tilden II and Vincent Richards, 6-3, 6-0, 6-4.

1923—UNITED STATES d. AUSTRALASIA, 4-1
    West Side Tennis Club, Forest Hills, N.Y.
    (Captains: Australasia, Gerald L. Patterson;
        U.S., R. Norris Williams II)
    Sixteen challenging nations entered competition.
James O. Anderson (A) d. William M. Johnston, 4-6, 6-2, 2-6, 7-5, 6-2; William T. Tilden II (U.S.) d. John B. Hawkes, 6-4, 6-2, 6-1; William M. Johnston (U.S.) d. John B. Hawkes, 6-0, 6-2, 6-1; William T. Tilden II (U.S.) d. James O. Anderson, 6-2, 6-3, 1-6, 7-5; William T. Tilden II and R. Norris Williams II (U.S.) d. James O. Anderson and John B. Hawkes, 17-15, 11-13, 2-6, 6-3, 6-2.

1924—UNITED STATES d. AUSTRALASIA, 5-0
    Germantown Cricket Club, Philadelphia, Pa.
    (Captains: Australasia, Gerald L. Patterson;
        U.S., R. Norris Williams II)
    Twenty-two nations entered competition.
William T. Tilden II (U.S.) d. Gerald L. Patterson, 6-4, 6-2, 6-2; Vincent Richards (U.S.) d. Pat O'Hara Wood, 6-3, 6-2, 6-4; William T. Tilden II (U.S.) d. Pat O'Hara Wood, 6-2, 6-1, 6-1; Vincent Richards (U.S.) d. Gerald L. Patterson, 6-3, 7-5, 6-4; William T. Tilden II and William M. Johnston (U.S.) d. Gerald L. Patterson and Pat O'Hara Wood, 5-7, 6-3, 6-4, 6-1.

1925—UNITED STATES d. FRANCE, 5-0
    Germantown Cricket Club, Philadelphia, Pa.
    (Captains: France, Max Décugis; U.S., R. Norris Williams II)
    Twenty-two nations entered competition.
William T. Tilden II (U.S.) d. Jean Borotra, 4-6, 6-0, 2-6, 9-7, 6-4; William M. Johnston (U.S.) d. Jean René Lacoste, 6-1, 6-8, 6-3; William T. Tilden II (U.S.) d. Jean René Lacoste, 3-6, 10-12, 8-6, 7-5, 6-2; William M. Johnston (U.S.) d. Jean Borotra, 6-1, 6-4, 6-0; Vincent Richards and R. Norris Williams II (U.S.) d. Jean René Lacoste and Jean Borotra, 6-4, 6-4, 6-3.

The 1928 United States Davis Cup team sails for the Inter-Zone matches aboard the *Ile de France: (left to right)* Wilbur Coen, George Lott, Samuel Peacock (manager), Bill Tilden, and John Hennessey. In the Challenge Round, Francis T. Hunter replaced Coen on the team. Incidentally, Coen was the youngest American player to play in a Davis Cup match.

1926—UNITED STATES d. FRANCE, 4-1

Germantown Cricket Club, Philadelphia, Pa.

(Captains: France, Pierre Gillou; U.S., R. Norris Williams II)

Twenty-three challenging nations entered competition.

William M. Johnston (U.S.) d. Jean René Lacoste, 6-0, 6-4, 0-6, 6-0; William T. Tilden II (U.S.) d. Jean Borotra, 6-2, 6-3, 6-3; William M. Johnston (U.S.) d. Jean Borotra, 8-6, 6-4, 9-7; Jean René Lacoste (F) d. William T. Tilden II, 4-6, 6-4, 8-6, 8-6; R. Norris Williams II and Vincent Richards (U.S.) d. Henri Cochet and Jacques Brugnon, 6-4, 6-4, 6-2.

1927—FRANCE d. UNITED STATES, 3-2

Germantown Cricket Club, Philadelphia, Pa.

(Captains: France, Pierre Gillou; U.S., Charles Garland)

Twenty-three challenging nations entered competition.

Jean René Lacoste (F) d. William M. Johnston, 6-3, 6-2, 6-2; William T. Tilden II (U.S.) d. Henri Cochet, 6-4, 2-6, 6-2, 8-6; Jean René Lacoste (F) d. William T. Tilden II, 6-3, 4-6, 6-3, 6-2; Henri Cochet (F) d. William M. Johnston, 6-4, 4-6, 6-2, 6-4; William T. Tilden II and Francis T. Hunter (U.S.) d. Jean Borotra and Jacques Brugnon, 3-6, 6-3, 6-3, 4-6, 6-0.

1928—FRANCE d. UNITED STATES, 4-1

Stade Roland Garros, Auteuil, Paris

(Captains: U.S., Joseph Wear; France, Pierre Gillou)

Thirty-three challenging nations entered competition.

William T. Tilden II (U.S.) d. Jean René Lacoste, 1-6, 6-4, 6-4, 2-6, 6-3; Henri Cochet (F) d. John F. Hennessey, 5-7, 9-7, 6-3, 6-0; Henri Cochet (F) d.

William T. Tilden II, 9-7, 8-6, 6-4; Jean René Lacoste (F) d. John F. Hennessey, 4-6, 6-1, 7-5, 6-3; Henri Cochet and Jean Borotra (F) d. William T. Tilden II and Francis T. Hunter, 6-4, 6-8, 7-5, 4-6, 6-2.

1929—FRANCE d. UNITED STATES, 3-2
    Stade Roland Garros, Auteuil, Paris
    (Captains: U.S., Fitz-Eugene Dixon; France, Pierre Gillou)
    Twenty-eight challenging nations entered competition.

Henri Cochet (F) d. William T. Tilden II, 6-3, 6-1, 6-2; Jean Borotra (F) d. George M. Lott, Jr., 6-1, 3-6, 6-4, 7-5; William T. Tilden II (U.S.) d. Jean Borotra, 4-6, 6-1, 6-4, 7-5; Henri Cochet (F) d. George M. Lott, Jr., 6-1, 3-6, 6-0, 6-3; John Van Ryn and Wilmer L. Allison (U.S.) d. Henri Cochet and Jean Borotra, 6-1, 8-6, 6-4.

1930—FRANCE d. UNITED STATES, 4-1
    Stade Roland Garros, Auteuil, Paris
    (Captains: U.S., Fitz-Eugene Dixon; France, Pierre Gillou)
    Twenty-seven challenging nations entered competition.

William T. Tilden II (U.S.) d. Jean Borotra, 2-6, 7-5, 6-4, 7-5; Henri Cochet (F) d. George M. Lott, Jr., 6-4, 6-2, 6-2; Jean Borotra (F) d. George M. Lott, Jr., 5-7, 6-3, 2-6, 6-2, 8-6; Henri Cochet (F) d. William T. Tilden II, 4-6, 6-3, 6-1, 7-5; Henri Cochet and Jacques Brugnon (F) d. Wilmer L. Allison and John Van Ryn, 6-3, 7-5, 1-6, 6-2.

1931—FRANCE d. GREAT BRITAIN, 3-2
    Stade Roland Garros, Auteuil, Paris
    (Captains: Britain, Herbert Roper Barrett; France, Jean René Lacoste)
    Twenty-nine challenging nations entered competition.

The 1932 United States Davis Cup team: *(left to right)* Frank Shields, Wilmer Allison, Bernon Prentice (captain), John Van Ryn, Ellsworth Vines, Jr.

Davis Cup Challenge Rounds—1931 *(cont.)*

Henri Cochet (F) d. Henry W. Austin, 3-6, 11-9, 6-2, 6-4; Frederick J. Perry (G.B.) d. Jean Borotra, 4-6, 10-8, 6-0, 4-6, 6-4; Henry W. Austin (G.B.) d. Jean Borotra, 7-5, 6-3, 3-6, 7-5; Henri Cochet (F) d. Frederick J. Perry, 6-4, 1-6, 9-7, 6-3; Henri Cochet and Jacques Brugnon (F) d. George P. Hughes and Charles H. Kingsley, 6-1, 5-7, 6-3, 8-6.

1932—FRANCE d. UNITED STATES, 3-2
Stade Roland Garros, Auteuil, Paris
(Captains: U.S., Bernon Prentice; France, Jean René Lacoste)
Twenty-eight challenging nations entered competition.

Jean Borotra (F) d. H Ellsworth Vines, Jr., 6-4, 6-2, 3-6, 6-4; Henri Cochet (F) d. Wilmer L. Allison, 5-7, 7-5, 7-5, 6-2; Jean Borotra (F) d. Wilmer L. Allison, 1-6, 3-6, 6-4, 6-2, 7-5; H. Ellsworth Vines,

The 1937 United States Davis Cup team: *(left to right)* Wayne Sabin, Bryan (Bitsy) Grant, Donald Budge, Gene Mako, Walter Pate (captain), Frank Parker.

Jr. (U.S.) d. Henri Cochet, 4-6, 0-6, 7-5, 8-6, 6-2; Wilmer L. Allison and John Van Ryn (U.S.) d. Henri Cochet and Jacques Brugnon, 6-3, 11-13, 7-5, 4-6, 6-4.

1933—GREAT BRITAIN d. FRANCE, 3-2
    Stade Roland Garros, Auteuil, Paris
    (Captains: Britain, Herbert Roper Barrett; France, Jean René Lacoste)
    Twenty-nine challenging nations entered competition.

Henry W. Austin (G.B.) d. André Merlin, 6-3, 6-4, 6-0; Frederick J. Perry (G.B.) d. Henri Cochet, 8-10, 6-4, 8-6, 3-6, 6-1; Henri Cochet (F) d. Henry W. Austin, 5-7, 6-4, 4-6, 6-4, 6-4; Frederick J. Perry (G.B.) d. André Merlin, 4-6, 8-6, 6-2, 7-5; Jean Borotra and Jacques Brugnon (F) d. George P. Hughes and Harold G. N. Lee, 6-3, 8-6, 6-2.

1934—GREAT BRITAIN d. UNITED STATES, 4-1
    Wimbledon, London
    (Captains: U.S., R. Norris Williams II; Britain, Herbert Roper Barrett)
    Twenty-six challenging nations entered competition.

Henry W. Austin (G.B.) d. Francis X. Shields, 6-4, 6-4, 6-1; Frederick J. Perry (G.B.) d. Sidney B. Wood, Jr., 6-1, 4-6, 5-7, 6-0, 6-3; Frederick J. Perry (G.B.) d. Francis X. Shields, 6-4, 4-6, 6-2, 15-13; Henry W. Austin (G.B.) d. Sidney B. Wood, Jr., 6-4, 6-0, 6-8, 6-3; George M. Lott, Jr., and Lester R. Stoefen (U.S.) d. George P. Hughes and Harold G. N. Lee, 7-5, 6-0, 4-6, 9-7.

1935—GREAT BRITAIN d. UNITED STATES, 5-0
    Wimbledon, London
    (Captains: U.S., Joseph Wear; Britain, Herbert Roper Barrett)
    Twenty-seven challenging nations entered competition.

Henry W. Austin (G.B.) d. Wilmer L. Allison, 6-2, 2-6, 4-6, 6-3, 7-5; Frederick J. Perry (G.B.) d. J. Donald Budge, 6-0, 6-8, 6-3, 6-4; Henry W. Austin (G.B.) d. J. Donald Budge, 6-2, 6-4, 6-8, 7-5; Frederick J. Perry (G.B.) d. Wilmer L. Allison, 4-6, 6-4, 7-5, 6-3; George P. Hughes and Charles R. D. Tuckey (G.B.) d. Wilmer L. Allison and John Van Ryn, 6-2, 1-6, 6-8, 6-3, 6-3.

1936—GREAT BRITAIN d. AUSTRALIA, 3-2
    Wimbledon, London
    (Captains: Australia, Cliff Sproule; Britain, Herbert Roper Barrett)

Twenty-three challenging nations entered competition.

Henry W. Austin (G.B.) d. John H. Crawford, 4-6, 6-3, 6-1, 6-1; Frederick J. Perry (G.B.) d. Adrian K. Quist, 6-1, 4-6, 7-5, 6-2; Adrian K. Quist (A) d. Henry W. Austin, 6-4, 3-6, 7-5, 6-3; Frederick J. Perry (G.B.) d. John H. Crawford, 6-2, 6-3, 6-3; John H. Crawford and Adrian K. Quist (A) d. George P. Hughes and Charles R. D. Tuckey, 6-4, 2-6, 7-5, 10-8.

1937—UNITED STATES d. GREAT BRITAIN, 4-1
    Wimbledon, London
    (Captains: U.S., Walter Pate; Britain, Herbert Roper Barrett)
    Twenty-four challenging nations entered competition.

Henry W. Austin (G.B.) d. Frank A. Parker, 6-3, 6-2, 7-5; J. Donald Budge (U.S.) d. Charles E. Hare, 15-13, 6-1, 6-2; Frank A. Parker (U.S.) d. Charles E. Hare, 6-2, 6-4, 6-2; J. Donald Budge (U.S.) d. Henry W. Austin, 8-6, 3-6, 6-4, 6-3; J. Donald Budge and C. Gene Mako (U.S.) d. Charles R. D. Tuckey and Frank H. D. Wilde, 6-3, 7-5, 7-9, 12-10.

1938—UNITED STATES d. AUSTRALIA, 3-2
    Germantown Cricket Club, Philadelphia, Pa.
    (Captains: Australia, Harry Hopman; U.S., Walter Pate)
    Twenty-three challenging nations entered competition.

Robert L. Riggs (U.S.) d. Adrian K. Quist, 4-6, 6-0, 8-6, 6-1; J. Donald Budge (U.S.) d. John E. Bromwich, 6-2, 6-3, 4-6, 7-5; J. Donald Budge (U.S.) d. Adrian K. Quist, 8-6, 6-1, 6-2; John E. Bromwich (A) d. Robert L. Riggs, 6-4, 4-6, 6-0, 6-2; Adrian K. Quist and John E. Bromwich (A) d. J. Donald Budge and C. Gene Mako, 0-6, 6-3, 6-4, 6-2.

1939—AUSTRALIA d. UNITED STATES, 3-2
    Merion Cricket Club, Haverford, Pa.
    (Captains: Australia, Harry Hopman; U.S., Walter Pate)
    Twenty-five challenging nations entered competition.

Robert L. Riggs (U.S.) d. John E. Bromwich, 6-4, 6-0, 7-5; Frank A. Parker (U.S.) d. Adrian K. Quist, 6-3, 6-4, 1-6, 7-5; Adrian K. Quist (A) d. Robert L. Riggs, 6-1, 6-4, 3-6, 3-6, 6-4; John E. Bromwich (A) d. Frank A. Parker, 6-0, 6-3, 6-1; Adrian K. Quist

Davis Cup Challenge Rounds—1939 *(cont.)*

and John E. Bromwich (A) d. John A. Kramer and Joseph R. Hunt, 5-7, 6-2, 7-5, 6-2.

1940–1945—no matches, World War II

1946—UNITED STATES d. AUSTRALIA, 5-0

Kooyong Tennis Club, Melbourne, Australia

(Captains: U.S., Walter Pate; Australia, Gerald L. Patterson)

Eighteen challenging nations entered competition.

Frederick R. Schroeder, Jr. (U.S.) d. John E. Bromwich, 3-6, 6-1, 6-2, 0-6, 6-3; John A. Kramer (U.S.) d. Dinny Pails, 8-6, 6-2, 9-7; John A. Kramer (U.S.) d. John E. Bromwich, 8-6, 6-4, 6-4; Gardnar Mulloy (U.S.) d. Dinny Pails, 6-3, 6-3, 6-4; John A. Kramer, and Frederick R. Schroeder, Jr. (U.S.) d. John E. Bromwich and Adrian K. Quist, 6-2, 7-5, 6-4.

1947—UNITED STATES d. AUSTRALIA, 4-1

West Side Tennis Club, Forest Hills, N.Y.

(Captains: Australia, Roy Cowling; U.S., Alrick Man)

Twenty-one challenging nations entered competition.

John A. Kramer (U.S.) d. Dinny Pails, 6-2, 6-1, 6-2; Frederick R. Schroeder, Jr. (U.S.) d. John E. Bromwich, 6-4, 5-7, 6-3, 6-4; Frederick R. Schroeder, Jr. (U.S.) d. Dinny Pails, 6-3, 8-6, 4-6, 9-11, 10-8; John A. Kramer (U.S.) d. John E. Bromwich, 6-3, 6-2, 6-2; John E. Bromwich and Colin Long (A) d. John A. Kramer and Frederick A. Schroeder, Jr., 6-4, 2-6, 6-2, 6-4.

1948—UNITED STATES d. AUSTRALIA, 5-0

West Side Tennis Club, Forest Hills, N.Y.

(Captains: Australia, Adrian K. Quist; U.S., Alrick Man).

Twenty-eight challenging nations entered competition.

Frank A. Parker (U.S.) d. O. William Sidwell, 6-4,

The 1946 United States Davis Cup team: *(left to right)* Gardnar Mulloy, William Talbert, Walter Pate (captain), Frank Parker, and Jack Kramer.

6-4, 6-4; Frederick R. Schroeder, Jr. (U.S.) d. O. William Sidwell, 6-2, 6-1, 6-1; Frank A. Parker (U.S.) d. Adrian K. Quist, 6-2, 6-2, 6-3; Frederick R. Schroeder, Jr. (U.S.) d. Adrian K. Quist, 6-3, 4-6, 6-0, 6-0; William F. Talbert and Gardnar Mulloy (U.S.) d. O. William Sidwell and Colin Long, 8-6, 9-7, 2-6, 7-5.

1949—UNITED STATES d. AUSTRALIA, 4-1
    West Side Tennis Club, Forest Hills, N.Y.
    (Captains: Australia, John Bromwich; U.S., Alrick Man)
    Twenty-six challenging nations entered competition.
Frederick R. Schroeder, Jr. (U.S.) d. O. William Sidwell, 6-1, 5-7, 4-6, 6-2, 6-3; Richard Gonzalez (U.S.) d. Frank Sedgman, 8-6, 6-4, 9-7; Frederick R. Schroeder, Jr. (U.S.) d. Frank Sedgman, 6-4, 6-3, 6-3; Richard Gonzalez (U.S.) d. O. William Sidwell, 6-1, 6-3, 6-3; O. William Sidwell and John Bromwich (A) d. William F. Talbert and Gardnar Mulloy, 3-6, 4-6, 10-8, 9-7, 9-7.

1950—AUSTRALIA d. UNITED STATES, 4-1
    West Side Tennis Club, Forest Hills, N.Y.
    (Captains: Australia, Harry Hopman; U.S., Alrick Man)
    Twenty-five challenging nations entered competition.
Frank Sedgman (A) d. Thomas P. Brown, Jr. 6-0, 8-6, 9-7; Kenneth McGregor (A) d. Frederick R. Schroeder, Jr., 13-11, 6-3, 6-4; Frank Sedgman (A) d. Frederick R. Schroeder, Jr., 6-2, 6-2, 6-2; Thomas P. Brown, Jr. (U.S.) d. Kenneth McGregor, 9-11, 8-10, 11-9, 6-1, 6-4; Frank Sedgman and John Bromwich (A) d. Frederick R. Schroeder, Jr., and Gardnar Mulloy, 4-6, 6-4, 6-2, 4-6, 6-4.

1951—AUSTRALIA d. UNITED STATES, 3-2
    White City Courts, Sydney, Australia
    (Captains: U.S. Frank Shields; Australia, Harry Hopman)
    Twenty-six challenging nations entered competition.
E. Victor Seixas, Jr., (U.S.) d. Mervyn Rose, 6-3, 6-4, 9-7; Frank Sedgman (A) d. Frederick R. Schroeder, Jr., 6-4, 6-3, 4-6, 6-4; Frederick R. Schroeder, Jr. (U.S.) d. Mervyn Rose, 6-4, 13-11, 7-5; Frank Sedgman (A) d. E. Victor Seixas, Jr., 6-4, 6-2, 6-2; Kenneth McGregor and Frank Sedgman (A) d. Frederick R. Schroeder, Jr. and Tony Trabert, 6-2, 9-7, 6-3.

1952—AUSTRALIA d. UNITED STATES, 4-1
    Memorial Drive Courts, Adelaide, Australia
    (Captains: U.S., E. Victor Seixas, Jr.; Australia, Harry Hopman)
    Twenty-seven challenging nations entered competition.
Frank Sedgman (A) d. E. Victor Seixas, Jr., 6-3, 6-4, 6-2; Kenneth McGregor (A) d. Tony Trabert, 11-9, 6-4, 6-1; Frank Sedgman (A) d. Tony Trabert, 7-5, 6-4, 10-8; E. Victor Seixas, Jr. (U.S.) d. Kenneth McGregor, 6-3, 8-6, 6-8, 6-3; Kenneth McGregor and Frank Sedgman (A) d. E. Victor Seixas, Jr., and Tony Trabert, 6-3, 6-4, 1-6, 6-2.

1953—AUSTRALIA d. UNITED STATES, 3-2
    Kooyong Stadium, Melbourne, Australia
    (Captains: U.S., William Talbert; Australia, Harry Hopman)
    Twenty-eight challenging nations entered competition.
Lewis Hoad (A) d. E. Victor Seixas, Jr., 6-4, 6-2, 6-3; Tony Trabert (U.S.) d. Kenneth Rosewall, 6-3, 6-4, 6-4; Lewis Hoad (A) d. Tony Trabert, 13-11, 6-3, 2-6, 3-6, 7-5; Kenneth Rosewall (A) d. E. Victor Seixas, Jr., 6-2, 2-6, 6-3, 6-4; E. Victor Seixas, Jr. and Tony Trabert (U.S.) d. Rex Hartwig and Lewis Hoad, 6-2, 6-4, 6-4.

1954—UNITED STATES d. AUSTRALIA, 3-2
    White City Stadium, Sydney, Australia
    (Captains: U.S., William Talbert; Australia, Harry Hopman)
    Thirty challenging nations entered competition.
Tony Trabert (U.S.) d. Lewis Hoad, 6-4, 2-6, 12-10, 6-3; E. Victor Seixas, Jr. (U.S.) d. Kenneth Rosewall, 8-6, 6-8, 6-4, 6-3; Kenneth Rosewall (A) d. Tony Trabert, 9-7, 7-5, 6-3; Rex Hartwig (A) d. E. Victor Seixas, Jr., 4-6, 6-3, 6-2, 6-3; E. Victor Seixas, Jr. and Tony Trabert (U.S.) d. Lewis Hoad and Kenneth Rosewall, 6-2, 4-6, 6-2, 10-8.

1955—AUSTRALIA d. UNITED STATES, 5-0
    West Side Tennis Club, Forest Hills, N.Y.
    (Captains: Australia, Harry Hopman; U.S., William Talbert)
    Thirty-four challenging nations entered competition.
Kenneth Rosewall (A) d. E. Victor Seixas, Jr., 6-3, 10-8, 4-6, 6-2; Lewis Hoad (A) d. Tony Trabert, 4-6, 6-3, 6-3, 8-6; Lewis Hoad (A) d. E. Victor

Davis Cup Challenge Rounds—1955 *(cont.)*

Seixas, Jr., 7-9, 6-1, 6-4; Kenneth Rosewall (A) d. Hamilton Richardson, 6-4, 3-6, 6-1, 6-4; Lewis Hoad and Rex Hartwig (A) d. Tony Trabert and E. Victor Seixas, Jr., 12-14, 6-4, 6-3, 3-6, 7-5.

1956—AUSTRALIA d. UNITED STATES, 5-0

    Memorial Drive Stadium, Adelaide, Australia

    (Captains: U.S., William Talbert; Australia, Harry Hopman)

    Thirty-two challenging nations entered competition.

Lewis Hoad (A) d. Herbert Flam, 6-2, 6-3, 6-3; Kenneth Rosewall (A) d. E. Victor Seixas, Jr., 6-1, 6-4, 4-6, 6-1; Kenneth Rosewall (A) d. Samuel Giammalva, 4-6, 6-1, 8-6, 7-5; Lewis Hoad (A) d. E. Victor Seixas, Jr., 6-2, 7-5, 6-3; Lewis Hoad and Kenneth Rosewall (A) d. Samuel Giammalva and E. Victor Seixas, Jr., 1-6, 6-1, 7-5, 6-4.

1957—AUSTRALIA d. UNITED STATES, 3-2

    Kooyong Stadium, Melbourne, Australia

    (Captains: U.S., William Talbert; Australia, Harry Hopman)

    Thirty-five challenging nations entered competition.

Malcolm J. Anderson (A) d. Barry MacKay, 6-3, 7-5, 3-6, 7-9, 6-3; Ashley J. Cooper (A) d. E. Victor Seixas, Jr., 3-6, 7-5, 6-1, 1-6, 6-3; E. Victor Seixas, Jr. (U.S.) d. Malcolm I. Anderson, 6-3, 4-6, 6-3, 0-6, 13-11; Barry MacKay (U.S.) d. Ashley J. Cooper, 6-4, 1-6, 4-6, 6-4, 6-3; Malcolm J. Anderson and Mervyn Rose (A) d. Barry MacKay and E. Victor Seixas, Jr., 6-4, 6-4, 8-6.

1958—UNITED STATES d. AUSTRALIA, 3-2

    Milton Courts, Brisbane, Australia

    (Captains: U.S., Perry Jones; Australia, Harry Hopman)

    Thirty-six challenging nations entered competition.

Alejandro Olmedo (U.S.) d. Malcolm J. Anderson,

Frank Parker *(left)* of the United States defeats Billy Sidwell (Australia) in the first match of the 1948 challenge round. The United States swept all matches.

8-6, 2-6, 9-7, 8-6; Ashley J. Cooper (A) d. Barry MacKay, 4-6, 6-3, 6-2, 6-4; Alejandro Olmedo (U.S.) d. Ashley J. Cooper, 6-3, 4-6, 6-4, 8-6; Malcolm J. Anderson (A) d. Barry MacKay, 7-5, 13-11, 11-9; Alejandro Olmedo and Hamilton Richardson (U.S.) d. Malcolm J. Anderson and Neale Fraser, 10-12, 3-6, 16-14, 6-3, 7-5.

1959—AUSTRALIA d. UNITED STATES, 3-2

> West Side Tennis Club, Forest Hills, N.Y.
> (Captains: Australia, Harry Hopman; U.S., Perry Jones)
> Thirty-nine challenging nations entered competition.

Neale A. Fraser (A) d. Alejandro Olmedo, 8-6, 6-8, 6-4, 8-6; Barry MacKay (U.S.) d. Rodney Laver, 7-5, 6-4, 6-1; Alejandro Olmedo (U.S.) d. Rodney Laver, 9-7, 4-6, 10-8, 12-10; Neale A. Fraser (A) d. Barry MacKay, 8-6, 3-6, 6-2, 6-4; Neale A. Fraser and Roy Emerson (A) d. Alejandro Olmedo and Earl Buchholz, Jr., 7-5, 7-5, 6-4.

1960—AUSTRALIA d. ITALY, 4-1

> White City Stadium, Sydney, Australia
> (Captains: Italy, Vanni Canapele; Australia, Harry Hopman)
> Forty challenging nations entered competition.

Neale A. Fraser (A) d. Orlando Sirola, 4-6, 6-3, 6-3, 6-3; Rodney G. Laver (A) d. Nicola Pietrangeli, 8-6, 6-4, 6-3; Rodney G. Laver (A) d. Orlando Sirola, 9-7, 6-2, 6-3; Nicola Pietrangeli (I) d. Neale A. Fraser, 11-9, 6-3, 1-6, 6-2; Neale A. Fraser and Roy Emerson (A) d. Nicola Pietrangeli and Orlando Sirola, 10-8, 5-7, 6-2, 6-4.

The 1963 United States Davis Cup team presents the Cup to President Johnson. *(left to right)* Bob Kelleher (captain), Dennis Ralston, Chuck McKinley, the President, Mrs. McKinley, Marty Riessen, and Edward Turville, President of USLTA. Two other members of the team, Frank Froehling and Gene Scott, were unable to be present at the ceremony.

The 1968 United States Davis Cup team: *(left to right)* Stan Smith, Jim Osborne, Clark Graebner, Donald Dell (captain), Arthur Ashe, Jr., Robert Lutz, Charles Pasarell.

Two reasons Romania challenged the United States in 1969 and 1971: Ilie Nastase *(left)* and Ion Tiriac *(right)*.

Davis Cup Challenge Rounds *(cont.)*

1961—AUSTRALIA d. ITALY, 5-0
Kooyong Stadium, Melbourne, Australia
(Captains: Italy, Vanni Canapele; Australia, Harry Hopman)
Forty-two challenging nations entered competition.
Roy Emerson (A) d. Nicola Pietrangeli, 8-6, 6-4, 6-0; Rodney G. Laver (A) d. Orlando Sirola, 6-1, 6-4, 6-3; Rodney G. Laver (A) d. Nicola Pietrangeli, 6-3, 3-6, 4-6, 6-3, 8-6; Roy Emerson (A) d. Orlando Sirola, 6-3, 6-3, 4-6, 6-2; Neale A. Fraser and RoyEmerson (A) d. Nicola Pietrangeli and Orlando Sirola, 6-2, 6-3, 6-4.

1962—AUSTRALIA d. MEXICO, 5-0
Milton Courts, Brisbane, Australia
(Captains: Mexico, Francisco Contreras; Australia, Harry Hopman)
Forty-one challenging nations entered competition.
Rodney G. Laver (A) d. Rafael Osuna, 6-2, 6-1, 7-5; Neale A. Fraser (A) d. Antonio Palafox, 7-9, 6-3, 6-4, 11-9; Neale A. Fraser (A) d. Rafael Osuna, 3-6, 11-9, 6-1, 3-6, 6-4; Rodney G. Laver (A) d. Antonio Palafox, 6-1, 4-6, 6-4, 8-6; Roy Emerson and Rodney G. Laver (A) d. Rafael Osuna and Antonio Palafox, 7-5, 6-2, 6-4.

1963—UNITED STATES d. AUSTRALIA, 3-2
Memorial Drive Stadium, Adelaide, Australia
(Captains: U.S., Robert Kelleher; Australia, Harry Hopman)
Forty-eight challenging nations entered competition.
R. Dennis Ralston (U.S.) d. John Newcombe, 6-4, 6-1, 3-6, 4-6, 7-5; Roy Emerson (A) d. Charles R. McKinley, 6-3, 3-6, 7-5, 7-5; Roy Emerson (A) d. R. Dennis Ralston, 6-2, 6-3, 3-6, 6-2; Charles R. McKinley (U.S.) d. John Newcombe, 10-12, 6-2, 9-7, 6-2; Charles R. McKinley and R. Dennis Ralston (U.S.) d. Roy Emerson and Neale A. Fraser, 6-3, 4-6, 11-9, 11-9.

1964—AUSTRALIA d. UNITED STATES, 3-2
Harold T. Clark Courts, Cleveland Heights, Ohio
(Captains: Australia, Harry Hopman; U.S., E. Victor Seixas, Jr.)
Forty-eight challenging nations entered competition.
Charles R. McKinley (U.S.) d. Fred Stolle, 6-1, 9-7, 4-6, 6-2; Roy Emerson (A) d. R. Dennis Ralston, 6-3, 6-4, 6-2; Fred Stolle (A) d. R. Dennis Ralston, 7-5, 6-3, 3-6, 9-11; 6-4; Roy Emerson (A) d. Charles R. McKinley, 3-6, 6-2, 6-4, 6-4; Charles R. McKinley and R. Dennis Ralston (U.S.) d. Roy Emerson and Fred Stolle, 6-4, 4-6, 4-6, 6-3, 6-4.

1965—AUSTRALIA d. SPAIN, 4-1
White City Stadium, Sydney, Australia
(Captains: Spain, Jaime Bartoli; Australia, Harry Hopman)
Forty-three challenging nations entered competition.
Fred Stolle (A) d. Manuel Santana, 10-12, 3-6, 6-1, 6-4, 7-5; Roy Emerson (A) d. Juan Gisbert, 6-3, 6-2, 6-2; Manuel Santana (S) d. Roy Emerson, 2-6, 6-3, 6-4, 15-13; Fred Stolle (A) d. Juan Gisbert, 6-2, 6-4, 8-6; John Newcombe and Tony Roche (A) d. Jose Luis Arilla and Manuel Santana, 6-3, 4-6, 7-5, 6-2.

1966—AUSTRALIA d. INDIA, 4-1
Kooyong Stadium, Melbourne, Australia
(Captains: India, Raj Kanna; Australia, Harry Hopman)
Forty-five challenging nations entered competition.
Fred Stolle (A) d. Ramanathan Krishnan, 6-3, 6-2, 6-4; Roy Emerson (A) d. Jaidip Mukerjea, 7-5, 6-4, 6-2; Roy Emerson (A) d. Ramanathan Krishnan, 6-0, 6-2, 10-8; Fred Stolle (A) d. Jaidip Mukerjea, 7-5, 6-8, 6-3, 5-7, 6-3; Ramanathan Krishnan and Jaidip Mukerjea (I) d. John Newcombe and Tony Roche, 4-6, 7-5, 6-4, 6-4.

1967—AUSTRALIA d. SPAIN, 4-1
Milton Courts, Brisbane, Australia
(Captains: Spain, Jaime Bartroli; Australia, Harry Hopman)
Forty-seven challenging nations entered competition.
Roy Emerson (A) d. Manuel Santana, 6-4, 6-1, 6-1; John Newcombe (A) d. Manuel Orantes, 6-3, 6-3, 6-2; Manuel Santana (S) d. John Newcombe, 7-5, 6-4, 6-2; Roy Emerson (A) d. Manuel Orantes, 6-1, 6-1, 2-6, 6-4; Roy Emerson and John Newcombe (A) d. Manuel Orantes and Manuel Santana, 6-4, 6-4, 6-4.

Davis Cup Challenge Rounds (*cont.*)

1968—UNITED STATES d. AUSTRALIA, 4-1
  Memorial Drive Stadium, Adelaide, Australia
  (Captains: U.S., Donald Dell; Australia, Harry Hopman)
  Forty-nine challenging nations entered competition.
Clark Graebner (U.S.) d. William Bowrey, 8-10, 6-4, 8-6, 3-6, 6-1; Arthur Ashe, Jr. (U.S.) d. Ray Ruffels, 6-8, 7-5, 6-3, 6-3; Clark Graebner (U.S.) d. Ray Ruffels, 3-6, 8-6, 2-6, 6-3, 6-1; William Bowrey (A) d. Arthur Ashe, Jr., 2-6, 6-3, 11-9, 8-6; Robert Lutz and Stan Smith (U.S.) d. John Alexander and Ray Ruffels, 6-4, 6-4, 6-2.
1969—UNITED STATES d. ROMANIA, 5-0
  Harold T. Clark Courts, Cleveland Heights, Ohio
  (Captains: Romania, Georgy Cobzucs; U.S., Donald Dell)
  Fifty challenging nations entered competition.
Arthur Ashe, Jr. (U.S.) d. Ilie Nastase, 6-2, 15-13, 7-5; Stan Smith (U.S.) d. Ion Tiriac, 6-8, 6-3, 5-7, 6-4, 6-4; Stan Smith (U.S.) d. Ilie Nastase, 4-6, 4-6, 6-4, 6-1, 11-9; Arthur Ashe, Jr. (U.S.) d. Ion Tiriac, 6-3, 8-6, 3-6, 4-0, def.; Robert Lutz and Stan Smith (U.S.) d. Ilie Nastase and Ion Tiriac, 8-6, 6-1, 11-9.
1970—UNITED STATES d. WEST GERMANY, 5-0
  Harold T. Clark Courts, Cleveland Heights, Ohio
  (Captains: West Germany, Ferdinance Henkel; U.S., Edward Turville)
  Fifty challenging nations entered competition.
Arthur Ashe, Jr. (U.S.) d. Wilhelm Bungert, 6-2, 10-8, 6-2; Cliff Richey (U.S.) d. Christian Kuhnke, 6-3, 6-4, 6-2; Cliff Richey (U.S.) d. Wilhelm Bungert, 6-4, 6-4, 7-5; Arthur Ashe, Jr. (U.S.) d. Christian Kuhnke, 6-8, 10-12, 9-7, 13-11, 6-4; Bob Lutz and Stan Smith (U.S.) d. Christian Kuhnke and Wilhelm Bungert, 6-3, 7-5, 6-4.
1971—UNITED STATES d. ROMANIA, 3-2
  Julian Clark Stadium, Charlotte, N.C.
  (Captains: Romania, Stefan Georgescu; U.S., Edward Turville)
  Fifty challenging nations entered competition.

Stan Smith (U.S.) d. Ilie Nastase, 7-5, 6-3, 6-1; Frank Froehling (U.S.) d. Ion Tiriac, 3-6, 1-6, 6-1, 6-3, 8-6; Stan Smith (U.S.) d. Ion Tiriac, 8-6, 6-3, 6-0; Ilie Nastase (R) d. Frank Froehling, 6-3, 6-1, 4-6, 6-4; Ilie Nastase and Ion Tiriac (R) d. Stan Smith and Erik van Dillen, 6-3, 6-1, 4-6, 6-4.

Final Rounds Beginning in 1972, the Challenge Round was replaced by the Final Round. The defending nation could no longer stand out of the competition and play the survivor of the Interzonal round. All teams were required to play through the draw, including the Cup-holding nation. Eligibility rules in the competition were loosened to permit all but contract pros to play and, in 1973 (for the 1974 competition), touring professionals were also admitted with only the proviso that they be "in good standing with their national association."

Following are the results of the Final Rounds of the Davis Cup (1972–1980):
1972—UNITED STATES d. ROMANIA, 3-2
  Progresul Club, Bucharest, Romania
  (Captains: Romania, Stefan Georgescu; U.S., Dennis Ralston)
  Fifty-four nations entered the competition.
Stan Smith (U.S.) d. Ilie Nastase, 11-9, 6-2, 6-3; Ion Tiriac (R) d. Tom Gorman, 4-6, 2-6, 6-4, 6-3, 6-2; Smith and Erik van Dillen (U.S.) d. Nastase and Tiriac, 6-2, 6-0, 6-3; Smith d. Tiriac, 4-6, 6-2, 6-4, 2-6, 6-0; Nastase d. Gorman, 6-1, 6-2, 5-7, 10-8.
1973—AUSTRALIA d. UNITED STATES, 5-0
  Public Auditorium, Cleveland, O.
  (Captains: Aust., Neale Fraser; U.S., Dennis Ralston)
  Fifty-three nations entered the competition.
John Newcombe (A) d. Stan Smith, 6-1, 3-6, 6-3, 3-6, 6-4; Rod Laver (A) d. Tom Gorman, 8-10, 8-6, 6-8, 6-3, 6-1; Newcombe and Laver (A) d. Erik van Dillen and Smith, 6-1, 6-2, 6-4; Newcombe (A) d. Gorman, 6-2, 6-1, 6-3; Laver (A) d. Smith, 6-3, 6-4, 3-6, 6-2.
1974—SOUTH AFRICA d. INDIA, default
  India refused to play the Final as a protest against the South Africa governmental policies.
  (Captains—South Africa, Claude Lister; India, Ramanathan Krishnan)
  Fifty-six nations entered the competition.

The 1959 Junior Davis Cup team: *(left to right)* Paul Palmer, Martin Riessen, William Bond, Dennis Ralston, Ramsey Earnhart, and Charles McKinley. Three members of this team—Marty Riessen, Denny Ralston, and Chuck McKinley—later played for the famed Cup.

Teams for the Final: South Africa—Bob Hewitt, Frew McMillan, Ray Moore, Rob Maud; India—Vijay Amritraj, Anand Amritraj; Jasjit Singh, Sashi Menon.

1975—SWEDEN d. CZECHOSLOVAKIA, 3-2
  Kungliga Tennishallen, Stockholm, Sweden
  (Captains—Sweden, Lennart Bergelin; Czechoslovakia, Antonin Bolardt)
  Fifty-six nations entered the competition.
Bjorn Borg (S) d. Jiri Hrebec, 6-1, 6-3, 6-0; Jan Kodes (C) d. Ove Bengston, 4-6, 6-2, 7-5, 6-4; Borg and Bengston (S) d. Kodes and Vladimir Zednik, 6-4, 6-4, 6-4; Borg (S) d. Kodes, 6-4, 6-2, 6-2; Hrebec (C) d. Bengston, 1-6, 6-3, 6-1, 6-4.

1976—ITALY d. CHILE, 4-1
  Estadio Nacional, Santiago, Chile
  (Captains—Italy, Nicola Pietrangeli; Chile, Luis Ayala)
  Fifty-eight nations entered the competition.
Corrado Barazzutti (I) d. Jaime Fillol, 7-5, 4-6, 7-5, 6-1; Adriano Panatta (I) d. Patricio Cornejo, 6-3, 6-1, 6-3; Panatta and Paoli Bertolucci (I) d. Fillol and Cornejo, 3-6, 6-2, 9-7, 6-3; Panatta (I) d. Fillol, 8-6, 6-4, 3-6, 10-8; Belus Prajoux (C) d. Antonio Zugarelli, 6-4, 6-4, 6-2.

1977—AUSTRALIA d. ITALY, 3-1
  White City Stadium, Sydney, Australia
  (Captains—Aust., Neale Fraser; Italy, Nicola Pietrangeli)
  Fifty-nine nations entered the competition.
  Tony Roche (A) d. Adriano Panatta, 6-3, 6-4, 6-4; John Alexander (A) d. Corrado Barazzutti, 6-2, 8-6, 4-6, 6-2; Panatta and Paolo Bertolucci (I) d. Alexander and Phil

Davis Cup Challenge Rounds—1977 *(cont.)*

Dent, 6-4, 6-4, 7-5; Alexander (A) d. Panatta, 6-4, 4-6, 2-6, 8-6, 11-9; Roche (A) and Barazzutti (I), 12-12, abandoned.

1978—UNITED STATES d. GREAT BRITAIN, 4–1
Mission Hills Country Club, Rancho Mirage, Calif.
(Captains—U.S., Tony Trabert; Great Britain, Paul Hutchins)
Fifty nations entered the competition.
John McEnroe (U.S.) d. John Lloyd, 6–1, 6-2, 6-2; Christopher Mottram (G.B.) d. Brian Gottfried, 4-6, 2-6, 10-8, 6-4, 6-3; McEnroe (U.S.) d. Mottram, 6-2, 6-2, 6-1; Gottfried (U.S.) d. Lloyd, 6-1, 6-2, 6-4; Stan Smith and Bob Lutz (U.S.) d. David Lloyd and Mark Cox, 6-2, 6-2, 6-3.

1979—UNITED STATES d. ITALY, 5-0
Civic Auditorium, San Francisco.
(Captains—U.S., Tony Trabert; Italy, Vittorio Crotta)
Fifty-two nations entered the competition.
Vitas Gerulaitis (U.S.) d. Corrado Barazzutti, 6-3, 3-2 ret.; John McEnroe (U.S.) d. Adriano Panatta, 6-2, 6-3, 6-4; Gerulaitis (U.S.) d. Panatta, 6-1, 6-3, 6-3; McEnroe (U.S.) d. Antonio Zugarelli, 6-4, 6-3, 6-1; Stan Smith and Bob Lutz (U.S.) d. Panatta and Paolo Bertolucci, 6-4, 12-10, 6-2.

1980—CZECHOSLOVAKIA d. ITALY, 4-1
Ice Stadium, Prague.
(Captains—Czech., Antonin Bolardt; Italy, Vittorio Crotta)
Fifty-two nations entered the competition.
Tomas Smid (Cz.) d. Adriano Panatta, 3-6, 3-6, 6-3, 6-4, 6-4; Ivan Lendl (Cz.) d. Corrado Barazzutti, 4-6, 6-1, 6-1, 6-2; Barazzutti (I.) d. Smid, 3-6, 6-3, 6-2; Lendl (Cz.) d. Gianni Ocleppo, 6-3, 6-3; Lendl and Smid (Cz.) d. Panatta and Paolo Bertolucci, 3-6, 6-3, 3-6, 6-3, 6-4.

CHALLENGE AND FINAL ROUND STANDINGS

	Won	Lost	Percent
Czechoslovakia	1	0	1.000
France	6	3	.667
Australia	22	15	.563
Great Britain	9	8	.529
United States	26	25	.510
Belgium	0	1	.000
Japan	0	1	.000
Mexico	0	1	.000
India	0	1	.000
West Germany	0	2	.000
Romania	0	1	.000
Italy	0	4	.000
Spain	0	2	.000

U.S. DAVIS CUP CAPTAINS AND THEIR RECORDS

Captains (Years), 1900–1971	Total Years	Total Matches	Finals* Won	Finals* Lost	Other Rounds Won	Other Rounds Lost	Total Won	Total Lost
Dwight F. Davis (1900)	1	1	1	0	0	0	1	0
Malcolm D. Whitman (1902)	1	1	1	0	0	0	1	0
William A. Larned (1903, 1909, 1911)	3	5	0	3	2	0	2	3
Paul Dashiel (1905)	1	3	0	1	2	0	2	1
Beals Wright (1906–07–08)	3	5	0	2	2	1	2	3
Harold Hacket (1913)	1	4	1	0	3	0	4	0
Maurice McLoughlin (1914)	1	1	0	1	0	0	0	1
Sam Hardy (1920, 1931)	2	5	1	0	3	1	4	1

Captains (Years), 1900–1971	Total Years	Total Matches	Finals* Won	Lost	Other Rounds Won	Lost	Total Won	Lost
R. Norris Williams (1921–26, 1934)	7	10	6	1	3	0	9	1
Charles Garland (1927)	1	1	0	1	0	0	0	1
Bill Tilden (1928)	1	3	0	0	3	0	3	0
Joseph Wear (1928, 1935)	2	4	0	2	2	0	2	2
Fitz-Eugene Dixon (1929–30, 1932)	3	10	0	2	8	0	8	2
Bernon Prentice (1931–32–33)	3	8	0	1	6	1	6	2
Wilmer Allison (1933, 1936)	2	4	0	0	4	0	4	0
Walter Pate (1935–39, 1946)	6	12	3	1	7	1	10	2
Walter Chandler (1937)	1	1	0	0	1	0	1	0
Alrick Mann (1947–50)	4	4	3	1	0	0	3	1
Frank Shields (1951)	1	5	0	1	4	0	4	1
Billy Talbert (1952–57)	6	16	1	4	11	0	12	4
Gardnar Mulloy (1952–53)	2	2	0	0	2	0	2	0
E. Victor Seixas (1952, 1957, 1964)	3	5	0	2	3	0	3	2
Tony Trabert (1953, 1976–78)	4	8	0	0	6	2	6	2
Lawrence Baker (1953)	1	1	0	0	1	0	1	0
Ham Richardson (1954)	1	2	0	0	2	0	2	0
Perry Jones (1958–59)	2	6	1	1	4	0	5	1
Dave Freed (1960–61)	2	10	0	0	8	2	8	2
Bob Kelleher (1962–63)	2	7	1	0	5	1	6	1
C. Alphonso Smith (1963)	1	1	0	0	1	0	1	0
George MacCall (1965–67)	3	9	0	0	6	3	6	3
Donald Dell (1968–69)	2	7	2	0	5	0	7	0
Edward Turville (1970–71)	2	2	2	0	0	0	2	0
Dennis Ralston (1972–75)	4	12	1	1	8	2	9	3
Tony Trabert (1976–80)	5	16	2	0	11	3	13	3
U.S. Totals, *1900–80	67	191	26	25	123	17	149	42

*Challenge rounds

CAPTAINS' RECORDS

Most Cups Won—R. Norris Williams (1921–26), 6.

Most Matches Won—Tony Trabert (1976–80), 13; Billy Talbert (1952–57), 12; Walter Pate (1935–39, 1946), 10; R. Norris Williams (1921–26, 1934) and Dennis Ralston (1972–75), 9.

Most Years—R. Norris Williams (1921–26, 1934), 7.

Most Matches—Billy Talbert (1952–57) and Tony Trabert (1976–80), 16.

UNITED STATES RIVALRIES

	Final Rounds and Challenge Rounds U.S. Won	U.S. Lost	Zone Matches U.S. Won	U.S. Lost	Overall U.S. Won	U.S. Lost
Australia (was Australasia—Australia and New Zealand—until 1924)	13	15	7	2	20	17
Britain	5	5	5	2	10	7
France	2	5	2	0	4	5
Romania	3	0	1	0	4	0
Japan	1	0	6	0	7	0

UNITED STATES RIVALRIES (cont.)

	Final Rounds and Challenge Rounds		Zone Matches		Overall	
	U.S. Won	U.S. Lost	U.S. Won	U.S. Lost	U.S. Won	U.S. Lost
Australia (was Australasia—Australia	13	15	7	2	20	17
Italy	1	0	5	2	6	2
Mexico	—	—	23	3	23	3
Canada	—	—	15	0	15	0
Caribbean Commonwealth (formerly British West Indies)	—	—	9	0	9	0
Germany	1	0	5	0	6	0
Venezuela	—	—	6	0	6	0
India	—	—	4	0	4	0
Sweden	—	—	4	0	4	0
Ecuador	—	—	2	1	2	1
Philippines	—	—	3	0	3	0
Belgium	—	—	2	0	2	0
Spain	—	—	2	1	2	1
Brazil	—	—	2	1	2	1
China	—	—	2	0	2	0
Cuba	—	—	3	0	3	0
Argentina	—	—	4	2	4	2
Iran	—	—	1	0	1	0
Chile	—	—	3	0	3	0
South Africa	—	—	2	0	2	0
Colombia	—	—	1	1	1	1
Total	26	25	119	15	145	40

The 1969 Federation Cup team: (left to right) Mrs. Donna Floyd Fales (captain), Nancy Richey, Peaches Bartkowicz, and Julie Heldman.

The Federation Cup

The Federation Cup was launched in 1963 by the International Lawn Tennis Federation as a worldwide team competition for women in the spirit of the Davis Cup but with a slightly different format. All entrants gather at one site to play an elimination tournament. Unlike Davis Cup, the champion nation does not stand out until the final. Two singles and one doubles constitute a match. The championship is completed in a week or less. The team of Billie Jean Moffitt (now Mrs. King), Darlene Hard, and Carole Caldwell (now Mrs. Graebner) won the first Federation Cup in London over Australia in the final, 2-1. United States captain was William Kellogg. Although the first matches were played in June of 1963 at Queens Club, they took place indoors because of rain.

Australia, with five victories, and the United States, with four, are the only countries to win the Cup. The Federation Cup Championship finals are as follows:

1963—UNITED STATES d. AUSTRALIA, 2-1
Queens Club, London
Margaret Smith (A) d. Darlene Hard, 6-3, 6-0; Billie Jean Moffitt (U.S.) d. Lesley Turner, 5-7, 6-0, 6-3; Darlene Hard and Billie Jean Moffitt (U.S.) d. Margaret Smith and Lesley Turner, 3-6, 13-11, 6-3.

1964—AUSTRALIA d. UNITED STATES, 2-1
Germantown Cricket Club, Philadelphia, Pa.
Margaret Smith (A) d. Billie Jean Moffitt, 6-2, 6-3; Lesley Turner (A) d. Nancy Richey, 7-5, 6-1; Billie Jean Moffitt and Mrs. Karen Hantze Susman (U.S.) d. Margaret Smith and Lesley Turner, 4-6, 7-5, 6-1.

1965—AUSTRALIA d. UNITED STATES, 2-1
Melbourne, Australia
Lesley Turner (A) d. Mrs. Carole C. Graebner, 6-3, 2-6, 6-3; Margaret Smith (A) d. Billie Jean Moffitt, 6-4, 8-6; Billie Jean Moffitt and Mrs. Carole C. Graebner (U.S.) d. Margaret Smith and Judy Tegart, 7-5, 4-6, 6-4.

1966—UNITED STATES d. WEST GERMANY, 3-0
Turin, Italy
Julie M. Heldman (U.S.) d. Helga Niessen, 4-6, 7-5, 6-1; Mrs. Billie Jean King (U.S.) d. Edda Buding, 6-3, 3-6, 6-1; Mrs. Carole C. Graebner and Mrs. Billie Jean King (U.S.) d. Helga Schultz and Edda Buding, 6-4, 6-2.

1967—UNITED STATES d. ENGLAND, 2-0
Berlin, Germany
Rosemary Casals d. Virginia Wade, 9-7, 8-6; Mrs. Billie Jean King d. Mrs. Ann H. Jones, 6-3, 6-4; doubles match called at set-all.

1968—AUSTRALIA d. NETHERLANDS, 3-0
Paris, France
Kerry Melville (A) d. Marijke Jansen, 4-6, 7-5, 6-3; Mrs. Margaret S. Court (A) d. Astrid Suurbeek, 6-1, 6-3; Mrs. Margaret S. Court and Kerry Melville d. Astrid Suurbeek and L. J. Venneboar, 6-3, 6-8, 7-5.

1969—UNITED STATES d. AUSTRALIA, 2-1
Athens, Greece
Nancy Richey (U.S.) d. Kerry Melville, 6-4, 6-3; Mrs. Margaret S. Court (A) d. Julie M. Heldman, 6-1, 8-6; Peaches Bartkowicz and Nancy Richey (U.S.) d. Mrs. Margaret S. Court and Judy Tegart, 6-4, 6-4.

1970—AUSTRALIA d. WEST GERMANY, 3-0
Freiburg, West Germany
Karen Krantzcke (A) d. Helga Schultz Hoesl, 6-2, 6-3; Judy Tegart Dalton (A) d. Helga Niessen, 4-6, 6-3, 6-3; Karen Krantzke and Judy Tegart Dalton (A) d. Helga Schultz Hoesl and Helga Niessen, 6-2, 7-5.

1971—AUSTRALIA d. GREAT BRITAIN, 3-0
Perth, Australia
Margaret Smith Court (A) d. Ann H. Jones, 6-8, 6-3, 6-2; Evonne Goolagong (A) d. Virginia Wade, 6-4, 6-1; Margaret Smith Court and Lesley Hunt (A) d. Virginia Wade and Winnie Shaw, 6-4, 6-4.

1972—SOUTH AFRICA d. GREAT BRITAIN, 2-1
Johannesburg, S.A.
Virginia Wade (G.B.) d. Pat Pretorius, 6-3, 6-2; Brenda Kirk (S.A.) d. Winnie Shaw, 4-6, 7-5, 6-0; Kirk and Pretorius (S.A.) d. Wade and Shaw, 6-1, 7-5.

1973—AUSTRALIA d. SOUTH AFRICA, 3-0
Bad Homburg, West Germany
Evonne Goolagong (A) d. Pat Pretorius, 6-0, 6-2; Patti Coleman (A) d. Brenda Kirk, 10-8, 6-0; Goolagong and Janet Young (A) d. Kirk and Pretorius, 6-1, 6-2.

1974—AUSTRALIA d. UNITED STATES, 2-1
Naples, Italy
Evonne Goolagong (A) d. Julie Heldman, 6-1, 7-5; Chris Evert (U.S.) d. Dianne Fromholtz, 2-6, 7-5, 6-4; Goolagong and Janet Young (A) d. Heldman and Sharon Walsh, 7-5, 8-6.

The 1971 Federation Cup winners: the Australian team *(left to right)* Lesley Hunt, captain, Mrs. Margaret Court, and Evonne Goolagong.

UNITED STATES FEDERATION CUP RIVALRIES (with 21 other nations)

	Final Matches		Other Rounds		Overall	
	U.S. Won	U.S. Lost	U.S. Won	U.S. Lost	U.S. Won	U.S. Lost
Argentina	—	—	1	0	1	0
Australia	7	3	0	1	7	4
France	—	—	5	0	5	0
Great Britain	1	0	5	1	6	1
Ireland	—	—	1	0	1	0
Italy	—	—	5	0	5	0
Netherlands	—	—	5	1	5	1
Rhodesia	—	—	2	0	2	0
South Africa	—	—	4	1	4	1
Sweden	—	—	2	0	2	0
Switzerland	—	—	4	0	4	0
West Germany	1	0	3	2	4	2
Yugoslavia	—	—	4	0	4	0
Austria	—	—	1	0	1	0
Poland	—	—	2	0	2	0
South Korea	—	—	2	0	2	0
Uruguay	—	—	1	0	1	0
Israel	—	—	1	0	1	0
New Zealand	—	—	2	0	2	0
U.S.S.R.	—	—	2	0	2	0
Czechoslovakia	—	—	1	0	1	0
Totals (1963–80)	9	3	53	6	62	9

FEDERATION CUP FINALS: 1963–1977

Nation	Won	Lost	Pct.
Czechoslovakia	1	0	1.000
United States	9	3	.750
Australia	7	8	.583
South Africa	1	1	.500
The Netherlands	0	1	.000
West Germany	0	2	.000
Great Britain	0	3	.000

U.S. Record in Final Round: vs. Australia, Won 7, Lost 3; Great Britain, Won 1, Lost 0; West Germany, Won 1, Lost 0.

1975—CZECHOSLOVAKIA d. AUSTRALIA, 3-0
Aix-en-Provence, France
Martina Navratilova (C) d. Evonne Goolagong, 6-3, 6-4; Renata Tomanova (C) d. Helen Gourlay, 6-4, 6-2; Navratilova and Tomanova (C) d. Dianne Fromholtz and Gourlay, 6-3, 6-1.

1976—UNITED STATES d. AUSTRALIA, 2-1
The Spectrum, Philadelphia
Kerry Reid (A) d. Rosemary Casals, 1-6, 6-3, 7-5; Billie Jean King (U.S.) d. Evonne Goolagong, 7-6, 6-4; King and Casals (U.S.) d. Goolagong and Reid, 7-5, 6-3.

1977—UNITED STATES d. AUSTRALIA, 2-1
Eastbourne, England
Billie Jean King (U.S. d. Dianne Fromholtz, 6-1, 2-6, 6-2; Chris Evert (U.S.) d. Kerry Reid, 7-5, 6-3; Reid and Wendy Turnbull (A) d. Evert and Rosemary Casals, 6-3, 6-3.

1978—UNITED STATES d. AUSTRALIA, 2-1
Melbourne, Australia
Kerry M. Reid (A.) d. Tracy Austin, 6-3, 6-3; Chris Evert (U.S.) d. Wendy Turnbull, 3-6, 6-1, 6-1; Evert and Bille Jean King (U.S.) d. Turnbull and Reid, 4-6, 6-1, 6-4.

1979—UNITED STATES d. AUSTRALIA, 3-0
    Madrid, Spain
Tracy Austin (U.S.) d. Kerry M. Reid, 6-3, 6-0;
Chris Evert Lloyd (U.S.) d. Dianne Fromholtz,
2-6, 6-3, 8-6; Billie Jean King and Rosemary Casals
(U.S.) d. Reid and Wendy Turnbull, 3-6, 6-3, 8-6.
1980—UNITED STATES d. AUSTRALIA, 3-0
    Berlin, West Germany
Chris Evert Lloyd (U.S.) d. Dianne Fromholtz,
4-6, 6-1, 6-1; Tracy Austin (U.S.) d. Wendy Turn-
bull, 6-2, 6-3; Kathy Jordan and Rosemary Casals
(U.S.) d. Sue Leo and Fromholtz, 2-6, 6-4, 6-4.

Wightman Cup

In 1923 Mrs. George W. Wightman of Boston, the
former Hazel Hotchkiss, who stands as one of the
game's all-time champions, presented a sterling
vase to the USLTA for international women's
team competition. Great Britain challenged the
United States for the cup that year, and the match
was the first to be played in the newly constructed
stadium of the West Side Tennis Club at Forest
Hills, N.Y. This began a rivalry that found favor in
both countries, and it was decided that the trophy,
known as the Wightman Cup, would be confined
to an annual match between British and American women. Mrs. Wightman captained the United
States team and joined Eleanor Goss to make a
doubles point in the opener, won by the U.S., 7-0.

The United States leads in the series, 36 mat-
ches to 7:
1923—UNITED STATES d. GREAT BRITAIN, 7-0
    West Side Tennis Club, Forest Hills, N.Y.
    (Captains: Britain, Anthony Sabelli; U.S.,
    Mrs. George W. Wightman)
Helen Wills (U.S.) d. Kathleen McKane, 6-2, 7-5;
Mrs. Molla B. Mallory (U.S.) d. Mrs. R. C. Clayton,
6-1, 8-6; Eleanor Goss (U.S.) d. Mrs. W. Geraldine
Beamish, 6-2, 0-6, 7-5; Helen Wills (U.S.) d. Mrs. R.
C. Clayton, 6-2, 6-3; Mrs. Molla B. Mallory (U.S.) d.
Kathleen McKane, 6-2, 6-3; Mrs. George W.
Wightman and Eleanor Goss (U.S.) d. Kathleen
McKane and Mrs. B. C. Covell, 10-8, 5-7, 6-4; Mrs.
Molla B. Mallory and Helen Willis (U.S.) d. Mrs. W.
Geraldine Beamish and Mrs. R. C. Clayton, 6-3,
6-2.

1924—GREAT BRITAIN d. UNITED STATES, 6-1
    Wimbledon, London
    (Captains: Britain, Mrs. Lambert Cham-
    bers; U.S., Mrs. George W. Wightman)
Mrs. B. C. Covell (G.B.) d. Helen Wills, 6-2, 6-4;
Kathleen McKane (G.B.) d. Mrs. Molla B. Mallory,
6-3, 6-3; Kathleen McKane (G.B.) d. Helen Wills,
6-2, 6-2; Mrs. B. C. Covell (G.B.) d. Mrs. Molla B.
Mallory, 6-2, 5-7, 6-3; Mrs. W. Geraldine Beamish
(G.B.) d. Eleanor Goss, 6-1, 8-10, 6-3; Mrs. B. C.
Covell and Mrs. D. C. Shepherd-Barron (G.B.) d.
Mrs. Marion Z. Jessup and Eleanor Goss, 6-2, 6-2;
Mrs. George W. Wightman and Helen Wills (U.S.)
d. Kathleen McKane and Evelyn L. Colyer, 2-6,
6-2, 6-4.

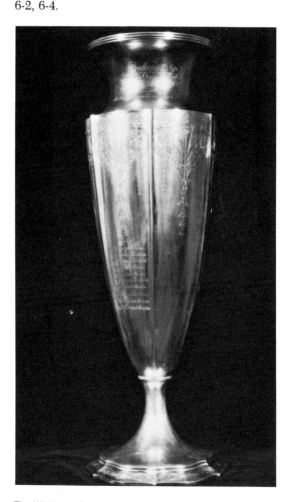

The Wightman Cup.

Wightman Cup *(cont.)*

1925—GREAT BRITAIN d. UNITED STATES, 4-3
West Side Tennis Club, Forest Hills, N.Y.
(Captains: Britain, Mrs. Lambert Chambers; U.S., Mary K. Browne)
Kathleen McKane (G.B.) d. Mrs. Molla B. Mallory, 6-4, 5-7, 6-0; Helen Wills (U.S.) d. Joan C. Fry, 6-0, 7-5; Mrs. Lambert Chambers (G.B.) d. Eleanor Goss, 7-5, 3-6, 6-1; Helen Wills (U.S.) d. Kathleen McKane, 6-1, 1-6, 9-7; Mrs. Molla B. Mallory (U.S.) d. Joan C. Fry, 6-3, 6-0; Mrs. Lambert Chambers and Ermyntrude H. Harvey (G.B.) d. Mrs. Molla B. Mallory and Mrs. May Sutton Bundy, 10-8, 6-1; Kathleen McKane and Evelyn L. Colyer (G.B.) d. Helen Wills and Mary K. Browne, 6-0, 6-3.

1926—UNITED STATES d. GREAT BRITAIN, 4-3
Wimbledon, London
(Captains: Britain, Mrs. Lambert Chambers, U.S., Mary K. Browne)
Elizabeth Ryan (U.S.) d. Joan C. Fry, 6-1, 6-3; Mrs. Kathleen McKane Godfree (G.B.) d. Mary K. Browne, 6-1, 7-5; Joan C. Fry (G.B.) d. Mary K. Browne, 3-6, 6-0, 6-4; Mrs. Kathleen McKane Godfree (G.B.) d. Elizabeth Ryan, 6-1, 5-7, 6-4; Mrs. Marion Z. Jessup and Eleanor Goss (U.S.) d. Mrs. Lambert Chambers and Mrs. D. C. Shepherd-Barron, 6-4, 6-2; Mary K. Browne and Elizabeth Ryan (U.S.) d. Mrs. Kathleen McKane Godfree and Evelyn L. Colyer, 3-6, 6-2, 6-4.

1927—UNITED STATES d. GREAT BRITAIN, 5-2
West Side Tennis Club, Forest Hills, N.Y.
(Captains: Britain, Maj. Dudley Larcombe; U.S., Mrs. George W. Wightman)
Helen N. Wills (U.S.) d. Joan Fry, 6-2, 6-0; Mrs. Molla B. Mallory (U.S.) d. Mrs. Kathleen McKane Godfree, 6-4, 6-2; Betty Nuthall (G.B.) d. Helen Jacobs, 6-3, 2-6, 6-1; Helen N. Wills (U.S.) d. Mrs. Kathleen McKane Godfree, 6-1, 6-1; Mrs. Molla B. Mallory (U.S.) d. Joan Fry, 6-2, 11-9; Gwendolyn Sterry and Mrs. John Hill (G.B.) d. Eleanor Goss and Mrs. Alfred H. Chapin, Jr., 5-7, 7-5, 7-5; Helen N. Wills and Mrs. George W. Wightman (U.S.) d. Mrs. Kathleen McKane Godfree and Ermyntrude Harvey, 6-4, 4-6, 6-3.

1928—GREAT BRITAIN d. UNITED STATES, 4-3
Wimbledon, London
(Captains: Britain, Ermyntrude H. Harvey; U.S., Eleanor Goss)
Helen N. Wills (U.S.) d. Mrs. P. Watson, 6-1, 6-2; Eileen Bennett (G.B.) d. Mrs. Molla B. Mallory, 6-1, 6-3; Helen N. Wills (U.S.) d. Eileen Bennett,

The United States Wightman Cup Squad of 1927—one of the strongest teams in history. *(left to right)* Helen Wills, Eleanor Goss, Mrs. J. Dallas Corbiere, Helen Jacobs, Mrs. Molla Mallory, Margaret Blake, Mrs. Charlotte Chapin, and Penelope Anderson.

6-3, 6-2; Mrs. P. Watson (G.B.) d. Mrs. Molla B. Mallory, 2-6, 6-1, 6-2; Helen Jacobs (U.S.) d. Betty Nuthall, 6-3, 6-1; Ermyntrude H. Harvey and Peggy Saunders (G.B.) d. Eleanor Goss and Helen Jacobs, 6-4, 6)1; Eileen Bennett and Mrs. P. Watson (G.B.) d. Helen N. Wills and Penelope Anderson, 6-2, 6-1.

1929—UNITED STATES d. GREAT BRITAIN, 4-3
West Side Tennis Club, Forest Hills, N.Y.
(Captains: Britain, Mrs. B. C. Covell; U.S.,
Mrs. George W. Wightman)
Helen N. Wills (U.S.) d. Mrs. P. Watson, 6-1, 6-4; Helen Jacobs (U.S.) d. Betty Nuthall, 7-5, 8-6; Mrs. A. G. Watson (G.B.) d. Helen Jacobs, 6-3, 6-2; Edith Cross (U.S.) d. Mrs. Peggy Saunders Michell, 6-3, 3-6, 6-3; Helen N. Wills (U.S.) d. Betty Nuthall, 8-6, 8-6; Mrs. P. Watson and Mrs. Peggy Saunders Michell (G.B.) d. Helen N. Wills and Edith Cross, 6-4, 6-1; Mrs. B. C. Covell and Mrs. D. C. Shepherd-Barron (G.B.) d. Mrs. George W. Wightman and Helen Jacobs, 6-2, 6-1.

1930—GREAT BRITAIN d. UNITED STATES, 4-3
Wimbledon, London
(Captains: Britain, Mrs. Phoebe Watson;
U.S., Mrs. Helen Wills Moody)
Mrs. Helen Wills Moody (U.S.) d. Joan Fry, 6-1, 6-1; Mrs. P. Watson (G.B.) d. Helen Jacobs, 2-6, 6-2, 6-4; Mrs. Helen Wills Moody (U.S.) d. Mrs. P. Watson, 7-5, 6-1; Helen Jacobs (U.S.) d. Joan Fry, 6-0, 6-3; Phyllis Mudford (G.B.) d. Sarah Palfrey, 6-0, 6-2; Joan Fry and Ermyntrude Harvey (G.B.) d. Sarah Palfrey and Edith Cross, 2-6, 6-2, 6-4; Mrs. P. Watson and Mrs. K. McK. Godfree (G.B.) d. Mrs. Helen Wills Moody and Helen Jacobs, 7-5, 1-6, 6-4.

1931—UNITED STATES d. GREAT BRITAIN, 5-2
West Side Tennis Club, Forest Hills, N.Y.
(Captains: Britain, Mrs. D. C. Shepherd-Barron; U.S., Mrs. George W. Wightman)
Mrs. Helen Wills Moody (U.S.) d. Phyllis Mudford, 6-1, 6-4; Helen Jacobs (U.S.) d. Betty Nuthall, 8-6, 6-4; Mrs. Lawrence A. Harper (U.S.) d. Dorothy E. Round, 6-3, 4-6, 9-7; Helen Jacobs (U.S.) d. Phyllis Mudford, 6-4, 6-2; Mrs. Helen Wills Moody (U.S.) d. Betty Nuthall, 6-4, 6-2; Phyllis Mudford and Mrs. D. C. Shepherd-Barron (G.B.) d. Sarah Palfrey and Mrs. George W. Wightman, 6-4, 10-8; Betty Nuthall and Mrs. Eileen Bennett Whittingstall (G.B.) d. Mrs. Helen Wills Moody and Mrs. Lawrence A. Harper, 8-6, 5-7, 6-3.

1932—UNITED STATES d. GREAT BRITAIN, 4-3
Wimbledon, London
(Captains: Britain, Mrs. D. C. Shepherd-Barron; U.S., Mrs. Helen Wills Moody)
Helen Jacobs (U.S.) d. Dorothy E. Round, 6-4, 6-3; Mrs. Helen Wills Moody (U.S.) d. Mrs. Eileen Bennett Whittingstall, 6-2, 6-4; Mrs. Helen Wills Moody (U.S.) d. Dorothy E. Round, 6-2, 6-3; Mrs. Eileen Bennett Whittingstall (G.B.) d. Helen Jacobs, 6-4, 2-6, 6-1; Mrs. Phyllis Mudford King (G.B.) d. Mrs. Lawrence A. Harper, 3-6, 6-3, 6-1; Mrs. Lawrence A. Harper and Helen Jacobs (U.S.) d. Mrs. Peggy Saunders Michell and Dorothy E. Round, 6-4, 6-1; Mrs. Eileen Bennett Whittingstall and Betty Nuthall (G.B.) d. Mrs. Helen Wills Moody and Sarah Palfrey, 6-3, 1-6, 10-8.

1933—UNITED STATES d. GREAT BRITAIN, 4-3
West Side Tennis Club, Forest Hills, N.Y.
(Captains: Britain, Malcolm Horn; U.S.,
Mrs. George W. Wightman)
Helen Jacobs (U.S.) d. Dorothy E. Round, 6-4, 6-2; Sarah Palfrey (U.S.) d. Margaret Scriven, 6-3, 6-1; Betty Nuthall (G.B.) d. Carolin Babcock, 1-6, 6-1, 6-3; Dorothy E. Round (G.B.) d. Sarah Palfrey, 6-4, 10-8; Helen Jacobs (U.S.) d. Margaret Scriven, 5-7, 7-2, 7-5; Helen Jacobs and Sarah Palfrey (U.S.) d. Dorothy E. Round and Mary Heeley, 6-4, 6-2; Betty Nuthall and Freda James (G.B.) d. Alice Marble and Mrs. Marjorie Gladman Van Ryn, 7-5, 6-2.

1934—UNITED STATES d. GREAT BRITAIN, 5-2
Wimbledon, London
(Captains: Britain, Malcolm Horn; U.S.,
James Cushman)
Sarah Palfrey (U.S.) d. Dorothy E. Round, 6-3, 3-6, 8-6; Helen Jacobs (U.S.) d. Margaret Scriven, 6-1, 6-1; Helen Jacobs (U.S.) d. Dorothy E. Round, 6-4, 6-4; Sarah Palfrey (U.S.) d. Margaret Scriven, 4-6, 6-2, 8-6; Betty Nuthall (G.B.) d. Carolin Babcock, 5-7, 6-3, 6-4; Nancy Lyle and Evelyn Dearman (G.B.) d. Carolin Babcock and Josephine Cruickshank, 7-5, 7-5; Helen Jacobs and Sarah Palfrey (U.S.) d. Mrs. Kathleen Godfree and Betty Nuthall, 5-7, 6-3, 6-2.

1935—UNITED STATES d. GREAT BRITAIN, 4-3
West Side Tennis Club, Forest Hills, N.Y.
(Captains: Britain, Malcolm Horn; U.S.,
Mrs. George W. Wightman)
Katharine Stammers (G.B.) d. Helen Jacobs, 5-7,

The 1935 British Wightman Cup team: *(left to right)* Freda James, Mrs. Phyllis Mudford King, Evelyn Dearman, Kay Stammers, Nancy Lyle, Dorothy Round.

Wightman Cup—1935 *(cont.)*

6-1, 9-7; Dorothy E. Round (G.B.) d. Mrs. Ethel Burkhardt Arnold, 6-0, 6-3; Mrs. Sarah Palfrey Fabyan (U.S.) d. Mrs. Phyllis Mudford King, 6-0, 6-3; Helen Jacobs (U.S.) d. Dorothy E. Round, 6-3, 6-2; Mrs. Ethel Burkhardt Arnold (U.S.) d. Katharine Stammers, 6-2, 1-6, 6-3; Helen Jacobs and Mrs. Sarah Palfrey Fabyan (U.S.) d. Katharine Stammers and Freda James, 6-3, 6-2; Nancy Lyle and Evelyn Dearman (G.B.) d. Mrs. Dorothy Andrus and Carolin Babcock, 3-6, 6-4, 6-1.

1936—UNITED STATES d. GREAT BRITAIN, 4-3
    Wimbledon, London
      (Captains: Britain, Malcolm Horn; U.S., James Cushman)

Katharine Stammers (G.B.) d. Helen Jacobs, 12-10, 6-1; Dorothy E. Round (G.B.) d. Mrs. Sarah Palfrey Fabyan, 6-3, 6-4; Mrs. Sarah Palfrey Fabyan (U.S.) d. Katharine Stammers, 6-3, 6-4; Dorothy E. Round (G.B.) d. Helen Jacobs, 6-3, 6-3; Carolin

Babcock (U.S.) d. Mary Hardwick, 6-4, 4-6, 6-2; Carolin Babcock and Mrs. Marjorie Gladman Van Ryn (U.S.) d. Evelyn Dearman and Nancy Lyle, 6-2, 1-6, 6-3; Helen Jacobs and Mrs. Sarah Palfrey Fabyan (U.S.) d. Katharine Stammers and Freda James, 1-6, 6-3, 7-5.

1937—UNITED STATES d. GREAT BRITAIN, 6-1
    West Side Tennis Club, Forest Hills, N.Y.
      (Captains: Britain, Malcolm Horn; U.S., Mrs. George W. Wightman)

Alice Marble (U.S.) d. Mary Hardwick, 4-6, 6-2, 6-4; Helen Jacobs (U.S.) d. Katharine Stammers, 6-1, 4-6, 6-4; Helen Jacobs (U.S.) d. Mary Hardwick, 2-6, 6-4, 6-2; Alice Marble (U.S.) d. Katharine Stammers, 6-3, 6-1; Mrs. Sarah Palfrey Fabyan (U.S.) d. Margot Lumb, 6-3, 6-1; Alice Marble and Mrs. Sarah Palfrey Fabyan (U.S.) d. Evelyn Dearman and Joan Ingram, 6-3, 6-2; Katharine Stammers and Freda James (G.B.) d. Mrs. Marjorie Van Ryan and Dorothy M. Bundy, 6-3, 10-8.

1938—UNITED STATES d. GREAT BRITAIN, 5-2
Wimbledon, London
(Captains: Britain, Mrs. M. C. King; U.S.,
Mrs. George W. Wightman) Katharine
Stammers (G.B.) d. Alice Marble, 3-6, 7-5,
6-3; Mrs. Helen Wills Moody (U.S.) d.
Margaret Scriven, 6-0, 7-5; Mrs. Sarah
Palfrey Fabyan (U.S.) d. Margot Lumb,
5-7, 6-2, 6-3; Alice Marble (U.S.) d. Marga-
ret Scriven, 6-3, 3-6, 6-0; Mrs. Helen Wills
Moody (U.S.) d. Katharine Stammers, 6-2,
3-6, 6-3; Alice Marble and Mrs. Sarah Pal-
frey Fabyan (U.S.) d. Margot Lumb and
Freda James, 6-4, 6-2; Evelyn M. Dear-
man and Joan Ingram (G.B.) d. Mrs.
Helen Wills Moody and Dorothy M.
Bundy, 6-2, 7-5.
1939—UNITED STATES d. GREAT BRITAIN, 5-2
West Side Tennis Club, Forest Hills, N.Y.
(Captains: Britain, Betty Nuthall; U.S., Mrs.
George W. Wightman)
Alice Marble (U.S.) d. Mary Hardwick, 6-3, 6-4;
Katharine Stammers (G.B.) d. Helen Jacobs, 6-2,
1-6, 6-3; Valerie Scott (G.B.) d. Mrs. Sarah Palfrey
Fabyan, 6-3, 6-4; Alice Marble (U.S.) d. Katharine
Stammers, 3-6, 6-3, 6-4; Helen Jacobs (U.S.) d.
Mary Hardwick, 6-2, 6-2; Dorothy M. Bundy and
Mary Arnold (U.S.) d. Betty Nuthall and Nina
Brown, 6-3, 6-1; Alice Marble and Mrs. Sarah Pal-
frey Fabyan (U.S.) d. Katharine Stammers and
Mrs. Freda James Hammersley, 7-5, 6-2.
1940–45—no matches, World War II
1946—UNITED STATES d. GREAT BRITAIN, 7-0
Wimbledon, London
(Captains: Britain, Mrs. Nancy Lyle Glover;
U.S., Mrs. Geroge W. Wightman)
Pauline Betz (U.S.) d. Mrs. Jean Bostock, 6-2, 6-4;
Margaret Osborne (U.S.) d. Mrs. Jean Bostock, 6-1,
6-4; Margaret Osborne (U.S.) d. Mrs. Kay Stam-
mers Menzies, 6-3, 6-2; A. Louise Brough (U.S.) d.
Joan Curry, 8-6, 6-3; Pauline Betz (U.S.) d. Mrs.
Kay Stammers Menzies, 6-4, 6-4; Margaret Os-
borne and A. Louise Brough (U.S.) d. Mrs. Jean
Bostock and Mrs. Mary Halford, 6-2, 6-1; Pauline
Betz and Doris Hart (U.S.) d. Mrs. Betty Passing-
ham and Molly Lincoln, 6-1, 6-3.

The Duchess of Kent presents the Wightman Cup to its donor, Mrs. George Wightman, captain of the 1938 United States team. The team members are *(left to right)* Mrs. Sarah Palfrey Fabyan, Dorothy Bundy, Mrs. Helen Wills Moody, and Alice Marble.

1947—UNITED STATES d. GREAT BRITAIN, 7-0
West Side Tennis Club, Forest Hills, N.Y.
(Captains: Britain, Ted Avory; U.S., Mrs. Geroge W. Wightman) Margaret Osborne (U.S.) d. Mrs. Jean Bostock, 6-4, 2-6, 6-2; A. Louise Brough (U.S.) d. Mrs. Kay Stammers Menzies, 6-4, 6-2; Doris Hart (U.S.) d. Mrs. Betty Hilton, 4-6, 6-3, 7-5; A. Louise Brough (U.S.) d. Mrs. Jean Bostock, 6-4, 6-4; Margaret Osborne (U.S.) d. Mrs. Kay Stammers Menzies, 7-5, 6-2; Doris Hart and Mrs. Patricia Todd (U.S.) d. Joy Gannon and Jean Quertier, 6-1, 6-2; Margaret Osborne and A. Louise Brough (U.S.) d. Mrs. Jean Bostock and Mrs. Betty Hilton, 6-1, 6-4.

1948—UNITED STATES d. GREAT BRITAIN, 6-1
Wimbledon, London
(Captains: Britain, Mrs. Kay Stammers Menzies; U.S., Mrs. George W. Wightman)
Mrs. Margaret Osborne du Pont (U.S.) d. Mrs. Jean Bostock, 6-4, 8-6; Louise Brough (U.S.) d. Mrs. Betty Hilton, 6-1, 6-1; Mrs. Margaret Osborne du Pont (U.S.) d. Mrs. Betty Hilton, 6-3, 6-4; A. Louise Brough (U.S.) d. Mrs. Jean Bostock, 6-3, 4-6, 7-5; Doris Hart (U.S.) d. Kay Stammers Menzies and Mrs. Betty Hilton, 6-2, 6-2; Mrs. Jean Bostock and Mrs. Molly Lincoln Blair (G.B.) d. Doris Hart and Mrs. Patricia Canning Todd, 6-3, 6-4.

The 1946 United States Wightman Cup team: *(left to right)* Mrs. Pat Todd, A. Louise Brough, Pauline Betz, Mrs. George Wightman (captain), Margaret Osborne, and Doris Hart.

1949—UNITED STATES d. GREAT BRITAIN, 7-0
Merion Cricket Club, Haverford, Pa.
(Captains: Britain, Mrs. Kay Stammers Menzies; U.S., Mrs. Marjorie Gladman Van Ryn Buck)
Doris Hart (U.S.) d. Mrs. Jean Walker-Smith, 6-3, 6-1; Mrs. Margaret Osborne du Pont (U.S.) d. Mrs. Betty Hilton, 6-1, 6-3; Doris Hart (U.S.) d. Mrs. Betty Hilton, 6-1, 6-3; Mrs. Margaret Osborne du Pont (U.S.) d. Mrs. Jean Walker-Smith, 6-4, 6-2; Beverly Baker (U.S.) d. Jean Quertier, 6-4, 7-5; Doris Hart and Shirley Fry (U.S.) d. Jean Quertier and Mrs. Molly Lincoln Blair, 6-1, 6-2; Gertrude Moran and Mrs. Patricia Canning Todd (U.S.) d. Mrs. Betty Hilton and Kay Tuckey, 6-4, 8-6.

1950—UNITED STATES d. GREAT BRITAIN, 7-0
Wimbledon, London
(Captains: Britain, Mrs. D. C. Shepherd-Barron; U.S., Mrs. Marjorie Gladman Van Ryn Buck)
Mrs. Margaret Osborne du Pont (U.S.) d. Mrs. Betty Hilton, 6-3, 6-4; Doris Hart (U.S.) d. Joan Curry, 6-2, 6-4; A. Louise Brough (U.S.) d. Mrs. Betty Hilton, 2-6, 6-2, 7-5; Mrs. Margaret Osborne du Pont (U.S.) d. Mrs. Jean Walker-Smith, 6-3, 6-2; A. Louise Brough (U.S.) d. Mrs. Jean Walker-Smith, 6-0, 6-0; Mrs. Patricia Canning Todd and Doris Hart (U.S.) d. Mrs. Jean Walker-Smith and Jean Quertier, 6-2, 6-3; A. Louise Brough and Mrs. Margaret Osborne du Pont (U.S.) d. Mrs. Betty Hilton and Kay Tuckey, 6-2, 6-0.

1951—UNITED STATES d. GREAT BRITAIN, 6-1
Longwood Cricket Club, Chestnut Hills, Mass.
(Captains: Britain, Mrs. D. C. Shepherd-Barron; U.S., Mrs. Marjorie Gladman Van Ryn Buck)
Doris Hart (U.S.) d. Jean Quertier, 6-4, 6-4; Shirley Fry (U.S.) d. Mrs. Jean Walker-Smith, 6-1, 6-4; Maureen Connolly (U.S.) d. Kay Tuckey, 6-1, 6-3; Doris Hart (U.S.) d. Mrs. Jean Walker-Smith, 6-4, 2-6, 7-5; Jean Quertier (G.B.) d. Shirley Fry, 6-3, 8-6; Mrs. Patricia Canning Todd and Nancy Chaffee (U.S.) d. Pat Ward and Mrs. Joy Gannon Mottram, 7-5, 6-3; Shirley Fry and Doris Hart (U.S.) d. Jean Quertier and Kay Tuckey, 6-3, 6-3.

1952—UNITED STATES d. GREAT BRITAIN, 7-0
Wimbledon, London
(Captains: Britain, Col. Duncan Macaulay;

U.S., Mrs. Marjorie Gladman Van Ryn Buck)

Doris Hart (U.S.) d. Mrs. Jean Quertier Rinkel, 6-3, 6-3; Maureen Connolly (U.S.) d. Mrs. Jean Walker-Smith, 3-6, 6-1, 7-5; Doris Hart (U.S.) d. Mrs. Jean Walker-Smith, 7-5, 6-2; Maureen Connolly (U.S.) d. Mrs. Jean Quertier Rinkel, 9-7, 6-2; Shirley Fry (U.S.) d. Susan Partridge, 6-0, 8-6; Shirley Fry and Doris Hart (U.S.) d. Helen Fletcher and Mrs. Jean Quertier Rinkel, 8-6, 6-4; A. Louise Brough and Maureen Connolly (U.S.) d. Mrs. Joy Gannon Mottram and Pat Ward, 6-0, 6-3.

1953—UNITED STATES d. GREAT BRITAIN, 7-0
Westchester Country Club, Rye, N.Y.
(Captains: Britain, Col. Duncan Macaulay;
U.S., Mrs. Margaret Osborne du Pont)

Maureen Connolly (U.S.) d. Angela Mortimer, 6-1, 6-1; Doris Hart (U.S.) d. Helen Fletcher, 6-4, 7-5; Shirley Fry (U.S.) d. Mrs. Jean Quertier Rinkel, 6-2, 6-4; Maureen Connolly (U.S.) d. Helen Fletcher, 6-1, 6-1; Doris Hart (U.S.) d. Angela Mortimer, 6-1, 6-1; Maureen Connolly and A. Louise Brough (U.S.) d. Angela Mortimer and Anne Shilcock, 6-2, 6-3; Doris Hart and Shirley Fry (U.S.) d. Mrs. Jean Quertier Rinkel and Helen Fletcher, 6-2, 6-1.

1954—UNITED STATES d. GREAT BRITAIN, 6-0
Wimbledon, London
(Captains: Britain, Mrs. Mary Halford; U.S.,
Mrs. Margaret Osborne du Pont)

Maureen Connolly (U.S.) d. Helen Fletcher, 6-1, 6-3; Doris Hart (U.S.) d. Anne Shilcock, 6-4, 6-1; Doris Hart (U.S.) d. Helen Fletcher, 6-1, 6-8, 6-2; A. Louise Brough (U.S.) d. Angela Buxton, 8-6, 6-2; Maureen Connolly (U.S.) d. Anne Shilcock, 6-2, 6-2; A. Louise Brough and Mrs. Margaret Osborne du Pont (U.S.) d. Angela Buxton and Pat Hird, 2-6, 6-4, 7-5; Helen Fletcher and Anne Shilcock (G.B.) vs. Shirley Fry and Doris Hart (U.S.), unplayed.

1955—UNITED STATES d. GREAT BRITAIN, 6-1
Westchester Country Club, Rye, N.Y.
(Captains: Britain, Mrs. Mary Halford; U.S.,
Mrs. Margaret Osborne du Pont)

Angela Mortimer (G.B.) d. Doris Hart, 6-4, 1-6, 7-5; A. Louise Brough (U.S.) d. Shirley Bloomer, 6-2, 6-4; A. Louise Brough (U.S.) d. Angela Mortimer, 6-0, 6-2; Mrs. DorothyHead Knode (U.S.) d. Angela Buxton, 6-3, 6-3; Doris Hart (U.S.) d. Shirley Bloomer, 7-5, 6-3; A. Louise Brough and Mrs.

Margaret Osborne du Pont (U.S.) d. Shirley Bloomer and Patricia Ward, 6-3, 6-3; Doris Hart and Shirley Fry (U.S.) d. Angela Mortimer and Angela Buxton, 3-6, 6-2, 7-5.

The 1955 British Wightman Cup team: *(left to right, kneeling)* Angela Buxton and Patricia Ward; *(standing)* Angela Mortimer, Shirley Bloomer, and Mrs. Mary Halford (captain).

1956—UNITED STATES d. GREAT BRITAIN, 5-2
Wimbledon, London
(Captains: Britain, Mrs. Mary Halford; U.S.,
A. Louise Brough)

A. Louise Brough (U.S.) d. Angela Mortimer, 3-6, 6-4, 7-5; Shirley Fry (U.S.) d. Angela Buxton, 6-2, 6-8, 7-5; A. Louise Brough (U.S.) d. Angela Buxton, 3-6, 6-3, 6-4; Shirley Bloomer (G.B.) d. Mrs. Dorothy Head Knode, 6-4, 6-4; Angela Mortimer (G.B.) d. Shirley Fry, 6-4, 6-3; Mrs. Dorothy Head Knode and Mrs. Beverly Baker Fleitz (U.S.) d. Shirley Bloomer and Patricia Ward, 6-1, 6-4; A. Louise Brough and Shirley Fry (U.S.) d. Angela Buxton and Angela Mortimer, 6-2, 6-2.

1957—UNITED STATES d. GREAT BRITAIN, 6-1
Edgeworth Club, Sewickley, Pa.
(Captains: Britain, Mrs. Mary Halford; U.S.,

Wightman Cup—1957 *(cont.)*

Mrs. Margaret Osborne du Pont)
Althea Gibson (U.S.) d. Shirley Bloomer, 6-4, 4-6,
6-2; Mrs. Dorothy Head Knode (U.S.) d. Christine
Truman, 6-2, 11-9; Ann Haydon (G.B.) d. Darlene
Hard, 6-3, 3-6, 6-4; Mrs. Dorothy Head Knode
(U.S.) d. Shirley Bloomer, 5-7, 6-1, 6-2; Althea Gib-
son (U.S.) d. Christine Truman, 6-4, 6-2; Althea
Gibson and Darlene Hard (U.S.) d. Shirley
Bloomer and Sheila Armstrong, 6-3, 6-4; A. Louise
Brough and Mrs. Margaret Osborne du Pont (U.S.)
d. Anne Shilcock and Ann Haydon, 6-4, 6-1.
1958—GREAT BRITAIN d. UNITED STATES, 4-3
    Wimbledon, London
      (Captains: Britain, Mrs. Mary Halford; U.S.,
      Mrs. Margaret Osborne du Pont)
Althea Gibson (U.S.) d. Shirley Bloomer, 6-3, 6-4;
Christine Truman (G.B.) d. Mrs. Dorothy Head
Knode, 6-4, 6-4; Mrs. Dorothy Head Knode (U.S.)
d. Shirley Bloomer, 6-4, 6-2; Christine Truman
(G.B.) d. Althea Gibson, 2-6, 6-3, 6-4; Ann Haydon
(G.B.) d. Miriam Arnold, 6-3, 5-7, 6-3; Christine
Truman and Shirley Bloomer (G.B.) d. Karol Fage-
ros and Mrs. Dorothy Head Knode, 6-2, 6-3; Al-
thea Gibson and Janet Hopps (U.S.) d. Anne Shil-
cock and Pat Ward, 6-4, 3-6, 6-3.
1959—UNITED STATES d. GREAT BRITAIN, 4-3
    Edgeworth Club, Sewickley, Pa.
      (Captains: Britain, Mrs. Bea Walter; U.S.,
      Janet Hopps)
Mrs. Beverly Baker Fleitz (U.S.) d. Angela Morti-
mer, 6-2, 6-1; Christine Truman (G.B.) d. Darlene
Hard, 6-4, 2-6, 6-3; Darlene Hard (U.S.) d. Angela
Mortimer, 6-3, 6-8, 6-4; Mrs. Beverly Baker Fleitz
(U.S.) d. Christine Truman, 6-4, 6-4; Ann Haydon
(G.B.) d. Sally Moore, 6-1, 6-1; Darlene Hard and
Jeanne Arth (U.S.) d. Christine Truman and Mrs.
Shirley Bloomer Brasher, 9-7, 9-7; Ann Haydon
and Angela Mortimer (G.B.) d. Janet Hopps and
Sally Moore, 6-2, 6-4.
1960—GREAT BRITAIN d. UNITED STATES, 4-3
    Wimbledon, London
      (Captains: Britain, Mrs. Bea Walter; U.S.,
      Janet Hopps)
Ann Haydon (G.B.) d. Karen Hantze, 2-6, 11-9,
6-1; Darlene Hard (U.S.) d. Christine Truman, 4-6,
6-3, 6-4; Darlene Hard (U.S.) d. Ann Haydon, 5-7,
6-2, 6-1; Christine Truman (G.B.) d. Karen

Hantze, 7-5, 6-3; Angela Mortimer (G.B.) d. Janet
Hopps, 6-8, 6-4, 6-1; Karen Hantze and Darlene
Hard (U.S.) d. Ann Haydon and Angela Mortimer,
6-0, 6-0; Christine Truman and Mrs. Shirley
Bloomer Brasher (G.B.) d. Janet Hopps and Mrs.
Dorothy Head Knode, 6-4, 9-7.
1961—UNITED STATES d. GREAT BRITAIN, 6-1
    Saddle and Cycle Club, Chicago, Ill.
      (Captains: Britain, Mrs. Bea Walter; U.S.,
      Mrs. Margaret Osborne du Pont)
Karen Hantze (U.S.) d. Christine Truman, 7-9, 6-1,
6-1; Billie Jean Moffitt (U.S.) d. Ann Haydon, 6-4,
6-4; Karen Hantze (U.S.) d. Ann Haydon, 6-1, 6-4;
Christine Truman (G.B.) d. Billie Jean Moffitt, 6-3,
6-2; Justina Bricka (U.S.) d. Angela Mortimer, 10-8,
4-6, 6-3; Karen Hantze and Billie Jean Moffitt
(U.S.) d. Christine Truman and Deirdre Catt, 7-5,
6-2; Mrs. Margaret Osborne du Pont and Margaret
Varner (U.S.) d. Angela Mortimer and Ann Haydon, default.
1962—UNITED STATES d. GREAT BRITAIN, 4-3
    Wimbledon, London
      (Captains: Britain, Mrs. Bea Walter; U.S.,
      Mrs. Margaret Osborne du Pont)
Darlene Hard (U.S.) d. Christine Truman, 6-2, 6-2;
Ann Haydon (G.B.) d. Mrs. Karen Hantze Susman,
10-8, 7-5; Deirdre Catt (G.B.) d. Nancy Richey,
6-1, 7-5; Darlene Hard (U.S.) d. Ann Haydon, 6-3,
6-8, 6-4; Mrs. Karen Hantze Susman (U.S.) d.
Christine Truman, 6-4, 7-5; Mrs. Margaret Osborne du Pont and Margaret Varner (U.S.) d. Deirdre Catt and Elizabeth Starkie, 6-2, 3-6, 6-2; Christine Truman and Ann Haydon (G.B.) d. Darlene
Hard and Billie Jean Moffitt, 6-4, 6-3.
1963—UNITED STATES d. GREAT BRITAIN, 6-1
    Cleveland Skating Club, Cleveland, Ohio
      (Captains: Britain, Mrs. Bea Walter; U.S.,
      Mrs. Margaret Osborne du Pont)
Mrs. Ann Haydon Jones (G.B.) d. Darlene Hard,
6-1, 0-6, 8-6; Billie Jean Moffitt (U.S.) d. Christine
Truman, 6-4, 19-17; Nancy Richey (U.S.) d. Deirdre Catt, 14-12, 6-3; Darlene Hard (U.S.) d. Christine Truman, 6-3, 6-0; Billie Jean Moffitt (U.S.) d.
Mrs. Ann Haydon Jones, 6-4, 4-6, 6-3; Darlene
Hard and Billie Jean Moffitt (U.S.) d. Christine
Truman and Mrs. Ann Haydon Jones, 4-6, 7-5, 6-2;
Nancy Richey and Mrs. Donna Floyd Fales (U.S.)
d. Deirdre Catt and Elizabeth Starkie, 6-4, 6-8,
6-2.

1964—UNITED STATES d. GREAT BRITAIN, 5-2
Wimbledon, London
(Captains: Britain, Angela Mortimer; U.S.,
Mrs. Donna Floyd Fales)
Nancy Richey (U.S.) d. Deirdre Catt, 4-6, 6-4, 7-5;
Billie Jean Moffitt (U.S.) d. Mrs. Ann Haydon Jones,
4-6, 6-2, 6-3; Carole Caldwell (U.S.) d. Elizabeth
Starkie, 6-4, 1-6, 6-3; Nancy Richey (U.S.) d. Mrs.
Ann Haydon Jones, 7-5, 11-9; Billie Jean Moffitt
(U.S.) d. Deirdre Catt, 6-3, 4-6, 6-3; Deirdre Catt
and Mrs. Ann Haydon Jones (G.B.) d. Carole Cald-
well and Billie Jean Moffitt, 6-2, 4-6, 6-0; Angela
Mortimer and Elizabeth Starkie (G.B.) d. Nancy
Richey and Mrs. Donna Floyd Fales, 2-6, 6-3, 6-4.

1965—UNITED STATES d. GREAT BRITAIN, 5-2
Harold T. Clark Stadium, Cleveland, Ohio
(Captains: Britain, Angela Mortimer; U.S.,
Mrs. Margaret Osborne du Pont)
Mrs. Ann Haydon Jones (G.B.) d. Billie Jean
Moffitt, 6-2, 6-4; Nancy Richey (U.S.) d. Elizabeth
Starkie, 6-1, 6-0; Mrs. Carole Caldwell Graebner
(U.S.) d. Virginia Wade, 3-6, 10-8, 6-4; Billie Jean
Moffitt (U.S.) d. Elizabeth Starkie, 6-3, 6-2; Mrs.
Ann Haydon Jones (G.B.) d. Nancy Richey, 6-4,
8-6; Mrs. Carole Caldwell Graebner and Nancy
Richey (U.S.) d. Nell Truman and Elizabeth
Starkie, 6-1, 6-0; Billie Jean Moffitt and Mrs. Karen
Hantze Susman (U.S.) d. Mrs. Ann Haydon Jones
and Virginia Wade, 6-3, 8-6.

1966—UNITED STATES d. GREAT BRITAIN, 4-3
Wimbledon, London
(Captains: Britain, Angela Mortimer; U.S.,
Margaret Varner)
Mrs. Ann Haydon Jones (G.B.) d. Nancy Richey,
2-6, 6-4, 6-3; Mrs. Billie Jean King (U.S.) d. Virginia
Wade, 6-2, 6-3; Winnie Shaw (G.B.) d. Mary Ann
Eisel, 6-3, 6-3; Nancy Richey (U.S.) d. Virginia
Wade, 2-6, 6-2, 7-5; Mrs. Billie Jean King (U.S.) d.
Mrs. Ann Haydon Jones, 5-7, 7-2, 6-3; Mrs. Ann
Haydon Jones and Virginia Wade (G.B.) d. Mrs.
Billie Jean King and Jane Albert, 7-5, 6-2; Nancy
Richey and Mary Ann Eisel (U.S.) d. Rita Bentley
and Elizabeth Starkie, 6-1, 6-2.

1967—UNITED STATES d. GREAT BRITAIN, 6-1
Harold T. Clark Stadium, Cleveland, Ohio
(Captains: Britain, Mrs. Angela Mortimer
Barrett; U.S., Mrs. Betty Rosenquest
Pratt)
Mrs. Billie Jean King (U.S.) d. Virginia Wade, 6-3,

6-2; Nancy Richey (U.S.) d. Mrs. Ann H. Jones, 6-2,
6-2; Christine Truman (G.B.) d. Rosemary Casals,
3-6, 7-5, 6-1; Nancy Richey (U.S.) d. Virginia
Wade, 3-6, 8-6, 6-2; Mrs. Billie Jean King (U.S.) d.
Mrs. Ann H. Jones, 6-1, 6-2; Rosemary Casals and
Mrs. Billie Jean King (U.S.) d. Mrs. Ann H. Jones
and Virginia Wade, 10-8, 6-4; Mary Ann Eisel and
Mrs. Carole C. Graebner (U.S.) d. Winnie Shaw
and Joyce Williams, 8-6, 12-10.

1968—GREAT BRITAIN d. UNITED STATES, 4-3
Wimbledon, London
(Captains: Britain, Mrs. Angela Mortimer
Barrett; U.S., Mrs. Betty Rosenquest
Pratt)
Nancy Richey (U.S.) d. Mrs. Christine T. Janes, 6-1,
8-6; Virginia Wade (G.B.) d. Mary Ann Eisel, 6-0,
6-1; Jane Bartkowicz (U.S.) d. Winnie Shaw, 7-5,
3-6, 6-4; Mary Ann Eisel (U.S.) d. Mrs. Christine T.
Janes, 6-4, 6-3; Virginia Wade (G.B.) d. Nancy Ri-
chey, 6-4, 2-6, 6-3; Virginia Wade and Winnie
Shaw (G.B.) d. Nancy Richey and Mary Ann Eisel,
5-7, 6-4, 6-3; Nell Truman and Mrs. Christine
Janes (G.B.) d. Stephanie DeFina and Kathy
Harter, 6-3, 2-6, 6-3.

1969—UNITED STATES d. GREAT BRITAIN, 5-2
Harold T. Clark Courts, Cleveland Heights,
Ohio
(Captains: Britain, Mrs. Angela Mortimer
Barrett; U.S., Mrs. Betty Rosenquest
Pratt)
Julie M. Heldman (U.S.) d. Virginia Wade, 3-6, 6-1,
8-6; Nancy Richey (U.S.) d. Winnie Shaw, 8-6, 6-2;
Peaches Bartkowicz (U.S.) d. Mrs. Christine Tru-
man Janes, 8-6, 6-0; Mrs. Christine T. Janes and
Nell Truman(G.B.) d. Mrs. Mary Ann E. Curtis and
Valerie Ziegenfuss, 6-1, 3-6, 6-4; Virginia Wade
(G.B.) d. Nancy Richey, 6-3, 2-6, 6-4; Julie M. Held-
man (U.S.) d. Winnie Shaw, 6-3, 6-4; Julie Held-
man and Peaches Bartkowicz (U.S.) d. Winnie
Shaw and Virginia Wade, 6-4, 6-2.

1970—UNITED STATES d. GREAT BRITAIN, 4-3
Wimbledon, London
(Captains: Britain, Mrs. Angela Mortimer
Barrett; U.S., Doris Hart)
Mrs. Billie Jean King (U.S.) d. Virginia Wade, 8-6,
6-4; Mrs. Ann H. Jones (G.B.) d. Nancy Richey, 6-3,
6-3; Julie M. Heldmano (U.S.) d. Joyce Williams,
6-3, 6-2; Virginia Wade (G.B.) d. Nancy Richey,
6-3, 6-2; Mrs. Billie Jean King (U.S.) d. Mrs. Ann H.

The 1970 United States Wightman Cup team: *(left to right)* Nancy Richey, Mrs. Billie Jean King, Doris Hart (captain), Peaches Bartkowicz, Julie Heldman, and Mary Ann Curtis.

The 1962 Junior Wightman Cup Squad: *(left to right)* Joyce Davenport, Susan Behlmar, Carole Caldwell, Judy Alvarez, Carol Hanks, Chris Safford, Connie Jaster, Tory Fretz, Marilyn Montgomery, and Carol Southmayd.

Wightman Cup—1970 (cont.)

Jones, 6-4, 6-2; Mrs. Ann H. Jones and Joyce Williams (G.B.) d. Mrs. Mary Ann E. Curtis and Julie M. Heldman, 6-3, 6-2; Mrs. Billie Jean King and Peaches Bartkowicz (U.S.) d. Virginia Wade and Winnie Shaw, 7-5, 6-8, 6-2.

1971—UNITED STATES d. GREAT BRITAIN, 4-3
Harold T. Clark Courts, Cleveland Heights, Ohio
(Captains: Britain, Mrs. Ann Haydon Jones; U.S., Mrs. Carole Caldwell Graebner)

Chris Evert (U.S.) d. Winnie Shaw, 6-0, 6-4; Virginia Wade (G.B.) d. Julie M. Heldman, 7-5, 7-5; Joyce Williams (G.B.) d. Kristy Pigeon, 7-5, 3-6, 6-4; Mary Ann Eisel and Valerie Ziegenfuss (U.S.) d. Mrs. Christine T. Janes and Nell Truman, 6-1, 6-4; Valerie Ziegenfuss (U.S.) d. Winnie Shaw, 6-4, 4-6, 6-3; Chris Evert (U.S.) d. Virginia Wade, 6-1, 6-1; Virginia Wade and Winnie Shaw (G.B.) d. Chris Evert and Mrs. Carole C. Graebner, 10-8, 4-6, 6-1.

1972—UNITED STATES d. GREAT BRITAIN, 5-2
Wimbledon, London
(Captains—Britain, Mrs. Ann Haydon Jones; U.S., Mrs. Edythe Ann Sullivan McGoldrick)

Joyce Williams (G.B.) d. Wendy Overton, 6-3, 3-6, 6-3; Chris Evert (U.S.) d. Virginia Wade, 6-4, 6-4; C. Evert and Patti Hogan (U.S.) d. Winnie Shaw and Nell Truman, 7-5, 6-4; Hogan (U.S.) d. Corinne Molesworth, 6-8, 6-4, 6-2; C. Evert (U.S.) d. Williams, 6-2, 6-3; Wade (G.B.) d. Overton, 8-6, 7-5; Valerie Ziegenfuss and Overton (U.S.) d. Wade and Williams, 6-3, 6-3.

1973—UNITED STATES d. GREAT BRITAIN, 5-2
Longwood Cricket Club, Brookline, Mass.
(Captains—Britain, Virginia Wade; U.S., Mrs. Edythe Ann Sullivan McGoldrick)

Chris Evert (U.S.) d. Virginia Wade, 6-4, 6-2; Patti Hogan (U.S.) d. Veronica Burton, 6-4, 6-3; Linda Tuero (U.S.) d. Glynis Coles, 7-5, 6-2; Wade and Coles (G.B.) d. C. Evert and Marita Redondo, 6-3, 6-4; Evert (U.S.) d. Burton, 6-3, 6-0; Wade (G.B.) d. Hogan, 6-2, 6-2; Hogan and Jeanne Evert (U.S.) d. Lindsey Beaven and Lesley Charles, 6-3, 4-6, 8-6.

1974—GREAT BRITAIN d. UNITED STATES, 6-1
Deeside Leisure Center, Queensferry, North Wales

(Captains—Britain, Virginia Wade; U.S., Julie Heldman)

Virginia Wade (G.B.) d. Julie Heldman, 5-7, 9-7, 6-4; Glynis Coles (G.B.) d. Janet Newberry, 4-6, 6-1, 6-3; Sue Barker (G.B.) d. Jeanne Evert, 4-6, 6-4, 6-1; Lesley Charles and Barker (G.B.) d. Newberry and Betsy Nagelson, 4-6, 6-2, 6-1; Coles (G.B.) d. Heldman, 6-0, 6-4; Wade (G.B.) d. Newberry, 6-1, 6-3; Heldman and Mona Schallau (U.S.) d. Wade and Coles, 7-5, 6-4.

1975—GREAT BRITAIN d. UNITED STATES, 5-2
Public Auditorium, Cleveland, O.
(Captains—Britain, Virginia Wade; U.S., Julie Heldman)

Virginia Wade (G.B.) d. Mona Schallau, 6-2, 6-2; Chris Evert (U.S.) d. Glynis Coles, 6-4, 6-1; Sue Barker (G.B.) d. Janet Newberry, 6-4, 7-5; Wade and Mrs. Ann Haydon Jones (G.B.) d. Newberry and Julie Anthony, 6-2, 6-3; C. Evert (U.S.) d. Wade, 6-3, 7-5; Coles (G.B.) d. Mona Schallau, 6-3, 7-6; Coles and Barker (G.B.) d. C. Evert and Schallau, 7-5, 6-4.

1976—UNITED STATES d. GREAT BRITAIN, 5-2
Crystal Palace Sports Centre, London
(Captains—Britain, Virginia Wade; U.S., Vicki Berner)

Chris Evert (U.S.) d. Virginia Wade, 6-2, 3-6, 6-3; Sue Barker (G.B.) d. Rosemary Casals, 1-6, 6-3, 6-2; Terry Holladay (U.S.) d. Glynis Coles, 3-6, 6-1, 6-4; C. Evert and Casals (U.S.) d. Wade and Barker, 6-0, 5-7, 6-1; Wade (G.B.) d. Casals, 3-6, 9-7, ret.; C. Evert (U.S.) d. Sue Barker, 2-6, 6-2, 6-2; Ann Kiyomura and Mona Schallau (U.S.) d. Sue Mappin and Lesley Charles, 6-2, 6-2.

1977—UNITED STATES d. GREAT BRITAIN, 7-0
Oakland Coliseum Arena, Oakland, Calif.
(Captains—Britain, Virginia Wade; U.S., Vicki Berner)

Chris Evert (U.S.) d. Virginia Wade, 7-5, 7-6; Billie Jean King (U.S.) d. Sue Barker, 6-1, 6-4; Rosemary Casals (U.S.) d. Michele Tyler, 6-2, 3-6, 6-4; King and JoAnne Russell (U.S.) d. Sue Mappin and Lesley Charles, 6-0, 6-1; King (U.S.) d. Wade, 6-4, 3-6, 8-6; C. Evert (U.S.) d. Barker, 6-1, 6-2; C. Evert and Casals (U.S.) d. Wade and Barker, 6-2, 6-4.

1978—GREAT BRITAIN d. UNITED STATES, 4-3
Royal Albert Hall, London.
(Captains—Great Britain, Virginia Wade; U.S., Vicki Berner)

Wightman Cup—1978 (*cont.*)

Chris Evert (U.S.) d. Sue Barker, 6–2, 6-1; Michelle Tyler (G.B.) d. Pam Shriver, 5-7, 6-3, 6-3; Virginia Wade (G.B.) d. Tracy Austin, 3-6, 7-5, 6-3; Billie Jean King and Austin (U.S.) d. Anne Hobbs and Sue Mappin, 6-2, 4-6, 6-2; Evert (U.S.) d. Wade, 6-0, 6-1; Barker (G.B.) d. Austin, 6-3, 3-6, 6-1; Barker and Wade (G.B.) d. Evert and Shriver, 6-0, 5-7, 6-4.

1979—UNITED STATES d. GREAT BRITAIN, 7–0
        Wellington, West Palm Beach, Fla.
          (Captains—Great Britain, Virginia Wade; U.S., Vicki Berner)
Chris Evert Lloyd (U.S.) d. Barker, 7–5, 6-2; Kathy Jordan (U.S.) d. Anne Hobbs, 6-4, 6-7, 6-2; Tracy Austin (U.S.) d. Virginia Wade, 6-1, 6-4; Tracy Austin and Ann Kiyomura (U.S.) d. Jo Durie and Debbie Jevans, 6-3, 6-1; Austin (U.S.) d. Barker, 6-4, 6-2; Lloyd (U.S.) d. Wade, 6-1, 6-1; Lloyd and Rosemary Casals (U.S.) d. Wade and Barker, 6-0, 6-1.

1980—UNITED STATES d. GREAT BRITAIN, 6–1
        Royal Albert Hall, London.
          (Captains—Great Britain, Virginia Wade; U.S., Chris Evert Lloyd)
Chris Evert Lloyd (U.S.) d. Sue Barker, 6-1, 6-2; Kathy Jordan (U.S.) d. Anne Hobbs, 4-6, 6-4, 6-1; Andrea Jaeger (U.S.) d. Virginia Wade, 3-6, 6-3, 6-2; Lloyd and Rosemary Casals (U.S.) d. Hobbs and Glynis Coles, 6-3, 6-3; Barker (G.B.) d. Jaeger, 5-7, 6-3, 6-3; Lloyd (U.S.) d. Wade, 7-5, 3-6, 7-5; Jordan and Anne Smith (U.S.) d. Barker and Wade, 6-4, 7-5.

        (The United States leads the series, 42 wins to 10.)

King's Cup

The King's Cup—the men's international team championship on indoor courts of Europe—is formally "H. M. King Gustav V of Sweden Cup." Here are the winning countries since its inception in 1936:

1936	France
1937	France
1938	Germany
1939–51	not held
1952	Denmark
1953	Denmark
1954	Denmark
1955	Sweden
1956	Sweden
1957	Sweden
1958	Sweden
1959	Denmark
1960	Denmark
1961	Sweden
1962	Denmark
1963	Yugoslavia
1964	Great Britain
1965	Great Britain
1966	Great Britain
1967	Great Britain
1968	Sweden
1969	Czechoslovakia
1970	France
1971	France
1972	Spain
1973	Sweden
1974	Italy

(Format changed to European indoor league competition.)

King Gustav V Adolph of Sweden, who died in 1973, presented the King's Cup to indoor tennis.

The 1969 United States Dubler Cup team: *(left to right)* Gardnar Mulloy, Nicholas E. Powell (captain), Leon Dubler (donor of the Cup), Emery Neale, and Robert Sherman.

1975 no competition	1960 Italy d. Switzerland, 5-0
1976 Hungary	1961 Italy d. Austria, 4-1
1977 Sweden	1962 Italy d. France, 3-2
1978 Sweden	1963 Italy d. Belgium, 4-1
1979 Czechoslovakia	1964 Italy d. Germany, 5-0
1980 Czechoslovakia	1965 Italy d. Sweden, 3-0
	1966 Sweden d. Italy, 4-1

Dubler Cup

The Dubler Cup, commonly known throughout the world as "The Davis Cup for Veterans," was offered by Leon Dubler of Switzerland for competition by members of the Veteran International Tennis Association (VITA). This association consists of some twenty-five nations including such far-away places as Pakistan, Israel, China, Japan, Brazil, and the Philippines, Australia, and New Zealand. The United States joined VITA in 1968. Matches were inaugurated in 1958, with the following challenge round results:

1958   Italy d. Germany, 3-1
1959   Switzerland d. Italy, 4-1

1967   France d. Sweden, 3-2
1968   United States d. France, 5-0
1969   United States d. Sweden, 4-1
1970   United States d. Sweden, 4-1
1971   United States d. Sweden, 4-1
1972   United States d. France, 4-1
1973   Australia d. United States, 3-1
1974   United States d. Australia, 3-2
1975   Australia d. United States, 5-0
1976   Italy d. Canada, 3-2
1977   United States d. France, 4-1
1978   United States d. Australia, 4-1
1979   Austria d. United States, 3-2
1980   Sweden d. Austria, 2-1

Stevens Cup

For the first six years of its existence (1964 to 1969), the Stevens Cup, donated by Richard Stevens in honor of his father—who in the years 1892–1905 was eight times nationally ranked in the top ten players—was as an international senior team competition, involving teams from the United States, Canada, Mexico, Great Britain, and India. In 1971, the Stevens was rededicated as the "World Senior Tennis Championships," and pits a team from the North American continent, composed of the top seniors in all age brackets, against its counterpart from the European continent. This competition is under the auspices of USLTA and VITA and follows international cup-match rules. The results of the Stevens Cup are as follows:

Year	Winner	Runner-up
1964	United States	India
1965	United States	Canada
1966	United States	Canada
1967	United States	Canada
1968	United States	Canada
1969	United States	Canada
1970	United States	Great Britain
1971	United States	Australia
1972	United States	Mexico
1973	United States	Sweden
1974	no competition	
1975	United States	Australia
1976	Canada	United States
1977	Canada	Australia
1978	not held	
1979	Canada	United States

Mitre Cup

The Mitre Cup is the Davis Cup of South American lawn tennis. The winning nations since it was first played in 1921 are as follows:

1921	Argentina
1922	Argentina
1923	Chile
1924	Argentina
1925	Argentina
1926	Argentina
1927	Argentina
1928	Argentina
1929	Argentina
1930	Argentina
1931	Argentina
1932	Brazil
1933	Argentina
1934	Brazil
1935	Brazil
1936	Argentina
1937	no competition
1938	Argentina
1939	no competition
1940	Argentina
1941–43	no competition
1944	Argentina
1945–46	no competition
1947	Argentina
1948	Peru
1949	Argentina
1950	Argentina
1951	Chile
1952	Chile
1953	Chile
1954	Chile
1955	Chile
1956	no competition
1957	Argentina

1958	Chile
1959	Brazil
1960	Chile
1961	Argentina
1962	Ecuador
1963	Chile
1964	Brazil
1965	Brazil
1966	Brazil
1967	Chile
1968	Chile
1969	Chile
1970	Chile
1971	Chile
1972	Argentina
1973	Chile
1974	Venezuela
1975	not held
1976	Chile
1977	Argentina
1978	Brazil
1979	Argentina
1980	Chile

Bonne Bell Cup

An international team competition, begun in 1972, which was expanded to a nine-match series in 1973, for Australian and American women.

1972	Australia d. United States, 5-2
1973	Australia d. United States, 6-3
1974	United States d. Australia, 5-4
1975–80	not played

World Cup

An annual team competition between professionals from the United States and Australia, the World Cup was originally donated by the Sportsman's Tennis Club of Boston. In 1972, the sponsorship was taken over by the Aetna Life and Casualty Insurance Co. and the tournament moved to Hartford, Conn. The matches were played at New Haven, Conn., in 1978 and 1979 before returning to Hartford in 1980.

1970	Australia d. United States, 5-2
1971	United States d. Australia, 4-3
1972	Australia d. United States, 6-1
1973	Australia d. United States, 5-2
1974	Australia d. United States, 5-2
1975	Australia d. United States, 4-3
1976	United States d. Australia, 6-1
1977	United States d. Australia, 7-0
1978	United States d. Australia, 6-1
1979	United States d. Australia, 7-0
1980	United States d. Australia, (United States leads series, 6-5)

RECORDS

Leading Yearly Money Winners

The annual money-winning leaders since the start of the Open tennis era follow (totals include all competitive winnings, tournaments, playoffs, and bonus money, but not endorsements, advertising or other earnings): * indicates estimate.

Year	Men		Women	
1968	Rod Laver	$100,000*		$
1969	Rod Laver	123,405		
1970	Rod Laver	201,453	Margaret Smith Court	60,000*
1971	Rod Laver	292,717	Billie Jean King	117,000
1972	Ilie Nastase	176,000	Billie Jean King	119,000
1973	Ilie Nastase	228,750	Margaret Smith Court	204,400
1974	Jimmy Connors	281,309	Chris Evert	261,460
1975	Jimmy Connors	600,273	Chris Evert	412,977
1976	Jimmy Connors	687,335	Chris Evert	343,165
1977	Jimmy Connors	922,657	Chris Evert	503,134
1978	Eddie Dibbs	582,872	Martina Narratilova	450,757
1979	Bjorn Borg	1,019,345	Martina Narratilova	747,548
1980	John McEnroe	1,206,383	Tracy Austin	683,787

Attendance Records
World Exhibition

30,472—(Mixed Singles) Mrs. Billie Jean King vs. Bobby Riggs, Astrodome, Houston, Tex., Sept. 20, 1973. Mrs. King won, 6-4, 6-3, 6-3.

Davis Cup

25,578—(Challenge Round) United States vs. Australia, White City, Stadium, Sydney, Aust., Dec. 27, 28 and 29, 1954. U.S. won, 3-2.

Tournament

37,999—(Single day, including guest passes)—U.S. Open, National Tennis Center, September 4, 1980.
364,370—(23 sessions, including guest passes) U.S. Open, 1980.

United States
Men's Event

19,108—(Grand Prix Masters) Bjorn Borg vs. John McEnroe, round-robin match, Madison Square Garden, New York, Jan. 15, 1981. Borg won, 6-4, 6-7, 7-6.

Women's Event

14,688—(Avon Finals) Martina Navratilova vs. Andrea Jaeger, Madison Square Garden, New York, March 29, 1981. Miss Navratilova won, 6-3, 7-6.

Tournament
U.S. Open Championships

Largest total tournament—364,370 (1980, 23 sessions including guest passes)

Largest paid tournament—331,140 (1980, 23 sessions)

Largest single session (day)—20,172, Sunday, Sept. 7, 1980 (18,551 Paid, 1,621 guests and working press)

Largest single session (night)—20,027, Thursday, Sept. 4, 1980 (18,606 paid)

Largest one-day total—37,999, Thursday, Sept. 4, 1980 (17,972 afternoon, 20,027 evening)

Largest Yearly Totals (Paid)

331,140—1980, National Tennis Center
305,311—1979, National Tennis Center
275,300—1978, National Tennis Center (21 sessions)
250,880—1976, West Side Tennis Club (20 sessions)
218,480—1977, West Side Tennis Club (21 sessions)
216,683—1975, West Side Tennis Club (20 sessions)

Tennis Greats

NATIONAL TENNIS
HALL OF FAME

The Tennis Hall of Fame and Tennis Museum was founded in 1954 and it was decided that its headquarters should be in the historic buildings of the Newport Casino, Newport, R.I. It must be remembered that it was with the building of the Newport Casino that the history of Championship Lawn Tennis in the United States really began. The Casino was built in 1880 under the sponsorship of James Gordon Bennett, owner of the New York *Herald.* As the result of a controversy with the Newport Reading Room, an old and conservative men's club, he engaged Stanford White, the noted architect of the firm of McKim, Mead and White, to design the buildings for a new club to be located opposite his residence on Bellevue Avenue. Upon completion, the club was turned over to the "Newport Casino" corporation formed by a group of summer residents.

The opening of the Casino coincided with the organization of the United States Lawn Tennis Association in 1881, and it was decided to hold their first official championship tournament at the Casino in August of that year. The National Men's Singles Championships were held there through 1914, and an important Invitation Tournament including many of the world's leading amateur tennis players was continued annually through

1967. An annual Professional Tournament has been held there since 1965.

The idea of the Tennis Hall of Fame originated with James H. Van Alen in 1952. A dedicated tennis player and enthusiast, and president of the Newport Casino, Van Alen considered the Casino, as the cradle of American Lawn Tennis, to be the logical place for a national museum. The United States Lawn Tennis Association gave official permission for its establishment in 1954. At an organizational meeting in New York in September of that year, the name of National Lawn Tennis Hall of Fame and Tennis Museum, Inc. was selected, and William J. Clothier, National Champion in 1906, was chosen to be the first president.

Later in 1954 an appeal was made through tennis organizations and interested individuals, which resulted in the donation of a significant collection of tennis trophies and other memorabilia, as well as financial support. A part of the south wing of the Casino was renovated to house the museum collection and set up an office. The museum has since received many gifts of championship trophies, antique rackets, and other historic tennis equipment, photographs, books, statuary, a model court tennis court, and other interesting items associated with the games of lawn tennis and court tennis. Today, thousands of people from all over the world visit this shrine of American lawn tennis each year to browse among the ever-

433

A lawn tennis tournament at Newport in the 1880s as viewed from the upper balcony of the Casino.

expanding display of tennis memorabilia, and to view the notable Stanford White architecture and the beautiful grass tennis courts of the Newport Casino.

Mr. Clothier retired as president in 1957 and was succeeded by Mr. Van Alen. In 1975 the Hall of Fame became an international institution, inducting into membership tennis figures from all nations. Two years later, the International Tennis Hall of Fame was merged with the National Tennis Foundation as a single administrative entity.

In 1979, William McChesney Martin, former chairman of the Federal Reserve Board and once president of the New York Stock Exchange, succeeded Mr. Van Alen as president of the Hall of Fame.

In the late 1970s, a $1 million renovation of the Casino building was undertaken. Included was a reconstruction of the Court tennis court, damaged in a 1939 fire, where the fabled Tom Pettitt played and coached for decades before his death in 1946.

One of the most important features of Tennis Week at the Casino in August of each year is the enshrinement ceremonies. Selection for enshrinement in the Tennis Hall of Fame is based on sportsmanship, skill, character, and contribution to the game of tennis. The following American lawn tennis players have been elected to enshrinement in the Hall of Fame:

1955

OLIVER SAMUEL CAMPBELL (born February 25, 1871; died July 11, 1953). He was National Singles Champion 1890, 1891, and 1892. At age 19 years, 6 months, 9 days, Campbell has been the youngest man ever to win the United States Singles Cham-

Robert Duffield Wrenn.

Joseph Sill Clark.

pionship. He was National Doubles Champion with Valentine G. Hall in 1888, and with Robert P. Huntington, Jr., in 1891 and 1892. He was ranked first in 1890, 1891, 1892; third in 1889, and eighth in 1888. Campbell is generally considered to be America's first net-rusher.

JOSEPH SILL CLARK (born November 30, 1861; died April 14, 1956). He was the first winner of the intercollegiate in 1883. In that year, with his brother C. M. Clark, he defeated R. D. Sears and Dr. James Dwight in doubles trials, first in Boston and then in New York. The Clark brothers played the first international tennis match against the Renshaw brothers at Wimbledon, losing in four sets. Joseph Clark was National Doubles Champion with R. D. Sears in 1885 and was ranked in the top ten from 1885 to 1889. He was secretary of the USNLTA in 1885 and 1886; vice-president in 1887 and 1888 and from 1894 to 1901; and president from 1889 to 1891.

DR. JAMES DWIGHT (born July 14, 1852; died July 13, 1917). He is generally considered to be the "father" of American lawn tennis. Ranked sec-ond to R. D. Sears in 1885 and 1886, Dr. Dwight was doubles champion with him in 1882, 1883, 1884, 1886, and 1887. He was a member of the first Executive Committee of USNLTA and was president of the Association from 1882 to 1884, and from 1894 to 1911.

RICHARD DUDLEY SEARS (born October 26, 1861; died April 8, 1943). He was the first United States Singles Champion, and the only man to win that title seven consecutive years, 1881 to 1887 inclusive, retiring undefeated. He also won the United States Doubles title with Dr. James Dwight in 1882, 1883, and 1884; with Joseph S. Clark in 1885; and again with Dr. Dwight in 1886 and 1887. He was president of the USNLTA in 1887 and 1888.

HENRY WARNER SLOCUM, JR. (born May 28, 1862; died January 22, 1948). He was National Singles Champion in 1888 and 1889. After winning the All-Comers Round in 1887, he was ranked second to R. D. Sears in that year. The next two years, of course, he was ranked number one in the United States. He was secretary of the USN-

William J. Clothier.

dent of the USNLTA from 1902–1911 and president from 1912 to 1915.

1956

MRS. MAY SUTTON BUNDY (born September 25, 1887; died October 4, 1975). Mrs. Bundy was the first woman to be enshrined in the Tennis Hall of Fame and was the first American to win at Wimbledon. She won the Women's Singles championship there in 1905 and 1907, having won the championship of the United States in 1904. For several years thereafter, though not competing in the national championship or abroad, she was considered the strongest woman player. When she later resumed national tournament play, she ranked fourth in 1921 and fifth in 1922 and 1928.

WILLIAM J. CLOTHIER (born September 27, 1881; died September 4, 1962). He was Singles Champion of the United States in 1900, and won the All-Comers in 1909. He was a member of the first Davis Cup Team to go across in 1905 and played on the team for two years. He ranked first in 1905, second in 1904 and 1909; third in 1903 and 1913; fourth in 1905, 1908, and 1912; and fifth in 1902 and 1914. He was elected president of the National Lawn Tennis Hall of Fame in 1954.

LTA in 1887; treasurer in 1888; vice-president from 1889 to 1891, and again in 1912 and 1913; president in 1892 and 1893. For many years, he represented the Association in international negotiations.

MALCOLM D. WHITMAN (born March 15, 1877; died December 28, 1932). He was National Singles Champion in 1898, 1899, and 1900. He represented the United States in Davis Cup matches in 1900 and 1902 in singles, without a defeat.

ROBERT DUFFIELD WRENN (born September 20, 1873; died November 12, 1952). He was National Singles Champion in 1893, 1894, 1896 and 1897 and was National Doubles Champion with Malcolm G. Chace in 1895. Wrenn was six times in the best-ten rankings. He played on the United States Davis Cup Team in 1903 singles, and with George L. Wrenn in doubles. He was vice-presi-

Dwight Filley Davis.

Holcombe Ward.

DWIGHT FILLEY DAVIS (born July 5, 1879; died November 28, 1945). He was the donor of International Lawn Tennis Challenge Bowl (the Davis Cup); United States Doubles Champion with Holcombe Ward in 1899, 1900, and 1901, retiring undefeated; won the All-Comers doubles at Wimbledon in 1901. In singles he ranked fourth in 1898; second in 1899 and 1900; and fourth in 1902, when he retired. He played on the winning first two Davis Cup Teams in 1900 and 1902. He was president of the USLTA in 1923. He served as Governor General of the Philippine Islands and as Secretary of War, and was a Major-General in World War II.

WILLIAM A. LARNED (born December 30, 1872; died December 16, 1926). He was seven times United States Singles Champion, retiring undefeated in 1911; ranked first in the United States eight times; second five times; third four times; fifth and sixth once, continuously from 1892 to 1911, except when absent in the Spanish War in 1898. He played four times in the Davis Cup Challenge Round.

HOLCOMBE WARD (born November 23, 1878; died January 23, 1967). He was six times Doubles Champion of the United States; first with Dwight F. Davis in 1899, 1900, and 1901 (with whom he also won the All-Comers title at Wimbledon); and with Beals C. Wright in 1904, 1905, 1906 (retiring undefeated); he was United States Singles Champion in 1904, and played four years in the Davis Cup Challenge Round. He was president of the USLTA from 1937 to 1947.

BEALS COLEMAN WRIGHT (born December 19, 1879; died August 19, 1961). He was singles champion of the United States in 1905, and doubles champion with H. Ward in 1904, 1905, and 1906. He won the All-Comers in 1908. He represented the United States four years in Davis Cup play, and beat A. F. Wilding and N. E. Brookes in singles in the Challenge Round in Australia in 1908, and (with K. Behr) beat them in doubles of the Final Tie in England in 1907. He ranked first in 1905; fourth in 1900, 1903, 1904; second in 1901, 1907, and 1908; and third in 1902, 1906, and 1910.

1957

MARY K. BROWNE (born 1897; died 1971). Played one of the best games of any American woman tennis champion. Miss Browne ranks among the finest volleyers developed in the women's ranks. She was one of the most popular champions, particularly with her fellow players. Her racket was always at service in a worthy cause. She went on tour with Suzanne Lenglen for the benefit of the Fund for Devastated France following World War I. During World War II she worked overseas with the American Red Cross.

Miss Browne won the National Women's Championship in 1912, 1913, and 1914, and was runner-up to Mrs. Molla Mallory in 1921. She won the National Doubles title in 1912, 1913, 1914, 1921, and 1925, the last year with Helen Wills. She won many other titles, including National Mixed Doubles. She was ranked first in 1913 and 1914, second in 1921 and 1924, and sixth in 1925. She played on the Wightman Cup Team in 1925 and 1926.

Tennis Hall 1957 Enshrinement Ceremony: *(left to right)* R. Norris Williams II, Mary K. Browne, Hazel H. Wightman, Maurice McLoughlin, with James H. Van Alen.

MAURICE EVANS MCLOUGHLIN (born January 7, 1890; died December 10, 1957). Known as the California Comet, he was one of the most spectacular of America's tennis champions. His tremendous service, behind which he was fairly irresistible with the volley, was one of the most effective, and he was decisive overhead. His service was a big factor in his most celebrated victory over Norman Brookes of Australia at Forest Hills in 1914. The first set went to the record score of 17-15 and Brookes never was able to break through service.

McLoughlin was National Champion in 1912 and 1913 and runner-up in 1911, 1914, and 1915. He won the National Doubles with Thomas Bundy in 1912, 1913, and 1914. He played in the Davis Cup Challenge Round in 1909, 1911, 1913, and 1914. He was ranked in the first ten from 1909 through 1915. He was No. 1 in 1912, 1913, and 1914. McLoughlin's career as a tournament

player was relatively short. He did not compete after World War I. The general belief was that he had "burned himself out" with his fiery style of play.

RICHARD NORRIS WILLIAMS II (born January 29, 1892; died 1968). He was one of the most daring players ever to win the National Championship. In his heyday his blinding brilliance was almost unbelievable as he stood in close and took the ball on the rise and volleyed and half-volleyed from positions that are untenable for most players. Because of the riskiness of his attack, with its narrow margin of safety as he played for the lines and a winning shot, errors marred his game when he did not have the "touch." But when he was at his best he was unbeatable.

Williams won the National Championship in 1914 and 1916 after having survived the *Titanic* disaster in 1912. He was runner-up to McLoughlin

William M. Johnston.

in 1913. He won the National Doubles with Vincent Richards in 1925 and 1926. These same two years he and Richards played the Davis Cup doubles against France. He also paired with William Tilden in the 1923 Davis Cup Challenge Round against Australia, and with Watson Washburn in 1921 against Japan. Williams played singles in the Challenge Rounds of 1913 against the British Isles and 1914 against Australia. Ten times Williams was ranked in the first ten, from 1912 through 1916 and, after the war, from 1919 through 1923. He was ranked first in 1916. In 1914 he was ranked second to McLoughlin despite the fact that he won the national title, and there was a considerable furor over this. This is the only time this occurred.

MRS. HAZEL HOTCHKISS WIGHTMAN (born December 20, 1886; died December 5, 1974). Hazel Wightman, donor of the Wightman Cup, has one of the most remarkable records ever compiled in tennis. She started winning National Championships in 1909 and she is still active and winning tournaments in Senior competition. At the same time she has worked with young players and helped to bring them to the top, and her hospital-

ity in taking players into her home during tournaments at the Longwood Cricket Club near Boston is known across the country.

Mrs. Wightman won the National Championship in 1909, 1910, 1911, and 1919. She was runner-up to Molla Bjurstedt (later Mrs. Mallory) in 1915. She won the National Doubles in 1909, 1910, 1911, 1915, 1924, and 1928, Helen Wills being her partner the last two years. She won the Mixed Doubles five times, the indoor singles twice, the indoor doubles nine times, and the Senior Doubles eleven times. The last time was in 1954. In all, she has won approximately fifty na-

Mrs. Molla Bjurstedt Mallory.

tional titles. She was ranked in the first ten, first instituted for women in 1913, in 1915, 1918, and 1919. The international team match between women's teams representing Great Britain and the United States for the Wightman Cup was started in 1923, when Mrs. Wightman put up the trophy. She played on the first team and again in 1924, 1927, 1929, and 1931, each time in doubles.

1958

WILLIAM M. JOHNSTON (born November 2, 1894; died May 1, 1946). Known as "Little Bill," he won the National Championship in 1915, defeating the defending champion, Maurice McLoughlin. He won again in 1919 over a rising player answering to the name of William T. Tilden II. In 1920, 1922, 1923, 1924, and 1925, Johnston was runner-up to Tilden. In 1923 Johnston won the Wimbledon title, defeating Francis T. Hunter in the final.

A Californian, Johnston ranked in the first ten of the country twelve times in fourteen years. His first appearance was at number four in 1913. He ranked first in 1915 and 1919, and second in 1916 and from 1920 to 1923, and also in 1925. He won three National Doubles Championships in 1915, 1916 and 1920, with Clarence J. Griffin. He won the National Mixed Doubles in 1921 with Mary K. Browne, and the National Clay Court title in 1919. He was Pacific Coast Champion seven times between 1913 and 1922. Johnston was a member of the celebrated team which brought back the Davis Cup from Australia in 1920. His overall Davis Cup Challenge Round record included thirteen wins and three losses. He died in 1946 at the age of 51. One of the greatest volleyers the game has known, and armed with a mighty Western topspin forehand drive, Johnston ranks among the world's all-time giants of the court, although he was one of the smallest men to win the championship. He was also one of the game's most beloved players, a sportsman of the first rank.

MRS. MOLLA BJURSTEDT MALLORY (born 1892; died November 22, 1959). She won the National title seven times and also won the Patriotic Tournament that took the place of the Championship in 1917. She was champion in 1915, 1916, and 1918 as Molla Bjurstedt, and in 1920, 1921, 1922, and 1926 after her marriage to Franklin Mallory. In 1922 she defeated Helen Wills for the title, and

in 1923 and 1924 she was runner-up to Miss Wills. With Eleanora Sears she won the National Doubles crown in 1916 and 1917. She and Irving C. Wright were National Mixed Doubles Champions in 1917, and she won with William Tilden in 1922 and 1923. Mrs. Mallory played on five Wightman Cup teams in the years 1923 through 1928. In 1922 she was a finalist at Wimbledon, losing to Suzanne Lenglen. She defeated the great French player at Forest Hills in the 1921 championship, Mlle. Lenglen defaulting after losing the first set of one of the most famous matches in tennis history. Mrs. Mallory was ranked in the first ten thirteen times between 1915 and 1928. She was first seven times. Her winning of the National title seven times has been equaled only by Mrs. Helen Wills Moody.

Mrs. Mallory's forehand and her fighting heart won her a place among the greatest players. She had a tremendous competitive spirit.

ROBERT LINDLEY MURRAY (born November 3, 1893; died 1970). He won the Patriotic Tournament of 1917 and the National Championship in 1918, defeating Tilden in the final. He was left-handed and his service was one of the strongest points of his game. He ranked fourth in 1914 and 1916, first in 1918, and fourth in 1919.

MRS. MAUD BARGER WALLACH (born 1871; died April 2, 1954). She won the Women's Singles Championship in 1908. She was runner-up in 1906. There were no women's rankings until 1913, and she was fifth in 1915 and tenth the following year. Mrs. Barger Wallach maintained a keen interest in tennis for many years, up to the time of her death in 1954. She was a patron of the game and gave her support particularly to the Newport Invitation Tournament.

1959

MRS. HELEN WILLS MOODY ROARK (born October 6, 1905). By capturing the English Ladies' 1938 Singles Championship at Wimbledon, Mrs. Roark (then Mrs. Moody) brought to a climax a tennis career which had covered a period of eighteen years; which had kept her in the front rank of women tennis players of the world during a majority of that time and enabled her to win more than thirty National and International championships. She won her first national championship,

Girls' Singles and Doubles, at fifteen. She reached the finals of the women's singles in 1922 and won the doubles with Mrs. Jessup. The next year she won her first Women's Singles at Forest Hills, defeating players many years her senior, including Kitty McKane, the English star, and Mrs. Mallory, then for several years the holder, in the final. She visited Europe for the first time in 1924 as a member of the United States Olympic team, won the Olympic singles and doubles in Paris, and reached the final of the Wimbledon singles; successfully defended her American singles title, won the doubles with Mrs. Wightman and the mixed doubles with Vincent Richards. In 1925 she retired her first singles trophy, and won the doubles and mixed doubles again. Her first setback came the following year in the famous match against Suzanne Lenglen at Cannes, following which she underwent an appendicitis operation in Paris and was unable to play either in England or the United States the remainder of the season. Her great triumph in 1927 was her first Wimbledon win, being the second American woman ever to win the English title (Mrs. May Sutton Bundy was the first in 1905). But Mrs. Moody made a record by winning the United States title again the same year. She bettered this in 1928 by adding the French title to the other two, a feat never equaled by any other woman player. Moreover she never lost a set in the doing. By this time a lost set for Miss Wills would have been front-page news. She repeated herself in 1929, three major titles without the loss of a set. In 1930 she defended her French and English titles successfully but did not defend at Forest Hills. Back again in 1931 she regained her American title and made a trip to Japan, a renowned celebrity. Her playing in 1932 was confined to England and the Continent, dominating major and minor tournaments as usual.

Illness called a halt to her 1933 activities. After winning the Wimbledon championship for the sixth time she was forced to withdraw from Wightman Cup play (she had played in No. 1 position in these matches 1923–1932 with the exception of 1927) and defaulted to Helen Jacobs midway in the American championship final. Two years later she entered the Wimbledon championships, defeating Miss Jacobs in a sensational recovery when within one point of defeat.

Most tennis "experts" agree that Helen Wills Roark is the greatest woman player in the annals of lawn tennis. Always a shrewd and methodical performer, she seemed, as one writer said, to look at each match as a separate rung to the ladder, carefully apportioning the requisite amount of effort needed to outplay each opponent and not allowing herself to be drawn into wasting an ounce of energy, knowing accurately just when to raise her game to an attacking force and when to let a rival defeat herself.

WILLIAM TATEM TILDEN II (born February 10, 1893; died June 5, 1953). He ruled the game in the 1920s, "Sport's Golden Age." He won the United States Singles Championship seven times—1920–1925 inclusive and 1929—equaling the records of Richard D. Sears and William A. Larned. In addition he was five times the National Doubles Champion (three times with Vincent Richards and once with Brian I. C. Norton and Francis T. Hunter), four times the National Mixed Doubles Champion (twice each with Mary K. Browne and Mrs. Molla Bjurstedt Mallory). Tilden also won the United States Clay Championship seven times, Indoor Singles Championship once, and Indoor Doubles four times. He was the first American player to win the men's singles at Wimbledon, in 1920, by defeating Zenzo Shimizer of Japan in the All-Comers and Gerald L. Patterson of Australia in the Challenge Round. He won the Wimbledon Singles Championship two more times and the Doubles once. He was also Singles, Doubles, and Mixed Doubles Champion of Australia in 1930; Singles and Doubles Champion of Holland in 1920 and 1930; Singles Champion of New Zealand in 1921 and of Italy in 1930. He was ranked in the first ten 12 times (ten times at No. 1, twice at No. 2) in the years 1918 to 1929. He turned professional in 1930 and was a great pro until the late 1940s.

"Big Bill" Tilden and "Little Bill" Johnston were the twin aces who won the Davis Cup from Australasia in 1920 and kept it in this country through 1926, with assistance from Vincent Richards, R. Norris Williams II, and Watson Washburn. In those seven years Tilden lost only one match in singles in the challenge round. Overall, he won 17 out of 22 Davis Cup Singles matches he played from 1920 to 1930, and in addition won four Davis

Cup Doubles matches.

There are many who rank Tilden as the greatest player of all time. He had tremendous hitting power from both forehand and backhand. He had one of the finest services the game has known. He was a master of spin and of tactics. He had a marvelous physique for the game and raced across the court on the nimblest of feet. He was the absolute master of the tennis world from 1920 through 1925.

1960
No enshrinements

1961

FRED BEASLEY ALEXANDER (born August 14, 1880; died 1969). After winning the Intercollegiate Doubles Championship in 1900 and Intercollegiate Singles Championship in 1901, he went on to win the United States Doubles with Harold H. Hackett from 1907 to 1910. He also won the Doubles Championship of the Patriotic Tournament with Harold A. Throckmorton. In addition, in that 1917 tournament, he was Captain and Manager of the players who played in tournaments and exhibition matches and who raised funds to purchase ambulances and personnel to man them under the direction of the United States Lawn Tennis Association for the benefit of the Red Cross. All of the tournaments and championships of that year were called Patriotic Tournaments and Championships and all of the profits were devoted to supplying the ambulances and personnel to the Red Cross. Each club that contributed a prescribed amount had a plate placed upon the ambulance with the club name. When the war was over these plates were returned to the Club that gave the ambulance. Fred Alexander did a magnificent job as leader to the various players that participated.

HAROLD HUMPHREY HACKETT (born July 17, 1878; died November 20, 1937). He was a member of the famous doubles team of Alexander and Hackett which won four National Doubles Championships four successive years (1907 to 1910). He also captured the 1912 Davis Cup team which defeated the British Isles 3 matches to 2. He won the deciding doubles match with Maurice McLoughlin in a close five-set match.

Fred Beasley Alexander.

FRANCIS TOWNSEND HUNTER (born June 28, 1894). He was National Indoors Singles Champion in 1922 and 1930, and Indoors Doubles Champion with Vincent Richards in 1922, 1924 and 1929. He was National Champion with Bill Tilden in 1927. In 1924 Paris Olympic Games, he and Richards

Francis Townsend Hunter.

John Hope Doeg.

won the doubles gold medal, while in 1928 he won the International Championship which was held in connection with the Olympic Games in Holland, defeating Jean Borotra in the final round in straight sets. He was on two Davis Cup teams (1927 and 1928), which were defeated by France in the Challenge Round. He joined Tilden in the professional ranks in 1931.

VINCENT RICHARDS (born March 20, 1903; died September 28, 1959). He won most of the United States titles—both amateur and professional—except National Singles. He won his first USNLTA doubles title with Bill Tilden at the age of 15 years, 4 months and 26 days—the youngest player to win a National Championship. He won the Doubles crown four more times—twice with Tilden and twice with R. Norris Williams. He won the National Mixed Doubles with Marion Ainderstein in 1919 and with Helen Wills in 1928. He won the Indoors Singles in 1919, 1923, and 1924 and Doubles in 1919, 1920, 1921, 1923, and 1924. He was ranked five times in the top ten.

Richards played in the first international match in 1922 against Australasia, defeating Gerald Patterson. He had a record in Davis Cup competition of two victories in singles and three in doubles. He was never beaten in Davis Cup play. He also won two gold medals—singles and doubles—in the 1924 Olympic Games in Paris.

Richards was the United States' first "name" player to turn professional (1926) and won most of the world's professional titles. His last one, in 1945, was the United States Professional Doubles Title with Bill Tilden.

1962

JOHN HOPE DOEG (born December 7, 1908; died April 27, 1978). He won the national title in 1930, defeating William T. Tilden in the semifinals and Francis X. Shields in the final. He was the Junior Champion of the country in 1926, and ranked Number 8 nationally the following year and in 1928. In 1929 he moved up to third place, and headed the ranking the following year. He won the National Doubles Title for two years in succession (1929 and 1930) with George M. Lott, Jr., and was runner-up for the Wimbledon doubles in 1930 with I. G. Collins, the British player. A slashing, fighting lefthander, Doeg is best remembered for his powerful serve and topspin forehand, and for his great courage and endurance as a match player.

HELEN HULL JACOBS (born August 8, 1908). She was a famous number two who eventually won most of the big ones herself. From 1927 to 1941, with the exception of two years of noncompetition, she was at or near the top of the national rankings. For four straight years (1932–1935) she ranked first, and she was in the Number 2 slot no less than ten times. Her celebrated rivalry with Helen Wills (now Mrs. Helen Wills Roark) went back as far as 1928, when Miss Wills beat her in the Forest Hills final. In 1933, Miss Jacobs lost the Wimbledon final to the same opponent, but in 1933 she beat her for the United States Championship. All told, Miss Jacobs won the National Singles four times and was runner-up an equal number. She was four-time Wimbledon finalist, finally carrying off the Championship there in 1936 by defeating Fraulein Sperling. Other national titles in her long record include: U.S. Girls' Singles, 1924–25; National Doubles with Sarah Palfrey (1932, '33, and '35); and National Mixed Doubles in 1934 with George Lott.

Helen Hull Jacobs.

In Wightman Cup play, during twelve years, Miss Jacobs has an overall record in singles and doubles of 18 victories and 11 defeats. She developed the chop forehand to a high level of accuracy and steadiness. She hit a classic, sweeping backhand and excelled in both serve and volley. Her match play and sportsmanship were both exemplary.

HENRY ELLSWORTH VINES, JR. (born September 28, 1911). He hit the ball as hard and fast as any man ever did. He was the United States Singles Champion in 1931 and 1932, beating Lott and Henri Cochet in the respective finals. He won the National Clay Court title in 1931 and the Wimbledon Championship over H. W. (Bunny) Austin a year later. Wimbledon finalist again in 1933, he lost to Jack Crawford, the great Australian. Paired with Keith Gladhill, he held the Junior Doubles Championship in 1929 and the National title, as well as the Clay Court title, two years later. In the Davis Cup Challenge Round of 1932, Vines beat Cochet in five sets but lost to Jean Borotra in four.

In his short, meteoric career, he ranked Number 8 in the country in 1930, and first for the two succeeding years. He turned professional in 1933 and later gained new fame as a professional golfer. Vines had every shot in the game and hit them

with every ounce of strength in his lean frame. His smash, serve, and forehand are perhaps best remembered.

1963

WILMER LAWSON ALLISON (born December 8, 1904; died April 30, 1977). He was United States national champion in 1935. In the final he beat Fred Perry of England. In 1930 he was runner-up to Tilden at Wimbledon after he had beaten the great Henri Cochet of France. He won the doubles championship of the United States with John Van Ryn in 1931 and 1935, and they were finalists in 1930, 1932, 1934, and 1936. They were Wimbledon titlists in 1929 and 1930 and runners-up in 1935. Allison was ranked third in 1930, second in 1932 and 1933, and first in 1934 and 1935.

MRS. SARAH PALFREY DANZIG (born September 18, 1912). Mrs. Danzig was one of the world's leading women players for many years. She ranked in the first ten thirteen times between 1929 and 1945. She was National Champion in 1941 and 1945—and runner-up in 1934 and 1935 to Helen Jacobs. She had a remarkable record in doubles, winning the title nine times. With Alice Marble she won the Wimbledon crown twice, 1938 and 1939. She was a winner of seven Wight-

Wilmer Lawson Allison.

John William Van Ryn with his wife, the former Marjorie Gladman— a fine player in her own right.

man Cup matches with Miss Jacobs from 1933 to 1936, and with Miss Marble from 1937 to 1939. Mrs. Danzig was best known for her sweeping backhand and keen competitive spirit.

JULIAN S. MYRICK (born March 1, 1880; died January 4, 1969). The elder statesman of tennis was president of the United States Lawn Tennis Association, chairman of the Davis Cup and Wightman Cup committees. He was a leader of international prominence in the vast development and growth of the game. During his administration programs for the development of junior boys' and girls' tennis were started and the number of clubs in the USLTA was increased all across the nation. He was largely responsible for the inauguration of the international women's matches with Britain for the Wightman Cup. Through the years he was a steadfast advocate of strict amateurism and the highest standards of sportsmanship.

JOHN WILLIAM VAN RYN (born June 30, 1906). He was one of the great doubles players of his time, and with Wilmer Allison formed one of the most famous combinations the game has known. With Allison he won the United States Doubles title in 1931 and 1935 and was a finalist in 1930, 1932, 1934, and 1936. They were Wimbledon champions in 1929 and 1930 and runners-up in 1935. In the Davis Cup Challenge Round they defeated Henri Cochet and Jean Borotra in 1929 and Cochet and Jacques Brugnon in 1932. In addition to the honors he gained with Allison, Van Ryn won the Wimbledon and French doubles championships with George Lott in 1931. He was ranked sixth in singles in 1927 and 1928, fifth in 1929, ninth in 1930, and fourth in 1931.

1964

GEORGE T. ADEE (born 1874; died 1948). He was famous as a Yale football player before he gained renown in tennis. He was named all-American quarterback by Walter Camp in 1894. He gave many years of devoted service to tennis. He was chairman of the Davis Cup Committee and Amateur Rule Committee and served on numerous other committees. He was also president of the USTA from 1916–1920, although he took a leave of absence for military service in World War I.

George T. Adee.

George Martin Lott, Jr.

JOHN DONALD BUDGE (born June 13, 1915). He ranks among the greatest men champions of all time. Budge is particularly famous for scoring the first grand slam in tennis. In 1938 he swept the world's four major championships—Wimbledon, Forest Hills, the French, and the Australian. He was champion of the United States in 1937 and won Wimbledon that year also. With Gene Mako he won the Wimbledon doubles in 1937 and 1938 and the United States doubles in 1936 and 1938. He was a member of the team that won the Davis Cup in 1937 and that successfully defended it in 1938. He ranked in the first ten five times before turning professional late in 1938 and was ranked first in 1936, 1937, and 1938. In 1937, he was the first tennis player to receive the James E. Sullivan Memorial Trophy for being America's top amateur athlete.

ALICE MARBLE (born September 28, 1913). Miss Marble was national champion four times, in 1936, 1938, 1939, and 1940, and was noted for her volleying ability and aggressive style of play. She was Wimbledon champion in 1939. With Sarah Palfrey Danzig she won the national doubles title from 1937 through 1940 and the Wimbledon doubles with Helen Jacobs in 1938 and 1939. She was a member of four winning Wightman Cup teams in 1933, 1937, 1938, and 1939. She ranked in the top ten seven times and was Number 1 from 1936 through 1940. Miss Marble ranks among the greatest women champions of all time.

GEORGE MARTIN LOTT, JR. (born October 16, 1906). Lott is rated as one of the greatest doubles players and he was finalist in the singles against Ellsworth Vines in 1931. He won the national doubles five times with three different partners. They were John Doeg (twice), Lester Stoefen (twice), and John Hennessey. He won the Wimbledon doubles with John Van Ryn in 1931 and with Stoefen in 1934 and in 1931 also won the French doubles with Van Ryn. He played in the Davis Cup challenge round in 1929, 1930, and 1934 and ranked in the first ten nine times.

FRANCIS X. SHIELDS (born November 18, 1910; died August 19, 1975). Shields won international fame early. He was runner-up to John Doeg for the national championship in 1930. In 1931 he got to the final at Wimbledon but had to default to Wood owing to an ankle injury suffered in the semifinals. He was on the Davis Cup challenge round team in 1934 and he ranked in the first ten eight times.

Francis Xavier Shields.

Sidney B. Wood, Jr.

Mrs. Pauline Betz Addie.

SIDNEY B. WOOD, JR. (born November 1, 1911). He was Wimbledon champion in 1931 and runner-up to Wilmer Allison for the national title in 1935. He played in the Davis Cup challenge round in 1934 and ranked in the first ten no less than ten times.

1965

MRS. PAULINE BETZ ADDIE (born August 6, 1919). She was perhaps the most agile of the American players who dominated the women's game during World War II. She was champion of the United States four times—in 1942, 1943, 1944, and 1946. She was runner-up to Sarah Palfrey in 1941 and 1945. In 1946 Mrs. Addie won the Wimbledon crown without losing a set, and won her two singles matches and the doubles with Doris Hart in the Wightman Cup matches. She also won the French Mixed Doubles championship with Budge Patty in 1946. Mrs. Addie ranked in the first ten eight times and was first four times.

MRS. ELLEN FORDE HANSELL ALLERDICE (born September 18, 1869; died 1937). She was the first winner of the women's United States

championship in 1887. She was honored, with Richard D. Sears, the first men's champion, at the Golden Jubilee celebration of the USLTA in 1931 at Forest Hills, New York.

W. DONALD MCNEILL (born April 30, 1918). He won the French championship in 1939 in singles and in doubles with Charles Harris. In 1944 he was doubles champion of the United States with Robert Falkenburg, and in 1946 he was runner-up with Frank Guernsey. He was the United States Singles Indoor Champion in 1938 and 1940, and was Indoor Doubles Champion in 1941, 1949, 1950, and 1951. McNeill ranked in the first ten six times and was number one in 1940. His career was interrupted by World War II, and the Davis Cup matches were suspended when he was in his prime.

JAMES H. VAN ALEN (born September 19, 1902). He won distinction in both lawn tennis and court tennis, the ancient forerunner of the modern game. Both sports are encompassed in the National Lawn Tennis Hall of Fame and Tennis Museum. In court tennis Van Alen was national champion repeatedly. His skill was not comparable in lawn tennis, but he has won his greatest fame for his distinguished service to lawn tennis.

As President of the Newport Casino, Van Alen was responsible for the establishment of the Hall

The first Men's Singles champion (Richard D. Sears, 1881) and the first Women's Singles champion (Mrs. Ellen Hansell Allerdice, 1887) receiving championship medallions from Secretary of Navy Charles Francis Adams during the Golden Jubilee celebration of the USLTA.

of Fame there. Following his election as president of the THF, succeeding William J. Clothier, Sr., he assured the permanence of the Casino home by gaining controlling shares for the Hall of Fame as donations from stockholders. Also as Casino president he became the director of the Newport Invitation Tournament and infused new life into it when it seemed it might be dropped permanently and the Casino might be sold. He has been a benefactor too of court tennis, and he has won wide attention recently for his VASSS (Van Alen Simplified Scoring System).

WATSON WASHBURN (born June 13, 1894; died 1973). He was a high-ranking player who represented the United States on Davis Cup and Olympic Teams and for many years he rendered valuable service to the USLTA. With Richard Norris Williams II, he won the Davis Cup Challenge Round doubles in 1921, and they were runners-up in the United States doubles in 1921 and 1923 and at Wimbledon in 1924. He ranked in the first ten seven times. He has served on many USLTA com-

mittees, and was chairman of the Constitution and Rules Committee, the Ball Committee, and the Intercollegiate Committee.

1966

JOSEPH R. HUNT (born February 17, 1919; died February 2, 1944). Hunt, a graduate of the United States Naval Academy, won the National championship in 1943. He was a lieutenant in the Navy at the time and played in the championship on a brief leave after serving as a deck officer in the Atlantic theater of the war and before starting training as a pilot. He was killed in training in Florida.

Hunt played in the 1939 Davis Cup challenge round against Australia, pairing in the doubles with Jack Kramer. He ranked in the first ten five times.

W. Donald McNeill.

FRANK A. PARKER (born January 31, 1916). He ranked in the first ten seventeen consecutive years from 1933 through 1949 and won the championship in 1944 and 1945 as an Army sergeant. He was French champion in 1948 and 1949 and won the Wimbledon and French doubles with Richard (Pancho) Gonzalez in 1949 and the United States doubles with Kramer in 1943. Parker won United States Clay Court Singles Championship 1933, 1939, 1941, 1946, and 1947 and the Doubles in 1939. He was the United States Indoor Champion with G. S. Mangin. He played singles with Donald Budge on the team that won the Davis Cup for the United States in 1937 for the first time since 1927. He was also a member of the team that lost the cup to Australia in 1939 and again on the winning team in 1949.

THEODORE R. PELL (born 1879; died 1967). Pell, who ranked in the first ten five times from 1910 to 1918 and was national indoor champion three times, is particularly famous for his backhand. It was rated as the greatest the game had seen. He is honored not only for his playing ability but also for the esteem in which he has been held for half a century.

FREDERICK R. [TED] SCHROEDER (born July 20, 1921). He was national champion in 1942 and Wimbledon champion in 1949. He won the United States doubles with Jack Kramer in 1940, 1941, and 1947 and the mixed doubles with Louise Brough in 1942. Schroeder was United States Clay Court Doubles champion in 1941 and 1947. He was a member of the winning Davis Cup team in 1946, 1947, 1948, and 1949 and was also on the 1950 and 1951 teams that lost to Australia. He ranked in the first ten eight times.

1967

MRS. A. LOUISE BROUGH CLAPP (born March 11, 1923). She was one of the greatest athletes women's tennis has ever known. She captured four Wimbledon Singles titles (1948, 1949, 1950, 1955) and was runner-up three times. She won the United States Singles crown in 1947 and was runner-up five times. She won the Australian Singles once in 1950. In Women's Doubles she won Wimbledon five times (1946, 1948, 1949, 1950, 1954), United States 12 times (1942–1950, 1955–1957), Australia once (1950), and France three times

(1946, 1947, 1949), a total of 21. In Mixed Doubles she won Wimbledon four times and United States four times. In Wightman Cup play from 1946 to 1957, she played in 22 matches and won all 22. She was ranked in the first ten each year commencing with 1941, excepting 1951, a total of 16 times. [This exceeds all male records also excepting Bill Larned (19) and Frankie Parker (17).] In 1948 she was named as the winner of the Service Bowl, which is awarded annually to the woman making the most outstanding contribution to tennis.

MRS. MARGARET OSBORNE DUPONT (born March 4, 1918). An excellent volleyer, she was National Champion in 1948, 1949, and 1950, and runner-up in 1944 and 1947. In Doubles she and Mrs. Louise Brough Clapp won the National Doubles title 12 times from 1942 to 1950, and 1955 through 1957. Mrs. duPont also won with Mrs. Sarah Palfrey Danzig in 1941. She was Wimbledon Champion in 1947 and finalist in 1949 and 1950, and Champion of France in 1946 and 1949. She and Mrs. Clapp won the Wimbledon Doubles in 1946, 1948, 1949, 1950, and 1954, and the French Doubles in 1946, 1947, and 1949. In Wightman Cup competition Mrs. duPont won both of her singles matches in 1946 and 1950, and doubles with Mrs. Clapp in 1946, 1947, 1948, 1950, 1954, 1955, and 1957, and with Margaret Varner in 1961 and 1962. She was ranked in the first ten fourteen times. She was seventh in 1938, fourth in 1941, third in 1942, fourth in 1943, second in 1944, third in 1945, second in 1946 and 1947, first in 1948, 1949, and 1950, fifth in 1953, fourth in 1956, and fifth in 1958.

ROBERT LORIMER RIGGS (born February 25, 1918). He was one of the cleverest and strongest defensive players the game has known. Riggs won the Singles Championship of the United States in 1939 and 1941, and was Mixed Doubles champion with Alice Marble in 1940. He was Champion of Wimbledon in 1939, the last year the tournament was held before the war forced its cancellation until 1946, and Doubles Champion with Elwood Cooke. He was United States Clay Court Singles Champion in 1936, 1937, and 1938 and was doubles champion with Wayne Sabin in 1936. He also won the United States indoor singles, doubles, and mixed doubles championships in 1940. He was a member of the victorious Davis Cup Team in 1935 with Don Budge, defeating Adrian Quist and losing to John Bromwich. In 1939 Riggs defeated Bromwich and bowed to Quist as the United States lost the Cup. He ranked fourth in 1936, second in 1937, 1938, and 1940, and first in 1939 and 1941.

WILLIAM F. TALBERT (born September 4, 1918). He was one of the world's outstanding doubles players and an authority on the tactics of that form of the game. With Gardnar Mulloy he won the United States doubles crown in 1942, 1945, 1946, and 1948. He won the United States Clay Court doubles in 1942 (with William Reedy), 1944 and 1945 (with Francisco Segura), and 1946 (with Gardnar Mulloy). Talbert with three different partners won the Indoor doubles championships in 1949–1952 and in 1954. With Tony Trabert he won French and Italian doubles in 1950. With Margaret Osborne he captured the United States Mixed Doubles title four times (1943–1946). He was United States Indoor Singles Champion in 1948. Talbert won the Davis Cup Challenge Round Doubles match with Mulloy in 1948 against Australia and lost the Doubles in 1949. He ranked in the first ten thirteen times. He was tenth in 1941, fifth in 1942, 1947, 1950, 1951, fourth in 1943 and 1948, second in 1944 and 1945, third in 1949, sixth in 1946, 1952, and ninth in 1954.

1968

MRS. MAUREEN CONNOLLY BRINKER (born September 17, 1934; died June 21, 1969). The brief but amazing record of "Little Mo" Connolly ranks her easily among the top 10 women who have played the game. Winner of three consecutive United States singles titles (1951–1953), beginning at the age of 17, as well as three successive Wimbledon titles (1952–1954). In 1953, she won the grand slam of tennis—Australian, French, Wimbledon, and United States singles titles. She also won the Italian championship in 1954 as well as the French doubles and mixed doubles. She also was United States clay court singles champion in 1953 and 1954, and won the doubles with Doris Hart in 1954. Besides being the Australian doubles champion in 1954, she won nine out of nine Wightman Cup matches from 1951 to 1954. In

national rankings, she was No. 10 in 1950, No. 1 in 1951 to 1953. If an unfortunate accident to her leg hadn't cruelly cut short her career, there is no telling how many titles she might eventually have racked up.

ALLISON DANZIG (born February 27, 1898). He was the highly respected dean of United States tennis writers while with the *New York Times* for over 45 years. Danzig wrote with a keen awareness and appreciation of the game, all embellished by a lovely fluent prose that made his accounts a rare pleasure to read. He also performed many a distinguished service for tennis, in recognition of which he was inducted into the Hall of Fame, the first writer to be so honored.

Danzig, a graduate of Cornell University, also covered rowing sports and collegiate football with the same graceful style and authored several authoritative books on sports. Cornell and Columbia —a school whose sports activities he covered extensively—now compete each spring for the Allison Danzig Cup in tennis.

RICHARD A. GONZALES (born May 9, 1928). He won the United States singles crown in 1948 at age nineteen and repeated in 1949. Also he won the French doubles championship in 1949 (with Frank Parker), United States Clay Court Singles in 1948 and 1949, and United States Indoor Singles in 1949. He played in 1949 Davis Cup Challenge Round, winning two singles matches without losing a set. He turned pro in 1949. After a few years there, he became the undisputed world champion for the incredible span of more than a decade.

JACK ALBERT KRAMER (born August 5, 1921). His big serve-and-volley game did more than anyone else's to perfect the modern, postwar attacking game, bringing it down to fine science. He won the United States singles championship in 1946 and 1947, and the Wimbledon crown in 1947. He won the United States doubles in 1940, 1941, and 1947 with Frederick Schroeder and in 1943 with Frank Parker. At Wimbledon, Kramer won the doubles in 1946 (with Tom Brown) and in 1947 (with Bob Falkenburg). In 1941, he won the United States Mixed Doubles with Mrs. Sarah Palfrey Cooke. He also was United States Clay Court doubles champion in 1941 and Indoor champion in both singles and doubles in 1947. After being in the top ten of the national rankings five times

Jack Albert Kramer *(left)* and Frank Parker *(right)*.

(twice as No. 1), he became a professional in 1947 and later became the leading impresario of the professional game.

ELEANORA SEARS (born 1881; died July 9, 1967). The daughter of a Boston "Brahmin" family, she was an unusually gifted sportswoman who won more than 240 trophies on the tennis and squash courts and in horse show rings. In tennis, she was four times national doubles champion (1911, 1915–1917).

1969

KARL HOWELL BEHR (born May 30, 1885; died October 15, 1949). He was ranked in the first ten seven times from 1906 through 1915. With Beals Wright he went to England in 1907 as the United States Davis Cup team to play Australasia. After Brookes defeated Wright, he lost to Wilding after leading two sets to one. He and Wright beat Brookes and Wilding in the doubles, and on the final day Wright defeated Wilding and Behr lost to Brookes after volleying sensationally to win the first set.

When on his game, Behr was phenomenally brilliant and in 1907 he scored several victories over William Larned, seven-time winner of the national championship.

DORIS J. HART (born June 20, 1925). She won each of the four major singles championships, Australia (1949), France (1950, 1952), Great Britain (1951), and United States (1954, 1955), plus those of Italy (1951, 1953) and South Africa (1952). She

also has won United States Clay Courts singles (1950), and British hard court championships (1951–1954). She won the women's doubles championship at Wimbledon three times with Shirley Fry and once with Mrs. Patricia C. Todd; the French doubles title once with Mrs. Todd and four times with Miss Fry; and the United States doubles four years also with Miss Fry. In 1954, she did

Doris J. Hart.

"the hat trick" by winning the United States singles, doubles, and mixed doubles (with Vic Seixas). It was her fourth offensive win of the mixed doubles (three with Seixas and two with Frank Sedgman). Miss Hart also has won the Wimbledon mixed doubles title four times (twice with Sedgman and twice with Seixas) and the French mixed doubles three times (twice with Sedgman, once with Seixas). She also won the Australian doubles (1950), Australian mixed doubles (1949, 1950), Italian doubles (1951), Italian mixed doubles (1953), South African doubles (1950, 1952), and South African mixed doubles (1950). She also won the United States Clay Courts doubles (1950, 1954), United States Indoors doubles (1947, 1948) and mixed doubles (1947, 1948) and British hard court doubles (1951–1954) and mixed doubles (1951, 1954). Miss Hart was a member of the Wightman Cup Team from 1946 through 1955 and lost one match in the ten years. Fourteen consecutive years (1942–1955) she ranked in the first ten.

CHARLES S. GARLAND (born October 29, 1898; died January 28, 1971). He was a member of the Davis Cup team in 1920 when the United States won back the trophy from Australia and began its seven-year reign as champion nation. He ranked in the first ten in 1918, 1919 and 1920, and in 1920 he won the Wimbledon doubles with Richard Norris Williams II, Bill Tilden and Bill Johnston falling before them in the semifinals. Garland won prominence not only as a player but also as an officer of the United States Lawn Tennis Association and a committeeman. He served as secretary in 1921 and 1922 and vice-president in 1942 and 1943. The Davis Cup Committee was among those on which he served.

ARTHUR LARSEN (born April 6, 1925). He was champion of the United States in 1950 and with Enrique Morea won the Italian doubles the same year. He was United States Clay Court champion in 1952 and the next year he added the indoor title. With Herb Flam in 1950 and Grant Golden in 1953 he took the United States Clay Court title while with K. Nielsen in 1953, he won United States doubles championship. He played in Davis Cup competition in 1951 and 1952, winning four out of four matches. Ranked in the top ten eight times from 1949 through 1956, his career on the

Marie Wagner.

courts was ended prematurely when he was badly injured while riding his motor-scooter. Small in size, Larsen lacked power and the big serve but he was a clever touch player and excelled in tactical play and volleying skill.

MARIE WAGNER (born February 3, 1883; died April 1, 1975). She was very popular and one of the best-known figures in tennis in the Metropolitan New York area for nearly half a century as a player and as a member of tournament and ranking committees. She was runner-up to Mary K. Browne for the United States championship in 1914 and she won the United States indoor title six times, a record, between 1908 and 1917. She ranked in the top ten eight times between 1913 and 1922 and might have been ranked many times more had the ranking started before 1913. She won the United States Indoor doubles title four times (1910, 1913, 1916, 1917).

1970

CLARENCE J. GRIFFIN (born Sept. 4, 1888; died 1973). Better known as "Peck," he and "Little Bill" Johnston won the doubles championship in

1915, 1916, and 1920. "Peck," whose brothers, Elmer and Mervyn, were also tennis players of note, won the United States clay court championship in 1914 and the doubles title with John Strachan. He ranked seventh in 1915, sixth in 1916 and 1920, and tenth in 1924.

SHIRLEY FRY IRVIN (born June 30, 1927). She was champion of the United States and Wimbledon in 1956 and runner-up in both in 1951, when she won the French title. She also won the United States clay court (1956), the South African (1950) and Australian (1957) championships. With Doris Hart, she won the United States doubles in 1951–54 and the Wimbledon doubles in 1951–53. With various doubles partners, Mrs. Irvin won the French (1950–53), British hard court (1951–1953), United States clay court (1946, 1950, 1956), Italian (1951), Australian (1957), and South African (1950 and 1952) championships. She also won the Wimbledon mixed doubles with Vic Seixas in 1956 and Italian mixed doubles with Felicissmo Ampon in 1951. Mrs. Irvin was a member of the Wightman Cup Team from 1949 through 1956, except in 1950. She ranked in the top ten from 1944 through 1956, being No. 1 in 1956, second in 1955, and third in 1951, 1952, and 1953.

PERRY JONES (born May 6, 1888; died February 16, 1970). Known as "Mr. Tennis" on the Pacific Coast, he devoted his adult life to the service of tennis. He did more for the development of junior tennis than probably anyone else in the history of tennis in southern California. He raised funds and marshalled the help of ranking players and club and civic officials in providing equipment and instruction for boys and girls in clinics, and he set standards of sportsmanship and personal neatness for the youth. Most of the young players who came East from southern California to win national and world renown were started on their way by Jones.

MARION ANTHONY TRABERT (born August 16, 1930). He won the championship of the United States in 1953 and 1955, and was the last player of this country to do so until Arthur Ashe triumphed in 1968. Trabert also won at Wimbledon in 1955, and was champion of France in 1954 and 1955. He was a member of the Davis Cup Team from 1951 through 1955. He won the United States doubles with Victor Seixas in 1954, the French doubles in

1954 and 1955, and the Australian doubles in 1955. He won the French and Italian doubles with William Talbert in 1950. Trabert won the United States clay court singles title in 1951 and 1955, and the doubles in 1954 and 1955. He also captured the United States indoor singles championship in 1955 and doubles in 1954 and 1955. He was ranked first in the United States in 1953 and 1955, second in 1954, and third in 1951. He served in the Navy in 1952 and left the amateur ranks after the 1955 season.

1971

ALTHEA GIBSON DARBEN (born August 25, 1927). Won both the United States and Wimbledon championships in 1957 and 1958, the first black player to be crowned. She was runner-up for the United States title in 1956, when she won the French and Italian championships. She won the Wimbledon Doubles with Angela Buxton in 1956, with Darlene Hard in 1957 and Maria Bueno in 1958; the French Doubles with Miss Buxton in 1956; and the Australian Doubles with Shirley Fry in 1957. Mrs. Darben was a member of the Wightman Cup team in 1957 and 1958. She ranked in the first ten 6 times between 1952 and 1958 and was No. 1 in 1957 and 1958.

ELISABETH MOORE (born June 6, 1876; died July 29, 1944). Won the Women's Championship of the United States in 1896, 1901, 1903, and 1905. She was runner-up for the title four times, in 1892, 1902, 1904, and 1906. She was Doubles Champion with Juliette Atkinson in 1896 and with Carrie Neely in 1903.

ARTHUR NIELSEN (born January 2, 1894). Chairman of the A. C. Nielsen Company, worldwide marketing research organization, he has been one of the most generous philanthropists to contribute to tennis. He and his wife gave a four-court indoor tennis building to the Park District in the village of Winnetka, Illinois, and following this, in 1966, he offered more than a million dollars to the University of Wisconsin for the construction of a building for tennis and squash courts. His gifts are estimated to total more than $3,000,000. He was captain of the Wisconsin tennis team from 1916 to 1918.

ELIAS VICTOR SEIXAS, JR. (born August 30, 1923) won the championships of the United States in 1954 and was runner-up in 1951 and 1953. He won the National Doubles with Mervyn Rose of Australia in 1952 and with Tony Trabert in 1954. He was Wimbledon Champion in 1953 and he won the French and Australian Doubles titles with Trabert. Seixas played on the United States Davis Cup team from 1951 through 1957. He ranked in the first ten 12 times between 1948 and 1966 and was No. 1 in 1951, 1954, and 1957.

1972

BRYAN M. (BITSY) GRANT, JR. (born December 25, 1910). A native of Atlanta, where a major tennis facility is named for him. Over a twenty-two-year period, from 1927 to 1949, won the Southern Tennis Association singles a record ten times including four straight years, 1927–30. Compiled an impressive 8-2 record in singles for United States Davis Cup teams in 1935, 1936, 1937, and 1938. In 1966 won the USTA Men's 55 Singles title and in 1969 played with Henry Crawford on the Men's 55 Doubles championship team. One of the first outstanding players produced in the South. Ranked seven times in United States top ten.

GARDNAR MULLOY (born November 22, 1914). A Miami native, he is one of the outstanding doubles players in American history. Mulloy played seven times in Davis Cup competition for the United States, winning eleven of his fourteen matches, including his only Challenge Round singles match (against Dinny Pails, 1946). In combination with Billy Talbert, Mulloy four times played on the winning United States National Championship Doubles team at Forest Hills. Three times made the finals at Wimbledon in doubles, winning in 1957 (with Budge Patty).

ELIZABETH RYAN (born February 5, 1892; died July 6, 1979). Often celebrated as "the best player never to win a major singles title," she was a runner-up twice at Wimbledon singles and lost the 1926 singles title to Molla Mallory at Forest Hills. She excelled in doubles, winning nineteen titles at Wimbledon (twelve women's doubles and seven mixed) and played on winning doubles teams at Forest Hills (1926) and France (1930, 1932, 1933, and 1934). Twice ranked United States No. 2 behind Helen Wills (1925) and Molla Mallory (1926).

Her record of 19 Wimbledon titles was surpassed after 31 years on the day following her death by Mrs. Billie Jean King, who was part of a winning women's double pair in 1979. During her final hours, Miss Ryan, a native of Anaheim, Calif., who lived for many years in London, had dined at the All-England Club where she had triumphed so often.

1973

DARLENE HARD (born January 6, 1936). The USTA Women's Intercollegiate Champion in 1958 playing for Pomona College, Miss Hard was a finalist in the women's singles at Forest Hills the same year. From 1954 to 1963, she was ranked ten times in the United States top ten and was United States No. 1 four times (1960–1963). Miss Hard won the United States National Singles at Forest Hills in 1960 and 1961 and Doubles in 1958, 1959, 1960, 1961, 1962, and 1969 with a variety of partners. She also won the 1960 French Singles and 1957 and 1960 Doubles at Roland Garros. In 1962 she played a winning doubles pair at the Italian Championship and won a total of seven titles at Wimbledon (four in women's doubles and three in mixed). She was the losing singles finalist at Wimbledon in 1957 and 1959. In 1963 Miss Hard played on the first United States Federation Cup team and was 6-1 in her matches as the United States won the initial championship (3-1 singles, 3-0 doubles). She also played on five Wightman Cup teams, winning ten of fourteen matches.

C. GENE MAKO (born January 24, 1916). A standout doubles player and later leading tennis official, Gene Mako was born in Budapest, Hungary, but emigrated to the United States at an early age. He was the United States Doubles Champion in 1936 and 1938, winning the mixed doubles (with Alice Marble) in 1936 as well. In 1937 and 1938, he played on the winning doubles team at Wimbledon. His first major title was the United States Clay Court Doubles in 1934, and he won it again in 1939. Mako was a member of the United States Davis Cup team from 1935 to 1938, playing eight matches with a 6-3 record. He paired with Don Budge to win the 1937 and 1938 doubles at Wimbledon.

ALASTAIR B. MARTIN (born March 11, 1915) is a leading business executive and major supporter of tennis, who was president of the USTA in 1969 and 1970, guiding it through the difficult early years of open tennis. In 1972 he became president of the National Tennis Foundation. In this capacity, Mr. Martin greatly broadened the scope of the NTF, increasing its support to tennis programs in major cities, organizing a joint program with the Boy Scouts of America, and merging the NTF with the International Tennis Hall of Fame at Newport, Rhode Island, to strengthen both organizations.

1974

JULIETTE P. ATKINSON of Brooklyn, N.Y., was one of the earliest outstanding United States Women Champions. During the height of her dominance, Miss Atkinson was a singles finalist in the United States Nationals five straight years, winning in 1895, 1897, and 1898. She was the first woman ever to win the singles title three times, and thus she retired the silver tennis girl then given as a trophy in the National Championship. In doubles she won ten national titles, seven in women's doubles from 1894 to 1902, including five in succession (1894 to 1898) and three in mixed (with Edwin P. Fischer) in 1894–96.

ROBERT FALKENBERG (born January 29, 1926) was a native of Los Angeles who later played in Davis Cup competition for Brazil. The highlight of his American career was his singles victory in 1948 at Wimbledon, where he had been a quarterfinalist in 1947. He was a semifinalist at Forest Hills in 1946 but never played Davis Cup for the United States. He later was a member of the Brazilian team for eleven matches (1954–55), winning three singles matches and one doubles.

FRED HOVEY (born October 7, 1868; died, October 18, 1945) was a singles finalist four times during the years that the United States Nationals were staged at Newport. He won the championship in 1895 by unseating the defender, R. D. Wrenn. He also won the National Doubles title twice (1893 and 1894) paired with Clarence Hobart.

BERTHA TOWNSEND TOULMIN (born March 7, 1869; died May 12, 1909) was one of the original "Big Four" from Philadelphia who dominated the early days of the National Women's Championship in the United States and were, indeed, instrumental in beginning the competition. She became the second women's titleholder in United States

history when she won the event in 1888 and became the first to win the championship two years in a row with another victory in the 1889 tournament.

1975

LAWRENCE A. BAKER (born June 20, 1890; died October 15, 1980) was a long-time official of the USTA. He served as president for three years (1948–1950) after having been an official of the national association for fifteen years as secretary, treasurer, and vice-president. Baker also served briefly as captain of the United States Davis Cup team, captaining the victory over Canada (5-0) at Montreal in 1953.

FRED J. PERRY (born May 18, 1909) was the first man to win three straight singles at Wimbledon since 1913, when he turned the trick in 1934–36. He was also the first man ever to win at Wimbledon, Australia, France, and the United States, although not in the same year. He was the United States Singles Champion in 1933 and 1934, French in 1935, and Australian in 1934. Thought by many to be the greatest British male player ever, he won forty-five of fifty-two matches representing Britain in Davis Cup play from 1933 to 1936, when his team won the Cup four years running. He is the only man ever to play through the draw and win Wimbledon three times. No British man won the title during the next four decades.

ELLEN C. ROOSEVELT (born 1868; died September 26, 1954) was another of the pioneering women of the early days of ladies' tournament tennis in the United States. She won the fourth National Women's Championship ever staged in 1890 by defeating her sister in the singles final. Miss Roosevelt also won the doubles title that year, in combination with sister Grace.

1976

JEAN BOROTRA (born August 13, 1898) had one of the longest careers in the history of international tennis. First appearing in Davis Cup play for France in 1922, he made his final appearance in 1947, winning forty-four of the fifty-four matches he played. A vital member of the championship Cup teams from 1927 to 1932, Borotra continued to play competitive tennis when well into his 70s. He was particularly active in the International Club series between France and Britain. Borotra (another of the "Four Musketeers" of French tennis) is perhaps the finest indoor player ever produced by his country. He won the French indoor title twelve times, the British eleven, and the United States four (1925, 1927, 1929, and 1931). He also won the Wimbledon singles in 1924 and 1926, the Australian in 1928, and the French in 1924 and 1931.

JACQUES BRUGNON (born June 11, 1895; died March 20, 1978) incredibly made the third round in doubles at Wimbledon in 1948 when he was 53. Long one of the world's finest doubles players, he narrowly missed winning the French doubles title, when he was 44, with Borotra (who was then 40). In 1928 he won the Australian, Wimbledon, and French doubles. In all, he won four doubles titles at Wimbledon and five in France. Brugnon also reached the semifinals at Wimbledon in 1926 in singles. He played Davis Cup (primarily doubles) for France from 1921 to 1934.

MABEL E. CAHILL was a native of Ireland who joined the New York Tennis Club upon coming to the United States. During her years in the U.S. she proved to be one of the dominant players of women's tennis. From 1890 to 1893, she scored a succession of triumphs in local and regional events (including the Middle States singles in 1890) and then won five U.S. National titles before returning to Ireland. In 1891, Miss Cahill won both the singles and doubles titles and repeated that sweep the following year when she also annexed the mixed doubles crown (with Clarence Hobart). Her Challenge Round win over Elisabeth Moore in 1892 was one of the most stirring women's finals seen up to that time, Miss Cahill winning, 5–7, 6-3, 6-4, 4-6, 6-2. Mabel Cahill was a quick, strong player considering the cumbersome costumes of the time and was characterized by her close-cropped dark hair in an almost masculine style.

HENRI COCHET (born December 14, 1901) was another of the famed French "Musketeers" who wrested the Davis Cup from the United States in 1927 and helped defend it successfully from 1928 to 1932. In his twenty-six matches in Cup play from 1922 to 1933, Cochet won 44 of 58 matches. He also twice won the singles title at Wimbledon (1927 and 1929), once at Forest Hills (1928), and

was five times the singles champion of France between 1922 and 1932. Although he turned professional in 1933, Cochet was reinstated as an amateur after World War II. He also won two doubles at Wimbledon and three at Roland Garros.

RENE LACOSTE (born July 2, 1905) was, perhaps more than any other man, responsible for France's taking possession of the Davis Cup in 1927, winning crucial singles matches against both Bill Tilden and Bill Johnston as the French team upset the United States defenders in the Challenge Round. LaCoste had a distinguished career as a singles player, winning Forest Hills in 1926 and 1927, Wimbledon in 1925 and 1928, and France in 1925, 1927, and 1928. Considered the best groundstroker player of his era, he was also a fine doubles partner and with Jean Borotra won the men's event at Wimbledon in 1925 and at Paris in 1924, 1925, and 1929. He played in fifty-one Davis Cup matches representing France between 1923 and 1928, when ill health forced his early retirement. He later became a very successful businessman in France.

RICHARD SAVITT (born March 4, 1927) reached the semifinals at Forest Hills in 1950 and, though he lost, the confidence he gained by getting to that point (with victories over Vic Seixas and John Bromwich) set the stage for his impressive 1951. That year, Savitt won both the United States and Wimbledon singles titles (beating Ken McGregor in both finals). With a promising basketball career cut short by an injury, Savitt concentrated on tennis from 1949 on. He was selected for the U.S. Davis Cup team that reached the Challenge Round against Australia in 1951, when he was ranked No. 2 in the U.S. (his highest ranking).

1977

MANUEL ALONSO (born November 12, 1895) was a native of San Sebastian, Spain, who became one of the first foreign-born players ever to achieve top-ten ranking by the USTA. In 1925 he was rated No. 5, moving up to No. 2 in 1926 and earning No. 4 in 1921. In 1920 he made the semifinals of the French championship and in 1921, was a semifinalist at Wimbledon. He and his brother Jose came to the United States in 1923, and he resided in the country for many years before returning to Spain.

SIR NORMAN E. BROOKES (born November 14, 1877; died; January 10, 1968) was one of the first great Australian players and still ranks among the best lefthanded players of tennis history. He was the first non-Briton to win at Wimbledon (1907) and annexed his second title there in 1914. He was also a fine doubles player, winning two doubles titles at Wimbledon and the United States championship in 1919. He won the Australian singles in 1911 and the doubles in 1924. Brookes was also a great Davis Cup player, representing Australia (or Australasia) on nine squads between 1905 and 1920. He captained Australia's team in 1935 and served as president of the Australian Lawn Tennis Association for twenty-nine years before retiring in 1955. He was a captain in the British Army during World War I. Awarded French Legion of Honor in 1928 and knighted by King George VI in 1939.

BARON GOTTFRIED VON CRAMM (born July 7, 1909; died November 8, 1976) was the finest player ever developed in Germany. Three times (1935–37) he was the Wimbledon singles runner-up. Lost United States final to Don Budge in 1937 and also lost crucial Davis Cup interzone match to Budge in the same year, 6-8, 5-7, 6-4, 6-2, 8-6. He was leading 5-2 in the fifth set. Von Cramm won the French singles in 1934 and 1936 and the German four straight years, beginning in 1932. He won the West German singles in 1948 and 1949 after service on the Eastern front in the German Army during the Second World War. Played Davis Cup for Germany from 1932 to 1953. In 1938 he was arrested by the Gestapo for criticism of the Nazi regime and spent two months in jail. His term was shortened due to international condemnation, led by Budge, of his arrest and trial.

BETTY NUTHALL (born May 23, 1911), though now Mrs. F. C. Shoemaker of New York, was born in Surbiton, Surrey, England, and became the first "pin-up girl" of British tennis. At age 19, she also became the first non-American winner of the women's title in the United States, winning at Forest Hills in 1930. Previously, she had been the runner-up to Helen Wills in 1927. She had great success in the United States Doubles, playing on the winning team in 1930, 1931, and 1933. Miss Nuthall was the runner-up for the French championship in 1931 and played on the British Wight-man Cup team in 1927, 1929, 1931–34, and 1939. She later became an American citizen and a highly successful executive in the travel field.

BUDGE PATTY (born February 11, 1924) was born in Arkansas, raised in California, and lived most of his life in Paris, where he won the French championship in 1950. The same year, Patty was the singles champion at Wimbledon and was a member of the United States Davis Cup team in 1951. With Gardnar Mulloy, he won the doubles at Wimbledon in 1957. For the United States, he won both his matches in 1951 Davis Cup play, but an injury curtailed his participation. In 1953 he engaged in a 93-game, 4-hour, 23-minute third-round match at Wimbledon, losing to Jaroslav Drobny. It was the longest match played up to that time at Wimbledon.

1978

MARIA BUENO (born October 11, 1939). A native of São Paulo, Brazil, Miss Bueno epitomized the combination of grace and skill that distinguishes a great woman champion. At age 20, she captured the first of her three United States singles titles, defending successfully in 1960 and winning again in 1964. She also won three Wimbledon singles titles (1959, 1960, and 1964). Miss Bueno was also an excellent doubles player and among her titles were included the U.S. in 1960, 1962, 1966 and the U.S. Open in 1968 as well as the Wimbledon doubles in 1958, 1960, 1963, 1965 and 1966. She won the French crown in doubles and mixed doubles in 1960.

PIERRE ETCHEBASTER (born October 11, 1893; died March 24, 1980). Born in St. Jean de Luiz in France's Basque country, Etchebaster became the greatest champion of court tennis in this century. Although he played the Basque games of pelota and pala until he was nearly 30, Etchebaster reigned as the world champion of court tennis from 1928 to 1954, an unprecedented span of 27 years before retiring. During many years of his championship era and for many thereafter, he was a teacher and coach of court tennis, primarily at New York's Racquet and Tennis Club (1927–66).

KITTY MCKANE GODFREE (born May 7, 1897) was among the finest British women players of the 1920s and early 1930s, twice winning Wimbledon singles titles. She scored a notable victory over

Helen Wills to take the title in 1924 despite trailing by a set midway through the match, and repeated in 1926 although down 1–3 in the third. In 1923 and 1927, she won the doubles titles at the United States championships and took the mixed doubles in the U.S. in 1925 with John B. Hawkes. She later paired with her husband, Leslie Godfree, to win the second of her two Wimbledon mixed crowns (in 1926). Her quick game was suited to indoor play and she captured the U.S. Indoor title in doubles in 1922 and 1923. Later, Mrs. Godfree won three doubles titles in the German championships (in 1930 and 1931). She played in seven Wightman Cup matches for Britain from 1923 to 1934.

HARRY C. HOPMAN (born December 8, 1906) was a fine doubles player who gained his greatest fame as the nonplaying captain of the Australian Davis Cup team. From 1950 to December, 1969, he served in that capacity. Along with an earlier tour as a playing captain (1938–39), Hopman steered the Australian teams to 16 wins in 26 tries for the Cup. He and his wife, Nell, won four Australian mixed doubles titles before he turned to coaching. Hopman also wrote a column for the Melbourne *Herald* for 23 years entitled "Talking Sport" which encompassed a variety of sports beside tennis. As a player, he was the United States doubles champion in 1939, the Australian doubles titlist in 1929 and 1930 and the German champion in doubles in 1932. He won the Australian mixed crown in 1930, 1936–37, and 1939 and the Italian in 1935.

SUZANNE LENGLEN (born May 24, 1899; died May 27, 1938) was one of the greatest women champions in tennis history although her temperamental outbursts of petulance rivaled those of great operatic *divas*. Although Mlle. Lenglen never won a United States championship (losing in her only try to Molla B. Mallory), she was the dominant force at Wimbledon and her native France from the end of World War I until she turned pro in 1927. She won the Wimbledon singles five straight years (1919–23) and again in 1925. She partnered on winning women's doubles during the same years and won mixed titles in 1920, 1922, and 1925. She did not compete in 1924 due to illness. Suzanne Lenglen, who came from Compiegne, burst onto the world tennis scene in 1914 when she swept through the French championships, winning singles, doubles and mixed doubles, and repeated the performance in singles and doubles at the world hard courts. She was the Olympic champion in 1920 in singles and mixed doubles but was unable to defend in 1924 when the Games were held in Paris.

Mlle Lenglen won a total of 21 titles in the French championships, gaining the women's singles, and doubles and mixed doubles in all of the following years—1914, 1920–23, 1925, 1926. She won the singles and mixed doubles championships in the world hard courts in 1921, 1922, and 1923, adding to her singles and doubles crowns of 1914. She also won the doubles in 1921 and 1922.

In the completeness of her game, few players of any era have been her equal. She was, however, often her own worst enemy in terms of the pressures she placed upon herself to perform. In an era when professionals were held outside the realm of major tennis events, her pro efforts (including the famous 1927 tour against Mary K. Browne) were less than successful.

ANTHONY F. WILDING (born October 31, 1883; died May 9, 1915) was the first great champion produced by New Zealand. He won four straight Wimbledon singles from 1910 to 1913 and was the Australian singles titlist in 1906 and 1909. He also won the doubles at Wimbledon in 1907–08, 1910, and 1914 and in Australia in 1906 and Germany in 1905. It was in Davis Cup play, however, that Wilding captured the attention of the world. New Zealand then played a combined team with Australia under the name of Australasia. In concert with Australian Norman Brookes, Wilding led that team to five Davis Cup victories in six Challenge Round attempts from 1907 to 1914. The first of those victories (over Great Britain, 3–2), enabled Australasia to become the first team except Britain or the U.S. to win the Cup. Wilding died tragically in action during World War I on May 9, 1915, in France at age 32.

1979

MARGARET SMITH COURT (born July 16, 1942) stood out as one of the premier women players during the final years before open tennis and scored one of only two women's Grand Slams in history during the 1970 campaign. She also scored one in 1963 in mixed doubles with Ken Fletcher. Margaret Smith was born in Albury, N.S.W., and won her first Australian singles championship at age 18 in 1960. Subsequently, she won singles titles in every major event then contested, including the United States five times (1962, 1965, 1968–70), Wimbledon three times (1963, 1965, 1970), France five times (1962, 1964, 1969–70, 1973), Australia 11 times (1960–66, 1969–71, 1973), Italy three times (1962–64), Germany three times (1964–66), South Africa four times (1968–71), Canada (1970), Ireland (1968), and Wales (1969). She also won innumerable doubles titles, on many occasions sweeping all three championships available at major events. In 1970, she won the singles, doubles and mixed doubles at the U.S. Open, a feat she had also performed at Wimbledon in 1965 and France in 1964. Miss Smith, who became Mrs. Barry Court in 1967, played Federation Cup for Australia from 1963 to 1971 and led her team to victories in two of the first three competitions (1964 and 1965). In winning her Grand Slam, she won easily at Australia and France, but struggled against Americans at Wimbledon and the U.S. Open. In England, she prevailed over Mrs. Billie Jean King, 14–12, 11–9, in an epic struggle and then went three sets against Rosemary Casals (before winning the U.S. title at Forest Hills.)

JOHN HERBERT CRAWFORD (born March 22, 1908) was a native of Albury, N.S.W., the same town which—34 years later—was to produce Margaret Smith Court. He never won a United States singles title, but his narrow miss at Forest Hills in 1933 cost him a Grand Slam. His Wimbledon victory over Ellsworth Vines that year is still considered one of the greatest finals ever seen there (4-6, 11-9, 6-2, 2-6, 6-4). A few weeks later, Jack Crawford went to the finals of the U.S. championship against Britain's Fred Perry but lost, 6–3, 11-13, 4-6, 6-0, 6-1, fading badly after gaining a one-set lead. He had previously beaten Henri Cochet in straight sets to win at Paris and came back to sweep Ken Gledhill after dropping the first set in the Australian final. Crawford never won another Wimbledon singles although he did take the doubles title in 1935 and had won the mixed doubles in 1930. He was the Australian singles champion three straight years (1931–33) and won four doubles titles there (1929–30, 1932, 1935). He was a member of the Australian Davis Cup team from 1928 to 1937.

GLADYS MEDALIE HELDMAN (born May 13, 1922) founded *World Tennis* magazine (along with Gardnar Mulloy) in June, 1953, and built it into one of the world's leading periodicals on the sport before selling it to CBS Publishing. Her other major contribution to changing the face of tennis came on September 23, 1970, when Mrs. Heldman signed nine of the world's leading women players to contract professional agreements (for one dollar each) in Houston and launched what was to become the Virginia Slims circuit for women. Her daughter, Julie, was a world class player who was ranked No. 5 in the world in 1969. Mrs. Heldman has been a longtime active amateur player.

AL LANEY (born January 11, 1896). Among the first of America's regular tennis writers, Laney began his newspaper career with the Pensacola *Journal* in his native city. After beginning his sportswriting efforts on baseball's spring training, he moved into golf and tennis—becoming a recognized authority on both sports. Following newspaper jobs in Dallas and Minneapolis, Laney joined the U.S. Army during World War I and in 1920 became a sportswriter for the New York *Evening Mail.* After the *Mail* was sold to the rival *Evening Telegram,* he joined the staff of the New York *Herald Tribune* in Paris in 1925, writing for both the New York and European editions. He continued with the *Herald Tribune* until its closure in 1965. While with the *Herald Tribune,* Laney covered the Wimbledon championships continuously from 1926 through 1939 as well as other major European tournaments. He was a fixture at the National Singles at the West Side Tennis Club for 40 years until his retirement. From 1940 on, Laney covered leading tennis events throughout the U.S. in addition to golf, baseball, and hockey. He also authored several books, including a notable one on tennis, *Covering the Court.*

RAFAEL OSUNA (born September 13, 1938; died 1969) came from Mexico City but learned his tennis in California. Osuna first gained world notice with a peculiar doubles triumph at Wimbledon in 1960. He teamed with American Dennis Ralston on the spot, the two having never paired before.

They won the championship against a rugged field but not before having to survive a 16–14 fifth set against qualifiers Gerald Oakley and Humphrey Truman. Osuna won his only major singles title in 1963 in the United States championships and was ranked No. 1 in the world that year in large part as a result of his Forest Hills victory. He teamed with countryman Antonio Palafox to win the U.S. doubles in 1962 (with Ralston on the losing team) and the Wimbledon doubles in 1963. In 1962, he won the NCAA singles championship while playing for the University of Southern California. From 1958 to 1968, Osuna played 59 Davis Cup singles matches for Mexico before being killed in an air crash at Monterrey, Mexico, in 1969.

FRANK SEDGMAN (born October 29, 1927) was an athletic player with a fine volleying touch who came from Mount Albert, Victoria, Australia and was twice singles champion of his country (1949–50). He (with fellow Australian Ken McGregor) achieved a Grand Slam in doubles in 1951. He was also a United States singles champion in 1951 and 1952 and won the Wimbledon singles in 1952 as well. He played for the Australian Davis Cup squad from 1949 to 1952 and won a remarkable 25 of 28 matches played. Sedgman was the world's No. 1 ranked player in 1951 and 1952 and might have achieved an even more impressive record of victories in major world tournaments had he not turned professional in 1953, an action which at that time ended attempts to win the principal world tournaments, which were reserved for amateurs.

1980

HUGH LAWRENCE DOHERTY (born October 8, 1876; died August 11, 1919) was the first non-American to win the United States singles championship. He turned the trick in 1903 at the Newport Casino while on a tour of the U.S. with his brother. The previous year, he had teamed with his brother to win the U.S. doubles title and repeated that feat in 1903. Doherty won five straight Wimbledon singles titles starting in 1902 and was part of one of the most formidable doubles pairings of his time. He and his brother dominated doubles in England by winning the Wimbledon competition in 1897–1901 and 1903–05.

"Laurie" Doherty was also the British indoor champion in singles from 1901 to 1906. He was 12–0 in Davis Cup play.

REGINALD FRANK DOHERTY (born October 16, 1874; died December 29, 1910) often paired with his younger brother in a fearsome doubles team but was also a fine singles player in his own right. Doherty won the Wimbledon singles title four years running (1897–1900) and was the South African champion in both singles and doubles in 1909. His doubles triumphs included Wimbledon from 1897 to 1905, failing to win only in 1902 during that period. He also combined with Laurie Doherty to win the United States doubles crown in 1902 and 1903. Considered a more sensitive player than his brother, Reggie Doherty was less powerful than Laurie, who became one of the great players in the game's history.

LEWIS A. HOAD (born November 23, 1934). Hoad was easily the world's No. 1 player in 1956 when, at the top of his game, he became a professional and was forced off the world scene. He did return briefly in 1968 when many of the tournaments he had won as an amateur became open and admitted professionals. Hoad won the United States doubles in 1956, the singles titles at Wimbledon, France, Australia, and Germany as well as the doubles at Wimbledon, Australia, Italy, and Germany. All told, he won two Wimbledon singles (1956–57), three doubles (1953, 1955–56) and three French titles (singles, 1956; doubles, 1953; mixed doubles, 1954). Hoad had a powerful service that was the heart of his game although he was also a skillful volleyer. He played Davis Cup for Australia from 1953 to 1956 and later became a teaching pro in Spain.

KING GUSTAV V (born June 16, 1858; died 1950) was king of Sweden for longer than any ruler in the nation's history. He followed his father Oscar II to the throne on December 8, 1907, beginning a reign of nearly 43 years. He was such a popular monarch that, on his 80th birthday in 1938, he was presented with a personal gift of $1 million collected and presented by the Swedish people. Throughout his life, King Gustav was an enthusiastic tennis player and supporter of the game. In 1936, he donated the King's Cup for European internation competition. When Germany won the third annual competition in 1938, the original

Cup went to Berlin and was destroyed in an air raid during the late stages of World War II. Competition was renewed the year of the king's death with a new trophy. During the war, Gustav devoted much energy to assisting tennis players caught in the hostile atmosphere of the conflict. When Baron Gottfried von Cramm, the famed German champion, was jailed by the Nazi government, Gustav was able to secure his release and provided him with refuge in Sweden. Although officially neutral during both World Wars, Gustav's Sweden heavily favored the Allied cause in them and lent considerable support short of jeopardizing the formal neutrality.

KENNETH R. ROSEWALL (born November 2, 1934) was a native of Sydney who was Australian singles champion in 1953 and 1955 but enjoyed some of his finest moments at the United States championships. He won the singles title at Forest Hills in 1956 as well as the doubles and the mixed doubles. Then he turned professional, leaving the world circuit. When the open era enabled him to return, he remarkably won the U.S. Open singles in 1970 at 35. He was also a Wimbledon doubles champion in 1953 and 1956 and won the French singles in 1953. Rosewall was an Australian Davis Cup player from 1953 to 1956.

Kenneth R. Rosewall.

WORLD TENNIS ROLL OF HONOR

The following are the all-time greats of tennis— foreign players and those Americans not already elected to the Hall of Fame—and a listing of their major victories:

ANDERSON, JAMES O. (Australia); born September 17, 1895, at Enfield, New South Wales; died July 19, 1960.

Wimbledon champion, doubles 1924. Australian champion, singles 1922, 1924, 1925; doubles 1924. Member of Davis Cup team.

ANDERSON, MALCOLM JAMES (Australia); born March 5, 1935, at Rockhampton, Queensland.

United States champion, singles 1957. Australian champion, mixed doubles (with F. Muller) 1957. French champion, doubles (with A. J. Cooper) 1957. Member of Davis Cup team 1957, 1958.

ASHE, ARTHUR ROBERT (United States); born July 10, 1943, in Richmond, Va.

United States champion singles 1968. United States Open champion, singles 1968. United States clay court champion, singles 1968. United States Hard Court champion, singles 1963. United States Indoor champion, doubles 1967, 1970. United States Clay Court Open champion, doubles, 1970. Australian champion, singles, 1970. Member of Davis Cup team 1963 to 1968.

AUSSEM, CILLY (Germany); born January 4, 1909, in Cologne, Germany; died March 22, 1963.

Wimbledon champion, singles 1931. French champion, singles 1931; mixed doubles (with W. T. Tilden) 1930. German champion, singles 1927, 1930, 1931; mixed doubles 1926, 1928, 1935.

AUSTIN, TRACY ANN (United States); born December 12, 1962, in Redondo Beach, Calif.

United States Open champion, singles, 1979. Italian Open champion, singles, 1979. Wimbledon champion, mixed doubles, 1980. Colgate Series champion, 1980. Ranked No. 1 in United States, 1980.

Youngest-ever singles champion at U.S. Open (16 years, 9 months) and was youngest ever accepted to compete at Wimbledon (14 years, 6 months) in 1977. Losing semifinalist at Wimbledon in 1979.

Turned pro in October, 1978, and won first pro title at Stuttgart. In 1980, she earned $683,787 to

Perhaps one of the outstanding players in the game's history, Sweden's Bjorn Borg became the dominant Men's Singles performer in the late 1970's.

lead all women players and became the fastest ever to reach $1 million in career earnings.

Won U.S. Girls' 18 singles, 1977, 1978; U.S. 16 singles, 1978; U.S. 14 singles, 1975, 1976; U.S. 12 singles, 1974. Also won 16 other U.S. age group championships, eight each in singles and doubles, 1974–78.

BADDELEY, WILFRED (Great Britain); born January 11, 1872; died January 30, 1929.

Wimbledon champion, singles 1891, 1892, 1895; doubles (with his twin brother Herbert) 1891, 1894–96. The youngest men's singles winner of Wimbledon. He was 19 years 5 months 23 days old when he won the title in 1891.

BERNARD, MARCEL (France); born May 18, 1914, in Lille, France.

French champion, singles 1946; doubles 1936, 1946; mixed doubles 1935, 1936. Member of Davis Cup team 1935 to 1956.

BOLTON, MRS. NANCYE WYNNE (Australia); born June 10, 1917, in Melbourne.

Australian champion, singles 1937, 1940, 1946–1948, 1951; doubles 1936–1940, 1947–1949, 1952; mixed doubles 1940, 1947, 1948.

BORG, BJORN (Sweden); born June 6, 1956, in Sodertlage, Sweden.

Wimbledon champion, singles, 1976, 1977, 1978, 1979, 1980. French champion, singles, 1974, 1975, 1978, 1979, 1980. Italian champion, singles, 1974, 1978. United States Indoor champion, singles, 1977. Winner of Pepsi Grand Slam, 1977, 1978.

Won Grand Prix Masters, 1979, 1980.

Led Sweden to first victory ever in Davis Cup final at Stockholm, 1975.

Won men's record $1,019,345 in 1979. Married to former Romanian player Mariana Simionescu and living in Monte Carlo since 1976.

BOWREY, MRS. LESLEY TURNER (Australia); born August 16, 1942, in New South Wales.

United States champion, doubles, 1961. Wimbledon champion, doubles 1964; mixed doubles 1961, 1964. French champion, singles 1963, 1965; doubles 1964, 1965. Australian champion, doubles 1964, 1965, 1967; mixed doubles 1962, 1967. Italian champion singles 1967, 1968; doubles 1961, 1964, 1967; mixed doubles 1962, 1967. German champion, doubles 1962, 1964, 1965, 1967; mixed doubles 1962, 1963.

Earl H. Buchholz.

BOWREY, WILLIAM W. (Australia); born December 25, 1943, in Sydney.

Australian champion, singles 1968.

BRASHER, MRS. SHIRLEY BLOOMER (Great Britain); born June 13, 1934, at Grimsby.

French champion, singles 1957; doubles 1957; mixed doubles 1958. Italian champion, singles 1957; doubles 1958; mixed doubles 1958. Scandinavian covered court champion, doubles 1958; mixed doubles 1958. British hard court champion, singles 1957, 1958; doubles 1955, 1957; mixed doubles 1958–60. British covered court champion, doubles 1960; mixed 1960.

BROMWICH, JOHN EDWARD (Australia); born November 14, 1918, at New South Wales.

United States champion, doubles 1939, 1949, 1950; mixed doubles 1947. Wimbledon champion, doubles 1948, 1950; mixed doubles 1947, 1948; Australian champion, singles 1939, 1946; doubles 1938–40; 1946–50; mixed doubles 1938. Member of Davis Cup team 1937 to 1950.

BROWN, TOM (United States); born November 26, 1922, in San Francisco, Calif.

United States champion, mixed doubles 1948; Wimbledon champion, doubles 1946; mixed doubles 1946. Member of Davis Cup team 1950, 1953.

BUCHHOLZ, EARL H. (United States); born September 16, 1940, in St. Louis, Mo.

South African champion, singles 1960; Member of Davis Cup team 1959, 1960. Achieved a unique record as a junior when he won the junior titles of Australia, France, Wimbledon, and United States in sequence 1958–1959.

CASALS, ROSEMARY (United States); born September 16, 1948, in San Francisco, Calif.

United States champion, doubles 1967, 1971. United States Hard Court, singles 1965; doubles 1966, 1967; mixed doubles 1966. United States Indoor, doubles 1966, 1967, 1968. Wimbledon champion, doubles 1967, 1968, 1970, 1971; mixed doubles 1970. Italian champion, doubles 1967, 1970. South African champion, doubles 1967–1970. Irish champion, doubles, 1968. Welsh champion, doubles 1970; mixed doubles 1970. Canadian champion, doubles 1970. Swiss champion, singles 1970; doubles 1970. Swedish champion, doubles 1970. Argentine champion, doubles 1968. Member of Wightman Cup (1967, 1976, 1977, 1979, 1980) and Federation Cup teams (1967, 1976, 1977, 1978, 1979, 1980).

CAWLEY, MRS. EVONNE GOOLAGONG (Australia); born July 31, 1951. Wimbledon Champion, Singles 1971, 1980; doubles, 1974. French Champion, singles 1971. Italian Champion, singles, 1973. Australian Champion, singles, 1974, 1975, 1976, 1977, 1978; doubles, 1974, 1975, 1976, 1978. Canadian Champion, singles, 1972, 1973.

CHAMBERS, DOROTHEA LAMBERT DOUGLAS (Great Britain); born 1872, in Ealing; died October 4, 1960.

Wimbledon champion, singles 1903, 1904, 1906, 1910, 1911, 1913, 1914; doubles 1903, 1904; mixed doubles 1903, 1906.

CONNORS, JIMMY (United States); born September 2, 1952, in East St. Louis, Illinois.

United States champion, singles, 1974, 1976, 1978; singles runner-up 1975, 1977; doubles champion, 1975. Wimbledon champion, singles, 1974; doubles, 1973. Australian champion, singles, 1974. South African champion, singles, 1973, 1974. French champion, doubles, 1973.

Greatest money winner in history of tennis with career total of $3 million through 1980. Ranked as undisputed No. 1 in world in 1974, winning virtually every major tournament entered. Denied entry to French and Italian Opens, 1974, due to

Dorothea Lambert Douglas Chambers.

Ashley John Cooper.

contract with World Team Tennis club (Baltimore Banners). Suits against French Federation and ITF settled out of court.

Grand Prix Masters champion, 1977. WCT singles champion, 1977, 1980. United States Indoor champion, singles, 1973, 1974, 1975. United States Clay Court champion, singles, 1974, 1976, 1978, 1979. Member United States Davis Cup team, 1971 and 1975.

Ranked No. 1 in United States, 1973 (co-ranked with Stan Smith), 1974, 1976, 1977, 1978. Won $922,657 in 1977, a single-season record. In 1976 won 106 of 118 matches played.

COOPER, ASHLEY JOHN (Australia); born September 15, 1936, in Melbourne.

United States champion, singles 1958; doubles 1957. Wimbledon champion, singles 1958. French champion, doubles 1957, 1958. Australian champion, singles 1957, 1958; doubles 1958. Member of Davis Cup team in 1957, 1958.

COURT, MARGARET SMITH (Australia); born July 16, 1942, in Albury, New South Wales.

United States, singles 1962, 1965, 1968, 1969; doubles 1963, 1968, 1969; mixed doubles 1963–1965. United States Open, singles 1969, 1970; doubles 1968, 1970; mixed doubles, 1969, 1970.

Wimbledon champion, singles 1963, 1965, 1970; doubles 1964, 1965, 1969; mixed doubles 1963, 1965, 1966, 1968, 1975. French champion, singles 1962, 1964, 1969, 1970, 1973; doubles 1964, 1965, 1973; mixed doubles 1963–1965, 1969. Australian champion, singles 1960–1966, 1969–1971, 1973; doubles 1961–1963, 1965, 1969–1971, 1973; mixed doubles 1963, 1964. Italian champion, singles 1962–1964; doubles 1963, 1964, 1968; mixed 1961, 1968. Canadian champion, singles 1970; doubles 1970, 1975. German champion, singles 1964–1966; doubles 1964–1969; mixed 1965, 1966. Irish champion, singles 1968. South African champion, singles 1968–1971; doubles 1966; mixed doubles 1966. Welsh champion, singles 1969. Member of Federation Cup team from 1963 to 1971.

CRAWFORD, JOHN HERBERT (Australia); born March 22, 1908, in Albury, New South Wales.

Wimbledon champion, singles 1933; doubles 1935; mixed doubles 1930. French champion, singles 1933; doubles 1935; mixed 1933. Australian champion, singles 1931–33; doubles 1929, 1930, 1932, 1935; mixed 1931–33. Member of Davis Cup team from 1928 to 1937.

DAVIDSON, SVEN (Sweden); born July 13, 1928, in Boras.

Wimbledon champion, doubles 1958. French champion, singles 1957. German champion, singles 1958. Member of Davis Cup team from 1950 to 1960.

DECUGIS, MAX (France); born February 21, 1882, at Paris; died September 6, 1978.

Wimbledon champion, doubles 1911. French champion, singles 1903, 1904, 1907–1909, 1912–1914; doubles 1902–1909, 1911–1914, 1920; mixed doubles 1904–1910, 1912–1914, 1920, 1921. German champion, singles 1901, 1902. Member of Davis Cup team.

DIBBS, EDDIE (United States); born February 23, 1951, in Brooklyn, New York.

German champion, singles, 1973, 1974, 1976. Iranian champion, singles, 1975. Ranked No. 2 in United States, 1976.

Ranked No. 4 in U.S. in 1978 when he was world money-earnings leader with $582,872.

DOD, CHARLOTTE (Great Britain); born September 24, 1871, at Bebington; died October 10, 1962.

Wimbledon champion, singles 1887, 1888, 1891–1893; ("Lottie" Dod was Wimbledon's youngest champion when, in 1887, she won the title at 15 years 10 months); doubles, 1886–1888; mixed doubles 1889, 1892. Irish champion, singles 1887; mixed doubles 1887.

DROBNY, JAROSLAV (Czechoslovakia); born October 12, 1921, at Prague.

Wimbledon champion, singles 1954. French champion, singles 1951, 1952; doubles 1948; mixed doubles 1948. Italian champion, singles 1950, 1951, 1953; doubles 1951, 1952, 1954, 1956. German champion, singles 1950; doubles 1952. South African champion 1954. Member of Davis Cup team 1946 to 1949.

DRYSDALE, CLIFFORD (South Africa); born May 26, 1941, at Nelsprint, Transvaal.

German champion, singles 1965. South African champion, singles 1965; doubles 1964.

DU PLOOY, MRS. ANNETTE VAN ZYL (South Africa); born September 25, 1943, at Pretoria.

French champion, mixed doubles 1966. Italian champion, doubles 1965, 1966. German champion, singles 1968; doubles 1963, 1968; mixed doubles 1968. South African champion, singles 1963; doubles 1962, 1963, 1965, 1966, 1968.

DURR, FRANÇOISE (France); born December 25, 1942, at Beziers.

French champion, singles 1967; doubles 1967–1971; mixed doubles 1968, 1971. German champion, singles 1967.

EMERSON, ROY (Australia); born November 3, 1936, at Kingsway, Queensland.

United States champion, 1961, 1964; doubles 1959, 1960, 1965, 1966. Wimbledon champion, singles 1964, 1965; doubles 1959, 1961. French champion, singles 1963, 1967; doubles 1960–1965. Australian champion, singles 1961, 1963–1967; doubles 1962, 1966, 1969. Italian champion, doubles 1959, 1961, 1966; mixed doubles 1961. German champion, singles 1967; doubles 1960. South African champion, singles 1966; doubles 1966. Member of Davis Cup team from 1957 to 1967.

FLETCHER, KENNETH (Australia); born June 15, 1940, in Queensland.

United States champion, mixed doubles 1963. Wimbledon champion, doubles 1966; mixed doubles 1963, 1965, 1966, 1968. French champion, doubles 1964; mixed doubles 1963–1965. Aus-

Roy Emerson.

tralian champion, mixed doubles 1963, 1964; German champion, mixed doubles 1962.

FRASER, NEALE ANDREW (Australia); born October 3, 1933 at St. Kilda, Melbourne.

United States champion, singles 1959, 1960; doubles 1957, 1959, 1960; mixed doubles 1958–1960. Wimbledon champion, singles 1960; doubles 1959, 1961; mixed doubles 1962. French champion, doubles 1958, 1960, 1962. Australian champion, doubles 1957, 1958, 1962; mixed 1956. Italian champion, doubles 1959, 1961. German champion, doubles 1960. Member of Davis Cup team from 1958 to 1963.

GERULAITIS, VITAS K. (United States); born July 26, 1954, in Brooklyn, New York.

Wimbledon champion, doubles, 1975. Italian champion, singles, 1977, 1979. Australian champion, singles, 1978. Member, United States Davis Cup team, 1976–80.

GORE, ARTHUR WENTWORTH (Great Britain); born January 2, 1868, at Lyndhurst, Hampshire; died December 1, 1928.

Wimbledon champion, singles 1901, 1908, 1909; doubles 1909. Member of Davis Cup team in 1900, 1907, and 1912.

GOTTFRIED, BRIAN (United States); born January 27, 1952, in Baltimore, Maryland.

Top doubles player. Wimbledon champion, doubles 1976. Italian champion, doubles 1974, 1975, 1976. French champion, doubles 1975, 1977. South African champion, doubles 1976. Japan champion, doubles 1975. United States Clay Court champion, doubles 1976.

GRAEBNER, MRS. CAROLE CALDWELL (United States); born June 24, 1943, at Pittsburgh, Pa.

United States champion, doubles 1965. Australian champion, doubles 1966. United States clay court champion, doubles 1964, 1965. Member of Wightman Cup (1964, 1965, 1967) and Federation Cup (1963, 1965, 1966) teams.

GRAEBNER, CLARK EDWARD (United States); born November 4, 1943, at Cleveland, Ohio.

French champion, doubles 1966. United States Clay court champion, singles 1968; doubles 1963, 1965–1967, 1969, 1970. United States Indoor champion, singles 1971. United States Hard Court, singles 1969. Member of Davis Cup team 1963 to 1970.

HAYGARTH, MRS. RENÉE SCHNUURMAN (South Africa); born October 26, 1939, at Durban, Natal.

French champion, doubles 1959, 1961–1963; mixed doubles 1962. Australian champion, doubles 1959. South African champion, doubles 1958, 1960, 1961. German champion, singles 1963; doubles 1961. United States clay court champion, doubles 1959.

HENKEL, HENNER ERNST OTTO (Germany); born October 9, 1915, at Posen; killed at Stalingrad, 1942.

United States champion, doubles 1937. French champion, singles 1937; doubles 1937. German champion singles 1937, 1939; doubles 1935, 1939; mixed doubles 1935. Member of Davis Cup team 1934 to 1939.

HEWITT, ROBERT A. J. (South Africa); born January 12, 1940, in New South Wales, Australia.

United States Open champion, doubles, 1977. U.S. Open Champion, mixed doubles, 1979. Wimbledon champion, doubles 1962; 1964, 1967, 1972, 1978; mixed doubles, 1977, 1979. Australian champion, doubles, 1963, 1964; mixed 1961.

Clark Graebner.

French champion, doubles, 1972; mixed doubles, 1979. Italian champion, doubles 1963, 1964, 1967. German champion, doubles 1961–63, 1967, 1977. South African champion, doubles 1967. United States clay court champion, doubles 1960. Canadian champion, doubles, 1976, 1977.

HILLYARD, MRS. BLANCHE BINGLEY (Great Britain); born November 3, 1863, at Greenford, Middlesex; died November 16, 1938.

Wimbledon champion, singles 1886, 1889, 1894, 1897, 1899, 1900; doubles 1893–1897, 1906, 1907; mixed doubles 1888, 1893, 1907. German champion, singles 1897, 1900. Irish champion, singles 1888, 1894, 1897. Welsh champion, singles 1888.

HUGHES, GEORGE PATRICK (Great Britain); born December 21, 1902, at Sutton, Coldfield.

Wimbledon champion, doubles 1936. French champion, doubles 1933. Australian champion, doubles 1934. Member of Davis Cup team.

JANES, MRS. CHRISTINE TRUMAN (Great Britain); born January 16, 1941, at Loughton, Essex.

French champion, singles 1959. Australian champion, doubles 1960. Italian champion, singles 1959; doubles 1958. German champion, doubles 1960. Member of Wightman Cup team.

JONES, MRS. ADRIANNE SHIRLEY HARDON (Great Britain); born October 17, 1938, at Birmingham.

Wimbledon champion, singles 1969; mixed doubles 1969. French champion, singles 1961, 1966; doubles 1963, 1968, 1969. Italian champion, singles 1966; doubles 1969. Member of Wightman Cup team 1957 to 1971.

KING, MRS. BILLIE JEAN MOFFITT (United States); born November 22, 1943, at Long Beach, Calif.

United States champion, singles 1967, 1971, 1972, 1974; doubles 1964, 1967, 1974, 1978, 1980; mixed 1967, 1973, 1976. Wimbledon champion, singles 1966–1968, 1972–73, 1975; doubles 1961, 1962, 1965, 1967, 1968, 1970, 1971–73, 1979; mixed doubles 1967, 1973–74. Australian champion, singles 1968; mixed doubles 1968. French champion, singles 1972; mixed doubles 1967, 1970. German champion, singles 1971; doubles 1971. Italian champion, singles 1970; doubles 1970. South African champion, singles 1966, 1967, 1969; doubles 1967–1970, mixed doubles 1967. Irish champion, singles 1963–1969; doubles, 1963; mixed doubles 1969. New Zealand champion, doubles 1969. Argentine champion, singles 1967. Swiss champion, doubles 1969. United States indoor champion, singles 1966–1967; doubles 1966, 1967, 1971; mixed doubles 1966, 1967. United States hard court champion, singles 1966; doubles, 1966. United States clay court champion, doubles 1960. Member of Wightman Cup (1961–67, 1970, 1978) and Federation Cup (1963–67, 1976–79) teams.

KNODE, MRS. DOROTHY HEAD (United States); born July 4, 1925, at Richmond, Calif.

German champion, singles 1950; doubles 1950, 1952; mixed doubles 1952. United States clay court champion, singles 1955, 1958, 1960; doubles 1955, 1956, 1958. Member of Wightman Cup team.

LARCOMBE, MRS. ETHEL THOMSON (Great Britain); born June 22, 1879, at Hampton Hill, Middlesex; died August 11, 1965.

Wimbledon champion, singles 1912; doubles 1911–13; mixed doubles 1912, 1914.

LAVER, RODNEY GEORGE (Australia); born August 9, 1938, at Rockhampton, Queensland.

United States champion, singles 1962. United States Open champion, singles 1969. Wimbledon champion, singles 1961, 1962, 1968, 1969; doubles 1971; mixed doubles 1959, 1960. Canadian champion, singles 1970. French champion, singles 1962, 1969; doubles 1961; mixed doubles 1962. German champion, singles 1961, 1962. Australian champion, singles 1960, 1962, 1969; doubles 1959–1961, 1969. Italian champion, singles 1962, 1971; doubles 1962. South African champion, singles 1969, 1970. Member of Davis Cup team 1959 to 1962.

LITTLE, MRS. DOROTHY ROUND (Great Britain); born July 13, 1909, at Dudley, Worcestershire.

Mrs. Dorothy Head Knode.

Wimbledon champion, singles 1934, 1937; mixed doubles 1934, 1935, 1937. Australian champion, singles 1935. Member of Wightman Cup team.

LLOYD, MRS. CHRIS EVERT (United States); born December 21, 1954, in Fort Lauderdale, Florida.

United States Open champion, singles, 1975, 1976, 1977, 1978, after being a losing semifinalist four years in a row (the first time at age 16). Wimbledon champion, singles 1974, 1976; doubles, 1976. French champion, singles 1974, 1975, 1979, 1980; doubles, 1974, 1975. Italian champion, singles, 1974, 1975, 1980; doubles, 1974, 1975. Canadian champion, singles, 1974.

United States Clay Court champion, singles, 1972, 1973, 1974, 1975, 1979, 1980. Won Family Circle Cup, 1974, 1975, 1976, 1977; doubles, 1977. Won Colgate Inaugural, 1976. Won L'Eggs World Series, 1975, 1976, 1977. Virginia Slims champion 1972, 1973, 1975, 1977, and runner-up 1974, 1976.

Over four-year span from 1974 through 1977, won 94 percent of matches played (342 of 364), including 103 of 110 in 1974 and 94 of 100 in 1975. Began open tournament play in 1969 and won 500th match on June 23, 1977, in third round at Wimbledon (over Mrs. Winnie Shaw Wooldridge, 6-0, 6-2). Turned pro on eighteenth birthday after spurning over $50,000 in prize money, but then won $142,949 in 1973. Earned women's world record $503,134 in 1977. In first seven years as a pro, won $2,742,621, becoming first woman to earn more than $1 million in tennis career.

Member Wightman Cup team nine times (1971–73, 1975–80) and United States Federation Cup championship team in 1977, 1979, 1980. Won United States 14 in 1968, United States 16 in 1970, United States 18 in 1971.

Won first major pro tourney (Lady Gotham Classic) in New York, 1973, and won her 100th pro tournament (Lynda Carter Classic) at Deerfield Beach, Fla., Oct. 19, 1980. Ranked United States No. 1, 1975, 1976, 1977, 1978, winning 93 of 157 tournaments entered during the span from 1973 to 1979. Before losing to Tracy Austin in the 1979 Italian semifinals, she won 125 straight matches on clay.

Full name Christine Marie Evert. Father,

teaching pro, James Evert, was Canadian champion, singles, 1947; doubles, 1947. Sister, Jeanne, played Virginia Slims Circuit for several years and was twice on U.S. Wightman Cup squad. Her husband, John Lloyd, played for Britain in the Davis Cup final against the U.S. in 1979.

LONG, MRS. THELMA COYNE (Australia); born May 30, 1918, at Sydney.

Australian champion, singles 1952, 1954; doubles 1936–40, 1947–49, 1951, 1952, 1956, 1958; mixed doubles 1951, 1952, 1954, 1955. German champion, singles 1956. Irish champion, singles 1949. Italian champion, doubles 1952, 1956, 1957; mixed doubles 1956, 1957.

LUTZ, ROBERT CHARLES (United States); born August 29, 1947, at Lancaster, Pa.

United States champion, doubles 1968. United States Open champion, doubles 1968. Australian champion, doubles 1970. United States indoor champion, doubles 1966–69. United States clay court champion, doubles 1968. United States hard court champion, doubles 1966, 1969. Member of Davis Cup team, 1968–70, 1975, 1977–79.

MACKAY, BARRY BRUCE (United States); born August 31, 1935 at Cincinnati, Ohio.

Italian champion, singles 1960. United States clay court champion, singles 1960; doubles 1958. United States indoor champion, singles 1960, doubles 1957–1959. Member of Davis Cup team 1956 to 1960.

MAKO, C. GENE (United States); born January 24, 1916, in Budapest, Hungary.

United States champion, doubles 1936, 1938; mixed doubles 1936. Wimbledon champion, doubles 1937, 1938. United States clay court champion, doubles 1934, 1939. Member of Davis Cup team 1935 to 1938.

MATHIEU, MRS. RENÉ SIMONE (France); born January 31, 1908, at Neuilly-sur-Seine.

Wimbledon champion, doubles 1933, 1934, 1937. French champion, singles 1938, 1939; doubles 1933, 1934, 1936–39; mixed doubles 1937, 1938.

McENROE, JOHN (United States); born February 15, 1959, at New York.

United States Open champion, singles 1979, 1980. United States Open champion, doubles 1979. Wimbledon champion, doubles 1979. Grand Prix Masters champion, 1978. WCT Finals champion, 1979.

René Simone Mathieu.

Led Grand Prix, 1979, 1980. Earned $1,005,238 in 1979 and led world in money winnings with $1,026,383, then a record, in 1980. Ranked No. 1 in the United States in 1979, 1980.

Reached quarterfinals at Wimbledon at age 18 in 1977, won NCAA singles title in 1978 as freshman for Stanford, only third man ever to do so, and turned pro that June, finishing year ranked No. 4 in U.S. and winning four Grand Prix events.

Led U.S. to Davis Cup in 1978 and 1979 by winning first 11 matches and first 31 sets he played before losing twice when U.S. was eliminated by Argentina in the 1980 American Zone final. Member of Davis Cup team, 1978–80.

MCGRATH, VIVIAN (Australia); born February 17, 1916, in New South Wales.

Australian champion, singles 1937; doubles 1935. Italian champion, doubles 1935. German champion, doubles 1937. Member of Davis Cup team.

MCGREGOR, KEN (Australia); born June 2, 1929, at Adelaide.

United States champion, doubles 1951; mixed doubles 1950. Wimbledon champion, doubles 1951, 1952. Australian champion, singles 1952; doubles 1951, 1952. French champion, doubles 1951, 1952. Member of Davis Cup team 1950 to 1952.

MCKINLEY, CHARLES (United States); born January 5, 1941, at St. Louis, Mo.

United States champion, doubles 1961, 1963, 1964. Wimbledon champion, singles 1963. United States clay court champion, singles 1962, 1963; doubles 1961, 1964. United States indoor champion, singles 1962, 1964; doubles 1962, 1963, 1965. Member of Davis Cup team 1960 to 1965.

MCMILLAN, FREW DONALD (South Africa); May 20, 1942, at Springs.

United States champion, doubles, 1977; mixed doubles, 1977, 1978. Wimbledon champion, doubles 1967, 1972, 1978; mixed doubles, 1978. South African champion, doubles 1965, 1967; mixed doubles 1965. German champion, doubles 1967. Italian champion, doubles 1967. Member of Davis Cup team 1965 to 1978.

MENZIES, MRS. KAY STAMMERS (Great Britain); born April 3, 1914, St. Albans, Hertfordshire.

Wimbledon champion, doubles 1935, 1936; French champion, doubles 1935; South African champion, doubles 1948. Member of Wightman Cup team.

MORTIMER, ANGELA (Great Britain); born April 21, 1932, at Plymouth.

Wimbledon champion, singles 1961; doubles 1955; French champion, singles 1955; Australian champion, singles 1958; German champion, doubles 1957. Welsh champion, singles 1951, 1957–

Gardnar Mulloy.

tralian champion, doubles 1965, 1967, 1970, 1971; doubles 1965, 1966, 1968–70. Italian champion, singles 1969; doubles 1971; mixed doubles 1964. German champion, singles 1968; mixed doubles 1966. Welsh champion, singles 1967. Canadian champion, doubles 1969. Wimbledon champion, singles 1970, 1971. Member of Davis Cup team 1963 to 1967.

NIELSEN, KURT (Denmark); born November 19, 1930, at Copenhagen.

United States champion, mixed doubles 1957. United States indoor champion, singles 1957; doubles 1953. Member of Davis Cup team from 1948 to 1960.

NUTHALL, BETTY MAY (Great Britain); born May 23, 1911, at Surbiton.

United States champion, singles 1930; doubles 1930, 1931, 1933; mixed doubles 1929, 1931. French champion, doubles 1931; mixed doubles 1931, 1932. Member of Wightman Cup team.

OKKER, TOM (Netherlands); born February 22, 1944, at Haarlem.

60. Member of Wightman Cup team.

MULLOY, GARDNAR (United States); born November 22, 1914, at Miami, Fla.

United States champion, doubles 1942, 1945, 1946, 1948. Wimbledon champion, doubles 1957. United States clay court champion, doubles 1946. Member of Davis Cup team 1946 to 1957.

NAVRATILOVA, MARTINA (United States); born October 18, 1956, in Prague, Czechoslovakia.

Czechoslovakian champion, singles 1972, 1973, 1974. United States Open champion, doubles 1977, 1978, 1980. Wimbledon champion, singles 1978, 1979, doubles 1976, 1979. French champion, doubles 1975. Italian champion, doubles 1975. Scottish champion, singles 1977. Virginia Slims champion, 1978.

Defected to United States during 1975 United States Open, creating international sensation. Settled in Dallas, Texas, and became U.S. citizen.

In 1979, she won 13 tournaments of 25 entered, was ranked No. 1 in the world and set a single-season women's record for winnings with $747,-548.

NEWCOMBE, JOHN (Australia); born May 23, 1944, at Sydney, New South Wales.

United States champion, singles 1967; doubles 1967. French champion, doubles 1967, 1969. Aus-

Martina Navratilova, a former Czechoslovak star who became an American citizen, unleashes one of the powerful strokes that mark her strong style.

Italian champion, singles 1968; doubles 1968. German champion, singles 1970; doubles 1968; mixed doubles 1967. South African champion, singles 1968; doubles 1968. Irish champion, singles 1968. Member of Davis Cup team 1964 to 1968.

OLMEDO, ALEJANDRO (Peru); born March 24, 1936, at Arequipa.

United States champion, doubles 1958. Wimbledon champion, singles 1959. Australian champion, singles 1959. United States clay court champion, doubles 1956. United States indoor champion, singles 1959; doubles 1959. Member of United States Davis Cup team 1958, 1959.

PARKE, JAMES CECIL (Great Britain); born July 26, 1881, at Clones, Ireland; died 1942.

Wimbledon champion, mixed doubles 1910, 1912, 1914. Australian champion, singles 1912; doubles 1912. Member of Davis Cup team.

PATTERSON, GERALD L. (Australia); born December 17, 1895, at Melbourne; died June 13, 1967.

United States champion, doubles 1919. Wimbledon champion, singles 1919, 1922; mixed doubles 1920. Australian champion, singles 1927; doubles 1914, 1922, 1925–1927. Member of Davis Cup team 1919 to 1928.

PATTY, J. EDWARD [BUDGE] (United States); born February 11, 1924, at Little Rock, Ark.

Wimbledon champion, singles 1950; doubles 1957. French champion, singles 1950; mixed doubles 1946. Italian champion, singles 1954. German champion, singles 1953, 1954; doubles 1953–55. South African champion, doubles 1954. United States indoor champion, mixed doubles, 1950. Member of Davis Cup team 1951.

PETRA, YVAN (France); born March 18, 1916, in Indo-China.

Wimbledon champion, singles 1946. French champion, singles 1945; doubles 1938, 1946; mixed doubles 1937. Member of Davis Cup team 1937 to 1947.

PIETRANGELI, NICOLA (Italy); born September 11, 1933, in Tunis.

French champion, singles 1959, 1960; doubles 1959; mixed doubles 1958. Italian champion, singles 1957, 1961. German champion, singles 1960. South African champion, mixed doubles 1962. Member of Davis Cup team 1954 to 1968.

PIM, JOSHUA (Great Britain); born May 20,

Tom Okker.

1869, in Ireland; died April 15, 1942.

Wimbledon champion, singles 1893, 1894; doubles 1890, 1893. Irish champion, singles 1893–95; doubles 1890, 1891, 1893–95. Member of Davis Cup team 1902.

PRICE, MRS. SANDRA REYNOLDS (South Africa); born March 4, 1939, at Bloemfontein.

French champion, doubles 1959, 1961, 1962. Australian champion, doubles 1959; mixed 1959. German champion, singles 1960–62; doubles 1961. South African champion, singles 1959, 1961; doubles 1959–61; mixed 1962. United States clay court champion 1959.

QUIST, ADRIAN KARL (Australia); born August 4, 1913, at Medindia, South Australia.

United States champion, doubles 1939. Wimbledon champion, doubles 1935, 1950. French champion, doubles 1935. Australian champion, singles 1936, 1940, 1948; doubles 1936–40, 1946–50. German champion, doubles 1934. Member of Davis Cup team 1933 to 1948.

RALSTON, RICHARD DENNIS (United States); born July 27, 1942, at Bakersfield, Calif.

William Renshaw and Ernest Renshaw.

Canadian champion, singles 1969. Argentine champion, singles 1966, 1967. United States clay court champion, singles 1966; United States clay court champion, singles 1966. United States indoor champion, singles 1968. Member of Davis Cup team 1966 to 1970.

RIESSEN, MARTIN CLARE (United States); born December 4, 1941, at Hinsdale, Ill.

United States champion, mixed doubles 1969, 1970. Italian champion, doubles 1968; mixed doubles 1968. German champion, doubles 1969; mixed doubles 1969. Canadian champion, doubles 1970. Swiss champion, doubles 1969. French champion, mixed doubles 1969. South African champion, mixed doubles 1968. Member of Davis Cup team 1961 to 1967.

ROCHE, ANTHONY DALTON (Australia); born May 17, 1945, at Tarcutta, New South Wales.

United States champion, doubles 1967. Wimbledon, 1965, 1968–1970. French champion, singles 1966; doubles 1967, 1969. Australian

United States champion, doubles 1961, 1963, 1964. Wimbledon champion, doubles 1960. French champion, doubles 1966. Argentine champion, doubles 1966. United States clay court champion, singles 1964, 1965; doubles 1961, 1964, 1966. United States hard court champion singles 1964, 1965; doubles 1964, 1965. United States indoor champion, 1963; doubles 1963–65.

RENSHAW, ERNEST (Great Britain); born January 3, 1861; died September 2, 1899.

Wimbledon champion, singles 1888; doubles 1880, 1881, 1884–86, 1888, 1889; mixed doubles 1888. Irish champion, singles 1883, 1887, 1888, 1892; doubles 1881, 1883–85.

RENSHAW, WILLIAM (Great Britain); born January 3, 1861; died August 12, 1904.

Wimbledon champion, singles 1881–86, 1889; doubles 1880, 1881, 1884–86, 1888, 1889. Irish champion, singles 1880–82; doubles 1881, 1883–85.

RICHEY, GEORGE CLIFFORD, JR. (United States); born December 31, 1946, San Angelo, Tex.

Martin Riessen.

Anthony Dalton Roche.

champion, singles 1951. Italian champion, doubles 1951. United States indoor champion, singles 1952, 1958, 1961. Member of Davis Cup team in 1951.

SEGURA, FRANCISCO (Ecuador); born June 20, 1921, at Guayaquil.

United States clay court champion, singles 1944; doubles 1945. United States indoor champion, singles 1946.

SMITH, STANLEY ROGER (United States); born December 14, 1946, at Pasadena, Calif.

United States champion, singles 1971, doubles 1968, 1971. Australian champion, doubles 1970. United States indoor champion, singles 1969, 1970, 1966–70. United States Open indoor champion, doubles 1970. United States clay court, doubles 1968. United States hard court, singles 1966–68; doubles 1966. Member of Davis Cup team 1968–73, 1975, 1977–79.

SOLOMON, HAROLD (United States); born September 17, 1952, in Washington, D.C.

champion, doubles 1965, 1967. Italian champion, singles 1966. Swiss champion, singles 1970. Irish champion, singles 1970. United States Pro Championship, singles 1970. Member of Davis Cup team 1965 to 1967.

ROSE, MERVYN (Australia); born January 23, 1930, at Coffs Harbor, New South Wales.

United States champion, doubles 1952, 1953. Wimbledon champion, doubles 1954; mixed 1957. Australian champion, singles 1954; doubles 1954. French champion, singles 1958. Italian champion, singles 1958. German champion, singles 1957; doubles 1957; mixed 1957. Member of Davis Cup team 1951 to 1957.

SANTANA, MANUEL (Spain); born May 10, 1938, at Madrid.

United States champion, singles 1965. Wimbledon champion, singles 1966. French champion, singles 1961, 1964; doubles 1963. South African champion, singles 1967. United States indoor champion, doubles 1964. Member of Davis Cup team 1958 to 1968.

SAVITT, RICHARD (United States); born March 4, 1927, at Bayonne, N.J.

Wimbledon champion, singles 1951. Australian

Manuel Santana.

South African champion, singles 1975, 1976. United States Amateur Clay Court champion, singles, 1971. Ranked in United States first ten six times from 1971 to 1977.

SPERLING, MRS. HILDA KRAHWINKEL (Germany and Denmark); born March 26, 1908.

Wimbledon champion, mixed doubles 1933. French champion, singles 1935. German champion, singles 1934, 1935, 1937–39; doubles 1932, 1937; mixed doubles 1932–34.

STERRY, MRS. CHARLOTTE COOPER (Great Britain); born September 12, 1870, at Ealing; died October 10, 1970.

Wimbledon champion, singles 1895, 1896, 1898, 1901, 1908; doubles 1908; mixed doubles 1894–98, 1900, 1908. German champion, singles 1899. Irish champion, singles 1895, 1898.

STOEFEN, LESTER ROLLO (United States); born March 30, 1911, at Des Moines, Iowa; died February 10, 1970.

United States champion, doubles 1933, 1934. Wimbledon champion, doubles 1934. United States indoor champion, singles 1934; doubles 1934.

STOLLE, FRED (Australia); born October 8, 1938 at Hornsby, New South Wales.

United States champion, singles 1966; doubles 1965, 1966; mixed doubles 1962, 1965. Wimbledon champion, doubles 1962, 1964; mixed doubles 1961, 1964. French champion, singles 1965; doubles 1965, 1968. Australian champion, doubles 1963, 1964, 1966; mixed doubles 1962. Italian champion, doubles 1963, 1964; mixed doubles 1962. German champion, singles 1966; doubles 1961, 1963, 1966; mixed doubles 1963. South African champion, doubles 1966; mixed doubles 1966.

STURGESS, ERIC (South Africa); born May 10, 1920, at Johannesburg.

United States champion, mixed doubles 1949. Wimbledon champion, mixed doubles 1949, 1950. French champion, doubles 1947; mixed doubles 1947, 1949. German champion, singles 1952; mixed doubles 1952. South African champion, singles 1939, 1940, 1946, 1948–54, 1957; doubles 1946–48, 1951–53, 1955, 1957; mixed doubles 1940, 1946–48, 1951, 1953. Member of Davis Cup team 1947 to 1951.

SUSMAN, MRS. KAREN HANTZE (United States); born December, 1942, at San Diego, Calif.

United States champion, doubles 1964; Wimbledon champion, singles 1962; doubles 1961, 1962. Member of Wightman Cup team.

TANNER, ROSCOE (United States); born October 15, 1951, at Chattanooga, Tennessee.

Japanese champion, singles, 1976. Australian champion, singles, 1977. Losing semifinalist at Wimbledon, singles, 1975, 1976, losing finalist (to Borg in five sets), 1979.

Bullet-like service (clocked at 140 mph) helped him become semifinalist at U.S. Open, 1974, 1979.

TODD, MRS. PATRICIA CANNING (United States); born July 22, 1922, at San Francisco, Calif.

Wimbledon champion, doubles 1947. French champion, singles 1947; doubles 1948; mixed doubles 1948. United States clay court champion, doubles 1951. United States indoor champion 1942, 1948; doubles 1952. Member of Wightman Cup team.

VILAS, GUILLERMO (Argentina) born August 17, 1952, at Mar del Plata, Argentina.

United States Open champion, singles, 1977. Canadian Open champion, singles, 1974, 1976; doubles, 1974. French champion, singles, 1977. Won South American championship, singles, 1973, 1974, 1975, 1976, 1977, 1978. Australian champion, singles 1978, 1979. Italian Open champion, singles 1980. First in Grand Prix standings, 1974, 1975, 1977.

VIVIEN, MRS. MARGARET CRAFT SCRIVEN (Great Britain); born August 18, 1912, at Leeds.

French champion, singles 1933, 1934; doubles 1935; mixed doubles 1933. Member of Wightman Cup team.

WADE, SARAH VIRGINIA (Great Britain); born October 7, 1945, at Bournemouth.

United States Open champion, singles, 1968. Wimbledon champion, singles, 1977. Italian champion, singles 1971; doubles 1968, 1971. Member of Wightman Cup team 1965 to 1971.

WATSON, MAUD (Great Britain); born 1863; died November 16, 1934.

Wimbledon champion, singles 1884, 1885. Irish champion, singles 1884, 1885.

USTA National Tennis Center, Flushing Meadow Park, N.Y.

Elizabeth Ryan.

LEADING TENNIS PLAYERS OF TODAY

Name	Country	Date of Birth
John Alexander	Australia	July 4, 1951
Victor Amaya	U.S.A.	July 2, 1954
Vijay Amritraj	India	December 14, 1953
Helena Anliot	Sweden	September 26, 1956
Julie Anthony	U.S.A.	January 13, 1948
Lea Antonoplis	U.S.A.	January 20, 1959
Arthur Ashe	U.S.A.	July 10, 1943
Tracy Ann Austin	U.S.A.	December 12, 1962
Syd Ball	Australia	January 24, 1950
Corrado Barazzutti	Italy	February 19, 1953
Sue Barker	Great Britain	April 19, 1956
Ove Bengston	Sweden	April 5, 1945
Paolo Bertolucci	Italy	August 3, 1951
Byron Bertram	South Africa	October 29, 1952
Fiorella Bonicelli	Uruguay	December 21, 1951
Bjorn Borg	Sweden	June 6, 1956
Jeff Borowiak	U.S.A.	September 25, 1949
Linky Boshoff	South Africa	November 12, 1956
Maria Bueno	Brazil	October 11, 1939
Martine Bureau	France	June 26, 1960
Ricardo Cano	Argentina	February 26, 1951
Mary Carillo	U.S.A.	March 15, 1957
Claudia Casablanca	Argentina	March 21, 1960
Rosemary Casals	U.S.A.	September 14, 1948
Jean Caujolle	France	March 31, 1953
Evonne Goolagong Cawley	Australia	July 31, 1951
Helen Gourlay Cawley	Australia	December 23, 1946
Lesley Charles	Great Britain	July 15, 1952
Natasha Chmyreva	U.S.S.R.	May 28, 1958
Glynis Coles	Great Britain	February 20, 1954
Jimmy Connors	U.S.A.	September 2, 1952
Patrick Cornejo	Chile	June 6, 1944
Mark Cox	Great Britain	July 5, 1943
Dick Crealy	Australia	September 18, 1944
Brigette Cuypers	South Africa	December 3, 1955
Scott Davis	U.S.A.	August 27, 1965
Eric Deblicker	France	April 17, 1959
Petra Delhees	Switzerland	March 28, 1959
Phil Dent	Australia	February 14, 1950
Diane Desfor	U.S.A.	June 15, 1955
Eddie Dibbs	U.S.A.	February 3, 1951
Colin Dibley	Australia	September 19, 1944
Steve Docherty	U.S.A.	May 6, 1950
Cynthia Doerner	Australia	February 11, 1951
Patrice Dominguez	France	January 12, 1950
Colin Dowdeswell	Rhodesia	May 12, 1955
Cliff Drysdale	South Africa	May 26, 1941
Laura DuPont	U.S.A.	May 4, 1949
Patrick DuPre	U.S.A.	September 16, 1954
Francoise Durr Browning	France	December 25, 1942
Katja Ebbinghaus	West Germany	June 1, 1948
Mark Edmondson	Australia	June 28, 1954
Roy Emerson	Australia	November 3, 1936
Chris Evert Lloyd	U.S.A.	December 21, 1954
Rick Fagel	U.S.A.	November 29, 1953
Brian Fairlie	New Zealand	June 13, 1948

Name	Country	Date of Birth
Jurgen Fassbender	West Germany	May 21, 1948
Anthony Fawcett	Rhodesia	June 29, 1951
Wojtek Fibak	Poland	August 30, 1952
Jaime Fillol	Chile	June 3, 1946
Mike Fishbach	U.S.A.	December 1, 1954
Pete Fleming	U.S.A.	January 21, 1955
Lele Forood	U.S.A.	September 10, 1956
Zeljko Franulovic	Yugoslavia	June 13, 1947
Diane Fromholtz	Australia	August 10, 1956
Frank Gebert	West Germany	November 6, 1952
Vitas Gerulaitis	U.S.A.	July 26, 1954
Hans Gildemeister	Chile	February 9, 1956
Raquel Giscafre	Argentina	May 15, 1949
Pancho Gonzalez	U.S.A.	May 9, 1928
Tom Gorman	U.S.A.	January 19, 1946
Brian Gottfried	U.S.A.	January 27, 1952
Larry Gottfried	U.S.A.	December 8, 1958
Georges Goven	France	April 27, 1948
Jiri Granat	Czechoslovakia	January 28, 1955
Mona Guerrant	U.S.A.	November 28, 1948
Zan Guerry	U.S.A.	February 12, 1949
Tim Gullikson	U.S.A.	September 8, 1951
Tom Gullikson	U.S.A.	September 8, 1951
Nancy Richey Gunter	U.S.A.	August 23, 1942
Barbara Hallquist	U.S.A.	May 1, 1957
Mary Hamm	U.S.A.	September 7, 1954
Sylvia Hanika	West Germany	November 30, 1959
Kathy Harter	U.S.A.	October 27, 1946
Bob Hewitt	South Africa	January 12, 1940
Jose Higueras	Spain	March 1, 1953
Terry Holladay	U.S.A.	November 28, 1955
Jiri Hrebec	Czechoslovakia	September 19, 1950
Lesley Hunt	Australia	May 29, 1950
Erick Iskersky	U.S.A.	January 25, 1958
Andrea Jaeger	U.S.A.	June 4, 1965
Francoise Jauffret	France	February 9, 1942
Mima Jausovec	Yugoslavia	July 20, 1956
Kjell Johansson	Sweden	February 12, 1951
Kathryn Jordan	U.S.A.	December 3, 1959
Hans Kary	Austria	February 23, 1949
Billie Jean King	U.S.A.	November 22, 1943
Ann Kiyomura	U.S.A.	August 22, 1955
Ilana Kloss	South Africa	March 22, 1956
Jan Kodes	Czechoslovakia	March 1, 1946
Marise Krueger	South Africa	July 17, 1958
Kathy Kuykendall	U.S.A.	November 23, 1956
Marcelo Lara	Mexico	October 5, 1947
Kate Latham	U.S.A.	October 25, 1952
Ivan Lendl	Czechoslovakia	March 7, 1960
Chris Lewis	U.S.A.	April 2, 1956
Zenda Liess	U.S.A.	December 13, 1959
John Lloyd	Great Britain	August 27, 1954
Mareen (Peanut) Louie	U.S.A.	August 15, 1960
Marcie Louie	U.S.A.	September 10, 1953
Bob Lutz	U.S.A.	August 29, 1947
Peter McNamara	Australia	May 7, 1955

LEADING TENNIS PLAYERS OF TODAY *(cont.)*

Name	Country	Date of Birth
Paul McNamee	Australia	November 12, 1954
Hana Mandlikova	Czechoslovakia	February 19, 1962
Bruce Manson	U.S.A.	March 20, 1956
Sue Mappin	Great Britain	November 7, 1947
Regina Marsikova	Czechoslovakia	December 11, 1958
Billy Martin	U.S.A.	December 25, 1956
Geoff Masters	Australia	May 19, 1950
Kathy May	U.S.A.	June 18, 1956
Sandy Mayer	U.S.A.	April 5, 1952
John McEnroe	U.S.A.	February 16, 1959
Frew McMillan	South Africa	May 20, 1952
Frederick McNair	U.S.A.	July 22, 1950
Paul McNamee	Australia	November 12, 1954
Karl Meiler	West Germany	April 30, 1949
Carrie Meyer	U.S.A.	August 22, 1955
Florenza Mihai	Romania	September 2, 1955
Bernie Mitton	South Africa	November 9, 1954
Ivan Molina	Colombia	June 16, 1946
Terry Moor	U.S.A.	April 23, 1952
Buster Mottram	Great Britain	April 25, 1955
Linda Mottram	Great Britain	May 17, 1957
Betsy Nagelsen	U.S.A.	October 23, 1956
Ilie Nastase	Romania	July 19, 1946
Martina Navratilova	U.S.A.	October 18, 1956
Janet Newberry	U.S.A.	August 6, 1953
John Newcombe	Australia	May 23, 1944
Yannick Noah	France	May 16, 1960
Tom Okker	The Netherlands	February 22, 1944
Manuel Orantes	Spain	February 6, 1944
Adriano Panatta	Italy	July 9, 1950
Charles Pasarell	U.S.A.	February 12, 1944
Andrew Pattison	Rhodesia	January 30, 1949
Victor Pecci	Paraguay	October 15, 1955
Hank Pfister	U.S.A.	October 8, 1953
Mary Lou Piatek	U.S.A.	August 6, 1961
Nikki Pilic	Yugoslavia	August 27, 1939
Marie Pinterova	Egypt	August 16, 1946
Pascal Portes	France	May 29, 1959
Patrick Proisy	France	September 10, 1949
Raul Ramirez	Mexico	June 20, 1953
Marita Redondo	U.S.A.	February 19, 1956
Kerry Melville Reid	Australia	August 7, 1947
Renee Richards	U.S.A.	August 19, 1934
Keith Richardson	U.S.A.	September 18, 1953
Cliff Richey	U.S.A.	December 31, 1946
Iris Riedel	West Germany	March 16, 1954
Marty Riessen	U.S.A.	December 4, 1941
Tony Roche	Australia	May 17, 1945
Lucia Romanov	Romania	April 28, 1959
Ken Rosewall	Australia	November 2, 1934
Maria Rothschild	U.S.A.	April 24, 1960
JoAnne Russell	U.S.A.	October 30, 1954
Virginia Ruzici	Romania	January 31, 1955
Toshiro Sakai	Japan	November 23, 1947
Nick Saviano	U.S.A.	June 5, 1956
Bill Scanlon	U.S.A.	November 13, 1956

Name	Country	Date of Birth
Howard Schoenfield	U.S.A.	November 15, 1957
Ismail el Shafei	Egypt	November 15, 1947
Kristien K. Shaw	U.S.A.	July 25, 1952
Tomaz Smid	Czechoslovakia	May 20, 1956
Anne Smith	U.S.A.	July 1, 1959
Stan Smith	U.S.A.	December 14, 1946
Harold Solomon	U.S.A.	September 17, 1952
Greer Stevens	South Africa	February 15, 1957
Sherwood Stewart	U.S.A.	June 6, 1946
Dick Stockton	U.S.A.	February 18, 1951
Caroline Stoll	U.S.A.	November 4, 1960
Betty Stove	The Netherlands	June 24, 1945
Hana Strachanova	Czechoslovakia	January 2, 1961
Mary Struthers	U.S.A.	July 21, 1950
Roscoe Tanner	U.S.A.	October 15, 1951
Balazs Taroczy	Hungary	May 9, 1954
Roger Taylor	Great Britain	October 14, 1941
Brian Teacher	U.S.A.	December 23, 1954
Pam Teeguarden	U.S.A.	April 17, 1951
Eliot Teltscher	U.S.A.	March 15, 1959
Renata Tomanova	Czechoslovakia	December 9, 1954
Wendy Turnbull	Australia	November 26, 1952
Michele Tyler	Great Britain	July 8, 1958
Erik Van Dillen	U.S.A.	February 21, 1951
Robert Van't Hof	U.S.A.	April 10, 1959
Robbie Venter	South Africa	May 7, 1960
Yvonne Vermaak	South Africa	December 18, 1956
Guillermo Vilas	Argentina	August 17, 1952
Virginia Wade	Great Britain	July 10, 1945
Sharon Walsh	U.S.A.	February 24, 1952
Butch Walts	U.S.A.	June 4, 1955
Kim Warwick	Australia	April 8, 1952
Van Winitsky	U.S.A.	March 12, 1959
Valerie Ziegenfuss	U.S.A.	June 29, 1949
Antonio Zugarelli	Italy	January 17, 1950

(left to right) Yannick Noah of France, Ivan Lendl of Czechoslovakia, and Peter Fleming of the United States.

AGE OF MEN NATIONAL CHAMPIONS

There is no predicting when a man will be ready to win the United States singles championship. Several have arrived as teenagers—Oliver Campbell, Dick Sears (our first champion, 1881), Bob Wrenn, and Ellsworth Vines winning at 19. Another, Vic Seixas, persisted until seven days after his thirty-first birthday before he became champion. The traditional entry to manhood—age 21—most frequently has been the breakthrough year for first championships. Six men—Ted Schroeder, Malcolm Whitman, Johnny Doeg, Bobby Riggs, Ken Rosewall, Ashley Cooper—made it at 21. In winning the USLTA's first seven tourneys, Dick Sears reigned through his twenty-fifth year. Bill Larned also won seven titles, although his success did not begin until 1901 when he was 28. This made Bill our oldest National champion, in 1911, at 38.

USTA RANKINGS

When the first Top Ten was determined in 1885 by the USLTA men's ranking committee, with national champion Dick Sears of Boston in the foremost position, the competition was not so extensive as today. The first national championship, at the Newport (R.I.) Casino, had been held only four years before, Sears felling Briton W. E. Glyn in the final. Now, room at the top is greatly sought. Hundreds of players, competing in scores of tournaments, are scheming to crash the Top Ten. In 1970, for example, the USTA ranked 57 men and 31 women, and the lowliest of those is an exceptional player. It is something to have been ranked at all, but to be in the Top Ten—that is arrival, an accomplishment to be cherished.

Men's Ranking

1885

1. R. D. Sears
2. James Dwight
3. W. V. R. Berry
4. G. M. Brinley
5. J. S. Clark
6. A. Moffat
7. R. L. Beeckman
8. H. A. Taylor
9. F. S. Mansfield
10. W. P. Knapp

1886

1. R. D. Sears
2. James Dwight
3. R. L. Beeckman
4. H. A. Taylor
5. J. S. Clark
6. H. W. Slocum
7. G. M. Brinley
8. F. S. Mansfield
9. A. Moffat
10. J. S. Conover

1887

1. R. D. Sears
2. H. W. Slocum
3. R. L. Beeckman
4. H. A. Taylor
5. J. S. Clark
6. F. S. Mansfield
7. P. S. Sears
8. G. M. Brinley
9. E. P. MacMullen
10. Q. A. Shaw, Jr.

1888

1. H. W. Slocum
2. H. A. Taylor
3. James Dwight
4. J. S. Clark
5. C. A. Chase
6. P. S. Sears
7. E. P. MacMullen
8. O. S. Campbell
9. R. L. Beeckman
10. F. S. Mansfield

1889

1. H. W. Slocum
2. W. A. Shaw, Jr.
3. O. S. Campbell
4. H. A. Taylor
5. C. A. Chase
6. J. S. Clark
7. W. P. Knapp
8. R. P. Huntington, Jr.
9. R. S. Sears
10. F. S. Mansfield

1890

1. O. S. Campbell
2. R. P. Huntington, Jr.
3. W. P. Knapp
4. H. W. Slocum
5. F. H. Hovey
6. Clarence Hobart
7. P. S. Sears
8. H. A. Taylor
9. C. A. Chase
10. V. G. Hall

1891

1. O. S. Campbell
2. Clarence Hobart
3. R. P. Huntington, Jr.
4. F. H. Hovey
5. E. L. Hall
6. V. G. Hall
7. P. S. Sears
8. S. T. Chase
9. C. T. Lee
10. M. D. Smith

1892

1. O. S. Campbell
2. E. L. Hall
3. E. P. Knapp
4. Clarence Hobart
5. F. H. Hovey
6. W. A. Larned
7. M. G. Chace
8. R. D. Wrenn
9. Richard Stevens
10. C. P. Hubbard

1893

1. R. D. Wrenn
2. Clarence Hobart
3. F. H. Hovey
4. M. G. Chace
5. W. A. Larned
6. E. L. Hall
7. Richard Stevens
8. A. E. Foote
9. John Howland
10. C. R. Budlong

1894

1. R. D. Wrenn
2. W. A. Larned
3. M. F. Goodbody*
4. F. H. Hovey
5. M. G. Chace
6. Clarence Hobart
7. Richard Stevens
8. C. R. Budlong
9. A. E. Foote
10. W. G. Parker

1895

1. F. H. Hovey
2. W. A. Larned
3. M. G. Chace
4. John Howland
5. R. D. Wrenn
6. C. B. Neel
7. Clarence Hobart
8. Richard Stevens
9. A. E. Foote
10. C. R. Budlong

1896

1. R. D. Wrenn
2. W. A. Larned
3. C. B. Neel
4. F. H. Hovey
5. E. P. Fisher
6. G. L. Wrenn, Jr.
7. Richard Stevens
8. M. D. Whitman
9. L. E. Ware
10. G. P. Sheldon, Jr.

1897

1. R. D. Wrenn
2. W. A. Larned
3. W. V. Eaves*
4. H. A. Nisbet*
5. H. S. Mahoney*
6. G. L. Wrenn, Jr.
7. M. D. Whitman
8. Kreigh Collins
9. E. P. Fisher
10. W. S. Bond

1898

1. M. D. Whitman
2. L. E. Ware
3. W. S. Bond
4. D. F. Davis
5. C. R. Budlong
6. E. P. Fisher
7. G. L. Wrenn, Jr.
8. Richard Stevens
9. S. C. Millett
10. G. K. Belden

1899

1. M. D. Whitman
2. D. F. Davis
3. W. A. Larned
4. J. P. Paret
5. Kreigh Collins
6. G. L. Wrenn, Jr.
7. L. E. Ware
8. B. C. Wright
9. Holcombe Ward
10. R. P. Huntington, Jr.

1900

1. M. D. Whitman
2. D. F. Davis
3. W. A. Larned
4. B. C. Wright
5. Kreigh Collins
6. G. L. Wrenn, Jr.
7. Holcombe Ward
8. L. E. Ware
9. J. A. Allen
10. R. D. Little

1901

1. W. A. Larned
2. B. C. Wright
3. D. F. Davis
4. L. E. Ware
5. Clarence Hobart
6. R. D. Little
7. Holcombe Ward
8. Kreigh Collins
9. E. P. Fisher
10. W. J. Clothier

1902

1. W. A. Larned
2. M. D. Whitman
3. B. C. Wright
4. Holcombe Ward
5. W. J. Clothier
6. L. E. Ware
7. R. D. Little
8. Kreigh Collins
9. H. H. Hackett
10. Clarence Hobart

*Foreign players included in USTA ranking.

USTA Rankings—Men *(cont.)*

1903

1. W. A. Larned
2. Holcombe Ward
3. W. J. Clothier
4. B. C. Wright
5. Kreigh Collins
6. E. P. Larned
7. H. F. Allen
8. E. W. Leonard
9. R. H. Carleton
10. Kenneth Horton

1904

1. Holcombe Ward
2. W. J. Clothier
3. W. A. Larned
4. B. C. Wright
5. Kreigh Collins
6. R. D. Little
7. F. B. Alexander
8. Richard Stevens
9. A. E. Bell
10. E. W. Leonard

1905

1. B. C. Wright
2. Holcombe Ward
3. W. A. Larned
4. W. J. Clothier
5. F. B. Alexander
6. Clarence Hobart
7. Richard Stevens
8. Kreigh Collins
9. R. D. Little
10. F. G. Anderson

1906

1. W. J. Clothier
2. W. A. Larned
3. B. C. Wright
4. F. B. Alexander
5. K. H. Behr
6. R. D. Little
7. H. H. Hackett
8. F. G. Anderson
9. E. B. Dewhurst
10. I. C. Wright

1907

1. W. A. Larned
2. B. C. Wright
3. K. H. Behr
4. R. D. Little
5. Robert LeRoy
6. Clarence Hobart
7. E. P. Larned
8. R. C. Seaver
9. I. C. Wright
10. F. C. Colston

1908

1. W. A. Larned
2. B. C. Wright
3. F. B. Alexander
4. W. J. Clothier
5. R. D. Little
6. Robert LeRoy
7. Nat Emerson
8. N. W. Niles
9. W. F. Johnson
10. R. H. Palmer

1909

1. W. A. Larned
2. W. J. Clothier
3. W. F. Johnson
4. N. W. Niles
5. R. D. Little
6. M. E. McLoughlin
7. M. H. Long
8. K. H. Behr
9. E. P. Larned
10. Robert LeRoy

1910

1. W. A. Larned
2. T. C. Bundy
3. B. C. Wright
4. M. E. McLoughlin
5. M. H. Long
6. N. W. Niles
7. G. F. Touchard
8. T. R. Pell
9. F. C. Colston
10. C. R. Gardner

1911

1. W. A. Larned
2. M. E. McLoughlin
3. T. C. Bundy
4. G. F. Touchard
5. M. H. Long
6. N. W. Niles
7. T. R. Pell
8. R. D. Little
9. K. H. Behr
10. W. M. Hall

1912

1. M. E. McLoughlin
2. R. N. Williams II
3. W. F. Johnson
4. W. J. Clothier
5. N. W. Niles
6. T. C. Bundy
7. K. H. Behr
8. R. D. Little
9. G. P. Gardner, Jr.
10. G. F. Touchard

1913

1. M. E. McLoughlin
2. R. N. Williams II
3. W. J. Clothier
4. W. M. Johnston
5. T. R. Pell
6. N. W. Niles
7. W. F. Johnson
8. G. F. Touchard
9. G. P. Gardner, Jr.
10. J. R. Strachan

1914

1. M. E. McLoughlin
2. R. N. Williams II
3. K. G. Behr
4. R. L. Murray
5. W. J. Clothier
6. W. M. Johnston
7. G. M. Church
8. F. B. Alexander
9. W. M. Washburn
10. E. F. Fottrell

1915

1. W. M. Johnston
2. R. N. Williams II
3. M. E. McLoughlin
4. K. H. Behr
5. T. R. Pell
6. N. W. Niles
7. C. J. Griffin
8. W. M. Washburn
9. G. M. Church
10. W. M. Hall

1916

1. R. N. Williams II
2. W. M. Johnston
3. G. M. Church
4. R. L. Murray
5. Ichiya Kumagae*
6. C. J. Griffin
7. W. M. Washburn
8. W. E. Davis
9. J. J. Armstrong
10. Dean Mathey

As only Patriotic Tournaments were held in 1917, no ranking was made for that year.

1918

1. R. L. Murray
2. W. T. Tilden II
3. F. B. Alexander
4. W. M. Hall
5. W. T. Hayes
6. N. H. Niles
7. Ichiya Kumagae*
8. C. S. Garland
9. S. H. Voshell
10. T. R. Pell

1919

1. W. M. Johnston
2. W. T. Tilden II
3. Ichiya Kumagae*
4. R. L. Murray
5. W. F. Johnson
6. R. N. Williams II
7. Roland Roberts
8. C. S. Garland
9. W. T. Hayes
10. W. M. Washburn

1920

1. W. T. Tilden II
2. W. M. Johnston
3. R. N. Williams II
4. Ichiya Kumagae*
5. W. E. Davis
6. C. J. Griffin
7. W. M. Washburn
8. C. S. Garland
9. N. W. Niles
10. W. F. Johnson

1921

1. W. T. Tilden II
2. W. M. Johnston
3. Vincent Richards
4. W. F. Johnson
5. W. M. Washburn
6. R. N. Williams II
7. Ichiya Kumagae*
8. S. H. Voshell
9. L. B. Rice
10. N. W. Niles

1922

1. W. T. Tilden II
2. W. M. Johnston
3. Vincent Richards
4. R. N. Williams II
5. W. F. Johnson
6. Robert Kinsey
7. Zenzo Shimizu*
8. Howard Kinsey
9. Francis T. Hunter
10. W. M. Washburn

1923

1. W. T. Tilden II
2. W. M. Johnston
3. R. N. Williams II
4. Vincent Richards
5. Francis T. Hunter
6. Howard Kinsey
7. Carl Fischer
8. Brian I. C. Norton*
9. Harvey Snodgrass
10. Robert Kinsey

1924

1. W. T. Tilden II
2. Vincent Richards
3. W. M. Johnston
4. Howard Kinsey
5. W. F. Johnson
6. Harvey Snodgrass
7. John F. Hennessey
8. Brian I. C. Norton*
9. Geo. M. Lott, Jr.
10. C. J. Griffin

1925

1. W. T. Tilden II
2. W. M. Johnston
3. Vincent Richards
4. R. N. Williams II
5. Manuel Alonso*
6. Howard Kinsey
7. Takeichi Harada*
8. Cranston W. Holman
9. Brian I. C. Norton*
10. Wray D. Brown

1926

1. W. T. Tilden II
2. Manuel Alonso*
3. Takeichi Harada*
4. W. M. Johnston
5. Edw. G. Chandler
6. Lewis N. White
7. A. J. Chapin, Jr.
8. Brian I. C. Norton*
9. Geo. M. Lott, Jr.
10. George King

*Foreign players included in USTA ranking.

USTA Rankings—Men *(cont.)*

1927
1. W. T. Tilden II
2. Francis T. Hunter
3. Geo. M. Lott, Jr.
4. Manuel Alonso*
5. John F. Hennessey
6. John Van Ryn
7. Arnold W. Jones
8. John H. Doeg
9. Lewis N. White
10. Cranston W. Holman

1928
1. W. T. Tilden II
2. Francis T. Hunter
3. Geo. M. Lott, Jr.
4. John F. Hennessey
5. Wilmer L. Allison
6. John Van Ryn
7. Frederick Mercur
8. John H. Doeg
9. Julius Seligson
10. Frank X. Shields

1929
1. W. T. Tilden II
2. Francis T. Hunter
3. John H. Doeg
4. George M. Lott, Jr.
5. John Van Ryn
6. Frederick Mercur
7. Wilmer L. Allison
8. Wilber F. Coen, Jr.
9. R. Berkeley Bell
10. Gregory S. Mangin

1930
1. John H. Doeg
2. Frank X. Shields
3. Wilmer L. Allison
4. Sidney B. Wood, Jr.
5. Clifford S. Sutter
6. Gregory S. Mangin
7. George M. Lott, Jr.
8. H. Ellsworth Vines, Jr.
9. John Van Ryn
10. Bryan M. Grant, Jr.

1931
1. H. Ellsworth Vines, Jr.
2. Geo. M. Lott, Jr.
3. Frank X. Shields
4. John Van Ryn
5. John H. Doeg
6. Clifford S. Sutter
7. Sidney B. Wood, Jr.
8. Keith Gledhill
9. Wilmer L. Allison
10. R. Berkeley Bell

1932
1. H. Ellsworth Vines, Jr.
2. Wilmer L. Allison
3. Clifford S. Sutter
4. Sidney B. Wood, Jr.
5. Frank X. Shields
6. Lester R. Stoefen
7. Gregory S. Mangin
8. Keith Gledhill
9. John Van Ryn
10. David N. Jones

1933
1. Frank X. Shields
2. Wilmer L. Allison
3. Lester R. Stoefen
4. Clifford S. Sutter
5. Gregory S. Mangin
6. Sidney B. Wood, Jr.
7. Bryan M. Grant, Jr.
8. Frank A. Parker
9. Keith Gledhill
10. George M. Lott, Jr.

1934
1. Wilmer L. Allison
2. Sidney B. Wood, Jr.
3. Frank X. Shields
4. Frank A. Parker
5. Lester R. Stoefen
6. Geo. M. Lott, Jr.
7. R. Berkeley Bell
8. Clifford S. Sutter
9. J. Donald Budge
10. Bryan M. Grant, Jr.

1935
1. Wilmer L. Allison
2. J. Donald Budge
3. Bryan M. Grant, Jr.
4. Frank X. Shields
5. Sidney B. Wood, Jr.
6. Gregory S. Mangin
7. Frank A. Parker
8. J. Gilbert Hall
9. Wilmer M. Hines
10. R. Berkeley Bell

1936
1. J. Donald Budge
2. Frank A. Parker
3. Bryan M. Grant, Jr.
4. Robert L. Riggs
5. Gregory S. Mangin
6. John Van Ryn
7. John McDiarmid
8. Charles R. Harris
9. Joseph R. Hunt
10. Arthur H. Hendrix

1937
1. J. Donald Budge
2. Robert L. Riggs
3. Frank A. Parker
4. Bryan M. Grant, Jr.
5. Joseph R. Hunt
6. Wayne R. Sabin
7. Harold Surface, Jr.
8. C. Gene Mako
9. W. Donald McNeill
10. John Van Ryn

1938
1. J. Donald Budge
2. Robert L. Riggs
3. C. Gene Mako
4. Sidney B. Wood, Jr.
5. Joseph R. Hunt
6. Bryan M. Grant, Jr.
7. Elwood T. Cooke
8. Frank A. Parker
9. Gilbert A. Hunt, Jr.
10. Francis L. Kovacs II

*Foreign players included in USTA ranking.

1939

1. Robert L. Riggs
2. Frank A. Parker
3. W. Donald McNeill
4. S. Welby Van Horn
5. Wayne R. Sabin
6. Elwood T. Cooke
7. Bryan M. Grant, Jr.
8. Gardnar Mulloy
9. Gilbert A. Hunt, Jr.
10. Henry J. Prusoff

1940

1. W. Donald McNeill
2. Robert L. Riggs
3. Francis L. Kovacs II
4. Joseph R. Hunt
5. Frank A. Parker
6. John A. Kramer
7. Gardnar Mulloy
8. Henry J. Prusoff
9. Elwood T. Cooke
10. F. R. Schroeder, Jr.

1941

1. Robert L. Riggs
2. Francis L. Kovacs II
3. Frank A. Parker
4. W. Donald McNeill
5. F. R. Schroeder, Jr.
6. Wayne R. Sabin
7. Gardnar Mulloy
8. Bryan M. Grant, Jr.
9. John A. Kramer
10. William F. Talbert

1942

1. F. R. Schroeder, Jr.
2. Frank A. Parker
3. Gardnar Mulloy
4. Francisco Segura*
5. William F. Talbert
6. Sidney B. Wood, Jr.
7. Seymour Greenberg
8. George Richards
9. E. Victor Seixas, Jr.
10. Ladislav Hecht*

1943

1. Joseph R. Hunt
2. John A. Kramer
3. Francisco Segura*
4. William F. Talbert
5. Seymour Greenberg
6. Sidney B. Wood, Jr.
7. Robert Falkenberg
8. Frank A. Parker
9. James Brink
10. Jack Tuero

1944

1. Frank A. Parker
2. William F. Talbert
3. Francisco Segura*
4. W. Donald McNeill
5. Seymour Greenberg
6. Robert Falkenberg
7. Jack Jossi
8. Charles W. Oliver
9. Jack McManis
10. J. Gilbert Hall

1945

1. Sgt. Frank A. Parker
2. William F. Talbert
3. Francisco Segura*
4. Elwood T. Cooke
5. Sidney B. Wood, Jr.
6. Lt. Gardnar Mulloy
7. Frank X. Shields
8. Lt. Harold Surface, Jr.
9. Lt. Seymour Greenberg
10. Jack McManis

1946

1. John A. Kramer
2. F. R. Schroeder, Jr.
3. Frank A. Parker
4. Thos. P. Brown, Jr.
5. Gardnar Mulloy
6. William F. Talbert
7. W. Donald McNeill
8. Robert Falkenberg
9. Edward Moulan
10. Francisco Segura*

1947

1. John A. Kramer
2. Frank A. Parker
3. F. R. Schroeder, Jr.
4. Gardnar Mulloy
5. William F. Talbert
6. Francisco Segura*
7. Robert Falkenberg
8. Edward Moylan
9. Earl H. Cochell
10. Seymour Greenberg

1948

1. Richard A. Gonzalez
2. F. R. Schroeder, Jr.
3. Frank A. Parker
4. William F. Talbert
5. Robert Falkenberg
6. Earl H. Cochell
7. E. Victor Seixas, Jr.
8. Gardnar Mulloy
9. Herbert Flam
10. Harry E. Likas, Jr.

1949

1. Richard A. Gonzalez
2. F. R. Schroeder, Jr.
3. William F. Talbert
4. Frank A. Parker
5. Gardnar Mulloy
6. Arthur D. Larsen
7. Earl H. Cochell
8. Samuel Match
9. Edward Moylan
10. Herbert Flam

1950

1. Arthur D. Larsen
2. Herbert Flam
3. F. R. Schroeder, Jr.
4. Gardnar Mulloy
5. William F. Talbert
6. Richard Savitt
7. Earl H. Cochell
8. E. Victor Seixas, Jr.
9. Thos. P. Brown, Jr.
10. Samuel Match

*Foreign players included in USTA ranking.

USTA Rankings—Men *(cont.)*

1951

1. E. Victor Seixas, Jr.
2. Richard Savitt
3. Tony Trabert
4. Herbert Flam
5. William F. Talbert
6. Arthur D. Larsen
7. F. R. Schroeder, Jr.
8. Gardnar Mulloy
9. Hamilton Richardson
10. J. Ed. (Budge) Patty

1952

1. Gardnar Mulloy
2. E. Victor Seixas, Jr.
3. Arthur D. Larsen
4. Richard D. Savitt
5. Herbert Flam
6. William F. Talbert
7. Hamilton Richardson
8. Thos. P. Brown, Jr.
9. Noel Brown
10. Harry E. Likas, Jr.

1953

1. Tony Trabert
2. E. Victor Seixas, Jr.
3. Arthur D. Larsen
4. Gardnar Mulloy
5. L. Straight Clark
6. Hamilton Richardson
7. Bernard Bartzen
8. Thos. P. Brown, Jr.
9. Noel Brown
10. Grant Golden

1954

1. E. Victor Seixas, Jr.
2. Tony Trabert
3. Hamilton Richardson
4. Arthur D. Larsen
5. Gardnar Mulloy
6. Thos. P. Brown, Jr.
7. Edward Moylan
8. Bernard Bartzen
9. William F. Talbert
10. Gilbert J. Shea

1955

1. Tony Trabert
2. E. Victor Seixas, Jr.
3. Arthur D. Larsen
4. Bernard Bartzen
5. Edward Moylan
6. Gilbert J. Shea
7. Hamilton Richardson
8. Herbert Flam
9. Samuel Giammalva
10. Thos. P. Brown, Jr.

1956

1. Hamilton Richardson
2. Herbert Flam
3. E. Victor Seixas, Jr.
4. Edward Moylan
5. Bernard Bartzen
6. Robert M. Perry
7. Samuel Giammalva
8. Arthur D. Larsen
9. Gilbert J. Shea
10. Grant Golden

1957

1. E. Victor Seixas, Jr.
2. Herbert Flam
3. Richard Savitt
4. Gilbert J. Shea
5. Barry MacKay
6. Ronald Holmberg
7. Thos. P. Brown, Jr.
8. Whitney Reed
9. Bernard Bartzen
10. William Quillian

1958

1. Hamilton Richardson
2. Alejandro Olmedo*
3. Barry MacKay
4. Bernard Bartzen
5. Herbert Flam
6. Richard Savitt
7. Samuel Giammalva
8. E. Victor Seixas, Jr.
9. Earl Buchholz, Jr.
10. Thos. P. Brown, Jr.

1959

1. Alejandro Olmedo*
2. Bernard Bartzen
3. Barry MacKay
4. Ronald Holmberg
5. Richard Savitt
6. Earl Buchholz, Jr.
7. Myron J. Franks
8. Noel Brown
9. Whitney Reed
10. E. Victor Seixas, Jr.

1960

1. Barry MacKay
2. Bernard Bartzen
3. Earl Buchholz, Jr.
4. Charles McKinley
5. R. Dennis Ralston
6. Jon Douglas
7. Ronald Holmberg
8. Whitney Reed
9. Donald Dell
10. Chris Crawford

1961

1. Whitney Reed
2. Charles McKinley
3. Bernard Bartzen
4. Jon Douglas
5. Donald Dell
6. F. Froehling III
7. Ronald Holmberg
8. Allen Fox
9. Jack Frost
10. William Bond

1962

1. Charles R. McKinley
2. F. A. Froehling, III
3. Hamilton Richardson
4. Allen E. Fox
5. Jon A. Douglas
6. Whitney R. Reed
7. Donald L. Dell
8. Eugene L. Scott
9. Martin Riessen
10. Charles Pasarell

*Foreign players included in USTA ranking.

1963

1. Charles R. McKinley
2. R. Dennis Ralston
3. F. A. Froehling, III
4. Eugene L. Scott
5. Martin Riessen
6. Arthur Ashe, Jr.
7. Hamilton Richardson
8. Allen Fox
9. Tom Edlefsen
10. Charles Pasarell

1964

1. R. Dennis Ralston
2. Charles R. McKinley
3. Arthur Ashe, Jr.
4. F. A. Froehling III
5. Eugene L. Scott
6. Ronald Holmberg
7. Hamilton Richardson
8. Allen E. Fox
9. Clark Graebner
10. Martin Riessen

1965

1. R. Dennis Ralston
2. Arthur Ashe, Jr.
3. Cliff Richey
4. Charles R. McKinley
5. Charles Pasarell
6. Hamilton Richardson
7. Mike Belkin
8. Martin Riessen
9. Ronald E. Holmberg
10. Tom Edlefsen

1966

1. R. Dennis Ralston
2. Arthur Ashe, Jr.
3. Clark Graebner
4. Charles Pasarell
5. Cliff Richey
6. Ronald E. Holmberg
7. Martin Riessen
8. F. A. Froehling III
9. E. Victor Seixas, Jr.
10. Charles R. McKinley

1967

1. Charles Pasarell
2. Arthur Ashe, Jr.
3. Cliff Richey
4. Clark Graebner
5. Martin Riessen
6. Ronald E. Holmberg
7. Stan Smith
8. Allen E. Fox
9. Eugene L. Scott
10. Robert Lutz

1968

1. Arthur Ashe, Jr.
2. Clark Graebner
3. Stan Smith
4. Cliff Richey
5. Robert Lutz
6. Ronald Holmberg
7. Charles Pasarell
8. James Osborne
9. James McManus
10. Eugene Scott

1969

1. Stan Smith
2. Arthur Ashe, Jr.
3. Cliff Richey
4. Clark Graebner
5. Charles Pasarell
6. Robert Lutz
7. Tom Edlefsen
8. Roy Barth
9. Jim Osborne
10. Jim McManus

1970

1. Cliff Richey
2. Stan Smith
3. Arthur Ashe, Jr.
4. Clark Graebner
5. Bob Lutz
6. Tom Gorman
7. Jim Osborne
8. Jim McManus
9. Barry MacKay
10. Charles Pasarell

1971

1. Stan Smith
2. Cliff Richey
3. Clark Graebner
4. Tom Gorman
5. Jimmy Connors
6. Erik Van Dillen
7. F. A. Froehling III
8. Roscoe Tanner
9. Alex Olmedo
10. Harold Solomon

1972

1. Stan Smith
2. Tom Gorman
3. Jimmy Connors
4. Dick Stockton
5. Roscoc Tanner
6. Harold Solomon
7. Erik van Dillen
8. Clark Graebner
9. Pancho Gonzalez
10. Brian Gottfried

1973

1. Jimmy Connors
   and Stan Smith
3. Arthur Ashe, Jr.
4. Tom Gorman
5. Cliff Richey
6. Charles Pasarell
7. Marty Riessen
8. Erik van Dillen
9. Brian Gottfried
10. Bob Lutz

1974

1. Jimmy Connors
2. Stan Smith
3. Marty Riessen
4. Roscoe Tanner
5. Arthur Ashe
6. Tom Gorman
7. Dick Stockton
8. Harold Solomon
9. Charles Pasarell
10. Jeff Borowiak

*Foreign players included in USTA ranking.

1975

1. Arthur Ashe
2. Jimmy Connors
3. Roscoe Tanner
4. Vitas Gerulaitis
5. Eddie Dibbs
6. Brian Gottfried
7. Harold Solomon
8. Bob Lutz
9. Cliff Richey
10. Dick Stockton

1976

1. Jimmy Connors
2. Eddie Dibbs
3. Arthur Ashe
4. Harold Solomon
5. Eddie Dibbs
6. Roscoe Tanner
7. Dick Stockton
8. Stan Smith
9. Vitas Gerulaitis
10. Bob Lutz

1977

1. Jimmy Connors
2. Brian Gottfried
3. Vitas Gerulaitis
4. Eddie Dibbs
5. Dick Stockton
6. Harold Solomon
7. Stan Smith
8. Roscoe Tanner
9. Bob Lutz
10. John McEnroe

1978

1. Jimmy Connors
2. Vitas Gerulaitis
3. Brian Gottfried
4. Eddie Dibbs
5. John McEnroe
6. Gene Mayer
7. Roscoe Tanner
8. Harold Solomon
9. Arthur Ashe, Jr.
10. Dick Stockton

1979

1. John McEnroe
2. Jimmy Connors
3. Roscoe Tanner
4. Vitas Gerulaitis
5. Arthur Ashe, Jr.
6. Eddie Dibbs
7. Harold Solomon
8. Peter Fleming
9. Gene Mayer
10. Brian Gottfried

1980

1. John McEnroe
2. Jimmy Connors
3. Gene Mayer
4. Vitas Gerulaitis
5. Harold Solomon
6. Brian Gottfried
7. Eddie Dibbs
8. Roscoe Tanner
9. Eliot Teltscher
10. Stan Smith

John McEnroe.

Women's Ranking

Not until 1913 did the ladies begin social climbing with racket in hand. Although their first national championship was held in 1887, there was no feminine Top Ten for 26 years. Mary K. Browne became the first leading lady by defeating Dorothy Green in the 1913 final.

1913

1. Mary K. Browne
2. Mrs. Ethel Sutton Bruce
3. Florence Sutton
4. Mrs. Helen Homans McLean
5. Mrs. Louise Williams
6. Marie Wagner
7. Mrs. Dorothy Green Briggs
8. Edith E. Rotch
9. Anita Myers
10. Gwendolyn Rees

1914
1. Mary K. Browne
2. Florence Sutton
3. Marie Wagner
4. Mrs. Louise H. Raymond
5. Edith E. Rotch
6. Eleanora Sears
7. Mrs. Louise Williams
8. Mrs. Sarita Van Viet Wood
9. Mrs. H. A. Niemeyer
10. Sara Livingstone

1915
1. Molla Bjurstedt
2. Mrs. Hazel H. Wightman
3. Mrs. Helen Homans McLean
4. Florence Sutton
5. Mrs. Maud Barger-Wallach
6. Marie Wagner
7. Anita Myers
8. Sara Livingstone
9. Clare Cassel
10. Eleanora Sears

1916
1. Molla Bjurstedt
2. Mrs. Louise H. Raymond
3. Evelyn Sears
4. Anita Myers
5. Sara Livingstone
6. Marie Wagner
7. Mrs. Homer S. Green
8. Martha Gunthrie
9. Eleanora Sears
10. Mrs. Maud Barger-Wallach

1917
As only Patriotic Tournaments were held in 1917, no ranking was made for that year.

1918
1. Molla Bjurstedt
2. Mrs. Hazel H. Wightman
3. Mrs. Homer S. Green
4. Eleanor Goss
5. Marie Wagner
6. Carrie B. Neely
7. Corinne Gould
8. Helene Pollak
9. Edith B. Handy
10. Clare Cassel

1919
1. Mrs. Hazel H. Wightman
2. Eleanor Goss
3. Mrs. Molla B. Mallory
4. Marion Zinderstein
5. Helen Baker
6. Mrs. Louise H. Raymond
7. Helen Gilleaudeau
8. Marie Wagner
9. Corinne Gould
10. Helene Pollak

1920
1. Mrs. Molla B. Mallory
2. Marion Zinderstein
3. Eleanor Tennant
4. Helen Baker
5. Eleanor Goss
6. Mrs. Louise H. Raymond
7. Marie Wagner
8. Mrs. Helene Pollak Falk
9. Edith Siguorney
10. Margaret Grove

1921
1. Mrs. Molla B. Mallory
2. Mary K. Browne
3. Mrs. Marion Z. Jessup
4. Mrs. May Sutton Bundy
5. Eleanor Goss
6. Helen Gilleaudeau
7. Mrs. B. E. Cole
8. Leslie Bancroft
9. Mrs. Louise H. Raymond
10. Margaret Grove

1922
1. Mrs. Molla B. Mallory
2. Leslie Bancroft
3. Helen N. Wills
4. Mrs. Marion Z. Jessup
5. Mrs. May Sutton Bundy
6. Martha Bayard
7. Helen Gilleaudeau
8. Mollie D. Thayer
9. Marie Wagner
10. Florence A. Ballin

1923
1. Helen N. Wills
2. Mrs. Molla B. Mallory
3. Eleanor Goss
4. Lillian Scharman
5. Mrs. Helen G. Lockhorn
6. Mayme MacDonald
7. Edith Sigourney
8. Leslie Bancroft
9. Martha Bayard
10. Helen Hooker

1924
1. Helen N. Wills
2. Mary K. Browne
3. Mrs. Molla B. Mallory
4. Eleanor Goss
5. Mrs. Marion Z. Jessup
6. Martha Bayard
7. Mayme MacDonald
8. Mrs. B. E. Cole
9. Mollie B. Thayer
10. Leslie Bancroft

1925
1. Helen N. Wills
2. Elizabeth Ryan
3. Mrs. Molla B. Mallory
4. Mrs. Marion Z. Jessup
5. Eleanor Goss
6. Mary K. Browne
7. Martha Bayard
8. Mrs. May Sutton Bundy
9. Charlotte Hosmer
10. Edith Sigourney

USTA Rankings—Women *(cont.)*

1926
1. Mrs. Molla B. Mallory
2. Elizabeth Ryan
3. Eleanor Goss
4. Martha Bayard
5. Mrs. Charlotte H. Chapin
6. Mrs. J. Dallas Corbiere
7. Margaret Blake
8. Penelope Anderson
9. Mrs. Edna Houselt Roeser
10. Mrs. William Endicott

1927
1. Helen N. Wills
2. Mrs. Molla B. Mallory
3. Mrs. Charlotte H. Chapin
4. Helen Jacobs
5. Eleanor Goss
6. Mrs. J. Dallas Corbiere
7. Penelope Anderson
8. Margaret Blake
9. Mrs. Edna H. Roeser
10. Alice Francis

1928
1. Helen N. Wills
2. Helen Jacobs
3. Edith Cross
4. Mrs. Molla B. Mallory
5. Mrs. May Sutton Bundy
6. Marjorie Morrill
7. Marjorie K. Gladman
8. Mrs. Anna McCune Harper
9. Mrs. Charlotte H. Chapin
10. Mrs. J. Dallas Corbiere

1929
1. Mrs. Helen Wills Moody
2. Helen Jacobs
3. Edith Cross
4. Sarah Palfrey
5. Mrs. Anna McC. Harper
6. Mary Greef
7. Eleanor Goss
8. Ethel Burkhardt
9. Marjorie K. Gladman
10. Josephine Cruickshank

1930
1. Mrs. Anna McC. Harper
2. Marjorie Morrill
3. Dorothy Weisel
4. Virginia Hilleary
5. Josephine Cruikshank
6. Ethel Burkhardt
7. Mrs. Marjorie G. Van Ryn
8. Sarah Palfrey
9. Mary Greef
10. Edith Cross

1931
1. Mrs. Helen W. Moody
2. Helen Jacobs
3. Mrs. Anna McC. Harper
4. Mrs. Marion Z. Jessup
5. Mary Greef
6. Marjorie Morrill
7. Sarah Palfrey
8. Mrs. Marjorie G. Van Ryn
9. Virginia Hilleary
10. Mrs. Dorothy Andrus Burke

1932
1. Helen Jacobs
2. Mrs. Anna McC. Harper
3. Carolin Babcock
4. Mrs. Marjorie M. Painter
5. Josephine Cruickshank
6. Virginia Hilleary
7. Alice Marble
8. Mrs. Marjorie G. Van Ryn
9. Virginia Rice
10. Marjorie Sachs

1933
1. Helen Jacobs
2. Mrs. Helen W. Moody
3. Alice Marble
4. Sarah Palfrey
5. Carolin Babcock
6. Josephine Cruickshank
7. Baroness Maud Levi
8. Mrs. Majorie G. Van Ryn
9. Virginia Rice
10. Mrs. Agnes S. Lamme

1934
1. Helen Jacobs
2. Mrs. Sarah P. Fabyan
3. Carolin Babcock
4. Mrs. Dorothy Andrus
5. Baroness Maud Levi
6. Jane Sharp
7. Mrs. Marjorie M. Painter
8. Mrs. Mary Greef Harris
9. Marjorie Sachs
10. Catherine Wolf

1935
1. Helen Jacobs
2. Mrs. E. Burkhardt Arnold
3. Mrs. Sarah P. Fabyan
4. Carolin Babcock
5. Mrs. Marjorie G. Van Ryn
6. Gracyn W. Wheeler
7. Mrs. Mary G. Harris
8. Mrs. Agnes S. Lamme
9. Mrs. Dorothy Andrus
10. Catherine Wolf

1936
1. Alice Marble
2. Helen Jacobs
3. Mrs. Sarah P. Fabyan
4. Gracyn W. Wheeler
5. Carolin Babcock
6. Helen A. Pedersen
7. Mrs. Marjorie G. Van Ryn
8. Dorothy M. Bundy
9. Katharine Winthrop
10. Mrs. Mary G. Harris

1937
1. Alice Marble
2. Helen Jacobs
3. Dorothy M. Bundy
4. Mrs. Marjorie G. Van Ryn
5. Gracyn W. Wheeler
6. Mrs. Sarah P. Fabyan
7. Mrs. Dorothy Andrus
8. Helen A. Pedersen
9. Katharine Winthrop
10. Mrs. Carolin Babcock Stark

1938

1. Alice Marble
2. Mrs. Sarah P. Fabyan
3. Dorothy M. Bundy
4. Barbara A. Winslow
5. Gracyn W. Wheeler
6. Dorothy E. Workman
7. Margaret E. Osborne
8. Helen A. Pedersen
9. Virginia Wolfenden
10. Katharine Winthrop

1939

1. Alice Marble
2. Helen Jacobs
3. Mrs. Sarah P. Fabyan
4. Helen I. Bernhard
5. Virginia Wolfenden
6. Dorothy M. Bundy
7. Dorothy E. Workman
8. Pauline Betz
9. Katharine Winthrop
10. Mary Arnold

1940

1. Alice Marble
2. Helen Jacobs
3. Pauline Betz
4. Dorothy M. Bundy
5. Mrs. Gracyn W. Kelleher
6. Mrs. Sarah P. Cooke
7. Virginia Wolfenden
8. Helen I. Bernhard
9. Mary Arnold
10. Hope Knowles

1941

1. Mrs. Sarah P. Cooke
2. Pauline Betz
3. Dorothy M. Bundy
4. Margaret Osborne
5. Helen Jacobs
6. Helen I. Bernhard
7. Hope Knowles
8. Mary Arnold
9. Mrs. Virginia W. Kovacs
10. A. Louise Brough

1942

1. Pauline Betz
2. A. Louise Brough
3. Margaret Osborne
4. Helen I. Bernhard
5. Mary Arnold
6. Doris Hart
7. Mrs. Patricia C. Todd
8. Mrs. Helen P. Rihbany
9. Mrs. Madge H. Vosters
10. Katharine Winthrop

1943

1. Pauline Betz
2. A. Louise Brough
3. Doris Hart
4. Margaret Osborne
5. Dorothy M. Bundy
6. Mary Arnold
7. Dorothy Head
8. Helen I. Bernhard
9. Mrs. Helen P. Rihbany
10. Katharine Winthrop

1944

1. Pauline Betz
2. Margaret Osborne
3. A. Louise Brough
4. Dorothy M. Bundy
5. Mary Arnold
6. Doris Hart
7. Mrs. Virginia W. Kovacs
8. Shirley J. Fry
9. Mrs. Patricia C. Todd
10. Dorothy Head

1945

1. Mrs. Sarah P. Cooke
2. Pauline Betz
3. Margaret Osborne
4. A. Louise Brough
5. Mrs. Patricia C. Todd
6. Doris Hart
7. Shirley J. Fry
8. Mrs. Mary A. Prentiss
9. Dorothy M. Bundy
10. Mrs. Helen P. Rihbany

1946

1. Pauline Betz
2. Margaret Osborne
3. A. Louise Brough
4. Doris Hart
5. Mrs. Patricia C. Todd
6. Mrs. Dorothy B. Cheney
7. Shirley J. Fry
8. Mrs. Mary A. Prentiss
9. Mrs. Virginia W. Kovacs
10. Dorothy Head

1947

1. A. Louise Brough
2. Mrs. Margaret O. du Pont
3. Doris Hart
4. Mrs. Patricia C. Todd
5. Shirley J. Fry
6. Barbara Krase
7. Dorothy Head
8. Mrs. Mary A. Prentiss
9. Gertrude Moran
10. Mrs. Helen P. Rihbany

1948

1. Mrs. Margaret O. du Pont
2. A. Louise Brough
3. Doris Hart
4. Gertrude Moran
5. Beverly Baker
6. Mrs. Patricia C. Todd
7. Shirley J. Fry
8. Mrs. Helen Pastall Perez
9. Mrs. Virginia W. Kovacs
10. Mrs. Helen P. Rihbany

1949

1. Mrs. Margaret O. du Pont
2. A. Louise Brough
3. Doris Hart
4. Mrs. Patricia C. Todd
5. Mrs. Helen Pastall Perez
6. Shirley J. Fry
7. Gertrude Moran
8. Mrs. Beverly B. Beckett
9. Dorothy Head
10. Barbara Scofield

USTA Rankings—Women *(cont.)*

1950
1. Mrs. Margaret O. du Pont
2. Doris Hart
3. A. Louise Brough
4. Beverly Baker
5. Mrs. Patricia C. Todd
6. Nancy Chaffee
7. Barbara Scofield
8. Shirley J. Fry
9. Mrs. Helen Pastall Perez
10. Maureen Connolly

1951
1. Maureen Connolly
2. Doris Hart
3. Shirley J. Fry
4. Mrs. Nancy Chaffee Kiner
5. Mrs. Patricia C. Todd
6. Mrs. Beverly Baker Fleitz
7. Dorothy Head
8. Mrs. Betty R. Pratt
9. Mrs. Magda Rurac
10. Mrs. Baba M. Lewis

1952
1. Maureen Connolly
2. Doris Hart
3. Shirley J. Fry
4. A. Louise Brough
5. Mrs. Nancy C. Kiner
6. Anita Kaner
7. Mrs. Patricia C. Todd
8. Mrs. Baba M. Lewis
9. Althea Gibson
10. Julia Ann Sampson

1953
1. Maureen Connolly
2. Doris Hart
3. Shirley J. Fry
4. A. Louise Brough
5. Mrs. Margaret O. du Pont
6. Mrs. Helen Pastall Perez
7. Althea Gibson
8. Mrs. Baba M. Lewis
9. Anita Kanter
10. Julia Ann Sampson

1954
1. Doris Hart
2. A. Louise Brough
3. Mrs. Beverly B. Fleitz
4. Shirley J. Fry
5. Mrs. Betty R. Pratt
6. Barbara Breit
7. Darlene Hard
8. Lois Felix
9. Mrs. Helen Pastall Perez
10. Mrs. Barbara S. Davidson

1955
1. Doris Hart
2. Shirley J. Fry
3. A. Louise Brough
4. Mrs. Dorothy Head Knode
5. Mrs. Beverly B. Fleitz
6. Mrs. Barbara S. Davidson
7. Barbara Breit
8. Althea Gibson
9. Darlene Hard
10. Mrs. Dorothy B. Cheney

1956
1. Shirley J. Fry
2. Althea Gibson
3. A. Louise Brough
4. Mrs. Margaret O. du Pont
5. Mrs. Betty R. Pratt
6. Mrs. Dorothy H. Knode
7. Darlene Hard
8. Karol Fageros
9. Janet S. Hopps
10. Miriam Arnold

1957
1. Althea Gibson
2. A. Louise Brough
3. Mrs. Dorothy H. Knode
4. Darlene Hard
5. Karol Fageros
6. Miriam Arnold
7. Jeanne Arth
8. Sally M. Moore
9. Janet S. Hopps
10. Mary Ann Mitchell

1958
1. Althea Gibson
2. Mrs. Beverly B. Fleitz
3. Darlene Hard
4. Mrs. Dorothy H. Knode
5. Mrs. Margaret O. du Pont
6. Jeanne Arth
7. Janet S. Hopps
8. Sally M. Moore
9. Gwyneth Thomas
10. Mary Ann Mitchell

1959
1. Mrs. Beverly B. Fleitz
2. Darlene Hard
3. Mrs. Dorothy H. Knode
4. Sally M. Moore
5. Janet S. Hopps
6. Karen J. Hantze
7. Mrs. Barbara G. Weigandt
8. Karol Fageros
9. Miriam Arnold
10. Lois Felix

1960
1. Darlene Hard
2. Karen Hantze
3. Nancy Richey
4. Billie Jean Moffitt
5. Donna Floyd
6. Janet Hopps
7. Gwyneth Thomas
8. Victoria Palmer
9. Kathy Chabot
10. Carol Hanks

1961
1. Darlene Hard
2. Karen Hantze
3. Billie Jean Moffitt
4. Katherine Chabot
5. Justina Bricka
6. Gwyneth Thomas
7. Marilyn Montgomery
8. Judy Alvarez
9. Carole Caldwell
10. Donna Floyd

1962
1. Darlene Hard
2. Mrs. Karen H. Susman
3. Billie Jean Moffitt
4. Carole Caldwell
5. Donna Floyd
6. Nancy Richey
7. Victoria Palmer
8. Gwyneth Thomas
9. Justina Bricka
10. Judy Alvarez

1963
1. Darlene Hard
2. Billie Jean Moffitt
3. Nancy Richey
4. Carole Caldwell
5. Gwyneth Thomas
6. Judy Alvarez
7. Carol Hanks
8. Tory A. Fretz
9. Mrs. Donna F. Fales
10. Carole Hanks

1964
1. Nancy Richey
2. Billie Jean Moffitt
3. Mrs. Carole C. Graebner
4. Mrs. Karen H. Susman
5. Mrs. Carol H. Aucamp
6. Jane Albert
7. Julie Heldman
8. Justina Bricka
9. Tory Fretz
10. Mary Ann Eisel

1965
1. Mrs. Billie Jean M. King
2. Nancy Richey
3. Mrs. Carole C. Graebner
4. Jane Albert
5. Mary Ann Eisel
6. Mrs. Carol H. Aucamp
7. Kathleen Harter
8. Julie M. Heldman
9. Tory Ann Fretz
10. Mrs. Donna F. Fales

1966
1. Mrs. Billie Jean King
2. Nancy Richey
3. Rosemary Casals
4. Tory Fretz
5. Jane Bartkowicz
6. Mary Ann Eisel
7. Mrs. Donna F. Fales
8. Mrs. Carol H. Aucamp
9. Stephanie DeFina
10. Peachy Kellmeyer

1967
1. Mrs. Billie Jean King
2. Nancy Richey
3. Mary Ann Eisel
4. Jane Bartkowicz
5. Rosemary Casals
6. Mrs. Carole C. Graebner
7. Stephanie DeFina
8. Kathleen M. Harter
9. Lynne Abbes
10. Vicky Rogers

1968
1. Nancy Richey
2. Julie Heldman
3. Vicky Rogers
4. Mary Ann Eisel
5. Kathleen Harter
6. Kristie Pigeon
7. Jane Bartkowicz
8. Linda Tuero
9. Stephanie DeFina
10. Patti Hogan

1969
1. Nancy Richey
2. Julie Heldman
3. Mrs. Mary Ann E. Curtis
4. Jane Bartkowicz
5. Patti Hogan
6. Kristie Pigeon
7. Betty Ann Grubb
8. Denise Carter
9. Valerie Ziegenfuss
10. Linda Tuero

1970
1. Mrs. Billie Jean M. King
2. Rosemary Casals
3. Mrs. Nancy Richey Gunter
4. Mrs. Mary Ann E. Curtis
5. Patti St. Ann Hogan
6. Jane Bartkowicz
7. Valerie Jean Ziegenfuss
8. Kristie Sue Pigeon
9. Mrs. Stephanie Johnson
10. Mrs. Denise Carter Triolo

1971
1. Mrs. Billie Jean M. King
2. Rosemary Casals
3. Chris Evert
4. Mrs. Nancy Richey Gunter
5. Mary Ann Eisel
6. Julie Heldman
7. Jane Bartkowicz
8. Linda Tuero
9. Patti St. Ann Hogan
10. Mrs. Denise Carter Triolo

1972
1. Mrs. Billie Jean King
2. Mrs. Nancy Richey Gunter
3. Chris Evert
4. Rosemary Casals
5. Wendy Overton
6. Patti Hogan
7. Linda Tuero
8. Julie M. Heldman
9. Pam Teegarden
10. Janet Newberry

1973
1. Mrs. Billie Jean King
2. Chris Evert
3. Rosemary Casals
4. Mrs. Nancy Richey Gunter
5. Julie M. Heldman
6. Pam Teegarden
7. Kristien Kemmer
8. Janet Newberry
9. Valerie Ziegenfuss
10. Wendy Overton

USTA Rankings—Women *(cont.)*

1974

1. Chris Evert
2. Mrs. Billie Jean King
3. Rosemary Casals
4. Mrs. Nancy Richey Gunter
5. Julie M. Heldman
6. Kathy Kuykendall
7. Pam Teegarden
8. Valerie Ziegenfuss
9. Jeanne Evert
10. Marcelyn Louie

1975

1. Chris Evert
2. Mrs. Nancy Richey Gunter
3. Julie M. Heldman
4. Wendy Overton
5. Marcelyn Louie
6. Mona Schallau
7. Kathy Kuykendall
8. Janet Newberry
9. Terry Holladay
10. Rosemary Casals

1976

1. Chris Evert
2. Rosemary Casals
3. Mrs. Nancy Richey Gunter
4. Terry Holladay
5. Marita Redondo
6. Mrs. Mona S. Guerrant
7. Kathy May
8. JoAnne Russell
9. Janet Newberry
10. Kathy Kuykendall

1977

1. Chris Evert
2. Mrs. Billie Jean King
3. Rosemary Casals
4. Tracy Austin
5. JoAnne Russell
6. Kathy May
7. Terry Holladay
8. Mrs. Kristien K. Shaw
9. Janet Newberry
10. Laura DuPont

1978

1. Chris Evert
2. Mrs. Billie Jean King
3. Tracy Austin
4. Rosemary Casals
5. Pam Shriver
6. Marita Redondo
7. Kathy May
8. Anne Smith
9. Jeanne DuVall
10. Stacy Margolin

1979

1. Martina Navratilova
2. Mrs. Chris Evert Lloyd
3. Tracy Austin
4. Mrs. Billie Jean King
5. Kathy Jordan
6. Ann Kiyomura
7. Carolina Stoll
8. Mrs. Kathy May Teacher
9. Kate Latham
10. Terry Holladay

1980

1. Tracy Austin
2. Mrs. Chris Evert Lloyd
3. Martina Navratilova
4. Andrea Jaeger
5. Mrs. Billie Jean King
6. Pam Shriver
7. Kathy Jordan
8. Bettina Bunge
9. Terry Holladay
10. Mary Lou Piatek

Tracy Austin.

ALL-AMERICAN TOP TEN

In 1970 and 1971, the USTA made an All-American ranking for men, selecting the top ten players regardless of their status as amateurs or professionals, or whether they are independent or contract professionals. The All-American ranking was an adjunct to the usual USTA rankings which include only players (amateur and independent pros) under the jurisdiction of the USTA during the ranking period.

1970

1. G. Clifford Richey, Jr.
2. Stanley R. Smith
3. Martin C. Riessen
4. Arthur R. Ashe, Jr.
5. R. Dennis Ralston
6. Richard A. Gonzales
7. Clark E. Graebner
8. Robert C. Lutz
9. Thomas W. Gorman
10. Earl Buchholz, Jr.

1971

1. Stanley R. Smith
2. Arthur R. Ashe, Jr.
3. Martin C. Riessen
4. G. Clifford Richey, Jr.
5. Clark E. Graebner
6. Thomas W. Gorman
7. James Connors
8. Erik Van Dillen
9. F. A. Froehling III
10. Robert C. Lutz

Bill Larned *(left)* and Mrs. Louise Brough Clapp *(right)* have appeared on the Men's and Women's USTA top-ten ranks the most of any players.

WORLD RANKINGS

Until recently, there has not been an "official" world ranking of tennis players. The rankings that appear here from 1914 through 1938 were made by A. Wallis Myers of the London *Daily Telegraph*. There were no rankings from 1915 to 1918, and the ladies were first rated by Myers in 1925. Sir F. Gordon Lowe did the ranking in 1939. No rankings were given from 1940 through 1945. Pierre Gillow made the rankings in 1946 and 1951, while John Dlliff did them from 1947 to 1950. Since 1952, Lance Tingay of the London *Daily Telegraph* has made the rankings. The world rankings by this group are as follows:

Men's Ranking

1914

1. Maurice E. McLoughlin (U.S.A.)
2. N. E. Brookes (Australia)
3. A. F. Wilding (New Zealand)
4. O. Froitzheim (Germany)
5. R. N. Williams (U.S.A.)
6. J. C. Parke (Ireland)
7. A. H. Lowe (England)
8. F. G. Lowe (England)
9. H. Kleinschroth (Germany)
10. M. Decugis (France)

1919

1. G. L. Patterson (Australia)
2. W. M. Johnston (U.S.A.)
3. A. H. Gobert (France)
4. W. T. Tilden (U.S.A.)
5. N. E. Brookes (Australia)
6. A. R. F. Kingscote (England)
7. R. N. Williams (U.S.A.)
8. P. M. Davson (England)
9. Willis Davis (U.S.A.)
10. W. H. Laurentz (France)

1920

1. William T. Tilden (U.S.A.)
2. W. M. Johnston (U.S.A.)
3. A. R. F. Kingscote (England)
4. J. C. Parke (Ireland)
5. A. H. Gobert (France)
6. N. E. Brookes (Australia)
7. R. N. Williams (U.S.A.)
8. W. H. Laurentz (France)
9. Z. Shimizu (Japan)
10. G. L. Patterson (Australia)

1921

1. William T. Tilden (U.S.A.)
2. W. M. Johnston (U.S.A.)
3. Vincent Richards (U.S.A.)
4. Z. Shimizu (Japan)
5. G. L. Patterson (Australia)
6. J. O. Anderson (Australia)
7. B. I. C. Norton (S. Africa)
8. M. Alonso (Spain)
9. R. N. Williams (U.S.A.)
10. A. H. Gobert (France)

1922

1. William T. Tilden (U.S.A.)
2. W. M. Johnston (U.S.A.)
3. G. L. Patterson (Australia)
4. Vincent Richards (U.S.A.)
5. J. O. Anderson (Australia)
6. H. Cochet (France)
7. P. O'Hara Wood (Australia)
8. R. N. Williams (U.S.A.)
9. A. R. F. Kingscote (England)
10. A. H. Gobert (France)

1923

1. William T. Tilden (U.S.A.)
2. W. M. Johnston (U.S.A.)
3. J. O. Anderson (Australia)
4. R. N. Williams (U.S.A.)
5. F. T. Hunter (U.S.A.)
6. Vincent Richards (U.S.A.)
7. B. I. C. Norton (S. Africa)
8. M. Alonso (Spain)
9. J. Washer (Belgium)
10. H. Cochet (France)

1924

1. William T. Tilden (U.S.A.)
2. Vincent Richards (U.S.A.)
3. J. O. Anderson (Australia)
4. W. M. Johnston (U.S.A.)
5. R. Lacoste (France)
6. J. Borotra (France)
7. H. Kinsey (U.S.A.)
8. G. L. Patterson (Australia)
9. H. Cochet (France)
10. M. Alonso (Spain)

1925

1. William T. Tilden (U.S.A.)
2. W. M. Johnston (U.S.A.)
3. Vincent Richards (U.S.A.)
4. R. Lacoste (France)
5. R. N. Williams (U.S.A.)
6. J. Borotra (France)
7. G. L. Patterson (Australia)
8. M. Alonso (Spain)
9. B. I. C. Norton (S. Africa)
10. T. Harada (Japan)

1926

1. René Lacoste (France)
2. J. Borotra (France)
3. H. Cochet (France)
4. W. M. Johnston (U.S.A.)
5. W. T. Tilden (U.S.A.)
6. Vincent Richards (U.S.A.)
7. T. Harada (Japan)
8. M. Alonso (Spain)
9. H. Kingsey (U.S.A.)
10. J. Brugnon (France)

1927

1. René Lacoste (France)
2. W. T. Tilden (U.S.A.)
3. H. Cochet (France)
4. J. Borotra (France)
5. M. Alonso (Spain)
6. F. T. Hunter (U.S.A.)
7. G. M. Lott (U.S.A.)
8. J. F. Hennessey (U.S.A.)
9. J. Brugnon (France)
10. J. Koseluh (Czechoslovakia)

1928

1. Henri Cochet (France)
2. R. Lacoste (France)
3. W. T. Tilden (U.S.A.)
4. F. T. Hunter (U.S.A.)
5. J. Borotra (France)
6. G. M. Lott (U.S.A.)
7. H. W. Austin (England)
8. J. F. Hennessey (U.S.A.)
9. H. L. de Morpurgo (Italy)
10. J. B. Hawkes (Australia)

1929

1. Henri Cochet (France)
2. R. Lacoste (France)
3. J. Borotra (France)
4. W. T. Tilden (U.S.A.)
5. F. T. Hunter (U.S.A.)
6. G. M. Lott (U.S.A.)
7. J. Doeg (U.S.A.)
8. J. Van Ryn (U.S.A.)
9. H. W. Austin (England)
10. H. L. de Morpurgo (Italy)

1930

1. Henri Cochet (France)
2. W. T. Tilden (U.S.A.)
3. J. Borotra (France)
4. J. H. Doeg (U.S.A.)
5. F. X. Shields (U.S.A.)
6. W. L. Allison (U.S.A.)
7. G. M. Lott (U.S.A.)
8. H. L. de Morpurgo (Italy)
9. S. Boussus (France)
10. H. W. Austin (England)

1931

1. Henri Cochet (France)
2. H. W. Austin (England)
3. H. E. Vines (U.S.A.)
4. F. J. Perry (England)
5. F. X. Shields (U.S.A.)
6. S. B. Wood (U.S.A.)
7. J. Borotra (France)
8. G. M. Lott (U.S.A.)
9. J. Satoh (Japan)
10. J. Van Ryn (U.S.A.)

1932

1. Ellsworth Vines (U.S.A.)
2. H. Cochet (France)
3. J. Borotra (France)
4. W. L. Allison (U.S.A.)
5. C. Sutter (U.S.A.)
6. D. Prenn (Germany)
7. F. J. Perry (England)
8. G. von Cramm (Germany)
9. H. W. Austin (England)
10. J. H. Crawford (Australia)

1933

1. J. H. Crawford (Australia)
2. F. J. Perry (England)
3. J. Satoh (Japan)
4. W. H. Austin (England)
5. H. E. Vines (U.S.A.)
6. H. Cochet (France)
7. F. X. Shields (U.S.A.)
8. S. B. Wood (U.S.A.)
9. G. von Cramm (Germany)
10. L. R. Stoefen (U.S.A.)

1934

1. Fred J. Perry (England)
2. J. H. Crawford (Australia)
3. G. von Cramm (Germany)
4. H. W. Austin (England)
5. W. L. Allison (U.S.A.)
6. S. B. Wood (U.S.A.)
7. R. Menzel (Czechoslovakia)
8. F. X. Shields (U.S.A.)
9. G. de Stefani (Italy)
10. C. Boussus (France)

1935

1. Fred J. Perry (England)
2. J. H. Crawford (Australia)
3. G. von Cramm (Germany)
4. W. L. Allison (U.S.A.)
5. H. W. Austin (England)
6. J. D. Budge (U.S.A.)
7. F. X. Shields (U.S.A.)
8. V. B. McGrath (Australia)
9. C. Boussus (France)
10. S. B. Wood (U.S.A.)

1936

1. Fred J. Perry (England)
2. G. von Cramm (Germany)
3. J. D. Budge (U.S.A.)
4. A. K. Quist (Australia)
5. H. W. Austin (England)
6. J. H. Crawford (Australia)
7. W. L. Allison (U.S.A.)
8. B. M. Grant (U.S.A.)
9. H. Henkel (Germany)
10. V. B. McGrath (Australia)

1937

1. Don Budge (U.S.A.)
2. G. von Cramm (Germany)
3. H. Henkel (Germany)
4. H. W. Austin (England)
5. R. L. Riggs (U.S.A.)
6. B. M. Grant (U.S.A.)
7. J. H. Crawford (Australia)
8. R. Menzel (Czechoslovakia)
9. F. A. Parker (U.S.A.)
10. C. E. Hare (England)

1938

1. Don Budge (U.S.A.)
2. H. W. Austin (England)
3. J. Bromwich (Australia)
4. R. L. Riggs (U.S.A.)
5. S. B. Wood (U.S.A.)
6. A. K. Quist (Australia)
7. R. Menzel (Czechoslovakia)
8. J. Yamagishi (Japan)
9. G. G. Mako (U.S.A.)
10. F. Puncec (Yugoslavia)

World Rankings—Men *(cont.)*

1939

1. Bobby Riggs (U.S.A.)
2. J. E. Bromwich (Australia)
3. A. K. Quist (Australia)
4. F. Puncec (Yugoslavia)
5. Frank A. Parker (U.S.A.)
6. H. Henkel (Germany)
7. W. D. McNeill (U.S.A.)
8. Elwood T. Cooke (U.S.A.)
9. Welby Van Horn (U.S.A.)
10. Joseph R. Hunt (U.S.A.)

1946

1. Jack Kramer (U.S.A.)
2. F. R. Schroeder (U.S.A.)
3. J. Drobny (Czechoslovakia)
4. Y. Petra (France)
5. M. Bernard (France)
6. J. Bromwich (Australia)
7. T. Brown (U.S.A.)
9. F. Parker (U.S.A.)
10. G. Brown (Australia)

1947

1. Jack Kramer (U.S.A.)
2. F. R. Schroeder (U.S.A.)
3. F. Parker (U.S.A.)
4. J. E. Bromwich (Australia)
5. J. Drobny (Czechoslovakia)
6. D. Pails (Australia)
7. T. Brown (U.S.A.)
8. B. Patty (U.S.A.)
9. J. Asboth (Hungary)
10. G. Mulloy (U.S.A.)

1948

1. Frank Parker (U.S.A.)
2. R. F. Schroeder (U.S.A.)
3. R. Gonzalez (U.S.A.)
4. J. E. Bromwich (Australia)
5. J. Drobny (Czechoslovakia)
6. E. W. Sturgess (S. Africa)
7. R. Falkenburg (U.S.A.)
8. J. Asboth (Hungary)
9. L. Bergelin (Sweden)
10. A. K. Quist (Australia)

1949

1. Pancho Gonzalez (U.S.A.)
2. F. R. Schroeder (U.S.A.)
3. W. F. Talbert (U.S.A.)
4. F. Sedgman (Australia)
5. R. Parker (U.S.A.)
6. E. W. Sturgess (S. Africa)
7. J. Drobny (Czechoslovakia)
8. B. Patty (U.S.A.)
9. G. Mulloy (U.S.A.)
10. O. W. Sidwell (Australia)

1950

1. Budge Patty (U.S.A.)
2. F. Sedgman (Australia)
3. A. Larsen (U.S.A.)
4. J. Drobny (Egypt)
5. H. Flam (U.S.A.)
6. F. R. Schroeder (U.S.A.)
7. E. V. Seixas (U.S.A.)
8. K. McGregor (Australia)
9. W. F. Talbert (U.S.A.)
10. E. W. Sturgess (S. Africa)

1951

1. Frank Sedgman (Australia)
2. R. Savitt (U.S.A.)
3. J. Drobny (Egypt)
4. E. V. Seixas (U.S.A.)
5. T. Trabert (U.S.A.)
6. F. R. Schroeder (U.S.A.)
7. K. McGregor (Australia)
8. H. Flam (U.S.A.)
9. A. Larsen (U.S.A.)
10. M. G. Rose (Australia)

1952

1. Frank Sedgman (Australia)
2. J. Drobny (Egypt)
3. K. McGregor (Australia)
4. M. G. Rose (Australia)
5. E. V. Seixas (U.S.A.)
6. H. Flam (U.S.A.)
7. G. Mulloy (U.S.A.)
8. E. W. Sturgess (S. Africa)
9. R. Savitt (U.S.A.)
10. K. Rosewall (Australia),
    L. Hoad (Australia)

1953

1. Tony Trabert (U.S.A.)
2. K. Rosewall (Australia)
3. E. V. Seixas (U.S.A.)
4. J. Drobny (Egypt)
5. L. Hoad (Australia)
6. M. G. Rose (Australia)
7. K. Nielsen (Denmark)
8. B. Patty (U.S.A.)
9. S. Davidson (Sweden)
10. E. Morea (Argentina)

1954

1. Jaroslav Drobny (Egypt)
2. T. Trabert (U.S.A.)
3. K. Rosewall (Australia)
4. E. V. Seixas (U.S.A.)
5. R. Hartwig (Australia)
6. M. G. Rose (Australia)
7. L. Hoad (Australia)
8. B. Patty (U.S.A.)
9. A. Larsen (U.S.A.)
10. E. Morea (Argentina),
    H. Richardson (U.S.A.),
    S. Davidson (Sweden)

1955

1. Tony Trabert (U.S.A.)
2. K. Rosewall (Australia)
3. L. Hoad (Australia)
4. E. V. Seixas (U.S.A.)
5. R. Hartwig (Australia)
6. B. Patty (U.S.A.)
7. H. Richardson (U.S.A.)
8. K. Nielsen (Denmark)
9. J. Drobny (Egypt)
10. S. Davidson (Sweden),
    M. G. Rose (Australia)

1956

1. Lew Hoad (Australia)
2. K. Rosewall (Australia)
3. H. Richardson (U.S.A.)
4. E. V. Seixas (U.S.A.)
5. S. Davidson (Sweden)
6. N. A. Fraser (Australia)
7. A. J. Cooper (Australia)

8. R. Savitt (U.S.A.)
9. H. Flam (U.S.A.)
10. B. Patty (U.S.A.),
  N. Pietrangeli (Italy)

1957

1. A. J. Cooper (Australia)
2. M. J. Anderson (Australia)
3. S. Davidson (Sweden)
4. H. Flam (U.S.A.)
5. N. A. Fraser (Australia)
6. M. G. Rose (Australia)
7. E. V. Seixas (U.S.A.)
8. B. Patty (U.S.A.)
9. N. Pietrangeli (Italy)
10. R. Savitt (U.S.A.)

1958

1. A. J. Cooper (Australia)
2. M. J. Anderson (Australia)
3. M. G. Rose (Australia)
4. N. A. Fraser (Australia)
5. L. Ayala (Chile)
6. H. Richardson (U.S.A.)
7. N. Pietrangeli (Italy)
8. U. Schmidt (Sweden)
9. B. MacKay (U.S.A.)
10. S. Davidson (Sweden)

1959

1. Neal A. Fraser (Australia)
2. A. Olmedo (U.S.A.)
3. N. Pietrangeli (Italy)
4. B. MacKay (U.S.A.)
5. R. Laver (Australia)
6. L. Ayala (Chile)
7. R. Emerson (Australia)
8. R. Bartzen (U.S.A.)
9. R. Krishnan (India)
10. I. Vermaak (S. Africa)

1960

1. Neal A. Fraser (Australia)
2. R. Laver (Australia)
3. N. Pietrangeli (Italy)
4. B. MacKay (U.S.A.)
5. E. Buchholz (U.S.A.)

6. R. Emerson (Australia)
7. L. Ayala (Chile)
8. R. Krishnan (India)
9. J. E. Lundquist (Sweden)
10. R. D. Ralston (U.S.A.)

1961

1. Rod Laver (Australia)
2. R. Emerson (Australia)
3. M. Santana (Spain)
4. N. Pietrangeli (Italy)
5. C. McKinley (U.S.A.)
6. R. Krishnan (India)
7. L. Ayala (Chile)
8. N. A. Fraser (Australia)
9. J. E. Lundquist (Sweden)
10. U. Schmidt (Sweden)

1962

1. Rod Laver (Australia)
2. R. Emerson (Australia)
3. M. Santana (Spain)
4. N. A. Fraser (Australia)
5. C. McKinley (U.S.A.)
6. R. H. Osuna (Mexico)
7. M. F. Mulligan (Australia)
8. R. Hewitt (Australia)
9. R. Krishnan (India)
10. W. Bungert (Germany)

1963

1. Rafael H. Osuna (Mexico)
2. C. McKinley (U.S.A.)
3. R. Emerson (Australia)
4. M. Santana (Spain)
5. F. S. Stolle (Australia)
6. F. Froehling (U.S.A.)
7. R. D. Ralston (U.S.A.)
8. B. Jovanovic (Yugoslavia)
9. M. J. Sangster (England)
10. M. F. Mulligan (Australia)

1964

1. Roy Emerson (Australia)
2. F. S. Stolle (Australia)
3. J. E. Lundquist (Sweden)
4. W. Bungert (Germany)

5. C. McKinley (U.S.A.)
6. M. Santana (Spain)
7. N. Pietrangeli (Italy)
8. C. Kuhnke (Germany)
9. R. D. Ralston (U.S.A.)
10. R. H. Osuna (Mexico)

1965

1. Roy Emerson (Australia)
2. M. Santana (Spain)
3. F. S. Stolle (Australia)
4. C. Drysdale (S. Africa)
5. R. D. Ralston (U.S.A.)
6. M. F. Mulligan (Australia)
7. J. E. Lundquist (Sweden)
8. A. D. Roche (Australia)
9. J. Newcombe (Australia)
10. A. R. Ashe (U.S.A.)

1966

1. Manuel Santana (Spain)
2. F. S. Stolle (Australia)
3. R. Emerson (Australia)
4. A. D. Roche (Australia)
5. R. D. Ralston (U.S.A.)
6. J. Newcombe (Australia)
7. A. R. Ashe (U.S.A.)
8. I. Gulyas (Hungary)
9. C. Drysdale (S. Africa)
10. K. Fletcher (Australia)

1967

1. John Newcombe (Australia)
2. R. Emerson (Australia)
3. M. Santana (Spain)
4. Marty Mulligan (Australia)
5. A. D. Roche (Australia)
6. Bob Hewitt (S. Africa)
7. N. Pilic (Yugoslavia)
8. C. Graebner (U.S.A.)
9. A. R. Ashe (U.S.A.)
10. J. Leschly (Denmark)
  W. Bungert (Germany)
  C. Drysdale (S. Africa)

World Rankings—Men *(cont.)*

1968

1. Rod Laver (Australia)
2. A. R. Ashe (U.S.A.)
3. K. R. Rosewall (Australia)
4. T. Okker (Netherlands)
5. A. D. Roche (Australia)
6. J. Newcombe (Australia)
7. C. Graebner (U.S.A.)
8. R. D. Ralston (U.S.A.)
9. Cliff Drysdale (S. Africa)
10. R. Gonzalez (U.S.A.)

1969

1. Rod Laver (Australia)
2. A. D. Roche (Australia)
3. John Newcombe (Australia)
4. T. Okker (Netherlands)
5. K. R. Rosewall (Australia)
6. A. R. Ashe (U.S.A.)
7. Cliff Drysdale (S. Africa)
8. R. Gonzalez (U.S.A.)
9. A. Gimeno (Spain)
10. F. S. Stolle (Australia)

1970

1. John Newcombe (Australia)
2. K. R. Rosewall (Australia)
3. A. D. Roche (Australia)
4. Rod Laver (Australia)
5. A. R. Ashe (U.S.A.)
6. I. Nastase (Romania)
7. T. Okker (Netherlands)
8. R. Taylor (Great Britain)
9. J. Kodes (Czechoslovakia)
10. C. Richey (U.S.A.)

1971

1. John Newcombe (Australia)
2. S. R. Smith (U.S.A.)
3. Rod Laver (Australia)
4. K. R. Rosewall (Australia)
5. J. Kodes (Czechoslovakia)
6. A. R. Ashe (U.S.A.)
7. T. Okker (Netherlands)
8. Marty C. Riessen (U.S.A.)
9. Cliff Drysdale (South Africa)
10. I. Nastase (Romania)

1972

1. Stan Smith (U.S.A.)
2. Ilie Nastase (Romania)
3. Ken Rosewall (Australia)
4. Rod Laver (Australia)
5. Arthur Ashe (U.S.A.)
6. John Newcombe (Australia)
7. Cliff Richey (U.S.A.)
8. Manuel Orantes (Spain)
9. Andres Gimeno (Spain)
10. Jan Kodes (Czechoslovakia)

1973

1. John Newcombe (Australia)
2. Stan Smith (U.S.A.)
3. Ilie Nastase (Romania)
4. Jan Kodes (Czechoslovakia)
5. Arthur Ashe (U.S.A.)
6. Ken Rosewall (Australia)
7. Rod Laver (Australia)
8. Tom Gorman (U.S.A.)
9. Jimmy Connors (U.S.A.)
10. Tom Okker (Netherlands)

1974

1. Jimmy Connors (U.S.A.)
2. Ken Rosewall (Australia)
3. John Newcombe (Australia)
4. Bjorn Borg (Sweden)
5. Ilie Nastase (Romania)
6. Stan Smith (U.S.A.)
7. Rod Laver (Australia)
8. Manuel Orantes (Spain)
9. Alex Metreveli (U.S.S.R.)
10. Guillermo Vilas (Argentina)

1975

1. Arthur Ashe (U.S.A.)
2. Manuel Orantes (Spain)
3. Jimmy Connors (U.S.A.)
4. Bjorn Borg (Sweden)
5. Guillermo Vilas (Argentina)
6. Ilie Nastase (Romania)
7. Raul Ramirez (Mexico)
8. John Newcombe (Australia)
9. Rod Laver (Australia)
10. Roscoe Tanner (U.S.A.)

1976

1. Jimmy Connors (U.S.A.)
2. Bjorn Borg (Sweden)
3. Adriano Panatta (Italy)
4. Ilie Nastase (Romania)
5. Guillermo Vilas (Argentina)
6. Eddie Dibbs (U.S.A.)
7. Harold Solomon (U.S.A.)
8. Manuel Orantes (Spain)
9. Raul Ramirez (Mexico)
10. Roscoe Tanner (U.S.A.)

1977

1. Bjorn Borg (Sweden)
2. Guillermo Vilas (Argentina)
3. Jimmy Connors (U.S.A.)
4. Vitas Gerulaitis (U.S.A.)
5. Brian Gottfried (U.S.A.)
6. Dick Stockton (U.S.A.)
7. Eddie Dibbs (U.S.A.)
8. Raul Ramirez (Mexico)
9. Harold Solomon (U.S.A.)
10. Roscoe Tanner (U.S.A.)

1978

1. Bjorn Borg (Sweden)
2. Jimmy Connors (U.S.A.)
3. Vitas Gerulaitis (U.S.A.)
4. Guillermo Vilas (Argentina)
5. Eddie Dibbs (U.S.A.)
6. Raul Ramirez (Mexico)
7. Brian Gottfried (U.S.A.)
8. Corrado Barazzutti (Italy)
9. Sandy Mayer (U.S.A.)
10. John McEnroe (U.S.A.)

1979

1. Bjorn Borg (Sweden)
2. John McEnroe (U.S.A.)
3. Jimmy Connors (U.S.A.)
4. Vitas Gerulaitis (U.S.A.)
5. Roscoe Tanner (U.S.A.)
6. Guillermo Vilas (Argentina)
7. Victor Pecci (Paraguay)
8. Jose Higueras (Spain)
9. Eddie Dibbs (U.S.A.)
10. Harold Solomon (U.S.A.)

1980

1. Bjorn Borg (Sweden)
2. John McEnroe (U.S.A.)
3. Jimmy Connors (U.S.A.)
4. Guillermo Vilas (Argentina)
5. Vitas Gerulaitis (U.S.A.)
6. Ivan Lendl (Czechoslovakia)
7. Harold Solomon (U.S.A.)
8. Gene Mayer (U.S.A.)
9. Elliot Teltscher (U.S.A.)
10. Brian Gottfried (U.S.A.)

Women's Ranking

1925

1. Suzanne Lenglen (France)
2. H. Wills (U.S.A.)
3. K. McKane (England)
4. E. Ryan (U.S.A.)
5. Mrs. M. B. Mallory (U.S.A.)
6. E. Goss (U.S.A.)
7. Mrs. Lambert Chambers (England)
8. J. Fry (England)
9. Mrs. B. Billout (France)
10. Mrs. M. Z. Jessup (U.S.A.)

1926

1. Suzanne Lenglen (France)
2. Mrs. K. M. Godfree (England)
3. L. d'Alvarez (Spain)
4. Mrs. M. B. Mallory (U.S.A.)
5. E. Ryan (U.S.A.)
6. M. Browne (U.S.A.)
7. J. Fry (England)
8. Mrs. P. H. Watson (England)
9. Mrs. M. Z. Jessup (U.S.A.)
10. D. Vlasto (France)

1927

1. Helen Wills (U.S.A.)
2. L. d'Alvarez (Spain)
3. E. Ryan (U.S.A.)

4. Mrs. M. B. Mallory (U.S.A.)
5. Mrs. K. M. Godfree (England)
6. B. Nuthall (England)
7. E. L. Heine (S. Africa)
8. J. Fry (England)
9. K. Bouman (Holland)
10. Mrs. C. H. Chapin (U.S.A.)

1928

1. Helen Wills (U.S.A.)
2. L. d'Alvarez (Spain)
3. D. Akhurst (Australia)
4. E. Bennett (England)
5. Mrs. P. H. Watson (England)
6. E. Ryan (U.S.A.)
7. C. Aussem (Germany)
8. K. Bouman (Holland)
9. H. Jacobs (U.S.A.)
10. E. Boyd (Australia)

1929

1. Helen Wills (U.S.A.)
2. Mrs. P. H. Watson (England)
3. H. Jacobs (U.S.A.)
4. B. Nuthall (England)
5. E. L. Heine (S. Africa)
6. Mrs. R. Mathieu (France)
7. E. Bennett (England)
8. P. von Reznicek (Germany)
9. Mrs. L. R. Michell (England)
10. E. A. Goldsack (England)

1930

1. Mrs. H. W. Moody (U.S.A.)
2. C. Aussem (Germany)
3. Mrs. P. H. Watson (England)
4. E. Ryan (U.S.A.)
5. Mrs. R. Mathieu (France)
6. H. Jacobs (U.S.A.)
7. J. Mudford (England)
8. L. d'Alvarez (Spain)
9. B. Nuthall (England)
10. H. Krahwinkel (Germany)

1931

1. Mrs. H. W. Moody (U.S.A.)

2. C. Aussem (Germany)
3. Mrs. F. Whittingstall (England)
4. H. Jacobs (U.S.A.)
5. B. Nuthall (England)
6. H. Krahwinkel (Germany)
7. Mrs. R. Mathieu (France)
8. L. d'Alvarez (Spain)
9. P. Mudford (England)
10. Mrs. E. A. G. Pittman (England)

1932

1. Mrs. H. W. Moody (U.S.A.)
2. H. Jacobs (U.S.A.)
3. Mrs. R. Mathieu (France)
4. L. Payot (Switzerland)
5. H. Krahwinkel (Germany)
6. M. Heeley (England)
7. Mrs. J. Whittingstall (England)
8. M. Horn (Germany)
9. K. Stammers (England)
10. J. Sigart (Belgium)

1933

1. Mrs. H. W. Moody (U.S.A.)
2. H. Jacobs (U.S.A.)
3. D. E. Round (England)
4. H. Krahwinkel (Germany)
5. M. C. Scriven (England)
6. Mrs. R. Mathieu (France)
7. S. Palfrey (U.S.A.)
8. B. Nuthall (England)
9. L. Payot (Switzerland)
10. A. Marble (U.S.A.)

1934

1. Dorothy E. Round (England)
2. H. Jacobs (U.S.A.)
3. Mrs. H. K. Sperling (Denmark)
4. S. Palfrey (U.S.A.)
5. M. C. Scriven (England)
6. Mrs. R. Mathieu (France)
7. L. Payot (Switzerland)
8. J. Hartigan (Australia)

Pam Shriver.

USTA National Tennis Center, Flushing Meadow Park, N.Y.

World Rankings—Women *(cont.)*

9. C. Aussem (Germany)
10. C. Babcock (U.S.A.)

1935

1. Mrs. H. W. Moody (U.S.A.)
2. H. Jacobs (U.S.A.)
3. K. Stammers (England)
4. Mrs. H. K. Sperling (Denmark)
5. Mrs. S. P. Fabyan (U.S.A.)
6. D. E. Round (England)
7. Mrs. H. Ardnold (U.S.A.)
8. Mrs. R. Mathieu (France)
9. J. Hartigan (Australia)
10. M. C. Scriven (England)

1936

1. Helen Jacobs (U.S.A.)

2. Mrs. H. K. Sperling (Denmark)
3. D. E. Round (England)
4. A. Marble (U.S.A.)
5. Mrs. R. Mathieu (France)
6. J. Jedrzejowska (Poland)
7. K. Stammers (England)
8. A. Lizana (Chile)
9. Mrs. S. P. Fabyan (U.S.A.)
10. C. Babcock (U.S.A.)

1937

1. Alice Lizana (Chile)
2. Mrs. K. Little (England)
3. J. Jedrzejowska (Poland)
4. Mrs. H. K. Sperling (Denmark)
5. Mrs. R. Mathieu (France)
6. H. Jacobs (U.S.A.)
7. A. Marble (U.S.A.)
8. M. Horn (Germany)
9. R. M. Hardwick (England)
10. D. M. Bundy (U.S.A.)

1938

1. Mrs. H. W. Moody (U.S.A.)
2. H. Jacobs (U.S.A.)
3. A. Marble (U.S.A.)
4. Mrs. H. K. Sperling (Denmark)
5. Mrs. R. Mathieu (France)
6. J. Jedrzejowska (Poland)
7. Mrs. S. P. Fabyan (U.S.A.)

8. Mrs. H. Miller (S. Africa)
9. K. Stammers (England)
10. N. Wynne (Australia)

1939

1. Alice Marble (U.S.A.)
2. K. Stammers (England)
3. H. Jacobs (U.S.A.)
4. Mrs. H. K. Sperling (Denmark)
5. Mrs. R. Mathieu (France)
6. Mrs. S. P. Fabyan (U.S.A.)
7. J. Jedrzejowska (Poland)
8. R. M. Hardwick (England)
9. V. E. Scott (England)
10. V. Wolfenden (U.S.A.)

1946

1. Pauline Betz (U.S.A.)
2. M. Osborne (U.S.A.)
3. A. L. Brough (U.S.A.)
4. D. Hart (U.S.A.)
5. Mrs. P. C. Todd (U.S.A.)
6. D. Bundy (U.S.A.)
7. Mrs. N. Landry (France)
8. Mrs. M. Menzies (England)
9. S. J. Fry (U.S.A.)
10. Mrs. F. Kovacs (U.S.A.)

1947

1. Margaret Osborne (U.S.A.)
2. A. L. Brough (U.S.A.)
3. D. Hart (U.S.A.)
4. Mrs. N. Bolton (Australia)
5. Mrs. P. C. Todd (U.S.A.)
6. Mrs. S. Summers (S. Africa)
7. Mrs. W. A. Bostock (England)
8. B. Krase (U.S.A.)
9. Mrs. B. Hilton (England)
10. Mrs. M. Rurac (Rumania)

1948

1. Mrs. Margaret O. du Pont (U.S.A.)

2. A. L. Brough (U.S.A.)
3. Mrs. D. Hart (U.S.A.)
4. Mrs. N. Bolton (Australia)
5. Mrs. P. C. Todd (U.S.A.)
6. Mrs. E. W. A. Bostock (England)
7. Mrs. S. Summers (S. Africa)
8. S. J. Fry (U.S.A.)
9. Mrs. M. Rurac (Rumania)
10. Mrs. N. Landry (France)

1949

1. Mrs. Margaret O. du Pont (U.S.A.)
2. A. L. Brough (U.S.A.)
3. D. Hart (U.S.A.)
4. Mrs. N. Bolton (Australia)
5. Mrs. P. C. Todd (U.S.A.)
6. Mrs. B. Hilton (England)
7. Mrs. S. Summers (S. Africa)
8. Mrs. A. Bossi (Italy)
9. Mrs. P. J. Curry (England)
10. Mrs. J. J. Walker-Smith (England)

1950

1. Mrs. Margaret O. du Pont (U.S.A.)
2. A. L. Brough (U.S.A.)
3. D. Hart (U.S.A.)
4. Mrs. P. C. Todd (U.S.A.)
5. Mrs. B. Scofield (U.S.A.)
6. N. Chaffee (U.S.A.)
7. B. Baker (U.S.A.)
8. S. J. Fry (U.S.A.)
9. Mrs. A. Bossi (Italy)
10. Mrs. H. Weiss (Argentina)

1951

1. Doris Hart (U.S.A.)
2. M. Connolly (U.S.A.)
3. S. J. Fry (U.S.A.)
4. Mrs. N. C. Kiner (U.S.A.)
5. Mrs. Walker-Smith (England)

6. J. Quertier (England)
7. A. L. Brough (U.S.A.)
8. Mrs. J. Fleitz (U.S.A.)
9. Mrs. P. C. Todd (U.S.A.)
10. Mrs. J. Maule (England)

1952

1. Maureen Connolly (U.S.A.)
2. D. Hart (U.S.A.)
3. A. L. Brough (U.S.A.)
4. S. J. Fry (U.S.A.)
5. Mrs. P. C. Todd (U.S.A.)
6. Mrs. N. C. Kiner (U.S.A.)
7. Mrs. T. C. Long (Australia)
8. Mrs. J. Walker-Smith (England)
9. Mrs. I. Rinkel-Quertier (England)
10. Mrs. D. Knode (U.S.A.)

1953

1. Maureen Connolly (U.S.A.)
2. D. Hart (U.S.A.)
3. A. L. Brough (U.S.A.)
4. S. J. Fry (U.S.A.)
5. Mrs. W. du Pont (U.S.A.)
6. Mrs. D. Knode (U.S.A.)
7. Mrs. S. Kormoczy (Hungary)
8. A. Mortimer (England)
9. H. Fletcher (England)
10. Mrs. I. Rinkel-Quertier (England)

1954

1. Maureen Connolly (U.S.A.)
2. D. Hart (U.S.A.)
3. Mrs. B. Fleitz (U.S.A.)
4. A. L. Brough (U.S.A.)
5. Mrs. W. du Pont (U.S.A.)
6. S. J. Fry (U.S.A.)
7. Mrs. S. Pratt (Jamaica)
8. H. Fletcher (England)
9. A. Mortimer (England)
10. Mrs. T. C. Long (Australia)

World Rankings—Women *(cont.)*

1955

1. A. Louise Brough (U.S.A.)
2. D. Hart (U.S.A.)
3. Mrs. B. Fleitz (U.S.A.)
4. A. Mortimer (England)
5. Mrs. D. Knode (U.S.A.)
6. B. Breit (U.S.A.)
7. D. Hard (U.S.A.)
8. B. Penrose (Australia)
9. P. E. Ward (England)
10. Mrs. S. Kormoczy (Hungary)
    S. J. Fry (U.S.A.)

1956

1. Shirley J. Fry (U.S.A.)
2. A. Gibson (U.S.A.)
3. A. L. Brough (U.S.A.)
4. A. Mortimer (England)
5. Mrs. S. Kormoczy (Hungary)
6. A. Buxton (England)
7. S. J. Bloomer (England)
8. P. E. Ward (England)
9. Mrs. S. Pratt (Jamaica)
10. Mrs. W. du Pont (U.S.A.) D. Hard (U.S.A.)

1957

1. Althea Gibson (U.S.A.)
2. D. Hard (U.S.A.)
3. S. J. Bloomer (England)
4. A. L. Brough (U.S.A.)
5. Mrs. D. Knode (U.S.A.)
6. V. Puzejova (Czechoslovakia)
7. A. Haydon (England)
8. Y. Ramirez (Mexico)
9. C. C. Truman (England)
10. Mrs. W. du Pont (U.S.A.)

1958

1. Althea Gibson (U.S.A.)
2. Mrs. S. Kormoczy (Hungary)
3. Mrs. B. Fleitz (U.S.A.)
4. D. Hart (U.S.A.)
5. S. Bloomer (England)
6. C. C. Truman (England)
7. A. Mortimer (England)
8. A. S. Haydon (England)
9. M. E. Bueno (Brazil)
10. Mrs. D. Knode (U.S.A.)

1959

1. Maria E. Bueno (Brazil)
2. C. C. Truman (England)
3. D. Hard (U.S.A.)
4. Mrs. B. Fleitz (U.S.A.)
5. S. Reynolds (S. Africa)
6. A. Mortimer (England)
7. A. S. Haydon (England)
8. Mrs. S. Kormoczy (Hungary)
9. S. Moore (U.S.A.)
10. Y. Ramirez (Mexico)

1960

1. Maria E. Bueno (Brazil)
2. D. Hard (U.S.A.)
3. S. Reynolds (S. Africa)
4. C. C. Truman (England)
5. Mrs. S. Kormoczy (Hungary)
6. A. S. Haydon (England)
7. A. Mortimer (England)
8. J. Lehane (Australia)
9. Y. Ramirez (Mexico)
10. R. Schuurman (S. Africa)

1961

1. Angela Mortimer (England)
2. D. Hard (U.S.A.)
3. A. S. Haydon (England)
4. M. Smith (Australia)
5. S. Reynolds (S. Africa)
6. Y. Ramirez (Mexico)
7. C. C. Truman (England)
8. Mrs. S. Kormoczy (Hungary)
9. R. Schuurman (S. Africa)
10. K. Hantze (U.S.A.)

1962

1. Margaret Smith (Australia)
2. M. E. Bueno (Brazil)
3. D. Hard (U.S.A.)
4. Mrs. J. R. Susman (U.S.A.)
5. Mrs. V. Sukova (Czechoslovakia)
6. Mrs. L. Price (S. Africa)
7. L. Turner (S. Africa)
8. A. S. Haydon (England)
9. R. Schuurman (S. Africa)
10. A. Mortimer (England)

1963

1. Margaret Smith (Australia)
2. L. Turner (Australia)
3. M. E. Bueno (Brazil)
4. B. J. Moffitt (U.S.A.)
5. A. H. Jones (England)
6. D. Hard (U.S.A.)
7. J. Lehane (Australia)
8. R. Schuurman (S. Africa)
9. N. Richey (U.S.A.)
10. Mrs. V. Sukova (Czechoslovakia)

1964

1. Margaret Smith (Australia)
2. M. E. Bueno (Brazil)
3. L. Turner (Australia)
4. Mrs. C. Graebner (U.S.A.)
5. H. Schultze (Germany)
6. N. Richey (U.S.A.)
7. B. J. Moffitt (U.S.A.)
8. Mrs. R. J. Susman (U.S.A.)
9. R. Ebbern (Australia)
10. J. Lehane (Australia)

1965

1. Margaret Smith (Australia)
2. M. E. Bueno (Brazil)
3. L. Turner (Australia)
4. B. J. Moffitt (U.S.A.)
5. Mrs. A. H. Jones (England)
6. A. Van Zyl (S. Africa)
7. C. C. Truman (England)
8. N. Richey (U.S.A.)
9. Mrs. C. Graebner (U.S.A.)
10. F. Durr (France)

1966

1. Mrs. Billie Jean King (U.S.A.)

2. M. Smith (Australia)
3. M. E. Bueno (Brazil)
4. Mrs. A. H. Jones (England)
5. N. Richey (U.S.A.)
6. A. Van Zyl (S. Africa)
7. N. Baylon (Argentina)
8. F. Durr (France)
9. R. Casals (U.S.A.)
10. K. Melville (Australia)

1967

1. Mrs. Billie Jean King (U.S.A.)
2. Mrs. A. H. Jones (England)
3. F. Durr (France)
4. N. Richey (U.S.A.)
5. L. Turner (Australia)
6. R. Casals (U.S.A.)
7. M. E. Bueno (Brazil)
8. S. V. Wade (England)
9. K. Melville (Australia)
10. J. A. M. Tegart (Australia)

1968

1. Mrs. Billie Jean King (U.S.A.)
2. Miss S. V. Wade (England)
3. N. Richey (U.S.A.)
4. M. E. Bueno (Brazil)
5. M. S. Court (Australia)
6. Mrs. A. H. Jones (England)
7. J. A. M. Tegart (Australia)
8. Mrs. J. du Plooy (S. Africa)
9. Mrs. W. W. Bowrey (Australia)
10. R. Casals (U.S.A.)

1969

1. Mrs. Margaret S. Court (Australia)
2. Mrs. A. H. Jones (England)
3. Mrs. B. J. King (U.S.A.)
4. N. Richey (U.S.A.)
5. J. Heldman (U.S.A.)
6. R. Casals (U.S.A.)
7. K. Melville (Australia)
8. J. Bartkowicz (U.S.A.)
9. S. V. Wade (England)
10. Mrs. W. W. Bowrey (Australia)

1970

1. Mrs. Margaret S. Court (Australia)
2. Mrs. B. J. King (U.S.A.)
3. R. Casals (U.S.A.)
4. S. V. Wade (England)
5. H. Niessen (Germany)
6. K. Melville (Australia)
7. J. Heldman (U.S.A.)
8. K. Krantzcke (Australia)
9. F. Durr (France)
10. Mrs. N. R. Gunter (U.S.A.)

1971

1. Evonne Goolagong (Australia)
2. Mrs. B. J. King (U.S.A.)
3. Mrs. M. S. Court (Australia)
4. R. Casals (U.S.A.)
5. S. V. Wade (England)
6. F. Durr (France)
7. Mrs. H. N. Masthoff (Germany)
8. K. Melville (Australia)
9. Mrs. N. R. Gunter (U.S.A.)
10. Mrs. J. T. Dalton (Australia)

1972

1. Mrs. Billie Jean King (U.S.A.)
2. Evonne Goolagong (Australia)
3. Chris Evert (U.S.A.)
4. Mrs. Margaret S. Court (Australia)
5. Kerry Melville (Australia)
6. Virginia Wade (Britain)
7. Rosemary Casals (U.S.A.)
8. Mrs. Nancy Richey Gunter (U.S.A.)
9. Francoise Durr (France)
10. Linda Tuero (U.S.A.)

1973

1. Mrs. Margaret S. Court (Australia)

2. Mrs. Billie Jean King (U.S.A.)
3. Chris Evert (U.S.A.)
4. Evonne Goolagong (Australia)
5. Kerry Melville (Australia)
6. Virginia Wade (Britain)
7. Rosemary Casals (U.S.A.)
8. Mrs. Helga N. Masthoff (W. Germany)
9. Olga Morozova (U.S.S.R.)
10. Betty Stove (Netherlands)

1974

1. Chris Evert (U.S.A.)
2. Mrs. Billie Jean King (U.S.A.)
3. Evonne Goolagong (Australia)
4. Olga Morozova (U.S.S.R.)
5. Kerry Melville (Australia)
6. Rosemary Casals (U.S.A.)
7. Virginia Wade (Britain)
8. Mrs. Helga N. Masthoff (W. Germany)
9. Julie Heldman (U.S.A.)
10. Mrs. Nancy Richey Gunter (U.S.A.)

1975

1. Chris Evert (U.S.A.)
2. Mrs. Billie Jean King (U.S.A.)
3. Mrs. Evonne Goolagong Cawley (Australia)
4. Martina Navratilova (Czechoslovakia)
5. Virginia Wade (Britain)
6. Mrs. Margaret S. Court (Australia)
7. Olga Morozova (U.S.S.R.)
8. Kazuko Sawamatsu (Japan)
9. Julie Heldman (U.S.A.)
10. Mrs. Kerry M. Reid (Australia)

World Rankings—Women *(cont.)*

1976

1. Chris Evert (U.S.A.)
2. Mrs. Evonne Goolagong Cawley (Australia)
3. Virginia Wade (Britain)
4. Rosemary Casals (U.S.A.)
5. Martina Navratilova (Czechoslovakia)
6. Dianne Fromholtz (Australia)
7. Mrs. Kerry M. Reid (Australia)
8. Sue Barker (Britain)
9. Mima Jausovec (Yugoslavia)
10. Olga Morozova (U.S.S.R.)

1977

1. Chris Evert (U.S.A.)
2. Virginia Wade (Great Britain)
3. Mrs. Billie Jean King (U.S.A.)
4. Martina Navratilova (U.S.A.)
5. Sue Barker (Great Britain)
6. Mrs. Kerry M. Reid (Australia)
7. Wendy Turnbull (Australia)
8. Rosemary Casals (U.S.A.)
9. Betty Stove (The Netherlands)
10. Mima Jausovec (Yugoslavia)

1978

1. Martina Navratilova (U.S.A.)
2. Chris Evert (U.S.A.)
3. Mrs. Evonne G. Cawley (Australia)
4. Virginia Wade (Great Britain)
5. Mrs. Billie Jean King (U.S.A.)
6. Wendy Turnbull (Australia)
7. Virginia Ruzici (Romania)
8. Mima Jausovec (Yugoslavia)
9. Regina Marsikova (Czechoslovakia)
10. Pam Shriver (U.S.A.)

1979

1. Martina Navratilova (U.S.A.)
2. Tracy Austin (U.S.A.)
3. Mrs. Chris Evert Lloyd (U.S.A.)
4. Mrs. Billie Jean King (U.S.A.)
5. Mrs. Evonne G. Cawley (Australia)
6. Virginia Wade (Great Britain)
7. Dianne Fromholtz (Australia)
8. Wendy Turnbull (Australia)
9. Virginia Ruzici (Romania)
10. Sylvia Hanika (West Germany)

1980

1. Mrs. Chris Evert Lloyd (U.S.A.)
2. Mrs. Evonne G. Cawley (Australia)
3. Tracy Austin (U.S.A.)
4. Martina Navratilova (U.S.A.)
5. Hana Mandlikova (Czechoslovakia)
6. Mrs. Billie Jean King (U.S.A.)
7. Virginia Ruzici (Romania)
8. Andrea Jaeger (U.S.A.)
9. Wendy Turnbull (Australia)
10. Kathy Jordan (U.S.A.)

LEADING MEMBERS OF THE FIRST TEN: 1885–1980

Men	Total Years	Between	Years No. 1
Bill Larned	19	1892–1911	8
Frank Parker	17	1933–1949	2
Arthur Ashe, Jr.	13	1963–1976	2
Gardnar Mulloy	14	1939–1954	1
Vic Seixas	13	1942–1966	3
Bill Talbert	13	1941–1954	0
Bill Tilden	12	1918–1929	10
Bill Johnson	12	1913–1926	2
Women			
Billie Jean Moffitt King	17	1960–1980	7
A. Louise Brough	16	1941–1957	1
Nancy Richey Gunter	16	1960–1976	4
Margaret Osborne duPont	14	1938–1958	3
Doris Hart	14	1942–1955	2
Helen Jacobs	13	1927–1941	4
Molla Bjurstedt Mallory	13	1915–1928	7
Sarah Palfrey Fabyan Cooke	13	1929–1945	2
Shirley Fry	13	1944–1956	1

Mrs. Ann Haydon Jones *(left)* has been in the world's first ten for 12 years, while H. W. "Bunny" Austin *(right)* has appeared for 11 years, but neither has been ranked number one. Austin never won a major international event; however, he was an outstanding player in the 1930s.

ALL-TIME RECORDS

With "sudden death" play (see page 208) in use, most of the following records will remain intact:

Men's Singles

126 games. Roger Taylor, England, d. Wieslaw Gasiorek, Poland, 27-29, 31-29, 6-4. King's Cup match, Warsaw, 1966.

112 games. Pancho Gonzales, Los Angeles, d. Charlie Pasarell, Santurce, P.R., 22-24, 1-6, 16-14, 6-3, 11-9. First round, Wimbledon, 1969.

107 games. Dick Knight, Seattle, d. Mike Sprengelmeyer, Dubuque, Iowa, 32-30, 3-6, 19-17. Qualifying round, Meadow Club Invitation, Southampton, N.Y., 1967.

100 games. F. D. Robbins, Salt Lake City, d. Dick Dell, Bethesda, Md., 22-20, 9-7, 6-8, 8-10, 6-4. First round, U.S. Open, Forest Hills, 1969.

100 games (not completed). Jaroslav Drobny, Czechoslovakia, tied with Budge Patty, France, 21-19, 8-10, 21-21. Lyons Covered Courts Invitation, Lyons, France, 1955.

95 games. Vic Seixas, Philadelphia, d. Bill Bowrey, Australia, 32-34, 6-4, 10-8. Third round. Pennsylvania Grass Championships, Merion Cricket Club, Philadelphia, 1966.

94 games. Dennis Ralston, Bakersfield, Calif., d. John Newcombe, Australia, 19-17, 20-18, 4-6, 6-4. Quarterfinal, Australian Open, Sydney, 1970.

93 games. Jaroslav Drobny d. Budge Patty, 8-6, 16-18, 3-6, 8-6, 2-10. Third round, Wimbledon, 1953.

92 games. Allan Stone, Australia, d. Phil Dent, Australia, 6-3, 20-22, 6-1, 8-10, 9-7. First round, Victorian Championships, Melbourne, 1968.

90 games. Rod Laver, Australia, d. Tony Roche, Australia, 7-5, 22-20, 9-11, 1-6, 6-3. Semifinal, Australian Open, Brisbane, 1969.

Women's Singles

62 games. Kathy Blake, Pacific Palisades, Calif., d. Elena Subirats, Mexico, 12-10, 6-8, 14-12. First round, Piping Rock, Locust Valley, N.Y., 1966.

60 games. Kristie Pigeon, Danville, Calif., d. Karen Krantzcke, Australia, 17-15, 2-6, 11-9. First round, Kingston Invitation, Kingston, Jamaica, 1969.

56 games. Helen Jacobs, Berkeley, Calif., d. Ellen Whittingstall, England, 9-11, 6-2, 15-13. Quarterfinal, British Hard Courts, Bournemouth, 1933.

54 games. A. Weiwers, France, d. Mrs. O. Anderson, U.S., 8-10, 14-12, 6-4. Second round, Wimbledon, 1948.

53 games. Mary Ann Eisel, St. Louis, d. Karen Krantzcke, Australia, 3-6, 16-14, 8-6. Final, Piping Rock, 1968.

53 games. Corinne Molesworth, England, d. Pam Teeguarden, Los Angeles, 3-6, 7-5, 17-15. Third round, Palace Indoor, Torquay, England, 1968.

51 games. Juliette Atkinson d. Marion Jones, 6-3, 5-7, 6-4, 2-6, 7-5 (best of 5 sets). Final, National Singles, Philadelphia Cricket Club, Philadelphia, 1898.

54 games. Molly Hannas, Kansas City, Mo., d. Lourdes Diaz, Mexico, 9-7, 13-15, 6-4. First round, National Girls 18 Championships, Philadelphia Cricket Club, Philadelphia, 1969.

49 games. Mabel Cahill d. Elizabeth Moore, 5-7, 6-3, 6-4, 4-6, 6-2 (best of 5 sets). Final, National Singles, Philadelphia, 1891.

48 games. Mrs. Margaret Osborne du Pont, Wilmington, Del., d. Louise Brough, Beverly Hills, Calif., 4-6, 6-4, 15-13. Final, National Singles, West Side Tennis Club, Forest Hills, 1948.

48 games. Janet Hopps, Seattle, d. Mary Ann Mitchell, San Leandro, Calif., 4-6, 6-4, 15-13. Seattle Championships, 1956. Seattle, Wash.

Men's Doubles

147 games. Dick Leach, Arcadia, Calif., and Dick Dell, Bethesda, Md., d. Len Schloss, Baltimore, and Tom Mozur, Sweetwater, Tenn., 3-6, 49-47, 22-20. Second round, Newport Casino, Newport, R.I., 1967.

144 games. Bobby Wilson and Mark Cox, both England, d. Ron Holmberg, Highland Falls, N.Y., and Charlie Pasarell, Santurce, P.R., 26-24, 17-19, 30-28. Quarterfinal, National Indoors, Salisbury, Md., 1968.

134 games. Ted Schroeder, La Crescenta, Calif., and Bob Falkenburg, Los Angeles, d. Pancho Gonzales, Los Angeles, and Hugh Stewart, San Marino, Calif., 36-34, 2-6, 4-6, 6-4, 19-17. Final, Southern California Champions, Los Angeles, 1949.

106 games. Len Schloss and Tom Mozur d. Chris Bovett, England, and Butch Seewagen, Bayside, N.Y., 7-5, 48-46. Second round, Meadow Club, 1967.

105 games. Cliff Drysdale and Ray Moore, both South Africa, d. Roy Emerson, Australia, and Ron Barnes, Brazil, 29-31, 8-6, 3-6, 8-6, 6-2. Quarterfinal, National Doubles, Longwood Cricket Club, Boston. 1967.

105 games. Jim Osborne, Honolulu, and Bill Bowrey, Australia, d. Terry Addison and Ray Keldie, both Australia, 3-6, 43-41, 7-5. Semifinal, Pennsylvania Grass, Merion Cricket Club, Philadelphia, 1969.

105 games. Joaquin Loyo-Mayo and Marcelo Lara, both of Mexico, d. Manolo Santana, Spain, and Luis Garcia, Mexico, 10-12, 24-22, 11-9, 3-6, 6-2. Third round, National Doubles, Longwood, 1966.

102 games. Don White, Coronado, Calif., and Bob Galloway, La Jolla, Calif., d. Hugh Sweeney and Lamar Roemer, both Houston, 6-4, 17-15, 4-6, 18-20, 7-5. First round, National Doubles, Longwood, 1964.

102 games. Russell Bobbitt and Bitsy Grant, both Atlanta, d. Ed Amark, San Francisco, and Robin Hippenstiel, San Bernardino, Calif., 14-12, 15-17, 6-4, 4-6, 13-11. Second round, National Doubles, Longwood 1941.

100 games. Bob Lutz, Los Angeles, Joaquin Loyo-Mayo, Mexico, d. Bill Bond, La Jolla, Calif., and Dick Leach, 19-17, 33-31. Quarterfinal, Thunderbird, Phoenix, 1969.

Women's Doubles

81 games. Nancy Richey, San Angelo, Tex., and Mrs. Carole Caldwell Graebner, New York, d. Justina Bricka and Carol Hanks, both St. Louis, 31-33, 6-1, 6-4. Semifinal Eastern Grass, Orange Lawn Tennis Club, South Orange, N.J., 1964.

48 games. Pat Brazier and Christabel Wheatcroft, both England, d. Mildred Nonweiller and Betty Soames, both England, 11-9, 5-7, 9-7. First round, Wimbledon, 1933.

48 games. Mrs. Billie Jean Moffitt King, Long Beach, Calif., and Rosie Casals, San Francisco, d. Mrs. Ann Haydon Jones, England, and Françoise Durr, France, 6-8, 8-6, 11-9. Final Pacific Southwest Open, Los Angeles, 1969.

Mixed Doubles

71 games. Mrs. Margaret Osborne duPont, Wilmington, Del., and Bill Talbert, New York, d. Gussie Moran, Santa Monica, Calif., and Bob Falkenburg, Los Angeles, 27-25, 5-7, 6-1. Semifinal, National Mixed, West Side Tennis Club, Forest Hills, 1948.

61 games. Jane Albert, Pebble Beach, Calif., and Dave Reed, Glendale, Calif., d. Kathy Blake, Pacific Palisades, Calif., and Gene Scott, New York, 6-3, 7-9, 19-17. Semifinal, Thunderbird, Phoenix, Ariz., 1965.

58 games. Virginia Wade, England, and Dick Crealy, Australia, d. Mrs. Joyce Barclay Williams and Bob Howe, both England, 7-5, 17-19, 6-4. Third round, U.S. Open, Forest Hills, 1969.

52 games. C. Lyon and W. Dixon, both England, d. Ann Barclay, Canada, and O. K. French, Australia, 2-6, 9-7, 15-13. Second Round, Wimbledon, 1963.

Longest Sets (Men's Singles)

70 games. John Brown, Australia, d. Bill Brown, Omaha, *36-34*, 6-1. Third round, Heart of America, Kansas City, Mo., 1968.

66 games. Vic Seixas d. Bill Bowrey, *32-34*, 6-4, 10-8. Merion.

64 games. Roger Taylor d. Taddeus Nowicki, Poland, *33-31*, 6-1. King's Cup, 1966.

One of the greatest professional matches of all times was Pancho Gonzales's five-set victory over favored Rod Laver in the final match of the 1969 Madison Square Garden Classic. *(above)* Gonzales serves in the fourth set.

62 games. Dick Knight d. Mike Sprengelmeyer, *32-30*, 3-6, 19-17. Southampton, 1967.

56-60 games. Roger Taylor d. Wieslaw Gasiorek, *27-29, 31-29*, 6-4. King's Cup, 1966.

54 games. Frank Froehling III, Coral Gables, Fla., d. Marty Riessen, Evanston, Ill., 7-5, *28-26*. Quarterfinal, Pennsylvania Grass, Merion, Philadelphia, 1964.

Longest Sets (Women's Singles)

36 games. Billie Jean Moffitt d. Christine Truman, England, 6-4, *19-17*. Wightman Cup, Cleveland Skating Club, Cleveland, 1963.

34 games. Lesley Hunt, Australia, d. Cerzsebat Polgar, Hungary, *18-16,* 6-3. Semifinal, Montana Invitation, Montana, Switzerland, 1969.

32 games. Kristie Pigeon d. Karen Krantzcke, *17-15,* 2-6, 11-9. Kingston, Jamaica, 1969.

Longest Sets (Men's Doubles)

96 games. Dick Leach and Dick Dell d. Len Schloss and Tom Mozur, 3-6, *49-47,* 22–20. Newport, 1966.

94 games. Schloss and Mozur d. Chris Bovett and Butch Seewagen, 7-5, *48-46.* Southampton, 1967.

84 games. Jim Osborne and Bill Bowrey d. Terry Addison and Ray Keldie, 3-6, *43–41,* 7-5. Merion, 1969.

70 games. Ted Schroeder and Bob Falkenburg d. Pancho Gonzales and Hugh Stewart, *36-34,* 3-6, 4-6, 6-4, 19-17. Southern California, 1949.

64 games. Bob Lutz and Joaquin Loyo-Mayo d. Bill Bond and Dick Leach, 19-17, *33–31.* Thunderbird, 1969.

62 games. Pancho Segura and Alex Olmedo, both Los Angeles, d. Abe Segal and Gordon Forbes, both South Africa, *32-30,* 5-7, 6-4, 6-4. Second round, Wimbledon, 1968.

60 games. Budge Patty, Paris, and Tony Trabert, Cincinnati, d. Frank Sedgman and Ken McGregor, both Australia, 6-4, *31–29,* 7-9, 6-2. Quarterfinal, Wimbledon, 1950.

60 games. Cliff Drysdale and Ray Moore d. Roy Emerson and Ron Barnes, *29-31,* 8-6, 3-6, 8-6, 6-2. National Doubles, 1967.

Longest Sets (Women's Doubles)

64 games. Nancy Richey and Mrs. Carole Caldwell Graebner d. Justina Bricka and Carol Hanks, *31-33,* 6-1, 6-4. Easterns, 1964.

Most Games Won in Succession

In two successive 1925 tournaments—Nassau Country Club and Agawam Hunt—William T. Tilden II won 57 games in a row and 63 games out of 64 played in this streak. This remarkable run began in the final match at Nassau when, playing Alfred Chapin, Jr., he was 3-4 in the first set and did not lose another game. He had previously won two love sets from Takeichi Harada. Going on to Providence for the Agawam tournament, Tilden won his first three matches without the loss of a game. He then won the first set from Carl Fischer at love, making his fifty-seventh.

Shortest Set in a Tournament Match

In 1925, *American Lawn Tennis* magazine recorded a 6-0 set that required only nine minutes. Ray Casey, United States, beat Pat Wheatley, Great Britain, in an international match at Eastbourne. The score, 6-0, 6-1, 6-3. "It is doubtful," commented ALT at the time, "whether there is any authenticated case of a set being won in less than nine minutes."

It is interesting to examine the problem involved in winning a set in less than nine minutes. The following analysis appeared in *ALT:*

A 6-0 set requires a minimum of 24 points. There must be three changes of sides. If the winner of the 6-0 set serves first, he can win three service games with four service aces in each, or 12 in all. He can also win the three in which his opponent serves by aceing the 12 serves. That is 24 strokes plus the 12 in the other three games, or 36 strokes in all. This is assuming that the first serve in each game is good. Players have served four consecutive aces in a game. Tilden, Anderson, and Williams have all done so; and McLoughlin aced four first services of Wilding in one game in 1914.

If the minimum of 24 points and 36 strokes is achieved it is still somewhat of a feat to crowd them into nine minutes. Even if the three changes of sides are not taken into consideration, that is 15 seconds to a stroke. Fast work!

Of course, there has never been such an achievement as 24 consecutive points scored in a set, each of the first services being good and each of the returns of service being an ace. Mrs. Hazel Hotchkiss Wightman did win a 6-0, 6-0 tournament match in which her opponent failed to win a point, but no record was kept of the point details of the two sets.

THE GRAND SLAMS OF TENNIS

First to win a traditional Grand Slam—the championships of Australia, France, England, and the United States in the same season—was Don Budge of Oakland, Calif., in 1938. Then came Maureen Connolly of San Diego in 1953 and Rod Laver, the Australian, in 1962, as an amateur, and again in 1969 when the Slam first became open to all competitors. Margaret Smith Court won the Grand Slam of women's tennis in 1970. Slams also have been made in doubles by Frank Sedgman and Ken McGregor, Australians, in 1951, and in mixed doubles by Margaret Smith Court and Ken Fletcher, Australians, in 1963.

The complete record of all Grand Slams follows:

Don Budge, 1938, Singles

AUSTRALIA, at Adelaide: d. Les Hancock, 6-2, 6-3, 6-4; H. Whillans, 6-1, 6-0, 6-1; L. A. Schwarts, 6-4, 6-3, 10-8; Adrian Quist, 5-7, 6-4, 6-1, 6-2; John Bromwich, 6-4, 6-2, 6-1.

FRANCE, at Roland Garros, Paris: d. Antoine Gentien, 6-1, 6-2, 6-4; Ghaus Mohammed, 6-1, 6-1, 5-7, 6-0; Franz Kukuljevic, 6-2, 8-6, 2-6, 1-6, 6-1; Bernard Destremeau, 6-4, 6-3, 6-4; Josip Pallada, 6-2, 6-3, 6-3; Roderic Menzel, 6-3, 6-2, 6-4.

ENGLAND, at Wimbledon, London: d. Kenneth Gandar-Dower, 6-2, 6-3, 6-3; Henry Billington, 7-5, 6-1, 6-1; George Lyttleton Rogers, 6-0, 7-5, 6-1; Ronald Shayes, 6-3, 6-4, 6-1; Franz Cejnar, 6-3, 6-0, 7-5; Henner Henkel, 6-2, 6-4, 6-0; Henry Austin, 6-1, 6-0, 6-3.

UNITED STATES, at Forest Hills: d. Welby Van Horn, 6-0, 6-0, 6-1; Bob Kamrath, 6-3, 7-5, 9-7; Charles Hare, 6-3, 6-4, 6-0; Harry Hopman, 6-3, 6-1, 6-3; Sidney Wood, 6-3, 6-3, 6-3; Gene Mako, 6-3, 6-8, 6-2, 6-1.

Maureen Connolly, 1953, Singles

AUSTRALIA, at Kooyong, Melbourne: d. C. Boreilli, 6-0, 6-1; Mrs. R. W. Baker, 6-1, 6-0; P. Southcombe, 6-0, 6-1; Mary Hawton, 6-2, 6-1; Julie Sampson, 6-3, 6-2.

FRANCE, at Roland Garros, Paris: d. Christiane Mercelis, 6-1, 6-3; Raymonde Verber Jones, 6-3, 6-1; Susan Patridge Chatrier, 3-6, 6-2, 6-2; Dorothy Head Knode, 6-3, 6-3; Doris Hart, 6-2, 6-4.

ENGLAND, at Wimbledon, London: d. D. Killian, 6-0, 6-0; J. M. Petchell, 6-1, 6-1; Anne Shilcock, 6-0, 6-1; Erika Vollmer, 6-3, 6-0; Shirley Fry, 6-1, 6-1; Doris Hart, 8-6, 7-5.

Don Budge was the first player to complete the Grand Slam of Tennis.

UNITED STATES, at Forest Hills: d. Jean Fallot, 6-1, 6-0; Pat Stewart, 6-3, 6-1; Jeanne Arth, 6-1, 6-3; Althea Gibson, 6-2, 6-3; Shirley Fry, 6-1, 6-1; Doris Hart, 6-2, 6-4.

Rod Laver, 1962, Singles

AUSTRALIA, at White City, Sydney: d. Fred Sherriff, 8-6, 6-2, 6-4; Geoff Pares, 10-8, 18-16, 7-9, 7-5; Owen Davidson, 6-4, 9-7, 6-4; Bob Hewitt, 6-1, 4-6, 6-4, 7-5; Roy Emerson, 8-6, 0-6, 6-4, 6-4.

FRANCE, at Roland Garros, Paris: d. Michele Pirro, 6-4, 6-0, 6-2; Tony Pickard, 6-2, 9-7, 4-6, 6-1; Sergio Jacobini, 4-6, 6-3, 7-5, 6-1; Marty Mulligan, 6-4, 3-6, 2-6, 10-8, 6-2; Neale Fraser, 3-6, 6-3, 6-2, 3-6, 7-5; Roy Emerson, 3-6, 2-6, 6-3, 9-7, 6-2.

ENGLAND, at Wimbledon, London: d. Naresh Kumar, 7-5, 6-1, 6-2; Tony Pickard, 6-1, 6-2, 6-2; Whitney Reed, 6-4, 6-1, 6-4; Pierre Darmon, 6-3, 6-2, 13-11; Manolo Santana, 14-16, 9-7, 6-2; Neale Fraser, 10-8, 6-1, 7-5; Marty Mulligan, 6-2, 6-2, 6-1.

UNITED STATES, at Forest Hills: d. Eleazar Davidman, 6-3, 6-2, 6-3; Eduardo Zuleta, 6-3, 6-3, 6-1; Bodo Nitsche, 9-7, 6-1, 6-1; Tonio Palafox, 6-1, 6-2, 6-2; Frank Froehling, 6-3, 13-11, 4-6, 6-3; Rafe Osuna, 6-1, 6-3, 6-4; Roy Emerson, 6-2, 6-4, 5-7, 6-4.

Rod Laver, 1969 Singles

AUSTRALIA, at Milton Courts, Brisbane: d. Massimo di Domenico, 6-2, 6-3, 6-3; Roy Emerson, 6-2, 6-3, 3-6, 9-7; Fred Stolle, 6-4, 18-16, 6-2; Tony Roche, 7-5, 22-20, 9-11, 1-6, 6-3; Andres Gimeno, 6-3, 6-4, 7-5.

FRENCH, at Roland Garros, Paris: d. Koji Watanabe, 6-1, 6-1, 6-1; Dick Crealy, 3-6, 7-9, 6-2, 6-2, 6-4; Pietro Marzano, 6-1, 6-0, 8-6; Stan Smith, 6-4, 6-2, 6-4; Andres Gimeno, 3-6, 6-3, 6-4, 6-3; Tom Okker, 4-6, 6-0, 6-2, 6-4; Ken Rosewall, 6-4, 6-3, 6-4.

BRITISH, at Wimbledon, London: d. Nicola Pietrangeli, 6-1, 6-2, 6-2; Premjit Lall, 3-6, 4-6, 6-3, 6-0, 6-0; Jan Leschly, 6-3, 6-3, 6-3; Stan Smith, 6-4, 6-2, 7-9, 3-6, 6-3; Cliff Drysdale, 6-4, 6-2, 6-3; Arthur Ashe, 2-6, 6-2, 9-7, 6-0; John Newcombe, 6-4, 5-7, 6-4, 6-4.

UNITED STATES, at Forest Hills: d. Luis Garcia, 6-2, 6-4, 6-2; Jaime Pinto-Bravo, 6-4, 7-5, 6-2; Jaime Fillol, 8-6, 6-1, 6-2; Dennis Ralston, 6-4, 4-6, 4-6, 6-2, 6-3; Roy Emerson, 4-6, 8-6, 13-11, 6-4; Arthur Ashe, 8-6, 6-3, 14-12; Tony Roche, 7-9, 6-1, 6-2, 6-2.

Margaret Smith Court, 1970 Singles

AUSTRALIA, at White City, Sydney: d. Evonne Goolagong, 6-3, 6-1; Karen Krantzcke, 6-1, 6-3; Kerry Melville, 6-3, 6-1.

FRENCH, at Roland Garros, Paris: d. Marijke Jansen Schaar, 6-1, 6-1; Olga Morozova, 3-6, 8-6, 6-1; Lesley Hunt, 6-2, 6-1; Rosie Casals, 7-5, 6-2; Julie Heldman, 6-0, 6-2; Helga Niessen, 6-2, 6-4.

BRITISH, at Wimbledon, London: d. Sue Alexander, 6-0, 6-1; Maria Guzman, 6-0, 6-1; Vlasta Vopickvoa, 6-3, 6-3; Helga Niessen, 6-8, 6-0, 6-0; Rosie Casals, 6-4, 6-1; Billie Jean Moffitt King, 14-2, 11-9.

UNITED STATES, at Forest Hills, New York: d. Pam Austin, 6-1, 6-0; Patti Hogan, 6-1, 6-1; Pat Faulkner, 6-0, 6-2; Helen Gourlay, 6-2, 6-2; Nancy Richey, 6-1, 6-3; Rosie Casals, 6-2, 2-6, 6-1.

Frank Sedgman and Ken McGregor, 1951 Doubles

AUSTRALIAN, at White City, Sydney: d. Rocavert and J. Gilchrist, 6-1, 6-3, 13-11; J. A. Mehaffey and Clive Wilderspin, 6-4, 6-4, 6-3; Merv Rose and

Don Candy, 8-6, 6-4, 6-3; Adrian Quist and John Bromwich, 11-9, 2-6, 6-3, 4-6, 6-3.

FRENCH, at Roland Garros, Paris: d. A. Gentien and P. Grandguillot, 6-0, 6-0, 6-0; M. Bergamo and Beppe Meriod, 6-3, 7-5, 6-1; Bob Abdesselam and Paul Remy, 6-2, 6-2, 4-6, 6-3; Merv Rose and Ham Richardson, 6-3, 7-5, 6-2; Gardnar Mulloy and Dick Savitt, 6-2, 2-6, 9-7, 7-5.

ENGLISH, at Wimbledon, London: d. Vladmir Petrovic and P. Milojkovic, 6-1, 6-1, 6-3; Raymundo Deyro and Gene Garrett, 6-4, 6-4, 6-3; Bernard Destremeau and Torsten Johansson, 3-6, 6-3, 6-2, 9-7; Gianni Cucelli and Marcello del Bello, 6-4, 7-5, 16-14; Budge Patty and Ham Richardson, 6-4, 6-2, 6-3; Eric Sturgess and Jaroslav Drobny, 3-6, 6-2, 6-3, 3-6, 6-3.

UNITED STATES, at Longwood Cricket Club, Boston: d. Harrison Rowbotham and Sumner Rodman, 6-2, 6-3, 6-3; Dave Mesker and Ed Wesely, 6-1, 6-1, 6-1; Earl Cochell and Merv Rose, 10-8, 4-6, 6-4, 7-5 (final round match played at Forest Hills, moved from Boston because of heavy rains).

Margaret Smith and Ken Fletcher, 1963 Mixed Doubles

AUSTRALIAN, at Memorial Drive, Adelaide: d. Faye Toyne and Bill Bowry, 6-2, 6-2; Jill Blackman and Roger Taylor, 6-3, 6-3; Liz Starkie and Mark Cox, 7-5, 6-4; Lesley Turner and Fred Stolle, 7-5, 5-7, 6-4.

FRENCH, at Roland Garros, Paris: d. C. Rouire and M. Lagard, 6-2, 6-1; d. Marie Dusapt and Ion Tiriac, 6-0, 6-2; Mary Habicht and Peter Strobl, 6-3, 6-0; Margaret Hunt and Cliff Drysdale, 7-5, 4-6, 6-1; Judy Tegart and Ed Rubinoff, 6-3, 6-1; Lesley Turner and Fred Stolle, 6-1, 6-2.

ENGLISH, at Wimbledon, London: d. Judy Tegart and Ed Rubinoff, 6-2, 6-2; Judy Alvarez and John Fraser, 6-2, 9-7; Senor and Senora Alfonso Ochoa, 6-4, 6-4; Renée Schuurman and Wilhelm Bungert, 6-2, 6-1; Ann Jones and Dennis Ralston, 6-1, 7-5; Darlene Hard and Bob Hewitt, 11-9, 6-4.

UNITED STATES, at Forest Hills: d. Heidi Schilnecht and Peter Scholl, 6-2, 6-3; Mr. and Mrs. Alan Mills, 6-4, 3-6, 6-1; Robyn Ebbern and Owen Davidson, 6-2, 6-2; Billie Jean Moffitt and Donald Dell, 5-7, 8-6, 6-4; Judy Tegart and Ed Rubinoff, 3-6, 8-6, 6-2.

USTA TENNIS AWARDS

The William M. Johnston Award

The William M. Johnston Trophy is awarded to that man player who by his character, sportsmanship, manners, spirit of cooperation, and contribution to the growth of the game ranks first in the opinion of the Selection Committee for the year ending at the time of the USTA Men's Singles Championship. This includes help which the player renders not only to players in his own class, but to the Junior players as well.

The award is the result of a suggestion by the late "Little Bill" Johnston, who gave one of his championship cups to the International Lawn Tennis Club of the United States to be used for this purpose. The name of the winner of the award is engraved on the trophy and a small silver tray suitably inscribed is given to the recipient as a memento of the award.

The William M. Johnston Trophy has been awarded to the following:

1947   John A. Kramer
1948   E. Victor Seixas, Jr.
1949   Frederick R. Schroeder
1950   J. Gilbert Hall
1951   W. Donald McNeill
1952   Francis X. Shields
1953   William F. Talbert
1954   L. Straight Clark
1955   Chauncey Depew Steele, Jr.
1956   Hamilton Richardson
1957   not awarded
1958   Thomas P. Brown, Jr.
1959   Bernard V. Bartzen
1960   not awarded
1961   Eugene Scott
1962   Jon A. Douglas
1963   Martin Riessen
1964   Arthur Ashe, Jr.
1965   Charles R. McKinley
1966   R. Dennis Ralston
1967   not awarded
1968   Stanley R. Smith
1969   Charles Pasarell
1970   Tom Gorman
1971   Jim McManus
1972   Roscoe Tanner

The 1969 winner of the William M. Johnston award was Charles Pasarell.

1973–79   not presented
1980   Brian Gottfried

USTA Junior and Boys' Sportsmanship Award

In 1957, shortly after the death of Dr. Allen B. Stowe, a long-time director of the National Junior and Boys' Tennis Championships, a group of Kalamazoo tennis enthusiasts sought to establish a fitting and lasting memorial to the former Kalamazoo College professor and tennis coach. The group contributed a sum of money for a trophy to be presented annually to the Junior player who, in the opinion of the National Junior and Boys' Championships Committee, best combined the qualities of outstanding sportsmanship and outstanding ability. Past winners are:

1958   Paul Palmer
1959   Bill Lenoir
1960   Charles Pasarell
1961   Davis Reed
1962   Jim Bests
1963   George Seewagen
1964   Armistead Neely

1965	Roy Barth
1966	Mac Claflin
1967	Bill Colson
1968	Charles Owens
1969	Danny Birchmore
1970	Brian Gottfried
1971	Compton Russell
1972	Fred DeJesus
1973	Bruce Nichols
1974	Earl Prince
1975	Ben McKown
1976	Walter Redondo
1977	Robert Van't Hof
1978	Brent Crymes
1979	Billy Nealon
1980	Mark Mees

USTA Girls' Sportsmanship Trophy Award

The United States Tennis Association Girls' Sportsmanship Trophy is awarded annually at the close of the United States Tennis Association Girls' Championship to the player in the Championship who, in the opinion of the Committee of Judges, most nearly approaches the ideal in Sportsmanship, Appearance, Court Manners, and Tactics. The Trophy was presented in 1936 by Mrs. Harrison Smith and the award has been made annually ever since.

The trophy is a sterling-silver plate. The name of the recipient of the award is engraved on the trophy each year and she receives a small silver plate similar to the trophy in design and engraving. The following players have received the award:

1936	Eleanor Dawson
1937	Mary Olivia Morrill
1938	Helen Irene Bernhard
1939	Dorothy Wightman
1940	Mary Jane Metcalf
1941	Barbara Krase
1942	Judy Atterbury
1943	Doris Jane Hart*
	Betty Rosenquest*
1944	Barbara Van Alen Scofield
1945	Shirley June Fry
1946	Nancy Anne Chaffee
	Mary Cunningham†
1947	Doris Marie Newcomer
	Martha Miller†

1948	Barbara Jane Scarlett
1949	Rosalie Meluney
1950	Natalie Cobough
1951	Elaine Marie Lewicki*
	Bonnie Jean MacKay*
1952	Judy Iselin
1953	Jeanne Arth
	Mary Ann Eilenberger†
	Gwenyth Howell Johnson†
1954	Mary Elizabeth Wellford
1955	Patricia Jean Shaffer
1956	Rosa Maria Reyes
1957	Susan Hodgman
1958	Gwyneth Thomas
	Albertina C. Rodl†
1959	Karen Hantze
1960	Pamela Davis
1961	Katherine D. Chabot
1962	Peachy Kellmeyer
1963	Nancy L. Falkenberg
1964	Kathleen M. Harter*
	Kathleen A. Blake*
1965	Wendy Overton
	Gretchen A. Vosters†
1966	Patsy Rippy
	Julia K. Anthony
1967	Valerie Ziengenfuss*
	Lynn Abbes*
	Vicki Rogers†
1968	Betty Ann Grubb
1969	Gail Hansen
1970	Sharon Walsh
1971	Ann Kiyomura
1972	Laurie Fleming
1973	Kathy May
1974	Betsy Nagelson
1975	Beth Norton
1976	Sheila McInerney
1977	Mareen Louie
1978	Wendy White
1979	Heather Ludloff
1980	Kathleen Horvath

*Joint Award
†Honorable Mention

Sam Hardy was an outstanding player in the early 1920s.

The Samuel Hardy Award

The Samuel Hardy Award is made each year by the USTA at its Annual Meeting by the Directors of the National Tennis Educational Foundation, Inc., for outstanding service rendered to the tennis educational program.

The Hardy Award is a large sterling tray commemorating numerous events won by Samuel Hardy in competition on the French Riviera and given by him to the USTA. The name of each winner of the award is engraved on the tray and the recipient receives a small silver tray, suitably inscribed as a memento of the award.

Following are the winners of the Samuel Hardy Award:

1953   Dr. Allen B. Stowe
1954   Mrs. Harrison Smith
1955   Perry T. Jones
1956   William Matson Tobin
1957   Percy C. Rogers
1958   Dr. Howard Z. Dredge
1959   Lawrence A. Baker
1960   Victor Denny
1961   Martin L. Tressel
1962   George E. Barnes
1963   James B. Moffet

1964   David L. Freed
1965   Robert H. Pease
1966   Harrison F. Rowbotham
1967   Mr. and Mrs. Monroe C. Lewis
1968   William J. Clothier II
1969   Edward A. Turville
1970   Robert J. Kelleher
1971   Daniel S. Johnson
1972   Frank G. Roberts
1973   Alastair B. Martin
1974   Robert B. Colwell
1975   Walter E. Elcock
1976   Col. N. E. Powel
1977   not awarded
1978   W. E. Hester, Jr.
1979   Stanley Malless
1980   Joseph E. Carrico

The Harold A. Lebair Memorial Trophy

The Harold A. Lebair Memorial Trophy is to be awarded annually at the National Open Tennis Championships to that player, man or woman, who by virtue of his or her sportsmanship, conduct on and off the court, and playing of the game, best exemplifies the finest traditions of tennis. The trophy is a perpetual one and will be inscribed with the winner's name and year of award. A small replica, suitably inscribed, will be given annually to the recipient of the award. The winner is to be named by a vote of the Lebair Memorial Trophy Committee, appointed each year by the President of the USTA from officials of the USTA, press representatives, and other knowledgeable and interested persons. The following have received the trophy:

1968   Arthur Ashe, Jr.
1969   Stanley R. Smith
1970   Ken Rosewall
1971   Chris Evert
1972   Tom Gorman
1973   award discontinued

The John T. McGovern Umpires' Award

The late John T. (Terry) McGovern was a well-known leader in amateur sports. He was for many years legal advisor to the United States Olympic Committee, a former president of the Cornell

University Alumni Association, and president of the Sandlot Baseball Association. Almost from the inception of the USTA Umpires Association, he was a devoted tennis linesman.

In 1949 he presented a beautiful gold-plated trophy for annual award to that umpire or linesman who contributed most to the cause of tennis officiating during the previous year. In addition to the perpetual trophy, Mr. McGovern contributed gold-plated medalettes to be given annually for the permanent possession of the recipient, as well as silver-plated medalettes to be given on a similar basis to junior officials. The Committee of Award consists of the chairman of the USTA Umpires Committee and all previous recipients of the award.

This trophy has been awarded to:

1949	Donald M. Dickson
1950	Craufurd Kent
1951	Harold A. Lebair
1952	David S. Niles
1953	Louis W. Shaw
1954	Frank J. Tybeskey
1955	Hubert J. Quinn
1956	H. LeVan Richards
1957	Winslow Blanchard
1958	Edward Mellor
1959	Harold E. Ammerman
1960	J. Clarence Davies, Jr.
1961	Herbert J. Lewis
1962	Frank Dowling
1963	John G. Kroel
1964	William Macassin
1965	Ernest J. Oberlaender, Jr.
1966	John B. Stahr
1967	S. R. Bumann
1968	John Coman
1969	Frank Hammond
1970	E. Brooks Keffer
1971	Titus Sparrow
1972	Col. Raymond Skinner
1973	Sydow Nieman
1974	Douglas B. Stewart
1975	Mrs. Florence Blanchard
1976	Sam Cox
1977	S. C. William Ackerman
1978	Harry Maiden
1979	Roy Dance
1980	John H. Sternbach

The Service Bowl Award

"To the Player Who Yearly Makes the Most Notable Contribution to the Sportsmanship, Fellowship, and Service of Tennis." This inscription is engraved on The Service Bowl trophy which, after being limited for four years to women players in New England, has been awarded on a nationwide basis since 1944 during the week of the National Doubles Championships at the Longwood Cricket Club, with the president of the New England Tennis Association acting as Master of Ceremonies. The award is the outgrowth of an association of thirty New England women players who earlier had been organized informally for a number of years in an annual "tennis party" given by the donor of the award, Mrs. Lyman H. B. Olmstead. The award has been made to the following:

New England Winners:

1940	Mrs. Hazel H. Wightman
1941	Mrs. William S. Shedden
1942	Mrs. J. Lewis Bremer
1943	Mrs. Marjorie Morrill Painter

National Winners:

1944	Mrs. Dorothy Bundy Cheney
1945	Mrs. Margaret Osborne du Pont
1946	Mrs. Hazel H. Wightman
1947	Mrs. John B. Prizer
1948	A. Louise Brough
1949	Mrs. Madge Harshaw Vosters
1950	Nancy P. Norton
1951	Mrs. Gladys Medalie Heldman
1952	Mrs. Maureen Connolly Brinker
1953	Mrs. John B. Moore
1954	Mrs. Marjorie Gladman Buck
1955	Doris Hart
1956	Mrs. Patricia Henry Yeomans
1957	Mrs. Dorothy Head Knode
1958	Katharine Hubbell
1959	Mrs. Barbara Krase Chandler
1960	Mrs. Sylvia K. Simonin
1961	Mrs. Gail Stewart
1962	Mimi Arnolds
1963	Marilyn Montgomery

1964 Mrs. Helen Fulton Shockley and
     Mrs. Theodore Hackett (co-winners)
1965 Mrs. Rosalind Greenwood
1966 Mrs. Billie Jean Moffitt King
1967 Mrs. Donna Floyd Fales
1968 Mrs. Betty R. Pratt
1969 Mrs. Doris Harrison
1970 Mrs. Nancy Jeffett
1971 Mrs. Ruth Lay
1972 Nancy Neeld
1973 Mrs. Edythe Ann McGoldrick
1974 Mary Arnold Prentiss
1975 Julie M. Heldman
1976 Mrs. Mary Hardwick Hare
1977 Catherine Sample
1978 Carol Schneider
1979 Marion Baird
1980 Evelyn Houseman

Seniors' Service Award

A perpetual trophy for service to Senior tennis is awarded each year at the National Championships to the individual who, in the judgment of the USTA Senior's Committee, has been, through his efforts, willingness, cooperation, and participation, most deserving of the respect and honor of all Seniors, either in play or organizational work for the betterment and furtherance of Senior Competition. Each year the winner's name and the year are engraved on the trophy and a replica of the trophy is given to the winners, who are as follows:

1958 W. Dickson Cunningham
1959 William L. Nassau, Jr.
1960 Henry L. Benisch
1961 Dr. Irving Bricker
1962 Monte L. Ganger
1963 Caspar H. Nannes
1964 Joseph Lipshutz
1965 Gardnar Mulloy
1966 J. Clarence Davies, Jr.
1967 C. Alphonso Smith
1968 Col. Nicholas E. Powel
1969 Robert L. Galloway
1970 E. Jefferson Mendal
1971 Emery Neale
1972 Alvin W. Bunis
1973 W. E. (Slew) Hester

1974 Richard C. Sorlien
1975 Jay Freeman
1976 Henry Crawford
1977 not awarded
1978 L. Roe Campbell
1979 A. W. (Buck) Archer
1980 John Powless

The Colonel James H. Bishop Award

The Colonel James H. Bishop Award is made during the USTA Men's Singles Championships to that U.S. Junior Davis Cup squad member who, in the opinion of his captain and teammates, has best exemplified during the year the objectives of the Junior Davis Cup Program in regard to highest standards of character, conduct, sportsmanship, appearance, amateurism on and off the tennis court, and tennis accomplishment.

The award, a sterling-silver tray, was donated by Dorothy W. and Thomas E. Price to the USTA in the memory of the late Colonel James H. Bishop—the founder of the Junior Davis Cup Program in 1937 (the forerunner of the Junior Wightman Cup Program in 1938) and a well-known and highly regarded friend of youth, educator, and tennis leader until his untimely death in 1961.

The name of the recipient of the award is engraved on the tray and a suitably inscribed small silver replica is given to the recipient as a memento of the award. The following U.S. Junior Davis Cup squad members have earned this award:

1962 David Reed
1963 James Parker
1964 David Power
1965 Jim Pickens
1966 Stan Smith
1967 James Osborne
1968 Robert McKinley
1969 Richard Stockton
1970 not awarded
1971 Roscoe Tanner
1972 Alexander Mayer, Jr.
1973 Jim Delaney
1974 John Whitlinger
1975 Brian Teacher
1976 not awarded

1977   Bruce Manson
1978   Bruce Nichols
1979   Larry Stefanki
1980   Billy Nealon

Tennis Educational Merit Award

The Tennis Educational Merit Award is made annually by the USTA to the person selected by the Directors of the National Tennis Educational Foundation, Inc., for outstanding service rendered to the tennis educational program by a teaching professional and/or instructor.

It is the desire of the USTA to honor and recognize such services to the development of the game through leadership, inspiration, and junior programs in the schools, colleges, clubs, parks, and playgrounds benefiting the nation's youth. Winners of the award are as follows:

1967   Harry A. Leighton
1968   William C. Lufler
1969   Dennis Van der Meer
1970   Harry James
1971   John Conroy
1972   Harry Fogelman
1973   Bill and Chet Murphy
1974   Victor K. Braden and Paul Xanthos
1975   Rolla Anderson and Clarence Mabry
1976   Robert Sassano
1977   not awarded
1978   Jack Barnaby
1979   Ed Faulkner
1980   George Basco

The Ralph W. Westcott Award

This award was initiated by Martin L. Tressel, president of the USTA, in 1965 to emphasize that tennis is a family game. Ralph W. Westcott donated a large silver tray as a Perpetual Award. This trophy was given by him upon retiring as president of the Chicago District Tennis Association. He has also been president of the Western Sectional Association and secretary of the USTA.

The award is made annually to the family who has done the most to promote amateur tennis during the past twelve months. The names of the recipients are engraved on this tray and a small silver replica suitably inscribed is given to the National Tennis Family of the Year as a memento of the award. Each District, each Section, and each Region selects a Tennis Family of the Year. From the four Regional finalists a National Winner is selected by a committee appointed by the president of the USTA. The trophy is presented at the USTA Singles Championships at Forest Hills in September.

The Ralph Westcott Trophy has been awarded to the following:

1965   The John F. Sullivan Family
1966   The Will Rompf Family
1967   The Charles Pasarell Family
1968   The Bundy-Cheney Family
1969–70   not awarded
1971   The James M. Gray family
1972   not awarded
1973   The George Acker family
1974   The Forest A. Hainline, Jr., family
1975   The Joseph Garcia family
1976   The Francis Wilson family
1977   not awarded
1978   The Herbert B. Gengler family
1979   The John Vest family
1980   The Leo Power family

The Leadership Award for Women

The Leadership Award for Women is made annually to the woman physical educator who has made outstanding contributions to the development and growth of tennis for girls and women. The recipient is named at the USTA Women's Collegiate Championships.

A large permanent silver trophy has been donated by Judy Barta upon which the name of the recipient is engraved. A smaller replica is given to the awardee. Winners are as follows:

1969   Mrs. Luell Weed Guthrie
1970   Mrs. Jean Johnson
1971   not awarded
1972   Elaine Mason
1973   award discontinued

The Maureen Connolly Brinker Award

The Maureen Connolly Brinker Outstanding Junior Girl Award was approved in February, 1969, at the annual meeting of the USTA. The award created by the Maureen Connolly Brinker Foundation, Inc., will be presented each year following the finals of the National Girls' 18 Championships in Philadelphia at the Philadelphia Cricket Club.

The award and the foundation were the dream of the late Maureen Connolly Brinker. This award will be presented each year to the girl player considered by the committee to have had the most outstanding full season performance. She must be exceptional in ability, sportsmanship, and in competitive spirit.

The magnificent silver bowl which will be kept at the Philadelphia Cricket Club will have inscribed the name of each year's winner. The recipient of the award will receive a small engraved silver tray and a lifetime enrollment in the USTA. Winners are as follows:

1969 Eliza Pande
1970 Sharon Walsh
1971 Chris Evert
1972 Marita Redondo
1973 Betsy Nagelson
1974 Kathy May
1975 Beth Norton
1976 Lynn Epstein
1977 Anne Smith
1978 Tracy Austin
1979 Mary Lou Piatek
1980 Susan Mascarin

NTF Special Educational Merit Award for Women

The National Tennis Foundation presents this award annually. The selection of the recipient is made by the NTF directors, and the presentation is made at the USTA annual meeting. The winner must exemplify those qualities of personal unselfishness and devotion to the game which have been an inspiration to others. The winners:

1972 Mrs. Lewis S. Kraft
1973 Mrs. Marion Wood Huey
1974 Mrs. Margaret Osborne duPont
1975 Mrs. Helen Lewis
1976 Pat Freebody
1977 Dr. Anne Pittman

1978 Peggy Mann
1979 Mrs. Sarah Palfrey Danzig
1980 Lois Blackburn

The Harry Fogelman Memorial Trophy

Dedicated to the memory of Harry Fogelman, outstanding tennis coach and director of the National 12 and 14 Champions for several years before his death in December, 1972, this award is presented annually by the USTA. It was donated by the Boys' 12 1973 National Championships Committee at the Knoxville (Tennessee) Racquet Club.

It is awarded to the boy who, in the opinion of the Tournament Committee, exemplifies outstanding sportsmanship, conduct, character, and tennis ability. The winners:

1973 Paul Crozier
1974 Mark Mees
1975 Derk Pardoe
1976 Derek Weiss
1977 Richie Reneberg
1978 Robby Weiss
1979 Robby Weiss
1980 Stephen Enochs

Women's National Collegiate Awards

Singles winner (The Treesh Bowl). 1974—Carrie Meyer, Marymount; 1975—Stephanie Tolleson, Trinity U.; 1976—Barbara Hallquist, U.S.C.; 1977—Barbara Hallquist, U.S.C.; 1978—Stacy Margolin, U.S.C.; 1979—Kathy Jordan, Stanford; 1980—Wendy White, Stanford.

Doubles winners (Pat Yoemans Bowl): 1974—Ann Lebedoff and Karen Reinke, San Diego State; 1975—JoAnne Russell and Donna Stockton, Trinity U.; 1976—Susan Hagey and Diane Morrison, Stanford; 1977—Jodi Applebaum and Terry Salganik, Miami (Fla.); 1978—Sherry and Judy Acker, U. of Florida; 1979—Kathy Jordan and Alycia Moulton, Stanford; 1980—

Team champion (Catherine Sample Bowl): 1974—Arizona State; 1975—Trinity U.; 1976—Trinity U.; 1977—Trinity U.; 1978—U.S.C.; 1979—U.S.C.; 1980—U.S.C.

LEADING ACHIEVERS IN DAVIS CUP PLAY

Davis Cup Stalwarts of All Times

Although Nikki Pietrangeli was unable to win the Davis Cup for Italy, he did retire with the distinction of having played more Cup matches for his homeland than any other man in the competition stretching back 70 years. In 66 international battles he appeared on the court 164 times in singles and doubles, winning 120 times. Twice, in 1960 and 1961, Pietrangeli led Italy to the Challenge Round final. Nobody in the list of Davis Cup stalwarts is close to him, and among them only Ilie Nastase, Tomas Koch and Ion Tiriac remain active. It is unlikely that non-Europeans will crack the list since more matches are involved for those playing in the larger European Zones.

	TOTAL GAMES		SINGLES		DOUBLES		
	Played	Won	Played	Won	Played	Won	Matches
Nikki Pietrangeli (Italy, 1954–72)	164	120	110	78	54	42	66
Manolo Santana (Spain, 1958–73)	121	92	86	69	35	23	46
Jackie Brichant (Belgium, 1949–65)	120	71	79	52	41	19	42
Ilie Nastase (Romania, 1966–77)	115	90	75	60	40	30	40
Tomas Koch (Brazil, 1962–77)	109	73	70	44	39	29	33
Ion Tiriac (Romania, 1959–77)	109	70	68	40	41	30	43
Edison Mandarino (Brazil, 1951–76)	108	50	70	39	38	27	38
Gottfried von Cramm (Germany, 1932–53)	102	82	69	58	33	24	37
Ulf Schmidt (Sweden, 1954–64)	102	66	69	44	33	22	38
Philippe Washer (Belgium, 1946–61)	102	66	64	46	38	20	39
Willy Bungert (W. Germany, 1958–71)	101	65	77	52	24	13	43
Torben Ulrich (Denmark, 1948–1968)	100	45	64	31	36	14	39
Ram Krishnan (India, 1953–69)	97	69	69	50	28	19	39
Kurt Nielsen (Denmark, 1948–60)	96	53	65	42	31	11	33
Jan Lundquist (Sweden, 1957–69)	89	64	61	47	28	17	34
Orlando Sirola (Italy, 1953–69)	89	57	46	22	43	35	45
Lennart Bergelin (Sweden, 1946–65)	88	62	60	43	28	19	36
Roderic Menzel (Czechoslovakia, 1928–38) (Germany, 1939)	84	61	60	47	24	14	35
Sven Davidson (Sweden, 1950–60)	84	61	53	39	31	22	35

Davis Cup Stalwarts Among the Leaders

Of the four nations who have won the cup more than once—the United States, Australia, Great Britain, and France—the United States has played with 96 men, while only 52 played for Australia. 71 have played for Great Britain, and 38 for France. (Incidentally, the 1977 American Zone Final was the 176th Davis Cup match for the United States—no other nation has had so many.)

Of the four winning nations, Bobby Wilson of Great Britain and Pierre Darmon of France have played in the most matches.

		TOTAL GAMES		SINGLES		DOUBLES		
		Played	Won	Played	Won	Played	Won	Matches
Australia								
Jack Crawford	1928–37	58	36	40	23	18	13	23
Adrian Quist	1933–48	55	42	33	23	22	19	28
John Bromwich	1937–50	52	39	31	19	21	20	23
Gerald Patterson	1919–28	46	32	31	21	15	11	16
Roy Emerson	1959–67	40	36	24	22	16	14	18
Great Britain								
Mike Sangster	1960–68	65	43	48	29	17	14	26
Bobby Wilson	1955–68	62	41	29	16	33	25	34
Tony Mottram	1947–55	56	36	38	25	18	11	19
Fred Perry	1930–36	52	45	38	34	14	11	20
Bunny Austin	1929–37	48	36	48	36	0	0	24
France								
Pierre Darmon	1956–67	69	47	62	44	7	3	34
Henri Cochet	1922–33	58	44	42	34	16	10	26
Jean Borotra	1922–47	54	36	31	19	23	17	32
Paul Remy	1949–58	53	33	29	16	24	16	25
René Lacoste	1923–28	51	40	40	32	11	8	26
United States								
Vic Seixas	1951–57	55	38	36	24	19	14	19
Wilmer Allison	1929–36	45	32	29	18	16	14	20
Bill Tilden	1920–30	41	34	30	25	11	9	17
Chuck McKinley	1960–65	38	30	22	17	16	13	16
Tony Trabert	1951–55	35	27	21	16	14	11	14
Dennis Ralston	1960–66	35	25	20	14	15	11	15

Four Davis Cup doubles players: *(left to right)* Quist, Schroeder, Kramer, and Bromwich, of 1946 challenge round, anxiously watch the fall of Australian Adrian Quist's racket to decide first service. The Australians won the toss, but Jack Kramer and Ted Schroeder won the match and the Davis Cup for the United States.

Challenge Round Stalwarts

In Challenge Rounds, that English notable at the turn of the century, Laurie Doherty, leads with a perfect record of 12 singles and doubles victories in five Challenge appearances. Bill Tilden, the legendary American who appeared in more Challenge Rounds than anyone else (11), won 21 of 28 matches. With the change in Davis Cup format (see page 395) all of the following challenge-round records will stand:

	Matches Played	Won	Average	Challenge Rounds
Hugh (Laurie) Doherty (Great Britain, 1902–06)	12	12	1.000	5
Fred Perry (Great Britain, 1931–36)	10	9	.900	5
Roy Emerson (Australia, 1959–67)	18	15	.833	9
Bill Johnston (United States, 1920–27)	16	13	.813	8
Frank Sedgman (Australia, 1949–52)	11	9	.818	4
Bill Tilden (United States, 1920–30)	28	21	.750	11
Neale Fraser (Australia, 1958–63)	11	8	.727	6
Lew Hoad (Australia, 1953–56)	11	8	.727	4
Henri Cochet (France, 1926–33)	20	14	.700	8
Ken Rosewall (Australia, 1953–56)	10	7	.700	4
Norman Brookes (Australia, 1907–20)	22	15	.682	8
Tony Wilding (Australia, 1907–14)	12	8	.667	4
Bunny Austin (Great Britain, 1931–37)	12	8	.667	6
Ted Schroeder (United States, 1946–51)	15	9	.600	6
John Bromwich (Australia, 1938–50)	14	7	.500	6
Adrian Quist (Australia, 1936–48)	12	5	.417	5
Maurice McLoughlin (United States, 1909–14)	11	4	.364	4
Jean Borotra (France, 1925–33)	17	6	.353	9
Gerald Patterson (Australia, 1919–24)	12	4	.333	4
Tony Trabert (United States, 1951–55)	12	4	.333	5
Vic Seixas (United States, 1951–57)	20	6	.300	7

Vital Challenge Round Matches

Laurie Doherty also leads in "vital" Challenge or Final Round matches—that is, those matches played while the issue was still in doubt. He was flawless, winning nine for nine.

	Matches Played	Won	Average
Laurie Doherty	9	9	1.000
Fred Perry	9	8	.889
Ray Emerson	15	13	.867
Stan Smith	14	11	.786
Bill Tilden	18	14	.778
Frank Sedgman	9	7	.778
Neale Fraser	9	7	.778
Bill Johnston	12	9	.750
Rod Laver	8	6	.750
Henri Cochet	17	12	.706
Tony Wilding	10	7	.700
Norman Brookes	19	13	.684
Lew Hoad	9	6	.667
John Newcombe	8	5	.625
Bunny Austin	8	5	.625
Ted Schroeder	13	8	.615
Ken Rosewall	7	4	.571
John Bromwich	11	6	.545
Jean Borotra	13	6	.462
Adrian Quist	11	5	.455
Gerald Patterson	10	4	.400
Tony Trabert	10	4	.400
Maurice McLoughlin	8	3	.375
Vic Seixas	15	4	.267

Longest Davis Cup Matches

Singles

86 Games. Arthur Ashe, U.S. d. Christian Kuhnke, Germany, 6-8, 10-12, 9-7, 13-11, 6-4. Challenge Round, Cleveland, 1970.

85 Games. Dale Powers, Canada d. Alvaro Betancur, Colombia, 6-4, 22-24, 2-6, 6-3, 7-5. Zone Match, Montreal, 1975.

83 Games. Arthur Ashe, U.S. d. Manolo Santana, Spain, 11-13, 7-5, 6-3, 13-15, 6-4. Zone Match, Cleveland, 1968.

80 Games. John Alexander, Australia d. Vijay Amritraj, India, 14-12, 17-15, 6-8, 6-2. Zone Match, Calcutta, 1974.

79 Games. Barry MacKay, U.S. d. Nicola Pietrangeli, Italy, 8-6, 3-6, 8-10, 8-6, 13-11. Zone Match, Perth, Australia, 1960.

78 Games. Jaroslav Drobny, Czechoslovakia d. Adrian Quist, Australia, 6-8, 3-6, 18-16, 6-3, 7-5. Zone Match, Boston, 1948.

75 Games. Tom Brown, U.S. d. Ken McGregor, Australia, 9-11, 8-10, 11-9, 6-1, 6-4. Challenge Round, New York, 1950.

Doubles

122 Games. Erik van Dillen and Stan Smith, U.S. d. Pat Cornejo and Jaime Fillol, Chile, 7-9, 37-39, 8-6, 6-1, 6-3. Zone Match, Little Rock, Arkansas, 1973.

99 Games. Anand Amritraj and Vijay Amritraj, India d. John Alexander and Colin Dibley, Australia, 17-15, 6-8, 16-18, 6-4, 6-3. Zone Match, Calcutta, 1974.

95 games. Wilhelm Bungert and Christian Kuhnke, Germany d. Mark Cox and Peter Curtis, England, 10-8, 17-19, 13-11, 3-6, 6-2. Zone Match, Birmingham, England, 1969.

94 Games. Roy Emerson and Fred Stolle, Australia d. Rafe Osuna and Antonio Palafox, Mexico, 18-16, 7-9, 7-9, 6-4, 10-8. Zone Match, Mexico City, 1964.

85 Games. Anand Amritraj and Vijay Amritraj, India d. Alex Metreveli and Vladimir Korotkov, U.S.S.R., 13-15, 7-5, 19-17, 6-3. Zone Match, Poona, India, 1974.

82 Games. Alex Olmedo and Ham Richardson, U.S. d. Neal Fraser and Mal Anderson, Australia, 10-12, 3-6, 16-14, 6-3, 7-5. Challenge Round, Brisbane, Australia, 1958.

81 Games. Bill Tilden and Dick William, U.S. d. Jim Anderson and John Hawkes, Australia, 17-15, 11-13, 2-6, 6-3, 6-2. Challenge Round, New York, 1923.

United States Davis Cup Who's Who

Ninety-six men are on America's tennis honor roll, having played for their country in the Davis Cup since the first balls were struck August 8, 1900, in Boston by Malcolm Whitman of the home side and the loser, A. W. Gore of Britain. Of this number, 54 have played in the grand final, the Challenge Round. Most illustrious of course was "Big Bill" Tilden, whose 11 years of Challenge Rounds are high for American players. No one of any other country has surpassed his 11 Challenge Round appearances (during which the United States won the Cup seven times), nor his number of individual victories (21) and matches (28). Only Roy Emerson of Australia played on more Cup-winning teams than Tilden—eight.

MALCOLM WHITMAN, 1900, '02. Challenge Rounds (2): 3-0 in singles, 1-0 in doubles.

DWIGHT DAVIS, 1900, '02. Challenge Rounds (2): 1-0 in singles, 1-1 in doubles.

HOLCOMBE WARD, 1900, '02, '05, '06. Challenge Rounds (4): 0-3 in singles, 1-3 in doubles. Zone Matches (3): 3-1 in singles, 3-0 in doubles. Overall: 7-7 for 7 matches.

BOB WRENN, 1903. Challenge Round (1): 0-2 in singles, 0-1 in doubles.

BILL LARNED, 1902, '03, '05, '08, '09, '11. Challenge Rounds (4): 2-5 in singles. Zone Matches (4): 8-0 in singles. Overall: 10-5 for 8 matches.

GEORGE WRENN, 1903. Challenge Round (1): 0-1 in doubles.

BEALS WRIGHT, 1905, '07, '08, '11. Challenge Rounds (3): 2-2 in singles, 0-3 in doubles. Zone Matches (4): 6-2 in singles, 3-0 in doubles. Overall: 11-7 for 7 matches.

BILL CLOTHIER, 1905, '09. Challenge Round (1): 0-1 in singles. Zone Matches (2): 4-0 in singles. Overall: 4-1 for 3 matches.

RAYMOND LITTLE, 1906, '09, '11. Challenge Round (1): 0-2 in singles, 0-1 in doubles. Zone Matches (3): 1-1 in singles, 2-1 in doubles. Overall: 3-5 for 4 matches.

KARL BEHR, 1907. Zone Match (1): 0-2 in singles, 1-0 in doubles.

FRED ALEXANDER, 1908. Challenge Round (1): 0-2 in singles, 0-1 in doubles. Zone Match (1): 1-0 in doubles. Overall: 1-3 for 2 matches.

HAROLD HACKETT, 1908, '09, '13. Challenge Round (1): 0-1 in doubles. Zone Matches (5): 4-1 in doubles. Overall: 5-1 for 6 matches.

MELVILLE LONG, 1909. Challenge Round (1): 0-2 in singles, 0-1 in doubles.

MAURICE MCLOUGHLIN, 1909, '11, '13, '14. Challenge Rounds (4): 3-4 in singles, 1-3 in doubles. Zone Matches (4): 6-0 in singles, 2-1 in doubles. Overall: 12-8 for 8 matches.

TOM BUNDY, 1911, '14. Challenge Round (1): 0-1 in doubles. Zone Match (1): 0-1 in doubles. Overall: 0-2 for 2 matches.

RICHARD WILLIAMS, 1913, '14, '21, '23, '25, '26. Challenge Rounds (6): 1-3 in singles, 4-0 in doubles. Zone Matches (3): 5-0 in singles. Overall: 10-3 for 9 matches.

WALLACE JOHNSON, 1913. Zone Match (1): 1-0 in singles.

BILL JOHNSTON, 1920 through 1927. Challenge Rounds (8): 11-3 in singles, 2-0 in doubles. Zone Matches (2): 3-0 in singles, 2-0 in doubles. Overall: 18-3 for 10 matches.

BILL TILDEN, 1920 through 1930. Challenge Rounds (11): 17-5 in singles, 5-1 in doubles. Zone Matches (6): 8-0 in singles, 5-0 in doubles. Overall: 35-6 for 17 matches.

WATSON WASHBURN, 1921. Challenge Round (1): 1-0 in doubles.

VINCENT RICHARDS, 1922, '24, '25, '26. Challenge Rounds (4): 2-0 in singles, 3-0 in doubles.

FRANK HUNTER, 1927, '28, '29. Challenge Rounds (2): 1-1 in doubles. Zone Matches (2): 3-1 in singles. Overall: 4-2 for 4 matches.

ARNOLD JONES, 1928. Zone Match (1): 1-0 in doubles.

JOHN HENNESSEY, 1928, '29. Challenge Round (1): 0-2 in singles. Zone Matches (7): 10-0 in singles, 3-0 in doubles. Overall: 13-2 for 8 matches.

GEORGE LOTT, 1928 through 1931, '33, '34. Challenge Rounds (3): 0-4 in singles, 1-0 in doubles. Zone Matches (14): 7-0 in singles, 10-0 in doubles. Overall: 18-4 for 17 matches.

WILBUR COEN, 1928. Zone Matches (2): 1-0 in singles, 1-0 in doubles.

JOHN VAN RYN, 1929 through 1936. Challenge Rounds (4): 2-2 in doubles. Zone Matches (20): 7-1 in singles, 9-0 in doubles. Overall 18-3 for 24 matches.

WILMER ALLISON, 1929 through 1933, '35, '36. Challenge Rounds (4): 0-4 in singles, 2-2 in doubles. Zone Matches (19): 17-6 in singles, 12-0 in doubles. Overall: 31-12 for 23 matches.

JOHN DOEG, 1930. Zone Matches (2): 2-0 in singles.

FRANK SHIELDS, 1931, '32, '34. Challenge Round (1): 0-2 in singles. Zone Matches (12): 16-4 in singles, 3-0 in doubles. Overall: 19-6 for 13 matches.

SIDNEY WOOD, 1931, '34. Challenge Round (1): 0-2 in singles. Zone Matches (6): 5-4 in singles, 3-0 in doubles. Overall: 8-6 for 7 matches.

CLIFF SUTTER, 1931, '33. Zone Matches (2): 3-0 in singles.

ELLSWORTH VINES, 1932, '33. Challenge Round (1): 1-1 in singles. Zone Matches (7): 12-2 in singles. Overall: 13-3 for 8 matches.

LES STOEFEN, 1934. Challenge Round (1): 1-0 in doubles. Zone Matches (2): 3-0 in singles, 2-0 in doubles. Overall: 6-0 for 4 matches.

BRYAN (BITSY) GRANT, 1935 through 1938. Zone Matches (5): 8-2 in singles.

DON BUDGE, 1935 through 1938. Challenge Rounds (3): 4-2 in singles, 1-1 in doubles. Zone Matches (8): 15-0 in singles, 5-1 in doubles. Overall: 25-4 for 11 matches.

GENE MAKO, 1935 through 1938. Challenge Rounds (2): 1-1 in doubles. Zone Matches (6): 0-1 in singles, 5-1 in doubles. Overall: 6-3 for 8 matches.

FRANK PARKER, 1937, '39, '46, '48. Challenge Rounds (3): 4-2 in singles. Zone Matches (4): 8-0 in singles. Overall: 12-2 for 7 matches.

BOBBY RIGGS, 1938, '39. Challenge Rounds (2): 2-2 in singles.

JOE HUNT, 1939. Challenge Round (1): 0-1 in doubles.

JACK KRAMER, 1939, '46, '47. Challenge Rounds (3): 3-0 in singles, 1-2 in doubles. Zone Match (1): 2-0 in singles. Overall: 6-2 for 4 matches.

BILL TALBERT, 1946, '48, '49, '51, '52, '53. Challenge Rounds (2): 1-1 in doubles. Zone Matches (6): 2-0 in singles, 6-0 in doubles. Overall: 9-1 for 8 matches.

TED SCHROEDER, 1946 through 1951. Challenge Rounds (6): 9-3 in singles, 1-3 in doubles. Zone Matches (2): 2-0 in singles, 1-0 in doubles. Overall: 13-6 for 8 matches.

GARDNAR MULLOY, 1946, '48, '49, '50, '52, '53, '57. Challenge Rounds (4): 1-0 in singles, 1-2 in doubles. Zone Matches (8): 2-0 in singles, 7-1 in doubles. Overall: 11-3 for 12 matches.

RICHARD (PANCHO) GONZALES, 1949. Challenge Round (1): 2-0 in singles.

TOM BROWN, 1950, '53. Challenge Round (1): 1-1 in singles. Zone Match (1): 1-1 in singles, 1-0 in doubles. Overall: 3-2 for 2 matches.

DICK SAVITT, 1951. Zone Matches (2): 3-0 in singles.

HERB FLAM, 1951, '52, '56, '57. Challenge Round (1): 0-1 in singles. Zone Matches (7): 10-1 in singles, 2-0 in doubles. Overall: 12-2 for 8 matches.

TONY TRABERT, 1951 through 1955. Challenge Rounds (5): 2-5 in singles, 2-3 in doubles. Zone Matches (9): 14-0 in singles, 9-0 in doubles. Overall: 27-8 for 14 matches.

ART LARSEN, 1951, '52. Zone Matches (3): 4-0 in singles.

VIC SEIXAS, 1951 through 1957. Challenge Rounds (7): 4-10 in singles, 2-4 in doubles. Zone Matches (16): 20-2 in singles, 12-1 in doubles. Overall: 38-17 for 23 matches.

BUDGE PATTY, 1951. Zone Match (1): 1-0 in singles, 1-0 in doubles.

HUGH STEWART, 1952, '61. Zone Matches (2): 2-0 in singles, 2-0 in doubles.

BERNARD BARTZEN, 1952, '53, '57, '60, '61. Zone Matches (9): 15-0 in singles, 1-0 in doubles.

BOB PERRY, 1952, '53. Zone Matches (2): 1-1 in singles, 1-0 in doubles.

HAMILTON RICHARDSON, 1952 through 1956, '58, '65. Challenge Rounds (2): 0-1 in singles, 1-0 in doubles. Zone Matches (12): 17-0 in singles, 2-1 in doubles. Overall: 20-2 for 14 matches.

RON HOLMBERG, 1956. Zone Match (1): 1-0 in doubles.

STRAIGHT CLARK, 1953, '54. Zone Matches (3): 3-0 in singles, 2-0 in doubles.

HAL BURROWS, 1954. Zone Matches (2): 2-0 in singles, 2-0 in doubles.

BARRY MACKAY, 1956 through 1960. Challenge Rounds (3): 2-4 in singles, 0-1 in doubles. Zone Matches (12): 15-3 in singles, 5-1 in doubles. Overall: 22-9 for 15 matches.

SAM GIAMMALVA, 1956, '57, '58. Challenge Round (1): 0-1 in singles, 0-1 in doubles. Zone Matches (6): 4-0 in singles, 3-1 in doubles. Overall: 7-3 for 7 matches.

MIKE GREEN, 1956, '57. Zone Matches (3): 1-2 in singles.

GRANT GOLDEN, 1957. Zone Matches (2): 1-1 in singles, 1-0 in doubles.

BILL QUILLIAN, 1958. Zone Match (1): 1-0 in singles, 1-0 in doubles.

WHITNEY REED, 1958, '61. Zone Matches (3): 2-3 in singles, 0-1 in doubles.

JACK DOUGLAS, 1959, '61, '62. Zone Matches (5): 5-3 in singles, 1-0 in doubles.

Most Challenge Round Individual Matches

28 Bill Tilden
20 Vic Seixas, 1951 through 1957

Most Zone Matches

20 John Van Ryn, 1929 through 1936
19 Wilmer Allison, 1929 through 1933, 1935, 1936

Most Zone Match Individual Wins

32 Vic Seixas—20 in singles, 12 in doubles
29 Wilmer Allison—17 in singles, 12 in doubles

Most Team Matches Overall

24 John Van Ryn
24 Wilmer Allison
24 Vic Seixas

Most Individual Wins Overall

38 Vic Seixas—24 in singles, 14 in doubles
35 Bill Tilden—25 in singles, 10 in doubles

Wightman Cup Leaders

Playing for their country in the Wightman Cup Series have been 60 American and 60 British women. Most successful of these was American Louise Brough, who played nine years and was unbeaten in 22 matches—12 singles and 10 doubles. Helen Jacobs of the United States and Ann Haydon Jones of Great Britain were selected the most times—12. Miss Jacobs and Helen Wills Moody appeared on court the most times for the United States in 30 singles and doubles matches. But Virginia Wade holds the record for both sides with 35 matches. Of those Miss Wade won 16, high for Great Britain.

The longest Wightman match, 46 games, was a singles won by Billie Jean Moffitt of the United States (now Mrs. King) over Christine Truman (now Mrs. Janes), 19-17, 6-4 in 1963. Hazel Hotchkiss Wightman, donor of the Cup, played in and won the longest doubles, 40 games, alongside Eleanor Goss of the United States when they defeated Mrs. B. C. Covell and Kathleen McKane, 10-8, 5-7, 6-4, in the series opener of 1923.

United States Wightman Cup Who's Who

HELEN WILLS MOODY, 1923, '24, '25, '27 through '32, '38. 18-2 in singles, 3-7 in doubles. Overall: 21-9 for 10 matches.
MOLLA BJURSTEDT MALLORY, 1923, '24, '25, '27, '28. 5-5 in singles, 1-1 in doubles. Overall: 6-6 for 5 matches.
ELEANOR GOSS, 1923 through 1928. 1-2 in singles, 2-3 in doubles. Overall: 3-5 for 6 matches.
HAZEL HOTCHKISS WIGHTMAN, 1923, '24, '27, '29, '31. 3-2 in doubles.
MARION ZINDERSTEIN JESSUP, 1924, '26. 1-0 in singles, 1-1 in doubles. Overall: 2-1 for 2 matches.
MAY SUTTON BUNDY, 1925. 0-1 in doubles.
MARY K. BROWNE, 1925, '26. 0-2 in singles, 1-1 in doubles. Overall: 1-3 for 2 matches.
ELIZABETH RYAN, 1926. 1-1 in singles, 1-0 in doubles.
HELEN JACOBS, 1927 through 1937, '39. 14-7 in singles, 5-4 in doubles. Overall: 19-11 for 12 matches.
CHARLOTTE HOSMER CHAPIN, 1927. 0-1 in doubles.
PENELOPE ANDERSON, 1928. 0-1 in doubles.
EDITH CROSS, 1929, '30. 1-0 in singles, 0-2 in doubles. Overall: 1-2 for 2 matches.
SARAH PALFREY FABYAN, 1930 through 1939. 7-4 in singles, 7-3 in doubles. Overall: 14-7 for 10 matches.
ANNA MCCUNE HARPER, 1931, '32. 1-1 in singles, 1-1 in doubles. Overall: 2-2 for 2 matches.
CAROLIN BABCOCK, 1933 through 1936. 1-2 in singles, 1-2 in doubles. Overall: 2-4 for 4 matches.
ALICE MARBLE, 1933, '37, '38, '39. 5-1 in singles, 3-1 in doubles. Overall 8-2 for 4 matches.
MARJORIE GLADMAN VAN RYN, 1933, '36, '37. 1-2 in doubles.
JOSEPHINE CRUICKSHANK, 1934. 0-1 in doubles.
ETHEL BURKHARDT ARNOLD, 1935. 1-1 in singles.
DOROTHY ANDRUS, 1935. 0-1 in doubles.
DOROTHY BUNDY, 1937, '38, '39. 1-2 in doubles.

MARY ARNOLD, 1939. 0-1 in doubles.

PAULINE BETZ, 1946. 2-0 in singles, 1-0 in doubles.

MARGARET OSBORNE DUPONT, 1946 through 1950, '54, '55, '57, '62. 10-0 in singles, 8-0 in doubles. Overall: 18-0 for 9 matches.

LOUISE BROUGH, 1946, '47, '48, '50, '52 through '57. 12-0 in singles, 10-0 in doubles. Overall: 22-0 for 10 matches.

DORIS HART, 1946 through 1955. 14-0 in singles, 8-1 in doubles. Overall: 22-1 for 10 matches.

PATRICIA CANNING TODD, 1947 through 1951. 4-1 in doubles.

BEVERLY BAKER FLEITZ, 1949, '56, '59. 3-0 in singles, 1-0 in doubles.

SHIRLEY FRY, 1949, '51, '52, '53, '55, '56. 4-2 in singles, 6-0 in doubles. Overall: 10-2 for 6 matches.

GERTRUDE MORAN, 1949. 1-0 in doubles.

MAUREEN CONNOLLY, 1951 through 1954. 7-0 in singles, 2-0 in doubles. Overall: 9-0 for 4 matches.

NANCY CHAFFEE, 1951. 1-0 in doubles.

DOROTHY HEAD KNODE, 1955, '56, '57, '58, '60. 4-2 in singles, 1-2 in doubles. Overall: 5-4 for 5 matches.

ALTHEA GIBSON, 1957, '58. 3-1 in singles, 2-0 in doubles. Overall: 5-1 for 2 matches.

DARLENE HARD, 1957, '59, '60, '62, 63. 6–3 in singles, 4-1 in doubles. Overall 10-4 for 5 matches.

MIRIAM ARNOLD, 1958. 0-1 in singles.

KAROL FAGEROS, 1958. 0-1 in doubles.

JANET HOPPS, 1958, '59, '60. 0-1 in singles, 1-2 in doubles. Overall: 1-3 for 3 matches.

SALLY MOORE, 1959. 0-1 in singles, 0-1 in doubles.

JEANNE ARTH, 1959. 0-1 in doubles.

KAREN HANTZ SUSMAN, 1960, '61, '62, '65. 3-3 in singles, 3-0 in doubles. Overall: 6-3 for 4 matches.

BILLIE JEAN MOFFITT KING, 1961 through 1967, 1970, 1977, 1978. 14-2 in singles, 7-3 in doubles. Overall: 21-5 for 10 matches.

JUSTINA BRICKA, 1961. 1-0 in singles.

MARGARET VARNER, 1961, '62. 1-0 in doubles.

NANCY RICHEY GUNTER, 1962 through 1969, 1977. 9-8 in singles, 3-2 in doubles. Overall: 12-10 for 8 matches.

DONNA FLOYD FALES, 1963, '64. 1-1 in doubles.

CAROLE CALDWELL GRAEBNER, 1964, '65, '67. 2-0 in singles, 2-1 in doubles. Overall: 4-1 for 4 matches.

MARY ANN EISEL CURTIS, 1966 through 1971. 1-2 in singles, 3-3 in doubles. Overall: 4-5 for 6 matches.

JANE ALBERT, 1966. 0-1 in doubles.

ROSEMARY CASALS, 1967, 1976, 1977, 1979, 1980. 1-3 in singles, 5-0 in doubles.

JANE BARTKOWICZ, 1968, '69, '70. 2-0 in singles, 2-0 in doubles. Overall: 4-0 for 3 matches.

STEPHANIE DEFINA JOHNSON, 1968. 0-1 in doubles.

KATHLEEN HARTER, 1968. 0-1 in doubles.

JULIE HELDMAN, 1969, '70, '71. 3-1 in singles, 1-1 in doubles. Overall: 4-2 for 3 matches.

VALERIE ZIEGENFUSS, 1969, '71, '72. 1-0 in singles, 2-1 in doubles. Overall: 3-1 for 3 matches.

KRISTIE PIGEON, 1971. 0-1 in singles.

CHRIS EVERT, 1971, '72, '73, 1975–80. 18-0 in singles, 5–4 in doubles. Overall: 20–4 for 9 matches.

WENDY OVERTON, 1972. 0-2 in singles, 1-0 in doubles.

PATTI HOGAN, 1972, '73. 2-1 in singles, 2-0 in doubles.

LINDA TUERO, 1973. 1-0 in singles.

MARITA REDONDO, 1973. 0-1 in doubles.

JEANNE EVERT, 1973, '74. 0-1 in singles, 1-0 in doubles. Overall: 1-1 for 2 matches.

JANET NEWBERRY, 1974, '75. 0-3 in singles, 0-2 in doubles. Overall: 0-5 for 2 matches.

BETSY NAGELSEN, 1974. 0-1 in doubles.

JULIE ANTHONY, 1975. 0-1 in doubles.

TERRY HOLLADAY, 1976. 1-0 in singles.

ANN KIYOMURA, 1976, '79. 2-0 in doubles.

MONA SCHALLAU GUERRANT, 1974–76. 0–2 in singles, 2–1 in doubles.

JOANNE RUSSELL, 1977. 1-0 in singles.

TRACY AUSTIN, 1978–79. 2–2 in singles, 2–0 in doubles. Overall: 4–2 in 2 matches.

PAM SHRIVER, 1978. 0–1 in singles, 0–1 in doubles.

KATHY JORDAN, 1979–80. 2–0 in singles, 1–0 in doubles.

ANDREA JAEGER, 1980. 1–1 in singles.

ANNE SMITH, 1980. 1–0 in doubles.

Leading British Wightman Cup Players

KATHLEEN MCKANE GODFREE, 1923–27, '30, '34. 5-5 in singles, 2-5 in doubles, Overall: 7-10 for 7 matches.

Two of the outstanding Wightman Cup players of the late 1930s period: Alice Marble of the United States *(left)* and Mrs. Kay Stammers Menzies of Great Britain *(right)*.

BETTY NUTHALL, 1927, '28, '29, '31, '32, '33, '34, '39. 3-5 in singles, 3-2 in doubles. Overall: 6-7 for 8 matches.

PHOEBE WATSON, 1928, '29, '30. 3-3 in singles, 3-0 in doubles. Overall: 6-3 for 3 matches.

KAY STAMMERS MENZIES, 1935–39, '46, '47, '48. 4-9 in singles, 1-4 in doubles. Overall: 5-13 for 8 matches.

ANGELA MORTIMER, 1953, '55, '56, '59, '60, '61. 3-7 in singles, 2-4 in doubles. Overall: 5-11 for 6 matches.

ANN HAYDON JONES, 1957 through 1967, 1970, 1975. 10-11 in singles, 6-5 in doubles. Overall: 16-16 for 13 matches.

CHRISTINE TRUMAN JANES, 1957 through 1963, '67, '68, '69. 5-11 in singles, 5-3 in doubles. Overall: 10-14 for 10 matches.

VIRGINIA WADE, 1965–80. 12–17 in singles, 6–9 in doubles. Overall: 18–29 for 16 matches.

SUE BARKER, 1974–80. 5–7 in singles, 3–4 in doubles. Overall: 8–11 for 7 matches.

Federation Cup Leaders

Eighteen women have competed for the United States in Federation Cup. Mrs. Billie Jean Moffitt King in seven years played 25 engagements against other countries and won 46 of 50 matches.

U.S. Federation Cup Who's Who

DARLENE HARD, 1963. 3-1 in singles, 3-0 in doubles.

MRS. BILLIE JEAN MOFFITT KING, 1963 through 1967, 1976, 1977–79. 25-4 in singles, 29–0 in doubles. Overall: 52–4 for 36 matches.

MRS. CAROLE CALDWELL GRAEBNER, 1963, '65, '66. 2-1 in singles, 10-0 in doubles. Overall: 12-1 for 10 matches.

MRS. NANCY RICHEY GUNTER, 1964, '68, '69. 10-1 in singles, 5-1 in doubles. Overall: 15–2 for 11 matches.

MRS. KAREN HANTZE SUSMAN, 1964. 4-0 in doubles. Overall: 4-4 for 4 matches.

JULIE HELDMAN, 1966, '69, '70, '74, '75. 12-6 in singles, 7-3 in doubles. Overall: 19-9 for 15 matches.

ROSIE CASALS, 1967, 1976–80. 8-1 in singles, 21–1 in doubles. Overall: 29-2 for 20 matches.

MRS. MARY ANN EISEL CURTIS, 1968, '70. 1-2 in singles, 4-2 in doubles. Overall: 5-4 for 6 matches.

KATHY HARTER, 1968. 1-0 in doubles.

JANE (PEACHES) BARTKOWICZ, 1969, '70. 3-0 in singles, 4-0 in doubles. Overall: 7-0 for 7 matches.

SHARON WALSH, 1971 through 1974. 1-2 in singles, 9-4 in doubles. Overall: 10-6 for 12 matches.

PATTI HOGAN, 1971, '73. 3-3 in singles, 4-1 in doubles. Overall: 7-4 for 6 matches.

LINDA TUERO, 1972, '73. 5-2 in singles.

VALERIE ZIEGENFUSS, 1972. 4-0 in singles, 2-1 in doubles. Overall: 6-1 for 4 matches.

JANICE METCALF, 1973. 0-1 in doubles.

KATHY KUYKENDALL, 1975. 3-1 in singles.

JANET NEWBERRY, 1975. 3-1 in doubles.

CHRIS EVERT, 1977–80. 18–0 in singles, 10–1 in doubles. Overall: 28–1 in 18 matches.

TRACY AUSTIN, 1978, '80. 13–1 in singles.
KATHY JORDAN, 1980. 1–0 in singles, 5–0 in doubles.

All-Time Federation Leading Players (Based on number of victories)

MRS. BILLIE JEAN MOFFITT KING, United States, 1963 through 1967, '76, '77. 25-4 in singles, 21-0 in doubles. Overall: 46-4 for 25 matches.
MRS. MARGARET SMITH COURT, Australia, 1963, '64, '65, '68, '69, '71, '77. 22-0 in singles, 15-5 in doubles. Overall: 37-5 for 21 matches.
MRS. ANN HAYDON JONES, Britain, 1963 through 1967, 1971. 11-8 in singles, 13-7 in doubles. Overall: 24-15 for 19 matches.
VIRGINIA WADE, Britain, 1967 through 1976. 24-9 in singles, 15-8 in doubles. Overall: 39-17 for 33 matches.
MRS. JUDY TEGART DALTON, Australia, 1965, '66, '67, '69, '70. 6-1 in singles, 11-3 in doubles. Overall: 17-4 for 14 matches.
FRANÇOISE DURR, France, 1963 through 1967, 1971, 1977. 14-0 in singles, 13-9 in doubles. Overall: 27-19 for 17 matches.

EVONNE GOOLAGONG CAWLEY, Australia, 1971 through 1976. 19-2 in singles, 10-2 in doubles. Overall: 29-4 for 21 matches.

Longest Federation Cup Matches

Lenna Mutanen of Finland defeated Beatriz Araujo of Argentina in a 44-game match in 1972, 9-7, 8-10, 6-4. It was the longest singles match in Federation Cup history and only once did a doubles match exceed it.

Also in 1972, Betty Stove and Trudy Groenmann Walhof defeated Marilyn Pryde and R. Hunt of New Zealand, 15-13, 10-8.

Andrée Martin of Canada won the second-longest Federation Cup singles match, 41 games, over Katalin Borka of Hungary, 3-6, 7-5, 11-9, in 1969. The longest Cup match involving an American was Billie Jean King's 38-game victory over Norma Baylon of Argentina in 1964, 12-10, 9-7.

Prize Money List (Men's)

1969 was the first time all the leading men players were competing for prize money, in opens, pro tournaments, or "player" events. The ten leading money winners from 1969 on are as follows:

Cliff Richey *(left)* won the Pepsi Grand Prix of Tennis in 1970, but Stan Smith *(right)* captured the Masters' Round Robin.

1969

1. Rod Laver $124,000
2. Tony Roche 75,045
3. Tom Okker 65,451
4. Roy Emerson 62,629
5. John Newcombe 52,610
6. Ken Rosewall 46,796
7. Pancho Gonzalez 46,288
8. Marty Riessen 43,441
9. Fred Stolle 43,160
10. Arthur Ashe 42,030

1970

1. Rod Laver $201,453
2. Arthur Ashe 141,018
3. Ken Rosewall 140,455
4. Cliff Richey 97,000
5. Roy Emerson 96,485
6. Stan Smith 95,251
7. John Newcombe 78,251
8. Pancho Gonzalez 77,365
9. Clark Graebner 68,000
10. Tony Roche 67,232

1971

1. Rod Laver $292,717
2. Ken Rosewall 138,317
3. Tom Okker 120,465
4. Ilie Nastase 114,000
5. Arthur Ashe 104,642
6. Stan Smith 103,806
7. John Newcombe 101,514
8. Marty Riessen 87,310
9. Clark Graebner 75,400
10. Cliff Richey 75,000

1972

1. Ilie Nastase $176,000
2. Stan Smith 142,300
3. Ken Rosewall 132,950
4. John Newcombe 120,600
5. Arthur Ashe 119,775
6. Rod Laver 100,200
7. Tom Okker 90,004
8. Jimmy Connors 90,000
9. Marty Riessen 74,436
10. Cliff Drysdale 68,433

1973

1. Ilie Nastase $228,750
2. Stan Smith 218,647
3. Tom Okker 178,215
4. Jimmy Connors 156,400
5. John Newcombe 151,675

6. Arthur Ashe 141,206
7. Rod Laver 140,325
8. Ken Rosewall 120,420
9. Manuel Orantes 97,175
10. Brian Gottfried 87,710

1974

1. Jimmy Connors $281,309
2. Guillermo Vilas 274,327
3. John Newcombe 273,299
4. Bjorn Borg 215,229
5. Ilie Nastase 190,752
6. Arthur Ashe 165,194
7. Stan Smith 163,326
8. Manuel Orantes 139,857
9. Rod Laver 134,600
10. Raul Ramirez 127,425

1975

Men	Tournament Prizes	Other Winnings	Total Earned
1. Jimmy Connors	$158,023	$442,250	$600,273
2. Arthur Ashe	243,379	94,958	338,337
3. Manuel Orantes	186,066	85,000	271,066
4. Guillermo Vilas	143,622	103,750	247,372
5. Bjorn Borg	174,875	55,000	229,875
6. Raul Ramirez	156,850	54,000	210,850
7. Ilie Nastase	158,293	52,500	210,793
8. Brian Gottfried	129,630	41,500	171,130
9. Rod Laver	104,571	60,750	165,321
10. John Alexander	120,900	37,750	158,650
11. Roscoe Tanner	109,659	36,000	145,659
12. Harold Solomon	119,200	21,000	140,200

1976

Men	Tournament Prizes	Other Winnings	Total Earned
1. Jimmy Connors	$303,335	$384,000	$687,335
2. Ilie Nastase	345,205	231,500	576,705
3. Raul Ramirez	253,422	212,500	465,942
4. Bjorn Borg	218,420	206,000	424,420
5. Arthur Ashe	243,636	130,250	373,886
6. Manuel Orantes	205,884	156,000	361,884
7. Harold Solomon	193,182	60,250	253,432
8. Guillermo Vilas	201,226	49,500	250,726
9. Eddie Dibbs	171,571	68,250	239,821
10. Wojtek Fibak	176,539	57,500	234,039
11. Brian Gottfried	168,033	58,500	226,533
12. Roscoe Tanner	178,906	34,500	213,406

Sandy Mayer.

1977

1. Jimmy Connors	$922,657
2. Guillermo Vilas	800,642
3. Bjorn Borg	480,661
4. Brian Gottfried	478,988
5. Dick Stockton	311,856
6. Ilie Nastase	306,956
7. Vitas Gerulaitis	294,324
8. Eddie Dibbs	283,691
9. Roscoe Tanner	281,131
10. Raul Ramirez	245,007

1978

1. Eddie Dibbs	$582,872
2. Raul Ramirez	450,110
3. John McEnroe	445,024
4. Wojtek Fibak	383,843
5. Ilie Nastase	367,422
6. Vitas Gerulaitis	359,095
7. Harold Solomon	354,372
8. Jimmy Connors	353,307
9. Bjorn Borg	348,386
10. Brian Gottfried	312,205

1979

1. Bjorn Borg	$1,019,345
2. John McEnroe	1,005,238
3. Jimmy Connors	701,340
4. Vitas Gerulaitis	414,515
5. Guillermo Vilas	374,195
6. Peter Fleming	353,315
7. Roscoe Tanner	263,433
8. Eddie Dibbs	249,293
9. Wojtek Fibak	234,452
10. Harold Solomon	222,078

1980

1. John McEnroe	$1,026,383
2. Bjorn Borg	723,212
3. Jimmy Connors	604,641
4. Ivan Lendl	568,911
5. Gene Mayer	384,719
6. Guillermo Vilas	378,601
7. Vitas Gerulaitis	344,666
8. Wojtek Fibak	319,887
9. Brian Gottfried	294,579
10. Jose-Luis Clerc	277,234

Prize Money List (Women's)

The women professional tennis players came into their own in 1971 with their tour. It proved to be a great success, and Mrs. Billie Jean King became the first woman professional athlete to win over $100,000 in one season. The leading money winners in the 1971 to 1977:

1971

1. Mrs. Billie Jean M. King	$117,000
2. Françoise Durr	65,000
3. Rosemary Casals	62,000
4. Mrs. Judy Dalton	33,867
5. Kerry Melville	29,767
6. Mrs. Dan H. Jones	26,148
7. Virginia Wade	24,000
8. Mrs. Nancy R. Gunter	15,300
9. Mary Ann Eisel	15,000
10. Valerie Ziegenfuss	14,000

1972

1. Mrs. Billie Jean King	$119,000
2. Rosemary Casals	70,000
3. Kerry Melville	55,000
4. Mrs. Nancy Richey Gunter	50,800
5. Mrs. Margaret S. Court	47,000
6. Françoise Durr	46,000
7. Evonne Goolagong	42,000

8. Virginia Wade	32,800
9. Wendy Overton	30,000
10. Karen Krantzcke	19,312

1973

1. Mrs. Margaret S. Court	$204,400
2. Mrs. Billie Jean King	194,700
3. Chris Evert	152,002
4. Evonne Goolagong	108,127
5. Rosemary Casals	104,375
6. Kerry Melville	61,200
7. Virginia Wade	60,100
8. Mrs. Nancy Richey Gunter	48,292

9. Françoise Durr	40,727
10. Betty Stove	40,019

1974

1. Chris Evert	$261,460
2. Billie Jean King	173,225
3. Evonne Goolagong	102,506
4. Virginia Wade	85,389
5. Rosemary Casals	72,389
6. Julie Heldman	60,511
7. Kerry Melville	56,022
8. Françoise Durr	41,227
9. Olga Morozova	40,927
10. Betty Stove	40,249

1975

Women	Tournament Prizes	Other Winnings	Total Earned
1. Chris Evert	$323,977	$89,000	$412,977
2. Martina Navratilova	184,518	1,000	185,518
3. Virginia Wade	138,576	15,000	153,576
4. Evonne Goolagong	132,754	12,500	145,254
5. Mrs. Billie Jean King	99,900	25,000	124,900
6. Mrs. Margaret S. Court	105,646	—0—	105,646

1976

1. Chris Evert	$289,165	$54,000	$343,165
2. Evonne Goolagong Cawley	173,285	36,667	209,952
3. Virginia Wade	126,380	32,833	159,213
4. Rosemary Casals	102,185	26,500	128,685
4. Martina Navratilova	96,035	32,500	128,535
6. Betty Stove	95,025	3,333	98,358

1977

1. Chris Evert	$503,134
2. Martina Navratilova	300,317
3. Virginia Wade	258,746
4. Betty Stove	229,162
5. Billie Jean King	193,194
6. Sue Barker	190,498
7. Kerry Reid	156,234
8. Rosemary Casals	126,193
9. Dianne Fromholtz	106,410
10. Wendy Turnbull	98,568

3. Virginia Wade	270,027
4. Kerry M. Reid	208,766
5. Wendy Turnbull	189,583
6. Betty Stove	177,243
7. Evonne Goolagong Cawley	160,844
8. Virginia Ruzici	151,379
9. Billie Jean King	149,492
10. Regina Marsikova	88,894

1978

1. Martina Navratilova	$450,757
2. Chris Evert	354,486

1979

1. Martina Navratilova	$747,548
2. Chris Evert Lloyd	564,398
3. Tracy Austin	541,676
4. Wendy Turnbull	317,463

5. Dianne Fromholtz	265,990
6. Bille Jean King	185,804
7. Betty Stove	182,006
8. Sue Barker	175,452
9. Evonne Goolagong Cawley	171,573
10. Virginia Wade	146,283

1980

1. Tracy Austin	$683,787
2. Martina Navratilova	674,400
3. Chris Evert Lloyd	427,705
4. Hana Mandlikova	376,430
5. Bille Jean King	321,309
6. Wendy Turnbull	315,573
7. Andrea Jaeger	258,431
8. Evonne Goolagong Cawley	210,080
9. Virginia Ruzici	194,113
10. Pam Shriver	182,649

CAREER MONEY-WINNING LEADERS

THROUGH 1980

Men

1. Jimmy Connors, 1972–80	$3,347,262
2. Bjorn Borg, 1973–80	3,139,228
3. John McEnroe, 1978–80	2,476,644
4. Guillermo Vilas, 1972–80	2,440,055
5. Ilie Nastase, 1969–80	2,262,341
6. Raul Ramirez, 1973–80	1,939,298
7. Brian Gottfried, 1972–80	1,858,792
8. Stan Smith, 1969–80	1,771,826
9. Eddie Dibbs, 1972–80	1,768,071
10. Arthur Ashe, 1969–79	1,711,373

Women

1. Chris Evert Lloyd, 1973–80	$2,826,327
2. Martina Navratilova, 1973–80	2,465,967
3. Bille Jean King, 1968–80	1,690,953
4. Virginia Wade, 1968–80	1,443,496
5. Tracy Austin, 1978–80	1,295,088
6. Evonne Goolagong Cawley	1,189,484

(All of the above records were compiled by the USTA to include tournament prize purses, recognized bonus money and national team competition or pro tour money only. Challenge matches, team tennis, exhibitions or special events involving less than eight players not included.)

Hana Mandlikova of Czechoslovakia reached the final of the U.S. Open Singles in 1980 at the age of 18, losing to Chris Evert Lloyd.

Although only 15, Andrea Jaeger turned pro in 1980 and was the losing finalist to Tracy Austin in the Colgate Series Championship.

Glossary of Tennis Terms

Tennis is a wonderful game . . . and it is fascinating to speculate just who originated the various terms that are so common to everyone who has ever swung a racket. For instance, as was stated in Section I, the name first applied to court tennis and later to lawn tennis is elusive and mysterious. Its origin, long said to be "unknown," is obscure. The word that began as *tenes* and ended as *tennis* has passed through twenty-four transformations, four variations of five letters, twelve of six letters, seven of seven letters, and one of eight letters. It would almost seem as though the word changed its form to escape the etymologists.

As noted in the first English treatise on tennis, published anonymously in 1822 and later attributed to one R. Lukin: "The unsettled state . . . of our orthography at that period [fifteenth century] forbids these varieties from becoming the ground-work of any speculations; nor does it seem at all expedient to lengthen out this note . . . by offering conjectures, which the reader may multiply at pleasure without much hope perhaps of arriving at the truth."

There are certain derivations that have never been substantiated, and may be disposed of at the outset to avoid confusion. Lukin himself offers two theories not found elsewhere: one that tennis came from the French word *tente,* referring to a covered building in which the game was played, and another that it came from an old Norman word meaning "bound," this referring to the "cords or tendons" which were formerly wound around the hand to protect it in playing *jeu de paume* (tennis).

Other authors have claimed that tennis comes from the Latin word *teniludium,* meaning "play of tennis," and from a so-called Greek word *phennis.* The word *teniludium* is not endorsed by the leading Latin scholars, although *teniludus* and *teniludius* appear in a compilation of medieval expressions by a Dominican friar of Norfolk, England, in 1440. There is not a shadow of Greek authority, however, for the word *phennis* as indicating tennis.

Other theories to be consigned to the realm of the imagination are: one, that tennis comes from the German *tanz,* the bounding or ricochet motion of the tennis ball, being a "tanz" or dance of the ball around the court; another, that *tenne* is German for threshing floor, which was used at an early time for a primitive tennis court; another, that tennis is old English for *tens,* and that the game is really double fives; another, that *tence* (tennis) meant combat or batting to and fro, and hence knocking a ball back and forth with a racket, it being said that *tence* is used with this meaning in early English works; another that, as Tennyson and Denison have been found to be the same originally, Saint Denis was probably Saint Tennis, who became a patron saint, and lent his name to the game.

The most accepted etymology, however, is that

tennis in English comes from the French word *tenez.* But, the derivation from the French *tenez* really rests upon the assumption that this expression was used by the French when they were about to strike the ball. Let us examine the evidence. From 1324, and all through the fourteenth century thereafter, the word *tennis* in its various forms appears, but during this period no French literature records any mention of the players calling *tenez* at the beginning of play. The first literature that makes such a suggestion does not appear in France but in England, and it does not appear until the seventeenth century. In 1617 a London lexicographer made a vast compilation in eleven languages, and this compilation contains the following: "Tennis, play . . . *tenez* . . . which word the Frenchmen, the only tennis players, use to speak when they strike the ball, at tennis."

Like so many words in our language, while the weight of authority favors the *tenez* theory, the more the subject is studied the less satisfactory the theory becomes. It fails to convince a great many students of tennis history. The French had a universally adopted name for their game before *tenez* appeared in their literature. *Jeu de paume,* meaning tennis, was mentioned as early as 1200, and probably began to take form from 1150 to 1200. It is difficult to believe that an established name should have been changed from a mere exclamation at play. Furthermore, the transition from *tenez* to *tennis* is not an easy one.

Are you bewildered or confused? Then how about the origin of scoring? Most players of today who call the scores so glibly may be surprised to know that they speak a language which has been a puzzle for centuries. While the use of "fifteen" in tennis scoring still remains obscure, as pointed out in Section IV, the use of the word *love* is the great mystery. It is so mysterious that it is not discussed in an authoritative way by any of the historians. Although of comparatively recent origin, for the word has no foreign equivalent and was first used by the English, no one really knows why it was used, nor exactly when it was first used. Only a few casual references or bold assertions appear in tennis literature. For example, one author states didactically that the word comes from an old Scotch word *luff,* meaning "nothing," and this has been repeatedly quoted. According to the authorities, however, no such word has been used at any time in the Scotch language. Most writers who mention "love" at all dismiss it with a hopeless gesture. There are, however, certain theories, legendary and otherwise, that are interesting to consider.

One of these, which has come down by word of mouth for many years, is to the effect that the French, the earliest exponents of court tennis, in marking up a zero to indicate no score, wrote the figure in an elliptical form. This figure often had the appearance of an egg, and so the French called it *l'oeuf* (the egg). It has been said that when the English learned the game from the French they heard the French calling *l'oeuf* for no score, and this sounded to them like the word *love,* so they called it "love," and have continued to do so ever since.

To support this theory an analogy is drawn from the game of cricket. In that game the zero or "0" placed against the batsman's name in the scoring sheet when he fails to score is used to designate "nothing," and this score for a long time has been called "the duck's egg" or "duck egg." An analogy is also drawn from the slang expression "goose egg" as applied in other games. It is said that this expression originated in the United States, *The New York Times* being referred to as giving the following description of a baseball game in 1886: "The New York players presented the Boston men with nine unpalatable goose eggs in their (baseball) contest on the Polo Grounds yesterday."

While most lexicographers believe the use by the French of *l'oeuf* to indicate "no score" is the basis of *love* in today's tennis, there are other theories, too. For example, the use of the word *love* to suggest "nothing" is as old as the English language. In the year 971 we find the equivalent of the expression "neither for love nor money," "ne for feu, ne for nanes mannes lufou." Similar expressions have been in common use for centuries. Later, by an easy antithesis, there developed the expression in competitive games "to play for love," meaning "to play for nothing," as contrasted with playing for money. Similarly, a labor of love, though originally meaning a labor one delights in, came to mean a labor done for favor, for love, or for nothing.

In fact, it is quite usual to say, "Let's play for

love," when we mean to play for nothing, and in view of the antiquity of this expression it would seem most natural for the English to have used the word to indicate no score when they first began to play the game.

As you go further in the language of tennis, you will find every phase of the sport has words of interesting derivations. A study of the service, for instance, naturally leads to a consideration of the let, because the word *let* is most often applied to a service, otherwise good, that touches the net. The word *let* means literally "obstruction." It is now almost obsolete, but appears in the current expression "without let or hindrance." It is easy to see how the word was used to apply to a ball that was hindered or obstructed by a person or object in such a way that the point had to be played over again.

The rules in the first two editions of Major Wingfield's *Sphairistike* in December, 1873, and November, 1874, make no mention of the let. Further, the first official rules of lawn tennis adopted by the Marylebone Cricket Club in 1875 provide that "it is a good service or return, although the ball touches the net or either of the posts." By 1878 the words "or either of the posts" were omitted, according to Jefferies' modern rules published in that year. In fact, the first mention of a *let* in lawn tennis appears in 1878, where it is stated that a *let* should be allowed for outside obstruction or interference, such as "an obtrusive dog running across the court, or anything of that kind," but should not be allowed "for anything which constitutes a part of court." In other words, no *let* was allowed for a service that touched the net.

In 1880, however, the Marylebone Cricket Club and the All-English Croquet and Lawn Tennis Club definitely established the *let* in their decision that "if the ball served touch the net, the service, provided it be otherwise good, counts for nothing." This rule was adopted in substance in the United States in 1881.

We could go on almost indefinitely on the derivations of tennis words. For the uninitiated, however, this could become bewildering and rather confusing. Instead, for those who are not familiar with the vocabulary of this sport, the following is a glossary of common tennis terms.

Ace. An earned point as distinguished from one scored by opponent's error.

Ace on service. A point earned on serving a ball that cannot be returned.

Ad in. The server's advantage.

Ad out. The receiver's advantage.

Advantage. A point won by player after deuce. If he wins the next point, he wins the game; if he loses it, the score returns to deuce.

All. An equal score. For example, "thirty-all" refers to points in a game; or "one-all" refers to games (sometimes called *games all*) in a set.

All-court game. A term usually applied to ability of a player to play all the strokes, from any part of the court. *All-around* play means a good ground game supplemented by a good net game.

Alley. The area on each side of the singles court employed to enlarge the court for doubles play.

Amateur. One who does not receive, or has not received, directly or indirectly, pecuniary advantage by the playing, teaching, demonstrating, or pursuit of the game of tennis.

American twist. A type of serve in which the racket strikes the ball with an upward motion, causing the ball to spin in its flight and to take a high bounce when it hits the ground.

Angle game. A style of play in which the angles of the court are used. Specifically, it refers to the short angles. E.g, the player hits a forehand cross court which lands inside his opponent's service line and close to the opponent's forehand sideline.

Angle volley. A volleying stroke angled past an opponent.

Anticipatory position. A position assumed while waiting for the ball to be served or returned. Same as a *waiting* or *readiness position.*

Approach shot. A hard, deep-to-the-corner shot that puts an opponent on the defensive. A type of forcing shot.

Australian formation. A positioning of players in a doubles game in which the server's partner stands on the same side of court from which he is serving.

Backcourt. The area between the base line and service line.

Backhand. A stroke made with the playing arm

and racket across the body. Any stroke played on the left side of a righthanded player, or on the right side of a lefthanded player.

Back room. The space between the base line and the court's backstop or fence. Also called *run-back.*

Backspin. The reverse or backward rotation of the ball while in its flight. The spinning of the ball caused by a straight cut or a chop stroke, the ball spinning back toward the striker. Opposite of *forward spin.*

Backstop. The netting or other obstruction behind the court to prevent the balls from rolling away.

Backswing. The initial swing of the racket in a backward direction in preparation for the forward stroking movement. Also called *racket-back position.*

Bad ball. A ball that does not land in the playing court area.

Ball. The cloth-covered sphere used in playing tennis. Also the term used for the result of a stroke. Thus, a "good-length ball" is a stroke which makes the ball hit the ground near the base line.

Ball boy. A person who retrieves the balls for the players.

Band. The strip of canvas attached to the top of the net.

Base line. The back line at either end of the court.

Base-line game. A style of play in which the player stays on or near the base line and seldom moves into the forecourt. Same as *baseline player.*

Being beaten by the ball. Arriving too late; being passed or almost passed; or too late for optimal position.

Big game. A style of play in which the emphasis is on a big service and a net attack.

Big server. A player with a powerful service.

Blocked ball. A ball returned without the swing of a racket, by simply meeting it with a stiff wrist and stationary racket; generally, a "stop-volley."

Bound. The rising of the ball from the court surface. Also the trajectory from first and second impact on the court surface.

Break. The action of a bounding ball as it leaves the ground; used chiefly in speaking of cut or twist strokes, when the ball bounds unnaturally.

Broken service. A game won by the opponent of the server.

Bullet. A hard-hit ball.

Bye. The right to enter the next round without playing, given by chance in the drawing to players for whom there is no antagonist. Same as a *walk-in.*

Cannonball. An extremely fast, flat service.

Center mark. The mark bisecting the base line, defining one of the limits of the service position.

Center service line. The line dividing the service court into halves and separating the right and left service courts.

Center strop. Two-inch-wide piece of canvas that secures the net at the center of the court on some surfaces.

Chalk. The white material often used to mark lines on some tennis surfaces. When a ball strikes exactly on a line, white dust often flies into the air, and players then speak of *seeing chalk*, meaning that a disputed ball was good because it raised white dust.

Challenge cups. Trophies offered in lawn tennis, the holders of which are open to challenge for their possession. The customary requirements are that the holder must meet the winner of an event held once each year, and if the trophy be won three times by the same player, it passes into his permanent possession. In England, some of these cups must be won three times in succession, but this is not the case in America.

Challenger. The player who wins an event for which there is a challenge cup, or title, and thus earns the right to challenge the holder for the trophy.

Challenge round. The extra round in which a match is played between the challenger and holder for any trophy or title.

Champion barred. The conditions of most events for championships, the holder of the title being debarred from entering for the prizes, and meeting the winner in the challenge round.

Championship. The title held by virtue of winning any tournament held for supremacy of any given section. Also, the event held for the right to challenge for the title or trophy.

Change of length. Shots that are made with varying lengths; one deep, followed by a short shot, or vice versa.

Change of pace. The game strategy or tactic of changing the speed of your shots or reversing the spin on the ball.

Changing courts. The process whereby players, at the end of every odd game during a set, change to opposite sides of the net.

Chip. A short, angled shot, often sliced, to return a serve.

Choke. To grip the racket handle up toward the head rather than at its end.

Chop. A slicing stroke made by drawing the racket down sharply with a chopping motion when striking the ball, giving it a sharp backspin or underspin.

Circuit. Term used when referring to the various tournaments on a player's schedule. Same as *tour.*

Closed-face racket. A racket whose face is tilted forward in the direction of the oncoming ball.

Consolation. A prize event, or match, open (in America) to any player beaten in the first match actually played, or (in England) generally to all players beaten in the first and second rounds. Similar to *plate*, as used abroad.

Continental grip. Used to maintain the same grip for forehand and backhand; sometimes called the *service grip.*

Conventional stroking. In the orthodox manner.

Court. The playing area on which the game of tennis is played.

Court material. The surface of the court—grass, clay, hard, synthetic, etc.

Cover. Turning the face of the racket from the perpendicular forward, usually giving topspin to the ball.

Covered court. An indoor court for winter play, generally with wood or synthetic surface, always with roof—used chiefly in England. In the United States, called an *indoor court.*

Crack. A slang expression abbreviated from "crack-a-Jack," meaning a very expert player.

Cross-court. A stroke that drives the ball across the court diagonally from one side to the other.

Curl. The twist, cut, or spin on a ball resulting from a sharp cut stroke.

Cut. The twist, spin, or curl of a ball when it has been sliced in hitting.

Cut stroke. A stroke in which the racket strikes a glancing blow and is drawn sharply to one side or another in striking.

Dead. A ball is dead after it has ceased to be "in play"; that is, when it has hit the ground twice anywhere or once out of court, when it has fallen into the net, or when either player has lost the point by any infraction of the rules. Also said of a ball that has been placed or smashed out of the reach of an antagonist; a "killed" ball.

Deep-court game. A style of play in which the player stays deep or in the backcourt.

Deep shot. A shot that bounces near the base line or deep into the playing area.

Default. The victory given to a player whose opponent is absent or declines to play; also, the absence or act of declining to play. Same as *walk-over.*

Defensive volley. A volleying stroke made from below the level of the net. Also called *low volley.*

Delivery. A service.

Deuce. An even score after six points of a game or ten games of a set.

Die. Descriptive of a ball that scarcely bounces at all.

Dink. A ball hit easily (usually close to the net) so that the opponent cannot reach it before it bounces twice. Also called *softie.*

Dipping balls. Balls that barely clear the net, then drop fast and short.

Double fault. Two successive faults in serving.

Double hit. A ball stroked twice on the same play —an illegal play.

Doubles. A game of four players (two on each side).

Down-the-line shot. A ball hit parallel and close to a side line.

Draft. The draw; the list of players entered for any event written out and bracketed in the order in which they are drawn to play.

Draw. The act of deciding by chance the order in which the players in any tournament will play, and against whom they will play. Also, the draft; the list of players entered.

Drive. A hard-hit groundstroke, either by forehand or backhand.

Drive volley.   A hard-hit volleying stroke, either by forehand or backhand.

Drop.   The unnatural down curve of a ball when hit with a "lifting" stroke that gives a top curl or forward spin.

Drop stroke.   A stroke made with a sharp lift of the racket as it meets the ball, which makes the ball twist forward rapidly and "drop" unnaturally after it crosses the net. Also, a short stroke made so that the ball drops just over the net.

Drop volley.   A volleying stroke hit softly and easily just over the net.

Duffer.   A poor player.

Earned point.   A point won by skillful play rather than by an opponent's error or fault.

Eastern grip.   The most common grip for a racket, (see page 110).

Echelon formation.   A positioning of players in a doubles game in which one player stands close to the net and his partner plays deep.

Error.   Failure to make a legal return after the ball touches the racket.

Event.   Any complete competition on the program of a tournament.

Face.   Either side of the stringing of a racket; the flat surface in the head or blade of a racket which is strung.

Falls.   Dies; the second bound of a ball in play, or its first bound if out of court.

Fast court.   A court on which a moderately hard-hit ball tends to have a long skid and low bounce and on which a ball with spin is not greatly diverted.

Fault.   A served ball that does not strike in the proper court or is not properly served.

Feeder stroke.   A drop-and-hit swing used in practicing or to return a ball to the server after a point.

Fifteen.   One point scored for either player.

Fifteen-all.   The score when each side has won one stroke.

Fifteen- (thirty-, or forty-) love.   The score when the server has won one (fifteen), two (thirty), or three (forty) points and the opponent none.

Final round.   The last round, in which the two surviving players or teams are opposed to each other; commonly referred to as the "finals."

Finishing shot.   A shot that cannot be returned by an opponent.

First return.   The first stroke made by the "striker-out," in returning the service.

Flat serve.   A service hit very hard with little or no spin. Same as *cannonball serve.*

Flat shot.   A very hard-hit shot that travels almost in a straight, flat line with little or no spin. Same as *plain shot.*

Flub.   To miss an easy shot.

Fluke.   A slang expression meaning an accidental return, or one that was intended in some other way. Also, the victory of a poorer player over a stronger player, through chance or luck; an "upset."

Follow-through.   The completion of the swing after impact. Same as *follow-after.*

Foot-fault.   An improper or illegal position or movement of the feet before or during the service.

Forced error.   An error made by a player because of a good shot on the part of his opponent.

Forcing shot.   A shot or series of shots that keep the opponent on the defensive or out of position.

Forecourt.   The area between the service line and the net.

Forehand.   A stroke used to hit a ball by a player on his right if righthanded; on his left if lefthanded.

Fork.   An iron upright stuck in the ground at the center of the court to keep the net at exactly the required height.

Form.   The style in which a player carries him- and makes his strokes. Also, his playing skill.

Forty.   Three points scored for either player.

Forward impulse.   The straight forward portion of the swing of any shot.

Forward spin.   A forward rotation of the ball in the direction of its flight. Opposite of "backspin."

Forward swing.   The motion of the racket toward and through the ball.

Frame.   The wooden or metal portion of the racket which holds the strings.

Full stroke.   Any stroke in which the player swings arm, racket, and body to the fullest extent possible.

Gallery. The spectators watching any game or match.

Gallery play. A slang expression meaning fancy strokes made for the purpose of attracting the attention of the spectators, or a spectacular stroke made in the regular course of a game.

Game. The unit of scoring next higher than the point; scored when either player has won four points, unless the other player has meantime won three; in that case (deuce score) the player first gaining a lead of two points.

Game point. The point which, if won by the player who is ahead, wins the game.

Games-all. The score of a set when the games are even at five-all, six-all, or higher. Same as "deuce" in the score of a set.

Game score. Points are reckoned as "15," "30," "40," and "game" rather than "1," "2," "3," and "4." A player must win a game by at least two points. Therefore, if each player has three points, the score is called "deuce" or "40-40" or "40-all." The player who wins the next point has "advantage" (not "50-40"). If he loses the next point, the score goes back to deuce.

Good. A ball that strikes in the proper court. Same as *good ball.*

Grip. The manner of holding a racket in the hand. Also the racket handle covering, generally made of leather.

Grooved stroke. A stroke with which the player is so familiar that he performs it automatically.

Ground game. A style of play that depends mainly on groundstrokes and is played in the backcourt.

Groundstroke. A stroke used to hit a ball after it has bounced on the playing surface. Opposite of volley.

Gut. An animal product (generally from lambs or hogs) sometimes used to string tennis rackets.

Guy-rope. The rope stays used to support the poles between which the net is suspended.

Hack. To make a clumsy swing at a ball.

Half-court line. The line dividing the service court into halves and separating the right and left service courts. Same as *center service line.*

Half volley. A stroke hit just as a ball is leaving the ground. Sometimes called *pickup shot.*

Handicap. Odds given or owed to a poorer player to equalize skill. Also, an event or match in which odds are assigned to unequal players, in order to equalize the chances of winning.

Handle. The end of the racket by which it is held.

Head. The upper part of a racket in which the stringing is fastened. Same as *blade.*

Hit out on the line of flight. A return on the same line as the shot received.

Hitting deep. Hitting to an area on or within 2 or 3 feet of the base line.

Hitting short. Hitting into an area in the vicinity of the service line.

Hold service. The winning of a game by the person who is serving. Opposite of *break service.*

Hop. The bound of the ball.

How? The call of a player for the decision of the linesman or umpire on any doubtful ball.

In. A ball that strikes in the proper court. Same as *good* or *right.*

Invitation tournament. A meeting which is open only to players who are invited to enter.

ITF. Abbreviation for International Tennis Federation.

Kill. To place a ball into some part of the opponent's court where it cannot be returned, or to smash it so fast that he cannot return it.

Knock-up. Practice play generally to warm up before a match, and often played without serving or scoring; sometimes only knocking the balls back and forth over the net regardless of the court lines.

Latitudinally. From side to side.

Length. The distance a ball travels after crossing the net; specifically, how close it strikes to the base line.

Let. A served ball that touches the net and yet goes into the proper court. It is then played over again without penalty. Also any stroke that does not count and is played over. Same as *net-cord stroke.*

Let it touch! The warning called out by a player to his partner in doubles, when he thinks a ball is going out.

Lift stroke. A stroke made with the racket nearly

or quite vertical, and drawn up sharply as it meets the ball, apparently lifting the ball over the net.

Line ball. A ball that strikes any portion of the line (outside edge, middle, or inside edge). Such a ball is considered to be good.

Line of flight. The direction of the shot.

Line pass. A stroke made from the side of the court so as to drive the ball past the player at the net, the ball passing parallel with and inside the side line.

Lines. The various lines or markings that indicate the boundaries and playing areas on a tennis court.

Linesman. An official of the match, whose duty it is to decide whether balls are inside or outside side lines and base lines.

Live hand. A firm but not viselike grip; not frozen or tightened up. Same as *life-in-the-hand.*

Lob. A stroke in which the ball is lifted high in the air. An *offensive lob* is a ball stroked high into the air, deep into the opponent's court. A *defensive lob* is a ball hit high into the air enabling a player to regain his proper court position.

Lob volley. A volleying stroke hit over the head of an opponent.

Long. Refers to a service or groundstroke which lands outside the base line or the service line.

Longitudinally. From back to front.

Loop drive. A groundstroke that is hit softer than the conventional drive. The ball travels in an arc rather than on a direct line.

Love. A scoring term indicating zero.

Love-fifteen (-thirty, or -forty). A term used in scoring to indicate that the server has not made a point and the opponent has made one (fifteen), two (thirty), or three (forty) points.

Love game. A game in which one side has not scored a point.

Love-one, (-two, -three, -four, or -five). A term used in scoring sets to indicate that the server has not won a game.

Love-set. A set in which one side did not win a single game. In England, winning six successive games is called a love set, even though the antagonist had already scored when the run began.

Marker. An implement for marking out the lines of the court. Also, a person who keeps the score.

Match. A predetermined number of sets, usually two out of three or three out of five sets, which decide the winner. Also a competition arranged between two clubs, teams, counties, states, nations, or other bodies, each being represented by an equal number of players who play a series of matches (as per first definition) against each other.

Match point. The final point of a match. Same as *match ball.*

Mid-court. The central area of a player's court in front of and behind the service line.

Miss. Failure to hit the ball with the racket.

Mixed doubles. A match between two teams each consisting of a male and a female.

Mix-up. Changing the pace of play; varying your shots.

Modifying the stroke. Adapting the stroke to incorrect body position in relation to the ball.

Net. The netting placed across the middle of the court. It is suspended by a cord or metal cable, the ends of which are attached to two posts.

Net ball. After the service, a ball that touches the net; the ball remains in play.

Net game. A game strategy in which a player plays in the forecourt, close to the net, and volleys.

Net man. The partner in doubles play who stays close to the net while his teammate serves. Same as *net player.*

Net play. The action which takes place near the net.

Net stick. Used to support the net during singles play at 42 inches when placed on singles side line. Same as *singles stick* or *side stick.*

No-man's land. The area on the court between the base line and the service line in which a player should not stand while waiting for the ball.

Nonporous court. A court on which water does not penetrate, but runs off the surface. Same as an *impervious court.*

Not up. The call made by the official when a player narrowly misses reaching a ball before it touches down a second time; often, informally called "two bounces" or "double bounce." Also applies to balls hit near the ground that go from the racket to the ground and *then* over the net.

Objective hit.   A planned shot carefully directed to a point in the opposite court to do the striker most good and the opponent least good.

Offensive volley.   A volleying stroke made from above net level. Also called *high volley.*

One- (two-, three-, etc.) love.   A term used in scoring to indicate that the server has one (two, three, etc.) games and the opponent none.

Open-face racket.   A racket whose face is tilted backward from the direction of the oncoming ball. The opposite of "covering" the ball.

Opening.   A defensive lapse or mistake which permits a player an opportunity to score a point.

Open tennis.   Refers to tournaments in which both amateurs and professionals may compete.

Out.   A term applied to a ball which lands outside of the playing area.

Out-of-position shot.   A stroke made when not in the optimal position.

Overdrive.   To stroke or drive the ball over the opponent's base line so that it lands outside of the playing court for an error.

Overhand.   With the racket above the shoulder.

Overhead.   With the racket above the head.

Overhead shot.   A ball hit in the air above one's head, generally off a lob.

Overhead smash.   Shot made with a hard overhead stroke so that the ball comes down sharply into the opponent's court. This shot is usually referred to as the "smash" or "kill."

Overspin.   The motion of a ball hit with the racket starting below the ball and coming up over it, imparting accentuated forward motion. Same as *topspin.*

Pace.   The speed or amount of speed of play.

Parallel formation.   A positioning of players in a doubles game in which the partners keep abreast of each other on the court.

Pass.   To hit the ball past an opponent so that he cannot return it. Also a stroke that drives the ball past an opponent at the net, inside the court, but beyond his reach, as a *passing shot.*

Pat-ball delivery.   A soft service.

Permanent fixtures.   The umpire, linesmen, and spectators and their chairs or stands, net, posts, back and side stops, and any other objects situated around the court.

Place.   To hit the ball accurately to a desired location on the court.

Placement.   A shot placed where an opponent cannot reach or return the ball.

Play.   A warning called by the server just before serving. Also, the response of a linesman or umpire when appealed to for a decision on a ball that is good; an order to continue play.

Played.   An abbreviation of "well played." Used as applause for a clever stroke. Also, the manner in which a ball is returned.

Player.   A participant in the game of tennis. Also, according to ILTF rules, a "player" is one who has reached the age of 18 years, accepts the authority of his national lawn tennis association at all times, and is authorized to derive pecuniary advantage from tennis.

Plugging the side line.   A game strategy or tactic in which the player keeps playing his opponent's backhand until he is moved sufficiently out of position to be vulnerable for a forehand drop shot.

Poach.   To hit a ball in doubles that should have been played by one's partner, usually applied to play at the net.

Point.   The smallest unit of the score. Four points scored win a game, unless both sides have won three points, when the score is deuce and one player must gain a lead of two points to win the game.

Point of impact.   The point at which the racket meets the ball.

Porous court.   A court which permits water to filter through the surface. Same as a *pervious court.*

Position.   Where a player stands in relation to the lines of the court, the net, the opponent, and the ball.

Position play.   Playing each shot in such a manner so as to get an opponent out of position. Playing to create an opening.

Post.   One of the wooden or metal uprights supporting the net. Same as *pole.*

Precision hitting.   Clear clean-cut hitting off the center of the racket.

Preliminary round.   In tournament play, the first series of matches when the number of entries does not exactly equal a power of two. Same as *first round.*

Press. To force, to attack. Also a device used to hold the racket firmly so that it will not warp.

Professional. One who receives pecuniary advantage by playing, teaching, demonstrating or pursuit of the game of tennis. There are two major classes: (1) *Independent* or *registered professional*—one who has reached the age of 18 years, accepts the authority of his national lawn tennis association at all times, and is authorized to derive pecuniary advantage from tennis; and (2) *touring* or *contract professional*—one who is under contract with an organization other than a national lawn tennis association or its affiliated bodies and who gains pecuniary advantage from taking part in events which are not organized by the national association of the country where they are held.

Put away. To hit so well that no return is made.

Racket. The implement used to strike or hit the ball. The *rough side* of a racket is that on which the thin binding strings at the throat and at the top form loops around the regular stringing. The other side is known as the *smooth side*.

Rallying. A prolonged series of strokes (groundstrokes and/or volleys). Also playing the ball to each other for practice or for warming up.

Ranking. A process by which players are listed according to their performances of the preceding year.

Reaching up and out. Making the service swing at the length of the arm and over the right (or left) shoulder.

Ready position. Ready for any stroke—weight on toes, knees bent, shoulders hunched.

Receiver. The player who receives the service.

Referee. The official in charge of a tournament.

Retire. For one player to give his opponent a "walk-over," or allow him to win by default by refusing to continue a match.

Retrieve. To make a good return of a ball which is difficult to handle or reach.

Retriever. A player whose style is primarily defensive and relies on running down and returning shots rather than putting away.

Return. To knock a ball back over the net while in play.

Reverse twist. A stroke made by drawing the racket across the body in striking the ball.

Round. A series of matches in a tournament, the winners of which must equal an even power of two.

Round robin. A method of playing a tournament by which each player meets all of the others in turn.

Runner-up. The loser in the final round of any tournament or event.

Running-in shot. A stroke made and followed to the net.

Rush. To advance to the net.

Rushing the net. A game strategy in which the player runs up close to the net after hitting the ball in hopes that the opponent's return can be killed from this vantage spot.

Seeding. Placing the most highly skilled performers in tournament competition in such a way as to prevent their meeting in early-round play; in effect, allowing the tournament committee a chance to pick or predict the winner by seeding him number one.

Semifinal round. The round preceding the final round.

Semifinals. The two matches in the round before the finals; the matches of the semifinal round.

Serve. To deliver the ball from the base line by throwing it into the air with the hand and knocking it into the opponent's service court; the opening stroke of each point; the act of putting the ball into play.

Server. The player whose privilege it is to serve, or put the ball in play.

Service. The ball that has been served.

Service ace. An ace scored by service; a point earned by a served ball that is placed out of the reach of the striker-out but in the right court.

Service break. See *broken service.*

Service court. The space on each side of the net between the service line and the net, and between the singles side lines. The *center line* divides this area into two equal parts—the *right service court* and the *left service court*.

Service line. The line 21 feet from the net that bounds the service courts.

Set. The unit of scoring next higher than the game, scored when either player has won six games, unless the other player has meantime won five; in that case (a deuce set) the player first gaining a lead of two games wins.

Setless. Without a set; when a player loses a match in *"straight sets."*

Set point. That game point which, if won, will also win the set.

Setup. An easy shot, usually a short, high ball, which a competent player can hit away for an outright winner.

Shadow tennis. A practice procedure in footwork and strokes done without the use of a ball. Similar to shadow boxing performed by prize fighters.

Shag. To collect or retrieve idle balls knocked out of the court; the work of the ball boys.

Short ball. A ball that drops just over the net when the opponent is back in his court, intended to win because it is out of his reach. Generally a "stop volley."

Side line. The line at either side of the court that marks the outside edge of the playing surface.

Side pass. A stroke that drives the ball along the side of the court, out of the reach of an opponent at the net. Same as *line* pass.

Side service line. The line forming the boundary of the service courts at the right and left sides. In singles the side service lines are also part of the side lines.

Side spin. A spin, usually accomplished by a slice stroke, that causes the ball to bounce to one side or the other.

Singles. A game in which only two players take part, one on each side of the court.

Skittles. A contemptuous slang expression to describe the poor play in a game where the ball is knocked back and forth with little attempt to win.

Slap-dash shots. Not objective hitting.

Slice. A stroke hit with the racket that imparts a side spin. Also a type of service.

Slow court. A court on which a moderately hard-hit ball tends not to skid very much and the bounce is generally higher than on a fast court. The ball hit with spin is considerably diverted.

Smash. A hard, overhead swing on a descending ball.

Spikes. Shoes in which nails protrude from the soles or heels to keep the player from slipping. Same as steel points.

Spin. The rotation or twist of a ball in its flight.

Spinning. A method of determining which player serves first, and from which side of the net. It is accomplished by one player spinning his racket rapidly and letting it fall to the ground. While the racket is spinning, the other player calls "rough" or "smooth," referring to the manner in which the trimming cord at the top and throat of the racket face is wound around the stringing. See also *toss*.

Stop volley. A volleying stroke intended to drop the ball barely over the net.

Straight sets. A match won without losing a set; setless.

Strap. A canvas strap in the center of the net which is anchored to the ground to hold the net secure and at its proper height (3 feet at the center).

Strategy. The general plan of play in a specific match usually based on the opponent's weaknesses. Also called *game strategy*.

Striker or striker-out. The player whose turn it is to return the service.

Stringing. The filament (animal gut, nylon, or silk) in the head of the racket.

Stroke. The act of striking or hitting the ball with the racket.

Sudden death. An expression meaning a set decided by one game, after the score has been even at five-all, in contradistinction to playing deuce-and-vantage sets.

Tactics. The carrying out of the strategical plans; the ways and means used in the presence of the opponent.

Take the net. To move in close to the net.

Tape. The "band" of canvas bound on the top of the net. Also, the court line (derived from the occasional use of tapes for lines on clay courts).

Tennis elbow. An inflammation and swelling of the elbow joint, resulting from too much playing.

Tennis leg. A rupture of some of the muscle fibers in the calf of the leg, resulting from a sudden twist or strain.

Tennis stroke. A stroke made by cutting or slicing the ball under so that it twists backward. Same as *cut stroke*.

Thirty. A term used in scoring to denote two points. Also, in handicap matches, two points given on every game.

Thirty-all. A term used in scoring to denote that each side has scored two points.

Three (or two) straight. A match won in successive sets; a setless victory. Same as *straight sets.*

Throat. The portion of the racket where the head meets the handle.

Top. To hit the ball on top, causing it to spin downward; the ball tends to bounce backward when it hits the ground.

Topspin. Forward revolving motion of the ball. Same as *forward spin, overspin,* or *top curl.*

Toss. A method to determine which player serves first, and from which side of the net. This is usually accomplished by spinning a racket and the player who wins the toss has his choice of serving or receiving, or the choice of side. He cannot choose both. Also throwing a ball into the air to start a serve.

Touch. A term used to describe a player who hits a ball with style and grace, as if *he* were actually touching it rather than the racket. Also the act of the ball when it strikes the ground. Also the feeling of the ball with a player's racket.

Tournament. An official competition.

Twist. The spin that is applied to curve the service ball.

Umpire. The official in charge of a tournament.

Undercut. To hit the ball on the bottom, thus causing reverse spin. Same as an *underspin* or *backspin.*

Underhand. A stroke made with the racket below the level of the shoulders.

Up. An equal score; same as *all.*

USTA. Abbreviation for United States Tennis Association.

Vantage. The score of a game after either side has won a point from "deuce." Same as *advantage.*

Vantage-all. A term used in scoring, when the usual method of deuce-and-vantage games or sets is not used. When the best two out of three points (for games) or games (for sets) decide the game or set, the score is vantage-all when each side has won one point or game after deuce.

Vantage game. The next game won by either side in a deuce-and-vantage set, after the score of games has been at deuce.

Vantage-in. A term used to indicate that the server has won the "vantage" point (opposite of "vantage-out"). Same as *vantage-server.*

Vantage-out. A term used in scoring to indicate that the striker-out has won the "vantage" point (opposite of "vantage-in"). Same as *vantage-striker.*

Vantage sets. Sets in which deuce-and-vantage has been or is to be played.

VASSS. Abbreviation for Van Alen Simplified Scoring System.

Veteran. A player over (men) 45 years of age; (women) 40 years of age. Same as *senior player.*

Volley. A stroke made by hitting the ball before it has touched the ground.

Volleyer. A player who uses the "net game"; one who volleys by preference (opposite to a baseline player).

Western grip. A method of gripping the racket. (see page 111).

Wide. A term generally given to a ball that lands out of the playing court beyond the side lines.

Wide-breaking slice. A slice service with so much spin that it pulls the receiver into or beyond the alley.

Wood shot. A shot in which the ball strikes the wooden portion of the racket rather than on the stringing. While this shot is legal, it is not a desirable one.

Wrist action. The "action" imparted by the wrist to any stroke.

Illustration Credits are listed by page numbers. The illustrations on pages 109 through 150 except those on pages 126 and 144 are through the courtesy of Russ Adams Productions; all other illustrations courtesy of United States Tennis Association except those listed below.

2 Tennis Hall of Fame
3 Australian News and Information Bureau
5 Tennis Hall of Fame
7 Tennis Hall of Fame
8 Tennis Hall of Fame
14 Tennis Hall of Fame
16 (left) Edwin Levick; (right) Edwin Levick
17 (left) Wide World Photos; (right) Tennis Hall of Fame
20 U.S. Army Signal Corps
24 Paul Thompson
25 (left) Edwin Levick
26 Edwin Levick
27 World Wide Photos
29 (left) William Fox
32 (top) International Film Service, Inc.; (bottom) Tennis Hall of Fame
33 Edwin Levick
34 (top) Edwin Levick; (bottom) Tennis Hall of Fame
36 (top) Edwin Levick; (bottom) Wide World Photos
37 Acme News
39 (left) International Film Service, Inc.
40 (top) Acme News; (bottom) Edwin Levick
41 (top) Edwin Levick; (bottom) Edwin Levick
42 Wide World Photos
44 (top) French Lines
45 (bottom) Edwin Levick
46 Wide World Photos
47 Charles Baulard
52 Russel Kingman
56 Max Peter Haas
62 Acme News
63 Edwin Levick
66 Max Peter Haas
68 Thelner Hoover
73 Derek Bayes
74 (bottom) Derek Bayes
77 Madison Square Garden Corp.
82 Russ Adams Productions
88 Chemold Corporation
89 (left) Bancroft Sporting Goods Company; (center) Garcia Ski and Tennis Corporation; (right) Charger Corporation
93 Ball-Boy Company
96 (top) Prince Manufacturing Company; (bottom) Bancroft Ski and Tennis Corporation
104 (top) Kalamazoo *Gazette*; (bottom) Sheltair, Inc.
107 Philadelphia *Sunday Bulletin*
126 (left) Central Press Photos, Ltd.
144 Mary Puschak

153 Madison Square Garden Corp.
172 Australian News and Information Bureau
173 Australian News and Information Bureau
177 Australian News and Information Bureau
178 Australian News and Information Bureau
185 Robert F. Warner, Inc.
186 (top) Robert F. Warner, Inc.
188 (top) Madison Square Garden Corp.; (bottom) British Travel Association
243 Madison Square Garden Corp.
259 Barbara Dodge
274 Rotofotos, Inc.
309 (left) Les Walsh; (right) Whitestone Photos
317 Russ Adams Productions
330 Telegraph Newspare Company, Ltd.
340 (left) Derek Bayes; (right) Fox Photos, Ltd.
344 (right) Le-Roye Productions, Ltd.
345 (top) Keystone View Company
347 Australian News and Information Bureau
352 Edwin Levick
368 Robert Stuart
371 Madison Square Garden Corp.
399 Henry Miller
404 Max Peter Haas
406 Acme News
407 Wide World Photos
411 Max Peter Haas
418 Edwin Levick
420 Edwin Levick
422 Ben Schnall
423 Cunard Line
426 (bottom) Max Peter Haas
434 Tennis Hall of Fame
437 Tennis Hall of Fame
438 Tennis Hall of Fame
439 (top) Edwin Levick; (bottom) Edwin Levick
442 (top) Edwin Levick
444 (left) Edwin Levick; (right) Edwin Levick
445 (left) Edwin Levick; (right) London *Daily Mirror*
446 Edwin Levick
447 (left) Edwin Levick; (right) Morris Engel
448 (top) European Picture Service
451 (top, right) International News Photos; (bottom) Ben Schnall
452 Edwin Levick
467 Max Peter Haas
470 (right) Russ Adams Productions
471 Russ Adams Productions
472 (top) Tennis Hall of Fame
473 (top) Chemold Corporation; (bottom) Russ Adams Productions
475 (left) Wide World Photos
479 Russ Adams Productions
495 (right) Max Peter Haas
508 (right) Sport & General Press Agency, Ltd.
510 Madison Square Garden Corp.
522 Press Association, Inc.
537 (left) Russ Adams Productions; (right) Russ Adams Productions

Index